The

WORLD
TREASURY

Of

RELIGIOUS
QUOTATIONS

The

WORLD TREASURY

Of

RELIGIOUS QUOTATIONS

*Diverse Beliefs, Convictions, Comments, Dissents and
Opinions from Ancient and Modern Sources*

COMPILED AND EDITED BY RALPH L. WOODS

GARLAND BOOKS, 95 Madison Avenue

New York City

THE WORLD TREASURY OF RELIGIOUS QUOTATIONS

This edition published by arrangement with Hawthorn Books, Inc.

ACKNOWLEDGMENTS

In the body of this book specific acknowledgment is made to authors and volumes quoted. In addition, special acknowledgment is made below to publishers, authors, copyright owners, and agents whose works have been heavily drawn upon, and whose cooperation in allowing such generous use of protected material is gratefully appreciated.

ABINGDON PRESS: *Sermons Preached in a University Church* (copyright © 1959 by Abingdon Press), *Prayer* (copyright 1942 by Whitmore and Stone [Abingdon Press]), and *Christ and History* (copyright © 1963 by Abingdon Press) by George A. Buttrick; *The Modern Rival of Christian Faith* (copyright 1952 by Pierce and Smith [Abingdon Press]) by Georgia Harkness; *Christianity, Communism and History* (copyright 1954 by Pierce and Washabaugh [Abingdon Press]) by William Hordern; *Victorious Living* (copyright renewed 1964 by E. Stanley Jones, used by permission of Abingdon Press) by E. Stanley Jones; *Modern Science and Christian Belief* (copyright © 1955 by Arthur F. Smethurst, used by permission of Abingdon Press) by Arthur F. Smethurst; *Christianity, Diplomacy and War* (1953) by Herbert Butterfield.

GEORGE MATTHEWS ADAMS SERVICE: *Ways to Happiness* (1953) by Fulton J. Sheen.

GEORGE ALLEN & UNWIN LTD.: *Mysticism and Logic* (1925) by Bertrand Russell; *The Spiritual Heritage of India* (1963) by Swami Prabhavananda; *The Church and Its Function in Society* (1937) by J. H. Oldham and W. A. Visser 't Hooft.

THE AMERICA PRESS: reprinted with permission from *America,* The National Catholic Weekly Review, 920 Broadway, New York, N.Y. 10010, from issues of October 10 and 19, 1959; November 7, 1959; December 12, 1959; January 23, 1960; February 20, 1960; January 30, 1960; March 31, 1962; September 29, 1962; November 3, 1962; *Philosophy of Catholic Education* (1951) by William J. McGucken.

THE AMERICAN ACADEMY OF POLITICAL AND SOCIAL SCIENCE: *The Annals* (March, 1948) by John Courtney Murray.

APPLETON-CENTURY, PUBLISHERS: *An Ethical Philosophy of Life* (1918) by Felix Adler; *Reason and Emotion* (1935) by John Macmurray; Fulton J. Sheen's *Three to Get Married* (1951) by Fulton J. Sheen; passages from Sabine, Murray, Hoagland, Mather and Dobzhansky in *Science Ponders Religion* (1960) by Harlow Shapley.

ASSOCIATION PRESS: *Sex and Religion Today* (1953), ed. S. Doniger, quotations from Bettocci, Fletcher, Hiltman, Howe; *Creative Society* (1938) by John Macmurray; *Prayer and Worship* (1938) by Douglas V. Steere; *The South and Christian Ethics* (1962) by James Sellars.

BEACON PRESS: *Religious Liberals Reply* (copyright 1947 by Beacon Press) by Wieman et al.

G. BELL AND SONS, LTD.: *Christianity and History* (1949) by Herbert Butterfield.

BENZIGER BROTHERS INC.: *Works of St. Thomas Aquinas,* trans. by the Fathers of the Dominican Province, England; *The Things Immortal* (1919) by E. F. Garesche.

A. AND C. BLACK LTD. and DACRE PRESS: *Jew and Greek* (1953) and *The Shape of the Liturgy* (1945) by Gregory Dix.

BLACKFRIARS PUBLICATIONS: *Life of the Spirit* (February–March, 1954).

BASIL BLACKWELL, PUBISHER: *From a Friar's Cell* (1923) by Vincent McNabb.

GEOFFREY BLES LTD.: *Slavery and Freedom* (1944), *Freedom and the Spirit* (1935), and *True Humanism* (1936) by Jacques Maritain; *Destiny of Man* (1937) by Nicolas Berdyaev; *Divided Christendom* (1939) by Yves Congar.

BLOOMSBURY PUBLISHING COMPANY, LTD.: *Companions for Eternity* (1947) by A. Carré.

THE BOBBS-MERRILL CO. INC.: *Christianity and Modern Man* (copyright 1961 by Albert T. Mollegen) by Albert T. Mollegen; *Near to the Heart of God* (copyright 1954 by the Bobbs-Merrill Co. Inc.) by C. B. McAfee; *Communism and the Conscience of the West* (copyright 1948 by Fulton J. Sheen) by Fulton J. Sheen.

THE BODLEY HEAD LTD.: *Christianity and Freedom* (1952) by Gustave Thibon; *Heretics* (1905) by G. K. Chesterton.

CHARLES S. BRADEN: *These Also Believe* (1949), *Jesus Compared: A Study of Jesus and Other Great Founders of Religions* (1957), *Christian Science Today* (1958), *Man's Quest for Salvation* (1941), *The Scriptures of Mankind* (1952), *Varieties of American Religion* (1936), ed. Charles S. Braden, *Procession of the Gods* (1948; written with Gaius Glenn Atkins), and "The Christian Encounter with World Religions," *Church and State Magazine* (Autumn 1965), all by Charles S. Braden.

GEORGE BRAZILLER, INC.: *Protestantism* (1962), ed. J. L. Dunstan; *The Humanity of Man* (1956) by Ralph Barton Perry; *Islam* (1963), ed. J. A. Williams; *Judaism* (1961), ed. Arthur Hertzberg; *Catholicism* (1962), ed. George Brantl; *Buddhism* (1963), ed. R. A. Gard; *Hinduism* (1963), ed. Louis Renou.

CURTIS BROWN, LTD.: *Science Today* (1934) by Sir John A. Thompson and J. G. Crowther.

BRUCE PUBLISHING COMPANY: *Theology and Race Relations* (1964) by Joseph T. Leonard.

DR. MARTIN BUBER: *At the Turning* (1952) and *Jewish Mysticism and the Legend of Bal Shem* (1916) by Dr. Martin Buber.

BURNS AND OATES LTD.: *Critical and Constructive Essays* (1934) by Richard Downey; *Christian Inheritance* (1896) by J. C. Hedley; *God's Way of Mercy* (1938) and *The Craft of Prayer* (1951) by Vincent McNabb.

CAMBRIDGE UNIVERSITY PRESS: from *The Nature of the Physical World* by A. S. Eddington, 1929; *The Right to Believe* by J. S. Whale, 1938.

REV. J. V. LANGMEAD CASSERLEY: *The Bent World* (1955), *The Fate of Modern Culture* (1940), and *Retreat from Christianity in the Modern World* (1952) by Rev. J. V. Langmead Casserley.

CATHOLIC ASSOCIATION FOR INTERNATIONAL PEACE: *Secularism's Attack on World Order* (1944) by John LaFarge; *Timeless Rights: International Ethics* (1942); *Ethics of Atomic War* (1947) by W. J. Parson.

THE CATHOLIC TRUTH SOCIETY OF LONDON: *Miracles* (1929) by Ronald A. Knox; *Meditations for Layfolk* (1955) by Bede Jarrett.

THE CATHOLIC UNIVERSITY OF AMERICA PRESS: *The Morality of the Color Line* (1929) by Francis J. Gilligan.

ACKNOWLEDGMENTS

CENTER FOR THE STUDY OF DEMOCRATIC INSTITUTIONS: *Religion and the Free Society* (1958) by William Clancy.

CHAPMAN AND HALL LTD.: *Man and Matter* (1951) by F. Sherwood Taylor.

THE CHRISTIAN CENTURY FOUNDATION: *Living Without Gloves* by Halford Luccock, (copyright 1957 by The Christian Century Foundation, reprinted by permission from the issue of November 6, 1957, of *The Christian Century*) by Halford Luccock; also from the following issues of *The Christian Century:* February 18, 1915; January 24, 1920; January 31, 1924; April 22, 1926; February 14, 1934; May 2, 1934; March 10, 1937; October 26, 1938; January 25, 1939; December, 1941; August 29, 1945; April 17, 1946; April 9, 1947; November 26, 1947; January 6, 1954; March 31, 1954; November 17, 1954; September 28, 1955; January 26, 1957; August 26, 1957; February 3, 1960; August 3, 1960; March 8, 1961.

T. AND T. CLARK: *History of Creeds and Confessions* (1911) by W. A. Curtis; *I and Thou* (1923) by Martin Buber.

WILLIAM COLLINS SONS & CO.: *Soul and Psyche* (1960) by Victor White; *The Divine Milieu* (1960) and *The Phenomenon of Man* (1955) by Teilhard de Chardin; Julian Huxley's Introduction to *The Phenomenon of Man* by Teilhard de Chardin.

COLUMBIA UNIVERSITY PRESS: *An Essay on Nature* (1940) by F. J. E. Woodbridge.

THE CRITIC: from issues of August–September, 1961; December, 1961; January, 1962; August–September, 1962; November, 1963.

J. M. DENT AND SONS LTD.: *Ethics* (1910) by Baruch Spinoza (trans. Boyle, Everyman Library Edition).

DIVINE WORD PUBLICATIONS: *Meditations for the Layman* (formerly titled *The Looking Glass;* copyright 1951 by J. S. Paluch Co. Inc.) by Walter Farrell.

HAROLD W. DODDS: from *Ladies' Home Journal* (December, 1961).

DOUBLEDAY & COMPANY, INC.: *Community, Church and State* (copyright © 1960 by the National Student Christian Federation) by Karl Barth; *An American Dialogue* (copyright © 1960 by Gustave Weigel and Robert McAfee Brown) by Gustave Weigel and Robert McAfee Brown; *The Precarious Vision* (copyright © 1961 by Peter L. Berger) by Peter L. Berger; *Makers of Heaven and Earth* (copyright © 1959 by Langdon Gilkey) by Langdon Gilkey; *From State Church to Pluralism* (copyright © 1962 by Franklin Hamlin Littell) by Franklin H. Littell; *The Renewal of Man* (copyright © 1955 by Alexander Miller) by Alexander Miller; *Chapters for the Orthodox* (copyright 1921 by D. Appleton-Century Company, Inc.; copyright 1934 by Don Marquis; copyright 1954 by Doubleday & Company, Inc.) by Don Marquis; *Disputed Questions* by Anton C. Pegis; *Religion and Freedom of Thought* (copyright 1954 by the Union Theological Seminary) by Nathan M. Pusey; *How to Believe* (copyright 1953 by Ralph W. Sockman) by Ralph W. Sockman; *The Spiritual Heritage of India* by Swami Prabhavananda. All used by permission of Doubleday & Company, Inc.

DUKE UNIVERSITY PRESS: *War and the Christian Conscience* (1961) by Paul Ramsey.

DUQUESNE UNIVERSITY PRESS: *Faith and the World* (1962) by Albert Dondeyne.

E. P. DUTTON AND CO. INC.: *Ethics* (1910) by Baruch Spinoza (trans. Boyle, Everyman Library Edition); *Life of the Spirit and Life Today* (1923) by Evelyn Underhill; *Samuel Butler's Notebooks* (1913), ed. H. F. Jones; *Essays and Addresses on the Philosophy of Religion* (1st series, 1925, 2nd series, 1926), *The Mystical Element of Religion* (1908), and *Selected Letters* (1933) by Baron Friedrich von Hügel.

EDITIONS ALBIN MICHEL: *Jean Christophe* (1910, 1938) by Romain Rolland, trans. Gilbert Cannan.

THE EPWORTH PRESS: *Christianity, Diplomacy and War* (1953) by Herbert Butterfield.

WM. B. ERDMAN'S PUBLISHING CO.: *Life Crucified* (1959) by Oswald J. C. Hoffman; *Communism and Christian Faith* (1956) by L. DeKoster.

FABER AND FABER, LTD.: *God Was in Christ* (1948) by D. M. Baillie.

FARRAR, STRAUS & GIROUX, INC.: *After Black Coffee* (copyright 1947 by Declan X. McMullen Co.) by Robert I. Gannon; *Judaism and Modern Man* (copyright 1951 by Will Herberg) by Will Herberg; *Recollections* (copyright 1950 by McMullen Books, Inc.) by A. Sertillanges; *The Sabbath* (copyright 1951 by Abraham Joseph Heschel) by A. J. Heschel; *An American Amen* (copyright © 1958 by John LaFarge) by John LaFarge; *What I Believe* (copyright © 1963 by Farrar, Straus & Company) by François Mauriac.

FIDES PUBLISHERS, INC.: *The Church Today* (copyright 1953 by Fides Publishers, Inc.) by Emmanuel Suhard.

HARCOURT, BRACE & WORLD, INC.: *Christian Thought and Action* (copyright 1951, © 1956, 1958 by Aelred Graham) by Aelred Graham; *Religion and the Rise of Capitalism* (copyright 1926 by Harcourt, Brace & World, Inc.; renewed 1954 by R. H. Tawney) by R. H. Tawney; *The Idea of a Christian Society* (copyright 1940 by T. S. Eliot) and *Selected Essays* (copyright 1932, 1936, 1950 by Harcourt, Brace & World, Inc.; copyright 1960, 1964 by T. S. Eliot) by T. S. Eliot; *Modern Man in Search of a Soul* (1933) by C. G. Jung; *The Modern Temper* (1929) by Joseph Wood Krutch; *The Four Loves* (1960) by C. S. Lewis; *The Waters of Siloe* (1949) by Thomas Merton; *Faith for Living* (1940) and *The Condition of Man* (1944) by Lewis Mumford; *The Anatomy of Faith* (1960) and *A Believing Jew* (1951) by Milton Steinberg; *The Third Revolution* (1954) by Karl Stern; *Flight to Arras* (1942) by Antoine de Saint-Exupery.

HARPER & ROW, PUBLISHERS: *Theism and Human Nature* (1915) by A. J. Balfour; *Do What You Will* (1929), *Those Barren Leaves* (1925), *The Perennial Philosophy* (1944), *Ends and Means* (1937), and *The Devils of Louden* (1952) by Aldous Huxley; *The Kingdom of God in America* (copyright by Harper & Brothers, 1937) by H. Richard Niebuhr; quotations from Aron, Shinn and Parr in *The Ethics of Power* (1962), ed. H. D. Lasswell and Harlan Cleveland; *Perspective on a Troubled Decade* (1950), ed. L. Bryson et al.; quotations from Brown and Greenberg in *Patterns of Faith in America* (1957), ed. F. Ernest Johnson; *Christian Faith and the Common Life* (1938) by Nils Ehrenstrom; *Theology of the Old Testament* by Edmund Jacob, 1955; *The Divine Milieu* (1960) and *The Phenomenon of Man* (1955) by Teilhard de Chardin; *Soul and Psyche* (1960) by Victor White; *A Testament of Devotion* (1941) by Thomas R. Kelly; *A Philosophy of the Christian Revelation* (1940) by Edwin Lewis; *Protestant Thought Before Kant* (1941) by A. C. McGiffert; *Interpretation of Christian Ethics* (1935) by Reinhold Niebuhr; *In Praise of Gratitude* (1961) by Robert Raynolds; *Faith and Ethics: The Theology of H. Richard Niebuhr* (1957), ed. Paul Ramsey; *Modern Literature and the Religious Frontier* (1958) by Nathan A. Scott; *Doors into Life* (1948) by Douglas V. Steere; *The Philosophy of Religion* (1957) by D. E. Trueblood; *Dynamics of Faith* (1957) by Paul Tillich; *Liberal Learning and Religion* by Amos N. Wilder; *Behold the Glory* (1955) by Chad Walsh; *Man: The Bridge Between Two Worlds* (1940) by Franz E. Winkler; 1940; *Meister Eckhart* (1941) by Eckhart, trans. E. B. Blakney; *Man's Disorder and God's Design* (1948) by World Conference of Churches, Amsterdam; *Life Together* (1938) by Dietrich Bonhoeffer; *Still Shine the Stars* (1941) by Bernard Iddings Bell; quotations from Sorokin, Haydon, Schlipp, Montagu and Cole in *This is My Faith* (1946), ed. S. G. Cole; *Man the Unknown* (1935) by Alexis Carrel; *In Place of Folly* (1961) by Norman Cousins; *Impact of American Religious Liberalism* (1962) by Kenneth Cautheen; *On the Road to Unity* (1961) by Samuel McC. Cavert; *Ethics in a Business Society* (1954) by Marquis Childs and Douglas Cater; *On Being a Real Person* (1943), *Adventurous Religion* (1926), *The Hope of the World* (1933) and *As I See Religion* (1932) by Harry Emerson Fosdick; *What Man Can Make of Man* (1942) and *The Coming of World Civilization* (1956) by William E. Hocking; *The Racial Problem in Christian Perspective* (1959) by Kyle Haselden; *The Social Gospel Re-Examined* (1940) by Ernest Johnson; *The Purpose of the Church and Its Ministry* (1956) by H. Richard Niebuhr; *The Logic of Belief* (1942) by D. E. Trueblood; *The Great Tradition of the American Churches* (1953) by W. S. Hudson; *The New Shape of American Religion* (1958) by Martin E. Marty; *Christian Theology* (1955) by Walter Horton; *Personal Experience and the Historic Faith* (1959) by A. Victor Murray.

HARVARD UNIVERSITY PRESS: *Theology and Modern Literature* (1958) by Amos N. Wilder; *Religion in the Twentieth Century* (1952) by H. W. Schneider; *St. Basil's Address to Young Men,* from the Loeb Classical Library, published by Harvard University Press.

ACKNOWLEDGMENTS

HAWTHORN BOOKS, INC.: *The Catholic Bookman's Guide* (copyright © 1962) by Sister M. Regis, I.H.M.; *Psychiatry and the Christian* (copyright © 1962) by J. Dominian; *Love in Marriage* (copyright © 1964) by Henri Gibert; *Christian Music* (copyright © 1961) by Alec Robertson; *Who Is the Devil?* (copyright © 1958 by Nicolas Corte).

B. HERDER BOOK CO.: *Meditations for Layfolks* (1915) by Bede Jarrett; *Christian Perfection and Contemplation* (1937) by Garrigou-Lagrange.

HERDER AND HERDER: *The Prison Meditations of Father Delp* (1963).

HOLT, RINEHART AND WINSTON, INC.: *Personality: A Psychological Interpretation* (1937) by Gordon W. Allport; *Jean-Christophe* (trans. Gilbert Cannan, copyright 1910, 1938 by Holt, Rinehart and Winston, Inc., and reprinted with their permission) by Romain Rolland; *Two Sources of Morality and Religion* (1935) by Henri Bergson; *Living Joyously* (1950) by Kirby Page; trans. from Formstacher, Mendelssohn and the Talmud, and passages from H. J. Schoep in his *The Jewish-Christian Argument* (1961).

HODDER AND STOUGHTON, LTD.: *Theology of the Old Testament* (1955) by Edmund Jacob.

IONA COMMUNITY PUBLISHING DEPARTMENT: *Only One Way Left* (1956) by George Macleod.

P. J. KENNEDY AND SONS: quotations from Aumann, Braceland, Stern and Allers in *Faith, Reason and Psychiatry* (1955), ed. F. J. Braceland; quotations from Ternus, Leiege, Congar, Saudee, Romana, Huby and Dondeyne, and a trans. from St. Vincent of Lerins, in *God, Man and Universe* (1950), ed. Saudee; *The Three-Dimensional Man* (1956) by A. M. Sullivan; *Be of Good Heart* (1924) by Joseph McAorley; *Back to Jesus* (1959) by Jacques Leclercq; *The Meaning of Evil* (1961) by Charles Journet; *The Law of Love* (1954) by Francis Devas, ed. Philip Caraman.

ALFRED A. KNOPF, INC.: *A Little Book in C Major* (1916) by H. L. Mencken.

J. B. LIPPINCOTT COMPANY: *The Hemlock and the Cross* (copyright 1963 by Geddes McGregor) by Geddes McGregor; *Religion and the Modern Mind* (copyright 1929 by W. T. Stace) by W. T. Stace.

LITTLE, BROWN AND COMPANY: *The Public Philosophy* (copyright 1955 by Walter Lippmann) and *The Good Society* (copyright 1936, 1937, 1943 by Walter Lippmann) by Walter Lippmann; *Dialogues of Alfred North Whitehead* (copyright 1954 by Lucien Price), as recorded by Lucien Price.

LONGMANS, GREEN AND CO. LTD.: *Retreat from Christianity in the Modern World* (1952) by J. V. Langmead Casserley.

LOOK MAGAZINE: "What Can I Believe?" by Samuel H. Miller, *Look* (December 19, 1961).

LUTTERWORTH PRESS: *Christian Vocation* (1951) by W. R. Forester; *Reformation Writings of Martin Luther* (1956), trans. B. Woolf; *The Divine Imperative* (1937) by Emil Brunner.

LUZAC AND COMPANY, LTD.: *Readings of the Mystics of Islam* (1950) by Margaret Smith.

McGRAW-HILL BOOK COMPANY: *Religion Today: A Challenging Enigma* (copyright 1933 by A. L. Swift), ed. A. L. Swift; *Peace of Soul* (copyright 1949 by Fulton J. Sheen) by Fulton J. Sheen; *A Man Called Peter* (copyright 1951 by Catherine Marshall) by Catherine Marshall.

DAVID McKAY CO. INC.: *The Eucharist* (1944) by François Mauriac; *Human Destiny* (1947) by Lecomte du Noüy; *Religion Without God* (1928) by Fulton J. Sheen; *Catholicism and the World Today* (1952) by Aelred Graham; *The Catholic Bedside Book* (1953), ed. C. C. Martindale; *Fruits of the Spirit* (1942) by Evelyn Underhill; *True Morality and Its Counterfeits* (1955) by Dietrich von Hildebrandt.

THE MACMILLAN COMPANY: *The Tragic Sense of Life* (1921) by Miguel de Unamuno; quotations from Cate, Wagoner, Bridston, Hyslop, Mudge, E. Adler, U. K. Than and Paul in *Unity in Mid-Career* (1963), ed. Bridston and Wagoner; *Religion in the Making* (1927), *Science in the Modern World* (1927), and *Adventure in Ideas* (1933) by Alfred North Whitehead; *The Abolition of Man* (1947), *Christian Behavior* (1943), *The Problem of Pain* (1940), *The Case of Christianity* (1943) by C. S. Lewis; *Hourglass* (1952) by John W. Lynch; *The Christian Significance of Karl Marx* (1947) by Alexander Miller; *The Ramparts We Guard* (1950) by R. M. MacIver; *The Religious Consciousness* (1921) by J. B. Pratt; *Theology for the Social Gospel* (1917) by Walter Rauschenbusch; *The Contemporary Christ* (1938) by R. Roberts; *The Highway of God* (1941) by Ralph W. Sockman; *Reality* (1926) and *The Spirit* (1919) by Burnett H. Streeter; *The Meaning and End of Religion* (1963) by Wilfred C. Smith; *The Spirit of Catholicism* (1924) by Karl Adam; *The Individual and His Religion* (1950) by Gordon W. Allport; *Ethics* (1955) by D. Bonhoeffer; *Dream and Reality* (1939) by Nicolas Berdyaev; *The Diary of a Country Priest* (1937) by Georges Bernanos; *The Catholic Church and Conversion* (1926) by G. K. Chesterton; *Minister* (1963) by J. B. Coburn; *The Possessed* and *The Brothers Karamazov* by Feodor Dostoevsky (trans. Constance Garnett); *A Call to What is Vital* (1949), *The Radiant Life* (1944), *The Eternal Gospel* (1938) by Rufus M. Jones; *The Sleepwalkers* (1959) and *The Trial of the Dinosaur and Other Essays* (1955), by Arthur Koestler; *The Future of the American Jew* (1948) by Mordecai Kaplan; *Jesus of Nazareth* (1929) by Joseph Klausner; *Preface to Morals* (1929) by Walter Lippmann.

METHUEN AND CO. LTD.: *The Faith of the Roman Church* (1937) by C. C. Martindale; *Existentialism and Humanism* (1948) by J. P. Sartre.

WILLIAM MORROW AND CO.: *Man's Right to be Human* (1959) by George W. Anderson; *Makers of the American Mind* (1964) by Robert C. Whittemore.

MUEHLENBERG PRESS: *Works of Martin Luther* (Vol. 51, trans. J. W. Doberstein).

THE NATIONAL COUNCIL OF CATHOLIC MEN and THE CATHOLIC HOUR: Fulton J. Sheen's radio sermons published under the title *The Fullness of Christ* (1935) and *The Eternal Galilean* (1934); Francis J. Connell's radio sermons published under the title *Morality and Government* (1949).

THE NEWMAN PRESS: *Paradoxes* (1948) by Henri de Lubac; *The Intellectual Life* (1946) by Antonin Sertillanges.

W. W. NORTON & COMPANY, INC. *Liberty* (copyright 1930 by W. W. Norton & Company, Inc.; renewed 1958 by Daphne Mason) by Everett Dean Martin; *The Mature Mind* (copyright 1949, © 1959 by W. W. Norton & Company, Inc.) by H. A. Overstreet.

OUR SUNDAY VISITOR: *The Woman* (1951) by Fulton J. Sheen.

OXFORD UNIVERSITY PRESS, London: *The Sense of the Presence of God* (1962) by John Baillie.

OXFORD UNIVERSITY PRESS, New York: *Faith, Reason and Existence* (1956) by John Hutchison; *Fact, Fiction and Faith* (1940) by James A. Martin, Jr.; *The Sikh Religion* (1909) by M. A. MacAuliffe, 6 vols.; *The Idea of God* (1917) A. S. Pringle-Pattison; A. J. Toynbee's *A Study of History, Reconsiderations* (1961), Vol. V (1939), Vol IX (1946), The Somerville one-volume abridgement of *A Study of History; An Historian's Approach to Religion* (1956) and *Civilization on Trial* (1948) by A. J. Toynbee.

PAULIST PRESS: from pamphlets, booklets and books; *The Spiritual Life* (1914) by Walter Elliott; *The Divine Romance* (1952) by Ignatius Cox; *Secularism* (1947) by J. D. Fee; *Catholics, Race and Law* (1947) by F. J. Haas; *God in Education* (1943) by Robert I. Gannon; *God in Government* (1943) by James M. Gillis; *The Problem of Evil* (1928, 1951) by M. C. D'Arcy; *God: Can We Find Him?* (1942), *The Origin of Man* (1947), and *Religion: Does It Matter?* (1944) by John A. O'Brien.

PENGUIN BOOKS, LTD.: *The Orthodox Church* (copyright 1963 by Timothy Ware) by Timothy Ware.

PHILOSOPHICAL LIBRARY: *The Christian Way* (1949) by Sydney Cave: *Out of My Later Years* (1950) by Albert Einstein; *Science and the Human Imagination* (1955) by Mary B. Hesse; *Art and Poetry* (1943) by Jacques Maritain; *Words of Faith* (1955) by François

ACKNOWLEDGMENTS

Mauriac; *Scientific Autobiography and Other Papers* (1949) by Max Planck; *Between Heaven and Earth* (1944) by Franz Werfel; *Letters to My God* (1958) by Dagobert D. Runes.

POCKET BOOKS, INC.: *Man, Nature and God* (copyright 1962 by Pocket Books, Inc.) by F. S. C. Northrop.

PRENTICE-HALL, INC.: *The Small Needle of Dr. Large* (copyright 1962 by John Ellis Large) by John E. Large; *Nine Modern Moralists* (copyright 1962) by Paul Ramsey.

PRINCETON UNIVERSITY PRESS: *Pages from an Oxford Diary* (1937) and *The Catholic Faith* (1931) by Paul Elmer More; *The Church and the Liberal Society* (1944) by John Emmet Hughes; *Either/Or, Works of Love, Postscript to Philosophical Fragments, Sickness unto Death,* and *Self-Examination,* as quoted in *A Kierkegaard Anthology* (1951), ed. Robert Bretall, trans. Lowrie.

FREDERICK PUSTET CO., INC.: *Marriage and the Family* (1941) by Jacques Leclercq.

G. P. PUTNAM'S SONS: *What I Believe* (1941) by Sholem Asch; *From a College Window* (1906) by A. C. Benson; *Cain: Where Is Your Brother?* (1962) by François Mauriac; quotations from Rust, Horrigan, Galloway and Tenney in *Science and Religion* (1962), ed. J. C. Monsma.

RANDOM HOUSE, INC.: *The Time Is Now* (1963) by John Rock, M.D.; *Basic Verities* (1943) by Charles Peguy; *Notebooks* (1950) by Albert Camus.

THE READER'S DIGEST: "Married Love" (March, 1941) and "Prayer Is Power" (July, 1939) by Alexis Carrel; "A Christian Manifesto" (July, 1948) by Francis B. Sayers; "Sermon from the Shows" (April, 1939) by A. J. Cronin.

HENRY REGNERY COMPANY: *The Last Essays of Georges Bernanos* (1955), trans. Barry and Joan Ulanov; *The Lord of History* (1958) by Jean Danielou; lines from the poem "Sermons We See" in *Collected Verse of Edgar A. Guest* (copyright 1934, 1962 by Reilly and Lee).

SCHOCKEN BOOKS INC.: *Israel and the World* (copyright © 1948 by Schocken Books, Inc.) by Martin Buber; *Dearest Father: Stories and Other Writings* (copyright © 1954) by Franz Kafka, trans. Ernst Kaiser and Eithne Wilkins.

CHARLES SCRIBNER'S SONS: *The Mind of the Catholic Layman* (1963) by Daniel Callahan; *Joy in Believing* (1956) and *The Meaning of the Cross* (1931) by Henry Sloan Coffin; *The Mysterious Human Nature* (1956) by James M. Gillis; *The Spirit of Medieval Philosophy* (1936) by Etienne Gilson; *In Search of Maturity* (1943) by Fritz Kunkel; *The Range of Reason* (1952), *Ransoming the Time* (1941), and *The Person and the Common Good* (1947) by Jacques Maritain; *Beyond Tragedy* (1937), *Faith and History* (1949), *The Nature and Destiny of Man, I* (1943) by Reinhold Niebuhr; *Beyond Anxiety* (1953) by James A. Pike; *Soliloquies in England and Later Soliloquies* (1922), *The Realm of Truth* (1937), and *The Realm of Essence* (1928) by George Santayana; *Christianity and the Problems of History* (1953) by Roger L. Shinn; *The Shaking of the Foundations* (1948) and *The New Being* (1955) by Paul Tillich; "The Prison and the Angel" in *The Builders* (1897) by Henry van Dyke; *God Was in Christ* (1948) by D. M. Baillie; *The Sense of the Presence of God* (1962) by John Baillie; *Church Dogmatics* by Karl Barth; *Slavery and Freedom* by Nicholas Berdyaev (1944); *I and Thou* (1958) by Martin Buber; *Christianity and History* (1949) by Herbert Butterfield; *Preaching in a Scientific Age* (1954) by A. C. Craig.

SHEED AND WARD, LTD., London: *Freedom in the Modern World* (1935) by Jacques Maritain.

SHEED AND WARD, INC., New York: *Window in the Wall* (copyright 1956 by Sheed and Ward, Inc., with the kind permission of Mr. Evelyn Waugh) and *Retreat for Priests* (copyright 1946 by Sheed and Ward, Inc., with the kind permission of Mr. Evelyn Waugh) by Ronald Knox; *Nature and Grace* (copyright 1964 by Sheed and Ward, Inc.) by Karl Rahner; *Sheed and Ward Trumpet* (Fall, 1962; Spring, 1964) by Philip Scharper; *Society and Sanity* (copyright 1953 by Sheed and Ward, Inc.) by F. J. Sheed; *The Divine Pity* (copyright 1946 by Sheed and Ward, Inc.) and *The Water and the Fire* (copyright 1954 by Sheed and Ward, Inc.)

by Gerald Vann, O.P.; *The Bible and the Church* (copyright 1959 by Sheed and Ward, Inc.) by Bruce Vawter, C.M.; *The Splendour of the Liturgy* by Maurice Zundel; *Catholicism* by Henri de Lubac; *Complete Works of St. Teresa,* in the critical edition of P. Silvio de Santa Teresa, C.C., trans. and ed. by E. Allison Peers (3 vols.); *The Church of the Word Incarnate* by Charles Journet; *Men and Tendencies* by E. I. Watkins; *Progress and Religion, The Judgment of the Nations* (copyright 1942 by Sheed and Ward, Inc.), and *Religion and Culture* (copyright 1948 by Sheed and Ward, Inc.) by Christopher Dawson; *God and the Supernatural,* ed. Father Cuthbert, O.F.M. Cap.; *The Spiritual Letters of Dom John Chapman; The Nature of Belief* by M. C. D'Arcy; *The Church and the Catholic* and *The Spirit of the Liturgy* (copyright 1948 by Sheed and Ward, Inc.) by Romano Guardini; *A Treasury of Russian Spirituality* (copyright 1948 by Sheed and Ward, Inc.), ed. G. P. Fedotov; *The Council: Reform and Reunion* (copyright by Sheed and Ward, Ltd.) by Hans Küng; *The Meaning of Man* (copyright 1948 by Sheed and Ward, Inc.) and *The Christian Experience* (copyright 1954 by Sheed and Ward, Inc.) by Jean Mouroux; *God and Mammon* by François Mauriac; *We Hold These Truths* (copyright 1950 by Sheed and Ward) by John Courtney Murray.

SIMON AND SCHUSTER, INC.: *This I Believe* (1954) by various authors; *Living Philosophies* (1931) by various authors; *Peace of Mind* (1946) by Joshua Loth Liebman; *Caesar and Christ* (1944), *The Age of Faith* (1956), and *The Age of Reason* (1961) by Will Durant.

R. R. SMITH, INC.: *Under Orders* (copyright 1944 by Richard R. Smith, Inc., Peterborough, N.H.) by William L. Sullivan.

THE SOCIETY OF AUTHORS: *Religion in the Modern State* (1935) and *The Modern Dilemma* (1932) by Christopher Dawson, with the additional permission of Mr. Christopher Dawson; *Back to Methuselah* (1921), *Androcles and the Lion* (1914), *St. Joan* (1926) by Bernard Snaw.

SOCIETY FOR PROMOTING CHRISTIAN KNOWLEDGE: "On the Spirit and the Letter" by St. Augustine, trans. W. J. S. Simpson, in *Translations of Christian Literature* (Series II, 1926); *St. Seraphim of Sarov* (1936) by F. Dobie-Bateman.

VINCENT STUART, PUBLISHERS, LTD.: *Meister Eckhart* by C. de B. Evans, trans. Franz Pfeiffer.

STUDENT CHRISTIAN MOVEMENT PRESS: *Preaching in a Scientific Age* (1954) by A. C. Craig; *The Nature of the Church,* ed. R. Newton Flew; *The Second World Conference on Faith and Order* (1938), ed. L. Hodgson; *The Divine Revolution* (1927) by W. G. Peck.

THEOLOGY DIGEST: quotations from J. L. Conway, J. C. Ford and P. Zamayon (Winter, 1957).

UNIVERSITY OF CHICAGO PRESS: *The Protestant Era* (copyright 1948 by Paul Tillich) by Paul Tillich; *Galilei: Dialogue on the Great World Systems* (copyright 1953 by University of Chicago Press), trans. by Giorgio de Santillana; *Systematic Theology,* Vols. I, II and III (copyright 1951, 1957 and 1964 by Paul Tillich), by Paul Tillich.

UNIVERSITY OF NORTH CAROLINA PRESS: *Science and Christian Belief* (1955) by C. A. Coulson; *Science and the Idea of God* (1945) by William E. Hocking.

UNIVERSITY OF PENNSYLVANIA PRESS: *Epigrams and Criticisms in Miniature* (1936) by William L. Sullivan.

THE VANGUARD PRESS: *Puritanism and Democracy* (1944) by Ralph Barton Perry.

THE VEDANTA PRESS OF CALIFORNIA: *The Upanishad* (1947), trans. Swami Prabhavananda and Frederick Manchester.

THE VIKING PRESS, INC.: *Two Roads to Truth* (copyright 1953 by Edmund W. Sinnott) and *Biology of the Spirit* (copyright © 1955 by Edmund W. Sinnott) by Edmund W. Sinnott; *The Portable Renaissance Reader* (copyright 1953 by the Viking Press, Inc.).

WAY MAGAZINE: from issues of August, September, 1961; October, 1962; January–February, May, June, 1963.

ACKNOWLEDGMENTS

THE WESTMINSTER PRESS: *The Divine Imperative* (1937) by Emil Brunner; *Cyril of Jerusalem and Nemesius of Emesa*, Vol. IV, LCC (1955), ed. William Telfer; *Luther: Letters of Spiritual Counsel* (1955), ed. T. G. Tappert; *Calvin: Institutes of the Christian Religion* (copyright © 1960 by W. L. Jenkins), ed. John T. McNeill, trans. Ford Lewis Battles; *Advocates of Reform* (1953), ed. Matthew Spinka; *Meditations of Kierkegaard* (copyright 1955 by W. L. Jenkins), ed. T. H. Croxall; *Honest to God* (copyright © 1963 by SCM Press Ltd.) by John A. T. Robinson; *Promise of Science and Power of Faith* (copyright © 1958 by W. L. Jenkins) by M. Holmes Hartshorne.

WORLD PUBLISHING COMPANY: *Nuclear Policy for War and Peace* (1960) by Thomas E. Murray.

YALE UNIVERSITY PRESS: *A Common Faith* (1934) by John Dewey; *The Freedom of Man* (1935) by Arthur Compton; *The Meaning of God in Human Experience* (1912) by William E. Hocking; *Belief Unbound* (1930) by W. P. Montagu.

PREFACE

Some years ago I had occasional need for religious quotations on various subjects. The standard reference sources usually failed to supply what I sought. When I found there was no one volume offering a wide range of religious quotations on both timeless questions and contemporary problems, I began to gather and hoard religious quotations for my immediate purposes.

When I no longer had a need for this kind of quotations I nevertheless continued to gather more of them. It was a challenging and interesting diversion, which after several years became a resolution to devote full time to compiling and editing the kind of book this is.

The guidelines then established to accomplish this goal will help the reader to a fuller understanding of this volume's purpose, scope and usefulness. The intent has been to gather from every available source—ancient and modern—meaningful, interesting, provocative and significant quotations of a spiritual and religious nature on any subject of relevance to life today, as well as on the great questions which have always perplexed, troubled and challenged man through the ages.

The first rule was that the book be *nondenominational,* and yet, paradoxically, to be made so by including quotations from every sectarian whose words were judged worthy of admission. And, of course, it was also necessary to include hundreds of memorable passages from philosophers, scientists and writers of no specific religious persuasion, and a lesser number of important statements by acknowledged agnostics and atheists.

Another determination was that, while the volume should have a great diversity of beliefs, opinions and points of view, it should exclude invective, keep polemics to the irreducible minimum, and give as little space as possible to the apologetic and didactic. If these rules have in a few instances been breached, I am nevertheless confident that the volume is happily free of the old-time free-wheeling religious controversies that produced little more than mutual hatred. There is here a rich abundance of conflicting beliefs and opinions. But there are no abusive attacks upon one religion by spokesmen of another religion.

The book contains only two quotations from the New Testament, and none from the Old Testament, except where several authors quote a few words from the Bible. Moreover, there are only a few passages of an exegetical nature. Because of the many books of Biblical quotations and of Biblical commentary it would be superfluous to include such material in this book, particularly since it would result in the exclusion of an equal number of significant but less available quotations on a host of other subjects of a religious nature.

On the other hand, the volume does contain numerous quotations from the sacred writings of Buddhism, Hinduism, Taoism, Confucianism, Islam, Zoroastrianism, and other less familiar sects, as well as from the Talmud and similar books of Jewish commentary. These inclusions are justified by the fact that they are less well known and less available than their Christian counterparts.

Incidentally, it is inevitable that this volume should have a predominantly Christian

emphasis; Christianity is a fundament of western civilization, and my research consequently produced a much greater abundance of Christian quotations. I have, however,
striven for objectivity, although I am aware that a compiler's constant judging and
choosing continually threatens, and no doubt sometimes defeats, strict impartiality.

It was decided that no poetry would be in the book, since there are numerous compila-
tions of religious verse. But of course the rule was flouted on a few appropriate occasions.

An effort has been made to date every quotation. Whenever possible, the earliest date
of a quotation is given. In instances where the exact date is unobtainable, the approximate date is given. When the approximate date was not determined, the author's birth
and death dates are shown. And when even an author's dates are not known, the century
or an approximation of the century is given.

The quotations are presented under some 1500 subject-headings. Complete cross-
references at the end of each subject-heading make it possible for the reader to explore
related aspects of a subject without having to consult cumbersome indexes. The Index of
Authors at the end of the book supplies whatever further guidance one may seek.

It will be noticed that the quotations are arranged chronologically under the subject-
headings. In addition to being a logical method of presentation, this has the added value
of often showing the development of an idea or the evolution of a concept over a long
period of time. Less often it may indicate the rigidity of thinking on a particular question.

It would be an inexcusable dereliction if I failed to make generous acknowledgment
of the assistance of my wife, Lillias Watt Woods, who devoted uncounted hours to the
organization of masses of material and data, and who helped with the formidable task
of cross-referencing and indexing. I am deeply grateful to Norman White, who selflessly
came to my rescue at a critical juncture during the final preparation of the manuscript.
Mary W. Lightfoot did a good deal of expert typing. And it was the Reverend Edward S.
Cooke whose genial prodding encouraged me to follow through on my original idea.

After this book was *apparently* completed, it was showered with additional riches and
given a greater measure of authority when the manuscript was placed in the hands of
Charles S. Braden, Professor Emeritus, History and Literatures of Religions, North-
western University, and author of not a few books in the field, for his critical inspection
and commentary. Professor Braden, presently Resident Scholar at Perkins School of
Theology, Southern Methodist University, Dallas, Texas, paid the work the generous
compliment of devoting many extra weeks of work to supply literally hundreds of quotations from scholarly sources on subjects he correctly judged lacked their rightful share
of quotable passages of significance and appeal. Moreover, Professor Braden's acute
comments sent me scurrying back to numerous volumes for additional passages to fill in
still other lacunae in the manuscript. He was especially interested in seeing to it that the
volume gave more attention to passages from the riches of Oriental religions, past and
present, although his contributions were by no means limited to these sources.

In acknowledging with pleasure and gratitude Professor Braden's generous and scholarly dedication to making this a better book, I should emphasize that whatever shortcomings might still remain are mine.

Naturally I look forward—though again with some trepidation—to the response this
volume evokes. Perhaps I shall be chided for this omission or that commission. But if
the consensus should be that this is a unique and useful collection, then I shall rest
content that my work has been to a good purpose, and that the volume will not only
fascinate and challenge many readers, but will find a more or less permanent place
among the valuable reference books.

Ralph L. Woods

How about war? - It is murder to order young men to go out to kill innocent lives + get killed themselves

other young strange soldier

ABANDONMENT

We require great confidence to abandon ourselves, without any reserve, to Divine Providence; but when we do abandon all, Our Lord takes care of all, and disposes of all.

ST. FRANCIS OF SALES (1567–1622), *Consoling Thoughts of,* ed. Huguet

See also Acceptance; Contemplation; Detachment; Man's Unity with God; Mystical Experience; Prayer: Defined and Explained; Providence; Religion: Its Nature and Function; Renunciation; Resignation; Self-Giving; Selflessness; Self-Sacrifice; Spirituality; Submission; Worship.

ABORTION

If the damsel being ashamed of the people shall destroy the fruit in her womb, the sin is on both the father and herself, the murder is on both the father and herself; both the father and herself shall pay the penalty for wilful murder.

Vendidad, 6th century B.C.

A woman convicted of abortion is an infanticide.

FLAVIUS JOSEPHUS, *Against Apion,* c. 93 A.D.

We say that those women who use drugs to bring on abortion commit murder and will have to give an account to God for the abortion.

ATHENAGORAS OF ATHENS, *Apologia,* c. 177 A.D.

Prevention of birth is a precipitation of murder. He also is a man who is about to be one.

TERTULLIAN, *Apologeticus,* 197 A.D.

It is a capital crime to destroy an embryo in the womb.

ISHMAEL, *Talmud: Sanhedrin,* 57b, c. 500 A.D.

Every human being, even a child in the mother's womb, has a right to life *directly* from God and not from the parents or from any human society or authority. Hence there is no man, no human authority, no science, no medical, eugenic, social, economic or moral "indication" that can offer or produce a valid juridical title to a *direct* deliberate disposal of an innocent human life.

ROMAN CATHOLIC CHURCH HOLY OFFICE, *Decree,* December 2, 1940

Innocent human life, in whatever condition it may be, is, from the first instant of its existence, to be preserved from any direct voluntary attack. This is a fundamental right of the human person.

POPE PIUS XII, *Address,* November 27, 1951

The materialist opinion is that the embryo before birth is a portion of the mother—not a moral or personal being, since it lacks freedom, self-determination, rationality, the ability to choose either ends or means, and knowledge of circumstances—which may be excised if it threatens her life.

JOSEPH FLETCHER, *Morals and Medicine,* 1954

The simple fact is that God certainly intended to create a human being and that this nascent human being has been deliberately deprived of his life. And that is nothing but murder.

DIETRICH BONHOEFFER, *Ethics,* 1955

With regard to the killing of the foetus in cases where the mother is in danger of losing her life . . . the life of the mother is in the hands of God, but the life of the child is arbitrarily extinguished. The question whether the life of the mother or the life of the child is of greater value can hardly be a matter for human decision.

DIETRICH BONHOEFFER, *Ethics,* 1955

Induced abortion may now be permitted in Norway in cases "where it is necessary in

abortion

They is why they are against abortion

I

The rich Command!— The church as with them! The poor are sent out to kill order to protect the life and health of the woman against serious dangers. In evaluating such danger any special disposition of the woman with regard to physical or psychical diseases should be considered as well as her living conditions and other circumstances likely to make her ill or contribute to give her a physical or psychical breakdown." Reported in *Christianity and Crisis*, March 6, 1961

See also Birth Control; Fetus: Death of through Surgery; Killing; Mother and Child, Life of; Pregnancy, Termination of; Sterilization.

ABSOLUTE, THE

The intelligence of each soul capable of receiving the soul's inheritance is enraptured at beholding the Absolute, is fulfilled and rejoices.
PLATO, *Phaedrus*, c. 370 B.C.

In religion God always tends to pass beyond himself. He is necessarily led to end in the Absolute, which for religion is not God.
F. H. BRADLEY, *Appearance and Reality*, 1897

Short of the Absolute, God cannot rest, and, having reached that goal, he is lost and religion with him.
F. H. BRADLEY, *Appearance and Reality*, 1897

In order to approach the Absolute, mystics must withdraw from everything, even themselves.
E. RECÉJAC, *Essay on the Basis of the Mystical Knowledge*, 1899

We long for the Absolute only in so far as in us the Absolute also longs, and seeks, through our very temporal striving, the peace that is nowhere in Time, but only, and yet Absolutely, in Eternity.
JOSIAH ROYCE, *The World and the Individual*, Vol. 2, 1900

Knowledge, science, and power have been our gods and they were clothed with a glory of the infinite and absolute. Today it begins to be revealed just how far we can really reach. *We cannot reach the absolute.*
C. F. VON WEIZSÄCKER, *Theologie und Physik*, 1951

See also Fact; the various rubrics under God; Liberalism and Religion; Reality.

ABSOLUTES

The old view that the principles of right and wrong are immutable and eternal is no longer tenable. The moral world is as little exempt as the physical world from the law of ceaseless change, of perpetual flux.
JAMES FRAZER, *The Golden Bough*, Vol. 11, p. vi, 1915

The first lesson of pragmatism: damn the absolute!
HENRY STEELE COMMAGER, *Freedom, Loyalty, Dissent*, 1954

He [H. S. Commager] refers to what he calls "the first lesson of pragmatism: damn the absolute!" . . . The philosophy that damns the absolute is thus strangely revealed as the absolute philosophy.
J. V. L. CASSERLEY, *The Bent World*, 1955

I am not sure whether what the philosophers call ethical absolutes exist, but I am sure that we have to act as if they existed. Ethics must be freed from its utilitarian chains.
ARTHUR KOESTLER, *The Trail of the Dinosaur and Other Essays*, 1955

Gone are the ultimates, absolutes, and finalities of the earlier ages. The steely rigidities of eternal truth are replaced by a view of reality as plastic, and therefore capable of being molded by good will and intelligence to the purposes of man.
A. EUSTACE HAYDON, *This Is My Faith*, ed. S. G. Cole, 1956

See also Agnosticism; Certainty; Ethics; Evil: Its Nature; Expediency; Humanism; Pragmatism; Relativity; Right; Right and Wrong; Sin; Skepticism; Truth; Values; Values, Spiritual.

ABSOLUTISM

Religion, like every other form of absolutism, should be above justification.
HEINRICH HEINE, *Germany from Luther to Kant,* 1834

ABSTINENCE

We regard voluntary total abstinence from all intoxicants as the obligation of the citizen, and the complete legal prohibition of the traffic in alcoholic drinks as the duty of civil government.
The Doctrines and Discipline of the Methodist Episcopal Church, 1832

Abstinence from spiritous liquors is the best safeguard of morals and health.
ROBERT E. LEE, *Letter to S. G. M. Miller,* December 9, 1869

Given the tremendous abuses of alcohol which are widespread in the United States, total abstinence is a peculiarly fitting and appropriate method of self-denial and self-discipline.
JOHN C. FORD, *Sanctity and Success in Marriage,* 1956

See also Alcohol; Discipline; Drunkenness; Moderation; Self-Denial; Sobriety; Temperance; Wine.

ACADEMIC FREEDOM

Anyone in a cap and gown can blast the presuppositions of life, can rob our sons and daughters of all the principles on which civilization depends—but let him as much as whisper "academic freedom, I've got my fingers crossed," and no profes-

sional educator dares to say a word of criticism.
ROBERT I. GANNON, *After Black Coffee,* 1946

Academic freedom means the right, long accepted in the academic world, to study, discuss, and write about facts and ideas without restrictions, other than those imposed by conscience and morality.
Report, Yale University, Advisory Committee's survey of "The Intellectual and Spiritual Welfare of the University, Its Students and Its Faculty, *New York Times,* February 18, 1952

See also Education; Freedom.

ACCEPTANCE

There is no estate of life in this world as to yield a Christian the perfection of content: and yet there is no state of life so wretched in this world, but a Christian must be content with it.
ARTHUR WARWICK, *Spare Minutes,* 1637

See also Abandonment; Adversity; Cross; Fatalism; Obedience; Patience; Resignation; Serenity; Submission; Suffering.

ACCIDENTAL, THE

Nothing in life is accidental. He who believes in accident does not believe in God.
ALEXANDER YELCHANINOV (1881–1934), *Fragments of a Diary*

ACHIEVEMENT

All attainment is immortal in that it fashions the actual ideals which are God in the world as it is now. Every act leaves the world with a deeper or a fainter impress of God.
ALFRED NORTH WHITEHEAD, *Religion in the Making,* 1927

3

See also Action; Acts; Ambition; Aspiration; Temporal.

ACTION

Action is far inferior to the devotion of the mind. In that devotion seek shelter.
Bhagavad-Gita, c. 5th century B.C.

Let not the fruit of action be your motive to action. Your business is with action alone, not with the fruit of action.
Bhagavad-Gita, c. 5th century B.C.

Perform all necessary acts, for action is better than inaction; none can live by sitting still and doing nought; it is by action only that a man attains immunity from action.
Bhagavad-Gita, c. 5th century B.C.

The most excellent of all actions is to befriend any one on God's account, and to be at enmity with whosoever is the enemy of God.
MOHAMMED, *Speeches and Table-Talk of,* 7th century A.D.

God, who, as first being, is the cause of all being, as first mover must be the cause of all action so that He produces in us the action itself, just as He placed in us the power to act. And the created action does not cease to be an action because it was produced by God.
J. B. BOSSUET (1627–1704), *Treatise on Free Will*

We were made for action, and for right action—for thought, and for true thought. Let us live while we live, let us be alive and doing; let us act on what we have, since we have not what we wish. Let us believe what we do not see and know. Let us forestall knowledge by faith.
JOHN HENRY NEWMAN, *Essays and Sketches,* Vol. 1, 1838

Action and not knowledge is man's destiny and duty in this life; and his highest principles, both in philosophy and in religion, have reference to this end.
DEAN MANSEL, *The Limits of Religious Thought,* 1859

When the measure of iniquity is full, and it seems that another day might bring repentance and redemption,—"Put ye in the sickle, for the harvest is ripe." (Joel 3:13) When the young life has been wasted all away, and the eyes are just opening upon the tracks of ruin, and the faint resolution rising in the heart for nobler things—"Put ye in the sickle."
JOHN RUSKIN, *Modern Painters,* V, 1860

The greatest of all the mysteries of life, and the most terrible, is the corruption of even the sincerest religion, which is not daily founded on rational, effective, humble, and helpful action.
JOHN RUSKIN, *Sesame and Lilies,* 1865

Every man feels instinctively that all the beautiful sentiments in the world weigh less than a single lovely action.
JAMES RUSSELL LOWELL, *Rousseau and the Sentimentalists,* 1870

Action is the normal completion of the act of will which begins as prayer. That action is not always external, but it is always some kind of effective energy.
W. R. INGE, *Speculum Animae,* 1911

Through faith man experiences the meaning of the world; through action he is to give to it a meaning.
LEO BAECK, *Essence of Judaism,* 1922

Men, who are driven by their nature as living creatures to act, are also compelled by their nature as free spirits to relate their actions to, and bring them into conformity with, some total scheme of meaning.
REINHOLD NIEBUHR, *Religion and the Modern World,* 1941

Because collective action is the only effective action, it is the only virtuous action.
J. D. BERNAL, *Modern Quarterly,* 1947

Man's action is enclosed in God's action, but it is still real action.

MARTIN BUBER, *Hasidism*, 1948

Pray to God, but row for the shore.

Russian Proverb

See also Achievement; Action and Prayer; Actions, Actions and Convictions; Acts; Apathy; Duty; Free Will; Idleness; Inaction; Social Action; Will.

ACTION AND PRAYER

If there is anything we do and we cannot rehearse it in prayer, then it is something that should not be done.

VINCENT MCNABB, *The Craft of Prayer*, 1951

See also Action; Acts; Prayer.

ACTIONS

Activity is better than inertia. Act, but with self-control. . . . The world is imprisoned in its own activity, except when actions are performed as worship of God.

Bhagavad-Gita, 5th century B.C.

Whatsoever thou dost affect, whatsoever thou dost reject, so do, and so project all, as one who, for aught thou knowest, may at this very present depart out of this life.

MARCUS AURELIUS, *Meditations*, c. 170 A.D.

It is in our power to stretch out our arms and, by doing good in our actions, to seize life and set it in our soul. This life of which Christ said, "I am the Life."

ORIGEN, *On the Soul*, c. 240 A.D.

It is not those who commit the least faults who are the most holy, but those who have the greatest courage, the greatest generosity, the greatest love, who make the boldest efforts to overcome themselves,

and are not immoderately apprehensive of tripping.

ST. FRANCIS OF SALES (1567–1622), *Consoling Thoughts of*, ed. Huguet

We have left undone those things which we ought to have done; and we have done those things which we ought not to have done.

The Book of Common Prayer, 1662

Actions are right in proportion as they tend to promote happiness; wrong as they tend to produce the reverse of happiness. By happiness is intended pleasure.

J. S. MILL, *Utilitarianism*, 1863

If . . . there be a nobler life in us than in the strangely moving atoms . . . it must be shown, by each of us in his appointed place, not merely in the patience, but in the activity of our hope . . . our labor.

JOHN RUSKIN, *The Ethics of the Dust*, 1866

Religion is full of difficulties, but if we are often puzzled what to think, we need seldom be in doubt what to do.

JOHN LUBBOCK, *Pleasures of Life*, 1887

All our external religious activities—services, communions, formal devotions, good works—these are either the expressions or the support of the inward life of loving adherence.

EVELYN UNDERHILL, *Concerning the Inner Life*, 1926

The question "Are we doing well?" is unrealistic; there are no measures. The test is: "Are we doing right?" For that, there is a measure—what Christ has told us to do.

FRANK J. SHEED, *Sheed and Ward Trumpet*, Spring, 1964

Whether a person be Jew or Gentile . . . according to his acts does the Divine Spirit rest upon him.

Proverb

See also Achievement; Acts; Deeds; Determinism; Duties; Election; Prayer: Defined and Explained.

ACTIONS AND CONVICTIONS

The relation is very close between our capacity to act at all and our conviction that the action we are taking is right. This does not mean, of course, that the action *is* necessarily right. What is necessary to continuous action is that it shall be *believed* to be right.

> WALTER LIPPMANN, *The Public Philosophy,* 1954

See also Commitment; Conviction; Duties.

ACTIVE LIFE

When theologians speak of the active life as contrasted with that of contemplation, . . . what they call active life is the life of good works.

> ALDOUS HUXLEY, *Grey Eminence,* 1941

See also Life; Work; Works.

ACTORS

Concerning the charioteers who belong to the faithful, we have decreed that, as long as they continue to drive, they be debarred from communion. Concerning the strolling players, we have decreed that, as long as they act, they be debarred from communion.

> *Decisions of the Council of Arles,* 314 A.D.

Besides legal proscriptions . . . the actor is also bound by strictly moral obligations flowing from divine and ecclesiastical laws. . . . If the performance is indecent by reason of place, dress, action or speech, no Catholic can take part, for to do so would make him a material cooperator.

> *The Maryknoll Catholic Dictionary,* 1965

ACTS

Mencius said: Men must be decided on what they will not do, and then they are able to act with vigor in what they ought to do.

> MENCIUS, *Works of* (371–288 B.C.)

Thou wilt find rest from vain fancies if thou dost every act in life as though it were thy last.

> MARCUS AURELIUS, *Mediations of,* c. 170 A.D.

An action, to have moral worth, must be done from duty.

> IMMANUEL KANT, *Metaphysics of Morals,* 1785

An action done from duty must wholly exclude the influence of inclination, and with it every object of the will.

> IMMANUEL KANT, *Metaphysics of Morals,* 1785

But how can it be *known* that you are in earnest
If the act follows not upon the word?

> J. C. F. VON SCHILLER, *The Piccolomini,* 1799

A human act once set in motion flows on for ever to the great account.

> GEORGE MEREDITH, *Rhoda Fleming,* 1865

No human act can be wholly spiritual. We ascend by a law of our nature, from the visible to the invisible, from the sensible to the supersensible.

> JOHN LANCASTER SPALDING, *Essays and Reviews,* 1877

A charitable act, an impulse of real pity sings for him the divine praises.

> LEON BLOY, *Pilgrim of the Absolute, Selected Writings of,* 1909

Every moral act of love, of mercy, and of sacrifice brings to pass the end of the world where hatred, cruelty and selfishness reign supreme.

NICHOLAS BERDYAEV, *Dream and Reality,* 1939

If our conscience tells us that we ought to perform a particular act, it is our moral duty to perform it.

FREDERICK COPLESTON, *Aquinas,* 1955

An act of faith is an act of a finite being who is grasped by and turned to the infinite.

PAUL TILLICH, *Dynamics of Faith,* 1957

See also Achievement; Action; Actions; Deeds; Duty; Free Will; Inaction; Practice; Will.

ACTS OF THE APOSTLES.
See NEW TESTAMENT

ACTUALITY

On watching our thoughts we see how impossible it is to get rid of the consciousness of an Actuality lying behind Appearances, and how from this impossibility results our indestructible belief in that Actuality.

HERBERT SPENCER, *First Principles,* 1862

See also the various rubrics under God, Reality.

ADAM

Adam himself is now spread out over the whole face of the earth. Originally one, he has fallen, and, breaking up as it were, he has filled the whole earth with the pieces.

ST. AUGUSTINE, *In Psalm* 95 c. 415 A.D.

When he had created the entire world as a fully-formed body without a soul so that it was like an unpolished mirror, and since it is a rule of the Divine Activity to prepare no locus which does not receive a Divine

spirit . . . Adam became the polish of that mirror, and the spirit of that body.

MUHYĪ AL-DĪN IBN AL-'ARABĪ (died 1240 A.D.), *Fusūs al-Hikam*

The only reason why sin is found in the sons of Adam is this, it is because Adam of earthly flesh and blood cannot bring forth a holy Angel out of himself, but must beget children of the same nature and condition with himself. . . . All the laborious volumes on God's imputing Adam's sin to his posterity ought to be considered as waste paper.

WILLIAM LAW, *The Spirit of Prayer,* 1749

Surely no man is bound to admit that Adam's body was created in the proper sense of the word. In our rigid interpretation of Genesis, we are accustomed to refer to it as having been formed from the earth. The only part of man that is immediately created is the human soul.

P. H. KEHOE, *The Church and Evolution,* 1937

Adam sinned when he fell from Contemplation. Since then, there has been division in man.

JACQUES MARITAIN, *Art and Scholasticism,* 1946

Adam ate the apple, and our teeth still ache.

Hungarian Proverb

See also Creation; Evolution; Fall, the; Genesis; Man; Man: His Self-Deification; Original Sin; Science and Creation.

ADOLESCENCE

Of all the curable illnesses that afflict mankind, the hardest to cure, and the one most likely to leave its victim a chronic invalid, is adolescence.

BONARO W. OVERSTREET, *Understanding Fear,* 1951

See also Youth.

ADORATION

The simple adoration of a God has preceded all the systems in the world.
> VOLTAIRE, *Philosophical Dictionary,* II, 1764

As religion consists in the recognition of God as our Creator and the end of all creatures, so its immediate and formal expression is adoration.
> F. HETTINGER, *Natural Religion,* 1898

Adoration is the use of intellect, feeling, will and imagination in making acts of devotion directed towards God in his personal aspect or as incarnated in human form.
> ALDOUS HUXLEY, *The Perennial Philosophy,* 1944

Adoration is the surge of the spirit of man upward and Godward.
> GEORGIA HARKNESS, *Prayer and the Common Life,* 1948

Adoration means that you put yourself in the attitude of him who is nothing before Him who is everything. It means total submission, even *annihilation* before the object of your adoration.
> JACQUES LECLERCQ, *Back to Jesus,* 1959

See also Blessed Sacrament; Church: Its work; Contemplation; Mystic; Praise; Prayer; Research; Worship.

ADULTERY

Four things does a reckless man gain who covets his neighbor's wife—a bad reputation, an uncomfortable bed, thirdly punishment, and lastly hell.
> *Dhammapada,* c. 5th century B.C.

For by adultery is caused a mixture of the castes among men, thence follows sin, which cuts up even the roots and causes the destruction of everything.
> *Laws of Manu,* c. 500 B.C.

Men who commit adultry with the wives of others, the king shall cause to be marked by punishments which cause terror and afterwards banish.
> *Laws of Manu,* c. 500 B.C.

God has bidden us to refrain not only from other men's wives, but also from the common women of the town; when two bodies are joined together, He says, they are made into one. So the man who plunges into filth must of necessity with filthiness be stained.
> LACTANTIUS, *Divine Institutes,* c. 310

A man is guilty of adultery if he marries a divorced woman; and so is he who divorces his wife, save on the ground of misconduct, in order to marry again.
> LACTANTIUS, *Divine Institutes,* c. 310

It is wrong to leave a wife who is sterile in order to take another by whom children may be had. Anyone doing this is guilty of adultery.
> ST. AUGUSTINE, *Conjugal Adultery,* c. 400

If a man leaves his wife and she marries another, she commits adultery.
> ST. AUGUSTINE, *On the Good of Marriage,* c. 401

There is nothing which Allah abhors more than adultery. The eye and the tongue can commit adultery.
> *Koran,* c. 625

I should not regard physical infidelity as a very grave cause and should teach people that it is to be expected and tolerated.
> BERTRAND RUSSELL, *Letter to Judge B. J. Lindsey,* quoted in latter's *The Companionate Marriage,* 1927

Society, when it rules "thumbs down" on extramarital relations, is guarding itself against destruction.
> MARIO A. CASTALLO, *Reader's Digest,* June, 1948

Adultery is indeed the form that love will assume as long as the institution of marriage lasts.

SIMONE DE BEAUVOIR, *The Second Sex,* 1949

See also Artificial Insemination; Divorce; Fornication; Infidelity; Lust; Marriage; Sexual Ethics; Sexual Intercourse; Sexual Sin.

ADVERSITY

The misfortune of evil does not kill you but instructs you; human tribulation teaches you, it does not destroy you. The more we are afflicted in this world, the greater is our assurance for the next; the more we sorrow in the present, the greater will be our joy in the future.

ST. ISIDORE OF SEVILLE (560–636), *Dialogue Between Erring Soul and Reason*

All the assaults of dark and evil fortune contribute to the salvation of those who receive them with thankfulness and are assuredly ambassadors of help.

ST. JOHN DAMASCENE (700?–754?), *Exposition of the Orthodox Faith*

Thought shall be the harder, heart the keener, courage the greater, as our strength fails.

Battle of Maldon, 10th century England

Why art thou troubled, that all things come not to thee as thou willest or desirest? who is he that hath all things at his own will? . . . There is no man in this world without some manner of tribulation or anguish, though he be king or pope.

THOMAS À KEMPIS, *Imitation of Christ,* 1441

How should thy patience be crowned in heaven if none adversity should befall to thee in earth? If thou wilt suffer none adversity how mayest thou be the friend of Christ?

THOMAS À KEMPIS, *Imitation of Christ,* 1441

Death, afflictions, labors, which, by the just ordinances of God, are the punishments of sin, are also, by His sweet mercy, so many ladders to ascend to heaven, so many means to increase in grace, so many merits to obtain glory.

ST. FRANCIS OF SALES (1567–1622), *Consoling Thoughts of,* ed. Huguet

Every one knows how to be resigned amid the joys and happiness of prosperity, but to be so amid storms and tempests is peculiar to the children of God.

ST. FRANCIS OF SALES (1567–1622), *Consoling Thoughts of,* ed. Huguet

Adversity in the things of this world opens the door for spiritual salvation.

A. J. TOYNBEE, *New York Times Magazine,* December 26, 1954

See also Acceptance; Affliction; Calamity; Misery; Misfortune; Pain; Poor, the; Poverty; Prosperity; Sickness; Sorrow; Suffering; Tribulations; Troubles.

ADVERTISING

Advertising is the organized effort to extend and intensify craving—to extend and intensify . . . the working of that force which is the principal cause of suffering and wrong-doing and the greatest obstacle between the human soul and its divine Ground.

ALDOUS HUXLEY, *The Perennial Philosophy,* 1945

Millions of dollars are spent annually to entice people to dedicate themselves to the "cult of things," nice things which are phony, valueless, glamorous, sinful . . . all of which are capable of stimulating the passions, beclouding the power of value-judgment.

ROLAN SIMONITSCH, *Sanctity and Success in Marriage,* 1956

See also Desires; Worldliness.

AFFECTIONS

Although to true religion there must indeed be something else beside affections; yet true religion consists so much in the affections, that there can be no true religion without them. He who has no religious affection is in a state of spiritual death.

JONATHAN EDWARDS, *Religious Affections,* 1818

The moment we exercise our affections, the earth is metamorphosed; there is no winter, and no night; all tragedies, all ennuis vanish;—all furies even.

RALPH WALDO EMERSON, "Friendship," *Essays,* 1844

See also Agape; Brotherhood; Love, Human.

AFFIRMATION

In the profoundest form of world-and-life affirmation, in which man lives his life on the loftiest spiritual and ethical plane, he attains to inner freedom from the world and becomes capable of sacrificing his life for some end.

ALBERT SCHWEITZER, *Indian Thoughts,* 1936

See also Belief; Commitment; Faith.

AFFLICTION

Affliction is a *treasure,* and scarce any man hath *enough* of it. No man hath *affliction* enough that is not matured and ripened by it, and made fit for God by that *affliction.*

JOHN DONNE (1573–1631), *Devotions,* XVIII

Times of great affliction are ordinarily times of great temptations, and it is usual with Satan then to charge us with more sins than we are really guilty of.

JOHN FLAVEL, *A Token for Mourners,* 1674

We cannot be guilty of a greater act of uncharitableness, than to interpret the afflictions which befall our neighbors, as *punishment* and *judgments.*

JOSEPH ADDISON, *The Spectator,* 1714

How naturally does affliction make us Christians!

WILLIAM COWPER, *Letter to Lady Hesketh,* July 4, 1765

Affliction is able to drown out every earthly voice . . . but the voice of eternity within a man it cannot drown.

SÖREN KIERKEGAARD, *Christian Discourses,* 1847

See also Adversity; Anxiety; Bereavement; Cross; Grief; Misery; Misfortune; Pain; Peace of Mind; Poverty; Religion: Its Nature and Function; Sadness; Sickness; Sorrow; Suffering; Tribulations; Troubles.

AGAPE

The whole point of the primitive Christian idea of Agape is that it is sinners God loves—that is, those who in disobedience and rebellion have turned away from him.

ANDERS NYGREN, *Agape and Eros,* 1930

The Greek New Testament word for this overflowing divine love is *agape* . . . God's own love spontaneously to all creatures, not by reason of their worth or merit, not moved by any gain for himself, not caused by any external force or value, but coming freely from his boundless generosity.

PAUL E. JOHNSON, *Christian Love,* 1951

Agape translated in the New Testament variously as charity (and as love) comes to us as a quite new creation of Christianity. . . . Without it nothing that is Christian would be Christian. Agape is Christianity's own original basic conception.

ANDERS NYGREN, *Agape and Eros,* 1953

The Christian idea of love, called *agape*, I interpret as a kind of affectionate, perceptive concern for other people.

CHARLES P. TAFT, *Ladies' Home Journal*, December, 1961

Divine *agape* or "charity" provides the supreme and controlling determination of what the Christian should do, or of what he thinks in ethics.

PAUL RAMSEY, *Nine Modern Moralists*, 1962

See also Affections; Brotherhood; Charity; Christian Life; Love, Human; Neighbor.

AGE

The heart of the old is always young in two things, in love for the world and length of hope.

MOHAMMED, *Speeches and Table-Talk of*, 7th century A.D.

Age is not all decay; it is the ripening, the swelling, of the fresh life within, that withers and bursts the husks.

GEORGE MACDONALD, *The Marquess of Lossie*, 1877

See also Old Age.

AGES

All ages of belief have been great; all of unbelief have been mean.

RALPH WALDO EMERSON, *North American Review*, May, 1878

AGGRESSION

The evil projected by the aggressor into the souls of those he aims to destroy or oppress comes back upon him and kills him.

GUSTAVE THIBON, *War and Love*, 1946

The challenge of aggressive evil can be met only by the power of aggressive good.

SWAMI NIKHILANANDER, *Perspectives on a Troubled Decade*, ed. Bryson, Finklestein, and MacIver, 1950

The only way that we can solve the problem of aggression is the way that Jesus advocated: "Father, forgive them for they know not what they do." Again it was said by Buddha: "If one man conquer in battle a thousand times thousand men, and if another conquer himself, he is the greatest of conquerors."

SWAMI AKHILANANDA, *Mental Health and Hindu Psychology*, 1951

See also Armaments; Atomic Bomb; Force; Nuclear War; Self-Defense; War, Condemnation of; War, Defense of; War, Just.

AGNOSTICISM

It is wrong for a man to say that he is certain of the objective truth of any proposition unless he can produce evidence which logically justifies that certainty. This is what Agnosticism asserts.

T. H. HUXLEY, *Essays Upon Controversial Questions*, 1889

Agnosticism should have its ritual no less than faith. It has sown its martyrs, it should reap its saints, and praise God daily for having hidden Himself from man.

OSCAR WILDE, *De Profundis*, 1896

We, too, have our religion, and it is this: Help for the living, hope for the dead.

ROBERT G. INGERSOLL (1833–1899), *Address at a Child's Grave*

The mistake of agnosticism, it seems to me, has been that it has said not merely, "I do not know," but "I will not consider."

G. LOWES DICKINSON, *Religion*, 1905

Agnosticism is the everlasting perhaps.

FRANCIS THOMPSON, *Paganism Old and New*, 1910

I do not pretend to know where many ignorant men are sure—that is all that agnosticism means.

CLARENCE DARROW, at Scopes Trial, July 13, 1925

Modern agnosticism is a tragic and shattering state of mind.
> BRONISLAW MALINOWSKI, *Science and Religion: A Symposium*, 1931

We sympathize with almost everything in the agnostic except his pride. He ought not to be proud. To call himself agnostic is to confess his ignorance.
> J. V. MOLDENHAWER, *Religion Today*, ed. A. L. Swift, 1933

A shadow cast by the eclipse of the supernatural. . . . Its meaning departs when the intellectual outlook is directed wholly to the natural world.
> JOHN DEWEY, *A Common Faith*, 1934

Agnosticism denies to the human mind a power of attaining knowledge which it does possess. . . . Agnosticism, as such, is a theory about knowledge and not about religion.
> RICHARD DOWNEY, *Critical and Constructive Essays*, 1934

When they call themselves agnostics they go beyond the humility involved in "We do not know" to the dogmatism involved in "We cannot know." . . . Agnosticism is necessarily a limited creed, since, if it goes beyond a certain stage, it is self-defeating.
> D. E. TRUEBLOOD, *The Logic of Belief*, 1942

Agnosticism is not open-mindedness; it is culpable inaction.
> NELS F. S. FERRÉ, *Faith and Reason*, 1946

Defensible agnosticism is that of the person who admits that he does not know, and is consequently open to learning.
> DAVID E. TRUEBLOOD, *Philosophy of Religion*, 1957

See also Absolutes; Agnostics; Atheism; Belief; Blasphemy; Despair; Doubt; God, Blasphemous Statements about; God, Unorthodox Comments about; Humanism; Knowledge; Man, Modern; Religion; Religion, Caustic Comments about; Religion: Its Decline; Secularism; Skepticism; Social Atheism; Truth; Unbelief.

AGNOSTICS

People who, like myself, confess themselves to be hopelessly ignorant concerning a variety of matters, about which metaphysicians and theologians, both orthodox and heterodox, dogmatize with the utmost confidence.
> HERBERT SPENCER, quoted in *Notes and Queries*, 1863

I belong to the Great Church which holds the world within its starlit aisles; that claims the great and good of every race and clime; that finds with joy the grain of gold in every creed and floods with light and love the germs of good in every soul.
> ROBERT G. INGERSOLL, *North American Review*, 1888

There never was on this earth a body of educated and cultured men so thoroughly agnostic and atheistic as the mass of Confucian scholars.
> ARTHUR H. SMITH, *Chinese Characteristics*, 1892

Our modern demand, "Prove it to me," easily becomes cowardice. That kind of mind sits at home to receive all arguments about God. . . . When the guests have gone it ponders the arguments, and concludes: "I find no convincing proof; I am an agnostic."
> GEORGE A. BUTTRICK, *Prayer*, 1942

We need to be agnostics first and then there is some chance at arriving at a sensible system of belief.
> D. E. TRUEBLOOD, *The Logic of Belief*, 1942

See also Absolutes; Agnosticism; Atheism; Atheists; Belief; Believer; Doubt; Knowledge; Religion; Truth; Unbelief.

AGREEMENT

There is a wider and deeper agreement among all Christians upon the characteristic elements of the Christian faith than either the detached outsider or the violent partisan within has been able to see.
> J. V. MOLDENHAWER, *Religion Today,* ed. A. L. Swift, 1933

See also Ecumenism; Unity.

AGRICULTURE

Those who labor on the earth are the chosen people of God, if ever he had a chosen people, whose breasts he has made his peculiar deposit for substantial and genuine virtue. It is the focus in which he keeps alive that sacred fire, which otherwise might escape from the face of the earth.
> THOMAS JEFFERSON (1743–1826), *Works,* Washington ed. VIII, 405

AIM

We only lose our way when we lose our own aim.
> FRANÇOIS FÉNELON (1651–1715), *Spiritual Letters*

ALCOHOL

When Heaven sends down its terrors, and our people are thereby greatly disorganized and lose their virtue, this may be traced invariably to their indulgence in spirits; yea the ruin of states small and great [by these terrors] has been caused invariably by their guilt in the use of spirits.
> KING WAU, *The Shu-Ching, Book* X, 6th century B.C.

The man who is master of himself drinks gravely and wisely.
> CONFUCIUS, *The Book of Poetry,* c. 500 B.C.

Everything which inebriates is an intoxicant and every intoxicant is unlawful. Even a little of that which when taken in quantity produces intoxication is unlawful.
> *Miskat-u Masabih,* "Hadith," c. 7th century A.D.

That I call immoderation that is beside or beyond that order of good things for which God hath given us the use of drink.
> JEREMY TAYLOR, *The Rule and Exercises of Holy Living,* 1650

Neither may we gain by hurting our neighbor in his body. We may not sell anything which tends to impair health; such is evidently all that liquid fire, commonly called drams or spirituous liquors.
> JOHN WESLEY (1703–1791), *Sermon* on "The Use of Money," quoted in *Methodism,* ed. W. K. Anderson, 1947

The blacksmith did ignorantly conduct this burglar into his family's heart. It was the Bottle Conjuror. Upon the opening of that fatal cork, forth flew the fiend, and shriveled up his home.
> HERMAN MELVILLE, *Moby Dick,* 1851

The morale that comes out of a bottle is not the morale to put into a battle.
> PETER MARSHALL, quoted by Catherine Marshall in her *A Man Called Peter,* 1951

Our Church reasserts its long-established conviction that intoxicating liquor cannot be legalized without sin. The Church of Jesus Christ from its very nature stands at variance with the liquor traffic.
> *Doctrine and Discipline of the Methodist Church,* 1952

No one can define what moderate drinking is for each individual. It is a delicate, personal decision each one has to make for himself with the light of God's grace.
> JOHN C. FORD, *Sanctity and Success in Marriage,* 1956

It is not permitted to a human being to make himself incapable of acting like a human being. Excessive drinking offends God because it is a mutilation of the mind to a greater or lesser degree.

> JOHN C. FORD, *Sanctity and Success in Marriage,* 1956

The alcohol problem confronts us today with one of the worst evils of our sensate culture. No form of human suffering is more tragic and none involves more people.

> ALBION R. KING, *Christian Century,* March 8, 1961

Morally, and in view of our Lord's first recorded miracle, it is not tenable to maintain, as some do, that alcohol is an evil and its consumption innately wrong.

> J. DOMINIAN, *Psychiatry and the Christian,* 1962

See also Abstinence; Desires; Discipline; Dissipation; Drunkenness; Hedonism; Immorality; Pleasure; Sensuality; Sobriety; Temperance.

ALCOHOLICS

Objectively alcoholics are responsible for their condition. . . . But subjectively it seems to me, not many are morally guilty. . . . Very few foresee addiction. . . . Very few believe they will ever become drunks. They succeed in deceiving themselves.

> JOHN FORD, *Depth Psychology, Morality and Alcoholism,* 1951

There is today much more understanding and concern for alcoholics among abstaining Christians than among the respectable denizens of cocktail bars.

> ALBION R. KING, *Christian Century,* March 8, 1961

We shall live in the All and the All will live in each of us.

> H. G. WELLS, *Anatomy of Frustration,* 1936

See also Absolutes, the various rubrics under God; Man and God; One; Religion Defined; Soul and God; Universe.

ALLAH

Allah! There is no God save Him, the living, the eternal! Neither slumber nor sleep overtaketh Him, unto Him belong whatsoever is in the earth. . . . He knoweth that which is in front of them and that which is behind them. . . . His throne includeth the heavens and the earth, and He is never weary of preserving them. He is the Sublime, the Tremendous.

> *Koran,* ii, c. 625 A.D.

Allah guideth whosoever he pleaseth, by grace, and he leadeth by justice.

> *Akbar,* II, 10th century A.D.

See also The various rubrics under God; Islam.

ALLEGIANCE

If the power of the ruler opposes the divine commandments, and wishes to make me share in its war against God, then with unrestrained voice I answer that God must be preferred before any man on earth. . . . To kill a tyrant is not merely lawful, but right and just.

> JOHN OF SALISBURY, *Polycraticus,* 1159

Our first duties are not to our country. Our first allegiance is not due to its laws. We belong first to God, and next to our race.

> WILLIAM ELLERY CHANNING (1780–1842), *Works*

It is a high crime indeed to withdraw allegiance from God in order to please men.

> POPE LEO XIII, *Sapientiae Christianae,* 1890

Partial allegiance to a perfect god is almost the last thing in futility and dreariness.

Nothing but thoroughness can save us here.

> WILLIAM F. McDOWELL, *This Mind,* 1922

Hebraic religion . . . says *no* to society or the state or the church when any of these dares to exalt itself and call for the worship of total allegiance.

> WILL HERBERG, *Judaism and Modern Man,* 1951

See also Conscience; Government; Patriotism; Rebellion; Rulers; Tyrants.

ALMSGIVING

He who gives alms in secret is greater than Moses.

> *Talmud,* c. 200

If you give alms publicly, it is well; but it is better to give them secretly. Allah knows what you do.

> *Koran,* c. 625

A man's giving in alms one piece of silver in his lifetime is better for him than giving one hundred when he is about to die.

> MOHAMMED (570–632), *Speeches and Table-Talk of,* ed. S. P. Lane

To pray for those who are in mortal sin is the best kind of almsgiving.

> ST. TERESA OF ÁVILA, *The Interior Castle,* 1577

Every almshouse in Massachusetts shows that the churches have not done their duty, that the Christians lie when they call Jesus "master" and men "brothers!"

> THEODORE PARKER, *Sermon,* Boston, 1846

Essentially it is a mere act of justice; it is not anything which has merit in it over and above justice, because justice requires that the strong help the weak, if you are

approaching the matter from the Christian end at all.

> WILLIAM TEMPLE, *The Church Looks Forward,* 1944

See also Beggars; Brotherhood; Charity; Liberality; Mercy; Neighbor; Poor, the; Poverty; Rich, the; Riches; Selfishness.

ALONE

When you have shut your doors and darkened your room, remember never to say that you are alone, for you are not alone, but God is within, and your genius is within.

> EPICTETUS, *Discourses of,* c. 110 A.D.

The flight of the Alone to the Alone.

> PLOTINUS (205–270, A.D.), *Ennead,* vi, 9

It is a dreadful thing, when a man is alone, to feel that he really is alone! That is the most devastating consequence of irreligion.

> HARRY EMERSON FOSDICK, *Radio Address,* January 6, 1946

See also Man and God; Solitary; Solitude.

AMBITION

There is no guilt greater than to sanction ambition.

> *Tao Tê Ching,* between 6th and 3rd century B.C.

A secret poison, the father of livor [spite, malignity], and mother of hypocrisy, the moth of holiness, and cause of madness, crucifying and disquieting all that it takes hold of.

> ST. BERNARD OF CLAIRVAUX (1091–1153), *Epistle* 126

I charge thee, fling away ambition:
By that sin fell the angels.

> WILLIAM SHAKESPEARE, *King Henry VIII,* c. 1611

Ambition tyrannizes over our souls.
>ROBERT BURTON, *Anatomy of Melancholy,* II, 1621

Ambition is a very dangerous thing; without it, in some degree a man would soon grow weary, and with it he is likely to be led away.
>FRANÇOIS FÉNELON (1651–1715), *Spiritual Letters*

Ambition is to the mind what the cap is to the falcon; it blinds us first, and then compels us to tower by reason of our blindness.
>CHARLES CALEB COLTON, *Lacon,* 1822

Ambition, commensurate with the powers which each man can discover in himself, should be frankly recognized as a part of Christian duty.
>LORD CHARNWOOD, *Abraham Lincoln,* 1916

Christianity, in fundamental contrast to Buddhism, recognizes that ambition is of the essence of religion.
>J. H. OLDHAM, *International Review of Missions,* January, 1921

Anyone who has lost his own soul feels that he must gain the whole world.
>HEYWOOD BROUN, *Collected Edition of,* c. 1938

See also Aspiration; Power.

AMERICA

The government of the United States of America is not, in any sense, founded on the Christian religion.
>Attributed to *Treaty between the U.S. and Tripoli,* XI, 1797, authorship ascribed to Joel Barlow, but an Italian translation of the original Arabic does not show the article in question.

There is no country in the world where the Christian religion retains a greater influence over the souls of men than in America.
>ALEXIS DE TOCQUEVILLE, *Democracy in America,* I, 1839

In the United States religion exercises but little influence upon the laws and upon the details of public opinion; but it directs the customs of the community, and, by regulating domestic life, it regulates the state.
>ALEXIS DE TOCQUEVILLE, *Democracy in America,* I, 1839

Religion and conscience have been a constantly active force in the American Commonwealth . . . not indeed strong enough to avert many moral and political evils, yet at the worst times inspiring a minority with a courage and ardor by which moral and political evils have been held at bay and, in the long run, overcome.
>JAMES BRYCE, *The American Commonwealth,* Vol. II, 1888

What America requires is not an American-made, but a God-made religion.
>JOHN IRELAND, *Address,* August 11, 1913

Storms from abroad directly challenge three institutions indispensable to Americans, now as always. The first is religion. . . . Religion, by teaching man his relationship to God, gives the individual a sense of his own dignity and teaches him to respect himself by respecting his neighbors.
>FRANKLIN D. ROOSEVELT, *Address to Congress,* January, 1939

As long as we *all* stand up *together,* God will bless America. For whether God blesses America or not does not depend so much upon God as it does upon us Americans.
>CARL HEATH KOPF, *Windows on Life,* 1941

America, as I found it, may be described as a land where the Common Man is perpetually bidding his fellow to go to hell, and at the same time doing his best to get him into heaven.

L. P. JACKS, *Confession of an Octogenarian,* 1942

When America begins to have saints, her own saints, born on her soil, canonizations at Rome will roll off the assembly line.

R. L. BRUCKBERGER, *One Sky to Share,* 1951

The international responsibilities of our maturing power have become such that the age on whose threshold we now stand must be, for our own salvation, the age of America's soul.

LAURENCE J. MCGINLEY, *Address,* May 25, 1952

The new religiosity pervading America seems to be very largely the religious validation of the social patterns and cultural values associated with the American Way of Life.

WILL HERBERG, *Protestant, Catholic, Jew,* 1955

The place of religion in our society is an exalted one, achieved through a long tradition of reliance on the home, the church and the inviolable citadel of the individual heart and mind. We have come to recognize through bitter experience that it is not within the power of government to invade that citadel, whether its purpose or effect be to aid or oppose, to advance or retard.

JUSTICE TOM C. CLARK, Majority Decision, U. S. Supreme Court, *Prayer and Bible Reading in Public Schools,* June 17, 1963

See also Church and State; Government and Religion; Secularism.

AMERICAN PEOPLE

I do not know how a man can be an American, even if he is not a Christian, and not catch something with regard to God's purpose as to this great land.

PHILLIPS BROOKS, *National Needs and Remedies,* 1890

We are a religious people whose institutions presuppose a supreme being.

U.S. SUPREME COURT, *Zorach v. Clauson,* 343 U.S. 306, 313, 1952

Because we [Americans] are out of the will of God we have lost the will to do right.

BILLY GRAHAM, *Sermon,* New York, May, 1957

I would say that we are "religious people" only in the sense that we are a "reverential" people who have escaped the dogmatic anti-religion which has infected large portions of European society.

WILLIAM CLANCY, *Religion and the Free Society,* 1958

The idea that the American people were once Christian and have subsequently declined is false. . . . America has never been a Christian nation except in the nominal sense. . . . The time of the Founding Fathers was not an age of Christian virtue.

FRANKLIN H. LITTELL, *From State Church to Pluralism,* 1962

A national examination of conscience would reveal today that we are in danger of becoming a people weakened by secularism in our social philosophy, materialism in our concept of the good life, and expediency in our moral code.

ROMAN CATHOLIC BISHOPS OF THE U. S., *Bonds of Union,* November, 1963

See also Church and State; Government and Religion; Secularism.

AMUSEMENTS

I am a great friend to public amusements; for they keep people from vice.

SAMUEL JOHNSON, *Boswell's Life of,* 1772

17

I do not think the glory of God best promoted by a rigid abstinence from amusements.

> JOHN KEBLE (1817), *Letters of Spiritual Counsel and Guidance,* XII, ed. R. F. Wilson, 1881

All amusements become a metaphysical trick to deceive our anguish; amusements disengage that fearful, devouring complex of gears which bind us to God's love and to our neighbor's love.

> JEAN C. DE MENASCE, *The Commonweal Reader,* ed. E. S. Skillin, 1950

See also Desires; Jest; Jesters; Laughter; Pleasure; Worldliness.

ANARCHIST

The anarchist and the Christian have the same ancestry.

> F. W. NIETZSCHE, *The Antichrist,* 1888

ANGELS

We should pray to the angels, for they are given to us as guardians.

> ST. AMBROSE, *On Bereavement,* c. 380

As for angels, seeing there is no compulsion drawing them to sin, and that they are by nature exempt from bodily passions, needs, and pleasures, there is plain reason why they cannot claim pardon by repenting.

> MEMESIUS OF EMESA, *Of the Nature of Man,* c. 395

The angels are the dispensers and administrators of the Divine beneficence toward us; they regard our safety, undertake our defense, direct our ways, and exercise a constant solicitude that no evil befall us.

> JOHN CALVIN, *Institutes,* I, 1536

An angel is a spiritual creature created by God without a body, for the service of Christendom and of the Church.

> MARTIN LUTHER (1483–1546), *Table-Talk*

Therefore for Spirits, I am so far from denying their existence that I could easily believe, that not only whole Countries, but particular persons, have their Tutelary and Guardian Angels.

> THOMAS BROWNE, *Religio Medici,* 1635

Every breath of air and ray of light and heat, every beautiful prospect, is, as it were, the skirts of their garments, the waving of the robes of those whose faces see God.

> JOHN HENRY NEWMAN, *Sermon,* Michaelmas Day, 1831

See also Devil; Guardian Angel; Spirit.

ANGER

He who holds back rising anger like a rolling chariot, him I call a real driver; other people are but holding the reins.

> *Dhammapada,* c. 5th century B.C.

Anger deprives a sage of his wisdom, a prophet of his vision.

> SIMEON, B. LAKISH, *The Talmud: Peshaim,* c. 500 A.D.

Reason opposes evil the more effectively when anger ministers at her side.

> POPE ST. GREGORY THE GREAT, *Morals on the Book of Job,* 584

As long as anger lives, she continues to be the fruitful mother of many unhappy children.

> ST. JOHN CLIMACUS (525–600), *Climax*

It is a universal poison of an infinite object; for no man was ever so amorous as to love a toad, none so envious as to repine at a condition of the miserable, no man so timorous as to fear a dead bee; but anger is troubled at every thing, and every man, and every accident.

> JEREMY TAYLOR, *Holy Living,* 1650

There is a holy anger, excited by zeal, which moves us to reprove with warmth

those whom our mildness failed to correct.
St. Jean Baptiste de la Salle, *Les devoirs du chrétien*, 1703

"Black grace." An influx of extraordinary powers, an almost infinite growth of energy, can be observed in angry men.
Alexander Yelchaninov (1881–1934), *Fragments of a Diary*

God clearly cannot be angry—at least in the crude sense of being in a rage, and losing his temper and throwing things at people—for to suffer such anger is limitation, and God is unlimited.
Christopher Hollis, *The Noble Castle*, 1941

He is a fool who cannot be angry: but he is a wise man who will not.
Proverb

See also Bitterness; Fanaticism; God: His Wrath; Hatred; Passions; Vengeance; Zeal.

ANIMALS

I believe where the love of God is verily perfected, and the true spirit of government watchfully attended to, a tenderness towards all creatures made subject to us will be experienced, and a care felt in us that we do not lessen the sweetness of life in the animal creation.
John Woolman, *Journal*, 1774

See also Creatures; Cruelty; Man.

ANIMISM

Animism, as a theory of belief, assumes a quality of reasoning which transcends the horizon of primitive man.
Morris Jastrow, *The Study of Religion*, 1911

ANNIHILATION

He that hath faith hath wisdom; he that hath wisdom hath peace. He that hath no wisdom and no faith, whose soul is one of doubt, is destroyed.
Mahabharata, c. 800 B.C.

And if He withdrew His efficient power from things, they would have no more being than they had ere they were created: Ere they were, I mean in eternity, not in time.
St. Augustine, *City of God*, XI.25, 426

If God were to reduce something real into nothingness, this would not take place through an operation, but through his ceasing to operate.
St. Thomas Aquinas, *Summa Theologica*, i, 1043 ad. 3, 1272

If man's goal is the grave, Christianity is the greatest imposture the world has known.
Martin J. Scott, *Prove There Is a Soul That Lasts Forever*, 1941

See also Death; God: His Omnipotence; Immortality; Nirvana.

ANONYMITY

To be nameless in worthy deeds exceeds an infamous history. . . . Who had not rather have been the good thief, than Pilate?
Thomas Browne, *Urn Burial*, 1658

See also Oblivion.

ANTHROPOMORPHISM

If oxen and horses had hands, and could paint with their hands, and produce works of art as men do, horses would paint the forms of the gods like horses, and oxen like oxen.
Xenophanes of Colophon (c. 576–480 B.C.), in *Early Greek Philosophy*, by John Burnet, 1892

Anthropomorphism is the road along which the believing mind has traveled from superstition to noble creeds.

> W. R. MATTHEWS, *God in Christian Thought and Experience*, 1930

See also God: Considered as Personal; God: What He Is Not.

ANTICHRIST

At first he will feign mildness and will appear to be a learned and understanding man, with pretended prudence and kindness. . . . And afterwards his character will be written large in evil deeds of inhumanity and lawlessness of every kind, so as to outdo all wicked and godless men that were before him. He will display a murderous, most absolute, pitiless and unstable temper towards all men, but especially towards Christians.

> ST. CYRIL OF JERUSALEM, *Catechetical Lectures*, 350

This is the great Antichrist, which is neither better nor worse nor anything else but the spirit of Satan working against Christ in the strength and subtlety of earthly wisdom.

> WILLIAM LAW (1686–1761), *Selected Mystical Writings of*

Just as a man without sight can be persuaded that night is day and day is night, so can we, who have lost our eyes, be made to believe that Antichrist is not here, that we are not smouldering in the glow of his eyes, that we are not standing in the shadow of his wings.

> JOSEPH ROTH, *The Anti-Christ*, 1935

Anti-Christ is not a *being*, not even a metaphysical entity, except in so far as the principle of negation may be so described.

> EDWIN LEWIS, *A Philosophy of the Christian Revelation*, 1940

A world organization might become the most deadly and impregnable of tyrannies, the final establishment of the reign of anti-Christ.

> *The Era of Atomic Power*, Student Christian Movement Press, London, 1946

The Church is always in danger of becoming Anti-Christ because it is not sufficiently eschatological. It lives too little by faith and hope and too much by the pretensions of its righteousness.

> REINHOLD NIEBUHR, *Faith and History*, 1949

One understands nothing of the traditional notion of Antichrist unless one simultaneously thinks that there is a guilt which happened in primordial times and whose effects are at work upon historical ages, that there is original and hereditary sin.

> JOSEF PIEPER, *The End of Time*, 1954

The Antichrist is to be conceived as a figure exercising political power over the whole of mankind; as a *world ruler*. Once, and as soon as, world dominion in the full sense has become possible, the Antichrist has become possible.

> JOSEF PIEPER, *The End of Time*, 1954

The most powerful embodiment of evil in human history, the Antichrist, might well appear in the guise of a great ascetic.

> JOSEF PIEPER, *Justice*, 1955

See also Blasphemy; Totalitarianism.

ANTI-GOD TOTALITARIANS

We see today what was never before seen in history, the satanical banners of war against God and against religion brazenly unfurled to the winds in the midst of all peoples and in all parts of the earth.

> POPE PIUS XI, *Caritate Christi Compulsi*, May 3, 1932

A Soviet teacher . . . is obliged not only to be an unbeliever himself, but also to be an active propagandist of Godlessness among others, to be the bearer of the ideas of militant proletarian atheism. . . . The Soviet teacher must expose and overcome religious prejudices in the course of his activity in school and outside school, day in and day out.

F. N. OLESCHUK (Secretary of the League of Militant Atheists), *Uchitelskaya Gazeta,* November, 1949

Why do the full-fledged totalitarians, Lenin, Hitler, Stalin, not shrink from the means they adopt to achieve their ends? . . . They have been known as atheists. But in fact God was their enemy, not because they did not believe in the Deity, but because they themselves were assuming His functions and claiming His prerogatives.

WALTER LIPPMANN, *The Public Philosophy,* 1954

See also Atheism; Blasphemy; Communism; Dictatorship; God; Blasphemous Statements about; Government and God; Totalitarianism.

ANTI-INTELLECTUALISM

This anti-intellectual brief for revealed religion is a sign of doubt rather than a sign of faith.

WILLARD L. SPERRY, *Jesus Then and Now,* 1949

See also Education; Intellect; Knowledge; Mind.

ANTI-SEMITISM

Oh, monstrous doctrine! O, what infernal counsel! contrary to prophets, hostile to apostles, practically subversive to all piety and grace!—a sacrilegious harlot of a doctrine, impregnated with the very spirit of falsehood, conceiving anguish, and bringing forth iniquity!

ST. BERNARD OF CLAIRVAUX (1091–1153), to a German Monk who preached "Death for Jews," *Epistle* 365

My lord, I only hope this—that not one man in England who calls himself a civilized or Christian man will have it in his heart to add by a single word to that which this great and ancient and noble people suffer; but that we shall do all we can by labor, by speech, and by prayer to lessen if it be possible, or at least to keep ourselves from sharing in sympathy with these atrocious deeds.

HENRY EDWARD MANNING, *Address on Anti-Semitism,* February 1, 1882

Strange inconsistency! to persecute in the name of religion those who had given the religion.

MADISON C. PETERS, *Justice to the Jew,* 1899

Anti-Semitism is a form of Christian hypocrisy. The Christian whitewashes himself by attributing his views to the Jew.

BERNARD LAZARE, *Anti-Semitism,* 1903

Of all the bigotries that ravage the human temper there is none so stupid as the anti-Semitic. It has no basis in reason, it is not rooted in faith, it aspires to no ideal.

LLOYD GEORGE, *Hearst Newspapers,* July 22, 1923

In large part, anti-Semitism is the direct result of religious indoctrination.

MILTON STEINBERG, *The Making of the Modern Jew,* 1934

Anti-Semitism is . . . a movement in which we, as Christians, cannot have any part whatever.

POPE PIUS XI, to Belgian pilgrims, September, 1938

It is not possible for Christians to take part in anti-Semitism. We are Semites spiritually.

POPE PIUS XI, *Address,* September, 1938

We declare anti-semitism to be a plain denial of the spirit of our Lord who was Himself a Hebrew according to the flesh and who taught us that all men are brothers.

FEDERAL COUNCIL OF CHURCHES OF CHRIST IN AMERICA, *Report,* 1938

Perhaps the saddest thing to admit is that those who rejected the Cross have to carry it, while those who welcomed it are so often engaged in crucifying others.

NICHOLAS BERDYAEV, *Christianity and Anti-Semitism,* 1938

If we avoid a unilateral selection of texts, and if there were sufficient acquaintance with the philosophy of history, it would be understood that neither the policy adopted at certain periods regarding the Jews by medieval Christendom, nor the supervening mistakes and abuses which may have occurred, prove that the Catholic Church is bound to anti-Semitism.

JACQUES MARITAIN, *Anti-Semitism,* 1939 1939

Anti-Semitism in any form is a barbaric insult to our culture and our civilization, which have been moulded by Christianity, and as a breakdown of Christian values, which have become confused and lacking in humanity.

KARL BARTH, *Community, Church and State,* 1946

Anti-Semitism is, at the bottom, the revolt of the pagan against the God of Israel and his absolute demand. This was obvious in pre-Christian anti-Semitism, but it is equally true of anti-Semitism in the Christian world.

WILL HERBERG, *Judaism and Modern Man,* 1951

See also Bigots; Brotherhood; Charity; Class Distinctions; Discrimination; Equality; Exclusiveness; Fanaticism; Genocide; Ghettoes; Hatred; Hypocrisy; Intolerance; Israel; Jews; Jews and Christians; Judaism; Love; Persecution; Prejudice; Racial Conflict; Racial Injustice; Racial Prejudice; Tolerance.

ANXIETY

There is an exceeding difference between suffering and trouble of mind. Simple suffering is a purgatory; but a troubled mind is a hell. Suffering without unfaithfulness is calm and peaceful, by reason of the entire purpose of the soul to accept the pain sent by God. But trouble and anxiety are a revolt against God.

FRANÇOIS FÉNELON, *Spiritual Letters of,* c. 1700

The reason why our public life is so disordered and our private life so hampered by anxiety is because we will not be still and know God.

A. MAUDE ROYDEN, *Federal Council Bulletin,* January, 1931

Though serious anxiety may need the help of a psychiatrist because it springs from unconscious levels of the mind, for most of us there is real help in the Christian religion.

LESLIE D. WEATHERHEAD, *Prescriptions for Anxiety,* 1956

See also Affliction; Despair; Misfortune; Peace; Serenity; Suffering; Tribulations; Troubles; Worry.

APARTHEID

The white man makes himself the agent of God's will and the interpreter of His providence in assigning the range and determining the bounds of non-white development. One trembles at the blasphemy of this attributing to God the offenses against charity and justice that are apartheid's necessary accompaniment.

STATEMENT OF CATHOLIC BISHOPS OF SOUTH AFRICA, July, 1957

The cardinal error of apartheid is that it never regards human beings as individuals. It persists in ignoring their personal worth because it always treats them as members of a particular ethnic group, and in so doing personifies the racial group, the tribe, the race.

AMBROSE REEVES, *Church and Race in South Africa,* ed. D. M. Paton, 1958

See also Brotherhood; Charity; Race; Racial Conflict; Racial Equality; Racial Injustice; Racial Prejudice.

APATHY

The forces of good in the world are immobilized less by their adversaries, than by their sleep.

E. M. POTEAT, *These Shared His Passion,* 1940

See also Actions; Acts; Complacency; Conformity; Duties; Ease; Inaction; Practice; Smugness; Spiritual Lethargy.

APOSTLES

The Apostles for our sake received the gospel from the Lord Jesus Christ; Jesus Christ was sent from God. Christ then is from God, and the Apostles from Christ. Both therefore came in due order from the will of God.

ST. CLEMENT OF ROME, *Epistle to the Corinthians,* c. 100

What sane man will believe that they were ignorant of anything, these whom Christ had set up as masters, who were His companions, His disciples, His intimates, to whom He privately explained all difficulties, saying that it was given to them to know things hidden from others.

TERTULLIAN, *De Praescriptione,* XXII; 2, 3, 8, c. 206

Although the Blessed Virgin Mary was more worthy, higher, than all the Apostles, it was not yet to her but to them that the Lord gave the keys of the Kingdom of Heaven.

POPE INNOCENT III (1198–1216), cited in the *Decretals,* lib. V, tit. xxxviii, cap. x

See also Jesus Christ; New Testament; Priests; Tradition; Unity.

APOSTLES' CREED

Only a presumptuous madness will suppose that anything devised today could take its [the Apostles' Creed's] place . . . only a soul aridly unimaginative can miss the thrill of awe, the ecstasy of spirit joining spirit to go out together in the supreme venture of faith.

PAUL ELMER MORE, *The Catholic Faith,* 1931

See also Creeds; Unity.

APOSTOLIC SUCCESSION

If what the Apostles had received from Christ was not transmitted to others; if on the contrary offices of a new type took their place, how can one possibly still speak of the *one Church* having maintained its identity through the changes of history?

F. M. BRAUN, *Neues Licht auf des Kirche,* 1946

Just as in the Gospel, the Lord's so disposing St. Peter and the other Apostles constitutes one apostolic college, so in a similar way the Roman Pontiff, the successor of Peter, and the Bishops, the successors of the Apostles, are joined together.

Constitution on the Church, Second Vatican Council, November, 1964

See also Bishop; Priesthood; Tradition.

APPEASEMENT

Woe to him whom this world charms from Gospel duty! Woe to him who seeks to pour oil upon the waters when God has brewed them into a gale! Woe to him who seeks to please rather than to appal!

HERMAN MELVILLE, *Moby Dick,* 1851

ARCHBISHOP

Archbishop—A Christian ecclesiastic of a rank superior to that attained by Christ.

> H. L. MENCKEN, *A Little Book in C Major,* 1916

ARCHITECTURE

Architecture paves the way, as it were, for the adequate realization of the God, toiling and wrestling in his service with external nature, and seeking to extricate it from the chaos of finitude, and the abortiveness of chance.

> G. W. F. HEGEL (1770–1831), *The Philosophy of Art,* publ. posth.

Good architecture is essentially religious— the production of a faithful and virtuous, not of an infidel and corrupted people. . . . Good architecture is the work of good and believing men. . . . Every great national architecture has been the result and exponent of a great national religion. . . . It is the manly language of a people inspired by resolute and common purpose, and rendering resolute and common fidelity to the legible laws of an undoubted God.

> JOHN RUSKIN, *The Crown of Wild Olives,* 1864

See also Art and Religion; Cathedral; Church: Edifice; Gothic Architecture.

ARISTOTLE

My heart is grieved to see how many of the best Christians this accursed, proud, knavish heathen has fooled and led astray with his false words. God sent him as a plague for our sins.

> MARTIN LUTHER, *Address to the Christian Nobility of the German Nation,* 1520

Aristotle was regarded [by the Schoolmen of the twelfth century] as a fore-runner of Christian truth, a John the Baptist in method and knowledge of natural things.

> PHILLIP SCHAFF, *History of the Christian Church,* V, 1892

ARMAMENTS

It is only the war-like power of a civilized people that can give peace to the world.

> THEODORE ROOSEVELT, *Independent,* December 21, 1899

To hold that the destructive power of atomic bombs will stop war is equivalent to a belief that the more devilish the devil is, the more saintly he becomes.

> PITIRIM SOROKIN, *The Reconstruction of Humanity,* 1948

It is not atomic bombs that we need fear, but atomic men—the men who have built a civilization in which bombs might be used.

> FULTON J. SHEEN, *Way to Happiness,* 1953

There must be a discipline which is determined to use the possession of megaton weapons and the upper ranges of kiloton weapons as deterrents only, and only in a discriminating way.

> *Christians and the Prevention of War in an Atomic Age,* World Council of Churches, August, 1958

Put in the mythological language of Biblical folklore, perhaps The Bomb is the *second* apple!

> DANIEL E. TAYLOR, *God and the H-Bomb,* ed. D. Keys, 1960

For the last decade or more our weapons program has been dictated by what we *can* do, scientifically and technologically, rather than by what we *ought* to do, militarily, politically, and morally.

> THOMAS E. MURRAY, *Nuclear Policy for War and Peace,* 1960

Any weapon whose every use must be for the purpose of directly killing non-combatants as a means of attaining some supposed good and incidentally hitting some military target is a weapon whose every use would be wholly immoral. . . .The manufacture and possession of a weapon whose every use is that just described, and the political employment of it for the sake of deterrence, is likewise immoral.

PAUL RAMSEY, *War and the Christian Conscience,* 1961

The moralist who . . . affirms universal imperatives and implores individuals to recognize in every man all humanity, can from now on pass from the individual ethic to the collective by invoking the fact of nuclear armaments.

R. RAYMOND ARON, *The Ethic of Power,* 1962, ed. Lasswell and Cleveland, 1962

How can a nation live with its conscience and know that it is preparing to kill twenty million children in another nation if the worst should come to the worst?

JOHN C. BENNETT, *Nuclear Weapons and the Conflict of Conscience,* 1962

As Christians we affirm that we cannot under any circumstances sanction the use of nuclear and other mass-destruction weapons, nor can we sanction using the threat of massive retaliation by these weapons for so-called deterrence.

FIVE HUNDRED MINISTERS AND LAYMEN, *Statement* issued by Church Peace Mission, New York City, April, 1962

"Right must be done even if the heavens fall"—that was the high point of Roman paganism. Now that the heavens may indeed fall, it is still true. If the use of the Bomb is immoral we must not use it; if its possession is immoral we must not possess it. As Christians we dare not say that we cannot face the consequences of acting morally.

T. D. ROBERTS, Preface to *Nuclear Weapons,* ed. W. Stein, 1962

Justice, right reason and humanity, urgently demand that the arms race should cease; that the stockpiles which exist in various countries should be reduced equally and simultaneously by the parties concerned; that nuclear weapons should be banned, and that a general agreement should eventually be reached about progressive disarmament and an effective method of control.

POPE JOHN XXIII, *Pacem in Terris,* April, 1963

The complacency with which the nation approves preparations for blasting and incinerating scores of millions of human beings indicates how completely we have slipped our ethical moorings.

W. H. FERRY, *Cross Currents,* Summer, 1963

If you wish to be brothers, let the arms fall from your hands. One cannot love while holding offensive arms.

POPE PAUL VI, *Address to the United Nations,* October, 1965

The arms race is an utterly treacherous trap for humanity, and one which ensnares the poor to an intolerable degree. It is much to be feared that if this race persists, it will eventually spawn all the lethal ruins whose path it is now making ready.

SECOND VATICAN COUNCIL, *The Church in the Modern World,* December, 1965

See also Aggression; Atomic Bomb; Force; Military Service; Mobilization; Nuclear Energy; Nuclear War; Pacifism; Pacifists; Peace; Self-Defense; War; War, Condemnation of.

ART

Your art is as it were a grandchild of God.

DANTE, *Inferno,* XI, 104, 1320

Seeing that the art of painting and carving . . . cometh from God, I require that the practice of art should be kept pure and lawful. Therefore men should not paint nor carve anything but such as can be seen with the eye.

> JOHN CALVIN, *Institutes,* III, 1536

Good art is nothing but a replica of the perfection of God and a reflection of His art.

> MICHELANGELO, *Dialogues,* 1538

All the sacred play of art is only a distant copying of that infinite play of the world, that work of art which is eternally fashioning itself.

> FRIEDRICH SCHLEGEL, *Gespräch über die Poesie,* 1800

All great art is the expression of man's delight in God's work, not in *his own.*

> JOHN RUSKIN, *Modern Painters,* V, 1860

God creates Art by man, having for a tool the human intellect. The great Workman has made this tool for himself; he has no other.

> VICTOR HUGO, *William Shakespeare,* 1864

So from Art's being immoral, in the ultimate power of it, nothing but Art is moral: Life without Industry is sin, and Industry without Art, brutality.

> JOHN RUSKIN, *Epilogue, Modern Painters,* V, 1888

By recalling the supreme exemplar of all beauty, God, from Whom all the beauty of nature derives, the arts will more securely withdraw from unworthy concepts and more effectively rise to express the master idea which is the life of all art.

> POPE PIUS X, *Motu Proprio,* November 22, 1903

If art can reveal the truth, art can also lie. An artist can be not only divinely inspired, but diabolically inspired.

> GEORGE BERNARD SHAW, *The Christian Commonwealth,* October 14, 1908

All ignoble, decadent and vacuous art breathes the atomosphere of the chambers of sleep and death.

> A. R. ORAGE, *Nietzsche in Outline and Aphorism,* 1910

A single-minded attempt to render the highest kind of justice to the visible universe, by bringing to light the truth, manifold and one, underlying its aspect.

> JOSEPH CONRAD, Preface, *The Nigger of the Narcissus,* 1914

Art is the stored honey of the human soul, gathered on wings of misery and travail.

> THEODORE DREISER, *Seven Arts,* February, 1917

If a thing uplifts and delights the Soul by the very fact of being granted to its intuition, it is good to lay hold of, it is beautiful.

> JACQUES MARITAIN, *The Philosophy of Art,* 1923

Art is concerned not with botany but with flowers, not with root causes but with ultimate values, not with sex but with love, not (I will dare to add) with human values but with human beings.

> GERALD BULLETT, *Modern English Fiction,* 1926

Art is revelation. If a painting shows only what is there, it is not art. Art like fine music or high literature must carry the beholder beyond this world and all that appears in it, transport him to the shores of the eternal world and enable him to see and hear the things not given to the tongue of man to utter.

> JAMES M. GILLIS, *If Not Christianity, What?,* 1935

Art is not a caricature of creation, it *continues* creation, "creates as it were in the second stage."

> JACQUES MARITAIN, *Art and Poetry,* 1943

There is no great art without reverence.

GERALD VANN, *The Heart of Man,* 1945

Art is a fundamental necessity in the human state. "No man," says St. Thomas following Aristotle, "can live without pleasure." Therefore a man deprived of the pleasures of the spirit goes over to the pleasures of the flesh.

JACQUES MARITAIN, *Art and Scholasticism,* 1946

We have an art that can apparently offer us nothing better than a confirmation of our own disintegration.

KARL BARTH, *Community, Church and State,* 1946

The role of art is to express through the body the mystery of a soul. Through the body—that is to say by way of all the signs—visual, audible, mobile.

JEAN MOUROUX, *The Meaning of Man,* 1948

When frozen faith melts again, when it is once more love and freedom, then will be the time that art will light up again at the new kindling of the fire of the spirit.

WLADIMIR WEIDLE, *The Dilemma of the Arts,* 1948

Art is an exercise of the whole being of man, not to compete with God but to coincide better with the order of Creation, to love it better, and to reestablish ourselves in it.

DENIS DE ROUGEMENT, *Address,* May, 1950, quoted by S. R. Hooper, *Spiritual Problems in Contemporary Literature,* 1952

The function of all art lies in fact in breaking through the narrow and tortuous enclosure of the finite, in which man is immersed while living here below, and in providing a window on the infinite for his hungry soul.

POPE PIUS XII, *Address,* April 8, 1952

The soul is asking for a home again. The mind rebels against its own emptiness. The hands, those precious wonderful instruments, ask for some creative occupation.

FRITZ EICHENBERG, *Art and Faith,* 1952

Modern art, modern poetry, at their best say to me: You must change your life! Such art represents a demand, even a rebuke. It sees through us.

AMOS N. WILDER, *Theology and Modern Literature,* 1958

Art *is* an act of attempted justice and in its responsible exercise stirs the ultimate issues even when it cannot decide them.

WILLIAM ERNEST HOCKING, *Strength of Men and Nations,* 1959

See also Architecture; Artists; Artistry; Arts; Beautiful, the; Creativity; Freedom of Thought and Speech; Images; Imagination; Literature; Music; Poems and Poets; Poetry.

ART AND CHRISTIANITY

Of all the religions which have ever existed, the Christian religion is the most poetical, the most human, the most favorable to freedom, to art, and to literature.

FRANÇOIS RÉNE DE CHATEAUBRIAND, *The Genius of Christianity,* 1802

Art's highest mission is to reveal to the world Jesus Christ in His birth, in His life, in His death, in His beautiful and perfect conception of the divine mind. . . . As the Christian religion is the fullest revelation of the soul, it ought to produce the highest art.

JOHN LANCASTER SPALDING, *Essays and Reviews,* 1877

Those who by their art desire to serve the Truth which is Christ are not pursuing a particular human end but a divine end, an end as universal as God Himself.

JACQUES MARITAIN, *Art and Scholasticism,* 1946

From the moment it reaches in its own line a certain level of greatness and purity, art heralds without understanding them the invisible order and glory of which all beauty is but a sign; Chinese or Egyptian, it is already Christian in hope and in symbol.

> JACQUES MARITAIN, *Art and Faith,* 1948

The real problem, evidently, is that of the alienation of the artist and the creative writer from the Christian tradition as a whole.

> AMOS N. WILDER, *Theology and Modern Literature,* 1958

So long as the secret of art remains undeciphered, the Christian has only one instrument at his disposal, his conscience; but he has a conscience as a Christian and one as an artist, and these two consciences are not always in agreement.

> HEINRICH BÖLL, *Art and Religion,* 1959

See also Gothic Architecture; Images; Liturgy.

ART AND MORALITY

The liberation of art from the moral obligations of life . . . [makes] human nature coterminous with the bestial in man.

> PAUL ELMER MORE, *Humanism and America,* ed. R. Forester, 1930

The essential purpose of art, its *raison d'être,* is to assist in the perfection of the moral personality which is man, and for this reason it must itself be moral.

> POPE PIUS XI, *Vigilanti Cura,* July 2, 1936

Art's vocation is to elevate the whole man, body and spirit, for God's sake, rather than to glamorize self-indulgence for the flesh's sake.

> DAVID ROSS KING, *The Commonweal Reader,* ed. E. S. Skillin, 1950

And because an artist is a man before being an artist, the autonomous world of morality is simply superior to (and more inclusive than) the autonomous world of art. . . . Art is indirectly and extrinsically subordinate to morality.

> JACQUES MARITAIN, *The Responsibility of the Artist,* 1960

Human life is in need of that very Beauty and intellectual creativity, where art has the last word; and art exercises itself in the midst of that very human life, those human needs and human ends, where morality has the last word.

> JACQUES MARITAIN, *The Responsibility of the Artist,* 1960

The total artistic judgment, the complete critical evaluation of a piece of art, includes a moral dimension.

> HAROLD C. GARDINER, *Movies, Morals and Art,* 1961

See also Art; Morality.

ART AND NATURE

Art owes its origin to Nature herself, that this beautiful creation the world supplied the first model, while the original teacher was that divine intelligence which has not only made us superior to the other animals, but like to Himself.

> GIORGIO VASARI, *The Lives of the Painters,* 1550

Nature is not at variance with Art, nor Art with Nature, they both being servants of His Providence. Art is the perfection of Nature. . . . Nature is the Art of GOD.

> THOMAS BROWNE, *Religio Medici,* 1635

See also Art; Nature.

ART AND RELIGION

Religion and art are allies. Between them there is no antagonism, as there is none between theology and science.

> JOHN LANCASTER SPALDING, *Essays and Reviews,* 1877

All noble art, with all noble religion, breathes gratitude for life. . . . Great art is a song of praise, an overflowing of life back to its source, a dithyramb of thanksgiving and gratitude.

A. R. ORAGE, *Nietzsche in Outline and Aphorism,* 1910

Religious art must, by its very nature, be a social art. That is, it must grow out of the common faith, thought, experience, life, and not least of all, the common worship of the Church.

ILDEFONS HERWEGEN, *Liturgical Art,* I, 1931–32

Herein are faith and hope and love at white heat, fit for the worship of God because they are at once so devoted to and so critical of what is man's.

ROBERT L. CALHOUN, *God and the Common Life,* 1935

It is not a question of prejudice or pious belief; it is not even a thesis in dispute; it is the verdict of history that art owes its origin to religion.

P. J. GANNON, *Studies,* December, 1942

Art is not religion. . . . Its object is esthetic beauty; that of religion is truth and moral beauty. Both are or should be spiritual. . . . Art, no less than religion, should mirror the essential, the ideal and the eternal. It should seek truth, but truth under the aspect of beauty.

P. J. GANNON, *Studies,* December, 1942

Religion is the everlasting dialogue between humanity and God. Art is its soliloquy.

FRANZ WERFEL, *Between Heaven and Earth,* 1944

It is the real with which religion deals, while art deals with symbols of the real.

WILLIAM ERNEST HOCKING, *Science and the Idea of God,* 1945

In so far as the liturgy, the common prayer of God's faithful people, does not

become incarnate in works of art . . . does not animate harmoniously space, matter, sound, poetry . . . it is not completely itself and its fruitfulness in souls finds itself compromised.

ILDEFONS HERWEGEN, *L'Art Sacra,* 1947

If there were no other proof of the infinite patience of God with men, a very good one could be found in His toleration of the pictures that are painted of Him and of the noise that proceeds from musical instruments under the pretext of being in His "honor."

THOMAS MERTON, *The Commonweal Reader,* ed. E. S. Skillin, 1950

Through art the senses, far from weighing down the soul and nailing it to earth, should serve it as wings on which to rise above transient trifles and paltriness toward that which is eternal, true, beautiful, toward the only real good . . . toward God.

POPE PIUS XII, *Address,* March 9, 1950

It is the function and duty of sacred art, by reason of its very definition, to enhance the beauty of the house of God and foster the faith and piety of those who gather in the church to assist at the divine service.

Sacred Congregation of the Holy Office to the Bishops of the World, June 30, 1952

As soon as religion becomes prosaic or perfunctory art appears somewhere else.

SUZANNE K. LANGER, *Feeling and Form,* 1953

Music and art and poetry attune the soul to God because they induce a kind of contact with the Creator and Ruler of the Universe.

THOMAS MERTON, *No Man Is an Island,* 1955

In our own period the most radically religious movements in literature and painting and music may gain expression in strangely uncanonical terms—in despairing maledictions and in apocalyptic visions of the "abyss" of disintegration that threatens the word today.

NATHAN A. SCOTT, *Modern Literature and the Religious Frontier,* 1958

Any true bridge-building between religion and the arts will require . . . a better theology and a better aesthetic.

AMOS N. WILDER, *Theology and Modern Literature,* 1958

See also Art and Morality, Art and Theology; Artists; Gothic Architecture; Images; Liturgy.

ART AND THEOLOGY

It is one of the laws of great art that its greatness is in direct proportion to the worth of its philosophy and its theology.

THEODOR HAECKER, *Virgil, Father of the West,* 1934

There is an interesting analogy between the surgical acerbity of much modern art and the inexorable sobriety of neo-orthodox theology.

AMOS N. WILDER, *Theology and Modern Literature,* 1958

See also Images.

ARTIFICIAL INSEMINATION

Artifical insemination outside marriage is to be condemned purely and simply as immoral. . . . Artificial insemination in marriage with the use of an active element from a third person is equally immoral. . . . The active element can never be lawfully attained by acts that are contrary to nature. . . . Artificial insemination is something which must not just be regarded with extreme reserve, but must be utterly rejected.

POPE PIUS XII, May, 1956

See also Adultery; Marriage; Sexual Intercourse.

ARTISTRY

The art-gift itself is only the result of the moral character of generations. A bad woman may have a sweet voice; but that sweetness of voice comes from the past morality of her race.

JOHN RUSKIN, *Sesame and Lilies,* 1865

ARTISTS

It is for artists to remind humanity of the unconquerable and to assert the eternity of ideas.

JOHN OLIVER HOBBES, *The Dream and the Business,* 1906

When an artist deserts the side of the angels, it is the most odious of treasons.

ALDOUS HUXLEY, *Do What You Will,* 1929

All great artists who have the subtle, spiritual appeal, convey a stillness, a remoteness, a sense of the beyond, the far away.

SRI RADHAKRISHNAN, *The Spirit in Man,* 1941

What joy to the artist who sees shining forth in every creature the resplendent light of the Creator! How noble the mission of the artist who helps the less sensitive, the less gifted, to see, to appreciate the natural beauty of the humblest things and through them the beauty of God!

POPE PIUS XII, *Address,* May 19, 1948

The light with which an artist sees inclines to affect the justness of his observations. . . . The artist who takes up his location in Plato's cave has not the same chance as he who sets up shop by Christ's open tomb.

S. L. BETHELL, *Essays on Literary Criticism and the English Tradition,* 1948

The highest experience of the artist penetrates not only beyond the sensibile surface of things into their inmost reality, but even beyond that to God Himself.

THOMAS MERTON, *The Commonweal Reader*, ed. E. S. Skillin, 1950

The right hand of the artist withers when he forgets the sovereignty of God.

ABRAHAM JOSHUA HESCHEL, *Religious Symbolism*, ed. F. E. Johnson, 1955

The modern artist of our world under judgment has exposed his nerves and heart to the fury and desolation of these decades, and can provide meaning for those who have the same intuition.

AMOS N. WILDER, *Theology and Modern Literature*, 1958

The Churches may still be entitled to decide whether some one is a Christian (the Recording Angel can confirm or annul the verdict): but the Churches are not entitled to decide whether some one is an artist.

HEINRICH BÖLL, *Art and Religion*, 1959

See also Art; Art and Christianity; Art and Morality; Art and Nature; Art and Religion.

ARTS

A young person who neglects the liberal arts may be both pious and pure; but so long as he has to live among men, I do not see how anyone can call him happy.

ST. AUGUSTINE, *De Ordine*, c. 395

Today, in a secular world, it is almost wholly through the arts that we have a living reminder of the terror and nobility of what we are.

J. ROBERT OPPENHEIMER, *Address*, New York City, March, 1963

ASCETICISM

The holy law imposes not asceticism. It demands that we . . . grant each mental and physical faculty its due.

JUDAH HALEVI, *Seter ha-Kuzari*, c. 1135 A.D.

Prayer, fasting, vigils, and all other Christian practices . . . do not constitute the aim of our Christian life: they are but the indispensable means of attaining that aim. *For the true aim of the Christian life is the acquisition of the Holy Spirit of God.*

SAINT SERAPHIM OF SAROV (1759– 1833), quoted by N. Matilov in *Conversation of Saint Seraphim on the Aim of the Christian Life*

Asceticism is the denial of the will to live.

ARTHUR SCHOPENHAUER, "On the Sufferings of the World," *Essays*, 1851

The ideal of asceticism represents moral effort as essentially sacrifice, the sacrifice of one part of human nature to another, that it may live the more completely in what survives of it.

WALTER PATER, *Marius the Epicurean*, 1885

[Jainism is] one of the most emphatic protests the world has ever known against accounting luxury, wealth or comfort as the main things in life.

M. STEVENSON, *The Heart of Jainism*, 1915

The "dark night of the Soul," the tragic asceticism that is one of the phases of dogmatic belief, is not the necessary accompaniment of the presence of God, though it has often been a very beautiful one.

WYNDHAM LEWIS, *Time and Western Man*, 1927

The Protestant asceticism of the 17th and 18th century did not lead men to fly from the world and give up all their goods to the poor and to the Church, as in the Middle Ages. It inculcated the duty of unremitting industry and thrift, while at the same time it discouraged rigorously every kind of indulgence and extravagance in the expenditure of what it had gained.

CHRISTOPHER DAWSON, *Progress and Religion*, 1929

Asceticism, or the sacrifice of one's personal inclinations, is unquestionably the heart of the Christian religion and of all great religions.

HENRY C. LINK, *The Return to Religion,* 1936

Asceticism prepares the soul for the mystical union, which then renders the exercise of the virtues and our apostolate much more supernatural and fruitful.

REGINALD GARRIGOU-LAGRANGE, *Christian Perfection and Contemplation,* 1937

It is his merit [the ascetic in India] to practice asceticism; it is the merit of others to give to him so that his simple wants may never lack supply, and thus on both sides asceticism ministers to spiritual profit, to the actual gain of the ascetic himself . . . and to the store of merit which by his generosity trusted to accumulate for himself, so as to win a higher position and birth in the next existence.

Encyclopedia of Religion and Ethics, II, 1951

The purpose of Calvary was not the death of Christ but the resurrection, and the purpose of asceticism is not to annihilate life but to increase it, to further the life of grace and the life of rational nature as well.

LOUIS COGNET, *Christian Asceticism and Modern Man,* 1955

See also Moderation; Mysticism; Sacrifice; Self-Conquest; Self-Denial; Selflessness; Self-Sacrifice.

ASCETICS

The well-intentioned ascetic may be in some danger of becoming the sanctified egoist.

ALFRED GRAHAM, *Christian Thought and Action,* 1951

See also Asceticism

ASPIRATION

If you aspire to the highest place it is no disgrace to stop at the second, or even the third.

CICERO, *De Oratore,* c. 80 B.C.

Dost thou wish to rise? Begin by descending. You plan a tower that shall pierce the clouds? Lay first the foundations on humility.

ST. AUGUSTINE (354–430), *Sermon 10 on the Words of God*

To love the beautiful, to desire the good, to do the best.

MOTTO OF MOSES MENDELSSOHN (1729–1786)

A certain glorious sorrow must ever mingle with our life; all our actual is transcended by our possible; our visionary faculty is an overmatch for our experience; like the caged bird, we break ourselves against the bars of the finite, with a wing that quivers for the infinite.

JAMES MARTINEAU, *Hours of Thought on Sacred Things,* 1879

The very child that misses the mother's appreciating love is introduced, by his first tears, to that thirst of the heart which is the early movement of piety.

JAMES MARTINEAU, *Hours of Thought on Sacred Things,* 1879

A man's reach should exceed his grasp, or what's a heaven for?

ROBERT BROWNING (1812–1889), "Andrea del Sarto"

It will not do for any one of us to make up his mind that he cannot be any good and noble thing, until first he has asked himself whether it is as impossible in God's sight as in his.

PHILLIPS BROOKS, *Perennials,* 1898

Whatever is capable of aspiring must be troubled that it may wake and aspire;—

then troubled still—that it may hold fast, be itself, and aspire still.

GEORGE MACDONALD (1824–1905), *Selections from,* ed. Dewey

Aspirations for the infinite constantly act upon us. They are more deeply rooted than desires on the surface of experience, and nothing in this world can ever satisfy them.

E. LE ROY, *The Problem of God,* 1929

We think we must climb to a certain height of goodness before we can reach God. But . . . He says "I am the Way." . . . If you are in a hole, the Way begins in a hole. The moment we set our face in the same direction as His, we are walking with God.

HELENE WODEHOUSE, *Inner Light,* First Series, 1931

Aspiration shows us the goal and the distance to it; inspiration encourages with a view to how far we have come. Aspiration gives us the map of the journey; inspiration furnishes the music to keep us marching.

RALPH W. SOCKMAN, *The Highway of God,* 1941

To walk always in the way of the cross remains for the best of men an aspiration rather than an achievement.

GEORGIA HARKNESS, *The Modern Rival of Christian Faith,* 1953

Neither pleasure nor knowledge nor art can satisfy our aspirations which are infinite in scope. They carry us irresistibly beyond what is human, to God, the final end, in which alone our heart can find utter peace and joy.

REGIS JOLIVET, *The God of Reason,* 1958

See also Ambition; Call; Inspiration; Prayer: Defined and Explained; Religion: Its Nature and Function; Spiritual; Vision; Vocation.

ASSIMILATION

What I understand by assimilation is loss of identity.

SOLOMON SCHECHTER, *Seminary Addresses,* 1915

Total assimilation is a great sin and a terrible danger.

LUDWIG LEWISOHN, *The American Jew,* 1950

American assimilation on the "folksy" level is destructive of every value by which Jews must live, if they would survive in any guise except the guise of apes and fools.

LUDWIG LEWISOHN, *The American Jew,* 1950

See also Jew; Jews.

ASSUMPTION OF MARY

We pronounce, declare, and define it to be a divinely revealed dogma; that the Immaculate Mother of God, the ever Virgin Mary, having completed the course of her earthly life, assumed body and soul into heavenly glory.

POPE PIUS XII, *Munificentissimus Deus,* November 2, 1950

See also Mary, the Mother of Jesus.

ASTROLOGY

That astrologers not infrequently forecast the truth by observing the stars may be explained in two ways. First, because a great number of men follow their bodily passions, so that their actions are for the most part disposed in accordance with the inclination of the heavenly bodies; while there are a few—namely the wise ones—who moderate these inclinations by their reason. . . . Secondly, because of the interference of demons. . . . Human actions are not subject to the action of heavenly bodies save accidentally and indirectly.

ST. THOMAS AQUINAS, *Summa Theologica*, 1272

Believing as they [the prophets] did in an all-powerful God who ruled the world on a basis of just reward and punishment, they had no room for a sidereal fatalism which made human lives helplessly subject to the influence of the heavenly bodies.

Universal Jewish Encyclopedia, I, 1939

ASTRONOMERS

How happy are those to whom it is given to rise to heaven by study. . . . It is there, above all, that they see God's work, and considering it they are filled with happiness and joy.

JOHANNES KEPLER, *Mysterium Cosmographium*, 1596

See also Scientists.

ASTRONOMY

Astronomy compels the soul to look upwards and leads us from this world to another.

PLATO, *The Republic*, c. 370 B.C.

See also Science; Science and Religion.

ATHANASIAN CREED

The Athanasian Creed is the most splendid ecclesiastical lyric ever poured forth by the genius of man.

BENJAMIN DISRAELI, *Lothair*, 1870

See also Creeds.

ATHEISM

Atheism is the source of all iniquities.

PHILO (20 B.C.?–20 A.D.?), *Decalog*

The causes of atheism are divisions in religion, if they be many; for any one main division added zeal to both sides, but many divisions introduce atheism. Another, is scandal of priests.

FRANCIS BACON, "Of Atheism," *Essays*, 1597

A little or superficial knowledge of philosophy may incline the mind of man to atheism, but a further proceeding therein doth bring the mind back again to religion.

FRANCIS BACON, *Advancement of Learning*, 1605

Atheism doth utterly root out of men's minds all the fear of doing evil.

JEAN BODIN, *The Republic*, 1606

I would fain ask one of these bigoted infidels, supposing all the great points of atheism . . . were laid together and formed into a kind of creed, . . . whether it would not require an infinitely greater measure of faith than any set of articles which they so violently oppose?

JOSEPH ADDISON, *The Spectator*, 1714

Atheism is aristocratic.

M. M. I. ROBESPIERRE, *Speech*, Paris, November 1, 1793

Atheism is an inhuman, bloody, ferocious system, equally hostile to every useful restraint and to every virtuous affection. . . . Its first object is to dethrone God.

ROBERT HALL, *Modern Infidelity*, 1801

The owlet Atheism,
Sailing on obscene wings athwart the moon,
Drops his blue fringed lids, and holds them close,
And hooting at the glorious Sun in Heaven,
Cries out, "Where is it?"

S. T. COLERIDGE (1772–1834), "Fears in Solitude"

Practical atheism, seeing no guidance for human affairs but its own limited foresight, endeavors itself to play the god, and decide what will be good for mankind and what bad.

> HERBERT SPENCER, *Social Statics,* IV, 1851

Outside man and nature nothing exists, and the higher beings which our religious phantasies have created are only the fantastic reflection of our individuality.

> FRIEDRICH ENGELS, *Feuerbach,* 1888

Atheism in art, as well as in life, has only to be pressed to its last consequences in order to become ridiculous.

> COVENTRY PATMORE, *Emotional Art,* 1889

Atheism is a natural and inseparable part of Marxism.

> NIKOLAI LENIN, *Religion,* 1905

My atheism, like that of Spinoza, is true piety towards the universe and denies only gods fashioned by men in their own image, to be servants of their human interests.

> GEORGE SANTAYANA, *Soliloquies in England,* 1922

There is no more evangelical cult in modern times than the American Association for the Advancement of Atheism. . . . Philosophically, it is religious, for it makes a huge religious ceremony of denying God.

> CHARLES W. FERGUSON, *The Confusion of Tongues,* 1928

The hour to overthrow the Church has come. Arise, ye prisoners of the priest! Strike down the God superstition! The Clergy are powerful because you are on your knees, Stand up! Cast aside supernatural faith and fear! Be men!

> *Bulletin,* American Association for the Advancement of Atheism, 1928

We have found putting over Atheism in the United States much easier than we anticipated.

> *Second Annual Report,* American Association for the Advancement of Atheism, February, 1929

Atheism leads not to badness but only to an incurable sadness and loneliness.

> W. P. MONTAGUE, *Belief Unbound,* 1930

Atheism if it could be lived down to its ultimate roots in the will, would disorganize and kill the will metaphysically. . . . Every absolute experience of atheism, if it is conscientiously and rigorously followed, ends by provoking its psychical dissolution in suicide.

> JACQUES MARITAIN, *True Humanism,* 1936

The core of real atheism expresses itself in that individualism which makes a man feel alone and isolated in a world against which he must defend himself.

> JOHN MACMURRAY, *Creative Society* 1938

We refine God away, we simplify him, strip him of his attributes, accept his silence and passivity. We agree that everything in this world takes place as though he never existed. All we ask of him is that we keep his name.

> JEAN ROSTAND, *Pensées d'un biologiste,* 1939

The more assertive it is, the more clearly we see in its features traces of past religious experience. . . . A man wills to be not religious, but the very volition makes him religious. He may flee the face of God, he will never escape him.

> G. W. VAN DER LEEUW, *L'homme primitif et la religion,* 1940

The existence of God, immortality, disembodied souls or spirits, cosmic purpose or design, as these have customarily been interpreted by the great institutional religions, are denied by naturalists for the same generic reasons that they deny the existence of fairies, elves, leprechauns.

SIDNEY HOOK, *Partisan Review,* January–February, 1943

"Atheist" professors don't practice atheism at home or in their social relationships. Atheism remains in the lecture hall, the classroom, the seminar. Take it outside, put it into operation and society would disintegrate.

JAMES M. GILLIS, *God in Government,* 1943

Of two men who have no experience of God, he who denies Him is perhaps nearer to Him than the other.

SIMONE WEIL, *Gravity and Grace,* 1947

Organized atheism has never produced anything better than Communism or the French Revolution, or the destruction of human liberty. Its history in the past, as in Russia today, is one of intolerance, of persecution, of ruthless cruelty.

J. F. NOLL, *Christian Faith Before the Bar of Reason,* 1948

It is only the conception of God as suffering, and yearning for the Other, and as sacrificed, which subdues atheism and the fight against God.

NICHOLAS BERDYAEV, *The Divine and the Human,* 1949

Often we find atheism both in individual and society a necessary passage to deeper religious and spiritual truth: one has sometimes to deny God in order to find Him.

SRI AUROBINDO, *The Human Cycle,* 1950

Fervid atheism is usually a screen for repressed religion.

WILHELM STEKEL, *Autobiography,* 1950

All things must speak of God, refer to God, or they are atheistic.

HENRY P. VAN DUSEN, *God in Education,* 1951

Atheism has often been the expression of the vitality of religion, its quest for reality in religion. The fact that man is unable or unwilling to acknowledge God, means only that he cannot accept the ideas and beliefs about God framed by men, the false gods which obscure the living and ineffable God. Today the world is very sick, for it is passing through a crisis of the birth of a new religion.

S. RADHAKRISHNAN, *The Philosophy of,* ed. by P. A. Schlipp, 1952

By positive atheism I mean an active struggle against everything that reminds us of God—that is to say, antitheism rather than atheism.

JACQUES MARITAIN, *The Range of Reason,* 1952

This is the first time in history that atheism as a philosophy of government has the support of a powerful sovereign state [Soviet Russia], which is still arming to the teeth for international application of its anti-God revolution.

EDMUND A. WALSH, *Address,* July 27, 1952

The really destructive atheism is not the denial of God; for that denial, if it is honest, keeps a man in the company of Job and other men of integrity. The really destructive atheism is fear of facts.

ALEXANDER MILLER, *The Renewal of Man,* 1955

The atheism of the heart consists in the living rejection of what we have here found to be God's command and promise to man.

JOHN HUTCHISON, *Faith, Reason and Existence,* 1956

Atheism can only mean the attempt to remove any ultimate concern—to remain unconcerned about the meaning of one's existence.

PAUL TILLICH, *Dynamics of Faith,* 1957

The unbelief of today is more affirmative than the shallow skepticism of yesterday.

The poignant atheism is more pregnant than the dogmatic rationalism of yesterday.
> AMOS N. WILDER, *Theology and Modern Literature,* 1958

Even atheism must define itself by theism: it is a-theism, that is to say, not theism.
> GEORGE A. BUTTRICK, *Sermons Preached in a University Church,* 1959

In the end, how a man thinks must affect how he acts; atheism must finally, if not in one generation then in several, remake the conduct of atheists in the light of its own logic.
> MILTON STEINBERG, *Anatomy of Faith,* 1960

There is no equivalent word in Sanskrit for the word atheism. In the Gita mention is made of those who do not believe in God, the intelligent principle, but these are spoken of merely as of "deluded intellect."
> SWAMI PRABHAVANANDA, *The Spiritual Heritage of India,* 1963

If you do not lie in idleness and ignorance, the gloom of your atheism will dilate the pupil of your eyes in order to strive to read in the dark the answer to the why and wherefore of things.
> POPE PAUL VI, *Easter Sermon,* 1964

See also Agnostic; Agnosticism; Anti-God Totalitarians; Atheists; Belief; Believing; Blasphemy; Buddhism and Christianity; Despair; Devil; Doubt; Education, Secularized; Existentialism; God: Blasphemous Statements about; God, Nonexistence of; God, Unorthodox Comments about; Man, Modern; Religion, Caustic Comments about; Religion: Its Decline; Secularism; Social Atheism; Unbelief.

ATHEISTS

We are called atheists. And yes, we confess it, we are atheists of those so-called gods.
> ST. JUSTIN MARTYR, *First Apology,* VI, c. 150

A man may meet an atheist as soon in his study as in the street.
> ROBERT BURTON, *Anatomy of Melancholy,* III, 1621

By night an atheist half believes a God.
> EDWARD YOUNG, *Night Thoughts,* 1742

Some are atheists by neglect; others are so by affectation; they that think there is no God at some times do not think so at all times.
> BENJAMIN WHICHCOTE, *Moral and Religious Aphorisms,* 1753

I shall always maintain that whoso says in his heart, "There is no God," while he takes the name of God upon his lips, is either a liar or a madman.
> JEAN JACQUES ROUSSEAU, *Émile,* 1762

The atheists are for the most part impudent and misguided scholars who reason badly, and who, not being able to understand the Creation, the origin of evil, and other difficulties, have recourse to the hypothesis of the eternity of things and of inevitability.
> VOLTAIRE, *Philosophical Dictionary,* 1764

No one is so much alone in the universe as a denier of God. With an orphaned heart, which has lost the greatest of fathers, he stands mourning by the immeasurable corpse of the universe.
> JEAN PAUL RICHTER, *Flower, Fruit and Thorn Pieces,* 1796

No man in a thousand has the strength of mind or goodness of heart to be an atheist.
> S. T. COLERIDGE, *Letter to Thomas Allsop,* c. 1820

The three great apostles of practical atheism, that make converts without persecuting, and retain them without preaching, are wealth, health, and power.
> C. C. COLTON, *Lacon,* 1820

An atheist . . . I can never be.
> THOMAS JEFFERSON, *Letter to John Adams*, 1823

The true atheist is not the man who denies God, the subject; it is the man for whom the attributes of divinity, such as love, wisdom, and justice, are nothing.
> LUDWIG FEUERBACH, *The Essence of Christianity*, 1841

An atheist is a man who believes himself an accident.
> FRANCIS THOMPSON, *Paganism Old and New*, 1910

What saves the atheist from the stigma of insanity is the fact that God is real, not like a dream but like an enemy at his door.
> FULTON J. SHEEN, *Religion Without God*, 1928

The energy of atheists, their tireless propaganda, their spirited discourses, testify to a belief in God which puts to shame mere lip worshippers. They are always thinking of God.
> FULTON J. SHEEN, *Religion Without God*, 1928

A few may echo the hesitation of the youth who affirmed, "God forgive me, but I'm an atheist."
> LOUIS I. NEWMAN, *Religion Today*, ed. A. L. Swift, 1933

Almost all atheists seem to imagine that a group of theologians met together in secret session and said to one another, "Let us concoct a dogma and impose it on the people."
> JAMES M. GILLIS, *If Not Christianity, What?* 1935

A man who has no invisible means of support.
> JOHN BUCHAN, *Reader's Digest*, October, 1941, p. 84

All atheists would be fools fighting against imaginary windmills if God did not exist.
> FULTON J. SHEEN, *Communism and the Conscience of the West*, 1948

There are only practical atheists. Their atheism consists, not in denying the truth of God's existence, but in failing to realize God in their actions.
> JULES LAGNEAU, *Célèbres leçons et Fragments*, 1950

Today . . . we have the first group of real atheists in all history. They have no doubts whatever. . . . The materialist philosophers of today have lost the last vestige of belief. They are satisfied with atheism and are at peace with it.
> JOHN A. CASS, *Quest of Certainty*, 1950

If he doesn't believe in God he doesn't believe that God decides and that means he has to decide everything for himself. And *that* means that he's God himself.
> Said by Anisetta, in Aubrey Mennen's novel *The Backward Bride*, 1950

Pseudo-atheists . . . believe that they do not believe in God but . . . in actual fact unconsciously believe in Him, because the God whose existence they deny is not God but something else.
> JACQUES MARITAIN, *The Range of Reason*, 1952

Absolute atheists . . . have chosen to stake their lives against divine Transcendence and any vestige of Transcendence whatsoever.
> JACQUES MARITAIN, *The Range of Reason*, 1952

A man does not become an absolute atheist as a result of some inquiry into the problem of God carried on by speculative reason. . . . The starting point of absolute atheism is . . . a basic act of moral choice, a crucial free determination.
> JACQUES MARITAIN, *The Range of Reason*, 1952

He [God] stands lovingly and laughingly by the desk of the atheist who is writing a book to prove that God does not exist.

CHAD WALSH, *Behold the Glory,* 1955

A young man who wishes to remain an Atheist cannot be too careful of his reading.

C. S. LEWIS, *Surprised by Joy,* 1955

It is entirely possible for a man to be related to God without being conscious of the relation. This, we maintain, is precisely the position of the honest atheist.

JOHN HUTCHISON, *Faith, Reason and Existence,* 1956

The atheist frequently poses as a philosophical optimist. Having given up all hope in the very existence of a human soul, he pretends to a glowing faith in man's innate goodness.

FRANZ E. WINKLER, *Man: The Bridge Between Two Worlds,* 1960

An atheist's most embarrassing moment is when he feels profoundly thankful for something, but can't think of anybody to thank for it.

ANONYMOUS

Someone has quoted an unnamed Irishman as saying: "And sure if we were all atheists, then we would probably live together as Christians."

See also Atheism and the various rubrics there referred to.

ATOMIC BOMB

An explosive has gone up, morality has gone down.

J. F. C. ALLEN, *Army Ordnance,* July-August, 1945

The atomic bomb can fairly be said to have struck Christianity itself.

EDITORIAL, *Christian Century,* August 29, 1945

The most terrible crime ever committed by a "Christian" nation against the Mystical Body of Christ.

JOHN J. HUGO, *Catholic Worker,* September, 1945

As American Christians we are deeply penitent for the irresponsible use already made of the atomic bomb. We are agreed that, whatever be one's judgment of the ethics of war in principle, the surprise bombings of Hiroshima and Nagasaki are morally indefensible. . . . As the power that first used the atomic bomb under these circumstances, we have sinned grievously against the laws of God, and against the people of Japan.

Report of Commission of Christian Scholars to Federal Council of Churches of Christ in America, 1945

Force means war. War means Atomic bombs. And Atomic bombs mean suicide.

ROBERT M. HUTCHINS, *Bulletin of the Atomic Scientists,* March 1, 1946

In some sort of crude sense which no vulgarity, no humor, no overstatement can quite extinguish, the physicists have known sin: and this is a knowledge which they cannot lose.

J. ROBERT OPPENHEIMER, quoted in *Time,* November 8, 1948

Our scientists have developed *The Thing,* but we don't know what to do with it. *The Thing* wiped out Hiroshima but the scientists and we, caring not for ultimate ends and uses, are left with a machine that we cannot drive. To act without conscious or ultimate ends is to act inhumanly. We are guilty of inhuman activity in making *The Thing.*

WILLIAM T. COSTELLO, *Address,* December, 1948

Not the clergy but the scientists instructed the American people in the moral consequences of the use of the atomic bomb.

HENRY STEELE COMMAGER, *The American Mind,* 1950

As I watched, two things that looked like great big hideous lizards crawled in slowly, making croaking, groaning sounds. Others followed. I was paralyzed with horror for minutes. Then the light got a little stronger and I could see they were human beings—skinned alive by fire or heat, their bodies all smashed where they had been thrown against something hard.

TAKASHI NAGAI, *We of Nagasaki,* 1951

The world has abandoned God and cast its lot with nature divorced from Nature's God. Such is the meaning of the atomic bomb.

FULTON J. SHEEN, *The Woman,* 1951

Only when our labors were finally completed when the bomb dropped on Japan, only then or a little bit before maybe, did we start thinking about the moral implications.

HANS BETHE, *In the Matter of J. Robert Oppenheimer,* Transcript before Personnel Security Board, Washington, 1954

The [A-] bomb as a portent of man's sin as dark a portent as any man could wish—or never wish—but the bomb as the sign of death has made no change. To die wholesale is not different from dying retail, for each of us must die each for himself.

GEORGE A. BUTTRICK, *Sermons Preached in a University Church,* 1959

See also Aggression; Armaments; Nuclear Energy; Nuclear War; War, Condemnation of.

ATOMIC ENERGY.
See NUCLEAR ENERGY

ATONEMENT

On the day of Atonement the pious Jew becomes forgetful of the flesh and its wants and, banishing hatred, ill-feeling and all ignoble thoughts, seeks to be occupied exclusively with things spiritual.

The Jewish Encyclopedia, II, 1909

The process of recovering the sinful personality into a life with God, and of neutralizing the moral wrong done by man to man, through the power of self-sacrificing love.

EUGENE W. LYMAN, *Theology and Human Problems,* 1910

Christ's atonement in no way relieves any man from the full moral responsibility for his own sinful acts nor from the necessity of making good, as far as he can, the evil he has done.

FATHER CUTHBERT, *God and the Supernatural,* 1920

To atone is to be *at one* with God, to sink self into the not-self, to achieve a mystic unity with the source of being, wiping out all error and finding peace in self-submergence.

ISAAC GOLDBERG, *The Wonder of Words,* 1938

There is an atonement, an expiation, in the heart of God Himself, and out of this comes the forgiveness of our sins.

D. M. BAILLIE, *God Was in Christ,* 1948

See also Adam; Calvary; Confession; Contrition; Cross; Forgiveness; Incarnation; Jesus Christ: His Passion and Death; Jesus Christ as Saviour; Salvation; Saviour; Sin; Suffering; Unitarians.

AUGUSTINE, SAINT

Augustine . . . held that Adam's act of disobedience started a long train of psychic inheritance. . . . There was no attempt at research or rigorous experiment. . . . Augustine's position was so flagrantly a projection upon the whole human race of his own uncontrollable lusts that a modern psychologist would have thrown out his contentions as untrustworthy and misconceived. . . . It was Augustine who denied to our species the healthy blessing of self-respect.

H. A. OVERSTREET, *The Mature Mind,* 1949

AUTHOR

That an author's work is the mirror of his mind is a position that has led to very false conclusions. If Satan were to write a book it would be in praise of virtue, because the good would purchase it for use, and the bad for ostentation.

C. C. COLTON, *Lacon,* 1822

The closer an author approaches the realization that sin is an offense to God, the greater will his work be.

HAROLD C. GARDINER, *Tenets for Readers and Reviewers,* 1944

Each literary man who comes along is equipped with his own universal remedy and thus assumes a special importance; his head swells, and his prestige increases in proportion as his faith decreases.

FRANÇOIS MAURIAC, *God and Mammon,* 1946

In order for the Christian writer . . . to assert his identity in the modern world, it has been necessary for him to do so *against* his environment and his culture.

NATHAN A. SCOTT, *Modern Literature and the Religious Frontier,* 1958

See also Bible: Its Inspiration; Books; Literature; Poems and Poets.

AUTHORITARIANISM

The result of . . . authoritarianism is to put all values on one dead level, those that are enduringly important, along with those that are trivial, transitory, or totally irrelevant.

W. P. MONTAGUE, *Belief Unbound,* 1930

This issue of authoritarianism *vs.* liberty— to put it far too simply—affects outlooks on education, marriage legislation, Church-State relations, methods of church administration. It derives from fundamentally different conceptions of the manner in which God deals with men, and from a radically different concept of what a man really is.

BERNARD LEEMING, *America,* November 3, 1962

See also Communism; Dictatorship; State, the; Totalitarianism; Tyrants.

AUTHORITY

Authority sometimes proceeds from reason, but reason never from authority. For all authority that is not approved by true reason seems weak. But true reason, since it rests on its own strength, needs no reinforcement by any authority.

JOHANNES SCOTUS ERIGENA, *De Divisione Naturae,* 861

Authority is the source of knowledge, but our own reason remains the norm by which all authority must be judged.

JOHANNES SCOTUS ERIGENA, *De Divisione Naturae,* 861

You, however captivated by . . . authority, follow your halter. For what else should authority be called than a halter? Those who are now counted authorities gained their reputation by following reason, not authority.

ADELARD OF BATH, *Quaestiones naturales,* c. 1130

Anyone who conducts an argument by appealing to Authority is not using his intelligence; he is just using his memory.

LEONARDO DA VINCI (1452–1519), *The Literary Works of,* ed. J. P. Richter

The only general persuasive in matters of conduct is authority; that is (when truth is in question), a judgment which we feel to be superior to our own.

JOHN HENRY NEWMAN, *An Essay on the Development of Christian Doctrine,* 1845

Authority has its roots in the organic conditions of the life of the species, and its end is the formation of the individual. . . . Like every good teacher, authority should labor to render itself useless.

AUGUSTE SABATIER, *Religion of Authority and the Religion of the Spirit,* 1904

The only authority that both sides to an argument must necessarily recognize will have to be an authority residing in the very nature of humanity. . . . It is reason.

JAMES BISSETT PRATT, *Religious Liberals Reply,* 1947

There is only one final and absolute authority for the faith and life of the Church, and therefore for the faith and life of the individual members within it: namely, the living Christ speaking through the Holy Spirit . . . and the authority of the Bible being bound up with the authority of the living Christ himself, cannot be a different authority from his.

H. H. FARMER, *Interpreter's Bible,* Vol. I, 1952

Authority permeates, guides, shapes our lives. The acceptance of authority is the acceptance of what is given by those who have more than we.

PAUL TILLICH, *The New Being,* 1955

If faith is needed, there is another commitment not less so. *We must refuse to accept the authority of the defeated.*

ARDIS WHITMAN, *A New Image of Man,* 1955

It is the opposition to authority in the matter both of motives and of norms which most frequently alienates those who reject a morality based on religion.

JOHN E. SMITH, *Reason and God,* 1961

When Protestants put the seat of authority in religion within man himself, linking it with man's free spirit, and make it essential for each individual to follow the dictates of his own mind and conscience,

illumined and guided by the Scripture, they establish a form of Christian faith in which every difference between people is bound to carry great weight.

J. LESLIE DUNSTAN, *Protestantism,* 1962

Since it is the power to command according to right reason, authority must derive its obligatory force from the moral order, which in turn has God for its first source and final end.

POPE JOHN XXIII, *Pacem in Terris,* April, 1963

Ecclesiastical authority must always realize that, although the people of the Church are duty-bound in their obedience to that authority, they are not therefore devoid of all rights over the ecclesiastical authority. Those in authority must also remember that not all of their actions are necessarily correct, or willed by God.

KARL RAHNER, *Herder Correspondence Feature Service,* July, 1965

See also Belief; Bible; Bible and the Church; Bible and Doctrine; Books, Prohibited; Catholicism; Church: Its Authority; Church and State; Divine Right of Kings; Government; Government and God; Government and Religion; Infallibility; Obedience; Rebellion; Rulers; State, the; Tradition; Treason.

AUTOMATION. See MACHINES

AVARICE

Avaricious men do not reach heaven, so they are fools, who give no regard to charity.

Udanavarga (Buddhist Text), 300 B.C.

Avarice is the spur of industry.

DAVID HUME, "Of Civil Liberty," *Essays,* 1741

See also Gambling; Greed; Money; Traders; Wealth.

AVATARA

The Avatara or Saviour is the messenger of God. . . . Whenever there is a decline of religion in any part of the world, God sends his Avatara there. It is one and the same Avatara that, having plunged into the ocean of life, rises up in one place and is known as Krishna, and diving down again rises up in another place and is known as Christ.

SRI RAMAKRISHNA, *His Life and Sayings,* ed. F. M. Muller, 1899

BACHELORHOOD

He who remains unmarried impairs the divine image.

AKIBA, *Talmud: Yebamot,* 63b, c. 500 A.D.

BAPTISM

They who are born again through divine Baptism are placed in Paradise, that is, the Church, to do spiritual works that are interior.

ORIGEN (185–254), *Selecta in Genes*

Great is this baptism to which you are coming; it is ransom to captives and remission of sins. It is the death of sin and the soul's regeneration. It is a garment of light and a holy seal that can never be dissolved.

ST. CYRIL OF JERUSALEM, *Catechetical Lectures,* 350

Baptism is for the captives the ransom price, the remission of debts, the death of sin, the regeneration of the soul, a shining garment, an unbreakable seal, the vehicle to heaven, the public agent of the Kingdom, the gift of adoption.

ST. BASIL (330–379), *Homiliae,* 13, 5

From the child just born to the decrepit old man, so none is to be prohibited from Baptism, so none is there who does not die to sin in Baptism.

ST. AUGUSTINE, *Enchiridion de Fide,* 421

All those who were regenerated in Christ, are also made king with the sign of the cross and consecrated priest with the anointing of the Holy Spirit.

POPE ST. LEO THE GREAT (440–461), quoted by Pope John XXIII on November 11, 1961

With the grace received through baptism aiding and cooperating, all who are baptized in Christ can and ought, if they will strive faithfully, to fulfill what pertains to the salvation of the soul.

Church Council of Orange, 529

Baptism is a living, saving water on account of the Word of God which is in it.

MARTIN LUTHER, *Sermons on the Catechism,* 1528

Therefore let the conclusion be that baptism remains always good and its essence unimpaired even though one be baptized without true faith; for God's ordinance and Word cannot be changed nor perverted by mankind.

MARTIN LUTHER, *Larger Catechism,* c. 1529

Infants are not barred from the Kingdom of Heaven just because they happen to depart the present life before they have been immersed in water.

JOHN CALVIN, *Institutes,* IV, 1536

At whatever time we are baptized, we are at once for all washed and purged for our whole life.

JOHN CALVIN, *Institutes,* IV, 1536

Baptism is a sign of initiation, by which we are admitted into the society of the Church, in order that, being incorporated into Christ, we may be numbered among the children of God.

JOHN CALVIN, *Institutes,* IV, ch. xv, 1536

Baptism is God's Wardrobe; in Baptism we put on Christ; there we are invested, apparelled in Christ.

JOHN DONNE, *Sermon,* Spring, 1618

Baptismal grace is so great, so necessary, so life-giving for man, that it will never be taken away even from the heretic until his very death.

ST. SERAPHIM OF SAROV (1759–1833), *Conversation With Nicholas Motovilov*

Grace and salvation are not so inseparably annexed unto it as that no person can be regenerated or saved without it.

Constitution of the Presbyterian Church in U.S.A., 1930

In Baptism the Holy Spirit, which in the beginning of creation "moved upon the face of the waters," renews its hidden action on water as a primordial and representative element of the material world.

VLADIMIR SOLOVIEV, *God, Man and the Church, The Spiritual Foundations of Life,* 1938

At the hour of our baptism, Christ engraves an indelible character upon our soul, we receive the pledge of the Divine spirit.

COLUMBA MARMION, *Words of Life,* 1939

It is not just an abstract knowledge of truth that is given in the sacrament of Baptism; it is the abiding presence of the Truth. God is with us, and in us.

GERALD VANN, *the Divine Pity,* 1946

It is not the act of baptism, submitted to by one person and administered by another that brings about the remission of sins or provides salvation. It is a symbol and only a symbol. . . . When one accepts Jesus Christ by faith he is saved with all that salvation means. Therefore, nothing that comes after faith is essential to one's salvation.

AUSTIN CROUCH, *Is Baptism Essential to Salvation?,* 1953

Baptism does not produce faith and a new heart. . . . Regeneration is by the Holy Ghost alone and should precede baptism.

E. T. HISCOX, *The New Directory for Baptist Churches,* 1954

Not merely a token of the Christian profession . . . but it is also a sign of internal ablution or the new birth.

The Discipline of the Evangelical United Brethren, 1955

Baptism establishes a sacramental bond of unity which links all who have been reborn by it. But of itself baptism is only a beginning. . . . Baptism, therefore, envisages a complete profession of faith, complete incorporation in the system of salvation such as Christ willed it to be.

Constitution on the Church, Second Vatican Council, November, 1964

See also Catholic; Church: Its Membership; Fall, the; Original Sin; Sacraments; Sin.

BARBARISM

It is a Christian theological intuition, confirmed by all of historical experience, that man lives both his personal and his social life always more or less close to the brink of barbarism.

JOHN COURTNEY MURRAY, *Religion in America,* ed. John Cogley, 1958

See also Civilization; Pleasure; Worldliness.

BATTLE

I know of no true measure of men except the total of human energy they embody. . . . The final test of this energy is battle in some form.

OLIVER WENDELL HOLMES, *Speeches of,* 1934

See also Combat; Discord; War.

BEACONS

The glow of great souls revolves around the horizon only to show men how to fly from the tempest, or to govern their ship in the tempest.

ÉLIE FAURE, *The Dance over Fire and Water,* 1926

BEATIFIC VISION

The Vision of God is the greatest happiness to which man can attain. . . . Our imprisonment in bodies of clay and water and entanglement in the things of sense constitute a veil which hides the Vision of God from us.

AL-GHAZZALI (born 1058 A.D.), quoted in *The Sufi Path of Love,* ed. by Margaret Smith, 1954

In the Beatific Vision God manifests Himself to the elect in a general epiphany which, nevertheless, assumes various forms corresponding to the mental conceptions of God formed by the faithful on earth.

IBN-ARABI (1165–1240 A.D.), quoted by Miguel Asin Palacio, *Islam and the Divine Comedy,* 1926

My sight, becoming pure, was entering more and more through the radiance of the lofty Light which of itself is true. Thenceforward my vision was greater than our speech, which yields to such a sight, and the memory yields to such excess.

DANTE, *The Divine Comedy,* c. 1310

The eyes beloved and revered by God, fixed on the speaker, showed to us how pleasing unto her are devout prayers. Then to the Eternal Light were they directed, on which it is not to be believed that eye so clear is turned by any creature. And I, who to the end of all desires was approaching, even as I ought, ended within myself the ardor of my longings.

DANTE, *The Divine Comedy,* c. 1310

Thus my mind, wholly rapt, was gazing fixed, motionless, and intent, and ever with gazing grew enkindled. In that Light one becomes such that it is impossible he should ever consent to turn himself from it for other sight; because the Good which is the object of the will is all collected in it, and outside of it that is defective which is perfect there.

DANTE, *The Divine Comedy,* c. 1310

In Heaven the souls of the blessed enjoy an intuitive and face-to-face vision of the Divine Essence, without the intermediary of any creature heretofore known: the Divine Essence reveals itself unveiled, in perfect light and these blessed souls enjoy it always and for eternity.

POPE BENEDICT XII, *Constit. Benedictus Deus,* 1336

At the end of woe suddenly our eyes shall be opened, and in clearness of light our sight shall be full; which Light is God.

JULIANA OF NORWICH (1343–1443), *Revelation of Divine Love*

In the Beatific Vision God Himself is the idea, God Himself is in the mind; and here we have the radical difference between the Beatific Vision and every other kind of divine knowledge, however sublime. . . . The vision of God, enjoyed by the Blessed, is the vision of the totality of God.

ANSCAR VONIER, *The Human Soul,* 1913

See also Death; Ecstasy; Eternal Life; the various rubrics under God; Happiness; Heaven; Immortality; Light; Man and God; Man's Unity with God; Soul and God; Supernatural; Vision.

BEAUTIFUL, THE

A soft, smooth, slippery thing, and therefore of a nature which easily slips in and permeates our souls. For I affirm that the good is the beautiful.

PLATO, "Lysis, or Friendship," *Dialogues,* c. 370 B.C.

He who loves the Beautiful is called a lover because he partakes of that inspiration.

PLATO, *Phaedrus*, c. 370 B.C.

The first of all beautiful things is the continual possession of God.

ST. GREGORY NAZIANZEN (325–390 A.D.), *Epistolae*, 212

Being beautiful one should not be charmed by it: it is the light of the Lord, that shines in all bodies.

ARJAN, *The Adi Granth*, c. 1600

The Beautiful is that which apart from concepts is represented as the object of a universal satisfaction. . . . The beautiful is the symbol of the morally Good.

IMMANUEL KANT, *Critique of Judgment*, 1790

All which is the type of God's attributes— which in any way or in any degree—can turn the human soul from gazing upon itself . . . and fix the spirit—in all humility—on the type of that which is to be its food for eternity—this and this only is in the pure and right sense of the word BEAUTIFUL.

JOHN RUSKIN, written prior to 1845, publ. posth. in *Works*, IV, ed. Cook and Wedderburn

The beautiful is as useful as the useful. Perhaps more so.

VICTOR HUGO, *Les Misérables*, 1862

The effect which great beauty has upon us today is in a large measure that of exasperating our nerves, of making us restless and ultimately miserable. For we are paying the penalty for dissociating the beautiful from the moral.

LAWRENCE HYDE, *The Prospects of Humanism*, 1931

Nothing in human life, least of all in religion, is ever right until it is beautiful.

HARRY EMERSON FOSDICK, *As I See Religion*, 1932

The beautiful is holiness visible, holiness seen, heard, touched, holiness tasted.

ERIC GILL, *Last Essays*, 1942

See also Art; God: His Attributes; Good.

BEAUTY

Beloved Pan, and all ye other gods who haunt this place, give me beauty in the inward soul.

SOCRATES' PRAYER, *Phaedrus*, Plato, *Dialogues*, c. 399 B.C.

The Divine beauty is not adorned with any shape or endowment of form, or with any beauty of color, but is contemplated as excellence in unspeakable bliss.

ST. GREGORY OF NYSSA (c. 335–c. 395), *On the Making of Man*

Would you see true beauty? Look at the pious man or woman in whom spirit dominates matter; watch him when he prays, when a ray of the divine beauty glows upon him when his prayer is ended; you will see the beauty of God shining in his face.

GIROLAMO SAVONAROLA, *28th Sermon on Ezekiel*, c. 1489

In the Primal Solitude, while yet Existence gave no sign of being, and the universe lay hid in the negation of itself, Something was. . . . It was Beauty absolute, showing Herself to Herself alone, and by Her own light. . . . So Beauty Eternal came forth from the Holy Places of Mystery to beam on all horizons and all souls and a single ray darting from Her, struck Earth and its Heavens; and so she was revealed in the mirror of created things.

Muru'd-Din Abd-er-Rahman Jami (died 1492), quoted in A. U. Pope's *Masterpieces of Persian Art*

Beauty, I believe, comes from God; therefore there can be no beauty without goodness.

BALDASSARE CASTIGLIONE, *Libro del Cortegiano*, 1518

The beauty, the grace and the attractiveness of creatures, when compared in their entirety with the beauty of God, are utterly ugly and horrible.

ST. JOHN OF THE CROSS (1542–1591), *Ascent of Mount Carmel*

That is truly excellent which God hath caused to shine with the glory of His own rays; wheresoever there is beauty, I can never doubt of goodness.

ALGERNON SIDNEY (1622–1683), *Of Love*

We see the most proper image of the beauty of Christ when we see beauty in the human soul.

JONATHAN EDWARDS (1703–1758), *Representative Selections*

If the vision of a beautiful woman, or of any lovely thing, comes suddenly to a man's eyes, let him ask himself: whence this beauty if not from the divine force which permeates the world?

BAAL SHEM, *Tzavaat Ribash,* 1797

I can never feel certain of any truth, but from a clear perception of its beauty.

JOHN KEATS, *Letter to George Keats,* 1818

Beauty is merely the Spiritual making itself known sensuously.

G. W. F. HEGEL (1770–1831), *The Philosophy of Religion,* publ. posth.

A more secret, sweet and overpowering beauty appears to man when his heart and mind open to the sentiment of virtue. Then he is instructed in what is above him.

RALPH WALDO EMERSON, *Divinity School Address,* July 15, 1838

God has not made some beautiful things, but Beauty is the creator of the universe.

R. W. EMERSON, *The Poet,* 1844

Beauty is undoubtedly the signature of the Master to the work in which he has put his soul; it is the divine spirit manifested.

HONORÉ DE BALZAC (1799–1850), *Treasure Bits from,* ed. Porter

The perception of beauty is a moral test.

HENRY DAVID THOREAU, *Journal,* June 21, 1852

It is not the worship of beauty we need so much as the beauty of holiness.

MICHAEL FAIRLESS, *The Roadmender,* 1895

There is nothing in the whole world that can vie with the soul in its eagerness for beauty, or in the ready power wherewith it adopts beauty unto itself.

MAURICE MAETERLINCK, *The Treasure of the Humble,* 1895

The natural and primitive relationship of soul to soul is a relationship of beauty. For beauty is the only language of the soul. . . . It has no other life, it can produce nothing else.

MAURICE MAETERLINCK, *The Treasure of the Humble,* 1895

Beauty is a pledge of the possible conformity between the soul and nature, and consequently a ground of faith in the supremacy of good.

GEORGE SANTAYANA, *The Sense of Beauty,* 1896

Oh son of dust! Be blind that thou mayest behold my beauty. . . . Be blind, that is, to all save my beauty; be deaf to all except my word; be ignorant to all but my knowledge; thus thou shalt enter my Presence with pure eyes, keen ears, and a purified heart.

BAHAULLAH, *Hidden Words,* late 19th century

As it is only in a theistic setting that beauty can retain its deepest meaning, and live its brightest lustre, so these great truths of aesthetics and ethics are but half-truths, isolated and imperfect, unless we add to them yet a third.

A. J. BALFOUR, *Theism and Humanism,* 1915

Wisdom is needed for the governance of this world, but beauty is needed for its existence. . . . No faith can live that is not beautiful.

DONN BYRNE, *Marco Polo*, 1920

Beauty is eternity gazing at itself in a mirror.

KAHLIL GIBRAN, *The Prophet*, 1923

Nothing that is in itself unbeautiful can have the least vital relation to religion; and, conversely, anything that is beautiful in itself or ministers to the sense of beauty is essentially religious.

W. J. DAWSON, *The Autobiography of a Mind*, 1925

In every man's heart there is a secret nerve that answers to the vibrations of beauty.

CHRISTOPHER MORLEY, *Essays*, 1928

All earthly beauty hath one cause and proof,
To lead the pilgrim soul to beauty above.

ROBERT BRIDGES, *Testament of Beauty*, 1929

Beauty is the distilled essence of love— love which suffers and aspires.

JOHN ELOF BOODIN, *God and Creation*, 1934

Moral beauty is an exceptional and very striking phenomenon. He who has contemplated it but once never forgets its aspect. This form of beauty is far more impressive than the beauty of nature and of science. It gives to those who possess its divine gifts, a strange, an inexplicable power.

ALEXIS CARREL, *Man, the Unknown*, 1935

The love of the beauty of this and that can be the lotus-flower that lulls us to forgetfulness of the One, of whom they are only a partial mirroring.

GERALD VANN, *The Heart of Man*, 1945

Beauty is a bitter, galling thing, as shocking as sin: in the sanctuary, when it proves a mirage enticing the heart to the embrace of emptiness or evil.

WALTER FARRELL, *My Way of Life*, 1952

"Beauty" *is not a biblical notion or term. The Scriptures speak . . . but very little or not at all of beauty. They do not tell us that God is Beauty, but that God is Love. Neither does Christ say that He is the Beauty, but that He is the Way. . . . This Way is not beautiful, but rough and painful.*

STANLEY R. HOOPER, *Spiritual Problems in Contemporary Literature*, 1952

See also Art; Art and Morality; Beautiful, the; God: His Attributes; Good; Holiness; Moral Beauty.

BEGGARS

Acts of begging are scratches and wounds by which a man woundeth his own face; then he who wisheth to guard his face from scratches and wounds must not beg, unless that a man asketh from his prince, or in an affair in which there is no remedy.

MOHAMMED, *Speeches and Table-Talk of*, 7th century A.D.

As for idle beggars, happy for them if fewer people spent their foolish pity upon their bodies, and if more shewed some wise compassion upon their souls.

RICHARD STEELE, *The Tradesman's Calling*, 1684

See also Almsgiving; Charity; Compassion; Poor, the; Poverty.

BEHAVIOR

The human race is tolerated in the universe only on strict condition of good behavior.

L. P. JACKS, *Constructive Citizenship*, 1928

The penalty for wrong biological behavior is pain. Failure to attain those moral and spiritual goals which the experience of the race has found to be the highest brings more subtle forms of pain and grief.

EDMUND W. SINNOTT, *Matter, Mind and Man,* 1957

My generation of radicals and breakers-down never found anything to take the place of the old virtues of work and courage and the old graces of courtesy and politeness.

F. SCOTT FITZGERALD (1896–1940), *Letter to his daughter,* in *The Letters of,* 1963

See also Conduct; Morality; Morals; Practice; Religion: Its Nature and Function; Virtue.

BEHAVIORISM

Reductive Materialism in general, and strict Behaviorism in particular . . . are instances of the numerous class of theories which are so preposterously silly that only very learned men could have thought of them.

C. D. BROAD, *The Mind and Its Place in Nature,* 1925

The behaviorist thinks that there is no thinking—a most peculiar paradox, and in strict consistency he ought no longer to make up his mind to anything.

GEORGIA HARKNESS, *Conflicts in Religious Thought,* 1929

BEING

All things come from being, and being comes from non-being.

LAO-TZU, *Tao Tê Ching,* 6th century B.C.

Being is as it were a torrent, in and out of which all bodies pass, coalescing and co-operating with the whole, as the various parts in us do with one another.

MARCUS AURELIUS, *Meditations,* c. 170

In Buddhism being cannot strictly be predicated of anything, or of any god or animal or man—each is really only becoming.

A footnote, Vol. 36, pp. 101–102 of *Sacred Books of the East,* explaining the saying in *Questions of King Milanda* (probably 2nd century A.D.): "And in the highest sense there is no such thing as being possessed of being."

Being is perfection of power to be.

JOHN DEWEY, *Experience and Nature,* 1925

See also Energy; God: His Existence; God: His Nature; God: His Omnipresence; God as Being; Humanity; Reality; Universe; Universe: Its Creation; Universe and God.

BELIEF

For what is believed unknown cannot be called found, nor is any one capable of finding God, unless he first believes that he will eventually find Him.

ST. AUGUSTINE, *On Free Will,* II, 2, 6, c. 400

A person can do other things against his will; but belief is possible only in one who is willing.

ST. AUGUSTINE, *Tractate* XXVI *in Joann.,* c. 416

Understanding is the reward of faith. Therefore seek not to understand that thou mayest believe, but believe that thou mayest understand.

ST. AUGUSTINE, *On the Gospel of St. John,* XXIX, c. 416

Those who believe and do not obscure their faith with wrong, they are those who shall have security and they are guided.

Koran, 7th century A.D.

That belief should be accorded sacraments where reason fails is but what Christ has deserved of us by his many benefits and great miracles.

JOHN OF SALISBURY, *Policraticus,* 1159

The Torah does not oblige us to believe absurdities.

JOSEPH ALBO, *Ikkarim,* 1428

We should always be disposed to believe that which appears to us to be white is really black, if the hierarchy of the Church so decides.

ST. IGNATIUS LOYOLA, *Spiritual Exercises,* 1541

We believe nothing so firmly as what we least know.

MICHEL DE MONTAIGNE, *Essays,* 1580

The human understanding is no dry light, but receives an infusion from the will and affections. . . . What a man had rather were true he more readily believes.

FRANCIS BACON, *Novum Organum,* 1620

It is your own assent to yourself, and the constant voice of your own reason, and not of others, that should make you believe.

BLAISE PASCAL, *Pensées,* 1670

Belief consists not in the nature and order of our ideas, but in the manner of their conception, and in their feeling to the mind. . . . something *felt* by the mind, which distinguishes the ideas of the judgment from the fictions of the imagination.

DAVID HUME, *Of the Understanding,* 1748

The belief of a God, so far from having any thing of mystery in it, is of all beliefs the most easy, because it arises to us . . . out of necessity.

THOMAS PAINE, *The Age of Reason,* 1795

Man, to behave, has no need of problems, but of beliefs. His cradle must be surrounded by dogmas, and when his reason awakes, it is necessary that he find all his opinions made.

JOSEPH DE MAISTRE (1753–1821), *Étude sur la Souveraineté*

And the belief in a God All Powerful wise and good, is so essential to the moral order of the World and to the happiness of man, that arguments which enforce it cannot be drawn from too many sources.

JAMES MADISON, *Letter to Frederick Beasley,* November 20, 1825

In this, as in all other revelations of God's relation to man, we must be content to believe without aspiring to comprehend.

HENRY MANSEL, *Prolegomena Logica,* 1851

All those things are to be believed by divine and Catholic faith which are contained in the written and unwritten word of God, and which are proposed by the Church as divinely revealed, either by a solemn definition or in the exercise of its ordinary and universal Magisterium.

VATICAN COUNCIL, Sess. iii, cap. 3, 1870

The belief in God has often been advanced as . . . the most complete of all distinctions between man and the lower animals. It is, however, impossible . . . to maintain that this belief is innate or instinctive in man.

CHARLES DARWIN, *The Descent of Man,* 1871

Strong beliefs win strong men, and then make them stronger.

WALTER BAGEHOT, *Physics and Politics,* 1876

Believe to the end, even if all men went astray and you were left the only one faithful; bring your offering even then and praise God in your loneliness.

FATHER ZOSSIMA, in Feodor Dostoevsky, *The Brothers Karamazov,* 1880

If a scholar arrives at a belief in these profound and lofty subjects which does not correspond to the belief of the majority of Jews, he is not therefore an apostate.

S. D. LUZZATTO, *Penine Shadal,* 1883

If we would find God in that full satisfaction of all our desires which He promises, we must believe extravagantly, i.e., as the Church and the Saints do: and must not be afraid to follow the doctrine of the Incarnation into all its natural consequences.

COVENTRY PATMORE, *The Rod, the Root and the Flower,* 1895

We are driven in mere self-defense to hold that behind these non-rational forces, and above them, guiding them by slow degrees, and, as it were, with difficulty, *stands that supreme Reason in whom we must believe, if we are to believe anything.*

A. J. BALFOUR, *Foundations of Belief,* 1895

It is always easier to believe than to deny. Our minds are naturally affirmative.

JOHN BURROUGHS, *The Light of Day,* 1900

There is no mere "will to believe"; a merely willed belief is a sham belief; it is no real belief.

ROBERT FLINT, *Agnosticism,* 1903

The Bible never commands us to believe, though it commends belief. Such a command would be useless. Belief cannot be coerced.

MORRIS JOSEPH, *Judaism as Creed and Life,* 1903

Belief is thought at rest.

CHARLES S. PEIRCE (1839–1914), *Collected Papers*

Belief is the demi-cadence which closes a musical phrase in the symphony of our intellectual life.

CHARLES S. PEIRCE (1839–1914), *Collected Papers*

One great gain that the scientific use of the comparative method in religion has brought us is the duty of genuine reverence for other men's beliefs. . . . Whatever thoughts any human soul is seeking to live by, deserve the reverence of every other human soul.

WILLIAM TEMPLE, *The Universality of Christ,* 1921

I cannot agree with those philosophers who maintain that religion is based on the will to believe. The two are clearly connected, but it would be truer to say that the will to believe is based on religion. . . . God is not a product, but the author and living principle of the will to believe.

L. P. JACKS, *Religious Perplexities,* 1922

No church can fulfill its functions or be faithful to the religion, unless it can be said of it with utter truth that it has no belief at all.

JOHN HAYNES HOLMES, *Sermon,* reported in *New York Times,* January 28, 1924

To tip the scales by the will to believe is childish foolishness since things will generally continue to weigh what they do despite this tipping.

MORRIS R. COHEN, *Journal of Philosophy and Scientific Method,* 1925

The argument that we should believe certain things because they are helpful to what we have assumed to be practical interests, is a wilful confusion between what may be pleasant for the time being and what is determined by the weight of rational evidence.

MORRIS R. COHEN, *Journal of Philosophy and Scientific Method,* 1925

Belief in a personal moral God has led all too frequently to a theoretical dogmatism and practical intolerance.

ALDOUS HUXLEY, *Ends and Means,* 1937

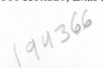

Belief in God, whatever else it may involve, at least includes the capacity to live as part of the whole of things in a world which is unified.

JOHN MACMURRAY, *Creative Society,* 1938

Religious belief is a total assertion which has for its subject the whole world order.

J. L. STOCKS, *Reason and Intuition,* 1939

Faith is belief, and belief has, over and above its intellectual character, an aspect of firmness, persistence, and subjective certainty.

RALPH BARTON PERRY, *Puritanism and Democracy,* 1944

True belief transcends itself; it is belief in something—in a truth which is not determined by faith, but which, on the contrary, determines faith.

ERICH FRANK, *Philosophic Understanding and Religious Truths,* 1945

Belief in God is acceptance of the basic principle that the universe makes sense, that there is behind it an ultimate purpose.

CARL WALLACE MILLER, *A Scientist's Approach to Religion,* 1947

Belief in God is not always beneficial to human life. Falsely used, it may become an escape from reality or a justification for a dogmatic arrogance that destroys the very fibre of human community.

EDW. LEROY LONG, JR., *Religious Beliefs of American Scientists,* 1952

While pleading the common ignorance, I also share the common hope. This subject touches the pathos of life so closely, . . . that if I had only negations to offer I should remain silent. . . . My philosophy tells me that even in default of knowledge belief is sometimes justified by the insistence or depth of the need which it satisfies.

RALPH BARTON PERRY, *The Humanity of Man,* 1956

Belief in God means believing . . . that the ideals . . . we cherish are real, that justice, peace, brotherhood, compassion and honesty . . . actually emerge out of the very structure of the universe.

IRA EISENSTEIN, *Judaism under Freedom,* 1956

Belief cannot argue with unbelief: it can only preach to it.

ALEXANDER MACINTYRE, *Metaphysical Beliefs,* 1957

Belief is the natural possession of beings possessing minds.

MARTIN C. D'ARCY, *The Nature of Belief,* 1958

Could it not be, with many of us, that the time we employ in denouncing, let us say, the evils of Russian atheism, would be more profitably devoted to asking what sort of God it is that we ourselves believe in?

AELRED GRAHAM, *Address,* Pittsburgh, Pa., April, 1960

See also Affirmation; Agnosticism; Agnostics; Atheism; Atheists; Believing; Coercion; Commitment; Creeds; Doctrine; Dogma; Doubt; Experience, Religious; Faith; Faith, Definitions of; Freedom, Religious; Knowledge; Libido; Loyalty; Miracles; Orthodoxy; Paths; Practice; Pragmatism; Reason; Religion Defined; Religion, Necessity of; Science and God; Skepticism; Spiritual Struggle; Theism; Theist; Tolerance; Tradition; Truth; Unbelief; Vision; Worship.

BELIEVING

All believers are brothers.

Koran, c. 625

One who believes but is guilty of some breach of the laws is a believing sinner, and God will do as He wishes about him:

punish him if He wills, and forgive him if He wills.

ABŪ HANĪFA (died 924), *Epistle to 'Uthmān al-Batti*

A man may be a heretic to the truth if he believes things only because his pastor says so, or the assembly so determines, without knowing other reason; though his belief be true, yet the very truth he holds becomes his heresy.

JOHN MILTON, *Aeropagitica,* 1644

To say a man is bound to believe, is neither truth nor sense.

JONATHAN SWIFT, *Thoughts on Religion,* 1728

He does not believe that does not live according to his belief.

THOMAS FULLER, *Gnomologia,* 1732

As cowards, that are well backed, will appear boldest, he that believes as the Church believes is more violent, though he knows not what it is.

SAMUEL BUTLER, *Remains,* 1759

My son, keep your spirit always in such a state as to desire that there be a God, and you will never doubt it.

JEAN JACQUES ROUSSEAU, *Émile,* 1762

He is less remote from the truth who believes nothing, than he who believes what is wrong.

THOMAS JEFFERSON, *Notes on the State of Virginia,* 1781

I believe in one God, Creator of the Universe. That He governs it by His Providence. That He ought to be worshipped. That the most acceptable service we render Him is doing good to His other children. That the soul of man is immortal, and will be treated with justice in another life respecting its conduct in this.

BENJAMIN FRANKLIN, *Letter to Ezra Stiles,* 1790

I believe in God—this is a fine, praiseworthy thing to say. But to acknowledge God wherever and however He manifest Himself, that in truth is heavenly bliss on earth.

J. W. VON GOETHE (1749–1832), *Maxims and Reflections*

A man lives by believing something; not by debating and arguing about many things.

THOMAS CARLYLE, *Heroes and Hero Worship,* 1840

Do you think that I should possess the gift of causing you to believe in God, if the germ of that belief did not exist in the depths of your heart, if there were not in your soul that which Tertullian called *a testimony naturally Christian?*

JEAN BAPTISTE LACORDAIRE, *Conferences of,* c. 1850

What takes place in us when we believe is a phenomenon of intimate and superhuman light.

JEAN BAPTISTE LACORDAIRE, *Conferences de Notre Dame de Paris,* 17th conference, 1850

We are born believing. A man bears beliefs, as a tree bears apples.

RALPH WALDO EMERSON, "Worship," *Conduct of Life,* 1860

We believe willingly what we love, and rarely what we love not. To the question of divine faith is united the question of divine virtue.

JEAN BAPTISTE LACORDAIRE (1802–1861), *Thoughts and Teachings of,* 1902

Man is a being born to believe, and if no church comes forward with all the title deeds of truth, . . . he will find altars and idols in his own heart and his own imagination.

BENJAMIN DISRAELI, *Speech,* Oxford, November 25, 1864

It is simply absurd to say you believe, or even want to believe, if you do not anything He tells you.

GEORGE MACDONALD, *Unspoken Sermons,* 2nd Series, 1886

Travellers from one religion to another, people who have lost their spiritual nationality, may often retain a neutral and confused residuum of belief, which they may egregiously regard as the essence of all religion.

GEORGE SANTAYANA, *Reason in Religion,* 1905

If there exists a man of faith in God joined to a life of purity and moral elevation, it is not so much the believing in God that makes him good, as the being good, thanks to God, that makes him believe in Him.

MIGUEL DE UNAMUNO Y JUGO, *Tragic Sense of Life,* 1921

I have never known a thinking man who did not believe in God. . . . Everyone who reflects at all believes, in one way or another, in God. . . . To me it is unthinkable that a real atheist should exist at all.

ROBERT A. MILLIKAN, *World's Work,* April, 1926

It is not really a question of what a man is made to believe but of what he must believe; what he cannot help believing.

G. K. CHESTERTON, *The Catholic Church and Conversion,* 1926

I cannot quite understand how a human being can face life without a belief in a Supreme Power, a Personality with whom communion can be a real thing.

MARY E. WOOLEY, *On the Meaning of Life,* ed. Will Durant, 1932

Men in the nineteenth century were sad that they could no longer believe in God; they are more deeply saddened now by the fact that they can no longer believe in man.

IRWIN EDMAN, *Candle in the Dark,* 1939

They dare not believe because they are afraid that what they most deeply want is not true.

NELS F. S. FERRÉ, *Faith and Reason,* 1946

To believe in God must mean to live in such a manner that life could not possibly be lived if God did not exist.

JACQUES MARITAIN, *The Review of Politics,* July, 1949

Every believer has to come to Christ through some other believer, and so the chain that goes back ultimately links each one of us with the life of our Lord on earth.

C. T. CRAIG, *The One Church,* 1951

The average man who goes wrong in belief does it when he forgets that there are other truths besides his favorite one.

CLELAND B. McAFEE, *Near to the Heart of God,* 1954

And this I do believe above all, especially in times of greater discouragement, that I must BELIEVE—that I must believe in my fellow men—that I must believe in myself—that I must believe in God—if life is to have any meaning.

MARGARET CHASE SMITH, *This I Believe,* 1954

Psychiatrists have sharp, taut, documentary proof that what a person believes about God is a vital ingredient in an individual's mental and emotional health.

GEORGE C. ANDERSON, *Man's Right to Be Human,* 1959

A religious man who says in his heart there is a God receives his life daily by divine appointment as a gift and a task set before him.

> PAUL RAMSEY, *Nine Modern Moralists,* 1962

Men may be compelled to do many things against their will, but no person can be compelled to believe.

> JOSEPH CARDINAL RITTER, *The Advocate* (organ of Newark, N.J., Roman Catholic archdiocese), October 31, 1963

See also Agnostics; Atheists; Belief; Coercion; Communion of Saints; Doubt; Indifference; Man; Practice.

BELLS

A bell is the Devil's instrument.

> MOHAMMED, *Speeches and Table-Talk of,* 7th century A.D.

Bells are the publicity of God. In France people say, "God is advertising Himself."

> R. L. BRUCKBERGER, *One Sky to Share,* 1951

BEREAVEMENT

I never prayed the gods that my son should be long lived. . . . But this rather was my prayer, that they would vouchsafe him the grace to be a good man, and to love and serve his country well.

> XENOPHON (4th century B.C.) upon learning of his son's death in battle, recalled by Plutarch in a letter of consolation to Apollonius

If we have been bereaved of our choicest blessings, we have enjoyed them, too. To be bereft is the lot of all: to enjoy is not the lot of many.

> POPE ST. GREGORY THE GREAT, (590–604), *Sepulchral Epigrams*

Our life is not so pleasant that those who escape from it need to be much lamented.

> ST. FRANCIS OF SALES (1567–1622), *Consoling Thoughts,* ed. Huguet

A family which allows one of its members to die without being wept for shows by that very fact that it lacks moral unity and cohesion; it abdicates, it renounces its existence.

> ÉMILE DURKHEIM, *The Elementary Forms of the Religious Life,* 1915

Since we hope he is gone to God and to rest, it is an ill expression of our love to them that we weep for their good fortune.

> JEREMY TAYLOR, *Holy Living,* 1650

Bereavement is the deepest initiation into the mysteries of human life, an initiation more searching and profound than even happy love. . . . Bereavement is the sharpest challenge to our trust in God; if faith can overcome this, there is no mountain which it cannot remove.

> W. R. INGE, *Survival and Immortality,* 1919

When the cold hand of death is laid upon those whom you love, and your heart seems torn in twain, climb to the Hill of Calvary to be consoled by the Mother of Sorrows who is also the Cause of our Joy.

> FULTON J. SHEEN, *The Fullness of Christ,* 1935

See also Affliction; Death; Grief; Mourning; Sadness; Tragedy.

BIBLE

If we cannot find explanations of all things which require investigation in the Scriptures, let us not seek for a second god beyond the One who is.

> ST. IRENAEUS, *Against Heresies,* c. 175

If anyone read the Scriptures . . . he will be both a perfect disciple and like unto a householder who brings forth out of his treasure new things and old.

> ST. IRENAEUS, *Against Heresies,* c. 175

Who shall understand the marrow of Scripture better than the school of Christ itself, whom the Lord had adopted as His disciples, namely to be taught of all things, and has set as masters over us, namely to teach all things?

TERTULLIAN, *Scorpiace,* c. 209

The study of inspired Scripture is the chief way of finding our duty.

ST. BASIL (330–379), *Letter to Gregory of Nazianzen*

One element the two Testaments have in common. They were established without any abrupt or instantaneous transformation. . . . God did not wish us to be coerced, but persuaded.

ST. GREGORY OF NAZIANZEN, *Fifth Theological Discourse,* c. 380

As in Paradise, God walks in the Holy Scriptures, seeking man. When a sinner reads these Scriptures, he hears God's voice saying, "Adam, where art thou?"

ST. AMBROSE, *de Paradiso,* c. 390

If there is anything in this life which sustains a wise man and induces him to maintain his serenity amidst the tribulations and adversities of the world, it is in the first place, I consider, the meditation and knowledge of the Scriptures.

ST. JEROME, *In Ephesius,* c. 400

Let sleep find you holding your Bible and when your head nods let it be resting on the sacred page.

ST. JEROME, *to Eustochium,* c. 405

Whatever they can really demonstrate to be true of physical nature we must show to be capable of reconciliation with our Scriptures; and whatever they assert in their treatises which is contrary to these Scriptures of ours, that is to the Catholic faith, we must either prove it as well as we can to be entirely false, or at all events we must, without the smallest hesitation, believe it to be so.

ST. AUGUSTINE, *De Genesi ad litteratum,* 415

In regard to the figure of the heavens the inspired writers knew what is naturally true (or considered as such in their time); but that the Spirit of God, speaking with their lips, did not will to teach men such things as were not directly useful to their eternal salvation.

ST. AUGUSTINE, *De Genesi ad litteratum,* 415

We ought to listen to the Scriptures with the greatest caution, for as far as understanding of them goes we are as but little children.

ST. AUGUSTINE, *Tractate* XVIII *in Joann.,* P.L. XXXV, c. 416

Love the Bible and wisdom will love you; and it will preserve you; honor it and it will embrace you; these are jewels which you should wear on your breasts and in your ears.

ST. JEROME (340–420), *Epist.* CXXX, 20

When you are really instructed in the Divine Scriptures, and have realized that its laws and testimonies are the bonds of truth, you can contend with adversaries.

ST. JEROME (340–420), *Epist.* LXXVIII, 30

In the Law is the shadow, in the Gospel is the Truth. . . . in the former we are slaves, in the latter the Lord Who is present speaks; in the former are promises, in the latter the fulfillment; in the former are the beginnings, in the latter their completion.

ST. JEROME (340–420), *Adv. Pelag.* I.31, P.L. XXIII

Everything in the Sacred Books shines and glistens, even in its outer shell: but the marrow of it is sweeter: if you want the kernel, you must break the shell.

ST. JEROME (340–420), *Epist.* LXIX

Ignorance of the Bible means ignorance of Christ.

> St. Jerome (340–420), *Prol. in Comment. in Isa.*

If in these books I meet anything which seems contrary to truth I shall not hesitate to conclude that the text is faulty, or that the translator has not expressed the meaning of that passage, or that I myself do not understand.

> St. Augustine (345–430), to St. Jerome, *Ep.* LXXVII, I

For what page, or what discourse, of Divine authority of the Old or the New Testament is not a most perfect rule for human life?

> St. Benedict of Nursia (c. 480–c. 533), *Rule of*

There is nothing empty and nothing idle in divine literature, but what is said is always said for some useful purpose in order that this purpose may be received in its proper meaning and bring salvation.

> Cassiodorus, *The Divine Letters,* c. 550

It is, as it were, a kind of river, if I may so liken it, which is both shallow and deep, wherein both the lamb may find a footing and the elephant float at large.

> Pope St. Gregory the Great, *Magna Moralia,* 584

The Bible is not the sole basis of our religion, for in addition to it we have two other bases. One of these is anterior to it: namely, the fountain of reason. The second is posterior to it: namely, the source of tradition. Whatever, therefore, we may not find in the Bible, we can find in the two other sources.

> Saadia ben Joseph (892–942), *The Book of Beliefs and Opinions*

Do not despise what is lowly in God's word, for by lowliness you will be enlightened to divinity. The outward form of God's word seems to you, perhaps like dirt. . . . But hear! that dirt, which you trample, opened the eyes of the blind.

> Hugh of St. Victor, *De Scripturis,* c. 1125

The Scriptures inculcate chiefly the necessity of repairing what was lost by sin and of reconstructing the broken order of things.

> St. Bonaventure, *The Journey of the Mind to God,* 1259

By the Mosaic Law men may be said to be purified, and by the prophetic revelations they are enlightened, and by the evangelical message they are brought to perfection.

> St. Bonaventure, *The Journey of Mind to God,* 1259

It is one of the glories of the Bible that it can enshrine many meanings in a single passage. . . . Each man marvels to find in the divine Scriptures truths which he has himself thought out.

> St. Thomas Aquinas, *De Potentia,* 1263

I wish to show that there is one wisdom which is perfect, and that this is contained in the Scriptures.

> Roger Bacon, *Opus Maius,* 1267

Holy Scripture is so exalted that there is no one in the world . . . wise enough to understand it so fully that his intellect is not overcome by it. Nevertheless, man can stammer something about it.

> Blessed Angela of Foligno (1248–1309), *Book of Vision and Instructions*

The Bible is for the government of the people, by the people, and for the people.

> John Wycliff, Preface to his translation of *The Bible,* 1384

Each place of holy writ, both open and dark, teaches meekness and charity; and therefore he that keepeth meekness and charity hath the true understanding and perfection of all holy writ. . . . Therefore no simple man of wit be afraid unmeasurably to study in the text of holy writ.

JOHN WYCLIFF, Preface to his translation of *The Bible,* 1384

If thou wilt profit by reading of Scripture, read meekly, simply, and faithfully, and never desire to have thereby the name of cunning.

THOMAS À KEMPIS, *Imitation of Christ,* 1441

You will feel yourself breathed upon by divine will, affected, seized, transfigured, in an ineffable manner, if you approach Scripture religiously with veneration, humbly.

DESIDERIUS ERASMUS, *Enchiridion,* 1501

I utterly dissent from those who are unwilling that the sacred Scriptures should be read by the unlearned translated into their vulgar tongue, as though Christ had taught such subtleties that can scarcely be understood even by a few theologians, or as though the strength of the Christian religion consisted in men's ignorance of it.

DESIDERIUS ERASMUS, *Introduction to Novum Instrumentum,* 1516

The soul can do without everything, except the word of God, without which none at all of its wants are provided for.

MARTIN LUTHER, *On Christian Liberty,* 1520

Of the whole of Scripture there are two parts: the law and the gospel. The law indicates the sickness, the gospel the remedy.

PHILIP MELANCHTHON, *Common Topics,* 1521

These words give us all a sure medicine . . . by which we shall keep from sickness, not the body . . . but the soul, which here preserved from the sickness of sin, shall after this eternally live in joy.

ST. THOMAS MORE, *The Four Last Things,* 1522

The Spirit is needed for the understanding of all Scripture and every part of Scripture.

MARTIN LUTHER, *Bondage of the Will,* 1525

What God has so plainly declared to the world is in some parts of Scripture stated in plain words, while in other parts it still lies hidden under obscure words.

MARTIN LUTHER, *Bondage of the Will,* 1525

For except a man first believe, that holy scripture is the word of God, and that the word of God is true, how can a man take any comfort of that, that the scripture telleth him therein?

ST. THOMAS MORE, *Dialogue of Comfort against Tribulation,* 1535

We believe and confess that the Canonical Scriptures of the Old and New Testaments are the true Word of God, and have sufficient authority in and of themselves, and not from men. . . . They contain all that is necessary to a saving faith and a holy life; and hence nothing could be added to or taken from them.

HENRY BULLINGER, *The Helvetic Confession,* 1536

They who have been inwardly taught by the Spirit, feel an entire acquiescence in the scripture.

JOHN CALVIN, *Institutes,* I, 1536

It is only in the scriptures that the Lord hath been pleased to preserve his truth in perpetual remembrance; it obtains the same complete credit and authority with believers, where they are satisfied of its divine origin, as if they heard the very words pronounced by God Himself.

JOHN CALVIN, *Institutes,* I, 1536

On any of the secret mysteries of the Scripture, we ought to philosophize with great sobriety and moderation; and also with extreme caution, lest either our ideas or our language should proceed beyond the limits of the divine word.

JOHN CALVIN, *Institutes,* I, 1536

The Scripture, collecting in our minds the otherwise confused notions of Deity, dispels the darkness and gives us a clear view of the true God.

JOHN CALVIN, *Institutes,* Bk. I, 1536

Scripture is the school of the Holy Spirit, in which, as nothing is omitted that is both necessary and useful to know, so nothing is taught but what is expedient to know.

JOHN CALVIN, *Institutes,* III, 1536

I have made a covenant with my Lord God that He send me neither visions nor dreams, nor even angels. For I am well satisfied with the gift of Holy Scriptures, which gives me abundant instruction and all that I need to know both for this life and for that which is to come.

MARTIN LUTHER (1483–1546) quoted in *What Luther Says*

It teaches us to see, feel, grasp, and comprehend faith, hope, and charity far otherwise than mere human reason can; and when evil oppresses us it teaches how these virtues throw light upon the darkness, and how, after this poor, miserable existence of ours on earth, there is another and eternal life.

MARTIN LUTHER (1483–1546), *Table-Talk*

All men now presume to criticize the Bible; almost every old doting fool or prating sophist must, forsooth, be a doctor of divinity.

MARTIN LUTHER (1483–1546), *Table-Talk*

The devil can cite Scripture for his purpose.

WILLIAM SHAKESPEARE, *The Merchant of Venice,* c. 1595

Prosperity is the blessing of the Old Testament; adversity is the blessing of the New.

FRANCIS BACON, *Essays,* 1597

For the Bible is not chained in every expression to conditions as strict as those which govern all physical effects; nor is God any less excellently revealed in Nature's actions than in the sacred statements of the Bible.

GALILEO, *Letter to Castelli,* December, 1613

I believe that the intention of Holy Writ was to persuade men of the truths necessary to salvation; such as neither science nor other means could render credible, but only the voice of the Holy Spirit.

GALILEO, *Letter to Father Benedetto Castelli,* 1613

Unspeakable mysteries in the Scriptures are often delivered in a vulgar and illustrative way; and being written unto man, are delivered, not as they truly are, but as they may be understood.

THOMAS BROWNE, *Religio Medici,* 1635

I have sometimes seen more in a line of the Bible than I could well tell how to stand under, and yet another time the whole Bible hath been to me as dry as a stick.

JOHN BUNYAN, *Grace Abounding,* 1666

Its object is not to convince the reason, but to attract and lay hold of the imagination.

BARUCH SPINOZA, *Tractatus Theologico-Politicus,* 1670

All Scripture was written primarily for an entire people, and secondarily for the whole human race; consequently its contents must necessarily be adapted, as far as possible, to the understanding of the masses.

 BARUCH SPINOZA, *Tractatus Theologico-Politicus,* 1670

Scripture does not aim at imparting scientific knowledge, and therefore it demands from men nothing but obedience, and censures obduracy but not ignorance.

 BARUCH SPINOZA, *Tractatus Theologico-Politicus,* XIV, 1670

Because they [the Scriptures] are only a declaration of the fountain and not the fountain itself, therefore they are not to be esteemed the principal ground of all truth and knowledge nor yet the adequate, primary rule of faith and manners.

 ROBERT BARCLAY, *Apology,* 1678

Sir, if the Bible be not true, I am as very a fool and madman as you can conceive; but if it be of God I am sober-minded.

 JOHN WESLEY, to a friend, 1735

Peruse the words of our philosophers with all their pomp of diction; how mean, how contemptible they are, compared with the Scriptures. Is it possible that a book at once so simple and so sublime should be merely the work of man?

 JEAN JACQUES ROUSSEAU, *Emilius and Sophia,* 1762

I am a Bible-bigot. I follow it in all things, both great and small.

 JOHN WESLEY, *Journal,* June 2, 1766

We understand that your religion is written in a book. If it was intended for us as well as you, why has not the Great Spirit given it to us, and not only to us, but why did he not give it to our forefathers, the knowledge of that book, with the means of understanding it rightly?

 SENECA INDIAN CHIEF RED JACKET, to delegate from Evangelical Mission Society of Massachusetts, 1805

I have made it a practice for several years to read the Bible through in the course of every year. I usually devote to this reading the first hour after I rise in the morning.

 JOHN QUINCY ADAMS, *Diary,* September 26, 1810

The Bible is a window in this prison-world, through which we may look into eternity.

 TIMOTHY DWIGHT (1752–1817), quoted in C. Hurd's *A Treasury of Great American Quotations*

The Bible becomes ever more beautiful the more it is understood.

 J. W. VON GOETHE, *Wilhelm Meister's Travels,* 1830

Scripture gives us no reason to believe that the traditions, thus originally delivered to mankind at large, have been secretly reanimated and enforced by new communications from the unseen world.

 JOHN HENRY NEWMAN, *The Arians of the Fourth Century,* 1833

Those who do not believe in the authenticity of the Bible nevertheless believe, in spite of themselves, that there is something more than common in the same Bible.

 VISCOUNT FRANÇOIS DE CHATEAUBRIAND, *Genius of Christianity,* 1802

The words of the Bible find me at greater depths of my being than any other book does. Whatever *finds me* brings with it an irresistible evidence of having proceeded from the Holy Spirit.

 SAMEUL TAYLOR COLERIDGE, *Confessions of an Inquiring Spirit,* 1840

What a book! great and wide as the world, rooted in the abysmal depths of creation and rising aloft into the blue mysteries of heaven. . . . Sunrise and sunset, promise and fulfillment, birth and death, the whole human drama, everything is in this book. . . . It is the book of books, *Biblia.*

 HEINRICH HEINE, *Ludwig Boerne,* 1840

We ought, indeed, to expect occasional obscurity in such a book as the Bible, . . . but God's wisdom is a pledge that whatever is necessary for *us,* and necessary for salvation, is revealed too plainly to be mistaken.

> WILLIAM ELLERY CHANNNG (1780–1842), *Works*

We believe that God never contradicts in one part of Scripture what He teaches in another; and never contradicts in revelation what He teaches in His works and providence.

> WILLIAM ELLERY CHANNING (1780–1842), *Works*

The Bible is a book of faith, and a book of doctrine, and a book of morals, and a book of religion, of especial revelation from God.

> DANIEL WEBSTER, *Address* at Bunker Hill Monument completion, June 17, 1843

The Bible, the greatest medicine chest of humanity.

> HEINRICH HEINE, *Ludwig Marcus,* 1844

Notice that the structure and style of Scripture is a structure so unsystematic and various, and a style so figurative and indirect, that no one would presume at first sight to say what is in it and what is not.

> JOHN HENRY NEWMAN, *An Essay on the Development of Christian Doctrine,* 1845

Great questions exist in the subject-matter of which Scripture treats which Scripture does not solve.

> JOHN HENRY NEWMAN, *An Essay on the Development of Christian Doctrine,* 1845

The whole Bible is a hymn to Justice,— that is, in the Hebrew style, to charity, to kindness to the weak on the part of the strong, to voluntary renunciation of the privilege of power.

> P. J. PROUDHON, *System of Economical Contradictions,* 1846

We have used the Bible as if it were the special constable's books—an opium dose for keeping beasts of burden patient while they were being overloaded, a mere book to keep the poor in order.

> CHARLES KINGSLEY, *Letter to Chartists,* 1848

The Bible is like an old Cremona; it has been played upon by the devotion of thousands of years until every word and parable is public and tunable.

> RALPH WALDO EMERSON, *Quotation and Originality,* 1859

This great book . . . is the best gift God has given to man. . . . But for it we could not know right from wrong.

> ABRAHAM LINCOLN, to a delegation that presented him with a Bible, August, 1864

Take all this book upon reason that you can, and the balance on faith, and you will live and die a happier and better man.

> ABRAHAM LINCOLN, *Letter to Speed,* 1864

Experience proves surely that the Bible does not answer a purpose for which it was never intended. It may be accidentally the means of the conversion of individuals; but a book, after all, cannot make a stand against the wild living intellect of man.

> JOHN HENRY NEWMAN, *Apologia pro Vita Sua,* 1864

It nowhere lays claim to be regarded as *the* Word, *the* Way, *the* Truth. The Bible leads us to Jesus, the inexhaustible, the ever unfolding Revelation of God.

> GEORGE MACDONALD, *Unspoken Sermons,* 1st Series, 1869

The books of the Old and New Testament, whole and entire, with all their parts, as enumerated by the decree of the same Council [Trent] and in the ancient Latin Vulgate, are to be received as sacred and canonical.

> *Council of the Vatican,* Session iii, c. ii, *de Rɛo.,* 1870

We are not left at liberty to pick and choose out of its contents according to our judgment, but must receive it all, as we find it, if we accept it at all.

> JOHN HENRY NEWMAN, *Grammar of Assent,* 1870

Is the Bible a book intelligible at all? Far from it; it is full of obscurities and difficulties, not only for the illiterate, but even for the learned.

> JAMES GIBBONS, *The Faith of Our Fathers,* 1876

The Bible . . . is the classical book of noble ethical sentiment. In it the mortal fear, the overflowing hope, the quivering longings of the human soul . . . have found their first, their freshest, their fittest utterance.

> F. ADLER, *Creed and Deed,* 1877

The Bible in its various transformations is the great book of consolation for humanity.

> ERNEST RENAN, *History of Israel,* 1888

The material record of the Bible . . . is no more important to our well being than the history of Europe and America; but the spiritual application bears upon our eternal life.

> MARY BAKER EDDY, *Miscellaneous Writings,* 1888

Throughout the history of the western world, the Scriptures . . . have been the greatest instigators of revolt against the worst forms of clerical and political despotism.

> T. H. HUXLEY, *Controverted Questions,* 1892

The sacred writers . . . did not seek to penetrate the secrets of nature, but rather described and dealt with things in more or less figurative language, or in terms which were commonly used at the time.

> POPE LEO XIII, *Holy Scripture,* 1893

In their eyes a profane book or ancient document is accepted without hesitation, whilst the Scripture, if they only find in it a suspicion of error, is set down with the slightest possible discussion as quite untrustworthy.

> POPE LEO XIII, *Holy Scripture,* 1893

No one should be so presumptuous as to think that he understands the whole of Scripture.

> POPE LEO XIII, *Holy Scripture,* 1893

For the saving and perfecting of ourselves and of others there is at hand the very best of help in the Holy Scriptures, as the Book of Psalms, among others, so constantly insists.

> POPE LEO XIII, *Holy Scripture,* 1893

Humanity can never deny the Bible in its heart, without the sacrifice of the best that it contains, faith in unity and hope for justice.

> JAMES DARMSTETER, *Selected Essays,* 1895

Sometimes, when I read spiritual treatises . . . my poor little mind grows weary, I close the learned book, . . . and I take the Holy Scriptures. Then all seems luminous, a single word opens up infinite horizons to my soul, perfection seems easy.

> ST. THÉRÈSE OF LISIEUX (1873–1897), *Autobiography,* publ. posth.

So far as such equality, liberty and fraternity are included under the democratic principles which assume the same names, the Bible is the most democratic book in the world.

> T. H. HUXLEY, *Science and the Christian Tradition,* 1902

In following these leadings of scientific revelation, the Bible was my only textbook. The Scriptures were illumined; reason and revelation were reconciled, and afterward the truth of Christian Science was demonstrated.

MARY BAKER EDDY, *Science and Health,* 1908

We have seen Scripture become mere plain philosophy, the words of Christ the words of a teacher who has seen the ultimate realities and speaks them very simply, with the simplicity of utter authority.

WOODROW WILSON, *Baccalaureate Address,* Princeton, June 12, 1910

This is the people's book of revelation, revelation of themselves not alone, but revelation of life and of peace.

WOODROW WILSON, *Address,* May, 1911

The recognition of the authority of the Bible was not an innovation; theoretically it had been supreme since an early day.

A. C. MCGIFFERT, *Protestant Thought Before Kant,* 1911

A man has found himself when he has found his relation to the rest of the universe, and here is the Book in which those relations are set forth.

WOODROW WILSON, *Speech,* May 7, 1911

It is the very marrow of a race of lions. Stout hearts are those that feed on it. Without the antidote of the Old Testament the Gospel is tasteless and unwholesome fare. The Bible is the bone and sinew of nations with the will to live.

ROMAIN ROLLAND, *Jean Christophe, The House,* 1911

The Bible is God's book because it is in a unique and universal sense Man's book. It is the record of and the vehicle for transmitting a great human experience, an experience of God, of human need, and of God's response to that need.

RICHARD BROOK, *Foundations,* ed. B. H. Streeter, 1912

To the plain man the Bible is no longer the Book of Books. . . . He has learnt that the Bible is not infallible in its statements of fact, in its ethical teaching or even in its theology.

RICHARD BROOK, *Foundations,* ed. B. H. Streeter, 1912

Although he did not read it in any religious spirit, the moral . . . vital energy of that Hebraic Iliad had been to him a spring in which, in the evenings, he washed his naked soul of the smoke and mud of Paris.

ROMAIN ROLLAND, *Jean Christophe in Paris; Market-Place,* 1912

The Bible is our patent of nobility.

SOLOMON SCHECHTER, *Seminary Addresses,* 1915

The more deeply we enter into the study the more effect the teachings of Holy Writ will have over our minds.

AIDAN GASQUET, *Preface to Catholic Student's Aid to Study of the Bible,* by Hugh Pope, Vol. 4, 1918

Even those who do not believe that the Bible is the revelation of God, will admit that it is the supreme revelation of man.

WILLIAM LYON PHELPS, *Reading the Bible,* 1919

And none can fail to see what profit and sweet tranquillity must result in well-disposed souls from such devout reading of the Bible. Whoever comes to it in piety, faith and humility, and with a determination to make progress in it, will assuredly find therein and will eat the "bread that comes down from heaven."

POPE BENEDICT XV, *Spiritus Paracletus,* 1920

Our one desire for all the Church's children is that, being saturated with the Bible, they may arrive at the all-surpassing knowledge of Jesus Christ.

POPE BENEDICT XV, *Spiritus Paracletus,* 1920

The Bible is by no means the simple and easily understood book which many imagine. If reading it with simple faith has brought consolation to many, it has also brought misunderstanding and dissension. It is easy for men to read their own meanings into it and then proclaim them as the word of God, equally binding on all men.

EVERETT DEAN MARTIN, *Liberty,* 1930

It furnished good Christians an armor for their warfare, a guide for their conduct, a solace in their sorrows, food for their souls.

GAIUS GLENN ATKINS, *Religion in Our Times,* 1932

You can learn more about human nature by reading the Bible than by living in New York.

WILLIAM LYON PHELPS, *Radio Speech,* 1933

All the obscurities of Scripture and all its flashes of light will fall together, dragging each other, on one slope or the other, according to which side your heart is.

JOSEPH MALÈGUE, *Augustin ou le Maître est là,* 1933

Every idea in the Bible started from primitive and childlike origins and, with however many setbacks and delays, grew in scope and height toward the culmination in Christ's Gospel.

HARRY EMERSON FOSDICK, *The Modern Use of the Bible,* 1934

Holy Scripture . . . is God's Word in that it is a memory of a past revelation of God and an expectation of future revelation.

ADOLPH KELLER, *Religion and the European Mind,* 1934

Man moves toward God and God moves toward man. The Old Testament is man's search for God, the New Testament is God's search for man.

E. STANLEY JONES, *Victorious Living,* 1936

The Bible has ceased to be an authority and has become a source book.

CARL S. PATTON, *Journal of Religion,* XVI, 1936

Consecutive reading of Biblical books forces everyone who wants to hear put to himself . . . where God has acted once and for all for the salvation of men. . . . We are torn out of our own existence and set down in the midst of the holy history of God on earth. There God dealt with us, and there He still deals with us, our needs and our sins, in judgment and grace.

DIETRICH BONHOEFFER, *Life Together,* 1938

The central ideas of Scripture, in whatever changing categories they may be phrased, seem to me the hope of man's individual and social life.

HARRY EMERSON FOSDICK, *A Guide to Understanding the Bible,* 1938

How many times one has laid the Bible aside in favor of what seemed more real and compelling . . . only to be driven back to it again by the great hunger to let the measured dignity and beauty of its language stir in him an emotion like that which comes in listening to classical music or in seeing a finely proportioned building.

DOUGLAS V. STEERE, *Prayer and Worship,* 1938

The trouble with the Bible has been its interpreters, who have scaled down and whittled down that sense of infinitude into finite and limited concepts.

ALFRED NORTH WHITEHEAD, December, 1939, *Dialogues of,* as recorded by Lucien Price

Its power to speak truth to the human heart, to interpret one to himself, to present life's highest values challengingly is enough to make it The Great Book.

FRITZ KUNKEL, *How Character Develops,* 1940

If we depend exclusively upon Scripture for our knowledge of Christ, and then seek in His light to interpret Scripture, we simply move in a circle. The circle is broken by a proper appreciation of the significance of Christian experience, of the guidance of the Holy Spirit, and of the function of the Church.

EDWIN LEWIS, *A Philosophy of the Christian Revelation,* 1940

Instead of spending so much time searching for keys to the Scriptures, we do better to use the Scriptures as the keys for unlocking the secrets of progressive revelation.

RALPH W. SOCKMAN, *The Highway of God,* 1941

The faithful, in particular those who are well-informed in the sciences sacred and profane, wish to know what God has told us in the Sacred Letters rather than what an ingenious orator or writer may suggest by a clever use of the Words of Scripture.

POPE PIUS XII, *Divino Afflante Spiritu,* 1943

The Sacred Books were not given to men by God to satisfy their curiosity or to provide them with material for study and research, but, as the Apostle observes, in order that these Divine Words might "instruct in justice, by the faith which is in Christ Jesus," and "that the man of God

may be perfect, equipped for every good work."

POPE PIUS XII, *Divino Afflante Spiritu,* September, 1943

But who in a world, where people believe in newspapers, still seriously believe in the Bible? It is a fact that modern man experiences less difficulty in lending faith to the lies of the day than to the eternal truths transmitted by holy books.

DENIS DE ROUGEMENT, *The Devil's Share,* 1944

The glory shines from Christ, but it shines back into the whole of Scripture, making it one glorious body, full of the Holy Spirit. Thus it is that the spiritual sense of Scripture is established.

R. KEHOE, *Eastern Churches Quarterly,* 1947

Holy Scripture is the unchangeable word of God to which man must bend himself, and not something which he can bend to his own personal ideas.

JEAN DANIELOU, *Les Divers Sens de l'Écriture,* 1948

The difference between the Old and the New Testaments is the difference between a man who said "There is nothing new under the sun" and a God who says "Behold, I make all things new."

RONALD A. KNOX, *Stimuli,* 1951

Although we may differ in the manner in which tradition, reason and natural law may be used in the interpretation of Scripture, any teaching that clearly contradicts the Biblical positions cannot be accepted as Christian.

ALAN RICHARDSON and W. SCHWEITZER, *Biblical Authority for Today,* 1951

BIBLE—A collection of different legends, mutually contradictory and written at different times and full of historical errors, issued by churches as a "holy" book.

Slovar Inostrannykh Slov (Dictionary of Foreign Words), publ. by Soviet government, Moscow, Russia, 1951

We believe the Bible to be the word of God, as far as it has been translated correctly; we also believe the Book of Mormon to be the word of God.

JAMES E. TALMAGE, *Articles of Faith* (Church of Jesus Christ of Latter-Day Saints), 1952

Since God is known by what He has done, the Bible exists as a confessional recital of His acts, together with the teaching accompanying those acts, or inferred from them in the light of specific situations which the faithful confronted.

G. E. WRIGHT, *God Who Acts,* 1952

The Gospel is eternal: from age to age we may catch new accents in God's Word to men, but the Word itself is from the foundation of the world.

Interpreter's Bible, I, 1952

It is when we think of the Bible in terms of Christ that we best understand what it is and what it is not.

JOHN J. WRIGHT, *Pastoral Letter,* 1952

We advise all who feel hemmed in by a closed and stifling world to open the Old and New Testaments. They will there find vistas, which will liberate them, and the excellent food of the only true God.

EMMANUEL SUHARD, *The Church Today,* 1953

While studying the literal sense we come to realize the prodigious fact of the slow historical growth of a complete religious literature through many centuries, culminating in the Person of Christ. . . . When studying the symbolic sense we find the equally prodigious fact that this whole literature is after all One Book, penetrated throughout by the mystery that is the Beginning and the End—and all eternity between.

SEBASTIAN BULLOUGH, *The Life of the Spirit,* February-March, 1954

You venture to judge the Bible and up to a point it submits to your judgment, and then you may find the roles reversed—you are in the dock and the Bible is the judge pronouncing sentence upon you.

A. C. CRAIG, *Preaching in a Scientific Age,* 1954

The Christian whose norm is Scripture must always have a particularly uneasy conscience.

A. ROY ECKARDT, *Christian Century,* November 17, 1954

The best way to get to know the Bible is to my mind to read it as a child, aloud, in common, either at home or in school.

NICOLETTE GRAY, *The Life of the Spirit,* February-March, 1954

The Bible experienced is God experienced in all the length and breadth and height and depth of His revelation and communication to man.

E. I. WATKIN, *The Life of the Spirit,* February-March, 1954

There are no words in the world more knowing, more disclosing and more indispensable, words both stern and graceful, heart-rending and healing.

ABRAHAM JOSHUA HESCHEL, *God in Search of Man,* 1955

What Dryden said about Chaucer applies in infinitely greater degree to the Bible: "Here is God's plenty."

ROBERT J. MCCRACKEN, *The Making of the Sermon,* 1956

To give final devotion to the Book is to deny the final claim of God. . . . To love the Book as the source of strength and of salvation is to practice an idolatry that can bring only confusion into life.

> H. RICHARD NIEBUHR, *The Purpose of the Church and Its Ministry,* 1956

In practice, concentration on the Book is ultimately self-corrective since the Bible faithfully studied allows none to make it the highest good or its glorification the final end. It always points beyond itself . . . to the Creator.

> H. RICHARD NIEBUHR, *The Purpose of the Church and Its Ministry,* 1956

Men suffer from intellectual dyspepsia when they attempt to swallow the Bible whole, accepting at face value the mathematics and rhetoric of a people who thought in poetry rather than in prose.

> A. M. SULLIVAN, *The Three-Dimensional Man,* 1956

The Old and New Testaments belong to one scheme of things, but mark two successive stages in its development.

> JEAN DANIELOU, *The Lord of History,* 1958

The most serious obstacle which modern men encounter in entering a discussion about the idea of the Bible, is the absence of the problem to which the Bible refers.

> ABRAHAM JOSHUA HESCHEL, *Religion in America,* ed. John Cogley, 1958

If Scripture has been given us "for our instruction," then, it is education of a very particular kind: supernatural, religious and nothing else.

> HENRI DANIEL-ROPS, *What Is the Bible?,* 1958

The fundamental attitude of mind in Scripture—aspiration towards God, love reaching out to Him, the ardent desire one day to possess Him—is the only thing which can enable us to penetrate its mystery.

> HENRI DANIEL-ROPS, *What Is the Bible?,* 1958

The great principle dominating the composition of Scripture is that of the ascent towards discovery.

> HENRI DANIEL-ROPS, *What Is the Bible?,* 1958

The Old Testament together with the New Testament enables us to see that the events related in the New Testament are events which are inseparably connected with that original event recorded in Gen. 1–3 which concerned humanity as a whole.

> GUSTAVE WINGREN, *Theology in Conflict,* 1958

The "Bible alone" formula was a novelty able to develop only after Christianity had grown old, only after the canon of Scripture was of such ancient standing that the grounds for its acceptance could be forgotten and it could be torn from the history that had given it being, to exist thenceforth without genealogy.

> BRUCE VAWATER, *The Bible in the Church,* 1959

One must read the Bible continually to prevent the image of truth being obscured in us.

> JULIAN GREEN, *Journal,* 1961

In these days of biblical revival we must be sure that we are assisting not at an exhumation but at a true resurrection.

> ALEXANDER JONES, *God's Living Word,* 1962

What the Bible affirms is not the primacy of the spirtual over the material, or the power of ideals in history, but the rule of God over all.

> PAUL RAMSEY, *Nine Modern Moralists,* 1962

If all who believe in Christ will read the Scriptures in prayerful meditation and incorporate its teaching into their lives, they

will not only be drawn closer to Christ, but
to one another.
>AUGUSTIN BEA, *Address,* Cambridge,
>Mass., March, 1963

Man in the Bible is always on tiptoe,
straining his eyes for the first light of
dawn.
>GEORGE A. BUTTRICK, *Christ and History,* 1963

When one rereads the Bible as a Jew,
Protestant, Orthodox or Roman Catholic,
he may read it as a mirror of his preconceptions; when encouraged to read it in the
contexts of other traditions, he is apt to
find something hitherto overlooked.
>MARTIN E. MARTY, *New York Times
>Book Review,* February 9, 1964

Sacred Scriptures provide for the work of
dialogue an instrument of the highest value
in the mighty hand of God for the attainment of that unity which the Saviour holds
out to all.
>*Constitution on the Church,* Second
>Vatican Council, November, 1964

Other books were given for our information, the Bible was given for our transformation.
>ANONYMOUS

See also Belief; Bible: Its Inspiration;
Bible: Its Interpretation; Bible and the
Church; Bible and Civilization; Bible and
Doctrine; Bible and History; Bible and
Morality; Bible and Prayer; Bible as Liter-
ature; Devil; Doctrine; Dogma; Evangel-
ism; Evolution; Faith; Fundamentalism;
Genesis; God: His Intervention in the
World; Israel; Jew; Jews; Job, Book of;
Man and God; Miracles; New Testament;
Old Testament; Preaching; Preaching and
the Bible; Private Judgment; Prophets;
Psalms; Religion; Religion, Revealed;
Revelation; Science and Creation; Science
and God; Science and Religion; Torah,
the; Tradition; Word, the.

BIBLE: ITS INSPIRATION

Since they wrote the things which He
showed and uttered to them, it cannot be
pretended that He is not the writer; for His
members executed what their head dictated.
>ST. AUGUSTINE (354–430), *De Con-
>sensu Evangel* 1

He then Himself wrote them, Who dictated the thing that should be written. He
did Himself write them Who both was
present as the Inspirer in the Saint's work,
and by the mouth of the writer has consigned to us His acts as patterns for our
imitation.
>POPE ST. GREGORY THE GREAT, *Magna
>Moralia,* 584

The Holy Roman Church professes one
and the same God to be author of both the
Old and New Testaments; because, having
been inspired by the Holy Spirit, the holy
writers of both Testaments have spoken.
>Council of Florence, 1443

The special and divine assistance which is
given to the author of every such book as
the Church receives for the Word of God
doth only extend itself to those things
which are doctrinal, or at least have some
near or necessary relation to them.
>H. HOLDEN, *The Analysis of Divine
>Faith,* 1658

Scripture is not inspired to convey mere
secular knowledge, whether about heaven,
or the earth, or the race of man.
>JOHN HENRY NEWMAN, *An Essay on
>the Inspiration of Holy Scripture,* 1861

The Church regards the books of Scripture
as sacred and canonical because, having
been composed by human industry, they
were afterwards approved by her authority, not merely because they contain revelation without error, but because, having

been written under the inspiration of the Holy Spirit, they have God for their Author, and as such, were handed down to the Church herself.

First Vatican Council, 1870

It is absolutely wrong and forbidden either to narrow inspiration to certain parts of Holy Scripture or to admit that the sacred writer has erred. . . . For all the books which the Church receives as sacred and canonical are written wholly and entirely, with all their parts, at the dictation of the Holy Ghost.

Pope Leo XIII, *Providentissimus Deus,* 1893

So far is it from being possible that any error can coexist with inspiration, that inspiration not only is essentially incompatible with error, but excludes and rejects it as absolutely and necessarily as it is impossible that God Himself, the Supreme Truth, can utter that which is not true.

Pope Leo XIII, *Providentissimus Deus,* 1893

The writer said just what God would have him say, and said it because God moved him to do so.

R. Clarke, *The Weekly Register,* October 28, 1899

We gratefully receive the Holy Scriptures, given by inspiration, to be the faithful record of God's gracious revelations and the sure witness to Christ, as the Word of God, the only infallible rule of faith and life.

Statement of the Reformed Faith by the General Assembly of the Presbyterian Church in the U.S.A., May, 1902

Though the English *words* of the Douai Bible are not inspired, the *truths* that these words contain are inspired, since they are the very self-same truths which are contained in the original.

John S. Vaughan, *Concerning the Holy Bible,* 1904

To be inspired for writing is to have one's knowledge so governed and one's powers so moved that the result shall be a document free from approved error.

William Barry, *The Tradition of Scripture,* 1906

It makes no difference at all that the Holy Ghost should have taken men to be as it were his tools in writing, as if forsooth the men who were inspired, but not the divine author, might let fall some error. Not so, for he himself so stirred and roused them by his supernatural power to write, and was so present to them in their writing that they conceived correctly, and were minded to write faithfully, and expressed fittingly with unfailing truth, all those things and those only which he bade them write.

Pope Benedict XV, *Spiritus Paraclitus,* 1920

The whole of the Bible is inspired, but we cannot venture to describe the mode or method of this inspiration, but accept it as a fact of which faith assures us.

Declaration of the United Lutheran Church in America, October 11, 1938

If the ancient authors of the Sacred Scriptures have taken something from popular accounts (which can be admitted), it must never be forgotten that they did so with the help of divine inspiration, which preserved them from all error in the choice and judgment of these documents.

Pope Pius XII, *Humani Generis,* August, 1950

The inspiration of the whole Bible cannot be known from the Bible, but only through the Church. For the biblical Canon can only be established by the Church.

William Leonard and Bernard Orchard, *A Catholic Commentary on Holy Scripture,* 1952

Since the Bible as salvation history is *primarily* God's self-revelation, God must be regarded as principal Author of Scripture. At the same time, and of necessity, the Bible, written by men, is an epiphany of those men's response of loving obedience and faith to God's message.

> DAVID M. STANLEY, *Proceedings* of the Twelfth Annual Convention of the Catholic Theological Society of America, 1959

See also God: His Intervention in the World; History; Holy Spirit; Inspiration; Old Testament; Prophets; Religion, Revealed; Revelation; Word, the.

BIBLE: ITS INTERPRETATION

For neither the prophets nor the Savior Himself announced the divine mysteries so simply as to be easily comprehended by all persons whatever. . . . All things are right to them that understand, says the Scripture: to those, that is, who perfectly preserve His revealed interpretations of the Scriptures, according to the Church's rule.

> ST. CLEMENT OF ALEXANDRIA, *Stromateis*, c. 193

Explain the Scriptures by the Scriptures.

> ST. CLEMENT OF ALEXANDRIA, *Stromateis*, c. 193

The science of the Scripture is the only one which all persons indiscriminately claim as their own! This science the babbling old woman, the doting old man, the worldly sophist, take upon themselves: they tear it to tatters and teach before they themselves have learned.

> ST. JEROME, *Epistula LIII ad Paulinum*, 340

You cannot make your way into the holy Scriptures without having someone to go before you and show you the road.

> ST. JEROME, *Epistula LIII ad Paulinum*, 340

What can be a greater sign of rashness and pride than to refuse to study the books of

the divine mysteries by the help of those who have interpreted them?

> ST. AUGUSTINE, *Ad Honorat,* 397

The interpreter should not be a lover of contention; but possess meekness in his piety.

> ST. AUGUSTINE, *Ad Honorat,* 397

He is mistaken, who gives to Scripture a meaning, however truthful or however edifying, which was not intended by the sacred author.

> ST. AUGUSTINE, *De Doct. Christ.* I, 35; 397

We must be on guard against giving interpretations of Scripture that are far-fetched or opposed to science, and so exposing the word of God to the ridicule of unbelievers.

> ST. AUGUSTINE, *De Genesi ad litteratum,* c. 415

The office of a commentator is to set forth not what he himself would prefer but what his author says.

> ST. JEROME (340–420), *Ad Pammachium*

Some, perhaps, may ask what need there is to join to Holy Scripture the authority of ecclesiastical interpretation. The reason is this—that the Scripture being of itself so deep and profound, all men do not understand it in one and the same sense, but divers men diversely.

> ST. VINCENT OF LERINS, *Commonitorium,* 434

Owing to the very depth of Holy Scripture itself, all do not receive it in one and the same sense; but one in one way and another in another interpret the declarations of the same writer, so that it seems possible to elicit from it as many opinions as there are men. Also in the Catholic Church itself we take great care that we hold that which has been believed everywhere, always, by all.

> ST. VINCENT OF LERINS, *Commonitorium,* 434

I hear the objection: "What need is there for interpretation when Scripture is entirely clear?" But if it is so clear, why have such eminent men groped so blindly and for so many centuries in such an important matter?

DESIDERIUS ERASMUS, *Of Free Will,* 1524

Wrestle with no such texts as might bring us in a doubt and perplexity of any of those articles wherein every good Christian man is clear.

ST. THOMAS MORE, *Dialogue Concerning Tyndale,* III, 16, 1533

We acknowledge only that interpretation as true and correct which is fairly derived from the spirit and language of the Scriptures themselves, in accordance with the circumstances and in harmony with other and plainer passages.

HENRY BULLINGER, *The Helvetic Confession,* 1536

If a theologian does not want to err, he must have all Scripture before his eyes, must compare apparently contradictory passages and, like the two cherubim facing each other from opposite sides, must find the agreement of the difference in the middle of the mercy seat.

MARTIN LUTHER (1483–1546), quoted in *What Luther Says*

In expounding the Bible, if one were always to confine oneself to the unadorned grammetical meaning, one might fall into error. Not only contradictions and propositions far from true might thus be made to appear in the Bible, but even grave heresies and follies. . . . For that reason . . . nothing physical which sense-experience . . . proves to us ought to be called in question (much less condemned) upon the testimony of biblical passages which may have some different meaning beneath the words.

GALILEO, *Letter to the Grand Duchess Christina,* 1614

The infallible rule of interpretation of Scripture is the Scripture itself.

Westminster Confession of Faith, formulary of the Presbyterian Church of Scotland, 1643

There have been too many commentators who are content not to understand a text themselves, if only they can make the readers believe they do.

S. T. COLERIDGE, *Aids to Reflection,* 1825

The testimony of Scripture . . . is plain and intelligible, when we are content to accept it as a fact for our practical guidance; it becomes incomprehensible only when we attempt to explain it as a theory capable of speculative analysis.

DEAN MANSEL, *Limits of Religious Thought,* 1859

In things of faith and morals, things that is, touching the building up of Christian doctrine, that is to be held as the true meaning of Holy Scripture which Holy Mother Church has held and holds; for it is hers to decide on the true meaning and interpretation of the Bible. Consequently no one is allowed to interpret Holy Scripture contrary to that meaning nor against the unanimous consent of the Fathers.

The Vatican Council, 1870

The language of the Bible is employed to express, under the inspiration of the Holy Ghost, many things which are beyond the power and scope of the reason of man— that is to say, divine mysteries and all that is related to them. There is sometimes in such passages a fullness and a hidden depth of meaning which the letter hardly expresses and which the laws of interpretation hardly warrant. Moreover, the literal sense itself frequently admits other senses, adapted to illustrate dogma or to confirm morality. Wherefore, it must be recognized that the sacred writings are wrapped in a certain religious obscurity, and that no one can enter into their interior without a guide.

POPE LEO XIII, *Holy Scripture,* 1893

The Catholic interpreter, although he should show that these facts of natural science which investigators affirm to be now quite certain are not contrary to the Scripture rightly explained, must, nevertheless, always bear in mind that much which has been held and proved as certain has afterwards been called in question and rejected.

POPE LEO XIII, *Providentissimus Deus,* 1893

Once the literal or historical sense has been established, it is time to investigate the inner and more sublime meaning. . . . Due moderation must be used in regard to the inner sense lest, seeking the richness of the spiritual, we should seem to despise the starkness of the mere historical.

POPE BENEDICT XV, *Spiritus Paraclitus,* 1920

Why not rid the Bible, as far as present knowledge will permit, of modes of interpretation justly calculated to fit the relatively childish and illiterate minds of primitive times, but which today only serve to obscure the true sense of the text and conceals its spiritual origin.

C. E. DE M. SAJOUS, *Strength of Religion as Shown by Science,* 1926

Private interpretation meant that any group of men, however ignorant, need only be able to read the Bible to be in possession of the ultimate, undeniable truth about almost any important question of human life.

EVERETT DEAN MARTIN, *Liberty,* 1930

They [the Church Fathers] interpreted the Bible by the tradition, and yet expounded that tradition out of the Bible.

G. L. PRESTIGE, *Fathers and Heretics,* 1940

Let the interpreters bear in mind that their foremost and greatest endeavor should be to discern and define clearly that sense of the biblical words which is called literal.

POPE PIUS XII, *Divino Afflante Spiritu,* 1943

As in our age indeed new questions and new difficulties are multiplied, so, by God's favor, new means and new aids to exegesis are also provided.

POPE PIUS XII, *Divino Afflante Spiritu,* 1943

The interpreter must, as it were, go back wholly in spirit to those remote centuries of the East and with the aid of history, archaeology, ethnology and other sciences, accurately determine what modes of writing, so to speak, the authors of that ancient period would be likely to use, and in fact did use.

POPE PIUS XII, *Divino Afflante Spiritu,* 1943

Allegoristic exegesis is almost purely subjective. He who uses it can find in the Holy Book anything he has already in mind.

J. LAWSON, *The Biblical Theology of St. Irenaeus,* 1948

The entire book of the Scriptures has been reoriented and reinterpreted. It becomes a new book. To the person who has been through this process of research the Bible emerges as a much greater book.

RUFUS M. JONES, *A Call to What Is Vital,* 1949

God abides, his Word abides, and his Holy Spirit coming imperceptibly like the morning light or in sudden lightning flash, is the best interpreter of his Word.

Interpreters Bible, I, 1952

The minister who is a faithful interpreter of the Word continues to exercise considerable authority because of the actual power of the Bible.

H. RICHARD NIEBUHR, *The Purpose of the Church and Its Ministry,* 1956

High among the devil's preferences in Holy Writ must be the verses that can be perversely warped out of their real meaning to make nice booby traps. Here is a beauty: "For you always have the poor with you."

HALFORD E. LUCCOCK, *Living Without Gloves,* 1957

See also Bible and Doctrine; Fundamentalism; Heresy; Heretics; Higher Criticism; New Testament; Private Judgment; Tradition.

BIBLE AND THE CHURCH

A man who is well grounded in the testimonies of the Scriptures is the bulwark of the Church.

ST. JEROME (340–420), *In Isaim.,* liv. 12

We are compelled to concede to the Papists that they have the Word of God, that we received it from them; and that without them we should have no knowledge of it at all.

MARTIN LUTHER, *Commentary on St. John,* ch. xiv, 1522

The Bible forms the theme of Christian meditation, Christian preaching, and Christian art: it is also the staple of the liturgy of the Church. It is a book to be meditated, and not gabbled over.

JOSEPH RICKABY, *Oxford Conferences,* 1897

The Bible is the Church's charter.

HUGE POPE, *The Catholic Church and the Bible,* 1929

That which had been given its character and value even its survival solely by the

authority and the power of the Catholic Church came, in the quarrel of the later Middle Ages and at its explosion in the sixteenth century, to be used as a principal weapon against the Church itself.

HILAIRE BELLOC, *Cranmer,* 1931

The Bible speaks primarily to the Church, but it also speaks through the Church to the world inasmuch as the whole world is claimed by the Church's Lord.

ALAN RICHARDSON and W. SCHWEITZER, *Biblical Authority for Today,* 1951

The Bible came out of the Church, not the Church out of the Bible. When finally the Gospels were written, they were secretarial reports of what was already believed.

FULTON J. SHEEN, *The Woman,* 1951

The Bible is itself a product of the saving activity of God and is not an authority apart from the Spirit and the Church.

R. NEWTON FLEW, *The Nature of the Church,* 1952

Scientific exegisis serves to prove that as the Bible did not develop in a vacuum, but in a Church that antedated it, it cannot be properly understood outside the tradition of the Church.

BRUCE VAWATER, *The Bible in the Church,* 1959

See also Bible: Its Inspiration; Bible: Its Interpretation; Bible and Doctrine; Bible and Prayer; New Testament.

BIBLE AND CIVILIZATION

The Bible is not only the foundation of modern English literature, it is the foundation of Anglo-Saxon civilization.

WILLIAM LYON PHELPS, *Reading the Bible,* 1919

Western civilization is founded upon the Bible; our ideas, our wisdom, our philosophy, our literature, our art, our ideals come more from the Bible than from all other books put together. It is a revelation of divinity and of humanity.

WILLIAM LYON PHELPS, *Human Nature in the Bible,* 1922

No individual, no Caesar or Napoleon, has had such a part in the world's history as this book. . . . If only shards and broken pieces of our civilization should remain, among them would still be found the Bible, whole and uninjured, The book that outlived the Roman Empire will outlive any destruction that impends.

E. S. BATES, *Biography of the Bible,* 1937

Conservative attachment to the eternal Gospel and liberal adaptation to modern needs and problems are not mutually inconsistent but equally necessary concerns. Without the first, Christianity becomes lost in its environment; without the second, its message does not reach the world for which Christ died.

WALTER M. HORTON, *Christian Theology, an Ecumenical Approach,* 1958

BIBLE AND DOCTRINE

Faith will totter if the authority of Sacred Scriptures wavers.

ST. AUGUSTINE, *De Doctrina Christiana,* 397

The Scriptures read are the same thing to us which the same doctrine was when it was preached by the disciples of our Blessed Lord; and we are to learn of either with the same dispositions.

JEROME TAYLOR, *Holy Living,* 1650

Obiter dictum means, as I understand it, a phrase or sentence which, whether a statement of literal fact or not, is not from the circumstances binding upon our faith. . . . There does not seem to be any serious

difficulty in admitting that they are found in Scripture.

JOHN HENRY NEWMAN, *The Nineteenth Century,* February, 1884

The holy Fathers, we say, are of supreme authority, whenever they all interpret in one and the same manner any text of the Bible, as pertaining to the doctrine of faith and morals; for their unanimity clearly evinces that such interpretation has come down from the apostles as a matter of Catholic faith.

POPE LEO XIII, *Providentissimus Deus,* 1893

The Church does not look at the beauty and dignity of a translation of the Bible so much as at its accuracy. Nor does she judge of accuracy according to the ordinary standards but solely by the standard of doctrine.

HUGH POPE, *The Catholic Church and the Bible,* 1929

So much is contained in the Bible that it is difficult to assert that certain particular truths of Christian faith and conduct are nowhere to be found in it.

W. LEONARD and B. ORCHARD, *A Catholic Commentary on Holy Scripture,* 1952

There is no universal precept, either divine or apostolic, that all the faithful—every man, woman and child—should personally read the Bible; Heaven is open to illiterates. It is the doctrine of the Bible that matters, not knowledge of the letter.

W. LEONARD and B. ORCHARD, *A Catholic Commentary on Holy Scripture,* 1952

Holy Scripture contains all things necessary to salvation; so that whatsoever is not read therein nor may be proved thereby, is not to be required of any man that it should be believed as an article of faith, or be thought requisite or necessary to salvation.

> *Doctrine and Discipline of the Methodist Church,* 1952

All teaching and all truth and all doctrine must be tested in the light of the Scriptures.

> D. MARTIN LLOYD-JONES, *Authority,* 1958

See also Belief; Bible: Its Inspiration; Bible: Its Interpretation; Bible and the Church; Dogma; New Testament.

BIBLE AND HISTORY

Scripture, which proves the truth of its historical statements by the accomplishment of its prophecies, gives no false information.

> ST. AUGUSTINE, *The City of God,* Book XVI, Ch. 9; 426

And what is the Bible after all but the history of a deliverer; of God proclaiming himself as man's deliverer from the state into which he is ever ready to sink,—a state of slavery to systems, superstitions, the world, himself, atheism?

> FREDERICK D. MAURICE, *Letter,* March 9, 1849

By the study of what other book could children be so much humanized and made to feel that each figure in the vast historical procession fills, like themselves but a momentary space in the interval between eternities.

> THOMAS HENRY HUXLEY, *The School Boards,* 1870

Throughout the history of the Western world the Scriptures have been the great instigators of revolt against the worst forms of clerical and political despotism. The Bible has been the Magna Charta of the poor and of the oppressed.

> THOMAS HENRY HUXLEY, *Controverted Questions,* 1892

The Bible makes an extraordinary impression on the historian . . . its concrete shape shrouded from the outset in the loftiest beliefs; then its stately expansion, its confident though hidden progress to a boundless and unpredictable end: nowhere else can be found anything in the least like it.

> HENRY DE LUBAC, *Catholicism,* 1927

When read intelligently, the Bible reveals itself as the immortal epic of a people's confused, faltering, but indomitable struggle after a nobler life in a happier world.

> LEWIS BROWNE, *The Graphic Bible,* 1928

The crucial truths revealed in the Bible are not timeless truths about God and man; they are rather historical truths, truths regarding events which took place in time but which were invested by God with eternal significance.

> JOHN A. MACKAY, *A Preface to Christian Theology,* 1941

If the words of the Great Book are not in full accord with *all known facts,* then we have been mistaken in calling it the Word of God.

> HARRY RIMMER, *The Harmony of Science and Scripture,* 1945

All human history as described in the Bible, may be summarized in one phrase, God in Search of Man.

> ABRAHAM JOSHUA HESCHEL, *God in Search of Man,* 1955

The supreme fact about the Bible is that it is substantially a history of the growth of the idea of God.

> ST. JOHN ERVINE, *Bernard Shaw,* 1956

The fundamental fact that the Bible was never the book of Israel lies so deeply below the historians' consciousness that today it is practically forgotten.

ERIC VOEGELIN, *Israel and Revelation,* 1956

The Bible is interested in what has happened in the world in so far as it is salvation history: and it has selected and arranged and described events in order to bring out this point of view . . . that God has acted to save men.

LEONARD JOHNSTON, *Witnesses to God,* 1961

The scriptural renascence is largely an effort to enable the Christian to hear the Word of God in the twentieth century as it was heard in the first—as salvation history, as the good news of God.

PHILIP SCHARPER, *The Critic,* August-September, 1962

Bible history is focused history. The forwardness climbs to a lighted hilltop, and all history beyond that point is in that light, moving on to the fulfillment of the light. The focal point is Christ; and the lighted hilltop, though the light is darkness, is Calvary.

GEORGE A. BUTTRICK, *Christ and History,* 1963

See also New Testament.

BIBLE AND MORALITY

Suppose a nation in some distant region should take the Bible for their only law-book, and every member should regulate his conduct by the precepts there exhibited! . . . What a Utopia; what a Paradise would this region be!

JOHN ADAMS, *Diary,* February 22, 1756

This is a book which reveals men unto themselves, not as creatures in bondage, not as men under human authority. . . . It reveals every man to himself as a dis-

tinct moral agent, responsible not to men, not even to those men who he has put over him in authority, but responsible though his own conscience to his Lord and Maker.

WOODROW WILSON, *Address,* May, 1911

The Sun of the Bible penetrates into the proudest palaces and the humblest shanties; . . . the Sun of the Bible radiates warmth and strength, and has called into being a system of morality which has become the corner-stone of human civilization.

I. FRIEDLANDER, *Past and Present,* 1919

The cynic who ignores, ridicules or denies the Bible, spurning its spiritual rewards and aesthetic excitement, contributes to his own moral anemia.

A. M. SULLIVAN, *The Three-Dimensional Man,* 1956

The whole of morality is based on the Bible; there is not a principle, however resolutely secular it would like to be, that did not originate, and often receive its final formulation, too, in Scripture.

HENRI DANIEL-ROPS, *What Is the Bible?,* 1958

See also Morality.

BIBLE AND PRAYER

Prayer, in its turn, needs to be sustained by reading Holy Scripture.

FRANÇOIS FÉNELON (1651–1715), *Spiritual Letters*

You can only understand Scripture on your knees.

MAURICE ZUNDEL, *The Splendor of the Liturgy,* 1934

It is only when our meditation on the Bible is brought into vital relation with our life of prayer that it begins to affect our lives. For these mysteries of faith are not shut up in a book; they are continuously operative in our lives.

BEDE GRIFFITH, *Life of the Spirit,* February-March, 1954

The liturgical worshipper prays the Bible, directly when he prays in the words of Scripture, indirectly when he reads or hears the lesson in the same attitude of prayer. . . . He who thus prays the Bible with the liturgy penetrates the letter of Scripture to its inner spirit.

E. I. WATKIN *The Life of the Spirit,* February-March, 1954

See also Prayer.

BIBLE AS LITERATURE

No man ever did or ever will become truly eloquent without being a constant reader of the Bible, and an admirer of the purity and sublimity of its language.

FISHER AMES (1758–1808), quoted in C. Hurd's *Treasury of Great American Quotations*

The English Bible is a book which, if everything else in our language should perish, would alone suffice to show the whole extent of its beauty and power.

THOMAS BABINGTON MACAULAY, *Edinburgh Review,* January, 1828

Intense study of the Bible will keep any writer from being vulgar in point of style.

S. T. COLERIDGE, *Table Talk,* June 14, 1830

. The language of the Bible is literary, not scientific language; language thrown out at any object of consciousness not fully grasped, which inspired emotion.

MATTHEW ARNOLD, *Literature and Dogma,* 1873

A collection of literature, containing in a pre-eminent measure the growth of the consciousness of God in the human soul, as interpreted by the pre-eminent religious leaders of a pre-eminently religious people.

LYMAN ABBOTT, *Theology of an Evolutionist,* 1897

Great consequences have flowed from the fact that the first truly popular literature in England—the first which stirred the hearts of all classes of people . . . was the literature comprised within the Bible.

JOHN FISKE, *The Beginnings of New England,* 1900

The bible is literature, not dogma.

GEORGE SANTAYANA, *Introduction to The Ethics of Spinoza,* 1910

The poetry of the Bible is not only the highest poetry to be found anywhere in literature, it contains the essence of all religion, so far as religion consists in aspiration.

WILLIAM LYON PHELPS, *Reading the Bible,* 1919

The Bible is not merely literature of the most wonderful kind, but it is God's literature.

HUGH POPE, *Catholic Church and the Bible,* 1929

Those who talk of the Bible as a "monument of English prose," are merely admiring it as a monument over the grave of Christianity.

T. S. ELIOT, "Religion and Literature," 1935, *Selected Prose*

The most stupendous book, the most sublime literature, even apart from its sacred character, in the history of the world.

BLANCHE MARY KELLY, *The Well of English,* 1936

The Bible as we now read it in the Authorized Version has had, and will continue to have, more influence upon the English language and upon English prose style than any other book.

R. W. CHAMBERS, *Man's Unconquerable Mind,* 1939

The literature of a great race, the literature of a great movement toward realizing the relation of God to man . . . But the Church does not ask you to make a formal statement of belief in the Bible.

GEORGE P. ATWATER, *The Episicopal Church,* 1952

The Old Testament and the New are imperishable masterpieces of literature largely because they speak frankly and powerfully the facts of life.

JAMES M. GILLIS, *This Mysterious Human Nature,* 1956

Those who make much of the Bible as literature are often really concerned to underline their emancipation from theology.

AMOS N. WILDER, *Theology and Modern Literature,* 1958

The Bible is indeed literature but not of a kind that can be forced into our usual Western categories.

AMOS N. WILDER, *Theology and Modern Literature,* 1958

See also Bible and Civilization; Books; Literature; New Testament.

BIGNESS

It is an injustice, a grave evil and a disturbance of right order for a larger and higher organization to arrogate to itself functions which can be performed efficiently by smaller and lower bodies. This is a fundamental principle of social philosophy, unshaken and unchangeable.

POPE PIUS XI, *Quadragesimo Anno,* 1931

See also Monopoly.

BIGOTS

There is nothing more dangerous than the conscience of a bigot.

GEORGE BERNARD SHAW, in 1904 while engaging in a political campaign, quoted in Stephen Winston's *Jesting Apostle, Life of G.B.S.,* 1956

Bigot, *v.t.* One who is obstinately and zealously attached to an opinion that you do not entertain.

AMBROSE BIERCE, *Devil's Dictionary,* 1906

See also Anti-Semitism; Christianity; Criticism of; Discrimination; Fanaticism; Hatred; Intolerance; Negroes; Opinions; Persecution; Prejudice; Tolerance; Zealots.

BIRTH

In the first minute that my soul is infused, the Image of God is imprinted in my soul; so forward is God in my behalf, and so early does he visit me. But yet Original sin is there, as soon as the Image of God is there. My soul is capable of God, as soon as it is capable of sin.

JOHN DONNE, *Sermon,* Spring, 1618

Birth is the sudden opening of a window, through which you look out upon a stupendous prospect. For what has happened? A miracle. You have exchanged nothing for the possibility of everything.

WILLIAM MACNEILE DIXON, *The Human Situation,* 1937

BIRTH CONTROL

Intercourse with even a lawful wife is unlawful and wicked if the conception of offspring be prevented.

ST. AUGUSTINE, *Conjugal Adultery,* c. 400

If government knew how, I should like to see it check, not multiply the population.

When it reaches its true law of action, every man that is born will be hailed as essential.

> RALPH WALDO EMERSON, *The Conduct of Life,* 1860

. . . condemns entirely the mechanical and chemical means to prevent conception, but admits that there may be cases in which a married pair may legitimately desire to limit the family. In these cases the Committee does not condemn those who reduce their marital relations to those parts of the month in which conception is less likely to take place.

> *Report of a Committee of Anglican Bishops,* 1913

. . . and emphatic warning against the use of unnatural means for the avoidance of conception.

> Lambeth Conference of Anglican Bishops, 1920

The thing the capitalist newspapers call "birth control" is not control at all. It is the idea that people should be in one respect completely and utterly uncontrolled, so long as they evade everything in that function that is positive and creative.

> G. K. CHESTERTON, *Social Reform versus Birth Control,* 1927

The practice of birth-control has robbed amorous indulgence of most of the sinfulness traditionally supposed to be inherent in it by robbing it of its socially disastrous effects.

> ALDOUS HUXLEY, *Do What You Will,* 1929

Where there is a clearly felt obligation to limit or avoid parenthood, the method must be decided on Christian principles. The primary and obvious method is complete abstinence from intercourse. . . . the Conference agrees that other methods may be used. . . . The Conference records its strong condemnation of the use of any methods of conception-control from motives of selfishness, luxury, or mere convenience.

> Lambeth Conferences of Anglican Bishops, Resolution 15, 1930

Since the conjugal act is destined primarily for the begetting of children, those who in exercising it deliberately frustrate its natural power and purpose sin against nature and commit a deed which is shameful and intrinsically vicious . . . an offense against the law of God and nature, and . . . a grave sin.

> POPE PIUS XI, *Casti Connubii,* 1930

The whole disgusting movement rests on the assumption of man's sameness with the brutes. . . . It is time to tell these pretentious mechanicians to stand aside. . . . Our public schools were not founded to furnish clinical opportunities for sex mad fanatics.

> WARREN CHANDLER, April 13, 1931, quoted in *A Catechism on Birth Control, a Sunday Visitor* booklet, 1955

We regard it as false and misleading to treat the question of birth control as though it were in itself obscene.

> *Report,* Federal Council of Churches of Christ in America, 1931

The time still endures when there are newly-wed couples who believe they can allow themselves at first a period of moral license and enjoy their rights without any concern for their duties. This is a grave sin.

> POPE PIUS XII, July 24, 1940

There is an act of will whose purpose is to prevent fertilization, whatever the method used may be. The real question, therefore, is only whether the intention to exercise birth control is sinful in itself in all circumstances.

> OTTO A. PIPER, *The Christian Interpretation of Sex,* 1941

As regards contraceptives, there is a paradoxical, negative sense in which all possible future generations are the patients or subjects of a power wielded by those already alive. By contraception simply, they are denied existence; by contraception used as a means of selective breeding, they are without their concurring voice.

C. S. LEWIS, *The Abolition of Man,* 1947

In the matter of sexual morality, it is not enough to condemn an action as wrong simply because it frustrates the natural purposes of the sexual faculty; an action is proved to be wrong only when it frustrates the nature of man.

D. J. B. HAWKINS, *Blackfriars,* 1951

Birth control is not an end in itself to be sure; but without it many persons cannot protect the other values open to them and their children.

PETER A. BERTOCCI, *Sex and Religion Today,* ed. S. Doniger, 1953

You will not find any reputable and responsible theologian who holds or teaches that *any* limitation of the family by self-restraint is a lack of trust in God. In fact the statement is false. . . . You will not find any theologian who holds that all families should have as many children as God sends.

THURSTON DAVIS, statement prepared for Maisie Ward and published in her *Be Not Solicitous,* 1953

A responsible attitude in regard to sex life within marriage cannot mean that "everything should be left to chance" in one of the more important relationships into which men and women enter.

GEORGE G. HOCKMAN, *Religion in Modern Life,* 1957

Contraception is wrong because it means attacking the primary purpose of the marriage act in the very manner of performing it.

DONALD F. MILLER, *For Wives and Husbands Only,* 1957

The procreation of children is not the sole purpose of Christian marriage. . . . Family planning, in such ways as are mutually acceptable to husband and wife in Christian conscience, and secure from the corruptions of sensuality and selfishness, is a right and important factor in Christian family life.

Encyclical Letter, Lambeth Conference of Anglican Bishops, 1958

Frustration of nature, far from being immoral, is man's vocation. . . . Man has always frustrated nature from the time he invented the first tool and will continue to do so until on his last day on earth he lays down his latest invention.

FREDERICK E. FLYNN, *Lecture* before Catholic Physicians' Guild of Southern California, May 15, 1960

Most of the Protestant Churches hold contraception and periodic continence to be morally right when the motives are right. . . . The general Protestant conviction is that motives, rather than methods, form the primary moral issue.

National Council of Churches of Christ in America, policy statement titled *Responsible Parenthood,* February 23, 1961

Having children is a venture in faith, requiring a measure of courage and confidence in God's goodness. Too cautious a reckoning of the costs may be as great an error as failure to lift the God-given power of procreation to the level of ethical decision.

National Council of Churches of Christ of America, policy statement titled *Responsible Parenthood,* February 23, 1961

The marriage act is a human act and, as such, is to be exercised in a reasonable manner. If cogent reasons indicate a limitation of family size, there should be no difficulty in admitting that the avoidance of pregnancy would be within the bounds of reason and morality.

JOHN A. GOODWINE, *Catholic Family Leader,* June, 1961

The education and welfare of the children are equally important as the primary end of marriage.

WILLIAM J. GIBBONS, *Milwaukee Journal,* September 16, 1961

Ultimately, according to responsible moral theologians, the obligation to procreate—to have a large family or a small one—is measured by the needs of the community and the human species, not merely by the needs or situation of the individual or couples.

LOUIS McKERNAN, *Population Bulletin,* November, 1961

The Catholic Church . . . teaches that there is, in principle, a right, or better, a duty, to practice a form of birth limitation based on careful thought, provided that this regulation is inspired solely by motives of genuine charity, and that it respects the order of values inherent in the sexual function and also the pattern of its structural factors.

STANISLAS DE LESTAPIS, *Family Planning and Modern Problems,* 1961

If it were true that the world is already disintegrating from a population explosion, and that the only alternative to chaos is an immediate crash program to effectuate birth prevention, opposition to its promotion would be patently unreasonable.

ANTHONY ZIMMERMAN, *Catholic Viewpoint on Over-Population,* 1961

A society which practices death control must at the same time practice birth control.

JOHN ROCK, *The Time Has Come,* 1963

American Catholics, from bishops down to the rank and file, must ponder with utmost seriousness the relationship between excessive fertility and excruciating, ruinous poverty in the nations of Asia, Latin America, and Africa, where two-thirds of the world's people live.

JOHN ROCK, *The Time Has Come,* 1963

Catholic theology insists that the marital embrace is a procreative act and must always retain this character. Hence contraceptive procedures are branded as always objectively immoral.

RICHARD A. McCORMICK, *America,* January 11, 1964

See also Abortion; Chastity; Continence; Love, Physical; Marriage; Population Explosion; Reproduction; Rhythm Method; Sex; Sexual Intercourse; Sexual Sin; Unchastity.

BISHOP

Our Apostles also knew through our Lord Jesus Christ that there would be strife over the name of the bishop's office. So for this reason, since they had perfect foreknowledge, they appointed the aforesaid persons and subsequently gave them permanence, so that, if they should fall asleep, other approved men should succeed to their ministry.

ST. CLEMENT OF ROME, *First Epistle to the Corinthians,* c. 100

For it will be no small sin on our part, if we depose from the episcopal office those who have in blameless and holy wise offered the gifts.

ST. CLEMENT OF ROME, *First Epistle to the Corinthians,* c. 100

Let no man do aught pertaining to the Church apart from the bishop. Let that eucharist be considered valid which is under the bishop or him to whom he commits it. Wheresoever the bishops appear, there let the people be. . . . Whatsoever he approves, that also is well-pleasing to God, that everything which you do may be secure and valid.

ST. IGNATIUS OF ANTIOCH, *To the Smyrnaeans,* c. 108

Every steward sent by the master to govern his house, should be received as if he were the sender; wherefore the bishop should be regarded as the Lord Himself.

ST. IGNATIUS OF ANTIOCH, *To the Ephesians,* c. 109

The bishop should be chosen in the presence of the people, who know most fully the lives of each, and are thoroughly acquainted with the character of every one from his conversation.

ST. CYPRIAN, *Epistle* LXVII, 254

The bishops are not to go beyond their dioceses to churches lying outside their bounds, nor bring confusion on churches.

Council of Constantinople, 381

The church of the City of Rome is not to be thought one church, and that of the whole world another. . . . Wherever there is a bishop, whether at Rome, or Eugubium, or Constantinople, or Rhegium, or Alexandria, or Tanis, he is of the same dignity and of the same priesthood. The power of the riches or the lowliness of poverty does not make him a higher bishop or a lower bishop, but all are successors of the Apostles.

ST. JEROME (c. 340–420), *Epistle* CXLVI

What I am for you terrifies me; what I am with you consoles me. For you I am a Bishop; but with you I am a Christian. The former is a duty; the latter a grace. The former is a danger; the latter, salvation.

ST. AUGUSTINE (354–430), *Sermon* 540.

How can the bishop properly enjoy the pastoral dignity, if he is himself engaged in those earthly occupations which he ought to blame in others?

POPE ST. GREGORY THE GREAT, *Pastoral Care,* 590

Nothing can be found in this world more lofty than priests or more sublime than bishops.

POPE GREGORY VII, *To the Bishop of Metz,* 1081

The Third Council of Carthage, at which Saint Augustine assisted, decided that all the furniture belonging to a bishop should be of low price and should reflect poverty.

ST. IGNATIUS LOYOLA, *Spiritual Exercises,* 1541

The Bishop of ——— is so like Judas that I now firmly believe in the apostolical succession.

SYDNEY SMITH, quoted in *A Memoir of Sydney Smith,* by his daughter, Lady Holland, 1855

Nearly all the evils in the church have arisen from bishops desiring power more than light; they want authority, not outlook.

JOHN RUSKIN, *Sesame and Lilies,* 1865

The bishops would lose the right and power to govern if they wilfully separated themselves from Peter or his successors.

POPE LEO XIII, *Satis Cognitum,* June 29, 1896

It is recorded that the praetorian prefect was so offended by St. Basil's freedom of speech that he declared that he had never in his life been spoken to in such a manner. "No doubt," replied St. Basil, "you have never met a Bishop."

CHRISTOPHER DAWSON, *A Monument to St. Augustine,* 1933

It has been said in jest that at the end of the apostolic age the church was like a locomotive going into a dark tunnel and that it emerged in the post-apostolic period with a bishop on its cowcatcher.

F. W. YOUNG, *Understanding the New Testament,* 1957

Bishops by divine institution have succeeded to the place of the Apostles, as shepherds of the Church, and he who hears them, hears Christ, and he who rejects them, rejects Christ and Him who sent Christ.

The Constitution of the Church, Second Vatican Council, November, 1964

Episcopal consecration, together with the office of teaching and of governing, . . . of its very nature, can be exercised only in hierarchical communion with the heads and members of the college. . . . But the college or body of Bishops has no authority unless it is understood together with the Roman Pontiff. . . . The Pope's power of primacy over all . . . remains whole and intact.

The Constitution of the Church, Second Vatican Council, November, 1963

The individual Bishops represent each his own church, but all of them together and with the Pope represent the entire Church. . . . The individual Bishops . . . exercise their pastoral government over the portion of the People of God committed to their care, and not over the churches nor over the universal Church.

The Constitution of the Church, Second Vatican Council, November, 1964

See *also* Apostolic Succession; Authority; Church: Its Authority; Hierarchy.

BITTERNESS

It were better to be of no Church, than to be bitter for any.

WILLIAM PENN, *Some Fruits of Solitude,* 1718

There may be pain and trouble and even a certain amount of rebellion in doing the will of God, but there should certainly not be bitterness. Cynicism cannot come from God.

HUBERT VAŃ ZELLER, *We Live with Our Eyes Open,* 1949

See *also* Anger; Fanaticism; Hatred.

BLASPHEMY

Blasphemy is . . . denying the being or providence of God, contumelious reproaches of our Saviour Christ, profane scoffing at the Holy Scripture, or exposing it to contempt or ridicule.

WILLIAM BLACKSTONE, *Commentaries on the Laws of England,* IV, 1765

One of the most blasphemous acts is a prayer describing the courageous sacrifice of Jesus Christ, offered by a compromising, comfortable clergyman who professes to accept the lordship of God's Son.

GERALD KENNEDY, *A Reader's Notebook,* 1953

See *also* Agnosticism; Antichrist; Anti-God Totalitarians; Atheism; Communism; Freedom of Thought and Speech; God, Blasphemous Statements about; God, Unorthodox Comments about.

BLESSEDNESS

Blessedness is one with divinity.

BOETHIUS, *Consolations of Philosophy,* c. 523

Blessedness lieth not in much and many, but in One and oneness.

Theologica Germanica, 14th century

He who thinks himself more blessed because he enjoys benefits which others do not, . . . is ignorant of true blessedness.

BARUCH SPINOZA, *Tractatus Theologico-Politicus,* 1670

Blessedness is nothing but the peace of mind which springs from the intuitive knowledge of God.
> BARUCH SPINOZA, *Ethics*, 1677

Blessedness is not the reward of virtue, but virtue itself.
> BARUCH SPINOZA, *Ethics*, 1677

There is in man a HIGHER than Love of Happiness: he can do without Happiness, and instead thereof find Blessedness!
> THOMAS CARLYLE, *Sartor Resartus*, 1836

See also Beatific Vision; Heaven; Saints; Sanctity.

BLESSED SACRAMENT

When we see the Blessed Sacrament enthroned, we should look up towards that white Disc which shines in the monstrance as towards a chink through which, just for a moment, the light of the other world shines through.
> RONALD A. KNOX, *The Window in the Wall*, 1956

See also Adoration; Eucharist.

BLESSINGS

The five blessings are long life, riches, serenity, the love of virtue, and the attainment of ambition.
> *Hung Fan*, c. 100 B.C.

Even God cannot make a creature in which a perfect blessing is found. Otherwise, God Himself would not be the highest blessing.
> MEISTER ECKHART (1260?–1327), *Meister Eckhart*

Experience teaches us that we do not always receive the blessings we ask for in prayer.
> MARY BAKER EDDY, *Science and Health*, 1908

BLISS

Perfect bliss
Grows only in the bosom tranquillized.
The spirit passionless, purged from offense,
Vowed to the Infinite. He who thus vows
His soul to the Supreme Soul, quitting sin,
Passes unhindered to the endless bliss
Of unity with Brahma.
> *The Song Celestial*, Sir Edwin Arnold's translation of *Bhagavad-Gita*, 5th to 2nd century B.C.

A man is born not to desire enjoyments in the world of the senses, but to realize the bliss of jivanmukti [liberation while living].
> SANKARA (c. 750 A.D.), *Sacred Books of the East*, XXXIV

BLOODSHED

Abstain from shedding blood . . . for blood that is spilt never sleeps.
> SALADIN, *Instruction to His Son*, 1193, quoted in S. LANE-POOLE's *Saladin*

It is impossible for the Christian and true church to subsist without the shedding of blood, for her adversary, the devil, is a liar and a murderer.
> MARTIN LUTHER (1483–1546), *Table Talk*

The blood of man should never be shed but to redeem the blood of man. It is well shed for our family, for our friends, for our God, for our country, for our kind. The rest is vanity; the rest is crime.
> EDMUND BURKE, *Letters on a Regicide Peace*, 1797

How easy it is to shed human blood; how easy it is to persuade ourselves that it is our duty to do so—and that the decision has cost us a severe struggle; how much in all ages have wounds and shrieks and tears been the cheap and vulgar resources of the rulers of mankind.

SYDNEY SMITH, *Peter Plymley's Letters*, 1808

The only gain of civilization for mankind is the greater capacity for variety of sensations. . . . And through the development of this many-sidedness man has come to finding enjoyment in bloodshed.

FEODOR DOSTOEVSKY, *Notes from the Underground*, 1864

See also Capital Punishment; Murder; Vengeance; Violence; War; War, Condemnation of.

BLUSHING

When you blush, it is notice to be careful.

E. W. HOWE, *Sinner Sermons*, 1926

BODY

He who knows that this body is like froth, and has learnt that it is as unsubstantial as a mirage, will break the flower-pointed arrow of Māra, and never see the king of death.

Dhammapada, c. 5th century B.C.

The body is a source of endless trouble to us. . . . It fills us full of loves, and lusts, and fears, and fancies of all kinds, and endless foolery, and in fact, as men say, takes away from us the power of thinking at all.

PLATO, *Phaedrus*, in *Dialogues*, 399 B.C.

"If my body," said Shun, "is not my own, pray whose is it?" "It is the bodily form entrusted to you by Heaven and Earth. Your life is not your own. It is a blended harmony, entrusted to you by Heaven and Earth" replied Ch'eng, his tutor.

CHUANG-TZU (4th century B.C.), *Texts of Taoism*, ed. J. Legge

These bodies are perishable; but the dwellers in these bodies are eternal, indestructible, and impenetrable.

Bhagavad-Gita, c. 2nd century B.C.

The body of a man is not a home but an inn—and that only briefly.

SENECA, *Epistulae morales ad Lucilium*, c. 63 A.D.

The body in every part should be despised by everyone who does not care to be buried in its pleasures, as it were in slime; or we ought to cleave to it only in so far as we obtain from it service for the pursuit of wisdom.

ST. BASIL THE GREAT, *Address to Young Men on the Reading of Greek Literature*, c. 370

Let us be pilgrims from the body lest we be pilgrims from Christ; though we are in the body, let us not follow the things of the body. . . . Nor let us abandon the law of nature.

ST. AMBROSE, *De Excessu Fratis Sui Satyri*, 375

The conception that the body and other things contained in the non-Self are our Self constitutes nescience [ignorance]: from it there spring desires with regard to whatever promotes the well-being of the body and so on, and aversions with regard to whatever tends to injure it: there further arise fear and confusion when we observe anything threatening to destroy it.

Vedanta Sutras, with commentary by Sankarakarya, c. 800 A.D.

Make thy body, which is only a morsel for death, thy beggar's coat, and faith thy rule of life and thy staff.

Japji, attributed to Guru Nanak (1496–1538)

The body is a vessel which He wrought, and into which He infused His workmanship and skill.

GURU NANAK (1496–1538), in *The Sikh Religion*, M. A. Macauliffe, I

When clothing our body, we ought to remember that it bears the imprint of sin; we ought therefore to cover it with decency in accordance with the law of God.

> ST. JOHN BAPTISTE DE LA SALLE, *The Rules of Christian Manners and Civility,* 1695

Tell me, tell yourselves fairly, is your flesh, your body, the part of yourself which you can see and handle, *You?*—You know that it is not.

> CHARLES KINGSLEY, *Sermons for the Times,* 1855

I must assert in the most unqualified way that it is primarily and mainly for the sake of saving the soul that I seek the salvation of the body.

> WILLIAM BOOTH, *In Darkest England and Way Out,* 1890

Some people believe that the Church is the enemy of the body! Why, she immortalizes it. Even here and now she divinizes it as the "temple of the Holy Ghost." She only forbids it to upset everything by the violence of its instincts, and the abuse of its own powers.

> ANTONIN SERTILLANGES, *Recollections,* 1950

If the body is evil to the core and belongs by right to hell, it follows that virtuous mastery of the body and its passions is impossible, that there is a limit to the grace of Christ who cannot redeem it, that one part of creation is condemned without recourse, and that the reality of the Incarnation of Christ is denied.

> R. L. BRUCKBERGER, *One Sky to Share,* 1951

My great religion is a belief in the blood, the flesh, as being wiser than the intellect. We can go wrong in our minds. But what our blood feels and believes and says, is always true.

> D. H. LAWRENCE, *Letter to Ernest Collings,* January 17, 1913, *Collected Letters of,* ed. H. T. Moore, 1962

Sometimes the body sits on a stump and has to be told by the happy Spirit, March on, brave one!

> ANONYMOUS

See also Body and Soul; Death; Evolution; Flesh; Immortality; Mind; Nudism; Passions; Pleasure; Resurrection; Spirit.

BODY AND SOUL

The body is the tomb of the soul.

> PLATO, *Cratylus,* c. 360 B.C.

Those are right who hold that the soul is neither independent of body nor itself a body; for it is not a body, but something belonging to the body, and therefore is present in a body, and a body of a certain kind.

> ARISTOTLE (384–322 B.C.), *De Anima*

The soul is born with the body, it grows and decays with the body, therefore it perishes with the body.

> LUCRETIUS, *De Rerum Natura,* Lib. III, c. 60 B.C.

Is not the soul a guest in our body, deserving of our kind hospitality? Today it is here, tomorrow it is gone.

> HILLEL, *Lev. R.* 34.3, c. 5 A.D.

The most perfect soul, says Heraclitus, is a dry light, which flies out of the body as lightning breaks from a cloud.

> PLUTARCH, *Lives,* c. 66 A.D.

The soul, incapable of death, suffers in the same manner in the body as birds that are kept in a cage.

> PLUTARCH, *Essays,* c. 66 A.D.

One ought not to be furnished out more elaborately than need requires, nor to be more solicitous for the body than is good for the soul.

> ST. BASIL THE GREAT, *Address to Young Men on the Reading of Greek Literature,* c. 370

The created soul is gifted with the knowledge which is proper to it; but after it is united to the body, it is withdrawn from receiving those impressions which are proper to it, by reason of the very darkness of the body.

    AVICEBRÓN (Solomon ben Judah ibn-Gabirol) (1021?–1058), *Fountain of Life*

This body, I say, is a tent, and a tent of Kedar, because, by its interference, it prevents the soul from beholding the infinite light.

    ST. BERNARD OF CLAIRVAUX (1091–1153), *Sermon on Death of Gerard*

They pretend decency and ornament; but let them take heed, that while they set out their bodies they do not damn their souls.

    ROBERT BURTON, *Anatomy of Melancholy,* Vol. 3, 1621

Man has no body distinct from his soul; for that called body is a portion of the soul discern'd by the five senses, the chief inlets of soul in this age.

    WILLIAM BLAKE, *The Marriage of Heaven and Hell,* 1790

The soul says, "Have dominion over all things to the ends of virtue"; the body would have the power over things to its own ends.

    RALPH WALDO EMERSON, "Compensation," *Essays,* 1841

Those who stunt their physical life are most certainly stunting their souls.

    RICHARD JEFFERIES, *The Story of My Heart,* 1882

There is nothing the body suffers that the soul may not profit by.

    GEORGE MEREDITH, *Diana of the Crossways,* 1885

The body is immersed in the soul, as a wick is dipped in oil; and its flame of active energy is increased or diminished by the strength or weakness of the fecundizing soul.

    FRANCIS THOMPSON, *Health and Holiness,* 1905

A tabernacle in which the transmissible human spirit is carried for a while, a shell for the immortal seed that dwells in it and has created it.

    GEORGE SANTAYANA, *Reason in Society,* 1906

When the flesh flourishes, the soul fades; when the flesh has full liberty, the soul is straitened; when the flesh is satiated, the soul hungers; when the flesh is adorned, the soul is deformed.

    ST. JOHN SERGIEFF OF CRONSTADT (1829–1908) *My Life in Christ*

The body is the Temple of the Holy Spirit, and it is the means whereby alone the soul can establish relation with the universe which constitutes man's earthly environment.

    HARRY ROBERTS, Letter, *New Statesman and Nation,* August 29, 1931

It was not the body that made the spirit sin; it was the spirit that brought death to the body.

    ÉTIENNE GILSON, *The Spirit of Medieval Philosophy,* 1936

The flesh never appears more beautiful than when, like a generous flow of blood always ready to be shed, it serves to glorify the spirit.

    PAUL CLAUDEL, *Discours et Remerciements,* 1947

The body is made for the soul, to express it, to open it out and to give it—*plenitudo animae*. But the soul is made for God.

    JEAN MOUROUX, *The Meaning of Man,* 1948

In no creature except man is there any act which involves such an interactivity of matter and spirit, body and soul.

    FULTON J. SHEEN, *Peace of Soul,* 1949

Body and soul are not two substances but one. They are man becoming aware of himself in two different ways.

C. F. VON WEIZSÄCHER, *The History of Nature,* 1949

The soul organizes the body as an expression of itself, as its instrument, as its intermediary with the outside world.

JOHN TERNUS, *God, Man and Universe,* ed. J. Bivort de la Saudée, 1950

There is something more menacing than the destruction of men's bodies, of their material environment, their comfort and security; and that is the voiding of the human spirit.

GERALD VANN, *The Water and the Fire,* 1954

This body of ours was sanctified by the Son of Man who Himself took it on and it is sanctified by the presence of the soul which enters it, which is able to receive God.

FRANÇOIS MAURIAC, *What I Believe,* 1962

See also Body; Celibacy; Chastity; Death; Health; Immortality; Resurrection; Soul; Spirit; Spirit, Human.

BOOKS

God hath said, "Like an ass laden with his books": burdensome is the knowledge that is not from himself.

JALLALUDIN RUMI (1207–1273), *Masnavi*

In books cherubim expand their wings, that the soul of the student may ascend and look around from pole to pole. . . . In them the most high and incomprehensible God Himself is contained and worshipped.

RICHARD DE BURY, *Philobiblon,* 1473

Whosoever therefore acknowledges himself to be a zealous follower of truth, of happi-

ness, of wisdom, of science, or even of the faith, must of necessity make himself a lover of books.

RICHARD DE BURY, *Philobiblon,* 1473

If you approach them, they are not asleep; if investigating, you interrogate them, they conceal nothing; if you mistake them, they never grumble; if you are ignorant, they cannot laugh at you.

RICHARD DE BURY, *Philobiblon,* 1473

The multitude of books is a great evil. There is no limit to this fever for writing; every one must be an author; some out of vanity, to acquire celebrity and raise up a name, others for the sake of mere gain.

MARTIN LUTHER (1483–1546), *Table Talk*

There is no book so bad but there is something good in it.

MIGUEL DE CERVANTES, *Don Quixote,* 1615

There are two Books from whence I collect my Divinity; besides that written one of GOD, another of His servant Nature, that universal and public Manuscript, that lies expans'd unto the Eyes of all.

THOMAS BROWNE, *Religio Medici,* 1635

A good Book is the precious life-blood of a master spirit, embalmed and treasured up on purpose to a life beyond life.

JOHN MILTON, *Aeropagitica,* 1644

Books should to one of these four ends conduce:
For wisdom, piety, delight, or use.

JOHN DENHAM, *Of Prudence,* 1650

A wicked book is the wickeder because it cannot repent.

THOMAS FULLER, *Gnomologia,* 1732

Books have always a secret influence on the understanding. . . . He that entertains himself with moral or religious treatises will imperceptibly advance in goodness.

SAMUEL JOHNSON, *The Adventurer,* February 26, 1753

Books are the best things, well used; abused, among the worst.

RALPH WALDO EMERSON, *The American Scholar,* 1837

Books are the true levellers. They give to all, who will faithfully use them, the society, the spiritual presence, of the best and greatest of our race.

WILLIAM ELLERY CHANNING, *Self-Culture,* 1838

All that mankind has done, thought, gained or been: it is lying as in magic preservation in the pages of books.

THOMAS CARLYLE, *Heroes and Hero-Worship,* 1840

There are in the world an innumerable quantity of books, nevertheless there are but six of them which have been venerated by nations as sacred. These are the Kings of China, the Vedas of India, the Zend-Avesta of the Persians, the Koran of the Arabs, the Law of the Jews, and the Gospel.

JEAN BAPTISTE LACORDAIRE, *Conferences of,* c. 1850

The essential ground of a new book or a new sermon is a new spirit.

RALPH WALDO EMERSON, *Address,* May 5, 1879

The most complicated and mightiest of all the miracles created by man on his path to the happiness and power of the future.

MAXIM GORKY, *Preface* to first catalogue of publishing house founded by Gorky under auspices of Bolshevik government, 1918

How often a man thinks he is carrying a book under his arm . . . and it turns out to be a load of dirt.

JOSEPH M. ESCRIVA, *The Way,* 1958

What nonsense! No one ever seduced by books? Since the invention of writing, people have been seduced by the power of the word into all kinds of virtues, follies, conspiracies and gallantries. They have been converted to religions, urged into sin and lured into salvation.

PHYLLIS MCGINLEY, *Ladies' Home Journal,* July, 1961

It takes three books to run a church—a hymn book, a prayer book, and a pocketbook.

ANONYMOUS

See also Author; Bible; Bible as Literature; Books, Prohibited; Knowledge; Literature; New Testament; Obscenity; Reading.

BOOKS, OBSCENE.
See OBSCENITY

BOOKS, PROHIBITED

Books of apostates, heretics, schismatics, and all other writers defending heresy or schism or in any way attacking the foundations of religion, are altogether prohibited.

POPE LEO XIII, *General Decrees Concerning the Prohibition and Censorship of Books,* January 25, 1897

Books which professedly treat of, narrate, or teach lewd or obscene subjects are prohibited.

POPE LEO XIII, *General Decrees Concerning the Prohibition and Censorship of Books,* January 25, 1897

See also Books; Censorship.

BOREDOM

Boredom is a vital problem for the moralist, since at least half the sins of mankind are caused by the fear of it.

BERTRAND RUSSELL, *The Conquest of Happiness,* 1930

BRAHMA

This shining, immortal Person who is in the earth, and, with reference to oneself, this shining, immortal Person—who is in the body—he, indeed, is just this Soul, this Immortal, this Brahma, this All.

Brihad-Aranyaka Upanishad, prior to 400 B.C.

BRAHMAN

East and other regions do not exist for Him [Brahman], nor across, nor below, nor above the Highest Self is not to be fixed.

Maitra-Brahmana Upanishad, Prapathaka, VI, probably prior to 6th century B.C.

He [Brahman] is the One God, hidden in all things, all-pervading, the Self within all beings, watching over all works, the Witness, the Perceiver, the only one free from qualities. . . . The wise who perceive Him within their self, to them belongs eternal happiness.

Svetasvatara Upanishad, Adhyaya VI, before 400 B.C.

Of that Brahman there are two conditions, one possessed of form, the other formless. . . . The undecaying is the highest Brahman; the decaying is this entire universe.

Visnu, The Puranas, c. 500 A.D.

A knower of Brahman becomes Brahman.

Mundaka Upanishad, prior to 400 B.C.

Meditate and you will realize that mind, matter, and Maya (the power which unites mind and matter) are but three aspects of Brahman, the one reality.

Svetasvatara Upanishad, before 400 B.C.

As you practice meditation, you may see in vision forms resembling snow, crystals, smoke, fire, lightning, fireflies, the sun, and moon. These are signs that you are on your way to the revelation of Brahman.

Svetasvatara Upanishad, before 400 B.C.

He from whom all works, all desires, all sweet odors and tastes proceed, who embraces all this, who never speaks and who is never surprised, he, my self within the heart, is that Brahman.

Chandogya Upanishad, prior to 400 B.C.

Brahman is supreme; he is self-luminous, he is beyond all thought. Subtler than the subtlest is he, farther than the farthest, nearer than the nearest. He resides in the heart of every being.

Chandogya Upanishad, prior to 400 B.C.

Within the city of Brahman, which is the body, there is the heart, and within the heart there is a little house. This house has the shape of a lotus, and within it dwells that which is to be sought after; inquired about, and realized.

Chandogya Upanishad, prior to 400 B.C.

He who is realized by transcending the world of cause and effect, in deep contemplation, is expressly declared by the scriptures to be the Supreme Brahman. He is the substance, all else the shadow. He is the imperishable.

Svetasvatara Upanishad, before 400 B.C.

No one who seeks Brahman ever comes to an evil end.

Bhagavad-Gita, between 500 and 200 B.C.

Utterly quiet,
Made clean of passion,
The mind of the yogi
Knows that Brahman,
His bliss is the highest.

Bhagavad-Gita, between 500 and 200 B.C.

Though One, Brahman is the cause of the many. There is no other cause. And yet

Brahman is independent of the law of causation. Such is Braman, and "thou art That." Meditate upon this truth within your consciousness.

SHANKARA (788–820), *Viveka-Chuda-mani*

Brahman resembles not the world, and (yet) apart from Brahman there is naught; all that which seems to exist outside of It (Brahman) cannot exist save in an illusory manner, like the semblance of water in the desert.

SHANKARA (788–820), quoted by René Guénon, *Man and His Becoming*

Supreme beyond the power of speech to express, Brahman may yet be apprehended by the eye of pure illumination. Pure, absolute and eternal Reality—such is Brahman and "thou art That."

SHANKARA (788–820), *Viveka-Chuda-mani*

The true knower knows that he who is Brahman is the personal God; that he who is impersonal, attributeless, and beyond the gunas, is again the personal God, the repository of all blessed qualities.

SRI RAMAKRISHNA (1834–1886), *Kath-amrta*, III, 11

See also Immortality, Belief in; Nirvana; Samadhi; Universe; Vision.

BRAHMANA

A man does not become a Brahmana by his plaited hair, by his family, or by birth; in whom there is truth and righteousness, he is blessed, he is a Brahmana.

Dhammapada, c. 5th century B.C.

Him I call a Brahmana from whom anger and hatred, pride and hypocrisy have dropped like a mustard seed from the point of a needle.

Dhammapada, c. 5th century B.C.

Him I call a Brahmana who without hurting any creature, whether feeble or strong, does not kill nor cause slaughter.

Dhammapada, c. 5th century B.C.

See also Vision.

BRAVERY

People glorify all sorts of bravery except the bravery they might show on behalf on their nearest neighbors.

GEORGE ELIOT, *Middlemarch,* 1872

It takes a brave man to look into the mirror of his own soul to see written there the disfigurements caused by his own misbehavior.

FULTON J. SHEEN, *Ways to Happiness,* 1953

See also Calvary; Courage; Cowardice; Valor.

BREAD

Bread for myself is a material question; bread for my neighbor is a spiritual question.

JACQUES MARITAIN, *Freedom in the Modern World,* 1936

See also Eucharist.

BRIBERY

It gives "great occasion to the enemies of God to blaspheme," that men of large wealth, however obtained, if they are lavish in its distribution, have no difficulty in finding ministers of the gospel to flatter them and in every possible way to elevate them so far as their influence can do it, in the communities in which they live.

JAMES MONROE BUCKLEY, *National Needs and Remedies,* 1890

See also Crookedness; Dishonesty.

BROTHERHOOD

Let the superior man never fail reverently to order his own conduct, and let him be respectful to others, and observant of property—then all within the four seas will be his brothers.

CONFUCIUS, *Analects*, 5th century B.C.

When you see your brother, you see God.

ST. CLEMENT OF ALEXANDRIA, *Stromateis*, 150

Let us be mutually mindful of each other, of one heart and one mind, let us ever on either side pray for one another. . . . And if one of us shall . . . depart hence the first, let our love continue in the presence of the Lord; let not prayer for our brethren and sisters cease in the presence of the mercy of the Father.

ST. CYPRIAN (200–258), *Epistle ad. Cornel*

There is no one in the whole human family to whom kindly affection is not due by reason of the bond of a common humanity, although it may not be due on the ground of reciprocal love.

ST. AUGUSTINE, *To Proba*, 412

He who bears another, is borne by another.

POPE ST. GREGORY THE GREAT (540–604), in *Ezech.*

Your brother needs your help, but you meanwhile mumble your little prayers to God, pretending not to see your brother's need.

DESIDERIUS ERASMUS, *Enchiridion*, 1501

The pious man owes to his brethren all that it is in his power to give.

JOHN CALVIN, *Institutes*, 1536

In proportion as you advance in fraternal charity, you are increasing in your love of God.

ST. TERESA OF ÁVILA, *The Interior Castle*, 1577

The dignity of resembling the Almighty is common to all men; we should then love them all as ourselves, as living images of the Deity. It is on this title that we belong to God.

ST. FRANCES OF SALES, *Treatise on the Love of God*, 1607

To love our neighbor with a love of charity is to love God in man or man in God and consequently, to love God alone for His own sake and creatures for the love of God.

ST. FRANCES OF SALES, *Treatise on the Love of God*, 1607

No man is an *Island*, entire of it self; every man is a piece of the *Continent*, a part of the *main* . . . any man's *death* diminishes *me*, because I am involved in *Mankind;* and therefore never send to know for whom the *bell* tolls; it tolls for *thee*.

JOHN DONNE (1573–1631), *Devotions Upon Mergent Occasions*

To consider mankind otherwise than brethren, to think favors are peculiar to one nation and exclude others plainly supposes a darkness in the understanding.

JOHN WOOLMAN, *Journal*, 1774

To pray together, in whatever tongue or ritual, is the most tender brotherhood of hope and sympathy that men can contract in this life.

ANNA LOUISE DE STAEL, *Corinne*, 1807

Brotherhood is Religion!

WILLIAM BLAKE, *Jerusalem*, 1820

Each man, simply because he exists, holds a right on other men or on society for existence.

THOMAS CHALMERS (1780–1847), *Selections from*, ed. by H. Hunter

I am hindered of meeting God in my brother, because he has shut his own temple doors, and recites fables merely of his brother's or his brother's brother's God.

RALPH WALDO EMERSON, "Self-Reliance," *Essays*, I, 1841

Oh! my dear fellow beings, why should we longer cherish any social acerbities, or know the slightest ill-humor or envy! Come; let us squeeze hands all round; nay, let us squeeze ourselves into each other; let us squeeze ourselves universally into the very milk and sperm of kindness.

HERMAN MELVILLE, *Moby Dick*, 1851

It is not by driving away our brother that we can be alone with God.

GEORGE MACDONALD, *Alec Forbes*, Vol. 2, 1865

There is a true Church wherever one hand meets another helpfully, and that is the only holy or Mother Church which ever was, or ever shall be.

JOHN RUSKIN, *Sesame and Lilies*, 1865

We shall never be able, I say, to rest in the bosom of the Father, till the fatherhood is fully revealed to us in the love of the brothers.

GEORGE MACDONALD, *Unspoken Sermons*, 1st Series, 1869

Until you become really, in actual fact, a brother to every one, brotherhood will not come to pass.

FEODOR DOSTOEVSKY, *The Brothers Karamazov*, 1880

Virtue requires self-restraint instead of self-assertion, respecting and helping one's fellows, instead of ruthless assertion, helping them instead of trampling on them and thrusting them aside.

THOMAS HENRY HUXLEY, *Ethics and Evolution*, 1894

You are a part of the Infinite. This is your nature. Hence you are your brother's keeper.

VIVEKANANDA (1863–1902), *Works of*

Only man helps man; only man pities; only man tries to save.

ROBERT BLATCHFORD, *God and My Neighbor*, 1903

God has given every man a duty towards his neighbor. Hence not only those in Holy Orders but all the faithful must work for God and souls; not indeed as isolated individuals but under the guidance of the bishops.

POPE PIUS X, *Supremi Apostolatus*, October 4, 1903

The true Christian will recognize his brethren not necessarily in the Church or sect to which he belongs, but in all who live humbly, purely, and lovingly, in dependence on the Great Father of all living.

ARTHUR CHRISTOPHER BENSON, *From a College Window*, 1906

The Fatherhood of God, as revealed by Jesus Christ, should lead us towards a Brotherhood which knows no restriction of race, sex or social class.

Friends [Quakers] in Great Britain, 1918

The Christian Church faces no more burning question than the problem of making brotherhood real.

NORMAN THOMAS, *Letter*, May 19, 1922

In order that we may come to a full realization that he and he alone is his brother's keeper, it is necessary that man should entirely give up the belief in personal superhuman causation.

JAMES LEUBA, *Psychology of Religious Mysticism*, 1925

Christianity holds that the inclination and will to practice brotherhood of man depends upon the constant adoration of God as father.

WILLARD L. SPERRY, *Reality in Worship*, 1925

We can never call one another "brother" until we have learned to call God "Father."

FULTON J. SHEEN, *Religion Without God*, 1928

There is a great spiritual brotherhood composed of Christians to which not only the Churches of the East and West belong, but also those whose wills are directed towards God and the divine, all in fact who aspire to some form of spiritual elevation.

NICHOLAS BERDYAEV, *Freedom and the Spirit,* 1935

Every step toward wider understanding and tolerance and good will is a step in the direction of that universal brotherhood Christ proclaimed.

H. G. WELLS, *Reader's Digest,* May, 1935

Our attitude to all men would be Christian if we regarded them as though they were dying, and determined our relation to them in the light of death, both of their death and of our own.

NICHOLAS BERDYAEV, *The Destiny of Man,* 1937

Christian brotherhood is not an ideal, but a divine reality . . . a spiritual and not a psychic reality.

DIETRICH BONHOEFFER, *Life Together,* 1938

Increase, O God, the spirit of neighborliness among us, that in peril we may uphold one another, in calamity serve one another, in suffering tend one another and in homeliness and loneliness in exile befriend one another. Grant us brave and enduring hearts that we may strengthen one another, till the disciplines and testing of these days be ended.

Prayer Used in Air Raid Shelters, England, World War II (1939–1945)

Only when two say to one another with all that they are, "It is *Thou,*" is the indwelling of the Present Being between them.

MARTIN BUBER, *Between Man and Men,* 1947

The word of him who wishes to speak with God without speaking with men goes astray.

MARTIN BUBER, *Between Man and Men,* 1947

The more we are induced to think of one another in the light of Christ's revelation of the brotherhood of men, the more we shall find ourselves to be, in *this sense,* involved in the sins of others.

H. D. LEWIS, *Morals and the New Theology,* 1947

It is possible to combine enthusiasm for the doctrine of universal brotherhood with inability to live in brotherly concord with anyone.

Man's Disorder and God's Design, II (Amsterdam Assembly Series), 1948

If you do not live, think, and suffer with the men of your time, as one of them, in vain will you pretend, when the moment comes to speak to them, to adapt your language to their ear.

HENRI DE LUBAC, *Paradoxes,* 1948

In a materialistic society which denies the existence and authority of God, the appeal for human brotherhood is a curious contradiction in terms.

CLARENCE MANION, *The Key to Peace,* 1950

Our separated brethren are not theological adversaries to be refuted, but friends seeking with us a deeper love of Christ.

BERNARD LEEMING, *Unitas,* XI, No. 2, 1952

I believe that if we really want human brotherhood to spread and increase until it makes life safe and sane, we must also be certain that there is no one true faith or path by which it may spread.

ADLAI E. STEVENSON, *This I Believe,* 1954

If we want the perfect host to take us into his eternal home when we come to knock at his door, he has told us himself what we have to do: we must be ready to open our own door to the earthly guests that come our way.

JEAN DANIELOU, *The Lord of History,* 1958

It is no doubt easy enough to love the fellow-creatures less and to imagine that this is happening because we are learning to love God more, when the real reason may be quite different. We may be only "mistaking the decays of nature for the increase of Grace."

C. S. LEWIS, *The Four Loves,* 1960

If men were only a little more aware of what they are all doing together this very moment, they would feel as if they were in church, singing in a chorus. How they all love one another without knowing it, and how beautiful it would be if they knew! If only they could do consciously what they now do unawares!

PAUL CLAUDEL, *I Believe in God,* 1963

All who have been justified by faith in Baptism are members of Christ's body, and have a right to be called Christian, and so are with solid reasons accepted as brothers by the children of the Catholic Church.

The Constitution of the Church, Second Vatican Council, November, 1963

See also Affections; Agape; Almsgiving; Anti-Semitism; Apartheid; Believing; Charity; Christian; Christian Life; Christianity; Christians; Church, Definitions of; Community; Compassion; Concord; Dialogue; Division; Ecumenism; Envy; Equality; Fellowship; Friendship; Humanity; Isolation; Loneliness; Love, Human; Love of Mankind; Mankind; Mercy; Neighbor; Pity; Prayer; Social Faith; Society; Solitude; Tolerance; Unity; Unity of Mankind; War; Worship.

BRUTALITY

The belief that human brutality is a vestigial remnant of man's animal or primitive past . . . [is] one of the dearest illusions of modern culture.

REINHOLD NIEBUHR, *Faith and History,* 1949

BUDDHA

One day as Gautama sat in deep meditation beneath the Bo tree, he saw a great light. In a moment he became the Buddha which means the Enlightened One. . . . There was one of the great climactic points in the history of the world. . . . There came to him the explanation of the world's suffering and pain, and this discovery sent him on a mission of release and peace to the troubled world about him.

CHARLES S. BRADEN, *The World's Religions,* 1954

BUDDHISM

Moreover, brethren, though robbers, who are highwaymen, would with a two-handed saw carve you in pieces limb by limb, yet if the mind of any one of you should be offended thereat, such an one is no follower of my gospel.

Buddha (6th century B.C.), *Some Sayings of,* tr. F. L. Woodward

Although I believe the articles of faith [of Buddhism] to be absolutely wrong . . . the rules and directions imposed on the will . . . not only prescribe hatred of vice, inculcate battling against passions, but what is more remarkable, lead men towards sublime and heroic perfection.

IPPOLITO DESIDERI, *An Account of Tibet,* publ. posth., 1808

Buddhist faith, devotion, moral discipline and religious zeal are worth more to their cause and to ours than all the books they have ever written.

DAVID SNELLGROVE, *Springs of Morality,* ed. J. M. Todd, 1956

The word used for religion in Buddhism is *brahma-cariya* which may be translated as "the ideal life"—any way of life which anyone may consider to be the ideal as a consequence of his holding a certain set of beliefs about the nature and destiny of man in the universe.

> G. P. MALALASEKERA and K. N. JAY-ATILLEKE, *Buddhism and the Race Question,* 1958

See also Buddhism and Christianity; Commandments; Dhamma; Immortality, Belief in; Immortality, Denial and Doubt of; Man and God.

BUDDHISM AND CHRISTIANITY

Buddhism, I think, at the last may be accepted as a preface to the Gospel . . . and as the most convincing argument withal that truth to be clearly known waits upon revelation.

> PAUL ELMER MORE, *The Catholic Faith,* 1931

Though Christianity from the start was more emotional in its temper than Buddhism, and though an element of nostalgia entered into it from an early period, it is at one in its final emphasis with the older religion. In both faiths this emphasis is on the peace that passeth understanding.

> IRVING BABBITT, *Dhammapada,* 1936

The modern development of Buddhism away from the atheism of its origin, points more and more in the direction of an emphasis on personality which finds its climax in Christianity.

> D. E. TRUEBLOOD, *The Logic of Belief,* 1942

BURDEN

God hath ordered it that we may learn to bear one another's burden; for no one is without fault, no one but hath a burden; no one is sufficient for himself.

> THOMAS À KEMPIS, *Imitation of Christ,* 1441

None knows the weight of another's burden.

> GEORGE HERBERT, *Outlandish Proverbs,* 1640

See also Charity.

BUREAUCRACY

It is futile for a non-Christian society to rail at bureaucracy. Bureaucracy is its sole substitute for virtue.

> WILLIAM A. ORTON, *Affirmations,* ed. B. I. Bell, 1938

BUREAUCRAT

The moral bureaucrat's standard word is, "That is no business of mine."

> DIETRICH VON HILDEBRAND, *True Morality and Its Counterfeits,* 1955

BURIAL

As for the burying of the body, whatever is bestowed on that is no aid of salvation, but an office of humanity.

> ST. AUGUSTINE, *On the Care to Be Had for the Dead,* c. 405

See also Dead; Death; Funerals.

BUS SERVICE, SCHOOL

If it could, in fairness, have been said that the expenditure [by the State of New Jersey for bus service for nonpublic school children] was a measure for the protection of the safety, health or morals of youngsters, it would not merely have been constitutional to grant it, it would have been unconstitutional to refuse it merely because he was a Catholic.

> JUSTICE JACKSON, dissenting opinion, U.S. Supreme Court, *Emerson vs. Board of Education of Township of Ewing, N.J.,* 1947

When a Catholic school child is denied the use of a public school bus an injustice is done not to the *Catholic* child, but to the *American* child who happens to be a Catholic. What is really involved is a violation not of religious liberty but of civic equality.

> FRANCIS SPELLMAN, *Justice or Bigotry?,* 1947

The reason for opposition to bus rides for all children is neither constitutional nor administrative. It is ideological. The opposition is not to bus rides but to parochial schools, to religious education, to the Catholic Church.

ROBERT C. HARTNETT, *Federal Aid to Education,* 1950

BUSINESS

Be wholly taken up in diligent business of your lawful callings when you are not exercised in the more immediate service of God.

RICHARD BAXTER, *Christian Directory,* 1673

To ask the individual to follow Christ in much of the business world today is almost like asking a man to live Christ while employed in a gambling house.

JEROME DAVIS, *Harper's Magazine,* January, 1937

The Church has not the function of telling people how to run their business; but it has the right and duty to tell businessmen what is right and wrong in the conduct of business.

JOHN LA FARGE, *Secularism's Attack on World Order,* 1945

See also Capitalism; Clergy; Competition; Economics and Christianity; Enterprise; Individualism; Money; Profit; Property; Success; Trade; Traders; Trust; Usury; Work.

BYZANTINE. See EAST

CALAMITY

Heaven-sent calamities you may stand up against, but you cannot survive those brought on by yourself.

SHU CHING, c. 490 B.C.

Calamity is virtue's opportunity.

SENECA, *De Providentia,* c. 64 A.D.

It is only when we are stricken by calamity that we are able to yield certain sparks, a certain sacred fire. This is the meaning of wars, revolutions, sickness.

ALEXANDER YELCHANINOV (1881–1934), *Fragments of a Diary*

See also Catastrophes.

CALCULATION

You are wrong, my friends, if you think a man with a spark of decency in him ought to calculate life or death; the only thing he ought to consider is whether he does right or wrong.

PLATO, *Apology,* 399 B.C.

See also Caution; Safety.

CALL

God did not call you to be canary-birds in a little cage, and to hop up and down on three sticks, within a space no larger than the size of the cage. God calls you to be eagles, and to fly from sun to sun, over continents.

HENRY WARD BEECHER, *Sermon,* 1887

The calling of man by God to his supernatural end is not simply a call from without. Before any call from without, the divine call has already sounded in the depths of human nature.

R. P. BRISBOIS, *Le désir de voir Dieu,* 1936

The idea of the Calling and of the Call is unintelligible apart from that of Divine Providence.

EMIL BRUNNER, *The Divine Imperative,* 1937

It is a vocation in an individually unrepeatable form to give an answer to the call of God and to put one's gifts to creative use.

NICHOLAS BERDYAEV, *Slavery and Freedom,* 1944

The proper use of the table napkin is not final evidence of a call to the ministry.

　CLELAND B. MCAFEE, *Near to the Heart of God,* 1954

The call to the ministry is not for our contemporaries first of all a mystic matter enacted in the solitariness of lonesome encounter; it is rather a call extended to social man, the member of a community, through the mediation of community.

　H. RICHARD NIEBUHR, *The Purpose of the Church and Its Ministry,* 1956

The call does not come to the ear, but to the heart. One does not "hear" it as much as he *knows* it.

　FULTON J. SHEEN, *Our Sunday Visitor,* March 11, 1962

See also Aspiration; Christian Life; Clergy; Community; Duties; Man and God; Minister; Ministry; Ordination; Priests; Priesthood; Providence; Service; Work.

CALUMNIES

The upright, if he suffer calumny to move him, fears the tongue of man more than the eye of God.

　C. C. COLTON, *Lacon,* 1822

Calumnies are diseases of others that break out in your body.

　FRIEDRICH NIETZSCHE, *Human, All Too Human,* 1878

See also Christianity, Criticism of; Falsehood; Gossip; Reputation; Words.

CALVARY

Calvary was too beautiful to be forgotten. It is remembered! It is commemorated! It is re-enacted! It is re-presented! It is prolonged through space and time—and its memorial is the Mass.

　FULTON J. SHEEN, *The Fullness of Christ,* 1935

We go to Calvary to learn how we may be forgiven, and to learn how to forgive others, to intercede on their behalf, to join the noble band of intercessors.

　S. J. REID, *The Seven Windows,* 1939

No man can know his true self, caught between this potential for depravity and this potential for divinity, except in the light of what happened on Calvary.

　STUART LEROY ANDERSON, *Way,* June, 1963

See also Atonement; Bereavement; Courage; Cross; Easter; Forgiveness; Incarnation; Jesus Christ: His Passion and Death; Jesus Christ: His Resurrection; Jesus Christ as Saviour; Mass, the; Redemption; Salvation; Suffering.

CAPACITY

God obligeth no man more than he hath given him ability to perform.

　Koran, c. 625 A.D.

CAPITAL PUNISHMENT

It does not please good people in the Catholic Church when an evil man, even a heretic, is put to death.

　ST. AUGUSTINE, *Contra Cresconium,* c. 406

Those who by God's commands have waged war, or who, wielding the public power, and in conformity with the divine laws, have put criminals to death, these have by no means violated the commandment *Thou shalt not kill.*

　ST. AUGUSTINE, *The City of God.* Lib. 1, cap. xxi; 426

If by the law of God all Christians are forbidden to kill . . . how can it be compatible for magistrates to shed blood? . . . The magistrate does not act at all from himself, but merely executes the judgments of God. . . . We can find no objection to the infliction of public vengeance, unless the justice of God be restrained from the punishment of crimes.

JOHN CALVIN, *Institutes,* 1536

Though every other man who wields a pen should turn himself into a commentator on the Scriptures—not all their united efforts, pursued through our united lives, could ever persuade me that Executions are a Christian law.

CHARLES DICKENS, Letter to *Daily News,* March 16, 1846

Assassination on the scaffold is the worst form of assassination, because there it is invested with the approval of society.

GEORGE BERNARD SHAW, *Man and Superman,* 1903

The verdict of capital punishment destroys the only indisputable human community there is, the community in the face of death.

ALBERT CAMUS, *Evergreen Review,* 1962

Religious values . . . are the only ones on which the death penalty can be based, since according to their own logic they prevent that penalty from being final and irreparable: it is justified only insofar as it is not supreme.

ALBERT CAMUS, *Evergreen Review,* 1962

See also Heresy; Lynching; Martyrdom; Vengeance.

CAPITALISM

The roots of modern religion are deeply imbedded in the social oppression of the working masses, and in their apparently complete helplessness before the blind forces of capitalism.

NICOLAI LENIN, *On Religion,* 1905

"The capitalist spirit" is as old as history. . . . But it found in certain aspects of later Puritanism a tonic which braced its energies and fortified its already vigorous temper.

RICHARD H. TAWNEY, *Religion and the Rise of Capitalism,* 1926

Capitalism was the social counterpart of Calvinism. The central idea is expressed in the characteristic phrase "a calling." . . . To the Calvinist, the calling is not a condition in which the individual is born, but a strenuous and exacting enterprise to be chosen by himself, and to be pursued with a sense of religious responsibility.

RICHARD H. TAWNEY, *Religion and the Rise of Capitalism,* 1926

The Catholic Church is a bulwark against Communism, but she is decidedly *not* a bulwark *for* Capitalism. She does not stand or fall with Capitalism.

JAMES M. GILLIS, *The Catholic World,* 1933

Capitalism is unthinkable as a "sacred" economy. It is the result of the secularization of economic life, and by it the hierarchical subordination of the material to the spiritual is inverted.

NICHOLAS BERDYAEV, *The End of Our Time,* 1933

Capitalism is not Christianity. The opposition of Christianity to communism is not unqualified and complete. Christianity has far more affinity for some of the basic principles of communism than for the corresponding principles of capitalism.

HUGH VERNON WHITE, *Christian Century,* February 14, 1934

Capitalism is above all anti-personal, the power of anonymity over human life, capitalism uses men as goods for sale. . . . Man is a wolf to man. The life of the capitalist world is lupine.

NICHOLAS BERDYAEV, *The Fate of Man in the Modern World,* 1935

The spirit of Capitalism considered objectively is a spirit of exaltation of active and inventive power, of the dynamic energies of man and of individual enterprise; but it is a spirit of hatred of poverty and of contempt of the poor.

> JACQUES MARITAIN, *Freedom in the Modern World,* 1936

Where "capitalism" . . . unduly claims for itself an unlimited right on property, without any subordination to the common good, the Church has reproved it as contrary to natural law.

> POPE PIUS XII, *Broadcast,* September 1, 1943

There are conflicts between Christianity and capitalism. . . . Capitalism tends to subordinate . . . the meeting of human needs to the economic advantages of those who have most power over its institutions. . . . It has developed a practical form of materialism in western nations in spite of their Christian background.

> *The Church and the Disorder of Society* (Amsterdam Report), 1948

American capitalism . . . now carries the burden of defending Christian civilization against its Eastern enemy.

> GARET GARRETT, *American Affairs,* Winter, 1949

The dehydrated moral notions of a capitalistic society [have] substituted mere caricatures for the fullness of the Christian virtues.

> GEORGE H. DUNNE, *The Commonweal Reader,* ed. E. S. Skillin, 1950

Perhaps one can say that the Church has one last reproach against modern Capitalism, namely, to have generated Marxism, which is another excess no less dangerous.

> EMMANUEL SUHARD, *The Church Today,* 1953

See also Business; Christianity; Communism; Competition; Enterprise; Industrialism; Labor; Laissez Faire; Machines; Mar-

ket Place; Marxism; Money; Ownership; Poverty; Profit; Property; Puritanism; Riches; Secularism; Wealth.

CATACOMBS

When Christianity came up from the catacombs to become the official religion of Rome, it left something precious down in the dark. It gained extension; it lost intensity. It gained in bulk; it lost in savor.

> HALFORD E. LUCCOCK, *Jesus and the American Mind,* 1930

CATASTROPHES

The Church is bidden in its mission to seek out the moments of opportunity and to interpret the catastrophes as the judgments of God which are the other side of His mercy.

> NORMAN GOODALL, *Missions Under the Cross,* 1953

See also Calamity; End of the World.

CATHEDRAL

Mankind was never so happily inspired as when it made a cathedral.

> ROBERT LOUIS STEVENSON, *An Inland Voyage,* 1878

He couldn't design a cathedral without it looking like the First Supernatural Bank.

> EUGENE O'NEILL, *The Great God Brown,* 1925

See also Architecture; Church: Edifice.

CATHOLIC AND NON-CATHOLIC

All that is pure in Protestant or Orthodox piety or in that *pietas Anglicana* which gives Anglicanism its peculiar ethos is a loss, not indeed to the substance of the Church but to the expression and embodiment of its life, or at least to the wholeness of that expression.

> YVES CONGAR, *Divided Christendom,* 1939

All our troubles today stem from the fact that Catholics love only God and Protestants only their neighbors.

> Unidentified person quoted by Bruce Marshall in *The World Crisis and the Catholic,* 1958

I do not believe that Catholics generally have anything that approaches an adequate understanding of what Protestantism actually is. Most of them know only what it is *not.* And this is a major failure in Catholic education.

> W. CLANCY, *Christianity and Crisis,* June 8, 1959

It is sometimes said that one great glory of the Church is that it can assimilate to itself truths discovered by those not of its fold. But it might just as fairly be said that the great triumph of non-Catholic thought is that it has been able to influence even so conservative a body as the Catholic Church.

> DANIEL CALLAHAN, *The Mind of the Catholic Layman,* 1963

See also the various rubrics under Church; Division; Ecumenism; Protestantism; Reformation, the; Unity.

CATHOLICISM

I believe in . . . the Holy Catholic [Universal] Church.

> *Apostles' Creed*—often printed in precisely this way in non–Roman Catholic versions.

It [the one, holy, Catholic church] is called Catholic because it extends over all the world, from one end of the earth to the other, and because it teaches universally and completely all the doctrines which ought to come to men's knowledge, concerning things both visible and invisible, heavenly and earthly.

> ST. CYRIL OF JERUSALEM, *Catechetical Lectures,* 350

You are not to be looked upon as holding the true Catholic faith if you do not teach that the faith of Rome is to be held.

> ST. AUGUSTINE (354–430), *Sermon* XX, CXX, n. 13

The Christian faith is not called catholic or universal because it embraces each individual of every kind, but because it embraces every kind of individual, for some have adhered to it from among every sort and conditions of men.

> ST. THOMAS AQUINAS, *Expositio Super Boetium De Trinitate,* 1258

The Catholic religion, even in the time of its most extravagance and atrocity, never wholly lost the spirit of the great Teacher whose precepts form the noblest code, as His conduct furnished the purest example, or moral excellence. It is of religions the most poetical.

> THOMAS BABINGTON MACAULAY, *Knight's Quarterly Magazine,* January, 1824

Modern Catholicism is nothing else but simply the legitimate growth and complement, that is, the natural and necessary development of the doctrine of the early Church.

> JOHN HENRY NEWMAN, *An Essay on the Development of Christian Doctrine,* 1845

Catholic Christendom is no simple exhibition of religious absolutism, but presents a continuous picture of Authority and Private Judgment alternately advancing and retreating in the ebb and flow of the tide.

> JOHN HENRY NEWMAN, *Apologia pro Vita Sua,* 1864

It is a vast assemblage of human beings with wilful intellects and wild passion, brought together into one by the beauty and majesty of a Superhuman Power.

> JOHN HENRY NEWMAN, *Apologia pro Vita Sua,* 1864

In her own eyes the Catholic Church is nothing at all if she be not *the* Church, *the* Body of Christ, *the* Kingdom of God.

KARL ADAM, *The Spirit of Catholicism,* 1924

No longer may a well-instructed Catholic lay the flattering unction to his soul that he has done all his religion demands when he takes a seat in the bark of Peter, paying his fare, and lets someone do all the rowing.

J. J. CANTWELL, *Address,* 1937

The Church is not Catholic because she is spread abroad over the whole of the earth and can reckon on a large number of members. She was already Catholic on the morning of Pentecost, when all her members could be contained in a small room.

HENRI DE LUBAC, *Catholicism,* 1937

The essence of Catholic Christianity is acceptance of a Supernatural Order, here and now, at every point and turn of daily life, impinging as it were on all we do, breaking through, always at hand, always real.

ROSALIND MURRAY, *The Good Pagan's Failure,* 1939

Only those are to be included as members of the Church who have been baptized and profess the true faith, and who have not been so unfortunate as to separate themselves from the unity of the Body, or been excluded by legitimate authority for grave faults committed.

POPE PIUS XII, *On the Mystical Body of Jesus Christ,* June 29, 1943

Catholic: universal or general. . . . Of or pertaining to the Church universal, specifically designating or pertaining to the ancient undivided Christian Church; or a Church or churches claiming historical continuity from it; hence the true apostolic Church; orthodox.

Webster's New International Dictionary, unabridged, 1945

Catholicism is sacramental through and through. Its worship is most characteristically a holy action of the Church. . . . The Church does not talk to people chiefly; it acts upon them or for them. It takes them up into its life.

ANGUS DUN, *Prospecting for a United Church,* 1948

Catholicism would falsify itself if it proved incapable of assimilating whatever there is of truth and goodness in religious and philosophical systems seemingly at odds with the Church.

AELRED GRAHAM, *Christian Thought and Action,* 1951

See also Catacombs; Christian; Christianity; the various rubrics under Church; Communion of Saints; Education, Catholic; Education, Parochial; Exclusiveness; Mary, the Mother of Jesus; Pope, the; Protestantism; Reformation, the; Roman Catholic Church.

CAUSE

It is obvious that there is some First Principle, and that the causes of things are not infinitely many . . . neither can the Final Cause recede to infinity.

ARISTOTLE, *Metaphysics,* II, 11, 1–2 c. 322 B.C.

The potency of a cause is greater, the more remote the effects to which it extends.

ST. THOMAS AQUINAS, *Summa c. Gent.* III, C. lxxxvii, 1260

It is for me easier to suppose that there are causes that elude, and must forever elude, our search, rather than to suppose that there are no causes at all.

E. N. da C. ANDRADE, *The Listener,* July 10, 1947

As the tiny mountain rivulet as well as the majestic lake and river, after many windings and turnings, all trace their course at last down to the ocean's mighty shore, so all things and all living creatures, all trace their origin and existence back to God, their Creator.

JOHN A. O'BRIEN, *The Origin of Man,* 1947

Man is forever climbing up the ladder of secondary causes to the First and Supreme Cause—God Himself.

JOHN A. O'BRIEN, *Truths Men Live By,* 1947

To ask the question, Who caused God, or Who caused the first cause, is to ask that a first cause be at one and the same time a secondary cause, which is a contradiction.

FULTON J. SHEEN, *The Philosophy of Religion,* 1948

The cause cannot necessitate the effect. If it did, the effect would exist when the cause did. What is normally termed a cause is only an antecedent condition.

PAUL WEISS, *Determinism and Freedom,* ed. Sidney Hook, 1958

The principle of causality, limited exclusively to explaining the interconnection of *phenomena,* and void of any *metaphysical* significance, has become incapable of making the mind pass from the world to God. Man's mind, if not his heart, has become godless, and knowledge, or science, has dethroned wisdom.

CHARLES JOURNET, *The Meaning of Evil,* 1961

See also Chance; Creation; Evolution; God: His Existence; God: His Nature; God: His Omnipotence; God: His Omniscience; God as Being; Matter; Nature and God; Science; Science and Creation; Science and God; Universe; Universe: Its Creation.

CAUTION

I hate your good careful men of the villages, lest they be confounded with the truly virtuous.

Mencius, c. 300 B.C.

He that hath a head of wax must not walk in the sun.

GEORGE HERBERT, *Outlandish Proverbs,* 1640

CELIBACY

In this world men have a liking for women; he who knows (and renounces) them will easily perform his duties as a monk.

Jaina Sutras, between 600 and 200 B.C.

The Law is my pond, celibacy is my bathing place, which is not turbid, and throughout clear for the soul; therein make ablutions; pure, clean and thoroughly cooled, I get rid of hatred (or impurity).

Jaina Sutras, between 600 and 200 B.C.

Bishops, presbyters, and deacons—indeed all clerics who have a place in the ministry (of the altar)—shall abstain from their wives and shall not beget children—this is a total prohibition; whoever does so let him forfeit his rank among the clergy.

Canons of the Council of Elvira, c. 305 A.D.

The great Synod altogether forbids any bishop, presbyter or deacon, or any one of the clergy, to have a woman dwelling with him except a mother, or sister, or aunt, or such persons only as are above all suspicions.

Canons of Nicea, 325 A.D.

If a presbyter marry, he is to be excluded from the clergy, if he fornicate or commit adultery, he is to be completely excommunicated and is to be brought to repentance.

Canons of Neocaesarea, c. 314–325 A.D.

The Church does not on any account admit a man living in the wedded state and having children, even though he have only one wife, to the orders of deacon, priest, bishop or sub-deacon; but only him whose wife be dead or who should abstain from the use of marriage.

ST. EPIPHANIUS (died 535), *Advers. Haer. Panar.*

He will possess an eminent degree of chastity so that the mind which is to consecrate the body of Christ may be pure and free from all defilement of the flesh.

ST. ISIDORE OF SEVILLE (560–636), *The Perfection of the Clergy*

Priests, after the order of priesthood received, as afore, may not marry, by the law of God.

Six Articles Act, Statutes of the Realm, Henry VIII, 1539

A preacher of the gospel, if he is able with a good conscience, to remain unmarried, let him so remain; but if he cannot abstain, living chastely, then let him take a wife; God has made this plaster for that sore.

MARTIN LUTHER (1483–1546), *Table Talk*

Bishops, priests and deacons are not commanded by God's law either to vow the estate of a single life, or to abstain from marriage.

The Thirty-nine Articles (Church of England), 1563

A single life doth well with churchmen, for charity will hardly water the ground when it must first fill a pool.

FRANCIS BACON, "Of Marriage and Single Life," *Essays,* 1597

It is an unnatural and impious thing to bar men of this Christian liberty, too severe and inhuman an edict.

ROBERT BURTON, *Anatomy of Melancholy,* III, 1621

If it was lawful for St. Peter to have a wife, why not lawful for another priest or preacher to have one?

LORENZO DOW, *Reflections on Matrimony,* 1833

Celibacy he [St. Paul] has no doubt is the ideal state, first because the time is short and detachment from the things of this age is required, and secondly because marriage diverts man and woman alike from the service of God.

C. H. DODD, *Evolution of Ethics,* ed. by E. H. Sneath, 1927

Since "God is a Spirit," it is only fitting that he who dedicates and consecrates himself to God's service should in some way "divest himself of the body."

POPE PIUS XI, *The Catholic Priesthood,* 1935

There are those called to be celibate because the requirements of God's Kingdom come first and must be met at any cost. . . . There are still tasks in the missionfield or in city slums which are best done by the unmarried, and those that do them are to be honored.

SYDNEY CAVE, *The Christian Way,* 1949

Not to practice something which is holy, which is meant by God to be the normal perfection of human nature, to give that up under the inspiration of the Holy Ghost —which is what we call vocation—is to be called, as a few are called in every generation.

FRANCIS DEVAS, *The Law of Love,* 1954

The self-glorification of celibacy by complacent celibates is an unlovely and sinful thing. But we cannot, because of the prev-

alence of this perverted attitude among celibates, deny the essential goodness and creativity of celibacy itself.
J. V. L. CASSERLEY, *The Bent World*, 1955

The law of celibacy does not arise from an organizational desire for efficiency and mobility. It is the result of a long spiritual maturation in the Church, meditating on the celibate witness of Christ's own priesthood.
EDITORIAL, *America*, March 28, 1964

Ultimately, the celibate's life taken on for God is an enacted prophecy, "shouting to the world that the world is passing away."
FRANCIS J. FILAS, *Chicago New World*, 1964

See also Chastity; Continence; Homosexuality; Marriage; Priesthood; Self-Conquest; Self-Denial; Self-Sacrifice; Sexual Intercourse; Virginity.

CENSORSHIP

Are we to have a censor whose imprimatur shall say what books may be sold and what we may buy? . . . Is a priest to be our inquisitor, or shall a layman, simple as ourselves, set up his reason as the rule for what we are to read and what we must believe? It is an insult to our citizens to question whether they are rational beings or not. . . . For God's sake let us hear both sides if we choose.
THOMAS JEFFERSON, *Letter to Dufief*, 1814

Men have a right freely and prudently to propagate throughout the State whatever things soever are true and honorable . . . but lying opinions, than which no mental plague is greater, and vices which corrupt the heart and moral life, should be diligently repressed by public authority, lest they insidiously work the ruin of the State.
POPE LEO XIII, *Libertas Humana*, 1888

A member of this Church [Christian Science] shall not patronize a publishing house or bookstore that has for sale obnoxious books.
Church Manual, Art. viii, section 12, First Church of Christ Scientist in Boston, 89th and final edition, 1910

The censor believes that he can hold back the mighty traffic of life with a tin whistle and a raised right hand. For after all, it is life with which he quarrels.
HEYWOOD BROUN (1888–1939), quoted by Ezra Goodman, *The Fifty Year Decline and Fall of Hollywood*, 1961

The state has no legitimate interest in protecting any or all religions from views distasteful to them which is sufficient to justify prior restraints upon the expression of those views.
JUSTICE TOM C. CLARK, unanimous decision of the U.S. Supreme Court, *Burstyn v. Wilson*, 1952

Morally, the Church can and does exercise what is called censorship. . . . Her decisions bind her people but her sanctions upon them are only spiritual and moral. She does, nevertheless, express her judgments to all men of good will, soliciting their reasoned understanding and their freely given acceptance and support.
Roman Catholic Bishops of U.S., 1957

Many supposedly innocuous popular novels and plays are far more toxic and censorable than the so-called pornographic paperbacks or the lowly comic strip.
AMOS N. WILDER, *Theology and Modern Literature*, 1958

The Churches have a stake both in the civil liberties aspect of censorship, and also in the moral and educational side of the question it raises. The task of the Church with its doctrines that creation is good, and that all life, including the sexual, is redeemed in Christ, is to steer a course

between the social repression of sexual feelings and an unprincipled release of them. The Church must recognize that legal censorship, being purely an act of restraint, compounds the problem rather than solving it.
> T. F. DRIVER, *Christianity and Crisis,* April 17, 1961

Generally censors have been notorious for partisanship and arbitrariness, and almost universally hated for a ruthless disregard of human rights and freedoms.
> J. M. MARTIN, *Christianity Today,* June 22, 1961

See also Motion Pictures; Obscenity.

CENSURE

Censure is the tax a man pays to the public for being eminent.
> JONATHAN SWIFT, *Thoughts on Various Subjects,* 1706

CEREMONY. See RITUAL

CERTAINTY

This restless, obstinate search after an unattainable certainty is very evidently the work of nature, not of grace.
> FRANÇOIS FÉNELON (1651–1715), *Spiritual Letters*

I am certain of nothing but of the holiness of the heart's affections, and the truth of the Imagination.
> JOHN KEATS, *Letter,* November 22, 1817

Man cannot accept certainties; he must discover them.
> JOHN MIDDLETON MURRY, *The Necessity of Art,* ed. A. Clutton-Brock, 1919

See also Absolutes; Faith; Relativity; Safety; Security.

CHALLENGE

O, do not pray for easy lives. Pray to be stronger men. Do not pray for tasks equal to your powers. Pray for powers equal to your tasks.
> PHILLIPS BROOKS, *Going Up to Jerusalem,* 1890

The first question to be answered by any individual or any social group, facing a hazardous situation, is whether the crisis is to be met as a challenge to strength or as an occasion for despair.
> HARRY EMERSON FOSDICK, *The Challenge of the Present Crisis,* 1917

How can any transcendental faith be accepted with conviction in the modern world? The question must be left unanswered until the answer comes spontaneously from the quality of life of the Christian community.
> MARY B. HESSE, *Science and the Human Imagination,* 1955

Once it was the skeptic, the critic of the status quo who had to make a great effort. Today the skeptic is the status quo. The one who must make the effort is the man who seeks to create a new moral order.
> JOHN W. GARDNER, *Self-Renewal,* 1963

CHANCE

Chance implies an absolute absence of any principle.
> CHUANG-TZU (4th century B.C.), *Texts of Taoism,* ed. J. Legge

All chances are governed by the secret counsel of God.
> JOHN CALVIN, *Institutes,* I, 1536

His Sacred Majesty, Chance, decides everything.
> VOLTAIRE, *Letter,* February 26, 1767

The doctrine of Chance in the eternal world corresponds to that of Free Will in the internal.

HENRY THOMAS BUCKLE, *History of Civilization in England*, Vol. I, 1913

Chance cannot possibly be the origin of things. For it presupposes an encounter of causal series. . . . Chance, that is to say, necessarily implies preordination. To hold that the universe can be explained by a primordial chance is self-contradictory.

JACQUES MARITAIN, *Metaphysics*, 1939

The way we face this factor of chance helps to determine the spirit and quality of our lives. When we count on chance in lieu of preparation and prudence we weaken our characters.

RALPH W. SOCKMAN, *The Meaning of Suffering*, 1961

See also Cause; Choice; Decision; Design; Destiny; Determinism; Election; Fatalism; Fate; Foreknowledge; Free Will; Necessity; Predestination.

CHANGE

The seen is the changing, the unseen is the unchanging.

PLATO, "Phaedrus," *Dialogues*, 399 B.C.

The changes which God causes in His lower creatures are almost always from worse to better, while the changes which God allows man to make in himself are very often quite the other way.

JOHN RUSKIN, *Lectures on Architecture and Painting*, 1853

Religion will not regain its old power until it can face change in the same spirit as does science. Its principles may be eternal, but the expression of those principles requires continual development.

ALFRED NORTH WHITEHEAD, *Science and the Modern World*, 1927

From 1945 to 1959, the human species has had to withstand and comprehend greater and more fundamental changes than have been recorded in all the histories since man first began to record his histories.

NORMAN COUSINS, *In Place of Folly*, 1961

See also Death.

CHAOS

For years past we have been sinking forward into a thoroughly modern chaos, a scholarly and documented chaos, worthy of our most Liberal and Progressive thinkers. For years past our universities of Europe and America have been hacking away at the twin foundations of their own house. Like men gone mad with pride they have recklessly attacked Christianity and Hellenism as though they could by some legerdemain preserve Western civilization and still destroy the two great traditions on which it rests.

ROBERT I. GANNON, *Address*, Fordham University, September, 1941

In our age, as never before, truth implies the courage to face chaos.

ERICH NEUMANN, *Man and Time*, ed. Jos. Campbell, 1957

See also Order.

CHARACTER

There is no more important element in the formation of a virtuous character than a rightly directed sense of pleasure and dislike; for pleasure and pain are coextensive with life, and they exercise a powerful influence in promoting virtue and happiness in life.

ARISTOTLE, *Nicomachean Ethics*, c. 340 B.C.

Character is higher than intellect. Thinking is the function. Living is the functionary.

JEAN PAUL RICHTER, *Titan,* 1803

Grandeur of character lies wholly in force of soul, not in the force of thought, moral principles, and love, and this may be found in the humblest conditions of life.

WILLIAM ELLERY CHANNING, *Self-Culture,* 1838

That which we call character is a reserved force which acts directly by presence, and without means. It is conceived of as a certain undemonstrable force, a familiar or genius, by whose impulses the man is guided, but whose counsels he cannot impart.

RALPH WALDO EMERSON, "Character," *Essays,* 1844

Character is what you are in the dark.

DWIGHT L. MOODY (1837–1899), *Sermons*

Do not think about your character. If you will think about what you ought to do for other people, your character will take care of itself. Character is a by-product and any man who devotes himself to its cultivation in his own case will become a selfish prig.

WOODROW WILSON, *Address,* October, 1914

Your character is developed according to your faith. This is the primary religious truth from which no one can escape.

ALFRED NORTH WHITEHEAD, *Religion in the Making,* 1927

While we inherit our temperament, we must build our character.

WILLIAM L. SULLIVAN, *Worry! Fear! Loneliness!* 1950

Out of our beliefs are born deeds. Out of our deeds we form habits; out of our habits grow our characters; and on our character we build our destination.

HENRY HANCOCK, *Alpha Xi Delta Magazine,* 1957

See also Education; Education and Religion; Integrity.

CHARITY

A disciple having asked for a definition of charity, the Master said LOVE ONE ANOTHER.

CONFUCIUS (5th century B.C.), *Gems of Chinese Literature,* translated by Giles

He who refuses a suppliant the aid which he has the power to give, is accountable to justice.

FLAVIUS JOSEPHUS, *Against Apion,* c. 93 A.D.

Let the rich minister aid to the poor; and let the poor give thanks to God, because He hath given him one through whom his wants may be supplied.

ST. CLEMENT OF ROME, *Epistle to the Corinthians,* c. 100

Of all your toil which God gives you, give in simplicity to all who need, not doubting to whom you shall give and to whom not; give to all, for to all God wishes gifts to be made of his own bounties.

Shepherd of Hermas, c. 148

If there is among them [the Christians] a man that is poor and needy, and they have not an abundance of necessaries, they fast two or three days that they may supply the needy with their necessary food.

ARISTEIDES, *Apology,* c. 150

Whosoever takes up the burden of his neighbor . . . and ministers unto those in need out of the abundance of things he has received and keeps out of God's bounty— this man becomes a god to those who receive from him, and this man is an imitator of God.

Epistle to Diognetus, c. 200

It would be a pious act to share our clothes and food even with the wicked.

For it is to the humanity in a man that we give, and not to his moral character.

JULIAN THE APOSTATE (332–363), *Letter to a Priest*

The bread that you store up belongs to the hungry; the cloak that lies in your chest belongs to the naked; and the gold that you have hidden in the ground belongs to the poor.

ST. BASIL, *Homilies*, c. 375

That money will be more profitable to you . . . if you so give it to a poor man that you actually bestow it on Christ.

ST. AMBROSE, *Exposit. Evan. Secundum Luc.*, 390

Let us relieve the poverty of those that beg of us, and if they do impose on us, let us not be overexact about it. For such a salvation is it that we ourselves require, one with pardon, with kindness, with much mercy along with it.

ST. JOHN CHRYSOSTOM, *Homilies on the Epistle to the Romans*, 391

There is no higher road than that of charity, and none but the humble walk therein.

ST. AUGUSTINE, *Enarratio in Ps. CXLI*, c. 415

The chill of charity is the silence of the heart: the flame of charity is the clamor of the heart.

ST. AUGUSTINE, *Enarratio in Ps. XXXVII*, c. 415

Charity knows no race no creed.

GITTIN, *Talmud*, c. 500 A.D.

There are eight rungs in charity. The highest is when you help a man to help himself.

MAIMONIDES, *Yad: Matnot Anigim*, 1180

The perfection of the Christian life principally and essentially consists in charity

. . . which in some sort unites or joins man to his end.

POPE JOHN XXII (1316–1334), the bull *Ad Conditorem*

The term justice may even be used for charity; for charity renders a man's will conformable to the whole law of God, and accordingly charity in a way contains within itself the sum of all the virtues.

LESSIUS, *De Justitia et Jure*, Lib. 11, cap. 1, 1605

This only is charity, to do all, all that we can.

JOHN DONNE (1572–1631), *Sermons of*

It is no greater Charity to clothe his body, than to apparel the nakedness of his Soul.

THOMAS BROWNE, *Religio Medici*, 1635

Faith in its obscurity attains God, while remaining as it were at a distance, in as much as faith is in things unseen. But charity attains immediately God in Himself, uniting itself intimately with that which lies hidden in faith.

JOHN OF ST. THOMAS (1589–1644), *Cursus Theologicus*, vi.

Christian Charity is Friendship to all the world; . . . friendship expanded like the face of the sun when it mounts above the eastern hills.

JEREMY TAYLOR, *Nature and Office of Friendship*, 1657

Charity is an universal benevolence whose fulfillment the wise carry out conformably to the dictates of reason so as to obtain the greatest good.

G. W. VON LEIBNIZ, *Letter to Arnauld*, March 23, 1690

God sends the Poor to try us, as well as he tries them by being such: And he that refuses them a little out of the great deal that God has given him, Lays up Poverty in Store for his own Posterity.

WILLIAM PENN, *Some Fruits of Solitude*, 1718

Charity is that sweet odor of Jesus Christ which evaporates and is lost the moment it is uncovered.

JEAN BAPTISTE MASSILLON (1663–1742), *Sermons*

You find people ready enough to do the Samaritan, without the oil and two-pence.

SYDNEY SMITH, *Lady Holland's Memoir*, I, 1855

His rich penitents and the pious women of D. had often contributed money for a beautiful new altar for monseigneur's oratory; but he had always taken the money and given it to the poor. "The most beautiful altar," said he, "is the soul of an unhappy man who is comforted, and thanks God."

VICTOR HUGO, *Les Miserables*, 1862

Ask not the name of him who asks you for a bed. It is especially he whose name is a burden to him who has need of an asylum.

VICTOR HUGO, *Les Miserables*, 1862

The dramatic Christianity of the organ and aisle, of dawn-service and twilight revival . . . this gaslighted, and gas-inspired Christianity, we are triumphant in. . . . You had better get rid of the smoke, and the organ pipes . . . and the Gothic windows and the painted glass . . . and look after Lazarus at the doorstep.

JOHN RUSKIN, *Works*, XXXVI, 1864

The active, habitual, and detailed charity of private persons, which is so conspicuous a feature in all Christian societies, was scarcely known in antiquity.

W. E. H. LECKY, *History of European Morals*, 1865

Christianity for the first time made charity a rudimentary virtue. . . . It effected a complete revolution in this sphere, by regarding the *poor as the special representatives of the Christian Founder* and thus making the love of Christ rather than the love of man the principle of charity.

W. E. H. LECKY, *History of European Morals*, 1865

Why all this apparatus of temples and meeting-houses to save men from perdition in a world which is to come, while never a helping hand stretched out to save them from the inferno of their present life?

WILLIAM BOOTH, *In Darkest England and the Way Out*, 1890

Whilst traces of divine power and wisdom appear even in the wicked man, charity, which, as it were is the special mark of the Holy Ghost, is shared in only by the just.

POPE LEO XIII, *The Holy Spirit*, 1904

It is a common error . . . to confuse charity, or supernatural desire, with devout feelings and religious sentiment.

CHRISTOPHER DAWSON, *God and the Supernatural*, 1920

Since Charity is the Queen and the soul of all virtues, every act inspired by it will have by far more merit than acts inspired by fear or by hope.

ADOLPHE TANQUERAY, *The Spiritual Life*, 1923

A clergyman wrote to a wealthy and influential businessman requesting a subscription to a worthy charity and soon received a curt refusal which ended, "As far as I can see, this Christian business is just one continuous Give, give, give." Replied the clergyman, "I wish to thank you for the best definition of the Christian life I have yet heard."

W. F. A. STRIDE, *Old Farmer's Almanac*, 1939

Woe to the false prophets of universal happiness, whose eyes consume themselves in a vision of the phantasm of complete and definitive justice on earth, and see in charity nothing but an importunate and intruding defamer of her regal sister!

POPE PIUS XII, *Address,* March 13, 1940

Charity is above all a hymn of love. Real, pure love is the gift of oneself; it is the desire of diffusion and complete donation that is an essential part of goodness.

POPE PIUS XII, *Address,* April 3, 1940

Charity is no substitute for justice, but it cannot be ignored or derided without failing utterly to comprehend its meaning and its potent influence in regulating and sublimating our social relations and responsibilities.

BISHOPS OF ADMINISTRATIVE BOARD OF NATIONAL CATHOLIC WELFARE COUNCIL, *The Church and Social Order,* 1940

Charity never humiliated him who profiteth from it, nor ever bound him by the chains of gratitude, since it was not to him but to God that the gift was made.

ANTOINE DE SAINT-EXUPÉRY, *Flight to Arras,* 1942

Everybody intent upon interfering with God's plan calls himself a charity worker.

MARTIN H. FISCHER, *Fischerisms,* 1943

I will have none of a Christian charity which would mean the constant capitulation of the spiritual before temporal powers.

CHARLES PÉGUY, *Basic Verities,* 1943

What the Church ultimately wants in the temporal order is to see there reflected in civic friendship the spirit of charity that is the primary expression of her faith.

JOHN COURTNEY MURRAY, *Address,* American Academy of Political and Social Science, *Annals,* March, 1948

Christian charity is the supernatural virtue of the love for God insofar as it extends from God to our fellow men. Love for God and for our neighbor are one and the same virtue.

EBERHARD WELBY, *A Handbook of Christian Social Ethics,* 1960

When one is motivated by Christian charity, he cannot but love others, and regard the needs, sufferings and joys of others as his own.

POPE JOHN XXIII, *Mater et Magistra,* May 15, 1961

See also Acts; Agape; Almsgiving; Beggars; Brotherhood; Burden; Christian Life; Christianity; Compassion; Fellowship; Friendship; Greed; Kindness; Liberality; Love; Love, Human; Love of Mankind; Malice; Mercy; Merit; Money; Negroes; Neighbor; Pacifism; Pacifists; Patience; Poor, the Poverty; Rich, the; Temptation; Tolerance; Unity; War.

CHASTITY

If anyone is able to abide in chastity to the honor of the flesh of the Lord, let him so abide without boasting.

ST. IGNATIUS OF ANTIOCH, *Letter to Polycarp,* c. 109

We Christians regard a stain upon our chastity as more dreadful than any punishment, or even than death itself.

TERTULLIAN, *Apologeticus,* 197

Salvation, in the case of men as well as of women, depends chiefly on the observance of chastity.

TERTULLIAN, *On Female Dress,* c. 220

The chastity of widows and virgins is above the chastity of marriage.

ST. AUGUSTINE, *On the Good of Marriage,* c. 401

The first degree of chastity is pure virginity; the second is faithful marriage.

Therefore the second species of virginity is the chaste love of matrimony.

> St. John Chrysostom (344–407), quoted by John Calvin in his *Institutes,* Bk. IV (1536)

Chastity takes its name from the fact that reason chastises concupiscence, which like a child, needs curbing.

> St. Thomas Aquinas, *Summa Theol.,* II, 2nd, q 41, art 1, 1272

Chastity without charity will be chained in hell.

> William Langland, *The Vision of Piers Plowman,* c. 1400

If you ask a chaste man why he is chaste, he should say, not on account of heaven or hell, and not on account of honour and disgrace, but solely because it would seem good to me and please me well even though it were not commanded.

> Martin Luther (1483–1546), *Works,* Vol. X

Nothing is beautiful but what is pure, and the purity of men is chastity.

> St. Francis of Sales, *Introduction to the Devout Life,* 1609

Chaste women are often proud and forward, as presuming upon the merit of their chastity.

> Francis Bacon, *Essays,* 1625

Chastity is the flowering of man; and what are called Genius, Heroism, Holiness, and the like, are but various fruits which succeed it.

> Henry David Thoreau, *Walden,* 1854

Chastity is the cement of civilization and progress.

> Mary Baker Eddy, *Science and Health,* 1908

Chastity is a wealth that comes from abundance of love.

> Rabindranath Tagore, *Stray Birds,* 1916

The moral idea of chastity is a direct corollary of our moral idea of love of neighbor. It is a supreme form of unselfishness.

> John M. Cooper, *Religion Outline for Colleges,* Vol. IV, 1930

Under the present arrangement of our country, as indeed of many other countries, conjugal chastity with its average parenthood has now become heroic virtue.

> Vincent McNabb, *Frontiers of Faith and Reason,* 1936

The Counsel of Chastity . . . means the spirit of poverty applied to our emotional life—all the clutch and feverishness of desire, the "I want" and "I must have" taken away and replaced by absolute single-mindedness, purity of heart.

> Evelyn Underhill, *The Fruits of the Spirit,* 1942

The Church puts such tremendous value on this vow of chastity precisely because the thing given up is one of the most precious things we have to give up.

> Francis Devas, *The Law of Love,* 1954

Christian chastity is as far from a mere masochistic abnegation of sex as is Christian humility from the disposition attributed to Uriah Heep.

> Geddes MacGregor, *The Hemlock and the Cross,* 1963

See also Adultery; Birth Control; Celibacy; Continence; Desires; Lust; Marriage; Modesty; Pity; Purity; Repression; Self-Conquest; Self-Denial; Sex; Sexual Intercourse; Unchastity; Virginity; Woman.

CHEATING

Every man takes care that his neighbor shall not cheat him; but a day comes when he begins to care that he does not cheat his neighbor. Then all goes well. He has changed his market-cart into a chariot of the sun.

> Ralph Waldo Emerson, *Uses of Great Men,* 1850

CHEERFULNESS

Not only does Religion allow but it obliges unto cheerfulness with Sobriety.

BENJAMIN COLMAN, *The Government and Improvement of Mirth,* 1707

Nothing contributes more to cheerfulness than the habit of looking at the good side of things. The good side is God's side of them.

W. B. ULLATHORNE, *Humility and Patience,* 1909

Christian cheerfulness is that modest, hopeful, and peaceful joy which springs from charity and is protected by patience.

F. X. LASANCE, *Remember-Thoughts,* 1936

The first sign of your becoming religious is that you are becoming cheerful.

SWAMI VIVEKANANDA (1863–1902), *Complete Works of,* I, 264; 1950

See also Amusements; Joy; Laughter; Melancholy; Pleasure.

CHILDREN

We take care of our possessions for our children. But of the children themselves we take no care at all. What an absurdity is this! Form the soul of thy son aright, and all the rest will be added hereafter.

ST. JOHN CHRYSOSTOM (340–407), *Select Library of Nicene and Post-Nicene Fathers,* Vol. 13, 1st Series

A child is a man in a small letter, yet the best copy of Adam before he tasted of Eve, or the Apple; . . . He is Nature's fresh picture newly drawn in oil, which time and much handling dims and defaces. His soul is yet a white paper unscribbled with observations of the world, wherewith at length it becomes a blurred notebook.

He is purely happy because he knows no evil.

JOHN EARLE, *Micro-Cosmographie,* 1628

Little boldnesses and looser words and wrangling for nuts, and lying for trifles, are of the same proportion to the malice of a child, as impudence and duels and injurious law-suits, and false witness in judgment and perjuries in men.

JEREMY TAYLOR, *Sermons,* 1651

Certainly Adam had not more sweet and curious apprehensions of the world, then I when I was a child.

THOMAS TRAHERNE (1634–1704), *Centuries of Meditation*

All children are by nature children of wrath, and are in danger of eternal damnation in Hell.

JONATHAN EDWARDS, *Sermon to Children,* 1740

He is destined to live in the past and future as well as in the present. His earthly being implies a past heaven; his birth makes a present heaven; in his soul he holds a future heaven. This threefold heaven, which you also bear within you, shines out on you through your child's eyes.

FRIEDRICH FROEBEL, *Mottoes and Commentaries of Mother-Play,* 1843

The child-soul is an ever-bubbling fountain in the world of humanity.

FRIEDRICH FROEBEL, (1782–1852), *Aphorisms*

Childish unconsciousness is rest in God.

FROEBEL (1782–1852), *Aphorisms*

The sublimest song to be heard on earth is the lisping of the human soul on the lips of children.

VICTOR HUGO, *Ninety-Three,* 1874

Children are not born either wholly good or neutral between good and evil, but with evil tendencies which grow into sin when responsible life begins.

WILLIAM NEWTON CLARKE, *An Outline of Christian Theology*, 1898

Know what it is to be a child? . . . It is to have a spirit yet streaming from the waters of baptism; it is to believe in love, to believe in loveliness, to believe in belief. . . . It is to know not yet that you are under sentence of life, nor petition that it be commuted to death.

FRANCIS THOMPSON, *Essay on Shelley,* 1909

Every child comes with the message that God is not yet discouraged of man.

RABINDRANATH TAGORE, *Stray Birds,* 1916

The first, the most fundamental right of childhood is the right to be loved. The child comes into the world alone, defenseless, without resource. Only love can stand between his infant helplessness and the savagery of a harsh world.

PAUL HANLY FURFEY, *The Church and the Child,* 1933

The unwarped child, with his spontaneous faith and confidence in goodness, is the best illustration of that spirit which fits the Kingdom of God.

RUFUS M. JONES, *The Testimony of the Soul,* 1936

Those who hold that the child is composed of a material body and an immortal soul will differ *toto coelo* from those who hold that the educand is merely a machine or a physico-chemical combination, or a bundle of S-R bonds or a product of the cosmic evolutionary process.

WILLIAM J. McGUCKEN, *The Philosophy of Catholic Education,* 1951

See also Christmas; Education; Family; Father; Illegitimate; Love, Human; Marriage; Mother; Parents.

CHOICE

There's small choice in rotten apples.

WILLIAM SHAKESPEARE, *The Taming of the Shrew,* 1594

It may be true that we can act as we choose, but can we *choose*? Is not our choice determined for us?

J. A. FROUDE, *Westminster Review,* 1855

If choice is real, if there really are alternatives, it follows that in choosing between them we are exhibiting our power as real agents, real causes and initiators of new departures in the flow of cosmic change, we thereby prove the existence of free causes.

F. C. S. VON SCHILLER, *Riddle of the Sphinx,* 1910

In any sense in which we can choose what action we shall do, we can choose what motive we shall act from.

C. S. PEIRCE (1839–1914), *Collected Papers,* ed. Hartshorne and Weiss

All choice, when one comes to think of it, is terrifying; liberty where there is no duty to guide it, terrifying.

ANDRÉ GIDE, *The Fruits of the Earth,* 1949

See also Chance; Commitment; Decision; Determinism; Discriminating; Fate; Free Will; Freedom; Individual Responsibility; Necessity; Predestination; Responsibility; Will.

CHOSEN PEOPLE

We are proud and happy in that the dread Unknown God of the infinite Universe has chosen our race as the medium by which to reveal His will to the world.

ISRAEL ZANGWILL, *Children of the Ghetto,* 1892

It is in no arrogant temper that we claim to be the chosen people. We thereby affirm, not that we are better than others, but that we ought to be better.

M. JOSEPH, *Judaism as Creed and Life*, 1903

A chosen people is really a choosing people. Not idly does Talmudical legend assert that the Law was offered first to all other nations and only Israel accepted the yoke.

ISRAEL ZANGWILL, *Menorah Journal*, IV, 1918

The Jews regarded themselves as the chosen people not because of their racial qualities, but because of having been selected to be the servants of God, to carry his moral law to the world.

ABBA HILLEL SILVER, *The World Crisis and Jewish Survival*, 1939

A people is not chosen because of any racial superiority; there is no such thing. . . . A people is chosen when it has the will to live in a way which would express God's spirit on earth.

DAVID ARONSON, *The Jewish Way of Life*, 1944

We . . . advocate the elimination from our own liturgy of all references to the doctrine of Israel as the Chosen People.

MORDECAI M. KAPLAN, *Future of the American Jew*, 1948

The Hebrew idea of the chosen nation is . . . continued in the new era of the Christian Church open to men of all peoples and tongues. From the New Testament standpoint it is this Christian Church which is now the chosen people of God.

J. V. L. CASSERLEY, *The Bent World*, 1955

Jews have regarded it as self-evident that the God of all the world had made them His priest-people, His "suffering servant,"

to live by the Law and to bear the burden of the woes that might come to them.

ARTHUR HERTZBERG, *Judaism*, 1961

See also Israel; Jew; Jews.

CHRIST. See JESUS CHRIST

CHRISTENING. See BAPTISM

CHRISTIAN

Look at the Christian! . . . If he is denounced [as a Christian] he glories in it; if he is accused, he does not defend himself; when he is questioned, he confesses without any pressure; when he is condemned, he renders thanks.

TERTULLIAN, *Apology*, 197

A man becomes a Christian, he is not born one.

TERTULLIAN, *Testimony of the Soul*, c. 210

You are called Christian. Be careful of that name. Let not our Lord Jesus Christ, the Son of God, be blasphemed on your account.

ST. CYRIL OF JERUSALEM, *Catechetical Lectures*, 350

The heathens, too, believe that Christ died; the belief, the faith in his resurrection makes the Christian Christian. . . . It is faith in this resurrection that justifies us.

ST. AUGUSTINE, *Contra Faustum Manichaeum*, XXIX; 400

If thou wilt be one of Christ's followers, be like Him in this. Learn to love thy enemies, and sinful men, for all these are thy neighbors.

WALTER HYLTON (died c. 1396), *Scale of Perfection*

May not the man be a Christian, who cannot explain philosophically how the activity of the Son differs from the procession of the Holy Spirit?

DESIDERIUS ERASMUS, *Letter to Archbishop of Palermo*, 1522

A Christian is not he that hath no sin, or feeleth no sin, but he to whom God imputeth not his sin because of his faith in Christ.

MARTIN LUTHER, *Commentary on Galatians*, 1531

There is no occupation or intent more worthy a good Christian, than by all means, studies and imaginations, carefully to endeavor, how to embellish, amplify and extend the truth of his belief and religion.

MICHEL DE MONTAIGNE, *Essays*, Bk. 2, ch. 12, 1580

Ah! though I am a Christian, the feelings of a man do not the less burn in my breast.

MOLIÈRE, *Le Tartuffe*, 1664

A Christian as such (according to the design of his Religion, and in proportion to his compliance with its dictates) is the most jocund, blithe and gay Person in the World; always in humor and full of cheer.

ISAAC BARROW, *Sermon*, 1686

To the distinguished character of Patriot, it should be our highest Glory to add the more distinguished character of Christian.

GEORGE WASHINGTON, *General Order*, Valley Forge, May 2, 1778

By a Christian, I mean one who so believes in Christ, as that sin hath no more dominion over him.

JOHN WESLEY (1703–1791), quoted by Southey in his *Life of John Wesley*, ii, 176

A Christian is God Almighty's good gentleman.

J. C. HARE, *Guesses at Truth*, 1827

If someone believes that he is a Christian and yet is indifferent to the fact that he is, then he truly is not a Christian.

SÖREN KIERKEGAARD (1813–1855), *Works of Love*

You are to accept as a Christian every one whose life and disposition are Christ-like, no matter how heretical the denomination may be to which he belongs.

HENRY WARD BEECHER, *Life Thoughts*, 1858

If a man cannot be a Christian in the place where he is, he cannot be a Christian anywhere.

HENRY WARD BEECHER, *Life Thoughts*, 1858

Before the twelfth century the nations were too savage to be Christian, and after the fifteenth too carnal to be Christian.

JOHN RUSKIN, *Val d'Arno*, 1874

Christian: One who believes that the New Testament is a divinely inspired book admirably suited to the spiritual needs of his neighbor. One who follows the teachings of Christ in so far as they are not inconsistent with a life of sin.

AMBROSE BIERCE, *Devil's Dictionary*, 1906

No man is a true Christian who does not think constantly of how he can lift his brother, how he can assist his friend, how he can enlighten mankind, how he can make virtue the rule of conduct in the circle in which he lives.

WOODROW WILSON, *Address*, October, 1914

The true Christian, product of a Christian education, is the supernatural man who thinks, judges, and acts consistently in accordance with right reason illumined by the supernatural light of the example and teaching of Christ.

POPE PIUS XI, *Encyclical on Christian Education*, 1931

The originators of the Christian movement . . . did not have an inalienable right to legislate for all generations that should choose to bear the name of "Christian."

J. GRESHAM MACHEN, *Christianity and Liberalism*, 1934

The Christian is a part of a whole, a citizen of the Kingdom of God, a child in the family of the Trinity, a cell in the organism of the Whole Christ and a member of the Mystical Body.

FULTON J. SHEEN, *The Fullness of Christ*, 1935

No age has the right to call itself Christian in the absolute sense: all stand under the same condemnation. The one merit of a relatively Christian age or culture—and it is no small one—is that it recognizes its spiritual indigence and stands open to God and the spiritual world.

CHRISTOPHER DAWSON, *Religion and the Modern State*, 1935

There is a deeper sense of the word "Christian" in which some who hold wrong beliefs may be more Christian than some who hold the right ones.

C. S. LEWIS, Preface, *Beyond Personality*, 1944

A maid, after she had been confirmed, was asked how she knew she was a Christian. "Because," she replied, "now I do not sweep the dirt under the rugs."

JOHN HOMER MILLER, *Why We Act That Way*, 1946

As long as there remains in the world a Christian worthy of the name—yes, even if there were only one—there will remain an inner life to which no police can ever force entry.

FRANÇOIS MAURIAC, *Words of Faith*, 1955

No one can become a Christian, no one is a Christian, save in the measure in which

he conforms himself by a mystical, but nonetheless real, incorporation into the one life that is all-sufficient, the life of Jesus.

R. L. BRUCKBERGER, *Toward the Summit*, 1956

It is not some religious act that makes a Christian what he is, but participation in the suffering of God in the light of the world.

DIETRICH BONHOEFFER, *Prisoner for God*, 1959

To be a Christian is not purely to serve God, but it is also an ethic, a service to mankind; it is not merely a theology but also an anthropology.

ALBERT DONDEYNE, *Faith and the World*, 1962

The Christian does not only bear responsibility for the whole Church; he bears it for the whole human family.

Joint Pastoral of the German Roman Catholic Bishops, September, 1962

I feel I am a Christian by the guilt separating me from God and by the faith in the means which the Church puts at my disposal in order to begin all over again.

FRANÇOIS MAURIAC, *What I Believe*, 1962

The Christian, for the sake of that which is in him, must be a man who leads on others with him. He must run towards Christ.

ROGER SCHUTZ, *Unity: Man's Tomorrow*, 1963

When a person is called to be a Christian he is at the same time sent to be a Christian.

JOHN B. COBURN, *Minister*, 1963

Whatever is truly Christian is never contrary to what genuinely belongs to faith; indeed, it can always bring a deeper realization of the mystery of Christ and the Church.

The Constitution of the Church, SECOND VATICAN COUNCIL, November, 1964

See also Brotherhood; Catholicism; Charity; Cheerfulness; Christian Life; Christianity; Christianity, Criticism of; Christians; Church, Criticism of; Citizen; Communion; Communism; Conversion; Jews and Christians; Obedience; Philosophy; Protestantism; Quakers; Unity; War, Condemnation of; World and Christianity.

CHRISTIAN LIFE

They [Christians] walk in humility and kindness, and falsehood is not found among them, and they love one another. They despise not the widow, and grieve not the orphan. He that hath distributeth liberally to him that hath not.

ARISTEIDES, Apology, c. 150

They [Christians] pass their time upon earth, but they have their citizenship in heaven. They obey the appointed laws, and they surpass the laws in their own lives. They love all men and are persecuted by all men. . . . They are put to death and they gain life. . . . They lack all things and have all things in abundance.

Epistle to Diognetus, c. 200

They [Christians] dwell in their own countries, but only as sojourners; they bear their share in all things as citizens, and they endure all hardships as strangers. . . . They have their meals in common, but not their wives. They find themselves in the flesh, and yet they live not after the flesh. . . . They are dishonored, yet they are glorified in their dishonor. They are evil spoken of, and yet they are vindicated. They are reviled, and they bless; they are insulted, and they respect. Doing good they are punished as evil-doers.

Epistle to Diognetus, c. 200

The Christian State is an invisible life in the Spirit of God, supported not by sensible goods, but the spiritual graces of Faith and Hope.

WILLIAM LAW, Christian Perfection, 1726

All Christians, as Christians, have the same calling, to live according to the excellency of the Christian spirit, and to make the sublime precepts of the gospel the rule and measure of all their tempers in common life. The one thing needful to one, is the one thing needful to all.

WILLIAM LAW, A Serious Call to the Devout and Holy Life, 1728

Prayer, fasting, watching, and all other Christian acts, however good they may be, do not alone constitute the aim of our Christian life, although they serve us as the indispensable means of reaching this aim.

ST. SERAPHIM OF SAROV (1759–1833), quoted in A. F. Robbie-Bateman's biography of St. Seraphim

One must either resolutely deny, combat and persecute Christianity, or one must really live it. What lies between is the cult of genius and deceit.

SÖREN KIERKEGAARD, Either-Or, 1843

It is distinctive of the Christian life, that while it grows more conscientious, it also grows less and less a task of duty and more and more a service of delight.

NEWMAN SMYTH, Christian Ethics, 1892

The Christian life consists in the reconciliation of the human will with the Divine— the control of the human will as it expresses itself in action.

WILLIAM CUNNINGHAM, Essays on Theological Questions, ed. H. B. Swete, 1905

The elementary law of Christian living, for laymen just as much as for the cleric, is

that, having come through Jesus to know the Father, we are put here on our honour to live such lives as match our discovery.
> W. M. MACGREGOR, *For Christ and the Kingdom*, 1932

Even when I act as a citizen of another city than the Church of Christ, the Christian life and truth should permeate my activity from within.
> JACQUES MARITAIN, *True Humanism*, 1936

The drama of the Christian's life is this: to die every day to his evil leanings so as to prevent the life of God from dying in him.
> A. CARRÉ, *Companions for Eternity*, 1947

A Christian does not live by practicing any ethic or moulding himself to any ideal, but by a faith in God which finally ascribes all good to Him. To detach the ethic from the whole context of the Christian secret is to make it irrelevant because it is impossible.
> D. M. BAILLIE, *God Was in Christ*, 1948

The intention of a Christian to follow a Christian way of life is not only the criterion for the sincerity of his belief in the assertions of Christianity, it is the criterion for the meaningfulness of his assertions.
> R. F. BRAITHWAITE, *An Empiricist's View of the Nature of Religion*, 1955

The Christian must plunge himself into the life of the godless world without attempting to gloss over its ungodliness with a veneer of religion, or trying to transfigure it. He must live a "worldly" life and so participate in the suffering God.
> DIETRICH BONHOEFFER, *Prisoner for God*, 1959

Though the ideals and high purposes of a Christian life are as valid as they were in the days when Christ walked the earth, the

execution of them might utterly destroy the patience of anything less than Divinity.
> RICHARD A. DUPREY, *The Critic*, December, 1961–January, 1962

See also Civilization and Christianity; Conduct; Duties.

CHRISTIAN PHILOSOPHY

A philosophy which intends to be a rational interpretation of data, but considers as the essential element of these data the religious Faith, the object of which is defined by the Christian revelation.
> ÉTIENNE GILSON, *The Philosophy of St. Thomas Aquinas*, 1939

See also Ethics.

CHRISTIAN SCIENCE

Healing the sick and reforming the sinner are one and the same thing in Christian Science. Both cures require the same method, and are inseparable in Truth.
> MARY BAKER EDDY, *Science and Health*, 1908

Christian Science explains all cause and effect as mental, not physical.
> MARY BAKER EDDY, *Science and Health*, 1908

Christian Science reveals incontrovertibly that Mind is All-in-all, that the only realities are the divine Mind and idea.
> MARY BAKER EDDY, *Science and Health*, 1908

To live so as to keep human consciousness in constant relation with the divine, the spiritual, and the eternal, is to individualize infinite power; and this is Christian Science.
> MARY BAKER EDDY, *The First Church of Christ, Scientist, and Miscellany*, publ. posth., 1914

"Christian Science is neither Christian nor Science."

An anonymous and frequently quoted statement.

Are Christian Scientists Christian? Of course they are. Traced historically Christian Science is an off-shoot of Protestant Christianity. Its basis is (in part) the Bible. It purports to be a recovery of the lost emphasis of primitive Christianity, especially in healing. . . . Christian Science is a modern restatement of the Christian faith developed by Mary Baker Eddy.

CHARLES S. BRADEN, *Christian Science Today*, 1958

See also Healing; Health; Mind; Suffering.

CHRISTIAN SOCIETY

A society has ceased to be Christian when religious practices have been abandoned, when behavior ceases to be regulated by reference to Christian principle, and when in effect prosperity in this world for the individual or for the group has become the sole conscious aim.

T. S. ELIOT, *The Idea of a Christian Society*, 1939

See also Civilization; Society.

CHRISTIANITY

Away with all attempts to produce a Stoic, Platonic, and dialectic Christianity! We want no curious disputation after possessing Jesus Christ, no inquisition after receiving the gospel!

TERTULLIAN, *De Praescriptione Haerticorum*, c. 206

Jesus Christ . . . instituted the observance of the divine Religion . . . to shed its brightness upon all nations and all peoples in such a way that the Truth . . . might through the Apostles' trumpet blast go out for the salvation of all men.

POPE ST. LEO I, *Letter to the Bishops of the Province of Vienne*, c. 448

Christianity is nothing but a continual exercise in feeling that you have no sin although you sin, but that your sins are thrown on Christ.

MARTIN LUTHER (1483–1546), *Works*, XL

A serious apprehension that Christianity may be true lays persons under the strictest obligations of a serious regard to it.

JOSEPH BUTLER, *Analogy of Religion*, 1736

Christianity is a scheme beyond our comprehension.

JOSEPH BUTLER, *Analogy of Religion*, 1736

Christianity must be divine since it has lasted 1,700 years despite the fact that it is so full of villainy and nonsense.

VOLTAIRE, *Essai sur les Moeurs*, 1756

Christianity as a religion is entirely spiritual, occupied solely with heavenly things; the country of the Christian is not of this world.

JEAN JACQUES ROUSSEAU, *The Social Contract*, 1762

The Christian religion is, above all the religions that ever prevailed, or existed in ancient or modern times, the religion of wisdom, equity, and humanity, let the blackguard Paine say what he will.

JOHN ADAMS, *Diary*, July 26, 1796

He, who begins by loving Christianity better than Truth, will proceed by loving his own sect or church better than Christianity, and end in loving himself better than all.

SAMUEL TAYLOR COLERIDGE, *Aids to Reflection*, 1825

The whole course of Christianity from the first, when we come to examine it, is but one series of troubles and disorders.

JOHN HENRY NEWMAN, *Via Media*, 1837

The more I examine Christianity, the more I am struck with its universality. I see in it a religion made for all regions and all times, for all classes and all stages of society.

WILLIAM ELLERY CHANNING (1780–1842), *Works*

Christianity would furnish a weapon against itself . . . should it claim the distinction of being the only light vouchsafed by God to men; for, in that case, it would represent a vast majority of the human race as left by their Creator without guidance or hope.

WILLIAM ELLERY CHANNING (1780–1842), *Works*

Christianity came to the nations as a beam of light shot into chaos; a strain of sweet music—so silvery and soft we know not we are listening—to him who wanders on amid the uncertain gloom, and charms him to the light, to the River of God and the Tree of Life.

THEODORE PARKER, *Discourse of Matters Pertaining to Religion*, 1842

Christianity is not a matter of opinion, but an external fact, entering into, carried out in, indivisible from, the history of the world.

JOHN HENRY NEWMAN, *Difficulties of Anglicans*, 1850

In all moments of laxness, sluggishness, dullness, when the sensuous nature of man predominates, Christianity seems madness, since it is incommensurable with any finite wherefore. What is the use of it, then? The answer is: Hold thy peace! It is the absolute!

SÖREN KIERKEGAARD, *Training in Christianity*, 1850

Unlike other religions, it is not a pure system of doctrine: its chief and essential feature is that it is a history, a series of events, a collection of facts, a statement of the actions and sufferings of individuals; it is this history which constitutes dogma, and belief in it is salvation.

ARTHUR SCHOPENHAUER, "The Christian System," *Essays*, 1851

If it could be proved . . . that the Gospels were the fabrication of designing and artful men, that Jesus of Nazareth had never lived, still Christianity would stand firm, and fear no evil. None of the doctrines of that religion would fall to the ground; for, if true, they stand by themselves.

THEODORE PARKER, *Views of Religion*, 1855

How did Christianity arise and spread abroad among men? . . . It arose in the mystic deeps of man's soul; and was spread abroad by the "preaching of the word," by simple, altogether natural and individual efforts; and flew, like hallowed fire, from heart to heart, till all were purified and illuminated by it.

THOMAS CARLYLE, *Critical and Miscellaneous Essays*, 1857

Silence the voice of Christianity, and the world is well-nigh dumb, for gone is that sweet music which kept in order the rulers of the people, which cheers the poor widow in her lonely toil, and comes like light through the windows of morning to men who sit stooping and feeble, with failing eyes and a hungering heart.

THEODORE PARKER (1810–1860), *Discourses of the Transient and Permanent in Christianity* (selected sermons)

The more knowledge advances, the more it has been, and will be, acknowledged that Christianity, as a real religion, must be viewed apart from connection with physical things.

BADEN POWELL, *Essays and Reviews*, 1861

To a world stricken with moral enervation Christianity offered its spectacle of an inspired self-sacrifice; to men who refused themselves nothing, it showed one who refused himself everything.

MATTHEW ARNOLD, *Culture and Anarchy,* 1869

Christianity has an external aspect and an internal, it is human without, divine within.

JOHN HENRY NEWMAN, *Essays Critical and Historical,* I

Christianity is at once a philosophy, a political power, and a religious rite: as a religion, it is Holy; as a philosophy, it is Apostolic; as a political power, it is imperial, that is, One and Catholic.

JOHN HENRY NEWMAN, in 1877 *Preface* to republication of *The Via Media or The Anglican Church*

Even those who have renounced Christianity and attack it, in their inmost being still follow the Christian ideal, for hitherto neither their subtlety nor the ardor of their hearts has been able to create a higher ideal of man and of virtue than the ideal given by Christ of old.

FEODOR DOSTOEVSKY, *The Brothers Karamazov,* 1880

Thus, whatever elements of truth, whatever broken and scattered rays of light the old religions contained, Christianity takes up into itself, explaining all, harmonizing all, by a divine alchemy transmuting all, yet immeasurably transcending all.

JOHN CAIRD, *An Introduction to the Philosophy of Religion,* 1880

It is the infusion into the Spiritual man of a New Life, of a quality unlike anything else in Nature. This constiutes the separate Kingdom of Christ, and gives to Christianity alone of all the religions of mankind the strange mark of Divinity.

HENRY DRUMMOND, *Natural Law in the Spiritual World,* 1883

Christianity is a battle, not a dream.

WENDELL PHILLIPS (1811–1884), quoted in C. Hurd's *Treasury of Great American Quotations*

People assert that Christianity must be the only true religion of the world, because the Christian nations are prosperous! But that assertion contradicts itself because the prosperity of the Christian nations depends upon the misfortune of un-Christian nations. There must be some to prey upon. Suppose the whole world were to become Christian; then the Christian nations would become poor, because there would be no non-Christian nations for them to prey upon.

SWAMI VIVEKANANDA (1863–1902), *The Yoga and Other Works,* ed. by Swami Nikhilananda

Christianity is always out of fashion because it is always sane; and all fashions are mild insanities.

G. K. CHESTERTON, *The Ball and the Cross,* 1909

The intrinsic greatness of Christianity is revealed in this capacity of development by which it advances with the advancing life of humanity.

GEORGE GALLOWAY, *The Philosophy of Religion,* 1922

It is to Christianity that we owe our deepest insight into the wondrously wide and varied range throughout the world, as we know it, of pain, suffering, evil.

FRIEDRICH VON HÜGEL, *Essays and Addresses on the Philosophy of Religion,* 1925

It can scarcely be denied that early Christianity was communistic, pacifistic, equalitarian, and inspired by hopes of a miraculous social cataclysm which would exalt those of low degree, overthrow the seats of the mighty, and establish a society in which the last should be first and the first last, and there should be no king but Christ.

EVERETT DEAN MARTIN, *Liberty*, 1930

It is primarily the conversion of all the ancient moral and mystic efforts of humanity into a higher religion, which in fulfilling their aspirations, transcends them.

EUGENE MASURE, *Bulletin des anciens élèves de Saint-Sulpice*, November 15, 1931

The worst enemies of Christianity are bad Christians.

W. R. INGE, *Living Philosophies*, 1931

A religion of spiritual redemption, not of social reform. . . . A religion of the spirit, a life of purity and holiness, of faith and love, . . . a brotherhood of men and women who find nothing hateful except hypocrisy, hard-heartedness, and calculating worldliness.

W. R. INGE, *Living Philosophies*, 1931

No interpretation of the life of mankind ever more exactly reflected the experience, or more effectively responded to the hopes of average men.

CARL L. BECKER, *Heavenly City of the 18th Century Philosophers*, 1932

Christianity is not merely a moral ideal or set of ideas. It is a concrete reality. It is the spiritual order incarnated in a historical person and in a historical society. . . . It is the function of Christianity to bring the spiritual order into contact and relation with the world of man.

CHRISTOPHER DAWSON, *The Modern Dilemma: The Problem of European Unity*, 1932

The Christian movement at its inception was not just a way of life in the modern sense, but a way of life founded upon a message It was based, not upon mere

feeling, not upon a mere program of work, but on an account of facts.

J. GRESHAM MACHEN, *Christianity and Liberalism*, 1934

The Christian faith does not arise out of the picture of the historical Jesus, but out of the testimony to Christ.

EMIL BRUNNER, *The Mediator*, 1934

We urgently need an interpretation of Christianity that will cut across both capitalism and communism and press for practical embodiment of its own reverence for personality.

HUGH VERNON WHITE, *Christian Century*, February 14, 1934

A century ago there was the tendency to treat Christianity as a kind of social sedative that kept the lower classes obedient and industrious, and the consequence of this was the Marxist denunciation of religion as the opium of the poor.

CHRISTOPHER DAWSON, *Religion and the Modern State*, 1935

Christianity places our conduct in this life on earth in its gigantic setting of infinity and eternity, and by opening our eyes to this vast spiritual vision it calls out our deepest spiritual energies.

ARNOLD J. TOYNBEE, *Christian Century*, March 10, 1937

Christianity alone continues to assert the transcendent destiny of man and the common destiny of mankind.

HENRI DE LUBAC, *Catholicism*, 1937

In this really very brief period of less than two thousand years Christianity has in fact produced greater spiritual effects in the world than have been produced in a comparable space of time by any other spiritual movement that we know of in history.

ARNOLD J. TOYNBEE, *Christian Century*, March 10, 1937

The Christian religion is true because it has pleased God, who alone can be the judge in this matter, to affirm it to be the true religion.

KARL BARTH, *Church Dogmatics,* 1938

The "Religion of the Commonplace": so the famous preacher of St. Paul's Cathedral described Christianity. The Christian religion is the religion of everyman, the religion for everyman, the religion of all conditions.

MAURICE ZUNDEL, *The Splendor of the Liturgy,* 1939

One has to speak of the end of Christianity in terms of a thousand years, but it has assumed so many forms in its history that I often speculate on its taking a new and perhaps final form here in America, coalescing with your democratic idea of life.

ALFRED NORTH WHITEHEAD, December, 1939, *Dialogues of,* as recorded by L. Price

The moment Christianity is made secondary to anything else, it has ceased to be Christianity in any proper sense, and has become simply one more of a competing number of possible views of existence.

EDWIN LEWIS, *A Philosophy of the Christian Revelation,* 1940

Christianity has compelled the mind of man not because it is the most cheering view of man's existence but because it is truest to the facts.

LORD DAVID CECIL, *The Fortnightly,* March, 1940

Its truth and greatness come to an end on the cross, at the moment when this man cries out that he has been forsaken. If we tear out these last pages of the New Testament, then what we see set forth is a religion of loneliness and grandeur. Certainly, its bitterness makes it unbearable. But that is its truth.

ALBERT CAMUS, *Notebooks,* 1935–1942

No person in the Western world can escape, by an act of deliberate choice, the facts of Christianity.

D. E. TRUEBLOOD, *The Logic of Belief,* 1942

The emergence of Christianity illuminates all other faiths, because it shows them as steps on the way, regardless of their dates of appearance.

D. E. TRUEBLOOD, *The Logic of Belief,* 1942

If Christianity be true at all, it is the most vital and important thing in the whole world, and its dominion, for those who accept it, must be universal.

LORD HALIFAX, *Address,* University of Laval, May, 1943

That a few simple men should in one generation have invented so powerful and appealing a personality, so lofty an ethic and so inspiring a vision of human brotherhood, would be a miracle far more incredible than any recorded in the Gospel.

WILL DURANT, *Caesar and Christ,* 1944

The darker the world and the deeper the virus of hate the more glowing must be our Christianity and the more triumphant the note of our faith.

RUFUS M. JONES, *The Radiant Life,* 1944

The Christian religion was true when it was delivered to the Apostles and therefore it cannot be improved or made more true since truth, like God, is eternal.

BRUCE MARSHALL, *Father Malachy's Miracle,* 1947

It is not the proper duty of Christianity to form leaders—that is, builders of the temporal—although a legion of Christian leaders is infinitely desirable. Christianity must generate saints—that is, witnesses to the eternal.

HENRI DE LUBAC, *Paradoxes,* 1948

The question is not to know whether Christians are always intelligent (we well know they are not) : it is to know whether Christianity is true.

HENRI DE LUBAC, *Paradoxes*, 1948

In other religions, one must be purified before he can knock at the door; in Christianity, one knocks on the door as a sinner, and He Who answers to us heals.

FULTON J. SHEEN, *Peace of Soul*, 1949

The Christian ideal, put into practice, can work like a ferment. Once before it turned the world upside down, or as Chesterton phrased it, turned the world right side up, and it can do it again.

ROBERT J. MCCRACKEN, *Questions People Ask*, 1951

The most stupid thing ever said about it is, that it is to a certain degree true.

SÖREN KIERKEGAARD (1813–1855), *The Living Thought of Kierkegaard*, ed. W. H. Auden, 1952

In the Christian religion we discern a transition from the religion of the cult to the prophetic religion of pure morals, from the religion of law to the religion of love, from the religion of priests to the religion of individual prayer and inward life, from the national God to the universal God.

SARVEPALLI RADHAKRISHNAN (born 1888), in *The Philosophy of*, ed. by P. A. Schlipp, 1952

It is non-Christian or sub-Christian religion rather than mere irreligion that contemporary Christendom must learn to recognize as its mortal foe.

J. V. L. CASSERLEY, *Retreat from Christianity in the Modern World*, 1952

Christianity always contains the latent dynamic of a potential return to the values of the early Christian era.

DAVID RIESMAN, "New Standards for Old," *Individualism Reconsidered*, 1953

Christianity, even if it cannot persuade men to rise to the contemplation of the spiritual things, embodies principles which may at least have the effect of bringing the dreamers down to earth. Because it confronts the problem of human sin, it can face our difficulties and dilemmas without evasions.

HERBERT BUTTERFIELD, *Christianity, Diplomacy and War*, 1953

The worst enemies of vital Christianity are those who have tried to regularize it, to take out its fantastic, peculiar qualities and leave it no different from anything else.

HALFORD E. LUCCOCK, *Like a Mighty Army*, 1954

It is the maturest fruit of Christian understanding to understand that Christianity, as such, is of no avail.

PAUL TILLICH, *The New Being*, 1955

Christendom represents the expression of an effort to build up and to organize temporal life in accordance with the principles of the Gospel.

R. L. BRUCKBERGER, *Toward the Summit*, 1956

There is a plain and pressing requirement for a reincarnation of Christianity in the form of these resurgent civilizations, the Oriental, the Near-Eastern, the African.

JEAN DANIELOU, *The Lord of History*, 1958

Christianity is an uneasy, a tragic, an impossible faith, in high tension between the real and the ideal, the "is" and the "ought"—that is one of the sources of its strength.

CRANE BRINTON, *A History of Western Morals*, 1959

For twelve centuries Christianity has been the religion of a culture—that is to say, it has had an organic relation with the social and moral structure of one particular society of people. It has held somewhat the same place in Europe that Islam has held in Western Asia, Hinduism in India, or Confucianism in China.

CHRISTOPHER DAWSON, *The Movement of World Revolution,* 1959

The call of Christianity is not primarily to service and good works, or even to faith, but to the Life.

OSWALD C. J. HOFFMANN, *Life Crucified,* 1959

It is one thing to say that men are free to believe what they choose, and another thing to say that it is all right for them to call anything they choose to believe "Christianity." Matters of fact are at stake here.

JAMES A. MARTIN, JR., *Fact, Fiction and Faith,* 1960

The great objection brought against Christianity in our time . . . is the suspicion that our religion makes its adherents *inhuman.*

PIERRE TEILHARD DE CHARDIN, *The Divine Milieu,* 1960

Is Christianity dying? Is the religion that gave morals, courage, and art to Western civilization suffering slow decay through the spread of knowledge, the widening of astronomic, geographical, and historical horizons, the realization of evil in history and the soul, the decline of faith in an afterlife and of trust in the benevolent guidance of the world? If this is so, it is the basic event of modern times, for the soul of a civilization is its religion, and it dies with its faith.

WILL DURANT, *The Age of Reason Begins,* 1961

Long after the fever and heat and self-righteousness of Communism has become a thing of past history, the Christian fellowship and the fruit of the Spirit, charity, shall be baptizing and remaking other cul-

tures. The Church has the courage to endure.

ALBERT T. MOLLEGEN, *Christianity and Modern Man,* 1961

Since Christianity is a message, great care must be taken to prevent it from ever losing its character of being a message. A message is something in the order of words, of testimony and dialogue. Violence, social pressure, and appeal to power are out of place in a message.

ALBERT DONDEYNE, *Faith and the World,* 1962

Christianity is not a mere garment that Western man can don or discard like a topcoat. It is the very fabric of his social and cultural being.

FRANCIS X. CANFIELD, *The Catholic Bookman's Guide,* ed. Sr. M. Regis, I.H.M., 1962

Christian faith does not consist in believing a list, long or short, of disparate and mutually detachable things. It is a single illumination, a single reception of and commitment to the light revealed.

JOHN BAILLIE, *The Sense of the Presence of God,* 1962

To make Christianity conform fully to the modern rational mood, it would have to cease to be Christianity.

BARBARA WARD, *Way,* January–February, 1963

Christianity teaches man how to fold his wings, hop out unnoticed and fly away, so that henceforward he may make a cage his home, but no cage his prison.

GEDDES MACGREGOR, *The Hemlock and the Cross,* 1963

A Christian who takes God seriously must surely recognize that God does not give a fig for Christianity. God is concerned with people, not with things.

WILFRED C. SMITH, *The Meaning and End of Religion,* 1963

Christianity is the name of a number of different religions.
ANONYMOUS

See also Art and Christianity; Bible and the Church; Brotherhood; Capitalism; Catholicism; Charity; Christian Life; Christianity: Criticism of; Christians; Church, Defined; Church: Its Work; Church and State; Civilization and Christianity; Civilization and Religion; Coercion; Communism; Community; Creeds; Culture and Christianity; Democracy; Ethics; Fall, the; Freedom and God; God: Considered as Personal; God: His Intervention in the World; Heresy; History; Humanism, Christian; Humanity; Immortality; Liberalism and Religion; Man and God; Marxism; Miracles; Morality; Morality and Religion; New Testament; Personality; Protestantism; Religion, Organized; Religion, Revealed; Roman Catholic Church; Secularism; Science and Religion; Society; Society and Religion; State, the; Unitarians; Universality; Universe; War; War, Condemnation of; War, Defense of; War, Just; Word, The; World and Christianity, World and the Church.

CHRISTIANITY, CRITICISM OF

Checked for the moment, this pernicious superstition again broke out, not only in Judea, the source of the evil, but even in Rome, that receptacle for everything that is sordid and degrading from every quarter of the globe.
TACITUS, *Annals*, XV, 44, c. 100 A.D.

Christianity is the bastard progeny of Judaism. It is the basest of all national religions.
CELSUS, *A True Discourse*, c. 178

They [Christians] have gathered from the lowest dregs of the populace ignorant men and credulous women—and women are naturally unstable—and have formed a rabble of impious conspirators; . . . They

are a secret tribe that lurks in darkness and shuns the light, silent in public, chattering in corners.
Speech of Caecilius, given in Minucius Felix's *The Octavius,* 3rd century

Beyond a few individuals who shun evil, what else is the whole assemblage of Christians but the bilge water of vice?
SALVIAN, *The Governance of God,* 5th century

Verily, the wild beasts deal more kindly with each other than Christians deal with Christians.
CANON GIESE, *Flosculorum Lutheranorum de fide et operibus,* 1525

True Christians are made to be slaves, and they know it and do not much mind: this short life counts for little in their eyes.
JEAN JACQUES ROUSSEAU, *The Social Contract,* Bk. IV, 1762

I condemn Christianity. I bring against it the most terrible of accusations that ever an accuser put into words. It is to me the greatest of all imaginable corruptions. . . . it has left nothing untouched by its depravity. It has made a worthlessness out of every value, a lie out of every truth, a sin out of everything straightforward, healthy and honest.
FRIEDRICH NIETZSCHE, *The Antichrist,* 1887

Christianity is essentially and thoroughly, the nausea and surfeit of Life for Life, . . . a longing for Nothingness, for the end, for rest, for the Sabbath of Sabbaths. . . . the most dangerous and most ominous of all possible forms of a "will to perish."
FRIEDRICH NIETZSCHE, *Ecce Homo,* 1889

I regard Christianity as the most fatal and seductive lie that has ever existed.
FRIEDRICH NIETZSCHE, *The Will to Power,* Vol. 1, 163, 1889

The shell of Christendom is broken. The unconquerable mind of the East, the pagan past, the industrial socialistic future confronts it with their equal authority. Our whole life and mind is saturated with the slow upward filtration of a new spirit—that of an emancipated, atheistic, international democracy.

GEORGE SANTAYANA, *Winds of Doctrine,* 1913

Christendom may be defined briefly as that part of the world in which, if any man stands up in public and solemnly swears that he is a Christian, all his auditors will laugh.

H. L. MENCKEN, *A Little Book in C Major,* 1916

Christianity is not the religion of Jesus; it is that of the followers of Jesus.

MAURICE GOGUEL, *Jesus the Nazarene —Myth or History?* 1926

We betray Christ today, when we accept the Christian Church and the Christian Faith as a means of preserving a particular social order which happens to maintain us in comfort and importance, while it condemns tens of thousands of our fellows, to an indecent scuffle for bread.

W. G. PECK, *The Divine Revolution,* 1927

This diluted "Christianity without tears" does, it is true, disarm opposition; you cannot feel much hostility to jelly, nor to an eiderdown.

ROSALIND MURRAY, *The Good Pagan's Failure,* 1939

Simply a "petrifaction" of an alien state of consciousness, projecting into the present from vanished ages.

HERMAN RAUSCHNING, *The Redemption of Democracy,* 1941

Among the Christian Churches now extant I know of none whose creed or profession

reproduces the original form of Christianity.

L. P. JACKS, *Confession of an Octogenarian,* 1942

Christianity itself, which is the religion of eternal salvation, is stuck in this mire, in the mire of rotten economic, industrial morality.

CHARLES PEGUY, *Basic Verities,* 1943

Traditional Christianity is disintegrating. . . . But the Christianity that can never die, that has functional value, is interwoven with all our democratic activities.

CONRAD HENRY MOEHLMAN, *School and Church: the American Way,* 1944

If the Christian faith be identified in the minds of our descendents with certain interpretations of it commonly heard today, not much will be heard about Christianity day after tomorrow.

JAMES BISSETT PRATT, *Religious Liberals Reply,* 1947

I am convinced that the New Supernaturalism and the old Fundamentalism are among the most insidious perils to twentieth-century Christianity.

JAMES BISSETT PRATT, *Religious Liberals Reply,* 1947

Christianity condemned man to a psychological hopelessness to which Christ himself bore no witness. It declared him to be basically impotent to work out his psychological salvation. . . . It encouraged him to distrust himself and malign himself. It encouraged him to cast himself upon a Power greater than himself.

H. A. OVERSTREET, *The Mature Mind,* 1949

Elijah can hardly be pictured as saying: "If you can't believe in the God of Israel, at least accept Baal." Many would say that this is precisely what has been wrong with the Christian tradition.

W. J. WOLF, *Man's Knowledge of God,* 1955

Professing in their speech-reactions the noblest precepts of the Sermon on the Mount, the Western Christian world has shown itself in its overt behavior to be the most belligerent, the most aggressive and the most power-drunk part of humanity.

PITIRIM A. SOROKIN, *This Is My Faith,* ed. S. G. Cole, 1956

Among Christian people today it must be admitted that Christianity is very largely inoffensive, politically, intellectually, and every way; but that sort of Christianity will never transform anything.

JEAN DANIELOU, *The Lord of History,* 1958

Despite all right thinking and orthodox belief we have arrived at a dead end. The Christian idea is no longer one of the leading and formative ideas today. The plundered human victim lies bleeding by the wayside—must it be a stranger that comes to the rescue?

ALFRED DELP, *The Prison Meditations of Father Alfred Delp,* 1963

One has even reached a point today where some Christians can speak of believing in Christianity (instead of believing in God and Christ); of preaching Christianity (instead of preaching good news, salvation, redemption); of practicing Christianity (instead of practicing love).

WILFRED C. SMITH, *The Meaning and End of Religion,* 1963

It is as Christians' faith in God has weakened that they have busied themselves with Christianity; and as their personal relation to Christ has virtually lapsed that they have turned to religion for solace.

WILFRED C. SMITH, *The Meaning and End of Religion,* 1963

See also Church, Criticism of; Clergy, Criticism of; Communism.

CHRISTIANS

Besides being put to death they [Christians] were made to serve as objects of amusement; they were clad in the hides of beasts and torn to death by dogs; others were crucified, others set on fire to serve to illuminate the night when daylight failed.

TACITUS, *Annals,* XV, 44, c. 100 A.D.

It is therefore meet that we not only be called Christians, but also be such.

ST. IGNATIUS OF ANTIOCH, *To the Magnesians,* c. 109

Because they acknowledge the goodness of God towards them, lo! on account of them there flows forth the beauty that is in the world.

ARISTEIDES, *Apology,* c. 150

Now the Christians, O King, by going about and seeking have found the truth, and as we have comprehended from their writings they are nearer the truth and to exact knowledge than the rest of the peoples. . . . They have the commandments of the Lord Jesus Christ engraven on their hearts, and these they observe looking for the resurrection of the dead and the life of the world to come.

ARISTEIDES, *Apology,* c. 150

For truly great and wonderful is their teaching to him that is willing to examine and understand it. And truly this people is a new people, and there is something divine mingled with it.

ARISTEIDES, *Apology,* c. 150

The Christians are unhappy men who are persuaded that they will survive death and live forever; in consequence, they despise death and are willing to sacrifice their lives to their faith.

LUCIAN, *On the Death of Peregrinus,* c. 166

We are a society with a common religious feeling, unity of discipline, a common bond of hope. We meet in gathering and congregation to approach God in prayer, massing our forces to surround Him.

TERTULLIAN, *Apology,* 197

Whether we be bond or free we are all one in Christ; and, under one God, we perform an equal service of subjection, for God is no respecter of persons. Only in this way is a distinction made by Him concerning us; if we are found humble and surpassing others in good works.

ST. BENEDICT OF NURSIA (c. 480–533), *Rule of*

Men of simple understanding, little inquisitive, and little instructed, make good Christians.

MICHEL DE MONTAIGNE, *Essays,* 1580

Those whom we see to be Christians without the knowledge of the prophets and evidences, nevertheless judge of their religion as well as those who have that knowledge. They judge it by the heart, as others judge of it by the intellect.

BLAISE PASCAL, *Pensées,* 1670

Sir, I think all Christians, whether Papists or Protestants, agree in the essential articles, and that their differences are trivial, and rather political than religious.

SAMUEL JOHNSON, *Boswell's Life of,* 1772

You say there is but one way to worship and serve the Great Spirit. If there is but one religion, why do you white people differ so much about it? Why not all agreed, as you can all read the book?

Seneca Indian Chief Red Jacket, to delegate from Evangelical Mission Society of Massachusetts, 1805

Penetrate a little beneath the diversity of circumstances, and it becomes evident that in Christians of different epochs . . .

there is veritably a single fundamental and identical spirit of piety and charity, common to those who have received grace; an inner state which before all things is one of love and humility, of infinite confidence in God, and of severity for one's self, accompanied with tenderness for others.

C. A. SAINTE-BEUVE, *Port Royal,* I, 1860

If you wish your children to be Christians you must really take the trouble to be Christians yourselves. Those are the only terms upon which the home will work the gracious miracle.

WOODROW WILSON, *Address,* October, 1904

It is assumed by many that there was a time when all who professed themselves Christians did actually keep the unity of the spirit and the bond of peace. As a matter of historical fact there never was such a time.

RICHARD DOWNEY, *Critical and Constructive Essays,* 1934

We Christians are not permitted to wash our hands in innocence, fearing contamination if we enter too deeply into a sick civilization.

PHILIP SCHARPER, *Sheed and Ward Trumpet,* Fall, 1962

Since Christians cannot deny the divinity of Christ and still be Christians, all of them—Catholics, Anglicans, Orthodox, Protestants—stand together this side of a great divide, and none of their internal differences equal their startling divergence from the world's common opinion.

BARBARA WARD, *Way,* January–February, 1963

The Church would do well to remember that Christians are *nowhere anything but pilgrims and strangers.*

ELIZABETH ADLER, *Unity in Mid-Career,* 1963

Christians have to face the fact that in the world at large they are a minority and possibly destined to become an even smaller one.

BARBARA WARD, *Way,* January–February, 1963

See also Citizenship; Persecution.

CHRISTMAS

When adoring the Birth of our Saviour, we are celebrating our own true origin. For indeed this generation of Christ in time is the source of the Christian People, and the birth of the Head is, too, that of His Mystical body.

ST. LEO (died 461), *Fourth Sermon on the Nativity*

The simple shepherds heard the voice of an angel and found their Lamb; the wise men saw the light of a star, and found their Wisdom.

FULTON J. SHEEN, *The Eternal Galilean,* 1934

Christmas . . . if it means anything, means the exaltation and glorification of the spirit of the child, which is just another word for humility.

FULTON J. SHEEN, *The Eternal Galilean,* 1934

The Christmas assurance supremely is that God has not forgotten human need.

CLELAND B. MCAFEE, *Near to the Heart of God,* 1954

Christ, light of light, is born today, and since He is born to us, He is born in us, and, therefore we also are born today. That is to say, our souls are born to new life and new light, by receiving Him Who is the Truth.

THOMAS MERTON, *A Thomas Merton Reader,* ed. T. P. McDonnell, 1963

CHURCH, CRITICISM OF

There is no doubt whatever among wise men that the Church must be purged.

ROGER BACON, *Compendium Studii Philosophiae,* 1271

Unless . . . Jesus lay to His hand with all speed, our most disordered Church cannot be far from death.

JOHN COLET, c. 1502, quoted in K. Seebohm's *The Oxford Reformers*

I endure the Church till the day I see a better one.

DESIDERIUS ERASMUS (1466–1536), *Hyperaspistes*

The Christian church has left nothing untouched by its depravity; it has turned every value into worthlessness, every truth into a lie, and every integrity into baseness of soul.

FRIEDRICH NIETZSCHE, *The Antichrist,* 1888

The churches are arrogance, violence, usurpation, rigidity, death; Christianity is humility, penitence, submissiveness, progress, life.

LEO TOLSTOY, *The Kingdom of God Is Within You,* 1893

For whatever it may be called, a totality of segregated and independent units, unknown both to themselves and to others, certainly has no attributes which entitle it to bear the name of church.

A. C. MCGIFFERT, *Protestant Thought Before Kant,* 1911

Wherever the church depends upon ancient forms and formulas for its influence over society, it must fail.

EDITORIAL, *Christian Century,* February 18, 1915

The social teaching of the Church has ceased to count, because the Church itself has ceased to think.

RICHARD H. TAWNEY, *Religion and the Rise of Capitalism,* 1926

The Church is nothing of what she was and she has become all that is most contrary to herself, all that is most contrary to her institution.

CHARLES PEGUY, *Basic Verities,* 1943

Christians are too content to regard the Church as a respectable and decorative institution, its wisdom somehow compatible with that of a self-corrupted humanity. That is not what the Church has been down the ages.

B. I. BELL, *Church in Disrepute,* 1943

It is not the university but the church that must become intellectually alive if they are to retain the allegiance of the graduates from state-supported institutions of higher learning in the United States.

HOWARD MUMFORD JONES, *Religion and Education,* ed. W. L. Sperry, 1945

Many and many a church today is more social center than shrine; many and many a minister of God is more sociologist than preacher.

Life editorial, December 26, 1949

Many a modern house of worship has become more a social club where one meets new people and makes new friends than an institution dedicated to help man in his quest of God.

BEN ZION BOKSAR, *Perspectives on a Troubled Decade,* ed. Bryson, Finklestein and MacIver, 1950

Does not the Church, in spite of her externally heightened prestige, often seem rather to be lingering on as a mere decoration for certain private and public occasions? How much does she really have to say, spiritually, in that central area of modern life where the questions essential to present and future are decided?

HANS KÜNG, *The Council, Reform and Reunion,* 1959

The Church has succumbed to the temptation to believe in the goodness and power of her own tradition, morality and religious activity. So the church has come to believe in images of man, of the world, and of God which she has fabricated of her own means.

KARL BARTH, *Christianity Today,* October, 1961

We must abandon our arrogant pretensions to reverence as a right. The Church must come to look upon herself far more as a sacrament, a way and a means, not as a goal and end in itself.

ALFRED DELP, *Prison Meditations of Father Alfred Delp,* 1963

The persistence of rigidity in the denominational structuring of the church is to a great extent responsible for the distortion of the local church into an increasingly parochial, self oriented, and isolated institution in the local community.

WILLIAM B. CATE, *Unity in Mid-Career,* 1963

The structure of the church as a religious club will inevitably find itself being squeezed out. If the efforts of the church are put into keeping it, it will survive as a museum piece, doomed to frustration. As the walls begin to fall, we'll discover whether this will find us exposed for death or stripped for action.

JOHN A. T. ROBINSON, quoted by Christopher S. Wren, *Look,* February 22, 1966

See also Authority; Christian; Christian Life; Christianity; Christians; Church, Definitions of; Clergy, Criticism of; Religion, Organized.

CHURCH, DEFINITIONS OF

The Church is a house of God built of living stones, a spiritual house for a holy priesthood.
ORIGEN, *In Joannem*, c. 232

Church in Greek means convocation, or assembly in Latin, because all are called to be members of it.
ST. ISIDORE, *Etymologies*, c. 634

For the Church (as our Saviour saith) is a place of prayer not of clattery and talking.
RICHARD WHYFORD, *Instruction to a Householder on Sunday Mass*, c. 1500

The congregation of saints in which the Gospel is rightly taught and the sacraments rightly administered.
PHILIP MELANCHTHON, *Augsburg Confession*, 1530

Wherever we see the Word of God purely preached and heard, and the sacraments administered according to Christ's institution, there, it is not to be doubted, a church of God exists.
JOHN CALVIN, *Institutes*, IV, 1536

I believe there is on earth, wide as the world is, not more than one holy general Christian Church, which is nothing else than the community or assembly of the saints.
MARTIN LUTHER (1483–1546), *Works*, Vol. XXII, p. 20

By the Church . . . we understand no other than only the visible Church. For preservation of Christianity there is not anything more needful, than that such as are of the visible Church have mutual fellowship and society one with another.
RICHARD HOOKER, *The Laws of Ecclesiastical Polity*, II, 1585

A voluntary society of men, joining themselves together of their own accord, in order to the public worshipping of God, in such a manner as they judge acceptable to him, and effectual to the salvation of their souls.
JOHN LOCKE, *The Spirit of Toleration*, 1690

The church is the society of the faithful collected into one and the same body, governed by its legitimate pastors, of whom Jesus Christ is the invisible head—the pope, the successor of St. Peter, being His representative on earth.
ST. JOHN BAPTISTE DE LA SALLE, *Les devoirs du chrétien*, 1703

The Church of Christ, as it is the door of salvation, is nothing else but Christ himself. Christ in us, or we in His Church, is the same thing.
WILLIAM LAW (1686–1761), *Selected Mystical Writings of*

Church is a place where one day's truce ought to be allowed to the dissensions and animosities of mankind.
EDMUND BURKE, *Reflections on the Revolution in France*, 1790

The Church is a collection of souls, brought together in one by God's secret grace, though that grace comes to them through visible instruments, and unites them to a visible hierarchy.
JOHN HENRY NEWMAN, *Sermons on Various Occasions*, 1881

The Church is a society *divine* in its origin, *supernatural* in its end and in the means proximately adapted to the attainment of that end; but it is a *human* community inasmuch as it is composed of men.
POPE LEO XIII, *Satis Cognitum*, 1896

The religious society tracing its origin historically from Jesus of Nazareth, and finding in Him its bond of union in common worship, work, and life, in which the revealing and redeeming influence of Christ is perpetuated.

WILLIAM ADAMS BROWN, *Outline of Christian Theology,* 1906

The Church is mankind embraced, taken up by the Son into the society of the Father and of the Son, entering through the Son into participation in this society, and entirely transformed, penetrated and surrounded by it.

A. GREA, *The Church,* 1907

The Church is that institution which affords proof of its utility, and is found elevating the race, rousing the dormant understanding from material beliefs to the apprehension of spiritual ideas and the demonstration of divine Science.

MARY BAKER EDDY, *Science and Health,* 1908

The Church is . . . the actual inner unity of redeemed humanity united with Christ.

KARL ADAM, *The Spirit of Catholicism,* 1924

The catholic or universal Church, which is invisible, consists of the whole number of the elect. . . . The visible Church, which is also catholic or universal under the gospel—not confined to one nation, as before under the law—consists of all those throughout the world that profess the true religion, together with their children.

Constitution of the Presbyterian Church in U.S.A., 1930

The Church is . . . the community of destiny operating under a divine mandate.

EDWARD J. JURJI, *The Christian Interpretation of Religion,* 1932

It is in the Church that the grass grows and the flowers blossom, for the Church is nothing less than the cosmos Christianized. . . . Christ entered the cosmos . . . and thereby all things were made new.

NICHOLAS BERDYAEV, *Freedom and Spirit,* 1935

When I am asked what the Church means to me, I answer that it is the Temple of Life in which I am a living stone; it is the Tree of Eternal Fruit of which I am a branch; it is the Mystical Body of Christ on earth of which I am a member.

FULTON J. SHEEN, *The Fullness of Christ,* 1935

What is the church save the assembly of the people before God, or the movement of those who, abandoning all relative and finite goals, turn toward the infinite end of life? It is the *ecclesia* which has been called out of the pluralism and the temporalism of the world to loyalty to the supreme reality and only good.

H. RICHARD NIEBUHR, *The Kingdom of God in America,* 1937

The Church is the people of the new covenant, fulfilling and transcending all that Israel under the old covenant foreshadowed. It is the household of God, the family in which the fatherhood of God and the brotherhood of man is to be realized in the children of his adoption.

The Second World Conference on Faith and Order, ed. L. Hodgson, 1938

It is the body of Christ, whose members derive their life and oneness from their one living Head; and thus it is nothing apart from Him, but is in all things dependent upon the power of salvation which God has committed to His Son.

The Second World Conference on Faith and Order, ed. L. Hodgson, 1938

The distinctive thing about the Church is that it is the community in which men share the process of total evaluation of every aspect of life, arrive at what they conceive to be spiritual judgments on their own lives in the light of an absolute imperative, formulate corporate ethical standards for their governance, and unify the entire experience in corporate worship.

ERNEST JOHNSON, *The Social Gospel Re-examined,* 1940

I mean by *the Church,* the Body of Christian believers and transmitters of Christ's mind and spirit through the centuries, rather than a specific organization, or institution, of a single concrete communion.
RUFUS JONES, *Religion and the Modern World,* 1941

The Church is the inner company of those who, under the leadership of Christ, and empowered by Him, insist on living, and if necessary dying, rather than surrender to the selfish, hateful folly of a perishing race of men.
B. I. BELL, *Church in Disrepute,* 1943

It is the messianic fellowship, the true Israel, the new covenant, *Kyrios-Christus* united with his own in the world.
GUSTAF AULÉN, *The Faith of the Christian Church,* 1948

The Church is the realizing of the Word of God. God is eternal. . . . Therefore the Church may be said to have a pre-existence in God.
P. A. LEIÉGÉ, *God, Man and the Universe,* 1950

A community of solitude before God.
RICHARD HOCKING, *Bulletin of General Theological Seminary,* June, 1951

The Church is more than an organization. The Church is also an organism. Joan of Arc expressed it perfectly five centuries ago before her judges when she cried: "I make no difference between Christ and His Church. It is all one."
JOHN J. WRIGHT, *The Tablet* (Brooklyn, N.Y.), November 17, 1951

There could never be a Church which is merely invisible. . . . Wherever the Word of God is preached and the sacraments are administered, there is the true Church of Jesus Christ.
ERICH H. WAHLSTROM, "Lutheran Church," *The Nature of the Church, World Conference on Faith and Order,* ed. R. N. Flew, 1952

The Church Universal is composed of all who accept Jesus Christ as Lord and Saviour, and which in the Apostles' Creed we declare to be the holy catholic Church.
Doctrines and Disciplines of the Methodist Church, 1952

The visible Church of Christ is a congregation of faithful men in which the pure word of God is preached, and the Sacraments duly administered.
Doctrines and Disciplines of the Methodist Church, 1952

A visible Church of Christ is a congregation of baptized believers, associated by a covenant in faith and fellowship of the Gospel; observing the ordinances of Christ; governed by His laws.
E. T. HISCOX, *The New Directory for Baptist Churches,* 1954

The Church is nothing but a section of humanity in which Christ has really taken form. The Church is the man in Christ, incarnate, sentenced and awakened to new life.
DIETRICH BONHOEFFER, *Ethics,* 1955

The Church is a worshipping, witnessing, confessing community of forgiven sinners who rejoice in the grace that has been given them and who proclaim the word of judgment and redemption to those who have not acknowledged the sovereignty of God over their lives.
KENNETH CAUTHEN, *The Impact of American Religious Liberalism,* 1962

See also Baptism.

CHURCH: EDIFICE

An instinctive taste teaches men to build their churches in flat countries, with spire steeples, which, as they cannot be referred to any object, point as with silent finger to the sky and star.
SAMUEL TAYLOR COLERIDGE, *The Friend,* Essay 14, 1818

Let all our churches be built plain and decent, and with free seats; but not more expensive than is absolutely unavoidable; otherwise the necessity of raising money will make rich men necessary to us.

> The Doctrines and Discipline of the Methodist Episcopal Church, South, II, 1846

A church is in many ways the house of God and the home of the Christian man. But in no way is it more truly God's house than in this, that it gathers the immortal souls of God's creation to hear about Himself and His Mysteries; nay, not to hear about them, but to witness them. For a church is a place of revelation; it is a Thabor, where glory is seen to shine, and awful words are heard.

> JOHN CUTHBERT HEDLEY, The Christian Inheritance, 1896

Church: A place in which gentlemen who have never been to Heaven brag about it to persons who will never get there.

> H. L. MENCKEN, A Little Book in C Major, 1916

Is not this the first Church to build: the invisible cathedral erected in our hearts to the silent Word?

> MAURICE ZUNDEL, The Splendor of the Liturgy, 1939

See also Architecture; Art and Religion; Cathedral; Devil; Gothic Architecture; Images.

CHURCH: ITS AUTHORITY

Since the East, shattered as it is by long-standing feuds between its peoples, is bit by bit tearing into shreds the seamless vest of the Lord . . . I think it my duty to consult the chair of Peter. . . . My words are spoken to the successor the fisherman, to the disciple of the Cross.

> ST. JEROME, to Pope Damascus, 376

What is held by the *whole Church* and what has been held *always,* even when not defined by the Councils, is rightly held to have been handed down by apostolical authority.

> ST. AUGUSTINE, De Baptismo Contra Donatistas, IV, cap. xxiv, c. 395

It is evident that the judgments of the Apostolic See, than which there is no authority greater, may be rejected by no one, nor is it lawful for anyone to pass judgment on its judgments.

> POPE NICHOLAS I, Letter to Emperor Michael, 865

The bishop of Rome has no more of essential sacerdotal authority than any other priest, even as the blessed Peter has no more than the other apostles. For all received this authority from Christ equally and immediately.

> MARSIGLIO OF PADUA (1280–1343), Defensor Pacis

The Church can have no other head than Christ. He is the one universal pastor of his flock, and has promised his presence to the end of the world. He needs, therefore, no vicar, for this would imply his absence.

> HENRY BULLINGER, The Helvetic Confession, 1536

The Church hath power to decree Rites or Ceremonies, and authority in Controversies of Faith.

> Thirty-nine Articles of Religion (Church of England)

In religious matters it is holiness which gives authority.

> S. T. COLERIDGE, Aids to Reflection, 1825

A revelation is not given if there be no authority to decide what it is that is given.

> JOHN HENRY NEWMAN, An Essay on the Development of Christian Doctrine, 1845

Just as the end at which the Church aims is by far the noblest of ends, so is its authority the most exalted of all authority, nor can it be looked upon as inferior to the civil power, or in any manner dependent upon it.

POPE LEO XIII, *The Christian Constitution of States,* 1885

The supreme pontifical authority, instituted by Jesus Christ and conferred on St. Peter and his legitimate successors, the Roman Pontiffs, cannot of its very nature, and by the will of its divine Founder, be subject to any earthly power, but should enjoy the most complete liberty for the exercise of its high functions.

POPE LEO XIII, *Letter to Cardinal Rampolla,* June 5, 1887

There is no other head of the Church but the Lord Jesus Christ.

Constitution of the Presbyterian Church in U.S.A., 1930

In the Church . . . the supreme judge, the highest instance of appeal, is never the community of the faithful. Therefore, there does not nor can there exist in the Church, as she was founded by Christ, a popular tribunal or a judicial power emanating from the people.

POPE PIUS XII, *Allocution,* October 2, 1945

Spiritual authority is not a dam to the river of thought, it is merely a levee which prevents thought from becoming riotous and destroying the countryside of sanity.

FULTON J. SHEEN, *The Effects of Conversion,* 1948

The perfect circle of the one universal Church requires a unique centre, not so much for its perfection as for its very existence.

VLADIMIR SOLOVIEV, *Russia and the Universal Church,* 1948

In the field of religion, we are all agreed that God and only God is the ultimate authority.

R. NEWTON FLEW, *The Nature of the Church,* 1952

In so far as the Church lives by the Word and Spirit, it has authority to proclaim, interpret and enforce the law of Christ, the King, in so far as given in Scripture.

R. NEWTON FLEW, *The Nature of the Church,* 1952

The authority of the Church is not the consecrated earthly image of the Heavenly Ruler of the Church, but it is a medium through which the Spiritual substance of our lives is preserved and protected and reborn.

PAUL TILLICH, *The New Being,* 1955

Any religious statement rests on some authority. It cannot rest on a referral to measurable public data of the empirical order because God is not of that order.

GUSTAVE WEIGEL, *Faith and Understanding in America,* 1959

I am convinced that the next big intramural task for Protestants is a lot of hardheaded re-thinking about the meaning of authority in Protestant terms.

ROBERT MCAFEE BROWN, *An American Dialogue,* 1960

See also Apostolic Succession; Authority; Belief; Bishops; Catholicism; Church and State; Exclusiveness; Government and God; Heresy; Holy Spirit; Infallibility; Obedience; Pope, the; Private Judgment; Tradition.

CHURCH: ITS MEMBERSHIP

How many sheep there are without, how many wolves within!

ST. AUGUSTINE, *Homilies on John,* 416

If entrance into the Church is not a step to a higher and holier life, the source of a larger and more perfect freedom, her claims do not merit a moment's consideration.

I. T. HECKER, *Aspects of Nature,* 1857

There can be no question but that Church membership has been made too cheap. It has become largely a convention . . . At present our churches draw and hold the settled and cramp or repel the venturesome, which is precisely the reverse of the New Testament Church.

HENRY SLOANE COFFIN, *The Meaning of the Cross,* 1931

The Herods of the world never find the Church as they never find Christ—not even in their attempt to slaughter it; and the reason is that men never feel a tug toward the Church until they have ceased to pull against it.

FULTON J. SHEEN, *The Eternal Galilean,* 1934

You join your church as you do your club. The Church cannot be so regarded. Membership in it is rather of the nature of membership in a family.

F. ERNEST JOHNSON, *The Social Gospel Re-examined,* 1940

We hold that every man of good faith and right will, provided he does not sin against the light and does not refuse the grace interiorly offered to him, belongs, as we put it, to the Soul of the Church . . . and partakes of her life, which is eternal life.

JACQUES MARITAIN, *Ransoming the Time,* 1941

Two categories of members alone are *wholly* within her—the newly baptized who have not yet sinned, and those souls who are consummated in sanctity, all absorbed by the light.

CHARLES JOURNET, *The Church of the Word Incarnate,* Vol. I, 1955

They are fully incorporated in the society of the Church who, possessing the Spirit of Christ, accept her entire system and all the means of salvation given to her. . . . Catechumens who, moved by the Holy Spirit, seek with explicit intention to be incorporated into the Church are by that very intention joined with her. . . . The Church recognizes that in many ways she is linked with those who, being baptized, are honored with the name of Christian, though they do not profess the faith in its entirety.

Constitution on the Church, Second Vatican Council, November, 1964

I don't think God is very interested in church attendance. The church's business isn't to tuck God into bed once a week. The trouble with the church is it has made God small.

ERNEST SOUTHCUTT, quoted by Christopher S. Wren, *Look,* February 22, 1966

See also Baptism; Believing; Catholicism; Clergy; Communion of Saints; Laity; Mystical Body of Christ.

CHURCH: ITS NATURE

Where the Church is, there is the Spirit of God; and where the Spirit of God is, there is the Church and all grace, and the Spirit is truth.

ST. IRENAEUS, *Contra Haereses,* III, c. 175

Thy refuge is the Church. It is higher than the heavens and wider than the earth. It never grows old, but is ever full of vigor. Wherefore holy writ pointing to its strength and stability calls it a mountain.

ST. JOHN CHRYSOSTOM, *Hom. De Capto Eutropio,* c. 388

He Who has His house very high in secret place, hath also on earth a tabernacle. His tabernacle on earth is the Church. It is here He is to be sought.

ST. AUGUSTINE, *Ennaration on Psalm XLI,* c. 415

The whole Church forms, in some sort, but one single person. As she is the same in all, so in each one is she whole and entire; and just as man is called a microcosm, so each one of the faithful is, so to say, the Church in miniature.

ST. PETER DAMIAN (1007–1072), *Liber qui appellatur Dominus vobiscum*

There is one true universal church of the faithful, outside of which no one can be saved, in which Jesus Christ Himself is the priest and sacrifice, whose body and blood are truly contained in the sacrament of the altar beneath the species of bread and wine.

Fourth Lateran Council, 1215

The Church of Christ is always new, because the Spirit who is her soul is always new.

JACQUES BÉNIGNE BOSSUET, *Sermon,* 1656

We look upon this visible church, though black and spotted, as the hospital and guest-house of sick, halt, maimed, and withered, over which Christ is Lord, Physician, and Master.

SAMUEL RUTHERFORD (1600–1661), *Letters of* (Letter CCCLXIV)

The poorer the church, the purer the church.

W. C. HAZLITT, *English Proverbs,* 1869

The Church is ever ailing, and lingers on in its weakness, "always bearing about in the body the dying of the Lord Jesus, that the life also of her Jesus might be made manifest in her body."

JOHN HENRY NEWMAN, *Via Media,* 1877

A church needs poor men and wicked men as much as it needs pure men and virtuous men and pious men.

HENRY WARD BEECHER (1813–1887), *Sermon*

In matters of faith and morals God has made the church a sharer in the divine magistracy, and granted her, by a special privilege, immunity from error.

POPE LEO XIII, *Libertas Praestantissimum,* June 20, 1888

It is only in relation to man that it is possible to recognize a division of the Church into visible and invisible; its unity is, in reality, true and absolute.

ALEXIS KHOMIAKOV, "The Church Is One," quoted by Birkbeck in *Russia and the English Church,* 1895

The Church is like a charioteer driving down the ages at breakneck speed, swerving now to the right, now to the left, always erect and undismayed.

MARTIN C. D'ARCY, *God and the Supernatural,* 1920

The true liberal Catholic thinker recognizes that though the Church is founded on a rock, men build thereon "gold, silver, precious stones, wood, hay, stubble." From time to time an examination has to be made not of the foundation "which is Christ Jesus" but of the lower courses of masonry laid down by man.

VINCENT MCNABB, *From a Friar's Cell,* 1923

For those who know the Church is divine her very infirmity and her exertions are the most incontrovertible and definite sign of her truth.

P. CHARLES, *La Robe sans Couture,* 1923

The Church is holy not because of the goodness of her members but because of the godliness of her begetting.

NATHAN MICKLEM, *What Is the Faith,* 1923

The Church is holy because her *Author* is holy and the very source of holiness; because her object is the *sanctification* of men; because the means which she uses, her dogmas, her moral doctrine, her Sacraments are holy in themselves and lead to holiness; because at all times *many of her members* have been distinguished for their sanctity.

W. DEVIVIER, *Christian Apologetics,* 1924

The Church is a seed which develops at the expense of its surroundings, living on those surroundings without belonging to them.

A. G. SERTILLANGES, *Catéchisme des Incroyants,* 1930

She is, indeed, immortal, through the fact that her life is bound up with that of her Lord.

BASIL MATTHEWS, *The Clash of World Forces,* 1931

By the *soul of the Church* is meant the invisible principle of the spiritual and supernatural life of the Church, that is to say the perpetual assistance of the Holy Spirit.

PIETRO GASPARRI, *Catholic Catechism,* 1932

It is the common faith of Christians that the Church owes its existence to an act of God in history. It derives its being from God. It draws its nourishment and sustenance from God.

W. A. VISSER 'T HOOFT and J. H. OLDHAM, *The Church and Its Function in Society,* 1937

The Church lives again the life of Christ. It has its period of obscurity and growth and its period of manifestation, and this is followed by the catastrophe of the Cross and the new birth that springs from failure.

CHRISTOPHER DAWSON, *Beyond Politics,* 1939

The Church is one in heaven and on earth. The stern of the vessel no doubt is still in the darkness. But the prow advances, shining into the living light of eternal glory.

MAURICE ZUNDEL, *The Splendour of the Liturgy,* 1939

The power of the Church embraces the whole of man, the inner man and the outer man, in view of the attainment of the supernatural end, inasmuch as he is entirely subject to the law of Christ of which the Church was made custodian.

POPE PIUS XII, *Allocution,* October 2, 1945

As her Master came not for the whole, but for the sick, so the Church in this world will always have her sick, will always have sores in her members, great and small.

KARL ADAM, *The Spirit of Catholicism,* 1946

The real Church is the lowliest, the poorest, the meanest, weakest thing that can possibly exist under God's heaven, gathered as it is around a manger and a Cross. . . . And the real Church is also the highest, richest, most radiant and mighty thing under God's heaven.

KARL BARTH, *Community, Church and State,* 1946

It is the character or property possessed by the Church to be at the same time rigorously one and limitlessly diverse.

YVES CONGAR, *Catholicisme,* ed. J. Jacquemet, 1948

From without, the Church is a visible society whose marks, as we designate them, are the windows through which the light streams. From within, once the door has been closed upon the darkness of unbelief, the Church is seen as a house of Light whose centre is the Real Presence.

JAMES EDWARD O'MAHONY, *As in a Mirror,* 1948

The existence of the Church hangs on a sovereignly free divine choice, whereby

God *gave* to men this particular form for their religious life.

JOHN COURTNEY MURRAY, *Address, American Academy of Political and Social Science, Annals of,* March, 1948

The Church is a sinful Church: that is a truth of faith, not just a fact of her primitive experience. And it is a shattering truth.

KARL RAHNER, *Kirche der Sünder,* 1948

The Christian Church as an institution may be left as the social heir of all other churches and all the civilizations.

ARNOLD J. TOYNBEE, *Civilization on Trial,* 1948

When St. Peter confessed Jesus to be the Christ, there was the beginning of the Church, the *ecclesia.*

SYDNEY CAVE, *The Christian Way,* 1949

The Church is not so much a continuously living thing, as something that has survived a thousand crucifixions through a thousand Resurrections.

FULTON J. SHEEN, *The Woman,* 1951

Since the New Testament documents were written in and for the Church and their acceptance as a sacred canon rests upon the decision of the Church, it is correct to say that the Church was normative for the New Testament.

R. NEWTON FLEW, *The Nature of the Church,* 1952

There is no place for a Church of aesthetes, an artificial construction of philosophers, or congregation of the millennium. The Church man needs is a church of human beings; divine, certainly, but including everything that goes to make up humanity, spirit and flesh, indeed earth.

ROMANO GUARDINI, *The Church and the Catholic,* 1953

The Church is *invisible* because the constitutive factor of the Church, faith in the heart, is invisible for men and known only to God. . . . All who declare the Church to be wholly visible—Romanists—or at least semi-visible—recent Lutherans—are perverting the nature of the Christian Church.

FRANCIS PIEPER, *Christian Dogmatics,* III, 1953

As with the disciples of Emmaus and the risen Christ, men walk the road with the Church and "cannot recognize" her.

EMMANUEL SUHARD, *The Church Today,* 1953

During her pilgrimage on earth the Church is in *via,* moving towards the heavenly Jerusalem; and the road is often a road of crucifixion.

EMMANUEL SUHARD, *The Church Today,* 1953

It is necessary to have the faith of the good thief to pick out fully the divinity of the Church from behind her earthly features.

EMMANUEL SUHARD, *The Church Today,* 1953

The fundamental Protestant idea is that the Church is not above judgment, inerrant and "self-authenticating" as though she were God Himself; she is the servant of God's Word, and must perpetually be judged by her degree of conformity to that Word.

WALTER M. HORTON, *Christian Theology,* 1955

In the midst of the evil and sin at war in each one of her children, the Church herself remains immaculate.

CHARLES JOURNET, *The Church of the Word Incarnate,* Vol. I, 1955

Everywhere the broken fragments of the Church's rusted weapons lie encumbering the path where she walked through history. Everywhere the tombs of her forgotten notables crumble by the wayside. . . . Within her, petty, narrow-minded, sinful men were always at work: assuming leadership, yet blocking progress. . . . The Church is the weary, dust-laden Pilgrim through the desert.

> HUGO RAHNER, *Address,* Cologne, Germany, October, 1956

The mystery of the Church consists in the very fact that *together* sinners become *something different* from what they are as individuals; this "something different" is the Body of Christ.

> J. MEYENDORFF, *Ecumenical Review,* 1960

The society structured with hierarchical organs and the Mystical Body of Christ, are not to be considered as two realities, nor are the visible assembly and the spiritual community, nor the earthly Church and the Church enriched with heavenly things; rather they form one complex reality which coalesces from a divine and a human element.

> *The Constitution of the Church,* Second Vatican Council, November, 1964

See also Catholicism; Communion of Saints; Contemplation; Devotion; Doctrine; Dogma; Fellowship; Holiness; Kingdom of Heaven; Man's Quest of God; Mystical Body of Christ; Protestantism; Religion, Revealed; Tradition; Unity.

CHURCH: ITS VITALITY

It will remain as long as the sun—as long as the sun rises and sets: that is, as long as the ages of time shall roll, the Church of God—the true body of Christ on earth—will not disappear.

> ST. AUGUSTINE, *In Psalm.* lxx, n. 8, c. 415

It is the peculiar property of the Church that when she is buffeted she is triumphant, when she is assaulted with argument she proves herself in the right, when she is deserted by her supporters she holds the field.

> ST. HILARY OF POITIERS (c. 315–367), *On the Trinity*

Her wonderful revivals, while the world was triumphing over her, is a further evidence of the absence of corruption in the system of doctrine and worship into which she has developed.

> JOHN HENRY NEWMAN, *Essay on the Development of Christian Doctrine,* 1845

The Latin church is the great fact which dominates the history of modern civilization.

> H. C. LEA, *A History of Sacerdotal Celibacy,* 1867

It is a miracle in itself that anything so huge and historic in date and design should be so fresh in the affections. It is as if a man should find his own parlor and fireside in the heart of the Great Pyramid.

> G. K. CHESTERTON, *Catholic Church and Conversion,* 1926

Not only must the Church exist today and continue always to exist, but it must ever be exactly the same as it was in the days of the Apostles. Otherwise we must say— which God forbid—that Christ has failed in His purpose, or that He erred when He asserted of His Church that the gates of hell should never prevail against it.

> POPE PIUS XI, *Mortalium Animos,* 1927

All churches, howsoever named or formed, ultimately derive from the primitive Church, the old Church, the historical Church, the great Church, the mother Church, which, however called, has come down and still continues unbroken only in the Roman Church.

> W. E. ORCHARD, *The Way of Simplicity,* 1934

The Church of the Prince of Peace is no mere mourner among the graves, no mere singer of songs by mouldering walls. Her voice is as vibrant today as when she stood unmoved as the ancient world perished.

MARTIN J. O'MALLEY, *The Peace of Christ,* 1939

See also Church, Criticism of.

CHURCH: ITS WORK

Since the Church has received this preaching and this faith, . . . although it is scattered throughout the whole world, diligently guards it as if it dwelt in one house; and likewise it believes these things as if it had one soul and one heart, and harmoniously it preaches, teaches, and believes these things as if possessing one mouth.

ST. IRENAEUS, *Against Heresies,* c. 175

In the same way that the will of God is an act and it is called the world, so his intention is the salvation of men, and it is called the Church.

ST. CLEMENT OF ALEXANDRIA, *Paedagog.* li. i, c. 220

Thus the Church, flooded with the light of the Lord, puts forth her rays through the whole world, with yet one light which is spread upon all places, where the "unity of the word" is not infringed.

ST. CYPRIAN, *On the Unity of the Catholic Church,* to the Council of Carthage, 251

The Church is well-named *Ecclesia* because it calls everyone out and assembles them together.

ST. CYRIL OF JERUSALEM, *Catechetical Lectures,* 350

The whole problem of the existence of an institution is to remain forever necessary, and therefore faithful to its original source.

PAUL DESJARDINS, *The Conversion of the Church,* 1894

The Church is bound to communicate without stint to all men, and to transmit through all ages, the salvation effected by Jesus Christ, and the blessings flowing therefrom. Wherefore, by the will of its Founder, it is necessary that this Church should be one in all lands and at all times.

POPE LEO XIII, *Satis Cognitum,* 1896

If the Church does nothing else for the world other than to keep open a house, symbolic of the homeland of the human soul, and where in season and out of season men reaffirm their faith in this universal fatherhood of God, it is doing the social order the greatest possible service.

WILLARD L. SPERRY, *Reality in Worship,* 1925

The church in the New Testament never thought of itself as being in a rest camp; it was obviously on a battle line.

HALFORD E. LUCCOCK, *Jesus and the American Mind,* 1930

The Church has the same scope and function as the Word; namely, that of offering to God the acceptable and pleasing sacrifice of re-establishing harmony between the creature and the Creator.

EMMANUELE CARONTI, *The Spirit of the Liturgy,* 1932

The Church . . . must never consider itself committed to any social order. It is the friend and critic of that which is evil. It is ready to cooperate with that which is good.

Federal Council of Churches of Christ in America, *Report,* 1935

The function of the Church is to glorify God in adoration and sacrificial service and to be God's missionary to the world. She is to bear witness to God's redeeming grace in Jesus Christ in her corporate life,

to proclaim the good news to every creature and to make disciples of all nations.
The Second World Conference on Faith and Order, ed. L. Hodgson, 1938

The first duty of the Church, and its greatest service to the world, is that it be in very deed the Church—confessing the true faith, committed to the fulfillment of the will of Christ, its only Lord, and united in him in a fellowship of love and service.
Official Reports of the Oxford Conference, ed. J. H. Oldham, 1938

The Church of Christ undertakes to change men, not systems. She knows that if men become what they ought, systems will become what they ought.
MARTIN J. O'MALLEY, *The Peace of Christ,* 1939

Although the Church may actually never yet have expressed Christianity to perfection, there is at least no inherent impediment here to the attainment of a perfect harmony, since the Church has been called into existence for this purpose and no other.
ARNOLD J. TOYNBEE, *A Study of History,* V, 1939

Because human beings and not animated machines toil in industry, therefore the Church cannot abdicate her right and duty to speak out in defense of the rights of human personality nor fail to declare uncompromisingly the moral obligations of industrial and economic life.
Bishops and Archbishops of the National Catholic Welfare Council, *The Church and Social Order,* 1940

Christ's death released a redemptive force in history which is peculiarly perpetrated by God's Holy Spirit through the redemptive fellowship which is the Church.
NELS F. S. FERRÉ, *The Christian Faith,* 1942

What organized institution is there, apart from the church, that has as its major purpose the fostering of Justice, Mercy, and Truth and the Freedom that they jointly make possible?
D. ELTON TRUEBLOOD, *The Predicament of Modern Man,* 1944

Bad and divided as the church may be, it is the only organization really working at the job of affecting men's lives in the deep way in which they must be affected if what we prize is to survive.
D. ELTON TRUEBLOOD, *The Predicament of Modern Man,* 1944

The Church has within her the power to assimilate and transform the whole of humanity, even to its deepest fibers, and it is her duty and her wish to display this power to its fullest extent.
Y. DE MONCHEUIL, *Aspects of the Church,* 1945

The Church cannot shut herself up and remain inert within the secrecy of her temples and by doing so desert the mission laid upon her by divine Providence, to form man and to form the whole man.
POPE PIUS XII, *Address to New Cardinals,* February 20, 1946

The Church is more than a company of preachers, or a teaching society, or a missionary board. It has not only to invite people, but also to introduce them into this New Life, to which it bears witness.
Man's Disorder and God's Design (Amsterdam Assembly Series), I, 1948

It brings the Christian past to each fresh individual. It confronts the spontaneous but limited immediate experience of each individual with the enduring experience of the great souls who have gone before him. . . . It draws his life into the great broad stream of Christian response to God.
DOUGLAS V. STEERE, *Door Into Life,* 1948

Every local church in Christendom ought to be a creative center of transforming life and love in its community.

> RUFUS M. JONES, *A Call to What Is Vital*, 1948

The arms proper to the Church are the arms of light. Her soldiers are apostles. They must conquer souls; that is, convert them through love and the illumination of their doctrine.

> R. L. BRUCKBERGER, *One Sky to Share*, 1951

The Church has need to stop regarding itself as an end to be served and to resume acting as an instrument for God to use in the rescue of human beings from worldliness, from self-centered incapacity.

> BERNARD IDDINGS BELL, *Crowd Culture*, 1952

In the light of the message entrusted to it the church is called to act as prophet, pastor and priest at the same time for the same people.

> JOHN C. BENNETT, *Christian Century*, January 6, 1954

No substitute can be found for the definition of the goal of the Church as *the increase among men of the love of God and neighbor.*

> H. RICHARD NIEBUHR, *The Purpose of the Church and Its Ministry*, 1956

The miracle is that the divine nature of the Church is not altogether obscured by the all too human nature of her members.

> WALTER MARSHALL HORTON, *Christian Theology*, 1958

Insofar as we are the Church, we must thrust Church into the center of the modern world, and from that position we must be able to listen to the modern world with exquisite attention, and then reply to that world in a language which it can understand.

> PHILIP SCHARPER, *The Critic*, August–September, 1962

The Church sometimes forgets that at least part of her divine commission is "to comfort the afflicted and to afflict the comfortable."

> JOHN E. LARGE, *The Small Needle of Doctor Large*, 1962

In times of prosperity the church administers; in times of adversity the church shepherds.

> FULTON J. SHEEN, *The Priest Is Not His Own*, 1963

Just as Christ carried out the work of redemption in poverty and oppression, so the Church is called to follow the same route that it might communicate the fruits of salvation to men. . . . The Church, although it needs human resources to carry out its mission, is not set up to seek earthly glory, but to proclaim, even by its own example, humility and self-sacrifice.

> *The Constitution of the Church*, Second Vatican Council, November, 1964

See also Adoration; Bible and the Church; Bible: Its Interpretation; Church, Criticism of; Salvation; War, Condemnation of; World and the Church.

CHURCH AND STATE

Since it is plain that when that religion is set at nought, in which is preserved the crowning reverence for the most celestial Being, great dangers are brought upon public affairs; but that, when legally adopted and safeguarded, it affords to the Roman name the greatest prosperity.

> EMPEROR CONSTANTINE to Anulinus; Eusebius, *Ecclesiastical History*, c. 325 A.D.

Intrude not yourself into ecclesiastical matters, neither give commands unto us concerning them, but learn from us. God hath put into your hands the kingdom; to us he hath entrusted the affairs of the Church.

> ST. HILIARY OF POITIERS, *First Epistle to Constantius*, 355

The power of the Church is as far above the civil power in value as heaven is above the earth, or rather it transcends it, even more.

ST. JOHN CHRYSOSTOM (347–407), *In II Cor. Hom.*, XV

Certain it is for us and our Empire that the only defense is in the favor of the God of heaven; and to deserve it our first care is to support the Christian faith and its venerable religion. Inasmuch then as the primacy of the Apostolic See is assured by the merit of St. Peter, prince of the episcopate, by the rank of the City of Rome, and also by the authority of a sacred Synod, let not presumption endeavor to attempt anything contrary to the authority of that See.

Edict of Valentinian, 445

God requireth not any uniformity of religion to be enacted and enforced in any civil state.

ROGER WILLIAMS, *The Bloudy Tenant of Persecution, 1644*

Both Commonwealth and Church are collective bodies, made up of many into one; and both so near allied that the one, the Church, can never subsist but in the other, the Commonwealth; nay, so near, that the same men, which in a temporal respect make the Commonwealth, do in a spiritual make the Church.

WILLIAM LAUD (1573–1645), *Works,* I

The dogmas of civil religion ought to be few, simple. . . . The existence of a mighty, intelligent, and beneficent Divinity, possessed of foresight and providence, the life to come, the happiness of the just, the punishment of the wicked, the sanctity of the social contract and the laws; these are its positive dogmas; its negative dogmas I confine to one, intolerance.

JEAN JACQUES ROUSSEAU, *The Social Contract, 1762*

The teaching of the divine law concerns the Church; but the teaching of the moral law belongs to the State.

L. R. C. LA CHALOTAIS, *Essay on National Education, 1763*

It is better that the commonwealth be fashioned to the setting forth of God's house, which is his church, than to accommodate the church to the civil state.

JOHN COTTON (1585–1652), quoted in *History of the Colony of Massachusetts Bay,* by Hutchinson, 1770

I cannot give up my guidance to the magistrate, because he knows no more of the way to Heaven than I do, and is less concerned to direct me right than I am to go right.

THOMAS JEFFERSON, *Notes on Religion, 1776*

To compel a man to furnish contributions of money for the propagation of opinions which he disbelieves and abhors is sinful and tyrannical.

THOMAS JEFFERSON, *Virginia Statutes of Religious Freedom, 1779*

Congress shall make no law respecting an establishment of religion, or prohibiting the free exercise thereof.

Constitution of the United States, Amendment I, December 15, 1791

Civil magistrates may not assume to themselves the administration of the Word and Sacraments. . . . It is the duty of civil magistrates to protect the Church of our common Lord, without giving their preference to any denomination of Christians above the rest.

Westminster Confession of Faith (1645–47), American edition as revised after the adoption of the Bill of Rights of the U.S. Constitution

The Power of the Civil Magistrate extendeth to all men, as well Clergy as laity, in all things temporal; but hath no authority in things purely spiritual.

> Protestant Episcopal Church in the United States, *Thirty-ninth Article,* American revision, 1801

I contemplate with sovereign reverence that act of the whole American people which declared that their legislature should "make no law respecting an establishment of religion, or prohibiting the free exercise thereof," thus building a wall of separation between Church and State.

> THOMAS JEFFERSON, *Letter to a Committee of Danbury Baptist Association,* Conn., January 1, 1802

We cannot prophesy happier results for religion and the civil power from the desires of those who call so vociferously for the separation of Church and State and the destruction of the agreement between the priesthood and the empire.

> POPE GREGORY XVI, *Mirari Vos,* August 15, 1832

So far from suffering from the want of state support, religion seems in the United States to stand all the firmer because, standing alone, she is seen to stand by her own strength.

> ALEXIS DE TOCQUEVILLE, *Democracy in America,* I, 1839

Religion in America takes no direct part in the government of society, but it must be regarded as the first of their political institutions. . . . Despotism may govern without faith, but liberty cannot.

> ALEXIS DE TOCQUEVILLE, *Democracy in America,* 1839

Christianity is not a part of the law of the land in any sense which entitles the courts to take notice of and base their judgments upon it, except in so far as they can find that its precepts and principles have been incorporated in and made a component part of the positive law of the state.

> THOMAS M. COOLEY, *Constitutional Limitations,* 1868

Leave the matter of religion to the family altar, the church and the private school, supported entirely by private contributions. Keep the church and the State for ever separate.

> ULYSSES S. GRANT, *Speech,* Des Moines, Iowa, 1875

No religion can long continue to maintain its purity when the church becomes the subservient vassal of the state.

> F. ADLER, *Creed and Deed,* 1877

To wish the Church to be subject to the civil power in the exercise of her duty is a great folly and a sheer injustice. Whenever this is the case, order is disturbed, for things natural are put above things supernatural.

> POPE LEO XIII, *The Christian Constitution of States,* 1885

The Almighty has given the charge of the human race to two powers, the ecclesiastical and the civil, the one being set over divine, and the other over human things. Each in its kind is supreme, each has fixed limits within which it is contained. . . . There must, accordingly, exist, between these two powers, a certain orderly connection.

> POPE LEO XIII, *The Christian Constitution of States,* 1885

To talk about any particular denomination as the Church . . . has no meaning, and betrays ignorance or conceit. . . . The American laws know no such institution as "the Church" but only separate and independent organizations.

> PHILIP SCHAFF, *Church and State in the U. S.,* 1888

Inasmuch as the destiny of the State depends mainly on the disposition of those who are at the head of affairs, it follows that the Church cannot give countenance or favor to those whom she knows to be imbued with a spirit of hostility to her; who refuse openly to respect her rights.

POPE LEO XIII, *Sapientiae Christianae*, 1890

Church and State both minister to something greater and larger than either. . . . And they find their true relation in this unity of aim and service. When the State supports morality by legal restraint, it cooperates with the voluntary moral power of the Church; but if it should seek to control the organization and influence of the Church by appointing its officers or interfering with its teaching, it would tamper with the seedpot of moral progress.

WALTER RAUSCHENBUSCH, *Christianity and the Social Crisis*, 1907

The separation of church and state in this country seems to Catholics the natural, the inevitable, the best conceivable plan, the one that would work best among us, both for the good of religion and of the state. . . . American Catholics rejoice in our separation of church and state; and I can conceive of no combination of circumstances likely to arise which should make a union desirable either to church or state.

JAMES GIBBONS, *A Retrospect of Fifty Years*, 1916

We have stood resolutely for the separation of state and church but with equal insistence we have stood for the continuous impact of the church upon the state.

National Council of Congregational Churches, *Minutes of*, 1917

While the humanistic religious sentiment which expresses itself by the catch in the throat at the last Evensong in the old school Chapel, the community singing of *Abide with Me* at a torchlight tattoo . . . can be utilized by totalitarianism, a religion which speaks of redemption by the incarnate Son of God . . . must be the declared enemy of all who see in the state the be-all and end-all of man's life.

HUMPHREY BEEVOR, *Peace and Pacifism*, 1936

Since the State is based on force, alliance with it contaminates the Church with the alien principle of force.

E. I. WATKIN, *Men and Tendencies*, 1937

"An establishment of religion" means a state church, such as for instance existed in Massachusetts for more than forty years after the adoption of the Constitution.

EDWARD S. CORWIN, *The Constitution and What It Means Today*, 1938

If the Church takes up its share of political responsibility, it must mean that it is taking that human initiative which the State cannot take; it is giving the State the impulse which it cannot give itself.

KARL BARTH, *Community, Church and State*, 1946

It was and is a sacrilege against the *totus Christus*, Christ in His integrity, and at the same time a fatal blow against the unity of mankind, whenever an attempt has been made or is being made to make the Church a prisoner and a slave of this or that particular people, to confine her to the narrow limits of a nation, as also to ban her from a nation.

POPE PIUS XII, *Allocution*, December 24, 1946

An absolutely rigorous separation of church and state [means] the secularization of the community.

REINHOLD NIEBUHR, *Christianity and Crisis*, September 15, 1947

The church is the organized institution of religion, as the state is the organized institution of political life. It is these two institutions that are to be kept separate. But it is a separation which leaves room for moral and spiritual and political interaction and responsiveness. . . . There must be no interlocking of their respective institutional processes by law or the administration of law.

Editorial, *Christian Century*, November 26, 1947

The "establishment of religion" clause of the First Amendment means at least this. Neither a State nor the Federal Government can set up a church. Neither can pass laws which aid one religion, aid all religion, or prefer one religion to another.

> JUSTICE BLACK, majority decision, U.S. Supreme Court, *Everson vs. Board of Education of Township of Ewing, N.J.,* 1947

It is not the purpose of the First Amendment "to cut off church schools from those services which are separate but indisputably marked off from religious functions." . . . State power is no more to be used so as to handicap religions than it is to favor them.

> JUSTICE BLACK, majority decision, U.S. Supreme Court, *Everson vs. Board of Education of Township of Ewing, N.J.* 1947

Undoubtedly the divine, supreme, fundamental reason for the existence of civil society is to enable the word of God to be taught and heard, and consequently to give the Christian community the chance to exist.

> KARL BARTH, *Against the Stream,* 1947

Our constitutional policy . . . does not deny the value or necessity for religious training, teaching or observance. Rather it secures their free exercise. But to that end it does deny that the state can undertake or sustain them in any form or degree.

> JUSTICE RUTLEDGE, dissenting opinion, *Everson v. Board of Education of Township of Ewing, N.J.,* 1947

Christianity has lived through innumerable persecutions and become stronger. But the successful corruption of the Church by the State will end the Christian era forever.

> DOROTHY THOMPSON, *Look,* January, 1948

No group in America is seeking union of Church and State; and least of all are Catholics. . . . If tomorrow Catholics constituted a majority in our country, they would not seek a union of Church and State. They would then, as now, uphold the Constitution and all its amendments, recognizing the moral obligation imposed on all Catholics to observe and defend the Constitution and its amendments.

> JOHN T. MCNICHOLAS, in 1948, quoted in *Federal Aid to Private Schools,* by N. S. McCluskey, 1950

Separation is a requirement to abstain from fusing functions of government and of religious sects, not merely to treat them all equally.

> JUSTICE FELIX FRANKFURTER, *McCollum v. Board of Education,* U.S. Supreme Court, 333 U.S., 19, 1948

The Constitution . . . prohibited the government common to all from becoming embroiled, however innocently, in the destructive religious conflicts of which the history of even this country records some dark pages.

> JUSTICE FELIX FRANKFURTER, *McCollum v. Board of Education,* U.S. Supreme Court, 333 U.S., 19, 1948

History and experience have brought the Church to ever more perfect respect for the autonomy of the State . . . and consequently to ever more purely spiritual assertions of her power in the temporal order.

> JOHN COURTNEY MURRAY, *Theological Studies,* X, 1949

The reconciliation of the spirit of freedom with the spirit of religious devotion or commitment has become a serious problem of public morality. Neither church nor state can now be indifferent to each other's moral structure.

> HERBERT WALLACE SCHNEIDER, *Religion in the 20th Century,* 1952

If the surrender of responsibility is successfully effected and the carefully devised equilibrium of church and state is destroyed, the consequence can only be a further emasculation of the churches and an increasing secularization of society.

W. S. HUDSON, *The Great Tradition of the American Churches,* 1953

When churches succumb to the pressures of secular life and fail to exhibit a distinctive quality of faith and life, the separation of church and state . . . loses its point.

W. S. HUDSON, *The Great Tradition of the American Churches,* 1953

The relation between the Church and State is not an abstract relation and cannot be. Its purpose is dynamic, to be fulfilled in the temporal order. The end in view is a certain management of society, the exertion of a spiritual influence—on that living action which is public order, the imparting of a moral direction to the total political movement.

JOHN COURTNEY MURRAY, *The Catholic Church in World Affairs,* ed. Gurian and Fitzsimmons, 1954

Whatever one may say about the separation of church and state in law, one cannot separate significant education from theology.

JAMES HASTINGS NICHOLS, *Religion in America,* ed. John Cogley, 1958

The "wall" of separation between Church and State, as it is conceived by most "absolute separationists" in America, is not really a constitutional concept. It is rather a private doctrine (of militant secularism in some cases, of one version of Christian theology in others) which a minority of Americans seem intent on imposing on all.

WILLIAM CLANCY, *Religion and the Free Society,* 1958

The democratic nature of our government precludes the imposition of sanctions in the field of religion; the religious nature of the governed sanctions the inclusion of

religion in the processes of democratic life; the dividing line between permitted accommodation and proscribed compulsion is a matter of degree, to be determined anew in each new fact situation.

JUSTICE BERNARD S. MEYER, N.Y. Supreme Court, August 24, 1959

If it be true that the First Amendment is to be given a theological interpretation and that therefore it must be "believed," made an object of religious faith, it would follow that a religious test has been thrust into the Constitution.

JOHN COURTNEY MURRAY, *We Hold These Truths,* 1960

I believe in an America where the separation of church and state is absolute, where no Catholic prelate would tell the President (should he be a Catholic) how to act and no Protestant minister would tell his parishioners for whom to vote.

JOHN F. KENNEDY, *Speech,* Houston, Tex., September 12, 1960

We repeat and again reaffirm that neither a state nor the Federal Government can constitutionally force a person "to profess a belief or disbelief in any religion." Neither can constitutionally pass laws or impose requirements which aid all religions as against non-believers, and neither can aid those religions based on a belief in the existence of God as against those religions founded on different beliefs.

JUSTICE HUGO L. BLACK, *Torcaso vs. Watkins,* U.S. Supreme Court, 1961

The constitutional prohibition against laws respecting an establishment of religion must at least mean that in this country it is no part of the business of Government to compose official prayers for any group of the American people to recite as part of a religious program carried on by Government.

JUSTICE HUGO L. BLACK, majority opinion of U.S. Supreme Court, N.Y. School Prayer Case, June 25, 1962

I cannot see how an "official religion" is established by letting those who want to say a prayer say it. On the contrary, I think that to deny the wish of these school children to join in reciting this prayer is to deny them the opportunity of sharing in the spiritual heritage of our nation.

> JUSTICE POTTER STEWART, dissenting opinion, U.S. Supreme Court, N.Y. School Prayer Case, June 25, 1962

The court's task in this as in all areas of constitutional adjudication, is not responsibly aided by the uncritical invocation of metaphors like the "wall of separation," a phrase nowhere to be found in the Constitution.

> JUSTICE POTTER STEWART, dissenting opinion, U.S. Supreme Court, N.Y. School Prayer Case, June 25, 1962

The recitation of prayers in the public schools, which is tantamount to the teaching of prayer, is not in conformity with the spirit of the American concept of the separation of church and state.

> New York Board of Rabbis, June, 1962

The Congress should at once submit an amendment to the Constitution which establishes the right to religious devotion in all governmental agencies—national, state or local.

> HERBERT C. HOOVER, *New York Times,* July 1, 1962

With us, separation of church and state was never intended to mean separation of religion from society.

> JAMES A. PIKE, *New York Times,* July 13, 1962

The First Amendment was adopted solely as a limitation upon the newly created national Government. The events leading to its adoption strongly suggest that the establishment clause was primarily an attempt to insure that Congress not only would be powerless to establish a national church, but would also be unable to interfere with existing state establishments.

> JUSTICE POTTER STEWART, dissenting opinion, U.S. Supreme Court, Prayer and Bible reading in the Public Schools, June 17, 1963

The claim advanced here in favor of Bible reading is sufficiently substantial to make simple reference to the constitutional phrase "establishment of religion" as inadequate an analysis of the cases before us as the ritualistic invocation of the nonconstitutional phrase "separation of church and state."

> JUSTICE POTTER STEWART, dissenting opinion, U.S. Supreme Court, Prayer and Bible reading in the Public Schools, June 17, 1963

The Founding Fathers unfailingly recognized a clear and elemental distinction which appears to elude the mind of the present Court—between religion as a well nigh universal concern of men and the several specific forms and institutions of "organized religion."

> HENRY P. VAN DUSEN, Letter, *New York Times,* July 7, 1963

See also America; American People; Authority; Church: Its Authority; Coercion; Constitution, U.S.; Democracy; Education; Education, Parents' Rights in; Education, Parochial; Education, Religious; Education and Religion; Freedom, Religious; Freedom and God; Government; Government and God; Government and Religion; Infallibility; Pluralism; President, U.S.; Religion; Religion, National; Religion, State; Religious Test for Office; Rulers; Secularism.

CIRCUMSTANCES

Somebody has said that if a letter were sent to that most influential person called "Circumstances," most of us could end it by saying, "I am, Sir, your most obedient servant."

E. STANLEY JONES, *Victorious Living,* 1936

CITIES, TWO

Two cities have been formed, by two loves; the earthly, the love of self, even to the contempt of God; the heavenly, by the love of God, even to the contempt of self. . . . The one seeks glory from men; but the greatest glory of the other is God, the witness of the conscience.

ST. AUGUSTINE, *The City of God,* Book XIV, 426

CITIZEN

Whatever makes men good Christians makes them good citizens.

DANIEL WEBSTER, *Speech,* December 22, 1820

The true Christian is the true citizen, lofty of purpose, resolute in endeavor, ready for a hero's deeds, but never looking down on his task because it is cast in the day of small things.

THEODORE ROOSEVELT, *Speech,* December 30, 1900

See also Allegiance; Collectivism.

CITIZENSHIP

It is the aim of the ecclesiastical authority by the use of spiritual means, to form good Christians in accordance with its own particular end and object; and in doing this it helps at the same time to form good citizens, and prepares them to meet their obligations as members of a civil society.

SILVIO ANTONIANO (1540–1603), *The Christian Education of Youth*

It is the right and duty of organized groups of Christians, such as congregations and synods, to direct and assist their members in the determination of their duty as Christian citizens and members of society.

Minutes of the United Lutheran Church, 1922

If the people as a group neglect those virtues that are required for good citizenship, the nation is doomed to decay and death.

FRANCIS J. CONNELL, *Morality and Government,* 1949

See also Allegiance; Education; Education, Catholic; Education, Parochial.

CITY

The Protestant churches, and more recently the Catholics and Jews, are simply abandoning the inner city to Pentecostal and Adventist sects and following the more choice consumers into the suburbs.

FRANKLIN H. LITTELL, *From State Church to Pluralism,* 1962

See also Suburbia.

CITY OF GOD

While this City of God is in exile on earth, it enrolls its citizens from men of all nations and tongues. It does not worry about differences in culture, laws and ways of life.

ST. AUGUSTINE, *The City of God,* Bk. XIX, 426

See also Community.

CIVIL RIGHTS

See Negroes; Nonviolence; Race; Racial Conflict; Racial Equality; Racial Injustice; Racial Prejudice; Rights.

CIVILIZATION

A decent provision for the poor is the true test of civilization.

SAMUEL JOHNSON, *Boswell's Life of,* 1772

If we neglect modern civilization, what right have we to stand and declaim against it as heretical or infidel?

ORESTES BROWNSON, *Brownson's Quarterly,* July, 1863

It [civilization] is the development of art out of nature, and of self-government out of passion, and of certainty out of opinion, and of faith out of reason.

JOHN HENRY NEWMAN, *Historical Sketches,* I, 1896

Civilization is the lamb's skin in which barbarism masquerades.

THOMAS BAILEY ALDRICH, *Ponkapog Papers,* 1903

Civilization is essentially the cooperation of regional societies under a common spiritual influence. This influence need not be religious in the ordinary sense of the word.

CHRISTOPHER DAWSON, *Sociological Review,* April, 1921

The alterations of civilization leave the heart of vital religion untouched as nothing else.

JAMES MOFFATT, *The Approach to the New Testament,* 1921

We are living in a completely secularized civilization which has lost the art of bringing its dominant motives under any kind of moral control.

REINHOLD NIEBUHR, *Christian Century,* April 22, 1926

Civilizations die from philosophical calm, irony, and the sense of fair play quite as surely as they die of debauchery.

JOSEPH WOOD KRUTCH, *The Modern Temper,* 1929

Civilization is in peril? Put it correctly. Civilization *is* peril! The higher it rises the more unstable and the more disastrous it falls. Its safety consists in increasing the peril and going on up.

WILLIAM L. SULLIVAN, *Epigrams and Criticisms in Miniature,* 1936

If our civilization should perish, this will come about in part, because it was not good enough to survive.

LEWIS MUMFORD, *Faith for Living,* 1940

A civilization is a heritage of beliefs, customs, and knowledge slowly accumulated in the course of centuries, elements difficult at times to justify by logic, but justifying themselves as paths when they lead somewhere, since they open for man his inner distance.

ANTOINE DE SAINT-EXUPÉRY, *Flight to Arras,* 1942

For civilization depends upon the vigorous pursuit of the highest values by people who are intelligent enough to know that their values are qualified by their interests and corrupted by their prejudices.

REINHOLD NIEBUHR, *Human Destiny,* 1943

What increases with civilization is not so much immorality of intent as opportunity of expression.

WILL DURANT, *Caesar and Christ,* 1944

Civilization is order and freedom promoting cultural activity. . . . Civilization begins with order, grows with liberty, and dies with chaos.

WILL DURANT, *Ladies Home Journal,* January, 1946

Civilization is the outcome of a spiritual work, it is born of man's need to fulfill himself by bringing the universe to fulfilment.

JEAN MOUROUX, *The Meaning of Man,* 1948

The only true hope for civilization—the conviction of the individual that his inner life can affect outward events and that, whether or not he does so, he is responsible for them.

STEPHEN SPENDER, *World Within World,* 1951

The most important fact about the civilized world today is not technology or mass production or atomic power or Russian aggression. It is the fact of mental and moral confusion. It is cultural instability.

VAN OGDEN VOGT, *Cult and Culture,* 1951

The civilization of the present day can be defined more accurately by a feature which marks it off from any civilization which has preceded it. It is an age without God.

EMMANUEL SUHARD, *The Church Today,* 1953

The more the world advances in time and the greater the progress of what is called civilization, the less does the soul act as a window overlooking creation.

JEAN HELLÉ, *Miracles,* 1593

The most primitive and dangerous idea ever held by the mind of man is the notion that it is somehow possible to preserve human civilization on this earth in the present condition of world anarchy.

NORMAN COUSINS, *In Place of Folly,* 1961

See also Bible and Civilization; Chaos; Christianity; Church: Its Vitality; Civilization and Christianity; Civilization and Religion; Communism; Devil; Ethics; Society; Technology.

CIVILIZATION AND CHRISTIANITY

The civilization of the world is Christian civilization; the more frankly Christian it is, so much is it more true, more lasting and more productive of precious fruit.

POPE PIUS XII, *Fermo Proposito,* June 11, 1905

A civilization of glaring inequalities, ostentatious display, shrieking advertisement, depending upon the fleets and armies and ready at any moment to assert its right to exist by wholesale bloodshed, is not the civilization of the Cross.

W. G. PECK, *The Divine Revolution,* 1927

Civilization is faced with the choice between a return to the spiritual traditions of Christianity or the renunciation of them in favor of complete social materialism.

CHRISTOPHER DAWSON, *The Modern Dilemma: The Problem of European Unity,* 1932

A post-Christian civilization which becomes conscious of its own powers and possibilities soon adopts an anti-Christian attitude; it seems to be forced to develop its own gospel of salvation, its own forms of worship, its own dogma and ethos.

NILS EHRENSTRÖM, *Christian Faith and the Common Life,* 1938

Our civilization, in spite of all its blemishes and its many ghastly failures, is still a Christian civilization. Take away the Christianity and the civilization will not remain what you and I mean by civilization.

J. S. WHALE, *The Right to Believe,* 1938

In the world as we know it I believe that civilization must have a Christian basis, and must ultimately rest on the Christian Church.

JOHN BUCHAN, *Pilgrim's Way,* 1940

As Western civilization loses its Christianity it loses its superiority. The ideology of communism rose out of the secularized remnants of a Western civilization whose soul was once Christian.

FULTON J. SHEEN, Preface, *Communism and the Conscience of the West,* 1948

We declare officially that ours is a Christian civilization, but when we construct an organization to save that civilization we dispense with Christ.

> JAMES M. GILLIS, *This Mysterious Human Nature*, 1956

Christianity is not essentially linked to any one form of cultural tradition; it is not even a product of civilization, but an historic act of God.

> JEAN DANIELOU, *The Lord of History*, 1958

The whole structure of Western civilization, its spirit and laws, its ideals, its very intellect and conscience are the product of a Graeco-Roman heritage infused and elevated by Christianity.

> FRANCIS X. CANFIELD, *The Catholic Bookman's Guide*, ed. Sr. M. Regis, I.H.M., 1962

See also Bible and Civilization; Christian Life; Civilization; Civilization and Religion; Culture and Christianity; Culture and Religion; World and Christianity.

CIVILIZATION AND RELIGION

The further we go back in the past, the more valuable is religion as an element in civilization; as we advance, it retreats more and more into the background, to be replaced by science.

> J. B. BURY, *A History of Freedom of Thought*, 1913

It is only when civilization is mature, when society becomes self-conscious and the struggle for bare survival is slackened, that the spiritual needs of man's nature exert their full power.

> CHRISTOPHER DAWSON, *God and the Supernatural*, 1920

However active the institutions of religion may be in our national life, there is no trace of ethical motive in our national conduct. . . . The social life of the West-

ern world is almost completely outside of ethical control.

> REINHOLD NIEBUHR, *Christian Century*, April 22, 1926

The civilization that finds no place for religion is a maimed culture that has lost its spiritual roots and is condemned to sterility and decadence.

> CHRISTOPHER DAWSON, *The Modern Dilemma: The Problem of European Unity*, 1932

The task of the present generation appears to lie in the liberation of the church from its bondage to a corrupt civilization.

> H. RICHARD NIEBUHR, *The Church Against the World*, 1935

It seems to be an inescapable law that all religious systems consciously designed to preserve civilizations prove unable to do so; while those that spring from some fresh, disinterested apprehension of superhuman Reality prove ultimately most powerful as social restoratives.

> WALTER MARSHALL HORTON, *Can Christianity Save Civilization*, 1940

The divorce of the practical and relative world of daily living from the astronomical sense of the high religions is surely one of the ultimate causes of the breakdown that has been going on so fast in our own generation.

> LEWIS MUMFORD, *Faith for Living*, 1940

If religion is a chariot, it looks as if the wheels on which it mounts toward Heaven may be the periodic downfalls of civilizations on Earth.

> ARNOLD J. TOYNBEE, *Civilization on Trial*, 1948

The preservation of civilization and culture is now one with the preservation of religion.

> FULTON J. SHEEN, *The Woman*, 1951

The great civilizations of the World do not produce the great religions as a kind of cultural by-product; in a very real sense, the great religions are the foundations on which the great civilizations rest.

> CHRISTOPHER DAWSON, *The Dynamics of World History,* 1957

I believe that civilization can be saved only by drawing on the resources of the higher religions as well as on those of civilization itself. I believe that human beings can save civilization by thus rising above it, but I do not believe that . . . this is bound to secure a future for civilization or for religion or for the human race.

> ARNOLD J. TOYNBEE, *A Study of History,* Vol. XII, *Reconsiderations,* 1961

One of the great spiritual tragedies of our day is the decidedly un-Christian, un-religious and unspiritual image of itself that the West has actually projected in its dealings with the rest of the world during the last century.

> NORRIS CLARK, *America,* March 31, 1962

One of the most disturbing things about the Western world of our time is that it is beginning to have much more in common with the Communist world than it has with the professedly Christian society of several centuries ago.

> THOMAS MERTON, *Commonweal,* February 9, 1962

We are no longer living in a Christian world. . . . It is therefore a serious error to imagine that because the West was once largely Christian, the cause of Western nations is now to be identified, without further qualification, with the cause of God.

> THOMAS MERTON, *Commonweal,* February 9, 1962

See also Bible and Civilization; Christian Life; Civilization and Christianity; Culture and Christianity; Culture and Religion; Machines; World and Christianity.

CLASS DISTINCTIONS

Rich and poor, capitalist and laboring men, are not classifications and distinctions made by the Church of Christ. To the church there are only two kinds of men— those who follow Christ and those who do not.

> FRANK MASON NORTH, *Address,* Philadelphia Meeting of Federal Council of Churches of Christ in America, 1908

See also Discrimination; Equality; Nobility; Prejudice; Vanity.

CLASS STRUGGLE

The doctrine of class-conscious struggle is opposed to the Christian ideal. It not only strikes at injustice by a greater and more savage injustice but tends in practice to the breaking up of society.

> Federal Council of Churches of Christ in America, *Report,* 1920

See also Class Distinctions.

CLERGY

Bishops, presbyters and deacons are not to leave their places in order to engage in trade; nor are they to go the round of their provinces in search of profitable markets.

> *Canons of the Council of Elvira,* c. 305

Those whom they are accustomed to call clerics—should once for all be kept absolutely free from all public offices, that they be not withdrawn away by any error or sacrilegious fault from the worship which they owe to the Divinity, but rather without any hindrance serve to the utmost their own law.

> EMPEROR CONSTANTINE to Anulinus, quoted in Eusebius, *Ecclesiastical History,* c. 325

Avoid, as you would the plague, a clergyman who is also a man of business.

ST. JEROME (340–420), *Letter to Nepotian*

Let those who are engaged in spiritual pursuits alone, adorn the Church. Let those guard her, who are not wearied even with the labors of the world. But let not him who now gleams with spiritual brightness within Holy Church, murmur against his superior, who is employed in worldly business.

POPE ST. GREGORY THE GREAT, *Magna Moralia,* 584

I do not see why all the clergy ought not to be content according to the rule of the apostles with food and clothing.

JOHN WYCLIF, *The Pastoral Office,* 1378

To a philosophic eye the vices of the clergy are far less dangerous than their virtues.

EDWARD GIBBON, *The Decline and Fall of the Roman Empire,* I, 1776

Discretion, gentle manners, common sense, and good nature are, in men of high ecclesiastical station, of far greater importance than the greatest skill in discriminating between sublapsarian and supralapsarian doctrines.

SYDNEY SMITH, *Edinburgh Review,* 1822

The clergy should be concerned primarily with teaching to the faithful the conduct they should follow in order to promote the well-being of the majority of the population.

C. H. SAINT-SIMON, *The New Christianity,* 1825

That which the *man* does not believe, the minister must never say. He does not serve his Lord if he becomes personally insincere in the service of the Church.

FRIEDRICH NAUMANN, *Briefe über Religion,* 1903

Clergyman, n. A man who undertakes the management of our spiritual affairs as a method of bettering his temporal ones.

AMBROSE BIERCE, *The Devil's Dictionary,* 1906

The clergy have lost their hold. In America a man in trouble now goes to his doctor.

ALFRED NORTH WHITEHEAD, *Dialogues of,* December, 1939, as recorded by L. Price

Dwelling in ivory towers may bring our ministers nearer to God; it doesn't bring them nearer the average man and his problems.

CHANNING POLLOCK, *American Mercury,* October, 1940

There is nothing the clergyman can know which the layman cannot know. Clergymen are not more adept than others at the art of worship and may be less so.

D. E. TRUEBLOOD, *The Logic of Belief,* 1942

Your problem and mine is to get behind the conventional fronts that sit row upon row in the pews.

PETER MARSHALL, quoted by Catherine Marshall in her *A Man Called Peter,* 1951

The institutional status and authority of the ministry are being modified in the direction of the democratic type of political, educational and economic executives of managerial authority.

H. RICHARD NIEBUHR, *The Purpose of the Church and Its Ministry,* 1956

If the preacher's hair is gray, he's too old; if he is a young man, he hasn't had much experience. If he has six children, he has too many; if he has none, he should have, and isn't setting a good example; if his wife sings in the choir, she is presuming; if she doesn't, she isn't interested in her husband's work. If a preacher reads from notes, he's a bore; if he speaks extemporaneously, he's superficial. If he stays at home in his study, he doesn't mix enough with the people; if he is seen outdoors, he ought to be home getting up a good sermon. If he calls on some poor family, he's pretending benevolence; if he calls at the home of the rich, he's a snob. Whatever he does, he can never satisfy his church members.

Anonymous

There are three classes of clergy: Nimrods, ramrods and fishing rods.

English Proverb

See also Bishops; Call; Celibacy; Clergy, Criticism of; Hierarchy; Laity; Minister; Ministry; Ordination; Pastor; Preachers; Preaching; Priesthood, Priests; Psychiatrists; Psychoanalysis; Theologians; Vocation.

CLERGY, CRITICISM OF

Idol-priests, play-actors, jockeys, and prostitutes can inherit property: clergymen and monks alone lie under a legal disability, a disability enacted not by persecutors, but by Christian emperors. I do not complain of the law, but I grieve that we have deserved a statute so harsh.

ST. JEROME, The Avarice of Clergy and Religious, c. 370

Many wear God's clothes that know not their Master.

JOSEPH HALL, Meditations and Vows, 1606

That Minister whose Life is not the Model of his Doctrine, is a Babler rather than a Preacher; a Quack rather than a Physician of Value.

WILLIAM PENN, Some Fruits of Solitude, 1718

A minister of the Church of England who may be possessed of good sense and some

hopes of preferment will seldom give up such substantial advantages for the empty pleasure of improving society.

OLIVER GOLDSMITH, The Bee, November 19, 1759

Indolent clergymen, pleasure-loving clergymen, money-loving clergymen, praise-loving clergymen, preferment-seeking clergymen; these are the wretches that cause the order in general to be condemned. These are the pests of the Christian world, the grand nuisance of mankind, a stink in the nostrils of God.

JOHN WESLEY, Sermon, September 25, 1789

There is in the clergy of all the Christian denominations a time-serving, cringing, subservient morality, as wide from the spirit of the Gospel as it is from the intrepid assertion and vindication of truth.

JOHN QUINCY ADAMS, Diary, May 27, 1838

I entertain no doubt that the time will come when the world will tolerate a life of luxury among those who are charged with the cure of souls as little as it tolerates priestly government.

ADOLF VON HARNACK, What Is Christianity, 1901

One shudders to see the light of the church turned off, all except the stream of light pouring down upon the pastor as he prays.

E. STANLEY JONES, Victorious Living, 1936

Oh, that more ministers of religions might abandon their platitudes, cease to be prudent and become sincere, forsake their empty churches and sally forth like soldiers to justify themselves in valiant conflict beneath the darkening sky. Then indeed might the world come back to sanity, and poor, bemused and tortured humanity back to God.

A. J. CRONIN, Reader's Digest, April, 1939

The clergy are in a special way tempted to take to themselves the sacredness that belongs to the things that they represent.
JOHN C. BENNETT, *Toward World-Wide Christianity,* ed. O. F. Nolde, 1946

Men who serve God professionally are apt to regard Him as a private preserve.
MORRIS WEST, *The Shoes of the Fisherman,* 1963

The clergy, as a whole, do not think theologically about the church. They have no clear image of the new shape the church should take. They are, therefore, unsheltered victims of environmental pressures that force the church, increasingly, to conform to secular concepts rather than to more constraining, theological images of the church.
WILLIAM B. CATE, *Unity in Mid-Career,* 1963

There can be no genuine cooperation between laity and clergy as long as the clergy are trained to believe that their word is law, that they are never required to consult the laity, that their ideas and direction must in all instances be decisive in the Church.
DANIEL CALLAHAN, *The Mind of the Catholic Layman,* 1963

The Protestant clergy in America are in such bondage to their local Mammon that even the most earnest and dedicated among them are victims to its demoralizing effect.
GEDDES MACGREGOR, *The Hemlock and the Cross,* 1963

See also Clergy.

CLERICALISM

To say that the Church has a mission in the temporal order is not to defend what is called "clericalism." It is simply to say that the virtualities of Christian faith are not exhausted by personal piety; they demand an attack on organized injustice in all its forms.
JOHN COURTNEY MURRAY, *Address,* American Academy of Political and Social Science, *Annals of,* March, 1948

What I call clericalism is the utilization of a church, a faith, and the discipline of the faithful for political ends.
R. L. BRUCKERGER, *One Sky to Share,* 1951

See also Priesthood, Priests.

COERCION

Let there be no compulsion in religion.
Koran, c. 625 A.D.

No Christian shall compel . . . Jews to accept baptism.
POPE INNOCENT III, *Epistle,* 1199

It is contrary to the Christian religion that any man, without willing it, and in spite of his absolute opposition, should be forced to become and remain a Christian.
POPE INNOCENT IV to Archbishop of Arles, *Decretals,* lib. III, c. 1250

Since belief or unbelief is a matter of everyone's conscience . . . the secular power should be content to attend to its own affairs, and permit men to believe one thing or another as they are able and willing, and constrain no one by force.
MARTIN LUTHER, *On Secular Authority,* 1522

No one is to be compelled to profess the faith, but no one must be allowed to injure it. . . . Even unbelievers should be forced to obey the Ten Commandments, attend church, and outwardly conform.
MARTIN LUTHER, *Letter to J. Metsch,* August 26, 1529

We neither can nor should force anyone into the faith.
MARTIN LUTHER, *Preface, Shorter Catechism,* 1531

We need only ask those who force consciences, "Would you like to have yours forced?" and immediately their own consciences, which are worth more than a thousand witnesses, will convict and make them dumb.

SEBASTIAN CASTELLIO (1513–1563), *Counsel to France in Her Distress*

Kings and bishops cannot command the wind, so they cannot command faith; and as the wind bloweth where it listeth, so it is [with] every man that is born of the Spirit.

LEONARD BUSHER, *Religious Peace*, 1614

No human power can force the impenetrable intrenchments of liberty in the human heart. Force can never persuade men; it can only make them hypocrites.

FRANÇOIS FÉNELON (1651–1715), *Selections from*, ed. Fellen

The man who says to me, "Believe as I do, or God will damn you," will presently say, "Believe as I do, or I shall assassinate you."

VOLTAIRE, *Treatise on Toleration*, 1766

Compulsion in religion is distinguished peculiarly from compulsion in every other thing. I may grow rich by an art I am compelled to follow; I may recover health by medicines I am compelled to take against my own judgment; but I cannot be saved by a worship I disbelieve and abhor.

THOMAS JEFFERSON, *Notes on Religion*, 1776

That Religion, or the duty which we owe to our Creator, and the manner of discharging it, can be directed only by reason and conviction, not by force or violence.

JAMES MADISON, *Journal of the Virginia Convention*, 1776

Millions of innocent men, women and children, since the introduction of Christianity, have been burned, tortured, fined and imprisoned, yet we have not advanced one inch toward uniformity. What has been the effect of coercion? To make one half of the world fools and the other half hypocrites.

THOMAS JEFFERSON, *Notes on Virginia*, 1782

The Church is wont to take earnest heed that no one shall be forced to embrace the Catholic faith against his will, for, as St. Augustine wisely reminds us, "Man cannot believe otherwise than of his own free will."

POPE LEO XIII, *The Christian Constitution of States*, 1885

Every time in history that man has tried to turn crucified Truth into coercive truth he has betrayed the fundamental principle of Christ.

NICHOLAS BERDYAEV, *Dostoevsky*, 1934

The lash may force men to physical labor; it cannot force them to spiritual creativity.

SHOLEM ASCH, *What I Believe*, 1941

God's redemptive dealing with men is not coercive. Accordingly, human attempts by legal enactment or by pressure of social custom to coerce or to eliminate faith are violations of the fundamental ways of God with men.

World Council of Churches, 1961

Since by nature all men are equal in human dignity, it follows that no one may be coerced to perform interior acts. That is in the power of God alone, Who sees and judges the hidden designs of men's hearts.

POPE JOHN XXIII, *Pacem in Terris*, April, 1963

See also Belief; Believing; Church and State; Force; Freedom; Freedom, Religious; Freedom and God; Freedom of Thought and Speech; Nonviolence; Rights.

COHABITATION.
See SEXUAL INTERCOURSE

COLD WAR

The cold war is a war of faiths. How much faith do we possess? Do we still know that each man and woman, in all this tormented world, is sacred? Do we still know that our most malignant enemies are also children of God, and that the more we hate them the more we diminish ourselves?

> HERBERT AGAR, New York *Herald Tribune Book Review,* March 8, 1953

The world-wide engagement which we call "cold war" is in fact a struggle for the soul of man, although the adversary denies that man has a soul.

> HERBERT AGAR, New York *Herald Tribune Book Review,* March 8, 1953

COLLECTIVISM

Collectivism is based on organized atrophy of personal existence.

> MARTIN BUBER, *Between Man and Man,* 1947

A state which seeks to subordinate the citizen wholly to itself and merges the person into an impersonal mass, commits a collective murder.

> C. C. MARTINDALE, *The Catholic Bedside Book,* 1953

Today the danger of an ecclesiastical collectivism is hard upon us; not by the church overstepping her limits, but by the individual not being able to hold out and bear his responsibility any longer, and clinging onto the church's apron strings.

> KARL RAHNER, *Nature and Grace,* 1964

COLONIALISM

Just as an individual man may not pursue his own interest to the detriment of other men, so, on the international level, one state may not develop itself by restricting or oppressing other states.

> POPE JOHN XXIII, *Pacem in Terris,* April, 1963

COMBAT

Regarding alike pleasure and pain, gain and loss, victory and defeat, fight thou the battle. Thus sin will not stain thee.

> *Bhagavad-Gita,* c. 2nd century B.C.

See also Battle; Discord; War.

COMFORT

Whatsoever I can desire or imagine for my comfort: I look for it not here, but hereafter. For if I might alone have all the comforts of the world and enjoy all its delights: it is certain that they could not long endure.

> ST. THOMAS À KEMPIS, *Imitation of Christ,* 1441

Happy is the soul that heareth the Lord speaking within her; and receiveth from His mouth the word of comfort.

> THOMAS À KEMPIS, *Imitation of Christ,* 1441

The lust for comfort, that stealthy thing that enters the house as a guest, and then becomes a host, and then a master.

> KAHLIL GIBRAN, *The Prophet,* 1923

In a world devoted to comfort it is fitting to have a comfortable religion. As one woman said ecstatically to another, "We have the most up-to-date church in the country. We have inner springs in the pew cushions." Evidently more attention to inner spring than to the inner man.

> HALFORD E. LUCCOCK, *Living Without Gloves,* 1957

See also Consolation; Ease; Luxury; Worldliness.

COMMANDMENTS

Let not one kill any living being. Let not one take what is not given to him. Let not one speak falsely. Let not one drink intoxicating drinks. Let not one be unchaste.
> Buddha (563–483 B.C.), "Five Moral Rules," quoted in R. C. Dutt, *Civilization of India*

Without commandments, obliging us to live after a certain fashion, our existence is that of the "unemployed." This is the terrible spiritual situation in which the best youth of the world finds itself today. By dint of feeling itself free, exempt from restrictions, it feels itself empty.
> JOSÉ ORTEGA Y GASSET, *Revolt of the Masses*, 1930

The old formulas, which we still regard as holy commandments . . . become empty words because they no longer fit the trend of time.
> HENRY LANZ, *In Quest of Morals*, 1941

There is no set of laws, not even the Ten Commandments, which came directly from heaven in finished form and to which we must conform. . . . There is also no such thing as sin in the technical sense.
> WALTER DONALD KRING, Sermon, *New York Times*, December 3, 1962

See also Obedience.

COMMERCE. See TRADE

COMMITMENT

Commitment does not stop with contemplation. It seeks issue in work. For the God discovered thus is a God at work, reconciling the world to Himself.
> ROBERT L. CALHOUN, *God and the Common Life*, 1935

There can be no true knowledge of ultimate things, that is to say, of God and man, of duty and destiny, that is not born in a concern and perfected in a commitment.
> JOHN MACKAY, *A Preface to Christian Theology*, 1941

COMMON MAN

So far from regarding the Common Man as representative of man in his fallen condition, he seemed to me rather the only man who is not fallen, the true Messiah, or Son of Man.
> L. P. JACKS, *Confession of an Octogenarian*, 1942

COMMUNION

They who do not repent nor testify sorrow for their sins . . . are to be altogether forbidden the hope of communion and peace, if in sickness and peril they begin to entreat for it; because not repentance for sin, but the warning of impending death, compels them to ask.
> ST. CYPRIAN, *Epistle LV*, c. 250

With regard to the Lord's body, its virtue is communicated to all who partake of it, provided that they receive this bread with a clean mind and an innocent conscience.
> ORIGEN (185–254), *Commentary on St. Matthew*

It is good and profitable to communicate even daily, and to partake of the holy body and blood of Christ who clearly says, "He that eateth my flesh and drinketh my blood hath everlasting life."
> ST. BASIL (330–379), *Epistle XCIII ad Caesariam*

You come to our feast, you join our hymn of praise, you place yourself among the faithful, and yet you communicate not? "I am unworthy" some one replies. Then you are also unworthy to join our prayers.
> ST. JOHN CHRYSOSTOM, *Epistle ad. Eph. c.l. Hom. iii*, c. 388

The effect of our communion in the Body and Blood of Christ is that we are transformed into what we consume, and that He in Whom we have died and in Whom we have risen from the dead, lives and is manifested in every movement of our body and our spirit.

St. Leo (390?–461), *Sermon LXIII, Patrologia Latina*, Vol. 84

In Holy Communion, the perfect Christian so participates in the Interior Life of Jesus Christ and in His Spirit that he is not only associated with Christ but enters into unity of spirit with Him.

Timothée Brianson de Raynier (1595–1681), *L'Homme Interieur*

It is neither logical nor consistent to celebrate the Holy Communion as a Christian while disclaiming the significance of that rite as it must have been felt by Christ and His Disciples.

Paul Elmer More, *The Catholic Faith*, 1931

To conceive of the Holy Communion as simply a meal of remembrance is to break decisively with Christian thought about the sacraments from the time when we first came in contact with such thought.

J. K. Mozley, *The Gospel Sacraments*, 1933

The Christian makes his way to eternity from communion to communion. At each stage in the journey, Christ is waiting for him in order that he may renew his strength and take heart again.

François Mauriac, *The Eucharist*, 1944

Any follower of Christ is invited to commune with us. . . . The Methodist Church admits to the Sacrament of the Lord's Supper all followers of Christ who desire to partake with us of the symbols of the body and blood of our Lord and Saviour Jesus Christ.

C. C. Selecman, *The Methodist Primer*, 1953

Holy Communion . . . is the medicine which enables the enfeebled soul to look steadily at the divine light, to breathe deeply of the unfamiliar air.

Ronald A. Knox, *The Window in the Wall*, 1956

It is the assertion of the "beyond" *in the midst of our life*, the holy *in* the common. The Holy Communion is *the* point at which the common, the communal, becomes the carrier of the unconditional.

J. A. T. Robinson, *Honest to God*, 1963

See also Eucharist; Man and God; Mass, the; Prayer: Defined and Explained; Unity.

COMMUNION OF SAINTS

There always was, now is, and shall be to the end of time, a Church or an assembly of believers and a communion of saints, called and gathered from the world, who know and worship the true God in Christ our Saviour.

Henry Bullinger, *The Helvetic Confession*, 1536

No man is ever alone in that vast communion which is named the Catholic Church and the Communion of Saints.

Susan L. Emery, *The Inner Life of the Soul*, 1903

A community of spirit and of spiritual goods among the saints on earth, that is among all those who are incorporated by faith and love in the one Head, Christ. . . . Also the vital communion of these faithful Christians with all those souls who have passed out of the world in the love of Christ.

Karl Adam, *The Spirit of Catholicism*, 1924

This *Communion of Saints* is the bond and life of the Church's mystical body, and gives it its note of sanctity, independent of the imperfections and faults of some, or of most, of the members of the visible Church.

RAISSA MARITAIN, *We Have Been Friends Together*, 1942

Every believer is a saint in so far as he belongs to the communion of saints, the new reality which is holy in its foundation.

PAUL TILLICH, *Systematic Theology*, I, 1951

To be Catholic is to be in the midst of a vast chorus, to be joined in perpetual choir, to be linked and bonded and accompanied. This is the tremendous social doctrine called the Communion of Saints.

JOHN W. LYNCH, *Hourglass*, 1952

The Communion of Saints is a real supernatural union whereby we are, here on earth, already in a certain sense in heaven.

W. H. VANDER POL, *The Christian Dilemma*, 1952

See also Church: Its Membership; Mystical Body of Christ; Saints.

COMMUNISM

Communism . . . is absolutely contrary to the natural law itself, and, if once adopted, would utterly destroy the rights, property, and possessions of all men, and even society itself.

POPE PIUS IX, *Qui Pluribus*, 1846

The fatal plague which insinuates itself into the very marrow of human society only to bring about its ruin.

POPE LEO XIII, *Quod Apostolici Muneris*, 1878

The modern proletariat ranges himself on the side of Socialism, which, with the help of science, is dispersing the fog of religion and is liberating the workers from their faith in a life after death.

NIKOLAI LENIN, *Socialism and Religion*, 1905

Religion and communism are incompatible in theory no less than in practice.

N. BUKHARIN and PREOBRAJENSKY, *The ABC of Communism*, 1923

The Communist lives by a faith in a power, which he calls in his own jargon "the process of history." . . . This simply means that Communism, whatever its exponents may say, has recovered that essential core of a real belief in God, which organized Christianity has in our day largely lost.

JOHN MACMURRAY, *Creative Society*, 1935

Communism strips man of his liberty, robs human personality of all its dignity, and removes all the moral restraints that check the eruptions of blind impulse.

POPE PIUS XI, *Atheistic Communism*, 1937

It is a system full of errors and sophisms. It is in opposition both to reason and to divine Revelation. It subverts the social order, because it means the destruction of its foundations; because it ignores the true origin and purpose of the state; because it denies the rights, dignity and liberty of human personality.

POPE PIUS XI, *Atheistic Communism*, 1937

A Christian heresy—the ultimate and altogether radical Christian heresy. . . . Collective revolution renewing history and society only for the life here—below.

JACQUES MARITAIN, *The Person and the Common Good*, 1947

Communism offers a means of integration to men whose souls and social structures are obviously disintegrating, who have lost their absolutes and hence are lonely and. afraid.

W. R. FORRESTER, *Christian Vocation*, 1951

Communism is an evil, but in the Providence of God, it may be the fertilizer of a new civilization, the death that is spread over the world in the winter of its discontent to prepare the dead earth to tell its secrets in flowers in the new springtime of the spirit.

FULTON J. SHEEN, *The Woman,* 1951

We face a fanatical foe who has become the high priest of a new religion. No middle-class virtue of respectability can steel us to this crisis. Only the strong God of religion, the real God, God personal to me, God intelligently believed in, prayed to and adored on bended knee, can give us wisdom commensurate with our strength.

LAURENCE J. MCGINELY, *Address,* March 25, 1952

Communism's success, so far as it has gone, looks like a portent of things to come. What it does tell us is that the present encounter between the world and the West is now moving off the technological plane onto the spiritual plane.

ARNOLD J. TOYNBEE, *The World and the West,* 1953

One of the attractions of communism is that . . . the will and conscience are reposed in a depository of granite solidity under a guardianship that resolves all ethical and moral problems.

MARQUIS W. CHILDS and DOUGLASS CATER, *Ethics in a Business Society,* 1954

Communism makes the disastrous mistake of believing that sin is the result of social organization. . . . Sin being the result of the social system, will disappear when the perfect social system is built.

WILLIAM HORDERN, *Christianity, Communism and History,* 1954

The old religion which communism has revived is the worship of collective human power.

ARNOLD J. TOYNBEE, *New York Times Magazine,* December 26, 1954

The adversity by which the Western world has been overtaken through the rise of militant communism will have been a blessing in transparent disguise if it compels us to regain a foothold on spiritual bedrock.

ARNOLD J. TOYNBEE, *New York Times Magazine,* December 26, 1954

In this society, there can be no room for love, or for friendship; for this would be static, it would mean accepting the opiate, it would be the end of dynamic contradiction—the end of process, which is death.

JOSEPH G. DAWSON, *Springs of Morality,* ed. J. M. Todd, 1956

The true price that must be paid for it is the unending rejection of God, because only God . . . could be greater than, and more important than, the group, the state, or the physical universe.

JOSEPH G. DAWSON, *Springs of Morality,* ed. J. M. Todd, 1956

Communism parallels secularism. Indeed it is the full-blown fruit of secularism. . . . There is thus an inherent affinity between secularism and Communism; their measures of value are intrinsically the same.

LESTER DE KOSTER, *Communism and Christian Faith,* 1956

The real "opium of the people," distracting men's minds from their essential task, is the communist myth of an earthly paradise.

JEAN DANIELOU, *The Lord of History,* 1958

No one would be bothered with the Communist conspiracy if its dynamism were not . . . an apostasy from civilization.

JOHN COURTNEY MURRAY, *We Hold These Truths,* 1960

It is a mistake to think of Communism as a vast undifferentiated and unchanging blot of evil to which the only response that is possible is one of undying hostility.

JOHN C. BENNETT, *Nuclear Weapons and the Conflict of Conscience*, 1962

See also Anti-God Totalitarians; Atheism; Blasphemy; Capitalism; Christianity; Civilization and Christianity; Dictatorship; Freedom; Government; Government and God; Government and Religion; Irreligion; Marxism; Religion, Caustic Comments about; Socialism; Soviet Russia; State, the.

COMMUNISM AND CHRISTIANITY

During the larger part of its history the Christian Church regarded communism as the only ideal life.

WALTER RAUSCHENBUSCH, *Christianity and the Social Crisis*, 1907

Christian love, which applies to all, even to one's enemies, is the worst adversary of Communism.

N. BUKHARIN, *Pravda*, March 30, 1934

Communism is intrinsically wrong, and no one who would save Christian civilization may collaborate with it in any undertaking whatsoever.

POPE PIUS XI, *Atheistic Communism*, 1937

It can surprise no one that the Communist fallacy should be spreading in a world already to a large extent de-Christianized.

POPE PIUS XI, *Atheistic Communism*, 1937

A Christian may, and in my opinion must, be a Socialist, but he can hardly be a Communist since he cannot accept Communism's pretense to being a complete and all-embracing world-view.

NICHOLAS BERDYAEV, *Religion in Life*, VIII, 1938

Christians should recognize with contrition that many churches are involved in the forms of economic injustice and racial discrimination which have created the conditions favorable to the growth of communism.

Report, Amsterdam Assembly of the World Council of Churches, 1948

Belief in Communism as an absolute movement of redemption in history, in the Communist society as a substitute for God, is . . . false from the Christian point of view and incompatible with the Christian's understanding of man's dependence upon God.

JOHN C. BENNETT, *Christianity and Communism*, 1948

What is necessary is the christianization and spiritualization of Communism, at the core of which we must know how to discern the positive elements of social justice.

NICHOLAS BERDYAEV, *Toward a New Epoch*, 1949

It sometimes seems that the inheritors of the zeal of the early Christians are not Catholics but Communists.

JAMES M. GILLIS, *This Our Day*, 1949

The faithful who profess the materialist and anti-Christian doctrine of the communists, and especially those who defend and propagate them, incur *ipso facto*, as apostates from the Catholic faith, excommunication specially reserved to the Holy See.

Decree of Supreme Congregation of the Holy Office, of the Roman Catholic Church, July 2, 1949

The Christian opposition to Russia and Communism must not be identified with the capitalistic opposition which now generates so much emotion in the United States.

JOHN C. BENNETT, *Perspectives on a Troubled Decade*, ed. Bryson, Finkle-stein and MacIver, 1950

The struggle against the Gospel and Christian legend must be conducted ruthlessly and with all the means at our disposal.

Radio Leningrad, Russia, August 27, 1950

It is wise that the Church leaders of Protestantism, while regarding with open eyes the spiritual dangers inherent in Communism, should refuse to be stampeded into a crusade against Communism as a political system.

W. R. FORRESTER, *Christian Vocation*, 1951

The Christian detects in the claim of the Communist party to be the sole judge of human existence another dangerous illusion and pretension. . . . A Chinese coolie has succinctly stated it in the remark: "God is my Creator and Judge, and, what is more, He is the Judge of Mao Tzetung."

C. T. LEBER, *World Faith in Action*, 1951

From New Testament times onward Christian faith has repeatedly given birth to communities which have practiced on a small and voluntary scale what Marx urged for vast economies.

ROGER L. SHINN, *Christianity and the Problem of History*, 1953

Men use the conflict in faith between Christianity and communism to give a Christian sanction to the most conservative interpretation of the American way of life.

JOHN C. BENNETT, *Christian Century*, January 6, 1954

The battle for the soul of the world . . . remains as one between the dogmatists, that is, between the Marxists and the Christians, both of whom have a deity, a beatific vision, a theory of revolution, a prophet, a body of doctrine, a missionary purpose, a moral code.

VICTOR J. GIESE, *The Apostolic Itch*, 1954

The want, injustice and oppression which Communism uses as steppingstones to power are the results of the failure of Christians to be Christians.

WILLIAM HORDERN, *Christianity, Communism and History*, 1954

In the modern struggle with Communism it is imperative that Christians weigh the strength of Communism as a religious alternative to Christianity. Otherwise we may go into battle unprepared.

WILLIAM HORDERN, *Christianity, Communism and History*, 1954

What we are fighting, as we oppose the march of Communism, is partly the fruit of past Christian selfishness.

LESTER DE KOSTER, *Communism and Christian Faith*, 1956

The most dangerous character of Communism is in its being a quasi-religion. . . . If religion is that interest or activity of man that places upon them a demand of ultimate commitment, then Communism qualifies. . . . It competes with any and all other ultimate loyalties, or religions for men's very souls.

MERRIMON CUNNINGHAM, ed. *Christianity and Communism*, 1958

See also Anti-God Totalitarians; Atheism; Civilization and Christianity; Communism; Communist Morality; Dictatorship; Government and God; Government and Religion; Irreligion; Marxism; Soviet Russia.

COMMUNIST MORALITY

We deny all morality taken from superhuman or non-class conceptions. We say that this is a deception, a swindle, a befogging of the minds of the workers and peasants in the interests of the landlords and capitalists.

NIKOLAI LENIN, *Speech*, October 2, 1920

We deny all morality borrowed from concepts exterior to class or even to humanity.

Our morality is entirely subordinated to the interests of the proletariat and the needs of the class struggle.

NIKOLAI LENIN, *Address*, Third All-Russian Congress of Communist Youth, 1920

All moral considerations in Communism are resolved down to a question of whether or not a certain action will help or hinder the achievement of the Marxian goal.

WILLIAM HORDERN, *Christianity, Communism and History*, 1954

COMMUNITY

We were born to unite with our fellow-men, and to join in community with the human race.

CICERO, *De Finibus*, c. 50 B.C.

Prayers for the community take precedence over those for ourselves. . . . and he who sets its claim above his private interests is especially acceptable to God.

FLAVIUS JOSEPHUS, *Against Apion*, c. 93 A.D.

Come together in common, one and all without exception in charity, in one faith and in one Jesus Christ, Who is of the race of David according to the flesh, the son of man and the Son of God, so that with undivided mind you may obey the bishop and the priests, and break one Bread which is the medicine of immortality and the antidote against death, enabling us to live for ever in Jesus Christ.

ST. IGNATIUS OF ANTIOCH, *To the Ephesians*, c. 109

Do not try to persuade yourselves that you can do anything good on your own; on the contrary, do all in common; one prayer, one petition, one mind, one hope in the unity of love and in innocent joy—this is Jesus Christ than whom there is nothing higher.

ST. IGNATIUS OF ANTIOCH, *Letter to the Magnesians*, c. 109

We who are united in heart and soul have no hesitation in sharing things. Among us all things are common except wives.

TERTULLIAN, *The Christian's Defense*, c. 215

For whence should the City of God originally begin or progressively develop or ultimately attain its end unless the life of the saints were a social one?

ST. AUGUSTINE, *The City of God*, xix, 426

The Gospel of Christ knows no religion but social, no holiness but social holiness.

JOHN WESLEY (1703–1791), *Preface, Methodist Hymn Book*

Not through imitating nor yet through loving any mere individual human being can we be saved, but only through loyalty to the "Beloved Community."

JOSIAH ROYCE, *The Problem of Christianity*, I, 1908

They all knelt together and suddenly—not a barrier of any kind remained, not a sundering distinction in the whole throng; but every life flamed into the other, and all flamed into the one Life and were hushed in ineffable peace.

ZEPHRINE HUMPHREY, *The Edge of the Woods and Other Papers*, 1913

It is one of the most beautiful features of a real and living corporate religion, that within it ordinary people at all levels help each other to be a little more supernatural than each would have been alone.

EVELYN UNDERHILL, *The Life of the Spirit and the Life of Today*, 1923

Goodness and devotion are more easily caught than taught; by association in groups, holy and strong souls.

EVELYN UNDERHILL, *The Life of the Spirit and the Life of Today*, 1923

Man finds his true self in the Church alone; not in the helplessness of spiritual isolation but in the strength of his communion with his brothers and with his Savior.

ALEXANDER YELCHANINOV (1881–1934), *Fragments of a Diary*

Our community with one another consists solely in what our Christ has done to both of us.

DIETRICH BONHOEFFER, *Life Together*, 1938

Because a man has to save his own soul, that does not destroy the fact that he must live in a commonwealth of souls.

WILLIAM L. SULLIVAN, *Under Orders*, 1944

The one really adequate instrument for learning about God is the whole Christian community, waiting for Him together.

C. S. LEWIS, *Beyond Personality*, 1945

Community is the being no longer side by side, but with one another.

MARTIN BUBER, *Between Man and Man*, 1947

The real beginning of a community is when its members have a common relation to the centre overriding all other relations.

MARTIN BUBER, *Paths in Utopia*, 1950

We are not isolated souls, singular, lonely, called and engaged in a solitary effort. We are members of a great Company, and whether we think it or not, we pray in Company.

JOHN W. LYNCH, *Hourglass*, 1952

A community of worship and service is the goal to which the Christian is committed, and to treat the contemplative and the practical as though they were alternatives . . . is to imperil both.

CHARLES E. RAVEN, *Theological Basis of Christian Pacifism*, 1952

Entirely by yourself as an individual you can go to hell, but alone you cannot go to heaven, for to go to heaven we need what one may call the natural grace of the mutual dependence on each other here on earth.

FRANCIS DEVAS, *The Law of Love*, ed. by Caraman, 1955

People are coming to church not simply to partake of the sacred but to partake of sacred community.

MILTON J. ROSENBERG, *Pastoral Psychology*, June, 1957

We hunger for a kind of group association in which, through being ourselves, we may get to something greater than ourselves. We long to touch the transcendent, and, furthermore, to do it in the company of others who, by sharing our experiences, verify and confirm them.

MILTON J. ROSENBERG, *Pastoral Psychology*, June 1957

In the Old Testament it is taken for granted that *man lives in a community*.

LUDWIG KÖHLER, *Old Testament Theology*, 1957

See also Aspiration; Brotherhood; Charity; Christian Life; Christianity; Christians; Church, Criticism of; Church, Definitions of; Church: Its Work; Communion of Saints; Congregation; Contemplation; Fellowship; Friendship; Jesus Christ and Christianity; Loneliness; Love, Human; Love of Mankind; Meeting; Neighbor; Prayer; Protestantism; Religion: Its Nature and Function; Social Faith; Society; Solitude; Tolerance; Unity.

COMPARATIVE RELIGION

The charm of study is in finding the agreements, the identities, in all religions of men.

RALPH WALDO EMERSON, *Speech*, May 28, 1869

A comparison of Christianity with Buddhism will be a great help to distinguish in both religions the essential from the accidental, the eternal from the transient, the truth from the allegory in which it has found its symbolic expression.

> PAUL CARUS, *The Gospel of the Buddha,* 1894

The professor of comparative religion is only comparatively religious.

> J. V. L. CASSERLEY, *Retreat from Christianity in the Modern World,* 1952

The Science of Comparative Religion so-called has proved thus far a very doubtful quantity. Usually it is only comparative theology or comparative ethics. . . . Very seldom does it discover a real basis of comparison.

> WILLIAM R. VAN BUSKIRK, *Saviors of Mankind,* 1929

A study of comparative religion gives insight into the values of the various faiths, values which transcend their differing symbols and creeds and in transcending penetrate to the depths of the spiritual consciousness where the symbols and formulas shrink into insignificance.

> SARVEPALLI RADHAKRISHNAN in *The Philosophy of Radhakrishnan,* ed. by P. A. Schlipp, 1952

COMPASSION

For though our Saviour's Passion is over, his Compassion is not.

> WILLIAM PENN, *Some Fruits of Solitude,* 1693

Who can look down upon the grave of even an enemy, and not feel a compunctious throb, that he should ever have warred with the poor handful of earth that lies mouldering before him.

> WASHINGTON IRVING, *The Sketch-Book,* 1820

Compassion is as natural as respiration.

> JOSEPH DE MAISTRE, *Les Soirées de Saint-Petersbourg,* 1821

The hidden and awful Wisdom which apportions the destinies of mankind is pleased so to humiliate and cast down the tender, good and wise; and to set up the selfish, the foolish, or the wicked. Oh, be humble, my brother, in your prosperity! Be gentle with those who are less lucky, if not more deserving.

> W. M. THACKERAY, *Vanity Fair,* ch. 57, 1848

If we could read the secret history of our enemies, we should find in each man's life sorrow and suffering enough to disarm all hostility.

> HENRY WADSWORTH LONGFELLOW, *Driftwood,* 1861

Compassion is the chief law of human existence.

> FEODOR DOSTOEVSKY, *The Idiot,* 1869

What is more harmful than any vice? Active compassion for all unsuccessful and weak ones—Christianity.

> FRIEDRICH NIETZSCHE, *The Anti-Christians,* 1867

Our lack of compassion, our ruthlessness towards other men, is an impenetrable curtain between ourselves and God.

> ALEXANDER YELCHANINOV (1881–1934), *Fragments of a Diary*

The existence of compassion in Man proves the existence of compassion in God.

> CHRISTOPHER HOLLIS, *The Noble Castle,* 1941

Compassion is not just an exhibition of pity; it is a virtue in the strict sense of being a habit. Compassion is suffering: constant willingness to share in the suffering of others.

> HUBERT VAN ZELLER, *Approach to Calvary,* 1961

See also Beggars; Brotherhood; Charity; Fellowship; Forgiveness; Kindness; Mercy;

Neighbor; Penitence; Pity; Poor, the; Punishment; Sinners; Sympathy.

COMPETITION

Every sect is a moral check on its neighbor. Competition is as wholesome in religion as in commerce.

W. S. LANDOR, *Imaginary Conversations,* 1824

Just as the unity of human society cannot be built upon class warfare, so the proper ordering of economic affairs cannot be left to free competition alone.

POPE PIUS XI, *Quadragesimo Anno,* 1931

The principle of competition appears to be nothing more than a partially conventionalized embodiment of primeval selfishness . . . the supremacy of the motive of self-interest. . . . The Christian conscience can be satisfied with nothing less than the complete substitution of motives of mutual helpfulness and goodwill for the motive of private gain.

Social Creed, Federal Council of Churches of Christ in America, 1932

The spiritual by-products of competition are far from the spirit of Christ; insincerity, suspicion, hatred, legalism, ruthless denial of the supreme worth of personality.

JEROME DAVIS, *Harper's Magazine,* January, 1937

COMPLACENCY

The Good Pagan and the Christian may often act in the same way, make the same moral judgments; they may both be virtuous, honorable and just, they may both be charitable and unselfish, they may be equally so, but the Pagan is satisfied, the Christian, not at all.

ROSALIND MURRAY, *The Good Pagan's Failure,* 1939

I am not opposed to the knowledge the behavioral sciences have to offer. I am not supercilious about the uses of pragmatism. Our problem is not that new learning was developed; our problem is that these new insights and discoveries have not been integrated with the Christian intellectual tradition.

JOHN COGLEY, *Commonweal,* March, 1960

See also Apathy; Conformity; Inaction; Nonconformity; Smugness; Spiritual Lethargy.

COMPLAINTS

Since we fulfil none of God's commands, why do we complain about God, who has more reason to complain about all of us? What is our reason for saying in sorrow that God does not heed us, when we ourselves do not heed Him? What is our reason for muttering that God does not look down towards earth, when we ourselves do not look up towards Heaven?

SALVIANUS, *The Governance of God,* 5th century A.D.

COMPULSION. See COERCION

COMTE, AUGUSTE

Auguste Comte, proponent of the "religion of humanity," finds disciples today in the advocates of a religion without a Personal God, a liturgy with phrases of a high thought instead of prayer, a program of service to mankind rather than of "otherworldliness."

LOUIS I. NEWMAN, *Religion Today,* Ed. A. L. Swift, 1933

See also Positivism.

CONCEIT

Conceit lies in thinking you want nothing.
EPICTETUS, *Moral Discourses,* c. 110 A.D.

I am glad I am guilty of some sins, else I might be guilty of one of the greatest sins of all—conceit.

M. HURWITZ, *Imre Noam,* 1877

Imagine a conceited boy trying to discover he is conceited, when his conceit makes him sure he is not conceited.

DAVID SEABURY, *What Makes Us Seem So Queer?,* 1934

See also Egoism; Pride; Self-Praise; Vainglory; Vanity.

CONCORD

Let us put on concord in meekness of spirit and in self-control, keeping ourselves far from all gossip and evil-speaking, being justified by works and not words.

ST. CLEMENT OF ROME, *Epistle to the Corinthians,* c. 100

Where there is concord there is God.

Montenegrin Proverb

See also Discord; Peace; Religious Conflict.

CONDEMNATION

If Judas was a traitor, that is no condemnation of the apostolate, but simply of his own life.

ST. JOHN CHRYSOSTOM (347–407), In *I Cor. Homil. IV*

No man is condemned for anything he has done; he is condemned for continuing to do wrong.

GEORGE MACDONALD, *Unspoken Sermons,* 3rd Series, 1887

See also Damnation; Punishment.

CONDUCT

Live with men as if God saw you; converse with God as if men heard you.

SENECA, *Epistulae Morales ad Lucilium,* c. 63 A.D.

Christian conduct is the operation of the rational soul in accordance with a correct judgment and aspiration after the truth, which attains its destined end through the body, the soul's consort and ally.

ST. CLEMENT OF ALEXANDRIA, *The Instructor,* ch. 13, c. 220

The true guide of our conduct is no outward authority, but the voice of God, who comes down to dwell in our souls, who knows all our thoughts.

J. E. E. DALBERG-ACTON (Lord Acton), *Address,* 1877

The highest conduct is that which conduces to the greatest length, breadth, and completeness of life.

HERBERT SPENCER, *Principles of Ethics,* 1893

If you deny that any principles of conduct at all are common to and admitted by all men who try to behave reasonably—well, I don't see how you can have any ethics or any ethical background for law.

FREDERICK POLLOCK, *Holmes-Pollock Letters,* 1874–1932

In modern civilization, the theoretical rules of conduct are based upon the remains of Christian morals. No one obeys them. Modern man has rejected all discipline of his appetites.

ALEXIS CARREL, *Man, the Unknown,* 1935

See also Behavior; Christian Life; Commitment; Conformity; Conscience; Deeds; Duties; Ethics; Humility; Hypocrisy; Inaction; Individual Responsibility; Judgment, God's; Moral Code; Morality; Natural Law; Practice; Religion: Its Nature and Function; Reward; Virtue.

CONFESSION

In proportion as a man who has done wrong, confesses it, even so far he is freed from guilt, as a snake from its slough.

Code of Manu, between 1200 and 500 B.C.

If we have sinned against the man who loves us, have ever wronged a brother, friend or comrade, the neighbor ever with us or a stranger, O Varuna, remove from us the trespass. . . . If we have done wrong unwittingly or sinned of purpose, cast all these sins away like loosened fetters, and Varuna, let us be thine beloved.
Rig-Veda, between 1000 and 600 B.C.

But if he be not a professor of the Religion of Mazda, not one who has been taught in it, then his sin is taken from him if he makes confession of the Religion of Mazda and resolves never to commit again such forbidden deeds.
Vendidad, 6th century B.C.

To confess a fault freely is the next thing to being innocent of it.
PUBLILIUS SYRUS, *Setentiae,* c. 50 B.C.

This act . . . whereby we confess our sin to the Lord, not indeed as if He were ignorant of it, but inasmuch as by confession satisfaction is settled, of confession repentance is born, by repentance God is appeased.
TERTULLIAN, *On Repentance,* c. 200 A.D.

While it abases the man, it raises him; while it covers him with squalor, it renders him more clean, while it accuses, it excuses; while it condemns, it absolves.
TERTULLIAN, *On Repentance,* c. 200 A.D.

To utter forth our sin, merits the remission of sin.
ORIGEN (185–254), *Hom. iii on Leviticus*

He who confesses his sins freely receives pardon from the priest by virtue of the grace of Christ.
ST. ATHANASIUS, *Contra Novatiani,* c. 350

To confess one's sins is to honor the Holy One.
JOSHUA B. LEVI, *Talmud: Sanhedrin,* c. 500

Confession heals, confession justifies, confession grants pardon of sin, all hope consists in confession, in confession there is a chance for mercy.
ST. ISIDORE OF SEVILLE (560–636), *Dialogue Between Erring Soul and Reason*

They who after they have done a base deed or committed a wrong against themselves, remember God, and implore forgiveness of their sins—and not persevere in what they have wittingly done amiss; as for these! Pardon from the Lord shall be their recompense.
Koran, 7th century A.D.

With regard to the precepts of the Torah, . . . if a person transgresses any of them, either wilfully or in error, and repents and turns away from his sin, he is under a duty to confess before God. . . . this means confess in *words.*
MAIMONIDES (1135–1204), *Repentance*

Privy confession made to priests . . . is not needful, but brought in late by the Fiend.
JOHN WYCLIF (c. 1320–1384), *English Works*

Private confession . . . is wholly commendable, useful and indeed necessary. I would not have it cease, but rather I rejoice that it exists in the Church of Christ, for it is the one and only remedy for troubled consciences.
MARTIN LUTHER, *The Babylonian Captivity,* 1520

Confession consists of two parts: first, to confess our sins, and secondly, to receive the absolution or forgiveness by the confessor, as from God Himself.
MARTIN LUTHER, *Luther's Catechism,* 1530

Auricular confession is expedient and necessary to be retained and continued, used and frequented in the Church of God.
Six Articles, Statutes of the Realm, HENRY VIII, 1539

A generous and free-minded confession doth disable a reproach and disarm an injury.

MICHEL DE MONTAIGNE, *Essays,* 1588

It is an abuse to confess any kind of sin, whether mortal or venial, without a will to be delivered from it, since confession was instituted for no other end.

ST. FRANCIS OF SALES, *Introduction to the Devout Life,* 1609

The Church of God, in all ages, hath commended, and, in most ages, enjoined, that we confess our sins, and discover the state and condition of our souls to such a person as we or our superiors may judge fit to help us.

JEREMY TAYLOR, *Holy Living,* 1650

We confess our little faults only to persuade others that we have no great ones.

LA ROCHEFOUCAULD, *Maxims,* 1665

Not God, but you, the maker of the confession, get to know something by your act of confession. Much that you are able to keep hidden in the dark, you first get to know by your opening it to the knowledge of the all-knowing.

SÖREN KIERKEGAARD, *Purity of Heart,* 1846

The Catholic practice of confession and absolution is in one of its aspects little more than a systematic method of keeping healthy-mindedness on top.

WILLIAM JAMES, *Varieties of Religious Experience,* 1902

For him who confesses, shams are over and realities have begun; he has exteriorized rottenness . . . he lives at least on a basis of veracity.

WILLIAM JAMES, *Varieties of Religious Experience,* 1902

The confessional, which Protestantism throws out the door, is coming back through the window in utterly new forms, to be sure, with new methods and with an entirely new intellectual explanation, appropriate to the Protestant churches but motivated by a real determination to help meet the inward problems of individuals.

HARRY EMERSON FOSDICK, *Literary Digest,* December 17, 1927

I often wonder if God ever speaks to us so intimately as when we are on our knees, speaking to Him about ourselves—in that Divine attitude of self-accusation—when God is speaking through us and to us.

VINCENT MCNABB, *God's Way of Mercy,* 1928

Protestantism needs to develop a better method of dealing with personal guilt than public confession of general sinfulness. There is a craving to particularize the guilt to get definitely rid of the burden, and this impulse at present is adequately recognized only by the Roman Catholic Confession.

E. R. GROVES and P. BLANCHARD, *Mental Hygiene,* 1930

If we are to climb the heights of spiritual creativity, we must confess our sins and bring forth fruit worthy of repentance.

KIRBY PAGE, *Living Creatively,* 1932

The great danger is that in the confession of any collective sin, one shall confess the sins of others and forget our own.

GEORGIA HARKNESS, *The Resources of Religion,* 1936

Promiscuous confession to promiscuous gatherings is not healthy. There are some things which God deals with in His private office.

E. STANLEY JONES, *Victorious Living,* 1936

Religious response to revelation is made quite as much in a confession of sin as in a confession of faith.

H. RICHARD NIEBUHR, *The Meaning of Revelation,* 1941

The purpose of sacramental Confession is atonement—at-one-ment—with God.
CARYLL HOUSELANDER, *Guilt,* 1941

Our confession has to bring to light the unknown, the unconscious darkness, and the undeveloped creativity of our deeper layers.
FRITZ KUNKEL, *In Search of Maturity,* 1943

Confession by its very nature serves to reinforce the inner guilt feelings.
JOSHUA LOTH LIEBMAN, *Peace of Mind,* 1946

Atonement, rather than growth, is the aim of the religious confessional, whereas psychotherapy does not require that you feel sorry for your sins so long as you outgrow them!
JOSHUA LOTH LIEBMAN, *Peace of Mind,* 1946

Jesus obliged us to confess our sins for our own sake rather than for His. . . . Confession is simply a Hospital of Souls, where the Good Samaritan, through the instrumentality of the priest, goes about binding up wounds and pouring in oil and wine; a hospital where the Divine Physician displays His healing art.
ALFRED WILSON, *Pardon and Peace,* 1947

The confessional in the humblest Catholic Church in the world is a more efficacious agency for a complete catharsis than the office of any psychoanalyst.
JOHN A. O'BRIEN, *Psychiatry and Confession,* 1948

If sin were merely a symptom of mental disease, the psychiatric clinic could and should be substituted for the confessional. Sacramental absolution is not intended to be a cure for disease. . . . The Sacrament of penance is primarily a sacrament of forgiveness. Consequently it presumes responsibility for sin and has no meaning outside of a context of responsibility.
JOHN R. CONNERY, *America,* January 23, 1960

See also Atonement; Conscience; Forgiveness; Grace; Justification; Penitence; Psychiatry; Psychoanalysis; Repentance; Sacraments; Sin.

CONFIDENCE

It is necessary to suppose that every good Christian is more ready to put a good interpretation on another's statement than to condemn it as false.
ST. IGNATIUS LOYOLA, *Spiritual Exercises,* 1541

Amid the greatest difficulties of my Administration, when I could not see any other resort, I would place my whole reliance in God, knowing that all would go well, and that he would decide for the right.
ABRAHAM LINCOLN, to a group of visitors in 1863

A little boy playing on the deck of a ship in a mighty storm was asked by a passenger if he wasn't afraid. "No, I'm not afraid. My father is the captain of the ship."
RUFUS M. JONES, *The Radiant Life,* 1944

How can a man be convinced of his own incompetency when he prays not alone but in the great Crowding that is the Church.
JOHN W. LYNCH, *Hourglass,* 1952

See also Despair; Faith; Fear; Hope; Prayer; Providence; Security; Self-Reliance; Trust.

CONFIRMATION

It is the custom of the churches for the Bishops to journey to those who have been baptized by priests and deacons at a distance from the greater cities, and to impose hands upon them to invoke the Holy Spirit.

ST. JEROME, *Adv. Lucifer*, 340

See also Sacraments.

CONFLICT

Never one fold and one shepherd, never one uniform culture for all mankind, never universal nobleness. Our virtue and our happiness can only flourish amid an active conflict with wrong.

WINWOOD READE, *The Martyrdom of Man*, 1872

The conflict of the future is between the absolute who is the God-man and the absolute which is the man-God; the God who became man and the man who makes himself God; between brothers in Christ and comrades in anti-Christ.

FULTON J. SHEEN, Radio Sermon, *Time*, February 3, 1947

See also Religious Conflicts; Spiritual Conflicts; Truths, Conflict of.

CONFORMITY

I fear yet this iron yoke of outward conformity hath left a slavish print upon our necks. . . . We do not see that while we still affect by all means a rigid external formality, we may as soon fall again into a gross conforming stupidity . . . which is more to the sudden degeneration of a Church than many . . . petty schisms.

JOHN MILTON, *Areopagitica*, 1644

It is reasonable to concur where Conscience does not forbid compliance; for Conformity is at least a Civic Virtue. . . . it is a Weakness in Religion and Government where it is carried to Things of an Indifferent Nature, since . . . Liberty is always the Price of it.

WILLIAM PENN, *Some Fruits of Solitude*, 1693

Whoso would be a man, must be a nonconformist.

RALPH WALDO EMERSON, *Self-Reliance*, 1841

He who lets the world, or his own portion of it, choose his plan of life for him has no need for any other faculty than the ape-like one of imitations.

JOHN STUART MILL, *On Liberty*, 1859

For us one of the saddest days in life is the day we allow the herd-fear to conquer the highest judgments and instincts of the soul.

E. STANLEY JONES, *Victorious Living*, 1936

The pseudo-conscience . . . demands not obedience to the inner law of our being, but conformity to super-imposed convention.

FRANCIS G. WICKES, *The Creative Process*, 1948

The casuistical resources of the mind determined to conform to social patterns rather than to obey God are well-nigh inexhaustible.

GEORGE H. DUNNE, *The Commonweal Reader*, ed. E. S. Skillin, 1950

Church of Christ—Stop this endeavor to harmonize yourself with modern culture and customs as though they were a standard and criterion. Rather, come out from among them. Only an independent standing ground from which to challenge modern culture can save either it or you.

HARRY EMERSON FOSDICK, *Riverside Sermons*, 1958

Life in the green pastures of church growth reveals the extent of religious conformity to secular ideals, patterns, and mores.

MARTIN E. MARTY, *The New Shape of American Religion*, 1958

CONGREGATION

See also Apathy; Authority; Complacency; Conduct; Criticism; Custom; Expediency; Nonconformity; Opinions.

CONGREGATION

The softness and peace, the benignant humanity that hovers over our assembly when it sits in the morning service in church, the cold gentleness of the women, the quietude of the men.

RALPH WALDO EMERSON, *The Heart of Emerson's Journal*, June 24, 1838

You can always count on the presence in your congregation of some soul in a crisis, crying out hungrily for the best you can give . . . or men and women fighting more devils than were ever cast out of Mary Magdalen; . . . of men and women sitting quietly in their pews who can scarcely keep the tears back as they reflect upon the little experiences through which they have been passing . . . some moral natures getting ready to flinch in the face of some hard duty. . . . The very thought of the spiritual possibilities dormant in any congregation is enough to shame any minister out of preaching a dull, cold, lifeless sermon, if by any measure of preparation and prayer he can do otherwise.

CHARLES R. BROWN, *The Art of Preaching*, 1922

A pastor should not complain about his congregation, certainly never to other people, but also not to God. A congregation has not been entrusted to him in order that he should become its accuser before God and men.

DIETRICH BONHOEFFER, *Life Together*, 1938

This minister thinks of the assembled people who face him on the Sabbath as a congregation who are to be led to the throne of grace. . . . Let the congregation remember that they should come to church to worship God—not to hear a weak, unskilled mortal man orate.

PETER MARSHALL, church bulletin, quoted by Catherine Marshall in her *A Man Called Peter*, 1951

Here they are. This is his congregation. This diversity is one of the problems of the pastoral ministry. These are areas in which specialists work—and sometimes disagree. Yet the pastor must minister to them all— to do so with power is his great privilege and responsibility.

CHARLES F. KEMP, *Pastoral Preaching*, 1963

The way the pastor views his congregation will largely determine his attitudes, the content of his message, even his tone of voice.

CHARLES F. KEMP, *Pastoral Preaching*, 1963

See also Brotherhood; Church, Definitions of; Community; Fellowship; Meeting; Preacher; Preaching; Sermons.

CONGREGATIONALISM

The Congregational Churches hold it to be the will of Christ that true believers should voluntarily assemble together to observe religious ordinances, to promote mutual edification and holiness, to perpetuate and propagate the gospel in the world, and to advance the glory and worship of God through Jesus Christ.

WILLESTON WALKER, *Creeds and Platforms of Congregationalism*, 1893

If a Congregationalist is asked, "What in general do Congregationalists believe?" he will answer, "There is no man or ecclesiastical body that has any right to put the Congregational denomination on record in answer to that question. But broadly speaking Congregationalists hold the evangelical faith common to Christian Churches, and have from time to time expressed that faith in confessions that

they use as a testimony and not as a test."
WILLIAM E. BARTON, *Congregational Creeds and Covenants,* 1917

A Congregational Church is not necessarily a church of Congregationalists; it is a church of Christians who are Congregationally governed.
WILLIAM E. BARTON, *Congregational Creeds and Covenants,* 1917

CONQUEST

Let a man overcome anger by love, let him overcome evil by good; let him overcome the greedy by liberality, the liar by truth!
Dhammapada, c. 5th century B.C.

To rejoice in conquest is to rejoice in murder.
LAO-TZE, *Tao Tê Ching,* c. 500 B.C.

See also Self-Discipline; Vengeance; Victory; War.

CONSCIENCE

There is no witness so terrible, no accuser so potent, as the conscience that dwells in every man's breast.
POLYBIUS, *Histories,* c. 125 B.C.

A good conscience enlists a multitude of friends; a bad conscience is distressed and anxious, even when alone.
SENECA (4 B.C.–65 A.D.), *Epistles* 43.5

God's law enters our mind and draws it to itself by stirring up conscience, which itself is called the law of our mind.
ST. JOHN DAMASCENE (700?–754?), *De Fide Orthodoxa,* 4.22

For thirty years my ear listened to nothing but my own conscience, but for thirty years since then my state has been such that my conscience has listened to none but God.
AL-MUHASIBI (died 857 A.D.), quoted in Margaret Smith's *An Early Mystic of Bagdad*

There is no man so bad that reason does not rebuke his conscience, branding some things as evil.
PETER OF POITIERS, *Sententiarum Libri,* V, 2, 21, 1179

He who acts against his conscience prepares for perdition.
Fourth Ecumenical Lateran Council, 1215

Every conscience, whether it be true or faulty, and whether it is concerned with bad acts or indifferent acts, is binding, and therefore anyone who acts against his conscience commits sin.
ST. THOMAS AQUINAS (1225–1274), *Quodlibet,* q. e, a. 22

O clear conscience, and upright! How doth a little failing wound thee sore.
DANTE, *"Purgatory," Divine Comedy,* c. 1310

To act against our conscience is neither safe for us, or open to us.
MARTIN LUTHER, *The Diet of Worms, Final Answer,* April 18, 1521

The afflicted and troubled conscience hath no remedy against desperation and eternal death, unless it takes hold of the promise of grace freely offered in Christ.
MARTIN LUTHER, *Commentary on Galatians,* 1531

For conscience, instead of allowing us to stifle our perceptions, and sleep on without interruption, acts as an inward witness and monitor, reminds us of what we owe to God, points out the distinction of good and evil, and thereby convicts us of departure from duty.
JOHN CALVIN, *Institutes,* II, 1536

Conscience is a thousand witnesses.
RICHARD TAVENER, *Proverbs,* 1539

More does God desire of thee the least degree of purity of conscience than all the works that thou canst perform.
ST. JOHN OF THE CROSS (1542–1591), *Spiritual Sentences and Maxims*

My conscience hath a thousand several tongues,
And every tongue brings in a several tale,
And every tale condemns me for a villain.
WILLIAM SHAKESPEARE, *King Richard III*, c. 1593

O coward conscience, how dost thou afflict me!
WILLIAM SHAKESPEARE, *King Richard III*, c. 1593

Conscience does make cowards of us all.
WILLIAM SHAKESPEARE, *Hamlet*, Act II, sc. 1, c. 1603

A peace above all earthly dignities,
A still and quiet conscience.
WILLIAM SHEAKSPEARE, *King Henry VIII*, c. 1611

It is the conscience alone which is a thousand witnesses to accuse us.
ROBERT BURTON, *Anatomy of Melancholy*, III, 1621

He that purchases a Manor, will think to have an exact Survey of the Land: But who think to have so exact a survey of his Conscience, how that money was got, that purchased that Manor?
JOHN DONNE, *Sermon,* Funeral of Sir William Cockayne, December 26, 1626

Conscience is a man's judgment of himself according to the judgment of God of him.
WILLIAM AMES, *Conscience with the Power and Cases Thereof,* 1643

God is especially present in the *consciences* of all persons, good and bad, by way of testimony and judgment: that is, He is there a remembrancer to call our actions to mind, a witness to bring them to judgment, and a judge to acquit or to condemn.
JEREMY TAYLOR, *Holy Living,* 1651

Men never do evil so fully and so happily as when they do it for conscience's sake.
BLAISE PASCAL, *Pensées* 1670

Conscience that can see without light sits in the areopagy and dark tribunal of our hearts, surveying our thoughts and condemning their obliquities.
THOMAS BROWNE, *Christian Morals,* c. 1680

Conscience is an actuated or reflex knowledge of a superior power and an equitable law; a law impressed, and a power above impressing it.
STEPHEN CHARNOCK (1628–1680), *Existence and Attributes of God*

The infallible way, which leads to life, is the delicate conscience of the worthy Christian.
LOUIS BOURDALOVE (1632–1704), *Sermons*

Whoever acts without conscience, or against conscience, though the very thing he does should be good, sins by doing it.
LOUIS BOURDALOVE (1632–1704), *Sermons*

A quiet conscience sleeps in thunder.
THOMAS FULLER, *Gnomologia,* 1732

Not to hear conscience is the way to silence it.
THOMAS FULLER, *Gnomologia,* 1732

It is always term-time in the court of conscience.
THOMAS FULLER, *Gnomologia,* 1732

The decrees of conscience are not judgments but feelings.
JEAN JACQUES ROUSSEAU, *Émile,* 1762

Conscience is an instinct to judge ourselves in the light of moral laws. It is not a mere faculty; it is an instinct.

IMMANUEL KANT, *Lecture at Konigsberg,* 1775

The work of conscience keeps the same hours as the owl.

J. C. F. VON SCHILLER, *Kabale und Liebe,* 1784

The moral sense, or conscience, is as much a part of man as his leg or arm.

THOMAS JEFFERSON, *Letter to Peter Carr,* 1787

A brave man hazards life, but not his conscience.

J. C. F. VON SCHILLER, *The Death of Wallenstein,* 1799

The wormwood of conscience embitters even sorrow.

JEAN PAUL RICHTER, *Titan,* 1803

The voice of conscience, which imposes on each his particular duty, is the light-beam on which we come forth from the bosom of the Infinite, and assume our place as particular individual beings; it fixes the limits of our personality.

J. G. FICHTE (1762–1814), *A Divine Government of the World*

There is nothing real, lasting, imperishable in me, but these two elements:—the voice of conscience, and my free obedience.

J. G. FICHTE (1762–1814), *The Vocation of Man*

If you would have a good conscience, you must by all means have so much light, so much knowledge of the will of God, as may regulate you, and show you your way, may teach you how to do, and to speak, and think, as in His presence.

S. T. COLERIDGE, *Aids to Reflection,* 1825

The guide of life, implanted in our nature, discriminating right from wrong, and in-

vesting right with authority and sway, is our Conscience, which Revelation does but enlighten, strengthen, and refine.

JOHN HENRY NEWMAN, *Essays and Sketches,* II, 1838

Conscience is an oracle of the Divinity.

WILLIAM ELLERY CHANNING (1780–1842), *Works*

Conscience is no longer recognized as an independent arbiter of actions . . . partly it is superseded in the minds of men by the so-called moral sense, which is regarded as the love of the beautiful; partly by the rule of expediency, which is forthwith substituted for it in the details of conduct.

JOHN HENRY NEWMAN, *Parochial and Plain Sermons,* 1843

Throughout eternity an infinite stillness reigns wherein the conscience may talk with the individual. . . . It must be heard.

SÖREN KIERKEGAARD, *Purity of Heart,* 1846

The most miserable pettifogging in the world is that of a man in the court of his own conscience.

H. W. BEECHER, *Life Thoughts,* 1858

Conscience is an imitation within ourselves of the government without us.

ALEXANDER BAIN, *The Emotions and the Will,* 1859

It is not because men's desires are strong that they act ill; it is because their consciences are weak. There is no natural connection between strong impulses and a weak conscience. The natural connection is the other way.

JOHN STUART MILL, *On Liberty,* 1859

We are never done with conscience. Choose your course by it, Brutus: choose your course by it, Cato. It is bottomless, being God.

VICTOR HUGO, *Les Miserables,* 1862

Conscience is a feeling in our own mind, a pain, more or less intense, attendant on violation of duty, which in properly cultivated moral natures rises, in the more serious cases, into shrinking from it as an impossibility.
JOHN STUART MILL, *Utilitarianism,* 1863

The phenomena of Conscience, as a dictate, avail to impress the imagination with the picture of a Supreme Governor, a Judge, holy, just, powerful, all-seeing, retributive, and is the creative principle of religion, as the Moral Sense is the principle of ethics.
JOHN HENRY NEWMAN, *Grammar of Assent,* 1870

Conscience does not repose on itself, but vaguely reaches forward to something beyond self, and dimly discerns a higher than self for its decisions.
JOHN HENRY NEWMAN, *Grammar of Assent,* 1870

The belief in authority is the source of conscience; which is therefore not the voice of God in the heart of man, but the voice of some men in man.
FRIEDRICH NIETZSCHE, *Human, All Too Human,* 1878

The disease of an evil conscience is beyond the practice of all physicians of all the countries in the world.
WILLIAM EWART GLADSTONE, *Speech,* 1878

This little flame should be the star of our life; it alone can guide our trembling ark across the tumult of the great waters.
HENRI AMIEL, *Journal,* 1882

The beautiful idea that every man has with him a Guardian Angel is true indeed: for Conscience is ever on the watch, ever ready to warn us of danger.
JOHN LUBBOCK, *The Pleasures of Life,* 1887

A mental possession of ours which enables us to pass some sort of judgment, correct or mistaken, upon moral questions as they arise. . . . your conscience is simply that ideal of life which constitutes your moral personality.
JOSIAH ROYCE, *The Philosophy of Loyalty,* 1908

Although we hold it wrong for a person to act against his conscience, we may at the same time blame him for having such a conscience as he has.
E. A. WESTERMARCK, *The Origin and Development of the Moral Ideas,* 1908

Conscience is simply my whole nature articulate. It is the voice, changing and never stationary, that results from my faith, my actual way of living, from my ideals, etc.
BEDE JARRETT, *Meditations for Layfolk,* 1915

Conscience: the Inner voice which warns you that someone may be looking.
H. L. MENCKEN, *A Little Book in C Major,* 1916

Conscience is the guardian in the individual of the rules which the community has evolved for its own preservation.
W. SOMERSET MAUGHAM, *The Moon and Sixpence,* 1919

It is the voice of our ideal self, our complete self, our real self, laying its call upon the will.
RUFUS JONES, *The Nature and Authority of Conscience,* 1920

Temptation is the voice of the suppressed evil; conscience is the voice of the repressed good.
J. A. HADFIELD, *Psychology and Morals,* 1923

Let none talk of conscience as a stable factor to be relied upon for telling the truest and the best. It can hesitate; be stifled, "talked down"; be distorted, falsified almost wholly. We have watched it. It is a ghastly spectacle.

C. C. MARTINDALE, *The Faith of the Roman Church*, 1927

Since conscience is the perfect interpreter of life, what it tells us is no question, no riddle, no problem, but a fact—the deepest, innermost, surest fact of life: God is righteous.

KARL BARTH, *The Word of God and the Word of Man*, 1928

It is still dubious as to just what conscience is and how it works, but that it is infallible, much less a divine and holy voice, is an idea no longer tenable.

JOHN HAYNES HOLMES, *Religion Today*, ed. A. L. Swift, 1933

We may ignore conscience, but we cannot dispute its existence.

RICHARD DOWNEY, *Critical and Constructive Essays*, 1934

A man's moral sense may be very low and shifty, but no man, whether in a state of savagery or of advanced civilization, escapes remorse if he commits an act flagrantly at variance with his code of right and wrong. . . . So far as we can judge from what men say of themselves, the teleology of conscience is universal.

PAUL ELMER MORE, *The Sceptical Approach to Religion*, 1934

Many are the devices and marvelous the elaborations by which men everywhere seek to avoid condemnation before that inner tribunal known as conscience.

ANTON T. BOISEN, *The Exploration of the Inner World*, 1936

While a jammed horn is recognized as abnormal, a jammed conscience is often regarded as the voice of God.

HARRY EMERSON FOSDICK, *On Being a Real Person*, 1943

Yet while conscience thus insists we do right, it does not by itself tell us what is right.

HARRY EMERSON FOSDICK, *On Being a Real Person*, 1943

Like an opiate, sin drugs a conscience to drowsiness and stupor. Prayer stabs it wide awake.

JOHN A. O'BRIEN, *The Test of Courage*, 1943

I am freeing men from the dirty and degrading chimaera called conscience and morality.

ADOLF HITLER (1889–1945), quoted in Erich Meissner's *Confusion of Faces*

Even Freud assumes that, when Freudian light has dawned upon us by Freudian psychoanalysis, we are under obligation to walk in the light. Thus Freud makes backdoor confession that we are responsible creatures; that is, people of conscience.

GEORGE A. BUTTRICK, *Christ and Man's Dilemma*, 1946

Conscience cannot be cajoled. It cannot be bribed. It cannot be coerced. It cannot be silenced. It can be disobeyed. For man is a free agent. But it cannot be disobeyed with impunity.

JOHN A. O'BRIEN, *Truths Men Live By*, 1947

More potent than all the brass-buttoned policemen in the land is the restraining power of conscience.

JOHN A. O'BRIEN, *Truths Men Live By*, 1947

The greatest event in natural history was the birth of conscience in the human mind. That was the moment when man put aside his strongest natural instinct, which was self-interest.

LECOMTE DU NOÜY, *Reader's Digest*, June, 1948

Everyone has an inner conscience. . . .
The cynic who ridicules conscience forgets
that his own cynicism has its reason not
unrelated to his conscience. The rabid behavior of the cynic is the expression of
defensive warfare against his "internal
enemy." He strikes others, but he is aiming
at himself.
> EDMUND BERGLER, *The Battle of the
> Conscience,* 1948

Our cosmic universe is not outside. Spiritual astronomy does not establish its observatories on mountains in California, but
in consciences.
> ANTONIN SERTILLANGES, *Recollections,*
> 1950

The Christian conscience is so wholly
molded in conformity to the Will of God
that the idea of a conscience without this
central essential for us can seem at first a
mere self-contradiction.
> ROSALIND MURRAY, *Columbia,* April,
> 1951

Religious conscience has undergone a radical reconstruction, which has brought it
closer to the issues of social morality and
has entangled the salvation of the soul in
affairs of the world.
> HERBERT WALLACE SCHNEIDER, *Reli-
> gion in the 20th Century,* 1952

Even if he should wish to do so, a man
could never shake off conscience. . . . He
will travel along the whole way of his life,
and likewise with it, a truthful and incorruptible witness, he will come up for God's
judgment.
> POPE PIUS XII, *Broadcast,* March 24,
> 1952

It is of the essence of the Protestant faith
that the individual conscience is supreme.
On all matters of political and social policy this means that the church may furnish
guidance but no directives.
> F. ERNEST JOHNSON, *The Nation,* July
> 25, 1953

If we are here for a solemn purpose, if
each man's life is a struggle to find God's
truth and to follow it, we can make no
terms with the smallest encroachment
upon conscience.
> HERBERT AGAR, New York *Herald Tri-
> bune Book Review,* March 8, 1953

A person may sometimes have a clear
conscience simply because his head is
empty.
> RALPH W. SOCKMAN, *How to Believe,*
> 1953

This still small voice [conscience] insistently has called to whatever is best in men
and led them on to deeds of uncalculating
devotion.
> EDMUND W. SINNOTT, *Two Roads to
> Truth,* 1953

Conscience can become hardened like
water becoming ice. . . . It films over
gradually, and at last becomes hard; and
then it can bear a weight of iniquity.
> SEBASTIAN MIKLAS, *Sanctify Your Emo-
> tions,* 1955

A conscience which is formed wholly on
abstract principles, if such a conscience is
possible, without reference to a personal
God is, from a Christian point of view, a
secular conscience.
> WALTER J. ONG, *Religion in America,*
> ed. John Cogley, 1958

A physical gratification bought at the expense of conscience is the bargain of a
fool.
> JOHN A. O'BRIEN, *Getting the Most Out
> of Marriage,* 1954

"Conscience" is, as it were, the *advocatus
Dei* in our soul.
> DIETRICH VON HILDEBRAND, *True Mo-
> rality and Its Counterfeits,* 1955

A scrupulous conscience can be one of the
worst kinds of emotional sickness.
> GEORGE C. ANDERSON, *Man's Right to
> Be Human,* 1959

Love is the source and substance of our conscience. . . . If it were not for our unquenchable need to love and to be loved there would be no conscience; there would remain only animal fear and animal aggression.

GREGORY ZILBOORG, *Psychoanalysis and Religion,* 1962

A man must obey his conscience. For conscience is the most immediate giver of moral imperatives, and can never be passed over. . . . Even in his obedience to his guiltlessly misinformed conscience, man is being obedient to God and paying homage to goodness.

KARL RAHNER, *Nature and Grace,* 1964

The conscience is not automatically infallible; it can easily make mistakes, and it is very difficult to distinguish its voice—the real voice of conscience—from the voice of precipitation, passion, convenience or self-will, or of moral primitiveness.

KARL RAHNER, *Nature and Grace,* 1964

In all his activity a man is bound to follow his conscience, in order that he may come to God, the end and purpose of life. It follows that he is not to be forced to act in a manner contrary to his conscience.

SECOND VATICAN COUNCIL, *A Declaration on Religious Freedom,* December, 1965

All too often a clear conscience is merely the result of a bad memory.

Proverb

Did you ever meet anyone who said he couldn't sleep because of his conscience?

Anonymous

A guilty conscience needs no accuser.

English Proverb

See also Act; Allegiance; Bigot; Coercion; Communism; Conduct; Confession; Courage; Duties; Freedom, Religious; Freedom

of Thought and Speech; God: His Intervention in the World; God: His Omniscience; Guilt; Happiness; Joy; Law; Man and God; Man Indwelt by God; Military Service; Obedience; Private Judgment; Psychiatry; Psychoanalysis; Repentance; Rights; Sin; Sin: Its Consequences; State, the; Superstition; Temptation; Unity; War.

CONSCIENCE AND LAW

Freedom of conscience is a natural right, both antecedent and superior to all human laws and institutions whatever: a right which laws never gave and which laws never take away.

JOHN GOODWIN, *Might and Right Well Met,* 1648

This principle of making the individual conscience the judge of law, and in last resorts the final justification of disobedience, is psychologically necessary for any free people.

EVERETT DEAN MARTIN, *Liberty,* 1930

How can human commerce go on, what store can be set by agreements, if conscience offers no security, if there is no faith in God and no fear of Him? Remove the foundation and the whole moral law collapses.

POPE PIUS XI, *Caritate Christi,* May 3, 1932

CONSCIENCE AND STATE

To pretend to dominion over the conscience is to usurp the prerogative of God. By the nature of things the power of sovereigns is confined to political government; they have no right of punishment except over those who disturb the public peace.

THEODORIC I, to Justin in 523 A.D., quoted by Cassiodorus in *Variae*

I am not bound to direct my conscience according to the council of one single kingdom against the general council of Christendom.

> St. Thomas More, to his judges after they had condemned him to death, 1535

My prison shall be my grave before I will budge a jot; for I owe my conscience to no mortal man.

> William Penn, in the Tower of London, 1669, *Passages from Writings of,* ed. T. P. Cope

Philip II and Isabella . . . inflicted more suffering in obedience to their consciences than Nero and Domitian in obedience to their lusts.

> W. E. H. Lecky, *History of European Morals,* I, 1906

The doctrine that there is a national conscience which must always be superior to individual conscience is the death of any vital religion and of any real sense of human brotherhood.

> Norman Thomas, *Letter,* August 15, 1917

The heavier the material sacrifices the State imposes on individuals and families, the more sacred and inviolate must it be to it the rights of consciences. The State can lay claim to property and life, but never to the soul, redeemed by God.

> Pope Pius XII, *Summi Pontificatus,* October, 1939

The State does not have the right to interfere with the judgment of conscience, even a wilfully erroneous conscience. . . . If the judgment of an erroneous conscience, however, leads to acts that are against the rights of others or the common good, the State has the right . . . to proscribe such rights.

> Catholic Association for International Peace, *Timeless Rights,* 1948

A person who holds for the moral authority of conscience will also hold for the individual's freedom to follow his conscience without interference from the State.

> Eric D'Arcy, *Conscience and Its Right of Freedom,* 1961

If civil authorities legislate or allow anything that is contrary to that [moral] order and therefore contrary to the will of God, neither the laws made nor the authorization granted can be binding on the consciences of citizens.

> Pope John XXIII, *Pacem in Terris,* April, 1963

Neither national hierarchies nor Christian individuals can give governments blank checks drawn on the bank of conscience.

> T. D. Roberts, *The Advocate* (organ of Newark, N.J., Roman Catholic Archdiocese), October 24, 1963

See also Art and Christianity; Conscientious Objector; Conscription; Judgment; Judgment, God's; Loyalty; Pacifism; Patriotism; Social Conscience; War.

CONSCIENTIOUS OBJECTOR

The conscientious objector . . . has no place in a republic like ours, and should be expelled from it, for a man who won't pull his weight in the boat has no right in the boat.

> Theodore Roosevelt, *Speech,* Baltimore, Md., September 28, 1918

We desire that all Christian people who though willing to risk their lives in noncombatant service are unwilling for conscience's sake to take human life in war, and shall have signified their intention by placing themselves on record at the national headquarters of their respective churches, be accorded by the U. S. Government the status in fact accorded to members of the Society of Friends [Quakers] as respects military service.

> *Resolution,* General Convention of the Episcopal Church, 1934

The conscientious objector is a "transcendent" egotist who is prepared to sacrifice to his ideal of *personal* perfection the most sacred interests—and even the very existence—of the community of which he is a part.

GUSTAVE THIBON, *War and Love,* 1946

Faced by the dilemma of participation in war, the individual Christian must decide prayerfully before God what is to be his course of action in relation thereto. What the Christian may not do is to obey men rather than God, or overlook the degree of compromise in our best acts, or gloss over the sinfulness of war. The Church must hold within its fellowship persons who sincerely differ at this point of critical decision, call all to repentance, mediate to all God's mercy.

Resolution, General Conference of the Methodist Church, 1952

We reaffirm the sacred obligation of every Christian to obey his conscience and . . . call upon all our people to maintain in the bonds of Christian love and fellowship those who in obedience to conscience refuse to participate.

Resolution, American Baptist Convention, 1953

It seems right that laws make humane provisions for the case of those who for reasons of conscience refuse to bear arms, provided, however, that they agree to serve the human community in some other way.

SECOND VATICAN COUNCIL, *The Church in the Modern World,* December, 1965

See also Conscription; Freedom; Military Service; Nuclear War; Pacifism; Pacifists; Patriotism; Soldier; War.

CONSCIOUSNESS

Man, created in the image of God, lost, it is said, his state of absolute contentment, by eating of the Tree of the knowledge of Good and Evil. Sin consists here only in Knowledge; this is the sinful element, and by it man is stated to have trifled away his Natural Happiness. This is a deep truth, that evil lies in consciousness.

G. W. F. HEGEL (1770–1831), *The Philosophy of History,* publ. posth.

We are obliged to regard every phenomenon as a manifestation of some Power by which we are acted upon; though Omnipresence is unthinkable, yet . . . we are unable to think of limits to the presence of this Power. . . . And this consciousness of an Incomprehensible Power . . . is just that consciousness on which Religion dwells.

HERBERT SPENCER, *First Principles,* 1862

When mystical activity is at its height, we find consciousness possessed by a sense of a being at once *excessive and identical* with the self: great enough to be God; interior enough to be me.

E. RECÉJAC, *Essay on the Being of the Mystical Knowledge,* 1899

I hold that it is in the Transcendental Feeling, manifested normally as Faith in the Value of Life, and ecstatically as a sense of Timeless Being, . . . that Consciousness comes nearest to the object of metaphysics, Ultimate Reality.

J. A. STEWART, *The Myth of Plato,* 1905

The theism of philosophical research in which the idea of God is arrived at by a process of reflective thought must give way to the theism of religious consciousness for which God is in some way an immediate object.

W. R. SORLEY, *Moral Values and the Idea of God,* 1915

Everywhere but in man, consciousness has come to a stand; in man alone it has kept on its way. . . . It is as if a vague and familiar being had sought to realize himself and had succeeded only by abandoning a part of himself on the way.

HENRI BERGSON, *Creative Evolution,* 1922

I incline to the idealistic theory that consciousness is fundamental, and that the material universe is derivative from consciousness. . . . In general the universe seems to me to be nearer to a great thought than to a great machine.

JAMES JEANS, to J. W. N. Sullivan, *Contemporary Mind: Some Modern Answers,* 1934

Consciousness is the inner light kindled in the soul . . . a music, strident or sweet, made by the friction of existence.

GEORGE SANTAYANA, *The Realm of Truth,* 1938

The consciousness of each of us is evolution looking at itself and reflecting.

PIERRE TEILHARD DE CHARDIN, *The Phenomenon of Man,* 1955

An expansion of the individual consciousness toward a harmony with Infinite Consciousness demands of the individual that he take on, commensurately, other characteristics of his Creator.

LEONARD E. READ, *The Freeman,* June, 1964

See also God: His Nature; Nirvana; Reality; Religion: Its Nature and Function; Soul Defined; World and Man.

CONSCRIPTION

It is part of the attempt to maintain peace by force, and . . . it is training in methods which are contrary to the highest moral standards recogniz d by man.

Statement on Conscription by Friends [Quakers] in Great Britain, 1945

The training of men to kill each other is a violation of the sacredness of personality,

for it is a crime against that of God in every man.

Statement on Conscription by Friends [Quakers] in Great Britain, 1945

See also Conscientious Objector; Military Service; Pacifism; Peace; Soldier; War.

CONSERVATION OF ENERGY

The most adequate formulation of this law [of the conservation of energy] creates the impression in every unbiased mind that nature is ruled by a rational, purposive will.

MAX PLANCK, *Scientific Autobiography and Other Papers,* 1949

CONSERVATISM

The "religious man" . . . in some considerable degree is at heart a conservative, for he appeals to an authority beyond the vanity of Demos or Expediency and he trusts in the wisdom of our ancestors and in enduring values.

RUSSELL KIRK, *A Program for Conservatives,* 1954

Two centuries ago the conservative could still believe that he could preserve the old regime and the ancient certainties. If he thinks so today, he is a romantic and deluded reactionary. The modern conservative has to . . . create the new forms in which the enduring truths and values can be carried on in a world that is being radically transformed.

WALTER LIPPMANN, New York *Herald Tribune,* August 4, 1964

CONSISTENCY

A consistent man believes in destiny, a capricious man in chance.

BENJAMIN DISRAELI, *Vivian Grey,* 1827

A foolish consistency is the hobgoblin of little minds, adored by little statesmen and philosophers and divines. With consistency a great soul has simply nothing to do. He may as well concern himself with his shadow on the wall. . . . If you would be a man, speak what you think today in words as hard as cannon balls, and tomorrow speak what tomorrow thinks in hard words again, though it contradict everything you said today.

> RALPH WALDO EMERSON, "Self-Reliance," *Essays,* 1841

Fear never but you shall be consistent in whatever variety of actions, so that they each be honest and natural in their hour. For of one will, the actions will be harmonious, however unlike they seem.

> RALPH WALDO EMERSON, "Self-Reliance," *Essays,* 1841

CONSOLATION

Too many people, Catholics included, appear to be seeking, not the God of consolation, but the consolation of God—a very different matter.

> AELRED GRAHAM, *Christian Thought and Action,* 1951

See also Bible; Comfort; Ease; Religion: Its Nature and Function.

CONSTANTS

The constants in all religion are the mystery of the universe, the nostalgia of the human spirit for an order beyond the show and flux of things to which it believes itself akin, and the belief that it has evidence of such an order.

> GAIUS GLENN ATKINS, *Religion Today,* ed. A. L. Swift, 1933

CONSTITUTION, U. S.

Our own republic in its Constitution and laws is of heavenly origin. It was not borrowed from Greece or Rome, but from the Bible.

> LYMAN BEECHER (1775–1863), *Works,* I

Our Constitution is the charter of all that is distinctively American in our national spirit. That document was written in a period as pagan as the Christian centuries had up to that time known. Yet, providentially that charter of ordered liberty was not written in the pagan spirit of that day.

> EDWARD MOONEY, *Address,* First National Catholic Social Action Conference, Milwaukee, 1938

See also Church and State.

CONTEMPLATION

Great becomes the fruit, great the advantage of earnest contemplation, when it is set round with upright conduct. Great becomes the fruit, great the advantage of intellect when it is set round with earnest contemplation.

> *Dialogues of the Buddha* (6th century B.C.), Part II

One may not be so given up to contemplation as to neglect the good of his neighbor, nor so taken up with the active life as to omit the contemplation of God.

> ST. AUGUSTINE, *The City of God,* XIX, 426

Those who wish to hold the fortress of contemplation, must first of all train in the camp of action.

> POPE ST. GREGORY THE GREAT, *Book of Morals,* 584

The contemplative life obtains a certain freedom of mind, for it thinks not of temporal but of eternal things.

> POPE ST. GREGORY THE GREAT, *Hom. III, in Ezech.,* c. 590

Do not defile in contemplation thought that is pure in his own nature.
But abide in the bliss of yourself and cease those torments.

> SARAHA, *Saraha's Treasury of Songs* (10th century)

When thou hast stabilized thine heart in right faith, and steadfast hope, and perfect love, then thou shalt heave up thine heart in high contemplation of thy Creator.
ST. EDMUND OF CANTERBURY, *Mirror of St. Edmund,* c. 1230

The life of work is necessary and the life of contemplation is good. In service the man gathers the harvest that has been sown in contemplation.
MEISTER ECKHART (1260?–1327?), *Meister Eckhart,* R. B. Blakney

To me it seems that contemplation is joyful song of God's love taken in mind, with sweetness of angels' praise. This is jubilation, this is the end of perfect prayer and high devotion in this life.
RICHARD ROLLE (c. 1300–1349), *The Mending of Life*

In the higher part of contemplative life, a man is above himself and under his God.
The Cloud of Unknowing, 14th century

There are many persons who desire the contemplative life, but they will not practice the things which lead to it.
THOMAS À KEMPIS, *Imitation of Christ,* 1441

The true inward lover of God that is free from all inordinate affections may anon turn himself freely to God, and in spirit lift himself up in contemplation and fruitfully rest him in Christ.
THOMAS À KEMPIS, *Imitation of Christ,* 1441

Because the earthly life of pious folk is nothing but a contemplation and kind of shadowing of that other, they sometimes feel a foretaste and a glow of the reward to come.
DESIDERIUS ERASMUS, *The Praise of Folly,* 1511

When God leads any one along the highest road of obscure contemplation and aridity, such an one will think himself lost.
ST. JOHN OF THE CROSS (1542–1591), *Ascent of Mount Carmel*

Let it be well understood that God does not lead to perfect contemplation all who give themselves resolutely to the interior life. Why is that? God alone knows.
ST. JOHN OF THE CROSS (1542–1591), *The Dark Night of the Soul*

A soul wholly lost in God wants to have only the virtue and the perfection that God wills it to have.
SAINT JEANNE FRANÇOISE DE CHANTAL (1572–1641), *Mystical Prayer According to*

The problem set before us is to bring our daily task into the temple of contemplation and ply it there, to act as in the presence of God, to interfuse one's little part with religion.
HENRI AMIEL, *Journal,* 1882

The world which asks of such saintly mortified souls hidden away in cloisters and convents: "What good do they do?" fails to understand that in the order of divine life they are doing for the wounded on the spiritual battlefields of the Church, that which, in the order of human life, nurses and doctors are doing on the battlefields of the world.
FULTON J. SHEEN, *The Fullness of Christ,* 1935

Contemplation may . . . be arid for a long time, during which one may be a contemplative without knowing it.
REGINALD GARRIGOU-LAGRANGE, *Christian Perfection and Contemplation,* 1937

Contemplation is the highest form of human life on condition that it is centered

upon the object, the knowledge of which is the end of that life.
ÉTIENNE GILSON, *The Philosophy of St. Thomas,* 1939

The highest activity possible to Man. . . . It is High Prayer. . . . because in this way man may rise highest above himself, reach the limit of his evolution . . . that creative glance whereby the creature becoming one with the Creator, achieves the constant interpretation of the apparent, temporal manifold into the Eternal One.
GERALD HEARD, *A Preface to Prayer,* 1944

Contemplation is that condition of alert passivity, in which the soul lays itself open to the divine Ground within and without, the immanent and transcendent Godhead.
ALDOUS HUXLEY, *The Perennial Philosophy,* 1945

This flowering of the contemplative life [in the U.S.] seems to be as important here as atomic research. Some days the prayers of the children of God will burst on the world like the bomb of Bikini.
R. L. BRUCKBERGER, *One Sky to Share,* 1951

Christian contemplation is not something esoteric and dangerous. It is simply the experience of God that is given to a soul purified by humility and faith.
THOMAS MERTON, *Commonweal,* October, 1958

Contemplation is an inward gaze into the depths of the soul and, for that very reason, beyond the soul to God.
HANS URS VON BALTHASAR, *Prayer,* 1961

The contemplative gaze always turns back to the humanity of Jesus.
HANS URS VON BALTHASAR, *Prayer,* 1962

See also Adoration; Brahma; Brahman; Experience, Religious; Happiness; Liturgy;

Love, Spiritual; Love of God; Man's Unity with God; Meditation; Mystical Experience; Prayer; Preachers; Self-Giving; Selflessness; Silence; Solitude; Spiritual; Spiritual Life; Vision; Worship.

CONTENTMENT

The sufficiency of contentment is an enduring and unchanging sufficiency.
Tao Tê Ching, between 6th and 3rd century B.C.

All mortal men's contentment is mortal.
MICHEL DE MONTAIGNE, *Essays,* Bk. 2, ch. 12, 1580

What though I am not so happy as I desire, 'tis well I am not so wretched as I deserve.
ARTHUR WARWICK, *Spare Minutes,* 1637

Contentment consisteth not in adding more fuel, but in taking away some fire; not in multiplying of wealth, but in subtracting men's desires.
THOMAS FULLER, *The Holy State,* 1642

Here is the wisdom of the contented man: to let God choose for him; for when we have given up our wills to Him . . . our spirits must needs rest while our conditions have for their security the power, the wisdom, and the charity of God.
JEREMY TAYLOR, *Holy Living,* 1650

Be content with your daily bread, and remember that in the desert manna gathered for a future day grew putrid at once.
FRANÇOIS FÉNELON (1651–1715), *Spiritual Letters*

Bad will be the day for every man when he becomes absolutely contented with the life that he is living . . . when there is not

forever beating at the doors of his soul some great desire to do something larger.
PHILLIPS BROOKS (1835–1893), *Perennials from*

True contentment is a real, even an active virtue—not only affirmative but creative. It is the power of getting out of any situation all there is in it.
G. K. CHESTERTON, *A Miscellany of Men*, 1912

See also Acceptance.

CONTEST

There is, in fact, only one contest in which everyone can win. That is the striving to lead a life that is pleasing to God.
RUPERT LANGENTSTEIN, *The Constant Cross*, 1954

CONTINENCE

Of all forms of continence, the bridling of the tongue is the most difficult.
PYTHAGORAS (6th century B.C.), *Pythagoras Source Book*, K. S. Guthrie

Continence is the pinnacle, as it were, and the consummation of all the virtues.
LACTANTIUS FIRMIANUS, *The Divine Institutes*, c. 310

Continence is a greater good than marriage.
ST. AUGUSTINE, *On the Good of Marriage*, c. 401

Continence is an angelic exercise.
ST. AUGUSTINE, *On the Good of Marriage*, c. 401

It is praiseworthy that even during the life of her husband, by his consent, a female vow continence unto Christ.
ST. AUGUSTINE, *On the Good of Widowhood*, c. 413

Continence even in the Old Testament was never called "clean"; it was called *holy*.
FRANCIS J. FILAS, *Chicago New World*, 1964

See also Birth Control; Chastity; Repression; Sexual Intercourse; Virginity.

CONTRACEPTION. See BIRTH CONTROL

CONTRIBUTIONS

The common response to the divine command is not, "Here I am, send me," but "Here is my check, Lord, send some one else," and many forget to offer the check as a substitute.
JOSIAH STRONG, *National Needs and Remedies*, 1890

Many are shocked by what they think is the worldly custom of collecting money in church. Woe to us, if we consider this from a worldly, commonplace point of view. . . . The "Christian outlook" is one whole. And within it, all matters are seen in their spiritual dimensions and significance.
ALEXANDER YELCHANINOV (1881–1934), *Fragments of a Diary*

CONTRITION

There is no moral awakening, no humility without a deep contrition, and thus it is likewise impossible to aspire to this awakening by means of sinning.
DIETRICH VON HILDEBRAND, *True Morality and Its Counterfeits*, 1955

See also Atonement; Compassion; Confession; Conscience; Forgiveness; Grace; Mercy; Penitence; Remorse; Repentance.

CONTROVERSY

Some Controverters in Divinity are like Swaggerers in a Tavern, that catch that which stands next to them, the candlestick or pots, turn everything into a weapon; ofttimes they fight blind-fold.

BEN JONSON, *Discoveries,* 1641

Dishonest controversy loves to confound the personal with the spiritual elements in the Church—to ignore the distinction between the sinful agents and the divine institution.

J. E. E. DALBERG-ACTON (Lord Acton), *Home and Foreign Review,* April, 1864

See also Discord; Disputation; Quarrels; Religious Conflict.

CONVERSATION

Absence of daily prayer is the disease of daily conversation.

Dhammapada, c. 5th century B.C.

Those are the happy Conversations, where only such things are spoken and heard as we can reflect upon afterward with Satisfaction; and without any Mixture either of Shame, or Repentance.

DESIDERIUS ERASMUS (1466?–1536), *Twenty Select Colloquies of,*

CONVERSION

It is only the simpletons, the ignoble, the senseless—slaves and women and children —whom Christians can persuade—wooldressers, and cobblers and fullers, the most uneducated and common men, whoever is a sinner—or a godforsaken fool.

CELSUS, quoted by Origen in his *Contra Celsus,* 246

Though we call those whom a robber chieftain would call, we call them . . . to bind up their wounds with our doctrines, to heal the festering wounds of their souls with the wholesome medicine of faith, nor do we say God calls only sinners.

ORIGEN, *Contra Celsus,* iii, LIX, 246

I am afraid to make hasty converts of educated men, lest they should not have counted the cost, and should have difficulties after they have entered the Church. . . . The Church must be prepared for converts, as well as converts prepared for the Church.

J. H. NEWMAN, a "private memorandum" prepared in 1863, quoted in *Three Cardinals,* by E. E. Reynolds, 1958

You have not converted a man because you have silenced him.

JOHN MORLEY, *On Compromise,* 1874

Conversion is primarily an unselfing.

E. T. STARBUCK, *The Psychology of Religion,* 1901

For one man conversion means the slaying of the beast within him; in another it brings the calm of conviction to an unquiet mind; for a third it is the entrance into a larger liberty and a more abundant life; and yet again it is the gathering into one of the forces of a soul at war within itself.

GEORGE JACKSON, *The Fact of Conversion,* 1908

Until a man realizes sin as the death of his own higher self and as a rebellion against the law of his true happiness, there is no true conversion of heart towards the higher life.

FATHER CUTHBERT, *God and the Supernatural,* 1920

There isn't any doubt about it, the human soul cannot go on for ever in sin without some desire to free itself. . . . Conversion simply means turning around.

VINCENT MCNABB, *God's Way of Mercy,* 1928

For all that psychology has to say, conversion might be what the convert thinks it is—the soul's discovery of God. . . . To say that "the subconscious did it" does not prevent one from saying "God did it." Both statements may be true at the same time. In conversion the deeps of the soul are stirred. True. But it is also true an angel may trouble the pool.

CHARLES A. BENNETT, *The Dilemma of Religious Knowledge*, 1931

There is no man, no "unbeliever," whose supernatural conversion to God is not possible from the dawn of reason onwards.

ÉTIENNE HUGUENY, *Le scandale édifiant d'une exposition missionaire*, 1933

The Christian purpose in the social and political spheres can be achieved only by those who have been converted to the Christian understanding of life.

W. A. VISSER 'T HOOFT and J. H. OLDHAM, *The Church and Its Function in Society*, 1937

If we are to convert the moral pagan, we must show him that the goodness he knows and values, the true human love of man for man, the true standard of personal honor and trust, is not ignored or lost, but carried further in the supernatural Christian goodness.

ROSALIND MURRAY, *Columbia*, April, 1951

Social teaching alone will not usually convert people to the Christian gospel. But the impression that Christianity is socially irrelevant can keep them away.

JOHN C. BENNETT, *Union Seminary Quarterly Review*, June, 1951

At conversion you do throw overboard your egocentricity, but you do not throw overboard what you are.

SAMUEL H. SHOEMAKER, *They're on the Way*, 1951

We do not try to convert non-Christians by showing them their errors, but by showing how the separate truths they hold ought to develop into the Oneness of truth.

BERNARD LEEMING, *Unitas*, XI, No. 2, 1952

Where a profound change in philosophy, ideology, or ethics occurs, the hidden but encompassing struggle is particularly significant. Thus conversion cannot be regarded as a sudden or dramatic event.

LEON SALZMAN, *Psychiatry*, 1953

It is impossible ever to do something morally evil in order to be led by it to a deep contrition and consequently to a conversion.

DIETRICH VON HILDEBRAND, *True Morality and Its Counterfeits*, 1955

When we stress, as we should, God's part in the experience of conversion, the more accurate word is "regeneration," literally "to be reborn."

JOHN SUTHERLAND BONNELL, *No Escape from Life*, 1958

Conversion is not expertness. It is not knowledge. It is not skill in the pursuit of theology. It is not church work. It is not the sacred ministry. It is not a feeling of pleasure. It is not enthusiasm. It is the process by which a man is received into the presence of God.

ERIK ROUTLEY, *The Gift of Conversion*, 1958

What man most needs now is to apply his conversion skills to those things that are essential for his survival. He needs to convert facts into logic, free will into purpose, conscience into decision. He needs to convert historical experience into a design for a sane world.

NORMAN COUSINS, *In Place of Folly*, 1961

The era in which religious statesmanship is conceived in terms of converting the world to one's own religion is over.

F. S. C. NORTHROP, *Man, Nature and God*, 1962

See also Commitment; Conviction; Experience, Religious; Prayer; Regeneration; Witness.

CONVICTION

Conviction, were it never so excellent, is worthless till it convert itself into Conduct.

THOMAS CARLYLE, *Sartor Resartus,* 1836

The important thing is not that two people should be inspired by the same convictions, but rather that each of them should hold his or her own convictions in a high and worthy spirit.

JOHN VISCOUNT MORLEY, *On Compromise,* 1874

He who begins life by stifling his convictions is in a fair way for ending it without any convictions to stifle.

JOHN VISCOUNT MORLEY, *On Compromise,* 1874

Religion at its best has supplied—and it can now supply—convictions by which men inwardly come to terms with themselves, gain spiritual peace and power, and come off more than conquerors.

HARRY EMERSON FOSDICK, *Adventurous Religion,* 1926

Convictions are the mainsprings of action, the driving powers of life. What a man lives are his convictions.

FRANCIS C. KELLEY, *Address,* Oklahoma City, November 28, 1933

He who holds convictions, respects convictions.

LEO BAECK, *Essence of Judaism,* 1936

See also Action; Commitment; Conduct; Conversion; Decision; Faith, Definitions of; Practice.

COOPERATION

Charity is not the watchword of the future faith. The watchword of the future faith is *association,* fraternal cooperation towards a common aim.

GIUSEPPE MAZZINI, *The Duties of Man,* 1858

The iron walls of the self may be torn down in a magnificent triumph of common purpose and common conscience as men discover they are but single cells in a larger and common body.

NORMAN COUSINS, *Saturday Review of Literature,* May 27, 1950

Cooperation among Christians should also employ every possible means to relieve the afflictions of our times such as famine and natural disasters, illiteracy and poverty, lack of housing and the unequal distribution of wealth.

Decree on Ecumenism, SECOND VATICAN COUNCIL, November, 1964

See also Social Cooperation.

CORRUPTION

Everything is good when it comes from the hands of the Almighty; everything degenerates in the hands of man.

JEAN JACQUES ROUSSEAU, *Émile,* 1762

It is my earnest belief that everything we see before us today is more or less polluted, diluted and devalued.

KARL BARTH, *Community, Church and State,* 1946

See also Original Sin.

COSMETICS

Against Him those women sin who torment their skin with potions, stain their cheeks with rouge, and extend the line of their eyes with black coloring. Doubtless they are dissatisfied with God's plastic skill. In their own persons they convict and censure the Artificer of all things.

TERTULLIAN, *Women's Dress,* c. 220

God has given you one face, and you make yourselves another.

WILLIAM SHAKESPEARE, *Hamlet,* c. 1601

A woman that paints puts up a bill that she is to be let.

THOMAS FULLER, *Gnomologia,* 1732

See also Vanity.

COSMOS. See UNIVERSE

COUNTRY

Your Country is the token of the mission which God has given you to fulfil in Humanity.

GIUSEPPE MAZZINI, *The Duties of Man,* 1858

A Country is a fellowship of free and equal men bound together in a brotherly concord of labor towards a single end.

GIUSEPPE MAZZINI, *The Duties of Man,* 1858

See also Nation; State, the.

COURAGE

The Master said: "To see what is right and not to do it, is want of courage."

CONFUCIUS, *Analects,* 5th century B.C.

The loving God never forsakes a hero on earth if his courage fail not.

Andreas, prior to 1100 A.D.

The strangest, most generous, and proudest of all virtues is true courage.

MICHEL DE MONTAIGNE, *Essays,* 1588

Courage is a virtue only in so far as it is directed by prudence.

FRANÇOIS FÉNELON, *Aventures de Télémaque,* 1699

Never can true courage dwell with them, who, playing tricks with conscience, dare not look at their own vices.

S. T. COLERIDGE (1772–1834), *Fears in Solitude*

Courage without conscience is a wild beast.

ROBERT G. INGERSOLL, *Speech,* May, 1882

The soul little suspects its own courage. . . . Take even a common man, the commonest, and beat and bruise him enough and you will see his soul rise God-like.

FRANK CRANE, *Human Confessions,* 1911

It is the lovely virtue—the rib of Himself that God sent down to His children.

JAMES M. BARRIE, *Courage,* 1922

As I by my courage in the face of life justify my particular existence, I supply the reason why myself, rather than Jones or Smith, exist in my place, here and now.

GRANT OVERTON, *American Nights Entertainment,* 1923

Courage is rightly esteemed the first of human qualities, because . . . it is the quality which guarantees all others.

WINSTON S. CHURCHILL, *Great Contemporaries,* 1937

On Calvary there was one man brave enough to die and one woman brave enough to go on living; so all men may know that life and death demand the same ingredient of courage.

WALTER FARRELL, *The Looking Glass,* 1951

Courage is never to let your actions be influenced by your fears.

ARTHUR KOESTLER, *Arrow in the Blue,* 1951

Courage: Fear that has said its prayers.

Author Unknown

See also Bravery; Cowardice; Fear; Heroism; Valor.

COURTSHIP

Courtship on the higher psychical level, by holding in leash the expression of the physical impulses, serves the extremely important function of deepening the channels of higher psychical and spiritual love.

> JOHN M. COOPER, *Religion Outline for Colleges,* Vol. IV, 1930

See also Love, Physical; Sex.

COVETOUSNESS

Covetousness makes a man miserable, because riches are not means to make a man happy.

> JEREMY TAYLOR, *Holy Living,* 1650

Covetousness is the greatest of monsters, as well as the root of all evil.

> WILLIAM PENN, *Some Fruits of Solitude,* 1693

See also Envy; Greed; Money; Property; Riches; Self-Interest; Selfishness; Wealth.

COWARDICE

To know what is right and not do it is the worst cowardice.

> CONFUCIUS, *Analects,* c. 500 B.C.

God will not have his work made manifest by cowards.

> RALPH WALDO EMERSON, "Self-Reliance," *Essays,* 1841

Wilt thou be a hero or a coward? No philosophy can relieve us from the responsibility of having to make that choice.

> L. P. JACKS, *Religious Perplexities,* 1922

All enchantments die; only cowards die with them.

> CHARLES MORGAN, *The Fountain,* 1932

See also Bravery; Conscience; Courage; Fear; Heroism.

CREATION

Who knows for certain? Who shall declare it? Whence was it born, and whence came this creation? The gods were born after this world's creation. Then who can know from whence it has arisen? . . . He who surveys it in the highest heaven, He only knows, or haply he may know not.

> *Rig-Veda,* between 1000 and 600 B.C.

This universe existed in the shape of Darkness, unperceived. . . . Then the divine Self-existent, himself indiscernible, but making all this, the great Elements and the rest, discernible, appeared with irresistible creative power, dispelling the darkness.

> *The Manu-Smriti,* c. 200 B.C.

For who that has understanding will suppose that the first, and second, and third day, and the evening and the morning, existed without a sun, and moon, and stars? And who is so foolish as to suppose that God, after the manner of a husbandman, planted a paradise in Eden, towards the east, and placed in it a tree of life, visible and palpable, so that one tasting of the fruit by bodily teeth obtained life.

> ORIGEN, *De Principiis,* Bk. IV, ch. 1, 16, c. 254 A.D.

Does God create as men do? . . . Perish the thought; we understand the term in one sense of God and in another of men. God creates in that He calls what is not into being, needing nothing thereunto; but men work some existing material.

> ST. ATHANASIUS (296–373), *De Decretis,* ch. 3, sec. 11

Love which works good to all things, pre-existing overflowingly in the Good . . . moved itself to creation, as befits the superabundance by which all things are generated. . . . The Good by being extends its goodness to all things.

> ST. AUGUSTINE, *De div. nom.,* c. 395

He but spoke the word, and by that intelligible and eternal one (not vocal or temporal) were all things created. . . . What was spoken was not spoken successively . . . but all things together and eternally.

ST. AUGUSTINE, *Confessions* XI.9, 397

To suppose that God formed man from the dust with bodily hands is very childish. . . . God neither formed man with bodily hands nor did he breathe upon him with throat and lips.

ST. AUGUSTINE, *Commentary on the Book of Genesis*, 415

Whatever bodily or seminal causes, then, may be used for the production of things . . . yet the natures themselves, which are thus variously affected, are the production of none but the most high God.

ST. AUGUSTINE, *City of God*, Bk. XII, ch. 25, 426

Hence it comes to pass that, if a dead man is raised to life, all men spring up in astonishment. Yet every day one that had no being is born, and no man wonders, though it is plain to all, without doubt, that it is a greater thing for that to be created, which was without being, than for that, which had being, to be restored.

POPE ST. GREGORY THE GREAT, *Morals on the Book of Job*, 584

Allah created man of congealed blood.
Koran, c. 625

But this model of things, which preceded their creation in the thought of the Creator, what else is it than a kind of expression of these things in His thought itself.

ST. ANSELM, *Monologium*, ch. X, c. 1077

Since every agent intends to induce its own likeness in the effect, so far as the effect can receive it, an agent will do this the more perfectly, the more perfect itself is. But God is the most perfect of agents; therefore it will belong to him to induce His likeness in creation most perfectly, so far as befits created nature.

ST. THOMAS AQUINAS, *Summa Contra Gentiles*, II, 45, 1260

According to Augustine, the passage "Let the earth bring forth the green herb" means, not that plants were then actually produced in their proper nature, but that a germinative power was given the earth to produce plants by the work of propagation.

ST. THOMAS AQUINAS (1226–1274), *Quaestiones Disputatae*, 1268

For He brought things into being in order that His goodness might be communicated to His creatures, and be represented by them, and because His goodness could not be adequately represented by one creature alone, He produced many and diverse creatures.

ST. THOMAS AQUINAS, *Summa Theologiae*, I, q. 47, art. 1, 1272

It is the intention of God that all created things should represent the likeness of God, so far as their proper nature will admit.

DANTE, *Of Monarchy*, c. 1300

When a certain shameless fellow mockingly asked a pious old man what God had done before the creation of the world, the latter aptly countered that he had been building hell for the curious.

JOHN CALVIN, *Institutes*, I, 1536

It is not difficult for one seal to make many impressions exactly alike, but to vary shapes almost infinitely, which is what God has done in creation, this is in truth a divine work.

ROBERT BELLARMINE, *De ascensione mentis in Deum per scalas creaturarum*, 1615

For God has not brought forth the creation, that he should be thereby perfect, but for his own Manifestation, *viz.* for the great Joy and Glory.

JAKOB BOEHME, *Signatura Rerum,* 1621

We ought to beware lest, in our presumption, we imagine that the ends which God proposed to Himself in the creation of the world are understood by us.

RENÉ DESCARTES, *Principles of Philosophy,* 1644

All things always *were,* in the Word of God, causally, in force and potency, beyond all places and times . . . beyond all forms and species known by sense and understanding. . . . But . . . before they flowed forth . . . they were not in generation, they were not in space, nor in time, nor in the proper forms and species to which accidents happen.

JOHN SCOTUS ERIGENA, *The Division of Nature,* 1681

In whatever manner God created the world, it would always have been regular and in a certain general order. God, however, has chosen the most perfect, that is to say, the one which is at the same time the simplest in hypothesis and the richest in phenomena.

G. W. VON LEIBNIZ, *Discourse on Metaphysics,* 1685

It is the presence of God that, without cessation, draws the creation from the abyss of its own nothingness above which His omnipotence holds it suspended, lest of its own weight it should fall back therein.

LA CROIX DE JESUS CHARDON (17th century), in Bremond's *History of Religious Thought in France*

Of old, in the beginning, there was the great chaos, without form and dark. . . . In the midst thereof there presented itself neither form nor sound. Thou, O Spiritual Sovereign, camest forth in Thy presidency, and first did divide the gross from the pure. . . . Thou madest heaven; Thou madest earth; Thou madest man. All things got their being, with their reproducing power.

Prayer offered during imperial sacrifice to Shang Ti (the Ruler over all, the Supreme Being). Taken from a 1700 version, but the prayer is much older than that.

God might, indeed, have refrained from creating, and continued alone, self-sufficient, and perfect to all eternity; but his infinite Goodness would by no means allow it.

WILLIAM KING, *Essay on the Origin of Evil,* 1702

The creation, or rather the development of Nature spreads by degrees . . . with a continuous advance to an even greater breadth, in order that, in the process of eternity, the infinity of space may be filled with worlds and systems of worlds.

IMMANUEL KANT, *Allgemeine Naturgeschichte,* 1755

The end of creation is that all things may return to the Creator and be united with Him.

EMMANUEL SWEDENBORG, *The Divine Love and Wisdom,* 1763

To produce from nothing, or the *Creation,* is a term which cannot give us the most slender idea of the formation of the universe; it presents no sense, upon which the mind can fasten itself. . . . as all the world are nearly agreed that matter can never be totally annihilated, or cease to exist, how can we understand, that which cannot cease to be, could ever have had a beginning.

P. H. D'HOLBACH, *The System of Nature,* 1770

I looked upon the works of God in this visible creation, and an awfulness covered me: my heart was tender and often contrite, and a universal love to my fellow creatures was increased in me.

JOHN WOOLMAN, *Journal,* 1774

The creation is the bible of the Deist. He there reads in the hand-writing of the Creator himself, the certainty of his existence, and the immutability of his power.

THOMAS PAINE, *The Age of Reason,* 1795

The creation speaketh a universal language. . . . It cannot be counterfeited; it cannot be lost; it cannot be suppressed. . . . It preaches to all nations and all worlds; and this Word of God reveals to man all that it is necessary for him to know.

THOMAS PAINE, *The Age of Reason,* 1795

There is a grandeur in this view of life, with its several powers, having been originally breathed by the Creator into a few forms or into one.

CHARLES DARWIN, *The Origin of Species,* 1859

The scientific investigator is wholly incompetent to say anything at all about the first origin of the material universe.

T. H. HUXLEY, *Science and Hebrew Tradition,* 1870

"Who made it?" asked noted agnostic Robert G. Ingersoll when he saw a beautiful globe portraying the constellations and stars of the heavens.

"Why colonel," replied Henry Ward Beecher (1813–1887), "nobody made it; it just happened."

Told by M. D. LANDON in *Kings of Platform and Pulpit*

The idea of creation by a simple word was never the product of a Semitic mind. . . . and since a transcendental effect demands a transcendental cause, the most rational

explanation of the Mosaic cosmogony is still Revelation.

MARIE-JOSEPH LAGRANGE, *Revue Biblique,* 1896

The will of God is *not driven into creation.* God creates because he *would* and not because he *must.*

O. A. CURTIS, *The Christian Faith,* 1905

There is, in truth, not one chance in countless millions of millions that the many unique properties of carbon, hydrogen, and oxygen, and especially of their stable compounds water and carbonic acid, which chiefly make up the atmosphere of a new planet, should simultaneously occur in the three elements otherwise than through the operation of a natural law which somehow connects them together.

L. J. HENDERSON, *The Fitness of the Environment,* 1913

We were intellectually intoxicated with the idea that the world could make itself without design, purpose, skill, or intelligence; in short, without life.

GEORGE BERNARD SHAW, *Preface, Back to Methuselah,* 1921

Not once in the dim past, but continuously by conscious mind is the miracle of the Creation wrought.

A. S. EDDINGTON, *The Nature of the Physical World,* 1929

Creation means the transformation of an otherwise chaotic world into a thing of order and beauty. It is the shaping of an indifferent matter into a world of value.

J. E. BOODIN, *God and Creation,* 1934

The spiritual interest in the doctrine of Creation lies solely in the assertion of the dependence of all existence upon the Will of God.

WILLIAM TEMPLE, *Nature, Man and God,* 1934

Creation took place in eternity as an interior act of the divine mystery of life. The biblical conception of creation is only the reflection of this interior act in the consciousness of primitive man.

NICHOLAS BERDYAEV, *Slavery and Freedom*, 1944

Creation means . . . that He has infused His own being into another thing which thereby has taken an independent existence of its own.

ERICH FRANK, *Philosophical Understanding and Religious Truth*, 1945

The only part of man that is immediately *created* is the human soul.

JOHN A. O'BRIEN, *Truths Men Live By*, 1946

By creating the first germinal forms of life and endowing them with potentialities which would evolve into successive higher forms in accordance with definite laws which He infused into them, God remains the Creator and Author of all living organisms just as truly and as really as if He had created them all at once in their different species and genera.

JOHN A. O'BRIEN, *The Origin of Man*, 1947

It may be difficult to believe in creation, but it is more difficult to believe that the first thing, even if only an atom, or an electron, was not created.

J. F. NOLL, *Christian Faith Before the Bar of Reason*, 1948

Why did God make the universe? . . . God is Good, and being Good He could not, as it were, contain Himself; consequently, He told the secret of His Goodness to nothingness and that was Creation. The world is the overflow of Divine Goodness. Begotten of the Goodness of God, the Goodness of God is in it.

FULTON J. SHEEN, *The Philosophy of Religion*, 1948

The Absolute neither creates nor is created —in the current sense of making or being made. We can speak of creation only in the sense of the Being becoming in form and movement what it already is in substance and status.

SRI AUROBINDO, *The Life Divine*, 1949

If we believe in revelation, we must believe that man is *imago Dei;* and if man is *imago Dei,* then the understanding which God has of Creation is not in principle closed to man also, though it may lie at the limit of an infinite series of approaches.

WILLIAM E. HOCKING, *Perspectives on a Troubled Decade,* ed. Bryson, Finklestein and MacIver, 1950

We could enjoy the story of creation if we were sure it were not true. . . . Faced with the fact that the story of creation is true, that God did indeed so call everything from nothingness, we are caught up breathless, almost incapable of protest.

WALTER FARRELL, *My Way of Life,* 1952

Creation is simply an overwhelming outpouring, the overflow of infinite goodness.

THOMAS J. HIGGINS, *Perfection Is for You,* 1953

By spreading out creation in time and space, there is no reduction in the mystery.

The British Journal for the Philosophy of Science, 1954

The primeval account of Adam and Eve in the plentitude of created and creative power . . . is a picture of such divine exhilaration in creation as forces us, if we are asked to say summarily why God made the world, to affirm that He made it for fun!

ALEXANDER MILLER, *The Renewal of Man,* 1955

Creation by the Word out of nothing describes the absolute independence of God as creator, the absolute dependence of creation, and the infinite gap between.

PAUL TILLICH, *Biblical Religion and the Search for Ultimate Reality,* 1955

The doctrine of creation is not a speculative cosmogony, but a confession of faith, of faith in God as Lord.

R. BULTMANN, *Primitive Christianity,* 1956

When one reflects on the stupendous complexity of the living organism, it is entirely reasonable to doubt that it could have arisen as the result of a chance event completely physical in character.

WILLIAM S. BECK, *Modern Science and the Nature of Life,* 1957

To assert that a world as intricate as ours emerged from chaos by chance is about as sensible as to claim that Shakespeare's dramas were composed by rioting monkeys in a print shop.

MERRILL C. TENNEY, *Science and Religion,* ed. J. C. Monsma, 1962

If living protoplasm began by the fortuitous combination of amino acids in some primeval pool, activated by a chance stroke of lightning, why has the same process never been repeated?

MERRILL C. TENNEY, *Science and Religion,* ed. J. C. Monsma, 1962

The notion of a World Soul, a universal reason, creating the world, is . . . in monstrous contradiction of natural science. . . . For the explanation of the universe, mankind does not need any fairy tales about a World Soul.

Social Science, textbook used in schools of Soviet Russia, 1963

See also Adam; Beauty; Cause; Darwinism; Design; Evolution; Genesis; Glory of God; God: Finding Him; God: His Existence; God: His Goodness; God: His Intervention in the World; God: His Omnipotence; God: His Omniscience; Life; Love, Divine; Man; Man: Defined and Interpeted; Man: His Destiny and Goal; Man and God; Man's Unity with God; Matter; Miracles; Natural Selection; Nature and God; Nuclear War; Providence; Religion, Natural; Sabbath; Science; Science and Creation; Soul; Soul and God; Universe; Universe and God; Universe: Its Creation; World, the; World and God; World, Praise of.

CREATIVITY

Men continue to be creative in poetry and art only so long as they are religious.

J. W. VON GOETHE, *Conversation with Riemer,* July, 1810

Man's chief end is not to be saved but to mount up creatively. For this creative upsurge salvation from sin and evil is necessary.

NICHOLAS BERDYAEV, *The Meaning of the Creative Act,* 1955

CREATOR

The creator . . . was good, and the good can never have any jealousy of anything. And being free from jealousy, he desired that all things should be as like himself as they could be.

PLATO "Timaeus," *Dialogues,* c. 360 B.C

I am moved with spiritual sweetness toward the Creator and Ruler of this world, and honor Him with greater veneration, when I behold the magnitude and beauty . . . of His creation.

VINCENT OF BEAUVAIS, *Image of the World,* 13th century

Modern scientific theory compels us to think of the Creator as working outside time and space, which are part of His creation, just as the artist is outside his canvas.

JAMES JEANS, *The Mysterious Universe,* 1930

The Biblical doctrine of the Creator, and the world as His creation is itself not a doctrine of revelation, but it is basic for the doctrine of revelation.

> REINHOLD NIEBUHR, *The Nature and Destiny of Man,* Vol. 1, 1941

Biological science robbed the God of traditional Christianity of his creator role.

> PAUL E. SABINE, *Science Ponders Religion,* ed. H. Shapley, 1960

See also Creation; Evolution; God: His Existence; God: His Omnipotence; Nature and God; Universe: Its Creation; Universe and God; World and God.

CREATURES

Since God is outside the whole order of creation and since all creatures are ordained to Him and not conversely, it is manifest that creatures are really related to God Himself.

> ST. THOMAS AQUINAS, *Contra Gentiles,* Lib. 2, 1260

Hence from out the great ring which represents the Eternal Godhead there flow forth . . . little rings, which may be taken to signify the high nobility of natural creatures.

> HENRY SUSO (c. 1295–1365), *Sermons*

A creature is descended from God, a most perfect Father; but from Nothing as its Mother, which is Imperfection.

> WILLIAM KING, *Essay on the Origin of Evil,* 1702

Although the creatures of God . . . are all good enough to afford matter for entertainment and praise, yet they cannot detain and give anchorage to the soul of man.

> JOHN MORRIS, *A Collection of Pieces,* 1706

See also Animals; Creation; Cruelty.

CREEDS

The creeds of the Churches have gradually to pass into the universal religion of reason, and so into a moral, that is, a Divine community on earth.

> IMMANUEL KANT, *Religion Within the Limits of Pure Reason,* 1793

As men's prayers are a disease of the will, so are their creeds a disease of the intellect.

> RALPH WALDO EMERSON, "Self-Reliance," *Essays,* 1841

When an age is found occupied in proving its creed, this is but a token that the age has ceased to have a proper belief in it.

> MARK PATTISON, *Tendencies of Religious Thought in England,* 1860

I am far from denying that every article of the Christian Creed is beset with intellectual difficulties. . . . But I have never been able to see a connection between apprehending those difficulties, however keenly, and multiplying them to any extent, and on the other hand doubting the doctrines to which they are attached.

> JOHN HENRY NEWMAN, *Apologia pro Vita Sua,* 1864

The creeds of the future will begin where the old ones end: upon the nature of man, his condition on earth, his social duties and civil obligations, the development of his reason, his spiritual nature, its range, possibilities, education.

> HENRY WARD BEECHER, *North American Review,* August, 1882

Creeds are the grammar of religion, they are to religion what grammar is to speech. Words are the expression of our wants; grammar is the theory formed afterwards.

> H. FIELDING, *The Hearts of Men,* 1902

Inability to rank all articles of the Creed on the same level in regard to historical evidence is not equivalent to the denial of any.

> FREDERIC CHASE, *Essays on Theological Questions,* ed. H. B. Swete, 1905

A thousand creeds have come and gone
But what is that to you or me?
Creeds are but branches of a tree
The root of love lives on and on.

> ELLA WHEELER WILCOX (1855–1919), *Poems of*

A religion without a creed, thought it may seem sufficient when life runs smoothly, does not suffice in a crisis when a man is brought face to face with the mystery and difficulty of life.

> FATHER CUTHBERT, Preface, *God and the Supernatural,* 1920

We need a confession of faith in which the essentials are implicit, rather than a creed which attempts to make them explicit.

> T. H. BINDLEY, *The Modern Churchman,* September, 1921

The creeds always breathe the air of worship. . . . In these terse recitations, as of the Apostles' Creed, or splendid rhapsodies, as of the Nicene Creed, we are really liberating expressions of faith which are akin to the best in the modern temper. In them we say enough without succumbing to the deadly temptation to say too much.

> J. V. MOLDENHAWER, *Religion Today,* ed. A. L. Swift, 1933

I do not believe in any creed, but I use the creeds to express, to conserve, and to deepen my belief in God.

> WILLIAM TEMPLE, *Nature, Man and God,* 1934

Man's creed is that he believes in God, and therefore in mankind, but not that he believes in creed.

> LEO BAECK, *Essence of Judaism,* 1936

It has been said that Protestants are often better than their creed, and Catholics never so good as their own.

> C. C. MARTINDALE, *The Gates of the Church,* 1936

The proper question to be asked about any creed is not, "Is it pleasant?" but, "Is it true?"

> DOROTHY L. SAYERS, *The Mind of the Maker,* 1941

A creed may divide men. It should not, for a great creed should be sung rather than debated.

> GEORGE A. BUTTRICK, *Prayer,* 1942

We believe not in a creed, but through a creed; we believe in a Person.

> GERALD VANN, *The High Green Hill,* 1951

There is not a single quotation from the Gospels in the Apostles' Creed. The early Christians of the first century were recording in that Creed certain facts of which the Gospels were the literary and fuller expression.

> FULTON J. SHEEN, *The Woman,* 1951

The making of creeds was not a matter of idle speculation or theological gamesmanship. From the very beginning of the Christian movement, the claim to be a Christian could be literally a matter of life and death.

> JAMES A. MARTIN, JR., *Fact, Fiction and Faith,* 1960

See also Apostles' Creed; Athanasian Creed; Belief; Faith; Religion, Definitions of; Unity.

CRIME

The Master said: "Love of daring, inflamed by poverty, leads to crime: a man without love, if deeply ill-treated, will turn to crime."

> CONFUCIUS, *Sayings of,* 5th century B.C.

Our distrust is expensive. The money in courts and prisons is very ill laid out. We make by distrust, the thief and burglar, and incendiary, and by our court and jail we keep him so. An acceptance of the sentiment of love throughout Christendom for a season would bring the felon and outcast to our side in tears, with devotion of his faculties to our service.

RALPH WALDO EMERSON, *The Reformer,* 1844

The real significance of crime is in its being a breach of faith with the community of mankind.

JOSEPH CONRAD, *Lord Jim,* 1900

See also Vice.

CRISES

We live amidst one of the greatest crises in human history. . . . All values are unsettled; all norms are broken. Mental, moral, aesthetic and social anarchy reigns supreme.

PITIRIM SOROKIN, *Man and Society in Calamity,* 1943

The terrible crisis we face may be nothing less than God's call to us to reach a new level of humanity.

SAMUEL H. MILLER, *Look,* December 19, 1961

CRITICISM

Let the people talk; stand like a firm tower, which never shakes its top for all the blowing of the winds.

Virgil to Dante, in Dante's *Purgatoria,* c. 1310

Literary criticism should be completed by criticism from a definite ethical and theological standpoint.

T. S. ELIOT, "Religion and Literature," 1935, *Selected Prose*

The "pure" literary critic, who pretends, in the cant phrase, to stay "inside" a work . . . cannot help smuggling unexamined moral and metaphysical judgments into his "close analyses."

LESLIE FIEDLER, *Kenyon Review,* Autumn, 1950

It is the nature of literature itself that compels the critic finally to move beyond the level of verbal analysis to the level of metaphysical and theological valuation.

NATHAN A. SCOTT, *Modern Literature and the Religious Frontier,* 1958

Criticism itself must, in the end, be theological.

NATHAN A. SCOTT, *Modern Literature and the Religious Frontier,* 1958

We do not have to give our assent and amen to *everything* in the Church. Criticism, indeed loud criticism, can be a duty.

HANS KÜNG, *The Council, Reform and Reunion,* 1962

As a Church of men, sinful men, the Church, though of divine foundation, needs criticizing; as the Church of God she is, more than any other institution, worth criticizing.

HANS KÜNG, *The Council, Reform and Reunion,* 1962

See also Books; Literature; Protestantism.

CROOKEDNESS

That God can write straight with crooked lines does not entitle creatures to write crooked lines in the book of their lives.

KARL RAHNER, *Stimmen der Zeit,* 1949

See also Bribery; Dishonesty.

CROSS

By the wood of the Cross the work of the Word of God was made manifest to all;

his hands are stretched out to gather all men together.

ST. IRENAEUS, *Against Heresies,* c. 175

By the wood of the Cross the bitterness of the Law is changed into the sweetness of spiritual understanding, and the people of God can quench its thirst.

ORIGEN (185–254), *In Exod.*

Take first, as an unassailable foundation the Cross and build on it the rest of thy faith. Deny not the Crucified for if thou deny Him, thou hast many to arraign thee.

ST. CYRIL OF JERSUALEM, *Catechetical Lectures,* 350

Let us not be ashamed of the cross of Christ. . . . Make this sign as you eat and drink, when you sit down, when you go to bed, when you get up again, while you are talking, while you are walking, in brief, at your every undertaking.

ST. CYRIL OF JERUSALEM, *Catechetical Lectures,* 350

The Cross is salvation; in the Cross is life; in the Cross is protection from enemies. In the Cross is infusion of heavenly sweetness.

THOMAS À KEMPIS, *Imitation of Christ,* 1441

If thou wilt gladly bear the cross, it shall bear thee, and bring thee to the end that thou desirest, where thou shalt never have anything to suffer.

THOMAS À KEMPIS, *The Imitation of Christ,* 1441

No man ought to lay a cross upon himself, or to adopt tribulation, as is done in popedom; but if a cross or tribulation comes upon him, then let him suffer it patiently, and know that it is good and profitable for him.

MARTIN LUTHER (1483–1546), *Table Talk*

Desire nothing but the cross, and without comfort, for the cross is perfect in itself.

ST. JOHN OF THE CROSS, *Steps to Perfection,* c. 1584

To take up one's cross cannot mean anything else than that we should receive and suffer all the pains, contradictions, afflictions, and mortifications that happen to us.

ST. FRANCIS OF SALES (1567–1622), *Consoling Thoughts of,* ed. Huguet

Our Lord has well shown us that it is not necessary we should choose our crosses, but that it is necessary we should take and carry such as are presented to us.

ST. FRANCIS OF SALES (1567–1622), *Consoling Thoughts of,* ed. Huguet

The good thief transformed a bad cross into a cross of Jesus Christ.

ST. FRANCIS OF SALES (1567–1622), *Consoling Thoughts of,* ed. Huguet

At the sight of a Cross or Crucifix I can dispense with my hat, but scarce with the thought of my Saviour.

THOMAS BROWNE, *Religio Medici,* 1635

The Cross on Golgotha cannot release thee from sin if it is not set up in thy heart, too.

ANGELUS SILESIUS (1624–1677), *Cherubic Pilgrim*

The Cross of Christ is the Jacob's ladder by which we ascend into the highest heaven.

THOMAS TRAHERNE (1634–1704), *Centuries of Meditation*

No Cross, No Crown.

THOMAS FULLER, *Gnomologia,* 1732

If some day the taming talisman, the cross, should crumble, the savagery of the old warriors will again burst forth, the insensate berserk rage, about which the Nordic poets sing and say so much. That talisman is rotting, and some day it will lamentably crumble. The old stone gods will rise from the ancient ruins and rub the millennial dust from their eyes. Thor with his giant hammer will spring aloft and shatter the Gothic cathedrals.

> HEINRICH HEINE, *A Contribution to the History of Religion and Philosophy in Germany,* 1834

In the Cross and Him who hung upon it, all things meet; all things subserve it, all things need it, it is their center and interpretation. For He was lifted up on it, that He might draw all men and all things to Him.

> JOHN HENRY NEWMAN, *Parochial and Plain Sermons,* VIII, 1843

We do not attach any intrinsic virtue to the Cross; this would be sinful and idolatrous. Our veneration is referred to Him who died upon it.

> JAMES GIBBONS, *Faith of Our Fathers,* 1876

What does the apotheosis of the Cross mean, if not the death of death, the defeat of sin, the beatification of martyrdom, the raising to the skies of voluntary sacrifice, the defiance of pain?

> HENRI AMIEL, *Journal,* 1882

The Cross may crumble into dust, but there were words spoken under its shadow in Galilee, the echo of which will forever vibrate in the human conscience.

> JAMES DARMESTETER, *Selected Essays,* 1895

The world is not divided into men who suffer and men who do not suffer, but into men who carry the cross and men who do not and will not carry the cross.

> JOSEPH RICKABY, *An Old Man's Jottings,* 1925

The Cross does not abolish suffering, but transforms it, sanctifies it, makes it fruit-

ful, bearable, even joyful, and finally victorious.

> JOSEPH RICKABY, *An Old Man's Jottings,* 1925

The Cross of Christ must be either the darkest spot of all in the mystery of existence, or a searchlight by the aid of which we may penetrate the surrounding gloom.

> B. H. STREETER, *Reality,* 1926

It is the symbol of an Elder Brother who went into the far country to manifest the Father's forgiving love.

> HENRY SLOANE COFFIN, *The Meaning of the Cross,* 1931

It was realized from the beginning that the doctrine of the cross was bound to be, as the old word has it, "offensive," but it could not be evaded. The idea which was shocking and absurd to a confident logic was somehow convincing and persuasive to apprehensive faith.

> J. V. MOLDENHAWER, *Religion Today,* ed. A. L. Swift, 1933

What a sight it would be—Christians bearing their cross, instead of simply singing about it!

> E. LEWIS, *A Christian Manifesto,* 1934

Without that tree of the Cross, life on Main Street or Park Avenue is not full. Its shadow falls athwart every threshold of man's abode. To bear the Cross is a necessity. To bear it cheerfully is the secret of the saints.

> JOHN B. DELAUNAY, *Joy in Religion,* 1937

It has been said that Crosses are fashioned of two pieces; the one, the will of God; the other, my own will. Place these two wills side by side and there is no Cross, but only pleasure. It is only when God's will is laid across my will that there is pain and sorrow.

> JOHN B. DELAUNAY, *Joy in Religion,* 1937

The Cross is the way; the Resurrection the goal. The Cross is of time; the Resurrection for eternity. And the Cross itself is primarily not the suffering of death, but the victorious struggle of Life over and through death.

E. I. WATKIN, *The Catholic Centre,* 1939

It is the Cross which is the only valid symbol for the life of good men. Without it they never see the limits of their goodness. Without it they never understand the arrogance of their righteousness.

J. C. SCHROEDER, *Modern Man and the Cross,* 1940

Perhaps the saddest thing to admit is that those who rejected the Cross have to carry it, while those who welcomed it are so often engaged in crucifying others.

NICHOLAS BERDYAEV, *Christianity and Anti-Semitism,* 1940

There is no such thing as living without a cross. We are free only to choose between crosses. . . . In seeking to live without the cross, we got a cross—not one of Christ's making or our own, but the devil's.

FULTON J. SHEEN, *Radio Sermon,* April 6, 1941

Who would have imagined that two pieces of wood placed one upon the other could assume as many shapes as there are individual destinies! And yet such is the case. Your cross is made to your measure, and you must stretch yourself on it whether you want to or not, whether with hatred and revolt or with submission and love.

FRANÇOIS MAURIAC, *God and Mammon,* 1946

If the tide of secularism which is now sweeping across the earth is to recede, the Cross must be restored to Christianity.

KIRBY PAGE, *Living Joyously,* 1950

A church near Broadway printed a plain cross on a white background and underneath inscribed the title of a clever, but twisted and ephemeral, play then having its Broadway "run"—Design for Living.

GEORGE A. BUTTRICK, *Faith and Education,* 1952

The cross is God's way of uniting suffering with love.

GEORGIA HARKNESS, *The Modern Rival of Christian Faith,* 1953

The Cross represents the inversion of all human values. The human is put to death; and out of the death comes life.

JOHN COURTNEY MURRAY, *Social Order,* 1953

The cross is a throne of God's revelation. The heavens do not declare his glory more than the cross; the firmament does not show his *handiwork* more fully than the cross.

CLELAND B. MCAFEE, *Near to the Heart of God,* 1954

In the cross of Christ God confronts the successful man with the sanctification of pain, sorrow, humility, failure, poverty, loneliness and despair.

DIETRICH BONHOEFFER, *Ethics,* 1955

The only shadow that the Cross casts over history is one of shelter and asylum.

AMOS N. WILDER, *Theology and Modern Literature,* 1958

It is set against the sky line of our raucous, anonymous cities. In our cemeteries it is a talisman against death. It quickens the world's finest art and music. Through it men have known that the bleakest tragedy may be the most piercing and healing light.

GEORGE A. BUTTRICK, *Sermons Preached in a University Church,* 1959

He who has surrendered himself to it knows that the way ends in the Cross— even when it is leading him through the jubilation of Gennersaret or the triumphal entry into Jerusalem.

DAG HAMMARSKJOLD, *Markings*, 1964

The Cross of Christ condemns us to be saints!
Attributed to an African native, by Ernest Wall in *The Sovereign Emblem*

See also Calvary; Civilization; Crucifixion; Images; Incarnation; Jesus Christ: His Passion and Death; Market Place; Militarism; Optimism; Pain; Suffering; Violence.

CRUCIFIXION. See CALVARY; JESUS CHRIST: HIS PASSION AND DEATH

CRUELTY

To say we love God as unseen and at the same time to practice cruelty toward the least creature moving by His life, or by life derived from Him was a contradiction in His life.

JOHN WOOLMAN, *Journal*, 1774

CRUSADERS

The Crusaders brought not peace but a sword; and the sword was to sever Christendom.

S. RUNCIMAN, *The Eastern Schism*, 1955

CULTS

The cults offer to do something that the regular churches make no pretense of doing. . . . They will solve any problem over night, and results are practically guaranteed.

CHARLES W. FERGUSON, *The Confusion of Tongues*, 1928

In general the cults represent the earnest attempt of millions of people to find the fulfillment of deep and legitimate needs of the human spirit which most of them have not found in the established churches.

CHARLES S. BRADEN, *These Also Believe*, 1949

CULTURE AND CHRISTIANITY

There is something different between the general atmosphere or savour of any society or person or literature which can be called Christian at all and those which are wholly lacking in any part of Christian doctrine.

HILAIRE BELLOC, *Essays of a Catholic*, 1931

The choice before us is between the formation of a new Christian culture, and the acceptance of a pagan one.

T. S. ELIOT, *The Idea of a Christian Society*, 1939

The utopian illusions and sentimental aberrations of modern liberal culture are really all derived from the basic error of negating the fact of original sin.

REINHOLD NIEBUHR, *Nature and Destiny of Man*, I, 1941

There can have been few times in our era when the continuity of the Christian tradition as a cultural fact has worn as thin as is the case today.

WILLARD L. SPERRY, *Religion and America*, 1946

We are witnessing the last convulsions of a dying world; a dying culture; and everything about the Church that intrinsically belongs to this particular culture dies with it.

JEAN DANIELOU, *The Lord of History*, 1958

There is a basic anomaly in the relation of the Gospel to human culture that it both condemns and nourishes it. The church both denies civilization and creates it.

AMOS N. WILDER, *Theology and Modern Literature*, 1958

Culture is religion externalized, and our culture bears the imprints of its molding by Christianity.

> EDMUND A. OPITZ, *The Freeman*, February, 1961

See also Civilization; Civilization and Christianity; Civilization and Religion; Literature; Secularism; Society.

CULTURE AND RELIGION

Culture preserves spiritual life from the unhealthy, eccentric, and one-sided elements with which it tends to get involved only too easily.

> ROMANO GUARDINI, *The Spirit of the Liturgy,* 1935

The adjustment of modern religion to the "mind" of modern culture inevitably involved capitulation to its thin "soul."

> REINHOLD NIEBUHR, *An Interpretation of Christian Ethics,* 1935

Culture, having lost its soul, becomes civilization. Spiritual matters are discounted; quantity displaces quality.

> NICHOLAS BERDYAEV, *The Meaning of History,* 1936

Church and society are one in their essential nature; for the substance of culture is religion and the form of religion is culture.

> PAUL TILLICH, *The Interpretation of History,* 1936

The refusal of religion by the modern poet, and by more than moderns and by more than poets, goes back to the apparent denial of human living by religion, to the supposed incompatibility of life with Life and of art with Faith.

> AMOS WILDER, *The Spiritual Aspects of the New Poetry,* 1940

Our culture has lost any clearly defined spiritual standards and aims, and our cultural values have become impoverished.

> CHRISTOPHER DAWSON, *The Judgment of the Nations,* 1942

It is of the essence of our position that religion is inseparably bound up with a culture as a whole.

> *Relation of Religion to Public Education,* Report, American Council on Education, April, 1947

History shows that the vital collaboration of religion and culture has been the normal condition of human society from the beginning.

> CHRISTOPHER DAWSON, *Religion and Culture,* 1947

We have a secularized scientific world culture which is a body without a soul; while on the one hand religion maintains its separate existence as a spirit without a body.

> CHRISTOPHER DAWSON, *Religion and Culture,* 1947

No cultural creation can hide its religious ground.

> PAUL TILLICH, *The Protestant Era,* 1948

A secular culture falsifies the world, for it ignores the highest level of significance in the drama of existence.

> BEN ZION BOKSAR, *Perspectives on a Troubled Decade,* ed. Bryson, Finkelstein and MacIver, 1950

The world of culture—man's achievement—exists within the world of grace—God's Kingdom.

> H. R. NIEBUHR, *Christ and Culture,* 1951

When the churches take courage and assume responsibility for the spiritual life of the community and begin once more to make a successful penetration of our culture, we shall not need to worry about a secular state or secular schools.

> W. S. HUDSON, *The Great Tradition of the American Churches,* 1953

A Main Street civilization has infected American religion with its own cultural insensitivity.

> AMOS N. WILDER, *Theology and Modern Literature,* 1958

See also Civilization; Civilization and Christianity; Civilization and Religion; Literature; Society.

CURIOSITY

Every man hath in his own life sins enough, in his own mind trouble enough; so that curiosity after the affairs of others cannot be without envy and evil mind.

> JEREMY TAYLOR, *Holy Living,* 1650

CUSTOM

It is nothing to the City of God what attire the citizens wear, or what rules they observe, so long as they contradict not God's holy precepts.

> ST. AUGUSTINE, *The City of God,* XIX, 426

Out of a hundred intelligent Anglo-Saxons there are seldom two who think precisely alike on any given subject, be that subject what it may,—art, politics, literature, or religion. Indeed, there is but one faith common to all, and that is custom.

> EDGAR E. SALTUS, *Philosophy of Disenchantment,* 1885

Custom forms the original content of duty.

> FRIEDRICH PAULSEN, *A System of Ethics,* I, 1903

Customs constitute moral standards.

> JOHN DEWEY, *Human Nature and Conduct,* 1922

See also Apathy; Complacency; Conformity; Nonconformity; Sin.

CYNICISM

Cynicism is intellectual dandyism.

> GEORGE MEREDITH, *The Egotist,* 1879

The temptation shared by all forms of intelligence: cynicism.

> ALBERT CAMUS, *Notebooks,* 1935–1942

See also Agnosticism; Doubt; Skepticism.

DAMNATION

Deceitfulness and arrogance and pride
Quickness to Anger, harsh and evil speech
. . .
These be the signs, my Prince! of him whose birth
Is fated for the region of the vile.

> *The Song Celestial,* Sir Edwin Arnold's translation of the *Bhagavad-Gita,* 5th to 2nd century B.C.

If a man by false teaching corrupt the faith of God, for the sake of which Jesus Christ was crucified, such a man shall go . . . to the unquenchable fire as also shall he who listens to him.

> SAINT IGNATIUS OF ANTIOCH, *Ad Ephes.* 16, 2., c. 109

We shall no more be condemned for visionary acts of sin, than we shall be crowned for imaginary martyrdom.

> TERTULLIAN, *The Soul's Testimony,* c. 210

The minds of the damned are so firmly established in evil that every movement of their free will is disordered and is a sin.

> ST. THOMAS AQUINAS, *De Veritate,* 1259

How improbable it is in itself that it is only by the *permission* and not by the *ordinance* of God that man has brought damnation upon himself. . . . God not only foresaw the fall of the first man, and thereby the ruin of all his posterity, but he also willed it.

> JOHN CALVIN, *Institutes,* III, 1536

Few are saved, infinitely more are damned.

> MARTIN LUTHER (1483–1546), *Table Talk*

Were it not for gold and women, there would be no damnation.

CYRIL TOURNEUR, *The Revenger's Tragedy,* 1607

Those who entertain an extreme and inordinate dread of being damned, show that they have more need of humility and submission than of understanding.

ST. FRANCIS OF SALES (1567–1622), *Consoling Thoughts of,* ed. Huguet

Lucifer is as immortal as Michael, and Judas as immortal as St. Peter: But that which we call immortality in the damned, is but a continual dying; howsoever it must be called life, it hath all the qualities of death, saving the ease, and the end, which death hath, and damnation hath not.

JOHN DONNE, *Sermon,* January 29, 1625

One of the confusions of the damned will be that they will be condemned by their own reason, which they now use to condemn Christianity.

BLAISE PASCAL, *Pensées,* 1670

It is impossible to live at peace with those we regard as damned; to love them would be to hate God who punishes them; we positively must either reclaim or torment them.

JEAN JACQUES ROUSSEAU, *The Social Contract,* 1762

A man may lose his money, and yet die rich. He may lose his health, and yet die of old age. But once he loses his immortal soul it's good-bye, John!

EDGAR W. (BILL) NYE (1850–1896)

How anyone can believe in eternal punishment, . . . or in any soul which God has made being "lost," and also believe in the love, nay, even in the justice, of God, is a mystery indeed.

C. G. MONTEFIORE, *Liberal Judaism,* 1903

Impenitent sinners after their death lose every possibility of changing for good, and therefore remain unalterably given up to everlasting torments (for sin cannot but be torment).

JOHN SERGIEFF OF CRONSTADT (1829–1908), *My Life in Christ*

It is apparently easier to accept damnation as poetic material than purgation or beatitude; less is involved that is strange to the modern mind.

T. S. ELIOT, "Dante," *Selected Essays,* 1917–1932

The damned come into fatal collision with God, the infinite Good, in whom their beatitude was to be found: that is the pain of damnation.

CHARLES JOURNET, *The Meaning of Evil,* 1961

See also Condemnation; Death; Despair; Devil; Election; Eternal Life; Evil; God: His Wrath; Hell; Immortality; Mercy; Predestination; Punishment; Religion, Necessity of; Salvation; Sin; Sin: Its Consequences; Soul; Soul and God.

DANDYISM

To be a dandy and get the name of being one ought, I maintain, to be considered by persons so inclined just as disgraceful as to keep company with harlots or to seduce other men's wives.

ST. BASIL THE GREAT (330–379), *Advice to Young Men*

DANGER

In the hour of danger a man is proven: the boaster hides, the egotist trembles, only he whose care is for honor and for others forgets to be afraid.

DONALD HANKEY, *A Student in Arms,* 1915

DARK AGES

Even the errors then prevalent, a persecuting spirit, for instance, fear of religious inquiry, bigotry, these were, after all, but perversions and excesses of real virtue, such as zeal and reverence; and we, instead of limiting and purifying them, have taken them away root and branch.

JOHN HENRY NEWMAN, *Parochial and Plain Sermons,* I, 1843

DARKNESS

Only the conviction that it is the darkness within us which makes the darkness without, can restore the lost peace of our souls.

FRIEDRICH FROEBEL, *Mottoes and Commentaries of Mother-Play,* 1843

If you have not clung to a broken piece of your old ship in the dark night of the soul, your faith may not have the sustaining power to carry you through to the end of the journey.

RUFUS M. JONES, *The Radiant Life,* 1944

See also Light.

DARWINISM

Darwinism endeavors to dethrone God.

WALTER MITCHELL, *Scientia Scientarum,* 1865

The Darwinian theory, even when carried out to its extreme logical conclusion, not only does not oppose, but lends a decided support to a belief in the spiritual nature of man.

A. R. WALLACE, *Darwinism,* 1889

Those who see in Darwinism the final destruction of religion fail to realize that religion does not rest upon a hypothesis concerning the origin of human beings any more than it rests upon an Aristotelian-Ptolemaic cosmology. . . . Living Religion has no biology and cosmology. It does not rest upon unexplainable natural events, but upon the experience of the heart.

VIRGILIUS FERM, *Encyclopedia of Religion,* 1945

In the dogma deriving from Darwin, or more accurately from the innumerable popularizers and vulgarizers of Darwinism, neither God nor man had very much to do with the human animal and the nature of the society he has organized.

MARQUIS W. CHILDS and DOUGLASS CATER, *Ethics in a Business Society,* 1954

See also Creation; Evolution; Science.

DAUGHTERS

Mothers, be specially warned to regulate your daughters well. . . . They ought to go from their father's house to marriage, as combatants from the school of exercise, furnished with all the necessary knowledge, and to be a leaven able to transform the whole lump to its own virtue.

ST. JOHN CHRYSOSTOM (340–407), *Nicene and Post-Nicene Fathers,* Vol. 13, First Series

DAWN

At dawn the mind perceives eternal and divine truths. At dawn we see more brightly and hear better the power which so wisely built this world, lighted the stars, and drew the frontiers of the sea. At dawn the senses are more alive to the meaning of the Almighty power, which infused the spirit into all.

LJUDEVIT VULIČEVIĆ, *Moja mati,* 1929

DAY

The same sun rises on this day, and enlightens it; yet, because that Sun of Righteousness arose upon it, and gave new life unto the world in it, and drew the strength of God's moral precept unto it, therefore justly do we sing with the Psalmist, This is the day which the Lord hath made.

JOSEPH HALL (1574–1656), *Epistle to Lord Denny*

Each day is a little life; every waking and rising a little birth, every fresh morning a little youth, every going to rest and sleep a little death.

ARTHUR SCHOPENHAUER, *Our Relation to Ourselves*, 1851

Only for this day are we to ask for our daily bread, and we are expressly bidden to take no thought for the morrow.

WILLIAM OSLER, *A Way of Life, Address to Yale Students,* April 20, 1913

Every day is a messenger of God.
Russian Proverb

See also Days; Sabbath; Weekdays.

DAYS

All days are his who gave time a beginning and continuance; yet some he hath made ours; not to command, but to use. In none may we forget him: in some, we must forget all besides him.

JOSEPH HALL (1574–1656), *Epistle to Lord Denny*

DEAD

If we treat the dead as if they were wholly dead, it shows want of affection; if we treat them as wholly alive it shows want of sense. Neither should be done.

CONFUCIUS, *The Book of Rites,* c. 500 B.C.

The life of the dead consists in being present in the minds of the living.

CICERO, *Orationes Phillipiae,* c. 60 B.C.

For ages, billions of fools, without number, in languages without number, have said again and again, with a knowing look, "When you're dead, you're dead."

GEORGE BERNANOS, *Last Essays of,* 1955

See also Burial; Death; Funerals.

DEATH

Possessed by delusion, a man toils for his wife and child; but whether he fulfills his purpose or not, he must surrender the enjoyment thereof. When one is blessed with children and flocks and his heart is clinging to them, Death carries him away as doth a tiger a sleeping deer.

Mahabharata, XII, c. 800 B.C.

When man is born, it is best that he should journey with all speed to the gates of Death, and, wrapping himself in a close covering of earth, should lie at rest.

THEOGNIS (sixth century B.C.), *Elegies*

Not in the sky, not in the midst of the sea, not even in the clefts of the mountains is there a spot in the whole world where, if a man abide there, death could not overtake him.

Dhammapada, c. 5th century B.C.

How do I know that the love of life is not a delusion; and that the dislike of death is not like a child that is lost and does not know the way home?

CHUANG-TZU (4th century B.C.), *Texts of Taoism,* ed. J. Legge

Truly is it said, "For the Wise Man life is conformity to the motions of Heaven, death is but part of the common law of Change."

CHUANG-TZU (4th century B.C.), *Three Ways of Thought in Ancient China*

And now, O my judges, I desire to prove to you that the real philosopher has reason to be of good cheer when he is about to die, and that after death he may hope to obtain the greatest good in the other world.

SOCRATES, "Phaedo," Plato, *Dialogues,* 399 B.C.

To whom the gods vouchsafe their love and grace,
He lives not long, but soon has run his race.

MENANDER (c. 342–292 B.C.), quoted by Plutarch in *Letter to Apollonius*

As a man casting off worn-out garments, taketh new ones, so the dweller in the body, casting off worn-out bodies, entereth into others that are new.

Bhagavad-Gita, c. 5th century B.C.

I look forward to my dissolution as to a secure haven, where I shall at length find a happy repose from the fatigues of a long journey.

CICERO, *Essay on Old Age,* 44 B.C.

None but those shadowed by death's approach are suffered to know that death is a blessing; the gods conceal this from those who have life before them, in order that they may go on living.

LUCAN, *De Bello Civili,* c. 48 A.D.

To die well is to die willingly.

SENECA, *Epistulae Morales ad Lucilium,* c. 63

Never say about anything, "I have lost it," but only "I have given it back." Is your child dead? It has been given back. Is your wife dead? She has been returned.

EPICTETUS, *Discourses,* c. 110

The act of dying is also one of the acts of life.

MARCUS AURELIUS, *Meditations,* c. 170

And as for death, if there be any gods, it is no grievous thing to leave the society of men. The gods will do thee no hurt, thou mayest be sure. But if it be so that there be no gods, or that they take no care of the world, why should I desire to live in a world void of gods, and of all divine providence.

MARCUS AURELIUS, *Meditations,* c. 170

Death ought to be a pleasure.

TERTULLIAN, *De spectaculis,* c. 200

With regard to death in the obvious sense, all men die; it is this death which we consider as a dissolution. Of this death no human soul dies.

ORIGEN, *On the Soul,* c. 240

It is God's law, that as things rose so they should fall, as they waxed so should grow old, the strong become weak, and the great become little, and when they have become weak and little, they end.

CYPRIAN (200–258), *To Demetrian*

By the death of One the world was redeemed. . . . We prove by this divine example that death alone found immortality and that death redeemed itself.

ST. AMBROSE, *Two Books on the Death of Satyrus,* 375

What, I pray you, is dying? Just what it is to put off a garment. For the body is about the soul as a garment; and after laying this aside for a short time by means of death, we shall resume it again with the more splendor.

ST. JOHN CHRYSOSTOM, *Homilies,* c. 388

The day of death is when two worlds meet with a kiss: this world going out, the future world coming in.

JOSE B. ABIN, *Talmud J: Yebamot,* c. 400

The sons of God, as long as they live in this body of death, are in conflict with death.

ST. AUGUSTINE, *Enchiridion,* 421

The death of the soul takes place when God forsakes it, as the death of the body when the soul forsakes it. Therefore the death of both—that is, of the whole man—occurs when the soul, forsaken by God, forsakes the body.
ST. AUGUSTINE, *The City of God*, 426

Every soul must taste of death.
Koran, c. 625

When the soul is taken from the body, the eyes follow it, and look toward it. On this account the eyes remain open.
MOHAMMED (570–632), *Speeches and Table-Talk of*, ed. S. P. Lane

The meaning of death is not the annihilation of the spirit, but its separation from the body, and that the resurrection and day of assembly do not mean a return to a new existence after annihilation, but the bestowal of a new form or frame to the spirit.
AL-GHAZALI (born 1058 A.D.), *Alchemy of Happiness*

The man of wisdom . . . rejoices at the prospect of death, when the soul is disenthralled from the body.
ABRAHAM HASDAI, *Sefer Ha Tapuah*, 1230

That which is the end of any natural thing, cannot be evil in itself; since that which is according to nature, is directed to an end by divine providence.
ST. THOMAS AQUINAS, *Summa Contra Gentiles*, III, 1260

The noble Soul in old age returns to God as to that port whence she set forth on the sea of this life. And as the good mariner, when he approaches port, furls his sails . . . so should we furl the sails of our worldly affairs and turn to God with our whole mind and heart, so that we may arrive at that port with all sweetness and peace.
DANTE, *The Convito*, c. 1310

A good death does honor to a whole life.
PETRARCH, *Canzoniere*, 1350

To save life it must be destroyed. When utterly destroyed, one dwells for the first time in peace.
Zenrin Kushu, ed. Toyo Eicho, c. 1500

As a well-spent day brings happy sleep, so life well used brings happy death.
LEONARDO DA VINCI (1452–1519), *Notebooks of*

For nothing is there that may more effectually withdraw the soul from the wretched affections of the body than may the remembrance of death.
ST. THOMAS MORE, *The Four Last Things*, 1522

No man dies before his hour. The time you leave behind was no more yours, than that which was before your birth, and concerneth you no more.
MICHEL DE MONTAIGNE, *Essays*, xix, 1580

Socrates answered one that told him, The Thirty Tyrants have condemned thee to death; *And Nature them*, said he.
MICHEL DE MONTAIGNE, *Essays*, xix, 1580

There is no evil in life, for him that hath well conceived, how the privation of life is no evil.
MICHEL DE MONTAIGNE, *Essays*, xix, 1580

It is uncertain where death looks for us; let us expect her everywhere: the premeditation of death is a forethinking of liberty.
MICHEL DE MONTAIGNE, *Essays*, xix, 1580

Whoever has learned to die, has forgotten what it is to be a slave.
MICHEL DE MONTAIGNE, *Essays*, 1580

It is as natural to die as to be born; and to a little infant, perhaps the one is as painful as the other.

FRANCIS BACON, *Essays,* 1597

All that live must die,
Passing through nature to eternity.

WILLIAM SHAKESPEARE, *Hamlet,* c. 1602

O eloquent, just and mighty Death! whom none could advise, thou hast persuaded; what none hath dared, thou hast done; and whom all the world hath flattered, thou only hast cast out of the world and despised.

WALTER RALEIGH, *Preface, History of the World,* 1614

There is a remedy to all things except Death.

MIGUEL DE CERVANTES, *Don Quixote,* 1615

I know death hath ten thousand doors For men to take their exit.

JOHN WEBSTER, *Duchess of Malfi,* c. 1618

We must die! These words are hard, but they are followed by a great happiness: it is in order to be with God that we die.

ST. FRANCIS OF SALES (1567–1622), *Consoling Thoughts of,* ed. Huguet

The name of death is terrible, as it is usually proposed to us, for some one says: "Your dear father is dead," or "Your son is dead." This is not well-spoken among Christians. We should say, "Your son or your father is gone to his country and to yours; and because necessity required it, he passed by the way of death, in which he lingered not."

ST. FRANCIS OF SALES (1567–1622), *Consoling Thoughts of,* ed. Huguet

Now that Sin hath made life so miserable, if God should deny us death, he multiplied our misery.

JOHN DONNE, *Sermon,* February 11, 1627

We have a winding sheet in our Mother's womb, which grows with us from our conception, and we come back into the world, wound up in that winding sheet, for we come to seek a grave.

JOHN DONNE, *Sermon,* February 29, 1627

If a man knew the *gain of death,* the *ease of death,* he would solicit, he would provoke *death* to assist him, by any hand, which he might use.

JOHN DONNE (1571–1631), *Devotions,* XVII

All *mankind* is of one *Author,* and is one *volume;* when one Man dies, one *Chapter* is not *torn* out of the *book,* but *translated* into a better *language;* and every *Chapter* must be so *translated.*

JOHN DONNE (1571–1631), *Devotions,* XVII

Each night is but the past day's funeral, and the morning his resurrection: why then should our funeral sleep be otherwise than our sleep at night?

ARTHUR WARWICK, *Spare Minutes,* 1637

If you have served God in a holy life, send away the women and the weepers; . . . and when thou art alone, or with fitting company, die as thou shouldest, but do not die impatiently, and like a fox caught in a trap.

JEREMY TAYLOR, *Holy Living,* 1650

If he died young he lost but little, for he understood but little, and had not capacities of great pleasures or great cares; but yet he died innocent, and before the sweetness of his soul was deflowered and ravished.

JEREMY TAYLOR, *Holy Living,* 1650

The very spirits of a man prey upon the daily portions of bread and flesh, and every meal is a rescue from one death, and lays up another; and while we think a thought, we die; and the clock strikes, and reckons on our portion of eternity; we form our words with the breath of our nostrils, we have the less to live upon for every word we speak.

JEREMY TAYLOR, *Holy Dying*, 1651

Old men go to death; death comes to young men.

GEORGE HERBERT, *Jacula Prudentum*, 1651

Death borders upon our birth, and our cradle stands in the grave.

JOSEPH HALL (1574–1656), *Epistles*

Whatsoever we lose in death, is not lost to God; as no creature could be made out of nothing but by Him, so can it not be reduced into nothing, but by the same.

JOHN PEARSON, *An Exposition of the Creed*, 1659

It [death] is not overcome by pride, soothed by flattery, tamed by entreaties, bribed by benefits, softened by lamentations, nor diverted by time. Wisdom, save this, can prevent and help everything.

WILLIAM DRUMMOND, *The Cypress Grove*, 1673

To die young, is to do that soon, and in some fewer days, which once thou must do; it is but the giving over of a game, that after never so many hazards must be lost.

WILLIAM DRUMMOND, *The Cypress Grove*, 1673

I am going to my Father's; and though with great difficulty I have got hither, yet now I do not repent me of all the trouble I have been to arrive where I am. My word I give to him that shall succeed me in my pilgrimage, and my courage and skill to him that can get it. My marks and scars I carry with me to be a witness for me that I have fought His battle who will now be my rewarder.

JOHN BUNYAN, Mr. Valiant for Truth in *Pilgrim's Progress*, 1678

It is right to wish for death, inasmuch as it is the consummation of our repentance, the entrance to blessedness, and our eternal reward.

FRANÇOIS FÉNELON, *Spiritual Letters of* c. 1700

For Death is no more than a turning of us over from Time to Eternity.

WILLIAM PENN, *Some Fruits of Solitude*, 1718

It is impossible that anything so natural, so necessary, and so universal as death should ever have been designed by Providence as an evil to mankind.

JONATHAN SWIFT, *Thoughts on Religion*, 1728

Choose any life, but the life of God and Heaven, and you choose death, for death is nothing else but the loss of the life of God.

WILLIAM LAW, *The Spirit of Prayer*, 1749

For if a system has, in the long period of its existence, exhausted all the diversity of which its constitution is capable . . . nothing is more fitting than that it should then play its final rôle in the cosmic spectacle of ever-lapsing change—the rôle which becomes every finite thing, that of paying its tribute to mortality.

IMMANUEL KANT, *Allgemeine Naturgeschichte*, 1755

It matters not how a man dies, but how he lives.

SAMUEL JOHNSON, *Boswell's Life of*, 1772

What could move the God who is not a God of the dead but of the living, to produce death. Infinitely more conceivable is it that out of death—which cannot be an absolute death, but only the death which has life concealed within it—should life arise, than that life should pass over into, should lose itself in death.

F. W. VON SCHELLING, *Denkmal de Schrift von den Göttlichem*, 1812

All Death in Nature is Birth, and in Death itself appears visibly the exaltation of Life.
  J. G. FICHTE (1762–1814), *The Vocation of Man*

Peace, Peace! He is not dead, he doth not sleep—
He hath awakened from the dream of life.
  PERCY BYSSHE SHELLEY, *Adonais*, 1820

He lives, he wakes—'tis Death is dead, not he.
  PERCY BYSSHE SHELLEY, *Adonais*, 1820

He has outsoared the shadow of our night.
  PERCY BYSSHE SHELLEY, *Adonais*, 1820

And death is a low mist which cannot blot
The brightness it may veil.
  PERCY BYSSHE SHELLEY, *Adonais*, 1820

He is a portion of the loveliness
Which once more he made lovely.
  PERCY BYSSHE SHELLEY, *Adonais*, 1820

Death is the liberator of him whom freedom cannot release, the physician of him whom medicine cannot cure, and the comforter of him whom time cannot console.
  C. C. COLTON, *Lacon*, 1822

We sometimes congratulate ourselves at the moment of waking from a troubled dream: it may be so at the moment of death.
  NATHANIEL HAWTHORNE, *Journal*, October 25, 1835

When Death strikes down the innocent and young, for every fragile form from which he lets the panting spirit free, a hundred virtues rise, in shapes of mercy, charity, and love, to walk the world, and bless it.
  CHARLES DICKENS, *The Old Curiosity Shop*, 1840

As a navigator who suddenly disembarks from the cold, wintry and lonely sea, upon a coast which is laden with the warm rich blossoms of spring, so with one leap from our little bark we pass at once from winter to eternal springtime.
  JEAN PAUL RICHTER, *Reminiscences of the Best Hours of Life*, 1841

Of all events which constitute a person's biography, there is scarcely one . . . to which the world so easily reconciles itself as to his death.
  NATHANIEL HAWTHORNE, *The House of the Seven Gables*, 1851

Death is only a launching into the region of the strange Untried; it is but the first salutation to the possibilities of the immense Remote, the Wild, the Watery, the Unshored.
  HERMAN MELVILLE, *Moby Dick*, 1851

Every mother who has lost an infant, has gained a child of immortal youth.
  GEORGE WILLIAM CURTIS, *Prue and I*, 1857

Death is not death if it kills no part of us, save that which hindered us from perfect life. Death is not death if it raises us in a moment from darkness to light, from weakness into strength, from sinfulness into holiness. Death is not death, if it brings us nearer to Christ.
  CHARLES KINGSLEY, *The Water of Life*, 1867

Let children walk with Nature, let them see the beautiful blendings and communions of death and life, their joyous inseparable unity, as taught in woods and meadows, . . . and they will learn that death is stingless indeed, and as beautiful as life.
  JOHN MUIR, *A Thousand Mile Walk to the Gulf*, 1867

From the voiceless lips of the unreplying dead there comes no word; but in the night of death hope sees a star, and listening love can hear the rustle of a wing.

ROBERT G. INGERSOLL, at his brother's grave, 1879

Dying is that breakdown in an organism which throws it out of correspondence with some necessary part of the environment. Death is the result produced, the want of correspondence—failure to adjust internal relations to external relations.

HENRY DRUMMOND, *Natural Law in the Spiritual World*, 1883

If you knew what He knows about death you would clap your listless hands.

GEORGE MACDONALD, *Unspoken Sermons*, 3rd series, 1887

O son of the Infinite! I made death for thee as glad tidings. Why grievest thou over it? I made light for thee as guidance. Why dost thou hide from it?

BAHA ULLAH (1817–1892), *Hidden Words*

Death is the enlightener. The essential thing concerning it must be that it opens the closed eyes, draws down the veil of blinding mortality, and lets the man see spiritual things.

PHILLIPS BROOKS, *Perennials*, 1898

Every cradle asks us "Whence," and every coffin, "Whither?" The poor barbarian, weeping above his dead, can answer these questions as intelligently as the robed priest of the most authentic creed.

ROBERT INGERSOLL (1833–1899), *Address at a Child's Grave*

Death is not the cessation of life, but an incident in it. It is but the "narrows," to use the Psalmist's striking expression, through which the soul passes on its fateful voyage.

MORRIS JOSEPH, *Judaism as Creed and Life*, 1903

As to what happens to us after death, we have no conception, and we form no theory.

C. G. MONTEFIORE, *Liberal Judaism*, 1903

In reality, man never dies.

MARY BAKER EDDY, *Science and Health*, 1908

Man, tree, and flower are supposed to die; but the fact remains that God's universe is spiritual and immortal.

MARY BAKER EDDY, *Science and Health*, 1908

Man is immortal and the body cannot die, because matter has no life to surrender. The human concept named matter, death, disease, sickness and sin are all that can be destroyed. Death is but another phase of the dream that existence can be material.

MARY BAKER EDDY, *Science and Health*, 1908

It is the falling star that trails light after it. It is the breaking wave, which has power. It is the passing shower that lets the rainbow appear.

FRANCIS THOMPSON, *Nature's Immortality*, 1910

If we are, at death, to enter the dream life stripped of its absurdities, I confess for one I rather like the prospect.

HENRY HOLT, *On the Cosmic Relations*, 1914

"You should not be discouraged; one does not die of a cold," the priest said to the bishop.

The old man smiled. "I shall not die of a cold, my son. I shall die of having lived."

WILLA CATHER, *Death Comes for the Archbishop*, 1927

Believing in a God of infinite love and of infinite power, I find it natural to believe that death is not a disastrous sundown but rather a spiritual sunrise, ushering in the unconjectured splendors of immortality.

ARCHIBALD RUTLEDGE, *Peace in the Heart,* 1927

Deep within life is the need to orient it toward death. The one incontrovertible item of our knowledge about death is that it gives notice of itself as motion, we go toward it, we go through it. It never loses its *goingness.*

MARY AUSTIN, *Experience Facing Death,* 1931

That the end of life should be death may sound sad; yet what other end can anything have?

GEORGE SANTAYANA, *Some Turns of Thought in Modern Philosophy,* 1933

You will wake up and search, and you will find no one. You will remember that you once could remember, but you will not be afraid. The words will be blotted out, but the rhythm will persist. You will know that death is one of the adventures that were promised you, and that immensity bears you and enfolds you as softly as the down of a bird's nest.

MRS. HENRY BREWSTER, *Via Lucis,* posth. selections from her thoughts, ed. by E. Rod, translated by Maurice Baring in his *Have You Anything to Declare?,* 1937; not otherwise identified

It is man only who is able to face his death consciously; that belongs to his greatness and dignity. . . . Man's knowledge that he has to die is also man's knowledge that he is above death.

PAUL TILLICH, *The Shaking of the Foundations,* 1948

The feeling has grown up that to speculate about what may lie beyond the embalmer's table is anti-social.

C. S. LEWIS, *Against the Skeptics,* 1949

Death is a detail. Death is nothing more than changing gears in the journey of life.

HUBERT VAN ZELLER, *We Die Standing Up,* 1949

When death is spoken of as a tearing asunder, we forget that it tears especially the veil of appearances and of deceptions which conceal from our view the depth of reality and of others and ourselves.

ANTONIN SERTILLANGES, *Recollections,* 1950

Christ promises a birth which shall be followed by no death. Buddha promises a death which shall be followed by no birth, and thus by no further death.

PAUL LUDWIG LANDSBERG, *The Experience of Death,* 1953

Death is not something which does not take place until the end of life. Rather, death is the signature of this so-called life.

EMIL BRUNNER, *Eternal Hope,* 1954

With Christ's death and resurrection something happened to death. . . . Christ's death has given it a new character, which does not change its form but does alter its meaning and restore it to what it should have been for the first man—the passage into a new, eternally human life.

ROMANO GUARDINI, *The Last Things,* 1954

In the last analysis, it is our conception of death which decides our answers to all the questions that life puts to us.

DAG HAMMARSKJOLD, *Markings,* 1964

See also Annihilation; Beatific Vision; Bereavement; Body; Body and Soul; Burial; Capital Punishment; Damnation; Death, Fear of; Devil; End of the World; Eternal Life; Euthanasia; Funerals; Grace; Grief; Heaven; Hell; Immortality; Immortality, Belief in; Jesus Christ: His Resurrection; Life; Life: Its Meaning; Life and Death; Martyr; Mourning; Nature; Nirvana; Oblivion; Original Sin; Predestination; Punishment; Sin: Its Consequences; Sorrow; Soul; Spirit; Spirit, Human; Tragedy.

DEATH, FEAR OF

The fear of death is indeed the pretense of wisdom, and not real wisdom, being a pretense of knowing the unknown; and no one knows whether death, which men in their fear apprehend to be the greatest evil, may not be the greatest good.

PLATO, "Apology," *Dialogues,* 399 B.C.

So long as we live death is absent from us; and when it is present, we shall not exist any more. So during our life and after death we have nothing to fear from death.

EPICURUS (340–270 B.C.,) *Epistle ad Menoeceum*

For certain is death for the born, and certain is birth for the dead; therefore over the inevitable thou shouldst not grieve.

Bhagavad-Gita, c. 2nd century B.C.

That day, which you fear as being the end of all things, is the birthday of your eternity.

SENECA, *Epistulae ad Lucilium, Epis.* c. 11, c. 63 A.D.

What is death at most? It is a journey for a season; a sleep longer than usual. If thou fearest death, thou shouldest also fear sleep.

ST. JOHN CHRYSOSTOM, *Homily,* c. 388

The first sign of love to God is not to be afraid of death, and to be always waiting for it. For death unites the friend to his friend—the seeker to the object which he seeks.

AL-GHAZALI (born 1058), *Alchemy of Happiness*

When the hour comes when life must be lost that you may find it in God, when danger of death is on you, and you see plainly that to obey God you must sacrifice life, then, I know not how, it comes to pass that what before seemed a very clear precept is involved in incredible darkness.

ST. FRANCIS XAVIER, *Letter to the Society of Jesus at Rome,* May, 1546

The end of our career is death, it is the necessary object of our aim: if it affrights us, how is it possible we should step one foot further without an ague?

MICHEL DE MONTAIGNE, *Essays,* xix, 1580

Men fear Death, as children fear to go in the dark. . . . Certainly the contemplation of death, as the wages of sin and passage to another world, is holy and religious; but the fear of it, as a tribute due unto nature, is weak.

FRANCIS BACON, *Essays,* 1597

Of all the evils of the world which are reproached with an evil character, death is the most innocent of its accusation.

JEREMY TAYLOR, *The Rule and Exercises of Holy Dying,* 1651

Men shun the thought of death as sad, but death will only be sad to those who have not thought of it. It must come sooner or later, and then he who has refused to seek the truth in life will be forced to face it in death.

FRANÇOIS FÉNELON, *Spiritual Letters of,* c. 1700

No one who is fit to live need fear to die. . . . To us here, death is the most terrible word we know. But when we have tasted its reality, it will mean to us birth, deliverance, a new creation of ourselves.

G. S. MERRIAM, *A Living Faith,* 1876

Death would be terrifying if there were not alongside it, resplendent immortality.

ADRIEN-EMANUEL ROQUETTE, *Propagateur Catholique,* 1882

To think of death and to prepare for death, is not a surrender; it is a victory over fear.

> PAUL WILHELM VON KEPPLER, *More Joy*, 1911

Why are happy people not afraid of Death, while the insatiable and the unhappy so abhor that grim feature?

> LOGAN PEARSALL SMITH, *Afterthoughts*, 1931

When we come to realize that death that crushes is but the tender clasp of God that loves, it loses all its terrors.

> VINCENT MCNABB, *Joy in Believing*, 1939

'Feared of dying? Were you 'feared of being born?

> *Old Farmer's Almanac*, 1943

The fear of dying is a thing lots of people have; I certainly have it, and I do not think there is any reason why you should regard yourself as a bad Christian if you have it too. It is very largely a matter of temperament.

> R. A. KNOX, *Retreat for Priests*, 1946

Death considered as a finality, physical death considered as the universal negation of our existence, is only the reflection of a despairing unbelief, a negation of the *person* by the *person*.

> PAUL-LUDWIG LANDSBERG, *The Experience of Death*, 1953

The attitude toward death is changing in our modern thinking. No longer is it something to be feared, but rather a giving of ourselves to God. It is the total gift of ourselves united with Christ.

> CLIFFORD HOWELL, *Address*, Seattle, Wash., August, 1962

See also Death; Fear; Immortality.

DECAY

All perishes and passes that we see with our eyes. The wealth of this world wanes into wretchedness. Robes and riches rot in the ditch. . . . Their gold and their treasure draw them to death.

> RICHARD ROLLE (c. 1300–1349), *Selected Works of*, ed. G. C. Heseltine

DECISION

When you have wandered a good deal, it is necessary either that you climb the heights of the blessed life carrying the weight of a wrongfully deferred labor or sink down inertly in the valley of your sins.

> PETRARCH, *Letter to Denis of Borgo San Sepolcro*, 1336

At every instant, at every step in life, the point has to be decided, our soul has to be saved, heaven has to be gained or lost. . . . At every step we must set down the foot and sound the trumpet. . . . The profit of every act should be this, that it was right for us to do it.

> ROBERT LOUIS STEVENSON, *Lay Morals*, 1898

Just because there are so many possible roads through time and eternity, do we need to choose one road; just because of the vastness of life, do we need a shelter?

> MAUDE PETRE, *My Way of Faith*, 1937

It is high time for the spiritually awake to acknowledge, "I dare not shirk the ultimate question without remaining a craven weakling on earth, having no firm foundation."

> FRANZ WERFEL, *Between Heaven and Earth*, 1944

The question of tentativeness in the search for the most high and the most good is often less a matter of reverence for truth than it is a desire to avoid responsible decision.

NELS F. S. FERRÉ, *Faith and Reason,* 1946

I believe that first we must look into the abyss and that we must be able to bear the sight of the void that opens before us. And I believe that this void does not signify an end but a call for decision.

C. F. VON WEIZSÄCKER, *Theologie und Physik,* 1951

Religion is commitment, decision, faith, personal responsibility. To be religious is to take a serious part in historical decisions.

HERBERT WALLACE SCHNEIDER, *Religion in the 20th Century,* 1952

The logic is clear that every decision is for or against God. And more than logic, we have our Lord's word for it: "Be ye perfect."

J. A. PIKE, *Doing the Truth,* 1955

See also Chance; Choice; Commitment; Conviction; Determinism; Free Will; Individual Responsibility.

DECLARATION OF INDEPENDENCE

We hold these truths to be self-evident, that all men are created equal, that they are endowed by their Creator with certain inalienable Rights, that among these are Life, Liberty and the pursuit of Happiness.

Declaration of Independence, United States of America, July 4, 1776

The Declaration of Independence was a leading event in the progress of the Gospel dispensation.

JOHN QUINCY ADAMS, *Letter to Rev. J. Edwards,* July 13, 1837

DEEDS

Seek ye for a store of good deeds, men and women! for a store of good deeds is full of salvation.

AOGEMADAECHA, *Zend-Avesta,* c. 700 B.C.

The Lord of this universe becomes pleased with him who is engaged in doing good to the world, since the Lord is its soul and refuge.

Mahanirvana Tantra (prior to 5th century B.C.)

An evil deed, like freshly drawn milk, does not turn sour at once.

Dhammapada, c. 5th century B.C.

That deed is not well done of which a man must repent, and the reward of which he receives crying and with a tearful face.

Dhammapada, c. 5th century B.C.

No noble deed has ever been done by men, without the Divine Word who visited the souls of those who were capable for a while of receiving Him.

ORIGEN, *Contra Celsum,* VI, 78, 246

Rabbi Eleazar used to say: One whose wisdom exceeds his deeds may be compared to a tree whereof the branches are many and the roots few, so that when the winds come it is uprooted and turned upon its face.

Pirke Aboth, Talmud, between 2nd and 4th century

It matters not whether a man does much or little, if only he directs his heart towards Heaven.

Berakot Talmud, c. 400 A.D.

The good deed drives away the evil deeds.

Koran, Sura II. 116, c. 625

God plays and laughs in good deeds, whereas all other deeds, which do not make for the glory of God, are like ashes before Him.

> MEISTER ECKHART (14th century), *Works*

If to do were as easy as to know what were good to do, chapels had been churches and poor men's cottages princes' palaces.

> PORTIA, in Shakespeare's *The Merchant of Venice*, c. 1595

It is not enough to do good; one must do it in the right way.

> JOHN VISCOUNT MORLEY, *On Compromise*, 1874

Not by the Creed but by the Deed.

> F. ADLER, *Motto of the Ethical Culture Society*

We have left undone those things which we ought to have done; and we have done those things which we ought not to have done.

> *Book of Common Prayer* (American version), first published 1876

If we are often puzzled what to think, we need seldom be in doubt what to do.

> JOHN LUBBOCK, *The Pleasures of Life*, 1887

No man can become a saint in his sleep.

> HENRY DRUMMOND, *The Greatest Thing in the World*, 1890

There is a vast difference between doing right and not doing wrong. . . . Indeed it is possible that to do what is definitely sinful may need more character than simply to do no wrong.

> B. W. MATURIN, *The Laws of the Spiritual Life*, 1907

Sick or well, blind or seeing, bond or free, we are here for a purpose and however we are situated, we please God better with useful deeds than with many prayers or pious resignation.

> HELEN KELLER, *My Religion*, 1927

Professors of religion spend too much of their energy on discussing the delivery of the goods and too little on the production of the goods to be delivered.

> L. P. JACKS, *Confession of an Octogenarian*, 1942

What makes Christ's teachings difficult is that they obligate us to do something about them.

> JOHN J. WADE, *Conquering with Christ*, 1942

What exasperates one in many Christians is that their deeds seem to stand in no relation at all to the faith they profess.

> GEDDES MACGREGOR, *The Hemlock and the Cross*, 1963

Good deeds are the best prayer.

> Serbian Proverb

See also Actions; Acts; Conduct; Determinism; Duties; Election; Inaction; Punishment; Will; Words.

DEFEAT

Defeat is a school in which Truth always grows strong.

> HENRY WARD BEECHER, *Life Thoughts*, 1858

Defeat is never anything but an invitation to have recourse to God.

> ANTONIN SERTILLANGES, *Recollections*, 1950

DEHUMANIZATION

When human atoms are knit into an organization in which they are used . . . as cogs and levers and rods, it matters little that their raw material is flesh and blood.

. . . The hour is very late, and the choice of good and evil knocks at our door.

NORBERT WIENER, *The Human Use of Human Beings*, 1954

DEISM

The great name of Deist, which is not sufficiently revered, is the only name one ought to take. The only gospel one ought to read is the great book of Nature, written by the hand of God and sealed with his seal. The only religion that ought to be professed is the religion of worshipping God and being a good man.

VOLTAIRE, *Bolingbroke*, 1736

The true deist has but one Deity; and his religion consists in contemplating the power, wisdom, and benignity of the Deity in his works, and in endeavoring to imitate him in every thing moral, scientifical, and mechanical.

THOMAS PAINE, *The Age of Reason*, 1795

Every person, of whatever religious denomination he may be, is a Deist in the first article of his Creed. Deism, from the Latin word Deus, God, is the belief of a God, and this belief is the first article of every man's creed.

THOMAS PAINE, *Prospect Papers*, 1804

You, O Deists, profess yourselves the Enemies of Christianity, and you are so: you are also the Enemies of the Human Race and of Universal Nature. . . . Deism, is the Worship of the God of this world by means of what you call Natural Religion and Natural Philosophy, and of Natural Morality or Self-Righteousness, the Selfish Virtues of the Natural Heart.

WILLIAM BLAKE, *Preface to Jerusalem*, 1820

Deism is nothing but a ghost of religion which haunts the grave of dead faith and lost hope.

CHRISTOPHER DAWSON, *The Judgment of the Nations*, 1942

There is the fact of the greatness of God over and above and through all the world, what the books call his *transcendence*. Push it too far and you have *deism*.

CLELAND B. MCAFEE, *Near to the Heart of God*, 1954

See also Democracy; God: Considered as Impersonal; Nature; Religion, Natural; Theism.

DELIGHT

Delight—top-gallant delight—is to him who acknowledges no law or lord but the Lord his God, and is only patriot to heaven.

HERMAN MELVILLE, *Moby Dick*, 1851

See also Pleasure.

DELIVERANCE

From lightning and tempest; from plague, pestilence and famine; from battle and murder, and from sudden death, Good Lord, deliver us.

The Book of Common Prayer, 1662

DEMOCRACY

This democratic idea is founded in human nature, and comes from the nature of God, who made human nature. To carry it out politically is to execute justice, which is the will of God.

THEODORE PARKER, *Sermon*, November 28, 1850

Religion, by devoting itself to the elevation of human character, becomes a prop and stay of free institutions.

CHARLES W. ELIOT, *Why the Republic May Endure*, 1894

The essential doctrine of democracy is that each man, as a free human soul, lives of his free will in the service of the whole people.

GILBERT MURRAY, *The League of Nations and the Democratic Idea*, 1918

Democracy is the very child of Jesus' teachings of the infinite worth of every personality.

> FRANCIS J. MCCONNELL, *Christian Principles and Industrial Reconstruction,* 1918

The institutions and the mentality which constitute modern democracy are a heritage from medieval churchmen.

> ALFRED O'RAHILLY, *Studies,* March, 1919

The Church originated representative institutions; the State adopted them.

> HENRY JONES FORD, *Representative Government,* 1924

Democracy is not simply a political system; it is a moral movement and it springs from adventurous faith in human possibilities.

> HARRY EMERSON FOSDICK, *Adventurous Religion,* 1926

Democracy in the last resort rests on a spiritual community. It arose in the West on a religious foundation. Even before the common man acquired political rights, he possessed a real kind of spiritual citizenship as a member of the universal Christian society.

> CHRISTOPHER DAWSON, *The Modern Dilemma,* 1932

The doctrines of modern democracy are not a scientific theory, but a moral and religious creed which owes more than was generally realized to the personal inspiration of Rousseau and is hardly separable from the mystical Deism with which it was originally associated.

> CHRISTOPHER DAWSON, *Science for a New World,* ed. Thompson and Crowther, 1934

We are justified, from the point of view of exegesis, in regarding the "democratic conception of the State" as a justifiable expansion of the thought of the New Testament.

> KARL BARTH, *Church and State,* 1939

Democracy, child of religion, heroically devoted vision of man, can part from that religious vision only at its mortal peril, like the nursling, torn from its mother's breast.

> WALDO FRANK, *Chart for Tough Water,* 1940

If we consider the extent and nature of the sacrifices demanded of all citizens, especially in our day when the activity of the state is so vast and decisive, the democratic form of government appears to many as a postulate of nature imposed by reason itself.

> POPE PIUS XII, *Christmas Message,* 1944

Man's capacity for justice makes democracy possible . . . his inclination to injustice makes democracy necessary.

> REINHOLD NIEBUHR, *The Children of Light and the Children of Darkness,* 1945

Democracy substitutes for our essential "sinfulness as making progress impossible," faith in man's essential loyalty to the ultimate good, for which democratic institutions exist.

> JAY WILLIAM HUDSON, *Religious Liberals Reply,* 1947

Christian education for democracy is an empty and hypocritical slogan . . . unless it means education for equality of opportunity.

> JAMES E. MURRAY, *Address,* March 31, 1948

The Catholic Church is not a democracy and democratic terms of reference are totally out of point in discussing her because the Catholic Church is not a political organization. . . . Christ did not come as the result of a plebiscite. . . . The

Incarnation and Redemption were not accomplished by democratic processes.

JOHN J. WRIGHT, *The Tablet* (Brooklyn, N.Y.) November 17, 1951

In a democracy, the state and its schools can never do much more than reflect the spiritual climate of the community at large.

W. S. HUDSON, *The Great Tradition of the American Churches,* 1953

The Christian line that follows from the gospel betrays a striking tendency to the side of what is generally called the "democratic State."

KARL BARTH, *Against the Stream,* 1954

Secularism is Democracy and Democracy is Secularism, both as a way of life and as a form of government.

HORACE M. KALLEN, *Secularism is the Will of God,* 1954

What the Deists hoped to achieve without a church has in large degree come to pass in the land of many churches. Indeed, the idea that religion is handmaiden to democracy has made such headway that American Catholicism, American Protestantism, and American Judaism appear like parallel shoots on a common stock.

ARTHUR MANN, *Commentary,* June, 1954

When democracy presents itself to the world and seeks to justify itself as a merely humanistic secularism, it cannot expect to secure the allegiance and support of a Christianity worthy of the name, of a Christianity reawakened.

J. V. L. CASSERLEY, *The Bent World,* 1955

I think that if Jesus had lived in our century he would have used the "democracy of God" in place of the "Kingdom of God." For even God can, after all, only choose those who first choose him.

PAUL ARTHUR SCHLIPP, *This Is My Faith,* ed. S. G. Cole, 1956

Although Christianity has never been the guarantee of a democratic state anywhere in the world, no democracy has ever thrived successfully for any period of time outside of Christian influence.

THEODORE H. WHITE, *The Making of the President—1960* (1961)

Democracy is . . . not the only possible form of society in which the Church can live and carry on her mission. But it is the best form of society for the modern world.

FRANZISKUS KOENIG, *Statement* to the National Catholic Welfare Council, July, 1964

See also Church: Its Authority; Church and State; Equality; Freedom, Religious; Government and God; Government and Religion; Religious Test for Office.

DEMOCRACY, RELIGION OF

Since service of God is in reality service of man, there will be sin in this new religion of democracy; it will be a failure to serve mankind. In other words it will be "disloyalty to society."

CHARLES A. ELLWOOD, *Reconstruction of Religion,* 1922

Democracy is good politics, but a poor religion.

NELS F. S. FERRÉ, *Learning and World Peace,* 1948

In this modern world there is only one faith that can sustain the unity of a people, the greater unity that gives free play to the richness of difference that makes the creative life of a community—and that is the faith of democracy.

R. M. MACIVER, *The Ramparts We Guard,* 1950

The power of this faith is that it does not depend on power, but on the consensus that leaves other faiths free and still provides a ground on which the diversities of faith can stand.

R. M. MACIVER, *The Ramparts We Guard,* 1950

Democracy must become an object of religious dedication.
J. PAUL WILLIAMS, *What Americans Believe and How They Worship*, 1952

Democracy can generate a system of moral principles . . . a secular morality.
AGNES MYER, *Address to American Unitarian Association*, 1954

The new danger is that a *non-Christian* democratic faith shall violate the conscience of many who yet adhere to a Christian faith in the sovereign God.
TUNIS ROMEIN, *Education and Responsibility*, 1955

As the state takes the place of the church in education, it must develop its own religion. Obviously that religion is democracy.
TUNIS ROMEIN, *Education and Responsibility*, 1955

The liberal humanist tendency toward an idolatrous absolutizing of democracy which transforms it into an ultimate ethic or even a higher religion, is . . . a ridiculous illusion.
J. V. L. CASSERLEY, *The Bent World*, 1955

DEMONOLOGY

Demonology is the shadow of theology.
RALPH WALDO EMERSON, *Demonology*, 1877

The demonology of the New Testament surpasses that of Judaism and paganism in that it places demons primarily in the moral sphere; that is, in their conflict against God and His Kingdom, and thus man, by his faith in Christ is freed from the constant fear of demons, which characterized the popular beliefs of old.
Encyclopedia Dictionary of the Bible, 1963

DEMONS

I will begin by asking, why should we not worship demons? They are the creatures of God, and the worshipper of God is right to serve those who have His authority.
CELSUS, *A True Discourse*, c. 178

Their great business is the ruin of mankind . . . Invisible and intangible . . . demons and angels breathe into the soul, and rouse up its corruptions with furious passions and vile excesses; or with cruel lusts accompanied by various errors.
TERTULLIAN, *Apology*, ch. xxii, 197

Demons are everywhere, and the cursing of them is universal.
TERTULLIAN, *The Testimony of the Christian Soul*, c. 210

Demons secretly work in [men's] inward parts, corrupt the health, hasten diseases, terrify their souls with dreams, harass their minds with frenzies.
LACTANTIUS, *The Divine Institutes*, c. 310

Demons have only that power which the secret decree of the Almighty allots to them.
ST. AUGUSTINE, *City of God*, II, 23, 426

According to Catholic belief demons or fallen angels retain their natural powers as intelligent beings, of acting in the material universe, and using material objects, and directing material forces for their own wicked ends; and this power which is in itself limited and is subject, of course, to the control of Divine Providence, is believed to have been allowed a wider scope for its activities in consequence of the sin of mankind.
Catholic Encyclopedia, V, 1913

I cannot rule it [the hypothesis of demon possessions] out as impossible, especially in regard to the far off days of the Biblical narrative and the far off places of the world where the power of Christ has yet had little chance of overcoming his enemies.

LESLIE D. WEATHERHEAD, *Psychology, Religion and Healing,* 1951

Demonic powers in history mean, then, that there are demons, purely spiritual beings, fallen angels, at work upon human history.

JOSEF PIEPER, *The End of Time,* 1954

There seems no reason *a priori* why we should reject the whole concept of demon possession. When the Gospels give us good evidence that it did take place, it is best to accept this.

J. D. DOUGLAS, ed. of *The New Bible Dictionary,* 1962

See also Devil; Dreams; Hell; Spirits; Evil.

DENOMINATIONALISM

I do not want the walls of separation between different orders of Christians to be destroyed, but only lowered, that we may shake hands a little easier over them.

ROWLAND HILL (1744–1833)

Denominationalism . . . represents the accommodation of Christianity to the caste-system of human society.

H. RICHARD NIEBUHR, *Social Sources of Denominationalism,* 1929

There is no establishment [in the denominational system], and no official connection of any church with the government. . . . All churches are free churches, all are equal before the law, all are separated from the state and the visible Church is frankly and confessedly divided. Histori-

cally it has been for the most part quite complacent about its divisions, glorying in the liberty of its parts.

WINIFRED E. GARRISON, *The Quest and Character of a United Church,* 1957

All denominations are, of course, in their various ways testifying to Christ. But their separate traditions make this witness less concentrated and distinct, and their insistence on continuing separateness beclouds the sole reason for His Church.

SAMUEL M. CAVERT, *On the Road to Christian Unity,* 1961

The dechristianization which has thrust deep into all communions makes denominational differences seem irrelevant to many people today, in comparison with the fundamental difference between Christain and non-Christian.

HANS KÜNG, *The Council, Reform and Reunion,* 1962

See also Division; Ecumenism; Paths; Pluralism; Religion; Religious Conflict; Rivalry; Sects and Sectarianism; Unity.

DEPRAVITY. See MAN: HIS WICKEDNESS

DESIGN

The idea of "design" has wholly disappeared from the vast province of science.

ERNEST HAECKEL, *The Riddle of the Universe,* 1901

For all that the lapsing of the old argument [from design] shows the world may be far more purposeful than Paley ever supposed. Probably it will be found that teleology is only driven from smaller fields to greater by the change.

WILLIAM NEWTON CLARKE, *The Christian View of God,* 1909

The chance that a world such as ours should occur without intelligent design becomes more and more remote as we learn of its wonders.

ARTHUR COMPTON, *Man's Destiny in Eternity,* 1949

See also Chance; Creation; God: His Existence; Nature and God; Science; Science and Creation; Universe; Universe: Its Creation.

DESIRE AND PRAYER

If you do not wish to cease praying, cease not to desire. Your continuing desire is your continuing voice.

ST. AUGUSTINE, *Enarratio in Ps.* 37, c. 415

If we desire from the heart, even though our tongues are still, we make clamor in our silence. Within, therefore, in our desires is our secret clamor which never comes to human ears, and yet it fills the hearing of our Maker.

POPE ST. GREGORY THE GREAT, *Moralium Lib.,* XXII, 584

To pray is to desire; but it is to desire what God would have us desire.

FRANÇOIS FÉNELON (1651–1715), *Advice Concerning Prayer*

Prayer is the expression of desire; its value comes from our inward aspirations, from their tenor and their strength. Take away desire, the prayer ceases; alter it, the prayer changes; increase or diminish its intensity, the prayer soars upward or has no wings.

ANTONIN SERTILLANGES, *The Intellectual Life,* 1946

See also Desires; Prayer.

DESIRES

Cut down the whole forest of desire, not just one tree only.

Dhammapada, c. 5th century B.C.

Not going naked, nor matted hair, nor dirt, nor fasting, nor sleeping on the ground, nor rolling in the dust, not sitting emotionless can purify one who has not overcome desire.

Dhammapada, c. 5th century B.C.

Craving is the hankering after pleasure, or existence, or success. It is the germ from which springs all human misery.

Vinaya, Mahavagga, between 5th and 1st century B.C.

When all desires of the heart shall cease, then man becomes immortal; then he attains to union with absolute being.

Katha Upanishad, prior to 400 B.C.

As a man's desire is, so is his destiny. For as his desire is, so is his will; as his will is, so is his deed; and as his deed is, so is his reward, whether good or bad.

Brhadaranyaka Upanishad, prior to 400 B.C.

If a man acts from the motive of Desire, he is not under compulsion because Desire is followed by pleasure; and what is done for the sake of pleasure is not compulsory.

ARISTOTLE (384 B.C.–322 B.C.), *Magna Moralia,* I, xii, 3–4

With the ceasing of craving, grasping ceases; with the ceasing of grasping, coming into existence ceases.

Upadana Sutra, c. 300 B.C.

That man attains peace who, abandoning all desires, moves about without attachment and longing, without the sense of "I" and "mine."

The Bhagavad-Gita, c. 2nd century B.C.

The fountainhead of evils . . . the progenitor of plunderings and robberies and repudiation of debts and false accusations and outrages, also seductions, adulteries, murders, and all wrong action, whether private or public.

PHILO JUDAEUS (born c. 10 B.C.), *De Specialibus Legibus*

Whensoever a man desireth aught above measure, immediately he becometh restless. The proud and avaricious man is never at rest; while the poor and the lowly of heart abide in the multitude of peace.

THOMAS À KEMPIS, *Imitation of Christ*, c. 1441

We are not to rely on a clear intellect, or on the gifts received from God, and then imagine that any affections or desires we may indulge in will not blind us, nor cause us to fall into a worse state, little by little.

ST. JOHN OF THE CROSS (1542–1591), *The Ascent of Mt. Carmel*

Oh that men knew how great a blessing, that of the Divine Light, this their blindness, the result of their desires, robs them of.

ST. JOHN OF THE CROSS (1542–1591), *The Ascent of Mt. Carmel*

What care I though I have not much, I have as much as I desire, if I have as much as I want; I have as much as the most, if I have as much as I desire.

ARTHUR WARWICK, *Spare Minutes*, 1637

A contented mind is the greatest blessing a man can enjoy in this world; and if in the present life his happiness arises from the subduing of his desires, it will arise in the next from the gratification of them.

JOSEPH ADDISON (1672–1719), *Selections from the Spectator*

Conquer desire and you will conquer fear. But as long as you are a slave you must be a coward.

JOHN WESLEY, *Letter to Samuel Furley*, February 21, 1756

Every desire is a viper in the bosom, who, while he was chill, was harmless; but when warmth gave him strength, exerted its poison.

SAMUEL JOHNSON, *Letter to James Boswell*, December 8, 1763

It is doubtful that any heavier curse could be imposed on man than the gratification of all his wishes without effort on his part, leaving nothing for his hopes, desires or struggles.

SAMUEL SMILES, *Self-Help*, 1859

All moral rules must be tested by examining whether they tend to realize ends that we desire. I say ends that we desire, not ends that we *ought* to desire. . . . Outside human desires there is no moral standard.

BERTRAND RUSSELL, *What I Believe*, 1925

That sorrow springs from desire was a real discovery, and a piece of genuine insight. . . . To strike at desire is to strike at the very root of sorrow. No wonder that this truth colored a large part of the teaching of primitive Buddhism.

J. B. PRATT, *The Pilgrimage of Buddhism*, 1928

Lust is repulsive. It shows as a beast. Desire is so compelling, so like true love to the inexperienced, so related to the glamour and poetry of life, that its poison is the more deadly. . . . Desire passes with satiety. Love includes but sublimates desire. Love shines more brightly and in varying lights as desire passes into its spiritual fulfillments.

Committee on Marriage and Home, Federal Council of Churches of Christ in America, 1929

The gist of all our religious, social and political desires: (1) Self-merger in a world order, (2) participation in an unending research and adventure, and (3) the attainment of a personal, shared and re-echoed happiness.

> H. G. WELLS, *Anatomy of Frustration*, 1936

If the comforts of the world are considered as paramount, then there will be desire for more and more comfort and pleasure. The result will be apprehension and anxiety.

> SWAMI AKHILANANDA, *Mental Health and Hindu Psychology*, 1951

See also Advertising; Amusements; Chastity; Conscience; Contentment; Desire and Prayer; Freedom; Greed; Hope; Love; Lust; Money; Pleasure; Poor, the; Possessions; Renunciation; Repression; Riches; Self-Denial; Self-Interest; Selfishness; Sex; Sexual Desire; Sexual Intercourse; Sexuality; Sin; Temptation; Wealth; Will; Worldliness.

DESPAIR

He who despairs of pardon for his sin, damns himself by despair rather than by the crime he has committed.

> ST. ISIDORE OF SEVILLE (560–636), *Dialogue between Erring Soul and Reason*

'Tis an epitome of hell, an extract, a quintessence, a compound, a mixture of all feral maladies, tyrannical tortures, plagues, and perplexities.

> ROBERT BURTON, *Anatomy of Melancholy*, III, 1621

Despair is one of Hell's catchpolls.

> THOMAS DEKKER, *The Honest Whore*, 1630

A man may be damned for despairing to be saved.

> JEREMY TAYLOR, *Holy Living*, 1650

Remember that despair belongs only to passionate fools or villains, such as were Achitopel and Judas, or else to devils and damned persons.

> JEREMY TAYLOR, *Holy Living*, 1650

The thought of the unattainableness of any good.

> JOHN LOCKE, *Essay Concerning Human Understanding*, 1690

Despair is the conclusion of fools.

> BENJAMIN DISRAELI, *Alroy*, 1833

When the sinner despairs of the forgiveness of sin, it is almost as if he were directly picking a quarrel with God.

> SÖREN KIERKEGAARD, *Sickness unto Death*, 1849

The torment of despair is precisely this: not to be able to die.

> SÖREN KIERKEGAARD, *Sickness unto Death*, 1849

If Religion was not wanted to keep bad men in check, it still would be wanted to keep good men from despair.

> *Old Farmer's Almanac*, 1851

The degeneracy of religious fear is despair of God's mercy, by which one persuades himself that his power of sinning is superior to God's power of forgiving.

> WALTER ELLIOTT, *The Spiritual Life*, 1914

God is more near in man's despair
Than man has wisdom to beware.

> JOHN MASEFIELD, *The Coming of Christ*, 1928

The fire of genius must burn out and saint and sinner alike yield up their bodies to the soil and to the air. The loftiest thoughts, the profoundest philosophy . . . the most enduring love, all are but concomitants of the long and never completely reversible chemical reaction known as life.

> CLIFFORD KILPATRICK, *Religion in Human Affairs*, 1929

Brief and powerless is man's life; on him and all his race the slow, sure doom falls pitiless and dark. Blind to good and evil, reckless of destruction, omnipotent matter rolls on its relentless way.

BERTRAND RUSSELL, *A Free Man's Worship*, 1929

Despair is the sin which cannot find—because it will not look for it—forgiveness.

HUBERT VAN ZELLER, *We Die Standing Up*, 1940

No man has the right to despair, since each was the messenger of a thing greater than himself. Despair was the rejection of God within oneself.

ANTOINE DE SAINT-EXUPÉRY, *Flight of Arras*, 1942

Ordinary man is at the end of his tether. Only a small, highly adaptable minority of the species can possibly survive.

H. G. WELLS, *Mind at the End of Its Tether*, 1945

A frightful queerness has come into life. . . . The writer is convinced that there is no way out, or around, or through the impasse. It is the end.

H. G. WELLS, *Mind at the End of Its Tether*, 1945

The Christian faith leaves no room for . . . despair, being based on the fact that the Kingdom of God is firmly established in Christ and will come by God's act despite all human failure.

The Church and the Disorder of Society, First Assembly of the World Council of Churches, Amsterdam, 1948

Despair is an ultimate or "boundary-line" situation. One cannot go beyond it. . . . No way out into the future appears. Nonbeing is felt absolutely victorious.

PAUL TILLICH, *The Courage to Be*, 1952

The pain of despair is that "being" is aware of itself as unable to affirm itself because of the power of non-being.

PAUL TILLICH, *The Courage to Be*, 1952

If there is no God, and everything, therefore, is permitted, the first thing permitted is despair.

FRANÇOIS MAURIAC, *Words of Faith*, 1955

Who then speaks most powerfully to and for the men of this generation? Those poets, artists, and philosophers who preach despair and sing of bleak encounter with silence and futility and nonbeing.

JULIAN N. HARTT, *Toward a Theology of Evangelism*, 1955

Despair is a significant aspect of this world's reality, and none of us escapes wholly its taint. But the realities of our world are judged by the actualities of God and his everlasting kingdom.

JULIAN N. HARTT, *Theology Today*, 1956

For many people life has gone dead and sour. To many others it is bleak, threatening, ominous. Our civilization is no longer a "neighborhood world." It is vast and bewildering. Everyman is an alien in it. . . . Wherefore duties and pleasures alike are compulsively pursued or evaded; and trivialities are endowed with transcendental significance which they can no longer endure; and when these overburdened trivialities crack and break as they do certainly, the gods of the depths revel obscenely in the breaches, and these gods are Fear and Despair.

JULIAN N. HARTT, *Theology Today*, 1956

Modern man's despair is not despair of God at all, but despair of all that is not God. Beyond that despair lies Christian hope, the certainty that God alone is enough for man.

WILLIAM MCNAMARA, *The Art of Being Human*, 1962

See also Anxiety; Atheism; Confidence; Damnation; Faith; Fear; Forgiveness;

Godlessness; Hell; Hope; Melancholy; Original Sin; Progress; Religion; Sin; Unbelief.

DESTINY

Life and Death, existence and non-existence, success and non-success, poverty and wealth, virtue and vice, good and evil report, hunger and thirst, warmth and cold,—these all revolve upon the changing wheel of Destiny.
Chuang-tzu, c. 300 B.C.

A disposing and bestowing abroad of that universal providence, by particulars. Therefore Providence is in God, and attributed to Him alone: Destiny is in the things, and to them is ascribed.
JUSTUS LIPSIUS, *Two Books of Constancie,* I ,1593

Men heap together the mistakes of their lives, and create a monster which they call Destiny.
JOHN OLIVER HOBBES, *The Sinner's Comedy,* 1892

Destiny, n. A tyrant's authority for crime and a fool's excuse for failure.
AMBROSE BIERCE, *Devil's Dictionary,* 1906

We are material in the hands of the Genius of the universe for a still larger destiny that we cannot see in the everlasting rhythm of worlds.
JOHN ELOF BOODIN, *Cosmic Evolution,* 1925

The highest moral ideal either for a people or for an individual is to be true to its destiny . . . to leave the known for the unknown.
CHRISTOPHER DAWSON, *The Sociological Review,* July, 1925

For God or against God, this once more is the alternative that will decide the destiny of all mankind, in politics, in business, in morals, in the sciences and arts, in civil and domestic society.
POPE PIUS XI, *Caritate Dei,* 1932

The Church Universal is not limited to humanity alone . . . the whole of creation . . . shares the destiny of man.
SERGIUS BULGAKOV, *The Orthodox Church,* 1935

Destiny waits in the hand of God.
T. S. ELIOT, *Murder in the Cathedral,* 1935

God has for no man a fixed and final destiny in the sense of either an inexorable fate or an assured security. . . . There is nothing in all creation that can separate us from God and his loving care.
GEORGIA HARKNESS, *The Providence of God,* 1960

See also Chance; Determinism; Fatalism; Fate; Foreknowledge; Free Will; various rubrics under God; Immortality; Man: His Destiny and Goal; Predestination; Providence.

DETACHMENT

The man who, casting off all desires, lives free from attachment; who is free from egoism and from the feeling that this or that is mine, obtains tranquillity.
Bhagavad-Gita, c. 5th century B.C.

He saw God's foot upon the treadle of the loom, and spoke it; and therefore his shipmates called him mad. So man's insanity is heaven's sense; and wandering from all mortal reason, man comes at last to that celestial thought, which to reason is absurd and frantic; and weal or woe, feels then uncompromised, indifferent as his God.
HERMAN MELVILLE, *Moby Dick,* 1851

Oh son of dust! Be blind that thou mayest behold my beauty—Be blind, that is, to all save my beauty; be deaf to all except my word; be ignorant to all but my knowledge; thus thou shalt enter my Presence with pure eyes, keen ears, and a purified heart.

BAHAULLAH, *Hidden Words,* late 19th century

The prophet and the martyr do not see the hooting throng. Their eyes are fixed on the eternities.

BENJAMIN CARDOZO, *Law and Literature,* 1931

The virtue of poverty means complete detachment; we are not to depend on things, but they on us. . . . You will get detachment from things and from self by merely giving yourself to God, and accepting yourself as you find yourself to be.

JOHN CHAPMAN, *Spiritual Letters,* 1935

Detachment, the foundation of all mystic techniques, may be compressed into the formula: I will not to will.

ARTHUR KOESTLER, *The Yogi and the Commissar,* 1945

Nothing short of religion will inspire self-detachment. A man will refuse for the sake of himself as a finite human animal to undergo the discipline to which he will gladly submit, once he is brought into conscious relation with God.

ROM LANDAU, *Sex, Life and Faith,* 1946

Detachment is not a denial of life but a denial of death; not a disintegration but the condition of wholeness; not a refusal to love but the determination to love truly, deeply and fully.

GERALD VANN, *Eve and the Gryphon,* 1946

See also Abandonment; Contemplation; Freedom; Happiness; Love; Love of God; Man's Unity with God; Mystical Experience; Piety; Prayer: Defined and Explained; Religion: Its Nature and Function; Renunciation; Sacrifice; Self-Giving; Selflessness; Self-Sacrifice; Spiritual; Worship.

DETERMINISM

When he [a man] goes away [dies] it is by the will of Fate he goes.

Vendidad, V, 6th century B.C.

No mischance chanceth either on earth or in your own persons, but ere we created them, it was in the Book [of our decrees], for easy is this for God.

Koran, 7th century A.D.

There is not one among you whose sitting-place is not written by God whether in the fire or in Paradise.

MOHAMMED, *Speeches and Table-Talk of,* 7th century A.D.

Those who . . . claim that everything is done by pure necessity, assert that God produces in all men not only good works but also bad. . . . If man has no claims to be considered the author of his good works, he also cannot be regarded as the author of his bad works.

DESIDERIUS ERASMUS, *Of Free Will,* 1524

God commands us to pray without ceasing, to watch, to struggle, and to contend for the reward of eternal life. Why does He wish to be prayed to endlessly for that which He has already decreed to grant or not to grant, since being immutable He cannot change His decrees?

DESIDERIUS ERASMUS, *Of Free Will,* 1524

Why do we hear so often of reward, if there is no merit? . . . Why does the Scripture so often mention judgment, if no account is taken of our merits?

DESIDERIUS ERASMUS, *Of Free Will,* 1524

There is no free will in the human mind: it is moved to this or that volition by some cause, and that cause has been determined by some other cause, and so on infinitely.

BARUCH SPINOZA, *Ethics,* 1677

Any other future complement than the one fixed from eternity is impossible. The whole is in each and every part, and welds it with the rest into an absolute unity, an iron block, in which there can be no equivocation or shadow of turning.

WILLIAM JAMES, *Unitarian Review,* September, 1884

Against the formidable array of cumulative evidence for Determinism, there is but one argument of real force: the immediate affirmation of consciousness in the moment of deliberate action.

HENRY SIDGWICK, *Method of Ethics,* 1906

Men are but automatons; a black crime or an act of sublime heroism are both as inevitable as the bursting of a rusty boiler. All is inevitable.

CLIFFORD KILPATRICK, *Religion in Human Affairs,* 1929

The Hegelians, the Marxians, the Pseudo-Darwinians, . . . Did they not have their histories to prove that men were less than men, emanations of the Absolute, pawns moved by the dialectic of history, animals struggling for survival, cells in a superorganism. . . . Having conceived man as a being without autonomy, they could not believe he had authentic purposes, inalienable rights, or binding obligations. . . . With man degraded to a bundle of conditioned reflexes . . . there remained only an aimless and turbulent moral relativity. . . . This denial of the human soul was the perfect preparation for the revival of tyranny.

WALTER LIPPMANN, *The Good Society,* 1937

Fortunately men believe in their will, and even if they are philosophically convinced of determinism, they will not make use of it in actual situations.

MAX WERTHEIMER, *Freedom, Its Meaning,* ed. R. Anshen, 1940

There has also been a propaganda of a soulless stupidity called Determinism, representing man as a dead object driven hither and thither by his environment, antecedents, circumstances, and so forth.

GEORGE BERNARD SHAW, Preface, *Androcles and the Lion,* 1941

The determinist's theory allows one to say that there is nothing wrong or right in holding to the theory and nothing wrong or right in opposing it. The formulation of the theory and the acceptance or rejection of it are, by that theory itself, predetermined.

PAUL WEISS, *Nature and Man,* 1947

How can a man be morally responsible, if his choices, like all other events in the universe could not have been otherwise than they in fact were?

P. H. NOWELL-SMITH, *Mind,* October, 1951

When the cards are dealt and you pick up your hand, that is determinism; there's nothing you can do except to play it out for whatever it may be worth. And the way you play your hand is free will.

JAWAHARLAL NEHRU, quoted in Norman Cousins, *Who Speaks For Man?,* 1953

If the theory of determinism is true, then no arguments against it have any force. But then, if it is true, no arguments in its favor have any force either. It is pretty clear that no one in normal society in fact holds this position in its fulness, for its consistent adoption would lead to insanity.

E. L. MASCALL, *Christian Theology and Natural Science,* 1956

There would be no sense in arguing about determinism or indeterminism if all our arguments were rigidly determined in advance.

MORRIS GINSBERG, *On the Diversity of Morals,* 1957

Determinism, if taken seriously, would involve the further notion that all intellectual judgment is itself determined, but this would have to apply even to the judgment that determinism is true.

D. E. TRUEBLOOD, *Philosophy of Religion,* 1957

Pure determinism had to be abandoned; . . . atomic physics has moved ever further away from the concept of determinism.

WERNER HEISENBERG, *The Physicist's Conception of Nature,* 1958

The falsity of determinism lies simply in the dogma that the future is already determinate. But if this were so there would be no future; the future would be already past.

JOHN MACMURRAY, *The Self as Agent,* 1958

The determinist scolds his children, but why?

GEORGE A. BUTTRICK, *Christ and History,* 1963

See also Chance; Choice; Despair; Election; Fatalism; Fate; Foreknowledge; Freedom; Free Will; God: His Intervention in the World; Liberalism; Man, Modern; Mechanism; Necessity; Philosophy; Predestination; Providence; Reason; Sin; Will.

DEVIL

Of the evil spirit [Ahriman] are the law of violence, the religion of sorcery, the weapons of fiendishness, and the perversion of God's [Ahura Mazda's] creations, and his desire is this: Inquire not concerning me, and do not understand me; for if ye ask about me and understand me, ye will not thereafter follow me.

Bunsahis, 7th century B.C.

But he who is the Prince
Of darkness, Mara—knowing this was
  Buddha
Who should deliver men . . .
Gave unto all his evil powers command.
Wherefore there trooped from every deep-
  est pit
The fiends who war with Wisdom and the
  Light
Nor knoweth one
Not even the wisest, how those fiends of
  Hell
Battled that night to keep the Truth from
  Buddha.

EDWIN ARNOLD, *The Light of Asia* (based largely on a late Buddhist epic), 1850

But the devil do not fear, for fearing the Lord you have power over the devil because there is no might in him.

Shepherd of Hermas, c. 148 A.D.

In divers ways the devil has shown hostility to the Truth. At times he has tried to shake it by pretending to defend it.

TERTULLIAN, *Against Praxeas,* c. 213

Satan transforms himself as it were into an angel of light, and often sets a snare for the faithful by means of the divine Scriptures themselves. Thus does he make heretics, thus weaken faith, thus attack the requirements of piety.

ST. AMBROSE, *Exposito in c.* iv *Lucas, n.* 26, 333

The devil has power to suggest evil, but he was not given the power to compel you against your will.

ST. CYRIL OF JERUSALEM, *Catechetical Lectures,* 350

The Devil often transforms himself into an angel to tempt men, some for their instruction and some for their ruin.

    Sт. Augustine, *The City of God*, xv, 426

The Evil Will lures man in this world, then testifies against him in the world to come.

    Jonathan b. Eleazar, *Talmud: Sukka*, c. 500

Undeniably, the Devil is the head of all sinners and they are all members of his head.

    Pope Sт. Gregory the Great (540–604), *Homily 16 on the Gospel*

Men should know that the will of Satan is always unrighteous but that his power is never unjust. The iniquities he proposes to commit, God allows in all justice.

    Pope Sт. Gregory (540–604), *P.L.* LXXV, 564

The devil is free to remain good, but there is no good in him.

    Sт. Thomas Aquinas, *De Malo*, q. XVI, 1268

The Evil One can not act *directly* on our higher faculties, the intellect and the will. God . . . alone can enter there and touch the mainspring of the will without doing violence to it.

    Adolphe Tanqueray, *The Spiritual Life*, 1490

It is one of the malicious devices of the devil to fill us with shame at the prospect of being defeated by evil preoccupations, so that we shall be hindered from lifting our eyes to God in contrition and praying to be freed of them.

    Sт. Nilus Sorsky (1433–1505), *The Monastic Rule*

The Devil seduces us at first by all the allurements of sin, in order thereafter to plunge us into despair; he pampers up the flesh, that he may by-and-by prostrate the spirit.

    Martin Luther (1483–1546), *Table Talk*

He is the most diligent preacher of all other; he is never out of his diocese.

    Hugh Latimer, *Sermons*, 1549

The prince of darkness is a gentleman.

    William Shakespeare, *King Lear*, 1605?

Where God hath a temple, the Devil will have a chapel.

    Robert Burton, *Anatomy of Melancholy*, III, 1621

The Devil is good when he is pleased.

    John Clarke, *Pareomiologia Anglo-Latina*, 1639

That there is a Devil is a thing doubted by none but such as are under the influence of the Devil.

    Cotton Mather, *A Discourse on Wonders of the Invisible World*, 1692

Wherever God erects a house of prayer,
The Devil always builds a chapel there;
And 'twill be found upon examination,
The latter has the largest congregation.

    Daniel Defoe, *The True-Born Englishman*, 1701

There is little in Satan's speeches that can give pain to a pious ear.

    Samuel Johnson, *Essay on Milton*, 1781

The devil's claims are fairly admitted, and his right to be here and take part in mundane affairs is unquestionable.

    Bronson Alcott, April 25, 1851, *Journal of*, ed. O. Shepard

I think if the devil doesn't exist, but man has created him, he has created him in his own image and likeness.

    Feodor Dostoevsky, *The Brothers Karamazov*, 1880

It is the devil's masterpiece to get us to accuse him.

> GEORGE MEREDITH, *Diana of the Crossways,* 1885

The Devil enters into me through impure, evil, blasphemous thoughts, through doubt, fear, pride, irritability, malice, avarice, envy; therefore his power over me entirely depends upon myself.

> JOHN SERGIEFF OF CRONSTADT (1829–1908), *My Life in Christ*

God may use Satan for His own purposes. Elements emerge from the chaos of evil and are built up into good.

> S. ALEXANDER, *Space, Time and Deity,* 1920

Never did Satan work, so to speak; he has never produced anything, but only tried to poison what the good God has created.

> ANSCAR VONIER, *The Art of Christ,* 1927

By a strange irony of fate, the Devil when cast down to oblivion has tended to drag down God Himself.

> CLIFFORD KILPATRICK, *Religion in Human Affairs,* 1929

Satan is too hard a master. He would never command as did the Other with divine simplicity: "Do likewise." The devil will have no victim resemble him. He permits only a rough caricature, impotent, abject, which has to serve as food for eternal irony, the mordant irony of the depths.

> GEORGE BERNANOS, *The Dairy of a Country Priest,* 1937

It is so stupid of modern civilization to have given up believing in the devil when he is the only explanation of it.

> RONALD A. KNOX, Mr. Battersby in *Let Dons Delight,* 1939

The Devil does not shock a saint into alertness by suggesting whopping crimes.

He starts off with little, almost inoffensive things to which even the heart of a saint would make only mild protests.

> WALTER FARRELL, *Companion to the Summa,* 1941

What we see in Satan is the horrible coexistence of a subtle and incessant intellectual activity with an incapacity to understand anything.

> C. S. LEWIS, *Preface* to *Paradise Lost,* 1942

If one believes in the truth of the Bible, it is impossible to doubt the reality of the Devil for a single moment.

> DENIS DE ROUGEMENT, *The Devil's Share,* 1944

The Devil *is* a myth, hence he exists and continues to be active. A myth is a story which describes and illustrates in dramatic form certain deep structures of reality.

> DENIS DE ROUGEMONT, *The Devil's Share,* 1944

Though contemporary atheism has not convinced us there is no God, it has convinced us that there is a devil.

> FULTON J. SHEEN, *Communism and the Conscience of the West,* 1948

Nowhere in Sacred Scripture do we find warrant for the popular myth of the Devil as a buffoon. . . . Rather is he described as an angel fallen from heaven, and as "the Prince of this world," whose business is to tell us that there is no other world.

> FULTON J. SHEEN, *Communism and the Conscience of the West,* 1948

It is in the highest interests of the devil to persuade the world that religious people are disagreeable.

> HUBERT VAN ZELLER, *We Live with Our Eyes Open,* 1949

At all times, too many Christians have behaved as though the devil were a First

Principle, on the same footing as God. They have paid more attention to evil and the problem of its eradication than to good.

ALDOUS HUXLEY, *The Devils of Loudon,* 1952

The devil tries to throw a veil over the face of Christ, by making us dwell on the enormity of our sin and nothing else.

R. J. H. STUART, *Spiritual Conferences of,* 1952

The Devil is sterile. He possesses the will to create, hence his pride; but is incapable of creating, hence his envy.

GERALD C. TREACY, *The Devil!,* 1952

The Devil cannot penetrate our intellects to make us reason crookedly, but can fire our imagination and arouse our passions to such an enjoyable degree that we do not wish to use our intellects.

GERALD C. TREACY, *The Devil!,* 1952

The Devil's cleverest wile is to make men believe that he does not exist.

GERALD C. TREACY, *The Devil!,* 1952

Belief in the Devil as an adversary playing havoc with God's plans is not a very satisfactory answer to the mystery of iniquity.

RALPH W. SOCKMAN, *How to Believe,* 1953

If Satan can be freed from the hatred of Christians, men would be freed for ever from Satan.

GIOVANNI PAPINI, *The Devil: Notes for a Future Diabology,* 1955

He is the accomplice if not the direct inspirer of all human crimes, from that of Cain down to those of our own time, and the instigator . . . of all that is evil and, as we say so glibly, "infernal" in our civilizations!

NICOLAS CORTE, *Who Is the Devil?,* 1958

The Prince of darkness shall not prevail as long as love reigns in the Church of Christ.

POPE JOHN XXIII, *Encyclical,* November 11, 1961

See also Antichrist; Damnation; Demons; Diabolism; Hell; Temptation; World, Condemnation of.

DEVOTION

There is no devotion without virtue.

Japji, attributed to Guru Nanak (1496–1538)

Of all devotions the best devotion is to utter the name of God.

ARJAN (died 1606), *The Sikh Religion,* III, M. A. Macauliffe

True devotion . . . presupposes love of God; rather, it is nothing else than the true love of God.

ST. FRANCIS OF SALES, *Introduction to the Devout Life,* 1609

It is thoroughly possible to use God as a necessary ingredient of a metaphysical structure, sometimes under the name of the Absolute, without the spirit of devotion.

D. E. TRUEBLOOD, *The Logic of Belief,* 1942

Devotion, which is a derivative of the Latin word for *to vow,* means to yield oneself, to commit oneself, to consecrate oneself to the object of devotion, without regard to the sacrifice or suffering involved.

DOUGLAS V. STEERE, *Door into Life,* 1948

Popular devotion is to religious life what the link with people and family, country and home, is to the natural life.

ROMANO GUARDINI, *Prayer in Practice,* 1957

The one universal God does not require one universal church in which to be worshipped, but one universal devotion.

Hillel Silver, *Where Judaism Differed*, 1957

See also Liturgy; Prayer; Ritual; Worship.

DEWEY, JOHN

Do our "experts" really believe that a young tough can be induced to self-restraint, kindness, and compassion just because John Dewey found moral deeds "refreshing"?

FRANZ E. WINKLER, *Man, The Bridge Between Two Worlds*, 1960

See also Education, Progressive.

DHAMMA

All the teachings of Buddha can be summed up in one word: dhamma. . . . It means truth, that which really is. It also means law, the law which exists in a man's own heart and mind. It is the principle of righteousness. . . . Dhamma . . . exists not only in a man's heart and mind; it exists in the universe also. All the universe is an embodiment and revelation of dhamma. Dhamma is the true nature of every existing thing.

VENERABLE U. THITTILA, *The Path of the Buddha*, ed. K. W. Morgan, 1956

DIABOLISM

That people should tour the country teaching onanism and preaching sin, that the law should allow adultery and almost a promiscuous exchange of married partners, that newspapers should give a tremendous amount of space to publicizing the circumstances of sexual sins indicate more than a purely secularistic attitude toward sex. They point to a diabolism that any truly Christian mind must sense immediately.

DEMETRIUS MANOUSOS, *Address*, March 14, 1950

See also Devil.

DIALECTICAL MAN

Dialectical Man is a frightening, if not revolting creature . . . he can be no more than a *material* man, because only matter is real. . . . He thus emerges as a kind of social puppet, deprived of individual dignity, exiled from the search for truth, and incompetent to choose between good and evil.

RUSSELL DAVENPORT, *The Dignity of Man*, 1955

See also Man.

DIALOGUE

Dialogue must be between persons who are fully persons by being committed, by having taken a stand in the world of persons. Otherwise it will degenerate into the mere talk of a television commercial.

WALTER J. ONG, *Religion in America*, ed. John Cogley, 1958

Dialogue can be a very dangerous pastime, for it may force us to give up some of our most cherished caricatures—and these die hard.

ROBERT McAFEE BROWN, *An American Dialogue*, 1960

Meetings and agreements in the various sectors of daily life between believers and those who do not believe, or believe insufficiently because they adhere to error, can be occasions for discovering truth and paying homage to it.

POPE JOHN XXIII, *Pacem in Terris*, April, 1963

There is a *kairos,* a moment full of potentialities, in Protestant-Catholic relations; and Protestant theology must become and remain conscious of it.

PAUL TILLICH, *Systematic Theology,* III, 1964

An ecumenical dialogue might start with discussion of the application of the Gospel to moral conduct.

Decree on Ecumenism, Second Vatican Council, November, 1964

In ecumenical dialogue, when Catholic theologians join with separated brethren in common studies of the divine mysteries, they should while standing fast by the teaching of the Church, pursue the work with love for the truth, with charity, and with humility.

Decree on Ecumenism, Second Vatican Council, November, 1964

Dialogue has a new connotation in contemporary religious discourse. Here attitudes of religious superiority are yielding place to those of humility, where men of different faiths share with one another what they have inherited from the past as well as their personal understanding and experience of that faith. This involves no compromise in matters of faith. Instead it results in personal religious enrichment between men of different religious tradition.

Religion and Society, 1964 (reporting a dialogue between Christians and Sikhs)

Dialogue [in the encounter of Christianity with non-Christian religions] represents a willingness on the part of representatives of different faiths to explain or illustrate the content of their faith in as clear and convincing a manner as possible, in order that out of such dialogue each may gain, or afford to the other, some deeper insight, or some larger measure of truth, or value. And really fruitful dialogue is impossible unless each party to the dialogue, however deeply committed to his own faith as he

understands it, is open to the possibility of some degree of change in his own outlook as a result of it.

CHARLES S. BRADEN, "The Christian Encounter with World Religions," *Church and State Magazine,* Autumn, 1965

See also Brotherhood; Charity; Community; Denominationalism; Disputation; Division; Ecumenism; Fellowship; Unity.

DICTATORSHIP

The scientific concept, dictatorship, means nothing more or less than power which directly rests on violence, which is not limited by any laws or restricted by any absolute rules. . . . Dictatorship means unlimited power, resting on violence and not on law.

JOSEPH STALIN, *Problems of Leninism,* 1929

Can men, acting like gods, be appointed to establish heaven on earth? If we believe that they can be, then the rest follows. To fulfill their mission they must assume a godlike omnipotence. They must be jealous gods, monopolizing power, destroying all rivals, compelling exclusive loyalty.

WALTER LIPPMANN, *The Public Philosophy,* 1954

See also Anti-God Totalitarians; Authoritarianism; Communism; Divine Right of Kings; Freedom; Government; Marxism; Rulers; State, the; Totalitarianism; Tyrants.

DIFFERENCES. See DIVISION

DIGNITY

And what is dignity to an unworthy man, but a gold ring in a swine's snout?

SALVIANUS, *De Gubernatione Dei. Lib.* 4, 5th century

DISAPPOINTMENTS

With most of us it is not so much great sorrows, disease, or death, but rather the little "daily dyings" which cloud over the sunshine of life.

JOHN LUBBOCK, *The Pleasures of Life,* 1887

DISARMAMENT.
See ARMAMENTS

DISCIPLINE

Vows and traditions concerning foods and days, and such like, instituted to merit grace and make satisfaction for sins, are useless and contrary to the Gospel.

PHILIP MELANCHTHON, *Augsburg Confession,* 1530

As the saving doctrine of Christ is the soul of the Church, so discipline forms the ligaments by which the members of the body are joined together and kept each in its proper place.

JOHN CALVIN, *Institutes,* IV, 1536

Man must be disciplined, for he is by nature raw and wild.

IMMANUEL KANT, *Lecture at Königsberg,* 1775

Discipline means power at command; mastery of the resources available for carrying through the actions undertaken. To know what one is to do and to move to do it promply and by the use of the requisite means is to be disciplined, whether we are thinking of an army or the mind. Discipline is positive.

JOHN DEWEY, *Democracy and Education,* 1916

See also Abstinence; Fasting; Moderation; Obedience; Repression; Self-Conquest; Self-Denial; Self-Discipline.

DISCORD

There are enough targets to aim at without firing at each other.

THEODORE ROOSEVELT. *Address,* National Federation of Churches, 1902

So long as we cling to any humanly devised definitions which we insist upon as articles of faith necessary to salvation, we shall inevitably insure discord for all time.

R. T. GRENFELL, *The Adventure of Life,* 1911

The discords of Christendom have drowned the finest strains of music in the human soul.

PETER AINSLIE, *The Message of the Disciples for the Union of the Church,* 1913

Disown the idea of an abiding God as the Creator and the ultimate end of all men, and you can only have peoples in various times and places, each working for its own ends in terms of their own time and place. Hence place must forever war against place, and time against time.

LOUIS J. A. MERCIER, *Address,* October 30, 1942

Let those who call themselves Catholics, or Protestant, or Jews recall that the function of their religion is to intensify the spiritual life of man and not to empty the vials of bitterness into hearts, stirring up one against another.

FULTON J. SHEEN, *Way to Happiness,* 1953

If the churches persist in presenting humanity with the spectacle of a Christendom at logger-heads with itself they might as well give up.

ALFRED DELP, *Prison Meditations of Father Alfred Delp,* 1963

See also Controversy; Disputation; Division; Order; Religious Conflict; War, Condemnation of.

DISCRIMINATING

Asses would prefer garbage to gold.
> HERACLITUS (535–475 B.C.), *Fragments*

The ability to discriminate between that which is true and that which is false is one of the last attainments of the human mind.
> JAMES FENIMORE COOPER, *The American Democrat*, 1838

See also Choice; Judgment; Taste.

DISCRIMINATION

The true way to overcome the evil in class distinctions is not to denounce them as revolutionists denounce them, but to ignore them as children ignore them.
> G. K. CHESTERTON, *Charles Dickens,* 1906

Anything that has any remote resemblance to discrimination is not only anti-American, but anti-Christian as well. Jesus Christ, the Son of God, declared that second only to the supreme law binding us to love our God is the law binding us to love our neighbor.
> FRANCIS J. HAAS, *Catholics, Race and Law,* 1947

If we press toward the exact center of the concentric circles of inclusion and exclusion we find there the lone individual in proud and splendid isolation from the rest of mankind.
> KYLE HASELDEN, *The Racial Problem in Christian Perspective,* 1959

Every type of discrimination whether social or cultural, whether based on sex, race, color, social condition, language or religion, is to be overcome and eradicated as contrary to God's intent.
> SECOND VATICAN COUNCIL, *The Church in the Modern World,* December, 1965

See also Anti-Semitism; Bigot; Class Distinctions; Equality; Exclusiveness; Intolerance; Negroes; Prejudice; Racial Conflict; Racial Injustice; Racial Prejudice.

DISHONESTY

Anyone who accepts the Christian principle that every civil official is God's representative will clearly perceive how wicked and degrading is any form of dishonesty by a person in public office.
> FRANCIS J. CONNELL, *Morality and Government,* 1949

See also Bribery; Crookedness; Liars and Lies.

DISOBEDIENCE

No civil rulers are to be obeyed when they enjoin things that are inconsistent with the commands of God; all such disobedience is lawful and glorious.
> JONATHAN MAYHEW, *Unlimited Submission and Non-Resistance to the Higher Powers,* 1755

See also Fall, the; Obedience; Original Sin; Rebellion; State, the.

DISORDERS

Some evil more deeply rooted in mankind than the Communist Revolution is causing these recurring disorders among the peoples of this earth.
> ROBERT C. HARTNETT, *Broadcast,* January 20, 1952

DISPUTATION

By mere disputation you will never succeed in convincing another of his error. When the grace of God descends on him, each one will understand his own mistakes.
> SRI RAMAKRISHNA, *Sayings of,* 1903

So long as a man quarrels and disputes about doctrines and dogmas, he has not tasted the nectar of true faith; when he has tasted it, he becomes quiet and full of peace.

SRI RAMAKRISHNA, *Sayings of,* 1903

I would no more quarrel with a man because of his religion than I would because of his art.

MARY BAKER EDDY (1821–1910), *Miscellany,* publ. posth., 1914

See also Controversy; Denominationalism; Dialogue; Discord; Division; Quarrels; Religious Conflict; Schisms; Sects and Sectarianism; Tolerance; Truths, Conflict of; Unity.

DISSATISFACTION

Let every dissatisfaction with the present be made not a discouragement, but an inspiration, by the continual consciousness of the great law of eternal growth.

PHILLIPS BROOKS, *Perennials,* 1898

DISSIPATION

The worst dissipation in the world is the dry-rot of morality, and the so-called piety which separates men of prosperity and of power from the poor and ignoble.

HENRY WARD BEECHER (1813–1887), *Sermon*

See also Alcohol; Drunkenness; Gluttony; Hedonism; Immorality; Lust; Pleasure; Sex; Sexual Sin.

DISTRIBUTIVE JUSTICE

Distributive justice is any principle sanctioned by conscience, or held morally valid, by which goods and evils are apportioned among the individual members or classes of society.

RALPH BARTON PERRY, *Puritanism and Democracy,* 1944

DISUNITY. See DIVISION

DIVINE

We may think of the Divine as a fire whose outgoing warmth pervades the Universe.

PLOTINUS (203–262 A.D.), *Enneads*

What is there of the divine in a load of brick? What . . . in a barber's shop? . . . Much. All.

RALPH WALDO EMERSON, *Journal,* July 18, 1834

The divine shall mean for us only such a primal reality as the individual feels impelled to respond to solemnly and gravely, and neither by a curse nor a jest.

WILLIAM JAMES, *Varieties of Religious Experience,* 1902

See also Divinity, various rubrics under God; Incarnation; Reality.

DIVINE LAW

That law which God has set to the actions of men, whether promulgated to them by the light of nature, or the voice of revelation.

JOHN LOCKE, *Essay Concerning the Human Understanding,* 1690

God is related to the universe, as Creator and Preserver; the laws by which He created all things are those by which He preserves them.

C. DE S. MONTESQUIEU, *Spirit of Laws,* I, 1748

The existence of a Divine Law-Giver is no less necessary to moral philosophy than the existence of a Divine Creator is to natural philosophy.

L. R. C. LA CHALOTAIS, *Essay on National Education,* 1763

See also Moral Law; Natural Law.

DIVINE RIGHT OF KINGS

Kings are justly called Gods, for that they exercise a manner or resemblance of Divine power upon earth.

JAMES I OF ENGLAND, *Speech,* 1609

The person of kings is sacred: they are the representatives of divine majesty, deputed by Providence to execute its designs.

JACQUES BOSSUET, *La Politique Tirée,* 1679

See also Authority; Dictatorship; Government; Government and God; Government and Religion; Kings; Law; Royalty; State, the; Totalitarianism.

DIVINITY

He who would see the Divinity must see him in his Children.

WILLIAM BLAKE, *Jerusalem,* 1820

Divinity is not something supernatural that ever and again invades the natural order in a crashing miracle. Divinity is not in some remote heaven, seated on a throne. Divinity is love. . . . Wherever goodness, beauty, truth, love, are—there is the divine.

HARRY EMERSON FOSDICK, *The Hope of the World,* 1933

See also Divine, various rubrics under God; Man Indwelt by God; Reality.

DIVINIZATION

It is the Christian faith which challenges me to believe that these few little motions of mine, seemingly lost in the mass, may be made eternal and divine as they are taken up into the plot which a good God is developing.

W. A. SMART, *The Contemporary Christ,* 1942

DIVISION

Whenever in any religious faith, dark or bright, we allow our minds to dwell upon the points in which we differ from other people, we are wrong, and in the devil's power.

JOHN RUSKIN, *Sesame and Lilies,* 1865

The causes of division lie deep in the past, and are by no means simple or wholly blameworthy. Yet none can doubt that self-will, ambition, lack of charity among Christians have been principal factors in the mingled process responsible for the breaches of Christendom.

LAMBETH CONFERENCE (of Anglican Bishops), 1920

Differences were meant by God not to divide but to enrich.

J. H. OLDHAM, *Faith and Order,* Lausanne, 1927

The divisions of Christendom may be a source of weakness in Christian countries, but in non-Christian lands they are a sin and a scandal.

V. S. A. ZARIAH, at Lausanne Conference on Faith and Order, 1927, quoted in *Proceedings of the World Conference*

America, settled by peoples of many regions, races, religions, colors, creeds, and cultures, should, by moral example, lead the way in helping "to make the world safe for differences." . . . Understanding religious differences makes for a better understanding of other differences and for an appreciation of the sacredness of human personality as basic to human freedom.

FRANK P. GRAHAM, *Christian Leadership and Today's World,* 1940

Christianity, with its primary inculcation of love of God and love of neighbor, is not divisive. Only those who teach hatred teach division.

American Catholic Bishops, November, 1955

Disunity in the Christian movement is disastrous above all because it hurts the Christian mission, and makes it hard for the world to accept Christ as the world's Savior.
> WALTER MARSHALL HORTON, *Christian Theology,* 1958

The fact today is not simply that we hold different views but that we have become different types of men, with different styles of interior life. We are therefore uneasy in one another's presence.
> JOHN COURTNEY MURRAY, *We Hold These Truths,* 1960

Each denomination is unconsciously saying to the world that it regards something else than Christ as justifying it in remaining apart from others who have the same loyalty to Him.
> SAMUEL MCCREA CAVERT, *On the Road to Christian Unity,* 1961

The widening of our horizons today has made Christianity painfully conscious that our divisions have become in the literal sense of the word a scandal for humanity, a stumbling-block for the mission the Christian faith has to fulfill in the world.
> BERNARD ALFRINK, *Address* to Interfederal Assembly of Pax Romana, Washington, D.C., July, 1964

See also Denominationalism; Dialogue; Disputation; Ecumenism; Education, Catholic; Education, Parochial; Opinions; Paths; Pluralism; Private Judgment; Protestantism; Religion; Religious Conflict; Rivalry; Schisms; Sects and Sectarianism; Tolerance; Truth and Religion; Truths, Conflict of; Unity.

DIVORCE

No man may divorce his wife unless he found her guilty of an immoral act.
> SHAMMAI SCHOOL, *Mishna: Gittin,* 1st century B.C.

Women who, without cause, leave their husbands and marry again, are not to be received into communion even at the last.
> *Canon of the Council of Elvira,* c. 305

A baptized woman who leaves a baptized husband on the ground of his adultery and marries again, is to be prohibited from marrying.
> *Canon of the Council of Elvira,* c. 305

The very altar sheds tears on him who divorces the wife of his youth.
> *Gittin, Talmud,* between 2nd and 4th century

The union of man and wife is from God, so divorce is from the devil.
> ST. AUGUSTINE, *On the Gospel of St. John,* Trac. VIII, c. 416.

Ye may divorce your wives twice; keep them honorably, or put them away with kindness.
> *Koran,* 7th century A.D.

Christ permitted divorce in case of fornication, and compelled no one to remain single; and Paul preferred us to marry rather than to burn, and seemed quite prepared to grant that a man may marry another woman in place of the one he has repudiated.
> MARTIN LUTHER, *The Babylonian Captivity,* 1520

What God has joined together, it is wrong to put asunder; for to those to whom God is a Father the Church is also a mother.
> JOHN CALVIN, *Institutes,* IV, 1536

There are two causes of divorce: first adultery, but first, Christians ought to labor and to use diligent persuasions to reconcile the married pair; sharply, withal, reproving the guilty person. The second cause is much like: when one runs away from the other, and after returning runs away again. Such have commonly mates in other places, and richly deserve to be punished.

MARTIN LUTHER (1483–1546), *Table Talk*

If anyone should say that on account of heresy or the hardships of co-habitation or a deliberate abuse of one party by the other the marriage tie may be loosened, let him be anathema.

Council of Trent, Sess. XXIV, cap. 5, 1563

The bond of matrimony cannot be dissolved on account of the adultery of one of the married parties, and both, even the innocent one who gave not occasion to the adultery, cannot contract another marriage during the lifetime of the other; and he is guilty of adultery who, having put away the adulteress, shall take another wife, as also she who, having put away the adulterer, shall take another husband.

Council of Trent, Sess. XXIV, 1563

Divorce is born of perverted morals, and leads, as experience shows, to vicious habits in public and private life.

POPE LEO XIII, *Arcanum divinae sapientae,* February 10, 1880

If Americans can be divorced for "incompatibility of temper" I cannot conceive why they are not all divorced. I have known many happy marriages, but never a compatible one.

G. K. CHESTERTON, *What Is Wrong with the World,* 1910

Remarriage after a divorce granted on grounds explicitly stated in Scripture or implicit in the gospel of Christ may be sanctioned in keeping with his redemptive gospel, when sufficient penitence for sin and failure is evident, and a firm purpose of an endeavor after Christian marriage is manifest.

Constitution of the Presbyterian Church in U.S.A., 1930

Any concept of marriage which from the first contemplates divorce is incompatible with the Christian ideal and the clearest lessons of human experience.

FEDERAL COUNCIL OF CHURCHES OF CHRIST IN AMERICA, *Report,* 1932

It is the function of the state to determine the grounds upon which a valid divorce may be granted. We recognize as lawful a divorce granted by the state.

The Doctrines and Discipline of the Methodist Episcopal Church, 1932

Where both parties to marriage are Christians, divorce is not thought of even as a possibility, for they have resources of spiritual power sufficient to keep their vow.

SYDNEY CAVE, *The Christian Way,* 1949

Each marriage in a divorcing society is a monogamous one so long as it lasts, but, since all marriages in such a society are permanent by accident rather than permanent in principle, what a divorcing society tends to produce is a kind of serialized polygamy and polyandry.

J. V. L. CASSERLEY, *The Bent World,* 1955

The foot-loose quester errs in believing he must marry a second wife when actually the first wife could reveal enough of God to blind him if he really looked at her.

CHAD WALSH, *Behold the Glory,* 1955

If the emotional and spiritual welfare of both parents and children in a particular family can be served best by divorce, wrong and cheapjack as divorce commonly is, then love requires it.

JOSEPH FLETCHER, *Harvard Divinity Bulletin,* October, 1959

People wouldn't get divorced for such trivial reasons, if they didn't get married for such trivial reasons.

Author unknown

See also Adultery; Marriage; Separation.

DOCTRINE

It is indeed harmful to come under the sway of utterly new and strange doctrines.
CONFUCIUS, *Sayings of,* 5th century B.C.

All doctrines which agree with that of the Apostolic churches . . . must be looked upon as the truth, holding without hesitation that the Church received it from the Apostles, the Apostles from Christ, and Christ from God.
TERTULLIAN, *De Praescript.,* c. 206

In-so-far as the rule of truth is prior in time, so far must all later doctrines be judged heresies.
TERTULLIAN, *Adversus Hermogenes,* I, c. 206

If it is a question of doctrines that claim to go back to the Apostles, and to have come down from them because they have existed ever since, we shall say: Let them show the succession of their bishops.
TERTULLIAN, *On Prescription Against Heresies,* c. 206

The holy Apostles . . . took certain doctrines . . . which they believed to be necessary ones, and delivered them in the plainest terms to all believers. . . . The grounds of their statements they left to be investigated by such as should merit the higher gifts of the Spirit.
ORIGEN, *De Principiis,* c. 254

It behooves Christian doctrine . . . to be consolidated by years, enlarged by time, refined by age, and yet, withal, to continue uncorrupt and unadulterate, complete and perfect in all the measurements of its parts.
ST. VINCENT OF LÉRINS, *A Commonitory,* 434

In doctrine and ceremonials among us there is nothing contrary to Scriptures or to the Catholic Church. . . . We have diligently taken heed that no new and godless doctrines should creep into our churches.
PHILIP MELANCHTHON, *Augsburg Confession,* Part II, Conclusion, 1530

For though a doctrine be never so reasonable in itself, this is no certain argument that it is from God if no testimony from heaven be given to it.
JOHN TILLOTSON (1630–1694), *Works,* Vol. III

There is no Doctrine of Faith, but it perfectly accords with the Principles of true Reason.
CHARLES CHAUNCY, *Minister Exhorted,* 1744

A purely doctrinal faith has a certain instability in itself, for it often deserts us in consequence of difficulties which meet us in our speculation, though we find ourselves inevitably returning to it again and again.
IMMANUEL KANT, *Critique of Pure Reason,* 1781

Religious doctrine is scientific poetry.
NOVALIS (1772–1801), *Fragments*

A false doctrine cannot be refuted; for it rests upon the conviction that the false is true.
J. W. VON GOETHE (1749–1832), *Maxims and Reflections*

No doctrine is defined until it is violated.
JOHN HENRY NEWMAN, *On the Development of Christian Doctrine,* 1845

Of no doctrine whatever, which does not actually contradict what has been delivered, can it be peremptorily asserted that it is not in the Scripture.
JOHN HENRY NEWMAN, *An Essay on the Development of Christian Doctrine,* 1845

Doctrine is nothing but the skin of truth set up and stuffed.

HENRY WARD BEECHER, *Life Thoughts,* 1858

It is clear that religion must have some doctrine, and it is clear again that such doctrine will not be ultimate truth.

F. H. BRADLEY, *Appearance and Reality,* 1894

The least one can demand of people who judge doctrine is that they should judge of it in the sense in which the teacher himself understood it.

LEO TOLSTOY, *What I Believe,* 1895

The evidence is overwhelming that the doctrines of Christianity have passed into the region of doubt.

LORD HUGH CECIL, *Speech,* House of Commons, March 14, 1904

There is no revealed doctrine proclaimed by the Church which is not contained in its exact substance in the sources of revelation, that is, in Scripture and Tradition. But it is not always expressly revealed in its specific content, and is often contained so to say wrapped up in other truths.

KARL ADAM, *The Spirit of Catholicism,* 1924

The official declaration of historic Lutheranism plainly declares that with new light and more adequate interpretation of the biblical writings, changes in doctrine are not only anticipated but necessary.

VERGILIUS FERM, *What is Lutheranism?,* 1930

A doctrine which is but a doctrine has a poor chance indeed of giving birth to the glowing enthusiasm, the illumination, the faith that moves mountains.

HENRI BERGSON, *The Two Sources of Morality and Religion,* 1935.

Accusations against the Church can only be substantiated by Church Doctrine!

ERIC GILL, *Autobiography,* 1941

I do not find that Jesus laid down any basic doctrine beyond that of a universal loving God and a universal brotherhood of man.

ALBERT JAY NOCK, *Memoirs of a Superfluous Man,* 1943

It is impossible to overlook the emphasis on the transmission of authoritative doctrine which is everywhere found in the New Testament.

J. N. D. KELLY, *Early Christian Creeds,* 1950

She [the Church] points us to the Scriptures not to "prove" her doctrine but to tell us how it became known to her.

E. C. RICH, *Spiritual Authority in the Church of England,* 1953

Religious doctrines were determined not by the logic of a few but by the needs of the many; they were a frame of belief within which the common man, inclined by nature to a hundred unsocial actions, could be formed into a being sufficiently disciplined and self-controlled to make society and civilization possible.

WILL DURANT, *The Reformation,* 1957

See also Belief; Bible; Bible: Its Interpretation; Bible and Doctrine; Church: Its Authority; Dogma; Dogmatism; Faith; Heresy; Infallibility; Miracles; New Testament; Obedience; Orthodoxy; Reform; Revelation; Tradition; Truth; Truth and Religion; Truths, Conflict of.

DOGMA

We reap from the planting of the wheat of doctrine the harvest of the wheat of dogma.

ST. VINCENT OF LÉRINS, *A Commonitory,* 434

The church is a faithful and ever watchful guardian of the dogmas which have been committed to her charge. In this sacred deposit she changed nothing, she takes nothing from it, she adds nothing to it.

> ST. VINCENT OF LÉRINS, *Commonitorium*, c. 450

It would be well if we thought less of our dogmas and more of the gospel.

> DESIDERIUS ERASMUS, *Letter to Peter Barbirius*, 1521

If by *religion* we are to understand *sectarian dogma*, in which no two of them agree, then your exclamation on that hypothesis is just, "that this would be the best of all possible worlds, if there were no religions in it."

> THOMAS JEFFERSON, *Letter to John Adams*, May 5, 1817

Theological dogmas are propositions expressive of the judgments which the mind forms, or the impressions which it receives, of revealed truth.

> JOHN HENRY NEWMAN, *Oxford University Sermons*, 1843

From the age of fifteen, dogma has been the fundamental principle of my religion. I know of no other religion.

> JOHN HENRY NEWMAN, *Apologia pro Vita Sua*, 1864

We do not deny dogma, but prefer to remit it to the sphere of individual conviction.

> FELIX ADLER, *Creed and Deed*, 1877

It is the uncompromisingness with which dogma is held and not in the dogma or want of dogma that the danger lies.

> SAMUEL BUTLER, *The Way of All Flesh*, 1884

Collect from the Bible all that Christ thought necessary for his disciples, and how little Dogma there is. Christianity is based, not on Dogma, but on Charity and Love.

> JOHN LUBBOCK, *The Pleasures of Life*, 1887

Religions, far from being really built on Dogmas, are too often weighed down and crushed by them.

> JOHN LUBBOCK, *The Pleasures of Life*, 1887

Dogma are the convictions of one man imposed authoritatively upon others.

> FELIX ADLER, An *Ethical Philosophy of Life*, 1918

From the literary standpoint Catholic dogma is merely the witness, under a special symbolism, of the enduring facts of human nature and the universe.

> ARTHUR MACHEN, *Hieroglyphics*, 1923

What is dogma to the ordinary man is experience to the pure in heart.

> S. RADHAKRISHNAN, *Indian Philosophy*, I, 1923

What the denouncer of dogma really means is not that dogma is bad; but rather that dogma is too good to be true.

> G. K. CHESTERTON, *The Everlasting Man*, 1925

Leave dogma to those who enjoy it; the true Christian is simply a member of Christ's society, of his party, one of his followers.

> WILLIAM LYON PHELPS, *Human Nature and the Gospel*, 1925

Today there is but one religious dogma in debate: What do you mean by "God"? . . . This is the fundamental religious dogma, and all the other dogmas are subsidiary to it.

> ALFRED NORTH WHITEHEAD, *Religion in the Making*, 1926

A system of dogmas may be the ark within which the Church floats safely down the flood-tide of history. But the Church will perish unless it opens its window and lets out the dove to search for an olive branch.

> ALFRED NORTH WHITEHEAD, *Religion in the Making*, 1926

All the simplifications of religious dogma are shipwrecked upon the rock of the problem of evil.

> ALFRED NORTH WHITEHEAD, *Religion in the Making,* 1926

To say we want no dogmas in religion is to assert a dogma.

> FULTON J. SHEEN, *Religion Without God,* 1928

The philosophy of St. Thomas is not a dogma; the Church can define as a truth *de fide* only what is contained at least implicitly, in the divine deposit of revelation.

> JACQUES MARITAIN, *St. Thomas Aquinas,* 1930

The word "dogma" is curiously unpopular. Any stigma is good enough to beat a dogma.

> W. R. INGE, *Science and Religion,* 1931

It is only truth—or dogma, to give it its other name—which can make prayer efficacious, and impregnate it with that austere, protective strength without which it degenerates into weakness.

> ROMANO GUARDINI, *The Spirit of the Liturgy,* 1935

In the literary order dogma must never be applied dogmatically.

> MARTIN TURNELL, *Poetry and Crisis,* 1938

Quarrels about dogma are quarrels about fact and not just about equally valid theories woven around unquestionable data.

> JOHN MCINTYRE, *Reformed Theological Review,* August, 1949

Scientism, like many of the anti-scientific attitudes against which it protests, resorts to its own type of dogmatism.

> E. LEROY LONG, JR., *Science and Christian Faith,* 1950

The most dangerous tendency of the modern world is the way in which bogus theories are given the force of dogma.

> JEAN DANIELOU, *The Lord of History,* 1958

Dogma is the belief of the Church as she herself has defined it. . . . The scholar does not submit dogma to criticism and examination because it is neither his office nor does it lie in his power to define what the Church believes; only the Church herself can do this.

> JOHN L. MCKENZIE, *The Critic,* August-September, 1961

Dogmas are nothing more or less than emergency measures to which the Church is driven by heresies.

> HANS KÜNG, *The Council in Action,* 1963

It is extremely necessary not to turn questions of current law or ceremonial into questions of dogma.

> HANS KÜNG, *The Council in Action,* 1963

See also Belief; Church: Its Authority; Doctrine; Dogmatism; Error; Faith; Heresy; Infallibility; Obedience; Orthodoxy; Theology; Tradition.

DOGMATISM

Dogmatism will not allow us to be ignorant of that of which we are ignorant.

> MICHEL DE MONTAIGNE, *Essays,* 1588

The view that truth consists in a proposition which is a fixed and final result, or again which is directly known.

> G. W. F. HEGEL, *Phenomenology of Mind,* 1807

The principle indeed of Dogmatism develops into Councils in the course of time; but it was active, nay sovereign from the first, in every part of Christendom. . . .

What Conscience is in the history of the individual mind, such was the dogmatic principle in the history of Christianity.

> JOHN HENRY NEWMAN, *The Development of Christian Doctrine*, 1878

Writers of the class to whom I fear you belong decry dogmatism, yet none are more dogmatic.

> EDWARD B. PUSEY, *Spiritual Letters of*, II, 1898

Dogmatism—uncritical thinking based on dogma. . . . Dogmatism is characteristic of religious beliefs, metaphysical points of view, and of all theoretical systems which are dying out, reactionary and fighting against the developing new ideas. Marxism-Leninism is foreign to any dogmatism.

> *Slovar Inostrannykh Slov* (*Dictionary of Foreign Words*), publ. by Soviet government, Moscow, Russia, 1951

The dogmatism of the local Vicar is not the dogmatism of the Church.

> J. V. L. CASSERLEY, *Retreat from Christianity in the Modern World*, 1952

Outside the practice of science itself, scientists have sometimes been the greatest offenders in adhering to dogmatic ideas against all the evidence.

> MARY B. HESSE, *Science and the Human Imagination*, 1955

See also Communism; Doctrine; Dogma; Tolerance.

DOUBLE STANDARDS

The Christian must reject as a deadly heresy the idea of two absolutely different standards, one for the Kingdom of God or the Church or the personal relations of men, and another for the economic order.

> JOHN C. BENNETT, *Goals of Economic Life*, ed. A. D. Ward, 1952

See also Economics and Christianity.

DOUBT

Let us doubt without unbelief of things to be believed.

> ST. AUGUSTINE, *De Trinitate*, c. 397

The first key to wisdom is assiduous and frequent questioning. . . . For by doubting we come to inquiry, and by inquiry we arrive at truth.

> PETER ABELARD, *Yes and No*, c. 1120

He that knows nothing doubts nothing.

> GEORGE HERBERT, *Outlandish Proverbs*, 1640

If you would be a real seeker after truth, it is necessary that at least once in your life you doubt, as far as possible, all things.

> RENÉ DESCARTES, *Principles of Philosophy*, 1644

Doubts are more cruel than the worst of truths.

> MOLIÈRE, *The Misanthrope*, 1666

Doubt is the trouble of a soul left to itself, which wants to see what God hides from it, and out of self-love seeks impossible securities.

> FRANÇOIS FÉNELON (1651–1715), *Spiritual Letters*

Never be afraid to doubt, if only you have the disposition to believe, and doubt in order that you may end in believing the truth.

> SAMUEL TAYLOR COLERIDGE, *Aids to Reflection*, 1825

Doubt itself may be the greatest blessing you ever had, may be the greatest striving of God's Spirit within you that you have ever known, may be the means of making every duty more real to you.

> FREDERICK D. MAURICE, *Letter*, April 14, 1863

Ten thousand difficulties do not make one doubt, as I understand the subject; difficulty and doubt are incommensurate.

JOHN HENRY NEWMAN, *Apologia pro Vita Sua,* 1864

Doubts must precede every deeper assurance; for uncertainties are what we see first when we look into a region hiterto unknown, unexplored, unannexed.

GEORGE MACDONALD, *Unspoken Sermons,* 1st Series, 1869

It is only after doubt has come that intellectual belief arises. To entertain reasons for believing in the existence of a thing presupposes the possibility of its nonexistence.

JAMES BISSET PRATT, *The Psychology of Religion and Belief,* 1907

To have doubted one's own first principles is the mark of a civilized man.

OLIVER WENDELL HOLMES, *Collected Legal Papers,* 1920

In 1890 the "liberal" was debating whether there were two Isaiahs; in 1930 the extreme "modernist" was debating whether there was a personal God.

GAIUS GLENN ATKINS, *Religion in Our Times,* 1932

Lift up your hands in the dark sanctuary of your soul when you are tempted to wonder what is the good of it all, and praise the Lord!

EVELYN UNDERHILL, *The Fruits of the Spirit,* 1942

Doubt is nothing but a trivial agitation on the surface of the soul, while deep down there is a calm certainty.

FRANÇOIS MAURIAC, *God and Mammon,* 1946

Once I heard a man say: "I spent twenty years trying to come to terms with my doubts. Then one day it dawned on me that I had better come to terms with my faith. Now I have passed from the agony of the questions I cannot answer into the agony of answers I cannot escape. And it's a great relief."

DAVID E. ROBERTS, *The Grandeur and Misery of Man,* 1955

There may be a measure of truth in the traditional doctrine that . . . all doubt is at bottom a dishonest rationalization of sin.

JOHN HUTCHISON, *Faith, Reason and Existence,* 1956

Serious doubt is confirmation of faith. It indicates the seriousness of the concern, its unconditional character.

PAUL TILLICH, *Dynamics of Faith,* 1957

See also Agnosticism; Agnostics; Atheism; Belief; Believing; Faith; Relativity; Risk; Security; Skepticism; Spiritual Struggle; Truth; Unbelief.

DREAMS

There is no divine energy which inspires dreams. . . . No visions of dreamers proceed from the agency of the gods. For the gods have for our own sake given us intellect sufficiently to provide for our own welfare.

CICERO, *On Divination,* 44 B.C.

If true dreams come from God, from whence come the false ones? For if these last do likewise come from God, what can be more inconsistent than God?

CICERO, *On Divination,* 44 B.C.

Dream is the *noblet* [the unripe fruit] of prophecy.

Beresbit Rabba, between 4th and 6th century A.D.

I call that a true dream which is caused by the celestial influences of the phantastic spirit, mind or body, being all well disposed.

HENRY CORNELIUS AGRIPPA, *Occult Philosophy,* 1530

If you suffer impressions to be made upon you by dreams, the devil hath the reins in his own hands, and can tempt you by that, which will abuse you, when you can make no resistance.

JEREMY TAYLOR, *Sermons,* 1651

As we often dream that we dream, and heap vision upon vision, it may well be that this life itself is but a dream, on which the others are grafted, from which we wake at death.

BLAISE PASCAL, *Pensées,* 1670

That there are demonical dreams we have little reason to doubt. Why may there not be Angelical?

THOMAS BROWNE (1605–1682), *On Dreams,* posth. publ.

As God has personally appeared to men in dreams, so have inferior spirits, and we have examples of this too in the Scripture.

DANIEL DEFOE, *The History and Reality of Apparitions,* 1727

Dreams have a poetic integrity and truth. . . . Wise and sometimes terrible hints shall in them be thrown to the man out of a quite unknown intelligence. . . . Why then should not symptoms, auguries, forebodings be, as one said, the moanings of the spirit?

RALPH WALDO EMERSON, *Demonology,* 1839

On the one side, the dream has claims to be considered part of an eternal life; on the other side . . . there may be in it . . . enough of the danger of excess to lead some very wise men to abstain.

HENRY HOLT, *On the Cosmic Relations,* 1914

If there be any truth in Freud's insistence upon the symbolic nature of normal dreams, it is the less surprising that the dream imagination of the Christian mystic should work up visions of a symbolic sort. . . . Our modern tendency to consider visions quite extraordinary and pathological is probably mistaken.

J. B. PRATT, *The Religious Consciousness,* 1921

See also Psychoanalysis; Vision.

DRINKING. See ALCOHOL

DRUNKENNESS

Drunkenness is the ruin of reason. It is premature old age. It is temporary death.

ST. BASIL, *Homilies,* c. 375

The drunken man is a living corpse.

ST. JOHN CHRYSOSTOM, *Homilies,* c. 388

Drunkenness is a vice which is painful and sickly in the very acting of it.

JEREMY TAYLOR, *Twenty-seven Sermons,* 1651

Drunkenness spoils health, dismounts the mind, and unmans man. It reveals secrets, is quarrelsome, lascivious, impudent, dangerous and mad.

WILLIAM PENN, *Fruits of Solitude,* 1693

Since the creation of this world there has been no tyrant like Intemperance, and no slaves so cruelly treated as his.

WILLIAM LLOYD GARRISON, *Life,* I, 1885

See also Abstinence; Alcohol; Dissipation; Gluttony; Pleasure; Temperance; Wine.

DUTIES

Let no one forget his own duty for the sake of another's, however great; let a man after he has discovered his own duty, be always attentive to his duty.

Dhammapada, c. 5th century B.C.

A man's own natural duty, even if it seems imperfectly done, is better than work not naturally his own, even if this is well performed.

> *Bhagavad-Gita,* between 5th and 2nd centuries B.C.

While still unable to do your duty to the living, how can you do your duty to the dead? . . . Not yet understanding life, how can you understand death?

> CONFUCIUS, *Analects,* 5th century B.C.

The path of duty lies in what is near, and men seek for it in what is remote. The work of duty lies in what is easy, and men seek for it in what is difficult.

> *Mencius,* c. 300 B.C.

Who does no more than his duty is not doing his duty.

> BAHYA, *Hobot HaLebabot,* 1040

God makes no limitations to His service, and how, then, does it happen that thy conscience is afflicted at having to do what He appoints for thee?

> JOHN TAULER (1300–1361), *Sermons and Conferences*

The duties of our Christianity, and our Religion must preponderate and weigh down the duties of all other places, and for all together.

> JOHN DONNE, *Sermon,* February 29, 1627

To do my duty in that state of life unto which it shall please God to call me.

> *The Book of Common Prayer,* 1662

Duties neither need nor can receive any stronger proof from miracles than what they have already from the evidence of right reason.

> MATTHEW TINDAL, *Christianity as Old as Creation,* 1730

An act of duty is law in practice.

> BENJAMIN WHICHCOTE, *Moral and Religious Aphorisms,* 1753

Duty is the necessity of acting out of respect for the law. . . . An action from duty must eliminate entirely the influence of inclinations and thus every object of the will.

> IMMANUEL KANT, *Metaphysics of Ethics,* 1785

Stern daughter of the voice of God.

> WILLIAM WORDSWORTH, *Ode to Duty,* 1807

In duty the individual finds his liberation; liberation from dependence on mere natural impulse.

> G. W. F. HEGEL, *The Philosophy of Right,* 1821

A sense of duty pursues us ever. It is omnipresent, like the Deity.

> DANIEL WEBSTER, *Argument,* at trial of J. F. Knapp, 1830

Our duties to God and man are not only duties done to Him, but they are means of enlightening our eyes and making our faith apprehensive.

> JOHN HENRY NEWMAN, *Parochial and Plain Sermons,* 6, 1843

Never to tire, never to grow cold; to be patient, sympathetic, tender; to look for the budding flower and the opening heart; to hope always, like God, to love always, —this is duty.

> H. F. AMIEL, *Journal,* May 27, 1849

We believe in the holy, inexorable, dominating idea of duty, the sole standard of life: duty that embraces family, fatherland, humanity . . . duty, without which no right exists.

> GIUSEPPE MAZZINI, *The Duties of Man and Other Essays,* 1858

"Learn what is true in order to do what is right," is the summary of the whole duty of man, for all who are unable to satisfy their mental hunger with the east wind of authority.

> THOMAS HENRY HUXLEY, *Lay Sermons,* 1870

Those who gain no experience are those who shirk the King's highway for fear of encountering Duty seated by the roadside.

GEORGE MACDONALD, *Thomas Wingfold*, 1876

In quiet fidelity to daily duty lies the only sure hope of reaching a high spiritual state . . . foregoing raptures if they are not granted him, seeking only to do his whole work in life honestly and well.

G. S. MERRIAM, *A Living Faith*, 1876

We want . . . not religion as a duty, but duty as a religion.

FELIX ADLER, *Creed and Deed*, 1877

The only prize which is infallibly gained by performing one duty well is the power of performing another.

F. W. H. MYERS, *Classical Essays*, 1883

Right is the faith of the individual. Duty is the common collective faith.

JOSEPH MAZZINI, *Essays*, 1887

Duty is what one expects from others—it is not what one does oneself.

OSCAR WILDE, *A Woman of No Importance*, 1893

The important thing is to know that there are gradations of duty and morality, that the duty of one state of life, in one set of circumstances, will not and cannot be that of another.

VIVEKANANDA (1863–1902), *Complete Works of*, I, 35

Duty becomes a disease with us; it drags us ever forward. . . . This duty, this idea of duty is the midday summer sun which scorches the innermost soul of mankind. . . . The only true duty is to be unattached and to work as free beings, to give up all work unto God.

VIVEKANANDA (1863–1902), *Works of*

Duty can only be defined as that action which will cause more good to exist in the universe than any possible alternative.

G. E. MOORE, *Principia Ethica*, 1903

When Elijah was waiting with impatience for the Divine Presence in the wilderness, he found that God was not clothed in the whirlwind or in the earthquake, but that He was in the still small voice of duty.

CHARLES E. GARMAN, *Letters, Lectures, Addresses*, 1909

The substitution of duty for a living creative love has drained all meaning from the precept "bear ye one another's burden."

FRANCIS G. WICKES, *The Inner World of Childhood*, 1927

The ability to weigh two duties, and balance them against each other, is the measure of human worth and dignity.

R. W. CHAMBERS, *Life of Sir Thomas More*, 1935

If a man like Hitler gained a position from which he had the power to do magnified harm, it is quite conceivable that he never could have reached it but for the minor sins and small delinquencies and petty lapses from duty on the part of multitudes of men.

HERBERT BUTTERFIELD, *Christianity, Diplomacy and War*, 1953

From the dawn of moral consciousness, we do not find it equally as easy to be true to our duty and to be false to it. . . . Movement toward moral perfection is upstream.

HAROLD DE WOLF, *Theology of the Living Church*, 1953

See also Action; Acts; Allegiance; Behavior; Commitment; Conduct; Conscience; Deeds; Determinism; Election; Ethics; Evil; Idleness; Inaction; Individual Responsibility; Morality; Perfection; Practice; Religion, Definitions of; Religion: Its Nature and Function; Responsibility; Vocation; War, Defense of; Work.

EARTH. See WORLD, THE

EASE

Who can for very shame desire to enter into the Kingdom of Christ with ease, when himself entered not into his own without pain?
> ST. THOMAS MORE, *Dialogue of Comfort*, 1535

We cannot go to Heaven on beds of down.
> RICHARD BRAITHWAITE, *The English Gentlemen*, 1631

God laughs at a man who says to his soul, Take thy ease.
> ABRAHAM COWLEY, *Of Myself*, 1665

Ease is the sluggard's dream of peace.
> HENRY STANLEY HASKINS, *Meditations in Wall Street*, 1940

Absorption in ease is one of the most reliable signs of present or impending decay.
> RICHARD WEAVER, *Ideas Have Consequences*, 1948

The adoption of the Christian view of the World has not, to put it mildly, made for greater simplicity and ease of living.
> C. E. M. JOAD, *The Recovery of Belief*, 1952

See also Apathy; Comfort; Inaction; Luxury; Wealth; Work; Worldliness.

EAST

And where did the Christianization of the world begin? In the East, the land of the Holy Places, of the Desert Fathers, of the Apologists, of the Councils, of the majestic liturgies, and of the decisive victories of orthodoxy over the Gnostic and christological heresies.
> F. VAN DER MEER, *Atlas of Western Civilization*, 1951

Were not the Byzantines the direct heirs of Paul and John, whose letters are still heard in the original language by the same congregations to whom they were originally addressed? Did not the majority of the bishoprics, and especially the most ancient, lie in the East?
> F. VAN DER MEER, *Atlas of Western Civilization*, 1951

EASTER

The great Easter truth is not that we are to live newly after death—that is not the great thing—but that . . . we are to, and may, live nobly now because we are to live forever.
> PHILLIPS BROOKS (1835–1893), *Perennials from*

Today one grave is open, and from it has risen a sun which will never be obscured, which will never set, a sun which creates new life. This new sun is the Crucified One, the Son of God.
> ST. JEAN VIANNEY, CURÉ D'ARS, *Sermon for Easter, Sermons for Sundays and Feasts*, 1901

Easter morning is not a mere declaration that we are immortal, but a declaration that we are *immortal children of God.*
> GEORGE MATHESON, *Studies in the Portrait of Christ*, 1902

The door of the Holy Sepulchre is the portal through which we enter the kingdom of God.
> HERBERT F. GALLAGHER, *The Life and Personality of Christ*, 1941

The great day does not merely arrive, like a date on a calendar; it explodes like an Event which the Faith has been keeping for a surprise.
> JOHN W. LYNCH, *Hourglass*, 1952

The indisputable Easter fact . . . is that Jesus was a more potent factor in Jerusalem in the weeks and months after His death on Calvary than when He rode into the city amid the crowds or sat with His disciples in the Upper Room.

HENRY SLOANE COFFIN, *Joy in Believing,* 1956

If Easter says anything to us today, it says this: You can put truth in a grave, but it won't stay there. You can nail it to a cross, wrap it in winding sheets and shut it up in a tomb, but it will rise!

CLARENCE W. HALL, *Reader's Digest,* April, 1957

Easter means that God has already taken the measure of evil at its very worst; that He has met the challenge at that crucial point; and that He routed the forces of darkness and thus settled the ultimate issue for those who say "Yes" to Him!

JOHN E. LARGE, *The Small Needle of Doctor Large,* 1962

See also Calvary; Immortality; Immortality, Belief in; Incarnation; Jesus Christ: His Divinity; Jesus Christ: His Passion and Death; Jesus Christ: His Resurrection; Resurrection, Sunday.

ECONOMIC CONTROL

As far as the first generation of reformers were concerned, there was no intention, among either Lutherans, or Calvinists, or Anglicans, of relaxing the rules of good conscience, which were supposed to control economic transactions and social relations.

RICHARD H. TAWNEY, *Religion and the Rise of Capitalism,* 1926

State activity in the economic field, no matter what its breadth or depth may be, ought not to be exercised in such a way as to curtail an individual's freedom of personal initiative.

POPE JOHN XXIII, *Pacem in Terris,* April, 1963

ECONOMICS AND CHRISTIANITY

The Christian ideal calls for hearty support of a planned economic system in which maximum social values shall be sought. It demands that cooperation shall supplant competition as the fundamental method.

FEDERAL COUNCIL OF CHURCHES OF CHRIST IN AMERICA, *Report,* 1932

For there are some who, while exteriorly faithful to the practice of their religion, yet in the field of labor and industry, in the professions, trade and business, permit a deplorable cleavage in their conscience, and live a life too little in conformity with the clear principles of justice and Christian charity. Such lives are a scandal to the weak and to the malicious a pretext to discredit the Church.

POPE PIUS XI, *Atheistic Communism,* 1937

In conformity with Christian principles, economic power must be subordinated to human welfare, both individual and social.

BISHOPS OF ADMINISTRATIVE BOARD OF NATIONAL CATHOLIC WELFARE COUNCIL, *The Church and Social Order,* 1940

May it not be that many Christian laymen resent the "interference" of the Church on economic issues, not because the Gospel has little to say about them, but because what it does say is so disturbing.

GEORGE F. THOMAS, *Christian Ethics and Moral Philosophy,* 1955

See also Business; Capitalism; Competition; Double Standards; Economic Control; Enterprise; Industrialism; Labor; Marketplace; Morality and Economics; Profit; Property; Puritanism; Success; Trade; Traders; Trust; Usury; Wages.

ECSTASY

The beginning of ecstasy is the lifting of the veil and the vision of the Divine

Guardian, and the presence of understanding, and the contemplation of the invisible, and the discoursing on secret things and perceiving the non-existent, and it means that you pass away from where you are.

> ZIYAD B. AL-ARABI (9th century), quoted in Margaret Smith's *Readings From the Mystics of Islam*

The soul is created in a place between Time and Eternity: with its highest powers it touches Eternity, with its lower Time.

> MEISTER ECKHART (1260–1327), *Sermons*

For when, through love, the soul goes beyond all work of the intellect and all images in the mind, and is rapt above itself (a favor only God can bestow), utterly leaving itself, it flows into God: then is God its peace and fullness. . . . It sinks down into the abyss of divine love, where, dead to itself, it lives in God.

> LOUIS DE BLOIS (1506–1566), *Works*

Ecstasy is from the contemplation of things vaster than the individual and imperfectly seen perhaps, by all those that still live.

> WILLIAM BUTLER YEATS, *Dramatis Personae*, 1935

Ecstasy means living in another. Here, you are living in the being you love; you are living in the race whose history you summarize, whose function you fulfill, whose life you gather in your hands and pass on to the future ages; you are living (if you have eyes to see), in God.

> GERALD VANN, *The Heart of Man*, 1945

No writers have insisted more strongly than the mystics themselves on the fact that ecstasy can be counterfeited by diabolic influences, or even by hysteria.

> RONALD A. KNOX, *Enthusiasm*, 1950

See also Beatific Vision; Contemplation; Experience, Religious; Mysticism; Sexual Intercourse.

ECUMENICAL

The word "ecumenical" is properly used to describe everything that is related to the whole task of the whole Church to bring the Gospel to the whold world.

> CENTRAL COMMITTEE, WORLD COUNCIL OF CHURCHES, 1951

See also Ecumenism.

ECUMENISM

It is only by remaining in one's confession, and by deepening and broadening it—that one can work towards universalism or supra-confessionalism.

> NICHOLAS BERDYAEV, *Freedom and the Spirit*, 1935

I distrust a friendship between believers of all denominations which is unaccompanied by any kind of compunction or sadness of soul.

> JACQUES MARITAIN, *Vie Intellectuelle*, August, 1939

Every single Christian community is as such an ecumenical (catholic) fellowship, that is, at one with the Christian communities in all other places, and lands.

> KARL BARTH, *Community, Church and State*, 1946

We may not be able to meet in the same pew—would to God we did—but we can meet on our knees.

> FULTON SHEEN, Radio Sermon, *Time*, February 3, 1947

The ecumenical leaven should revolutionize the international world.

> F. M. VAN ASBECK, *The Church and the International Disorder*, 1948

The modern Eucumenical Movement thus unites the Catholic ideal of Christian unity with the Protestant ideal of Christian liberty, and promises to break the tragic deadlock between those opposite but equally essential trends in Christian life and thought.

WALTER MARSHALL HORTON, *Christian Theology*, 1958

It is a matter of experience that the first effect of joining the Ecumenical Movement is to make everyone *more*, not *less*, conscious of his own special loyalties and traditions.

WALTER MARSHALL HORTON, *Christian Theology*, 1958

The ecumenical gatherings of the last decade and a half have brought Americans into close contact with men and women who are struggling and dying for the faith.

MARTIN E. MARTY, *The New Shape of American Religion*, 1958

The ecumenical movement, in its ultimate meaning is . . . people in the world-wide Christian fellowship, people bound together in Christian love, trying to reflect their common relation to Jesus Christ in their relation to one another.

SAMUEL MCCREA CAVERT, *On the Road to Christian Unity*, 1961

The churches have discovered the Church. This, far beyond every achievement in common Biblical interpretation, beyond every device for uniting separated ministries, is the heart of the new thing that the ecumenical movement has brought into being.

LEWIS S. MUDGE, JR., *Unity in Mid-Career*, 1963

National and regional commissions of the churches on international affairs . . . make an indispensable contribution to the formation of a truly ecumenical policy in international affairs and to its subsequent application to particular problems.

Statement from *Annual Report*, THE COMMISSION OF THE CHURCHES ON INTERNATIONAL AFFAIRS, 1963–1964

The ecumenical movement . . . is able to heal divisions which have become historically obsolete, to replace confessional fanaticism by interconfessional cooperation, to conquer denominational provincialism, and to produce a new vision of the unity of all churches in their foundation.

PAUL TILLICH, *Systematic Theology*, III, 1964

The sacred council exhorts all the Catholic faithful to recognize the signs of the times and to take an active and intelligent part in the work of ecumenism. . . . Catholics, in their ecumenical work, must assuredly be concerned for their separated brethren, praying for them, keeping them informed about the Church, making the first approaches toward them. But their primary duty is to make a careful and honest appraisal of the Catholic household itself.

SECOND VATICAN COUNCIL, Decree on Ecumenism, November, 1964

Catholics must gladly acknowledge and esteem the truly Christian endowments from our common heritage which are to be found among our separated brethren.

SECOND VATICAN COUNCIL, Decree on Ecumenism, November, 1964

Nothing is so foreign to the spirit of ecumenism as a false irenicism, in which the purity of Catholic doctrine suffers loss and its assured genuine meaning is clouded.

SECOND VATICAN COUNCIL, Decree on Ecumenism, November, 1964

The Church exhorts all her sons that through dialogue and collaboration with the followers of other religions, carried out with prudence and love and in witness to the Christian faith and life, they recognize, preserve and promote the good things, spiritual and moral, as well as the sociocultural values found among these men.

SECOND VATICAN COUNCIL, *Declaration on the Relation of the Church to Non-Christian Religions*, October, 1965

Non-Christians cannot simultaneously participate in the ecumenical movement and keep faith with their faith. The very definitions and stated goals of the World Council of Churches and the Catholic Church make this logically incompatible.

ABRAHAM B. HECHT, Letter, *New York Times*, December 15, 1965

See also Agreement; Brotherhood; Catholic and Non-Catholic; Christians; Denominationalism; Dialogue; Division; Dogmatism; Fellowship; Luther, Martin; Pluralism; Rivalry; Theology; Tolerance.

EDIFICATION

We do more for truth by edification than by wrangling. It is better to pray for the erring than to confute them.

FRANÇOIS FÉNELON, *Spiritual Letters*, c. 1700

EDUCATED

An American clergyman once asked Mahatma Gandhi what caused him most concern. "The hardness of heart of the educated," Gandhi replied.

LOUIS FISCHER, *The Life of Mahatma Gandhi*, 1950

EDUCATION

The principle of learning [higher education] consists in preserving man's clear character, in giving new life to the people, and in dwelling in perfection, or the ultimate good.

Ta Hsüeh, or *Great Learning*, attributed to Confucius, 5th century B.C.

The Way of Education lies in elucidating virtue, in the renovation of the people, and in stopping short of nothing but the *summum bonum*.

Ta Hsüeh, or *Great Learning*, attributed to Confucius, 5th century B.C.

Next to the care of our own souls a right education of our children is greatest.

JOHN BELLERS, *Epistles to Friends Concerning Education*, 1697

Education is nothing more than the polishing of each single link in the great chain that binds humanity together and gives it unity.

JOHANN HEINRICH PESTALOZZI (1746–1827), *The Education of Man: Aphorisms*

Why preserve unborn embryos of life, if we do not intend to watch over and protect them, and to expand their subsequent existence into usefulness and happiness?

HORACE MANN, *Common School Journal*, IX, 1847

Implies an action upon our mental nature, and the formation of a character; it is something individual and permanent, and is commonly spoken of in connection with Religion and virtue.

JOHN HENRY NEWMAN, *The Idea of a University*, 1852

Education is the leading human souls to what is best, and making what is best out of them; and these two objects are always attainable together, and by the same means.

JOHN RUSKIN, *Stones of Venice*, 1853

Education is the instruction of the intellect in the laws of Nature, under which name I include not merely things and their forces, but men and their ways; and the fashioning of the affections and of the will into an earnest and loving desire to move in harmony with those laws.

THOMAS HENRY HUXLEY, *Lay Sermons*, 1870

And what is the education of mankind if not the passage from faith in authority to personal conviction, and to the sustained practice of the intellectual duty to consent to no idea except by virtue of its recognized truth, to accept no fact until its reality has been, in one way or another, established.

AUGUSTE SABATIER, *The Religions of Authority and Religions of the Spirit,* 1904

Nothing in education is so astonishing as the amount of ignorance it accumulates in the form of inert facts.

HENRY ADAMS, *The Education of Henry Adams,* 1906

Society possesses an original and fundamental right in the education of children. We must accordingly reject without compromise and brush aside the claim of parents to impart through family education their narrow views to the minds of their offspring.

N. BUKHARIN and E. PREOBEASHENSKY, *The ABC of Communism,* 1922

The first thing education teaches you is to walk alone.

TRADER HORN, in *Trader Horn,* by A. A. Horn, 1927

Education—the process of driving a set of prejudices down your throats.

MARTIN H. FISCHER, *Fischerisms,* 1937

An educational system that would not respect the sacred place of the Christian family which is under the protection of the holy law of God, one that sapped its foundations, that barred from youth the way to Christ, to the Savior's springs of life and joy, and that considered apostasy from Christ and from the Church to be a symbol of fidelity to the people or to a specific class, would be pronouncing its own condemnation.

POPE PIUS XII, *Summi Pontificatus,* October, 1939

There is no common faith, no common body of principle, no common body of knowledge, no common moral and intel-

lectual discipline. . . . We have established a system of education in which we insist that while every one must be educated, yet there is nothing in particular that an educated man must know.

WALTER LIPPMANN, *Address,* American Association for the Advancement of Science, December 29, 1940

Modern secular education treats the transmission of religious tradition as either unnecessary or untouchable.

RALPH W. SOCKMAN, *The Highway of God,* 1941

For years past we have been sinking forward into a thoroughly modern chaos, a scholarly and documented chaos worthy of our most Liberal and Progressive thinkers.

ROBERT I. GANNON, *God in Education,* 1943

Institutions which devote themselves exclusively to relative and subordinate truths hardly deserve to be known as educational.

ROBERT I. GANNON, *God in Education,* 1943

Education of the child ceases to be education when it rifts soul from body, intellect from will; imagination, emotions, and senses from the guidance of the intellect or from the discipline of the will; time from eternity; the child from its Creator.

JOHN T. MCNICHOLAS, *No Wall Between God and the Child,* 1947

The perverted purposes to which education was put by totalitarian states has shattered our simple illusions about the essential goodness of education.

JAMES H. RYAN, *Moral Values in American Education,* 1947

The soul and mind and life are powers of living and can grow, but cannot be cut out or made. . . . One can indeed help the being to grow . . . but even so, the growth must still come from within.

SRI AUROBINDO, *The Life Divine,* 1949

A good education is not so much one which prepares a man to succeed in the world, as one which enables him to sustain failure.

> BERNARD IDDINGS BELL, *Life,* October 16, 1950

Reflection is easy and commitment is easy; but the two together—that is an educational task demanding the highest powers.

> HOWARD LOWRY, *The Mind's Adventure: Religion and the Higher Education,* 1950

The trouble with some Christian colleges is that they exist as promotional or maintenance institutions of the Church, and are not, in a high and holy sense, educational.

> NELS F. S. FERRÉ, *Christian Faith and Higher Education,* 1954

When we look at the troubled state of the present world . . . one thing becomes manifest. This is the failure of recent educational practice to prepare men in terms of heart and will to prevent the strife, misunderstanding, and willfulness that now arise.

> NATHAN M. PUSEY, *Religion and Freedom of Thought,* 1954

The Soviet dialectician is making every effort to apply educational methods designed to close man's vision forever to the existence of a nonmaterial reality.

> FRANZ E. WINKLER, *Man, The Bridge Between Two Worlds,* 1960

See also Academic Freedom; Chaos; Children; Democracy; Democracy, Religion of; Education, Catholic; Education, Jewish; Education, Parents' Rights in; Education, Parochial; Education, Progressive; Education, Religious; Education, Secularized; Education, State; Mind; Scholars; Teachers; Theology; Thinking; Truth; Universities; Values; Values, Spiritual.

EDUCATION, CATHOLIC

In order that the opportunity of reading and making progress may not be taken away from poor children . . . let some sufficient benefice be assigned in every cathedral church for a master who shall teach gratis the clerks of the same church, and poor scholars.

> THIRD COUNCIL OF THE LATERAN, 1179

The true Christian product of Christian education, is the supernatural man who thinks, judges and acts constantly and consistently in accordance with right reason illumined by the supernatural light of the example and teaching of Christ.

> POPE PIUS XI, *Christian Education of Youth,* 1929

It is the inalienable right as well as the indispensable duty of the Church, to watch over the entire education of her children, in all institutions, public or private, not merely in regard to the religious instruction there given, but . . . in so far as religion and morality are concerned.

> POPE PIUS XI, *Christian Education of Youth,* 1929

The subject of Christian education is man whole and entire, soul united to body in unity of nature, with all his faculties, natural and supernatural, such as right reason and revelation show him to be.

> POPE PIUS XI, *Encyclical on Christian Education,* 1931

Education consists essentially in preparing man for what he must do here below in order to attain the sublime end for which he was created.

> PIUS XI, *Encyclical on Christian Education,* 1931

Classical culture, Christian culture, the medieval synthesis of Thomas Aquinas, and modern science and modern thought

—these are the strands that the Catholic believes must be combined somehow into unity to provide a liberal education for the youth of our day, to place him in contact with truth, and beauty and goodness.
WILLIAM J. MCGUCKEN, *The Philosophy of Catholic Education,* 1951

All our modern teaching institutions have been created by the Catholic Church, not the State. The university dates from the early 13th century, and the high schools are an invention of the Jesuits, who organized the first one in the 16th century. Primary schools began to take shape in the 17th century when St. John Baptist de la Salle organized a teaching order specially destined to fight illiteracy in the mass of the population.
ÉTIENNE GILSON, *Ensign,* March, 1952

The role and object of Christian education is the formation of a new human being, reborn in baptism, into a perfect Christian.
POPE PIUS XII, *Broadcast,* March 24, 1952

This, I submit, is our mission, to educate men and women in the building of a civilization on earth as the vehicle of their dedication to heaven.
ANTON C. PEGIS, *Disputed Questions in Education,* 1954

To assume that because able and sagacious religious pour out their heart's blood in the effort to keep institutions going, the holiness of their graduates or their ability to move to the forefront of the scholarly procession will be guaranteed, is to run afoul of statistics.
GEORGE N. SHUSTER, *Education and Moral Wisdom,* 1960

See also Bus Service, School; Catholicism; Church and State; Education; Education, Parents' Rights in; Education, Parochial; Education, Religious; Education, Secularized; Education, State; Secularism; Sex Education.

EDUCATION, JEWISH

The aim [of Jewish education] is to develop a sincere faith in the holiness of life and a sense of responsibility for enabling the Jewish people to make its contribution to the achievement of the good life.
M. M. KAPLAN, *Future of the American Jew,* 1948

Where Jewish education is neglected, the whole content of Judaism is reduced to merely an awareness of anti-Semitism. Judaism ceases then to be a civilization, and becomes a complex.
M. M. KAPLAN, *Future of the American Jew,* 1948

See also Education; Education, Parochial; Education, Religious; Education, Secularized.

EDUCATION, PARENTS' RIGHTS IN

If anyone doubts that it is the peculiar and inalienable office of parents to educate their own children, let him go to the dens of beasts and the nests of birds and be wiser.
W. B. ULLATHORNE, *Characteristics from the Writings of,* 1889

The fundamental theory of liberty upon which all governments in this Union repose excludes any general power of the State to standardize its children by forcing them to accept instruction from public teachers only. The child is not the mere creature of the State; those who nurture him and direct his destiny have the right coupled with the duty, to recognize, and prepare him for additional duties.
U. S. SUPREME COURT, *Oregon School Case,* 1925

The parent has a right to say that no teacher paid by their money shall rob their children of faith in God and send them back to their homes skeptical, or infidels, or agnostics, or atheists.

WILLIAM JENNINGS BRYAN, *Testimony at Scopes Trial,* July 16, 1925

The family holds directly from the Creator the mission and hence the right to educate the offspring, . . . a right anterior to any right whatever of civil society and of the State, and therefore inviolable on the part of any power on earth.

POPE PIUS XI, *Christian Education of Youth,* 1929

It is the duty of the State to protect in its legislation, the prior rights . . . of the family as regards the Christian education of its offspring, and consequently also to respect the supernatural rights of the Church in this same realm of Christian education.

POPE PIUS XI, *Christian Education of Youth,* 1929

The God-given rights of parents either are not understood or are ignored by our secularist educators and by many school administrators who, in a delusion of sovereignty, act as though they, not the parents, have complete control of the education of the child.

JOHN T. MCNICHOLAS, *No Wall Between God and Child,* 1947

Parents have a prior right to choose the kind of education that shall be given to their children.

United Nations Universal Declaration of Human Rights, Article 26, 1948

See also Academic Freedom; Church and State; Education; Education, Catholic; Education, Parochial; Education, Religious; Education, State.

EDUCATION, PAROCHIAL

Encourage free schools and resolve that not one dollar appropriated for their support shall be appropriated to the support of any sectarian schools.

ULYSSES S. GRANT, *Address,* Des Moines, Iowa, 1875

It does seem unwise for a separate school system to be established, because that would lead to divisiveness in the community and mutual bigotry.

WILLIAM J. SANDERS, *The Public Schools and Spiritual Values,* 1944

Parochial education . . . cannot be said to meet the requirements of a democracy that rests upon a community of shared education experience.

WILLIAM CLAYTON BOWER, *Church and State in Education,* 1944

As for the parochial school of Christian and Jew, let us regard it as an element of American democracy and as an expression of the freedom of American culture. It is a means of preserving the diversity of cultures within our land.

JOSEPH H. LOOKSTEIN, *Jewish Education,* XXI, 1949

On a truly objective estimate of the contribution of parochial schools to American democracy—financially, educationally and religiously—we deserve much better of our nation than the begrudging right to exist.

ROBERT C. HARTNETT, *Federal Aid to Education,* 1950

We are unalterably opposed to the diversion of tax funds to the support of private and sectarian schools.

Doctrines and Discipline of the Methodist Church, 1952

When we speak of "Separate schools," let us not imagine that the Catholic schools once separated themselves from State-operated schools. The real "Separate" schools are those which the State separated from both Church and God, when, at the time of the French Revolution, it decided to open schools of its own.

ÉTIENNE GILSON, *Ensign,* March, 1952

The religious school is not divisive, because American unity is not monolithic, but essentially pluralistic, and the religious school fits in very well as an American institution into the emerging pattern of American religious pluralism.

WILL HERBERG, *Religion in America,* ed. John Cogley, 1958

See also Church and State; Education; Education, Catholic; Education, Religious; Education, Secularized; Education, State; Secularism; State, the.

EDUCATION, PROGRESSIVE

The true center of correlation on the school subjects is not science, nor literature, nor history, nor geography, but the child's own social activities.

JOHN DEWEY, "My Pedagogic Creed," *The School Journal,* 1897

The only true education comes through the stimulation of the child's powers by the demands of the social situations in which he finds himself.

JOHN DEWEY, "My Pedagogic Creed," *The School Journal,* 1897

The primary business of school is to train children in co-operative and mutually helpful living; to foster in them the consciousness of mutual interdependence.

JOHN DEWEY, *The School and Society,* 1899

To imposition from above is opposed [in progressive education] expression and cultivation of individuality; to external discipline is opposed free activity; to learning from texts and teachers, learning through experience; to acquisition of skills and techniques by drill, is opposed acquisition of them as means of attaining ends which

make a direct vital appeal; to preparation for a more or less remote future, is opposed the making the most of the opportunities of present life.

JOHN DEWEY, *Experience and Education,* 1938

Having begun by confusing traditional subject matters with traditional ways of teaching them, it has ended by providing a corps of teachers as learned in methods as they are ignorant of the contents of the subjects they supposedly teach. For all its emphasis on life-adjustment and the interests of the child, it has raised up a succession of generations of neurotics.

ROBERT C. WHITTEMORE, *Makers of the American Mind,* 1964

See also Dewey, John; Education.

EDUCATION, RELIGIOUS

But as for those who will not learn, let them be told that they deny Christ and are no Christians . . . let their parents or masters refuse them food and drink, and tell them that the prince will have such rude people driven from the land.

MARTIN LUTHER, Preface to *Luther's Catechism,* 1530

The greater the intellectual progress of the ages, the more fully will it be possible to employ the Bible not only as the Foundation of education, but as the instrument of education.

J. W. VON GOETHE (1749–1832), quoted in E. S. Bate's *The Bible to Be Read as Living Literature*

It is an honest and logical end to preserve Christian truth and morality among the people by fostering religion in the young. Nor is it any antagonism to the State; on the contrary, it is an honest end to give to the State better citizens by making them better Christians.

Third Plenary Council of Baltimore, of Roman Catholic Church in the United States, 1884

A child that is early taught that he is God's child, that he may live and move and have his being in God, and that he has, therefore, infinite strength at hand for the conquering of any difficulty, will take life more easily, and probably will make more of it.

EDWARD EVERETT HALE (1822–1909), quoted in E. D. Starbuck's *Psychology of Religion*

Religious education is the directed process of helping growing persons progressively to achieve the experience defined as religious. . . . It is not anything added to education nor something apart from it. It is a certain quality of education.

THEODORE G. SOARES, *Religious Education*, 1928

All too often a religious education fails to build up anything in the soul; it merely stamps it—brands it, so to speak—with the fear of death, the last judgment and hell.

GEORGE BERNANOS, *La Grande Peur des Bien Pensants*, 1932

In the domain of spirituality and in the moral training of children the Church must be supreme.

JOHN T. MCNICHOLAS, *No Wall Between God and Child*, 1947

Neither parents, nor State, nor any power on earth can rightly shut out God from the life of the child. Every attempt to separate the child from God by any civil constitution or legislative enactment is an attack on the Divine Creator of the child.

JOHN T. MCNICHOLAS, *No Wall Between God and Child*, 1947

It is essential for the moral development of the child to start with some form of belief in a divine order, whose framework he will at first take for Gospel truth until the spiritual content matures into symbolic interpretation.

ARTHUR KOESTLER, *The Trail of the Dinosaur and Other Essays*, 1955

It is thought virtuous to have Faith—that is to say, to have a conviction which cannot be shaken by contrary evidence. . . . The consequence is that the minds of the young are stunted and are filled with fanatical hostility.

BERTRAND RUSSELL, *Why I Am Not a Christian*, 1957

Religious education is . . . a God-centered business which so infuses child's entire life that it must move from the baptismal font and on to the altar, but with the core of its spirit in the continuing atmosphere of a Christian home.

JOHN E. LARGE, *The Small Needle of Doctor Large*, 1962

There are those parents who deprive a spirit-hungry child of the sacramental fellowship of the Church, on the grounds that he is too young to understand. Well, we're all too young to understand.

JOHN E. LARGE, *The Small Needle of Doctor Large*, 1962

See also Academic Freedom; Church and State; Education; Education, Catholic; Education, Jewish; Education, Parents' Rights in; Education, Parochial; Education, Secularized; Education, State; Government and God; Secularism; Seminaries; State, the; Sunday School.

EDUCATION, SECULARIZED

The vast populaton around us are limited to schools of secularism—and in this way secularism is fast becoming the religion of America.

JOHN IRELAND, *Address*, August 11, 1913

The mentality of the entire body of American Protestantism has thus been fashioned under the influence of the secularized public school.

CHARLES CLAYTON MORRISON, *Christian Century*, April 17, 1946

Our public school . . . is organized on the premise that secular education can be isolated from all religious teaching so that the school can inculcate all needed temporal knowledge and maintain a strict and lofty neutrality as to religion.

> JUSTICE JACKSON, dissenting opinion, U. S. Supreme Court, *Everson vs. Board of Education of Township of Ewing, N. J.,* 1947

The only group secular education actually pleases is the atheistic.

> FULTON J. SHEEN, *Communism and the Conscience of the West,* 1948

Any reference to God, His Christ, or to anything at all connected with any religion but pure atheistic secularism in the history of literature classes is positively illegal, and you've got the U. S. Supreme Court to back up your Constitutional protest.

> NEIL G. MCCLUSKEY, *Federal Aid to Education,* 1950

To the full extent that it educates, the State educates in view of itself. What, from the very beginning, had prompted the desire for a secularized education now shines forth with the unmistakable necessity of a principle. The only conceivable end of State-managed education is the State itself.

> ÉTIENNE GILSON, *Ensign,* March, 1952

The secularization of the schools was a positive movement to embody in American education the interaction of the real and the ideal, upon which both democracy and active Christianity depend.

> AGNES MYER, *Address to American Unitarian Association,* 1954

In no field has secularism done more damage than in education. . . . Our youth problem would not be so grave if the place of God were emphasized in the rearing of children.

> ROMAN CATHOLIC BISHOPS OF THE U.S., November, 1962

The complete secularization of public schools would not be merely unpopular—the Court always has to risk that—but it would offend the nation's natural piety and sense of its own past.

> Editorial, *Life,* March 15, 1963

And a refusal to permit religious exercises [in public schools] thus is seen, not as the realization of state neutrality, but rather as the establishment of a religion of secularism.

> JUSTICE POTTER STEWART, dissenting opinion, U. S. Supreme Court, Prayer and Bible Reading in the Public Schools, June 17, 1963

See also Church and State; Education; Education, Catholic; Education, Jewish; Education, Parents' Rights in; Education, Parochial; Education, Progressive; Education, Religious; Education, State; Protestantism; Secularism.

EDUCATION, STATE

The state has a right to insist that its citizens shall be educated.

> *Pastoral Letter of the American Roman Catholic Hierarchy,* February, 1920

Unjust and unlawful is any monopoly, educational or scholastic, which physically or morally forces families to make use of government schools, contrary to the dictates of their Christian conscience, or contrary to their legitimate preferences.

> POPE PIUS XI, 1931

Functionally viewed, American public education emancipated from sectarianism is indirectly the only universal teacher of religious values in the United States.

> CONRAD HENRY MOEHLMAN, *School and Church: The American Way,* 1944

The Catholic Church is not opposed to tax-supported schools. On the contrary, she heartily endorses our compulsory system of education in America; she sincerely commends the traditional freedom of American education, and also the generous spirit of America to make adequate provision for education.

> JOHN T. MCNICHOLAS, *No Wall Between God and the Child,* 1947

If we do not care to awaken some morning on the wrong side of the Iron Curtain, then we ought all to be interested in not letting the liberal State believe that it can indefinitely persist in educating children in view of nothing.

> ÉTIENNE GILSON, *Ensign,* March, 1952

The Public School is the chief vehicle for mutual love, forgiveness, and tolerance between all races, classes, and creeds, it becomes an act of vandalism to attack it and an act of piety to work towards its improvement.

> AGNES MYER, *Address to American Unitarian Association,* 1954

See also Church and State; Education; Education, Catholic; Education, Jewish; Education, Parents' Rights in; Education, Parochial; Education, Religious; Education, Secularized; Government and God; Secularism; State, the.

EDUCATION AND RELIGION

Religion, morality and knowledge being necessary to good government and the happiness of mankind, schools and the means of education shall forever be encouraged.

> *Northwest Ordinance,* passed by U. S. Congress, July 13, 1787

Without religious preparation in childhood, no true religion and no union with God is possible for men.

> FRIEDRICH FROEBEL (1782–1852), *Aphorisms*

Each religion sets before mankind a new educational idea as its aim; each is a

fragment, enveloped in symbols, of eternal truth.

> GIUSEPPE MAZZINI, *The Duties of Man and Other Essays,* 1858

To shut religion out of the school and keep it for home and church is, logically, to train up a generation that will consider religion good for home and the church, but not for the practical business of real life.

> *Third Plenary Council of Baltimore,* of Roman Catholic Church in the United States, 1884

If education in its highest forms pay no attention to religious truth, then I ask by what means shall the conscience of the nation be developed?

> JAMES GIBBONS, *Address,* Silver Jubilee of Catholic University of America, 1912

Education does not mean the impartation of information. It means the development of character. Without religion there can be no true education.

> COMMISSION ON CHURCH AND RELIGIOUS EDUCATION, FEDERAL COUNCIL OF CHURCHES OF CHRIST IN AMERICA, *Report,* 1912

No church can sincerely subscribe to the theory that questions of faith do not enter into the education of children.

> WALTER LIPPMANN, *A Preface to Morals,* 1929

When religion is banished from the school, from education and from public life, when the representatives of Christianity and its sacred rites are held up to ridicule, are we really not fostering the materialism which is the fertile soil of Communism?

> POPE PIUS XI, *Atheistic Communism,* 1937

In a Christian society education must be religious, not in the sense that it will be administered by ecclesiastics, still less in the sense that it will exercise pressure, or attempt to instruct everyone in theology, but in the sense that its aims will be directed by a Christian philosophy of life.

T. S. ELIOT, *The Idea of a Christian Society,* 1940

Education is typically carried out without specific and continuous reference to the central spiritual values of our culture and without the reverent cultivation of those values which it is the function of religion to maintain.

F. ERNEST JOHNSON, *The Social Gospel Re-Examined,* 1940

If . . . the inalienable rights of man and our American way of life cannot survive except through that faith in God the Creator which was at their source, then evidently the neutral school, since it cannot teach religion, is practically incapable by itself of safeguarding our American institutions.

LOUIS J. A. MERCIER, *Address,* October 30, 1942

The religious element in public education is everything that promotes faith in the higher values of life. Religion is not something apart but a continuous part of our experience.

CONRAD HENRY MOEHLMAN, *School and Church: the American Way,* 1944

And neither mind nor character can be made without a spiritual element. This is just the element that has grown weak, where it has not perished, in our education, and therefore in our civilization, with disastrous results.

RICHARD LIVINGSTONE, *On Education,* Part II, 1945

Unlike Catholicism, the Protestant churches . . . have given to the public school their consistent and unreserved devotion. The result is that their own children have been delivered back to their

churches with a mentality which is not only unintelligent about religion but relatively incapacitated even to ask the question out of which religion arises.

CHARLES CLAYTON MORRISON, *Christian Century,* April 17, 1946

The over-all situation with reference to religion and public education in America is not satisfactory and the exclusion of religious subject matter which so largely prevails is neither required on grounds of public policy nor consistent with sound educational principles.

Relation of Religion to Public Education, Report, American Council on Education, April, 1947

The first obligation of the school with reference to religion is, we believe, to facilitate intelligent contact with it.

Relation of Religion to Public Education, Report, American Council on Education, April, 1947

A philosophy of education which omits God, necessarily draws a plan of life in which God either has no place or is a strictly private concern of men.

CATHOLIC BISHOPS OF THE U. S., 1947

Only Christian education can save America from all the subversive teaching tolerated, permitted, or even encouraged in our country.

JOHN T. MCNICHOLAS, *No Wall Between God and Child,* 1947

The public schools have not been neutral towards religion. To deny or to disregard the supernatural revealed truths of religion is to bring religion into the classroom with a vengeance. The tacit assumption that the things of God are not as important as the things of this world is the dominant principle of public school philosophy as it expresses itself in the administrative practice of barring religion from the school curriculum.

JAMES H. RYAN, *Moral Values in American Education,* 1947

When public education omits faith in God from its teaching, the public school gives a distorted and untrue view of history, of literature and of human society.

LUTHER A. WEIGLE, *Social Action*, November, 1947

Every form of pedagogic naturalism which in any way excludes or weakens supernatural Christian formation in the teaching of youth, is false.

JOHN J. CAVANAUGH, *The Blasphemous Thing*, 1950

The illiteracy, immaturity, inertia, indifference, and antagonism of faculty people toward religion constitute serious obstacles to the religious enterprise in education.

BERNARD L. LOOMER, *Liberal Learning and Religion*, ed. A. N. Wilder, 1951

We believe that religion has a rightful place in the public school program, and that it is possible for public school teachers, without violating the traditional American principle of separation of church and state, to teach moral principles and spiritual values.

Doctrines and Discipline of the Methodist Church, 1952

The only reason why a State may not want children to be educated in view of God is that it wants them educated in view of itself.

ÉTIENNE GILSON, *Ensign*, March, 1952

What we need is a concentrated incarnation of the Spirit in the community of teaching and learning—a Pentecost in education.

NELS F. S. FERRÉ, *Christian Faith and Higher Education*, 1954

I have tried to suggest that freedom is the real goal of education, but that it will not be won without an undergirding of religious experience.

NATHAN M. PUSEY, *Religion and Freedom of Thought*, 1954

The greatest and most urgent task of educators today is to instill ineradicably into the young precisely the utility of the useless, the value of the things that produce no cash returns but that make the "soul worth saving."

GERALD VANN, *The Water and the Fire*, 1954

But if the living God of the Bible truly exists, then surely no educational system that ignores the fact of His existence can be regarded as an adequate educational system.

J. V. L. CASSERLEY, *The Bent World*, 1955

In some ways, the atheist school may even be preferable, from a Christian point of view, to the neutral school. Schools that teach a dogmatic atheism at least have the virtue of raising the religious issue in a direct, inescapable way.

J. V. L. CASSERLEY, *The Bent World*, 1955

When all specific forms of religion are omitted from the world of the schools, this is in itself a negative form of religious teaching; it strongly implies that religion is peripheral and dispensable as a matter of human concern.

JOHN C. BENNETT, *Christians and the State*, 1958

Twentieth century public school education is avowedly dealing with values and loyalties, that is to say, with theology and ethics.

JAMES HASTINGS NICHOLS, *Religion in America*, ed. John Cogley, 1958

Almighty God, we acknowledge our dependence upon Thee, and we beg Thy blessing upon our parents, our teachers and our country.

Prayer for Public Schools, devised by N. Y. State Board of Regents and ruled unconstitutional by the U. S. Supreme Court in 1962

When one recalls the tradition of prayer in the schools both before and after the inauguration of the public school system . . . and can point not only to a resolution, passed by Congress on the day after it passed the proposal which became the First Amendment calling for the designation of a "day of public thanksgiving and prayer," but also to recognition of that tradition going back to Plato and Plutarch, one must conclude that due process does not proscribe legislative permission to say a noncompulsory prayer in schools.

> JUSTICE BERNARD S. MEYER, N. Y. Supreme Court, decision of August 24, 1959

For years the Christian enterprise was under the mesmerizing spell of so-called progressive educators, with their gadgets and gimmicks and gobbledegook. But now the world over, Christian education is returning to a sacrament-centered program.

> JOHN E. LARGE, *The Small Needle of Doctor Large,* 1962

In our view the Supreme Court [ruling against prayers in the public schools] has rendered a service of the greatest importance to true religion as well as to the integrity of a democratic state. It has placed one more obstacle in the way of those who desire eventually to use the power of the state to enforce conformity to religious or political ideas.

> EDITORIAL, *The Christian Century,* July 4, 1962

A compulsory state educational system so structures a child's life that if religious exercises are held to be an impermissible activity in schools, religion is placed at an artificial and state created disadvantage.

> JUSTICE POTTER STEWART, dissenting opinion, U. S. Supreme Court, Prayer and Bible Reading in the Public Schools, June 17, 1963

Religious exercises are not constitutionally invalid if they simply reflect differences which exist in the society from which the school draws its pupils. They become constitutionally invalid only if their administration places the sanction of secular authority behind one or more particular religious or irreligious beliefs.

> JUSTICE POTTER STEWART, dissenting opinion, U. S. Supreme Court, Prayer and Bible Reading in the Public Schools, June 17, 1963

We fervently believe that prayers, Bible readings and sectarian practices should be fostered in the home, church and synagogue, that public institutions such as the public school should be free of such practices.

> URI MILLER FOR THE SYNAGOGUE COUNCIL OF AMERICA, *New York Times,* June 18, 1963

Teaching for religious commitment is the responsibility of the home and the community of faith (such as church or synagogue) rather than the public schools. . . . Neither the church nor the state should use the public school to compel acceptance of any creed or conformity to any specific religious practice.

> NATIONAL COUNCIL OF CHURCHES, *New York Times,* June 18, 1963

A good many people will obviously agree with it, others will disagree. . . . We have in this a very easy remedy, and that is to pray ourselves. And I would think it would be a welcome reminder to every American family that we can pray a good deal more at home. We can attend our churches with a good deal more fidelity. And I would hope that all of us would support the Constitution and the responsibility in interpreting it.

> PRESIDENT JOHN F. KENNEDY, commenting on the U. S. Supreme Court decision banning prayers in the public schools, June, 1963

One of the wholesome results of this decision [by the U. S. Supreme Court forbidding the reading of the Bible and prayers in the public schools] is unintentional so far as the court is concerned. It is not the role of the Supreme Court to purify religion, in part or in whole. Nevertheless this decision does just that. The reading of two verses—no more, no less—selected by one of the students at random, the reading being unaccompanied by any comment, degenerates into incantation. So to read the Bible is to turn it into a talisman which encourages superstition, or to make its recitation meaningless rote. The decision delivers public school children from such ritualistic, potentially harmful exposure to an abuse of Holy Scripture.

EDITORIAL, *Christian Century,* July 3, 1963

See also Church and State; Education, Catholic; Education, Jewish; Education, Parochial; Education, Religous; Education, Secularized; Education, State; Government and Religion; Secularism.

EGO

The freedom of the ego here and now, and its independence of the causal chain, is a truth that comes from the immediate dictate of the human consciousness.

MAX PLANCK, *Where Is Science Going?,* 1932

Religion is in no way an obliteration or suppression of the ego . . . but a conscious, rational and ethical relationship of the ego to what transcends not only the ego but the whole cosmos.

VICTOR WHITE, *Soul and Psyche,* 1960

See also False Love; Falsehood; Freudianism; Nirvana; Pride; Self-Love; Self-Praise; Self-Righteousness; Vanity.

EGOISM

To identify consciousness with that which merely reflects consciousness—this is egoism.

PATANJALI (2nd century B.C.), *Yoga Aphorisms*

Every man regards his own life as the New Year's Eve of time.

JEAN PAUL RICHTER, *Levana,* 1807

Only by the supernatural is man strong; nothing is so weak as an egotist.

RALPH WALDO EMERSON, *The Young American,* 1844

There is one kind of religion in which the more devoted a man is, the fewer proselytes he makes, the worship of himself.

GEORGE MACDONALD, *Alec Forbes,* Vol. 11, 1865

Egotism is a terrible malady; it deprives man of the acquaintance of God and bereaves him of the Sun of assurance.

BAHAULLAH, *Epistle to the Son of the Wolf,* late 19th century

See also Conceit; Ego; False Love; Falsehood; Glory; Hell; Idolatry; Pride; Self-Love; Self-Righteousness; Vainglory; Vanity.

ELECTION

If all men in general bowed the knee before Christ, election would be general.

JOHN CALVIN, *Institutes,* III, 1536

Although God knows who are his, and a "small number of the elect" is spoken of, yet we ought to hope well of all, and not rashly count any one among the reprobate.

HENRY BULLINGER, *The Helvetic Confession,* 1536

Election precedes faith, and so it comes to pass that those who are elect, and do not come to a knowledge of the faith, as *e.g.* children, nevertheless attain eternal blessedness, for it is election which makes them blessed.

> HULDREICH ZWINGLI (1484–1581), *Works,* Vol. IV, p. 123

By the decree of God, for the manifestation of His glory, some men and angels are predestined unto everlasting life, and others are foreordained to everlasting death. . . . Neither are any redeemed by Christ . . . but the elect only. The rest of mankind God was pleased . . . to pass by, and to ordain them to dishonor and wrath.

> *Westminster Confession of Faith,* Formulary of the Presbyterian Church of Scotland, 1643

Jesus Christ, by His death did purchase salvation for the elect that God gave unto Him; these only have interest in Him and fellowship with Him.

> *Baptist Confession of Faith,* 1646

The elect are whosoever will, and the non-elect whosoever won't.

> HENRY WARD BEECHER, *Life Thoughts,* 1858

When people get it into their heads that they are being specially favored by the Almighty they had better as a general rule mind their p's and q's.

> SAMUEL BUTLER, *The Way of All Flesh,* 1884

The elect of the New Testament, like the elect of the Old, are chosen and called of God that he may use them for the good of other men. . . . The elect are elect for the sake of the non-elect.

> W. N. CLARKE, *An Outline of Christian Theology,* 1898

We believe that all dying in infancy are included in the election of grace, and are regenerated and saved by Christ, through the Spirit, who works when and where and how he pleases.

> *Constitution of the Presbyterian Church,* 1930

Every intervention by God in history is an election: either when he chooses a place in which to make more especial manifestation of his presence, or when he chooses a people to carry out his intentions, or when he chooses a man to be his representative or his messenger.

> EDMOND JACOB, *Theology of the Old Testament,* 1955

Election is to be understood in the sense of election to *responsibility,* and not election to special privilege.

> ROBERT McAFEE BROWN, *Patterns of Faith in America Today,* ed. F. E. Johnson, 1957

See also Chance; Commitment; Determinism; Duties; Fatalism; Fate; Foreknowledge; Free Will; Freedom; God: His Intervention in the World; God: His Omniscience; God: His Wrath; Guilt; Hell; Individual Responsibility; Judgment, God's; Justice; Man: His Wickedness.

ELOQUENCE

It is not what the speaker says but who he is that gives weight to eloquence.

> EURIPEDES, *Hecuba,* c. 326 B.C.

He is an eloquent man who can treat subjects of an humble nature with delicacy, lofty things impressively, and moderate things temperately.

> CICERO, *De Oratore,* c. 80 B.C.

Eloquence is the painting of thought.

> BLAISE PASCAL, *Pensées,* 1670

See also Preachers; Preaching; Sermons; Speech; Words.

EMOTION

I ask that you turn from everything usually reckoned religion, and fix your regard on the inward emotions and dispositions.
    FRIEDRICH SCHLEIERMACHER, *On Religion, Speeches to Its Cultured Despisers,* 1799

There is no ground for assuming a simple abstract "religious emotion" to exist as a distinct elementary mental affection by itself, present in every religious experience without exception. . . . There thus seems to be no one elementary religious emotion, but only a common storehouse of emotions upon which religious objects may draw.
    WILLIAM JAMES, *Varieties of Religious Experience,* 1902

The emotion felt by a man in the presence of nature certainly counts for something in the origin of religions.
    HENRI BERGSON, *The Two Sources of Morality and Religion,* 1935

Emotion is not the Cinderella of our inner life, to be kept in her place among the cinders in the kitchen. Our emotional life is *us* in a way our intellectual life cannot be.
    JOHN MACMURRAY, *Reason and Emotion,* 1935

A great deal of highly emotional corporate religion consists in . . . tempting God.
    A. VICTOR MURRAY, *Personal Experience and the Historic Faith,* 1939

No religion that ministers only to the intellect and not also to the emotions can meet the needs of men, and this accounts in large measure for the failure of all essentially intellectual religions to gain popular favor.
    EDWIN GRANT CONKLIN, *Man, Real and Ideal,* 1940

Religion is never devoid of emotion, any more than love is. It is not a defect of religion, but rather its glory, that it speaks always the language of feeling.
    D. E. TRUEBLOOD, *The Logic of Belief,* 1942

Emotionalism never finds depths of truth, but depth of truth cannot be had apart from a full and free emotional response.
    NELS F. S. FERRÉ, *Faith and Reason,* 1946

Fine emotions can be cheapened, and cheap emotions can be refined, but no emotions can be, with safety, wallowed in.
    HUBERT VAN ZELLER, *We Die Standing Up,* 1949

The *unconscious* conversion of instinctual impulses into religious activity is ethically worthless, and often no more than an hysterical outburst, even though its products may be aesthetically valuable.
    C. G. JUNG, *Symbols of Transformation,* 1952

The spiritual life is not a thing without emotions. The saints weep at the thought of their own sins and the goodness of God; their hearts beat to the bursting point within them, they shout and dance for joy; they die to see God.
    JEAN MOUROUX, *Christian Experience,* 1954

See also Ecstasy; Enthusiasm; Evangelism; Experience, Religious; Feelings; Heart; Intellect; Mysticism; Prayer; Religion, Definitions of; Religious; Repression; Revelation; Revivalism; Sentimentalism.

EMPLOYEES

Religion teaches the rich man and employer that their work-people are not their slaves; that they must respect in every man his dignity as a man and as a Christian.
    POPE LEO XIII, *Encyclical,* May, 1891

The rights and interests of the laboring man will be protected and cared for—not by the labor agitators, but by the Christian men to whom God in his infinite wisdom has given control of the property interests of the country.

> GEORGE BAER, on United Mine Workers' strike against the Reading Co., of which he was president, in 1902

See also Labor; Labor Unions; Wages.

EMPLOYMENT

It is better to get ten men to work than to do ten men's work.

> DWIGHT L. MOODY, *D. L. Moody,* by Wm. R. Moody, 1930

See also Labor; Labor Unions.

ENCOURAGEMENT

Providence seldom vouchsafes to mortals any more than just that degree of encouragement which suffices to keep them at a reasonably full exertion of their powers.

> NATHANIEL HAWTHORNE, *The House of the Seven Gables,* 1851

ENCYCLICALS

It is not to be believed that what is set forth in encyclicals does not in itself claim assent.

> POPE PIUS XII, *Humani Generis,* August 12, 1950

END

Days end with the sun's setting; the night ends with the sun's rising; the end of pleasure is ever grief; the end of grief ever pleasure. All accumulations end in exhaustion; all ascents end in falls; all associations end in dissociations; and life ends in death.

> ANUZITA, c. 800 B.C.

See also End of the World; Eternal; Infinite; Nuclear Energy; Nuclear War; Progress; Time.

END OF THE WORLD

Other spectacles will come—the last eternal Day of Judgment . . . when all this old world and its generations shall be consumed in one fire. How vast the spectacle will be on that day!

> TERTULLIAN, *De Spectaculis,* c. 200

If the Judge delays our salvation, it is through love and not through indifference, by design, and not lack of power. . . . He is waiting until the number of our fellowship may be filled in to the very last one.

> ST. AUGUSTINE, *Ennar. in Psalms,* XXVIII, XVI, c. 415

All the noonday brightness of human genius are destined to extinction in the vast death of the solar system, and that the whole temple of man's achievement must inevitably be buried beneath the debris of a universe in ruins—all these things if not quite beyond dispute, are yet so nearly certain that no philosophy which rejects them can hope to stand.

> BERTRAND RUSSELL, *Mysticism and Logic,* 1925

The day will come when the silence of death will descend upon our planet. . . . Against this futility of an all-devouring time, the human soul rises up demanding eternity.

> E. I. WATKIN, *The Catholic Centre,* 1939

We have reached a point in history where the unchecked pursuit of truth, without regard to its social consequences, will bring to a swift end the pursuit of truth, without regard to its social consequences, will bring to a swift end the pursuit of truth, by wiping out the very civilization that has favored it. That would indeed be the judgment of God.

LEWIS MUMFORD, *Saturday Review,* January 15, 1950

Death has unexpectedly become a phenomenon that not only the person must face, but society or civilization itself.

FULTON J. SHEEN, *The Woman,* 1951

What until recently seemed to be only the apocalyptic fantasies of the Christian faith has today entered the sphere of the soberest scientific calculations; the sudden end of history.

EMIL BRUNNER, *Eternal Hope,* 1954

Judaism has never faltered in its conviction that the "end of days" is destined to arrive and that mankind will be here to experience its bliss.

SIMON GREENBERG, *Patterns of Faith in America Today,* ed. F. E. Johnson, 1957

We are living in an apocalyptic age, when the daily newscasts carry overtones of eternity. . . . I don't know whether these days are a sunrise or the world's last, dark dusk. But I do know that we must set our eyes toward dawning, and it will come if our faith be true enough.

DONALD S. HARRINGTON, *Sermon,* New York, N.Y., October 22, 1961

We live in an impenitent age; fearing . . . the same sort of world-catastrophe which our ancestors hoped for.

RONALD A. KNOX, *Lightning Meditations,* 1961

Perhaps for the last time, our turn has come again to drink this chalice which peoples have been passing from hand to hand since the time men first came upon the earth and began slaughtering one another.

FRANÇOIS MAURIAC, *Cain, Where Is Your Brother,* 1962

See also Catastrophes; Death; Eternal; History; Judgment, God's; Nuclear War; Salvation; Second Coming; Time; War; World; World and God.

ENEMY

The greatest concerns of men are these, to make him who is an enemy a friend, to make him who is wicked righteous, and to make him who is ignorant learned.

Zend-Avesta, 6th century B.C.

To be an enemy is a sin; to have one is a temptation.

BENJAMIN WHICHCOTE, *Moral and Religious Aphorisms,* 1753

He who loves his enemies betrays his friends; this surely is not what Jesus meant.

WILLIAM BLAKE, *The Everlasting Gospel,* 1810

God has enjoined on us enmity against the serpent alone.

ST. SERAPHIM OF SAROV (1759–1833), quoted in A. F. Dobbie-Bateman's biography of St. Seraphim

See also Bloodshed; Hatred; Malice; Vengeance.

ENERGY

We cannot possibly conceive a passage from not-being to being, . . . or from potential to actual existence, except through the operation of some energy which is already actual, before the process in question begins, and adequate to produce every result in which such a process may ultimately issue.

J. R. ILLINGWORTH, *The Doctrine of the Trinity,* 1909

Without the slightest doubt *there is something* through which material and spiritual energy hold together and are complementary. In last analysis, *somehow or other,* there must be a single energy operating in the world.

> PIERRE TEILHARD DE CHARDIN, *The Phenomenon of Man,* 1955

Modern developments in physics have indicated that the ultimate constituent of the universe is energy. If energy is the essential basis of the whole material world, this to the Christian is a clear manifestation of the active, creative Spirit of God.

> ARTHUR F. SMETHURST, *Modern Science and Christian Beliefs,* 1955

See also Cause; Existence; God: Considered as Impersonal; Nuclear Energy; Universe.

ENJOYMENT

If you wish to reach the stage of enjoying everything, then seek enjoyment in nothing.

> ST. JOHN OF THE CROSS, *Steps to Perfection,* c. 1584

See also Amusements; Dissipation; Pleasure; Worldliness.

ENLIGHTENMENT

In this world, aspirants may find enlightenment by two different paths. For the contemplative is the path of knowledge; for the active is the path of selfless action.

> *Bhagavad-Gita,* between 500 and 200 B.C.

Souls that have once had the experience of intellectual enlightenment can never thereafter find spiritual salvation by committing intellectual suicide.

> ARNOLD J. TOYNBEE, *A Study of History,* Vol. IX, 1946

See also Experience, Religious; Knowledge; Light; Truth.

ENTERPRISE

The virtues of enterprise, diligence, and thrift are the indispensable foundation of any complex and vigorous civilization. It was Puritanism which, by investing them with a supernatural sanction, turned them from an unsocial eccentricity into a habit, and a religion.

> RICHARD H. TAWNEY, *Religion and the Rise of Capitalism,* 1926

See also Business; Capitalism; Competition; Economics and Christianity; Puritanism; Trade.

ENVIRONMENT

Every child, youth, adult, and even the most mature man is wholly the product of the environment that nourishes and raised him—an inevitable, involuntary and consequently irresponsible product.

> M. O. BAKUNIN (1814–1876), *Political Philosophy of,* ed. G. P. Marimoff

Judas shows how futile is the finest environment unless responded to from within.

> GEORGE MATHESON, *Studies in the Portrait of Christ,* 1902

There is a *Jesus way of life* which is independent of the conditions under which it is lived. . . . It is a way of reacting to one's environment whatever the environment is.

> RALPH W. SOCKMAN, *The Highway of God,* 1941

The basic religious concept in any time or place, the "doctrine of God," has also been to some degree shaped by the environment. . . . America has always had a national concept of God and of its own relation to Him.

> MARTIN E. MARTY, *The New Shape of American Religion,* 1958

ENVY

Envy, the meanest of vices, creeps on the ground like a serpent.
OVID, *Epistulae ex Ponto,* c. 5 A.D.

He that envies is possessed of self-made hurts.
SHAIKH SAADI, *Gulistan,* c. 1265

'Tis the beginning of hell in this life, and a passion not to be excused.
ROBERT BURTON, *Anatomy of Melancholy,* I, 1621

Envy is uneasiness of the mind, caused by the consideration of a good we desire, obtained by one we think should not have it before us.
JOHN LOCKE, *Essay Concerning Human Understanding,* 1690

Envy is a criminal sorrow for the welfare of our neighbor.
ST. JOHN BAPTIST DE LA SALLE, *Les devoirs du chrétien,* 1703

There is but one man who can believe himself free from envy, and it is he who has never examined his own heart.
C. A. HELVETIUS, *De l'esprit,* 1758

There is not a passion so strongly rooted in the human heart as envy.
RICHARD BRINSLEY SHERIDAN, *The Critic,* 1779

Envy is a coal come hissing hot from hell.
PHILIP JAMES BAILEY, *Festus,* V, 1846

Envy's special aversion is successful covetousness.
HENRY S. HASKINS, *Meditations in Wall Street,* 1940

See also Brotherhood; Covetousness; Greed.

ENTHUSIASM

Enthusiasm though founded neither on reason nor divine revelation, but rising from the conceits of a warmed or overweening brain, works yet . . . more powerfully on the persuasions and actions of men, than either of those two, or both together.
JOHN LOCKE, *Essay Concerning Human Understanding,* IV, 1690

Enthusiasm is that temper of the mind in which the imagination has got the better of the judgment.
WILLIAM WARBURTON, *The Divine Legation of Moses,* 1737

The enthusiast will always react against any form of institutional religion, whether it be Catholic or Protestant.
RONALD A. KNOX, *Enthusiasm,* 1950

See also Emotion; Evangelism; Experience, Religious; Imagination.

EPISTLES. See NEW TESTAMENT

EQUALITY

Open the tombs and see the bones there mixed in mockery! Which dust was servant, which was lord's?—open the tomb and see!
SHAIKH SAADI, *Gulistan,* c. 1265

No reasonable man will think more highly of himself because he has office or power in this world; he is no more than a prisoner whom the chief gaoler has set over his fellow-prisoners, until the executioner's cart comes for him, too.
ST. THOMAS MORE, *The Four Last Things,* 1522

An earthly kingdom cannot exist without inequality of persons. Some must be free, others serf, some rulers, others subjects.
MARTIN LUTHER, *Works,* XVIII, 1525

Religion consisteth not in mere words; he who looketh on all men as equal is religious.

> GURU NANAK (1496–1538), *The Sikh Religion*, M. A. Macauliffe

Under the Guru's instruction regard all men as equal, since God's light is contained in the heart of each.

> ARJAN (died 1606), *The Sikh Religion*, M. A. Macauliffe

The yearning after equality is the offspring of envy and covetousness.

> WILLIAM GRAHAM SUMNER, *What Social Classes Owe to Each Other*, 1883

I believe that the more we think, the more we become convinced that the instinct which asks for equality is a low one, and that equality, if it were completely brought out, would furnish play for the lower instincts and impulses of man.

> PHILLIPS BROOKS, *New Starts in Life and Other Sermons*, 1897

Human society, as established by God, is composed of unequal elements, just as parts of the human body are unequal; to make them all equal is impossible, and would mean the destruction of human society itself.

> POPE PIUS X, *Apostolic Letter on Catholic Action*, December, 1903

It was the contemplation of God that created men who were equal, for it was in God that they were equal. . . . As the manifestation of God, they were equal in rights. As the servants of God, they were also equal in their duties.

> ANTOINE DE SAINT-EXUPÉRY, *Flight to Aras*, 1942

From the very beginning the modern mind has missed the real source of man's equality with man. It does not know what makes a Chinese coolie the equal of a Roman cardinal. It is the fact that they were both created by the same God to enjoy Him fully for all eternity, a destiny that dwarfs all accidentals, social, economic, intellectual . . . With the necessary grace they are equally capable of attaining it.

> ROBERT I. GANNON, *After Black Coffee*, 1946

The Church does not promise that complete equality which others proclaim; because she knows that the human community always and necessarily produces a scale of degrees and differences in physical and intellectual qualities, in inward dispositions and tendencies, in occupation and responsibilities. But at the same time, she does guarantee full equality in human dignity.

> POPE PIUS XII, *Address*, October 31, 1948

Equality today means "sameness," rather than "oneness."

> ERICH FROMM, *The Art of Loving*, 1956

The Christian view of man knows no graded scale of essential and fundamental worth; there is no divine right of whites which differ from the divine rights of Negroes.

> KYLE HASELDEN, *The Racial Problem in Christian Perspective*, 1959

It is not true that some human beings are by nature superior and others inferior. All men are equal in their natural dignity. Consequently there are no political communities which are superior by nature and none which are inferior by nature.

> POPE JOHN XXIII, *Pacem in Terris*, April, 1963

There is in Christ and in the Church no inequality on the basis of race or nationality, social condition or sex.

> SECOND VATICAN COUNCIL, *Constitution on the Church*, November, 1964

See also Anti-Semitism; Brotherhood; Bus Service, School; Class Distinctions; Coercion; Democracy; Discrimination; Exclusiveness; Fellowship; Office; Power; Prejudice; Racial Conflict; Racial Injustice; Racial Prejudice; Rights.

EROS

Eros, honoured without reservation and obeyed unconditionally, becomes a demon. And this is just how he claims to be honoured and obeyed.

    C. S. LEWIS, *The Four Loves,* 1960

See also Desires; Idolatry; Love, Human; Love, Physical; Marriage; Sex; Sexual Intercourse.

EROTIC

Mutual erotic love, erotic adoration, is the most natural religion.

    HENRY A. MURRAY, *Science Ponders Religion,* ed. H. Shapley, 1960

See also Desires; Idolatry; Love, Human; Love, Physical; Marriage; Sex; Sexual Intercourse.

ERROR

To err and not reform, this may indeed be called error.

    CONFUCIUS, *Analects,* 5th century B.C.

All men are liable to err; but when an error hath been made, that man is no longer witless or unblest who heals the ill into which he hath fallen, and remains not stubborn.

    SOPHOCLES (495–406 B.C.), *Antigone*

Error . . . is to follow something which does not lead to that at which we wish to arrive.

    ST. AUGUSTINE, *On the Free Will,* c. 400

Man is a being filled with error. This error is natural and, without grace, ineffaceable. Nothing shows him the truth; everything deceives him.

    BLAISE PASCAL, *Pensées,* 1670

There is no error in religion, of whatever nature, which is a sin when it is involuntary. . . . We have an inalienable right to profess those doctrines which we believe conformable to the pure truth.

    PIERRE BAYLE (1647–1706), *Critique Générale, Works,* II

That great Householder of his World who suffers not even a straw to fall to the ground uselessly . . . could not permit even error to remain unutilized in his great design, could not allow this wide region of thought to lie empty and joyless in the mind of man.

    J. F. VON SCHILLER, *Philosophische Briefe,* 1786

Error makes the circuit of the globe while Truth is pulling on her boots, and no error ever is or ever can be harmless. . . . Error has no rights, but the man who errs has equal rights with him who errs not.

    ORESTES BROWNSON, *Brownson's Quarterly,* July, 1864

As long as we honestly wish to arrive at truth we need not fear that we shall be punished for unintentional error.

    JOHN LUBBOCK, *The Pleasures of Life,* 1887

Error struggling on towards the living truth is more fruitful than dead truth.

    ROMAINE ROLLAND, *Jean Christophe,* 1912

If you shut your door to all errors truth will be shut out.

    RABINDRANATH TAGORE, *Stray Birds,* 1916

The answer to error is not terror, but the cleansing power of light and liberty under the moral law.

FRANK P. GRAHAM, *Christian Leadership and Today's World,* 1940

Error, falsehood, evil are cosmic powers, but relative in their nature, not absolute, since they depend for existence upon the perversion or contradiction of their opposites, and are not like truth and good, self-existing absolutes, inherent aspects of the Supreme Self-Existent.

SRI AUROBINDO, *The Life Divine,* 1949

It is a great gain when error becomes manifest, for it then ceases to deceive the simple.

ROGER J. McHUGH, *Christianity and the Sceptic,* 1950

Free expression of error should be tolerated, not as an approval of error itself, but because we love our neighbor so much that we do not want him to be a man who talks *as if* he knew the truth, but to be a man who knows it.

ÉTIENNE GILSON, *Dogmatism and Tolerance,* 1952

The duty of repressing moral and religious error cannot be an ultimate norm of action. It must be subordinate to higher and more general norms, which in some circumstances permit and even seem to indicate as the better policy, toleration of error in order to protect a greater good.

POPE PIUS XII, December 6, 1953

One must never confuse error and the person who errs, not even when there is a question of error or inadequate knowledge of truth in the moral or religious field.

POPE JOHN XXIII, *Pacem in Terris,* April, 1963

See also Bible: Its Inspiration; Doctrine; Dogma; Evil; Exclusiveness; Freedom, Religious; Ignorance; Infallibility; Knowledge; Truth; Truths, Conflict of.

ESCAPE

It would seem that almost all the people in the world could be divided into two classes: those who are running after something, and those who are running away from something.

R. L. EVANS, *Tonic for Our Times,* 1952

[The] evolutionary in man can no longer take refuge from his loneliness by creeping for shelter into the arms of a divinized father-figure whom he has himself created, nor escape from the responsibility of making decisions by sheltering under the umbrella of Divine Authority.

JULIAN S. HUXLEY, *The Humanist Frame,* 1961

ESTRANGEMENT

Man chooses self-realization and falls into the state of estrangement, and with him his world also falls. . . . The term "original sin" should be replaced by existential descriptions of the universal and tragic character of man's estrangement.

PAUL TILLICH, *Contemporary Problems in Religion,* ed. H. A. Basilius, 1956

ETERNAL

All things are eternal by their very nature.
Sutra-Krit-Anga, between 600 and 200 B.C.

Whatever that which feels, which has knowledge, which wills, which has the power of growth, it is celestial and divine, and for that reason must of necessity be eternal.

CICERO, *Tusculanae Disputationes,* Bk. I, ch. 27, 44 B.C.

In the eternal nothing passeth but the whole is present; whereas no time is all at once present.

ST. AUGUSTINE, *Confessions,* XI, 33, 397

It is not possible that we should remember that we existed before our body, for our body can bear no trace of such existence, neither can eternity be defined in terms of time or have any relation to time. But notwithstanding, we feel and know that we are eternal.

BARUCH SPINOZA, *Ethics,* 1677

In the mere clinging of human creatures to each other, nay! in one's own solitary self-pity, even amidst what might seem absolute loss I seem to touch the eternal.

WALTER PATER, *Marius the Epicurean,* 1885

It is from the very element of the eternal and the unlimited, which the materialist seeks to deny, that the true progress of the human race has sprung.

CHRISTOPHER DAWSON, *God and the Supernatural,* 1920

See also Beatific Vision; Damnation; Death; Eternal Life; Immortality; Life; Life: Its Meaning; Life and Death; Love of God; Nirvana; Soul; Soul and God; Time.

ETERNAL LIFE

Going back to the origin is called peace; it means reversion to destiny. Reversion to destiny is called eternity. He who knows eternity is called enlightened.

TAO TÊ CHING, c. 500 B.C.

Eternal life is the actual knowledge of the truth.

ST. AUGUSTINE, *De moribus Ecclesiae catholicae etc.,* 368

Eternity is the simultaneous and complete possession of infinite life.

BOETHIUS, *Consolations of Philosophy,* c. 524

The life to come will be better for thee than the life thou livest, for the bounty of the Lord shall come to thee.

Koran, c. 625

If an account were kept of what we owe the Creator, no man would ever receive reward in the world to come. He will receive it only by divine grace.

BAHYA BEN JOSEPH IBN PAKUDA, *Hobot HaLebabot,* 1040

The good which is stored up for the righteous is the life in the world to come, life unaccompanied by death, good unaccompanied by evil. . . . The reward of the righteous is that they will merit this pleasantness and goodness.

MAIMONIDES, *Mishneh Torah,* 1170

The conviction that faith brings with it eternal life, that is to say, the divine life of God himself, sums up the accumulated experience of centuries.

ST. THOMAS AQUINAS, *Summa Theologiae,* I–II, arts. 1 and 2, 1272

Drawing near her death, she [Monica] sent most pious thoughts as harbingers to heaven; and her soul saw a glimpse of happiness through the chinks of her sickness-broken body.

THOMAS FULLER, *The Holy State,* 1642

Our whole eternity is to take its color from those hours which we here employ in virtue or in vice.

JOSEPH ADDISON, *The Spectator,* 1712

All the sophistry of the Predestinarians rests on the false notion of eternity as a sort of time antecedent to time. It is timeless, present with and in all times.

SAMUEL TAYLOR COLERIDGE, *Aids to Reflections,* 1825

Peace, Rest and Bliss dwell only where there is no where and no when.

ARTHUR SCHOPENHAUER, *Parega und Paralipomena*, II, 1862

The eternal life is not the future life; it is life in harmony with the true order of things—life in God.

HENRI AMIEL, *Journal*, 1882

When once the sting of eternity has entered the heart, and the desire to behold things *sub specie aeternitatis*, when once the thirst of stability and repose has been felt, for that soul there is no longer content in the diversions of life.

PAUL ELMER MORE, *Shelburne Essays*, 6th Series, 1909

Man does, in eternity, not what God through an arbitrary disposition makes him do, but what man has made himself capable of doing through the grace of God in mortal life.

ANSCAR VONIER, *The Human Soul*, 1913

It is difficult to imagine a temporary Heaven, for if the souls in Heaven knew that their bliss would end, this knowledge alone would prevent their happiness from being perfect.

GERALD C. TREACY, *After Death— What?*, 1927

Since the moral law can rightfully command us to live as aspirants to eternity, eternity must really be our destination.

A. E. TAYLOR, *Faith of a Moralist*, 1930

The life beyond the world is, in very deed, the inspiration of the life that now is.

E. TROELTSCH, *The Social Teaching of the Christian Churches*, 1931

Eternal life is not an unending continuance of this life—that would perhaps be Hell—but eternal life is a quite different life, divine not mundane, perfect not earthly, true life not corrupt half-life.

EMIL BRUNNER, *Our Faith*, 1936

All the moments of the whole of time are present for the divine Eternity, who sees in its own instant, and hence always, everything creatures do, have done, will do in the very instant that it *happens,* and hence in an eternal freshness of life and newness.

JACQUES MARITAIN, *Ransoming the Time,* 1946

Eternal life is not a life for the future. By charity we start eternity right here below.

HENRI DE LUBAC, *Paradoxes,* 1948

The eternal life now put within the reach of man by the Word-made-flesh is the possession of God as He is in Himself, in a vision face to face, without the distorting, darkening "glass" of creatures interposed.

JOHN COURTNEY MURRAY, *Address,* American Academy of Political and Social Science, *Annals of,* March, 1948

Eternal life is not won by those who have their hearts set on this world and on things —even the beautiful things—of time; the destiny of man is achieved only by the full discipline of unworldliness and otherworldliness.

JOHN COURTNEY MURRAY, *Address,* American Academy of Political and Social Science, *Annals of,* March, 1948

Today, eternity enters into time, and time, sanctified, is caught up into eternity.

THOMAS MERTON, *A Thomas Merton Reader,* ed. T. P. McDonnell, 1963

Eternity is the lifetime of the Almighty.
Anonymous

See also Beatific Vision; Damnation; Death; Eternal; Immortality; Life; Life: Its Meaning; Life and Death; Love of God; Nirvana; Soul and God; Time.

ETHICS

The ethical progress of society depends, not on imitating the cosmic process, still less in running away from it, but in combating it.

THOMAS HENRY HUXLEY, *Evolution and Ethics*, 1893

The science which investigates the general principles for determining the true worth of the ultimate ends of human conduct.

REGINALD A. P. ROGERS, *A Short History of Ethics*, 1911

The next step in the development of an ethical theology must be the translation of the categories of divinity into terms compatible with democratic ethics. We must learn to think of God as the immanent coworker, always toiling with His children rather than as a sovereign to whom they are subject.

GERALD BINNEY SMITH, *Social Idealism and the Changing Theology*, 1913

It may be questioned whether . . . the ethical attitude is not taken over from the formerly dominant religion, and then justified by a philosophical construction.

CHRISTOPHER DAWSON, *The Sociological Review*, April, 1921

It is only an ethical movement which can rescue us from the slough of barbarism, and the ethical comes into existence only in individuals.

ALBERT SCHWEITZER, *The Decay and Restoration of Civilization*, 1923

A man is truly ethical only when he obeys the compulsion to help all life which he is able to assist, and shrinks from injuring anything that lives.

ALBERT SCHWEITZER, *Civilization and Ethics*, 1923

The domination of class and self-preservative church ethics over the ethics of the gospel must be held responsible for much of the moral ineffectiveness of Christianity in the West.

H. RICHARD NIEBUHR, *Social Sources of Denominationalism*, 1929

The church . . . by the very nature of its constitution is committed to the accommodation of its ethics to the ethics of civilization; it must represent the morality of the respectable majority, not of the heroic minority.

H. RICHARD NIEBUHR, *Social Sources of Denominationalism*, 1929

The ethic of Jesus seeks human development directly through the limitation of self-interest by mutual adjustment and mutual aid.

HARRY F. WARD, *Our Economic Morality and the Ethic of Jesus*, 1929

As to ethics, I have called them a body of imperfect social generalizations expressed in terms of emotions.

OLIVER WENDELL HOLMES, JR., *Holmes–Pollock Letters*, 1874–1932

Jewish ethics is rooted in the doctrine of human responsibility, that is, freedom of the will.

JOSEPH H. HERTZ, *The Pentateuch and Haftorahs*, 1936

There is no individual Christian ethic . . . God's command places us in relation to our neighbor, not to ourselves.

EMIL BRUNNER, *The Divine Imperative*, 1937

The distinctive element in Christian ethics is the primacy of love, the self-giving love that is known fully to Christian faith in the cross of Christ.

JOHN BENNETT, *Goals of Economic Life*, 1943

The ethics of the Gospel find their sanction upon no lower level than the eternal purpose of God.

F. C. GRANT, *The Practice of Religion*, 1946

In a market situation pervaded by . . . the "market mentality" control of the economy will carry with it, to an unusual degree, control of the ethical regime.

DAVID RIESMAN, *Commentary,* Vol. 6, no. 5, 1948

Outside the Roman Church, there is now no consensus of opinion in regard either to the method or the content of Christian ethics.

SYDNEY CAVE, *The Christian Way,* 1949

There may be systems of philosophical ethics: there can never be a system of Christian ethics, at least if it is true to its nature. . . . All legalism and moralism stand condemned under the judgment of the ever-dynamic and ever-new dimension of God's activity.

HENDRIK KRAEMER, *Contributions to a Social Ethic,* 1949

Science will never replace ethics; its subject matter is not continuous with moral actions, and the *ought* of ethics is foreign to the factual *is* of science.

HENRY MARGENAU, *Perspectives on a Troubled Decade,* ed. Bryson, Finklestein and MacIver, 1950

To say that there is no basis for personal and social ethics apart form one or another of the organized religions is untrue to observed fact and immensely derogatory to a God worth respect.

NORMAN THOMAS, *A Socialist's Faith,* 1951

To attempt to formulate a Christian philosophy or ethical system which should be valid independently of faith in Christ himself is an idle and presumptuous task.

AELRED GRAHAM, *A Catholic Commentary on Holy Scripture,* 1952

Christian ethics is the name given to the attempt to think through the implications of Christian faith for the moral life.

JOHN BENNETT, *Christian Values and Economic Life,* 1954

Christian ethics is not a scheme of codified conduct. It is a purposive effort to relate love to a world of relativities through a casuistry obedient to love.

JOSEPH FLETCHER, *Harvard Divinity Bulletin,* October, 1959

The highest and most authoritative source [of Catholic Social Ethics] is the Word of God as contained in the writings of the Old and New Testaments and the traditions of the Church.

EBERHARD WELBY, *A Handbook of Christian Social Ethics,* I, 1960

Protestant ethics, lacking the tough institutionalism and rigid legalisms of some systems, always runs the danger of sliding into irrelevant piety or of endorsing too readily the prevailing culture ethic.

ROGER L. SHINN, *The Ethics of Power,* ed. Lasswell and Cleveland, 1962

The outstanding problem for Christian social ethics is how we are to understand the relation between the law of nature and the righteousness of the covenant, or between justice and love.

PAUL RAMSEY, *Nine Modern Moralists,* 1963

See also Absolute, the; Behavior; Christian Life; Christianity; Civilization; Conduct; Duties; Jesus Christ: His Influence and Teaching; Judaism; Moral Law; Moral Order; Moral Standards; Morality; Morality and Freedom; New Testament; Religion; Religion, Definitions of; Religion: Its Nature and Function; Religion, Necessity of; Sexual Ethics; Society.

EUCHARIST

For not as common bread and common drink do we receive these; but in like manner as Jesus Christ our Saviour, having been made flesh by the word of God had both flesh and blood for our salvation, so likewise have we been taught that the food which is blessed by the word of prayer transmitted from Him . . . is the flesh and blood of that Jesus who was made flesh.

> St. Justin Martyr, *Apology*, c. 150

And on the Lord's Day, after you have come together, break bread and offer the Eucharist, having first confessed your offenses, so that your sacrifice may be pure. However, no one quarreling with his brother may join your meeting until they are reconciled; your sacrifice must not be defiled.

> *Didache, or Teaching of the Twelve Apostles* (Discovered at Constantinople in 1875, attributed to 2nd century)

As the bread and wine of the Eucharist, before the holy invocation of the adorable Trinity, were simple bread and wine, after the invocation the bread becomes Christ's body and the wine Christ's blood.

> St. Cyril of Jerusalem, *Cateches. Myst.,* 350

It is not the season of Lent or Epiphany which makes a man worthy to approach this Sacrament, but sincerity and purity of conscience. With this preparation . . . APPROACH ALWAYS; without it, never.

> St. John Chrysostom, *Ep. ad. Eph. cl, Hom. 111,* c. 388

The spiritual virtue of the sacrament is like light; on those on whom it falls it falls pure, and is in no way fouled by passing through foul things.

> St. Augustine, *In Evang. Joannis,* Tract 5, c. 416

The participation in the Body and Blood of Christ does nothing less than transform us into that which we consume, and we bear with us, in flesh and spirit, Him Himself in whom we died, were buried and were raised again.

> Pope St. Leo the Great (440–461), quoted by Pope John XXIII on November 11, 1961

Surely if men had faith, reverence and devotion, as they ought to have when they approach this Sacrament, they would not make themselves vile with so many errors, sins and wickedness, but would know all wisdom and wholesome truth in this life.

> Roger Bacon, *Compendium Studii Philosophiae,* c. 1266

Christ does not found his sacrament upon our use or abuse of it. What he says or ordains remains, no matter whether one uses it right or wrongly.

> Martin Luther, *Sermons on the Catechism,* 1528

The sacrament is not simply bread and wine, but the body and blood of Christ, as the words say. If you take away the words, you have only bread and wine. Hence the command of God is the greatest thing in the sacrament, as in the Lord's Prayer. . . . Our unbelief does not alter God's Word.

> Martin Luther, *Sermons on the Catechism,* 1528

The true body and blood of Christ are truly present in the Supper under the form of bread and wine and are there distributed and received.

> *Augsburg Confession,* 1530

In the most blessed Sacrament of the Altar, by the strength and efficacy of Christ's mighty word (it being spoken by the priest), is present really under the form of bread and wine, the natural body and blood of our Saviour Jesus Christ.

> *Six Articles Act, Statutes of the Realm,* Henry VIII, 1539

They say that Christ is corporally under the form of bread and wine; we say that Christ is not there, neither corporally nor spiritually; but in them that worthily eat and drink the bread and wine, he is spiritually, and in heaven corporally.

> Thomas Cranmer, *A Defense of the True and Catholic Doctrine,* Bk. III, 1550

In the sacred and holy sacrament of the eucharist the substance of the bread and wine remains conjointly with the Body and Blood of our Lord Jesus Christ . . . — the species only of the bread and wine remaining.

> Council of Trent, Canon 2, 1551

All of us therefore profess with one voice that by receiving the Sacrament with faith, according to the ordinance of the Lord, we truly become partakers of the very substance of the body and blood of Jesus Christ.

> JOHN CALVIN (1509–1564), Petit traile de lu saints cene

This is the sum of the greatest mystery of our religion; it is the copy of the passion, and the ministration of the great mystery of our redemption.

> JEREMY TAYLOR, Holy Living, 1650

How I hate this folly of not believing in the eucharist, etc.! If the gospel be true, if Jesus Christ be God, what difficulty is there?

> BLAISE PASCAL, Pensées, 1670

The Fathers teach us that the Eucharist is that daily bread for which we ask in the Lord's Prayer.

> FRANÇOIS FÉNELON (1651–1715), Spiritual Letters

Jesus has left Himself in the Most Holy Sacrament, first, that all may be able to find Him; secondly, to give audience to all; thirdly, to give His graces to all.

> ST. ALPHONSUS LIGUORI, Preface for Death, c. 1760

The Catholic Church presents to men the Blessed Sacrament as the answer of the deep cry of the soul after love.

> I. T. HECKER, Questions of the Soul, 1855

The Eucharist announces the reunion of mankind into one great family.

> FRANÇOIS DE CHATEAUBRIAND, Genius of Christianity, 1856

I gladly take . . . the Lord's Supper with members of my own family or nation who obey Him, and should be equally sure it was His giving, if I were myself worthy to receive it, whether the intermediate mortal hand were the Pope's, the Queen's, or a hedge-side gipsy's.

> JOHN RUSKIN, 1899, Works, XXXV

Just as those who ate the ancient manna found in it the flavor of the food each relished most, the blessed Manna of the Eucharist will supply the soul with a relish for that particular virtue it needs most.

> WALTER DWIGHT, Our Daily Bread, 1911

While the Eucharist unites us to Christ, it effects also a mysterious and ineffable union between the members of Christ.

> R. A. KEARNEY, Address, 1935

Here we have a perpetual witness to the fact that our faith rests on history. . . . In the Sacrament there is a corporate memory of the facts, going back by an unbroken chain of witness to a period earlier than any of our written records.

> C. H. DODD, Christian Worship, ed. by N. Micklen, 1936

Members of other denominations should be invited to participate in the Church's administration of the Lord's Supper.

> The Constitution and By-Laws of the Evangelical and Reformed Church, 1938

Eucharist, with its emphasis on the adoration of God, vanishes. Communion, with its emphasis on man's need, takes its place.

> EVELYN UNDERHILL, The Mystery of Sacrifice, 1938

The climax of Christian corporate prayer is the celebration of the Sacrament. That was the burning heart of worship in the Early Church. It seems to have the fire of Eternity.

> GEORGE A. BUTTRICK, Prayer, 1942

It is remarkable that in spite of the spread of worldliness and irreligion, the Eucharist has been more and more glorified and honored from century to century.

FRANÇOIS MAURIAC, *The Eucharist,* 1944

The "action" of the earthly church in the Eucharist only manifests within time the eternal act of Christ as the heavenly High Priest at the altar before the throne of God, perpetually pleading His accomplished and effectual sacrifice.

GREGORY DIX, *The Shape of the Liturgy,* 1945

The Holy Eucharist is for Christ's faithful people, not for anybody else. Not for those, however excellent their dispositions, however honest their difficulties, who are not visibly united to the corporate body of Christ's faithful people. . . . By separating ourselves in this way from the rest of the world, we unite ourselves more closely to one another.

R. A. KNOX, *Retreat for Priests,* 1946

It is the almost indispensable key to the messianic plan. It so declares the essence of the mission of Jesus and so communicates its effects that it becomes the central liturgical act of the Kingdom which Christ founded.

R. DYSON A. JONES, *The Kingdom of Promise,* 1946

The Eucharist . . . sums up in its richness everything which St. Paul in Eph. unites in the one word "Mystery"; that is to say the whole content of the designs of God upon the world, revealed and realized in Christ.

HENRI DE LUBAC, *Corpus Mysticum,* 1950

The means whereby the body of Christ is received and eaten in the Supper is faith.

Doctrines and Discipline of the Methodist Church, 1952

The Eucharist is the all-sufficient vehicle for appropriating the benefits of the joyful work of the descending and ascending Christ.

JOHN H. VRUWUNK, *The Lively Tradition,* 1952

The Eucharist is a personal encounter. It is the place where God and man meet— within the life of the Church.

OLIVE WYON, *The Altar Fire,* 1954

The Eucharist is central: because it gathers up, expresses, and makes effective the whole meaning of the spiritual life.

OLIVE WYON, *The Altar Fire,* 1954

Not merely a token of love and union . . . . but is rather a mystery or a representation of our redemption by the sufferings and death of Christ.

The Discipline of the Evangelical United Brethren, 1955

Here is the Christian soldier's iron ration.

HENRY SLOANE COFFIN, *Joy in Believing,* 1956

As our humanity assimilates the material world, and as the Host assimilates our humanity, the eucharistic transformation goes beyond and . . . irresistibly invades the universe.

PIERRE TEILHARD DE CHARDIN, *The Divine Milieu,* 1960

It is indeed strange that the Eucharist, which constitutes in the Christian mystery that which defies reason the most, helps me to believe, simplifies for me faith in that God who is reduced to the proportions of the most insignificant man and the poorest woman, to the degree of giving Himself to them as food if they want Him.

FRANÇOIS MAURIAC, *What I Believe,* 1962

Any attempt to make the celebration of the Eucharist approximate more closely to the Last Supper must be of the greatest ecumenical importance.

HANS KÜNG, *The Council in Action,* 1963

Really partaking of the body of the Lord in the breaking of the eucharistic bread, we are taken up into communion with Him and with one another.

The Constitution of the Church, Second Vatican Council, November, 1964

See also Bishops; Blessed Sacrament; Communion; Liturgy; Man and God; Mass, the; Mystery; Priesthood; Priests; Real Presence; Ritual; Sacraments; Sacrifice; Transubstantiation; Unity.

EUROPE

Europe will return to the faith, or she will perish. The faith is Europe. And Europe is the faith.

HILAIRE BELLOC, *Europe and the Faith,* 1939

EUTHANASIA

No unsolved problem in medicine or surgery is solved by killing the patient. To kill the sick man is the refuge of the lazy, the incompetent, the unscrupulous, who meet the problems by asserting no problem exists.

PAUL BLAKELY, *America,* November 14, 1939

Voluntary euthanasia violates nature, and violates the right of nature's Creator. Man has no right to destroy his own life. Consequently, he has no right to ask another to kill him, for he cannot transfer a right he does not possess. One who yields to such a request takes part in the invasion of the Creator's right, and so commits murder.

HILARY R. WERTS, *Linacre Quarterly,* April, 1947

If human life is ever to be held sacred, it should be only when that life is of value to its possessor and to society.

EARNEST A. HOOTON, quoted in interview, Boston *Traveler,* January 6, 1950

The public is readier to recognize the right to *die* than the right to *kill,* even though the latter be in mercy.

EUTHANASIA SOCIETY OF AMERICA, *Merciful Release,* 1950

Why not legalize euthanasia for all who are a burden to themselves and the community (including mental defectives and others incapable of consent) rather than merely for sufferers who themselves ask for euthanasia?

EUTHANASIA SOCIETY OF AMERICA, *Merciful Release,* 1950

The type of Christianity with which mercy-murder is compatible is so watered down as to be almost unrecognizable. It is a form of religion in which moral values have become subjective and sentimental, and religion itself largely humanitarian.

JOHN C. FORD, *Mercy Murder,* 1951

It is the savage who kills his old and his sick that they may no longer burden him. It is the Communist savage who deals as he will with human life in the slave camps of Siberia. It was the Nazi savage who did it in Germany.

JOHN C. FORD, *Mercy Murder,* 1951

To support the rightfulness of euthanasia with a number of essentially different arguments is to put oneself in the wrong from the outset by arguing that no single absolutely cogent argument exists.

DIETRICH BONHOEFFER, *Ethics,* 1955

See also Death; Murder; Pain; Suffering; Suicide.

EVANGELISM

It is due to evangelical influence, and not to scholasticism or the Protestantism of

the Reformation period that the authority of the Scriptures has meant so much to English and American Christians of modern times.
A. C. McGiffert, *Protestant Thought Before Kant*, 1911

Evangelism . . . sharpened the issue between Christianity and the modern age and promoted the notion that the faith of the fathers had no message for their children.
A. C. McGiffert, *Protestant Thought Before Kant*, 1911

Evangelism has come to mean the whole spiritual outlook of the church, both in the realm of the child and in the experience of the man and woman who have turned aside from the path of peace and virtue and need to be reclaimed.
Charles L. Goodsell, in *Report of Federal Council of the Churches of Christ in North America*, 1924

There is nothing so contagious as holiness, nothing more pervasive than Prayer. This is precisely what the traditional Church means by evangelism and what distinguishes it from recruitment.
Martin Thornton, *Pastoral Theology: a Reorientation*, 1956

Evangelism in the modern world must probe much deeper than the swift, immediately personal method of a revived traditional approach.
Cecil Northcott, *Christian Century*, June 26, 1957

The most potent evangelism is that which takes place daily, weekly, yearly through the work of the local church.
Georgia Harkness, *The Church and Its Laity*, 1962

Western Christianity has failed in its vocation. It is to be blamed for not evangelizing or for evangelizing only halfway. God needed men, and men exploited God.
François Mauriac, *What I Believe*, 1962

See also Emotion; Evangelists; Preachers; Preaching; Rhetoric; Sermons; Witness.

EVANGELISTS

The evangelists neither lied nor made any mistakes.
Origen, *In Joanen*, c. 232 A.D.

Evangelist, n. A bearer of good tidings, particularly (in a religious sense) such as assure us of our own salvation and the damnation of our neighbors.
Ambrose Bierce, *Devil's Dictionary*, 1906

Historians have nominated the evangelist —not the theologian or priest or layman— as the characteristic man of God in this nation.
Martin E. Marty, *The New Shape of Religion*, 1958

See also Emotion; Enthusiasm; Evangelism; Preachers; Preaching; Sermons; Witness.

EVE. See MARY, THE MOTHER OF JESUS

EVENTS

Faith and philosophy are air, but events are brass.
Herman Melville, *Pierre*, 1852

EVIL

Lo you now, how vainly mortal men do blame the gods! For of us they say comes evil, whereas they even of themselves, through the blindness of their own hearts, have sorrows beyond that which is ordained.
Zeus rebukes men, in Homer's *Odyssey*, between 12th and 9th century B.C.

Deal firmly, yet tenderly with evil, as if it were a disease in your own person, and the people will entirely put away their faults.
Shu-Ching, 6th century B.C.

Even if the water falls drop by drop, it will fill the pot; and the fool will become full of evil, even though he gather it little by little.

Dhammapada, c. 5th century B.C.

Even an evil-doer sees happiness so long as his evil deed does not ripen; but when his evil deed ripens, then does the evil-doer see evil.

Dhammapada, c. 5th century B.C.

The evil-doer suffers in this world, and he suffers in the next; he suffers in both. He suffers when he thinks of the evil he has done; he suffers more when going on the evil path.

Dhammapada, c. 5th century B.C.

No man voluntarily pursues evil, or that which he thinks to be evil. To prefer evil to good is not in human nature.

PLATO, "Protagoras," *Dialogues,* 399 B.C.

No evil can happen to a good man, either in life or after death.

SOCRATES in Plato's "'Georgics," *Dialogues,* c. 380 B.C.

One evil flows from another.

TERENCE, *Eunuchus,* 160 B.C.

The exit of evil works the entrance of virtue.

PHILO (20 B.C.?–20 A.D.?), *Sacrifices of Abel and Cain*

There neither were formerly, nor are there now, nor will there be again, more or fewer evils in the world [than have always been]. For the nature of all things is one and the same, and the generation of evils is always the same.

CELSUS, quoted by Origen in *Against Celsus,* Bk. 4, ch. 62, 246

We are not the principle of our evils and that evil does not come from ourselves, but that evil exists prior to ourselves; evil pos-

sesses man, and he possesses it in spite of himself.

PLOTINUS (203–262), *First Ennead*

Do you know that oftentimes a root has split a rock, when suffered to remain in it? Give no lodgment to the seed of evil, seeing that it will break up your faith.

ST. CYRIL OF JERUSALEM, *Catechetical Lectures,* 350

The evil man is neither an evil because he is a man, nor a good because he is unjust; he is a good because he is a man, an evil because he is unjust.

ST. AUGUSTINE, *Confessions,* VII, 397

No evil could exist where no good exists.

ST. AUGUSTINE, *Enchiridion,* 421

Repay evil with good and, lo, between whom and you there was enmity will become your warm friend.

Koran, c. 625

For as a picture is often more beautiful and worthy of commendation if some colors in themselves are included in it, than it would be if it were uniform and of a single color, so from an admixture of evil the universe is rendered more beautiful and worthy of commendation.

PIERRE ABELARD, *Epitome Theologiae Christianae,* c. 1135

Every prudent man tolerates a lesser evil for fear of preventing a greater good.

ST. THOMAS AQUINAS, *De Veritate,* q. 5, a.4, ad 4, 1259

Of two evils we should always choose the lesser.

THOMAS À KEMPIS, *Imitation of Christ,* 1441

The ancientest evil, if it be known to us, bears always lighter upon us than a new one of which we know but little.

MICHEL DE MONTAIGNE, *Essays,* 1580

It can never be said that evil happeneth to him, who falls accompanied with virtue.

PHILIP SIDNEY, *Arcadia,* I, 1590

No man is clever enough to know all the evil he does.

FRANÇOIS DE LA ROCHEFOUCAULD, *Maxims,* 1665

Men never do evil so completely and cheerfully as when they do it from religious conviction.

BLAISE PASCAL, *Pensées,* 1670

The source of evil must be sought in the very idea of a creature's nature . . . in the region of eternal truths.

G. W. VON LEIBNIZ, *Theodicy,* 1710

God makes all things good; man meddles with them and they become evil.

JEAN JACQUES ROUSSEAU, *Émile,* 1762

This is the curse of every evil deed,
That propagating still, it brings forth evil.

J. C. F. VON SCHILLER, *The Piccolomini,* 1799

The doing evil to avoid an evil
Cannot be good

J. C. F. VON SCHILLER, *The Death of Wallenstein,* 1799

A moral evil is an evil that has its origin in the Will.

SAMUEL TAYLOR COLERIDGE, *Aids to Reflection,* 1825

We shut our eyes to the beginnings of evil because they are small, and in this weakness is contained the germ of our defeat.

SAMUEL TAYLOR COLERIDGE, *Aids to Reflection,* 1825

Evil perpetually tends to disappear.

HERBERT SPENCER, *Social Statics,* 1850

They asked Ge-She-Pu-to-pa for instructions concerning how to deal with evil, and

he said, "Reflect frequently on death and impermanence. If you are conscious of the certainty of death, it will not be difficult for you to avoid evil and it will not be difficult for you to practice virtue."

Mirror of Kun-Zang-Le-Ma (a summary of Buddhist teaching, by an anonymous monk), 1850

As the most poisonous reptile of the marsh perpetuates his kind as inevitably as the sweetest songster of the grove; so equally with every felicity, all miserable events do naturally beget their like.

HERMAN MELVILLE, *Moby Dick,* 1851

Multitudes think they like to do evil; yet no man ever really enjoyed doing evil since God made the world.

JOHN RUSKIN, *Stones of Venice,* 1851

There are a thousand hacking at the branches of evil to one who is striking at the root.

HENRY DAVID THOREAU, *Walden,* 1854

It is because we children have inherited the good that we feel the evil.

GEORGE ELIOT, *Daniel Doronda,* 1876

No evil dooms us hopelessly except the evil we love, and desire to continue in, and make no effort to escape from.

GEORGE ELIOT, *Daniel Doronda,* 1876

"Man is evil"—so the wisest men told me to console me. Ah, if it were only still true! For evil is man's best strength.

FRIEDRICH NIETZSCHE, *Thus Spake Zarathustra,* 1883

There is only one way to put an end to evil, and that is to do good for evil.

LEO TOLSTOY, *What I Believe,* 1884

Do what you can, some evil will inhere in it; but do all without regard to personal result, give up all results to the Lord, then neither good nor evil will affect you.

SWAMI VIVEKENANANDA (1862–1902), *Complete Works of,* VII

Do not fear to come in contact with evil. Mix freely with it. Ah, my child, only those know what lies on the reverse side of the evil who have taken it in their own hands and turned it over.

RENÉ BAZIN, *Redemption,* 1908

There is no need to go searching for a remedy for the evils of the time. The remedy already exists—it is the gift of one's self to those who have fallen so low that even hope fails them. Open wide your heart.

RENÉ BAZIN, *Redemption,* 1908

The belief in a supernatural source of evil is not necessary; men alone are quite capable of every wickedness.

JOSEPH CONRAD, *Under Western Eyes,* 1911

God uses evil to educate His children for a place in His kingdom.

KAUFMAN KOHLER, *Jewish Theology,* 1918

It is a sin to believe evil of others, but it is seldom a mistake.

H. L. MENCKEN, *Prejudices,* 1919

The decreased sensibility to sin has produced an exaggerated notion that evil in all its forms is independent of free will.

E. I. WATKIN, *God and the Supernatural,* 1920

How shall we think of evil? We shall think ill of it.

L. P. JACKS, *Religious Foundations,* 1923

If we could see the amount of wretchedness, moral as well as physical, which each minute produces . . . our minds would

not stand the shock. If evil were not hidden like impure germs disseminated in our system, there would not be a single sane person on earth.

ERNEST DIMNET, *What We Live By,* 1932

The good that can be derived from evil is attained only by the way of suffering, and repudiation of evil.

NICHOLAS BERDYAEV, *Dostoevsky,* 1934

All evil is either sin or the consequence of sin.

ÉTIENNE GILSON, *The Spirit of Medieval Philosophy,* 1936

We use evil in every moment of our existence to hold evil in check.

REINHOLD NIEBUHR, *Radical Religion,* Winter, 1936

The existence of evil is not so much an obstacle to faith in God as a proof of God's existence, a challenge to turn towards that in which love triumphs over hatred, union over division, and eternal life over death.

NICHOLAS BERDYAEV, *Dream and Reality,* 1939

My faith is that we now understand evil as implicit in the world—and so we will bring courage and fortitude and strength, not panic, to the struggle against it. That we will see the struggle as one not to eradicate evil but to subdue and contain it.

BERNARD DEVOTO, *Harper's Magazine,* 1947

Towards the end of the Messianic era, in the very last days, the predominance of Evil over Good will be appalling.

R. J. LOENERTZ, *The Apocalypse of St. John,* 1948

At the cross it becomes evident that evil is that which God does not will, and does not do, and at the same time, that God has such power over this evil, which he does not will, that He is able to make it a part of his saving work.

EMIL BRUNNER, *The Christian Doctrine of Creation and Redemption,* 1948

Non-cooperation with evil is as much a duty as is cooperation with good.

MAHATMA GANDHI (1869–1948), quoted by Louis Fischer, *The Life of Mahatma Gandhi,* 1950

Evil, coming every minute into life, interrupting its peaceful course, breaking its equilibrium, forces the human being to a deeper and livelier consciousness and stimulates his reaction to defense.

PAUL SIWEK, *The Philosophy of Evil,* 1951

The gates have been opened to evil in part because of a terrible discrepancy between the human ideals and actual possibilities— terrible heresies concerning the nature of man and the structure of the historial universe.

HERBERT BUTTERFIELD, *Christianity, Diplomacy and War,* 1953

The evil of our day is not of the East or of the West, but of the world.

FULTON J. SHEEN, *Way to Happiness,* 1953

Vigilance in the face of evil may give rise to preoccupation with evil. And, as the Fathers of the Church taught, if we are unduly preoccupied with evil, we become evil.

KARL STERN, *The Third Revolution,* 1954

If evil appears in the form of light, beneficence, loyalty and renewal, if it conforms with historical necessity and social justice, then this . . . is a clear additional proof of its abysmal wickedness.

DIETRICH BONHOEFFER, *Ethics,* 1955

"Error and evil have no rights" is, in general, an accurate statement of the case, that there are no abstract rights to evil as there are to goods—such as virtue, knowledge, and good such as happiness.

H. J. McCLOSKEY, *Ethics,* April, 1959

If evil is due to ignorance, then all professors should be saints.

RICHARD S. EMRICH, *Detroit News,* June 25, 1961

When we deny the evil in ourselves, we dehumanize ourselves, and we deprive ourselves not only of our own destiny but of any possibility of dealing with the evil of others.

J. ROBERT OPPENHEIMER, *Address,* New York City, March, 1963

See also Atheism; Conscience; Damnation; Devil; Duties; Error; Evil: Its Nature; Evil, Problem of; Fear; Free Will; Good; Good and Evil; Malice; Man: His Wickedness; Moral Evil; Morality; Mystery; Pain; Power; Punishment; Right and Wrong; Sin; Wicked, the; World, the.

EVIL: ITS NATURE

It will never be possible to get rid of evil altogether, for there must always be something opposite to good.

PLATO, *Theaetetus,* c. 360 B.C.

It is always indeterminate and unstable, completely passive, never fulfilled, it is utter poverty; these are not the accidental attributes but, as it were, the very substance of evil.

PLOTINUS (203–262 A.D.), *1st Ennead*

It could not be said without impiety that evil has its origin in God, because contrary does not give rise to contrary. . . . Evil is not a living, animate being, but a disposition of the soul which is contrary to virtue and comes from a heedless desertion of good.

ST. BASIL (c. 329–379), *Hexaemeron*

What is evil, if not the lack of a good? It is from good things that bad ones come: indeed the only bad things are those deprived of good.

ST. AMBROSE, *De Isaac et anima,* c. 387

Evil is not a living substance but a perversion of mind and soul.

ST. AMBROSE, *Hexaemeron,* c. 389

Everything which is, is good; and the evil whose origin I sought is not a substance, for if it were a substance, it would be good.

ST. AUGUSTINE, *Confessions,* Bk. VII, 397

Wherever there is no privation of good there is no evil.

ST. AUGUSTINE, *Enchiridion,* IV, 421

It is no part of divine providence wholly to exclude from things the possibility of their falling short of good: but what *can* thus fall short, sometimes *will* do so; and the lack of good is evil.

ST. THOMAS AQUINAS, *Summa Contra Gentiles,* II, 45, 1260

Evil as such, is not a reality in things, but the privation of a particular good, inherent in a particular good.

ST. THOMAS AQUINAS, *De malo,* qu.1, a.1, 1268

By evil I understand that which we certainly know hinders us from possessing anything that is good.

BARUCH SPINOZA, *Ethics,* 1677

Evil can be taken metaphysically, physically and morally. *Metaphysical evil consists in simple imperfection,* physical evil is suffering, and moral evil is sin.

G. W. VON LEIBNIZ, *Essays in Theodicy,* 1710

Evil is the footstool of good, and there is no absolute evil.

RABBI ISRAEL BAAL-SHEM TOB (1700–1760), quoted in *Judaism,* ed. A. Hertzberg, 1961

There is no evil, no guilt, no deformity in any creature, but in its dividing and separating itself from something which God alone has given to be in union with it.

WILLIAM LAW (1686–1761), *Selected Mystical Writings of,* ed. S. Hobhouse

If evil is not from Him, as assuredly it is not, this is because evil has no substance of its own, but it is only the defect, excess, perversion, or corruption of that which has substance.

JOHN HENRY NEWMAN, *The Idea of a University,* 1852

Evil has no reality, it is neither person, place, nor being, but is simply a belief, an illusion of material sense.

MARY BAKER EDDY, *Science and Health,* 1908

Evil is not therefore wholly evil; it is misplaced good.

SAMUEL ALEXANDER, *Space, Time and Deity,* 1922

What is evil but good tortured by its own hunger and thirst?

KAHLIL GIBRAN, *The Prophet,* 1923

There is no such thing as an evil in itself. Evil is not a thing, but a wrong function; it is the use of a good impulse at the wrong time, in the wrong place, towards a wrong end, that constitutes an evil function.

J. A. HADFIELD, *Psychology and Morals,* 1923

The brute motive force of fragmentary purpose, disregarding the eternal vision. Evil is overruling, retarding, hurting.

ALFRED NORTH WHITEHEAD, *Science and the Modern World,* 1925

Evil is not a positive reality comparable with good, a peer or rival. It presupposes good as shadow light; it means subtraction, deprivation, failure. Therefore it is idle to speak of a principle of evil; what is intended must be either good or a loss of good.

> MARTIN C. D'ARCY, *The Problem of Evil,* 1928

Historians, moralists, even philosophers refuse to see anything but the criminal, they re-create evil in the image and likeness of humanity. They form no idea of essential evil, that vast yearning for the void, for emptiness.

> GEORGE BERNANOS, *The Diary of a Country Priest,* 1937

What is thus the power of evil? It is the very power of the good that evil wounds and preys upon. The more powerful this good is, the more powerful evil will be,— not by virtue of itself, but by virtue of this good.

> JACQUES MARITAIN, *St. Thomas and the Problem of Evil,* 1942

Evil is not being; it is a hole in being, a lack. That is why there can be no absolute evil: evil can exist only in what is itself good.

> YVES M. CONGAR, *God, Man and the Universe,* 1950

Evil comes, not from an Evil First Principle, but from an evil will which rebels against God's command. . . . The supreme moral evil is defiance of God: pride.

> RALPH RUSSELL, *The Springs of Morality,* ed. J. M. Todd, 1956

See also Evil; Good; Goodness; Mystery; Sin.

EVIL, PROBLEM OF

The Gods can either take away evil from the world and will not, or being willing to do so cannot; or they neither can nor will, or lastly, they are both able and willing. If they have the will to remove evil and cannot, then they are not omnipotent. If they can, but will not, then they are not benevolent. If they are neither able nor

willing, then they are neither omnipotent or benevolent. Lastly, if they are both able and willing to annihilate evil, how does it exist?

> EPICURUS, *Aphorisms,* c. 300 B.C.

Although evil, as far as it is evil, is not a good; yet the fact that evil as well as good exists, is a good. For if it were not a good, that evil should exist, its existence would not be permitted by the omnipotent God.

> ST. AUGUSTINE, *Enchiridion,* 421

Nothing can be evil on the part of God. For a thing is evil on our part only because we transgress the limit and bound set for us and do what we have no right to do. But the Creator is subject to no one and bound by no command.

> AL-ASH'ARI (died 935 A.D.), *Kitáb al-Luma'*

If evil were entirely excluded from the universe by divine providence, it would be necessary to lessen the multitude of good things. This ought not to be, since good is more powerful in goodness than evil in malice.

> ST. THOMAS AQUINAS, *Contra Gentiles,* III, 1260

Evil can no more be charged upon God than darkness can be charged upon the sun.

> WILLIAM LAW (1686–1761), *Selected Mystical Writings of,* ed. S. Hobhouse

Epicurus' old questions are still unanswered. Is Deity willing to prevent evil, but not able? Then he is impotent. Is he able but not willing? Then he is malevolent. Is he both able and willing? Whence then is evil?

> DAVID HUME, *Dialogues Concerning Natural Religion,* 1779

Evil must have had had a beginning, since otherwise it must either be God, or a co-eternal and co-equal rival of God; both impious notions, and the latter foolish to boot. . . . It could not originate in God; for if so, it would be at once evil and not evil, or God would be at once God, that is, infinite goodness, and not God—both alike impossible positions.

S. T. COLERIDGE, *Aids to Reflections,* 1825

Only the man who recognizes in its, at first, inconceivably wide extent, the permission given by God to evil . . . is able to understand the great phenomena of history, which are of a complexity often dark and strange, though he, too, can penetrate only a little way into the hidden and mysterious ways of Providence.

FRIEDRICH SCHLEGEL, *Philosophy of History,* 1829

The real mystery is, not that evil should never have an end, but that it should ever have had a beginning.

JOHN HENRY NEWMAN, *Parochial and Plain Sermons,* 1843

God and Evil . . . are contraries: if the problem of evil is altogether insoluble, there is an end of Theism: if God exists, there is nothing absolutely evil.

JAMES WARD, *The Realm of Ends,* 1911

The passive and active resistance of the Kingdom of Evil at every stage of its advance is so great, and the human resources of the Kingdom of God so slender, that no explanation can satisfy a religious mind which does not see the power of God in its movements.

WALTER RAUSCHENBUSCH, *Theology for the Social Gospel,* 1917

The spectacle of the ideally good man brought to an ideally bad end, as a consequence of his self-devotion to moral and religious reform, raises the problem of evil in its acutest form.

B. H. STREETER, *Reality,* 1926

The Problem of Evil is the problem how to reconcile suffering and sin with God's goodness. God being what He is, and man so finite, we cannot expect to escape mystery.

MARTIN C. D'ARCY, *The Problem of Evil,* 1928

The problem presupposes the existence of God—and rightly so. There is no problem if there is no God.

MARTIN C. D'ARCY, *The Problem of Evil,* 1928

The disproportion between the Infinite and the finite mind ever at the mercy of passing emotions is too great to allow of a comprehensive answer to the Problem of Evil.

MARTIN C. D'ARCY, *The Problem of Evil,* 1928

God would not be God and personified Perfection if He showed Himself indifferent or treated evil in the same way as good.

MARTIN C. D'ARCY, *The Problem of Evil,* 1928

The real problem of evil, the problem that justifies every assault upon war and poverty and disease, is to reduce it to amounts that can be spiritually assimilated.

LEWIS MUMFORD, *Living Philosophies,* 1931

To attribute the evil of the world to a plan of God's is to the ethically minded, nothing short of blasphemous.

J. E. BOODIN, *God and Creation,* 1934

Evil as such is the only thing I am able to do without God, by withdrawing myself, as it were, as if by an initiative emanating from my nothingness, from the current of Divine causality.

JACQUES MARITAIN, *Freedom in the Modern World,* 1935

In making himself independent of God he [man] becomes dependent on the power of evil; for there is no evil in itself, but only because there is God.

RUDOLF BULTMAN, "The Meaning of Christian Faith in Creation," 1936, in *Existence and Faith*, ed. S. M. Ogden

The very absence of evil would constitute a problem since there would, then, be nothing to jar us out of an attitude of self-sufficiency.

JOHN BENNETT, *Christian Realism*, 1941

The existence of evil is not the only obstacle to our faith in God, for it is equally a proof of the existence of God, and the proof that this world is not the only nor the ultimate one.

NICHOLAS BERDYAEV, *Freedom and the Spirit*, 1944

The problem of evil is not a necessary problem; it does not even exist for the unbeliever.

DAVID E. TRUEBLOOD, *Philosophy of Religion*, 1957

To find a rational explanation for evil would be to find a natural cause for it. But this would be to transform this whole Christian understanding of the nature of evil from a perversion into a necessity.

LANGDON GILKEY, *Maker of Heaven and Earth*, 1959

Evil, at least in some of its dimensions, is irrational; or at least we usually mean by "evil" some events of life which "make no sense whatever." If this is what we mean by the term, then a request to make sense of that which by definition does not make sense would be odd indeed. Yet this is just what many of us do when we ask for "answers" to the problem of evil.

JAMES A. MARTIN, JR., *Fact, Fiction and Faith*, 1960

If we reject God on this ground, we exchange obscurity for chaos and for a more inspissated darkness—for in a supposedly purposeless world we should be faced with a still more intractable problem, the problem of good.

ILLTYD TRETHOWAN, *The Basis of Belief*, 1961

See also Evil; Evil: Its Nature; Mystery; Sin; Suffering; War.

EVOLUTION

If the notion of a gradual rise in Beings from the meanest to the most High be not a vain imagination, it is not improbable that an Angel looks down upon a Man, as Man doeth upon a Creature which approaches the nearest to the rational Nature.

JOSEPH ADDISON, *The Spectator*, November 17, 1714

Evolution is an integration of matter and concomitant dissipation of motion.

HERBERT SPENCER, *First Principles*, 1862

A brutal philosophy—to wit, there is no God, and the ape is our Adam.

HENRY EDWARD MANNING, *Essays on Religion and Literature*, 1865

The more fully this conception of universal evolution is grasped, the more firmly a scientific doctrine of Providence will be established, and the stronger will be the presumption of a future progress.

W. H. LECKY, *History of the Rise and Influence of the Spirit of Rationalism*, I, 1868

Evolution can only end in the establishment of the greatest perfection and the most complete happiness.

HERBERT SPENCER, *First Principles*, 1880

It is an error to imagine that evolution signifies a constant tendency to increased perfection.

THOMAS HENRY HUXLEY, *The Struggle for Existence in Human Society*, 1888

The evolution of the body of man from some inferior animal and its subsequent endowment in the body by God of a rational soul is antagonistic to no dogma of faith and may be shown to be in harmony with the teaching of St. Thomas.

> JOHN A. ZAHM, *Bible, Science and Faith,* 1895

God has but one way of doing things . . . the way of growth, or development, or evolution.

> LYMAN ABBOTT, *The Theology of an Evolutionist,* 1898

The whole of evolution is, in reality, a process of self-realizing a moral purpose; the correlation of mind and brain is just the phenomenal aspect of the real correlation of our mind with the divine power which sustains us.

> GEORGE A. COE, *Education in Religion and Morals,* 1904

In itself the theory of evolution, which asserts the variability of species of animals and plants, is by no means opposed to religious truths. It neither includes a necessity of assuming the origin of the human soul from the essentially lower animal soul, nor is it an atheistic theory.

> J. DONAT, *The Freedom of Science,* 1914

In the light of this principle of the Christian interpretation of nature, the history of the animal and vegetable kingdoms on our planet is, as it were, a versicle in a volume of a million pages in which the natural development of the cosmos is described, and the finger of God is evident throughout.

> ERICH WASMANN, "Evolution," *Catholic Encyclopedia,* Vol. V, 1922

Speaking generally, we must reject *a priori* any interpretation which would make a text of Holy Writ a Divine instruction upon a subject belonging to the physical or natural sciences.

> HENRY DORDOLOT, *Darwinism and Catholic Thought,* 1922

Theistic evolution puts God so far away that he ceases to be a present influence in this life.

> WILLIAM JENNINGS BRYAN, *Letter, New York Times,* February 22, 1922

Evolution seems to close the heart to some of the plainest spiritual truths while it opens the mind to the wildest guesses advanced in the name of science.

> WILLIAM JENNINGS BRYAN, *Letter, New York Times,* February 22, 1922

Evolution by no means takes God out of the universe, as Mr. Bryan supposes, but it greatly increases the wonder, the mystery and the marvelous order which we call Natural Law pervading all nature.

> H. F. OSBORN, *New York Times,* March 5, 1922

It shall be unlawful for any teacher in . . . public schools in the state, . . . to teach the theory that denies the story of the divine creation of man as taught in the Bible, and to teach instead that man has descended from a lower order of animals.

> ACT OF THE LEGISLATURE OF TENNESSEE, March 21, 1925

There is no more reason to believe that man descended from some inferior animal than there is to believe that a stately mansion has descended from a small cottage.

> WILLIAM JENNINGS BRYAN, at Scopes Trial, 1925

If a minister believes and teaches evolution, he is a stinking skunk, a hypocrite, and a liar.

> W. A. "BILLY" SUNDAY, Statement to Press, 1925

Evolution involves no fundamental issue. It clashes with no theology or philosophy. . . . Evolution simply means continuous growth; a tree growing from a seedling is an example of evolution.

> HILAIRE BELLOC, *A Companion to H. G. Wells' "Outline of History,"* 1926

Evolution begins and ends with the purposes of God.

> HENRY FAIRFIELD OSBORN, *Evolution and Religion in Education*, 1926

There is nothing in this notion [evolution] intrinsically repugnant either to the scriptures or to Faith. She [the Church] will not affirm it, even supposing it were true, because it is not her business to make such affirmations.

> E. C. MESSENGER, *Evolution and Theology*, 1932

Only those who have discovered the path of evolution, what is its next step and how we are to co-operate with that development, can know themselves as part of a self-transcending purpose.

> GERALD HEARD, *Pain, Sex and Time*, 1939

Christians hold that if evolution should be a fact it owes its origin and process to an intelligent First Cause, the Creator God. This is termed Theistic evolution. It is not opposed in principle to Divine Revelation, provided it does not include the human soul.

> MARTIN J. SCOTT, *Science Helps the Church*, 1941

Evolution is far more of a philosophical concept than a strictly scientific one.

> D. E. TRUEBLOOD, *The Logic of Belief*, 1942

In the hands of an agnostic or atheistic teacher the theory [evolution] is always dangerous. It draws attention away from God and sets up in His place a new god of natural law.

> ULRICH A. HAUBER, *Creation and Evolution*, 1947

We cannot subscribe to the hypothesis that any subhuman animal organism gradually took on a human type of mind.

> ULRICH A. HAUBER, *Creation and Evolution*, 1947

Far from taking God out of the universe, it gives us a more sublime conception of God's creative act.

> JOHN A. O'BRIEN, *The Origin of Man*, 1947

Instead of lessening the dignity of man's origin, evolution actually exalts it, by placing it far above the moistened dust or mud of the earth to living creatures endowed by God with sentiency and a form of intelligence.

> JOHN A. O'BRIEN, *The Origin of Man*, 1947

Evolution is comprehensible only if we admit that it is demanded by finality.

> LECOMTE DU NOÜY, *Human Destiny*, 1947

Evolution as a method of creation fits a divine and spiritual interpretation as completely as creation by fiat does.

> RUFUS M. JONES, *A Call to What Is Vital*, 1949

The teaching authority of the Church does not forbid that, in conformity with the present state of science and theology, the doctrine of evolution should be examined and discussed by experts in both fields, in so far as it deals with research on the origin of the human body, which it states to come from pre-existent organic matter.

> POPE PIUS XII, *Humani generis*, August, 1950

The faithful cannot embrace this opinion which states that after Adam there existed here on earth real men who were not descended, by natural generation, from him, the forefather of all men; now, these statements cannot be reconciled with what the founts of revelation and the decrees of the authority of the Church teach us about original sin.

> POPE PIUS XII, *Humani generis*, August, 1950

Evolution, then, at most, can take us back to the moment of creation: it can never obliterate that moment when creation is necessary.

ANTONIO ROMANA, *God, Man and Universe,* ed. by Jacques Bivort de la Saudée, 1950

God's intervention in the forming of the body of the first man might be conceived as a special virtuality, placed in the primitive organism, which from the very first tended precisely to the production of the human body by way of an evolution willed and ordered by God.

JACQUES BIVORT DE LA SAUDÉE, footnote, *God, Man and Universe,* 1950

Though frightened for a moment by evolution, the Christian now perceives that what it offers him is nothing but a magnificent means of feeling more at one with God and of giving himself more to him.

PIERRE TEILHARD DE CHARDIN, *The Phenomenon of Man,* 1955

Evolution, the story of man, traced for us by the scientist, is seen as the travail of God's energy, creating man in His own image.

C. A. COULSON, *Science and Christian Belief,* 1955

Collaboration with God in the whole of evolution—this is a vision so new that it may even be regarded as dangerous in its sweep. For it is nothing less than at last to Christianize Atlas, to unchain Prometheus on his own recognizance, to create a greater Renaissance which shall not become pagan.

HENRY LUCE, in 1955, quoted in *The Fabulous Future; America in 1980*

Although the creationist . . . must of necessity hold that there was a "first man," it is of no consequence whether he looked like a Pithecanthropoid or a Caucasoid.

JAMES D. BUSWELL III, *Evolution and Christian Thought,* ed. R. L. Mixter, 1959

What began with Darwin as evolution has become *evolutionism,* the effort to interpret man and his universe in evolutionary concepts.

PHILIP SCHARPER, *The Critic,* August– September, 1962

See also Adam; Bible; Body; Cause; Creation; Creator; Darwinism; Free Will; Genesis; Immortality, Denial and Doubt of; Life; Man; Man: His Destiny and Goal; Man: His Potential; Matter; Mind; Natural Selection; Nature; Optimism; Perfection; Progress; Providence; Science; Science and God; Science and Religion; Soul; Spiritual Progress.

EXAMPLE

A good example is the best sermon.

THOMAS FULLER, *Gnomologia,* 1732

One fire kindles another; and without that overtrust in human worth which they show, the rest of us would lie in spiritual stagnancy.

WILLIAM JAMES, *Varieties of Religious Experience,* 1902

Someone has said . . . that the only bible which millions of people read today is the daily example of Christians—your example and mine.

JAMES E. MURRAY, *Address,* March 31, 1948

See also Preachers.

EXCELLENCE

Nor can the good man do otherwise than well and perfectly whatever he does; and he who does well must of necessity be happy and blessed.

SOCRATES, IN "GORGIAS," PLATO'S *Dialogues,* 395 B.C.

The love of excellence for its own sake! This is the attitude of mind, when acquired, which witnesses man's sharing in Creation.

LEONARD E. READ, *The Freeman*, June, 1964

See also Expediency.

EXCLUSIVENESS

Since the creator intended all men for eternal bliss, an exclusive religion cannot be the true one. . . . No revelation purporting to be alone capable of saving man can be the true revelation, for it does not harmonize with the purposes of the all-merciful creator.

MOSES MENDELSSOHN, *Letters to the Prince of Denmark*, 1770

I do not understand how people declare themselves to be believers in God, and at the same time think that God has handed over to a little body of men all truth, and that they are the guardians of the rest of humanity.

VIVEKANANDA (1863–1902), *Works of*

So far as Catholicism is genuinely universal and represents fully all religious values, it must be exclusive. But this exclusiveness is not the exclusiveness of narrowness, but of inexhaustible wealth.

F. HEILER, *Der Katholizismus, seine Idee, etc.*, 1923

Only because it is inclusive can Catholicism be exclusive; only because it comprehends all religious truth can it be intolerant of all error.

E. I. WATKIN, *The Catholic Center*, 1939

The Roman Catholic Church . . . must demand the right to freedom for herself alone, because such a right can only be possessed by truth, never by error. As to other religions, the Church will certainly never draw the sword, but she will require that by legitimate means they shall not be allowed to propagate false doctrine.

La Civiltà Cattolica, 1950

Infinitely better than *one* church would be *no* church; for given no church, we might find our civilizing influences in the creation of more and better churches or in utilizing other agencies of spirituality; but given only one church, we would use it to deprive ourselves of any felt need for becoming more civilized than we are.

T. V. SMITH, *Perspectives on a Troubled Decade*, ed. Bryson, Finklestein and MacIver, 1950

We lay no claim to exclusiveness in doctrines, rites or authority. We request only a place of fellowship and service in the ranks of those who love our Lord Jesus Christ in sincerity.

C. C. SELECMAN, *The Methodist Primer*, 1953

See also Catholicism, various rubrics under Church; Discrimination; Error; Pluralism; Revelation; Universality.

EXEGESIS. See BIBLE: ITS INTERPRETATION

EXPECTATION. See DESIRES; HOPE

EXPEDIENCY

A man who wishes to act entirely up to his professions of virtue soon meets with destruction amidst so much that is evil. . . . It is necessary for a prince who wishes to hold his own to know how to do wrong, and to make use of it or not according to necessity.

NICCOLÒ MACHIAVELLI, *The Prince*, 1513

The true, to put it very briefly, is only the expedient in the way of our thinking, just as the right is only the expedient in our way of behaving.

WILLIAM JAMES, *Pragmatism*, 1907

Here is the stupendous moral problem of our time. Is there an absolute morality, or is conduct simply to be regulated in such a way as to serve the present needs of society? The Christian and the Communist unhesitatingly give opposite answers: the fate of the world hangs on the outcome of their differences.

F. SHERWOOD TAYLOR, *Man and Matter,* 1951

If what is good, what is right, what is true, is only what the individual "chooses" to "invent," then we are outside the traditions of civility. We are back in the war of all men against all men.

WALTER LIPPMANN, *The Public Philosophy,* 1954

The conflict between expediency and morality . . . is at the root of our political and social crisis . . . it contains in a nutshell the challenge of our time.

ARTHUR KOESTLER, *The Trail of the Dinosaur and Other Essays,* 1955

The subordination of excellence to expediency or public opinion is a symptom of the decline in respect for moral excellence.

ADLAI STEVENSON, *Ladies' Home Journal,* December, 1961

See also Conformity; Morality; Pragmatism.

EXHORTATION

Exhort, v.t., In religious affairs, to put the conscience of another upon the spit and roast it to a nut-brown discomfort.

AMBROSE BIERCE, *Devil's Dictionary,* 1906

See also Preachers; Preaching; Rhetoric; Sermons; Speech; Words.

EXISTENCE

If there is existence, there must be non-existence. And if there was a time when nothing existed, there must have been a time before that—when even nothing did not exist. Suddenly, when nothing came into existence, could one really say whether it belonged to the category of existence or non-existence?

CHUANG-TZU, c. 300 B.C.

The entire aggregate of existence springs from the divine world, in greater beauty There because There unmingled but mingled here.

PLOTINUS (203–262 A.D.), *The Enneads*

Human existence is girt round with mystery: the narrow region of our experience is a small island in the midst of a boundless sea.

J. S. MILL, *Three Essays on Religion,* 1874

This thing we call existence—is it not a something which has its roots far down below in the dark, and its branches stretching out into the immensity above. . . . Not a chance jumble; a living thing, a One?

OLIVER SCHREINER, *The Story of an African Farm,* 1883

A temporal series of events or facts . . . a form of the appearance of the Real.

F. H. BRADLEY, *Appearance and Reality,* 1894

All existence is co-existence.

MARTIN HEIDEGGER, *Sein und Zeit,* 1927

As long as we look at our own existence as meaningless, there is no point whatever in desiring to effect anything in the world.

ALBERT SCHWEITZER, *The Anatomy of Frustration,* 1936

It is the stupidity of our minds that prevents us from seeing existence as a mystery wilder than the dreams of Devil or God.

LLEWELYN POWYS, *Earth Memories,* 1938

We are separated from the mystery, the depth, and the greatness of our existence. We hear the voice of that depth; but our ears are closed.

PAUL TILLICH, *The Shaking of the Foundations,* 1949

If nothing existed except receivers of existence, where would the existence come from?

FRANK J. SHEED, *The Advocate,* January, 1960

See also Energy; Existentialism; God: His Existence; God: His Nature; God as Being; Life; Love, Divine; Materialism; Matter; Mystery; Nonexistence; Science and Creation; Suicide.

EXISTENTIALISM

A vision of a man as a stranger in the universe—a stranger to himself and to others. The Sartre brand of Existentialism is an atheist who sees man as helpless, flung without knowing why or how into a world he cannot understand, endowed with liberty ("Man is liberty," says Sartre flatly) which he may betray but which he cannot deny, to make his way as best he can in fear and trembling, in uncertainty and anguish.

JOHN L. BROWN, *New York Times Magazine,* February 2, 1947

There are two kinds of existentialists; first, those who are Christian . . . and on the other hand the atheistic existentialists. . . . What they have in common is that they think that existence precedes essence, or, if you prefer, that subjectivity must be the starting point.

JEAN PAUL SARTRE, *Existentialism,* 1947

Its [existentialism's] method, as the name implies, is to leave the unchanging essence of things out of sight, and concentrates all its attention on particular existences.

POPE PIUS XII, *Humani Generis,* August 12, 1950

Existentialism is the philosophy, or to be more accurate, the substitute for religion of men who are lonelier and more isolated than human individuals have ever been before, "without hope and without God in this world."

AELRED GRAHAM, *Christian Thought and Action,* 1951

Atheistic existentialism . . . does not reflect the anguish of man confronting nothingness; it reflects and declares the longing of man for nothingness.

JACQUES MARITAIN, *The Range of Reason,* 1952

The philosophical existentialist inverts Descartes' "I think, therefore I am" by stating, "I am, therefore I think." But the religious existentialist will have to say, "I believe, therefore I am."

WILLIAM HUBBEN, *Four Prophets of Destiny,* 1952

The central preoccupation of existentialism can be defined in one phrase: the stature of man. Is he a god or a worm?

COLIN WILSON, *The Stature of Man,* 1959

The atheistic existentialism of our time is completely at variance with the Christian idea of providence. Such a portrayal of human existence may have value in puncturing over-optimistic illusions and shattering the complacency of the too comfortable; it cannot build faith and hope.

GEORGIA HARKNESS, *The Providence of God,* 1960

See also God, Nonexistence of; Philosophy; Unbelief.

EXPERIENCE

You cannot step twice into the same river; for other and ever other waters flow on.

HERACLITUS (535–475 B.C.), *Fragments*

He who has lived in the form of an experience looks back, while he who has entered into the substance of an experience looks forward. Live deeply and you must live hopefully.
PHILLIPS BROOKS, *Perennials,* 1898

All experience is an arch, to build upon.
HENRY ADAMS, *The Education of Henry Adams,* 1906

The person who chooses to believe that all of his experiences refer to ideas in his own mind, and not to anything beyond his mind, cannot be dislodged from his position, but it can be shown that he has no reason, on this basis, to assume the existence of other persons with whom to argue the point.
D. E. TRUEBLOOD, *The Logic of Belief,* 1942

The long experience of the church is more likely to lead to correct answers than is the experience of the lone individual.
D. E. TRUEBLOOD, *The Logic of Belief,* 1942

The spirit is always willing, always yearning for righteousness and love, but its purpose is deceived and betrayed by the delusions of experience.
WARNER ALLEN, *The Happy Issue,* 1948

See also Experience, Religious.

EXPERIENCE, RELIGIOUS

The light of undimmed experience of the divine is much too pure and radiant to fit the capacities of poor weak men.
J. W. VON GOETHE, *Conversations with Eckermann,* March 11, 1832

In all sad sincerity I think we must conclude that the attempt to demonstrate by purely intellectual processes the truth of the deliverances of direct religious experience is absolutely hopeless.
WILLIAM JAMES, *Varieties of Religious Experience,* 1902

If you, being orthodox Christians, ask me as a psychologist whether the reference of a phenomenon to a subliminal self does not exclude the notion of a direct presence of the Deity altogether, I have to say frankly that as a psychologist I do not see why it necessarily should.
WILLIAM JAMES, *Varieties of Religious Experience,* 1902

The centre of gravity in religion is shifting from authority to experience, the religious experience as it lives and develops in the life of prayer.
W. R. INGE, *Speculum Animae,* 1911

Religion as a matter of experience is held to be witness to its own validity. The experience itself is the final court of appeal, and its authority is supposed to be higher and more unerring than that of any logic.
HENRY JONES, *A Faith that Inquires,* 1921

Men have never believed in God only after they have proved His existence; on the contrary, they were certain they had experienced God before they sought for the rational meaning or the ground of that experience.
C. A. BECKWITH, *The Idea of God,* 1922

I experience in *myself,* in a manner which none other can teach me, the truth of the affirmation that God is.
K. B. BAMFIELD, *On Values,* 1922

The recrudescence of superstitious emotion (envisaged as "religious experience") . . . is part of the great pseudo-revolutionary movement *back* to the primitive world.
WYNDHAM LEWIS, *Time and Western Man,* 1927

All discussion of the validity of religious experience is but a beating of the air.
F. R. TENNANT, *Philosophical Theology,* 1928

The cosmic religious experience is the strongest and noblest driving force behind scientific research.

ALBERT EINSTEIN, *Cosmic Religion,* 1931

We are agreed in holding the personal experience of fellowship with God in Christ to be the supreme value in life and the foundation of any Christian program adequate for a fear-stricken and bewildered world.

Statement of 31 denominational heads, issued under sponsorship of Federal Council of Churches of Christ in America, in its *Report,* 1932

There are moments in the lives of all men when you feel yourself compeletely belonging to something larger, nobler, more permanent than yourself. This experience is the religious experience.

JOHN DEWEY, *A Common Faith,* 1934

We are both transcendent of experience and immanent in it. This union of transcendence and immanence is . . . the full fact about human personality.

JOHN MACMURRAY, *The Structure of Religious Experience,* 1936

No matter what the world thinks about religious experience, the one who has it possesses the great treasure of a thing that has provided him with a source of life, meaning and beauty and that has given a new splendor to the world and mankind.

CARL JUNG, *Psychology and Religion,* 1938

Experience of the spiritual world is not only possible in special moments of ecstasy but is waiting for us within every experience, however ordinary.

A. VICTOR MURRAY, *Personal Experience and the Historic Faith,* 1939

Religion must come to us through spiritual experience, but outer, visible manifesta-

tions of beauty will help us to catch its meaning.

FREDERICK K. STAMM, *Country Home Magazine,* December, 1939

To complain that man measures God by his own experience is a waste of time; he has no other yardstick.

DOROTHY L. SAYERS, *The Mind of the Maker,* 1941

The root experience, the experience that makes religious belief precious to sensitive men, appears to be a sense of oneness with an immense whole.

HERBERT J. MULLER, *Science and Criticism,* 1943

The presence and possession of God which are realized in religious experience can never be anything more than a preliminary sketch, a seed, a hope.

JEAN MOUROUX, *Christian Experience,* 1954

The importance attached to religious experience is due to a partition made in the past between religion and reason.

MARTIN C. D'ARCY, *The Nature of Belief,* 1958

If . . . natural theology is the attempt to reach God the Creator either through man's experience of the immanent coherence of the world or through his general religious experience, it can only uncover an idol, never the true God.

LANGDON GILKEY, *Maker of Heaven and Earth,* 1959

Nothing that comes from God, even the greatest miracle, proves out like 2 times 2. It touches one; it is seen and grasped when the heart is open and the spirit purged of self.

ROMANO GUARDINI, *Jesus Christus,* 1959

After having agreed that God is experienced rather than proved, theology too quickly forgot that it had recognized the usefulness of experience, and again fell back on abstract reasoning.

REMY CHAUVIN, *God of the Scientists— God of the Experiment,* 1960

Modern man no longer expects religious experience; he trusts his own reason and his own common sense. But when religious experience returns to him, it is not Christian experience, but primitive, demonic, and idolatrous.

ALBERT T. MOLLEGEN, *Christianity and Modern Man,* 1961

The proper name of religious experience is faith.

JOHN BAILLIE, *The Sense of the Presence of God,* 1962

See also Contemplation; Conversion; Ecstasy; Emotion; Enlightenment; Enthusiasm; Feelings; Fellowship; God: Finding Him; God: His Existence; Idealism; Light; Man and God; Man Indwelt by God; Man's Unity with God; Mystical Experience; Mysticism; Mystic; Phenomena; Prayer; Reality; Religion; Religion, Definitions of; Religious; Revelation; Transcendence; Vision; Worship.

EXPLOITATION

Christians must be more interested in abolishing the exploitation of man by man than any Communist can possibly be.

G. BROMLEY OXNAM, *Sermon,* World Council of Churches, 1954

EXTERNALS

Learn to despise outward things and give thyself to inward things, and thou shalt see the kingdom of God, come into thy soul.

THOMAS À KEMPIS, *Imitation of Christ,* 1441

EXTREMITY

Man's extremity is God's opportunity.

THOMAS ADAM, *Sermon,* 1629

EYES

The eyes are the windows of our souls, by which, as so many channels, all dishonest concupiscence gets into our hearts.

SALVIANUS, *De Providentia,* Lib. 3, 5th century

Eyes too old to see are not too old to weep.

Anonymous

FACT

Philosophers and theologians have yet to learn that a physical fact is as sacred as a moral principle.

LOUIS AGASSIZ, *Atlantic Monthly,* 1874

If facts are to be ultimate and real, there are no facts anywhere at all. There will be one single fact which is the Absolute.

F. H. BRADLEY, *Appearance and Reality,* 1897

Every fact is what it is, a fact of pleasure, of joy, of pain, or of suffering. In its union with God that fact is not a total loss, but on its finer side is an element to be woven immortally into the rhythm of mortal things.

ALFRED NORTH WHITEHEAD, *Religion in the Making,* 1926

Historically, the Christian religion is supposed to rest upon the rock of fact, not upon the shifting sands of pious speculation.

WILLARD L. SPERRY, *Jesus Then and Now,* 1949

See also Faith.

FAILURE

Man's historical experience has been one of steady failure and there are no grounds for supposing it will ever be anything else. Not one single project elaborated within the historical process has ever proved successful.

NICHOLAS BERDYAEV, *The Meaning of History*, 1936

If there is nothing but failure, be humble enough to offer that; if it is all we have to offer it is ourselves.

WILLIAM OF GLASSHAMPTON (1862–1937), quoted in *William of Glasshampton*, by Geoffrey Curtis, 1947

There is no failure so great that a Christian cannot rise from it, there is no defeat so final that he cannot convert it into a victory.

HELEN C. WHITE, *To the End of the World*, 1939

Man's historical experience is one of steady failure. Christianity, too, as a historical *world* religion, is a complete failure.

KARL LÖWITH, *Meaning in History*, 1949

See also Defeat; Success; Victory.

FAITH

Mencius said: If a scholar have not faith, how shall he take a firm hold of things.

Works of Mencius (371–288 B.C.)

I will not accept the Buddhahood if all who, with sincere faith, desire to be reborn in my Paradise are not to enter it. If all men save deadly sinners may not enter it, I will not enter Buddhahood.

VOW OF THE BODDHISATTVA AMITABHA, greatest of the Mahayana Buddhist Saviors; quoted from the *Sukhavati Vyuha* (in K. J. Saunders, *Lotuses of the Mahayana*, publ. 1924), of uncertain date; translated into Chinese late in the 2nd century

The state of faith allows no mention of impossibility.

TERTULLIAN, *De Corona*, c. 200 A.D.

Take thou, hold, learn, profess only that faith which is now delivered to thee by the Church, and which is fenced around by all the Scripture.

ST. CYRIL OF JERUSALEM, *Catecheses*, 350

Guard the deposit of faith. . . . It is a treasure entrusted to you. . . . It comes to you by teaching, not by research. . . . Hence you must not add new Truths to it, you must guard accepted truth; you must keep the treasure of the faith unplundered and undefiled.

ST. VINCENT OF LÉRINS, *Commonitorium*, 434

The integral and true Faith is a great bulwark to which nothing can be added or taken from by anyone; if the Faith is not single, it does not exist at all.

POPE ST. LEO THE GREAT (440–461), quoted by Pope John XXIII, November 11, 1961

Faith is required of thee, and a sincere life, not loftiness of intellect, nor deepness in the mysteries of God.

THOMAS À KEMPIS, *Imitation of Christ*, 1441

Believe that you have it, and you have it.

DESIDERIUS ERASMUS, *Letter to Thomas More*, c. 1500

God our Father has made all things depend on faith so that whoever has faith will have everything, and whoever does not have faith will have nothing.

MARTIN LUTHER, *Freedom of a Christian*, 1520

Above all things bear in mind what I have said, that faith alone without works justifies, sets free, and saves.

MARTIN LUTHER, *On Christian Liberty*, 1520

In the true faith, I include the whole doctrine handed down in the books of the prophets and apostles, and comprehended in the Apostles', Nicene, and Athanasian creeds.

PHILIP MELANCHTHON (1497–1560), *Corpus Reformatorum,* Vol. XI, p. 273

When God commands us to believe, he does not propose to have us search into his divine judgments, nor to inquire their reasons and causes, but demands an immutable faith. . . . Faith, therefore, excludes not only all doubt, but even the desire of subjecting its truth to demonstration.
Catechism of the Council of Trent, 1566

Faith alone is the proximate and proportionate means which can unite the soul to God.
ST. JOHN OF THE CROSS (1549–1591), *The Ascent of Mount Carmel,* Bk. II

It is therefore of great importance to give to faith no more than the things that are faith's.
FRANCIS BACON, *Novum Organum, Aphorism,* 1620

No man hath such a measure of faith, as that he needs no more, or that he may not lose at least some of that.
JOHN DONNE, *Sermon,* Funeral of Sir William Cockayne, December 26, 1626

Faith is the parent of charity; and whatsoever faith entertains must be apt to produce love to God.
JEREMY TAYLOR, *Holy Living,* 1650

No man could work a day's labor without faith; but because he believes he shall have his wages at the day's or week's end, he does his duty.
JEREMY TAYLOR, *Holy Living,* 1650

Faith tells what the senses do not tell, but not the contrary of what they see.
BLAISE PASCAL, *Pensées,* 1670

Faith is kept alive in us, and gathers strength, more from practice than from speculations.
JOSEPH ADDISON, *The Spectator,* August 23, 1712

It is neither necessary nor indeed possible, to understand any matter of faith farther than it is revealed.
BENJAMIN WHICHCOTE, *Moral and Religious Aphorisms,* 1753

In the affairs of this world, men are saved not by faith, but by want of it.
BENJAMIN FRANKLIN, *Poor Richard's Almanac,* 1758

Faith separate from love is not faith, but mere science, which in itself is void of spiritual life.
EMMANUEL SWEDENBORG, *Heaven and Hell,* 1758

Men in the dark endeavor to tread firmer than when they are in the light.
SAMUEL BUTLER, *Remains,* 1759

I have, therefore, found it necessary to deny *knowledge* of God, *freedom* and *immortality* in order to find a place for faith.
IMMANUEL KANT, *Critique of Pure Reason,* XXX, 1781

If you take faith away from the people you will end by producing nothing but highway robbers.
NAPOLEON BONAPARTE, at a session of the Council of State, Tuilleries, 1804–1805

Faith is a profound sense of security in regard to both the present and the future; and this assurance springs from confidence in an immense, all-powerful, and inscrutable Being. The firmness of this confidence is the one grand point. . . . Faith is a holy vessel into which every one stands ready to pour his feelings, his understanding, his imagination, as perfectly as he can.

J. W. VON GOETHE, *Autobiography*, II, 1822

Faith is private capital stored in one's own house. It is like a public savings-bank or loan office, from which individuals receive assistance in their days of need; but here the creditor quietly takes his interest for himself.

J. W. VON GOETHE (1749–1832), *Maxims and Reflections*

For man's well-being, Faith is properly the one thing needful; how, with it, Martyrs otherwise weak, can cheerfully endure the shame and the cross; and without it, Worldings puke up their sick existence, by suicide, in the midst of luxury.

THOMAS CARLYLE, *Sartor Resartus*, 1836

Why should we be unwilling to go by faith? We do all things in this world by faith in the word of others. By faith only we know our position in the world, our circumstances, our rights and privileges, our fortunes, our parents, our brothers and sisters, our age, our mortality. Why should Religion be an exception?

JOHN HENRY NEWMAN, *Essays and Sketches*, Vol. 1, 1838

Faith constitutes a sphere all by itself, and every misunderstanding of Christianity may at once be recognized by its transforming it into a doctrine, transferring it to the sphere of the intellectual.

SÖREN KIERKEGAARD, Postscript to *Philosophical Fragments*, 1846

Faith must make a venture and is rewarded by sight.

JOHN HENRY NEWMAN, *Loss and Gain*, 1848

Faith is the antiseptic of the soul.

WALT WHITMAN, Preface to *Leaves of Grass*, 1853

It is rather with matters of religious belief belonging to a higher and less conceivable class of truths, with the mysterious things of the unseen world, that faith owns a connection, and more readily associates itself with spiritual ideas than with external evidence, or physical events.

BADEN POWELL, *Essays and Reviews*, 1861

We cannot live on probabilities. The faith in which we can live bravely and die in peace must be a certainty, so far as it professes to be a faith at all, or it is nothing.

J. A. FROUDE, *A Plea for Free Discussion of Theological Difficulties*, 1863

Without faith a man can do nothing. But faith can stifle all science.

H. F. AMIEL, *Journal*, February 7, 1872

We cannot prove our faith by syllogisms. The argument refuses to form in the mind.

RALPH WALDO EMERSON, *Letters and Social Aims*, 1876

Faith is God's interpreter; without its enlightenment we understand nothing of the language of created things.

J. P. DE CAUSSADE, *Abandonment*, 1880

In the harsh face of life faith can read a bracing gospel.

ROBERT LOUIS STEVENSON, *Familiar Studies of Men and Books*, 1881

It is faith and not logic which is the supreme arbiter.

SAMUEL BUTLER, *The Way of All Flesh*, 1884

Faith requires an aim capable of embracing life as a whole, of concentrating all its manifestations, of directing its various modes of activity, or of repressing them all in favor of one alone.

JOSEPH MAZZINI, *Essays*, 1887

Every sort of energy and endurance, of courage and capacity for handling life's evils, is set free in those who have religious faith.

WILLIAM JAMES, *The Will to Believe,* 1895

You can keep a faith only as you can keep a plant, by rooting it into your life and making it grow there.

PHILLIPS BROOKS, *Perennials,* 1898

That man is perfect in faith who can come to God in the utter dearth of his feelings and desires, without a glow or an aspiration, with the weight of his low thoughts, failures, neglects, and wandering forgetfulness, and say to Him, "Thou art my refuge."

GEORGE MACDONALD (1824–1905), *George Macdonald: an Anthology,* ed. C. S. Lewis

If we are too stupid to ask for any meaning in our experience, . . . too frivolous to care seriously for what can only be cared for seriously, too gloomy to hope, or too wilful to learn, we are laboring under fatal disqualifications for the experience of Faith.

W. R. INGE, *Faith and Its Psychology,* 1910

Faith always contains an element of risk, of venture; and we are impelled to make the venture by the affinity and attraction which we feel in ourselves.

W. R. INGE, *Faith and Its Psychology,* 1910

You can do very little with faith, but you can do nothing without it.

SAMUEL BUTLER, *Notebooks of,* ed. H. F. Jones, 1912

Talk of faith as venture is legitimate only when what is meant by it is that faith *"ventures something."* "Not to venture *faith itself,* but to venture *in* faith."

RUDOLF BULTMAN, "Faith as Venture," 1918, in *Existence and Faith,* ed. S. M. Ogden

Faith is in no way contradictory of clear vision. . . . Faith as the knowledge of truth not yet fully understood, is true knowledge and a participation in the truth.

FATHER CUTHBERT, *God and the Supernatural,* 1920

Nothing in life is more wonderful than faith—the one great moving force which we can neither weigh in the balance nor test in the crucible.

WILLIAM OSLER, *Life of,* II, H. Cushing, 1925

Except with the eye of faith we have no measure either of life or of death.

J. A. SPENDER, *The Public Life,* 1925

In matters of faith it is not permitted to make a distinction between fundamental and so-called non-fundamental articles of faith, as if the first ought to be held by all and the second the faithful are free to accept or not.

POPE PIUS XI, *True Religious Unity,* January, 1928

Christian faith in God has its rooting in a venturesome moral attitude similar to that which is involved in every act of loyal devotion—a willingness to trust beyond the evidence.

WALTER MARSHALL HORTON, *Theism and the Modern Mood,* 1930

Something greater than divine philosophy must link the heights and depths for man. It is faith. Faith lowers the heavens to earth.

JAMES EDWARD O'MAHONY, *Romanticism of Holiness,* 1933

Faith is a free choice; wherever there is a desire of proof, . . . there is no faith.

ALEXANDER YELCHANINOV (1881–1934), *Fragments of a Diary*

There would be nothing paradoxical in the discovery that a religion which had lost its faith in God must be overwhelmed by a faith which had rejected religion.

JOHN MACMURRAY, *Creative Society*, 1935

Faith is not a thing which one "loses," we merely cease to shape our lives by it.

GEORGES BERNANOS, *Diary of a Country Priest*, 1937

Faith is not only a virtue, but also the divine entrance through which all virtues enter into the temple of the soul.

POPE PIUS XII, *Broadcast*, December 24, 1941

Of all mad faiths maddest is the faith that we can get rid of faith.

HARRY EMERSON FOSDICK, *On Being a Real Person*, 1943

Without faith man becomes sterile, hopeless, and afraid to the very core of his being.

ERICH FROMM, *Man for Himself*, 1947

Pure faith or "bare faith" must not be confused with the parroting of a purely literary belief, not truly informed by the mind. The latter is wholly exterior, the former reaches the secret depths of the soul.

HENRI DE LUBAC, *Paradoxes*, 1948

The light of faith confers upons us undreamed-of enhancement of our vision, an extension of our understanding, an enrichment of our natural powers beyond the power of words to convey.

ROSALIND MURRAY, *The Forsaken Fountain*, 1948

There can be no true faith that is not the free homage of the spirit to a truth greater than itself.

R. L. BRUCKBERGER, *One Sky to Share*, 1951

Faith *is* obscure. By faith a man moves through darkness; but he moves securely,

his hand in the hand of God. He is literally seeing through the eyes of God.

WALTER FARRELL, *The Looking Glass*, 1951

To rely on our faith would be idol-worship. We have only the right to rely on God.

ABRAHAM J. HESCHEL, *Man Is Not Alone*, 1951

Faith does not spring out of nothing. It comes with the discovery of the holy dimension of our existence.

ABRAHAM J. HESCHEL, *Man Is Not Alone*, 1951

Religious faith is not needed to tell us *what* is good, but it is needed to make us *want* it enough to do it.

JOSEPH FLETCHER, *Sex and Religion Today*, ed. S. Doniger, 1953

Those who might seem to have the most reason to distrust life because of its hardships are the ones who have come through with the strongest faith.

RALPH W. SOCKMAN, *How to Believe*, 1953

Faith in God may be an elective in our university of daily living. In the presence of death it assumes crucial significance.

SIDNEY GREENBERG, *Treasury of Comfort*, 1954

Faith will not be restored in the West because people believe it to be useful. It will return only when they find that it is true.

BARBARA WARD, *Faith and Freedom*, 1954

The real battles of faith are being fought in factories, shops, offices and farms, in political parties and government agencies, in countless homes, in the press, radio and television, in the relationship of nations.

WORLD CONFERENCE OF CHURCHES, Evanston, Ill., 1954

It is only when Christian faith is lost that man must himself make use of all means, even criminal ones, in order to secure by force the victory of his cause.

DIETRICH BONHOEFFER, *Ethics,* 1955

"Have I the right to keep my faith," said a student inquirer, "at the price of my intellectual integrity." The answer would have to be that the "faith" which is kept at such a price is no faith at all.

ALEXANDER MILLER, *The Renewal of Man,* 1955

The exploration of the earth in itself fails to bring any light or point out any solution to the most fundamental question. . . . The wider the problem seems to grow before my eyes, the more clearly I see that its solution can only be sought in a "faith" beyond all experience.

PIERRE TEILHARD DE CHARDIN, *Letters from a Traveler,* 1956

More necessary than faith in the gods is faith that man can give justice, brotherhood, peace and all his beloved moral values embodiment in human relations.

A. EUSTACE HAYDON, *This Is My Faith,* ed. S. G. Cole, 1956

Faith comes when Christ is recognized as divine and His word becomes the way and the truth and the life.

MARTIN C. D'ARCY, *The Nature of Belief,* 1958

We do not speak of faith unless the reality which we are to reach surpasses our own powers of discovery.

EUGÈNE JOLY, *What Is Faith?,* 1958

Faith thrives on reality and sickens in an atmosphere of sentiment illusion.

JOHN LAFARGE, *An American Amen,* 1958

The act of faith is both an affirmation and an act of love—a love which desires a Person, and which affirms that Person in order to possess Him.

JEAN MOUROUX, *I Believe,* 1960

Faith stands at the point where ultimate reality must be affirmed as a gamble, not a reasonable deduction.

SAMUEL H. MILLER, *Look,* December 19, 1961

Faith faces everything that makes the world uncomfortable—pain, fear, loneliness, shame, death—and acts with a compassion by which these things are transformed, even exalted.

SAMUEL H. MILLER, *Look,* December 19, 1961

Not to have faith is not a personal fault, it is a misfortune.

ÉTIENNE GILSON, *The Philosopher and Theology,* 1962

Like a tree, it shades the evil as well as the good. The crucial question is this: in what soil are you rooting your faith?

JOHN E. LARGE, *The Small Needle of Doctor Large,* 1962

Faith is not an easy virtue but in the broad world of man's total voyage through time to eternity, faith is not only a gracious companion, but an essential guide.

THEODORE M. HESBURGH, *Way,* June, 1963

My faith is an act that I make, myself, naked before God. . . . There is only my faith, and yours, and that of my Shinto friend, and my particular Jewish neighbor. . . . In the eyes of God each of us is a person, not a type. . . . There is nothing in heaven or on earth that can legitimately be called the Christian faith.

WILFRED C. SMITH, *The Meaning and End of Religion,* 1963

Man's response to God in faith must be free: no one therefore is to be forced to embrace the Christian faith against his own will. . . . The act of faith is of its very nature a free act. . . . God calls men to serve Him in spirit and in truth: hence they are bound in conscience but they stand under no compulsion.

SECOND VATICAN COUNCIL, *A Declaration on Religious Freedom,* December, 1965

Where faith is, there God is.
Marathi Proverb

See also Affirmation; Belief; Believing; Bible; Bible and Doctrine; Catholicism; Certainty; Christian; Christianity; Christianity, Criticism of; Church:Its Authority; Church: Its Nature; Coercion; Commitment; Confidence; Creeds; Despair; Doctrine; Dogma; Dogmatism; Doubt; Education and Religion; Election; Eucharist; Faith, Definitions of; Faith: Its Origin; Faith and Prayer; Faith and Reason; Fear; Forgiveness; Freedom, Religious; God: Knowledge About Him; Heart; Holy Spirit; Hope; Justification; Knowledge; Light; Man's Quest of God; Morality; Mysteries; New Testament; Optimism; Orthodoxy; Practice; Prayer, Methods and Time of; Preaching; Private Judgment; Predestination; Protestantism; Providence; Reason and God; Religion; Religion, Necessity of; Revelation; Risk; Salvation; Science; Science and Religion; Security; Skepticism; Social Faith; Spiritual Struggle; Superstition; Tradition; Trust; Truth; Truth and Religion; Unbelief; Vision; War, Defense of; Word, the; Works; Worship.

FAITH, DEFINITIONS OF

Faith is a voluntary anticipation.
ST. CLEMENT OF ALEXANDRIA, *Stromateis,* c. 193

Now it is faith to believe that which you do not yet see; and the reward of faith is to see that which you believe.
ST. AUGUSTINE (354–430), *Sermon* XLIII

Faith is the foretaste of that knowledge which hereafter will make us happy.
ST. THOMAS AQUINAS (1225–1274), *Opusc.* xiii, *Compendium Theologiae*

Faith is a theological virtue that inclines the mind, under the influence of the will and grace, to yield firm assent to revealed truths, because of the authority of God.
ADOLPHE TANQUERAY, *The Spiritual Life,* 1490

Faith is nothing else than trust in the divine mercy promised in Christ.
PHILIP MELANCHTHON, *Loci Communes,* 1521

This is the acme of faith, to believe that God, Who saves so few and condemns so many, is merciful; that He is just Who made us necessarily doomed to damnation.
MARTIN LUTHER, *De servo arbitrio,* 1525

Faith consists, not in ignorance, but in knowledge; and that, not only of God, but also of the divine will.
JOHN CALVIN, *Institutes,* I, 1536

As faith is the evidence of things not seen, so things that are seen are the perfection of faith.
ARTHUR WARWICK, *Spare Minutes,* 1637

True faith is confident, and will venture all the world upon the strength of its persuasion. Will you lay your life upon it, your estate, your reputation, that the doctrine of Jesus Christ is true in every article? Then you have true faith.
JEREMY TAYLOR, *Holy Living,* 1650

An outward and visible sign of an inward and spiritual grace.
The Book of Common Prayer, 1662

A certain beginning by which knowledge of the Creator begins to be produced in the rational nature.
JOHN SCOTUS ERIGENA, *The Division of Nature,* 1681

Faith is the assent to any proposition not thus made out by the deductions of reasons; but upon the credit of the proposer, as coming from God, in some extraordinary way of communication.

> JOHN LOCKE, *Essay Concerning Human Understanding,* 1690

Faith consists in believing not what seems true, but what seems false to our understanding. . . . Divine faith, . . . is evidently nothing more than incredulity brought under subjection, for we certainly have no other faculty than the understanding by which we can believe; and the objects of faiths are not those of the understanding.

> VOLTAIRE, *Philosophical Dictionary,* I, 1764

It consists in believing things because they are impossible.

> VOLTAIRE, *Philosophical Dictionary,* 1764

It is a free belief, not in that for which dogmatical proofs for the theoretically determinant Judgment are to be found, or in that to which we hold ourselves bound, but in that which we assume on behalf of a design in accordance with laws of freedom.

> IMMANUEL KANT, *Critique of Judgment,* 1790

Faith is that divine evidence whereby the spiritual man discerneth God and the things of God.

> JOHN WESLEY (1703–1791), *An Earnest Appeal to Men of Reason and Religion, Works,* XII

Authentic tidings of invisible things, of ebb and flow, and ever'during power, and central peace. Subsisting at the heart of endless agitation.

> WILLIAM WORDSWORTH, *The Prelude,* 1800

Faith is loyalty to some inspired teacher, some spiritual hero.

> THOMAS CARLYLE, *Heroes and Hero Worship,* 1840

Faith, which is the beginning of man's salvation, is a supernatural virtue, whereby, inspired and assisted by the grace of God, we believe that the things He has revealed are true.

> VATICAN COUNCIL, Session III, 1870

Faith is the soul's consciousness of its Divine relationship and exalted destiny.

> G. S. MERIAM, *A Living Faith,* 1876

Faith is the sense of life, that sense by virtue of which man does not destroy himself, but continues to live on. It is the force whereby we live.

> LEO TOLSTOY, *My Confession,* 1879

Faith is the light of time; it alone grasps the truth without seeing it; it touches what it does not feel; it sees this world as though it existed not, beholding quite other things than those which are visible.

> J. P. DE CAUSSADE, *Abandonment,* 1880

Faith means belief in something concerning which doubt is still theoretically possible; and as the test of belief is willingness to act, one may say that faith is the readiness to act in a cause the prosperous issue of which is not certified to us in advance.

> WILLIAM JAMES, *Princeton Review,* July, 1882

All human knowledge, human endeavor, earthly progress depends on faith that beyond what we know there is a great world of truth and good still to be discovered. And this is, in reality, faith in God.

> JAMES FREEMAN CLARKE, *Every Day Religion,* 1886

A man's religious faith (whatever more special items of doctrine it may involve) means for me essentially his faith in the existence of an unseen order of some kind in which the riddles of the natural order may be found explained.

> WILLIAM JAMES, *Address* to Harvard Y.M.C.A. publ. in *International Journal of Ethics*, October, 1895

If faith be provisionally defined as conviction apart from or in excess of proof, then it is upon faith that the maxims of daily life, not less than the loftiest creeds and the most far-reaching discoveries, must ultimately lean.

> A. J. BALFOUR, *The Foundations of Belief*, 1895

Faith, n. Belief without evidence in what is told by one who speaks without knowledge, of things without parallel.

> AMBROSE BIERCE, *Devil's Dictionary*, 1906

Faith is like the little night-light that burns in a sickroom; as long as it is there, the obscurity is not complete, we turn towards it and await the daylight.

> ABBÉ HUVELIN, interviewed by Adeline, Duchess of Bedford, *English Church Review*, 1911

Faith is a venture; it began as the resolution to stand or fall by the noblest hypothesis.

> W. R. INGE, *Proceedings of the Aristotelian Society*, 1923

Faith is obedience, nothing else; literally nothing else at all.

> EMIL BRUNNER, *Der Mittler*, 1927

The fundamental error commonly made lies in considering faith as a kind of knowledge. . . . Faith, however, is not a kind of knowledge, but rather a practical attitude of the will.

> JOHN MACMURRAY, *Adventure*, ed. B. H. Streeter, 1928

Knowledge of God far beyond all human possibilities.

> EMIL BRUNNER, *The Word and the World*, 1931

Faith is not a vision, if by vision we mean comprehension and intuition; it is rather the beginning of a new life, the discovery within and without of a new order, of a new and final definition.

> MARTIN C. D'ARCY, *The Nature of Belief*, 1931

That indispensable and therefore imperishable illusion of the heart of man that, though he may seem a mere worm on the earth, he nevertheless can make himself lord of the Universe.

> LEWIS BROWNE, *This Believing World*, 1933

Faith in the continued disclosing of truth through directed human endeavor is more religious in quality than is any faith in a completed revelation.

> JOHN DEWEY, *A Common Faith*, 1934

In Judaism faith is . . . the capacity to perceive the abiding . . . in the transitory, the invisible in the visible.

> LEO BAECK, *Essence of Judaism*, 1936

The faith of a Christian . . . is trust in God, in a good God who created a good world, though the world is not now good; in a good God, powerful and good enough finally to destroy the evil that men do and redeem them of their sins.

> REINHOLD NIEBUHR, *Beyond Tragedy*, 1937

Faith itself appears as a direct commerce, an intimate union with the interior word of God, and consequently with His interior life.

> REGINALD GARRIGOU-LAGRANGE, *Christian Perfection and Contemplation*, 1937

Faith is trust, and it is therefore primarily volitional and emotional. Belief, on the other hand, is primarily intellectual: it is the assent of the mind. But while belief is not itself faith, faith where there is no belief is something quite impossible.

EDWIN LEWIS, *A Philosophy of the Christian Revelation,* 1940

Faith is the final triumph over incongruity, the final assertion of the meaningfulness of existence. . . . Faith is the final assertion of the freedom of the human spirit, but also the final acceptance of the weakness of man and the final solution for the problem of life through the disavowal of any final solutions in the power of man.

REINHOLD NIEBUHR, *Discerning the Signs of the Time,* 1946

"Faith" is a word like the Japanese word *Degozaimes* that can apparently mean anything you happen to want it.

JAMES BISSETT PRATT, *Religious Liberals Reply,* 1947

The response of our spirits to the beckonings of the eternal.

G. A. BUTTRICK, *Speech,* Boston, Mass., reported in *New York Times,* January 14, 1947

Faith is a superior view opening on truths that only God could know. In itself faith perfects the mind of man far beyond anything else that can come to it in the universe.

WALTER FARRELL, *The Looking Glass,* 1951

Faith is an awareness of divine mutuality and companionship, a form of communion between God and man.

ABRAHAM J. HESCHEL, *Man Is Not Alone,* 1951

Faith is the acceptance of the *kerygma* not as mere cognizance of it and agreement with it but as that genuine obedience to it which includes a new understanding of one's self.

RUDOLF BULTMANN, *Theology of the New Testament,* Vol. 1, 1952

An evangelical grace wrought by the Spirit. . . . It is an assent of the mind and a consent of the heart, consisting mainly of belief and trust.

E. T. HISCOX, *The New Directory for Baptist Churches,* 1954

Faith means being grasped by a power that is greater than we are, a power that shakes us and turns us, and transforms and heals us. Surrender to this power is faith.

PAUL TILLICH, *The New Being,* 1955

Faith is more than intellectual acceptance of the revelation in Jesus Christ; it is whole-hearted trust in God and His promises, and committal of ourselves to Jesus Christ as Saviour and Lord.

WALTER M. HORTON, *Christian Theology,* 1955

We may define "faith" as a firm belief in something for which there is no evidence. . . . Where there is evidence, no one speaks of "faith." We only speak of faith when we wish to substitute emotion for evidence.

BERTRAND RUSSELL, *Human Society in Ethics and Politics,* 1955

Faith is the state of being ultimately concerned.

PAUL TILLICH, *Dynamics of Faith,* 1957

Faith, like the whole Christian life, is an encounter in which God takes and keeps the initiative.

EUGÈNE JOLY, *What Is Faith?,* 1958

Faith is apprehension through commitment.

JOHN BAILLIE, *The Sense of the Presence of God,* 1962

Faith is when you believe something you know ain't true.

Anonymous

See also Belief; Certainty; Doubt; Faith; Faith: Its Origin; Faith and Prayer; Faith and Reason; Knowledge; Light; Truth.

FAITH: ITS ORIGIN

Though our birth was not originally our own doing, yet in order that we may choose to follow what is pleasing to Him, He, by the reasonable faculties which He has bestowed on us, both persuades us, and leads us, to faith.

ST. JUSTIN MARTYR, First Apology, c. 150

The spirit of grace causes us to have faith, in order that through faith we may, on praying for it, obtain the ability to do what we are commanded.

ST. AUGUSTINE, Confessions of, 397

Since man by assenting to matters of faith, is raised above his nature, this must needs accrue to him from some supernatural principle moving him inwardly; and this is God.

ST. THOMAS AQUINAS, Summa Theologiae, IIa, IIae, q. b, 1272

Faith is a gift of God which man can neither give or take away by promise of rewards or menaces of torture.

THOMAS HOBBES, Leviathan, 1651

Faith is a gift of God; do not believe that we said it was a gift of reasoning.

BLAISE PASCAL Pensées, 1670

Faith is not found in man's nature, but it springs and grows from the previous seed, so that it is a gift to be waited for and obtained from God.

ISAAC PENNINGTON (1616–1679), Works, Vol. IV

Because God is its cause, faith is more certain than knowledge resulting from

purely natural action of the human faculties.

MORTIMER ADLER, Vital Speeches, December, 1949

Religious faith, on which sacred theology rests, is itself a supernatural act of the human intellect and is thus a divine gift.

MORTIMER ADLER, Vital Speeches, December, 1949

See also Belief; Fact; Faith; Faith, Definitions of; Faith and Reason; Grace; Reason; Truth; Vision.

FAITH AND PRAYER

Faith furnishes prayer with wings, without which it cannot soar to Heaven.

ST. JOHN CLIMACUS (525–600), Climax

[Faith is] to pray without doubting, without weariness, without faintness; entertaining no jealousies or suspicions of God, but being confident of God's hearing us, and of His return to us.

JEREMY TAYLOR, Holy Living, 1650

Religion has not arrived until faith in God has been translated into action, and the most intimate and outward action which emerges when faith in God is real is prayer.

HARRY EMERSON FOSDICK, Adventurous Religion, 1926

Without prayer faith remains a theoretical conviction; worship is only an external and formal act; moral action is without spiritual depth; man remains at a distance from God; an abyss yawns between the finite and the Infinite.

FRIEDRICH HEILER, Prayer, 1932

Faith is a gift—but you can ask for it!

FULTON OURSLER, Why I Know There Is a God, 1949

Faith is fulfilled only in prayer. Prayer is at once faith's direct act and daily food, faith's venture and certitude. Faith without prayer is dead.

> GEORGE A. BUTTRICK, *So We Believe, So We Pray,* 1951

Without faith a prayer has only form. Without faith a prayer has no heart or flame.

> GUY EVERTON TREMAINE, *The Prayer Life of Jesus,* 1954

See also Faith; Faith and Reason; Prayer.

FAITH AND REASON

I do not require a reason for Christ. If I am convinced by reason, I reject faith.

> ST. AMBROSE, *On Belief in the Resurrection,* c. 381

Reason is the greatest enemy that faith has: it never comes to the aid of spiritual things, but—more frequently than not—struggles against the divine Word, treating with contempt all that emanates from God.

> MARTIN LUTHER (1483–1546), *Table Talk*

I teach my haggard and unreclaimed Reason to stoop unto the lure of Faith.

> THOMAS BROWNE, *Religio Medici,* 1635

Nothing that is contrary to, and inconsistent with, the clear and self-evident dictates of reason, has a right to be urged or assented to as a matter of faith, wherein reason hath nothing to do.

> JOHN LOCKE, *Essay Concerning Human Understanding,* 1690

For till it be resolved how far we are to be guided by reason, and how far by faith, we shall in vain dispute, and endeavor to convince one another in matters of religion.

> JOHN LOCKE, *Essay Concerning Human Understanding,* 1690

Faith . . . can be nothing but the annihilation of reason, a silence of adoration at the contemplation of things absolutely incomprehensible. . . . Faith, therefore, is nothing but submissive or deferential incredulity.

> VOLTAIRE, *Philosophical Dictionary,* I, 1764

Whatever is against right reason, that no faith can oblige us to believe.

> SAMUEL TAYLOR COLERIDGE, *Aids to Reflection,* 1825

Faith is an intellectual act . . . done in a certain moral disposition. Faith is an act of Reason, viz. a reasoning upon presumptions; right Faith is a reasoning upon holy, devout, and enlightened presumptions.

> JOHN HENRY NEWMAN, *Difficulties of Anglicans,* 1850

It is always right that a man should be able to render a reason for the faith that is within him.

> SYDNEY SMITH, *Lady Holland's Memoirs,* I, 1855

Nothing in this world is so marvelous as the transformation that a soul undergoes when the light of faith descends upon the light of reason.

> W. BERNARD ULLATHORNE, *Endowments of Man,* 1889

The reason refuses to acknowledge that there can be anything over which it has not the right of judgment. . . . Here lies the real cause of man's antagonism to faith.

> EMIL BRUNNER, *The Theology of Crisis,* 1929

A man seeks the truth by the unaided effort of reason and is disappointed; it is offered him by faith and he accepts; and, having accepted, he finds that it satisfies his reason.

> ÉTIENNE GILSON, *The Spirit of Medieval Philosophy,* 1936

Faith is assent to something because it is revealed by God. . . . Faith implies assent of the intellect to that which the intellect does not see to be true, either as one of the first principles, or as one of their necessary conclusions. Consequently an act of faith cannot be caused by a rational evidence, but entails an intervention of the will.

ÉTIENNE GILSON, *Reason and Revelation in the Middle Ages*, 1938

Faith . . . is not a lord that tyrannizes over reason, nor does it contradict it: the seal of truth is impressed by God no differently upon faith than upon reason.

POPE PIUS XII, *Address*, December 3, 1939

Faith is not a dam which prevents the flow of the river of reason and thought; it is a levee which prevents unreason from flooding the countryside.

FULTON J. SHEEN, *Preface to Religion*, 1946

If faith can not be reconciled with rational thinking, it has to be eliminated as an anachronistic remnant of earlier stages of culture and replaced by science dealing with facts and theories which are intelligible and can be validated.

ERICH FROMM, *Man for Himself*, 1947

Reason is the precondition of faith; faith is the act in which reason reaches ecstatically beyond itself.

PAUL TILLICH, *Dynamics of Faith*, 1957

The contemporary divorce between faith and reason is not the result of a contest for power or for intellectual monopoly, but of a progressive estrangement without hostility or drama, and therefore all the more deadly.

ARTHUR KOESTLER, *The Sleepwalkers*, 1959

See also Faith; Faith, Definitions of; Knowledge; Light; Reason; Reason and God; Vision.

FALL, THE

Since Adam's fall, all men begotten after the common course of nature are born with sin, that is, without the fear of God, without trust in Him, and with fleshly appetites.

PHILIP MELANCHTHON, *Augsburg Confession*, 1530

God not only foresaw the fall of the first man, and in him the ruin of his posterity, but also at his own pleasure arranged it.

JOHN CALVIN, *Institutes*, 1536

By the fall the divine witness in man was extinguished as a candle is blown out and from our corrupt human nature no saving light proceeds.

ROBERT BARCLAY (1648–1690), *Works*, Vol. 1

All Adam's posterity, or mankind . . . is fallen, degenerated and dead . . . and is subject unto the power, nature, and seed of the Serpent.

ROBERT BARCLAY, *An Apology for the True Christian Divinity*, 1765

The fall of man is the very foundation of revealed religion. If this be taken away, the Christian system is subverted, nor will it deserve so honorable an appellation as that of a cunningly devised fable.

JOHN WESLEY (1703–1791), *Works*, Vol. I, p. 176

A Fall of some sort or other . . . is the fundamental postulate of the moral history of man. Without this hypothesis, man is unintelligible; with it, every phenomenon is explicable. The mystery itself is too profound for human insight.

SAMUEL TAYLOR COLERIDGE, *Table Talk*, May 1, 1830

The Fall is the eternal Mythus of Man . . . in fact, the very transition by which he becomes man.

G. W. F. HEGEL (1770–1831), *The Philosophy of History*, publ. posth.

Knowledge, as the disannulling of the unity of mere Nature, is the "Fall"; which is no casual conception, but the eternal history of Spirit. For the state of innocence, the paradisiacal condition, is that of the brute.

> G. W. F. HEGEL (1770–1831), *The Philosophy of History*, publ. posth.

To fall into the truth and rise a just man,—a transfiguring fall,—that is sublime.

> VICTOR HUGO, *William Shakespeare*, 1864

The old conceptions of the fall of man and of the total depravity of the race were good foundations for the *regime* of a beneficent despot, but not for the *regime* of self-governing freemen.

> CHARLES W. ELIOT, *Why the Republic May Endure*, 1894

While the legend of the Fall passes away, the doctrine of the Fall remains.

> WILLIAM N. RICE, *Christian Faith in an Age of Science*, 1903

In the Protestant theory . . . the Fall does not mean a relapse into Nature, and Redemption is not the ascent from Nature to Grace; rather the idea is that the Fall means the removal of Nature, and Redemption is its restoration.

> ERNEST TROELTSCH, *The Social Teaching of the Christian Churches*, 1931

The Fall is not occasioned by the transgression of Adam; but the transgression was presumably its first manifestation.

> KARL BARTH, *The Epistle to the Romans*, 1933

The Fall could not take place in the natural world, because this world is itself the result of the Fall. The Fall is an event in the spiritual world, and in this sense it is anterior to the world, for it took place before time and, in fact, produced time as we know it.

> NICHOLAS BERDYAEV, *Freedom and the Spirit*, 1935

The fall is not historical. It does not take place in any concrete human act. It is the presupposition of such acts.

> REINHOLD NIEBUHR, *Beyond Tragedy*, 1937

The "Fall" did not happen once and for all and become an inevitable fate, but it continually happens here and now in all its reality.

> MARTIN BUBER, *Israel and the World*, 1948

Unless this fact of the "Fall of Man"—or, if you will, the dogma of original sin—be admitted, Christianity simply collapses like a pricked balloon. . . . For without the Fall, there would be no need of the Incarnation and Redemption, the two cardinal points of Christian belief.

> WILLIAM J. McGUCKEN, *The Philosophy of Catholic Education*, 1951

The Fall is not from some superior grade of civilization or even from a better-developed body. It is wholly from a supernatural way of being, and no imaginable "natural" science can ever discover anything about it.

> C. C. MARTINDALE, *The Catholic Bedside Book*, 1953

The Fall did not extinguish the Light; it crept slowly back to that full Light which is Christ.

> C. C. MARTINDALE, *Duckett's Register*, September, 1959

See also Adam; Atonement; Baptism; Human Nature; Incarnation; Man: His Wickedness; Nature and Man; Original Sin; Predestination; Redemption; Salvation; Sin; Sin: Its Consequences.

FALSE, THE

The false can never grow into truth by growing into power.
> RABINDRANATH TAGORE, *Stray Birds,* 1916

See also Calumnies; Error; Falsehood; Gossip.

FALSE GODS

The false gods are obvious. The primary one is physical power and comfort.
> REINHOLD NIEBUHR, *Christianity Today,* October, 1961

The gods are many, but no matter how they are called, Zeus or atomic power, Venus or libido, Mars or war, they are natural powers and they are always the same. They cannot save, no matter in what era their aid is sought.
> GUSTAVE WEIGEL, *Christianity Today,* October, 1961

See also Idolatry.

FALSE LOVE

False love is the stuff of all sin, for it is egoism, and egoism is rooted in pride, and pride is the primal sin.
> GERALD VANN, *Eve and the Gryphon,* 1946

See also Ego; Egoism; Pride; Self-Love; Self-Praise; Vanity.

FALSE PROPHETS

The false prophet . . . begins with voluntary ignorance, he ends with involuntary madness of soul.
> Anonymous, quoted by Eusebius, *Ecclesiastical History,* early 4th century A.D.

See also Prophets.

FALSE RELIGIONS

The secular world, particularly in political forms, is finding that it cannot maintain its supremacy without some religious sanction, and consequently is busy manufacturing spurious religious faiths to bolster its own inadequacies.
> WHITNEY J. OATES, *The American School,* Summer, 1940

If morality be regarded as a mere convention, and God as the projection of men's hopes or fears, then the way is open for the false religions which relieve the maimed will of the many from the burden of decision.
> SYDNEY CAVE, *The Christian Way,* 1949

FALSEHOOD

False words are not only evil in themselves, but they infect the soul with evil.
> SOCRATES, in "Apology," Plato's *Dialogues,* 399 B.C.

Sweeter than truth which aims at ill
Is falsehood from a well-meant will.
> SHAIKH SAADI, *Gulistan,* c. 1265

The gravest sins are forbidden in Scripture once, but falsehood is forbidden many times.
> M. COHEN, *Sefer Hasidim Zuta,* 1573

See also Calumnies; Dishonesty; False, the; Gossip; Hypocrisy; Integrity; Liars and Lies; Speech; Truth; Truths, Conflict of; Veracity; Words.

FAME

Fame is like a river, that beareth up things light and swollen, and drowns things weighty and solid.
> FRANCIS BACON, *Of Praise,* 1597

Fame is a revenue payable only to our ghosts.

GEORGE MACKENZIE, *Essay on Preferring Solitude to Public Employment,* 1665

Fame is the undying brother of ephemeral honor. I speak, of course, of the highest kind of fame, that is, of fame in the true and genuine sense of the word; . . . fame means nothing but what a man is in comparison with others . . . it vanishes the moment other people become what the famous man is.

ARTHUR SCHOPENHAUER, "The Wisdom of Life," *Essays,* 1851

Fame as a noble mind conceives and desires it, . . . consists in the immortality of a man's work, his spirit, his efficacy, in the perpetual rejuvenation of his soul in the world. . . . Fame is thus the outward sign of recognition of an inward representative authority residing in genius or good fortune.

GEORGE SANTAYANA, *Reason in Society,* 1906

Fame is a food that dead men eat.

HENRY AUSTIN DOBSON (1840–1931), *Poems*

What's fame, after all, me la-ad? 'Tis apt to be what some wan writes on ye'er tombstone.

FINLEY PETER DUNNE (1867–1936), *Mr. Dooley*

Sometimes the pinnacle of fame and the height of folly are twin peaks.

Anonymous

See also Death; Honor; Idolatry; Oblivion; Office; Power; Reputation.

FAMILY

From the loving example of one family a whole state becomes loving.

The Great Learning, c. 500 B.C.

All happy families resemble one another; every unhappy family is unhappy in its own way.

LEO TOLSTOY, opening line of his novel *Anna Karenina,* 1876

The men and women who, for good reasons and bad, revolt against the family are, for good reasons and bad, simply revolting against mankind.

G. K. CHESTERTON, *Heretics,* 1905

For individuals the breakdown of the family means the gloomy despair of a life without happiness, of a life which not even pleasure can light up. For nations it means slow death through sterility, and it can even mean this for the human race.

JACQUES LECLERCQ, *Marriage and the Family,* 1941

In the Götterdämmerung which over-wise science and over-foolish statesmen are preparing for us, last man will spend his last hours searching for his wife and child.

RALPH LINTON, *The Family: Its Function and Destiny,* ed. Ruth Nanda Anshen, 1949

The only preserving and healing power counteracting any historical, intellectual or spiritual crisis no matter of what depth.

RUTH NANDA ANSHEN, in *The Family: Its Function and Destiny,* 1949

Where religion has grown weak the family has shown a corresponding tendency to disintegrate. When religion remains strong, it stands as a protective armor, safeguarding both individual and family.

ROMAN CATHOLIC BISHOPS OF THE U.S., 1957

The family, grounded on marriage freely contracted, monogamous and indissoluble, is and must be considered the first and essential cell of human society.

POPE JOHN XXIII, *Pacem in Terris,* April, 1963

FANATICISM

A fanaticism composed of superstition and ignorance has been the sickness of all the centuries.
VOLTAIRE, *Essai sur les Moeurs,* 1756

The effect of a false conscience, which makes religion subservient to the caprices of the imagination, and the excesses of the passions . . . Fanaticism is, in reference to superstition, what delirium is to fever, or rage to anger.
VOLTAIRE, *Philosophical Dictionary,* I, 1764

Atheism and fanaticism are two monsters, which may tear society to pieces; but the atheist preserves his reason, which checks his propensity to mischief, while the fanatic is under the influence of a madness which is constantly urging him on.
VOLTAIRE, "Atheist," *Philosophical Dictionary,* 1764

What is fanaticism today is the fashionable creed tomorrow, and trite as the multiplication table a week later.
WENDELL PHILLIPS (1811–1884), quoted in C. Hurd's *Treasury of Great American Quotations*

A fanatic is a man that does what he thinks th' Lord wud do if he knew th' facts in th' case.
FINLEY PETER DUNNE, *Mr. Dooley's Opinions,* 1902

Fanaticism (when not a mere expression of ecclesiastical ambition) is only loyalty caried to convulsive extreme.
WILLIAM JAMES, *Varieties of Religious Experience,* 1902

Fanaticism consists in redoubling your effort when you have forgotten your aim.
GEORGE SANTAYANA, *The Life of Reason,* 1905

Nothing is so sure of itself as fanaticism.
LUDWIG LEWISOHN, *Creative Life,* 1924

It is well that in all ages there have been the so-called fanatics who have understood these commands and the whole Sermon as a law to be literally fulfilled.
KARL BARTH, *Kirchlichte Dogmatik,* Vol. II, ii, p. 777, 1940

Religious fanaticism in the name of a rigorous monotheism is obviously possible only because men falsely identify historically contingent values with the God of their own devotion. . . . The inclination cannot be overcome by abolishing "religion."
REINHOLD NIEBUHR, *Religion and Freedom of Thought,* 1954

It is part of the nature of fanaticism that it loses sight of the totality of evil and rushes like a bull at the red cloth instead of at the man who holds it.
DIETRICH BONHOEFFER, *Ethics,* 1955

FASTING

Fasting is a medicine.
ST. JOHN CHRYSOSTOM, *Gen. Homilae,* c. 388

If your body is not strong enough to continue fasting all day, the wise man will reprove you; for we serve a gentle and merciful Lord who expects nothing from us beyond our strength.
ST. JOHN CHRYSOSTOM, *Gen. Homilae,* c. 388

There is no better rule for the wise and serious Christian in this matter, than to conform to the practices which he finds prevailing in the Church to which it may be his lot to come.

ST. AUGUSTINE, *To Januarius,* 400

If you have fasted for two days, do not think yourself better than one who has not fasted. You fast and are peevish; the other eats and is pleasant. You work off your irritability and hunger by quarreling; the other eats and gives thanks to God.

ST. JEROME, *To Eustochium,* c. 405

The prayer of him who fasts is as the offspring of the eagle flying against the heavens.

ST. NILUS (died c. 430), *De Octo Spiritibus Malitiae*

What we forego by fasting is to be given as alms to the poor.

POPE ST. LEO I, *Sermon XIII,* 461

Fasting is more effective than charity, for the latter is done with money, the former with one's person.

ELEAZAR B. PEDAT, *Talmud, Berakot,* c. 500

A keeper of fasts, who doth not abandon lying and slandering, God careth not about his leaving off eating and drinking.

MOHAMMAD, *Speeches and Table-Talk of,* 7th century A.D.

When war, pestilence or famine begin to rage, or any other calamity threatens a country and people, it is the duty of pastors to exhort the church to fasting, that they may deprecate the wrath of the Lord.

JOHN CALVIN, *Institutes,* 1536

By fasting we recover possession of our soul; by prayer we recover possession of God. By fasting we mortify the deeds of the flesh; by prayer we lift up our hearts to God. . . . Fasting puts us on the Cross;

prayer lifts up our hearts above the Cross. Fasting tries the patience, which prayer strengthens.

W. BERNARD ULLATHORNE, *Pastoral Letter,* February, 1863

Fasting is the general bequest of the East to religion—an aspect of the general ascetic discipline of sense life. It is a hard matter to trace to its hidden roots: they are in some general sense of the persuasion that the body is evil or mischievous and needs for the sake of the soul to be kept strongly in hand.

GAIUS GLENN ATKINS in *Procession of the Gods,* with Charles S. Braden, 1948

I often think the doctrine of fasting in Lent and having meatless days are old-fashioned. . . . It might be better to give up television. That would be a more meaningful self-denial in this day and age.

ARTHUR MICHAEL RAMSEY, *Sermon,* 1962

See also Discipline; Gluttony; Penitence; Self-Denial; Self-Discipline.

FATALISM

Fatalism is the wine-soaked premise of the earth-trapped mortal. . . . Fatalism is the device of a lazy and evasive thinker who denies the existence of a free will. Fatalism is futility in trust and the compensation for defeat.

A. M. SULLIVAN, *The Three-Dimensional Man,* 1956

Can anything be more unreasonable than to pretend that a blind fatality could be productive of intelligent beings?

MONTESQUIEU, *The Spirit of the Laws,* 1748

See also Chance; Choice; Destiny; Determinism; Election; Fate; Foreknowledge; Free Will; God: His Intervention in the World; Guilt; Judgment, God's; Man: His Destiny and Goal; Merit; Necessity; Predestination; Providence; Resignation; Will.

FATE

Fate is the Karma, good or bad, acquired by an embodied being in the past life.
Atmanushasana, c. 500 B.C.

Neither by prowess and wisdom, nor by magic and incantations can a man attain to that which he is not fated to receive: What is there to mourn for this?
Garuda Puranam, c. 500 B.C.–c. 50 B.C.

A man dies not before the appointed time, even if he is riddled with shafts. A wound from the tip of a Kusa sprout proves fatal at the right moment. A man receives that which he is fated to receive, goes only there where fate leads him, and finds only that much pleasure or pain he is destined to meet in this life: What is there to mourn for in this life?
Garuda Puranam, c. 500 B.C.–c. 50 B.C.

Even if fate were from the stars, the Maker of the stars could not be subject to their destiny. Moreover not only Christ had not what thou callest fate, but not even hast thou or I, or any human being whatsoever.
ST. AUGUSTINE, *Lectures or Tractates on the Gospel According to St. John,* c. 416

If by fate anyone means the will or power of God, let him keep his meaning but mend his language: for fate commonly means a necessary process which will have its way apart from the will of God and of men.
ST. AUGUSTINE, *The City of God,* c. 426

Fate is a disposition inherent in changeable things, by which Providence connecteth all things in their due order.
BOETHIUS, *Consolations of Philosophy,* c. 525

If from the Hill of Fate a rock roll down, The man of faith sits where he sate before.
SHAIKH SAADI, *Gulistan,* c. 1265

The pagan cannot come into relation with fate, for one instant it is necessity, the next instant it is chance. Nearer to fate than this, the pagan cannot come.
SÖREN KIERKEGAARD, *The Concept of Dread,* 1844

By heaven, man, we are turned round and round in this world, like yonder windlass, and Fate is the handspike.
HERMAN MELVILLE, *Moby Dick,* 1851

Fate is something outside us. What really plays the dickens with us is something in ourselves.
JOHN A. O'BRIEN, *The Test of Courage,* 1943

See also rubrics referred to under Fatalism.

FATHER

What a father says to his children is not heard by the world, but it will be heard by posterity.
JEAN PAUL RICHTER, *Levna,* 1807

The Christian renewal will take place only if the father, the head of the Christian home, regains effective spiritual leadership.
WILLIAM S. MORRIS, *The Father, The Head of the Home,* 1953

See also Children; Daughters; Family; Husband; Marriage; Mother; Parents; Son; Wife; Woman.

FAULTS

To see another's fault is easy; to see one's own is hard; Men winnow the faults of others like chaff; their own they hide as a crafty gambler hides a losing throw.
Dhammapada, c. 5th century B.C.

Not to alter one's faults is to be faulty indeed.
CONFUCIUS, *Sayings of,* 5th century B.C.

Be not concerned over men not knowing of you; be concerned rather over your failings.

CONFUCIUS, *Sayings of,* 5th century B.C.

He who overlooks one fault invites another.

PUBLILIUS SYRUS, *Sententiae,* c. 50 B.C.

Bad men excuse their faults; good men will leave them.

BEN JONSON, *Catilene,* 1611

We are surprised at falling: an evident mark that we scarcely know ourselves. We ought, on the contrary, to be surprised at not falling more frequently, and into more grievous faults.

ST. FRANCIS OF SALES (1567–1622), *Consoling Thoughts of,* ed. Huguet

If we had no faults, we should not take so much pleasure in noting those of others.

LA ROCHEFOUCAULD, *Maxims,* 1665

Almost all our faults are more pardonable than the methods we think up to hide them.

LA ROCHEFOUCAULD, *Maxims,* 1665

We can often do more for other men by correcting our own faults than by trying to correct theirs.

FRANÇOIS FÉNELON (1651–1715), *Spiritual Letters*

The greatest of faults, I should say, is to be conscious of none.

THOMAS CARLYLE, *Heroes and Hero-Worship,* 1840

See also Self-Knowledge.

FEAR

It is the fear of punishment either of the king, or of hell, or of society that keeps people away from sin.

Mahabharata, c. 800 B.C.

To live in fear and falsehood is worse than death.

Zend-Avesta, 6th century B.C.

When internal examination discovers nothing wrong, what is there to be anxious about, what is there to fear?

CONFUCIUS, (5th century B.C.), *The Chinese Classics,* translated by J. Legge, Vol. 1

Blest be the man in whose heart reigneth Holy Fear.

AESCHYLUS (525–456 B.C.), *The Eumenides*

Expectation of evil.

PLATO, "Protagoras," *Dialogues,* 4th century B.C.

God has sent me into the world to be his soldier and witness, to tell men that their sorrows and fears are vain, that to a good man no evil can befall, whether he live or die.

EPICTETUS, *Discourses,* c. 110 A.D.

The Christian should fear nothing so much as separation from the Body of Christ.

ST. AUGUSTINE, *In Joan Evang.,* Tract 26, c. 416

Everything on earth gives cause for fear, and the only freedom from fear is to be found in the renunciation of all desire.

BHARTRI-HARI (c. 7th century), quoted by Brian Brown, *Wisdom of the Hindus*

And if the Wuzzer dreaded God as he doth fear the King, with archangels of Paradise that man might soar and sing.

SHAIKH SAADI, *Gulistan,* 1265

After the time we ourselves repent, so willeth He that *we* forget our sin in regard to our stupid and our doubtful fears.

JULIANA OF NORWICH, *Revelations of Divine Love,* 15th century

In our fear let us remember Christ's painful agony that himself would for our comfort suffer before his passion to the intent that no fear should make us despair.

> ST. THOMAS MORE, *Dialogue of Comfort,* 1535

It is folly to fear God. God is good by his own nature, man by his industry.

> MICHEL DE MONTAIGNE, *Essays,* Bk. 2, ch. 12, 1580

First, my son, fear God; for, to fear God is wisdom, and, being wise, thou canst not err.

> MIGUEL DE CERVANTES, *Don Quixote,* 605

I can hardly think there was ever any scared into Heaven; they go the fairest way to Heaven that would serve GOD without a Hell.

> THOMAS BROWNE, *Religio Medici,* 1635

Fear of things invisible, is the natural seed of that which every one in himself calleth religion.

> THOMAS HOBBES, *Leviathan,* 1651

Fear is an uneasiness of the mind, upon the thought of future evil likely to befall us.

> JOHN LOCKE, *Essay Concerning Human Understanding,* 1690

One always needs a fear of the judgment of God as a counterpoise to the passions.

> FRANÇOIS FÉNELON (1651–1715), *Spiritual Letters*

It is fear that first made the gods.

> DAVID HUME, *Natural History of Religion,* 1755

The characteristic trait of a man who says: "There is no God," is to fear not God but man; they tremble for fear when there is no fear. For he who does not fear the only God fears all.

> ST. TYCHON OF ZADONSK (1724–1783), *Letters*

The man who is actually afraid, because he finds reasons for fear in himself, whilst conscious by his culpable disposition of offending against a Might whose will is irresistible and at the same time just, is not in the frame of mind for admiring the Divine greatness.

> IMMANUEL KANT, *Critique of Judgment,* 1790

The confidence that attends a Christian's belief makes the believer not fear men, to whom he answers, but still he fears his God.

> SAMUEL TAYLOR COLERIDGE, *Aids to Reflection,* 1825

Fear always springs from ignorance.

> RALPH WALDO EMERSON, *The American Scholar,* 1837

It is love which makes Christian fear differ from servile dread, and true faith differ from the faith of devils.

> JOHN HENRY NEWMAN, *The Development of Christian Doctrine,* 1845

The repentance which cuts off all moorings from evil, demands something more than selfish fear.

> GEORGE ELIOT, *Romola,* 1863

Until love, which is the truth towards God, is able to cast out fear, it is well that fear should hold.

> GEORGE MACDONALD, *Unspoken Sermons,* 1st Series, 1869

Fear is the parent of cruelty.

> JAMES ANTHONY FROUDE, *Short Studies in Great Subjects,* 1883

In religion fear and approval to some extent *must* always combine. . . . In religion approval implies devotion, and devotion seems hardly possible, unless there is some fear, if only the fear of estrangement.

> F. H. BRADLEY, *Appearance and Reality,* 1894

Has not Augustine said that fear is the needle that pierces us that it may carry a thread to bind us to heaven.

JAMES HASTINGS, *The Great Texts of the Bible,* 1912

Fear only two: God and him who fears not God.

JUDAH L. LAZEROV, *Enciklopedie Idishe Vitzen,* 1928

The only known cure for fear is faith.

WILLIAM S. SADLER, *The Mind at Mischief,* 1929

The predominant emphasis on the motive of fear for the enforcement of absolute commands has made religious morality develop the most intense cruelty that the human heart has known.

MORRIS R. COHEN, *Religion Today,* ed. A. L. Swift, 1933

But, we repeat, religion is less a fear than a reaction against fear.

HENRI BERGSON, *The Two Sources of Morality and Religion,* 1935

Fear is a necessary ingredient in our life and indeed in all spiritual life. A great soul is one who loves and loves aright and fears and fears aright.

VINCENT MCNABB, *Joy in Believing,* 1939

One of the strange phenomena of the last century is the spectacle of religion dropping the appeal to fear while other human interests have picked it up.

HARRY EMERSON FOSDICK, *On Being a Real Person,* 1943

Fear is fossilized greed.

GERALD HEARD, *A Preface to Prayer,* 1944

In a sense, you see, Fear is nevertheless the daughter of God, redeemed on the evening of Good Friday. She is not fair to look upon—No!—now mocked, now cursed, rejected by everyone. . . . Yet, make no mistake: she stands by the bedside of every death, she intercedes for man.

GEORGES BERNANOS, *La Joie,* 1946

We are slaves of fear, not because we have to die, but because we deserve to die!

PAUL TILLICH, *The Shaking of the Foundations,* 1948

"Fear of God," . . . never means to the Jews that they ought to be afraid of God, but that, trembling, they ought to be aware of his incomprehensibility. . . . Only through the fear of God does man enter so deep into the love of God that he cannot again be cast out of it.

MARTIN BUBER, *Israel and the World,* 1948

Most souls are afraid of God precisely because of His Goodness. . . . Our greatest fear is not that God may not love us enough but that He may love us too much.

FULTON J. SHEEN, *Peace of Soul,* 1949

"He began to be sorrowful: he began to be afraid." We live today in a world so haunted by fear that this story of Christ's agony must be very close to us.

GERALD VANN, *The High Green Hill,* 1951

One does not fear God because He is terrible, but because he is literally the soul of goodness and truth, because to do him wrong is to do wrong to some mysterious part of oneself.

JOYCE CARY, *Except the Lord,* 1953

Fear knocked at the door. Faith answered. No one was there.

On the front of the mantel in the ancient Hind's Head Hotel at Bray, England

See also Confidence; Courage; Cowardice; Death, Fear of; Despair; Evil; Faith;

Gloom; Heaven; Hell; Opinions; Peace; Persecution; Pessimism; Security; Serenity.

FEELINGS

There is no feeling which is not religious, save such as indicate an unhealthy condition in life.

> F. SCHLEIERMACHER, *Second Discourse on Religion*, 1831

The feelings of the purest and most mightily passioned human souls are likely to be the truest.

> JOHN RUSKIN, *The Ethics of the Dust*, 1866

Feeling is necessary in religion, but it is by the *content* or intelligent basis of a religion, and not by feeling, that its character and worth are to be determined.

> JOHN CAIRD, *Introduction to the Philosophy of Religion*, 1880

Religious feeling is as much a verity as any other part of human consciousness; and against it, on the subjective side, the waves of science beat in vain.

> JOHN TYNDALL, *Fragments of Science*, II, 1896

I do believe that feeling is the deeper source of religion, and that philosophic and theological formulas are secondary products, like translations of a text into another tongue.

> WILLIAM JAMES, *Varieties of Religious Experience*, 1902

Religious feeling itself suggests the notion of God which when elaborated by reflection is discovered to be that of the world big with deity.

> SAMUEL ALEXANDER, *Space, Time, and Deity*, 1920

It is an ancient insight that at least some "feelings" are unformed and inchoate cognitions. And this is the justification of the religious feelings of common men. . . .

They are a dim vision of the eternal, appearing in the guise of feelings, or even emotions.

> W. T. STACE, *Religion and the Modern Mind*, 1952

Absence of feeling cannot prevent the soul from ascending to God, nor can its presence ensure it, and when feeling is sought after and enjoyed for its own sake, it prevents it.

> JEAN MOUROUX, *Christian Experience*, 1954

Feeling, no less than experience, can be a source of spiritual knowledge just as intuition can at times be stronger and stranger than the stubborn conclusions of the intellect.

> MARCUS BACH, *Rotarian*, December, 1962

See also Emotion; Experience, Religious; Institution; Passions; Religion; Religious.

FELLOWSHIP

There is no fellowship with a fool.

> *Dhammapada*, c. 5th century B.C.

A branch cut off from its neighbor branch cannot but be cut off from the whole plant. In the very same way a man severed from one man has fallen away from the fellowship of all men.

> MARCUS AURELIUS, *Meditations*, c. 170 A.D.

God has created mankind for fellowship, and not for solitariness, which is clearly proved by this strong argument: God, in the creation of the world, created man and woman, to the end that the man in the woman should have a fellow.

> MARTIN LUTHER (1483–1546), *Table Talk*

Dost thou love and fear God? It is enough! I give thee the right hand of fellowship.

> Common greeting of JOHN WESLEY (1703–1791)

Fellowship is heaven, and lack of fellowship is hell; fellowship is life, and lack of fellowship is death; and the deeds that ye do upon the earth, it is for fellowship's sake that ye do them.

WILLIAM MORRIS, *A Dream of John Ball*, 1888

After justice has rendered impartial decision it is charity that brings men back to fellowship.

JAMES GIBBONS, *Pastoral Letter*, 1919

We believe that God wills fellowship. . . . We believe that it is God's purpose to manifest this fellowship . . . using God-given means of grace, and inspiring all its members to the world-wide service of the Kingdom of God. This is what we mean by the Catholic Church.

LAMBETH CONFERENCE (of Anglican Bishops), 1920

The distinctive thing about fellowship is its lesson of self-subordination.

GREGORY VLASTOS, *The Religious Way*, 1934

At rare moments of history the feeling of Christian fellowship overmasters the jealousies by which the Church of Christ is ever liable to be rent asunder.

H. A. L. FISHER, *A History of Europe*, 1935

The Church is the realization of true community. Its essential nature is fellowship between persons.

W. A. VISSER 'T HOOFT and J. H. OLDHAM, *The Church and Its Function in Society*, 1937

Central as is the relationship between the separate individual and God, each man needs an experience of life in the great family of God if he is to grow to understand the real nature of that love and the real character of his response to that love.

DOUGLAS V. STEERE, *Prayer and Worship*, 1938

The final grounds of holy Fellowship are in God. Persons in the Fellowship are related to one another through Him, as all mountains go down into the same earth. They get at one another through Him.

THOMAS R. KELLY, *A Testament of Devotion*, 1941

In the Fellowship cultural and educational and national and racial differences are leveled. . . . We find men with chilly theologies but with glowing hearts. We overleap the boundaries of church membership and find Lutherans and Roman Catholics, Jews and Christians, within the Fellowship.

THOMAS R. KELLY, *A Testament of Devotion*, 1941

The problem of good fellowship between members of the various religious families seems to me to be a cardinal one for the new age of civilization.

JACQUES MARITAIN, *Ransoming the Time*, 1941

We who have been created for fellowship with God repudiate it continually; and the whole of mankind does this along with us. Every man is his own Adam and all men are solidarily Adam.

JOHN WHALE, *Christian Doctrine*, 1941

In the Christian church we cannot interpret human nature except as fellowship.

KARL BARTH, *Church Dogmatics*, III:2, 1951

The all-important question is not whether human life will survive upon this planet. Rather, it is whether the souls of men will be fit to use God's gift of personal survival in an eternal fellowship.

GEORGIA HARKNESS, *The Modern Rival of Christian Faith*, 1953

See also Brotherhood; Charity; Christian Life; Christianity; Christians; Church, Definitions of; Church: Its Work; Community; Compassion; Division; Dogmatism; Ecumenism; Equality; Experience, Religious; Friendship; Israel; Kingdom of God; Loneliness; Love, Human; Love of Mankind; Mystical Body of Christ; Neighbor; Religion: Its Nature and Function; Social Faith; Society; Solitude; Unity; Worship.

FETUS, DEATH OF THROUGH SURGERY

If . . . the safeguarding of the life of the future mother, independently of her state of pregnancy, were to call for an urgent surgical intervention, or any other therapeutic application, which would have as an accessory consequence, in no way desired or intended but unavoidable, the death of the fetus, this could not be termed a direct attempt on innocent life. In these conditions the operation can be licit . . . provided the stake at issue is a high one, and that it is not possible to postpone it until after the birth of the child.

POPE PIUS XII, *Address,* November 27, 1951

See also Abortion.

FIGHT

For he who fights with love will win the battle.

LAO-TZU, *The Tao Tê Ching,* 6th century B.C.

Fight in the way of Allah against those who fight against you, but begin not hostilities. Allah loveth not aggressors.

Koran, ii, c. 625 A.D.

See also Aggression; Battle; Combat; War.

FLABBY

Ah, when some day the reckoning shall be made of the countless multitude of the human race, there will be found a greater number under the rubric "The flabby," than under all these rubrics taken together: "Thieves," "Robbers," "Murderers."

SÖREN KIERKEGAARD, *For Self-Examination and Judge for Yourselves,* 1944

FLATTERY

Flatterers look like friends, as wolves like dogs.

GEORGE CHAPMAN (1559–1634), *Byron's Conspiracy*

Sometimes we think we dislike flattery when it is only its method we dislike.

LA ROCHEFOUCAULD, *Maxims,* 1665

Among all the diseases of the mind there is not one more epidemical or more pernicious than the love of flattery.

RICHARD STEELE, *The Spectator,* December 3, 1791

The praise of a fool is incense to the wisest of us.

BENJAMIN DISRAELI, *Vivian Grey,* 1827

See also Praise.

FLESH

I do not understand the mortification of matter, which is the essence of Christianity. I think it a sacrilegious act to strike God's handiwork, and I cannot believe that the flesh is bad, since He has Himself formed it with His own fingers and in His own image.

THÉOPHILE GAUTIER, *Mademoiselle de Maupin,* 1835

Man must liberate himself from a bondage which is normal for animals, and, therefore, evil for him. The goal of man demands a complete mastery over the flesh.

LECOMTE DU NOÜY, *Human Destiny,* 1947

There is a law running through human nature, that he who does not spiritualize the flesh will carnalize his spirit.

FULTON J. SHEEN, *Three to Get Married,* 1951

See also Body; Body and Soul; Celibacy; Chastity; Sexual Intercourse.

FOLLY

Nothing is too high for the daring of
mortals;
We storm Heaven itself in our folly.

HORACE, *Carmina,* c. 20 B.C.

FOOLS

The fool who knows his foolishness is wise at least so far. But a fool who thinks himself wise, he is a fool indeed.

Dhammapada, c. 5th century B.C.

If a fool be associated with a wise man even all his life, he will perceive the truth as little as a spoon perceives the taste of the soup.

Dhammapada, c. 5th century B.C.

But, because we are subject to the temptations of this illusory world, the foolish keep on living their futile, indolent, weak and licentious life, which is a life in vain, a life not worth having.

Dhammapada, c. 5th century B.C.

FORCE

Where wisdom is called for, force is of little use.

HERODOTUS, *Histories,* II, c. 430 B.C.

To what purpose should the magistrates bear the sword, if it be not to serve God, who has committed it to them, to defend the good and punish the bad?

STEPHEN JUNIUS BRUTUS, *A Defense of Liberty Against Tyrants,* 1579

The recourse to force, however unavoidable, is a disclosure of the failure of civilization, either in the general society or in a remnant of individuals.

ALFRED NORTH WHITEHEAD, *Adventures of Ideas,* 1933

Whoever's attitude is so uncertain that he must convince himself of its absolute validity by force, is the enemy of civilization.

T. V. SMITH, *Perspectives on a Troubled Decade,* ed. Bryson, Finkelstein and MacIver, 1950

Any human society that is established on relations of force must be regarded as inhuman, inasmuch as the personality of its members is repressed or restricted.

POPE JOHN XXIII, *Pacem in Terris,* April, 1963

See also Aggression; Coercion; Militarism; Nonresistance; Pacifism; Pacifists; Punishment; Violence.

FOREIGN AID.
See INTERNATIONALISM

FOREKNOWLEDGE

You would not necessarily compel a man to sin by foreknowing his sin, though undoubtedly he would sin; otherwise you would not foreknow that this would happen.

ST. AUGUSTINE, *The Problem of Free Choice,* c. 400

If God's foreknowledge of anything could be the cause of its coming into being, then all things would have to be eternal, having existed always since God has always known them.

SAADIAH GAON (882–942), *The Book of Beliefs and Opinions*

Since he foresees the things which are to happen, simply because he has decreed that they are so to happen, it is vain to debate about prescience, while it is clear that all events take place by his sovereign appointment.

JOHN CALVIN, *Institutes*, 1536

When we attribute foreknowledge to God, we mean that all things have ever been, and perpetually remain, before his eyes, so that to his knowledge nothing is future or past, but all things are present.

JOHN CALVIN, *Institutes*, IV, 1536

Though we can have no conception how the future free actions of man may be known to the Deity, this is not a sufficient reason to conclude that they cannot be known.

THOMAS REID, *Essay on the Active Powers of the Human Mind*, 1822

See also Chance; Determinism; Election; Fatalism; Fate; Free Will; God: His Omniscience; Necessity; Original Sin; Predestination; Providence; Sin; Will.

FORGETFULNESS

The loftier soul must desire to come to a happy forgetfulness . . . all is best when human interest and the memory of them have been put out of the way.

PLOTINUS (205–271), *Ennead* 4

A retentive memory may be a good thing, but the ability to forget is the true token of greatness.

ELBERT HUBBARD (1859–1915), *Notebook*

FORGIVENESS

The remission of sins. For it is by this that the Church on earth stands: it is through this that what has been lost, and was found, is saved from being lost again.

ST. AUGUSTINE, *Enchiridion*, 421

He that thinks he lives without sin does not avoid sin but rather excludes all pardon. . . . And therefore I dare assert it is good that the proud should fall into some broad and disgraceful sin.

ST. AUGUSTINE, *City of God*, XIV, 426

Who more holy among the new people than the Apostles? And yet the Lord would have them pray *forgive us our trespasses*.

ST. AUGUSTINE (345–430), *Contra Duas Epist. Pelog.*, Lib. III

Allah, Most High, says: He who approaches near to me one span, I will approach to him one cubit; and he who approaches near to me one cubit, I will approach near to him one fathom; and whoever approaches me walking, I will come to him running, and he who meets me with sins equivalent to the whole world, I will greet him with forgiveness equal to it.

Mishkat-ul-Masabih, 7th century A.D.

No sin is too big for God to pardon, and none too small for habit to magnify.

BAHYA BEN JOSEPH IBN PAKUDA, *Hobot HaLebabot*, 1040

Oh, God, I say not hear my prayers! I say: Blot with forgiving pen my sins away!

SHAIKH SAADI, *Gulistan*, c. 1265

To speak of unforgivable sin is to impugn divine power.

ST. THOMAS AQUINAS (1225–1274), *Opusc.* xiii, *Compendium Theologiae*

It belongeth to the proper goodness of our Lord God courteously to excuse man.

JULIANA OF NORWICH, *Revelations of Divine Love*, 15th century

In the absolution . . . a distressed sinner is pardoned. By what authority is he pardoned? Not by human command, but by God's command.

MARTIN LUTHER, *Sermon*, 1528

Sin powerfully; God can forgive only a hearty sinner.
> MARTIN LUTHER (1483–1546), quoted by R. Bainton, *Here I Stand*

Where is the foolish person who would think it in his power to commit more than God could forgive?
> ST. FRANCIS OF SALES (1567–1622), *Consoling Thoughts of*, ed. Huguet

If a man do depart in some actions, for an exact obedience of God's will, upon infirmity, or human affection, and not a contempt, God passes it over oftentimes.
> JOHN DONNE, *Sermon*, Funeral of Sir William Cockayne, December 26, 1626

Disconsolate soul, dejected spirit, bruised and broke, ground and trodden, attenuated, evaporated, annihilated heart come back; hear thy reprieve and sue for thy pardon; God will not take thee away in thy sins, thou shalt have time to repent.
> JOHN DONNE, *Sermon*, February 11, 1627

We pardon in the degree that we love.
> LA ROCHEFOUCAULD, *Maxims*, 1665

If I am even with my enemy, the debt is paid; but if I forgive him, I oblige him for ever.
> WILLIAM PENN, *Some Fruits of Solitude*, 1693

Force may subdue, but Love gains; and he that forgives first, wins the laurel.
> WILLIAM PENN, *Some Fruits of Solitude*, 1693

To err is human, to forgive divine.
> ALEXANDER POPE, *An Essay on Criticism*, 1711

A wise man will make haste to forgive, because he knows the true value of time, and will not suffer it to pass away in unnecessary pain.
> SAMUEL JOHNSON, *The Rambler*, December 24, 1751

A man filled with rancor will not be forgiven by God, inasmuch as this man himself has not forgiven.
> ST. TYCHON OF ZADONSK, *Letter*, December 4, 1764

How could man live at all if he did not give absolution every night to himself and all his brothers?
> J. W. VON GOETHE (1749–1832), quoted in *Goethe and Faust*, by F. M. Stawell and G. L. Dickinson

"I can forgive, but I cannot forget," is only another way of saying, "I will not forgive." A forgiveness ought to be like a cancelled note, torn in two and burned up, so that it can never be shown against the man.
> HENRY WARD BEECHER, *Life Thoughts*, 1858

There is an ugly kind of forgiveness. . . . Men take one who has offended, and set him down before the blowpipe of their indignation, and scorch him, and burn his fault into him; and when they have kneaded him sufficiently with their fiery fists, then—they forgive him.
> HENRY WARD BEECHER, *Life Thoughts*, 1858

Not the Enthusiasm of Humanity alone, nor the great sentences of the Sermon on the Mount alone, but both together, the creative meeting of the Spirit and the Word, brought to life the new virtue of forgiveness.
> J. R. SEELEY, *Ecce Homo*, 1865

No man who will not forgive his neighbour, can believe that God is willing, yea wanting, to forgive *him*.
> GEORGE MACDONALD, *Unspoken Sermons*, 1st Series, 1869

The one thing that cannot be forgiven is the sin of choosing to be evil, of refusing deliverance. It is impossible to forgive that.
> GEORGE MACDONALD, *Unspoken Sermons*, 3rd Series, 1887

Revenge is of death and deadly. Forgiveness has taken *its* place, and forgiving is the giving, and so the receiving of life.

GEORGE MACDONALD (1824–1905), *Selections from,* ed. Dewey

I must practice unlimited forgiveness because, if I did not, I should be wanting in veracity to myself, for it would be acting as if I myself were not guilty in the same way as the other has been guilty towards me.

ALBERT SCHWEITZER, *Civilization and Ethics,* 1923

Jesus said, "Pray ye, Forgive us our trespasses, *as we forgive them that trespass against us.*" This can only mean that the reason we should urge for our own forgiveness is that we have forgiven others. It might even mean that the measure of forgiveness we should demand is the measure of forgiveness we have granted.

ROBERT KEABLE, *The Atlantic Monthly,* December, 1928

Penitence and confession are necessary if one is to possess the forgiving spirit, without which the full sense of forgiveness is impossible.

KIRBY PAGE, *Living Creatively,* 1932

Forgiving love is a possibility only for those who know they are not good, who feel themselves in need of divine mercy.

REINHOLD NIEBUHR, *An Interpretation of Christian Ethics,* 1935

Everyone says forgiveness is a lovely idea, until they have something to forgive.

C. S. LEWIS, *Christian Behavior,* 1943

God is too good, it is said, not to forgive. That is exactly what he does: everything, he forgives everything the moment the heart repents. If the devil repented he would immediately be forgiven. But sin without repentance *cannot* be pardoned.

JACQUES MARITAIN, *Art and Faith,* 1948

The really unforgiveable sin is the denial of sin, because, by its nature, there is now nothing to be forgiven.

FULTON J. SHEEN, *Peace of Soul,* 1949

We are not doomed forever to walk on this knife edge of eternity with the threat of utter loss on one side and some tentative human good on the other. God in his own way has enabled man to walk with faith, with love, and with hope. The way to the new life is forgiveness.

DANIEL D. WILLIAMS, *What Present-Day Theologians Are Thinking,* 1952

Forgiveness is the fragrance the violet sheds on the heel that has crushed it.

Author Unknown

See also Calvary; Compassion; Confession; Despair; Faith; God: His Goodness; God: His Wrath; Grace, Definitions of; Guilt; Jesus Christ as Saviour; Justification; Man and God; Mercy; Penitence; Pity; Providence; Repentance; Revenge; Sin; Sinners.

FORM

If we look at the mere empty shape of things and not at their essential nature, they do not speak to our hearts. We must read into them our own soul and spirit if they are to answer us.

F. W. VON SCHELLING, *Lecture on Relation of the Art of Form to Nature,* 1807

FORNICATION

Fornication is a lapse from one marriage into many.

ST. CLEMENT OF ALEXANDRIA, *Stromateis,* c. 193

The monstrosity of sexual intercourse outside marriage is that those who indulge in it are trying to isolate one kind of union (the sexual) from all other kinds of union which were intended to go along with it and make up the total union.

C. S. LEWIS, *Christian Behavior,* 1943

It is fairly common in both young men and women with high standards of conduct and integrity to have one or two love affairs, involving intercourse, before they find the person they will ultimately marry. . . . Where there is genuine tenderness, an openness to responsibility and the seed of commitment, God is surely not shut out.

> A group of the Religious Society of Friends, England, quoted in *Time*, March 22, 1963

See also Adultery; Premarital Sex; Sex; Sexual Ethics; Sexual Intercourse; Sexual Sin.

FORTITUDE

Nothing happens to anybody which he is not fitted by nature to bear.
> MARCUS AURELIUS, *Meditations of*, c. 170 A.D.

Religion does not say that everything is easy and comfortable, for religion is not meant to fill our minds with illusions but fortitude.
> WILLIAM LYON PHELPS, *Essay on Things*, 1930

FORTUNE

Fortune can take from us nothing but what she gave us.
> PUBLILIUS SYRUS, *Sententiae*, c. 50 B.C.

It is the business of moralists to detect the frauds of fortune, and to show that she imposes upon the careless eye by a quick succession of shadows, which will shrink to nothing in the gripe.
> SAMUEL JOHNSON, *Rambler*, October 6, 1750

See also Riches; Wealth.

FREE WILL

Where we are free to act, we are also free to refrain from acting, and where we are able to say No, we are also able to say Yes.
> ARISTOTLE, *Nicomachean Ethics*, Bk. 111, ch. 5, 340 B.C.

You may fetter my leg, but my will not even Zeus can overpower.
> EPICTETUS, *Discourses*, c. 110 A.D.

No one can rob us of free choice.
> EPICTETUS, *Encheiridion*, c. 110 A.D.

All is foreseen, yet man is endowed with free will.
> AKIBA (50–132 A.D.), *Mishna: Abot*

Not only in works, but also in faith, God has given man freedom of the will.
> ST. IRENAEUS, *Against Heresy*, c. 175

The power of choosing good and evil is within the reach of all.
> ORIGEN, *De principiis*, c. 254

Since He has foreknowledge of our will, that will must exist, of which he has the foreknowledge. . . . Nor could it be a will, if it were not in our power. So he has foreknowledge also of our power over it. My power is not taken away by His foreknowledge.
> ST. AUGUSTINE, *The Problem of Free Choice*, c. 400

Do we then by grace make void free will? God forbid! Nay, rather we establish free will . . . so free will is not made void through grace, but is established, since grace cures the will whereby righteousness is freely loved.
> ST. AUGUSTINE, *On the Spirit and the Letter*, 415

When man by his own free will sinned, then sin being victorious over him, the freedom of his will was lost . . . he who is the servant of sin is free to sin. And hence he will not be free to do right until, being freed from sin.
> ST. AUGUSTINE, *Enchiridion*, 421

It does not follow that, though there is for God a certain order of causes, there must therefore be nothing depending on the free exercise of our own wills, for our wills themselves are included in that order of causes which is certain to God, and is embraced by His foreknowledge.

ST. AUGUSTINE, *The City of God,* Vol. 1, Bk. V, ch. 9, 426

Free will is of itself sufficient for evil but, so far as good is concerned, it does nothing unless aided by all-powerful goodness.

ST. AUGUSTINE, *De correptione et gratia,* ch. 11, 427

A man is led the way he wishes to follow.

HUNA, *Talmud: Makkot,* c. 500

Foreknowledge cannot be held to be a cause for the necessity of future results, and therefore free will is not in any way shackled by foreknowlege.

BOETHIUS, *Consolations of Philosophy,* c. 523

Take away free will and there remaineth nothing to be saved. . . . Salvation is given by God alone, and it is given only to the free-will; even as it cannot be wrought without the consent of the receiver it cannot be wrought without the grace of the giver.

ST. BERNARD, *Treatise Concerning Grace and Free Will,* c. 1128

The theory of man's perfectly free will is one of the fundamental principles of the law of our teacher Moses, and of those who follow the Law.

MAIMONIDES, *Guide for the Perplexed,* 1190

Free will . . . has an essential and natural relation with the good; and a relation by defect and deviation from nature with evil.

ST. THOMAS AQUINAS, *Summa Theologiae,* III, 34, 3, ad. 1, 1272

There is no distinction between what flows from free will, and what is of predestination; as there is no distinction between what flows from a secondary cause and a first cause.

ST. THOMAS AQUINAS, *Summa Theologiae,* Ia, q. 23, 1272

The will remains mistress of its acts and can use it as it likes with reference to any object.

ST. THOMAS AQUINAS (1225–1274), *The Philosophy of St. Thomas Aquinas,* Étienne Gilson

If we mean by "The power of free will" the power which makes human beings fit subjects to be caught up by the Spirit and touched by God's grace, as creatures made for eternal life or eternal death, we should have a proper definition.

MARTIN LUTHER, *Bondage of the Will,* 1525

Even if it could be, I should not want "free-will" to be given me, nor anything to be left in my own hands to enable me to endeavor after salvation. . . . because, even were there no dangers, adversities, or devils, I should still be forced to labor, with no guarantee of success, and to beat my fists at the air.

MARTIN LUTHER, *Bondage of the Will,* 1525

God foresees, foreordains, and accomplishes all things by an unchanging, eternal, and efficacious will. By this thunderbolt free will sinks shattered in the dust.

MARTIN LUTHER, *De servo arbitrio,* 1525

Man is not possessed of free will for good works unless it be assisted by grace, and that special grace which is bestowed on the elect alone.

JOHN CALVIN, *Institutes,* 1536

I confess that mankind has a free-will, but it is to milk kine, to build houses, etc., and no further.

MARTIN LUTHER (1483–1546), *The Table Talk of Martin Luther*

Man, by his fall into a state of sin, hath wholly lost all ability of will to any spiritual good. . . . His grace alone enables him freely to will and to do that which is spiritually good.

> *Westminster Confession of Faith,* Formulary of the Presbyterian Church of Scotland, 1643

That our will is free is self-evident.

> RENÉ DESCARTES, *Principles of Philosophy,* 1644

There is no such thing as free will. The mind is induced to wish for this or that by some cause, and that cause is determined by another cause, and so on back to infinity.

> BARUCH SPINOZA, *Ethics,* 1677

We own no such thing as free will to do good in the fallen state. But the Spirit of the Lord changeth and reneweth the will in the day of His power.

> ISAAC PENNINGTON (1648–1690), *Works,* IV

He produces not only our choice, but also the very freedom that is in our choice. . . . In order to understand that God creates our free will in us, we must understand only that He wills us to be free. But He wills not only that we should be free in power, but that we should be free in its exercise.

> J. B. BOSSUET (1627–1704), *Treatise on Free Will*

If the free Will of God, which is above and superior to Nature, be communicated to the creature, then the creature's free Will must have the same power over its own nature that the Will of God has over that eternal nature which is His own manifestation.

> WILLIAM LAW, *Appeal to All That Doubt,* 1740

Will, then, is not a faculty which can be called free. "Free-will" is a word abso-

lutely devoid of sense, and that which scholars have called "indifference," that is to say, will without cause, is a chimera unworthy to be combated.

> VOLTAIRE, *Philosophical Dictionary,* I, 1764

All theory is against the freedom of the will; all experience for it.

> SAMUEL JOHNSON, *Boswell's Life,* April 15, 1778

The will of a rational being can be his own only if he acts on the idea that it is free, and therefore this idea must, as a practical matter, be ascribed to all rational beings.

> IMMANUEL KANT, *Grundlegung zur Metaphysik der Sitten,* 1785

What else can the freedom of the will be but autonomy, that is, the property of the will to be a law unto itself?

> IMMANUEL KANT, *Critique of Practical Reason,* 1788

The absolute freedom of the will, which we bring down with us from the Infinite into the world of Time, is the principle of this our life.

> J. G. FICHTE (1762–1814), *The Vocation of Man*

I believe that I am a free agent, inasmuch as, and so far as, I have a will, which renders me justly responsible for my actions, omissive as well as commissive.

> SAMUEL TAYLOR COLERIDGE, *Confessio Fidei,* 1816

Freedom is a fundamental character of the will, as weight is of matter. . . . That which is free is the will. Will without freedom is an empty word.

> G. W. F. HEGEL, *Grundlinien der Philosophie des Rechts,* 1821

Everywhere the human soul stands between a hemisphere of light and another of darkness; on the confines of two everlasting hostile empires, necessity and free will.

THOMAS CARLYLE, *Foreign Review,*
July, 1828

To deny the freedom of the will is to make morality impossible.

JAMES A. FROUDE, *Short Studies: Calvinism,* 1871

The more the will submits itself to grace, the more it does all that in it lies to make itself absolutely, fully, and constantly dependent, so much the more will it be free.

J. N. GROU, *Maximes Spirituelles,* 1872

Free Will does not say that everthing that is physically conceivable is also morally possible. It merely says that of alternatives that really *tempt* our will more than one is really possible.

WILLIAM JAMES, *Unitarian Review,*
September, 1884

Either free-will is a fact, or moral judgment a delusion.

JAMES MARTINEAU, *Types of Ethical Theory,* 1886

It is a moral postulate that what ought to be can be, and that bad acts cannot be fated, but that good ones must be possible in their place.

WILLIAM JAMES, *Principles of Psychology,* Vol. II, 1890

The question of free will is insoluble on strictly psychologic grounds.

WILLIAM JAMES, *Psychology, Briefer Course,* 1892

The human will has no more freedom than that of the higher animals, from which it differs only in degree, not in kind.

ERNEST HAECKEL, *The Riddle of the Universe,* 1899

Universal usage throughout civilization, and indeed in uncivilization, tells us that in every detail of intercourse among men we recognize the existence of free will. The

state of mind that denies it is not one of enlightenment, but of muddleheadedness.

THOMAS DWIGHT, *Thoughts of a Catholic Anatomist,* 1912

Evolution knows nothing of free will, all our actions are the necessary outcome of chemical processes.

I. I. METCHNIKOFF, *Nature of Man,* 1916

If God were in no way the cause of our choice, He would not have been able to foresee it infallibly from all eternity; for He alone is eternal, and our free acts are future from all eternity only because He decided to produce them in us and with us, or at least to permit them if they are bad.

REGINALD GARRIGOU-LAGRANGE, *Christian Perfection and Contemplation,* 1927

According to the Buddha the will is free, effort is worth while, man makes his own fate, deeds have consequences, knowledge is possible, the body is not the real self, and death is not its end.

J. B. PRATT, *The Pilgrimage of Buddhism,* 1928

Behind all faith . . . lies the plain fact that man, as a creature of free will, cannot shirk the ultimate responsibility for his own fate.

PAUL ELMER MORE, *The Catholic Faith,* 1931

God . . . created man; He has also created the circumstances under which he lives and acts; but still He has endowed man with discretion to choose how to act. . . . And as he can exercise his discretion or his will in doing a thing or not doing it, he is responsible for his own deeds, and made to suffer the consequences.

MUHAMMAD ALI, *The Religion of Islam,* 1936

A civilization denying free will naturally and inevitably produces slaves, not artists, and in such a civilization few men are artists.

ERIC GILL (1882–1940), *It All Goes Together, Selected Essays*

We can, perhaps, conceive of a world in which God corrected the results of this abuse of free will by his creatures at every moment; so that a wooden beam became soft as grass when it was used as a weapon. . . . But such a world would be one in which wrong actions were impossible, and in which, therefore, freedom of the will would be void.

C. S. LEWIS, *The Problem of Pain,* 1940

To deny free will is to make mankind nothing but driftwood on the inexorable river of fate, and how we jostle one another is beyond our power to help.

J. A. MCWILLIAMS, *Philosophy for the Millions,* 1942

There is little hope for universal and lasting peace simply because God will not destroy man's free will; and so long as man has a free will he has the power of being selfish.

JOHN J. WADE, *Conquering with Christ,* 1942

Free will, though it makes evil possible, is also the only thing that makes possible any love of goodness or joy worth having.

C. S. LEWIS, *The Case for Christianity,* 1943

The will is motivated; but since there is a conflict of motives, the choice is free. . . . Free will involves a genuine indeterminacy, but it is plainly distinct from chance or caprice.

D. J. B. HAWKINS, *Modern Schoolmen,* May, 1949

No amount of libido, or passion, no external force, and no inner prompting to sin can make the human action of man any-

thing but free. We are never tempted beyond our strength. Every moral failure is ours alone, because our choices are our own.

FULTON J. SHEEN, *Lift Up Your Hearts,* 1950

The denial that a man is free to decide means that he is not responsible for the course he adopts.

PAUL WEISS, *Man's Freedom,* 1950

Humanism believes, contrary to all theories of universal predestination, determinism or fatalism, that human beings possess true freedom of creative action and are, within reasonable limits, the masters of their own destiny.

CORLISS LAMONT, *The Independent Mind,* 1951

You can't examine free will in a test tube. Yet, much of what man does for weal or woe springs from this inner life of free choice. Nuclear energy can explode with uncontrollable force. The occasion for its explosion may be controlled by evil or by good men.

THOMAS E. MURRAY, *Address,* December 4, 1951

There is in human conduct an element of will and choice. Without it freedom and democracy are meaningless, scarcely the substance of a dream.

NORMAN THOMAS, *A Socialist's Faith,* 1951

God is not fate nor an impersonal detached determining power. We are not puppets moved hither and yonder by the blind impersonal necessity of omnipotent matter or the sovereignty of divine providence. . . . The future has yet to be made. Our present choices give a new form even to the past so that what it means depends on what we do now.

S. RADHAKRISHNAN, *The Philosophy of,* ed. by P. A. Schlipp, 1952

Learned professors of philosophy or psychology who deny the existence of free will do so only in their professional moments and in their studies and lecture rooms.

> W. T. STACE, *Religion and the Modern Mind,* 1952

Although prone to evil, man is a free agent. His spiritual powers were marred but not destroyed by the Fall.

> *The Salvation Army Handbook of Doctrine,* 1955

Man has a certain amount of free will and there is every possibility to mold his life or to modify his actions. Even the most vicious person can by his own free will and effort become the most virtuous person. One may at any moment change for the better or for the worse.

> VENERABLE U. THITTILA, *The Path of the Buddha,* ed. K. W. Morgan, 1956

A man can be said to exercise free will in a morally significant sense only in so far as his chosen act is one of which he is the sole cause or author, and only if—in the straightforward categorical sense of the phrase—he "could have chosen otherwise."

> CHARLES A. CAMPBELL, *On Selfhood and Godhood,* 1957

To possess free-will is simply to be able to determine the indeterminate; that is, the future—this is implied in the very conception of action. The Agent is the determiner. To deny free-will is to deny the possibility of action.

> JOHN MACMURRAY, *The Self as Agent,* 1958

Looked at from outside (objectively) the will is causally determined and looked at from the inside (subjectively) it is free.

> MAX PLANCK, *The New Science,* 1959

See also Action; Acts; Art; Blasphemy; Chance; Choice; Coercion; Commitment; Conscience; Decision; Democracy; Destiny; Determinism; Election; Evil; Evolution; Fatalism; Fate; Foreknowledge; Freedom; Freedom of Thought and Speech; Freud; God: His Omniscience; Good; Grace; Guilt; Independence; Individual Responsibility; Judgment, God's; Justification; Mechanism; Merit; Morality; Morality and Freedom; Necessity; Obedience; Original Sin; Personality; Predestination; Punishment; Responsibility; Salvation; Self-Will; Sin; Sinners; Will; Works.

FREEDOM

Those whose mind is well grounded in the seven elements of knowledge, who without clinging to anything, rejoice in freedom from attachment, whose appetites have been conquered, and who are full of light, they are free even in this world.

> *Dhammapada,* c. 5th century B.C.

The excess of liberty, whether in States or individuals, seems only to pass into excess of slavery.

> PLATO, *The Republic,* c. 370 B.C.

The good man always acts sensibly, and therefore, he alone is free.

> PHILO, *Every Good Man Is Free,* c. 10 A.D.

Let him then who wishes to be free not wish for anything or avoid anything that depends on others.

> EPICTETUS, *Manual of,* Sec. 14, c. 110 A.D.

He whose body is chained, and his soul unbound, is free.

> EPICTETUS (60–140 A.D.), *Moral Discourses of*

With the Holy Spirit, by whose gift we are justified, we take delight in this, that we sin not,—and that is liberty; without the Spirit we take delight in sin, and that is slavery.

> ST. AUGUSTINE, *De. Spiritu et. litt.,* XVI, 415

Man alone among mortals can resist the constraining power of nature, and he alone among earthly creatures is therefore free.
ST. BERNARD (1091–1153), *Serm. in Cant.*

Virtue cannot be fully attained without liberty and the absence of liberty proves that virtue in its full protection is wanting. Therefore a man is free in proportion to the measure of his virtues, and the extent to which he is free determines what his virtues can accomplish.
JOHN OF SALISBURY, *Policraticus,* 1159

Freedom (or this principle of freedom) is the greatest gift conferred by God on human nature; for through it we have our felicity here as men, through it we have our felicity elsewhere as deities.
DANTE, *De Monarchia,* c. 1300

All who allow themselves a wrong liberty make themselves their own aim and object.
HENRY SUSO (1300–1366), *Life of Blessed Henry Suso by Himself*

To renounce one's liberty is to renounce one's quality as a man, the rights and also the duties of humanity.
JEAN JACQUES ROUSSEAU, *The Social Contract,* 1762

Liberty is not and cannot be anything but the power of doing what we will.
VOLTAIRE, *Philosophical Dictionary, I,* 1764

Natural liberty is a gift of the beneficent Creator to the whole human race, and . . . civil liberty is founded in that, and cannot be wrested from any people without the most manifest violation of justice.
ALEXANDER HAMILTON, *The Farmer Refuted,* 1775

Liberty, rightly understood, is an inestimable blessing, but liberty without wisdom, and without justice, is no better than wild and savage licentiousness.
CHANCELLOR KENT, *Debate in the New York Constitutional Convention,* 1821

Man's freedom is his inner worth. . . . His guilt alone can rob him of it.
MICHAEL BEER, *Clytemnestra,* 1823

Nothing but the recognition and adoption of such universal substantial objects as Right and Law, and the production of a reality that is accordant with them—the State.
G. W. F. HEGEL (1770–1831), *The Philosophy of History,* publ. posth.

Let your cry be for free souls rather than for freedom. Moral liberty is the one really important liberty.
JOSEPH JOUBERT, *Pensées,* 1842

The only freedom which deserves the name, is that of pursuing our own good in our own way, so long as we do not attempt to deprive others of theirs, or impede their efforts to obtain it.
JOHN STUART MILL, *On Liberty,* 1859

To hazard the contradiction—freedom is necessary.
RALPH WALDO EMERSON, *The Conduct of Life,* 1860

Freedom is only necessity understood, and bondage to the highest is identical with true freedom.
WILLIAM JAMES, *Unitarian Review,* September, 1884

When it is established that man's soul is immortal and endowed with reason and not bound up with things material, the foundation of natural liberty is at once most firmly laid.
POPE LEO XIII, *Libertas Humana,* 1888

What do you suppose will satisfy the soul, except to walk free and own no superior?
WALT WHITMAN, "Laws for Creation," *Leaves of Grass,* 1892

Every man is free to do what he will, provided he infringes not upon the equal freedom of any other man.

HERBERT SPENCER, *The Principles of Ethics*, IV, 1898

A man's worst difficulties begin when he is able to do as he likes.

THOMAS HUXLEY, "Address on University Education," *Collected Essays*, 1902, III, 236

Everything that we perceive around us is struggling towards freedom. . . . When the line of action is not a proper one we call it evil, and when the manifestation of it is proper and high we call it good. But the impulse is the same, the struggle towards freedom.

SWAMI VIVEKANANDA (1863–1902), *Works of*

The soul is free, and it is its freedom that tells you every moment that you are free.

SWAMI VIVEKANANDA (1863–1902), *Works of*, I, 255

A man is said to act freely when he acts according to the ultimate ideal of his nature.

J. M. C. MCTAGGART, *Some Dogmas of Religion*, 1906

To be free from everything is to be—nothing. Only nothing is quite free, and freedom is abstract nothingness.

F. H. BRADLEY, *Ethical Studies*, 1927

Freedom simply means the power to carry out your own emotions.

CLARENCE DARROW, *Freedom in the Modern World*, ed. H. M. Kallen, 1928

Unrestrained indulgence kills not merely passion, but, in the end, even amusement. Too much liberty is as life-destroying as too much restraint. The present fashion in love-making is likely to be short, because

love that is psychologically too easy is not interesting.

ALDOUS HUXLEY, *Do What You Will*, 1929

When we have reached the point of measuring the stature of our freedom by the height of the pile of our discarded inhibitions, is anyone minded to die for this eviscerated ghost of that modern liberty which once was sacred because it was important?

WILLIAM ERNEST HOCKING, *What Man Can Make of Man*, 1942

The torch held high in the hand of Liberty scatters the darkness of natural inequality and reveals the royal kinship of all men in God.

ROBERT I. GANNON, *God in Education*, 1943

We shall be outwardly free when we unbind ourselves from slavery within.

NICHOLAS BERDYAEV, *Slavery and Freedom*, 1944

The sense of sharing a common fate, which is the basis of enduring comradeship and love, is also the firmest foundation for a free society.

HENRY ALONZO MYERS, *Are Men Equal?*, 1945

What was called freedom in the European age now past collapsed, and was bound to collapse, because for a long time and at an amazingly deep level it had degenerated into a freedom for godlessness and inhumanity.

KARL BARTH, *Community, Church and State*, 1946

Man is condemned to be free. Condemned, because he did not create himself, yet is nevertheless at liberty, and from the moment that he is thrown into this world he is responsible for everything he does.

JEAN PAUL SARTRE, *Existentialism and Humanism*, 1948

The price we pay for liberty is that so far as a man is free to do right he is also free to do wrong.

L. T. HOBHOUSE, *Elements of Social Justice,* 1949

We are neither free from all conditioning nor inexorably bound. We have neither too much nor too little freedom. We have just enough to be responsible.

PAUL WEISS, *Man's Freedom,* 1950

If freedom is now withering and threatened with extinction, we know the reason. It is because it is impossible for it to live in a materialistic climate where there are no moral principles.

HENRI DANIEL-ROPS, *Christianity and Freedom,* 1952

The more man trusts in and affirms his freedom the more likely he is to misuse the freedom which he confuses with absolute, i.e., divine, freedom.

EMIL BRUNNER, *Eternal Hope,* 1954

The root of freedom is what has been called man's self-transcendence, the capacity of the human mind to stand clear of itself. . . . to determine his action and to manipulate objects as he wills.

JOHN HUTCHISON, *Faith, Reason and Existence,* 1956

Christian freedom is neither the lonely rebellion of an atheistic existentialist nor the self-will of the rugged individualist. It is freedom-in-community.

ROGER L. SHINN, *Religious Education* April, 1958

There are virtually infinite possibilities, both material and moral, wherewith to vindicate freedom against unfreedom, joy of living against tyranny, man against all that is subhuman and inhuman, truth against darkness and falsehood and God against the devil and his works. The only

question is whether the realm of freedom will prove worthy of its possibilities.

CHARLES MALIK, *Address,* Washington, D. C., June 1, 1959

The freedom of the human self is a curse inasmuch as it is the source of spiritual evil in Man, but at the same time is an inestimable treasure inasmuch as it is also the source, the only source, in Man, of spiritual good.

ARNOLD J. TOYNBEE, *A Study of History,* Vol. XII, *Reconsiderations,* 1961

See also Choice; Coercion; Communism; Conscience; Conscience and Law; Conscience and State; Democracy; Desires; Detachment; Determinism; Dictatorship; Election; Fatalism; Fate; Free Will; Freedom, Religious; Freedom and God; Freedom of Thought and Speech; God: His Omniscience; Independence; Individual; Individual Responsibility; Liberties; Morality and Freedom; Natural Law; Necessity; Obscenity; Opinions; Power; Predestination; Reason; Responsibility; Rights; Selflessness; Slavery; Suicide; Truth; Will.

FREEDOM, RELIGIOUS

It is one of the rights of man and privileges of nature that everyone should worship according to his own convictions. One man's religion neither harms nor helps another's. It is no part of religion to compel religion.

TERTULLIAN, *Ad Scapulam,* c. 212

We, Constantine and Licinius the emperors, having met in concord at Milan and having set in order everything which pertains to the common good and public security, are of the opinion that among the various things which we perceived would profit men . . . was to be found the cultivation of religion; we should therefore give both to Christians and to all others free facility to follow the religion which each may desire.

Edict of Milan, March, 313

With regard to those who still hold themselves aloof from us, let them have, if they please, their temples of falsehood; *we* have the glorious edifice of thy truth. We pray, however, that they too may receive the same blessing which thou hast given in accordance with thy nature.

> EMPEROR CONSTANTINE, *Letter to the People of the Eastern Provinces,* quoted in Eusebius, *Ecclesiastical History,* c. 325

It is the will and command of God that . . . permission of the paganish, Jewish, Turkish, or anti-Christian consciences and worships be granted to all men in all nations and countries.

> ROGER WILLIAMS, *The Bloudy Tenant of Persecution,* 1644

Leave every church Independent; not Independent from brotherly Counsel, God forbid it that we should refuse that; but when it comes to power, that one Church shall have the power over the rest, then look for a Beast.

> JOHN COTTON, *An Exposition of the Thirteenth Chapter of the Revelation,* 1656

Rulers ought to employ a page to repeat to them every morning: "See that you do not torment anyone on account of his religious opinions, and that you do not extend the power of the sword to touch the conscience."

> JOSEPH GLANVILLE, *The Vanity of Dogmatizing,* 1661

For no man can, if he would, conform his faith to the dictates of another. All the life and power of true religion consists in the outward and full persuasion of the mind; and faith is not faith without believing.

> JOHN LOCKE, *A Letter Concerning Toleration,* 1685

The legitimate powers of government extend to such acts only as are injurious to others. But it does me no injury for my neighbor to say there are twenty Gods, or no God.

> THOMAS JEFFERSON, *Notes on Virginia,* 1779

Convinced that our Religious Liberties were as essential as our Civil, my endeavors have never been wanting to encourage and promote the one, while I have been contending for the other.

> GEORGE WASHINGTON, *To the Ministers, Elders, and Deacons of the Reformed Protestant Dutch Church, Kingston, N. Y.,* November 16, 1782

It is the duty of every man to render to the Creator such homage, and such only, as he believes to be acceptable to him. This duty is precedent both in order of time and degree of obligation, to the claims of the Civil Society.

> JAMES MADISON, *Memorials and Remonstrances,* 1785

Whilst we assert a freedom to embrace, to profess, and to observe the Religion which we believe to be of divine origin, we cannot deny an equal freedom to those whose minds have not yet yielded to the evidence which has convinced us.

> JAMES MADISON, *Memorials and Remonstrances,* 1785

The liberty enjoyed by the people of these States, of worshipping Almighty God agreeably to their consciences, is not only among the choicest of their blessings, but also of their rights.

> GEORGE WASHINGTON, *Reply to Address sent by the Religious Society called Quakers,* September 28, 1789 (Washington's reply undated)

If I could have entertained the slightest apprehension that the constitution framed in the convention, where I had the honor to preside, might possibly endanger the religious rights of any ecclesiastical society, certainly I would never have placed my signature to it.

GEORGE WASHINGTON, *Reply to Address sent by the General Committee of the United Baptists Churches in Virginia,* May, 1789

I consider the government of the United States as interdicted by the Constitution from intermeddling with religious institutions, their doctrines, disciples, or exercises.

THOMAS JEFFERSON, *Letter to Samuel Miller,* January 23, 1808

In France I had almost always seen the spirit of religion and the spirit of freedom marching in opposite directions. But in America I found they were intimately united and they reigned in common over the same country.

ALEXIS DE TOCQUEVILLE, *Democracy in America,* I, 1839

Religious liberty is possible only where the coexistence of different religions is admitted, with an equal right to govern themselves according to their several principles.

J. E. E. Dalberg-Acton (Lord Acton), *The Rambler,* 1862

The great rule of human affairs and human interests is left by any free government to individual enterprise and individual action. Religion is eminently one of these interests, lying outside the true and legitimate province of government.

OHIO SUPREME COURT, *Board of Education of Cincinnati v. Minor,* Ohio, 1872

The State is acting against the laws and dictates of nature whenever it permits the license of opinion and of action to lead minds astray from truth and souls away from the practice of virtue.

POPE LEO XIII, *The Christian Constitution of States,* 1885

Man indeed, is free to obey his reason, to seek moral good and to strive unswervingly after his last end. Yet he is free also to turn aside to all other things . . . and to fall headlong into the destruction which he has voluntarily chosen.

POPE LEO XIII, *Libertas Praestantissimum,* June 20, 1888

The essence of religious liberty is that men should feel that there is nothing whatever that stands between themselves and God.

ARTHUR CHRISTOPHER BENSON, *From a College Window,* 1906

Necessarily religious freedom is the basic life of America, the cement running through all its walls and battlements, the safeguard of its peace and prosperity.

JOHN IRELAND, *Address,* August 11, 1913

No citizen enjoys genuine freedom of religious conviction until the state is indifferent to every form of religious outlook from Atheism to Zoroastrianism.

HAROLD LASKI, *Grammar of Politics,* 1925

Everyone has the right to freedom of thought, conscience and religion; this right includes freedom to change his religion or belief, and freedom, either alone or in community with others, and in public or in private, to manifest his religion or belief in teaching, practice, worship and observance.

United Nations Universal Declaration of Human Rights, Article 18, 1948

Liberty of religion . . . is not something that state, or an absolutist church offers, but that which the citizen claims and the law protects.

CECIL NORTHCOTT, *Religious Liberty,* 1948

Some freedoms we prize so highly in a true democracy that they are exempted even from the unifying power of majority decision. Such is the freedom to worship God according to one's conscience and to have one's children instructed in the faith of their parents.

ROBERT C. HARTNETT, *The Right to Educate,* 1949

Let them hold to their dogmas, let them worship their Gods, but they do it with cleaner hands and with purer hearts if they refrain from the ironic falsehood that when they force others to do the same, that is for others liberty.

R. M. MacIver, *The Ramparts We Guard,* 1950

All Christian Churches . . . have a prophetic role to play within the national life. It is their duty so to sensitize the conscience of the nation and of all classes and institutions within it that no group of citizens shall arrogate to itself perpetual rights and privileges which it denies to others.

GENERAL ASSEMBLY OF NATIONAL COUNCIL OF CHURCHES, December, 1952

Practical political considerations stemming from the diversity of religious belief and practice in our society, together with an insistence upon the necessity of safeguarding civil liberties if democracy is to survive, now constitute the sole apologetic for the maintenance of the free church system in American life.

W. S. HUDSON, *The Great Tradition of the American Churches,* 1953

To require a man to do a thing which has nothing at all to do with religion is not prohibiting him from a free exercise of religion.

AUSTRALIAN HIGH COURT, *Krygger v. Williams,* 15 C.L.R., 1958 (ruling against a Jehovah's Witness who objected to military service on religious grounds)

It is consistent with the maintenance of religious freedom for the State to restrain actions and courses of conduct which are inconsistent with the maintenance of civil government or prejudicial to the continued existence of the community.

AUSTRALIAN HIGH COURT, *Krygger v. Williams,* 15 C.L.R., 1958 (ruling against a Jehovah's Witness who objected to military service on religious grounds)

A religious body which denies legitimate freedom is in danger of becoming a demonic institution which blasphemously claims to be an absolute.

W. NORMAN PITTENGER, *The Churchman,* September, 1958

Every individual . . . has a constitutional right personally to be free from religion but that right is a shield, not a sword, and may not be used to compel others to adopt the same attitude.

JUSTICE BERNARD S. MEYER, N. Y. Supreme Court, decision of August 24, 1959

Religious liberty includes freedom to change one's religion or belief without consequent social, economic and political disabilities. Implicit in this right is the right freely to maintain one's belief or disbelief without external coercion or disability.

WORLD COUNCIL OF CHURCHES, 1961

What our constitution indispensably protects is the freedom of each of us, be he Jew or agnostic, Christian or atheist, Buddhist or free thinker, to believe or disbelieve, to worship or not to worship, to pray or keep silent, according to his own conscience, uncoerced and unrestrained by government.

JUSTICE POTTER STEWART, dissenting opinion, U. S. Supreme Court, Prayer and Bible Reading in the Public Schools, June 17, 1963

Every human being has the right to honor God according to the dictates of an upright conscience, and therefore the right to worship God privately and publicly.

POPE JOHN XXIII, *Pacem in Terris,* April, 1963

The exercise of religion, of its very nature, consists before all else in those internal, voluntary, and free acts whereby man sets the course of his life directly toward God. No merely human power can either command or prohibit acts of this kind.

SECOND VATICAN COUNCIL, *A Declaration on Religious Freedom,* December, 1965

The right to religious freedom has its foundation, not in the subjective disposition of the person, but in his very nature. In consequence, the right to this immunity continues to exist even in those who do not live up to their obligation of seeking the truth and adhering to it and the exercise of this right is not to be impeded, provided that just public order be observed.

SECOND VATICAN COUNCIL, *A Declaration on Religious Freedom,* December, 1965

Every man has the duty, and therefore the right, to seek the truth in matters religious, in order that he may with prudence form for himself right and true judgments of conscience, under use of all suitable means.

SECOND VATICAN COUNCIL, *A Declaration on Religious Freedom,* December, 1965

See also Belief; Church and State; Coercion; Conscience; Conscientious Objector; Democracy; Dogmatism; Error; Faith; Free Will; Freedom; Freedom and God; Government; Heresy; Independence; Pacifism; Pluralism; Religion; Religious Test for Office; Rights; Rulers; State, the; Will; Worship.

FREEDOM AND GOD

The soul of man must needs be more free while it continues to gaze on the Divine mind.

BOETHIUS, *Consolations of Philosophy,* c. 525

God's service spells freedom.

JUDAH HALEVI, *Cuzari,* c. 1135

In regenerate state, man is free in the true and proper sense of the term. His intellect is enlightened by the Holy Spirit to understand the mysteries and the will of God; and the will is changed by the Spirit and endowed with the power freely to will and to do what is good.

HENRY BULLINGER, *The Helvetic Confession,* 1536

There can be no prescription old enough to supersede the law of nature, and the grant of God almighty, who has given to all men a natural right to be *free.*

JAMES OTIS, *Rights of the British Colonists Asserted and Proved,* 1764

And can the liberties of a nation be thought secure, when we have removed their only firm basis, a conviction in the minds of the people that these liberties are the gift of God? That they are not to be violated but by his wrath? Indeed, I tremble for my country when I reflect that God is just; that His justice cannot sleep forever.

THOMAS JEFFERSON, *Notes on Virginia,* 1784

If liberty is to be saved, it will not be by the doubters, the men of science, or the materialists; it will be by religious conviction, by the faith of individuals, who believe that God wills man to be free but also pure.

SAMUEL TAYLOR COLERIDGE, *Aids to Reflection,* 1825

God grants liberty to those who love it, are always ready to guard and defend it.
> DANIEL WEBSTER, *Address,* January 26, 1830

The more we are morally necessitated to the good, the more we shall be free as God is free, who is necessitated to good by His very nature.
> J. N. PÈRE GROU, *Maximes Spirituelles,* 1872

To reject the supreme authority of God, and to cast off all obedience to Him in public matters, or even in private and domestic affairs, is the greatest perversion of liberty.
> POPE LEO XIII, *Libertas Humana,* 1888

Freedom consists not in refusing to recognize anything above us, but in respecting something which is above us; for by respecting it, we raise ourselves to it, and by our very acknowledgement make manifest that we bear within ourselves what is higher, and are worthy to be on a level with it.
> J. W. VON GOETHE, *Maxims and Reflections,* ed. B. Saunders, 1892

No man in this world attains to freedom from any slavery except by entrance into some higher servitude. There is no such thing as an entirely free man conceivable.
> PHILLIPS BROOKS (1835–1893), *Perennials*

Christianity promises to make men free; it never promises to make them independent.
> W. R. INGE, *The Philosophy of Plotinus,* 1918

If man were free, God would cease to exist.
> GEORGES CLEMENCEAU, *In the Evening of My Thoughts,* 1929

There is in Christianity a strong sense, not only of the value but of the *moral necessity* of freedom. The Christian not only demanded liberty; he took it.
> EVERETT DEAN MARTIN, *Liberty,* 1930

When your immortal souls took on flesh, they became even as the Son of Man was—bound. No man is free—we are not free of one another—we can never be free of God.
> FATHER ANDREA in Pearl Buck's *The First Wife and Other Stories,* 1933

Freedom has opened the path of evil to man, it is proof of freedom, and man must pay the price. The price is suffering, and by it the freedom that has been spoiled and turned into its contrary is reborn and given back to man. Therefore is Christ the Saviour freedom itself.
> NICHOLAS BERDYAEV, *Dostoevsky,* 1934

There is no freedom without . . . fear of God.
> LEO BAECK, *Essence of Judaism,* 1936

Christian freedom is an inner or eschatological freedom for which it is irrelevant how far the State extends its claim in the sphere of the social life. The freedom of the natural man and his subordination to the commands of the State is a matter of political responsibility.
> *The Churches Survey Their Task: Report of the Conference at Oxford,* 1937

The liberty possessed by souls yielded up to God, brings them peace and deep joy; they know that God is a Father full of goodness, that He loves them and will bring them to Himself.
> DOM COLUMBA MARMION, *Words of Life,* 1939

The true freedom of the world—the only freedom that can free man in the depths of his personality—depends on keeping open the channels of revelation, preserving the Word of Truth and communicating the Spirit of Life.
> CHRISTOPHER DAWSON, *Dublin Review,* July, 1942

The moment a nation ceases to rest heavily upon God it turns the hands of the clock back to savagery. Religion is the bulwark of freedom.

> JOSEPH R. SIZOO, *On Guard,* 1942

Man's freedom is real but never beyond the measure of God's ultimate sovereignty.

> NELS F. S. FERRÉ, *Faith and Reason,* 1946

Liberty does not mean that we have the right to cast aside the laws of God and the legitimate regulations of those who govern us.

> FRANCIS J. McCONNELL, *Morality and Government,* 1949

In any context that separates man from the creative and sustaining hand of God there can be no freedom.

> CATHOLIC BISHOPS OF THE U. S., November, 1952

The recession of freedom coincides with the recession of *lived* Christianity, with the obliteration of the concept of one's neighbor and of that human brotherhood founded on the fatherhood of God.

> GUSTAVE THIBON, *Christianity and Freedom,* 1952

There is no greater possible assertion of human freedom than man's refusal to despair of his God.

> MICHAEL MASON, *The Centre of Hilarity,* 1959

Without God, there is no limit fixed to the ever renewed and restless *deployment* of human freedom.

> PAUL RAMSEY, *Nine Modern Moralists,* 1962

All in the Church must preserve unity in essentials. But let all, according to the gifts they have received enjoy a proper freedom, in their various forms of spiritual life and discipline, in their different liturgical rites, and even in their theological elaborations of revealed truth.

> SECOND VATICAN COUNCIL, *Decree on Ecumenism,* November, 1964

See also Christianity; Church and State; Coercion; Holy Spirit; Natural Law; Religion; State, the.

FREEDOM OF THOUGHT AND SPEECH

To speak freely what is dictated by a clear conscience befits the nobly born.

> PHILO (20 B.C.?–40 A.D.?), *Every Good Man Is Free*

In those things which do not come under the obligation of faith, the saints were at liberty to hold divergent views, just as we ourselves are.

> ST. THOMAS AQUINAS *In Sent.* II Dist. q. 1, a. 3, 1256

Preserve in everything freedom of mind. Never spare a thought for what men may think, but always keep your mind so free inwardly that you could always do the opposite.

> ST. IGNATIUS LOYOLA, *Spiritual Exercises,* 1548

Not only is freedom of thought and speech compatible with piety and the peace of the State, but it cannot be withheld without destroying at the same time both the peace of the State and piety itself.

> BARUCH SPINOZA, *Theological-Political Treatise,* 1670

Liberty of thought is in itself a good; but it gives an opening to false liberty.

> JOHN HENRY NEWMAN, *Apologia pro Vita Sua,* 1864

Judaism, which is throughout rationalistic, is the sole stronghold of free thought in the religious sphere.

> HEINRICH GRAETZ, *Jewish Quarterly Review,* 1888

If unbridled license of speech and of writing be granted to all, nothing will remain sacred and inviolate; even the highest and truest mandates of natures, justly held to be the common and noblest heritage of the human race, will not be spared.

POPE LEO XIII, *Libertas Humana,* 1888

No one has the right to blaspheme God, or to spread false reports about his fellow men, or to advocate treason. But the reasonable expression of one's opinions, including constructive criticism of the policy followed by public officials, belongs to every citizen as a free, intelligent being.

FRANCIS J. MCCONNELL, *Morality and Government,* 1949

In the most civilized and progressive countries freedom of discussion is recognized as a fundamental principle.

C. E. M. JOAD, *The Recovery of Belief,* 1952

There is no foundation in the supposed right to indiscriminate liberty in art and in the plea that thought and the imparting of information are free; higher values are at stake.

POPE PIUS XII, *Apostolic Letter,* January 1, 1954

See also Art; Blasphemy; Coercion; Conscience; Error; Judaism; Literature; Rights; Speech; Thinking; Thought; Truths, Conflict of.

FREUD

Freud has unfortunately overlooked the fact that man has never yet been able single-handed to hold his own against the powers of darkness—that is, of the unconscious. Man has always stood in need of the spiritual help which each individual's own religion held out to him. . . . It is this which lifts him out of his distress.

CARL JUNG, *Modern Man in Search of a Soul,* 1933

The man who has any insight at all into the Cross of Christ simply stands aghast at the thought that Christian men should feel that Freud has the secret which their religion fails to give.

A. VICTOR MURRAY, *Personal Experience and the Historic Faith,* 1939

Freud's discarding of moral values has contributed toward making the analyst just as blind as the patient.

KAREN HORNEY, *Our Inner Conflicts,* 1945

Freud's scientific label permits the nicest girl to discuss intimate sexual details with any man, the two stimulating each other erotically during the talk while wearing poker faces, and at the same time proving themselves learned and liberated.

EMIL LUDWIG, *Dr. Freud,* 1947

The new understanding of man which arose with Freud . . . can be ignored by the religious thinker with no more impunity than would attend his overlooking the discoveries of Darwin in the nineteenth century and Einstein in the twentieth.

ROLLO MAY, *Liberal Learning and Religion,* ed. A. N. Wilder, 1951

If Freud had told some of his patients, "What you call religion is actually your neurosis," instead of claiming that religion is a neurosis, he would have stated a frequently observed truth.

KARL STERN, *The Third Revolution,* 1954

What impresses me in reading Freud is not so much his negative attitude toward the truth and value of religion, but his preoccupation with religion as a power in human life.

SEWARD HILTNER, *Pastoral Psychology,* January, 1955

Nowhere in Freud's principal writings is there the slightest indication that he ever dreamed of what religion at its best means to men and women.

SAMUEL M. THOMPSON, *A Modern Philosophy of Religion,* 1955

Freud's basic beliefs require incorporation in any philosophy or theology that is to be relevant to the best knowledge and insight that man has into himself and his universe.

SEWARD HILTNER, *Pastoral Psychology,* November, 1956

Freud's selection of religious data is almost as unfair as could be arranged. All of his major illustrations are of three related kinds, the pathological, the primitive and the infantile.

DAVID E. TRUEBLOOD, *Philosophy of Religion,* 1957

However sincere our sympathy for the man who lives in frustration and turmoil because as a child he was not permitted to kill his father and possess his mother, we cannot help wondering how mankind could have managed so well before Freud discovered his "Oedipus Complex."

FRANZ E. WINKLER, *Man: The Bridge Between Two Worlds,* 1960

He showed . . . the enormous importance of man's unconscious in his everyday activities of thought and action. Carried to its extreme conclusion, Freud and his followers have seen in this discovery the end of free will.

J. DOMINIAN, *Psychiatry and the Christian,* 1962

See also Psychiatrists; Psychiatry; Psychoanalysis; Psychology; Unconscious Mind.

FREUDIANISM

The "one God" satisfied the narcissistic craving of the beloved Ego for an omnipotent projection of its own adoration.

CAVENDISH MOXON, *Freudian Essays on Religion and Science,* 1925

Freudianism is essentially even more anti-Christian in its implications than the ethical theory of Marxism. For, in setting up the infantile appetites as the basis of all life of the soul and the spirit it ranges virtue—to speak in Christian terminology—under sin, it places the ultimate origins of the recognition of the highest values in the flesh.

J. HUIZINGA, *In the Shadow of Tomorrow,* 1936

See also Dreams; Freud; Mind; Psychiatrist; Psychiatry; Psychoanalysis; Psychology; Unconscious Mind.

FRIENDSHIP

Friendship with a man is friendship with his virtue, and does not admit of assumptions of superiority.

Mencius, c. 300 B.C.

There is a superior friendship that is founded not on custom, but on reason, in which one loves a man because of loyalty and mutual good-will. . . . If we find anything superior to this, it is divine. Man begins to love God, and he will love nothing in man but God.

ST. AUGUSTINE (354–430), *Sermon,* 385.3

Take not the Jews and the Christian for friends. . . . Choose not your fathers nor your brothers for friends if they take pleasure in disbelief rather than in faith.

Koran, v and ix, c. 625

Holy Friendship that has medicine for all the wretchedness is not to be despised. From God it truly is, that amid the wretchedness of this exile, we be comforted with the counsel of friends until we come to Him.

RICHARD ROLLE (c. 1300–1349), *The Fire of Love,* Bk. 2

Christian Charity is Friendship to all the world . . . friendship expanded like the face of the sun when it mounts above the eastern hills.

JEREMY TAYLOR, *A Discourse of the Nature and Offices of Friendship,* 1657

Friendship . . . is an Union of Spirits, a Marriage of Hearts, and the Bond thereto Virtue.

WILLIAM PENN, *Fruits of Solitude,* 1693

I awoke this morning with devout thanksgiving for my friends, the old and the new. Shall I not call God, the Beautiful, who daily showeth himself so to me in his gifts.

RALPH WALDO EMERSON, "Friendship," *Essays,* 1844

Friendship is the only religion possible to moderns. Our God is a domestic God, and that fine sentiment which binds persons to each other is the only piety practical and efficient.

BRONSON ALCOTT (1799–1888), *The Journals of*

To become Love, Friendship needs what Morality needs to become Religion—the fire of emotion.

RICHARD GARNETT, Preface, *Der Flagello Myrteo,* 1897

The very possibility of friendship with God transfigures life. The religious convictions, thus, tend inevitably to deepen every human friendship, to make it vastly more significant.

HENRY CHURCHILL KING, *The Laws of Friendship,* 1909

See also Brotherhood; Charity; Community; Fellowship; Love, Human.

FRUSTRATION

The only way to escape from ultimate frustration for every living intelligence . . . lies through this formula: "I am life"

or what is practically the same thing, "I am Man."

H. G. WELLS, *Anatomy of Frustration,* 1936

A life without frustration is not to be imagined otherwise than a fanciful dream. . . . Frustration pertains to the very nature of the human situation. . . . There is no reason why a man should do "as he pleases."

RUDOLF ALLERS, *Perspectives on a Troubled Decade,* ed. Bryson, Finkelstein and MacIver, 1950

FULFILLMENT

Every facet of the Christian revelation . . . points to the impossibility of man fulfilling the true meaning of his life and reveals sin to be primarily derived from his abortive attempts to do so.

REINHOLD NIEBUHR, *Nature and Destiny of Man,* II, 1943

FUNDAMENTALISM

Militant fundamentalism is a twentieth century movement of protest and unrest; it is apocalyptic, prophetic, critical of modern life and apprehensive of the future.

HERBERT WALLACE SCHNEIDER, *Religion in the 20th Century,* 1952

The Fundamentalist position also served to justify the contention of the religiously emancipated that the churches, despite their pretensions to the contrary, did represent a culturally out-of-date way of thinking which modern man could not accept.

W. S. HUDSON, *The Great Tradition of the American Churches,* 1953

The crass literal interpretation of the Bible without regard for literary forms and literary background.

JOHN L. MCKENZIE, *The Two-Edged Sword,* 1956

Fundamentalism errs in assuming that God gives *information* about himself. The classical Protestant counters by asserting that God gives *himself*.

ROBERT MCAFEE BROWN, *Patterns of Faith in America Today*, ed. F. E. Johnson, 1957

The fault inherent in fundamentalism is the result of a misguided determination to cling to a superficial meaning of the Bible at all costs—even the cost of real understanding.

DAVID M. STANLEY, *Theological Studies*, Vol. 20, 1959

While the doctrine purported to come from Scripture, scrutiny showed that it derived from the conviction that possession of truth is the same thing as possession of virtue.

EDWARD J. CARNELL, *Christian Century*, August 26, 1959

From the standpoint of classical Christianity the Fundamentalist position is a new idolatry, "bibliolatry," which makes the Bible an object of faith at least alongside God, if not instead of him.

ALBERT T. MOLLEGEN, *Christianity and Modern Man*, 1961

See also Conservatism; Neo-Orthodoxy.

FUNERALS

We arrange our funerals as simply as our lives; we place no fading garland upon the grave, but await from God an undying crown of immortal flowers; quiet, modest, confident in the generosity of our God, we enliven our hope of future happiness by faith in His ever-present majesty.

MARCUS MINUCIUS FELIX, *Octavius*, 3rd century A.D.

Earth to earth, ashes to ashes, dust to dust; in sure and certain hope of the Resurrection.

The Book of Common Prayer (Burial Service), 1662

Nowhere is there a lack of concern in the matter of death, care of the dead, or readjustment of the individuals and groups involved. The conceptions of body and spirit, after-life, and after-world may and do vary greatly in different societies, in different religious beliefs, and in different continents. Yet the crisis of death is universally recognized wherever there is human society and culture. Consequently, ceremony and ritual give meaning to death and funerary behavior.

ROBERT W. HOBENSTEIN and WILLIAM M. LAMBERS, *Funeral Customs the World Over*, 1960

See also Burial; Dead; Death.

FURY

To be Furious in Religion is to be Irreligiously Religious.

WILLIAM PENN, *Some Fruits of Solitude*, 1718

FUTILITY

When I look upon the tombs of the great, every emotion of envy dies in me. . . . When I see kings lying by those who deposed them, when I consider rival wits placed side by side, or the holy men that divided the world with their contests and disputes, I reflect with sorrow and astonishment on the little competitions, factions, and debates of mankind.

JOSEPH ADDISON (1672–1719), *Meditations in Westminster Abbey*

If we are to be saved from our futility we must recover the faculty of being still: we must make an enclave of silence within our own souls.

GERALD VANN, *The High Green Hill*, 1951

FUTURE

The past and present are only our means; the future is always our end. Thus we

never really live, but only hope to live. Always looking forward to being happy, it is inevitable that we should never be so.
BLAISE PASCAL, *Pensées,* 1670

The future is lighted for us with the radiant colors of hope. Strife and sorrow shall disappear. Peace and love shall reign supreme.The dream of poets, the lesson of priest and prophet, the inspiration of the great musician, is confirmed in the light of modern knowledge.
JOHN FISKE, *The Destiny of Man,* 1884

The more one studies society, the more one feels that the future will belong either to Jesus Christ or to coercive mechanism.
SHAILER MATTHEWS, *Is God Emeritus?,* 1940

If the future logically pre-exists in the present state of the universe, why does it require a certain time to become present?
MILIC CAPEK, *Review of Metaphysics,* September, 1951

See also Determinism; Election; Eternal; Hope; Necessity; Predestination; Time.

GAMBLING

Gambling is the child of avarice, the brother of iniquity, and the father of mischief.
GEORGE WASHINGTON, *Letter,* January 15, 1783

Gambling promises the poor what property performs for the rich: something for nothing. That is why the Bishops dare not denounce it fundamentally.
GEORGE BERNARD SHAW, *Socialism of,* ed. J. Fuchs, 1926

We affirm again our vigorous opposition to gambling as an insidious menace both to personal character and social morality.
GENERAL BOARD OF NATIONAL COUNCIL OF CHURCHES, March 26, 1951

See also Avarice; Chance; Fatalism; Fate.

GEHENNA. See HELL

GENEROSITY. See LIBERALITY

GENESIS

Unless every one of these legends is a myth, involving, as I indeed believe, some secret interpretation, they are filled with blasphemies against God.
JULIAN THE APOSTATE (332–363), *Against the Galileans*

The book of Genesis contains a record of the dispensation of natural religion, or paganism, as well as of the patriarchal.
JOHN HENRY NEWMAN, *The Arians of the Fourth Century,* 1833

It is not history in the strict sense. . . . It is rather history surrounded with a halo of natural poetry—the traditional history of the nation in the poetic form it has assumed after passing for centuries through the fresh, creative national spirit.
ALEX R. GORDON, "The Religious Value of the Narratives in Genesis," *Hibbert Journal,* IV, 1906

We may not call in doubt the literal historical sense of Genesis with regard to the special creation of man.
BIBLICAL COMMISSION OF ROMAN CATHOLIC CHURCH, 1909

The conception of the order of creation in Genesis is also in principle correct: there has been an advance from a lower comparatively unorganized state of matter through a gradation of levels up to man. That the description does not tally in detail with the story in the rocks . . . detracts not in the least from the divine inspiration of the poet who gave us the true intuition—that to understand the origin of the world it requires more than primal matter, whatever that may be. It requires also divine Genius.
J. E. BOODIN, *God and Creation,* 1934

If a person prefers to interpret the words of Genesis literally and to believe that God made the body of Adam out of mud, fashioning it somewhat after the manner of a potter making a pot or pan, and then blowing upon the statue of mud, caused it suddenly to start walking and talking, he contradicts no dogma of the Christian faith.

JOHN A. O'BRIEN, *The Origin of Man,* 1947

To declare *a priori* that these narratives do not contain history in the modern sense of the word would easily lead to the idea that they do not contain history in any sense of the word, whereas they relate, in the language which is simple and figured and which is adapted to the minds of a less developed humanity, the fundamental truths presupposed in the economy of salvation, as well as a popular description of the origins of the human race and of the chosen people.

Letter of the Biblical Commission to Cardinal Suhard, 1948

Its [Genesis'] God is transcendent and yet so human; its man so earthly and yet so godlike. Its appeal is universal and yet reads as if it were intended for us alone. Its air is familiar and yet an immortal freshness rests upon it.

SOLOMON GOLDMAN, *In the Beginning,* 1949

It is Jewish genius brooding on God. It is the progenitors of the Jewish people examining and discarding the views of Creator and creation universally held in their day. It was an upheaval in the mind and conscience of man that occasioned the differences between the Biblical and the pagan narratives.

SOLOMON GOLDMAN, Preface, *In the Beginning,* 1949

See also Adam; Bible; Bible: Its Inspiration; Creation; Evolution; Nature and God; Old Testament; Science; Science and Creation.

GENIUS

What is genius but that productive power which leads to actions that can show their faces before God and men, and which for that very reason have results and duration.

J. W. VON GOETHE (1749–1832), *Goethe's Opinions,* ed. O. Wencksterns

To believe your own thoughts, to believe that what is true for you in your private heart is true for all men,—that is genius.

RALPH WALDO EMERSON, "Self-Reliance," *Essays,* 1841

Genius is the clearer presence of God Most High in a man. Dim, potential in all men, in this man it has become clear, actual.

THOMAS CARLYLE, *Past and Present,* 1843

Genius on earth is God giving Himself. Whenever a masterpiece appears, a distribution of God is taking place. The masterpiece is a variety of the miracle.

VICTOR HUGO, *William Shakespeare,* 1864

To Christ, genius was simply an instrument for service, to be displayed only so far as it might be useful.

WILLIAM H. CRAWSHAW, *The Genius of Christ,* 1917

See also Greatness; Intellect; Intellectuals; Mind; Privilege; Scholars.

GENOCIDE

Genocide . . . a denial of the right of existence of human groups . . . shocks the conscience of mankind, results in great losses to humanity . . . and is contrary to moral law and to the spirit and aims of the United Nations.

U. N. GENERAL ASSEMBLY, *Resolution 96,* December 11, 1946

If it were certain that without Jews the world would be a paradise, there could be no valid objection to Auschwitz; but if it is much more probable that the world resulting from such methods would be a hell, we can allow free play to our humanitarian revulsion against cruelty.

BERTRAND RUSSELL, *Philosophy and Politics,* 1947

See also Anti-Semitism; Hatred; Intolerance; Murder; Race.

GENTLENESS

The heart of the gentle is the throne where the Lord reposes.

ST. JOHN CLIMACUS (525–600), *Climax*

GEOLOGY AND SCRIPTURE

If only the Geologists would let me alone, I could do very well, but those dreadful Hammers! I hear the clink of them at the end of every cadence of the Bible verses.

JOHN RUSKIN, *Letters from Venice,* 1851–1852, ed. by J. L. Bradley

GEOMETRY

Geometry existed before the Creation, is co-eternal with the mind of God, *is God himself* (what exists in God that is not God himself?); geometry provided God with a model for the creation and was implanted into man together with God's own likeness—and not merely conveyed to his mind through the eyes.

JOHANNES KEPLER, *Harmonice Mundi,* Lib. iv, 1616

GHETTOS

Were I of Jew blood, I do not think I could ever forgive the Christians; the ghettos would get in my nostrils like mustard or lit gunpowder.

R. L. STEVENSON, 1891, quoted by J. L. Baron, *Stars and Sand,* 1943

See also Anti-Semitism; Intolerance; Racial Injustice; Racial Prejudice.

GIFTS

Just heaven is not so pleased with costly gifts, offered in hope of future recompense, as with the merest trifle set apart from honest gains, and sanctified by faith.

Mahabharata, c. 800 B.C.

Whatever you give to others, give with love and reverence. Gifts must be given in abundance, with joy, humility, and compassion.

Taittiriya Upanishad, prior to 400 B.C.

Although a man truly gives when he avoids evil, because he is acting freely, yet the truest giving is when he does good without being under the penalty of avoiding evil.

J. A. McWILLIAMS, *Philosophy for the Millions,* 1942

See also Almsgiving; Charity.

GLAMOUR

He may draw a crowd without drawing the Divine Presence . . . He may be personally magnetic without being spiritually dynamic.

RALPH W. SOCKMAN, *The Highway of God,* 1941

GLOOM

To see some people you would think that the essential of orthodox Christianity is to have a face so long you could eat oatmeal out of the end of a gas pipe.

WILLIAM A. (BILLY) SUNDAY, *Sermon,* New York, 1914

One of the very worst sins of religious people is that they go about the world looking as if God were dead.

A. MAUDE ROYDEN, *Federal Council Bulletin,* January, 1931

See also Bereavement; Enlightenment; Grief; Light; Pessimism; Sadness; Self-Pity; Sorrow; Tears; Unhappiness.

GLORY

We call that glory vain which we assume to ourselves, either for what is not in us, or for what is in us, and belongs to us, but deserves not that we should glory in it.
> St. Francis of Sales, *Introduction to the Devout Life*, 1609

We seek a perfection of honors on earth, when the fullness of glory is only in heaven. The honor on earth is full of degrees, but no degree admits a perfection: whereas the glory of heaven admits of degrees, but each degree affords a fullness.
> Arthur Warwick, *Spare Minutes*, 1637

What is glory without virtue? A great man without religion is no more than a great beast without a soul.
> Daniel Defoe, *The Instability of Human Glory*, c. 1710

The boast of heraldry, the pomp of pow'r,
And all that beauty, all that wealth e'er gave
Await alike the inevitable hour:
The paths of glory lead but to the grave.
> Thomas Grey, *Elegy in a Country Churchyard*, 1752

God deny you peace, and give you glory.
> Miguel de Unamuno, closing lines of *Tragic Sense of Life*, 1913

See also Egoism; Glory of God; Honor; Nature and God; Office; Pride; Vainglory; Vanity.

GLORY OF GOD

Every substance is like a whole world, and like a mirror of God or of the universe, which they portray. . . . Thus the universe is in some sort multiplied as many times as there are substances, and the glory of God in the same way is multiplied by as many wholly different representations of his work. . . . Every substance bears in some sort the character of God's infinite wisdom and omnipotence and imitates him as much as it can.
> G. W. von Leibniz, *Discourse on Metaphysics*, 1685

Men have dared to say, the glory of God: God created this world for His glory; not that the Supreme Being can have glory; but that men, having no expressions suitable to Him, use for Him those by which they are themselves most flattered.
> Voltaire, *Philosophical Dictionary*, I, 1764

Wherever in anything that God has made, in the glory of it, be it the sky or flower or human face, we see the glory of God, there a true imagination is beholding a truth of God.
> George MacDonald, *Unspoken Sermons*, Third Series, 1889

Light, I found, was a series of tiny electronic impulses sent through space from the sun and stars. . . . And the more I think of it as a scientist, the more do I feel that those gleams of light from the quiet stars which fell upon my eyes as I tended the oxen, were really messages to the soul, declaring the glory of God.
> Michael Pupin, *The American Magazine*, September, 1927

Here and whatever happens here is for the sake of Elsewhere—for God's glory, not for an earthly purpose.
> Frederick J. E. Woodbridge, *An Essay on Nature*, 1940

"The heavens declare the glory of God," they do not contain it. If a man would behold the glory of God, he must look beyond the world.

M. HOLMES HARTSHORNE, *The Promise of Science and the Power of Faith,* 1958

See also Nature; Nature and God; Universe.

GLUTTONY

Keep belly lightly loaded, if mind would
    wisdom see;
For bodies crammed to bursting, make
    empty souls to be.

SHAIKH SAADI, *Gulistan,* c. 1265

See also Alcohol; Desires; Dissipation; Drunkenness; Fasting; Greed; Hedonism; Lust; Pleasure; Sensuality; Wine; Worldliness.

GOAL

It is not a question of the victory of one system over another, but of helping souls to their fulfillment in the truth and in true Christian fellowship.

YVES M. CONGAR, *Divided Christendom,* 1939

We have lost any other basis for conduct than the will to survive, a will that becomes ever feebler and more subject to suicidal turnings upon itself, as a people loses its religious sense of a goal and a purpose beyond mere existence.

LEWIS MUMFORD, *Saturday Review,* January 15, 1950

GOD: APHORISMS AND SAYINGS ABOUT

There is for all mankind but one felicity
—a gracious God.

FLAVIUS JOSEPHUS, *Antiquities of the Jews,* 4.8.2., c. 75 A.D.

God never will be hidden, never will be wanting; always will be understood, always

be heard, always be seen, in such manner as he wishes.

TERTULLIAN, *De Testimonio animae,* c. 199

God is not what you imagine or what you think you understand. If you understand you have failed.

ST. AUGUSTINE, *In Boet. de Trinitate,* c. 397

We shall see Him face to face, if we now see Him by faith.

ST. AUGUSTINE, *Ennaration on Psalm XCVII,* c. 415

Since all those who think of God think of something living, only they can think of Him without absurdity who think of Him as life itself.

ST. AUGUSTINE, *On Christian Doctrine,* 427

All things can be said of God, yet is nothing worthily said of God.

ST. AUGUSTINE (354–430), *Sermon LII*

If anyone, having seen God, understands what he saw, he did not see Him, but some of His creatures that are existing and known.

DIONYSIUS THE PSEUDO-AREOPAGITE, c. 5th century A.D.

Almost everything said of God is unworthy, for the very reason that it is capable of being said.

POPE ST. GREGORY THE GREAT, *Magna moralia,* 584

If ye do not recognize God, at least recognize His signs.

AL-HALLAJ (10th century), quoted in A. J. Arberry, *Sufism*

The less theorizing you do about God, the more receptive you are to his inpouring.

MEISTER ECKHART (1260?–1327?), R. B. Blakney, *Meister Eckhart*

He may well be loved, but not thought. By love He be gotten and holden; but by thought never.
The Cloud of Unknowing, 14th century

God alone, who is eternal and incomprehensible, is the whole solace and comfort of the soul.
THOMAS À KEMPIS, *Imitation of Christ,* 1441

It is a peculiar property of His glory not to have any intercourse with iniquity and uncleanness.
JOHN CALVIN, *Institutes,* II, 1536

I fear God, yet am not afraid of Him.
THOMAS BROWNE, *Religio Medici,* 1642

What He has without measure He bestows with measure that our weakness may be able to bear it.
J. B. BOSSUET, *Discourse on Universal History,* II, 1675

Note that God has never exerted himself, nor rested: his work is rest, his rest is work.
ANGELUS SILESIUS (1624–1677), *Cherubic Pilgrim*

God is a spirit, a fire, an essence and a light; and yet again he is none of these things.
ANGELUS SILESIUS (1624–1677), *Cherubic Pilgrim*

In the opinion that there is a God, there are difficulties; but in the contrary opinion there are absurdities.
VOLTAIRE, *Traité de Metaphysique,* Ch. II, 1738

He will not suffer Himself to be transformed by men and be a nice . . . human God: He will transform men, and that He wills out of love.
SÖREN KIERKEGAARD, *Training in Christianity,* 1850

God is, and all is well.
J. G. WHITTIER, *My Birthday,* 1871

The beginning and end of all things is in God.
HEINRICH HEINE, *Romantic School,* Pref. April 2, 1833

I believe in God as the Supreme Being. I know not what the person of omnipotence and omnipresence is, or what infinite includes, therefore I worship that which I can conceive, first as Father and Mother; then as thought ascends the scale of being to diviner consciousness, God becomes to me . . . divine Principle—which I worship.
MARY BAKER EDDY, *Miscellaneous Writings: Prose Works Other than Science and Health,* 1896

Vedanta [Hindu] says there is nothing that is not God. . . . The living God is within you. . . . The only God to worship is the human soul in the human body. . . . Man is the greatest of all temples . . . the moment I have realized God sitting in the temple of every human body, that moment I stand in reverence before every human being and see God in him, that moment I am free from bondage, everything that binds vanishes and I am free.
SWAMI VIVEKANANDA, *Yoga and Other Works,* ed. by Swami Nikhilananda, from a speech delivered in London in 1896

To the masses who could not conceive anything higher than a Personal God he [Jesus] said: "Pray to your Father in Heaven." To others who could grasp a higher idea, He said: "I am the vine, and ye are the branches." But to His disciples to whom He revealed himself more fully, he proclaimed the highest truth, "I and the Father are one."
SWAMI VIVEKANANDA (1863–1902), *Yoga and Other Works,* ed. by Swami Nikhilananda

Most persons would "listen on their knees" to anyone who would make God absolutely real to them.

> RUFUS JONES, *Social Law in the Spiritual World,* 1904

The one Ego, the one Mind, or Spirit called God is infinite individuality, which supplies all form and comeliness and which reflects reality and divinity in individual spiritual man and things.

> MARY BAKER EDDY, *Science and Health,* 1908

I shall always be more certain that God is, than what He is.

> WILLIAM E. HOCKING, *The Meaning of God in Human Experience,* 1912

God is an Unutterable Sigh in the Human Heart, said the old German mystic.

> HAVELOCK ELLIS, *Impressions and Comments,* 1914

We must not infer that because God is good He is good-natured.

> MARGOT ASQUITH, *Autobiography,* III, 1922

God does not exist, because He is useful; He is useful, if you will, because He exists.

> FULTON J. SHEEN, *Religion Without God,* 1928

God . . . strange, isn't it, the obsession, the constant, overwhelming cloud with which that little word overcomes us?

> GAMALIEL BRADFORD, *Biography of the Human Heart,* 1929

I learned from a hillbilly revivalist that God is the *croupier;* and never loses.

> MARTIN H. FISCHER, *Fischerisms,* 1943

The God of the "other religions" is always an idol.

> EMIL BRUNNER, *Revelation and Reason,* 1946

God is of no importance unless He is of supreme importance.

> A. J. HESCHEL, *Man Is Not Alone,* 1951

A denial of God is practically always the result of shutting one eye. It may be for this reason that God gave us two.

> C. A. COULSON, *Science and Christian Belief,* 1955

Everything we say about God is symbolic. Such a statement is an assertion about God which itself is not symbolic.

> PAUL TILLICH, *Systematic Theology,* II, 1957

Nothing is easier than to use the word "God" and mean almost nothing by it.

> DAVID E. TRUEBLOOD, *Philosophy of Religion,* 1957

We affirm our belief in God as the Universal Wisdom, Love, Life, Truth, Power, Peace, Beauty and Joy, in whom we live and move and have our being.

> INTERNATIONAL NEW THOUGHT ALLIANCE, *Declaration of Principles,* 1960

The name of God is Truth.

> Hindu Proverb

The legs of those who require proofs of God's existence are made of wood.

> Persian Proverb

Sometimes a nation abolishes God, but fortunately God is more tolerant.

> ANONYMOUS

We cannot go where God is not, and where God is, all is well.

> ANONYMOUS

GOD: BLASPHEMOUS STATEMENTS ABOUT

Whereas the old God could not receive our homage without degrading Himself by a puerile vanity, the new God will only accept praise which is deserved and which will improve Him as much as ourselves.

AUGUSTE COMTE, *Positive Polity,* 1820

An honest God is the noblest work of man.

ROBERT G. INGERSOLL, *The Gods,* 1872

For the old gods came to an end long ago. And verily it was a good and joyful end of God!

FRIEDRICH NIETZSCHE, *Thus Spake Zarathustra,* 1883

I hate God as I do my personal enemies.

NIKOLAI LENIN, *New Life,* December 16, 1905

If I thought there was an omnipotent God who looked down on battles and deaths and all the waste and horror of this war—able to prevent these things—doing them to amuse Himself, I would spit in His empty face.

H. G. WELLS, *Mr. Britling Sees It Through,* 1916

The socialized human being looks with natural scepticism upon any proposition to the effect that there is a wholly good God.

W. E. HOCKING, *Human Nature and Its Re-Making,* 1918

God as actually possessing deity does not exist, but is an ideal, is always becoming.

S. ALEXANDER, *Mind,* October, 1921

For my own part, the sense of spiritual relief which comes from rejecting the idea of God as a supernatural being is enormous.

JULIAN HUXLEY, *Religion Without Revelation,* 1927

Operationally, God is beginning to resemble not a ruler but the last fading smile of a cosmic Cheshire cat.

JULIAN HUXLEY, *Religion Without Revelation,* 1927

See also Agnosticism; Agnostics; Anti-God Totalitarians; Atheism; Atheists; Blasphemy; Man: His Self-Deification; Rebellion; Religion, Caustic Comments About.

GOD: CONSIDERED AS IMPERSONAL

Call it nature, fate, fortune: all are but names of the one and the same God.

SENECA, *De beneficiis,* c. 63 A.D.

God is himself the Essence of all Essences; all is generated from Him and is originally from Him. And He is therefore called God, because He alone is the Good, the Heart, or [that which is] best; understand, He is the Light and Virtue [or Power] from whence Nature has its Origin.

JACOB BŒHME (1575–1624), *The Three Principles of Divine Essence*

I hold that God is the immanent, and not the extraneous, cause of all things. I say, All is in God; all lives and moves in God.

BARUCH SPINOZA (1632–1677), *Epistle 21, Letters of*

In all conversation between two persons, tacit reference is made as to a third party, to a common nature. That third party or common nature is not social; it is impersonal; is God.

RALPH WALDO EMERSON, "The Over-Soul," *Essays,* 1841

God is another name for human intelligence raised above all error and imperfection, and extended to all possible truth.

WILLIAM ELLERY CHANNING (1780–1842), *Works*

What the physical creation presents to us in itself is a piece of machinery, and . . . men speak of a Divine Intelligence as its Author. . . . the animating principle of a vast and complicated system. . . . It is an instinct or a soul of the world, or a vital power; it is not the Almighty God.

JOHN HENRY NEWMAN, *Parochial and Plain Sermons,* 1843

The latent EGO of the visible Infinite, that is God. God is the invisible made evident. The world concentrated, is God; God expanded, is the world.

VICTOR HUGO, *William Shakespeare,* 1864

There is an Inscrutable Existence everywhere manifested, to which he [the man of science] can neither find nor conceive either beginning or end. Amid the mysteries which become the more mysterious the more they are thought about, there will remain the one absolute certainty, that he is ever in presence of an Infinite and Eternal energy, from which all things proceed.

HERBERT SPENCER, *Principles of Sociology,* ch. 16, 1896

The Impersonal God is a living God, a Principle . . . [it] includes all personalities, is the sum total of everything in the universe, and infinitely more besides.

SWAMI VIVEKANANDA, *Yoga and Other Works,* ed. by Swami Nikhilananda, from a speech delivered in London in 1896

I wish you here to agree to my giving the name of God to the sum of the forces acting in the cosmos as perceived and grasped by human mind.

JULIAN S. HUXLEY, *Science and Religion,* ed. F. S. Marvin, 1923

The binding element in the world. The consciousness which is individual in us, is universal in him: the love which is partial in us is all-embracing in him. Apart from him there could be no world, because there could be no adjustment of individuality.

ALFRED NORTH WHITEHEAD, *Religion in the Making,* 1927

That character of events to which man must adjust himself in order to attain the greatest goods and avoid the greatest evils.

H. N. WIEMAN, *The Wrestle of Religion with Truth,* 1927

The antecedent condition of all being, the unitary ground of existence.

GEORGE HERBERT PALMER, *Autobiography of a Philosopher,* 1930

I am sustained by a sense of the worthwhileness of what I am doing; a trust in the good faith of the process which created and sustains me. That process I call God.

UPTON SINCLAIR, *What God Means to Me,* 1935

The stupidest of all inventions of nihilistic thinking is the so-called "impersonal God." . . . The impersonal God is the most wretched reflection of technologized and thought-weary brains, the modern old folk's home of senile pantheism.

FRANZ WERFEL, *Between Heaven and Earth,* 1944

We believe that God is to be thought of as the perfect fulfilment of all our capacities and powers, as the Perfect Person of our ideal; that this ideal is the supreme reality of life; that He ever exists on earth in the degree that life unfolds towards His perfection.

JAY WILLIAM HUDSON, *Religious Liberals Reply,* 1947

A conviction, akin to religious feeling, of the rationality or intelligibility of the world lies behind all scientific work of a higher order. This firm belief, a belief bound up with deep feeling, in a superior mind that reveals itself in the world of experience, represents my conception of God.

ALBERT EINSTEIN, *The American Weekly,* 1948

I find in the universe so many forms of order, organization, system, law, and adjustment of means to ends, that I believe in a cosmic intelligence and I conceive God as the life, mind, order, and law of the world.

WILL DURANT, *This I Believe,* 1954

See also Absolute, the; All; Deism; Energy; Geometry; God, Unorthodox comments about; Idolatry; Nature; Pantheism; Reality; Universe.

GOD: CONSIDERED AS PERSONAL

God is designated One to suit our comprehension, not to describe his character. *His character is capable of division, He Himself is not.* The words are different, the paths are many, but one thing is signified: the paths lead to one Person.

ST. BERNARD OF CLAIRVAUX, *De Consideratione,* Bk. v, cap. viii, c. 1150

To predicate personality of God is nothing else than to declare personality as the absolute essence.

LUDWIG FEUERBACH, *The Essence of Christianity,* 1841

God is an Individual, Self-dependent, All-perfect, Unchangeable Being; intelligent, living, personal, and present; almighty, all-seeing, all-remembering, between whom and His creatures there is an infinite gulf; who has no origin, who is all-sufficient for Himself who created and upholds the universe.

JOHN HENRY NEWMAN, *The Idea of a University,* 1852

Is it more unphilosophical to believe in a personal God, omnipotent, omniscient, than in natural forces unconscious and irresistible? Is it unphilosophical to combine power with intelligence?

BENJAMIN DISRAELI, the Paraclete in *Lothair,* 1870

It is essential that God be conceived as the deepest power in the universe; and second, he must be conceived under the form of a mental personality.

WILLIAM JAMES, *Unitarian Review,* October, 1881

God's personality is to be regarded, like any other personality, as something lying outside my own and other than me, and whose existence I simply come upon and find.

WILLIAM JAMES, *Unitarian Review,* October, 1881

There is only one kind of God who can satisfy the infinite variety of human beings —all their ideals, all their attractions, all their forecasts, all their lawful hopes. That God is the God of the Christian Mysteries.

JOHN CUTHBERT HEDLEY, *The Christian Inheritance,* 1896

To those who have once accepted the rationality of things, and most emphatically to those who have once accepted the faith in a personal God, the improbability that a being of such capacity should have been created to be simply the creature of a day, . . . has a most invariably amounted to an absolute impossibility.

HASTINGS RASHDALL, *The Theory of Good and Evil,* II, 1907

God must be either the personalized Whole, or, as I am forced rather to believe, the Person who, as over against our own personalities, expresses Himself in the Whole.

SHEILER MATHEWS, *The Gospel and Modern Man,* 1910

The existence of a supreme being as a personal external to ourselves and to the world, like a magnified human creature, is not affirmed by the religious consciousness, and if it were known to be a fact, would have no bearing on religion.

B. BOSANQUET, *Value and Destiny of the Individual,* 1913

The attribution of personality to God, though much truer, I think, than the denial of it, is manifestly inadequate to the full reality we are struggling to express.

A. J. BALFOUR, *Theism and Humanism,* 1915

The abandonment of the belief in a personal God and in personal immortality, though it involves the disappearance of existing religions, need not bring to an end religious life.

J. H. LEUBA, *The Belief in God and Immortality,* 1916

It is difficult to estimate the harm done by the conviction that for its ethical improvement society is dependent upon a personal God.

J. H. LEUBA, *Psychology of Religious Mysticism,* 1925

The demand that God shall be a person is only the last of the anthropomorphisms by which man has compromised God by the desire to worship him.

RALPH BARTON PERRY, *General Theory of Values,* 1926

God is to me that creative Force, behind and in the universe, who manifests Himself as energy, as life, as order, as beauty, as thought, as conscience, as love, and who is self-revealed supremely in the creative Person of Jesus of Nazareth.

HENRY SLOANE COFFIN, *My Idea of God,* ed. by Jos. Fort Newton, 1927

Either God is the Other One, the Wholly Other One, not as a neuter but as a person, or He is not really God; and if He *is* the Other One, it is He alone who can disclose His secret.

EMIL BRUNNER, *The Word and the World,* 1931

If the universe be a thought, as the present trends of science indicate, then it must exist in the Mind of an Eternal Thinker. If we accept this it is logical to invest the Thinker with a personality.

H. E. KIRK, *Stars, Atoms and God,* 1932

Conscious thought is imbedded in the very texture of the universe known to science; if God be less than a person, then is man His superior, just as consciousness is superior to unconsciousness.

H. E. KIRK, *Stars, Atoms and God,* 1932

God is more than a personality because the parts between which that interaction occurs which is God are personalities.

HENRY N. WIEMAN, *Is There a God,* 1932

I believe in a *personal* God; a power, operating at the center of this universe, which creates, maintains, and comprehends my personality, and all other personalities, . . . a power which causes my being . . . which sustains my being . . . which understands my being.

UPTON SINCLAIR, *What God Means to Me,* 1935

For the personal relation to God which gives all its meaning and worth to religion, God must be conceived as at least personal, although the mystery of His Being may not be fully manifested in personality.

ALFRED E. GARVIE, *The Christian Faith,* 1936

If there is no personal God, there can be no human person. If you merge God in nature, you must also merge man in nature. If a personal God is not the master, then impersonal men will be the slaves of the most ruthless.

LOUIS J. MERCIER, *Address,* October 30, 1942

God may be far *more* than personal, but if He is *less* than personal, faith in His existence is hardly worth all the trouble of laborious examination.

D. E. TRUEBLOOD, *The Logic of Belief,* 1942

The Christian God is not a force immanent in the world, a fine fiery air that penetrates all its fibres, but a personal God, a pure Spirit, distinct from the creatures He has called into existence.

JOSEPH HUBY, *God, Man and the Universe,* 1950

What we really mean when we say that God is personal is that He is more like a

person than He is like anything else in our experience.
KIRBY PAGE, *Living Joyously,* 1950

The God of the Hebraic religion is either a living, active, "feeling" God or He is nothing.
WILL HERBERG, *Judaism and Modern Man,* 1951

To deny the materiality of God's person is to deny God; for a thing without parts has no whole, and an immaterial body cannot exist. The Church of Jesus Christ of Latter-Day Saints proclaims against the incomprehensible God, devoid of body, parts, or passions.
JAMES E. TALMAGE, *Articles of Faith,* 1952

We have been assured by no less a theologian than Jane Russell [Hollywood movie star] that the Lord is a "livin' Doll," a right nice guy. Thus is the citizenry guided to divine-human chumminess.
A. ROY ECKARDT, *Christian Century,* November 17, 1954

The conception of a deity is the conception of a personal ground of all that we experience.
JOHN MACMURRAY, *The Self as Agent,* 1957

The Old Man in the Sky is only a mythological symbol for the Infinite Mind behind the scenes. . . . This whole way of thinking is wrong, and if such a Being did exist, he would be the very devil.
JOHN WREN-LEWIS, *They Become Anglicans,* 1959

See also Allah; Anthropomorphism; Belief; Believing; Brahma; Brahman; Christianity; Church, Definitions of; Communion; Conscience; Contemplation; Determinism; Election; Isis; Jesus Christ: see various rubrics under; Krishna; Reality; Trinity; Worship.

GOD, FATHERHOOD OF

We can part with every other good. We can endure the darkening of life's fairest prospects. But this bright, consoling doctrine of one God, even the Father, is dearer than life, and we cannot let it go.
WILLIAM ELLERY CHANNING (1780–1842), *Works*

He is the eternal Father, He is that in Himself. It is as such that He is then Father for us and reveals Himself to us and is the incomparable prototype of all human creaturely fatherhood.
KARL BARTH, *Credo,* 1935

The fatherhood of God, which is the greatest and most incredible concept of Christianity, has become one of the most usual and insignificant phrases of daily life.
PAUL TILLICH, *The Shaking of the Foundations,* 1948

See also Brotherhood; Church: Its Work; Determinism; Election; Love, Divine; Mercy; Providence; Trinity.

GOD: FINDING HIM

Know that all that is other than God veils you from Him. . . . If it were not for your alienation, you would look upon Him face to face.
AL-GHAZALI (fl. 1100 A.D.), quoted in Margaret Smith's *Al-Ghazali*

He alone is God who can never be sought in vain: not even when He cannot be found.
ST. BERNARD OF CLAIRVAUX, *De Consideratione,* c. 1150

Suppose a man in hiding and he stirs, he shows his whereabouts thereby; and God does the same. No one could ever have found God; he gives himself away.
MEISTER ECKHART (1260?–1327?), *Meister Eckhart*

For silence is not God, not speaking is not God, fasting is not God, nor eating is not God; loneliness is not God, nor company is not God; nor yet any of all the other two such contraries. He is hid between them, and may not be found by any work of thy soul, but all only by love of thine heart.

The Cloud of Unknowing, 14th century

Beginning with creatures of the lower grade and mounting up from the first step and the lower scale of nature, we gradually arrived at the genuine apprehension and knowledge of God, supremely mighty, supremely wise and supremely good.

RAYMOND DE SEBOND, *Thelogia Naturalis,* 1450

Not only has God planted in our minds this seed of religion, but has also manifested Himself in the whole fabric of His creation, so placing Himself before our view that we cannot open our eyes without being constrained to behold Him.

JOHN CALVIN, *Institutes,* I, V, i, 1536

I see the marks of God in the heavens and the earth; but how much more in a liberal intellect, in maganimity, in unconquerable rectitude, in a philanthropy which forgives every wrong, and which never despairs of the cause of Christ and human virtue.

WILLIAM ELLERY CHANNING (1780–1842), *Inscription from his Writings on Channing Memorial,* Boston

If we cannot find God in your house or in mine, upon the roadside or the margin of the sea; in the bursting seed of opening flower; in the day duty or the night musing; in the general laugh and the secret grief. . . . I do not think we should discern him any more on the grass of Eden, or beneath the moonlight of Gethsemane.

JAMES MARTINEAU, *Endeavours After a Christian Life,* 1847

God Himself does not speak prose, but communicates with us by hints, omens, inferences and dark resemblances in objects lying all around us.

RALPH WALDO EMERSON, *Poetry and Imagination,* 1876

Our God, the God of our fathers, is a hidden God; and not until we are bathed in sorrow are we enabled to discern him.

STEFAN ZWEIG, *Jeremiah,* 1917

I find the most convincing evidence of Him . . . in the quiet testimony of beauty, truth, love, goodness, peace, joy, self-sacrifice, and a consecration, which point to another kind of world within the one we see and touch.

RUFUS JONES, *My Idea of God,* ed. Jos. Fort Newton, 1927

Only if God is revealed in the rising of the sun and in the sky can He be revealed in the rising of a son of man from the dead; only if He is revealed in the history of the Syrians and Philistines can He be revealed in the history of Israel. Only if He chooses all men for His own can He choose any at all.

WILLIAM TEMPLE, *Nature, God and Man,* 1951

The Bible says "God is." To believe this is the first requisite in finding God.

E. S. WILLIAMS, *Systematic Theology,* 1954

The truth of God is so concealed in us and above us, that we need a special intuition, a supernatural light, light infused in our hearts by God Himself.

R. L. BRUCKBERGER, *Toward the Summit,* 1956

God is concealed behind the dusk of eternity, and only the silent voices of the deep-spirited reach His ear; only the worshipping arms of those who pray not for material things will draw His eyes.

DAGOBERT D. RUNES, *Letters to My God,* 1958

God, the unconditional, is to be found only in, with *and under* the conditioned relationships of this life: for he *is* their depth and ultimate significance.

J. A. T. ROBINSON, *Honest to God,* 1963

When men shout that "God is dead," this can only mean that He is not in the place where they are looking for Him.

W. A. VISSER 'T HOOFT, quoted in *New York Times,* December 20, 1965

See also Bible; Creation; Experience, Religious; Light; Man and God; Mystical Experience; Nature; Prayer; Religion; Religion, Definitions of; Religion: Its Nature and Function; Revelation; Science and God.

GOD: HIS ATTRIBUTES

When we hear that God wishes, loves, chooses, sees, hears . . . we should think nothing else than that His ineffable essence and power are being expressed by meanings co-natural with us.

JOHANNES SCOTUS ERIGENA, *The Division of Nature,* 867

All attributes ascribed to God are attributes of His acts, and do not imply that God has any qualities.

MAIMONIDES, *Guide for the Perplexed,* 1190

God cannot be conceived without His eternity, power, wisdom, goodness, truth, right and mercy.

JOHN CALVIN (1509–1564), *Commentary on the Epistle of St. Paul to the Romans*

[God is] a being consisting in infinite attributes, whereof each is infinite or supremely perfect, after its kind.

BARUCH SPINOZA, *Letter to Henry Oldenburg,* 1661

All that which we call the attributes of God are only so many human ways of our conceiving that abyssal All which can neither be spoken nor conceived by us.

WILLIAM LAW (1686–1761), *Selected Mystical Writings of,* ed. S. Hobhouse

All attributes which we ascribe to God are to be taken as denoting not something special in God, but only something special in the manner in which the feeling of absolute dependence is related to Him.

F. SCHLEIERMACHER, *The Christian Faith,* 1822

God's attributes are intelligible . . . these qualities are essentially the same in God and man, though differing in degree, in purity, and in extent of operation.

WILLIAM ELLERY CHANNING (1780–1842), *Works*

There is no higher idea of God than righteousness and perfection; to follow these is virtue and spirituality and the only reasonable service of God.

F. W. NEWMAN, *Theism,* 1858

God is beautiful. He is the most beautiful of all beings, because . . . His Beauty is without change or vicissitude, without increase or diminution.

JACQUES MARITAIN, *The Philosophy of Art,* 1923

The traits often assigned to Deity, the qualities of personality, of love, of truth, properly belong only to poetry and symbolism.

DAVID STARR JORDAN, *The Higher Foolishness,* 1927

We invest God with human qualities and even human emotions, such as tenderness and pity, patience and strength. These are, of course, metaphors, and it requires an unusual degree of stupidity, not to say irreligion, not to see this.

GEDDES MACGREGOR, *The Hemlock and the Cross,* 1963

See also Beautiful, the; God: Considered as Personal; Love, Divine.

GOD: HIS EXISTENCE

The earth, the sun and stars, and the universe itself; and the charming variety of the seasons, demonstrate the existence of a Divinity.

> PLATO, *De Legibus,* Lib. XI, 4th century B.C.

There is no race so wild and untamed as to be ignorant of the existence of God.

> CICERO, *De Natura Deorum,* 44 B.C.

Although we do not know what God is, we infer from the existence of the world that He is.

> JOHANNES SCOTUS ERIGENA, *The Division of Nature,* 867

No one who understands the reality that God is can think that God does not exist.

> ST. ANSELM OF CANTERBURY, *The Proslogion,* 1100

Therefore, Lord, not only are You that than which a greater cannot be thought, but You are also something greater than can be thought. For since such a being can be thought to exist, if You are not this being, then something greater than You can be thought—which is impossible.

> ST. ANSELM OF CANTERBURY, *Proslogion,* 1100

Now we see that in the world things of different natures accord in one order, not seldom or fortuitously, but always or for the most part. Therefore it follows that there is someone by whose providence the world is governed. And this we call God.

> ST. THOMAS AQUINAS, *Summa Contra Gentiles,* II, 1260

To know that God exists in a general and confused way is inplanted in us by nature, inasmuch as God is man's beatitude. For man naturally desires happiness, and what is naturally desired by man is naturally known by him.

> ST. THOMAS AQUINAS, *Summa,* la. l.v., 1272

Rama is the sun, the true Being, Consciousness, Bliss; him the night of Delusion touches not. He is the Fundamental Light, the Adorable: how shall there be a dawn of wisdom for him? . . . Rama, as all the world knows, is the Omnipresent, Absolute, Supreme Bliss, Lord over all, and everlasting.

> TULSIDAS (died 1623), *Ramacaritmanas*

It is absolutely necessary to conclude . . . that God exists; for though the idea of substance be in my mind owing to this,— that I myself am a substance,—I should not however have the idea of an infinite substance, seeing that I am a finite being, unless it were given me by some substance in reality infinite.

> RENÉ DESCARTES, *Meditations,* 1641

The metaphysical proofs of God are so remote from the reasoning of men and so complicated, that they make but little impression.

> BLAISE PASCAL, *Pensées,* 1670

No cause or reason can be given which prevents Him from existing, or which rules out His existence.

> BARUCH SPINOZA, *Ethics,* Prop. 11, 1677

The existence of a Being endowed with intelligence and wisdom is a necessary inference from a study of celestial mechanics.

> ISAAC NEWTON, *Principia,* 1687

I exist, hence something exists. If something exists, then something must have existed from all eternity; for whatever is, either exists through itself, or has received its being from something else. If through itself, it exists of necessity, it has always existed of necessity, it is God; if it has received its being from something else, and that something from a third, that from which the last has received its being must of necessity be God.

VOLTAIRE, *Traité de Metaphysique,* ch. II, 1738

It is necessary that one should be convinced of God's existence, but not so necessary that one should prove it.

IMMANUEL KANT, *The Only Possible Ground of Proof for a Demonstration of the Existence of God,* 1763

If God did not exist it would be necessary to invent Him.

VOLTAIRE, *Letter to M. Saurin,* November, 10, 1770

The *summum bonum* is possible . . . only on the supposition of a supreme Being having a causality corresponding to moral character. . . . The possibility of this *summum bonum* . . . is possible only on the condition of the existence of God; it inseparably connects the supposition of this with duty; that is, it is morally necessary to assume the existence of God.

IMMANUEL KANT, *The Critique of Pure Reason,* 1781

He does not prove the existence of God; existence *is* God!

J. W. VON GOETHE, *Letter to T. Jacobi,* June 9, 1785

We must assume a moral World-Cause (an Author of the world), in order to set before ourselves a final purpose consistent with the moral law . . . we must admit there is a God.

IMMANUEL KANT, *Critique of Judgment,* 1790

Almighty God exists more really and absolutely than any of those fellow-men whose existence is conveyed to us through the senses.

JOHN HENRY NEWMAN, *Parochial and Plain Sermons,* IV, 1843

In my most extreme fluctuations I have never been an atheist in the sense of denying the existence of God.

CHARLES DARWIN, *Life and Letters,* I, 1887

The existence and essence of God are one and the same.

C. G. MONTEFIORE, *Liberal Judaism,* 1903

Whether God exists or not, is not important to the nature of religion.

E. EUCKEN, *Truth of Religion,* 1911

On the basis of the knowledge of God through religious experience, one can scientifically assume *that* God is, although he may have as yet very little knowledge as to *what* God is.

DOUGLAS CLYDE MACINTOSH, *Theology as an Empirical Science,* 1919

He exists only in the striving of the world to realize his deity, and to help it as it were to birth. Morever, he is not a creature as in historical religions, but created.

S. ALEXANDER, *Science and Religion,* 1931

Proof of the existence of God is wasted on those who are perverse enough to deny God.

JAMES M. GILLIS, *If Not Christianity, What?,* 1935

The best proof of God's existence is what follows when we deny it.

WILLIAM L. SULLIVAN, *Epigrams and Criticisms in Miniature,* 1936

Jesus lived so intimately with God that he never thought of proving God's existence, as religious people are so feverishly doing in our day.

W. A. SMART, *The Contemporary Christ,* 1942

As far as proofs and reasons go, one might say the chances of God's existence are incomparably greater than the chances of his nonexistence; and men suspect as much.

> YVES M. CONGAR, *God, Man and the Universe,* 1950

If it is not easy, by natural reason alone, to arrive at absolute certitude about the existence of God, it is harder still to prove the nonexistence of God!

> ALBERT DONDEYNE, *God, Man and the Universe,* 1950

If the primitive experience of the ancients was able to offer sufficient arguments to reason to demonstrate the existence of God, now, with the amplification and deepening of the field of experience itself, the imprint of the Eternal upon the visible world is all the more splendid and radiantly visible.

> POPE PIUS XII, *Address,* November 22, 1951

God does not exist. He is being-itself beyond essence and existence. Therefore, to argue that God exists, is to deny him.

> PAUL TILLICH, *Systematic Theology,* I, 1951

To ask for a proof of the existence of God is on a par with asking for a proof of the existence of beauty. If God does not lie at the end of a telescope, neither does He lie at the end of any syllogism.

> WALTER T. STACE, *Time and Eternity,* 1952

However valid the proofs of God's existence may be in themselves, absolutely speaking, they can only be valid for us in so far as we accept them on our side, with honesty, moral rectitude and purity of heart.

> REGIS JOLIVET, *The God of Reason,* 1958

God does not have to receive existence, because He is existence.

> FRANK J. SHEED, *The Advocate,* January, 1960

All the objections brought against the various proofs of the existence of God are in vain; criticism can never invalidate them, for it can never get its teeth into the principle common to them all.

> HENRI DE LUBAC, *The Discovery of God,* 1961

We demand "proof" of God, forgetting that if we could prove God He would be within the compass of our rationalities, and that then our logical mind would be our own grotesque God.

> GEORGE A. BUTTRICK, *Christ and History,* 1963

See also Being; Belief; Believing; Bible; Cause; Christianity; Creation; Design; Evil, Problem of; Existence; Experience, Religious; Mystical Experience; Providence; Reality; Science and God; Theism; Theist; Universe.

GOD: HIS GOODNESS

God, if He be good, is not the author of all things, but of a few things only, and not of most things that occur to man.

> PLATO, *The Republic,* c. 370 B.C.

The Good which is above hearing and eye and heart must be that God which transcends the universe.

> ST. GREGORY OF NYSSA (c. 335–c. 395), *On the Soul and the Resurrection*

Nor is it right for a man to try to comprehend with his mind all the means of divine working, or to explain them in words. Let it be enough that we have seen that God, the Creator of all nature, directs and disposes all things for good.

> BOETHIUS, *Consolations of Philosophy,* c. 524

What we call goodness in creatures preexists in God in a far higher way. Whence it follows, not that God is good because He is the source of good, but rather, because He is good, He imparts goodness to all things else.

ST. THOMAS AQUINAS, *Summa Theologiae,* 1272

God is a thousand times more ready to give than to receive.

MEISTER ECKHART (14th century), *Works*

And if we will intently pray for the getting of good, let us cry, either with word or with desire, nought else and no more words, but this word GOD.

The Cloud of Unknowing, 14th century

If a good man be merciful to his beast; then surely a good God is bountiful and benign, and takes Pleasure that all his Creatures enjoy themselves that have Life and Sense, and are capable of any enjoyment.

HENRY MORE, *Antidote Against Atheism,* 1653

We state it as a fixed and immovable principle that God is the first and only cause of all our good and delivers us from all evil.

BARUCH SPINOZA, *Book of God,* c. 1662

God's creating decree is free: God is inclined to everything good; the good, and even the best, disposes him to act; but it does not necessitate him.

G. W. VON LEIBNIZ, *Theodicy,* 1710

The holy triune God has but one nature and intent towards all the creation which is to pour forth the riches and sweetness of His divine perfections upon everything that is capable of them and according to its capacity to receive them.

WILLIAM LAW (1686–1761), *Selected Mystical Writings of,* ed. S. Hobhouse

God is not made good by the Christian revelation, but only declared and shown to be good; he has always been good; he has always been the Father Almighty, and he always had purposes of grace concerning his children whether they knew him or not.

BORDEN P. BOWNE, *Personalism,* 1908

Two great influences have made goodness the outstanding characteristic in the conception of God. The first influence was Jesus of Nazareth; the second influence has been the growth of modern science, and particularly the growth of the theory of evolution.

ROBERT A. MILLIKAN, *Science and Life,* 1924

It is not from the contemplation of this world that logic derives its belief in the goodness of God. It derives it, to repeat the admirable saying of Dr. Johnson . . . from the absence of any reason for His being other.

CHRISTOPHER HOLLIS, *The Noble Castle,* 1941

Although God is good, this does not mean that he is goody-good, or that all he does is pleasant and agreeable to human tastes.

VICTOR WHITE, *Soul and Psyche,* 1960

See also Creation; Evil, Problem of; Forgiveness; God; Goodness; Grace; Grace, Definitions of; Hope; Immortality; Love, Divine; Nature; Providence; Redemption; Salvation.

GOD: HIS INFINITY

He, the universal God, is not born any time, nor does he ever die; nor will he ever cease to be. Unborn, everlasting, eternal.

Mahabharata, c. 800 B.C.

Only God is, not according to any measure of time, but according to an immovable and immutable eternity, not measured by time, nor subject to any declination, before whom nothing is, nor nothing shall be after, nor more new or more recent, but one really being: which by one only Now or Present, filleth the EVER, and there is nothing that truly is, but he alone.

> MICHEL DE MONTAIGNE, *Essays,* Bk. 2, ch. 12, 1580

God is a being absolutely infinite; a substance consisting of infinite attributes, each of which express His eternal and infinite essence.

> BARUCH SPINOZA, *Ethics,* 1677

God could not be infinite at all unless He be infinite in every one of His attributes.

> J. F. NOLL, *Christian Faith Before the Bar of Reason,* 1948

His Eternity, then, is something quite different from timelessness; it is a sovereign rule over Time and the temporal sphere, the freedom of Him who creates and gives us Time. . . . God includes and comprehends Time within His Presence; He does not eliminate it, but He fulfills it.

> EMIL BRUNNER, *The Christian Doctrine of God,* 1949

See also Beatific Vision; Eternal; Eternal Life.

GOD: HIS INTERVENTION IN THE WORLD

Man thinks, God directs.

> ALCUIN, *Epistles,* c. 800

God governs heaven and earth by His providence, and regulates all things in such a manner that nothing happens but according to His counsel.

> JOHN CALVIN, *Institutes,* I, 1536

The line of our days is drawn by night, and the various effects therein by a pencil that is invisible; wherein though we con-

fess our ignorance, I am sure we do not err if we say it is in the hand of GOD.

> THOMAS BROWNE, *Religio Medici,* 1635

God in his highest heaven holds the reins of all the kingdoms of earth. He holds the hearts of men in his hands.

> J. B. BOSSUET, *Discourses on Universal History,* 1675

This most elegant system of suns, planets and comets could only arise from the purpose and sovereignty of an intelligent and mighty being. . . . He rules them all, not as a soul of the world, but a sovereign lord of all things.

> ISAAC NEWTON, concluding scholium of *Principia,* 1687

[God] is a spirit who is intimately present to our minds, producing in them all that variety of ideas or sensations which continually affect us, on whom we have an absolute and entire dependence.

> GEORGE BERKELEY, *Principles of Human Knowledge,* 1710

Upon supposition that God exercises a moral government over the world, the analogy of His natural government suggests and makes it creditable that His moral government must be a scheme quite beyond our comprehension.

> JOSEPH BUTLER, *Analogy of Religion,* pt. I. ch. 7, 1736

God . . . is not a transcendent being living in a distant heaven whence from time to time he intervenes in the affairs of the earth. He is an ever-present spirit guiding all that happens to a wise and holy end.

> DAVID HUME, *Dialogues Concerning Natural Religion,* 1779

God acts upon earth only by means of superior, chosen men.

> JOHANN G. HERDER, *Philosophy of the History of Man,* 1791

Behind the dim unknown standeth God within the shadow, keeping watch above his own.

JAMES RUSSELL LOWELL, *The Present Crisis,* 1845

The order of God, the good pleasure of God, the will of God, the actions of God, the grace of God, all these are one and the same thing in this life. It is God laboring to render the soul like unto Him.

P. J. DE CAUSSADE, *Abandonment,* 1887

The God whom science recognizes must be a God of universal laws exclusively, a God who does a wholesale, not a retail business. He cannot accommodate his processes to the convenience of individuals.

WILLIAM JAMES, *Varieties of Religious Experience,* 1902

Divine Guidance must be postulated if we are to maintain the three great values—knowledge, love and beauty.

A. J. BALFOUR, *Theism and Thought,* 1923

The central conviction and doctrine of Christianity is the prevenience and condescension of the real God—is the penetration of spirit into sense, of the spaceless into space, of the eternal into time, of God into man.

FRIEDRICH VON HÜGEL, *Essays and Addresses, Second Series,* 1926

The fact that men have always believed in the possibility of Divine intervention is much more striking than attempts to explain that belief away are convincing.

CHRISTOPHER HOLLIS, *The Noble Castle,* 1941

God does not will everything that happens but he wills something in every thing that happens . . . even in relation to that which opposes him.

GUSTAFE AULEN, *Faith of the Christian Church,* 1948

God's acts occur with but never "in and under," always over and opposite to human action.

KARL BARTH, *Church Dogmatics,* III:4, 1951

The God of Judaism is not the unmoved mover, but the uncreated creator of everything and so there is absolutely nothing independent of His will.

SIMON GREENBERG, *Patterns of Faith in America Today,* ed. F. E. Johnson, 1957

The God who answers special prayers, the God who blesses cannon, the God who is the man upstairs, the God who is "my co-pilot" is very much dead, for this God never existed except in some wild imaginations. But to say that God is dead because some people have a very human concept of God is only to say, if we are truthful, that this particular idea of God is dead.

WALTER DONALD KRING, quoted in New York *Herald Tribune,* November 7, 1965

The God who deliberately sends sickness and death as a punishment for our sins—that God has died. The God who took all the joy out of Sunday and draped it in black, that God, I am glad to say, has died. It is not so much that He died as that He changed His name and thereafter was quite different for us. . . . He may have withdrawn for a while to teach us how to get along without Him. . . . Yet once in a while the clouds break through and He appears when we least expect Him.

THEODORE FERRIS, quoted in New York *Herald Tribune,* November 7, 1965

See also Art; Bible; Bible: Its Inspiration; Christianity; Church, Definitions of; Church: Its Nature; Church: Its Work; Conscience; Determinism; Election; Government and God; Grace; Grace, Definitions of; Holy Spirit; Mind; Miracles; Necessity; Old Testament; Prayer: Its Efficacy; Predestination; Prophets; Providence; Revelation; Transcendence; World and God.

GOD: HIS LOVE.
See LOVE, DIVINE

GOD: HIS NATURE

The Universal Being has infinite heads, unnumbered eyes, and unnumbered feet. Enveloping the universe on every side, he exists transcending it. All this is he—what has been and what shall be. . . . The whole series of universes—past, present and future—express his glory and power; but he transcends his own glory.

Samhitas, Rig-Veda, c. 1200 B.C.

God must not be thought of as a physical being, or as having any kind of body. He is pure mind. He moves and acts without needing any corporeal space, or size, or form, or color, or any other property of matter.

ORIGEN, *De principiis,* c. 254

He is invisible, for He is too bright for us to look upon. He is impalpable, for He is too pure for us to touch. He is incomprehensible, for He is beyond our ken—infinite, immense, and His real greatness is known to Himself alone. Our mind is too limited to understand Him.

MARCUS MINUCIUS FELIX, *Octavius,* 3rd century

God is self-existent, enclosing all things and enclosed by none; within all according to His goodness and power, yet without all in His proper nature.

ST. ATHANASIUS (296–373), *De Decretis,* ch. 3, sec. 11

What, then, art Thou, O my God . . . stable, yet contained of none; unchangeable, yet changing all things; never new, never old . . . always working yet ever at rest; gathering, yet needing nothing; sus-

training, pervading, and protecting; creating, nourishing, and developing; seeking, and yet possessing all things.

ST. AUGUSTINE, *Confessions of,* Bk. 1, ch. IV, 397

No essence at all is contrary to God, the chief essence, and cause of essence of all.

ST. AUGUSTINE, *City of God* XI.2, 426

I consider it insane folly to investigate the nature of God. . . . I shall observe a discreet silence concerning these questions, with the sole object that old and venerable beliefs may not be discredited.

PROCOPIUS, *History of the Wars,* 550 A.D.

There is nothing in existence which is self-subsistent, save the Living and Self-sustaining God, in Whom subsists all other things.

AL-GHAZALI (died 1111 A.D.), quoted in M. Watt's *Faith and Practice of Al-Ghazali*

A single and complete essence, which consists of no diversity of parts or of accidents. . . . The eternal Author is understood from the perpetuity of creatures; the omnipotent Author from the magnitude of creatures; the wise Author from their order and disposition; the good Author from their governance. All these relate to revealing the unity of Deity.

PETER LOMBARD, *Book of Sentences,* c. 1157

We firmly believe and honestly declare that there is only one true God . . . three Persons indeed, but only one absolutely simple divine essence, substance, or nature . . . one first cause of all things—the Creator of all things visible and invisible, spiritual and material.

FOURTH LATERAN COUNCIL OF ROMAN CATHOLIC CHURCH, 1215

The Perfect and Absolute Being, which is simply being, the first and the last, is principle and end of all creatures. Being eternal and omnipresent, it embraces and penetrates all durations: it is at once center and circumference.

ST. BONAVENTURE, *Itinerarium*, V, 1259

We cannot know in what consists the Essence of God . . . by this word [God] is signified that thing than which nothing greater can exist. . . . God is his Own Existence . . . God is the Prime Mover; and is Himself unmoved. Therefore it is clear God is not a body. . . . God is the First Being. . . . It is impossible that matter should exist in God. . . . He is the First and efficient Cause. He is therefore of His Essence a pure form; and not composed of matter and form.

ST. THOMAS AQUINAS, *Summa Theologiae* I, 11,21,30, 1272

True Christian divinity commandeth us not to search out the nature of God, but to know His will set out to us in Christ.

MARTIN LUTHER, *Commentary on Galatians*, 1531

There is but one God whose name is true, the Creator, devoid of fear and enmity, immortal, unborn, self-existent.

Japji, attributed to Guru Nanak (1496–1538)

When we say, that the infinity of ages, as well past as to come, is but an instant with God; that his wisdom, goodness and power, are one selfsame thing with his essence; our tongue speaks it, but our understanding can no whit apprehend it.

MICHEL DE MONTAIGNE, *Essays*, Bk. 2, ch. 12, 1580

By the name God I understand a substance infinite, eternal, immutable, independent, all-knowing, all-powerful, and by which I myself, and every other thing that exists,— if any such there be,—were created.

RENÉ DESCARTES, *Meditations*, 1641

I believe that a triangle, if it could speak, would in like manner say that God is eminently triangular, and a circle that the divine nature is eminently circular; and thus would every one ascribe his own attributes to God.

BARUCH SPINOZA (1632–1677), *Epistle 60, Correspondence of*

One ought not so much to call God a spirit, in order to express positively what He is, as in order to signify that He is not matter. . . . Neither ought we to imagine, that the Spirit of God has human ideas, or bears any resemblance to our spirit. . . . We ought rather to believe, that as He comprehends the perfections of matter without being material . . . He comprehends also the perfections of created spirits without being spirit, in the manner we conceive spirit.

N. P. MALEBRANCHE, *The Search for Truth,* 1688

The nature of God I affirm, from the infirmities of human understanding, to be altogether incomprehensible and unknown to us. The essence of that supreme mind, his attributes, the manner of his existence, the very nature of his duration . . . are mysterious to men.

DAVID HUME, *Concerning Natural Religion,* 1779

The best notion that we can conceive of God may be, that He is to the creation what the soul is to the body.

WILLIAM SHENSTONE, *Works,* II, 1791

The conviction that an infinite Being exists seems forced upon us by the manifest incompleteness of our finite knowledge; but we have no natural means whatever of determining *what* is the nature of that Being.

DEAN MANSEL, *The Limits of Religious Thought,* 1859

God is incorporeal, divine, supreme, infinite Mind, Spirit, Soul, Principle, Life, Truth, Love.

MARY BAKER EDDY, *Science and Health,* 1908

An essence whose spirituality transcends that of all other spirits, human, angelic, or archangelic; even as his immortality transcends that of man or angel.

WILLIAM G. T. SHEDD, *Dogmatic Theology*, I, 1891

All attempts of language, calling Him [God] Father, or Brother, or our dearest Friend, are attempts to objectify God, which cannot be done. He is the eternal subject of everything . . . the eternal Subject of my soul. How can you objectify Him, the Essence of your soul, the Reality of Everything?

SWAMI VIVEKANANDA, *The Yoga and Other Works*, from an address delivered in London, 1896

Men of acknowledged and pre-eminent saintliness agree very closely in what they tell us about God. . . . not based on inference, but on immediate experience, that God is a spirit with whom the human spirit can hold intercourse; that in Him meet all that they can imagine of goodness, truth and beauty.

W. R. INGE, *Christian Mysticism*, 1899

God is the Eternal Substance, and is known as such; God is also the Eternal Order of things; but God is That Which does whatever Substance is found to do.

WILLIAM E. HOCKING, *The Meaning of God in Human Experience,*1912

The difference between the Supreme as Spirit and the Supreme as person is one of standpoint, not of essence; between God as he is and God as he seems to us. When we consider the abstract and impersonal aspects of the Supreme we call it the Absolute; when we consider the Supreme as self-aware and self-blissful we get God. The real is beyond all conception of personality and impersonality.

S. RADHADKRISHNAN, *An Idealist View of Life*, 1929

The identifying mark of God is organic unity, found functioning preeminently in Jesus, which operates in the world to make us brothers; that is, functional members of one another.

HENRY NELSON WIEMAN, *Christian Century*, May 2, 1934

The infinite superabundance of the Divine Being, the transcendence of a glorious and exultant Deity, a transcendent life . . . His being is not only being and not only knowledge but also love. . . . He is indeed One and Incommunicable.

JACQUES MARITAIN, *A Preface to Metaphysics*, 1939

God, in His essence, is Pure Consciousness, incomprehensible to the senses and the mind. Neither being nor non-being, He is described as silence.

SWAMI NIKHILANANDA, *Perspectives on a Troubled Decade*, ed. Bryson, Finklestein and MacIver, 1950

The reality of God is a reality of spirit. . . . God cannot in any sense whatever be conceived as an object, not even as the very highest object. God is not to be found in the world of objects.

NICHOLAS BERDYAEV, *The Beginning and the End*, 1952

All conceptions of God which are incompatible with a movement of pure charity are false. All other conceptions of Him, in varying degree, are true.

SIMONE WEIL, *Letters to a Priest*, 1953

See also Beatific Vision; Being; Cause; Existence; Good; Goodness; Holy Spirit; Love, Divine; Mind; Spirit; Trinity.

GOD: HIS OMNIPOTENCE

According to the avowal of the whole human race, God is the Cause and Principle of things.

ARISTOTLE, *Metaphysics*, II, 11, 820 c. 322 B.C.

There is nothing which God cannot accomplish.

CICERO, *De divinatione,* c. 78 B.C.

The God and Father, who holds the universe together, is superior to every being that exists, for he imparts to each one from his own existence that which each one is.

ORIGEN, *De Principiis,* c. 254 A.D.

His wisdom and power in creating an ant or bee is no less than in the making of the sun and its spheres.

JUDAH HALEVI, *Cuzari,* c. 1135

God's power is infinite in a double sense. Quantitatively, it can never make so many things that it could not go on making yet more. Qualitatively, it never acts with such intensity that it could not act with greater intensity still.

ST. THOMAS AQUINAS, *De potentia,* qu. 1, a.2, 1263

We arrogate too much to ourselves, when we take it for granted that only the care of us is the adequate reason and limit, beyond which Divine Wisdom and Power does or disposes nothing.

GALILEO, *Dialogue on the Great World Systems,* 1632

It is the presence of God that, without cessation, draws the creation from the abyss of its own nothingness above which His omnipotence holds it suspended, lest of its own weight it should fall back therein.

LOUIS CHARDON (1595–1651), *Le Croix de Jésus*

Whatever we conceived to be in the power of God necessarily exists.

BARUCH SPINOZA, *Ethics,* Prop. 35, 1677

From the sovereign power of God, or from his infinite nature, an infinity of things in an infinity of modes, in other words everything, has necessarily flowed from it or follows it, always with the same necessity.

BARUCH SPINOZA, *Ethics,* 1677

An eternal, most powerful, and most knowing being; which whether any one will please to call God, it matters not.

JOHN LOCKE, *Essay Concerning Human-Understanding,* 1690

God Himself is not an absolute but a limited monarch, limited by the rule which infinite wisdom prescribes to infinite power.

HENRY BOLINGBROKE, *The Idea of a Patriot King,* 1749

Divine Wisdom, i.e. Reason, is one and the same in the great as in the little; and we must not imagine God to be too weak to exercise his wisdom on the grand scale.

G. W. F. HEGEL (1770–1831), *The Philosophy of History,* publ. posth.

The will of God prevails. In great contests, each party claims to act in accordance with the will of God. Both may be, and one must be, wrong. God cannot be for and against the same things at the same time.

ABRAHAM LINCOLN, *A meditation* written in 1862, copied and preserved by John Hay.

God must be shorn of the word omnipotence, in order that He may become less awe-inspiring, perhaps less mysterious, less removed from us and all our possibilities.

FRANCIS HOWE JOHNSON, *God in Evolution,* 1911

We limit God if we deny Him the power to create any other world than this; just as— though this is more subtle—we limit Him if we deny Him the right to create a world which was not the highest conceivable.

MARTIN C. D'ARCY, *Problem of Evil,* 1928

Plainly we cannot mean that God can do whatever we imagine, for we can imagine Him doing irrational and evil things. But in doing such things He would be contradicting His nature.
> W. R. MATTHEWS, *God in Christian Thought and Experience,* 1930

[Omnipotence] means power to do all that is intrinsically possible, not to do the intrinsically impossible. You may attribute miracles to Him, but not nonsense.
> C. S. LEWIS, *The Problem of Pain,* 1940

Whilst everything around me is ever-changing, ever-dying, there is underlying all that change a Living Power that is changeless, that holds all together, that creates, dissolves, and re-creates. That informing Power or Spirit is God.
> MOHANDAS K. GANDHI (1869–1948), quoted in C. F. Andrews' *Gandhi's Ideas*

If God is what everywhere brings form and order out of randomness and finally molds dead matter into something that gives birth to spirit, He can well be worshipped as Sovereign of the universe, of the lifeless as well as of the living.
> EDMUND W. SINNOTT, *The Biology of the Spirit,* 1955

See also Cause; Chance; Church: Its Authority; Creation; Determinism; Election; Evil, Problem of; Fatalism; Fate; Foreknowledge; Free Will; Miracles; Nature and God; Necessity; Obedience; Power; Prayer: Its Efficacy; Predestination; Providence; Science and Creation; Science and God; Will; World and God.

GOD: HIS OMNIPRESENCE

God, surrounding all things, is Himself not surrounded.
> PHILO (20 B.C.?–40 A.D.?), *Fugitives,* 14, *Allegories*

There is no God but he: the Living, the Self-subsisting; neither slumber seizeth him, nor sleep; his, whatsoever is in the heavens and whatsoever is in the earth! . . . His throne reacheth over the heavens and the earth, and the upholding of both burdeneth him not; and he is the High, the Great!
> *Koran,* c. 625 A.D.

God is the East and the West, and wherever ye turn, there is God's face.
> *Koran,* 7th century A.D.

God is everything that truly is, since He makes all things and is made in all things.
> JOHANNES SCOTUS ERIGENA, *On the Division of Nature,* 867

When we hear that God made everything, we ought to understand nothing other than God is in all things—i.e., subsists as the essence of all things.
> JOHANNES SCOTUS ERIGENA, *On the Division of Nature,* 867

And just as by moving natural causes He does not prevent their acts being natural, so by moving voluntary causes He does not deprive their actions of being voluntary: but rather is He the cause of this very thing in them; for He operates in each thing according to its own nature.
> ST. THOMAS AQUINAS, *Summa Theologial,* Ia, q. 83, 1272

God is the universal substance in existing things. He comprises all things. He is the fountain of all being. In Him exists everything that is.
> GIORDANO BRUNO, *Summa terminorum metaphysicorum,* 1590

Fall at the feet of the great God; He is not a stone. He liveth in water, in the dry land, in all things, and in all monarchs. He is in the sun, in the moon, in the sky. He is in fire, in wind, and beneath the earth. In what place is He not?
> GOBIND SINGH (died 1708), *The Sikh Religion,* M. A. Macauliffe, I

The true doctrine of omnipresence is that God reappears with all his parts in every moss and cobweb.
RALPH WALDO EMERSON, *Compensation*, 1841

God is in the world, or nowhere, creating continually in us and around us. This creative principle is everywhere, in animate and so-called inanimate matter.
ALFRED NORTH WHITEHEAD, November, 1947, *Dialogues of,* as recorded by L. Price

There is no place to which we could flee from God which is outside God.
PAUL TILLICH, *The Shaking of the Foundations,* 1948

The Divine that we adore is not only a remote extra-cosmic Reality, but a half-veiled Manifestation present and near to us here in the universe.
AUROBINDO, *Synthesis of Yoga,* 1950

See also Being; Cause; Creation; Man and God; Nature; Pantheism; Providence; Reality; Universe; World and God.

GOD: HIS OMNISCIENCE

God's knowledge does not vary. He does not foresee things to come as we do . . . He sees them, not by change in thought but immutably, be they past or not past.
ST. AUGUSTINE, *City of God,* X, 21, 426

God has knowledge of His Essence: His Knowledge, His Being Known and His Knowing are one and the same thing. He knows other than Himself, and all objects of knowledge. He knows all things by virtue of one knowledge.
AVICENNA (980–1037), *On Theology*

Divine wisdom is so high that it transcends the capacity of the soul and therefore is in that respect darkness.
ST. JOHN OF THE CROSS, *The Dark Night of the Soul,* Book II, c. 1580

Now these inferences, which our intellect apprehends with time and gradual motion, the Divine Wisdom, like light, penetrates in an instant, which is the same as to say, has them always all present.
GALILEO, *Dialogue on the Great World Systems,* 1632

Human wisdom understands some propositions as perfectly and is as absolutely certain thereof, as Nature herself; and such are the pure mathematical sciences, to wit, Geometry and Arithmetic. In these Divine Wisdom knows infinitely more propositions, because it knows them all.
GALILEO, *Dialogue on the Great World Systems,* 1632

Whatsoever is, is in God.
BARUCH SPINOZA, *Ethics,* 1677

God is infallible in His own nature: He cannot be subject to error or sin, for He is His own light, and His own law; reason is consubstantial with Him, He understands it perfectly, and loves it invincibly.
NICOLAS DE MALEBRANCHE, *Traité de morale,* 1684

If we grant freedom to man, there is an end to the omniscience of God; for if the Divinity knows how I shall act, I must act so perforce.
J. W. VON GOETHE, *Conversations with Eckermann,* June 11, 1825

See also Being; Cause; Creation; Man and God; Nature; Pantheism; Providence; Reality; Universe; World and God.

GOD: HIS WRATH

They are not as impious who deny the existence of God as are those who picture Him as inexorable.
DESIDERIUS ERASMUS (1466–1536), *On the Immense Mercy of God*

The God that holds you over the pit of hell, much as one holds a spider, or some loathsome insect, over the fire, abhors you, and is dreadfully provoked: his wrath towards you burns like fire; he looks upon you as worthy of nothing else, but to be cast into the fire.

JONATHAN EDWARDS, *Sinners in the Hands of an Angry God,* 1741

From eternity to eternity no spark of wrath was or ever will be in the holy triune God. If a wrath of God was anywhere it must be everywhere; if it burned once it must burn to all eternity.

WILLIAM LAW (1686–1761), *Selected Mystical Writings of,* ed. S. Hobhouse

Where the beauty and wisdom of the Divine working are most manifested, there also are manifested most clearly the terror of God's wrath, and inevitableness of His power.

JOHN RUSKIN, *Modern Painters,* IV, 1856

The worst God of all is the God of the older Christian theology; God the Father, the creator of evil, who in His all-power and all-knowledge deliberately plans a cruel universe bristling with traps for His creatures.

MAY SINCLAIR, *The New Idealism,* 1922

It is a fact of great significance that the history of religions nowhere presents us with the phenomena of a High God conceived as malevolent and definitely accepted by the Worshipper as such.

LEWIS FARNELL, *The Attributes of God,* 1925

The God of wrath is the God of love vindicating Himself in the death of those who will not live in love.

GREGORY VLASTOS, *Christian Faith and Democracy,* 1939

The Old Testament teaching about God's wrath finds its logical expression in the statement of the Psalmist: "His wrath is for a moment, his faithfulness life-long" (Psalms 30:6).

EDMOND JACOB, *Theology of the Old Testament,* 1955

See also Anger; Damnation; Election; Hell; Judgment, God's; Love, Divine; Mercy; Predestination.

GOD: KNOWLEDGE ABOUT HIM

Grasping without hands, hasting without feet, he sees without eyes, he hears without ears. He knows what can be known, but no one knows him; they call the first, the great person.

Svetasvatara Upanishad, before 400 B.C.

We cannot know God in His greatness, for the Father cannot be measured.

ST. IRENAEUS, *Adversus Haereses,* c. 175

What we say about God is not what should be said (for that is known only to Him) but only what human nature takes in, and only what our infirmity can bear. . . . Our chief theological knowledge is that we have none.

ST. CYRIL OF JERUSALEM, *Catechetical Lectures,* 350

We realize how majestic the nature of God is, not by understanding it but because it cannot be proved by any demonstration or grasped by our intellectual powers.

ST. GREGORY OF NYSSA (c. 335–c. 395), *In Cant. hom.* 12

We can know what God is not, but we cannot know what He is.

ST. AUGUSTINE, *De Trinitate,* c. 397

God is infinite and incomprehensible, and all that is incomprehensible about Him is His infinity and incomprehensibility.

ST. JOHN OF DAMASCUS (675–749), *On the Orthodox Faith*

We do not know what God is . . . because He is infinite and therefore objectively unknowable. God Himself does not know that He is because He is not anything. Therefore nothing can be predicated of God literally or affirmatively. Literally God is not, because He transcends being.
JOHANNES SCOTUS ERIGENA, *The Division of Nature,* 867

God Himself is comprehended by no intellect; neither is the secret essence of anything created by Him comprehensible. We perceive only accidents, not essences.
JOHANNES SCOTUS ERIGENA, *The Division of Nature,* 867

The highest knowledge we can have of God in this life is to know that He is above all we can think concerning Him.
ST. THOMAS AQUINAS, *De Veritate,* 1259

We cannot know what God is, but only what He is not.
ST. THOMAS AQUINAS, *Summa Theologiae,* 1272

If the soul is to know God, it must know him above time and outside of space; for God is neither this nor that, as are these manifold things. God is One!
MEISTER ECKHART (1260?–1327?), *Meister Eckhart*

A man may go into one field and say his prayer and be aware of God, or he may be in Church and be aware of God, but if he is more aware of Him because he is in a quiet place, that is his own deficiency and not due to God. . . . He knows God rightly who knows Him everywhere.
MEISTER ECKHART (1260?–1327?), *Sermons*

God cannot be known in this life or in the life to come. God alone knows Himself; He is as incomprehensible to creatures as infinite light is to darkness.
NICHOLAS OF CUSA, *Of Learned Ignorance,* c. 1438

It is Satan's wisdom to tell what God is, and by doing so he will draw you into the abyss. Therefore keep to revelation and do not try to understand.
JOHN CALVIN, *Institutes,* 1536

We cannot with propriety say, there is any knowledge of God, where there is no religion or piety.
JOHN CALVIN, *Institutes,* I, 1536

If any man shall think by view and inquiry into these sensible and material things to attain that light, whereby he may reveal unto himself the nature or will of God, then indeed is he spoiled by vain philosophy.
FRANCIS BACON, *Advancement of Learning,* 1605

If there is a God, He is infinitely incomprehensible, since, having neither parts nor limits, He has no affinity to us. We are then incapable of knowing either what He is or if He is.
BLAISE PASCAL, *Pensées,* 1670

The inner testimony of Spirit is that alone by which the true knowledge of God hath been, is and can be only revealed.
ROBERT BARCLAY, *Apology,* 1678

After all, is our idea of God anything more than personified incomprehensibility?
G. C. LICHTENBERG, *Reflections,* 1799

I believe in the incomprehensibility of God.
HONORÉ DE BALZAC, *Letter to Madame de Hanska,* 1837

If a man claims to know and speak of God, and carries you backward to the phraseology of some old mouldered nation in another country in another world, believe him not.
RALPH WALDO EMERSON, "Self-Reliance," *Essays,* 1841

I do not see much difference between avowing that there is no God, and implying that nothing definite can for certain be known about Him.

> JOHN HENRY NEWMAN, *On the Scope and Nature of University Education,* 1852

Our natural intuition of God is extrinsic, apprehensive, not comprehensive, and is a view of God as He is in relation to our intellect, . . . not as he is in himself.

> ORESTES BROWNSON, *Dignity of Human Reason,* 1857

We must remain content with the belief that we have the knowledge of God which is best adapted to our wants and training. How far that knowledge represents God as He is, we know not, and we have no need to know.

> DEAN MANSEL, *The Limits of Religious Thought,* 1859

Deity is unknowable just in so far as it is not manifested to consciousness through the phenomenal world,—knowable just in so far as it is thus manifested. . . . We may at least know all that it concerns us to know, as intelligent and responsible beings.

> JOHN FISKE, *Cosmic Philosophy,* II, 1874

The knowledge of God may be likened to a man, while love of God is like a woman. Knowledge has entry only to the outer rooms of God, and no one can enter into the inner mysteries of God save a lover.

> RAMAKRISHNA (1836–1886), quoted by Romain Rolland, *Prophets of the New India*

God then is immediately known, and permanently known, as the Other Mind which in creating Nature is also creating me.

> WILLIAM E. HOCKING, *The Meaning of God in Human Experience,* 1912

As it is not by the methods of the laboratory that we learn to know life, so it is not

by the methods of the intellect that we learn to know God.

> EVELYN UNDERHILL, *Practical Mysticism,* 1914

If I cannot completely know even a daisy, still less can I completely know God.

> FRIEDRICH VON HÜGEL, *Letters to a Niece,* 1928

Where God is known, it may be even imperfectly and through a distorting medium, there He has in some degree allowed Himself to become known, yes, made Himself known.

> NATHAN SODERBLOM, *The Nature of Revelation,* 1933

When we ask about the Creator, we have in so doing passed beyond all possibilities of human knowledge. The question could never even arise in our mind by our own evocation: it comes by the act of the Creator Himself.

> KARL HEIM, *God Transcendent,* 1935

Our concept of Him and his Word can be no more than a pointer to the limits of our conceiving.

> KARL BARTH, *Kirchliche Dogmatik,* I, i, 1938

The calm way in which the self-satisfied of all denominations, Catholics and Protestants, presume to know Him, tells you that He approves of this and does not approve of that, is a profound shock to the religiously-minded man.

> A. VICTOR MURRAY, *Personal Experience and the Historic Faith,* 1939

"A scientific knowledge of the Creator" is an utter contradiction in terms; indeed, it savors of sheer intellectual arrogance, to say nothing worse.

> EDWIN LEWIS, *A Philosophy of the Christian Revelation,* 1940

The best picture we can ever acquire of God is that afforded by the person of Jesus

Christ, the untarnished mirror of the Most High.

JOHN A. O'BRIEN, *God: Can We Find Him?*, 1942

The most perfect knowledge of God is that the nature of God *lies completely beyond* anything we can conceive in this life and that God *remains for us unknown.*

HANS MYER, *The Philosophy of St. Thomas Aquinas*, 1944

Inexhaustible in variety, God can be dimly thought, directly experienced and creatively realized.

BARBARA SPOFFORD MORGAN, *Skeptics' Search for God*, 1947

If we could really conceive God we could no longer believe in Him because our representation, being human, would inspire us with doubts.

LECOMTE DU NOÜY, *Human Destiny*, 1947

What is known by faith about God's nature and man's destiny is knowledge which exceeds the power of the human intellect to attain without God's revelation of Himself.

MORTIMER ADLER, *Vital Speeches*, December, 1949

See also Beatific Vision; Bible; Experience, Religious; Mystical Experience; Revelation; Science and God.

GOD, MERCY OF. See MERCY

See also Compassion; Damnation; Election; Evil, Problem of; Forgiveness; Grace; Grace, Definitions of; Hell; Hope; Immortality, Belief in; Predestination.

GOD, NONEXISTENCE OF

There is an unborn, an unoriginated, an unmade, an uncompounded; were there not, O mendicants, there would be no escape from the world of the born, the originated, the made, and the compounded.

BUDDHA (6th century B.C.), *Udana*, VIII

By denying the existence, or providence of God, men may shake off their ease, but not their yoke.

THOMAS HOBBES, *Leviathan*, 1651

To wish there should be no God is to wish that things which we love and strive to realize and make permanent, should be only temporary and doomed to frustration and destruction.

W. P. MONTAGUE, *Belief Unbound*, 1930

God can be denied only on the surface; but he cannot be denied where human experience reaches down beneath the surface of flat, vapid, commonplace existence.

NICHOLAS BERDYAEV, *Dream and Reality*, 1939

When God is denied, every foundation of morality is also shaken and there is a smothering or at least a great weakening of the voice of nature which teaches even the untaught, and peoples that have not yet reached civilization, what is good and what is bad, what is lawful and what is unlawful, and makes men feel responsible for his actions before a Supreme Judge.

POPE PIUS XII, *Summi Pontificatus*, October, 1939

The existentialist finds it very troublesome that God does not exist, because with Him disappears all possibility of finding values in an intelligible world. . . . We are precisely on a plane where nothing exists but men.

JEAN PAUL SARTRE, *Existentialisme est un Humanisme*, 1946

Everything is permissible if God does not exist, and as a result man is forlorn, because neither within him nor without does

he find anything to cling to. He can't start making excuses for himself.
JEAN PAUL SARTRE, *Existentialism,* 1947

If it is true that there is no God, then the whole of human life, both private and public, has to be reorganized on the basis of this new truth.
ÉTIENNE GILSON, *Ensign,* March, 1952

Where there is no God, there would be no personal identity, no persistent past and no realization of what is really possible.
PAUL WEISS, *Religious Experience and Truth,* 1962

See also Agnosticism; Agnostics; Atheism; Atheists; Godlessness; Religion, Caustic Comments about; Science and God.

GOD, PRAISE OF

What is beautiful is to be loved, and the Absolutely Beautiful is the One, who has no equal; the Unique, who has no opposite; the Eternal, who has no similitude; the Rich, who has no need; the Omnipotent, who does as he wishes, and judges as He will.
AL-GHAZALI (died 1111 A.D.), quoted in M. Watt's *Faith and Practice of Al-Ghazali*

Since his goodness is so great, his will so perfect, that he does what ought to be done, not unwilling, but spontaneously, he is so much the more completely to be loved because of his very nature, and the more to be glorified because this goodness of his belongs to him not by accident but substantially and immutably.
PIERRE ABELARD, *Epitome Theologiae Christianae,* c. 1135

God be prais'd, that to believing souls
Gives light in darkness, comfort in despair!
WILLIAM SHAKESPEARE, *King Henry VI,* 1592?

All the ends of the earth look up to Him. All human beings, all things on the earth, rejoice together in the Great Name.
Prayer offering during imperial sacrifice to Shang Ti (the Ruler over all, the Supreme Being). Taken from a 1700 version, but prayer is apparently much older than that.

There is a God. The plants of the valley, and the cedars of the mountain bless his name; the insect hums his praise; the elephant salutes him with the rising day; the bird glorifies him among the foliage; the lightning bespeaks his power, and the ocean declares his immensity. Man alone has said, "There is no God."
VICOMTE DE CHATEAUBRIAND, *The Genius of Christianity,* 1802

Delight is keener, suffering is richer, thought is more exciting, love and friendship are deeper, steadier in the long perspective of God.
BARBARA SPOFFORD MORGAN, *Skeptics' Search for God,* 1947

See also Love, Divine; Praise; Prayer; Worship.

GOD: UNORTHODOX COMMENTS ABOUT

God may be called the normal object of the mind's belief. Whether over and above this he be really the living truth is another question.
WILLIAM JAMES, *Unitarian Review,* October, 1881

I believe that the only God worthy of the name must be finite.
WILLIAM JAMES, *Pluralistic Universe,* 1909

It is probably true that it is best to avoid the term "God" in purely philosophical writing, just as in the critical discussion of poetry, we need not refer to the Muses.
J. MACKENZIE, *Hibbert Journal,* Vol. XXIV, 1916

[God] A force representing a sort of distillation of the best instincts of men, which inspires them and somehow triumphs in human events in the end.

H. G. WELLS, *Mr. Britling Sees It Through,* 1916

A deistically conceived God existing in solitary state before the world was, and to whom the finite world bears only a contingent relation, as called into existence by the word of His power is . . . a figment of the logical imagination. God exists only as a self-communicating Life.

A. S. PRINGLE-PATTISON, *The Idea of God,* 1917

Paul's God was an Oriental monarch; to the modern He is a cad.

R. W. SELLARS, *Next Step in Religion,* 1918

God is the whole world as possessing the quality of deity.

S. ALEXANDER, *Space, Time and Deity,* Vol. 2, 1920

Since God is a society of finite sentients and finite sentients are each and all evolved, the evolution of God is seen to be the compensation for that corruption of eternity in which the world process began.

DOUGLAS FAUCETT, *The Divine Imaging,* 1921

God is essentially a social God, a concentrated projection of all the qualities useful to the herd in a supreme supernatural personality—the supreme herd leader of humanity, just as the tribal gods were the tribal leaders.

A. G. TANSLEY, *The New Psychology and Its Relation to Life,* 1922

Though the traditional content of the term "God" is to be denied, the value of the term is not to be denied. Religion needs that word although it needs to overhaul its meaning.

JULIAN HUXLEY, *Essays of a Biologist,* 1923

We say to ourselves, it would be very nice if there were a God, who was both creator of the world and a benevolent providence, if there were a moral world order and a future life, but at the same time it is very odd that this is all just as we should wish it ourselves.

SIGMUND FREUD, *The Future of an Illusion,* 1928

[God is] that interaction between individual groups and ages which generates and promotes the greatest possible mutuality of good.

HENRY NELSON WIEMAN, *Is There a God?,* 1932

On one score the word can mean only a particular Being. On the other score it denotes the unity of all ideal ends arousing us to desire and actions. . . . It is this active relation between ideal and actual to which I would give the name "God." I would not insist that it must be given.

JOHN DEWEY, *A Common Faith,* 1934

Up to the dawn of social conscience . . . God held in his own hands the whole responsibility for the evolution of life upon this planet. Gradually this responsibility is being shifted to our shoulders.

ARTHUR H. COMPTON, *The Freedom of Man,* 1935

[God is] the sum of the animating, organizing forces and relationships which are forever making a cosmos out of chaos.

MORDECAI KAPLAN, *The Meaning of God in Modern Jewish Religion,* 1937

God is that character of events to which man must adjust himself in order to attain the highest goods and avoid the greatest evils.

H. N. WIEMAN, *The Source of Human Good,* 1946

"God" is a convenient way of expressing our wonder in the vast splendor of the universe, and our humility over the modesty of man's achievements.

BROOKS ATKINSON, *New York Times,* April 23, 1963

The greatest theological problem of our times is an understanding of the meaning of the death of God. . . . When a contemporary Christian confesses the death of God, he is giving witness to the fact that the Christian tradition is no longer meaningful to him, that the word is not present in its traditional form, and that God has died in the history which he lives.

THOMAS J. J. ALTIZER, *Theology Today,* Fall, 1965

The very God whose Incarnation represented a way out of darkness has become part of a new darkness. No longer can the Christian find security in an absolutely sovereign God who exercises a beneficent and providential dominion over the world. That God has disappeared from view, or rather He is visible in our history only insofar as He has become alien and lifeless, appearing as the God of an irrecoverable past, or an inhuman present.

THOMAS J. J. ALTIZER, *Address,* Emory University, November, 1965

The death of God as a cultural event is undeniable, but this is no reason to dance with joy at the funeral. What Dr. Altizer sees as an apocalyptic promise, the French existentialist philosophers—and I would agree with them—saw as anguish.

RICHARD L. RUBENSTEIN, quoted in *New York Times,* November 21, 1965

See also Agnosticism; Agnostics; Atheism; Atheists; Man: His Self-Deification; Pantheism; Religion, Caustic comments about.

GOD, VARIOUS OTHERWISE UNCATEGORIZED PASSAGES ABOUT

Above this visible nature there exists another, unseen and eternal, which, when all things created perish, does not perish.

Bhagavad-Gita, c. 200 B.C.

There is nothing higher than I [God], O winner of wealth. All this universe is strung upon me as rows of jewels upon a string.

Bhagavad-Gita, 2nd century B.C.

God never leaves off making; as it is the property of fire to burn and of snow to chill, so it is of God to make.

PHILO (20 B.C.?–40 A.D.?), *Allegorical Interpretation*

He is and there is with Him no before or after, nor above nor below, nor far nor near, nor union nor division, nor how nor where nor place. He is now as He was, He is the One without oneness and the Single without singleness. He is the very existence of the First and the very existence of the Last, and the very existence of the Outward and the very existence of the Inward.

IBN AL-ARABI (died 1240 A.D.), quoted by Margaret Smith, *Readings from the Mystics of Islam*

Do not get into the habit of exclaiming God! but speak always of "the Creator, blessed be He!"

ELIEZER HALEVI, *Tzavaah,* c. 1350

God according to the Persons is Eternal Work, but according to the Essence and Its perpetual stillness He is Eternal Rest.

JOHN RUYSBROECK (1293–1381), *De Septem Gradibus Amoris*

He may not be known by reason, He may not be gotten by thought, nor concluded understanding; but he may be loved and chosen with the true lovely will of thine heart.

An Epistle of Discretion, an old English tract, no date, possibly 14th century.

Otherwise esteemed theologians assert . . . that if no eternal life resulted from the love of God, then they would seek what is best for themselves; as though they could discover anything better than God!

BARUCH SPINOZA, *Ethics,* 1677

He who recognizes only a creating God, he who views in God only a Being infinitely powerful, and who sees in His creatures only wonderful machines, is not religious towards Him any more than a European, admiring the king of China, would thereby profess allegiance to that prince.

VOLTAIRE, *Philosophical Dictionary*, II, 1764

God . . . stands in no need of, cannot be profited by, or receive anything from the creature, or be truly hurt, or be the subject of any suffering or impair of his glory and felicity from any other being.

JONATHAN EDWARDS, *On the End in Creation*, I, i, 1765

The word "God" is a Theology in itself, indivisibly one, inexhaustibly various, from the vastness and simplicity of its meaning. Admit a God, and you introduce among the subjects of your knowledge, a fact encompassing, closing in upon, absorbing, every other fact conceivable.

JOHN HENRY NEWMAN, *The Idea of a University*, 1852

We have to find out that God is not in a book; that he *is;* that he must reveal himself to us.

FREDERICK D. MAURICE, *Letter, A*pril 14, 1863

The word [God] is used in most cases as by no means a term of science or exact knowledge, but a term of poetry and eloquence, a term *thrown out,* so to speak, at a not fully grasped object of the speaker to consciousness, a literary term, in short.

MATTHEW ARNOLD, *Literature and Dogma*, 1873

The universe gives us the scale of God, and Christ, His Spirit.

JAMES MARTINEAU, *Studies of Christianity*, 1873

The wise of all the earth have said in their hearts always, "God is, and there is none beside Him"; and the fools of all the earth have said in their hearts always, "I am, and there is none beside me."

JOHN RUSKIN, *Fors Clavigera*, 1880

There is no God but God, and Israel is His prophet; not Moses, not Christ, not Mohammed, but Israel, the race in whom God was revealed.

ISRAEL ZANGWILL, *North American Review*, April, 1895

You see many stars at night in the sky but find them not when the sun rises. . . . Because you behold not God in the days of your ignorance, say not there is no god.

SRI RAMAKRISHNA, *His Life and Sayings*, ed. F. M. Muller, 1899

The God of many men is little more than their court of appeal against the damnatory judgment passed on their failures by the opinion of this world.

WILLIAM JAMES, *Varieties of Religious Experience*, 1902

The prince of darkness may be a gentleman, as we are told he is, but whatever the God of earth and heaven is, He can surely be no gentleman. His menial services are needed in the dust of our human trials, even more than his dignity is needed in the empyrean.

WILLIAM JAMES, *Pragmatism*, 1907

Whatever may be true of men's creed, nothing is clearer than the fact that the personality and the sovereignty of God are not a large factor in the practical life and thought of our age.

CHARLES W. GARMAN, *Letters, Lectures, Addresses*, 1909

God is divided into two, through the created world and its actions. He is divided into the ultimate being of God, Elohut, which is remote and apart from creatures, and the Presence of God, his Glory, the Shekhina, which dwells in the world, wandering astray and scattered.

MARTIN BUBER, *Jewish Mysticism and Legends of Baalshem*, 1916

But my one unchanged obsession, where-
soe'er my feet have trod,
Is a keen, enormous, haunting, never-sated
thirst for God.
GAMALIEL BRADFORD, *Shadow Verses*,
1920

To define God is to limit Him. Still it
seems inevitable that man should do that
in order to get some edge to which his
mind may cling.
HEYWOOD BROUN, c. 1929, *Collected
Edition of*

To live is to believe in God, and to know
God is to become aware, by the very act of
awareness, of that which lies behind the
fact of living a human life.
E. LE ROY, *The Problem of God*, 1929

The anthropomorphic God of the ancient
world, the God of human passions, frailties, caprices, and whims is gone. . . .
The new God is the God of law and order,
the new duty to know that order and to get
into harmony with it.
ROBERT A. MILLIKAN, *Science and the
New Civilization*, 1930

The imagery of the heavens as being two
thousand million light-years in diameter is
awesome when compared to the tiny earth,
but trivial when compared to the imagery
of the "hand that measured the heavens."
FULTON J. SHEEN, *Old Errors and New
Labels*, 1931

God has been accepted as the highest,
remotest, most infinite, and final—*not* idea
or conception, *but*—emotional speculation
of which man is capable; and to reduce
God to nature is merely to shift words
about.
JOHN   GALSWORTHY   (1867–1933),
quoted in *The Life and Letters of John
Galsworthy*, ed. H. V. Manot

Good God or bad god, true God or false
god, kind God or cruel god, man will have

some god. The God-idea is indestructible.
JAMES M. GILLIS, *If Not Christianity,
What?*, 1935

Whatever the queer little word means, it
means something we can none of us quite
get away from, or at; something connected
with our deepest explosions.
D. H. LAWRENCE, *Phoenix: The Posthumous Papers of*, 1936

For every civilization or every period in
history it is true today: Show me what
kind of God you have and I will tell you
what kind of humanity you possess.
EMIL BRUNNER, *Man in Revolt*, 1939

There is no guarantee that the God whom
we proclaim is not our own idolized self,
which we adore in reality while paying lip
service to God.
I. MAYBAUM, *The Jewish Home*, 1946

The fact that God is wholly other refers to
that which distinguishes Him as Creator
from the creatures. He alone is Lord, He
alone is the Source of all Life.
EMIL BRUNNER, *The Christian Doctrine
of God*, 1949

The name of this infinite and inexhaustible
depth and ground of all being is God. That
depth is what the word God means. . . .
It . . speaks of the depths of your life, of
the source of your being. . . . If you
know that God means depth, you know
much about him.
PAUL TILLICH, *The Shaking of the
Foundations*, 1949

Whether we will it or not, we are being
confronted not with a choice between religions, but with the supreme alternative of
God or anti-God.
FULTON J. SHEEN, *The Woman*, 1951

God is the sculptor who chisels on the
rough block of stone the general outline of
what the finished piece will be.
THOMAS J. HIGGINS, *Perfection Is for
You*, 1953

If a purely metaphysical God is a cold abstraction, a wholly unmetaphysical God is a finite idol, whose worship violates the First Commandment.

> WALTER M. HORTON, *Christian Theology,* 1955

God is not a problem. He is the necessary and total solution of the problem posed by a universally absurd world.

> R. L. BRUCKBERGER, *Toward the Summit,* 1956

When God became the property of specialized theologians, generalized peddlers took Him over and redesigned Him for mass consumption.

> MARTIN E. MARTY, *The New Shape of American Religion,* 1958

See also Adoration; Art; Bible; Contemplation; Creation; Creator; Doctrine; Dogma; Faith; Glory of God; Good; Government and God; Grace; Happiness; Heaven; Holy Spirit; Humanity; Jesus Christ; Jesus Christ: His Divinity; Kingdom of God; Knowledge; Light; Man and God; Man Indwelt by God; Mind and God; Moral Law; Morality and God; Natural Law; New Testament; Obedience; One; Perfection; Prayer; Providence; Reality; Reason and God; Revelation; Revelation and Reason; Science and Creation; Science and God; Secularism; Silence; Sin; Soul; Soul and God; Spirit; Suffering; Thanksgiving; Theology; Trinity; Trust; Truth; Unity; Universe; Universe and God; Virtue; World and God; Worship.

GOD: WHAT HE IS NOT

God is not a capricious and cruel Oriental sultan, nor a magnified schoolmaster, nor the head of the clerical profession. The purification of the idea of God is a great gain.

> W. R. INGE, *Living Philosophies,* 1931

God is not a cosmic bell-boy for whom we can press a button to get things done.

> HARRY EMERSON FOSDICK, *Prayer,* 1943

God who creates and is nature, is very difficult to understand, but He is not arbitrary or malicious.

> ALBERT EINSTEIN (1879–1955), Words carved above the fireplace in a room at Fine Hall, Princeton

The Christian revelation pictures God as sovereign and majestic and holy. When he unveils Himself, "The Lord lays bare His holy arm." To suggest that He is a sort of folksy dodderer sitting in a rocker upstairs is the height of blasphemy.

> MARTIN E. MARTY, *The New Shape of American Religion,* 1958

GOD, WORD OF. See WORD, THE
GOD AND MAN. See MAN AND GOD
GOD AND REALITY. See REALITY

GOD AS BEING

Of the Heaven which is above the heavens . . . there abides the ultimate Being, with which truth is concerned: the Essence formless, intangible, colorless, visible only to Intelligence, the pilot of the soul.

> PLATO, *Phaedrus,* c. 370 B.C.

Life belongs to God. For the actuality of thought is life, and God is that actuality. . . . God is a living Being, eternal, most good; and therefore life and a continuous eternal existence belong to God, for that is what God is.

> ARISTOTLE, *Metaphysics,* XII, vii, 9, c. 322 B.C.

When it is stated that He is a Necessary Being, this means that he is a Being without a cause, and that He is the Cause of other than Himself.

> AVICENNA (980–1037), *On Theology*

How indeed could the human mind surmise that the particular things with which it comes in contact are defective and incomplete did it not possess some knowledge of a Being who is utterly devoid of imperfection?

ST. BONAVENTURE, *Journey of the Mind to God,* 1259

A being, however perfect, without dominion, cannot be said to be Lord God. . . . It is the dominion of a spiritual being which constitutes a God. . . . And from his true dominion it follows that the true God is a living, intelligent, and powerful Being.

ISAAC NEWTON, *Principia,* 1687

God is the absolutely perfect Being, and can, therefore, will nothing other than himself—his own Will.

G. W. F. HEGEL (1770–1831), *The Philosophy of History,* publ. posth.

Of all points of faith, the being of God is, to my own apprehension, encompassed with most difficulty, and yet borne in upon our minds with most power.

JOHN HENRY NEWMAN, *Apologia pro Vita Sua,* 1864

Above and beyond the beings whose existence is contingent there is a first Being whose existence is in no wise contingent; in other words, a Being whose very essence is existence, whom metaphysicians call the Self-Subsisting Being—the *Ens a se,*—the Necessary Being.

DÉSIRÉ JOSEPH MERCIER, *Retreat to His Priests,* 1912

There is but one God, and this God is Being, and that is the corner-stone of all Christian philosophy, and it was not Plato, it was not even Aristotle, it was Moses who put it in position.

ÉTIENNE GILSON, *Spirit of Medieval Philosophy,* 1932

So long as God remains a purposeful Being—and to faith He can be only that— He must be imagined as working out a design.

PAUL ELMER MORE, *The Sceptical Approach to Religion,* 1934

God in the mystery of his being is probably much greater than any wish we could have for him.

HENRY NELSON WIEMAN, *The Growth of Religion,* 1938

The statement that God is being-itself is a nonsymbolic statement. It does not point beyond itself.

PAUL TILLICH, *Systematic Theology,* I, 1951

To say that God exists *a se,* of and by reason of Himself, is to say that God is Being itself. This is the concept of Brahman as it is formulated in the Upanishads. It is the *I am that I am* of the Christian Scriptures.

S. RADHAKRISHNAN, *The Philosophy of,* ed. Paul Schlipp, 1952

A being *in* space and time could not account for the existence *of* space and time. Thus many philosophers and theologians have affirmed that God is not one being among others, *in* existence as other things are, but that he is *being-itself,* or that he is *true* existence which is the "ground" of spatio-temporal existence.

JAMES A. MARTIN, JR. *Fact, Fiction and Faith,* 1960

See also Allah; Being; Belief; Brahma; Brahman; Cause; Existence.

GODLESSNESS

Justice therefore forbids, and reason itself forbids, the State to be godless; or to adopt a line of action which would end in godlessness.

POPE LEO XIII, *Libertas Praestantissimum,* June 20, 1888

A Life lived on the plan of getting along without God, without a sense of the cosmic demand, is already, whether it knows it or not, sick, off from normal, its values infected with the dry rot of mortality, intrinsically unhappy because unreal.

WILLIAM ERNEST HOCKING, *Science and the Idea of God,* 1944

One must cite the open-stated denial that there is a God . . . made by certain men, even by certain States . . . as a scientifically established dogma. . . . For the first time since the beginning of the world, mankind is approaching the day when it will have to live alone, left to its own decisions and to its own resources, without the guidance of God, and, consequently, of any religion. This is the most tremendous revolution that ever took place in world history.

ÉTIENNE GILSON, *The Ensign*, March, 1952

See also Agnosticism; Atheism; Civilization; Despair; God, Blasphemous Statements about; God, Nonexistence of; God, Unorthodox Comments about; Irreligion; Religion; Religion, Caustic Comments about; Religion: Its Decline; Religion, Necessity of; Rootlessness; Secularism; Social Atheism; Unbelief.

GODLINESS

True godliness does not turn men out of the world, but enables them to live better in it, and excites their endeavors to mend it; not to hide their candle under a bushel, but to set it upon a table in a candlestick.

WILLIAM PENN, *Some Fruits of Solitude*, 1693

GOLD

Saint-seducing gold.

WILLIAM SHAKESPEARE, *Romeo and Juliet*, c. 1593

He who loves gold is a fool; he who fears it, is a slave; he who adores it, an idolater; he who hoards it up, a dunce; he who uses it, is the wise man.

Old Farmer's Almanac, 1840

Nothing is to be had for gold but mediocrity.

ARTHUR SCHOPENHAUER, Preface, 2nd ed., *The World as Will and Idea*, 1844

See also Greed; Idolatry; Money; Riches; Wealth.

GOLDEN RULE

Deal with others as thou wouldst thyself be dealt by. Do nothing to thy neighbor which thou wouldst not have him do to thee hereafter.

Mahabharata, c. 800 B.C.

That nature only is good when it shall not do unto another whatever is not good for its own self.

Dadistan-I dinik, Zend-Avesta, c. 700 B.C.

Hurt not others with that which pains yourself.

UDANA VARGA, c. 500 B.C.

Tuan-mu Tz'u said, "What I do not wish others to do unto me I also wish not to do unto others."

CONFUCIUS, *Sayings of*, 5th century B.C.

Do not unto others what you would not they should do unto you.

CONFUCIUS, *Analects of*, c. 5th century B.C.

Ponder well the maxim: Never do to other persons what would pain thyself.

Panchatantra, c. 200 B.C.

Whatsoever thou wouldst that men should not do to thee, do not do that to them. This is the whole law. The rest is only explanation.

HILLEL HA-BABLI, *The Sabbath*, c. 30 B.C.

As ye would that men should do to you, do ye also to them likewise.

St. Luke, VI, 31, c. 75

All things whatsoever ye would that men should do to you, do ye even so to them; for this is the law and the prophets.

St. Matthew, VII: 12, c. 75

Say not, if people are good to us, we will do good to them, and if people oppress us we will oppress them: but resolve that if people do good to you, you will do good to them, and if they oppress you, oppress them not again.

> MOHAMMED, *Speeches and Table-Talk of,* 7th century A.D.

There are two rules of life, the Golden Rule and the rule of gold.

> C. S. MACFARLAND, *Christian Service in the Modern World,* 1912

See also Revenge.

GOOD

To injure none by thought, word or deed, to give to others, and be kind to all—this is the constant duty of the good.

> *Mahabharata,* c. 800 B.C.

To the good I would be good; to the not-good I would also be good, in order to make them good.

> LAO-TZU (6th century B.C.), *Sayings of,* translated by Lionel Giles

The tendency of man's nature to good is like the tendency of water to flow downwards. There are none but have this tendency to good, just as all water flows downwards.

> MENCIUS, *Works of,* 4th century B.C.

Let no man think lightly of good, saying in his heart, it will not come nigh unto me. Even by the falling of water-drops a water-pot is filled; the wise man becomes full of good, even if he gathers it little by little.

> *Dhammapada,* c. 5th century B.C.

All are good at first, but few prove themselves to be so at the last.

> *Shu Ching,* c. 490 B.C.

Then let me put the word "good" in the place of the beautiful, and repeat the question once more: What does he who loves the good desire? "The possession of the good," I said. "And what does he gain who possesses the good?" "Happiness," I replied.

> SOCRATES' speech, "The Symposium," PLATO, *Dialogues,* 4th century B.C.

In the world of knowledge the idea of good appears . . . the universal Author of all things beautiful and right, parent of Light and Lord of Light in the visible world.

> PLATO, *The Republic,* Bk. VII, c. 370 B.C.

The idea of the good is the highest wisdom. All things are useful and helpful only when added to this. If we lack understanding of the Beautiful and the Good, though we learn all else to perfection, it profits us nothing.

> PLATO, *The Republic,* c. 370 B.C.

That which imparts truth to the known and the power of knowing to the knower is what I would have you term the idea of good.

> PLATO, *The Republic,* c. 370 B.C.

The time has now arrived at which they must raise the eye of the soul to the universal light which lightens all things, and behold the absolute good.

> PLATO, *The Republic,* c. 370 B.C.

Science and truth may be deemed to be like the good, but not the good; the good has a place of honor yet higher.

> PLATO, *The Republic,* c. 370 B.C.

The good of man comes to be a working of the soul in the way of the best and most perfect excellence in a complete life.

> ARISTOTLE, *Nicomachean Ethics,* c. 340 B.C.

He who does good to those who do him wrong alone deserves the epithet of good.

> *Panchatranta,* c. 200 B.C.

Nothing is ever advantageous if at the same time it is not morally good, and it is not because it is useful that it is morally good, but because it is morally good it is also useful.

CICERO, *De Officiis*, 78 B.C.

Nature does not bestow virtue; to be good is an art.

SENECA, *Epistulae Morales ad Lucilium*, c. 63 A.D.

God is beneficial. Good is also beneficial. It should seem, then, that where the essence of God is, there too is the essence of good. What, then, is the essence of God? . . . Intelligence? Knowledge? Right reason?—Certainly. Here then, without more ado, seek the essence of good.

EPICTETUS (60–140 A.D.), *Discourses of*

For as our sun, not by choosing or taking thought but by merely being, enlightens all things, so the Good . . . by its mere existence sends forth upon all things the beams of its goodness.

ST. AUGUSTINE, *De div. nom.*, c. 395

All things, when they are corrupted, are deprived of good. If they were deprived of all the good which is in them, they would absolutely cease to exist. Therefore, in so far as they exist, they are good.

ST. AUGUSTINE, *Confessions*, Bk. VII, 397

The will that turns away from the immutable good common to all, and turns towards its own good, whether outward to itself or downward, sins.

ST. AUGUSTINE, *De libero arbitrio*, c. 400

We say that there is no unchangeable good but the one, true, blessed God; that the things which He made are indeed good because from Him, yet mutable because not made out of Him; but out of nothing.

ST. AUGUSTINE, *City of God*, 426

The Good must be the beginning and the end even of all evil things. For the Good is the final Purpose of all things, good and bad alike.

DIONYSIUS THE AREOPAGITE, *The Divine Names*, c. 5th century

Regard as trifling the great good you did to others, and as enormous the little good others did to you.

Talmud: Derek Eretz, 1.29, c. 500

Every man has a natural good in him, because every mind desires to obtain the true good; but it is hindered by the transitory good, because it is more prone thereto.

BOETHIUS, *Consolations of Philosophy*, c. 525

For whatsoever every man chiefly loves above all other things, that, he persuades himself, is best for him, and that is his highest good.

BOETHIUS, *Consolations of Philosophy*, c. 525

Be constant in prayer and give alms, and what good ye have sent before for your souls ye shall find it with God.

Koran, c. 625

Human nature is originally good. Any evil in it results from the changes made upon it by [external] things.

LU WANG (Lu Hsian-Shan) (1139–1192) quoted in *Lu Hsian-Shan, A Twelfth Century Chinese Idealist Philosopher*, 1944

Whatsoever good there is in things below, since it cannot come from the matter itself, which only exists as potentiality, must come primarily from the artificer, God.

DANTE, *De Monarchia*, c. 1300

The greatest good is the knowledge of the union which the mind has with the whole of Nature.

BARUCH SPINOZA, *De Intellectus Emendatione*, 1665

My heart inclines wholly to know where is the true good, in order to follow it; nothing would be too dear to me for eternity.
BLAISE PASCAL, *Pensées*, 1670

By good I understand that which we certainly know is useful to us.
BARUCH SPINOZA, *Ethics*, 1677

By *good* I understand everything which we are certain is a mean by which we may approach nearer and nearer to the model of human nature we set before us.
BARUCH SPINOZA, *Ethics*, 1677

There would be less good than there is if there were nothing but virtue, if only rational creatures existed. . . . Midas was less rich when he possessed only gold.
G. W. LEIBNIZ, *Théodicé*, 1710

He who would do good to another, must do it in minute particulars.
WILLIAM BLAKE, *Jerusalem*, 1820

How indestructibly the Good grows, and propagates itself, even among the weedy entanglements of Evil!
THOMAS CARLYLE, *Sartor Resartus*, 1836

That there is a susceptibility to good, in every mind, fallen though it be, is to me beyond a reasonable question. The soul has that within it, which may be appealed to by what is right and holy.
HORACE BUSHNELL, *An Argument for the New Life*, 1858

The only thing that is really good is that Living Love that wills the blessedness of others.
HERMANN LOTZE, *Microcosmus*, II, 1858

I will call no being good who is not what I mean when I apply the epithet to my fellow creatures: and if such a being can sentence me to hell for not calling him so, to hell I will go.
JOHN STUART MILL, *Examination of Sir William Hamilton's Philosophy*, 1865

By desiring what is perfectly good, even when we don't quite know what it is and cannot do what we would, we are part of the divine power against evil—widening the skirt of light and making the struggle with darkness narrower.
GEORGE ELIOT, *Middlemarch*, 1872

Good is not a thing that can be made up by deferred payments.
BERNARD BOSANQUET, *Address*, Ethical Society, 1886

What is good? Everything that arouses in man the feeling of power, the desire for power, power itself.
FRIEDRICH NIETZSCHE, *The Anti-Christian*, 1887

There is an idea abroad among moral people that they should make their neighbors good. One person I have to make good: myself.
ROBERT LOUIS STEVENSON, *A Christmas Sermon*, 1893

The good is universally the pleasurable.
HERBERT SPENCER, *The Data of Ethics*, 1898

It is not because a higher power desires our good that it is incumbent on us to seek it; it is because we inevitably desire it ourselves.
PAUL GANET, *Theory of Morals*, 1898

Good is a product of the ethical and spiritual artistry of individuals; it cannot be mass-produced.
ALDOUS HUXLEY, *Grey Eminence*, 1942

Basically, man is good, not bad; or he would not feel remorse and he would not repent when the good in him has been temporarily defeated.
JAY WILLIAM HUDSON, *Religious Liberals Reply*, 1947

Good is that which contributes to the course of ascending evolution and leads us away from the animal toward freedom.
LECOMTE DU NOÜY, *Human Destiny*, 1947

There is a mysterious call ringing through the universe like the challenge of a trumpet. . . . It is the first and last sound that rings in the ears of a man; its promise is the first and last thing a man's eyes fix on; the first and last things his hands reach out for. . . . It is the call issued by the desirable thing which men call *good*.

WALTER FARRELL. *The Looking Glass,* 1951

Unless we train our children not merely to know the good with their minds but to cultivate the longing for it that is born in their hearts, the good society will never.

EDMUND W. SINNOTT, *Two Roads to Truth,* 1953

Only if man can do evil is there any meaning in doing good.

E. LAB. CHERBONNIER, *Hardness of Heart,* 1955

See also Beautiful, the; Devil; Evil; Evil: Its Nature; Evil, Problem of; Free Will; God: His Goodness; Good and Evil; Happiness; Holiness; Joy; Love; Man's Quest of God; Moral Beauty; Morality and God; Purity; Truth; Values; Virtue; Wisdom.

GOOD AND EVIL

If a man foolishly does me wrong, I will return to him the protection of my ungrudging love; the more evil comes from him, the more good shall go from me; the fragrance of goodness always comes to me, and the harmful air of evil goes to him.

BUDDHA, Sermon on "Abuse" in *Sutra of Forty-two Sections,* c. 5th century B.C.

Good and evil are so set, differing from each other just as reward and punishment are in opposition to each other: hence the rewards, which we see fall to the good, must correspond precisely to the punishment of the evil on the other side.

BOETHIUS, *Consolations of Philosophy,* c. 524

Where there is good there must be evil; [the transition from one to the other] is truly [like] the turning over of one's hand. Goodness, however, is so from the very beginning, whereas evil comes into existence only as a result of such a turning over.

LU WANG (Lu Hsian-Shan) (1139–1192), from *Lu Hsian-Shan, a Twelfth Century Chinese Idealist Philosopher,* 1944

We all measure good and evil by the pleasure or pain we feel at present, or expect hereafter.

THOMAS HOBBES, *Philosophical Rudiments Concerning Government and Society,* 1651

As to good and evil, neither of them point to anything positive in things . . . and are nothing other than modes of thinking or notions which we form because we compare things.

BARUCH SPINOZA, *Ethics,* IV, 1677

The good is that which is closer to God and the evil is that which is farther from Him. Evil is therefore a lower degree of good.

RABBI ISRAEL BAAL-SHEM TOB (1700–1760), quoted in *Judaism,* ed. A. Hertzberg, 1961

There no doubt is good in all the bitter woes that come upon us, because evil cannot proceed from God.

RABBI ISRAEL BAAL-SHEM TOB (1700–1760), quoted in *Judaism,* ed. A. Hertzberg, 1961

Pleasure is in itself a good; nay, even setting aside immunity to pain, the only good; pain is in itself an evil; and, indeed, without exception, the only evil; or else the words good and evil have no meaning.

JEREMY BENTHAM, *Principles of Morals and Legislation,* 1789

It is precisely the conflict between the good or divine principle, on the one hand,

and the evil or adverse principle on the other, which constitutes the meaning of human life and human history, from the beginning to the end of time.

FRIEDRICH SCHLEGEL, *Philosophy of History*, 1829

Not only is there "a soul of goodness in things evil," but generally also a soul of truth in things erroneous.

HERBERT SPENCER, *First Principles*, 1862

Nothing gives such force in getting rid of evil as this belief that the good is the only reality.

BERNARD BOSANQUET, *Address*, Ethical Society, 1886

Roaming in thought over the Universe, I
　　saw the little that is Good steadily
　　hastening toward immortality,
And the vast that is Evil I saw hastening to
　　merge itself and become lost and dead.

WALT WHITMAN, "Roaming in Thought After Reading Hegel," *Leaves of Grass*, 1892

To call Good Evil is the great sin—the sin of the Puritan and the Philistine. To call Evil Good is comparatively venial.

COVENTY PATMORE, *The Rod, the Root, and the Flower*, 1895

When good befalls a man he calls it Providence, when evil Fate.

KNUT HAMSUN, *Vagabonds*, 1909

Good and evil coexist and are blended. Each modifies the other.

WILLIAM NEWTON CLARKE, *The Christian Idea of God*, 1909

Evil is destroyed by the sense of good.

MARY BAKER EDDY, *Science and Health*, 1908

The perception of Good and Evil—whatever choice we may make—is the first requisite of spiritual life.

T. S. ELIOT, *After Strange Gods*, 1934

Unless one knows in addition that good and evil are constant realities in human life, all one's other intellectual acquisitions are valueless. The consciousness of this truth turns the trifler into a responsible personality.

LEWIS MUMFORD, *Faith for Living*, 1940

The power of evil . . . is the very power of the good that evil wounds and preys upon. The more powerful this good is, the more powerful evil will be—not by virtue of itself, but by virtue of this good.

JACQUES MARITAIN, *St. Thomas and the Power of Evil*, 1942

The creation of evil is therefore the index of God's glory and His power. That had to be so that the creation of good might be the index of man's glory and power. But by God's help. By His help, and in His Wisdom.

Jack Burden speaking in ROBERT PENN WARREN'S *All the King's Men*, 1946

If therapy for minds in distress requires a reorientation of perspective, it may well turn out that the historic religious conceptions of good and evil have a special merit for modern minds caught in the web of psychological terminology.

GORDON W. ALLPORT, *The Individual and His Religion*, 1950

It has always been my own belief that what can perpetuate itself is good and what is evil destroys itself, and that this is the principle on which all rational religious thought must be based.

LYMAN BRYSON, *Perspectives on a Troubled Decade*, ed. Bryson, Finklestein and MacIver, 1950

Is it not Satan's sophism for all time when he says to Eve: "You will be like God, knowing good and evil!" To possess all the light, you must also possess all the darkness! To "know life," you must have

abused it! To attain truth, you must have experienced error.
> NICOLAS CORTE, *Who Is the Devil?*, 1958

If even there was an apocalyptic era, in which the forces of good and evil, in the soul of every man as well as in the soul of every nation, were locked in a combat truly mortal, that era is ours.
> JOHN JULIAN RYAN, *America*, January 30, 1960

Today there is a new appreciation of our Lord's parable which depicted the good and the evil growing up together until the harvest.
> JOHN T. GALLOWAY, *Science and Religion*, ed. J. C. Monsma, 1962

See also Evil; Evil, Problem of; Good; Goodness; Justification; Nuclear Energy.

GOOD WILL

We cannot form the idea of an innocent and sensible being whose happiness we should not desire, or to whose misery, when distinctly brought home to the imagination, we should not have some degree of aversion.
> ADAM SMITH, *Theory of Moral Sentiments*, 1760

No degree of good will alone can cure a deficiency in glandular secretions.
> REINHOLD NIEBUHR, *An Interpretation of Christian Ethics*, 1925

GOODNESS

Good people shine from afar, like the peaks of the Himalayas.
> *Dhammapada*, c. 5th century B.C.

The scent of flowers does not travel against the wind, nor that of sandalwood, or of Tagara and Mallika flowers; but the odor of good people travels even against the wind; a good man pervades every place.
> *Dhammapada*, c. 5th century B.C.

When good men die their goodness does not perish,
But lives though they are gone.
> EURIPIDES, *Fragment*, 5th century B.C.

True goodness springs from a man's own heart. All men are born good.
> CONFUCIUS, *Sayings of*, 5th century B.C.

True goodness is loving your fellow men.
> CONFUCIUS, *Analects of*, c. 5th century B.C.

The subdual of self, and reversion to the natural laws governing conduct—this is true goodness.
> CONFUCIUS, *Analects of*, c. 5th century B.C.

Goodness does not come from possessions . . . goodness alone makes possessions or anything else worth having, whether in public or in private life.
> SOCRATES, speech at his trial, "Apology," PLATO, *Dialogues*, 399 B.C.

The tendency of man's nature to good is like the tendency of water to flow downwards.
> MENCIUS, *Works of*, 4th century B.C.

A good man doubles the length of his existence. To have lived so as to look back with pleasure on life is to have lived twice.
> MARTIAL, *Epigrams*, c. 95 A.D.

Put an end once for all to this discussion of what a good man should be, and be one.
> MARCUS AURELIUS, *Meditations*, c. 170

Men are not made good by possessing these so-called good things, but if men have become good otherwise, they make these things to be really good by using them well.
> ST. AUGUSTINE, *To Proba*, 412

Every being, to the extent that it is a being at all, must have, simply as a being, the attribute of goodness.
> ST. AUGUSTINE, *Enchiridion*, 421

Goodness needeth not to enter into the soul, for it is there already, only it is unperceived.

Theologica Germania, c. 1350

Of all virtues and dignities of the mind, goodness is the greatest.

FRANCIS BACON, "Of Goodness," *Essays*, 1597

There was never law, or sect, or opinion did so magnify goodness as the Christian religion doth.

FRANCIS BACON, *Essays*, 1597

No man deserves to be praised for his goodness unless he has the strength of character to be wicked. All other goodness is generally nothing but indolence or impotence of will.

LA ROCHEFOUCAULD, *Maxims*, 1665

Men who are good by reason—i.e., men who, under the guidance of reason, seek what is useful to them—desire nothing for themselves which they do not also desire for the rest of mankind.

BARUCH SPINOZA, *Ethics*, IV, 1677

None are known to be good until they have opportunity to be bad.

BENJAMIN WHICHCOTE, *Moral and Religious Aphorisms*, 1753

If there is a hamlet, to be good it must have a religion.

VOLTAIRE, "Religion," *Philosophic Dictionary*, 1764

I can lay but little stress upon that instinctive, that constitutional, goodness that is not founded upon principle.

SAMUEL JOHNSON, (1709–1784), quoted in James Boswell's *London Journal*, publ. posth.

An interest in the beauty of nature for its own sake is always a sign of goodness.

IMMANUEL KANT, *Critique of Judgment*, 1790

Truth and goodness have their basis in the natural disposition of every human being, both in his reason and in his heart.

IMMANUEL KANT, *Religion Within the Limits of Pure Reason*, 1793

Do not be too moral. You may cheat yourself out of much life so. Aim above morality. Be not simply good; be good for something.

HENRY DAVID THOREAU, *Letter to Mrs. B.*, March 27, 1848

He who does no good does evil enough.

R. C. TRENCH, *Lessons in Proverbs*, 1853

There is no odor so bad as that which arises from goodness tainted.

HENRY DAVID THOREAU, *Walden*, 1854

There is never an instant's truce between virtue and vice. Goodness is the only investment that never fails.

HENRY DAVID THOREAU, *Walden*, 1854

Only goodness meeting evil and not infected by it, conquers evil.

LEO TOLSTOY, *What I Believe*, 1882

The practice of . . . goodness or virtue involves a course of conduct which, in all respects, is opposed to that which leads to success in the cosmic struggle for existence.

THOMAS HENRY HUXLEY, *Evolution and Ethics*, 1894

Goodness has a nobler destiny than defeat. God has not taught us to dream of success, only to deceive us. Somewhere and somehow our noblest visions will be fulfilled.

MORRIS JOSEPH, *Judaism as Creed and Life*, 1903

To be good is not difficult, but to be always good is a gift that reflects the unending perfections of the Eternal.

BEDE JARRETT, *Meditations for Layfolk*, 1915

To realize the greatness of ourselves is not to minify God, but to magnify Him.
    W. S. RAINSFORD, *The Story of a Varied Life,* 1922

Every act of goodness which we perform bears witness to an ideal operating in us and that has no definite definable limits.
    RUFUS JONES, *Pathways to the Reality of God,* 1931

Goodness is the only value that seems in this world of appearances to have any claim to be an end in itself. Virtue is its own reward. I am ashamed to have reached so commonplace a conclusion.
    SOMERSET MAUGHAM, *The Summing Up,* 1938

I have found little that is "good" about human beings on the whole. In my experience most of them are trash, no matter whether they publicly subscribe to this or that ethical doctrine or to none at all.
    SIGMUND FREUD (1856–1939), *Psychoanalysis and Faith,* Letters Exchanged with Oskar Pfister, ed. H. Meng and E. L. Freud

O God, make all the bad people good and make all the good people nice!
    Child's prayer, quoted by Harry Emerson Fosdick, *On Being a Real Person,* 1943

The chief rival of goodness is not badness in itself, but the attractive spectacle of lives powerfully organized on low levels.
    HARRY EMERSON FOSDICK, *On Being a Real Person,* 1943

Goodness and nobility have an inherent power to attract, whereas self-seeking and evil inevitably repel.
    FRANCIS B. SAYRE, *Reader's Digest,* July, 1948

The modern world is witnessing the liquidation of the idea of the natural goodness of man.
    FULTON S. SHEEN, *Communism and the Conscience of the West,* 1948

Goodness in the Church is always individual and personal, . . . but it is enabled to be so because it is a community of goodness.
    WILLIAM LAWSON, *For Goodness Sake,* 1951

There is in many kinds of pagan goodness a form of zeal for an ideal of human perfection, of pity for human suffering that puts much nominal Christian love to shame.
    ROSALIND MURRAY, *Columbia,* April, 1951

Goodness is not theory or pious aspiration. It is action, and action prescribed.
    L. ROTH, *Jewish Thoughts,* 1954

The concentration on sheer unmitigated goodness in Christianity has brought with it an enormous advance in man's moral consciousness, but it has at the same time immeasurably deepened man's shadow and increased his load of quilt.
    VICTOR WHITE, *Soul and Psyche,* 1960

Whatever goodness may be manifested in individual action tends to be lost in mass action.
    LEONARD E. READ, *The Freeman,* March, 1962

See also Aspiration; Beauty; Evil; Evil, Problem of; God: His Goodness; Good; Good and Evil; Holiness; Jesus Christ; Justification; Moral Beauty; Morality; Morality and God; Perfection; Piety; Reward; Right and Wrong; Sanctity; Values; Virtue.

GOSPEL. See NEW TESTAMENT

GOSSIP

To engage in gossip is to cast aside Excellence.
    CONFUCIUS, *Sayings of,* 5th century B.C.

Evil-speaking is wicked; it is a restless devil, never making peace, but always living in strife.

Shepherd of Hermas, c. 148 A.D.

Althought it be with truth thou speakest evil, this also is a crime.

St. John Chrysostom, *Homilies,* c. 388

The gossiper stands in Syria and kills in Rome.

Talmud J. Peah. I.I., c. 500

Believe nothing against another but upon good Authority; nor report what may hurt another, unless it be a greater hurt to others to conceal it.

William Penn, *Some Fruits of Solitude,* 1718

There is something murderous in the conspiracy of Gossips.

Henry Edward Manning, *Pastime Papers,* 1892

This mixture of detraction and prophesy is the original sin of gossiping: and it has descended with rapid propagation to all races and languages among Christian men.

Henry Edward Manning, *Pastime Papers,* 1892

The sewing-circle—the Protestant confessional, where each one confesses, not her own sins, but the sins of her neighbors.

Charles B. Fairbanks, *My Unknown Chum,* 1912

See also Calumnies; Falsehood; Reputation; Scandal; Words.

GOTHIC ARCHITECTURE

You would not enter a Gothic church without feeling a kind of awe and a vague sentiment of Divinity. . . . everything excites a feeling of religious awe, of mystery, and of the Divinity.

Vicomte de Chateaubriand, *The Genius of Christianity,* 1802

Clothed with a power that can awe the mightiest, and exalt the loftiest of human spirits; an architecture that kindles every faculty in its workmen, and addresses every emotion in its beholder.

John Ruskin, *The Stones of Venice,* 1860

The special atmosphere, the hoarded beauty, the evocative yet often archaic symbolism of a Gothic Cathedral . . . its conservation of eternal truths—the intimate union in it of the sublime and homely, the successive and abiding aspects of reality—make it the most fitting of all images of the Church, regarded as the spiritual institution of humanity.

Evelyn Underhill, *The Life of the Spirit and the Life of Today,* 1923

See also Architecture; Art and Christianity; Art and Religion; Church: Edifice.

GOVERNMENT

He who governs by his spiritual power is like the Pole Star which abides in its place while all the stars bow towards it.

Confucius, *Analects of,* 5th century B.C.

Pray for the welfare of the government, since but for fear thereof men would swallow one another alive.

Pirke Aboth, *Talmud,* between 2nd and 4th century A.D.

It is the divine wisdom and not mere chance, that has ordained that there should be government, that some should command and others obey.

St. John Chrysostom, *Homil* XXIII, c. 388

The prince holds the power of legislating only so far as he represents the will of the people.

St. Thomas Aquinas, *Summa Theologial,* 1272

The right of the Empire to govern was derived not from the Church but from the natural law that social order requires government; and since natural law is the will of God, the state derives its powers from God.

DANTE, *De Monarchia*, c. 1300

Government is no other than the soul of a city or nation.

JAMES HARRINGTON, *The Commonwealth of Oceana*, 1656

Government is a true religion: it has its dogmas, its mysteries, its ministers.

JOSEPH DE MAITRE (1753–1821), *Étude sur la Souveraineté*

We admit of no government by divine right.

WILLIAM HENRY HARRISON, *Inaugural Address*, 1841

Catholics are free to prefer one form of government to another, precisely because none of these forms is in itself opposed either to the dictates of right reason or to the maxims of Christianity.

POPE LEO XIII, *Encyclical to the Clergy of France*, February 16, 1892

No man has yet invented a form of political machinery which the ingenuity of the devil would not find a way of exploiting for evil ends.

HERBERT BUTTERFIELD, *Christianity and History*, 1950

See also Allegiance; Authority; Church and State; Communism; Conscience and State; Democracy; Dictatorship; Dishonesty; Disobedience; Divine Right of Kings; Freedom, Religious; Government and God; Government and Religion; Kings; Natural Law; Obedience; Politics; Power; Rebellion; Rulers; State, the; Totalitarianism; Tyrants.

GOVERNMENT AND GOD

It is a law both divine and natural that we should obey the edicts and ordinances of him whom God has set in authority over us, providing his edicts are not contrary to God's law.

JEAN BODIN, *The Six Books of the Republic*, 1579

The powers that be are ordained of God; whosoever therefore resisteth the power resisteth the ordinance of God. For rules are not a terror to good works, but to evil.

WILLIAM PENN, *Frame of Government for Pennsylvania*, 1682

I have lived, Sir, a long time, and the longer I live, the more convincing proof I see of this truth—that God governs in the affairs of men.

BENJAMIN FRANKLIN, During the Constitutional Convention, 1787

The safety and prosperity of nations ultimately and essentially depend on the protection and the blessing of Almighty God.

JOHN ADAMS, *Proclamation* for a day of prayer, 1797

Whatever belongs to the authority of God, or to the laws of nature, is necessarily beyond the province and sphere of human institution and government.

HENRY GRATTAN, *Speech*, May 31, 1811

Whenever you take upon yourselves to legislate for God, though there may be truth in your enactments, you have no authority to enforce them. . . . When once man goes out of his sphere, and says he will legislate for God, he in fact makes himself God.

HENRY GRATTAN, *Speech*, May 31, 1811

Every philosopher and statesman who has discussed the subject of human governments, has acknowledged that there can be no stable society without justice, no justice without morality, no morality without religion, no religion without God.

JAMES GIBBONS, *Our Christian Heritage*, 1889

The genius or demon of politics lives in an inner tension with the god of love, as well as with the Christian God as expressed by the church. This tension can at any time lead to an irreconcilable conflict.

> MAX WEBER (1864–1920), *Politics as a Vocation*

Unless we are prepared to cut our life into two utterly separate halves we must admit that it is our duty to do all that in us lies to bring Caesar—the traditions and practices of government—to the recognition of his duty to God.

> *Report on the Universal Church and the World of Nations,* Oxford Conference, 1937

A constitution conformable to the Divine will gives a man a right to juridical security and accordingly grants him a sphere of rights immune from all arbitrary attack.

> POPE PIUS XII, *Christmas Message,* 1942

Men call upon God when they form a government. But they must continue to call upon Him to sustain what He and they have built.

> JAMES M. GILLIS, *God in Government,* 1943

We can have the assurance that we are being governed properly only when those who govern us are convinced that they have the obligation in conscience to give us honest, upright, faithful service, and that they are bound to do this by the law of Almighty God.

> FRANCIS J. MCCONNELL, *Morality and Government,* 1949

See also Anti-God Totalitarians; Authority; Church: Its Authority; Church and State; Communism; Democracy; Divine Right of Kings; Government; Government and Religion; Kings; Rulers; State, the.

GOVERNMENT AND RELIGION

They who advance in great excellence within the bosom of holy Church, ought not to despise the doings of their rulers, when they see that they are engaged in the business of the world. For that they penetrate in safety into secret mysteries, is owing to the help of those who buffet with the storms of this world from without.

> POPE ST. GREGORY THE GREAT, *Magna Moralia,* 584

Providence had designed two ends to be contemplated of man: the happiness of this life . . . and then the blessedness of life everlasting. . . . Wherefore a twofold directive agent was necessary to man, in accordance with the twofold end: the Supreme Pontiff to lead the human race by means of revelation, and the Emperor to guide it to temporal felicity.

> DANTE, *De Monarchia,* c. 1300

If the Christian religion had from the beginning been maintained according to the principles of its founder the Christian states and republics would have been much more united and happy than what they are.

> NICCOLÒ MACHIAVELLI, *Discourses,* c. 1519

As the observance of divine institutions is the cause of the greatness of republics, so the disregard of them produces their ruin; for where the fear of God is wanting, there the country will come to ruin, unless it be sustained by the fear of the prince, which may temporarily supply the want of religion.

> NICCOLÒ MACHIAVELLI, *Discourses,* c. 1519

It is the duty of godly kings and princes to sustain religion by laws, edicts, and judgments.

> JOHN CALVIN, *Institutes,* IV, 1536

That Form of Government wherein the power of the Civil Administration is denied unto unbelievers, and committed to the Saints, is the best Form of Government in a Christian Commonwealth.

> JOHN COTTON, *The Bloudy Tenant etc.,* 1647

It matters very much to the community that each citizen should have a religion. . . . But the dogmas of that religion concern the State and its members only so far as they have reference to morality and to the duties which he who professes them is bound to do to others.

JEAN JACQUES ROUSSEAU, *The Social Contract,* 1762

Of all the disposition and habits which lead to political prosperity, Religion and Morality are indispensable supports.

GEORGE WASHINGTON, *Address,* September 19, 1796

It is the duty of nations as well as of men to own their dependence upon the overruling power of God: to confess their sins and transgressions in humble sorrow, yet with assured hope that genuine repentance will lead to mercy and pardon.

ABRAHAM LINCOLN, *Proclamation,* March 30, 1863

The constitution and law in America must be written on ethical principles, so that the entire power of the spiritual world can be enlisted to hold the loyalty of the citizen, and to repel every enemy as by force of Nature.

RALPH WALDO EMERSON, *North American Review,* April, 1866

A civil ruler dabbling in religion is as reprehensible as a clergyman dabbling in politics. Both render themselves odious as well as ridiculous.

JAMES GIBBONS, *Faith of Our Fathers,* 1876

All things that are of a civil nature the Church acknowledges and declares to be under the power and authority of the ruler: and in things whereof for different reasons the decision belongs both to the sacred and to the civil power, the Church wishes that there should be harmony between the two.

POPE LEO XIII, *On Civil Government,* 1881

All who rule should hold in honor the holy name of God, and one of their chief duties must be to favor religion, to protect it, to shield it under the credit and sanction of the laws, and neither to organize nor enact any measure that may compromise its safety.

POPE LEO XIII, *The Christian Constitution of States,* 1885

So far from thinking their commonwealth godless, the Americans conceive that the religious character of a government consists in nothing but the religious belief of individual citizens, and the conformity of their conduct to that belief.

JAMES BRYCE, *The American Commonwealth,* II, 1888

We avow our sincere patriotism and our unquestioned loyalty to the nation that we love, but we claim for ourselves the right and the liberty to speak at any time contrary to those who may temporarily be in control of the government, if loyalty to Jesus Christ, as we apprehend it, demands such action.

The Reformed Church in the U.S., *Minutes of the General Synod,* 1926

Modern governments are not merely neutral as between rival churches. They draw to themselves much of the loyalty which was once given to the churches.

WALTER LIPPMANN, *A Preface to Morals,* 1929

It is the duty of the Church of Christ to assist the makers and administrators of just laws, that have as their objective the betterment of the morals of mankind.

General Conference of Methodist Episcopal Church, South, Message to President Hoover, in *Journal of the General Conference,* 1930

The Christian church is universal in its scope and purpose. The obligations which it recognizes and upholds . . . must continually transcend, and even sometimes contradict, the obligation to obey the will of the sovereign state.

Church Assembly, Church of England, *Church and State: Report of the Archbishops Commission on the Relation between Church and State,* 1935

The evils overwhelming the world today are exactly the final result of the idea current in the classic age according to which politics cannot and must not be Christian because it is a pure technique, an art intrinsically independent of ethics and religion.

JACQUES MARITAIN, *Religion and the Modern World,* 1941

Government tolerance of the widest diversity and variety in the field of religion is of the essence of political democracy. . . . But the institutions embodying these diversities should pay their own way. . . . It should be considered just as immoral for a church not to pay taxes as not to pay its ordinary debts.

Editorial, *Christian Century,* April 9, 1947

We are a religious people whose institutions presuppose a Supreme Being. . . . When the State encourages religious instruction or cooperates with religious authorities by adjusting the schedules of public events to sectarian needs, it follows the best of our traditions. For then it respects the religious nature of our people and accommodates the public service to their spiritual needs.

JUSTICE WILLIAM O. DOUGLAS, majority opinion, U.S. Supreme Court, *Zorach v. Clauson,* 1952

Government may not finance religious groups nor undertake religious instruction nor blend secular and sectarian education nor use secular instructions to force one or some religion on any person. But we find no constitutional requirement which makes it necessary for government to be hostile and to throw its weight against efforts to widen the effective scope of religious influence.

JUSTICE WILLIAM O. DOUGLAS, majority opinion, U.S. Supreme Court, *Zorach v. Clauson,* 1952

If a religious leaven is to be worked into the affairs of our people, it is to be done by individuals and groups, not by the Government.

U.S. Supreme Court, *McGowan v. Maryland,* 366 U.S. 420, 563 (dissenting opinion), 1961

Once government finances a religious exercise it inserts a divisive influence into our communities. . . . The philosophy is that if Government interferes in matters spiritual, it will be a divisive force.

JUSTICE WILLIAM O. DOUGLAS, concurring opinion, U.S. Supreme Court, N.Y. School Prayer Case, June 25, 1962

Government in this country, be it state or federal, is without power to prescribe by law any particular form of prayer which is to be used as an official prayer in carrying on any program of governmentally-sponsored religious activity.

JUSTICE HUGO L. BLACK, majority opinion, U.S. Supreme Court, N.Y. School Prayer Case, June 25, 1962

Spending Federal funds to employ chaplains for the armed forces might be said to violate the establishment clause. Yet a lonely soldier stationed at some faraway post could surely complain that a government which did not provide him the opportunity for pastoral guidance was affirmatively prohibiting the free exercise of his religion.

JUSTICE POTTER STEWART, dissenting opinion, U.S. Supreme Court, on Prayer and Bible Reading in Public Schools, June 17, 1963

We err in the first place if we do not recognize, as a matter of history and as a matter of the imperatives of our free society, that religion and government must necessarily interact in countless ways.

JUSTICE POTTER STEWART, dissenting opinion, U.S. Supreme Court, on Prayer and Bible Reading in the Public Schools, June 17, 1963

By no stretch of the imagination can the actual relations of government to religious institutions be defined as "strict neutrality, neither aiding nor opposing religion."

HENRY P. VAN DUSEN, Letter, *New York Times*, July 7, 1963

Injury is done to the human person and to the very order established by God for human life, if the free exercise of religion is denied in society, provided just public order is observed.

Second Vatican Council, *A Declaration on Religious Freedom*, December, 1965

A wrong is done when government imposes upon its people, by force or fear or other means, the profession or repudiation of any religion.

Second Vatican Council, *A Declaration on Religious Freedom*, December, 1965

See also America; American People; Authority; Church: Its Authority; Church and State; Communism; Democracy; Divine Right of Kings; Education, Religious; Government; Government and God; Intolerance; Kings; Morality and State; Religion; Religion, National; Religion, State; Rulers; Secularism; State, the.

GOVERNMENT INTERVENTION

Whenever the general interest of any particular class suffers or is threatened with injury which can in no other way be met or prevented, it is the duty of the public authority to intervene.

POPE LEO XIII, *Rerum Novarum*, 1891

GRACE

It is for God to grant His grace. Your task is to accept that grace and guard it.

SAINT CYRIL OF JERUSALEM (died 386), *Catechetical Orations*

It is grace alone that separates the redeemed from the lost, all having been involved in one common perdition through their common origin.

ST. AUGUSTINE, *Enchiridion*, 421

The law detects, grace alone conquers, sin.

ST. AUGUSTINE, *Of Continence*, c. 425

It is not in virtue of its liberty that the human will attains to grace, it is much rather by grace that it attains to liberty.

ST. AUGUSTINE, *De Corrupt. et Gracia*, VIII, 427

The grace of Christ clothes us, as it were, with gorgeous purple and raises us to a dignity that surpasses all knowledge.

ST. CYRIL OF ALEXANDRIA (412–444), *In Joan.*, cap. 1

O Christian soul! recognize your dignity! Know that as a Christian you surpass the angels not only in nature but also in grace!

ST. LEO (390?–461), *Serm. 1, De Nativitate Domini*

Usually grace begins by illuminating the soul with a deep awareness, with its own light.

DIODICUS, *Spiritual Perfection*, 5th century

The divinity is given us when grace penetrates our nature by a heavenly light, raising it above its natural condition by the greatness of glory.

ST. MAXIMUS, *Centur. Oeco.* 1,76, c. 626

Allah guideth whomsoever he pleaseth, by grace, and he leadeth astray whomsoever he pleaseth, by justice.

Fiqh Akbar, c. 10th century A.D.

Grace is necessary to salvation, free will is equally so; but grace in order to give salvation, free will in order to receive it.

ST. BERNARD, *De gratia et libero arbitrio,* c. 1150

Only those are deprived of grace, who place in themselves an obstacle to grace.

ST. THOMAS AQUINAS, *Contra Gentes,* Bk. 111, 1260

If it should happen that a creature cannot sin, this results from a gift of grace, not from the condition of its nature. . . . It is only in the divine will that sin cannot exist.

ST. THOMAS AQUINAS, *Summa Theological* I, qu. 63m a.l, 1272

Man's preparation for grace is from God, as Mover, and from the free will, as moved. . . . If God intends, while moving, that the one whose heart He moves should attain to grace, he will infallibly attain to it.

ST. THOMAS AQUINAS, *Summa Theol.,* Ia IIae, q. 112, 1272

The grace given us is the grace for struggle and not the grace for peace.

ADOLPHE TANQUERAY, *The Spiritual Life,* 1490

Grace is sufficient to enable us to be accounted entirely and completely righteous in God's sight.

MARTIN LUTHER, *Preface to Romans,* 1522

The holy man hath made God's grace germinate; the perverse have lost their capital.

GURU NANAK (1496–1538), *The Sikh Religion,* M. A. Macauliffe, I

If men do not resist his Grace, as God has begun in them the work of salvation, He will pursue its accomplishment by working in them both to will and to accomplish.

Council of Trent, Sess. VI, ch. 13, 1566

Grace is so gracious and so graciously seizes on our hearts to draw them, that it in no way offends the liberty of our will.

ST. FRANCIS OF SALES, *Treatise on the Love of God,* Bk. II, 1607

The chains of grace are so powerful, and yet so sweet, that though they attract our heart, they do not shackle our freedom.

ST. FRANCIS OF SALES, *Treatise on the Love of God,* 1607

Our loss has been our gain, since human nature has received more gifts of grace from its redemption by its Savior than it would ever have received from the innocence of Adam, if he had perservered in it.

ST. FRANCIS OF SALES, *Treatise on the Love of God,* 1607

To feel in ourselves the want of grace, and to be grieved for it, is grace itself.

ROBERT BURTON, *Anatomy of Melancholy,* III, 1621

God would not have given us souls capable of contemplating and desiring this holy eternity, if He had not intended to bestow on us the means of obtaining it.

ST. FRANCIS OF SALES, (1567–1622), *Consoling Thoughts of,* ed. Huguet

God will not judge you for your natural temperament, which you did not choose, and cannot lay aside at will. . . . What God does require of you is that you should really do what His Grace puts before you.

FRANÇOIS FÉNELON (1651–1715), *Spiritual Letters*

Grace only works effectively in us in proportion to our unremitting correspondence to it.

FRANÇOIS FÉNELON (1651–1715), *Spiritual Letters*

Divine graces works for an infinite and eternal good, which cannot fall under the dominion of the senses, and in consequence the mind moves the senses to deeds of virtue.

GIOVANNI VICO, *The New Science*, 1725

Every virtuous act done for Christ's sake gives us the grace of the Holy Spirit, but most of all is this given through prayer; for prayer is somehow always in our hands as an instrument for acquiring the grace of the Spirit.

ST. SERAPHIM OF SAROV (1759–1833), *Conversation with Micholas Motovilov*

Grace holds us in one world, nature draws us down again into the other.

FREDERICK W. FABER, *Growth in Holiness*, 1855

It is only by faith that the soul is so trusted to, and deposited in, the supernatural grace of God, as to be invested with His righteousness, or assimilated to it.

HORACE BUSHNELL, *Nature and the Supernatural*, 1861

In grace you have the pledge, indeed, the root of your future glorification in soul and body.

MATHIAS SCHEEBEN, *The Glories of Divine Grace*, 1886

Properly grace belongs only to the nature of God Himself. God cannot produce a created being that would by its nature possess grace; such a creature would not differ from God Himself.

MATHIAS SCHEEBEN, *The Glories of Divine Grace*, 1886

To receive grace we need only to love its Donor.

MATHIAS SCHEEBEN, *The Glories of Divine Grace*, 1886

Grace alone is inclosed by no limits. Being a ray of the Divine nature glorifying our soul, it has its measure and end only in the infinity of God.

MATHIAS SCHEEBEN, *The Glories of Divine Grace*, 1886

But for the grace of God, what sinner would have returned to God? For it is the nature of sin to darken our souls, to bind us hand and foot.

JOHN SERGIEFF OF CRONSTADT (1829–1908), *My Life in Christ*

It is the gift of God which is only given to us to draw us on to God Himself.

BEDE JARRETT, *Meditations for Layfolk*, 1915

God, who wishes all men to be saved, grants to all the graces they need for obtaining eternal life.

PIETRO GASPARRI, *Catechism for Adults*, 1932

Grace exists only for the sinner, and we only speak of sin in respect of grace, which is the central meaning of the principal dogma of the Reformation, justification by faith.

ADOLPH KELLER, *Religion and the European Mind*, 1934

Deification is not a physical or magical act of *man*, but an interior action, a work of grace *in* man. This work is accomplished in man with the cooperation of human liberty and not without his will.

SERGIUS BULGAKOV, *The Orthodox Church*, 1935

Not one of us knows to what extent he is living by the power of grace which flows into him through others—by the hidden prayer of the tranquil heart, the sacrifices offered up by persons unknown to him.

ROMANO GUARDINI, *The Church and the Catholic*, 1935

If grace takes hold of us and remakes us in the depths of our being, it is so that all our actions should feel its effects and be illuminated by it.

JACQUES MARITAIN, *True Humanism*, 1936

The world of sin confronts the world of grace like the reflected picture of a landscape in the blackness of very still, deep waters.

> GEORGE BERNANOS, *The Diary of a Country Priest,* 1937

Grace does not destroy our liberty by its certain efficacy; rather by that very efficacy divine grace moves the free will without doing violence to it.

> REGINALD GARRIGOU-LAGRANGE, *Christian Perfection and Contemplation,* 1937

In late Judaism there is an increasing emphasis upon the grace of God as the ultimate basis of salvation. Daily the Jew prays: "Not because of our righteous acts do we lay our supplication before Thee, but because of Thine abundant mercies." . . . Man's own merit requires to be supplemented by the grace of God.

> CHARLES S. BRADEN, *Man's Quest of Salvation,* 1941

What is in question in our world today is not the existence of grace, but the existence of nature and its helplessness apart from grace.

> FULTON J. SHEEN, *The Woman,* 1951

The problem of human life, in theological terms, is the struggle of the fallen nature of man to cooperate with the freely distributed graces of God and in this struggle to merit salvation.

> FRANCIS J. LALLY, *Letter, Saturday Review,* June 21, 1952

However great be the degree of a soul's grace and infused virtues at any given time, those great gifts may remain static and sterile if the individual does not cultivate the acquired virtues to such a degree that he can utilize the supernatural powers at his disposal.

> JORDAN AUMANN, in Broceland's *Faith, Reason and Psychiatry,* 1955

Nature can be considered perfect in its own sphere, but miracles come not from the natural but from the supernatural order—i.e., from grace. Grace but fulfills and perfects nature.

> ZSOLT ARADI, *The Book of Miracles,* 1956

Grace does not annul nor supplant human nature but heals and perfects it, empowering the Christian to merit by his daily life the reward of eternity with his Creator, which he already possesses in germ.

> EDWARD DUFF, *The Social Thought of the World Council of Churches,* 1956

Grace taken in itself—the divine transformation of the soul, the action of God upon the soul—is independent of what we feel.

> JACQUES LECLERCQ, *Back to Jesus,* 1959

The latter period of Judas' life is a frightening illustration of the power of the human will to resist grace. Judas looked upon Christ day after day; he talked with him and supped with him: he slept alongside him under the stars at night. . . . And yet, after more than two years of this, he refuses to open the doors of his soul to the rays of Christ's divine grace.

> RALPH GORMAN, *The Last Hours of Jesus,* 1960

Our prayer is the interior disposition which has gradually been established in us by the author of grace.

> GEORGES LEFEBVRE, *The Well-Springs of Prayer,* 1961

We belong truly to Christ only when we are interiorly identified with Him through the life of grace.

> RICHARD CUSHING, *Way,* October, 1962

No one expects grace by itself to restore a broken limb or heal a tuberculous lesion, yet it is expected that this is the only requirement to cure an obsessional neurosis, attacks of anxiety or a depressive illness. This is a grave misconception and springs from the inability to accept these disorders as truly genuine ailments.

J. DOMINIAN, *Psychiatry and the Christian,* 1962

See also Baptism; Confession; Eternal Life; Faith, Definitions of; Faith: Its Origin; Forgiveness; Free Will; God: His Goodness; God: His Intervention in the World; Grace, Definitions of; Holy Spirit; Justification; Light; Love, Divine; Man and God; Man's Unity with God; Mary, the Mother of Jesus; Mercy; New Testament; Obedience; Penitence; Prayer; Religion, Definitions of; Religion, Necessity of; Repentance; Reward; Sacraments; Saints; Salvation; Soul; Soul and God; Unbelief; Vice.

GRACE, DEFINITIONS OF

Sanctity or sanctifying grace is a divine gift, an inexpressible copy of the highest divinity and the highest goodness, by means of which we enter a divine rank through a heavenly generation.

PSEUDO-DIONYSIUS, *Ep. 2 ad. Caim.,* c. 500 A.D.

Grace is nothing else but a certain beginning of glory in us.

ST. THOMAS AQUINAS, *Summa Theologiae,* IIa, I, 1272

Grace is nothing else than the forgiveness or remission of sins.

PHILIP MELANCHTHON, *Loci Communes,* 1521

Grace I understand here properly as the favour of God as it should be understood, and not as a quality of soul.

MARTIN LUTHER (1483–1546), *Against Latomus*

Grace is like a deity or living image of Christ, which enters the soul and deifies it and is truly the soul of the soul.

LUIS DE LEON (1528?–1591), *The Names of Christ*

Grace is unconquerable love . . . waits not for merit to call it forth, but flows out to the most guilty, is the sinner's only hope.

WILLIAM ELLERY CHANNING (1780–1842), *Works*

What is grace? It is the inspiration from on high; it is the breath, *fiat ubi vult;* it is liberty. Grace is the spirit of law.

VICTOR HUGO, *Les Miserables,* 1862

The grace of God is a ray of Divine beauty, infused from Heaven into the soul of man, and penetrating its innermost nature with such a bright and beautiful light, that the soul delights the eye of God, is most tenderly loved by Him, is adopted as His child and spouse, is elevated above all limits of nature from earth to Heaven.

M. J. SCHEEBEN, *Glories of Divine Grace,* 1886

Grace is nothing but the heavenly light, which from the depths of the Divinity diffuses itself over the rational creatures.

M. J. SCHEEBEN, *Glories of Divine Grace,* 1886

Sanctifying grace is the fitness, divinely received, in the human soul, to see God one day, as He is in Himself, and to be happy in this vision of Him.

ANSCAR VONIER, *The Human Soul,* 1913

Grace is the germ of glory; it has the potencies of the beatific vision within it.

FULTON J. SHEEN, *Religion Without God,* 1928

The life of grace, which has been given us, is the seed of the life of heaven, and is the same life in its essence.

REGINALD GARRIGOU-LAGRANGE, *Christian Perfection and Contemplation,* 1937

The grace of God is the good which God puts into each concrete situation over and above all that man can do or plan or even imagine.

HENRY N. WIEMAN, *The Christian Century,* January 25, 1939

Grace is nothing if not the final power; and power is force if it is not grace.

JOHN OMAN, *Honest Religion,* 1941

Grace is light, and through the familiar shape of things it brings unknown and divine realities into view.

JEAN MOUROUX, *The Meaning of Man,* 1948

Grace is not something that comes in from the outside and says "No, you are doing it wrong, let me show you how to do it." Grace is not a kind of auxiliary steam, supplementing our feeble powers with a force not of the same character. Grace does not replace nature, it perfects nature, transmutes something that belongs to earth and makes it glow with the radiance of heaven.

RONALD A. KNOX, *Bridegroom and Bride,* 1957

The love that gives, that loves the unlovely and the unlovable, is given a special name in the New Testament, grace.

OSWALD C. J. HOFFMANN, *Life Crucified,* 1959

GRATIFICATION

The greatest part of human gratifications approach nearly to vice.

SAMUEL JOHNSON, *The Rambler,* September 28, 1751

GRATITUDE

Gratitude tries to return more than has been received.

ST. THOMAS AQUINAS, *Summa Theologiae* 2a-2ae. cvi. 6, 1272

The creator, Hormizd, demands two things from mankind, the one is that he should

not commit sin, and the other is that one should practice thanksgiving. . . . As to every one who is not grateful—the bread that he eats becomes unlawful, and it is not proper for any one to do good in connection with him.

Sad Dar, possibly late 16th century A.D.

Gratitude does nothing but love God because of the greatness of His bounty and proclaims His goodness unceasingly. . . . It will be a foretaste of heaven to us here below, if we are able to thank God for all His infinite goodness with all our heart.

OTTOKAR PROHASZKA, *Meditations on the Gospels,* 1937

Gratitude is a blessing we give to one another.

ROBERT RAYNOLDS, *In Praise of Gratitude,* 1961

Gratitude is the memory of the heart.

ANONYMOUS

See also Thanksgiving.

GRAVE

The grave is but a covered bridge leading from light to light, through a brief darkness.

HENRY WADSWORTH LONGFELLOW, *A Covered Bridge at Lucerne,* 1851

The grave of one who dies for truth is holy ground.

German Proverb

See also Burial; Death; Funerals.

GREATNESS

Great man is sparing in words but prodigal in deeds.

CONFUCIUS, *Sayings of,* 5th century B.C.

The great man is he who does not lose his child's heart.

Mencius, c. 300 B.C.

414

Greatness is the Creator's robe, and he who comes into His presence in this robe is thrown out.

BAHYA BEN JOSEPH IBN PAKUDA, *Hobot Halebabot,* 1040 A.D.

True greatness . . . is filled with awe and reverence in the face of dark and mysterious fate, it is mindful of the ever-rolling wheel of destiny, and never allows itself to be counted great or happy before its end.

J. G. FICHTE, *Address to the German Nation,* 1808

Great is he who enjoys his earthenware as if it were plate, and not less great is the man to whom his plate is no more than earthenware.

SAMUEL TAYLOR COLERIDGE, *Aids to Reflection,* 1825

Great men are they who see that spiritual is stronger than any material force; that thoughts rule the world.

RALPH WALDO EMERSON, *Phi Beta Kappa Address,* July 18, 1867

No man has come to true greatness who has not felt in some degree that his life belongs to his race, and that what God gives him, he gives him for mankind.

PHILLIPS BROOKS (1835–1893), *Perennials from*

Greatness, after all, in spite of its name, appears to be not so much a certain size as a certain quality in human lives. It may be present in lives whose range is very small.

PHILLIPS BROOKS (1835–1893), *Perennials from*

See also Genius; Honor.

GREED

From love comes grief, from greed comes fear; he who is free from greed knows neither grief nor fear.

Dhammapada, c. 5th century B.C.

Lust of possession, prestige and power have also burned their devastating way into the very citadels of our civilization and have not been afraid to invade our sanctuaries.

Federal Council of Churches of Christ in America, *Report,* 1932

The Judge will say, I was hungry and you gave me not to eat, and a thousand pork butchers will say, "That is all very well, but Lent did us real injury."

LEON BLOY, quoted in MARTIN C. D'ARCY, *The Nature of Belief,* 1958

See also Avarice; Covetousness; Desires; Envy; Evil; Gluttony; Gold; Lust; Money; Poor, the; Possessions; Renunciation; Rich, the; Riches; Self-Interest; Selfishness; Success; Wealth; Worldliness.

GREGORIAN CHANT. See MUSIC

GRIEF

Those griefs smart most which are seen to be of our own choice.

SOPHOCLES (495–406 B.C.), *Oedipus the King*

Krishna to Arjuna after the latter's declaration of grief at the thought of slaying men in battle:

Thou grievest where no grief should be!
Thou speakest
Words lacking in wisdom! for the wise in heart
Mourn not for those that live, nor those that die . . .
All that doth live, live always.

The Song Celestial, Sir Edwin Arnold's translation of the *Bhagavad-Gita,* 5th to 2nd century B.C.

Grief is more evil than all the spirits, and is most terrible to the servants of God, and corrupts man beyond all the spirits and wears out the Holy Spirit.

SHEPHERD OF HERMAS, c. 148 A.D.

Grief and death were born of sin, and devour sin.
ST. JOHN CHRYSOSTAN, *Homilies,* c. 388

No greater grief than to remember days
Of joy when misery is at hand.
FRANCESCA DA RIMINI, in Dante's *Inferno,* c. 1310

Thus there grows from my deepest sorrow
—his death—
The fruit of faith, the soul's daily bread.
VITTORIA COLONNA (1490–1547), *Sonnets*

So I exchange my grief for eternal bliss and strive ever upward. All at once the ray of God's grace strikes me with heavenly fire.
VITTORIA COLONNA (1490–1547), *Sonnets*

Grief is a species of idleness.
SAMUEL JOHNSON, *Letter to Mrs. Thrale,* March 17, 1773

Both the ancestry and posterity of Grief go further than the ancestry and posterity of Joy.
HERMAN MELVILLE, *Moby Dick,* 1851

Great grief is a divine and terrible radiance which transfigures the wretched.
VICTOR HUGO, *Les Miserables,* 1862

Only when grief finds its work done can God dispense us from it.
HENRI AMIEL, *Journal,* 1882

Love remembered and consecrated by grief belongs, more clearly than the happy intercourse of friends, to the eternal world; it has proved itself stronger than death.
W. R. INGE, *Personal Religion and the Life of Devotion,* 1924

See also Bereavement; Death; Gloom; Mourning; Sadness; Serenity; Sorrow; Tears.

GROUP

The idea that man belong only to the group and not to his Creator is one that already deals in death—if not today, then tomorrow!
PAUL RAMSEY, *Nine Modern Moralists,* 1962

GUARDIAN ANGEL

It is a universal Catholic belief that not merely every *just* man, every child of grace, but in fact *every single human being* here upon earth, whether Christian or non-Christian, whether in grace or sin, remains during its entire life under the care of a Guardian Angel.
JOSEPH HUSSLEIN, *Our Guardian Angels,* 1950

See also Angels; Conscience; Spirit.

By confession, repentance, by austerity, and by reciting the Veda a sinner is freed from guilt.
The Code of Manu, between 1200 and 500 B.C.

Guilt proceeds from the free will of the person who is reprobated and deserted by grace.
ST. THOMAS AQUINAS, *Summa Theologiae,* I, 22. 4, 1272

In law a man is guilty when he violates the rights of another. In ethics he is guilty if he only thinks of doing so.
IMMANUEL KANT, *Lecture at Königsberg,* 1775

It is not a gain that guilt should be wholly forgotten. On the contrary, it is loss and perdition. But it is a gain to win an inner intensity of heart through a deeper and deeper inner sorrowing over guilt.
SÖREN KIERKEGAARD, *Purity of Heart,* 1846

My child can be no more guilty or deserving of punishment for my sin than he can see with my eyes or feel with my nerves.

WASHINGTON GLADDEN, *How Much Is Left of the Old Doctrines,* 1900

The sense of guilt implies in some vague outline the ideas of a broken moral order and an offended God.

WILLIAM CUNNINGHAM, *Essays on Theological Questions,* ed. H. B. Swete, 1905

Either guilt has to be incurred deliberately or it has not. Sin cannot be in part the choice of the individual, in part the result of the fall or the "sin of man."

H. D. LEWIS, *Morals and the New Theology,* 1947

Every reliable Christian authority and every really sane man, is solidly on the side of deep, strong and abiding guilt feelings as we rational creatures stand before the almighty and most holy God.

VINCENT P. MCCORRY, *America,* February 20, 1960

A rational being feels guilty when he most certainly is guilty.

VINCENT P. MCCORRY, *America,* February 20, 1960

The Christian again contradicts no unequivocal psychological tenets when he insists that, besides pathological guilt, there is far more commonly in every human being the natural reaction from behavior which contravenes the sense of right and wrong.

J. DOMINIAN, *Psychiatry and the Christian,* 1962

The experience of guilt feelings is of crucial interest both to psychiatry and religion.

J. DOMINIAN, *Psychiatry and the Christian,* 1962

A public admission of our guilt and the ready acknowledgment of our need of *metanoia* as a group will give more powerful witness to the holiness of the Church than do the eager attempts to white-wash the past and to shirk our responsibility for history.

GREGORY BAUM, *Progress and Perspectives,* 1962

See also Confession; Conscience; Determinism; Election; Forgiveness; Free Will; Individual Responsibility; Judgment, God's; Justification; Necessity; Original Sin; Penitence; Punishment; Responsibility; Sin; Sinners; Will.

HAPPINESS

Wouldst thou be happy, be thou moderate.
Code of Manu, between 1200 and 500 B.C.

It is good to tame the mind, which is difficult to hold in and flighty, rushing wherever it listeth; a tamed mind brings happiness.
Dhammapada, c. 5th century B.C.

Full of love for all things in the world, practicing virtue, in order to benefit others, this man alone is happy.
Dhammapada, c. 5th century B.C.

He who, seeking his own happiness, does not punish or kill beings who long for happiness will find happiness after death.
Dhammapada, c. 5th century B.C.

The greatest happiness which a mortal man can imagine is the bond of marriage that ties together two loving hearts. But there is a greater happiness still: it is the embrace of truth. Death will separate husband and wife, but death will never affect him who has espoused the truth.
Fo Pen Hsing Chi Ching (A Chinese Life of Buddha) c. 5th century B.C.

Of no mortal say "That man is happy," till vexed by no grievous ill he pass Life's goal.
SOPHOCLES, *Oedipus Tyrannis,* 4th century B.C.

Happiness is gained by a use, and right use, of the things of life, and the right use of them, and good-fortune in the use of them is given by knowledge.

PLATO, "Euthydemus," *Dialogues,* c. 370 B.C.

True happiness flows from the possession of wisdom and virtue and not from the possession of external goods.

ARISTOTLE (384–322 B.C.), *Politics* (Book VII of the Analysis)

Perfect happiness is the absence of happiness.

Chuang-tzu, c. 300 B.C.

Pronounce no man happy before his death, for by his latter end shall a man be known.

Apocrypha: Ben Sira, ii, 28, c. 300–190 B.C.

Knowledge of Him is the consummation of happiness.

PHILO, *Special Laws,* c. 10 A.D.

The man is happy, we say, who knows no good that would be greater than that which he can give to himself.

SENECA (4. B.C.–65 A.D.), *De Vita Beata*

Happiness is, literally, god within, or good.

MARCUS AURELIUS, *Meditations,* c. 170

Who is more happy than he who enjoys the unshaken and immutable and most excellent truth? . . . This truth reveals all goods which are true, which men of understanding, each according to his capacity, choose singly or together to enjoy.

ST. AUGUSTINE, *On the Free Will,* c. 400

He is truly happy who has all that he wishes to have, and wishes to have nothing which he ought not to wish.

ST. AUGUSTINE, *To Proba,* 412

Here we are called happy when we have peace, such little peace as can be had in a good life; but that happiness, in comparison with our final happiness, is altogether misery.

ST. AUGUSTINE, *The City of God,* 426

It is that highest of all good things, and it embraces in itself all good things. . . . Wherefore happiness is a state which is made perfect by the union of all good things.

BOETHIUS, *The Consolations of Philosophy,* c. 525

Since happiness is nothing else but the enjoyment of the Supreme Good, and the Supreme Good is above us, no one can be happy who does not rise above himself.

ST. BONAVENTURE, *The Journey of the Mind to God,* 1259

The perfect happiness of man cannot be other than the vision of the divine essence.

ST. THOMAS AQUINAS, *Summa Theologiae,* 2a, 2ae, div. I, Q 111, 1272

Bless me in this life with but peace of my Conscience, command of my affections, the love of Thyself and my dearest friends, and I shall be happy enough to pity Caesar.

SIR THOMAS BROWNE, *Religio Medici,* 1635

Happiness is that pleasure which flows from the sense of virtue and from the consciousness of right deeds.

HENRY MORE, *Encheiridion Ethicum,* 1667

The one happiness is the Life, the Light, the Spirit of God, manifested in nature and creature.

WILLIAM LAW, *Serious Call to the Devout and Holy Life,* 1728

He that is endeavoring to subdue, and root out of his mind, all those passions of pride, envy and ambition, . . . is doing more to make himself happy . . . than he that is contriving means to indulge them.

WILLIAM LAW, *Serious Call to the Devout and Holy Life,* 1728

By *happiness* we are to understand the internal satisfaction of the soul, arising from the possession of good; and by good, whatever is suitable or agreeable to man for his preservation, perfection, conveniency, or pleasure.

> JEAN JACQUES BURLAMAQUI, *Works of,* I, ch. 2, 1763

As a result of our interrogation of history we find ourselves only too well convinced that the peoples of the world not only have never known true happiness but have never even followed the path that could lead them towards it.

> CHEVALIER DE CHASTELLUX, *On Public Felicity,* 1772

He who made all men hath made the truth necessary to human happiness obvious to all.

> SAMUEL ADAMS, *Speech,* August 1, 1776

The first and indispensable requisite of happiness is a clear conscience, unsullied by the reproach or remembrance of an unworthy action.

> EDWARD GIBBON, *Autobiography,* 1789

Anthony sought for happiness in love; Brutus in glory; Caesar in dominion; the first found disgrace, the second disgust, the last ingratitude, and each destruction.

> C. C. COLTON, *Lacon,* 1820

I believe in God—this is a fine, praiseworthy thing to say. But to acknowledge God wherever and however he manifests himself, that in truth is heavenly bliss on earth.

> J. W. VON GOETHE, *Maxims and Reflections,* 1829

The happiness which we receive from ourselves is greater than that which we obtain from our surroundings. . . . The world in which a man lives shapes itself chiefly by the way in which he looks at it.

> ARTHUR SCHOPENHAUER, *Essays,* 1841

The thought of God, and nothing short of it, is the happiness of man.

> JOHN HENRY NEWMAN, *Parochial and Plain Sermons,* 5, 1843

The first requisite for the happiness of the people is the abolition of religion.

> KARL MARX, *A Criticism of the Hegelian Philosophy of Right,* 1844

The supreme happiness of life is the conviction that we are loved.

> VICTOR HUGO, *Les Miserables,* 1862

He who never sacrificed a present to a future good, or a personal to a general one, can speak of happiness only as the blind do of colors.

> HORACE MANN, *Thoughts,* 1867

Those only are happy who have their minds fixed on some object other than their own happiness,—on the happiness of others, on the improvement of others, on the improvement of mankind, even on some art or pursuit, not as a means but as itself an ideal end.

> JOHN STUART MILL, *Autobiography,* 1873

Wondrous state of man! never so happy as when he has lost all private interests and regards, and exists only in obedience and love of the Author.

> RALPH WALDO EMERSON, *North American Review,* May, 1878

No one truly knows happiness who has not suffered, and the redeemed are happier than the elect.

> HENRI AMIEL, *Journal,* 1882

What is happiness? The feeling of growing power. . . . Not contentment but the urge for power; not peace in general, but war.

> FRIEDRICH NIETZSCHE, *The Anti-Christians,* 1887

It would be a great thing if people could be brought to realize that they can never add to the sum of their happiness by doing wrong.

JOHN LUBBOCK, *The Pleasures of Life*, 1887

What is happiness? The feeling that power increases, that resistance is overcome.

FRIEDRICH NIETZSCHE, *Anti-Christ*, 1889

Man's happiness is based upon there being for him an indisputable truth.

FRIEDRICH NIETZSCHE (1844–1900), *Die Unschuld des Werdens,* publ. posth.

He is the happiest man who best understands his happiness; for he is of all men most fully aware that it is only the lofty ideal, that separates gladness from sorrows.

MAURICE MAETERLINCK, *Thoughts from Maeterlinck,* 1903

Humanly speaking, it is only when the hair is white, when . . . life is almost over, that men begin to realize how hopelessly elusive is the happiness promised by wealth and fame.

JOSEPH MCSORLEY, *Be of Good Heart,* 1924

Happiness has so many forms, and human beings have so many desires, that to know happiness and to seek it involves not only the power to understand ends and the relation of means to ends but the ability to drive the steeds in the chariot of human nature.

THOMAS VERNER MOORE, *Dynamic Psychology,* 1924

Happiness is to "become portion of that around me." . . . We are happy only when the self achieves union with the not-self. Now both self and not-self are states of our consciousness.

ALDOUS HUXLEY, *Texts and Pretexts* 1932

Health alone does not suffice. To be happy, to become creative, man must always be strengthened by faith in the meaning of his own existence.

STEFAN ZWEIG, *Mental Healers,* 1932

Happiness is not something to be aimed for; it is the result of right living.

ALEXANDER YELCHANINOV (1881–1934), *Fragments of a Diary*

If happiness truly consisted in physical ease and freedom from care, then the happiest individual would not be either a man or a woman, it would be, I think, an American cow.

WILLIAM LYON PHELPS, *Happiness,* 1935

Happiness is essentially a state of going somewhere, wholeheartedly, one-directionally, without regret or reservation.

WILLIAM H. SHELDON, *Psychology and the Promethean Will,* 1936

There may be Peace without Joy, and Joy without Peace, but the two combined make Happiness.

JOHN BUCHAN, *Pilgrim's Way,* 1940

Our Savior has nowhere promised to make us infallibly happy in this world.

POPE PIUS XII, *Address,* July 2, 1941

We cannot be happy until we can love ourselves without egotism and our friends without tyranny.

CYRIL CONNOLLY, *The Condemned Playground: Essays,* 1927–1944

What is happiness other than the grace of being permitted to unfold to their fullest bloom all the spiritual powers planted within us.

FRANZ WERFEL, *Between Heaven and Earth,* 1944

Do not go as far as the new-thought student who committed suicide and left a note behind saying: "I'm tired of being so damned happy!"

PATRICK MAHONY, *You Can Find a Way,* 1950

A man is truly happy when he is rightly related to God and to people, because then his lower nature is rightly related to his higher self.

KIRBY PAGE, *Living Joyously,* 1950

The secret of a happy life is the moderation of our pleasures in exchange for an increase of joy.

FULTON J. SHEEN, *Way to Happiness,* 1953

When we try to reach real happiness on cheap terms, what we get is bound to be cheap.

DAVID ROBERTS, *The Grandeur and Misery of Man,* 1955

See also Beatific Vision; Contentment; Heaven; Joy; Laughter; Love; Peace; Pleasure; Utilitarianism.

HARDSHIP

If God puts or permits anything hard in our lives, be sure that the real peril, the real trouble, is what we shall lose if we flinch or rebel.

MALTBIE D. BABCOCK, *Thoughts for Everyday Living,* 1901

No Christian escapes a taste of the wilderness on the way to the Promised Land.

EVELYN UNDERHILL, *The Fruits of the Spirit,* 1942

HARM

It is our maxim that we can suffer harm from none, unless we be convicted as doers of evil, or proved to be wicked; you may indeed slay us, but hurt us you cannot.

ST. JUSTIN MARTYR, *First Apology,* c. 150

HARMONY

While there are no stirring of pleasure, anger, sorrow or joy, the mind may be said to be in a state of EQUILIBRIUM. When these feelings have been stirred, and they act in their due degree, there ensues what may be called the state of HARMONY. This EQUILIBRIUM is the great root *from which grow all the human actings* in the world, and this HARMONY is the Unique path *which they all should pursue.*

CONFUCIUS, *The Golden Mean,* 5th century B.C.

It is reasonably expected that there should be accord among those on earth who are citizens of Heaven.

BENJAMIN WHICHCOTE, *Moral and Religious Aphorisms,* 1753

The history of the world is not the theatre of happiness; periods of happiness are blank pages in it, for they are periods of harmony.

G. W. F. HEGEL (1770–1831), *Philosophy of History,* publ. posth.

The hurricane of miracles blows perpetually. Day and night the phenomenon surges around us on all sides, and (not least marvelous) without disturbing the majestic tranquillity of the Creation. This tumult is harmony.

VICTOR HUGO, *William Shakespeare,* 1864

Judaism from its inception always . . . demanded harmony between thought, feeling and deed.

AUGSBURG SYNOD, *Declaration,* July 17, 1871

I believe in the eternal harmony in which they say we shall one day be blended. I believe in the Word to Which the universe is striving, and Which Itself was "with God," and Which Itself is God, and so on, and soon, to infinity.

FEODOR DOSTOEVSKY, *The Brothers Karamazov,* 1880

Has any man ever attained inner harmony by pondering the experience of others?

Not since the world began. He must pass through the fire.

    NORMAN DOUGLAS, *South Wind,* 1917

See also Discord; Peace; Religious Conflict.

HATRED

Let a man overcome anger by kindness, evil by good. . . . Victory breeds hatred, for the conquered is unhappy. . . . Never in the world does hatred cease by hatred; hatred ceases by love.

    BUDDHA (563–483 B.C.), quoted by Radakrishnan in *Indian Philosophy*

For hatred does not cease by hatred at any time: Hatred ceases by love, this is an old rule.

    Dhammapada, c. 5th century B.C.

When a fool hates a man that has no hate,
Is purified and free from every blemish,
Such evil he will find come back on him,
As does fine dust thrown up against the wind.

    Dhammapada, c. 5th century B.C.

Just as he who has charity has God, so he who has hatred nourishes the devil.

    ST. BASIL (330–379), *Sermo III De Charitate*

Unprovoked hatred is worse than the three cardinal sins.

    Talmud: Yoma, 9b., c. 500

There would be no place for hatred among wise men. For who but the foolish would hate good men? And there is no cause to hate bad men. Vice is as a disease of the mind, just as feebleness shows ill-health to the body.

    BOETHIUS, *Consolations of Philosophy* c. 524

Die, ye who hate!
Since Death alone from such estate
Can free you.

    SHAIKH SAADI, *Gulistan,* c. 1265

We shall set the seal of our approval on no kind of life whatever if we hate the good members on account of the wicked ones.

    DESIDERIUS ERASMUS, Preface to *Psalms of Hayno,* 1534

My neighbor despises me, he is wrong, because he is of no more importance than I am, and God has forbidden him to despise me.

    JEAN GROU, *Meditations in the Form of a Retreat,* c. 1795

An hour spent in hate is an eternity withdrawn from love.

    LUDWIG BOERNE (1786–1837), *Fragmente and Aphorismen,* no. 191

God . . . is only father in the sense of father of all. . . . When I hate some one or deny that God is his father—it is not he who loses, but me; for then I have no father.

    SÖREN KIERKEGAARD (1813–1855), *Journals of*

Hatred of those whom they have counted their enemies,—this has been the too characteristic sign of men who have called themselves Christ's servants and soldiers.

    FREDERICK D. MAURICE (1805–1870), *Sermons*

Heaven does not open its doors to those who hate, even if the hatred be only directed against themselves or the material things of God's creation.

    B. W. MATURIN, *The Laws of the Spiritual Life,* 1907

The most malicious kind of hatred is that which is built upon a theological foundation.

    GEORGE SARTON, *History of Science,* 1927

Hatred, I consider, is just a standing reproach to the hated person, and owes all its meaning to a demand for love.

    IAN SUTTIE, *The Origins of Love and Hate,* 1935

He who condemns sin becomes part of it, espouses it. You hate this woman and feel yourself so far removed from her, when your hate and her sin are as two branches of the same tree.

GEORGES BERNANOS, *The Diary of a Country Priest,* 1937

We may fight against what is wrong, but if we allow ourselves to hate, that is to insure our spiritual defeat and our likeness to what we hate.

GEORGE WILLIAM RUSSELL, (Æ), *The Living Torch,* 1937

You cannot conquer the world for the God of love by a jihad of hate.

M. S. LAZARON, *Common Ground,* 1938

Christ came to heal, not to hurt. Prejudice wounds our fellow men. Christians especially should take particular care as we teach His Gospel to avoid sowing seeds of hatred towards those of His own background—or hatred toward any minority group. He died for all.

JAMES A. PIKE, *Look,* March 14, 1961

See also Anger; Anti-Semitism; Bigots; Bitterness; Charity; Christianity, Criticism of; Conflict; Discrimination; Enemy; Evil; Fanaticism; Genocide; Intolerance; Love, Human; Malice; Negroes; Prejudice; Racial Conflict; Racial Injustice; Revenge; Sin; Vengeance; Vice.

HEALING

One may heal with holiness, one may heal with the law, one may heal with the knife, one may heal with herbs, one may heal with the Holy Word; amongst all remedies this one is the healing one that heals with the Holy Word; this one is that will best drive away sickness from the body of the faithful.

Zend-Avesta, Part II, c. 550 B.C.

It is more necessary for the soul to be healed than the body; for it is better to die than to live ill.

EPICTETUS (1st century A.D.), *Enchiridion*

To impute our recovery to medicine, and to carry our view no further, is to rob God of His honor, and is saying in effect that He has parted with the keys of life and death, and, by giving to a drug the power to heal us, has placed our lives out of His own reach.

WILLIAM COWPER, *Letter to Lady Hesketh,* 1765

All the power of the occult healer lies in his conscious will and all his art consists in producing faith in the patient.

ELIPHAS LEVI, *Dogma et Rituel de la Haute Magie,* 1861

Miraculous cures seldom occur. Despite their small number, they prove the existence of organic and mental processes that we do not know. They show that certain mystic states, such as that of prayer, have definite effects.

ALEXIS CARREL, *Man, the Unknown,* 1935

The religious man, I take it, not only feels the spirit of worship welling up within him in the presence of healing by prayer, but feels the same spirit when he witnesses a recovery after a skilled surgeon's difficult operation.

GERALD KENNEDY, *A Reader's Notebook,* 1953

Healing and the healing of the whole man are creative acts of God, no matter what the agent may be. He who has healing in his hands, be he physician, surgeon, psychiatrist, pastor, or layman, may only thank God humbly that he is used in this ministry.

JOHN SUTHERLAND BONNELL, *No Escape from Life,* 1958

See also Christian Science; Health; Miracles; Prayer; Psychiatry; Psychoanalysis; Psychotherapy.

HEALTH

To keep the body in good health is a duty, for otherwise we shall not be able to trim the lamp of wisdom, and keep our mind strong and clear. Water surrounds the lotus flower, but does not wet its petals.

> BUDDHA, "Sermon at Benares," in Asvaghosha's *The Fo-Sho-Hing-Tsan-King,* c. 5th century B.C.

It is the part of a Christian to take care of his own body for the very purpose that by its soundness and well-being he may be enabled to labor, and to acquire and preserve property, for the aid of those who are in want.

> MARTIN LUTHER, *Christian Liberty,* 1520

It has been increasingly evident, as pointed out by doctors everywhere, that physical health is closely associated with, and often dependent upon, spiritual health.

> DR. LORING T. SWAIM, *Presidential Address,* 1942, before the American Rheumatism Association

"But of course your health must come first." Must it? Certainly not if there is anything better to put before it.

> HUBERT VAN ZELLER, *We Die Standing Up,* 1949

See also Body; Christian Science; Healing; Self-Preservation.

HEART

If by abyss we mean a great depth, is not man's heart an abyss? For what is there more profound than that abyss? . . . Whose thought, whose heart is seen into?

> ST. AUGUSTINE, In *Psalm XLI,* c. 415

God demands the *heart,* that matters are to be judged according to the intent of the heart.

> MAIMONIDES (1135–1204), *Letter to Hasdai ha-Levi*

Sins of the heart, such as infidelity, heresy, envy, hate, etc., are to be punished by the sword of the spirit, which is the Word of God.

> SEBASTIAN CASTELLIO, *Concerning Heretics,* 1554

The heart, without the tongue, may pierce the ears of heaven: the tongue, without the heart, speaks an unknown language.

> ARTHUR WARWICK, *Spare Minutes,* 1637

The heart of man is the place the Devil dwells in; I feel sometimes a Hell within myself.

> THOMAS BROWNE, *Religio Medici,* 1642

The hearts of holy men are temples in the truth of things, and, in type and shadow, they are heaven itself.

> JEREMY TAYLOR, *Holy Living,* 1650

It is the heart which experiences God, and not the reason. This, then, is faith. God felt by the heart, and not by the reason.

> BLAISE PASCAL, *Pensées* 1670

We know the truth, not only by the reason, but also by the heart.

> BLAISE PASCAL, *Pensées,* 1670

The heart has its reasons, which reason does not know. We feel it in a thousand things.

> BLAISE PASCAL, *Pensées,* 1670

A heart that is satisfied with time and place does not know its own infinity.

> ANGELUS SILESIUS (1624–1677), *Cherubic Pilgrim*

The Heart is like a viper hissing, and spitting poison at God.

JONATHAN EDWARDS, *The Freedom of the Will,* 1754

No man must go to Heaven who has not sent his heart thither before.

THOMAS WILSON, *Maxims of Piety and of Christianity,* 1755

When the mind and heart are united in prayer and the thoughts of the soul are not scattered, then the heart is warmed with a spiritual warmth.

ST. SERAPHIM OF SAROV (1759–1833), quoted in A. F. Robbie-Bateman's biography of St. Seraphim

One is not a Christian by means of the mind but only by means of the heart.

C. A. SAINTE-BEUVE, *Port-Royal,* III, 1848

God builds his temple in the heart on the ruins of churches and religions.

RALPH WALDO EMERSON, *Method of Nature,* 1849

What other dungeon is so dark as one's own heart!

NATHANIEL HAWTHORNE, *The House of the Seven Gables,* 1851

By the supremacy of the Heart, the Intellect, so far from being crushed, is elevated; for all its powers are consecrated to the service of the social instincts.

AUGUSTE COMTE, *A General View of Positivism,* 1851

Of all the things which God hath made, the human heart is that which sheds the most light, and, alas! most night!

VICTOR HUGO, *Les Miserables,* 1862

You must put your hand into a man's heart to find out how much he is worth, not into his pocket.

HENRY WARD BEECHER, *Eyes and Ears,* 1864

Man's limitation is God's occasion. Only God can fully satisfy the hungry heart of man.

HUGH BLACK, *Friendship,* 1898

The best people I have known were saved from folly not by the intellect but by the heart.

GEORGE GISSING, *The Private Papers of Henry Ryecroft,* 1903

Fed on the dry husks of facts the human heart has a hidden want which science cannot supply.

WILLIAM OSLER, *Science and Immortality,* 1904

The purer the heart, the larger it is, and the more able it is to find room within it for a greater number of beloved ones; whilst the more sinful it is, the more contracted it becomes, and the smaller number of beloved it can find room for, because it is limited by self-love.

JOHN SERGIEFF OF CRONSTADT (1829–1908), *My Life in Christ*

The sin of the heart is the beginning and, so to speak, the root of all sin; the word and deed that spring from it merely bring it to its full development.

ÉTIENNE GILSON, *The Spirit of Medieval Philosophy,* 1938

In each heart there is a secret garden which God made uniquely for Himself.

FULTON J. SHEEN, *Peace of Soul,* 1949

When God measures man, He puts the tape around his heart—not his head.

Guideposts, September, 1962

See also Emotion; Faith; Hypocrisy; Intellect; Man and God; Mind; Prayer; Sin; Sincerity; Truth.

HEAVEN

The great souls of departed saints, look ever down on earth, and are full of beauty, shining each in its own place, and with its own glory. Saints, and heroes who died in battle, wise kings, and hermits, were there, visible by thousands, angels by thousands, heavenly singers, like to the sun in glory.

Mahabharata, c. 800 B.C.

The righteous in Heaven are undecaying and immortal, unharmed, undistressed and undisturbed. Everywhere, they are full of glory, fragrant and joyful, full of delight and full of happiness.

Zend-Avesta, 6th century B.C.

In the heaven-world there is no fear; thou art not there, O Death, and no one is afraid on account of old age. Leaving behind both hunger and thirst, and out of the reach of sorrow, all rejoice in the world of heaven.

Katha Upanishad, before 400 B.C.

He who knows the joy of Heaven has no grievance against Heaven and no grudge against men; he is unembarrassed by things, and unrebuked by the spirits of the departed.

CHUANG-TZU (4th century B.C.), *Texts of Taoism,* ed. J. Legge

The peace of the celestial city is the perfectly ordered and harmonious enjoyment of God, and of one another in God.

ST. AUGUSTINE, *City of God,* Bk. XIX, ch. XIII, 426

But announce to those who believe and do the things that are right, that for them are gardens 'neath which the rivers flow! So oft as they are fed therefrom with fruit for sustenance, they shall say, "This same was for our sustenance of old." And they shall have its like given to them. Therein shall they have wives of perfect purity, and therein shall they abide for ever.

Koran, Sura, II.23, c. 625

The end of a reasonable creature is to attain beatitude, and that can only consist in the kingdom of God, which in turn is nothing else than the well-ordered society of those who enjoy the vision of God.

ST. THOMAS AQUINAS, *Contra Gentiles,* Lib. 2, 1260

But what is Paradise? All things that are; for all that is, is good and joyous. Therefore it is called a Paradise, and is so indeed. . . . All that is, is verily an outer court of the Eternal and of Eternity.

Theologica Germanica, 14th century

The way to Heaven out of all places is of like length and distance.

THOMAS MORE, *Utopia,* 1516

There has not been any good man, nor any holy mind, nor any faithful soul, from the very beginning of the world even to its end, whom you will not find there with God.

ULRICH ZWINGLI, *Christianae fidei brevis,* 1531

Heaven is above all yet; there sits a judge
That no king can corrupt.

WILLIAM SHAKESPEARE, *King Henry VIII,* c. 1611

Heaven-gates are not so highly arch'd
As princes' palaces; they that enter there
Must go upon their knees.

JOHN WEBSTER, *Duchess of Malfi,* c. 1618

All places are distant from heaven alike.

ROBERT BURTON, *Anatomy of Melancholy, II,* 1621

As star differs from star in brightness, so men will be different, one from the other, in glory, in proportion as they will have been different in graces and merits.

ST. FRANCIS OF SALES (1567–1622), *Consoling Thoughts of,* ed. Huguet

Here [on earth] one may be lower than another in honor, and yet the highest want glory: there, though one star differs from another in glory, they all shine as stars.

Here the greatest must want—there the least hath enough. Here all the earth may not be enough for one—there one heaven is enough for all.

ARTHUR WARWICK, *Spare Minutes,* 1637

Where the Soul hath the full measure and complement of happiness; where the boundless appetite of that spirit remains completely satisfied, that it can neither desire addition not alteration; that, I think, is truly Heaven.

THOMAS BROWNE, *Religio Medici,* 1643

The rewards of heaven are so great and glorious, and Christ's burden is so light, his yoke so easy, that it is a shameless impudence to expect so great glories at a less rate than so little a service, at a lower rate than a holy life.

JEREMY TAYLOR, *Holy Living,* 1650

No man was ever scared into Heaven.

THOMAS FULLER, *Gnomologia,* 1732

Heaven is a cheap purchase, whatever it cost.

THOMAS FULLER, *Gnomologia,* 1732

He will never get to Heaven who desires to go thither alone.

THOMAS FULLER, *Gnomologia,* 1732

All that is sweet, delightful, and amiable in this world . . . is nothing else but Heaven breaking through the veil of this world.

WILLIAM LAW (1686–1761), *Selected Mystical Writings of*

The happiness of an unembodied spirit will consist in a consciousness of the favor of God, in the contemplation of truth, and in the possession of felicitating ideas.

SAMUEL JOHNSON, *Boswell's Life,* March, 1772

Many might go to heaven with half the labor they go to hell, if they should venture their industry the right way.

BEN JONSON, *Discoveries,* 1841

All that is high and holy in human life meets in that faith which is born of the unveiling of a heaven that has always been; in that hope of a vision of the heaven that shall be; in that love which creates a heaven in the eternal Now.

FRIEDRICH FROEBEL, *Mottoes and Commentaries of Mother-Play,* 1843

Heaven at present is out of sight, but in due time, as snow melts and discovers what it lay upon, so will this visible creation fade away before those greater splendors which are behind it.

JOHN HENRY NEWMAN, *Parochial and Plain Sermons,* 4, 1843

The secret of heaven is kept from age to age. No imprudent, no sociable angel ever dropped an early syllable to answer the longings of saints, the fears of mortals.

RALPH WALDO EMERSON, Essay on Swedenborg in *Representative Men,* 1850

Heaven is the presence of God.

CHRISTINA ROSSETTI, *Seek and Find,* 1879

Heaven possesses all light, all goodness, all glory, all fragrance, all joy. . . . It is devoid of want, pain, distress, discomfort . . . the radiance and brightness of the souls in heaven are like the stars and the moon, and they sit on golden thrones. . . . and their state of happiness continues up to the day of resurrection.

M. N. DHALLA, *Zoroastrian Theology,* 1914

To rest in God eternally is the supreme joy of Heaven. Indeed, Heaven has no meaning but that.

BEDE JARRETT, *Meditations for Layfolk,* 1915

What I am interested in is a heaven for humanity—sweating, swearing, toiling, loving, lusting, hating, worshipping, wonderful humanity—unregenerate yet lovable.

BENJAMIN LINDSEY, *The Companionate Marriage,* 1927

Sometimes I see in heaven the shores without end covered with the shining peoples of joy. A great vessel, all gold, above me, flourishes its banners and pennants, multicolored in the morning breeze.

ARTHUR RIMBAUD, *Season in Hell*, 1931

There are only War Veterans in heaven, who have fought the good fight for the Kingdom of God.

FULTON J. SHEEN, *The Fullness of Christ*, 1935

Heaven is not thrown open exclusively to men of heroic calibre.

EDWARD LEEN, *In the Likeness of Christ*, 1936

The blessed in heaven can share in the essentially divine operations only because they participate in the divine nature.

REGINALD GARRIGOU-LAGRANGE, *Christian Perfection and Contemplation*, 1937

Poor creature of time and mundane limits, the mind of man shrinks back abashed before the task of portraying a bliss that shall endure without end.

J. H. RANDALL, *The Making of the Modern Mind*, 1940

That Oriental concept which makes the realms of bliss a place where a man may have three hundred and fifty excellent meals a day and as many wives as he wants would appear to be preferable to the celestial picture which exists in many Christian minds.

VINCENT P. McCORRY, *As We Ought*, 1949

Heaven, to those who truly love all, can be heaven only when it has emptied hell.

NELS F. S. FERRÉ, *The Christian Understanding of God*, 1951

See also Beatific Vision; Death; Eternal Life; Fear; Happiness; Hell; Immortality; Joy; Judgment, God's; Man and God;

Nirvana; Paradise; Peace; Reward; Reward and Punishment; Soul; Supernatural.

HEBREW. See JEW

HEGELIANISM

The displacement not only of Christianity, but of Deism by the pantheistic and hence atheistic philosophy of Hegel was the great intellectual revolution of the early 18th century.

LOUIS J. A. MERCIER, *Address*, October 30, 1942

HEDONISM

Could we act more contrary to God than by making that life a state of pleasure and indulgence, which He has laid under the curse of death?

WILLIAM LAW, *Christian Perfection*, 1726

It is a remarkable fact that in their hedonistic aims, materialism and a certain species of "joyful" Christianity join hands like brothers.

C. J. JUNG, *The Practice of Psychotherapy*, 1954

See also Alcohol; Dissipation; Gluttony; Lust; Luxury; Perversion; Sex; Sexual Intercourse; Sexuality; Sobriety; Worldliness.

HELL

A terrific hell awaits the wicked— profound abyss of utter misery—into the depths of which bad men shall fall headlong and mourn their doom for countless years.

Mahabharata, c. 800 B.C.

And let those who think and speak and do Evil Thoughts and Words and Deeds abide in Hell. For to all those who think Good

Thoughts, speak Good Words, and do Good Deeds, Heaven—the Best World—belongs.

Zend-Avesta, 6th century B.C.

It is the iron's own rust that destroys it. It is the sinner's own acts that bring him to hell.

Dhammapada, c. 5th century B.C.

Hell has three doors: lust, rage and greed.

Bhagavad-Gita, between 500 and 200 B.C.

The fire of Gehenna is sixty times as hot as the fire of this earth.

Talmud, Berachoth, c. 200 A.D.

All who go down to hell shall come up again, except these three: he who commits adultery, he who shames another in public, and he who gives another a bad name.

Baba Metzia, Talmud, between 2nd and 4th century

The fire of Hell is insupportable—who does not know it?—and its torments are awful. But if you were to heap a thousand hell-fires one on top of the other, it would be as nothing compared to the punishment of being excluded from the beatific glory of Heaven, hated by Christ and compelled to hear him say, "I know you not."

ST. JOHN CHRYSOSTOM, *Homily on Gospel of St. Matthew,* c. 388

Hell is paved with priests' skulls.

ST. JOHN CHRYSOSTOM, *De sacerdotio,* c. 390

And I have warned you of a fire that flames! None shall broil thereon, but the most wretched, who says it is a lie and turns his back. But the pious shall be kept away from it.

Koran, c. 625

They who believe not shall have garments of fire fitted unto them; boiling water shall be poured on their heads; their

bowels shall be dissolved thereby, and also their skins, and they shall be beaten with maces of iron.

Koran, c. 625

There shall not abide eternally in the Fire a single believer, but whoever has in his heart the weight of a single grain of faith shall be brought forth therefrom.

AL-GHAZALI (died 1111 A.D.), *Ihya*

The wicked with the devil will receive eternal punishment while the good with Christ will receive eternal glory.

The Fourth Lateran Council, 1215

That the saints may enjoy their beatitude and the grace of God more abundantly, they are permitted to see the punishment of the damned in Hell.

ST. THOMAS AQUINAS, *Summa Theologiae,* c. 1265

Through me one enters the sorrowful city; through me one enters into eternal pain; through me one enters among the lost race. Justice moved my high Maker; divine power made me . . . I endure eternally. All hope abandon, ye who enter here.

Inscription over the gate of Hell, in Dante's *Inferno,* c. 1310

Nothing burneth in hell but self-will.

Theologica Germanica, 14th century

Hell hath no limits, nor is circumscribed
In one self-place; for where we are is Hell,
And where Hell is, there must we ever be.

CHRISTOPHER MARLOWE, *The Jew of Malta,* c. 1591

Represent to yourself a city involved in darkness, burning with brimstone and stinking pitch, and full of inhabitants who cannot make their escape.

ST. FRANCIS OF SALES, *Introduction to the Devout Life,* 1609

The punishments of sinners in hell shall be very great, very many and very pure, to wit, mixed with no comforts and which shall increase their misery everlasting.

ROBERT BELLARMINE, *On the Ascent to God,* 1616

Hell is full of good meanings and wishings.

GEORGE HERBERT, *Jacula Prudentum,* 1640

I thank GOD, and with joy I mention it. I was never afraid of Hell, nor never grew pale at the description of that place. I have so fixed my contemplations on Heaven, that I have almost forgot the Idea of Hell.

THOMAS BROWNE, *Religio Medici,* 1642

When thou art scorching in thy flames, when thou art howling in thy torments, then God shall laugh, and His saints shall sing and rejoice, that His power and wrath are thus made known to thee.

CHRISTOPHER LOVE, *Hell's Torments,* c. 1650

Hell could not be Hell without the despair of accursed souls; for any hope were a refreshment, and a drop of water, which would help to allay, those flames, which as they burn intolerably, so they must burn forever.

JEREMY TAYLOR, *Twenty-Seven Sermons,* 1651

There is nothing that keeps wicked men at one moment out of Hell, but the mere pleasure of God.

JONATHAN EDWARDS, *Sinners in the Hands of an Angry God,* 1741

Hell is paved with good intentions.

SAMUEL JOHNSON, *Boswell's Life of,* 1772

A lake of fire and brimstone whose flames are unquenchable, and whose smoke ascendeth up forever and ever.

The Book of Mormon, 1830

For myself, I see no need of a local hell for the sinner after death.

WILLIAM ELLERY CHANNING (1780–1842), *Works*

What is hell? . . . The suffering that comes from the consciousness that one is no longer able to love.

ALOYSHA in Feodor Dostoevsky's *The Brothers Karamazov,* 1880

Even if there were material fire, they would be genuinely glad of it, for I fancy that in material agony the much more terrible spiritual agony would be forgotten, even though for a moment.

ALOYSHA in Feodor Dostoevsky's *The Brothers Karamazov,* 1880

The one principle of hell is "I am my own!"

GEORGE MACDONALD, *Unspoken Sermons,* 3rd Series, 1887

The hell to be endured hereafter, of which theology tells, is no worse than the hell we make for ourselves in this world by habitually fashioning our characters in the wrong way.

WILLIAM JAMES, *Psychology,* 1892

I don't believe any man was ever drawn into heaven for fear he would go to hell.

WOODROW WILSON, *Address,* October, 1904

Hell is the work of prigs, pedants and professional truth-tellers.

SAMUEL BUTLER, *Notebooks of,* ed. H. F. Jones, 1912

Hell is . . . deep, dark, vile—devoid of comfort and happiness—but Hell is not eternal, for there comes at last the day of resurrection and the period of renovation "when the world will be regenerated, and all will be saved by the compassionate Lord."

M. N. DHALLA, *Zoroastrian Theology,* 1914

If I have so much compassion on the most guilty wretch on earth that I cannot in my heart wish him so terrible an end, then God, whose love is infinite, must be still less willing to see men in such straits.

BEDE JARRETT, *Meditations for Layfolk,* 1915

In Hell there is no hope, and consequently no duty, no work, nothing to be gained by praying, nothing to be lost by doing what you like. Hell, in short, being a place where you have nothing to do but amuse yourself, is the paradise of the worthless.

GEORGE BERNARD SHAW, *Socialism of,* ed. J. Fuchs, 1926

The damned can love no more and therefore they are damned. Hell is the home of incurables.The disease that is beyond cure is their egoism.

J. P. ARENDZEN, *Eternal Punishment,* 1928

The one big difficulty is not why there is a Hell but why God chooses a world in which there should have to be one.

MARTIN C. D'ARCY, *Problem of Evil,* 1928

Hell is paved with great granite blocks hewn from the hearts of those who said, "I can do no other."

HEYWOOD BROUN, *Column,* January 20, 1934

Jehovah. Did I ever mention publicly how Hell got started? . . . I thought I'd do something nice for a lot of theologians who had, after all, been doing the best they could, according to their lights; so I gave them an enormous tract of Heaven to do what they pleased with—set it apart for them to inhabit and administer, I didn't pay any attention to it for a few thousand years, and when I looked at it again, they'd made it into Hell.

DON MARQUIS, *Chapters for the Orthodox,* 1934

Hell as a place of retribution for the wicked, which is a comfort to the good, is a fairy tale; there is not a shadow of reality about it; it is borrowed from our everyday world existence with its rewards and punishments. . . . From the point of view of God, there cannot be any hell. To admit hell would be to deny God.

NICHOLAS BERDYAEV, *The Destiny of Man,* 1937

The damned is no less an inmate of hell because he does not believe in it.

FRANZ WERFEL, *Between Heaven and Earth,* 1944

Hell is other people.

JEAN PAUL SARTRE, *Huis Clos,* 1945

Hell is oneself. Hell is alone, and the other figures in it merely projections. There is nothing to escape from and nothing to escape to. One is always alone. . . . the final desolation of solitude in the phantasmal world of imagination, shuffling memories, and desires.

T. S. ELIOT, *The Cocktail Party,* 1950

Hell begins on the day when God grants us a clear vision of all that we might have achieved, of all the gifts which we have wasted, of all that we might have done which we did not do. . . . For me, the conception of hell lies in two words: "too late."

GIAN-CARLO MENOTTI, *Saturday Review of Literature,* April 22, 1950

If eternal hell is real, love is eternally frustrated and heaven is a place of mourning and concern for the lost. Such joy and grief cannot go together. . . . Heaven can be heaven only when it has emptied hell, as surely as love is love and God is God.

NELS F. S. FERRÉ, *The Christian Understanding of God,* 1951

To deny hell in principle would be to deny man's freedom; to confine it to anything short of eternity would be to limit that freedom.

J. A. PIKE and W. N. PITTENGER, *The Faith of the Church,* 1951

We put ourselves there. The door to hell is locked from the inside.

JAMES A. PIKE, *Beyond Anxiety,* 1953

Hell is the ego, sated with its own satisfied wishes, having to consume itself forever with no hope of release.

FULTON J. SHEEN, *Way to Happiness,* 1953

There would be no hell for modern man if our men of letters were not calling attention to it.

ALLEN TATE, *The Forlorn Demon: Didactic and Critical Essays*, 1953

Hell-fire . . . is not literally physical fire. It is present pain of mind, spiritual torment which neither sleep nor time nor any distraction can alleviate.

R. V. C. BODLEY, *In Search of Serenity*, 1955

If there is no belief in hell the concept of Judgment also becomes meaningless; and then all that is left of Christianity is a system of ethics.

GEOFFREY GORER, *Exploring English Character*, 1955

It is evident that hell, for the devils and the damned, is above all a condition of life, a *spiritual state*.

CHARLES JOURNET, *The Meaning of Evil*, 1961

It is absurd, unworthy and hateful to think that God can draw pleasure from the sufferings endured in hell and that he can seek and find in revenge a means of satisfying his justice—and yet is any blasphemy about hell more common than this?

CHARLES JOURNET, *The Meaning of Evil*, 1961

Heaven has a road, but no one travels it; Hell has no gate but men will bore through to get there.

Chinese Proverb

He who is used to hell is as comfortable there as anywhere else.

ANONYMOUS (very old)

We all hope he is where we know he ain't.

Funeral sermon attributed to Negro preacher.

No, said the churchman in a small town, there's no chance of our two churches combining. This church believes there ain't no hell, and the other church says, "The hell there ain't!"

ANONYMOUS

See also Damnation; Death; Despair; Election; Eternal Life; Fear; God: His Wrath; Hatred; Heaven; Judgment, God's; Loneliness; Love; Man: His Wickedness; Misery; Pain; Predestination; Punishment; Reward and Punishment; Self-Will; Sin: Its Consequences; Sinners; Suffering; Time.

HERESY

The trouble and difficulty of ascertaining the truth have given rise to questioning, from whence spring vain and self-willed heresies.

ST. CLEMENT OF ALEXANDRIA, *Stromateis*, c. 193

The order of time shows that it is divine and true which has been handed down from the beginning; that that is alien and false which has been added later. That is the prescription which disposes of all the heresies started in later days—they can make no assured claim to the truth.

TERTULLIAN, *On Prescription Against Heresies*, c. 206

These are "the doctrines" of men and "of demons" produced for itching ears of the spirit of this world's wisdom.

TERTULLIAN, *On Prescription Against Heresies*, c. 206

Heresies have not arisen except when the good Scriptures were not well understood and what was not well understood in them was rashly and boldly asserted.

ST. AUGUSTINE, *In Joann. Fr.*, c. 416

The most dangerous heresy is that of a sovereign who separates himself from part of his subjects because they believe not according to his belief.

THEODORIC I, to Justin in 523 A.D., quoted by Cassiodorus in *Variae*

If forgers and malefactors are put to death by the secular power, there is much more reason for excommunicating and even putting to death one convicted of heresy.

ST. THOMAS AQUINAS, *Summa Theologiae,* 1272

In any case, the Apostle is to be believed when he says: *There must needs be heresies.*

MARTIN LUTHER, *Resolutiones Disputationum, etc.,* to Pope Leo X, 1518

Divers great learned men have been heretical, whilst they have sought to fly up to the secrets of Deity by the waxen wings of the senses.

FRANCIS BACON, *Advancement of Learning,* 1605

Heresies perish not with their Authors. but, like the river Arethusa, though they lose their currents in one place, they rise up again in another.

THOMAS BROWNE, *Religio Medici,* 1642

Heresy is an act of the will, not of reason; and is indeed a lie, not a mistake.

JOHN HALES, *A Treatise Concerning Schism and Schismatics,* 1642

All so-called Christian religions of the present time are nothing but heresies—that is to say, they do not aim directly at the quickest possible improvement of the well-being of the poorest class, which is the sole aim of Christianity.

C. H. SAINT-SIMON, *The New Christianity,* 1825

The law knows no heresy.

U.S. Supreme Court, *Watson vs. Jones,* 1871

The great heresy in the world of religion is a cold heart, not a luminous head.

HENRY WARD BEECHER (1813–1887), *Sermon*

The undivineness of the natural and the unnaturalness of the divine . . . the great heresy of popular thought about religion.

BORDEN P. BOWNE, *The Immanence of God,* 1905

There is only one fatal heresy about Christ, namely, the heresy called Docetic, which robs Him of all reality.

A. CLUTTON-BROCK, *Studies in Christianity,* 1918

The one utter heresy in Christianity is thus to believe that we have reached finality and can settle down with a completed system. That is the essential denial of the living God, who cannot have said his last word on any subject or have landed his last hammer-blow on any task.

HARRY EMERSON FOSDICK, *Adventurous Religion,* 1926

The dislocation of some complete and self-supporting scheme by the introduction of a novel denial of some essential part therein.

HILAIRE BELLOC, *The Great Heresies,* 1938

The real issue in a heresy case is never the soundness, or reverse, of the views held by the accused, but the vindication of ecclesiastical authority.

WILLIAM ADAMS BROWN, *A Teacher and His Times,* 1940

Even genuine heresy is an attack on the divinity of the divine. It gives to something finite infinite validity. It conditions the unconditional, for instance, by human morality or rationality.

PAUL TILLICH, *The Journal of Religion,* January, 1947

Why do you accept mildewed old heresies as bold and constructive contributions to modern Christian thought when any handbook on Church history will tell you where they came from?

DOROTHY L. SAYERS, *Current Religious Thought,* 1947

The right to profess a heresy of any character, on any theme, is an essential element of a liberal society.

SIDNEY HOOK, *New York Times Magazine,* July 9, 1950

The great heresy of our times is the worship of the State.

R. L. BRUCKBERGER, *One Sky to Share,* 1951

Nothing so easily lures Christians into heresy as the over-confident dogmatic assumption that men, themselves, of course, in particular, are in a position to know all about God.

J. V. L. CASSERLEY, *Retreat from Christianity in the Modern World,* 1952

But his main concern is with the "hidden heresy" special to now—things said privately that one would not print, "an esoteric teaching which is spread only by word of mouth," "an unformulated heresy which works by omissions and one-sided perspectives."

FRANK J. SHEED, *Sheed and Ward Trumpet,* Spring, 1964

What we may call the Honorius-heresy consists not in the teaching of actual error, but in the failure to teach all the truth that there is to be known.

FRANK J. SHEED, *Sheed and Ward Trumpet,* Spring, 1964

See also Communism; Doctrine; Dogma; Freedom, Religious; Immortality, Denial and Doubt of; Infallibility; Orthodoxy; Philosophy; Schisms; Tradition.

HERETICS

Avoid heretics like wild beasts; for they are mad dogs, biting secretly.

ST. IGNATIUS OF ANTIOCH, *To the Ephesians,* c. 109

Heretics, indeed, who bring a strange fire to the altar of God—that is, strange doctrines—will be consumed by fire from heaven.

ST. IRENAEUS OF LYONS, *Adversus Haereses,* c. 175

The heretics do away with the true doctrine of the Lord, not interpreting and transmitting the Scriptures agreeably to the dignity of God and of the Lord.

ST. CLEMENT OF ALEXANDRIA, *Stromateis,* c. 193

And formerly heretics were quite evident, but now the church is full of masked heretics. For men have deserted the truth and want to have their ears tickled. . . . Talk of changing one's life, and everyone makes off.

ST. CYRIL OF JERUSALEM, *Catechetical Lectures,* 350

The Catholic Church has been vindicated by heretics, and those that think rightly have been proved by those that think wrongly. For many things lay hid in the Scriptures, and when the heretics had been cut off, they troubled the Church of God with questions: those things were then opened up which lay hid, and the will of God was understood.

ST. AUGUSTINE *in Ps.* 54, 22, c. 415

Those who seek the truth with care and prudence, who are ready to accept it when discovered, are not to be counted among the heretics.

ST. AUGUSTINE (354–430), *Epist.* xliii, I

Whoever shall maintain that wrong is done to heretics and blasphemers in punishing them makes himself an accomplice in their crime.

JOHN CALVIN, *Defensio orthodoxae fidei,* 1554

'Tis a vain thing to talk of an heretic; for a man can think no otherwise than he does think.

JOHN SELDEN, *Table Talk,* 1689

What is called a heretic has a very good side. It is a man who wishes to see with his own eyes. The only question is whether he has good eyes.

> G. E. LESSING, *Education of the Human Race*, 1780

The heretics of fifty years ago are the saints of today.

> EMMANUEL SCHREIBER, *Reformed Judaism*, 1892

The only real heathen and heretics are the purely selfish.

> WILFRED T. GRENFELL, *The Adventure of Life*, 1911

A heretic in one generation would have been a saint if he had lived in another, and a heretic in one country would often be a hero in another.

> RUFUS M. JONES, *The Church's Debt to Heretics*, 1924

Christ Himself and His apostolic followers, by the standards existing in their day, were "heretical."

> RUFUS M. JONES, *The Church's Debt to Heretics*, 1924

Wherever there is a creed there is a heretic round the corner or in his grave.

> ALFRED NORTH WHITEHEAD, *Adventures of Ideas*, 1933

Too often the heretic has been a tender-hearted advocate of spiritual first aid.

> VINCENT MCNABB, *Frontiers of Faith and Reason*, 1936

A heretic is a peculiar and highly pronounced representative of ecclesiasticism, who is possessed by a desire to cut an exclusive ecclesiastical figure and to be alone in the right with regard to the religious truth he professes.

> NICHOLAS BERDYAEV, *Dream and Reality*, 1939

There is never a devout saint or believer in universal love who is not a "heretic" to some other believer, whether Christian or Buddhist.

> LIN YUTANG, Introduction to "Sermons by Buddha" in Lin's *The Wisdom of China and India*, 1942

In all ages the tendency of the heretic has been to single out one aspect of Christian life or doctrine, and treat it as if it were the whole.

> RONALD A. KNOX, *Enthusiasm*, 1950

If history is correct, any progress that has been made in ethics and religion has been made not by the conformers, but by the heretics.

> FREDERICK KELLER STAMM, *If This Be Religion*, 1950

They [heresiarchs] seized on a few facts as though they were all the facts, and from these framed theories to explain and interpret all. They put forward a meagre and immature conception as a full-grown representation of the Christian idea of life.

> HORTON DAVIES, *Christian Deviations*, 1954

See also Heresy.

HEROES

It is wars most peaceful, waged for the very peace of the soul, and men who therein have been valiant for truth . . . and for piety . . . that our record of those who order their lives according to God will inscribe on everlasting monuments.

> EUSEBIUS, *The Ecclesiastical History*, c. 192

Virtue hath her heroes too,
As well as fame and fortune.

> FRIEDRICH SCHILLER, *The Death of Wallenstein*, 1799

The hero is he who lives in the inward sphere of things, in the True, Divine, Eternal, which exists always. . . . His life is a piece of the everlasting heart of nature itself.

THOMAS CARLYLE, *Lectures on Heroes,* 1840

Life, misfortunes, isolation, abandonment, poverty, are battlefields which have their heroes; obscure heroes, sometimes greater than the illustrious heroes.

VICTOR HUGO, *Les Miserables,* 1862

We want no heroes of the Soviet type to shape our futures for us; reckless heroes who are ready to throw away their lives in defense of indefensible principles which they never understood in the first place. We want the enlightened bravery of Christian Humanism.

ROBERT I. GANNON, *Address,* Fordham University, September, 1941

HEROISM

Christian virtue, to be heroic, must make its possessor act readily, joyfully, and with ease in a way that is above the ordinary.

POPE BENEDICT XIV (1675–1758), *Heroic Virtue*

To stand held only by the invisible chains of higher duty, and, so standing, to let the fire creep up to the heart—that is the truer heroism.

PHILLIPS BROOKS (1835–1893), *Perennials from*

The true heroic faith is that of him who, conscious of having calmly taken stock of the situation, and done everything that is humanly possible to ensure success, leaves the event to God, if he believes in God,— or to what ever may be his substitute for God.

ESME WINGFIELD-STRATFORD, *New Minds for Old,* 1935

How many men will never have the least idea of what is meant by supernatural heroism, without which there can be no

inner life! Yet by that very same inner life shall they be judged.

GEORGE BERNANOS, *The Diary of a Country Priest,* 1937

One day or another all young lives are stirred by an urge which seems to compel; every pure young breast has depths which are raised to heroism.

GEORGE BERNANOS, *The diary of a Country Priest,* 1937

See also Bravery; Courage; Cowardice; Moral Heroism; Valor.

HIDDEN LIVES

The growing good of the world is partly dependent on unhistoric acts; and that things are not so ill with you and me as they might have been, is half owing to the number who lived faithfully a hidden life, and rest in unvisited tombs.

GEORGE ELIOT, *Middlemarch,* 1872

HIERARCHY

If any one shall say that there is not in the Catholic Church a hierarchy instituted by divine ordinance and comprising bishops, priests and ministers, let him be anathema.

Council of Trent, Session XXIII, 1562

The eyes of faith see in the hierarchy ambassadors and representatives of Jesus Christ.

GERARD PHILLIPS, *The Role of the Laity in the Church,* 1962

See also Bishops; Church: Its Authority; Clergy; Leaders; Ministry; Priests; Religion, Organized.

HIGHER CRITICISM

There has arisen . . . an inept method, dignified by the name of the "higher criticism," which pretends to judge the origin, integrity and authority of each book from internal indications alone. . . . This vaunted "higher criticism" will resolve it-self into the reflection of the bias and the prejudice of the critic. . . . Seeing that most of them are tainted with false philos-ophy and rationalism, it must lead to the elimination from the sacred writings of all prophecy and miracle, and of everything else that is outside the natural order.

POPE LEO XIII, *Holy Scripture*, 1893

The Higher Criticism simply asks about the books of the Bible: who wrote them, when and why were they written, and to whom.

HARRY EMERSON FOSDICK, *The Modern Use of the Bible*, 1934

In the enthusiasm of its discoveries the Higher Criticism has applied to the New Testament tests of authenticity so severe that by them a hundred ancient worthies— e.g., Hammurabi, David, Socrates—would fade into legend.

WILL DURANT, *Caesar and Christ*, 1944

See also Bible: Its Interpretation, New Testament.

HISTORY

In general, the development of Spirit in *Time*, as Nature is the development of the Idea in *Space*.

G. W. F. HEGEL (1770–1831), *The Philosophy of History*, publ. posth.

God governs the world; the actual working of His government—the carrying out of His plan—is the History of the World.

G. W. F. HEGEL (1770–1831), *The Philosophy of History*, publ. posth.

History is a voice forever sounding across the centuries the laws of right and wrong.

J. A. FROUDE, *The Science of History*, 1864

What is called the Philosophy of history is nothing else than a Theology of history, more or less disguised.

ROBERT FLINT, *History of the Philosophy of History*, London, 1893

There is one history, and that the most touching and most profound of all, . . . the history of the human soul in its rela-tions with its Maker; the history of its sin, and grief, and death, and of the way of its recovery to hope and life and to enduring joy.

ISAAC M. WISE, *Selected Writings*, 1900

Religion, occupying herself with personal destinies and keeping thus in contact with the only absolute realities which we know, must necessarily play an eternal part in human history.

WILLIAM JAMES, *Varieties of Religious Experience*, 1902

History is in truth the path to another world. It is in this sense that its content is religious.

NICHOLAS BERDYAEV, *The Meaning of History*, 1936

History is a movement towards the King-dom of God. . . . But it is absurd to think that it will come *in and as a part of* history, where good and evil are inextri-cably intertwined. . . . It will come at the end of history.

JACQUES MARITAIN, *True Humanism*, 1936

The victory that overcomes the world is not success but faith and it is only the eye of faith that understands the true value of history.

CHRISTOPHER DAWSON, *The Kingdom of God and History*, 1937

We have not formed the right theory of History until we see History itself as a spiritual drama, moving toward a signifi-cant dénouement and at the same time a process which has meaning and value as it goes on.

RUFUS JONES, *The Eternal Gospel*, 1938

In its profoundest insight the Christian faith sees the whole of human history as involved in guilt, and finds no release from guilt except in the grace of God. The Christian is freed by that grace to act in history.

REINHOLD NIEBUHR, *Christianity and Power Politics,* 1940

History in its deepest sense, does not consist merely of secular happenings but . . . is always and at the same time a sacred process, a spiritual happening.

PETER WUST, *Essays in Order,* 1940

The flittering tumult of history in all its multiplicity, waywardness and concreteness is only a breaking wave on the ocean of Absolute Being.

JOHN WHALE, *Christian Doctrine,* 1941

It is not the history of families, nor of races and nation, nor of cultures that holds within itself the final meaning of history, but only the history of the Salvation of persons in the Kingdom of God.

THEODOR HAECKER, *Dublin Review,* CCXIX, 1946

The modern conception of history has its roots in the Biblical story of Jahveh and of the world which He creates as the scene for the unfolding of a divine plan.

MORRIS R. COHEN, *The Meaning of Human History,* 1947

The Christian, who serves not the historic process but the living will of God, may be compelled to stand against the stream of history, even as a forlorn and protesting voice.

ALEXANDER MILLER, *The Christian Significance of Karl Marx,* 1947

There is a deadly danger for any philosophy or sociology or Theology which sets the end of history within history itself. . . . It involves the delusion that something *total* can be built in an order of things which of its nature is transitory, transitional and non-total, and that delusion breeds idolatrous and totalitarian claims.

ALEXANDER MILLER, *The Christian Significance of Karl Marx,* 1947

Is not history, in the last analysis, a vision of the whole universe on the move in the four-dimensional framework of space-time?

ARNOLD J. TOYNBEE, *New York Times Magazine,* September 21, 1947

The fact that Christianity comes down to us as an historical religion . . . is bound to provide certain bearings for the interpretation of the whole drama of human life on this earth, bound to affect for example any views or dim feelings that we may have concerning the scheme of things in time.

HERBERT BUTTERFIELD, *Christianity and History,* 1949

The importance of secular history decreases in direct proportion to the intensity of man's concern with God and himself. . . . The message of the New Testament is not an appeal to historical action but to repentance.

KARL LOWITH, *Meaning in History,* 1949

Either there is no pattern of history at all (in which case a cosmic caprice will finally destroy every sense of the meaning of life) or there is a pattern but it is beyond our comprehension and under a Sovereignty which we can only dimly discern.

REINHOLD NIEBUHR, *Christianity and Crisis,* 1949

The Christian view of history is not merely a belief in the direction of history by divine providence, it is a belief in the intervention by God in the life of mankind by direct action at certain definite points in time and place.

CHRISTOPHER DAWSON, *Blackfriars,* July-August, 1951

History, without God, is a chaos without design or end or aim.

HENRY P. VAN DUSEN, *God in Education,* 1951

Christianity is the revelation of Divine Truth from beyond all history and all time, but it is so only because it is the only fully historical religion. It is the only religion which actually depends entirely upon history.

GREGORY DIX, *Jew and Greek*, 1953

Traditional Christianity could not conceive history apart from the Last Judgment and the establishment of God's Kingdom in purity and power.

ROGER L. SHINN, *Christianity and the Problem of History*, 1953

For others a knowledge of the history of their people is a civic duty, while for Jews it is a sacred duty.

MAURICE SAMUEL, *The Professor and the Fossil*, 1956

The course of human history consists of a series of encounters between individual human beings and God in which each man or woman or child, in turn, is challenged by God to make his free choice between doing God's will and refusing to do it. When Man refuses, he is free to make his refusal and to take the consequences. When Man accepts, his reward for willing what is the will of God is that he finds himself taken by God into partnership in the doing of God's creative work.

ARNOLD J. TOYNBEE, *Collier's*, March 30, 1956

Sacred history is not restricted to the contents of the Bible, but is still going on; we are living in sacred history.

JEAN DANIELOU, *The Lord of History*, 1958

History is made as men respond to the disclosure of the divine will and purpose either in rebellion and disobedience or in faith and obedience.

KENNETH CAUTHEN, *The Impact of American Religious Liberalism*, 1962

History is Dialogue between God and man-in-pilgrimage in the language of Event;

and Christ is the Conversation's middle term, the key to the translation.

GEORGE A. BUTTRICK, *Christ and History*, 1963

See also Bible; Bible and Civilization; Demons; End of the World; God: His Intervention in the World; New Testament; Old Testament; Providence; Revelation.

HOLINESS

Holiness is the best of all good. Happy the man who is holy with perfect holiness.

Vendidad, Zend-Aresta, c. 700 B.C.

Holiness comes by holy deeds,
Not starving flesh of daily needs.

SHAIKH SAADI, *Gulistan*, c. 1265

When a man is made holy, it is from a mere and arbitrary grace: God may for ever deny holiness to the fallen creature as he pleases.

JONATHAN EDWARDS, *Sermon*, preached at Boston, 1731

Now the perfect accordance of the will to the moral law is *holiness,* a perfection of which no rational being of sensible world is capable at any moment of his existence.

IMMANUEL KANT, *Critique of Practical Reason*, 1788

When couriers come down into the country, the common home-bred people possibly think their habit strange; but they care not for that, it is the fashion at court. What need, then, that Christians should be so tender-foreheaded, as to be put out of countenance because the world looks on holiness as a singularity; it is the fashion in the highest court, yea, of the king of kings himself.

SAMUEL TAYLOR COLERIDGE, *Aids to Reflection*, 1825

A being who can create a race of men devoid of real freedom and inevitably foredoomed to be sinners, and then punish them for being what he has made them, may be omnipotent and various other things, but he is not what the English language has always intended by the adjective holy.

JOHN STUART MILL, *Examination of Sir William Hamilton's Philosophy*, 1865

The remedy for modern lassitude of body, for modern weakness of will, is Holiness. There alone is the energizing principle from which the modern world persists in divorcing itself.

FRANCIS THOMPSON, *Health and Holiness*, 1905

Not holiness alone, but the beauty of holiness, is required to bind our hearts, our whole souls to God.

BEDE JARRETT *Meditations for Layfolk*, 1915

At the sight of beauty love always awakes; at the appeal of holiness the divine witness within us at once responds.

PAUL SABATIER, *The Life of St. Francis of Assisi*, 1920

It was in this submission of Himself, in which His human will was at one with His divine will, that Christ in His human life realized the perfection of holiness: for Christ was not less holy on earth than He now is in heaven.

FATHER CUTHBERT, *God and the Supernatural*, 1920

Christ constituted the Church holy and the source of holiness, and all those who take her for guide and teacher must, according to the divine will, aim at holiness of life.

POPE PIUS XI, *Encyclical*, January 26, 1923

It would be a great error fraught with many dangers should the priest, carried away by a false zeal, neglect his own sanctification, and become over immersed in the external works, however holy, of the priestly ministry.

POPE PIUS XI, *The Catholic Priesthood*, 1935

The holy is above all aesthetic as well as moral and logical classifications—it is the "wholly other" transcending all worldly values.

I. MAYBAUM, *Synagogue and Society*, 1944

There is such a thing as the danger of a selfish pursuit of holiness.

GERALD VANN, *Eve and the Gryphon*, 1946

"Holy" has the same root as "wholly"; it means complete. A man is not complete in spiritual stature if all his mind, heart, soul, strength are not given to God.

R. J. H. STEWART, *Spiritual Conferences of*, 1952

The beauty of holiness has only rarely been exhibited by the principal artists of our period.

NATHAN A. SCOTT, *Modern Literature and the Religious Frontier*, 1958

A holy person is one who is sanctified by the presence and action of God within him.

THOMAS MERTON, *Life and Holiness*, 1963

In our era, the road to holiness necessarily passes through the world of action.

DAG HAMMARSKJOLD, *Markings*, 1964

See also Beautiful, the; Beauty; Church: Its Authority; Community; Goodness; Grace; Humility; Justice; Perfection; Piety; Prayer; Prudence; Sabbath; Sanctity; Spiritual Progress.

HOLLYWOOD

A dreary industrial town controlled by hoodlums of enormous wealth, the ethical sense of a pack of jackals, and taste so degraded that it befouled everything it touched.

S. J. PERELMAN, *Paris Review,* April, 1964

HOLY GHOST. See HOLY SPIRIT

HOLY ORDERS. See ORDINATION

HOLY SPIRIT

He whom the Spirit chooses for his own, only he can comprehend the Spirit. This Spirit is hidden in all beings.

Katha Upanishad, before 400 B.C.

Because it calculates not, Spirit shines in lonely glory in what is beyond the world. . . . Though Spirit lies beyond the world, it stays ever within them.

SENG-CHAO (388–414), A.D. *Book of Chaos*

For what is the office of the Paraclete but this: the direction of teaching, the revelation of the Scriptures, the reformation of the intellect, the advance towards better things.

TERTULLIAN, *Ad Scapulam,* c. 212 A.D.

We, the baptized, cleansed of the sins whose darkness imposed a barrier between us and the Holy Ghost, have the free, untrammeled eye of the Holy Spirit.

ST. CLEMENT OF ALEXANDRIA, *Paedagogi Lib.* I, c. 220

In regard to him [the Holy Spirit] it is not yet clearly known that he is to be thought of as begotten or unbegotten, or as being himself also a Son of God or not.

ORIGEN, *De Principiis,* c. 254

The Holy Ghost is by nature holiness, but the holiness of angels and men is a participation in His natural sanctity.

ST. BASIL, *Contra. Eunom.* I. 3, c. 363

Just as transparent substances, when subjected to light, themselves glitter and give off light, so does the soul, illuminated by the Holy Spirit, give light to others and itself become spiritual.

ST. BASIL, *De Spir. Sancto,* IX, c. 375

All truth, by whomever uttered, is from the Holy Spirit.

ST. AMBROSE (c. 340–397), *Comment in Epist. I Ad Cor.*

The Holy Spirit rests on him only who has a joyous heart.

Talmud J: Sukka, 5.1, c. 400

One stream flows out from the throne of God, and that is the Grace of the Holy Spirit, and that Grace of the Holy Spirit is in the Holy Scriptures, that is in the stream of the Scriptures.

ST. JEROME, *Tractate in Marcum,* c. 408

What our soul is to the body, the Holy Ghost is to the Body of Christ, which is the Church.

ST. AUGUSTINE (354–430), *Sermo 187, De Tempore*

If we have once quit the sensual life, is it not evident that, by surrendering to the Holy Spirit, and by uniting ourselves to the Holy Spirit, we are changed into a heavenly image and transformed, to a certain extent, into another nature?

ST. CYRIL OF ALEXANDRIA (412–444), *In Joan;* I, 11

The grace of the Holy Ghost is not bound by any law.

POPE ST. GREGORY THE GREAT (540–604), *Dialogues*

The Holy Spirit Who is the love whereby the Father loves the Son, is also the love whereby God loves creatures and imparts to them His goodness.

ST. THOMAS AQUINAS, *Commentary on the Sentences,* c. 1252

We do not get the Holy Spirit in temporal things. When a person turns from temporal things inwards, into himself, he becomes aware of a heavenly light.
> MEISTER ECKHART (1260?–1327?), *Meister Eckhart*

The Holy Ghost openeth the eye of the soul, and showeth to the soul the sight of Jesus wonderfully, and the knowledge of Him as well as the soul can suffer it by little and little.
> WALTER HYLTON (died c. 1396), *Scale of Perfection*

Nor shall I believe that you are in the Spirit except I behold in you the fruits of the Spirit.
> DESIDERIUS ERASMUS, *Enchiridion*, 1503

The Holy Spirit distributes to each according as He wills, and according to each one's disposition and cooperation.
> *Council of Trent*, Sess. vi, ch. 7, 1551

No man sins against the Holy Ghost, but he that wilfully and finally renounceth Christ, and condemneth him and his word to the last, without which there is no salvation.
> ROBERT BURTON, *Anatomy of Melancholy*, 1621

The Holy Ghost, who moves in thy darkness, and will bring light even out of that, knowledge out of thine ignorance, clearness out of thy scruples, and consolation out of thy Dejection of spirit.
> JOHN DONNE, *Sermon*, 1624

The Holy Spirit only gives its testimony in favor of works . . . and is in itself nothing but the mental acquiescence which follows a good action in our souls.
> BARUCH SPINOZA, *Tractatus Theologico-Politicus*, ch. XV, 1670

The testimony of the Spirit is that alone by which the true knowledge of God hath been, and can only be revealed. . . . These divine inward revelations . . . neither do nor can contradict the outward testimony of the Scriptures, or right and sound reason.
> ROBERT BARCLAY, *Apology for the Quakers*, 1678

Every good gift is from God, and is given to man by the Holy Ghost. By nature there is in us no good thing. And there can be none; but so far as it is wrought in us by that good Spirit.
> JOHN WESLEY (1703–1791), *Works*, VIII

What is the Divine Spirit? Is the Holy Ghost any other than an Intellectual fountain?
> WILLIAM BLAKE, *Jerusalem*, 1820

Though the assent of faith is by no means a blind action of the mind, still no man can assent to the Gospel teaching, as is necessary to obtain salvation, without the illumination and inspiration of the Holy Spirit.
> Vatican Council, Session III, 1870

As Christ is the Head of the Church, so is the Holy Ghost her soul.
> POPE LEO XIII, *The Holy Spirit*, May, 1897

The Holy Ghost . . . is the free reign of God in man himself, it is something intimate, which no synods can limit, and no pastor can convey.
> FRIEDRICH NAUMANN, *Briefe über Religion*, 1903

This soul is enriched a hundredfold by the infusion of the Holy Spirit. . . . for the flame of human love or active energy is substituted the intenser flame of Divine Love or Divine Energy. Rather it is not a substitution; but the higher is added to the lower.
> FRANCIS THOMPSON, *Health and Holiness*, 1905

The Father works from without, in Providence; the Holy Spirit from within—in conscience and inspiration, to lead a man to Christ, to the imitation of the Son, who is redemption.

JOANNES JORGENSEN, *Autobiography*, 1928

There is indeed a unity of God and man: God himself creates it. It is no other unity than his own eternal unity as Father and Son. This unity is the Holy Ghost.

KARL BARTH, *Credo*, 1935

Not every deadly sin willingly committed after Baptism is sin against the Holy Ghost.

Article 16, Anglican Articles, *Book of Common Prayer*, edition of 1935

The presence of the ascended Lord in the Church, His Body, is effected by the power of the one Spirit, who conveys to the whole fellowship the gifts of the ascended Lord.

The Second World Conference on Faith and Order, ed. L. Hodgson, 1938

Only the Spirit, if it breathes upon the clay, can create Man.

ANTOINE DE SAINT EXUPÉRY, *Wind, Sand and Stars*, 1939

The sins against the Spirit are those which destroy in man just that which places him at the disposal of mercy: repentance, hope, consent to truth.

JACQUES MARITAIN, *Art and Poetry*, 1943

What lifts the Christian society to a level that transcends the whole order of nature is the Spirit of our Redeemer—the Spirit who, as the source of all graces, gifts and charisms, is forever filling the Church in her inmost being, and energizing within her.

POPE PIUS XII, *Mystici Corporis*, 1943

The Holy Spirit is henceforth corporate, not an individual possession. Church and Holy Spirit are from this point on inseparable. . . . Apart from this corporate community, there is no gift of the Holy Spirit.

THEODORE WEDEL, *The Coming Great Church*, 1945

The Holy Ghost teaches, strengthens, and energizes you actually to relive Christ.

RICHARD L. ROONEY, *Our Gifted Selves*, 1947

Christ speaks; the Holy Ghost explains. Christ acts and lives; the Holy Ghost expounds, illuminates, interprets the significance of Christ's deeds.

RICHARD L. ROONEY, *Our Gifted Selves*, 1947

The Spirit operates through human personality, and a man is fulfilling the function for which he was designed only when the energy of the Spirit is flowing through him.

G. B. CAIRD, *The Truth of the Gospel*, 1950

Only when the members of the Church allow the Spirit to declare His presence within them will those outside the fold be convinced that here is the unmistakable witness to Christ.

AELRED GRAHAM, *Christian Thought and Action*, 1951

The true believer in the Holy Spirit is one who knows how to hoist the sail of his own spirit to catch the winds of God.

RALPH W. SOCKMAN, *How to Believe*, 1953

One might risk a comment in this sense about the mysterious "blasphemy against the Holy Ghost" which hath no forgiveness. . . . the sin against the Spirit of Truth . . . what can God Himself do with or for the man who will not acknowledge the truth he knows, or follow the light he sees?

ALEXANDER MILLER, *The Renewal of Man*, 1955

Seen in the full context of the history of salvation, the sequence of religious systems is not a mere succession, or a natural evolution, but a series of advances under the creative impulsion of the Holy Ghost.

JEAN DANIELOU, *The Lord of History*, 1958

See also Baptism; Bible; Bible: Its Inspiration; Bible as History; Church: Its Nature; Church: Its Work; Freedom and God; God: Considered as Personal; God: His Intervention in the World; Grace; Jesus Christ; Light; Man and God; Man Indwelt by God; Man's Unity with God; Mystical Body of Christ; New Testament; Pentecost; Preaching and the Bible; Private Judgment; Quakers; Revelation; Soul and God; Spirit; Tradition; Trinity; Truth and Religion; Unity; Word, the.

HOME

The happiness of the domestic fireside is the first boon of Heaven.

THOMAS JEFFERSON, *Letter to John Armstrong*, February, 1813

When men do not love their hearths, nor reverence their thresholds, it is a sign they have dishonored both, and that they have never acknowledged the true universality of that Christian worship which was indeed to supersede the idolatry, but not the piety, of the pagan. Our God is a household God, as well as a heavenly one; He has an altar in every man's dwelling.

JOHN RUSKIN, *The Seven Lamps of Architecture*, 1848

This is the true nature of home—it is the place of Peace; the shelter, not only from all injury, but from all terror, doubt, and division.

JOHN RUSKIN, *Sesame and Lilies*, 1865

The domestic household is antecedent, as well in idea as in fact, to the gathering of men into a community.

POPE LEO XIII, *Rerum Novarum*, 1891

Anyone can build an altar; it requires a God to provide the flame. *Anybody can build a house; we need the Lord for the creation of a home.*

JOHN HENRY JOWETT, *Thirsting for the Springs*, 1903

The sumptuously furnished house may be only an exquisitely sculptured tomb; the scantily furnished house may be the very hearthstone of the eternal God.

JOHN HENRY JOWETT, *Thirsting for the Springs*, 1903

A man travels the world over in search of what he needs and returns home to find it.

GEORGE MOORE, *The Brook Kerith*, 1916

The Christian home is the school of Christ.

EDWIN V. O'HARA, *The Parent-Educator*, Vol. V, 1944

A good home is authoritarian, for if a wise mother sees her young son about to eat poison berries, she stops him. She does not say: "I must not coerce him. He must make his own discovery of truth." . . . but a good home is also . . . an honoring of personality. So any sound education is both authoritarian and free.

GEORGE A. BUTTRICK, *Christ and Man's Dilemma*, 1946

Home is a necessity for man's existence. It imparts security and it assures that strength which a singleness and an aloofness is not able to impart in life. . . . It completes our incompleteness.

S. J. Jhabuala, *Catechism on Zoroastrianism* (contemporary, but no date)

See also Children; Family; Marriage; Parents.

HOMOSEXUALITY

Even if all nations committed such sins, they should all alike be held guilty by God's law which did not make men so that they should abuse each other thus. The friendship which is between God and us is violated when nature, whose author he is, is polluted and by so perverted a lust.
ST. AUGUSTINE, *Confessions*, 397

Our current moral code tells the homosexual that he must sublimate his homosexuality and embrace the celibate life. . . . But it is difficult for a society that does not honor celibacy in heterosexuals to insist on celibacy in the case of homosexuals with any real conviction and justice.
J. V. L. CASSERLEY, *The Bent World*, 1955

At present there are influential secularist thinkers making the same arguments about homosexuality that their forebears were making earlier in the century about birth control. They are ridiculing the Christian teaching on sexual perversion as another example of power of inherited inhibitions.
ROBERT HOYT, Kansas City–St. Joseph *Reporter*, December 25, 1959

Since he [the homosexual] possesses no innate evil, he deserves to be treated not as a perverted outcast but as a citizen no less worthy than others.
J. DOMINIAN, *Psychiatry and the Christian*, 1962

The state [of homosexuality] itself carries no stain of sin and offends neither God nor society. If this alone became clear in the minds of people, the homosexual's lot would ease immediately. . . . If he practices the Christian faith, he is still expected to resist all physical sexual contacts.
J. DOMINIAN, *Psychiatry and the Christian*, 1962

See also Impurity; Perversion; Sex; Sexual Sin.

HONESTY

Divine Providence has granted this gift to man, that those things which are honest are also the most advantageous.
QUINTILIAN, *Institutio Oratoria*, c. 90 A.D.

On honesty God's favor is bestowed,
I never saw one lost in a straight road.
SHAIKH SAADI, *Gulistan*, c. 1265

An honest man's the noblest work of God.
ALEXANDER POPE, *An Essay on Man*, 1734

To be employed in things connected with virtue is most agreeable with the character and inclinations of an honest man.
JOHN WOOLMAN, *Serious Considerations on Various Subjects*, 1773

"Honesty is the best policy," but he who acts on that principle is not an honest man.
RICHARD WHATELY, *Easy Lessons on Morals*, 1854

It is easy to be honest enough not to be hanged. To be *really* honest means to subdue one's party spirit, one's vanity, one's prepossessions, ideals—stating things fairly, not humoring your argument—doing justice to your enemies . . . making confession whether you can afford it or not; refusing unmerited praise; looking painful truths in the face.
AUBREY DE VERE, *Recollections*, 1897

The life of an honest man must be an apostasy and a perpetual desertion. . . . For the man who wishes to remain faithful to truth must make himself continually unfaithful to all the continual, successive, indefatigable renascent errors.
CHARLES PÉGUY, *Basic Verities*, 1943

See also Honor; Hypocrisy; Integrity; Veracity; Virtue.

HONOR

For my own part, I believe that honor and money nearly always go together, and that he who desires honor never hates money, while he who hates money cares little for honor.

ST. TERESA OF ÁVILA, *Way of Perfection,* 1565

To those whose god is honor, disgrace alone is sin.

J. C. and A. W. HARE, *Guesses at Truth,* 1827

Every noble crown is, and on earth forever will be, a crown of thorns.

THOMAS CARLYLE, *Past and Present,* 1843

When one has to seek the honor that comes from God only, he will take the withholding of the honor that comes from men very quietly indeed.

GEORGE MACDONALD (1824–1905), *Selections from,* ed. Dewey

See also Fame; Glory; Greatness; Honesty; Integrity; Office; Reputation.

HOPE

Hope is the source of all happiness. . . . None is to be considered a man who does not hope in God.

PHILO, *Rewards,* c. 10 A.D.

If you do not hope, you will not find what is beyond your hopes.

ST. CLEMENT OF ALEXANDRIA, *Stromateis,* c. 193

Found not thy hopes on thyself but on thy God. For if thou restest thy hopes on thyself, thy soul is troubled within thyself, for it has not yet found anything about thee that should make it secure.

ST. AUGUSTINE, *Enarrations in Psalms,* xli, 12, c. 415

Everything that is done in the world is done by hope.

MARTIN LUTHER (1483–1546), *Table Talk*

The miserable have no other medicine,
But only hope.

WILLIAM SHAKESPEARE, *Measure for Measure,* c. 1604

Without hope, it is impossible to pray; but hope makes our prayers reasonable, passionate, and religious.

JEREMY TAYLOR, *Holy Living,* 1650

This is a direct act of hope to look through the cloud and look for a beam of the light from God.

JEREMY TAYLOR, *Holy Living,* 1650

Hope is the poor man's bread.

GEORGE HERBERT, *Jacula Prudentum,* 1651

Of all the ills that men endure,/The only cheap and universal cure.

ABRAHAM COWLEY, (1618–1667), *The Mistress: For Hope*

Hope is but the dream of those that wake.

MATTHEW PRIOR, *Solomon on the Vanity of the World,* 1718

Hope itself is a species of happiness, and, perhaps, the chief happiness which this world affords; but, like all other pleasures immoderately enjoyed, the excesses of hope must be expiated by pain.

SAMUEL JOHNSON, June 8, 1762, *Letters of*

Hope is the soul of the unhappy.

J. W. VON GOETHE (1749–1832), *Maxims and Reflections,* ed. B. Saunders

It would appear that our nature is not, for any length of time, capable of perfect resignation. Hope will make its way into

the mind, and with hope, activity, and with activity, the realization of hope.
> J. W. VON GOETHE (1749–1832), *Maxims and Reflections of,* ed. B. Saunders

True hope seeks only the Kingdom of God, and is convinced that all earthly things necessary for this life will without doubt be given. . . . The heart cannot have peace until it acquires this hope.
> ST. SERAPHIM OF SAROV (1759–1833), quoted in A. F. Dobbie-Bateman's biography of St. Seraphim

In this vale of Death, God girds us round; and over our gloom, the sun of Righteousness still shines a beacon and a hope. If we bend down our eyes, the dark vale shows her mouldy soil; but if we lift them, the bright sun meets our glance half way, to cheer.
> HERMAN MELVILLE, *Moby Dick,* 1851

The mighty hopes that make us men.
> ALFRED TENNYSON, *In Memoriam,* 1851

Reality has but one shape; hope is many-shaped.
> J. W. VON GOETHE, *Goethe's Opinions,* ed. Otto Wencksterns, 1853

Hope is the belief, more or less strong, that joy will come; desire is the wish it may come. There is no word to designate the remembrance of joys past.
> SYDNEY SMITH, *Lady Holland's Memoirs,* I, 1855

There never yet was a generation of men (savage or civilized) whom taken as a body, so woefully fulfilled the words "having no hope, and without God in the world," as the present civilized European race.
> JOHN RUSKIN, *Modern Painters,* III, 1856

Hope is the parent of faith.
> C. A. BARTOL, *Radical Problems,* 1872

My antagonist has closed with me again. A protest comes, out of the very depth and dust of man's radically hopeless position in the world. . . . Dared one hope that there is a heart even as ours, in that Divine *Assistant* of one's thoughts—a heart even as mine, behind this vain show of things!
> WALTER PATER, *Marius the Epicurean,* 1885

The word which God has written on the brow of every man is Hope.
> VICTOR HUGO (1802–1885), *Treasure Bits from,* ed. Rose

Hope is the thing with feathers
That perches in the soul
And sings the tune without the words,
And never stops at all
And sweetest in the gale is heard.
> EMILY DICKINSON (1830–1886), *Poems*

If in the hour of death the conscience is at peace, the mind need not be troubled. The future is full of doubt, indeed, but fuller still of hope.
> JOHN LUBBOCK, *The Pleasures of Life,* 1887

Hope, n. Desire and expectation rolled into one.
> AMBROSE BIERCE, *Devil's Dictionary,* 1906

Prayer breathes hope, and a prayer without hope is a sinful prayer.
> JOHN SERGIEFF OF CRONSTADT (1829–1908), *My Life in Christ*

Within us we have a hope which always walks in front of our present narrow experience; it is the undying faith in the infinite in us.
> RABINDRANATH TAGORE, *Sādhāna,* 1913

A true Christian should have but one fear—lest he should not hope enough.
> WALTER ELLIOTT, *The Spiritual Life,* 1914

What enthusiasm is to the youth and ambition to the apprentice and peace of mind to the invalid, such is hope to the Christians.

JOSEPH MCSORLEY, *Be of Good Heart,* 1924

Give humanity hope and it will dare and suffer joyfully, not counting the cost—hope with laughter on her banner and on her face the fresh beauty of morning.

J. E. BOODIN, *God: A Cosmic Philosophy of Religion,* 1934

The sin against hope—the deadliest sin and perhaps also the most cherished, the most indulged.

GEORGES BERNANOS, *The Diary of a Country Priest,* 1937

Hope is some extraordinary spiritual grace that God gives us to control our fears, not to oust them.

VINCENT MCNABB, *Joy in Believing,* 1939

As it was preached by the first apostles, it meant nothing more or less than a confidence on the part of the Christian that he or she would attain happiness in a future life.

RONALD A. KNOX, *God and the Atom,* 1945

Rising above the false antithesis of "Idealism" and "Realism," of optimism and pessimism, is Christian hope. But hope presupposes faith. And here, for the world we live in, is the rub.

AELRED GRAHAM, *Christian Thought and Action,* 1951

Jeremiah could never believe that the national ruin was the end. True, he could see no cause for hope; but he never lost hope, because he never lost God.

JOHN BRIGHT, *The Kingdom of God,* 1953

Belief in progress as hope resting upon self-confidence is the opposite of the Christian hope, which is hope founded upon trust in God.

EMIL BRUNNER, *Eternal Hope,* 1954

Hope . . . is one of the ways in which what is merely future and potential is made vividly present and actual to us. Hope is the positive, as anxiety is the negative, mode of awaiting the future.

EMIL BRUNNER, *Eternal Hope,* 1954

While justice, prudence, or courage may very well be natural virtues of natural man, hope is a virtue *only* when it is a *theological* virtue; hope becomes a virtue precisely through that which renders it theological, supra-natural virtue.

JOSEF PIEPER, *The End of Time,* 1954

Into this world of flimsy, false, and dying hopes, comes the one hope that can endure. Christian hope faces all facts, and is trained by Christ to face them at their worst possible, where no room is left for any excuse of self-deception.

GEOFFREY FISHER, *Episcopal Church News,* April 1, 1956

The *Encyclopaedia Britannica* devotes many columns to the topic of love, and many more to faith. But hope, poor little hope! She is not even listed!

KARL MENNINGER, *American Journal of Psychiatry,* December, 1959

The Gospels . . . brought a new hope into the world—but it was the hope of another world, which often left this one only darker, by contrast, in the shadow of God's reprobation.

F. L. LUCAS, *The Greatest Problem,* 1960

True to the heart of Jewish religious belief, above both faith and reason, hope reigns supreme.

MILTON STEINBERG, *Anatomy of Faith,* 1960

See also Belief; Confidence; Despair; Eternal; Faith; God: His Goodness; Hell; Melancholy; Mercy; Optimism; Worship.

HOSPITALITY

Whosoever believeth in God and the Day of Resurrection must respect his guest, and the time of being kind to him is one day and one night, and the period of entertaining him is three days, and after that, if he doth it longer, he benefitteth him more. It is not right for a guest to stay in the house of the host so long as to inconvenience him.

MOHAMMED, *Speeches and Table-Talk of,* 7th century A.D.

To give our Lord perfect hospitality, Mary and Martha must combine.

ST. TERESA OF ÁVILA, *The Interior Castle,* 1577

HUMAN NATURE

As soon as the Christian religion discovers the principle that human nature is corrupted and fallen from God, this opens our eyes to see everywhere the character of this truth.

BLAISE PASCAL, *Pensées,* 1670

I derive nothing whatever from my own nature, nothing from the nature imagined by the philosophers—all comes from God and His decrees.

NICOLAS DE MALEBRANCHE (1638–1715), *Dialogue on Metaphysics and Religion*

By . . . acting on the external world and changing it, [man] at the same time changes his own nature.

KARL MARX, *Das Kapital,* Vol. 1, Pt. III, ch. VII, sec. 1, 1867

There is nothing in religion, there is nothing in Christianity, which has not its roots in human nature and in the fundamental affections of mankind.

PHILLIPS BROOKS, *National Needs and Remedies,* 1890

The great religions have spoken ill of original human nature; but they have never despaired of its possibilities.

WILLIAM HOCKING, *Human Nature and Its Remaking,* 1918

We see that Nature develops from stage to stage and in each new stage takes up its past and transforms it into stuff of its own new development. We see, too, that human nature is of the same make; all the earth-past is there in it. It has an element of matter taken up by life, an element of life taken up by mind, an element of mind which is being taken up by Spirit.

SRI AUROBINDO, *The Life Divine,* 1949

It is essential not to have faith in human nature. Such faith is a recent heresy and a very disastrous one.

HERBERT BUTTERFIELD, *Christianity and History,* 1950

Our real danger is our sentimental belief that human nature is naturally good. If human nature is good, we don't need either the wisdom of the Constitution or the Grace of God.

RICARD S. EMRICH, *Detroit News,* June 25, 1961

It is hard to believe we are born condemned. And yet the light shows me that human nature has been wounded. I can fight against the cause which faith assigns to this wound, but not against the fact that the wound bleeds, and that it bleeds at the heart of a nature capable of love, of that very love which involves the gift of love.

FRANÇOIS MAURIAC, *What I Believe,* 1962

See also Humanity; Man; Man: Defined and Interpreted; Mankind; Original Sin.

HUMANISM

Humanism . . . is not a single hypothesis or theorem, and it dwells on no new facts.

It is rather a slow shifting in the philosophic perspective, making things appear as from a new centre of interest or point of sight.

WILLIAM JAMES, *The Meaning of Truth*, 1909

The Humanist's religion, is the religion of one who says yea to the life here and now, of one who is self-reliant, fearless, intelligent and creative. . . . Its Goal is the mastery of things that they may become servants and instrumentalities to man's spiritual comradeship.

R. W. SELLARS, *The Next Step in Religion*, 1918

If you find examples of humanism which are antireligious, or at least in opposition to the religious faith of the place and time, then such humanism is purely destructive, for it has never found anything to replace what it has destroyed.

T. S. ELIOT, "Humanism of Irving Babbit," 1927, in *Selected Essays, 1917–1932*

Will not the humanist, unless he adds to his creed the faith and hope of religion, find himself at last, despite his protests, dragged back into the camp of the naturalist?

PAUL ELMER MORE, *On Being Human*, 1928

There is no institution in his [the humanist's] private life for regularly bringing his thoughts back to a centre from which he can derive sustenance and power, no routine for enforcing his flagging aspirations and resolutions. He has no means of symbolizing the unity of all in the One in terms of physical association.

LAURENCE HYDE, *The Prospects of Humanism*, 1931

Humanism sucks the egg of personality's value and then tries to hatch a higher religion out of it.

HARRY EMERSON FOSDICK, *As I See Religion*, 1932

A humanism which is sustained only by the obvious marks of common humanity breaks down when the hysteria of conflict destroys or obscures those obvious human ties.

REINHOLD NIEBUHR, *An Interpretation of Christian Ethics*, 1935

The highest and best thing that man can conceive is a human life nobly and beautifully lived—therefore his loyalties and energies should be devoted to the arrangement of conditions which make this possible. The sole issue is how to make this world a place conducive to the living of a noble human life, and then to help people in every possible way to live such lives.

JOHN H. DIETRICH, *Varieties of American Religion*, ed. Charles S. Braden, 1936

Agnosticism and materialism . . . are the fruits of that spiritual heresy of Humanism by which man came to see himself as a whole, instead of as a spiritual-social-biological organism in living relation to the real world of spirit, of other men and things.

V. A. DEMANT, *Christian Polity*, 1936

To the question, What is man, whence comes and whither goes he? humanism by its own lights is powerless to reply.

HENRI BREMOND, *A Literary History of Religious Thought in France*, I, 1937

The hope of humanism that a society will be constructed on earth . . . which will be the abode of secularist self-sanctified saints is doomed to disappointment. Death and sin can never be destroyed by any social order however wise.

E. I. WATKIN, *Men and Tendencies*, 1937

Humanity idolized as an absolute and sufficient value in the place of God . . . is . . . the idol of the humanist Utopians, of Russell and Shaw and Wells.

E. I. WATKIN, *Men and Tendencies*, 1937

The humanist stands in a mediating position—he has the ear of the general public and speaks directly to their comprehension as neither the theologian nor the scientist can do.

WALTER M. HORTON, *Approach to National Unity,* 1945

No age has more proudly asserted man's supremacy over nature, and yet the "humanism" which proclaimed man's self-sufficiency was accompanied by a sense of powerlessness and frustration.

SYDNEY CAVE, *The Christian Way,* 1949

Humanism needs Christianity to supplement it just as little as the Christian faith needs humanism. It may even feel that Christianity is an uncomfortable *disturbance to the self-assurance of the mind.*

RUDOLF BULTMANN, *Essays,* 1951

One would not go far wrong if one defined humanism as Puritanism with a sense of humor.

J. C. F. AUER and JULIAN HARTT, *Humanism vs. Theism,* 1951

Duty to Man has replaced Duty to God. It is the central point of Humanism.

ROSALIND MURRAY, *Columbia,* April, 1951

The end product of atheist humanism is the modern totalitatian state, in which the illusion of man's metaphysical freedom from divine government goes hand in hand with the reality of his political subjection.

J. V. L. CASSERLEY, *Retreat from Christianity in the Modern World,* 1952

There are still a few old-fashioned rationalists, free-thinkers, or professional atheists, who mourn the failures of humanitarianism as a universal religion, and who are therefore willing to call themselves religious humanists.

HERBERT WALLACE SCHNEIDER, *Religion in the 20th Century,* 1952

Scientism and anthropocentric humanism are the attractive blooms that adorn a nearly rootless society.

GEORGIA HARKNESS, *The Modern Rival of Christian Faith,* 1953

A scientific humanism frequently offends the dignity of man, which it ostensibly extols, by regarding human beings as subject to manipulation and as mere instruments of some "socially approved" ends.

REINHOLD NIEBUHR, *Christian Realism and Political Problems,* 1953

Both Buddhism and Jainism threw over wholly the ancient systems of gods. Both repudiated pantheism. Indeed both repudiated any means of achieving life's goal that was not to be formed within oneself.

CHARLES S. BRADEN, *The World's Religions,* 1954

Human existence has no such simple and direct meaning or goodness as the humanistic American dream. . . . A comfortable chair, a hi-fi set, a powerful car, the protection of a deodorant, a college romance and a paying job, cannot even in combination provide meaning for our life.

LANGDON GILKEY, *Maker of Heaven and Earth,* 1959

The Humanist is reconciled to reality and makes his home there, and has a horror of the black-and-white fantasy of heaven and hell.

H. J. BLACKHAM, *The Humanist Frame,* ed. J. Huxley, 1961

A humanist, as I understand the term, says, "This world is good enough for me, if only I can be good enough for it."

WILLIAM EMPSON, *Milton's God,* 1961

The failure of the Christian people to effect a real humanism was followed by the rise of what were practically new religions, or substitutes for religion.

SIR ROBERT FALCONER, *Christianity and Culture,* ed. J. S. Murphy, 1961

The greatest challenge to Christianity today is a popular, bland, respectable faith termed secular humanism. It is often called "The American Way of Life." It is not Godless, but it keeps God in His place—the pulpit. It equates the Christian moral code with such terms as decency, brotherhood, the Golden Rule. It is the orthodoxy of the nonbeliever, but it is a ready refuge for the half-believer too. . . . It simply says: "Take up your credit card and follow me."

> PAUL J. HALLINAN, *speech,* quoted in *Life,* September 15, 1961

The lineaments of the new religion that we can be sure will arise to serve the needs of the coming era. . . . Instead of worshipping supernatural rulers, it will sanctify the higher manifestations of human nature, in art and love, in intellectual comprehension and aspiring adoration, and will emphasize the fuller realization of life's possibilities as a sacred trust.

> JULIAN S. HUXLEY, *The Humanist Frame,* 1961

It will have nothing to do with Absolutes, including absolute truth, absolute morality, absolute perfection and absolute authority.

> JULIAN S. HUXLEY, *The Humanist Frame,* 1961

It rejects supernaturalism and moral absolutism, and argues that the best possibilities of human beings can be achieved only by a combination of informed intelligence and the candid recognition that man must bear the responsibility for whatever standards he adopts.

> CHARLES FRANKEL, *New York Times Book Review,* January 14, 1962

On issues of the greatest moral and practical importance Humanism is a fertile and liberating point of view, and one that is thoroughly compatible with a fervent devotion to the highest spiritual interests of mankind.

> CHARLES FRANKEL, *New York Times Book Review,* January 14, 1962

See also Agnosticism; Atheism; Humanism, Christian; Humanitarianism; Irreligion; Liberalism; Liberalism and Religion; Man: His Self-Deification; Materialism; Modernism; Naturalism; Rationalism; Religion, Caustic Comments about; Religion: Its Decline; Rootlessness; Secularism; Social Atheism; Society and Religion; Unbelief; Unbelievers.

HUMANISM, CHRISTIAN

For its theology, Christian Humanism accepts purely and simply that of the Church. Is it taken for a sect? It is nothing but a temper of mind. Without neglecting any of the essential truths of Christianity, it brings forward by preference those which appear the most consoling, encouraging, in a word human, which to it seem the most divine and the most conformed to Infinite Goodness.

> HENRI BREMOND, *A Literary History of Religious Thought in France,* I, 1937

In the Christian millennium from the 4th to the 14th century there was a practically unbroken chain of humanists who at the same time could feel and sing like artists, think and write like sages, and pray like saints.

> GERALD GROVELAND WALSH, *Thought,* March, 1943

It will perhaps be the great honor of our time to have undertaken what others will bring to a good issue, a humanism embracing the dimensions of the world and adequate to the designs of God.

> EMMANUEL SUHARD, *The Church Today,* 1953

Christian humanism is an attempt to get the natural and the supernatural back together in a well-balanced synthesis.

> PAUL B. STEINMETZ, *The Catholic Bookman's Guide,* ed. Sr. M. Regis, I.H.M., 1962

The basic idea of Christian humanism is that man can become fully human only by becoming divine through sanctifying grace. For this subordination of human nature to graces does not destroy human values; rather, it brings them to perfection.

> PAUL B. STEINMETZ, *The Catholic Bookman's Guide,* ed. Sr. M. Regis, I.H.M., 1962

Although the term "Christian humanism" may speak in an accent that has become strange to modern ears, it is the best term I know for the rich and varied legacy of theological scholarship upon which our entire culture has been built.

> JAROSLAV JAN PELIKAN, *Address,* May 19, 1964

See also Christianity; Humanism.

HUMANITARIANISM

Humanitarianism, left to itself, has a way of becoming disturbingly inhuman.

> AELRED GRAHAM, *Christian Thought and Action,* 1951

See also Humanism; Liberalism; Liberalism and Religion.

HUMANITY

The whole clay of humanity is a condemned clay.

> ST. AUGUSTINE, *The City of God,* xxi, 42b

The still sad music of humanity.

> WILLIAM WORDSWORTH, *Tintern Abbey,* 1798

To behold humanity within oneself, and never to lose sight of the vision when once found, is the only certain means of never straying from its sacred precincts.

> F. SCHLIERMACHER, *Soliloquies,* 1810

Every soul develops itself only by means of other souls, and there are no longer individual men, but only one humanity.

> J. G. FICHTE (1762–1814), *The Vocation of Man*

To love Humanity constitutes all healthy morality.

> AUGUSTE COMTE, *Positive Polity,* 1820

The universal reign of Humanity is to replace the provisory reign of God.

> AUGUSTE COMTE, *Positive Polity,* 1820

The superiority of demonstrated over revealed religion is shown by the substitution of love of Humanity for the love of God.

> AUGUSTE COMTE, *Positive Polity,* 1820

Humanity . . . is for us the only Great Being.

> AUGUSTE COMTE, *A General View of Positivism,* 1848

The true division of humanity is this: the luminous and the dark.

> VICTOR HUGO, *Les Miserables,* 1862

We see in every member of the human race something that looks like a glimmering at least of heavenly light. . . . The Divine Spirit is as wide in its workings as the Divine Providence.

> G. S. MERRIAM, *A Living Faith,* 1876

You may see the disc of Divinity quite clearly through the smoked glass of humanity, but not otherwise.

> COVENTRY PATMORE, *The Rod, the Root, and the Flower,* 1895

Only as men believe in God can they believe in humanity.

> CHARLES E. GARMAN, *Letters, Lectures, Addresses,* 1909

Those thinkers who cannot believe in any gods often assert that the love of humanity would be in itself sufficient for them; and so, perhaps, it would, if they had it.

> G. K. CHESTERTON, *Tremendous Trifles,* 1915

What humanity needs is not the promise of scientific immortality, but compassion-

ate pity in this life and infinite mercy on
the Day of Judgment.

> JOSEPH CONRAD, *Notes on Life and
> Letters,* 1921

Humanity's sinful nature . . . is an inherited mortgage and handicap on the whole
human family.

> HARRY EMERSON FOSDICK, *Christianity
> and Progress,* 1922

Social Christianity . . . will become di-
vested to a greater degree of vestigial
supernaturalism and thus replace service to
God by service to Humanity.

> CLIFFORD KILPATRICK, *Religion in Hu-
> man Affairs,* 1929

Humanity seems to have run like boys let
out of school away from the humanitarian,
idealistic, nineteenth century, from whose
morality—if we can speak at all of morality in this connection—our time represents a wide and wild reaction.

> THOMAS MANN, *Speech,* Berlin, October
> 17, 1930

The religious emotions must be largely or
entirely secularized and be put in the service of humanity. The religion of humanity
is surely the religion of the nearer future.

> J. C. FLUGEL, *Man, Morals and Society,*
> 1945

The perfection of humanity is the fullest
embodiment of deity.

> JOHN DILLENBERGER and CLAUDE
> WELCH, *Protestant Christianity,* 1954

From Comte and the Religion of Humanity to Freud and Kinsey and Hitler is only
a short and logical step.

> ALBERT T. MOLLEGEN, *Christianity and
> Modern Man,* 1961

See also Brotherhood; Fellowship; Human-
ism; Immortality, Denial and Doubt of;
Internationalism; Love; Man; Man: His
Destiny and Goal; Man: His Self-Deifica-
tion; Mankind; Rationalism; Society;
Wonder.

HUMILITY

Be humble and you will remain entire.
The sage does not display himself, therefore he shines.
He does not approve himself therefore he
  is noted.
He does not praise himself, therefore he
  has merit.
He does not glory in himself, therefore he
  excels.

> *Tao Tê Ching,* variously dated to 3rd
> century B.C.

Christ is with those of humble mind, not
with those who exalt themselves over his
flock.

> ST. CLEMENT OF ROME, *Epistle to Cor-
> inthians,* c. 100

Nothing is more scandalous than a man
who is proud of his humility.

> MARCUS AURELIUS, *Mediations of,* c.
> 170

One of the old men said, "When a man
saith unto his companion, 'Forgive me,'
and at the same time humbleth himself,
the devils are consumed."

> *The Paradise of the Fathers,* between
> 250 and 400 A.D.

There is something in humility which
strangely exalts the heart.

> ST. AUGUSTINE, *The City of God,* xiv,
> 42b

The humility of Christ is the medicine of
man's swollen pride.

> ST. AUGUSTINE (354–430), *Sermons on
> Selected Lessons of the New Testament*

Be humble, that you may not be humbled.

> *Talmud: Derek Eretz,* 1.27, c. 500

It is not true humility, if a man perceives
that it is God's will that he be above
others, for him to refuse it, but to submit

to God's will and decree, and to relinquish the vice of obstinacy.

POPE ST. GREGORY THE GREAT, *Pastoral Care,* 590

Humility is a Divine veil which covers our good deeds, and hides them from our eyes.

ST. JOHN CLIMACUS (525–600), *Climax*

The royal gateway, through which one approaches the inner courts.

ST. JOHN CLIMACUS (525–600), *Scala*

Since Adam's sons are moulded from the clay,
'Tis only mortal to be humble—pray!

SHAIKH SAADI, *Gulistan,* c. 1265

The more meek that a man is and the more subject to God the more wise shall he be in all things,—and the more patient.

THOMAS À KEMPIS, *Imitation of Christ,* 1441

In humility alone lies true greatness, and that knowledge and wisdom are profitable only in so far as our lives are governed by them.

NICHOLAS OF CUSA, *Dialogue on Peace,* 1452

The humility of hyprocrites is, of all pride, the greatest and most haughty.

MARTIN LUTHER (1483–1546), *Table Talk*

Humility must always be doing its work like a bee making its honey in the hive: without humility all will be lost.

ST. TERESA OF ÁVILA, *The Interior Castle,* 1577

True humility never makes a show of herself, nor uses many humble words.

ST. FRANCIS OF SALES, *Introduction to the Devout Life,* 1609

Someone asked one of those ancient Fathers how he might obtain true humil-ity, and he answered: "By keeping your eyes off other people's faults, and fixing them on your own."

ST. ALPHONSE RODRIGUEZ, *The Practice of Perfection and Christian Virtues,* 1611

Professions of humility are the very cream, the very essence of pride; the really humble man wishes to be, and not to appear so.

Quoted in J. P. CAMUS, *The Spirit of St. Francis de Sales,* 1641

There is some lack of humility in making so much of serving God by aridities.

SAINT JANE FRANCES OF CHANTAL (1575–1643), *Mystical Prayer According to*

Humility is the great ornament and jewel of Christian religion.

JEREMY TAYLOR, *Holy Living,* 1650

Humility is a virtue all preach, none practice, and yet every one is content to hear. The master thinks that it is good doctrine for his servant, the laity for the clergy, and the clergy for the laity.

JOHN SELDEN, *Table Talk,* 1689

Though humility be a virtue, an affected one is none.

WILLIAM PENN, *Fruits of Solitude,* 1693

Humility is nothing else but a right judgment of ourselves.

WILLIAM LAW, *Christian Perfection,* 1726

There is no true holiness without humility.

THOMAS FULLER, *Gnomologia,* 1732

Humility is the modesty of the soul. It is the antidote to pride.

VOLTAIRE, *Philosophical Dictionary,* II, 1764

There is small chance of truth at the goal where there is not a child-like humility at the starting-post.

SAMUEL TAYLOR COLERIDGE, *Aids to Reflection,* 1825

Viewed as a virtue of conduct . . . it is not only a voluntary relinquishment of the privileges of our station, but an actual participation or assumption of the condition of those to whom we stoop. . . . to feel and to behave as if we were low; not, to cherish a notion of our importance, while we affect a low position.

JOHN HENRY NEWMAN, *Idea of a University,* 1852

Humility like darkness reveals the heavenly lights.

HENRY DAVID THOREAU, *Walden,* 1854

A Christian prefers humility to hope, a moral virtue but not a divine one, favoring pious timidity at the expense of trustfulness towards God.

WALTER ELLIOTT, *The Spiritual Life,* 1914

Humility provides everyone, even him who despairs in solitude, with the strongest relationship to his fellow man.

FRANZ KAFKA (1883–1924), *Reflections*

The modern man is humble, not with the old humility which made a man doubt his power, but with the new humility that makes a man doubt his humanity.

FULTON J. SHEEN, *Old Errors and New Labels,* 1931

Genuine humility does not arise from the sense of our pitiable kinship with the dust that is unworthy of us but from the realization of our awful nearness to a magnificence of which we are unworthy.

ALISTAIR MACLEAN, *High Country,* 1934

Humility is the virtue of men, and their only defense; to walk humbly with God,

never doubting, whatever befall, that His will is good, and His law is right.

PAUL ELMER MORE, *Pages from an Oxford Diary,* 1937

As it obliged him to respect the presence of God in others, so it obliged him to respect the presence of God in himself, to make himself the messenger of God, or the path taken by God.

ANTOINE DE SAINT-EXUPÉRY, *Flight to Arras,* 1942

In Revelation it is the saints and elders nearest God who cast down their crowns when they adore Him. The lesser fry, further off, are quite content to go on wearing theirs.

EVELYN UNDERHILL, *The Fruits of the Spirit,* 1942

A country possessed of the might of the United States might do better to go into its closet and pray to its Father in secret rather than standing on the street corners parading its piety before men.

A. ROY ECKARDT, *Christian Century,* November 17, 1954

The necessity of getting reconciled with the idea of his possible extinction may breed a new humility and may rid man of that biological jingoism which made him regard himself as the crown of creation.

ARTHUR KOESTLER, *New York Times Magazine,* March 20, 1960

Another old monk who, asked to define humility, replied: "If you forgive a brother who has wronged you before he is penitent towards you."

GEDDES MACGREGOR, *The Hemlock and the Cross,* 1963

Among the ambiguities of a religion that has preached a gospel of humility is that all along it has bred more of such proud, stubborn, troublesome types than has any other religion.

HERBERT J. MULLER, *Religion and Freedom in the Modern World,* 1963

See also Conduct; Holiness; Hypocrisy; Meekness; Modesty; Neighbor; Pride; Resignation; Self-Contempt; Self-Deception; Self-Knowledge; Self-Love; Self-Praise; Sincerity; Spiritual Progress; Vanity; Virtue.

HUMOR

A sense of humor keen enough to show a man his own absurdities, as well as those of other people, will keep him from the commission of all sins, or nearly all, save those that are worth committing.
SAMUEL BUTLER, *Notebooks of,* ed. H. F. Jones, 1912

A case might be made for the potentially superior humor of the religious person who has settled once and for all what things are of ultimate value, sacred and untouchable. For then nothing else in the world need be taken seriously.
GORDON W. ALLPORT, *Personality,* 1937

I have never understood why it should be considered derogatory to the Creator to suppose that He has a sense of humor.
DEAN INGE, *A Rustic Moralist,* 1937

HUNGER

First bread, and then religion. We stuff them too much with religion, when the poor fellows have been starving. No dogmas will satisfy the cravings of hunger.
VIVEKANANDA (1863–1902), *Works of*

HUSBAND

A good husband and father, who is working because it is his duty to work for his family and because it is God's will, is really praying all the time.
VINCENT MCNABB, *The Craft of Prayer,* 1951

See also Family; Father; Marriage; Parents; Wife; Woman.

HUSBAND AND WIFE

Let mutual fidelity continue until death. This may be considered as the summary of the highest law for husband and wife.
Laws of Manu, ix, between 1000 and 500 B.C.

Husband and wife commune together through the flesh and in time, but above time and the flesh. They unite in a total offering and consecration in which are embraced a generosity and pure faith, a humble loyalty, chastity, and an exquisite modesty—in short an absolute religious reverence not far removed from adoration.
JEAN MOUROUX, *The Meaning of Man,* 1948

See also Husband; Love, Physical; Marriage; Sexual Intercourse; Wife.

HYPOCRISY

Hateful to me even as the gates of Hades is he that hideth one thing in his heart and uttereth another.
ACHILLES in Homer's *Iliad,* c. 10th century B.C.

When a scholar speaks what he ought not to speak by guile of speech to gain some end, and when he does not speak, by guile of silence to gain some end—both these cases are of a piece with breaking through a neighbor's wall.
MENCIUS, *Works of,* 4th century B.C.

The idolater worships one object, but there is no limit to the number of men the hypocrite worships.
BAHYA BEN JOSEPH IBN PAKUDA, *Hobot Halebabot,* 1040 A.D.

Let the Brothers take care that they do not present the appearance of hypocrites, with dark and castdown mein, but that they show themselves glad in the Lord, cheerful and worthy of love, and agreeable.
ST. FRANCIS OF ASSISI (1181?–1226), *Little Flowers of*

Hypocrisy is the homage which vice renders to virtue.

LA ROCHEFOUCAULD, *Maxims,* 1665

Hypocrisy itself does great honor, or rather justice, to religion, and tacitly acknowledges it to be an ornament to human nature.

JOSEPH ADDISON, *The Spectator,* December 8, 1711

Solemn prayers, rapturous devotions, are but repeated hypocrisies unless the heart and mind be comformable to them.

WILLIAM LAW, *Christian Perfection,* 1726

All is pure hypocrisy, which does not come from the heart, and so accustom the people to cultivate love to God and to their neighbors and to act from it as a motive.

P. J. SPENER, *Pia Desideria,* 1841

Hypocrite, n. One who, professing virtues that he does not respect, secures the advantage of seeming to be what he despises.

AMBROSE BIERCE, *Devil's Dictionary,* 1906

For so long as the world refuses to accept Jesus as entirely possible, entirely normal, entirely right, it is mere hypocrisy to regard Caiaphas and Pilate and Herod as exceptional monsters of evil.

W. G. PECK, *The Divine Revolution,* 1927

The characteristic modern malady is not plain and unvarnished materialism but sham spirituality.

IRVING BABBITT, *Living Philosophies,* 1931

A subtler and much more terrible kind of hypocrisy consists in the suppression of saintly unconventionality and the development of outward sanctimoniousness.

GEDDES MACGREGOR, *The Hemlock and the Cross,* 1963

The Creoles in New Orleans used to have a saying when a "pious cheat" entered a church: "When the Devil goes to Mass he hides his tail."

The person who doesn't go to church because so many hypocrites attend, does not hesitate to go to other places where there are just as many hypocrites.

ANONYMOUS

See also Anti-Semitism; Coercion; Conduct; Falsehood; Heart; Honesty; Humility; Integrity; Liars and Lies; Persecution; Pharisee; Practice; Pretense; Self-Knowledge; Sin; Sincerity; Vice.

IDEAL

Devotion to an ideal is worship; the higher the ideal, the nobler the worship.

F. W. NEWMAN, *Theism,* 1858

The human soul has still greater need of the ideal than of the real. It is by the real that we exist; it is by the ideal that we live.

VICTOR HUGO, *William Shakespeare,* 1864

The ideal life is in our blood, and never will be still. We feel the thing we ought to be beating through the thing we are.

PHILLIPS BROOKS, *Perennials,* 1898

The Christian ideal has not been tried and found wanting. It has been found difficult; and left untried.

G. K. CHESTERTON, *What's Wrong with the World,* 1910

The submergence of self in the pursuit of an ideal, the readiness to spend oneself without measure, prodigally, almost ecstatically, for something intuitively apprehended as great and noble, spend oneself one knows not why—some of us like to believe that this is what religion means.

BENJAMIN CARDOZO, *Values,* 1931

Every man possessed of an ideal which engrosses his whole being, is inevitably and continuously inclined to link its presence in his soul with the presence of the Spirit in the world.

ERNEST DIMNET, *What We Live By,* 1932

The ideal can lead to killing men for the glory of the Good in the expectation that the Good will be served and will appropriately bless the killer with a crown of glory.

F. J. E. WOODBRIDGE, *An Essay on Nature,* 1940

Christianity is not so much the pursuit of an ideal as an Ideal that pursues humanity, stooping down in an Incarnation to take up dwelling in the hearts of man.

JAMES EDWARD O'MAHONY, *As in a Mirror,* 1948

The ideal is, as it were, the projection before us of what is behind impelling us, of what is above guiding us, of what is within creating us.

ANTONIN SERTILLANGES, *Recollection,* 1950

Where an external code of behavior, be it the highest, takes the place of an inward ideal, the way is open to spiritual stagnation—of which the signs are the identification of religious practice with what is socially respectable.

AELRED GRAHAM, *Christian Thought and Action,* 1951

See also Idealism; Idealists; Ideals.

IDEALISM

Idealism is profoundly irreligious, because it is the perversion of religion into unreality.

JOHN MACMURRAY, *Creative Society,* 1935

Idealism tends to absorb all of objective reality into a system made up solely of experience. . . . Sooner or later the idealist has to admit that his experience touches something beyond its own content.

LANGDON GILKEY, *Maker of Heaven and Earth,* 1959

See also Ideal; Idealists; Ideals.

IDEALISTS

Idealist: one who, on noticing that a rose smells better than a cabbage, concludes that it is also more nourishing.

H. L. MENCKEN, *A Little Book in C Major,* 1916

When they come downstairs from their Ivory Towers, Idealists are apt to walk straight into the gutter.

LOGAN PEARSALL SMITH, *Afterthoughts,* 1931

It is the besetting sin of the idealist to sacrifice reality for his ideals; to reject life because it fails to come up to his ideal; and this vice is just as prevalent among religious idealists as secular ones.

CHRISTOPHER DAWSON, *The Judgment of the Nations,* 1942

See also Ideal; Idealism; Ideals.

IDEALS

Ideals are like stars; you will not succeed in touching them with your hands. But like the seafaring man on the desert waters, you choose them as your guides, and following them you will reach your destiny.

CARL SCHURZ, *Address,* Boston, April 18, 1859

Blessed is he who carries within himself a God, an ideal and who obeys it—ideal of art, ideal of science, ideal of the gospel virtues; therein lie the springs of great thought and great actions; they all reflect light from the Infinite.

LOUIS PASTEUR (1822–1895) quoted in *The Life of,* by René Vallery-Radot

The highest flights of charity, devotion, trust, patience, bravery, to which the wings of human nature have spread themselves have been flown for religious ideals.
> WILLIAM JAMES, *Varieties of Religious Experience*, 1902

Ideals are thoughts. So long as they exist merely as thoughts, the power latent in them remains ineffective.
> ALBERT SCHWEITZER, *Memories of Childhood and Youth*, 1931

If we hang beautiful pictures on the walls of our souls, mental images that establish us in the habitual companionship of the highest that we know, and live with them long enough, we cannot will evil.
> HARRY EMERSON FOSDICK, *The Hope of the World*, 1933

Ideals are ideas or beliefs when these are objects not only of contemplation or affirmation but also of hope, desire, endeavor, admiration, and resolve.
> RALPH BARTON PERRY, *Puritanism and Democracy*, 1944

See also Ideal; Idealism; Idealists.

IDENTITY

The complete loss of one's identity is, with all propriety of theological definition, hell. In diminished form it is insanity.
> JOHN COURTNEY MURRAY, *Religion in America*, ed. John Cogley, 1958

See also Personality.

IDEOLOGY

That ideology which captures the higher education of a nation will ultimately determine its mind and soul.
> HOWARD Y. MCCLUSKY, *Liberal Learning and Religion*, 1951

IDLENESS

Idleness is the enemy of the soul.
> ST. BENEDICT OF NURSIA (c. 480–c. 533), *Rule of*

The mother of vices.
> JOHN LYDGATE, *The Fall of Princes*, c. 1440

The nurse of sin.
> EDMUND SPENSER, *The Fairie Queene*, c. 1589

If thou hast nothing to do, thou shalt be haled in pieces with envy, lust, some passion or other.
> ROBERT BURTON, *Anatomy of Melancholy*, III, 1621

'Tis a bosom enemy, 'tis a delightful melancholy, a friend in show, but a secret devil, a sweet poison, it will in the end be his undoing.
> ROBERT BURTON, *Anatomy of Melancholy*, II, 1621

The idle person goeth to School to the Devil.
> RICHARD BAXTER, *A Christian Directory*, 1673

If the Devil finds a man idle he'll set him to work.
> JAMES KELLY, *Complete Collections of Scottish Proverbs*, 1721

He that is busy is tempted by but one devil; he that is idle, by a legion.
> THOMAS FULLER, *Gnomologia*, 1732

When we do ill the Devil tempteth us; when we do nothing, we tempt him.
> THOMAS FULLER, *Gnomologia*, 1732

The refuge of weak minds.
> EARL OF CHESTERFIELD (Philip Stanhope), *Advice to His Son*, July, 1749

Thomas AP-Morgan, the Welsh preacher, says, "We must look out for the devil; for if he finds anyone idle, he will set him at work; and who wants to do the devil's work?"

Old Farmer's Almanac, 1854

The devil tempts all men; but the idle man tempts the devil.

Old Farmer's Almanac, 1865

There are but few men who have character enough to lead lives of idleness.

HENRY WHEELER SHAW ("Josh Billings"), *Proverbial Philosophy,* 1877

Idleness does not consist in doing nothing, but in doing a great deal not recognized in the dogmatic formularies of the ruling class.

ROBERT LOUIS STEVENSON, *Virginibus Puerisque and Other Papers,* 1881

Idleness, n. A model farm where the devil experiments with seeds of new sins and promotes the growth of staple vices.

AMBROSE BIERCE, *Devil's Dictionary,* 1906

IDOLATRY

Not only the adoration of images is idolatry, but also trust in one's own righteousness, works and merits, and putting confidence in riches and power. As the latter is the commonest, so it also is the most noxious idolatry.

MARTIN LUTHER (1483–1546)

Oh senseless man, who cannot possibly make a worm, and yet will make gods by dozens.

MICHEL DE MONTAIGNE, *Essays,* Bk. 2, ch. 12, 1580

All men are idolaters, some of fame, others of self-interest, most of pleasure.

BALTASAR GRACIÀN, *The Art of Worldly Wisdom,* 1647

The modern idol maker goes not to the forest but to the laboratory, and there, with the help of scientific concepts moulds the kind of God he will adore.

FULTON J. SHEEN, *Religion Without God,* 1928

A naturalist attitude towards God, conceived of as a metaphysical transcendent Being, an immobile Substance, represents the latest form of idolatry in the history of the human spirit.

NICHOLAS BERDYAEV, *Freedom and the Spirit,* 1935

Not only is idolatry condemned in its gross form, which takes it for granted that an idol can cause benefit or do harm, but the idea is also controverted that there is any meaning underlying this gross form of worship.

MUHAMMAD ALI, *The Religion of Islam,* 1936

To worship the State or the man is idolatry, the sin that the Jews lived and died to destroy.

JAMES M. GILLIS, *God in Government,* 1943

Ultimately all idolatry is worship of the self projected and objectified: all idolization is self-idolization.

WILL HERBERG, *Judaism and Modern Man,* 1951

The laziest form of idolatry . . . simply turns to some finite and secular reality . . . and treats it as though it had the supremacy of God, nation, class or party, family, business or profession, even oneself.

J. V. L. CASSERLEY, *Retreat from Christianity in the Modern World,* 1952

I read in the morning paper that a local minister had proclaimed that God was depending upon President Einsenhower more than he had depended on any man in history! You see how easy it is to slip into the position of identifying God with our own particular system and beliefs. This is the fundamental sin, idolatry.

ALBERT T. MOLLEGEN, *Christianity and Modern Man,* 1961

See also Eros; False Gods; False Religions; Gold; Man: His Self-Deification; Mary, the Mother of Jesus; Money; Technology.

IGNORANCE

Fools dwelling in darkness, wise in their own conceit, and puffed up with vain knowledge, go round and round, staggering to and fro like men led by the blind.
Katha Upanishad, Adhyaya, probably prior to 6th century B.C.

But Ignorance, the child
Of Darkness, blinding mortal men, binds down
Their souls to stupor, sloth and drowsiness.
The Song Celestial, Sir Edwin Arnold's translation of the *Bhagavad-Gita,* c. 5th century B.C.

As imprisoned birds do not get out of their cage, so those ignorant of right or wrong do not get out of their misery.
Sutra-Krit-Anga, between 600 and 200 B.C.

The greatest ignorance is when a man hates that which he nevertheless thinks to be good and noble, and loves and embraces that which he knows to be unrighteous and evil.
PLATO, *Laws,* 360 B.C.

No pain is more troublesome than ignorance. People are enemies of that they are ignorant of. The ignorant man is a loser in whatever condition he may be.
ALI IBU ABU TALIB (died 661 A.D.), quoted in *Ali-the-Caliph,* by Mohammad Ali-Al-Haj Salman

Ignorance is the curse of God.
WILLIAM SHAKESPEARE, *Henry VI, Part II,* 1592?

I know no disease of the Soul, but Ignorance; not of the Arts and Sciences, but of itself. . . . Knowledge is the activity of the soul.
BEN JONSON, *Discoveries,* 1641

While all complain of our ignorance and error, everyone exempts himself.
JOSEPH GLANVILL, *The Vanity of Dogmatizing,* 1661

Ignorance is no more the mother of devotion, than the lying harlot, which pleaded before Solomon, was the mother of the living child.
THOMAS FULLER, *Worthies of England,* 1662

For after all, man knows mighty little, and may some day learn enough of his own ignorance to fall down again and pray.
HENRY ADAMS, *Letter to Brooks Adams,* 1895

See also Error; Knowledge; Learning; Superstition; Truth.

ILLEGITIMACY

There are no illegitimate children—only illegitimate parents.
JUDGE LEON R. YANKWICH, of the U.S. District Court for the Southern District of California, *Zipkin vs. Mozon,* June, 1928

ILLNESS. See SICKNESS

ILLUMINATION

If any illumination at all is to be had of our secret nightmares and the deepest issues of our perplexity, . . . it is likely to be gotten not from our philosophers or social scientists but from a few prophetic spirits in the theological community and from the major poets and novelists of our day.

> NATHAN A. SCOTT, *Modern Literature and the Religious Frontier,* 1958

IMAGES

There shall be no pictures in church, lest what is reverenced and adored shall be depicted on the walls.

> *Canons of the Council of Elvira,* c. 305

We do not make obeisance to the nature of wood, but we revere and do obeisance to Him who was crucified on the Cross. . . . When the two beams are joined together I adore the figure because of Christ who on the Cross was crucified, but if the beams are separated, I throw them away and burn them.

> LEONTIUS OF NEAPOLIS (died c. 650), in Migne, *Patrologia Graeca,* xciv

Just as the figure of the previous and life-giving Cross, so also the venerable and holy images, as well in painting and mosaic as of other fit materials, should be set forth in the holy churches of God and on the sacred vessels and on the vestments and hangings and in pictures both in houses and by the wayside. . . . For the honor which is paid to the images passes to that which the image represents, and he who reveres the image reveres in it the subject represented.

> *Council of Nicea,* 787

Pictures and ornaments in churches are the lessons and the scriptures of the laity. . . . For what writing supplieth to him which can read, that doth a picture supply to him which is unlearned, and can only look.

> WILLIAM DURANDUS (1273–1296), *Rationale divinorum officorum*

That images of Christ, the Virgin Mother of God, and other saints, are to be held and kept especially in churches; that due honor and reverence are to be paid to them, not that any divinity or power is thought to be in them, . . . or that anything can be asked of them, or that any trust may be put in images, but because the honor shown them is referred to the prototypes which they represent.

> *Second Council of Nicea,* 1543

The image is for us the way to the original; in it we touch at least the hem of the garment of the eternal idea.

> ODO CASEL, *Mysterium,* 1926

See also Art; Art and Christianity; Art and Religion; Art and Theology; Symbols.

IMAGINATION

The primary imagination I hold to be the living Power and prime agent of all human Perception, and as a repetition in the finite mind of the eternal act of creation in the infinite *I am.*

> SAMUEL TAYLOR COLERIDGE, *Biographia Literaria,* 1817

I know of no other Christianity and no other Gospel than the liberty both of body and mind to exercise the Divine Arts of Imagination.

> WILLIAM BLAKE, *Jerusalem,* 1820

Imagination is not only the creative source of artistic production, but also the root of religious experience. The Highest cannot be experienced, except in an imaginative fashion.

> RICHARD KRONER, *Perspectives on a Troubled Decade,* ed. Bryson, Finkle-stein and MacIver, 1950

See also Enthusiasm; Mind; Thinking; Thought; Vision.

IMMACULATE CONCEPTION

We declare, pronounce, and define that the doctrine which holds that the most blessed Virgin Mary, in the first instant of her conception, by a singular grace and privilege granted by almighty God, in view of the merits of Jesus Christ, the Savior of the human race, was preserved free from all stain of original sin, is a doctrine revealed by God and therefore to be believed firmly and constantly by all the faithful.

POPE PIUS IX, *Ineffabilis Deus,* December 8, 1854

See also Mary, the Mother of Jesus.

IMMORALITY

One of the greatest triumphs of the nineteenth century was to limit the connotation of the word "immoral" in such a way that, for practical purposes, only those were immoral who drank too much or made too copious love. Those who indulged in any or all of the other deadly sins could look down in righteous indignation on the lascivious and the gluttons.

ALDOUS HUXLEY, *Those Barren Leaves,* 1925

There is all the difference in the world between a system in which an immoral principle is admitted and one in which, though the immorality is practiced, the principle is denied.

HILAIRE BELLOC, *Essays of a Catholic,* 1931

Renunciation of immoral acts hurting both ourselves and other human beings in the circle of our influence is the true mark of maturity and nobility.

JOSHUA LOTH LIEBMAN, *Reader's Digest,* June, 1948

See also Alcohol; Civilization; Dissipation; Evil; Impurity; Morality; Morals; Obscenity; Sex; Sexual Intercourse; Unchastity; Vice.

IMMORTALITY

If men had been immortal, they would not have come into the world.

GALILEO, *Dialogue on the Great World Systems,* 1632

To look upon the soul as going on from strength to strength, to consider that she is to shine forever with new accessions of glory, and brighten to all eternity, that she will be still adding virtue to virtue and knowledge to knowledge; carries with it something that is wonderfully agreeable to that ambition which is natural to the mind of man.

JOSEPH ADDISON, *The Spectator,* 1711

The postulate of immortality . . . must lead to the supposition of the existence of a cause adequate to this effect; in other words, it must postulate the existence of a God.

IMMANUEL KANT, *Critique of Practical Reason,* 1788

Either we have an immortal soul, or we have not. If we have not, we are beasts; the first and wisest of beasts, it may be; but still true beasts.

SAMUEL TAYLOR COLERIDGE, *Table Talk,* January 3, 1823

All the philosophers, ancient and modern, who have attempted without the help of revelation to prove the immortality of man, from Plato down to Franklin, appear to us to have failed deplorably.

THOMAS BABINGTON MACAULAY, *Essay on Ranke's "History of the Popes,"* 1839

Neither a man nor a nation can live without a "higher idea," and there is only one such idea on earth, that of an immortal human soul; all the other "higher ideas" by which men live follow from that.

FEODOR DOSTOEVSKY (1821–1881), *Diary of a Writer*

God is the producer of immortality; and who ever has doubts of immortality is written down as an atheist without trial.

WILLIAM JAMES, *The Varieties of Religious Experience,* 1902

The less a man believes in the soul—that is to say in his conscious immortality, per-

sonal and concrete—the more he will exaggerate the worth of this poor transitory
life.

MIGUEL DE UNAMUNO, *Tragic Sense of
Life*, 1921

Those for whom the belief in immortality
is most vivid are the most likely to practice
the virtues which have a survival value and
the least likely to deviate into either those
virtues or those vices which are exclusively
human.

JOSEPH WOOD KRUTCH, *The Modern
Temper*, 1929

Apart from an adequate doctrine of God it
is, as I believe, impossible to find any
secure foundation for a doctrine of human
immortality or any ground for thinking the
prospect of such immortality unattractive.

A. E. TAYLOR, *The Faith of a Moralist*,
Vol. I, 1930

There is no escape—the man who denies
personal immortality must deny what Sir
Thomas Browne described as "the only
indisputable axiom in philosophy, *Nature
does nothing in vain.*"

RICHARD   DOWNEY,   *Critical   and
Constructive Essays*, 1934

Science cannot supply a definite answer to
this question. Immortality relates to an
aspect of life which is not physical, that is,
which cannot be detected and measured by
any instrument, and to which the application of the laws of science can at best be
only a well-considered guess.

ARTHUR H. COMPTON, *The Freedom of
Man*, 1935

The central theme of the New Testament
. . . is Immortality—not the immortality
of anybody and everybody, but of the
believer in Christ as risen from the dead.
This theme I found everywhere present.

L. P. JACKS, *Confession of an Octogenarian*, 1942

I have been greatly struck by the comparative silence which seems to have fallen on
the belief in immortality, as an essential
element of the Christian religion. . . .
The general practice seems to be, not indeed to disavow the belief, but to keep it in
cold storage for funeral occasions.

L. P. JACKS, *Confession of an Octogenarian*, 1942

Only faith in a life after death in a brighter
world where dear ones will meet again—
only that and the measured tramp of time
can give consolation.

WINSTON S. CHURCHILL, *Maxims and
Reflections*, 1947

Recognition of the immortality of man as
he builds himself into society does not
preclude the possibility that the mysterious
core of his personality, having served in
this life as a channel for mediating God's
bounty to others, may yet be redeployed
for future tasks.

CARL WALLACE MILLER, *A Scientist's
Approach to Religion*, 1947

When Judaism speaks of immortality . . .
its primary meaning is that man contains
something independent of the flesh and
surviving it; his consciousness and moral
capacity; his essential personality; a soul.

MILTON STEINBERG, *Basic Judaism*,
1947

The man who refuses firmly to entertain
the hope of immortality . . . is no more
brave and realistic than a man who refuses
to open the door of his dark room and
come out into the sunshine.

D. G. M. JACKSON, *Advocate* (Melbourne, Australia), November 3, 1949

We could probably prove that throughout
history those Christians who have accomplished the most practical benefit in this
world are those who have believed most
fervently in the next.

GORDON W. ALLPORT, *The Individual
and His Religion*, 1950

465

Like many others before me, I have experienced "intimations of immortality." I can no more explain these than the brown seed can explain the flowering tree.

ROBERT HILLYER, *This I Believe*, 1952

Immortality could not be, we believe, a commodity bought for us by a transaction between God and a supposed devil.

H. B. SCHOLEFIELD, *Guide to Unitarianism*, 1955

If, as many of us believe, there is a real immortality, it must necessarily be the natural continuation of life *per se*. The "devil" and "hell" have greatly enriched the vocabulary of abuse and humor, but they add nothing to the understanding of nature.

H. B. SCHOLEFIELD, *Guide to Unitarianism*, 1955

Men's views of immortality become a framework within which earthly ways of life are judged and changed, lived and abandoned.

MARGARET MEAD, *Garvin Free Lecture*, Scranton, Pa., December 3, 1956

Man can have a portion in the world to come, not because his soul *per se* is immortal any more than his body is immortal, but rather because God's justice and His mercy permits human beings to achieve immortality. Not every one achieves it.

SIMON GREENBERG, *Patterns of Faith in America Today*, ed. F. E. Johnson, 1957

It is the *idea* of immortality, not its detailed blueprinting, that is of supreme importance,

HYMAN J. SCHACHTEL, *The Shadowed Valley*, 1962

See also Annihilation; Beatific Vision; Belief; Body; Body and Soul; Communism; Damnation; Death; Destiny; Easter; Eter-nal Life; Heaven; Immortality, Arguments for; Immortality, Belief in; Immortality, Denial and Doubt of; Life: Its Meaning; Life and Death; Love; Love, Divine; Man; Man: His Destiny and Goal; Man and God; Man's Unity with God; Morality; Nirvana; Personality; Purgatory; Redemption; Religion: Its Nature and Function; Religion, Necessity of; Resurrection; Reward; Reward and Punishment; Salvation; Sin; Soul; Soul and God; Spirit; Spirit, Human; Spiritualism; Vision.

IMMORTALITY, ARGUMENTS FOR

Above the senses is the mind. Above the mind is the intellect. Above the intellect is the ego. Above the ego is the unmanifested seed, the Primal Cause. And verily beyond the unmanifested seed is the self, the unconditioned Knowing whom one attains to freedom and achieves immortality.

Katha Upanishads, prior to 400 B.C.

O mighty among men, he is fit to attain immortality who is serene and not afflicted by these sensations, but is the same in pleasure and pain.

Bhagavad-Gita, c. 2nd century B.C.

Whatever it is that feels, and knows and wills, and has the power of growth, is celestial and divine, and for that reason must be immortal.

CICERO, *Tusculanae disputationes*, 45 B.C.

Why should you not believe you will exist again after this existence, seeing you exist now after non-existence? . . . Is it harder for God . . . who made your body when it was not, to make it anew when it has been?

ST. IRENAEUS (130–c. 200), *Dem. Apost.* 34

The soul . . . comes directly from God in heaven. . . . The soul is not destroyed, as it does not require physical life for its activities.

MAIMONIDES (1135–1204), *Fundamental Principles of the Torah,* 4

Among other excellent arguments for the immortality of the soul, there is one drawn from the perpetual progress of the soul to its perfection, without a possibility of ever arriving at it.

JOSEPH ADDISON, *The Spectator,* 1711

Can we believe that a thinking being that is in perpetual progress of improvements, and travelling on from perfection to perfection, after having just looked abroad into the works of its Creator, and made a few discoveries of his infinite goodness, wisdom, and power, must perish at her first setting out.

JOSEPH ADDISON, *The Spectator,* 1713

There cannot be a stronger argument that God has designed us for a state of future happiness, . . . than that he has thus naturally qualified the soul for it, and made it a being capable of receiving so much bliss.

JOSEPH ADDISON, *The Spectator,* 1714

A proof, even a demonstrative one, of a future life would not be a proof of religion. . . . But as religion implies a future state, any presumption against such a state is a presumption against religion.

JOSEPH BUTLER, *The Analogy of Religion,* 1736

It is scarcely to be imagined that Infinite Benevolence would create a being capable of enjoying so much more than is here to be enjoyed and qualified by nature to prolong pain by remembrance and anticipate its terror, if he were not designed for something nobler and better.

SAMUEL JOHNSON, *The Adventurer,* December 29, 1753

Without wanting to deceive men, it can be said we have as much reason to believe in as to deny the immortality of the being that thinks.

VOLTAIRE, *Homélie sur l'athéisme,* 1763

I trouble not myself about the manner of future existence. I content myself with believing, even to positive conviction, that the power that gave me existence is able to continue it, in any form and manner he pleases, either with or without this body; and it appears more probable to me that I shall continue to exist hereafter than that I should have had existence, as I now have, before that existence began.

THOMAS PAINE, *The Age of Reason,* 1794

Our Creator would never have made such lovely days, and have given us the deep hearts to enjoy them, above and beyond all thought, unless we were meant to be immortal.

NATHANIEL HAWTHORNE, *Mosses from an Old Manse,* 1846

The blazing evidence of immortality is our dissatisfaction with any other solution.

RALPH WALDO EMERSON, *Journal,* July, 1855

What better can the Lord do for a man, than take him home when he has done his work?

CHARLES KINGSLEY, *Westward Ho!,* 1855

Socrates proved the immortality of the soul from the fact that sickness of the soul (sin) does not consume it as bodily sickness consumes the body.

SÖREN KIERKEGAARD (1813–1855), *Meditations From,* ed. T. H. Croxall, 1955

It cannot be that our life is a mere bubble cast up by eternity to float a moment on its waves and then sink into nothingness. Else why is it that the glorious aspirations which leap like angels from the temple of our heart are forever wandering unsatis-

fied. . . . There is a realm where the rainbow never fades; where the stars will be spread out before us like islands that slumber in the ocean, and where the beautiful beings which now pass before us like shadows will stay in our presence forever.
GEORGE D. PRENTICE, *Man's Higher Destiny*, 1860

Neither experience nor science has given man the idea of immortality. . . . The idea of immortality rises from the very depths of his soul—he feels, he sees, he knows that he is immortal.
FRANÇOIS GUIZOT, *Méditations et Études Morales*, 1883

I believe in the immortality of the soul, not in the sense in which I accept the demonstrable truths of science, but as a supreme act of faith in the reasonableness of God's work.
JOHN FISKE, *Destiny of Man*, 1884

The deeper our conviction of the rationality of the Universe, the stronger becomes our unwillingness to believe that such an order can be final and permanent. Hence it is that a sincere Theism has nearly always carried with it a belief in Immortality.
HASTINGS RASHDALL, *The Theory of Good and Evil*, II, 1907

If the Father deigns to touch with divine power the cold and pulseless heart of the buried acorn and to make it burst forth from its prison walls, will He leave neglected in the earth the soul of man made in the image of his Creator?
WILLIAM JENNINGS BRYAN, *The Prince of Peace*, 1909

Since in the course of our life here below virtue is not duly rewarded, there must be a future life in which a Sovereign Ruler completes His sanction of the moral order by giving to each according to his deserts.
DÉSIRÉ JOSEPH MERCIER, *Retreat to His Priests*, 1912

A psychological proof of post mortem existence has been found in the fact that immortality is an apprehension of human reason.
J. D. QUACKENBOS, *Body and Spirit*, 1916

Our deepest mature conviction is that finite and infinite interpenetrate, as time and eternity interpenetrate, and our problems must be solved in the light of that conviction.
LILY DOUGLAS, *Immortality*, ed. B. H. Streeter, 1917

It is the sense of boundless possibilities in man which justifies faith in personal immortality.
WILLIAM ADAMS BROWN, *The Life of Prayer in a World of Science*, 1927

The soul is not composed of parts, and therefore cannot perish by being resolved into constituents.
RICHARD DOWNEY, *Critical and Constructive Essays*, 1934

If God feels toward men as Christ felt, we simply ask ourselves whether such a God could conceivably call men into an existence like human life, and then let them pass out into nothingness.
FRANCIS J. MCCONNELL, *The Christlike God*, 1938

Unless we are willing to believe that the Creator and Ruler of the world is unjust, we must believe in a future life wherein He will render to everyone according to his deeds.
MARTIN J. SCOTT, *Prove There's a Soul That Will Last Forever*, 1941

See also Death: Fear of; Easter; God: His Goodness; Immortality; Immortality: Belief in; Immortality: Desire for; Jesus Christ: His Resurrection; New Testament; Personality; Resurrection; Soul; Soul and Immortality; Spirit.

IMMORTALITY, BELIEF IN

King Tety has not indeed died. He has become a glorious one in the sky; he abides in continuity. The lifetime of King Unis is eternity; his boundary is eternity. . . . Though thou sleepest, thou wakest again; though thou diest, thou livest again.
> Inscribed on a royal Egyptian Tomb, c. 2500 B.C.

The body dies but the spirit is not entombed.
Dhammapada, c. 5th century B.C.

Some people are born again; evil doers go to hell; righteous people go to heaven; those who are free from all worldly desires attain Nirvana.
Dhammapada, c. 5th century B.C.

As rivers flow into the sea and in so doing lose name and form, even so the wise man, freed from name and form, attains the Supreme Being, the Self-luminous, the Infinite.
Mundaka Upanishad, prior to 400 B.C.

The snarer who rules alone by his powers, who rules all the worlds by his powers, who is one and the same, while things arise and exist—they who know this are immortal.
Svetasvatara Upanishad, before 400 B.C.

Those who know beyond this the High Brahman, the vast, hidden in the bodies of all creatures, and alone enveloping everything, as the Lord, they become immortal.
Svetasvatara Upanishad, before 400 B.C.

When the soul returns into itself and reflects, it passes into . . . the region of that which is pure and everlasting, immortal and unchangeable.
PLATO, "Phaedo," *Dialogues,* 399 B.C.

Birthless and deathless and changeless remains the spirit forever;

Death has not touched it at all, dead though the house of it seems!
Bhagavad-Gita, c. 2nd century B.C.

He who, at the time of death, thinking of Me alone, goes forth, leaving the body, he attains unto my Being.
Bhagavad-Gita, c. 2nd century B.C.

Nor I, nor you, nor any one of these,
Ever was not, nor ever will not be,
Forever and forever afterwards,
All, that does live, lives always!
Bhagavad-Gita, c. 2nd century B.C.

Indestructible,
Learn thou! the Life is spreading life through all;
It cannot anywhere, by any means,
Be anywise diminished, stayed, or changed.
. . . These fleeting frames which it informs
With spirit deathless, endless, infinite,
They perish.
Bhagavad-Gita, 5th to 2nd century B.C.

In my better part I shall be raised to immortality above the lofty stars.
> OVID, (43 B.C.–17 A.D.), *Metamorphoses,* Bk. XV, 1.875

The soul lives forever: it is a portion of the Deity housed in our bodies.
> FLAVIUS JOSEPHUS, *The Jewish Wars,* c. 76 A.D.

We maintain that after life has passed away thou still remainest in existence, and lookest forward to a day of judgment, and according to thy deserts are assigned to misery or bliss.
> TERTULLIAN, *The Testimony of the Christian Soul,* c. 210

Souls in punishment will seek death. They prefer not to be, rather than to be punished. It is for this they shall seek death and not find it. In this sense, every human soul is immortal.
> ORIGEN, *On the Soul,* c. 240

We know that it [the soul] survives the body and that being set free from the bars of the body, it sees with clear gaze those things which before, dwelling in the body, it could not see.

> St. Ambrose (340?–397), *Two Books on the Death of Satyrus*

I believe with perfect faith that there will be a revival of the dead at the time when it shall please the Creator.

> Maimonides, *Commentary to Mishna: Sanhedrin*, 1168

There is a part of the soul that is untouched by time or mortality: it proceeds out of the Spirit and remains eternally in the Spirit and is divine.

> Meister Eckhart (1260?–1327?), *Meister Eckhart*

Here in this world He bids us come, there in the next He shall bid us Welcome.

> John Donne, *Sermon*, January 29, 1625

In sickness the soul begins to dress herself for immortality.

> Jeremy Taylor, *Holy Dying*, 1651

There is nothing strictly immortal, but immortality.

> Thomas Browne, *Urn Burial*, 1658

The sufficiency of Christian Immortality frustrates all earthly glory, and the quality of either state after death, makes a folly of posthumous memory.

> Thomas Browne, *Urn Burial*, 1658

Death is but crossing the world, as friends do the seas; they live in another still.

> Thomas Traherne (1636–1674), *Centuries of Meditation*

Death cannot kill what never dies.

> Thomas Traherne (1636–1674), *Centuries of Meditation*

After the end of this world every nature, whether corporeal or incorporeal, will seem to be only God, the integrity of the nature remaining, so that God, who is in himself incomprehensible, will be somehow comprehended in the creature.

> Johannes Scotus Erigena, *The Division of Nature*, 1681

The truest end of Life, is to know the Life that never ends.

> William Penn, *Some Fruits of Solitude*, 1718

The belief of immortality is impressed upon all men, and all men act under an impression of it, however they may talk, and though, perhaps, they may be scarcely sensible of it.

> Samuel Johnson, *Boswell's Life*, April 14, 1775

If I did not believe in a future state, I should believe in no God.

> John Adams, *Letter to Thomas Jefferson*, December 8, 1818

The term is not very distant at which we are to deposit in the same cerement our sorrows and suffering bodies, and to ascend in essence to an ecstatic meeting with the friends we have loved and lost, and whom we shall still love and never lose again.

> Thomas Jefferson, *Letter to John Adams*, 1818

If we have but once seen any child of Adam, we have seen an immortal soul. It has not passed away, as a breeze or sunshine, but it lives; it lives at this moment in one of those many places, whether in bliss or misery, in which all souls are reserved until the end.

> John Henry Newman, *Parochial and Plain Sermons*, 1843

Nor blame I Death, because he bare
The use of virtue out of earth:

I know transplanted human worth
Will bloom to profit, otherwise.
ALFRED, LORD TENNYSON, *In Memoriam,* 1850

The eternity of the spirit does not begin after death, but is, like God, always present.
MOSES HESS, *Rome and Jerusalem,* 1862

I am a better believer, and all serious souls are better believers in the immortality, than we can give grounds for.
RALPH WALDO EMERSON, *Letters and Social Aims,* 1876

I swear I think there is nothing but immortality.
WALT WHITMAN, "To Think of Time," *Leaves of Grass,* 1892

As I draw near the borderland . . . the wonderful light of the other life seems often to shine so joyfully into this one, that I almost forget the past and present, in an eager anticipation of the approaching awakening.
ELIZABETH BLACKWELL, January 2, 1887, quoted in *Pioneer Work for Women,* 1895

The doctrine of the immortality of the Soul is an integral part of the Jewish creed. It is more; it is a necessary ingredient of every consistent religious creed.
MORRIS JOSEPH, *Judaism as Creed and Life,* 1903

The notion of the survival of the spirit after death in some form, whether clear or vague, has ever existed in the human mind from the most primitive times to the present hour.
HENRY FRANK, *Modern Light on Immortality,* 1909

The word "death" never occurs in the Pyramid Texts except in the negative or applied to a foe. Over and over again we hear the indomitable assurance that the dead lives.
JAMES H. BREASTED, *Development of Religion and Thought in Ancient Egypt,* 1912

The question whether our conscious personality survives after death has been answered by almost all races of men in the affirmative. On this point skeptical or agnostic people are nearly, if not wholly unknown.
SIR JAMES G. FRAZER, *The Belief in Immortality,* Vol. 1, 1912

Buddhism . . . is so persuaded of survival after death as being the rule, that it grants only to rare and elect souls the privilege of at length laying down the burden of continuous life.
I. I. METCHNIKOFF, *The Nature of Man,* 1916

Only of this I am assured, that some time and in some way, spirit to spirit, face to face, I shall meet the great Lord of life, and, falling before Him, tell my gratitude for all He has done, and implore pardon for all that I have left undone.
PAUL ELMER MORE, *Pages from an Oxford Diary,* 1937

If an empty tomb is the sign of our journey's end, the presence of an Angel of Light sitting on the cerements of death is the pledge of all our hope of immortality.
HERBERT F. GALLAGHER, *The Life and Personality of Christ,* 1940

The root cause of a man's grief and delusion is the identification of the Soul with the body. Fear of death paralyzes him because he is ignorant of the Soul's true nature. The wise perform their duties in the world, cherishing always the knowledge of the Soul's deathlessness.
SWAMI NIKHILANANDA, *Perspectives on a Troubled Decade,* ed. Bryson, Finkle-stein and MacIver, 1950

The hope of immortality is the most subjective of experiences. No one can prove it for us and no philosophical argument can convince us. It is, of course, a matter of faith which Easter bestows on those who have accepted Jesus Christ as Lord.

GERALD KENNEDY, *A Second Reader's Notebook*, 1959

Everything science has taught me—and continues to teach me—strengthens my belief in the continuity of our spiritual existence after death.

WERNER VON BRAUN, *This Week*, January 24, 1960

The immortality in which I declare my faith is uncompromisingly religious in concept. . . . I mean a personal immortality of *this* soul, *this* consciousness after a physical death on earth.

HYMAN J. SCHACHTEL, *The Shadowed Valley*, 1962

See also Belief; Believing; Easter; God: His Goodness; Immortality; Immortality: Arguments for; Immortality: Desire for; New Testament; Nirvana; Personality; Resurrection; Soul; Spirit.

IMMORTALITY: DENIAL AND DOUBT OF

There are sixteen heresies teaching a *conscious* existence after death. Then there are eight heresies teaching that the soul, material or immaterial, or both, or neither, finite or infinite, or both, or neither, has an *unconscious* existence after death. And, finally, eight others, which teach that the soul, in the same eight ways, exists after death in a state of being, neither conscious nor unconscious.

BUDDHA (6th century B.C.), in Rhys-David, *Buddhism*

Mortal man thinks of himself as immortal because his race is immortal: he confuses the drop in the stream with the stream itself.

JEAN PAUL RICHTER, *Hesperus*, 1795

The Religion of Humanity transforms the coarse idea of objective immortality into the real objective immortality common to the whole race.

AUGUSTE COMTE, *Positive Polity*, 1820

Dust to the dust! but the pure spirit shall flow
Back to the burning fountain whence it came,
A portion of the Eternal, which must glow
Through time and change, unquenchably the same . . .

PERCY BYSSHE SHELLEY, *Adonais*, 1820

I neither deny nor affirm the immortality of man. I see no reason for believing in it, but, on the other hand, I have no means of disproving it.

THOMAS HENRY HUXLEY, *Letter to Charles Kingsley*, September 23, 1860

Virtue can have no recompense, save as its own recompense, and vice can have no real punishment, save as it is its own avenger. The hope of immortality, in so far as it is based on the supposed necessity of righting in a future state that which is wrong here, is therefore untenable, for it is based on the assumption of a wrong which exists in the imagination only.

FELIX ADLER, *Creed and Deed*, 1878

Immortality is but a way of saying that the determination of expectancy is the essential factor of rationality.

WILLIAM JAMES, *Princeton Review*, July, 1883

The great lie about immortality destroys every kind of reason, every kind of naturalness in the instincts.

FRIEDRICH NIETZSCHE, *The Anti-Christians*, 1887

The belief in immortality is not found in Buddhism, the religion that dominates thirty percent of the entire human race; it is not found in the ancient popular religion

472

of the Chinese, nor in the reformed religion of Confucius, which succeeded it; and what is still more significant, it is not found in the earlier and purer religion of the Jews.

ERNEST HAECKEL, *The Riddle of the Universe,* 1890

We . . . are in reality as unable to conceive the separate existence of our soul as . . . to comprehend the resurrection of our body.

M. FRIEDLANDER, *Jewish Religion,* 1891

The survival of personality is neither conceivable nor desirable.

MAX NORDAU, *What Happens After Death?,* 1916

Science speaks much less clearly on the question of immortality than on the related one of the existence of an order and a supreme Intelligence in nature. . . . Yet many who profess to speak for science have drawn the definite conclusion that death is the end of all.

ARTHUR H. COMPTON, *The Freedom of Man,* 1935

"Immortality," said a famous Chinese statesman, "is when a man dies but his words live."

CARL CROW, *Master King,* 1937

However desperate the chance for survival may be, the chance for collective survival in the sense of an endless material continuance of its race and its culture is more desperate by far.

W. P. MONTAGUE, *The Way of Things,* 1940

This concern with the immortality of the soul of man, with its survival in a place no one has ever seen, is part of the wasted energy of the mind.

BEN HECHT, *A Child of the Century,* 1954

IMMORTALITY, DESIRE FOR

So far as in us lies, we must play the immortal and do all in our power to live by the best element in our nature.

ARISTOTLE, *Nicomachean Ethics,* c. 340 B.C.

If I err in my belief that the souls of men are immortal, I err gladly, and I do not wish to lose so delightful an error.

CICERO, *De Senectute,* c. 78 B.C.

The supreme desire of everything, and that first given by Nature, is to return to its source; and since God is the source of our souls and Maker of them . . . to him this soul desires above all to return.

DANTE, *Il Convito,* c. 1310

We shall all, I hope, be happy in a future state, but we must not expect to be all happy in the same degree. It is enough, if we be happy according to our several capacities.

SAMUEL JOHNSON, *Boswell's Life of,* 1772

The surest means of acquiring a conviction of a life after death, is so to act in this life that ye can venture to wish for another.

J. G. FICHTE (1762–1814), *The Vocation of Man*

There can be no doubt that the idea of a happy immortality, serving as a harbor of refuge from the tempests of this mortal existence . . . carries with it inexpressible consolation to those who are wearied, burdened, and tormented by pain and suffering. To feel one's self individually cared for and protected by God gives a special dignity and beauty to life.

HENRI AMIEL, *Journal,* 1873

The more materialistic science becomes, the more angels shall I paint: their wings are my protest in favor of the immortality of the soul.

E. C. BURNE-JONES *To Oscar Wilde,* c. 1880

473

The only truly religious hope of immortality so lives with God now as to know that God is not the God of the dead but of the living.

 JOHN OMAN, *Grace and Personality,* 1919

Life implies its own continuation. The more intensely one lives, the more difficult it is to think of destruction.

 J. H. LEUBA, *The Belief in God and Immortality,* 1921

Millions long for immortality who do not know what to do with themselves on a rainy Sunday afternoon.

 SUSAN ERTZ, *Anger in the Sky,* 1943

If I find in myself a desire which no experience in this world can satisfy, the most probable explanation is that I was made for another world.

 C. S. LEWIS, *Christian Behavior,* 1943

See also Immortality; Immortality, Arguments for; Immortality, Belief in.

IMPERIALISM

Every kind of national egotism, where love of one's own nation leads to the suppression of other nationalities, is sin and rebellion against God.

 Official Report of the Oxford Conference, ed. J. H. Oldham, 1938

See also War, Unjust.

IMPURITY

The taking of life, killing, cutting, binding, stealing, lying, fraud and deception . . . this is impurity.

 Sutta-Nipata, 6th century B.C.

The impurity of the world is a dark covering before the face of the soul and it preventeth it from discerning spiritual wisdom.

 PALLADIUS OF EGYPT, *Paradise of the Fathers,* c. 300

Now true servants of God regard all impure pleasures and creaturely quests as the depths of an ancient cistern defiled with slime, whence the pure water has long since flowed away.

 PÈRE JOSEPH (1577–1638), *Method*

There is never a vice which more separates the sinner from God; there is never a vice which, after it has separated him from God, leaves him less resource for returning to Him; there is never a vice which renders the sinner more unsupportable to himself; finally, there is not one which renders him more contemptible in the eyes even of other men.

 JEAN BAPTISTE MASSILLON (1663–1742), *Sermons*

See also Hedonism; Homosexuality; Immorality; Lust; Pleasure; Purity; Sexual Intercourse; Sexual Sin.

INACTION

There is no more contemptible type of human character than that of the nerveless sentimentalist and dreamer who spends his life in a weltering sea of sensibility and emotion, but who never does a manly, concrete deed.

 WILLIAM JAMES, *Principles of Psychology,* 1890

The listless, uninterested and unoccupied life is the most dangerous of all. It is better to be interested in frivolities than to be interested in nothing at all. Life is too strong merely to be held in check.

 B. W. MATURIN, *The Laws of the Spiritual Life,* 1907

See also Action; Acts; Apathy; Complacency; Conduct; Duties; Ease; Idleness; Practice; Spiritual Lethargy.

INCARNATION

Born as a Son, led forth as a lamb, sacrificed as a sheep, buried as a man, he rose from the dead as God, being by nature God and man.

ST. MELITO, *Homily on the Passion,* 2nd century

The Son of God was made the son of man that the children of man might be made children of God.

ST. ATHANASIUS (296–373), *Cit. apud. Petavium,* I.c

God was made man, that man might be made God.

ST. AUGUSTINE (354–430), *Serm.* 13 de temp.

Abiding before all time, He began to be in time; the Lord of all things He obscured His immeasurable majesty and took on Him the form of a servant. Being God who cannot suffer, He did not disdain to be man that can and, immortal as He is, to subject Himself to the laws of death.

POPE ST. LEO THE GREAT, *Letter to Flavianus,* 449

Coming together in the single person, human nothingness was assumed by divine majesty, weakness by power, mortality by eternity. . . . The inviolable nature was united to a susceptible nature, in such a manner that as was indeed needed for our salvation . . . the man Jesus Christ, could indeed die to one nature, but not according to the other.

POPE ST. LEO THE GREAT, *Letter to Flavianus,* 449

We confess one and the same Son, our Lord Jesus Christ, perfect in Godhead, perfect in Manhood, truly God and truly man, of a rational soul and body, of one substance with the Father with respect to the Godhead, and of one substance with us in respect of the Manhood, like us in everything except sin.

Council of Chalcedon, 451

We acknowledge in one and the same Lord Jesus Christ two natures, a divine and a human, which are conjoined and united in one person without absorption or confusion and mixture.

HENRY BULLINGER, *The Helvetic Confession,* 1536

Through the mystery of the incarnation of his Son and his glorious resurrection according to the flesh, the Father has not only lent creatures a certain beauty but has also left them clad, as it were, in the perfect raiment of glory and majesty.

ST. JOHN OF THE CROSS, *Spiritual Canticle,* c. 1580

Christ is God clothed with human nature.

BENJAMIN WHICHCOTE, *Moral and Religious Aphorisms,* 1753

That a son of God was born from eternity, descended and assumed the human may be compared to the fables of the ancients.

EMMANUEL SWEDENBORG (1688–1772), quoted in R. F. Barrett's *The Question, What Are the Doctrines of the New Church?*

Among the external operations of God, the highest of all is the mystery of the Incarnation of the Word, in which the splendor of the divine perfections shines forth so brightly that nothing more sublime can even be imagined, nothing else could have been more salutary to the human race.

POPE LEO XIII, *Divinum Illud,* May, 1897

The incarnation is the center of all sane theology . . . man at his best can alone give us God at his best.

GEORGE A. GORDON, *The New Puritanism,* ed. R. W. Raymond, 1897

The Incarnation is an alliance contracted, not with that soul and that body only which was united in the unity of one Person with the Word made flesh, but likewise with all mankind by their entrance into the Church, in which that Word has dwelt amongst us.

JOSEPH RICKABY, *Notes on St. Paul,* 1898

Christ conceived as the Incarnate Son is a Person so possessed of the communicable life of God as to be the inexhaustible medium of its communication to man.

A. M. FAIRBAIRN, *The Place of Christ in Modern Theology,* 1902

In almost all other cases the historian is able to test his materials by some external criterion of probability. But in the case of the Incarnation, we have nothing with which to compare it; the only external criterion to which we can appeal is the judgment of the Christian Church.

W. R. INGE, *Contentio Veritatis,* 1916

Christ came in human form chiefly for the purpose of awakening man to a sense of divine possibilities.

JOSEPH MCSORLEY, *Be of Good Heart,* 1924

Faith only can recognize in the man Jesus the Son of God.

EMIL BRUNNER, *The Theology of Crisis,* 1929

Jesus is the bridge between Humanity and Divinity. In Him God is not only manifested to man, but vitally participated.

CHRISTOPHER DAWSON, *Christianity and the New Age,* 1931

The Incarnation implies a personal Deity, and some indefinable dualism in the Godhead which makes it possible that the divine personality should manifest itself in a human life while the essential Deity remains intact.

PAUL ELMER MORE, *The Catholic Faith,* 1931

It had to be that in the person of man the whole material creation should be made capable of getting back to its Creator and of being one with Him. . . . Else what would have been the use of the Incarnation?

PAUL CLAUDEL, *Ways and Crossways,* 1933

The Incarnation of God, the coming of the Son of God into the external order of this world, shows that the physical order is not a closed system incapable of being influenced from without.

NICHOLAS BERDYAEV, *Freedom and Spirit,* 1935

God in the aspect of God-the-Son descends into the abyss, into the *Ungrund,* into the depths of freedom out of which springs evil as well as every kind of good. This is the only possible interpretation of the mystery of the Incarnation.

NICHOLAS BERDYAEV, *The Destiny of Man,* 1937

I believe that Christ was very man made very God, the Incarnation of man's potential Divinity. Unfortunately, this is not Christianity as taught in any Church, but a neomonophysite heresy.

FRANCIS YEATS-BROWN, *Saver at Large,* 1937

I can find no key to the Incarnation unless it reveals God as a personality somehow involved in the failure of His own handiwork and somehow redeeming the evil of the world by participating in the penalties of imperfection.

PAUL ELMER MORE, *Pages from an Oxford Diary,* 1937

Since the essence of the divine consists in its unconditional character, and since the essence of the human lies in its conditional and contingent nature, it is not logically possible to assert both qualities of the same person.

REINHOLD NIEBUHR, *Beyond Tragedy,* 1937

The Incarnation does not destroy or supersede nature. It is analogous and complementary to it, since it restores and extends man's natural function as the bond of union between the material and spiritual worlds.

CHRISTOPHER DAWSON, *Progress and Religion,* 1938

In the great affirmation that "The Word was made flesh and we beheld his glory" is implicit a whole theory of the relation between spirit and matter.

WILLIAM TEMPLE, *Readings in St. John's Gospel,* 1st series, 1939

If we accept the truth of the Incarnation, it follows inevitably in logic that all other events in history derive ultimately their importance only from their relation to that supreme event.

CHRISTOPHER HOLLIS, *The Noble Castle,* 1941

Jesus Christ was perfectly human, precisely because his human nature was in unfailing communion with the Divine Nature. He was not less a man, but more a man, because He was also God.

GERALD GROVELAND WALSH, *Faith for Today,* 1941

It is almost literal fact that at the words *Et Incarnatus Est* the whole of Christendom fell upon its knees and remained there for a thousand years.

BLANCHE MARY KELLY, *The Well of English,* 1946

The conception of one solitary incarnation of deity is peculiar to Christianity.

N. SODERBLOM, in *Encyclopedia of Religion and Ethics,* vii, 184, 1951

At the moment when the Word was made flesh, the divine virtue was carried in some way into the very heart of the material Universe, to restore it, transform it, and sanctify it.

CHARLES JOURNET, *The Apostolic Hierarchy,* 1955

For if the technological age is of major importance in the "hominization" of the universe, this "hominization" itself reaches its apogee by being at once realized and transcended in the Person of Christ, the God-Man.

WALTER J. ONG, *Frontiers in American Catholicism,* 1957

See also Atonement; Calvary; Cross; Easter; Fall, the; Jesus Christ; Man and God; Redemption; Reincarnation; Resurrection; Salvation; Trinity; Universe and God; Word, the.

INDEPENDENCE

It is not my duty, I cannot so regard it, to attend the churches. My own spirit preaches sounder doctrine than I there hear, and I must listen to its divine teachings. . . . the Lord appeareth to me more visibly in other courts, and that there am I to seek and find Him, worshipping in the holy temple of Self.

BRONSON ALCOTT, December 20, 1836, *Journal of,* ed. O. Shepard, 1938

If God exists, all things depend on Him and I can do nothing outside His will. If He does not exist, all depends on me and I am bound to display my independence. . . . I shall kill myself to prove my independence and my terrible new freedom.

KIRILOV in Feodor Dostoevsky's *The Possessed,* 1871

Independence of judgment alone can enable a man to stand upright with godlike grace.

T. V. SMITH, *Perspectives on a Troubled Decade,* ed. Bryson, Finklestein and MacIver, 1950

No church can empower any man, or body of men, to do anything which will impair its independency.

J. M. PENDLETON, *Baptist Church Manual,* 1955

See also Coercion; Free Will; Freedom; Freedom, Religious; Individual; Individualism; Rootlessness.

INDIFFERENCE

To be of no church is dangerous. Religion, of which the rewards are distant, and which is animated only by faith and hope, will glide by degrees out of the mind unless it be invigorated and reimpressed by external ordinances, by stated calls to worship, and the salutary influence of example.

SAMUEL JOHNSON, *Life of Milton,* 1781

Indifferentism, i.e. the fatal opinion, spread abroad by the villainy of evil men, that the soul's eternal salvation can be obtained by any kind of profession of faith provided that morals conform to justice and probity.

POPE GREGORY XVI, *Mirari Vos,* August 15, 1832

If ignorance and passions are foes of popular morality, it must be confessed that moral indifference is the malady of the cultivated classes.

HENRI AMIEL, *Journal,* 1882

To hold, therefore, that there is no difference in matters of religion between forms that are unlike each other, and even contrary to each other, most clearly leads in the end to the rejection of all religion both in theory and practice.

LEO XIII, *Immortale Dei,* November 1, 1885

The worst sin towards our fellow-creatures is not to hate them, but to be indifferent to them; that's the essence of inhumanity.

GEORGE BERNARD SHAW, *Socialism of,* ed. J. Fuchs, 1926

The indifference of believers is something far more dreadful than the fact that unbelievers exist.

ALEXANDER YELCHANINOV (1881–1934), *Fragments of a Diary*

The vicious people in the world are numerically insignificant; the indifferent are like sands of the sea for number.

E. M. POTEAT, *These Shared His Passion,* 1940

Indifference is the greatest danger that Christianity or any other religion, has to fear.

JAMES BISSETT PRATT, *Can We Keep the Faith?,* 1941

The fact that man is physically free to worship God or not, should never be construed to mean that he is morally free to ignore his Creator.

JOHN A. O'BRIEN, *Religion—Does It Matter?,* 1944

Our quarrel is not with Jews who are different but with Jews who are indifferent.

STEPHEN S. WISE (1874–1949), *Rededication*

The moral indifferentism so common today, masquerading as toleration.

W. R. FORRESTER, *Christian Vocation,* 1951

By attempting to demonstrate the affinity of the Christian faith to what members of the intelligentsia had already accepted on other grounds, the churches succeeded only in demonstrating that they had so little of consequence to contribute that the person outside the church could justifiably remain indifferent.

W. S. HUDSON, *The Great Tradition of the American Churches,* 1953

See also Believing; Individual Responsibility; Tolerance.

INDIGENOUS CHURCH

If the indigenous church in each land means anything it means that there are likely to emerge forms and expressions of Christianity which we would not recognize as such.

HUGH VERNON WHITE, *Christian Century,* February 14, 1934

INDIGENOUS RELIGION

The Great Spirit has made us all, but he has made a great difference between his white and red children. He has given us different complexions and different customs. . . . Since he has made so great a difference between us in other things, why may we not conclude that he has given us a different religion according to our understanding?

SENECA INDIAN CHIEF RED JACKET, to delegate from Evangelical Mission Society of Massachusetts, 1805

INDIVIDUAL

One individual has more reality than all universals put together.

ROGER BACON, *Compendium Studii Philosophiae*, 1271

It is precisely individuality that is the original and eternal thing in men. . . . The cultivation and development of this individuality as one's highest vocation would be divine egoism.

FRIEDRICH SCHLEGEL, *Athenaeum*, III, 15, 1800

Unification pure and simple is the true content of the individual, and the individual's destiny is the living of a universal life.

G. W. F. HEGEL, *The Philosophy of Right*, 1821

A distinct universe walks about under your hat and under mine. . . . You and I are but a pair of infinite isolations, with some fellow islands a little more or less near to us.

WILLIAM MAKEPEACE THACKERAY, *The History of Pendennis*, 1850

Humanity is alone real; the individual is an abstraction.

AUGUSTE COMTE, *Catéchisme positiviste*, 1852

The initiation of all wise and noble things, comes and must come from individuals, generally at first from some one individual.

JOHN STUART MILL, *On Liberty*, 1859

Since every individual human being is a nucleus of living forces; since he is potentially capable of limitless perfecting . . . he cannot be valued too highly.

VLADIMIR SOLOVIEV (1853–1900), *The Meaning of Love*

The basic lie and evil . . . come from . . . disinclination to extend to others the recognition of an absolute worth rightly perceived by him in himself, but wrongly refused to others.

VLADIMIR SOLOVIEV (1853–1900), *The Meaning of Love*

Humanity does not exist outside of the individual man, nor without him; the individual man does not exist outside of humanity and without it. The individual and society are the object one of the other.

AUGUSTE SABATIER, *Religions of Authority and the Religion of the Spirit*, 1903

The isolated individual is marked by complete impotence and irreconcilable discord.

ALEKSEI KHOMYAKOV, *Satchineniya*, 1911

The happening-but-once is the eternity of the individual. For with his uniqueness he is engraved irrevocably in the heart of the universe.

MARTIN BUBER, *Jewish Mysticism and the Legends of Baalshem*, 1916

The more a man . . . is mastered by individuality, the deeper does the I sink into unreality.

MARTIN BUBER, *I and Thou*, 1923

In the atheistic conception of a self-existing universe in total evolution, in which man is conceived as but a part of the total becoming, the individual can only exist in terms of his social group, and hence, he can only be a mere tool of the state.

LOUIS J. A. MERCIER, *Address*, October 30, 1942

All the way through the Book the movement is away from the tribe and the group to this stark figure or that, daring to get to his feet, shaken loose before the Eternal.

P. SCHERER, *For We Have This Treasure,* 1944

As an individual, each of us is a fragment of a species, a part of the universe, a unique point in the immense web of the cosmic, ethnical, historical forces and influences—and bound by their laws. . . . Our whole being is an individual by reason of that in us which derives from matter, and a person by reason of that in us which derives from spirit.

JACQUES MARITAIN, *The Person and the Common Good,* 1947

Nowhere in the Christian life is the believer more an individual than in contemplative prayer.

HANS URS VON BALTHASAR, *Prayer,* 1961

See also Freedom; Individual Responsibility; Individualism; Man; Person; Personality; Rootlessness.

INDIVIDUAL RESPONSIBILITY

By one's self the evil is done, by one's self one suffers; by one's self evil is left undone, by one's self one is purified. The pure and the impure stand and fall by themselves, *no one can purify another.*

Dhammapada, c. 5th century B.C.

The world has fallen prey to scoundrels, who can rule it in all impunity, because people, in order to go to heaven, prefer to bear and bewail their abuses rather than punish them.

NICCOLÒ MACHIAVELLI, *Discourses,* c. 1519

Ah me! you must bear your own burthen, fashion your own faith, think your own thought, and pray your own prayer. . . . Who can weigh circumstances, passions, temptations, that go to our good and evil

account, save One, before whose awful wisdom we kneel, and at whose mercy we ask absolution.

ARTHUR PENDENNIS in William M. Thackeray's *Pendennis,* 1850

If a man cast the blame of his sloth and inefficiency upon others, he will end by sharing the pride of Satan and murmuring against God.

FATHER ZOSSIMA'S discourse, Feodor Dostoevsky, *The Brothers Karamazov,* 1880

Be assured that if thou failest, none other —not nature, nor man, nor angel, nor Creator—will render the service or bestow the love due from thee.

STANTON COIT, *Social Worship,* ed. Stanton Coit, 1913

Fate is something outside of us. What really plays the dickens with us is something in ourselves. Something that makes us go on doing the same sort of fool things, however many chances we get.

PURDIE in James M. Barrie's *Dear Brutus,* 1917

The peculiar character of an individual human being in distinction from an atom lies in this, that he is the owner of himself and responsible to himself.

MARTIN C. D'ARCY, *God and the Supernatural,* 1920

Naturalistic determinism has not yet found a place for the concept of individual responsibility.

RALPH H. GABRIEL, *The Course of American Democratic Thought,* 1940

Action, however far it spreads, comes back to its recorded page, black or white, to the one man that sent it forth, that he must read it to the last syllable in the Presence where there is no deceiving.

WILLIAM L. SULLIVAN, *Under Orders,* 1944

Outside the sphere of individual responsibility there is neither goodness nor badness. . . . Only where we ourselves are responsible for our own interests and are free to sacrifice them has our decision moral value.

FRIEDRICH A. HAYEK, *The Road to Serfdom,* 1945

So long as men and women believed themselves to be responsible beings, called to choose, and accountable to God for their choices, life might be tragic, but it was not trivial.

SYDNEY CAVE, *The Christian Way,* 1949

Does any one really believe he can escape from the responsibility for what he has done and thought in secret? . . . The centre of our whole being is involved in the centre of all being; and the centre of all being rests in the centre of our being.

PAUL TILLICH, *The Shaking of the Foundations,* 1949

Is there no such thing as moral responsibility and social accountability at all? Is every mean or vicious thing that you or I as ordinary individuals do, not sin, but rather an expression of "illness"? Who would seriously hold that a society could long endure which consistently subscribed to this flaccid doctrine?

O. HOBART MOWRER, *Address,* Cincinnati, Ohio, September, 1959

The nidus of the malady from which our civilization suffers lies in the individual soul and is only to be overcome within the individual soul.

WILHELM ROEPKE, *Modern Age,* Summer, 1959

The social pressures of today's complex life do not excuse from, but rather create a demand for, a greater exercise of personal responsibility. No man can be neutral on a moral cause.

CATHOLIC BISHOPS OF THE U.S., November, 1961

See also Conduct; Decision; Determinism; Duties; Election; Free Will; Freedom; Independence; Individual; Individualism; Man: Defined and Interpreted; Man: His Destiny and Goal; Predestination; Responsibility; Rights; Self; Society.

INDIVIDUALISM

We have been strangled by an exaggerated form of Individualism. But the coming century will show that human society is grander and nobler than anything merely individual.

HENRY E. MANNING, *Dignity and the Rights of Labor,* 1886

I do not see any promise of vitality either in the church or in society except upon the true basis of individualism.

WOODROW WILSON, *Address,* November 19, 1909

Such emphasis as Christianity has given to the individual soul has done much to create that spirit of individualism in the modern world which is the basis of our freedom.

EVERETT DEAN MARTIN, *Liberty,* 1930

The religious individualism of the last age, with its self-centred absorption in the question of personal salvation and private religious emotion, will not help us. The Christianity of the future must be a social Christianity that is embodied in a real society.

CHRISTOPHER DAWSON, *The Modern Dilemma: The Problem of European Unity,* 1932

Once men had accepted the axiom that the individual was capable of realizing his own spiritual salvation, the next step was already half-taken; the individual was equally competent to attain his own *economic* salvation.

JOHN EMMET HUGHES, *The Church and the Liberal Society,* 1944

The burly individualism of former years must be tempered by the consciousness of being a member of the body of Christ.

JACKSON JARMAN, *Address,* Consultation on Church Union held at Oberlin College, March, 1963

In one single field, that of moral conduct, individualism is growing unhealthily, and even writing a new charter, or rather anticharter. The essence here is the denial of moral laws binding upon all men—for no two men are alike, each is a special case.

F. J. SHEED, *Sheed and Ward Trumpet,* Spring, 1964

See also Freedom; Independence; Individual; Individual Responsibility; Person; Personality; Rootlessness; Society.

INDOCTRINATION

In our fear of indoctrination we have practiced a worse indoctrination: by our silences in secular education we have indoctrinated children to believe that God does not exist and that Jesus Christ does not matter.

GEORGE A. BUTTRICK, *Christ and Man's Dilemma,* 1946

Indoctrination is not an educational crime; it is an educational necessity, in religion as in table manners. The crime is to indoctrinate in such a way as to destroy the freedom and the responsibility of the pupil.

M. V. C. JEFFREYS, *Glaucon: An Inquiry into the Aims of Education,* 1950

INDULGENCES

Christ never commanded that indulgences be preached, but he emphatically commanded that the Gospel be preached.

MARTIN LUTHER, *Letter to the Archbishop of Mainz,* 1518

There is no doubt that Tetzel did . . . proclaim as Christian doctrine that noth-ing but an offering of money was required to gain the indulgence for the dead, without there being any question of contrition or confession. . . . There is no doubt that his doctrine was virtually that of the drastic proverb: "As soon as the money in the coffer rings, the soul from purgatory's fire springs." The papal bull of indulgence gave no sanction whatever to this proposition.

L. PASTOR, *History of the Popes,* VII, 1898

Luther began his work of reformation in an attack on what was called an Indulgence proclaimed by Pope Leo X. . . . So far as the common people were concerned, this indulgence meant that on the payment of certain specified· sums of money, spiritual privileges, incl·.ding the forgiveness of sins, could be obtained by the purchases.

THOMAS M. LINDSAY, *Luther and the German Reformation,* 1900

An indulgence is the remission of the temporal punishment due to sin, the guilt of which has been forgiven. . . . Once it is admitted that Christ left the Church the power to forgive sins, the power of granting indulgences is logically inferred.

Catholic Encyclopedia, VII, 1913

INDUSTRIALISM

Modern industry, particularly American industry, is not Christian. The economic forces which move it are hardly qualified at a single point by really ethical considerations.

REINHOLD NIEBUHR, *Leaves from the Notebook of a Tamed Cynic,* 1929

Modern industrialism could not have been born, and could not subsist if it had not been disposed to transgress the most elementary duties of morality.

GINA LOMBROSO, *The Tragedies of Progress,* 1931

As long as industry is organized, humanly, not for the service of the community but for the object of producing a purely financial result for some of its members it cannot be recognized as properly filling its social purpose.

Report on the Church and the Economic Order, Oxford Conference, 1937

The Christian Church throughout the formative decades of the industrial era showed little insight into what was befalling human society.

Report on the Lambeth Conference of Bishops of the Anglican Communion, 1948

We converted the world to industrialism, in which we believed, not to Christianity, in which we were becoming skeptical.

HERBERT AGAR, New York *Herald Tribune Book Review,* March 8, 1953

See also Business; Capitalism; Economics and Christianity; Machines; Profit; Property; Technology.

INFALLIBILITY

It could be maintained without absurdity that the Pope could go wrong when, for example, ordering things which, without being either good or evil in themselves, nor contrary to salvation, would be useless.

ST. ROBERT BELLARMINE (1542–1621), *De Romano Pontifice,* Lib. IV

The Church asks no more than do other governments, albeit it enjoys an immense superiority over them, since on the one side infallibility is *humanly supposed,* and on the other *divinely promised.*

JOSEPH DE MAISTRE, *Du Pape,* 1819

Sir Richard Steele has observed that there is this difference between the Church of Rome and the Church of England; the one professes to be infallible—the other to be never in the wrong.

C. C. COLTON, *Lacon,* 1822

A Roman Catholic is not bound to believe the [Vatican] Council infallible in making

civil and political regulations. Neither is he required to believe that the Council has any power or authority to make any such regulation, and if the Council should make it, he is not therefore bound to obey it.

JOHN ENGLAND, *U.S. Catholic Miscellany,* January 12, 1824

A Church that claims a divine origin, in order to be consistent must also claim to be unerring; for the idea of teaching error in the name of the Divinity is blasphemous.

I. T. HECKER, *Aspects of Nature,* 1857

The word of the Church is the word of the revelation. That the Church is the infallible oracle of the truth is the fundamental dogma of the Catholic religion.

JOHN HENRY NEWMAN, *Grammar of Assent,* 1870

Any supernatural religion that renounces its claim to this, . . . can claim to be a semi-revelation only. It is a hybrid thing, partly natural and partly supernatural.

WILLIAM H. MALLOCK, *Is Life Worth Living?,* 1877

The Christian will believe that he has an infallible authority in the mind of Christ; but he has no infallible means of ascertaining its application to given circumstances.

WILLIAM TEMPLE, *Nature, Man and God,* 1934

The enemies of the Papacy fail to make a distinction between infallibility and impeccability. Infallibility means freedom from error, impeccability means freedom from sin.

FULTON J. SHEEN, *The Fullness of Christ,* 1935

Any sect, by the very fact that it denies the possibility of an infallible Church, admits that it itself is fallible.

MARTIN J. SCOTT, *Hundreds of Churches,* 1941

It is a happy distinction which the Roman Catholic Church makes when it contrasts the Pope's infallibility in respect of faith and morals with the possibility of his falling into error on historical matters.

HERBERT BUTTERFIELD, *Christianity, Diplomacy and War,* 1953

If the religious and academic world would once clearly grasp the fact that the infallibility of the Church is concerned only with the message of Divine Revelation and not with science, art, or culture, then it would find no difficulty in reconciling infallibility with intellectual freedom.

KARL J. ALTER, *The Tablet* (Brooklyn, N.Y.), March 14, 1953

Formal exercise of their infallibility by Church or Pope, it must be admitted, has not yet seriously limited the freedom of men's minds.

EDMUND W. SINNOTT, *Two Roads to Truth,* 1953

In the Protestant understanding of the divine economy, no mortal man and no human institution was infallible, and any attempt to absolutize the fallible could only be interpreted as idolatry.

W. S. HUDSON, *The Great Tradition of the American Churches,* 1953

If the [Roman Catholic] Church is not infallible, then the Church cannot claim our allegiance. This is so because the Church insists, and has ever insisted, upon acceptance of her infallibility as a *sine qua non* of Christian allegiance.

B. C. BUTLER, *The Church and Infallibility,* 1954

The concept of the "infallibility" of a decision by a council or a bishop or a book excludes doubt as an element of faith in those who subject themselves to these authorities. . . . This faith has become static, a nonquestioning surrender.

PAUL TILLICH, *Dynamics of Faith,* 1957

The Protestant must record that to him the dogma of papal infallibility represents the ultimate expression of spiritual pride, i.e. the belief that a human being can be the perfect and uncorrupted transmitter of the Word of God. This is indeed to mistake the earthen vessel for the treasure.

ROBERT McAFEE BROWN, *An American Dialogue,* 1960

The Protestant . . . can only interpret it to mean that Roman Catholicism has become master of the gospel rather than its servant. Instead of believing that judgment must begin at the house of God, it has proclaimed that the house of God is one place, where there is no need for judgment.

ROBERT McAFEE .BROWN, *The Spirit of Protestantism,* 1961

Although the individual Bishops do not enjoy the prerogative of infallibility, they nevertheless proclaim Christ's doctrine infallibly whenever, even though dispersed through the world, but still maintaining the bond of communion among themselves and with the successor of Peter, and authentically teaching matters of faith and morals, they are in agreement on one position as definitively held.

Constitution on the Church, Second Vatican Council, November, 1964

See also Authority; Belief; Bishops; Church: Its Authority; Church: Its Nature; Church and State; Doctrine; Dogma; Error; Heresy; Pope, the; Revelation.

INFERIORITY

To know that you have done wrong is not the road to an inferiority complex. It will reveal that you are inferior. But you are.

SEBASTIAN MIKLAS, *Sanctify Your Emotions,* 1955

INFIDEL

I do not know, sir, that the fellow is an infidel, but if he is an infidel, he is an infidel as a dog is an infidel; that is to say, he has never thought upon the subject.

SAMUEL JOHNSON, *Boswell's Life of,* 1772

The lawbook is the nation's creed, the newspapers chant the actual liturgy and service of the day. What avails it that the priests call us "Christian" when the newspapers and the Congress prove us infidels.

THEODORE PARKER, *Sermon, on Conventional and Natural Sacraments,* 1849

Infidel, n. In New York, one who does not believe in the Christian religion; in Constantinople, one who does.

AMBROSE BIERCE, *Devil's Dictionary,* 1906

INFIDELITY

A sin so fearful that for the committing it both land and people must be destroyed, as it went with Jerusalem, with Rome, Greece, and other kingdoms.

MARTIN LUTHER (1483–1546), *Table Talk*

Sir, between a man and his Maker it is a different question: but between a man and his wife, a husband's infidelity is nothing. They are connected by children, by fortune, by serious considerations of community.

SAMUEL JOHNSON, *Boswell's Life of,* 1772

To form churches without reference to doctrinal opinion or experimental religion, and only by location within certain parish limits and by certain civil qualifications is the most pernicious infidelity that was ever broached.

LYMAN BEECHER, *Autobiography,* I, 1871

There are natures . . . which . . . bind us over to rectitude and purity by their pure beliefs about us, and our sins become

that worst kind of sacrilege which tears down the invisible altar of trust.

GEORGE ELIOT, *Middlemarch,* 1872

See also Adultery, Purity.

INFINITE

There is no bliss in anything finite. Infinity only is bliss. The Infinite rests in its own greatness.

Chandogya Upanishad, Prapathaka, prior to 400 B.C.

The Infinite is the source of joy. There is no joy in the finite. Only in the Infinite is there joy. Ask to know of the Infinite. . . . Infinite is immortal.

Chandogya Upanishad, prior to 400 B.C.

When I seek for a beginning, I find only infinite. When I look for an end I see only time infinite. Infinity of time past and to come implies no beginning, and is in accordance with the laws of material existences.

CHUANG-TZU (4th century B.C.), *Texts of Taoism,* ed. J. Legge

Infinity past and to come is a fathomless gulf, into which vanish all things.

MARCUS AURELIUS, *Meditations,* c. 170 A.D.

He who sees the Infinite in all things, sees God.

RICHARD HOOKER, *Ecclesiastical Polity,* 1585

If the doors of perception were cleansed everything would appear to man as it is, infinite.

WILLIAM BLAKE, *The Marriage of Heaven and Hell,* 1790

Whether we view religion from the human side or the divine—as the surrender of the soul to God, or as the life of God in the soul—in either aspect it is of its very essence that the Infinite has ceased to be a far-off vision, and has become a present reality.

> JOHN CAIRD, *Introduction to the Philosophy of Religion,* 1880

The works of the Magician of the Beautiful are not like ours and in the least fragment His artistry is no less present than in the stars. We may enter the infinite through the minute no less than through contemplation of the vast.

> GEORGE WILLIAM RUSSELL (*Æ*), *The Candle of Vision,* 1919

To admit the unattainableness of the end in a finite world by a finite being is the very condition of our acquiring the conviction that there is an infinite world, and that we . . . are included in it.

> FELIX ADLER, *The Reconstruction of the Spiritual Ideal,* 1924

Despite your every straining to find your ideals satisfied here below, the infinite torments you. . . . With your feet on earth, you dream of heaven; creature of time, you despise it; flower of a day, you seek to eternalize yourself.

> FULTON J. SHEEN, *Preface to Religion,* 1946

Since man cannot help seeking the infinite, he now seeks the meaning of his life in an infinity of things.

> EMIL BRUNNER, *The Divine Imperative,* 1947

If there is anything that modern man regards as infinite, it is no longer God; nor is it nature, let alone morality or culture; it is his own power.

> GUNTHERS ANDERS, *Dissent,* Spring, 1956

See also End; Eternal; Reality; Time.

INFIRMITY

I would rather be infirm than strong before God, for the infirm He takes into His arms, while the strong He leads by the hand.

> ST. FRANCIS OF SALES (1567–1622), *Letters to Religious*

INFORMER

If any believer appears as an informer, and through his information someone has been proscribed or killed, he shall not receive communion even at the last.

> *Canons of the Council of Elvira,* c. 305

INGRATITUDE

How sharper than a serpent's tooth it is
To have a thankless child!

> WILLIAM SHAKESPEARE, *Hamlet,* c. 1602

INHERITANCE

Man's natural right of possessing and transmitting property by inheritance must be kept intact and cannot be taken away by the state from man.

> POPE LEO XIII, *Rerum Novarum,* 1891

INJUSTICE

To do . . . injustice to another is a far greater evil for the doer of the injustice than it is for the victim.

> SOCRATES, PLATO, *Dialogues,* 399 B.C.

That amid our highest civilization men faint and die with want is not due to the niggardliness of nature, but to the injustice of man.

> HENRY GEORGE, *Progress and Poverty,* 1879

See also Economics and Christianity; Justice; Law; Right and Wrong; War, Just; War, Unjust.

INNOCENCE

The innocent are God's elect.

> ST. CLEMENT OF ROME, *First Epistle to the Corinthians,* c. 100

Perhaps thou art rather Innocent than Virtuous, and Owest more to thy Constitution, than thy Religion.

> WILLIAM PENN, *Some Fruits of Solitude*, 1718

Live innocently; God is here.

> CARL LINNAEUS (1707–1778), Inscribed over the door of his bedroom

Is not innocence, which in its essence is nothing but holy ignorance, the most ineffable mystery?

> FRANÇOIS RENÉ DE CHATEAUBRIAND, *Beauties of the Christian Religion*, 1802

INSPIRATION

By inspiration I mean all the affection, attraction, inward reproaches and regrets, perceptions and illuminations with which God moves, working in our hearts through His fatherly love and care, in order to awaken, to kindle, lead, and draw us to heavenly love and holy desires.

> ST. FRANCIS OF SALES (1567–1622), *A Diary of Meditations*

High art, high morals, high faith, are impossible among those who do not believe their own inspirations, but only court them for pleasure or profit.

> JAMES MARTINEAU, *Hours of Thought on Sacred Things*, 1879

The notion that inspiration is something that happened thousands of years ago, and was then finished and done with . . . the theory that God retired from business at that period and has not been heard from since, is as silly as it is blasphemous.

> GEORGE BERNARD SHAW, *The Quintessence of Ibsenism*, 1890

If there were such a thing as inspiration from a higher realm, it might well be that the neurotic temperament would furnish the chief condition of the requisite receptivity.

> WILLIAM JAMES, *Varieties of Religious Experience*, 1902

Inspiration presupposes revelation. Inspiration may be called the guardian of revelation.

> VINCENT MCNABB, *Frontiers of Faith and Reason*, 1936

Inspiration is not necessarily self-conscious. It is a subjective light.

> VINCENT MCNABB, *Frontiers of Faith and Reason*, 1936

Demonic inspiration . . . reveals the divine, but as a reality which it fears, which it cannot love, with which it cannot unite.

> PAUL TILLICH, *Interpretation of History*, 1936

[Defining a sacred book as one containing writings] that purport to have been produced under divine or extra-human inspiration or impulse and recognized by a substantial number of people as the basis of their religious faith . . . the authentic revelation of God to them and to the world. . . . Are there any modern sacred books? The answer is, "Yes, many"— found all over the world.

> CHARLES S. BRADEN, *The Scriptures of Mankind*, 1952

That portion of Hindu Sacred Literature known as "sruti" is regarded as the very word of God. It was given by verbal inspiration to the rishis or seers and gathered into a closed canon. From this nothing can be taken away and nothing may be added, and . . . in the course of time [it] came to be thought of as infallibile, incapable of error, because of its non-human character.

> CHARLES S. BRADEN, *The Scriptures of Mankind*, 1952

It usually happens that the more faithfully a person follows the inspirations he receives, the more does he experience new inspirations which ask increasingly more of him.

> JOSEPH DE GUIBERT, *Theology of the Spiritual Life*, 1953

The orthodox followers of Mrs. Eddy today believe "that her writing was the result of inspiration." God revealed it all to her. There are many references in her writings, in at least her later ones, clearly indicating that she herself looked upon her written works as inspired.

CHARLES S. BRADEN, *Christian Science Today,* 1958

See also Aspiration; Bible: Its Inspiration; Holy Spirit; Light; Mind; Poems and Poets; Poetry; Revelation; Thinking; Thought; Thoughts.

INSTINCT

The reasoned argument is but a surface exhibition. Instinct leads; intelligence does but follow. . . . Our passions and our mystical intuitions fix our beliefs beforehand.

WILLIAM JAMES, *Varieties of Religious Experience,* 1902

Certainly man has instincts, but those instincts do not have him. We have nothing against instincts, nor against a man's accepting them. But we hold that such acceptance must also presuppose the possibility of rejection.

VIKTO E. FRANKL, *The Doctor and the Soul,* 1955

See also Intuition.

INSTITUTIONALISM

All that can be expected from the most perfect institutions is that they should make it possible for individual excellence to develop itself.

HENRI AMIEL, *Journal,* 1882

There are men more willing to compromise God for the sake of an institution than to censure an institution for the sake of God.

WILLIAM L. SULLIVAN, *Under Orders,* 1944

Wherever the demon of organization invades and tyrannizes the human spirit, signs of false and abnormal orientation of social development come to light at once.

POPE PIUS XII, *Address,* December 24, 1952

During the past decades the work of the American religious bodies has become so specialized, organized, practical, that the very life of religions seems to be shifting from worship to "service" and from altar to office.

HERBERT WALLACE SCHNEIDER, *Religion in the 19th Century,* 1952

There is a dilemma that faces every religion. It is that of reconciling its original charismatic spirit with the institutional apparatus that it needs in order to survive and grow.

PEDRO MESEGUER, *America,* November 7, 1959

See also Religion, Organized; Rigidity.

INTEGRATION. See RACE, and also other rubrics under RACIAL

INTEGRITY

Never esteem anything as of advantage to thee that shall make thee break thy word or lose thy self-respect.

MARCUS AURELIUS, *Meditations,* c. 170

If everyone were clothed with integrity, if every heart were just, frank, kindly, the other virtues would be well-nigh useless, since their chief purpose is to make us bear with patience the injustice of our fellows.

MOLIÈRE, *Le Misanthrope,* 1666

"Hush, don't say that—you'll lose some of your friends." My answer is simple and final: If I don't say it, I'll lose my own soul.

E. STANLEY JONES, *Victorious Living,* 1936

Integrity is the clear allegiance of a transparent soul to its radical will, without being true to anything external.

GEORGE SANTAYANA, *The Realm of Truth,* 1938

Secular society loses one essential for its survival. For it is only religion which . . . can create the unpurchasable man. And it is only the man unpurchasable by any society that can create a sound society.

WILLIAM ERNEST HOCKING, *Saturday Review of Literature,* February 3, 1946

See also Honesty; Hypocrisy; Liars and Lies; Truth.

INTELLECT

When the intellect seeks to understand beyond its powers, it loses even that which it understood.

POPE ST. GREGORY THE GREAT, *Magna Moralia,* 584

The intellect is the link that joins us to God.

MAIMONIDES, *The Guide for the Perplexed,* III, 1190

When we consider how common it is in the world at large to consider the intellect as the characteristic part of our nature, the silence of Scripture in regard to it (not to mention its positive disparagement of it) is very striking.

JOHN HENRY NEWMAN, *Oxford University Sermons,* 1843

It too often happens that the religiously disposed are in the same degree intellectually deficient.

JOHN HENRY NEWMAN, *The Idea of a University,* 1852

Since it is in the very nature of man to follow the guide of reason in his actions, if his intellect sins at all his will soon follows; and thus it happens that looseness of

intellectual opinion influences human actions and perverts them.

POPE LEO XIII, *Scholastic Philosophy,* 1879

Not one word is said in the whole of the New Testament about our Lord's intellect; only always about His Heart.

ALEXANDER WHYTE, *Walk, Conversation and Character of Jesus Christ,* 1905

Faith in the intellect . . . is the only faith yet sanctioned by its fruits.

GEORGE SANTAYANA, *Reason in Science,* 1906

Intellect we shall put in its proper place as complementary to the subjective life of the Spirit.

WILLIAM KINGSLAND, *Our Infinite Life,* 1922

Modern philosophers have a message for the age, and that is the declaration of independence from the claims of the intellect.

FULTON J. SHEEN, *God and Intelligence,* 1925

The intellect has been given us as the appointed and natural path on which to make our approach to God.

WYNDHAM LEWIS, *Time and Western Man,* 1927

While I admit that intellect cannot go all the way, there can, for me, be no believing which the intellect cannot, so far as its writ runs, defend and justify.

C. E. M. JOAD, *The Recovery of Belief,* 1952

To say that our intellect naturally desires to see God is to say that it naturally desires a knowledge of which nature itself is incapable.

JACQUES MARITAIN, *Approach to God,* 1954

Religion is the last subject that the intellect begins to understand.

WILL DURANT, *The Reformation,* 1957

When intellect has become a full partner in man's inner and outer life, religion can fulfill its mission only if it is capable of satisfying the mind as well as the heart.

> FRANZ E. WINKLER, *Man: The Bridge Between Two Worlds,* 1960

See also Emotion; Genius; Heart; Knowledge; Mind; Mind and God; Reason; Skepticism; Spirit, Human.

INTELLECTUAL PRIDE

The care to increase in wisdom and knowledge was the first overthrow of mankind: It is the way whereby man hath headlong cast himself down into eternal damnation.

> MICHEL DE MONTAIGNE, *Essays,* Bk. 2, ch. 12, 1580

Intellectual pride . . . might be described as Original Sin in an academic hood and gown.

> JOHN HUTCHISON, *Faith, Reason and Existence,* 1956

See also Intellectuals; Pride.

INTELLECTUALS

The intellectual is constantly betrayed by his own vanity. Godlike, he blandly assumes that he can express everything in words.

> ANNE MORROW LINDBERGH, *The Wave of the Future,* 1940

An intellectual is someone whose mind watches itself.

> ALBERT CAMUS, *Notebooks,* 1935–1942

The intellectuals have given us Agnosticism, Anarchism, Communism, Darwinism, Fatalism, Empiricism, Individualism, Materialism, Nationalism, Nihilism, Positivism, Pragmatism, Racism, Rationalism, Skepticism, Socialism, Subjectivism, Utilitarianism, and dozens of other "isms" to make the modern mind a philosophical jungle, and create enormous ideological confusion.

> JOHN D. FEE, *Secularism,* 1947

A man may walk intellectually among the stars and grovel morally among the swine.

> JOHN A. O'BRIEN, *Why the Catholic School?,* 1947

The very original sin of the intellectual life is the "all or none" fallacy: man's attempt to be as absolute as God is, to know absolutely and to refuse the creaturehood of partial knowledge and of veiled choices.

> NELS F. S. FERRÉ, *Christian Faith and Higher Education,* 1954

One of the gravest dangers now confronting the contemporary Church is the possibility that it may be gradually transformed by the pressure of events into a kind of high-brow intellectual coterie.

> J. V. L. CASSERLEY, *The Bent World,* 1955

Of all the obstacles that Christianity encounters in the case of many intellectuals, the most serious is doubtless [that] . . . they have lost the sense of human weakness.

> FRANÇOIS MAURIAC, *Words of Faith,* 1955

The tragedy of our time is "the treason of the clerks," that is, the failure of our best minds to give themselves to contemplation of truth, and their undue preoccupation with immediate problems to the neglect of the deeper problems.

> BERNARD LEEMING, *America,* November 3, 1962

See also Genius; Intellect; Philosophers; Rationalism.

INTELLIGENCE

The more you extend intelligence, unless you extend the moral restraints and influences of the gospel at the same time, the more you sharpen the intellect for evil.

ORESTES BROWNSON, *Brownson's Views,* ed. H. F. Brownson, 1893

Whoever believes in God—"in a God, the almighty Father"—and a God "who is love"—might expect the initiatives of that love to surpass his understanding. His intelligence is transcended, but not contradicted.

L. DE GRANDMAISON, *Jésus dans l'histoire et dans le mysterie,* 1925

Intelligence alone is dangerous if it is not subjected to the intuitive or rational perception of moral values. It has led, not only to materialism, but to monstrosities.

LECOMTE DU NOÜY, *Human Destiny,* 1947

See also Reason.

INTEREST. See USURY

INTERFERENCE

I maintain that there is a moral interference with our fellow-creatures at home and abroad, not only to be asserted as a right, but binding as a duty.

W. E. CHANNING, *Letter to Jonathan Phillips,* 1839

INTERNATIONALISM

Even in war the church ought to stand for a form of society transcending nationalism and national boundaries.

NORMAN THOMAS, *Letter,* January, 1917

It is much to be desired . . . that all States, putting aside mutual suspicion, should unite in one league, or rather a sort of family of peoples, calculated both to maintain their own independence and to safeguard the order of human society.

POPE BENEDICT XV, *Pacem Dei Munus,* May 23, 1920

Since states are moral persons they are united by the same bonds of humanity as physical persons. Men do not cease to be brothers in the human family when they become grouped into states nor do they get rid of their obligations of universal charity when they take on the character of national citizens or national rulers.

Report, Catholic Association for International Peace, *International Ethics,* 1942

National sovereignty may not be interpreted as absolving a nation from its obligations in the international community.

Catholic Bishops of the U.S., November, 1944

We shall not have to fight *against* war and national sovereignty, but to arm ourselves for a legal order above the States, for an international law with binding force for "peace."

F. M. VAN ASBECK, *The Church and International Disorder,* 1948

The citizens of this country, and of all countries, have a responsibility to evaluate and judge the United Nations' deliberations and decisions according to objective norms of morality universally binding.

Catholic Bishops of the U.S., November, 1961

In the atomic age, each individual, each party, each state must feel itself responsible to humanity in its entirety and not merely to its own group or ideal.

R. RAYMOND ARON, *The Ethics of Power,* ed. Losswell and Cleveland, 1962

Since Christian beliefs are those of but a minority of the people in the world, it follows that we must root our international law in the living beliefs of *all* the religions of the world.

F. S. C. NORTHROP, *Man, Nature and God,* 1962

The universal common good poses problems of world wide dimensions which cannot be adequately tackled or solved except by . . . public authorities which are in a position to operate in an effective manner on a worldwide basis.

POPE JOHN XXIII, *Pacem in Terris,* April, 1963

It is our earnest wish that the United Nations Organization may become ever more equal to the magnitude and nobility of its tasks, and that the day may come when every human being will find therein an effective safeguard for the rights which derive directly from his dignity as a person, and which are therefore universal, inviolable and inalienable rights.

POPE JOHN XXIII, *Pacem in Terris,* April, 1963

In the world of our day the inter-dependence of nations is a reality. The ideal which the Christian seeks, along with all those interested in the promotion of human welfare, is a community of nations, wherein each nation can develop its own life only in the context of an active and just international association.

From a statement issued by the Commission of the Churches on International Affairs, in its *Annual Report* of 1963–1964

The edifice which you have constructed must never fall; it must be perfected, and made equal to the needs which world history will present. You mark a stage in the development of mankind, from which retreat must never be admitted, but from which it is necessary that advance be made.

POPE PAUL VI, *Address to United Nations,* October, 1965

See also Humanity; Mankind; Nuclear War; One World; Peace; War.

INTERPRETATION

The hardest of all lessons in interpretation is to believe that great men mean what they say.

BERNARD BOSANQUET, *True Conception of Another World,* 1886

INTOLERANCE

Discountenance and banish strange doctrines, in order to exalt the correct doctrine.

EMPEROR K'ANG-HE, *Sixteen Maxims,* 1723

There is a purely civil profession of faith of which the Sovereign should fix the articles . . . as social sentiments without which a man cannot be a good citizen. . . . While it can compel no one to believe them, it can banish . . . whoever does not believe them . . . not for impiety, but as an antisocial being.

JEAN JACQUES ROUSSEAU, *The Social Contract,* 1762

The supposed right of intolerance is absurd and barbaric. It is the right of the tiger; nay, it is far worse, for tigers do but tear in order to have food, while we rend each other for paragraphs.

VOLTAIRE, *Essay on Toleration,* 1766

When will the churches learn that intolerance, personal or ecclesiastical, is an evidence of weakness: The confident can afford to be calm and kindly; only the fearful must defame and exclude.

HARRY EMERSON FOSDICK, *Adventurous Religion,* 1926

Every Church which takes itself seriously must assert dogmatic intolerance. . . . It merely recognizes the primacy of truth and logic, [as conceived by itself] injures no one's rights.

MAX PROBILLA, *The Month,* October, 1950

See also Discord; Discrimination; Fanaticism; Genocide; Negroes; Opinions; Persecution; Prejudice; Religious Conflict; Tolerance.

INTUITION

Instinct is wonderful. But intuition is far more so, for it is the power of direct spiritual insight into the reason of things, which is acquired neither by knowledge nor by experience, and which is therefore superior to both.

J. GURNHILL, *Christian Philosophy,* 1921

It is true . . . that to claim an immediate intuition of God is contrary to Catholic teaching, but I have maintained that we have an "apprehension" of God which, although it has a character of directness, is nevertheless mediate.

ILLTYD TRETHOWAN, *The Basis of Belief,* 1961

See also Feelings; God: Knowledge about Him; Instinct; Light; Mind; Thinking; Thought; Vision.

INVINCIBLE IGNORANCE

He who does not know the true religion is guiltless in the sight of God so far as his ignorance is invincible.

POPE PIUS IX, *Allocution,* December 1, 1854

INVISIBLE WORLD

Invisibly, very near us, touching us all, is a real world of divine order and beauty, whose mission it is to bring order and beauty where they can, to mortal souls who are struggling for such things.

JOHN MASEFIELD, *Address,* London, 1931

IRRATIONALITY

Belief in the ultimate irrationality of everything is the quintessence of what is called the modern mind.

W. T. STACE, *Atlantic Monthly,* September, 1947

IRRELIGION

One perceives here the tremendous deprivation undergone by the person for whom definite religious faith and practice are no longer possible. As there are no rites and ceremonies in which he can participate, he loses the enormous privilege of associating his physical body with his most profound states of mind.

LAWRENCE HYDE, *The Prospects of Humanism,* 1931

Irreligion, when it is radical and complete, involves disbelief in life itself—its spiritual source, its ultimate meaning, its undergirding purpose, its eternal value.

HARRY EMERSON FOSDICK, *On Being a Real Person,* 1943

The imminent threat to our country comes not from religious divisiveness but from irreligious social decay.

Catholic Bishops of the U.S., November, 1952

There is as little reason to trust the judgment of the irreligious in regard to religion as to trust the unscientific in matters of science.

DAVID E. TRUEBLOOD, *Philosophy of Religion,* 1957

We beg those who have no religion or who are against religion to judge for themselves that they are laboring under the weight of irrational dogmas, of contradicting doubts that leave no peace, of absurdities without escape, of maledictions caused by despair and nothingness.

POPE PAUL VI, *Easter Sermon,* 1964

See also Godlessness; Humanism; Religion; Religion, Caustic Comments about; Religion: Its Decline; Religion, Necessity of; Rootlessness; Secularism.

ISIS

I am He that was, and is, and ever shall be, and my veil hath no one lifted.

Inscription in the Temple of Isis, Ancient Egypt

ISLAM

Islam is to believe in Allah and His Prophet, to recite the prescribed prayers, to give alms, to observe the fast of Ramadan, and to make pilgrimage to Mecca.

> MOHAMMED (570–632), quoted in Sir P. Sykes, *History of Persia, I*

Islam proclaims the fatalistic doctrine that everything that occurs is the inscrutable will of Allah, but this is not the language of Christian faith. . . . Faith refuses to attribute to God that which the Gospel attributes to Satan.

> GUSTAF AULEN, *Faith of the Christian Church,* 1948

Islamic culture is unquestionably one of the greater cultures in the history of mankind and of the world today. . . . Few others have managed so consistently to incorporate and accommodate so many disparate elements and minds. Within Islamic culture many ancient cultures have found a species of immortality.

> JAMES KRITZECK, Introduction to *Anthology of Islamic Literature,* 1964

See also Allah; Koran; Man and God; Missionaries.

ISOLATION

The verdict of the world is conclusive that those men cannot be good who in any part of the world cut themselves off from the rest of the world.

> ST. AUGUSTINE, *Contra Epistolam Parmeniani,* 400

For those who love to think of the visible universe as a cosey corner of God's footstool, there is something bleak and terrifying in the isolated position of man since science has postulated him as an infinitesimal bubble on an unimportant planet.

> JAMES GIBBONS HUNEKER, *Essays,* 1929

Only man is capable of separating himself alike from God and from nature, and making himself his last end and living a purely self-regarding and irreligious existence.

> CHRISTOPHER DAWSON, *Christianity and the New Age,* 1931

We all wish other men were better than they are. But likely we wouldn't like living alone.

> R. L. EVANS, *At This Same Hour,* 1949

There is no ultimate privacy or final isolation. . . . The most intimate motions within the depths of our souls are not completely our own. For they belong also to our friends, to mankind, to the universe, and to the Ground of all being, the aim of our life.

> PAUL TILLICH, *The Shaking of the Foundations,* 1949

No person can be religious alone, however rich may be the ecstasy or despair of his isolation. Authentic religion . . . is rather a relationship in which one person responds reverently to another person.

> P. E. JOHNSON, *Personality and Religion,* 1957

See also Brotherhood; Neighbor; Unity; Unity of Mankind.

ISRAEL

Israel can be reconciled to God only when all Jews are one brotherhood.

> *Talmud: Menahot,* 27a., c. 500 A.D.

Israelites are dearer to the Holy One than angels.

> *Talmud: Hullin,* 91b., c. 500 A.D.

By a miracle of Providence, which ought to astonish all Christians, this nation, hated and persecuted in all places for so many ages, still subsists in all parts of the world.

> JACQUES BASNAGE, *The History of the Jews from Jesus Christ to the Present Time,* 1708

As long as the world lasts, all who want to make progress in righteousness will come to Israel for inspiration.

MATTHEW ARNOLD, *Literature and Dogma,* 1873

When the nation who made the Bible shall have disappeared,—the race and the cult, —though leaving no visible trace of its passage upon earth, its imprint will remain in the depth of the heart of generations, who will, unconsciously perhaps, live upon what has thus been implanted in their breasts.

JAMES DARMESTETER, *Selected Essays,* 1895

The center and soul of all religion, the belief in a personal God, is the pillar of the religion of Israel.

C. H. CORNILL, *Culture of Ancient Israel,* 1914

A secular, non-religious Israel is a monstrosity.

C. G. MONTEFIORE, *Rabbinic Anthology,* 1938

It is the vocation of Israel which the world execrates. To be hated by the world is their glory.

JACQUES MARITAIN, *A Christian Looks at the Jews,* 1939

The State of Israel will be judged not by its riches or military power, nor by its technical skills, but by its moral worth and human values. . . . To be like other peoples is not enough. We may pridefully aspire to bring true the words of the prophet: "I the Lord . . . give thee for a covenant of the people to the Gentiles."

DAVID BEN GURION in the *Government Yearbook,* October, 1951, and in his *Rebirth and Destiny of Israel,* 1954

Nothing can surpass the Bible as lighting up the manifold problems of our life. . . . There can be no worthwhile political or military education about Israel without profound knowledge of the Bible.

DAVID BEN GURION, *Government Yearbook,* October, 1952, and in his *Rebirth and Destiny of Israel,* 1954

Israel has a divine and prophetic role to play in the concert of nations and in the progress of united humanity toward an era of universal justice and peace.

ABRAHAM J. NEUMAN, *Landmarks and Goals,* 1953

It is general theological doctrine that before the intra-temporal end of history, Jewry as a national totality will be converted to Christ.

JOSEF PIEPER, *The End of Time,* 1954

If modern Israel is to have any elements of greatness, then this quality must be vindicated in the spiritual realm.

ABBA EBAN, *Address,* Notre Dame University, 1955

Israel was made to be a "holy people." This is the essence of its dignity and the essence of its merit.

ABRAHAM J. HESCHEL, *God in Search of Man,* 1955

For us Jews there can be no fellowship with God without the fellowship with Israel. Abandoning Israel, we desert God.

ABRAHAM J. HESCHEL, *God in Search of Man,* 1955

Israel is not merely an ethnic group, a racial entity, or some historically conditioned society, but is indeed a servant of God.

SIMON GREENBERG, *Patterns of Faith in America Today,* ed. F. E. Johnson, 1957

The suffering of Israel, the true "servant of God," will not cease until Israel fulfills its historic role of being the prime mover in bringing all of mankind to the service of the Lord.

SIMON GREENBERG, *Patterns of Faith in America Today,* ed. F. E. Johnson, 1957

Israel according to the flesh, which wandered as an exile in the desert, was already called the Church of God. So likewise the new Israel which while living in this present age goes in search of a future and abiding city is called the Church of Christ.

The Constitution of the Church, Second Vatican Council, November, 1964

See also Anti-Semitism; Bible and History; Chosen People; Church, Definitions of; Jesus Christ and the Jews; Jew; Jews; Judaism; Messiah; Old Testament; Redemption; Synagogue; Torah; Usury.

JANSENISM

The main theme of Jansen was that ever since the Fall, man had become sinful utterly: that his only hope of escaping eternal demnation was through Grace; without Grace even the most virtuous of human acts are tainted with evil. Everyone does not possess Grace: it is God alone who confers Grace on his elect.

HAROLD NICOLSON, *Sainte-Beuve,* 1956

JEALOUSY

Jealousy is a kind of civil war in the soul, where judgment and imagination are at perpetual jars.

WILLIAM PENN, *Some Fruits of Solitude,* 1693

Jealousy is said to be the offspring of love. Yet unless the parent makes haste to strangle the child, the child will not rest till it has poisoned the parent.

J. C. HARE, *Guesses at Truth,* 1827

See also Covetousness; Desires; Greed; Possessions; Self-Interest; Selfishness.

JEHOVAH

Moses conceived the Deity as a Being who has always existed, does exist, and always will exist, and he therefore called him Jehovah, which in Hebrew signifies these three phases.

BARUCH SPINOZA, *Theological-Political Treatise,* 1670

See also various categories under God.

JEST

Jest not with the two-edged sword of God's word.

THOMAS FULLER, *The Holy State and the Profane State,* 1642

See also Amusements; Laughter; Pleasure.

JESTERS

Men of merry mouths, minstrels of heaven,
God's servants and God's jesters.

WILLIAM LANGLAND, *Piers Plowman,* 1362

See also Jest.

JESUS CHRIST

At that time lived Jesus, a holy man, if man he may be called, for he performed wonderful works, and taught men, and joyfully received the truth. And he was followed by many Jews and many Greeks. He was Messiah.

FLAVIUS JOSEPHUS, *Antiquities of the Jews,* 93 A.D. (Most Christian scholars assert this passage is an interpolation.)

Although Christ always remains the same in Himself, nevertheless the vision of Him that you see is not always of equal efficacy, but is patterned by the merits of the individuals whom He looks upon; into some He strikes fear, to others He brings comfort.

ST. GREGORY OF NYSSA (c. 335–c. 395), *Third Homily on the Canticle of Canticles*

Man is soon changed and lightly falleth away, but Christ abideth for ever and standeth strongly with his lover unto the end.

> THOMAS À KEMPIS, *Imitation of Christ*, 1441

Christ is rich, who will maintain you: He is a king, who will provide you: He is a sumptuous entertainer, who will feast you: He is beautiful, who will give in abundance all that can make you happy.

> EDMUND CAMPION, *Ten Reasons*, 1581

Know that Our Lord is called in Scripture the Prince of Peace, and hence, wherever He is absolute Master, He preserves peace.

> ST. FRANCIS OF SALES (1567–1622), *Consoling Thoughts of*, ed. Huguet

You are to conceive of the holy Jesus or the Word of God as the hidden treasure of every human soul, born as a seed of the Word in the birth of the soul.

> WILLIAM LAW (1686–1761), *Selected Mystical Writings of*, ed. S. Hobhouse

Jesus Christ belonged to the true race of prophets. He saw with open eye the mystery of the soul. Drawn by its severe harmony, ravished with its beauty, he lived in it, and had his being there. Alone in all history he estimated the greatness of man.

> RALPH WALDO EMERSON, *Divinity School Address*, July 15, 1838

Jesus astonishes and overpowers sensual people. They cannot unite Him to history or reconcile Him with themselves.

> RALPH WALDO EMERSON, "History," *Essays*, 1841

In an unpermissible and unlawful way people have become *knowing* about Christ, for the only permissible way is to be believing.

> SÖREN KIERKEGAARD, *Training in Christianity*, 1850

Whatever may be the surprises of the future, Jesus will never be surpassed. His worship will grow young without ceasing; his legend will call forth tears without end; his sufferings will melt the noblest hearts; all ages will proclaim that among the sons of men there is none born greater than Jesus.

> ERNEST RENAN, *St. Paul*, 1869

The son of God is unique. To appear for a moment, to flash forth a sympathetic but piercing radiance, to die very young, that is the life of a God.

> ERNEST RENAN, *St. Paul*, 1869

Everything that is tender, that is sensitive, that is movingly beautiful in modernity, comes from Christ.

> EDMOND and JULES DE GONCOURT, 1867, *Journals of*, 1851–1870

He who believes that Christ is the Truth, and that the Evangelists are truthful, believes all that He has said through them.

> JOHN HENRY NEWMAN, *Grammar of Assent*, 1870

Christ is rich, who will maintain you: He opens at once the eye of conscience to perceive and know the pure and holy God the Father that dwelt in him and made him so full of truth and grace.

> JAMES MARTINEAU, *Studies of Christianity*, 1873

Many, as has been well said, ran after Christ, not for the miracles, but for the loaves.

> JOHN LUBBOCK, *The Pleasures of Life*, 1887

That Christ should be and should be Christ appears the one reasonable, natural, certain thing in all the universe. In Him all broken lines unite; in Him all scattered sounds are gathered into harmony.

> PHILLIPS BROOKS, *The Light of the World*, 1890

The devotion of the leader to his men and to his cause, Jesus shared it. The devotion of the led to their leader—Jesus inspired it. He kindled a flame which was to burn more brightly after his death than ever before it in his lifetime.

C. G. MONTEFIORE, *Some Elements of the Religious Teaching of Jesus,* 1892

Christ did not love humanity. He never said that he loved humanity; He loved men.

G. K. CHESTERTON, *Twelve Types,* 1903

The Jesus of Nazareth who came forward publicly as the Messiah, who preached the ethic of the Kingdom of God, who founded the Kingdom of Heaven upon earth, and died to give His work its final consecration, never had any existence.

ALBERT SCHWEITZER, *The Quest of the Historical Jesus,* 1906

The truth is, it is not Jesus as historically known, but Jesus as spiritually arisen within men, that is significant for our time, and can help it.

ALBERT SCHWEITZER, *The Quest of the Historical Jesus,* 1906

If the character which is revealed by that Sufferer be the character of God Himself, then the love that is awakened towards Christ will also be the love of the Father whom in a supreme and unique way Christ reveals.

HASTINGS RASHDALL, *The Idea of Atonement in Christian Theology,* 1919

Sometimes in narrower, sometimes in broader channels, the purpose of love moves on till the Spirit finds in the Son of Man, the Anointed One, the perfect realization of the destiny of man, the manhood in which he can freely and fully work.

CHARLES GORE, *Lux Mundi,* 1921

He was exactly what the man with a delusion never is; he was wise; he was a good judge.

G. K. CHESTERTON, *The Everlasting Man,* 1925

There must surely have been something not only mysterious but many-sided about Christ if so many smaller Christs could be carved out of him.

G. K. CHESTERTON, *The Everlasting Man,* 1925

The mystery of Jesus remains, even so, as deep in its essence for a Paul or an Augustine, for an Aquinas or a Newman, as it is for the most resolute and determined unbeliever.

L. DE GRANDMAISON, *Jésus dans l'histoire et dans le mysterie,* 1925

Up to this day no one has ever been loved as much as Jesus Christ is loved and in the future likewise no one will ever be loved as much as He is loved.

POPE PIUS XI, *Encyclical Letter,* December 11, 1925

The Galilean has been too great for our small hearts.

H. G. WELLS, *Outline of History,* 1926

The basis of Christ's authority is not a prior belief in his divinity or miracles, but the impression which his Personality makes on us.

R. H. STRACHAN, *The Authority of Christian Experience,* 1929

There was in Him no world-weariness, no strengthless melancholy, no timid shrinking from the fray.

KARL ADAM, *Christ Our Brother,* 1931

In no one else in all history do you find an abiding hatred, an immortal hatred except against Our Lord. . . . The hatred against Christ has never weakened even after twenty centuries . . . because He is still an obstacle—an obstacle to sin, to selfishness, to godlessness, and to the spirit of the world.

FULTON J. SHEEN, *The Eternal Galilean,* 1934

The most unique thing to my mind about the Jesus of history is . . . a new and most wonderfully rich experience of God that apparently had been growing and deepening through all those silent background years.

J. S. BONNELL, *Pastoral Psychology,* 1935

He is all the world's hero, the desire of nations. But besides he is the hero of single souls.

GERARD MANLEY HOPKINS, *Notebook and Papers of,* 1937

Jesus of the Gospels is the contrary of an artificial and composite being. Here is the most moving of the great figures of history, and of all the great characters history places before us, the least logical because he is the most living.

FRANÇOIS MAURIAC, *Life of Jesus,* 1937

His real joy was to reveal himself to the poor men crushed under their habitual sins and to open under their feet an abyss of mercy and of pardon.

FRANÇOIS MAURIAC, *Life of Jesus,* 1937

Christ, who expresses both the infinite possibilities of love in human life and the infinite possibilities beyond human life, is . . . a true revelation of the total situation in which human life stands.

REINHOLD NIEBUHR, *Beyond Tragedy,* 1937

There is no single deed or saying of which we can be perfectly sure that He said or did precisely this or that.

WILLIAM TEMPLE, *Revelation,* 1937

His *life,* his spirit, his personality, is incomparably greater than anything he said, or did, or taught.

RUFUS M. JONES, *The Eternal Gospel,* 1938

Jesus marks the point in history at which it becomes possible for man to adopt consciously as his own purpose the purpose which is already inherent in his own nature.

JOHN MACMURRAY, *The Clue to History,* 1939

When we set out on this quest, we found ourselves moving in the midst of a mighty host, but, as we have pressed forward, the marchers, company by company, have fallen out of the race. . . . And now, as we stand and gaze with our eyes upon the farther shore, a single figure rises from the flood and straightway fills the whole horizon. There is the Savior.

A. J. TOYNBEE, *A Study of History,* 1939 (1 vol. abridgement by D. C. Somerwell)

Here is pictured for us all the spirit of Compassionate Goodness at the heart of reality.

HAROLD BLAKE WALKER, *Westminster Assembly Tercentenary Sermons,* 1942

Christ did not find heroism in everyone; whoever showed but a trace of good will, to him He tendered His hand and inspired him with courage.

POPE PIUS XII, *Allocution,* February 23, 1944

In considering the teachings of Jesus as a whole, we find that he was the Oriental of the Orientals. He was the ideal of typical Oriental life. In other words he was the embodiment of the ideals the Oriental people cherished and manifested in their thought and actions.

SWAMI AKHILANANDA, *Hindu View of Christ,* 1949

The way of Christ is not possible without Christ.

> WILLIAM RUSSELL MALTBY, *Obiter Scripta,* ed. F. B. James, 1952

[To an educated Hindu] Jesus is a supreme illustration of the growth from human origins to divine destiny. . . . He is the great hero who exemplifies the noblest characteristics of manhood, the revealer of the profoundest depths in ourselves, one who brings home to us the ideal of human perfection by embodying it in himself.

> RADHAKRISHNAN, *The Philosophy of,* ed. by P. A. Schlipp, 1952

He is an abyss filled with light. One must close one's eyes if one is not to fall into it.

> FRANZ KAFKA, "Conversations with Kafka," *Partisan Review,* March-April, 1953

Just as we find the real meaning of our personality in Christ, so in Christ we find the real meaning and character of our relationship with other persons.

> AELRED WATKIN, *The Heart of the World,* 1954

Let us not be confused by the modern argument about a changed position. We are still left where believers have always been left. It is still "Christ or the critics."

> D. MARTIN LLOYD-JONES, *Authority,* 1958

In every decade we instruct Christ as to what He was and is, instead of allowing ourselves to be instructed by Him.

> AMOS N. WILDER, *Theology and Modern Literature,* 1958

Two veils keep us from seeing the living truth of Jesus. One veil is our ignorance. . . . The other veil is that we think we know, but in truth we are just accustomed to hearing the same words, episodes, statements over and over again.

> ROMANO GUARDINI, *Jesus Christus,* 1959

See also Antichrist; Apostles; Art and Christianity; Baptism; Beauty; Believing; Bible; Calvary; Christian; Christianity, Criticism of; Christians; Christmas; Church, Definitions of; Church: Its Authority; Church: Its Nature; Church: Its Work; Communion; Communion of Saints; Community; Cross; Eucharist; Faith; Faith, Definitions of; God: His Goodness; Grace; Happiness; Holiness; Holy Spirit; Humility; Incarnation; Kingdom of God; Kingdom of Heaven; Logos; Love; Man and God; Man Indwelt by God; Mary, the Mother of Jesus; Mass, the; Messiah; Miracles; Morality; Mystical Body of Christ; New Testament; Perfection; Preachers; Preaching; Redemption; Religion; Religion, Revealed; Revelation; Rich, the; Salvation;. Second Coming; Sin; Suffering; Trinity; Truth and Religion; Unitarians; Unity; War, Condemnation of; Wisdom; Word, the; World, the; World and Christianity.

JESUS CHRIST: HIS DIVINITY

There is one Physician of flesh and spirit, begotten and unbegotten, God in man, true life in death, son of Mary and son of God, first suffering and then beyond suffering, Jesus Christ our Lord.

> ST. IGNATIUS OF ANTIOCH, *To the Ephesians,* c. 109

If Christ forgives sins, if Christ is Mediator between God and man, this is because He is really a divine person.

> ST. IRENAEUS, *Adver. Haer.,* III, c. 175

Lo, thou art far from God, O man, and God is far above man. Between them the God-man placed Himself. Acknowledge Christ, and through Him as Man ascend to God.

> ST. AUGUSTINE (354–430), *Sermon LXXXI*

If anyone say that the one Lord, Jesus Christ, was glorified by the Spirit, as though the power which He exercised was another's received through the Spirit, . . . be he anathema.

ST. CYRIL OF ALEXANDRIA (412–444), *Epistle* XVII

From our proper Ground, that is to say from the Father and all that which lives in Him, there shines an eternal Ray, the which is the Birth of the Son.

JOHN RUYSBROECK (1293–1381), *De Ornatus Spiritalium Nuptiarum*

If Jesus of Nazareth is not God, how is it that, without any help, this sacrilegious Seducer has prevailed against the laws of his country, against princes, against wise men, against the whole universe in opposition to him, against the powers of heaven and hell, in fine, against God Himself, even so far as to make himself equal to God, to receive honors due only to Divinity, and to fulfill with an infinite success, in spite of difficulties, and the contradictions generated by long centuries, all the prophecies.

JEROME SAVONAROLA, *The Triumph of the Cross,* 1497

Whatever other philosophers may have been, he alone is a teacher from heaven; he alone was able to teach certain and eternal wisdom; he alone taught things pertaining to our salvation, because he alone is its author; he alone absolutely practiced what he preached, and is able to make good what he promised.

DESIDERIUS ERASMUS, Introduction to *Novum Instrumentum,* 1516

The Son, according to his Divinity, is coequal and consubstantial with the Father; true God.

HENRY BULLINGER, *The Helvetic Confession,* 1536

Yes, if the life and death of Socrates were those of a sage, the life and death of JESUS are those of a God.

JEAN JACQUES ROUSSEAU, *Emilius and Sophia,* 1762

There is not a God in heaven, if a mere man was able to conceive and execute successfully the gigantic design of making himself the object of supreme worship, by usurping the name of God. Jesus alone dared to do this.

NAPOLEON BONAPARTE (1769–1821), *Napoleon's Argument for the Divinity of Christ* (in conversation with General Bertrand at St. Helena), published 1842

The Christian world, aghast at such awful beauty in the flesh, transfixed with wonder as such a spirit rises in heavenly flight, veils its face and says, It is a God.

THEODORE PARKER, *A Discourse of Matter Pertaining to Religion,* 1845

Whatever motives Jesus Christ might have had against calling himself God, he did call himself God; such is the fact.

JEAN BAPTISTE LACORDAIRE, *Jesus Christ,* 1869

What holds true, in all our experience of men, is inverted in him. He grows sacred, peculiar, wonderful, divine, as acquaintance reveals him. At first he is only a man, as the sense reports him to be; knowledge, observation, familiarity, raise him into the God-man.

HORACE BUSHNELL, *The Character of Jesus,* 1886

As the reality of Christ seems to fade away when He is regarded only as a manifestation of Divinity, so the results of His life become inexplicable when we refuse to see Divinity in His Manhood.

HENRY B. SWETE, *Essays on Theological Questions,* 1905

The assured conviction of the deity of Christ is coeval with Christianity. There never was a Christianity, neither in times of the Apostles or since, of which this was not a prime test.

BENJAMIN B. WARFIELD, *The Deity of Christ,* 1906

It is imperative to show that Christ is unique and that what dwelt in others as an informing spirit was in Him His very self.
　　W. E. ORCHARD, *The Necessity of Christ,* 1916

Unless the teaching of Christ does present itself to us as containing the eternally true pith and marrow of the moral idea, and a true representation of the essential character of God, we have no basis for any theory of Christ's divinity.
　　HASTINGS RASHDALL, *The Idea of Atonement in Christian Theology,* 1919

This calm assumption of Jesus that he is not a sinner will take hold of the wrists of any thoughtful mind and twist them till it must come to its knees.
　　WILLIAM A. QUAYLE, *The Healing Shadow,* 1923

To see the revelation of God in Christ is a gracious privilege of faith, of the believer and not of the historian.
　　EMIL BRUNNER, *The Theology of Crisis,* 1929

Either Jesus was and knew that He was, what He proclaimed Himself to be, or else He was a pitiable visionary.
　　LEONCE DE GRANDMAISON, *Jesus Christ,* 1930

If we are to find the secret of His Timelessness, the simplicity of His Wisdom, the transforming power of His Doctrine, we must go out beyond time to the Timelessness, beyond the complex to the Perfect, beyond Change to the Changeless, out beyond the margent of the world to the Perfect God.
　　FULTON J. SHEEN, *The Eternal Galilean,* 1934

The Christian Church stands or falls with this simple proposition: that Jesus is nothing less than God's self-communication to man, and the only certain source of our knowledge of God.
　　W. A. VISSER 'T HOOFT, *None Other Gods,* 1937

Christ is God or He is the world's greatest liar and impostor.
　　DORTHY DAY, *From Union Square to Rome,* 1938

What Christ brought to light in the unfolding of the Eternal Gospel is the Face, the personal aspect, the revelation of the Heart, the Love, the Grace, the Character-Nature of God. We *see* Him at last.
　　RUFUS M. JONES, *The Eternal Gospel,* 1938

The Kingly Rule of Christ extends not merely over the Church as the congregation of the faithful but, . . . over the whole of the universe in all its heights and depths; and it also confronts and overrules with sovereign dignity the principalities and powers and evil spirits of this world.
　　KARL BARTH, *A Letter to Great Britain, In This Christian Cause,* 1939

That God who gave life to the world by His Son should not have wholly withdrawn him from the world, that the flesh which saved it should still sustain it. . . . Does it not seem consistent with the very plan of the Incarnation?
　　M. J. LAGRANGE, *The Gospel of Jesus Christ,* I, 1939

The witnesses for the historical authentication and for the proofs of the Divinity of Jesus, from the earliest days, are far more comprehensive than the testimonies for the existence of many famous historical characters we accept without question.
　　HERBERT E. CORY, *The Emancipation of a Freethinker,* 1941

A man who was merely a man and said the sort of things Jesus said wouldn't be a great moral teacher. He'd either be a lunatic—on a level with a man who says he's a poached egg—or else he'd be the Devil of Hell. You must make your choice. Either this man was, and is, the Son of God, or else a madman or something worse.
　　C. S. LEWIS, *The Case for Christianity,* 1943

Through Christ, the Logos, not only the human race but the whole universe turns to God and responds to the divine need of love.

> NICHOLAS BERDYAEV, *Slavery and Freedom*, 1944

Christ exists and is Spirit and I myself am spirit too; since through the spirit I can reach Him, and through Him reach God, for He is both man and God and since, after all, I was conceived in God's likeness, and the presence of Christ in our midst is formal proof of this fact.

> C. F. RAMUZ, *What Is Man?*, 1948

Our age has fortunately rediscovered the extraordinarily brotherly character of the Son of Man but misses the mystery of the Son of God.

> EMMANUEL SUHARD, *The Church Today*, 1953

The belief that we are at this point and in this person in touch with God has increasingly been left to the religious minority that can still accept the old mythology as physically or metaphysically true.

> J. A. T. ROBINSON, *Honest to God*, 1963

I've jettisoned the Trinity, the Virgin Birth and the Incarnation.

> JAMES A. PIKE, to interviewer Christopher S. Wren, *Look*, February 22, 1966

Jesus is still unique because God who breaks through Him is unique, and Jesus is the standard by which all others are measured.

> JAMES A. PIKE, to interviewer Christopher S. Wren, *Look*, February 22, 1966

See also Easter; Eucharist; God: Considered as Personal; God: Knowledge about Him; Miracles; Revelation.

JESUS CHRIST: HIS INFLUENCE AND TEACHING

Truly the yoke of Christ would be sweet and his burden light, if petty human institutions added nothing to what he himself imposed.

> DESIDERIUS ERASMUS, *Greek Testament, Note to Matt.* 11: 30, 1516

When Jesus Christ utters a word, he opens his mouth so wide that it embraces all heaven and earth, even though the word be but a whisper.

> MARTIN LUTHER (1483–1546), *Table Talk*

Rarely, almost never, do we see the vast divinity within that soul, which, new though it was in the flesh, at one step goes before the world whole thousands of years; judges the race; decides for us questions we dare not agitate as yet, and breathes the very breath of heavenly love.

> THEODORE PARKER, *A Discourse of Matter Pertaining to Religion*, 1845

The peculiar office of Christ is to supply a new *moral* image of Providence.

> JAMES MARTINEAU, *Studies of Christianity*, 1873

The influence of His life, His words, and His death, have, from the first, been like leaven cast into the mass of humanity.

> CUNNINGHAM GEIKIE, *The Life and Words of Christ*, 1877

He bent over the corpse of the dead world, and whispered a word of faith . . . uttered words then unknown,—love, sacrifice, a heavenly origin. And the dead arose. A new life circulated through the clay, which philosophy had tried in vain to reanimate.

> JOSEPH MAZZINI, *Essays*, 1887

He proclaimed that to gain the whole world was nothing if the soul were injured, and yet he remained kind and sympathetic to every living thing. That is the most astonishing and the greatest fact about him!

ADOLF VON HARNACK, *What Is Christianity?*, 1901

The doctrines of Christ, if accepted by the world in their integrity—the virtues, that is, of humility, nonresistance and poverty —would . . . simply make an end of the whole social fabric . . . and there is every reason to believe that he [Christ] looked to see only a few chosen souls follow in his footsteps.

PAUL ELMER MORE, *Shelburne Essays*, 1904

Jesus knew that he had come to kindle a fire on earth. . . . He saw that what was exalted among man was an abomination before God.

WALTER RAUSCHENBUSCH, *Christianity and the Social Crisis*, 1907

Jesus . . . bore within him the germs of a new social and political order. He was too great to be the Saviour of a fractional part of human life.

WALTER RAUSCHENBUSCH, *Christianity and the Social Crisis*, 1907

Christ . . . does not really teach one anything, but by being brought into his presence one becomes something. And everybody is predestined to his presence. Once at least in his life each man walks with Christ to Emmaus.

OSCAR WILDE, *De Profundis*, 1909

With a width and wonder of imagination that fills one almost with awe, he took the entire world of the inarticulate, the voiceless world of pain, as his kingdom, and made of himself its external mouthpiece.

OSCAR WILDE, *De Profundis*, 1909

The quibblers who discard Jesus' social teachings as irrelevant to the modern age, because he never heard of elevator wells and sprinkler systems or even shoe factories, are more rabbinical than Christian.

GEORGE WALTER FISKE, *A Study of Jesus' Own Religion*, a lecture included in Fiske's *Life and Letters*, by J. S. Clarke, 1917

More and more, I believe the great spiritual dividing line between men will be the line between those who really accept Christ's ideals and those who do not.

HASTINGS RASHDALL, *The Idea of Atonement in Christian Theology*, 1919

His genius, though he wrote nothing, was that of a great literary artist; if it were not for the sound of the thing, one might say that he was the master rhetorician of religion.

PAUL ELMER MORE, *The Christ of the New Testament*, 1924

The whole teaching of Jesus is grounded in what may be termed an ethical mysticism. He is possessed with the thought of love and goodness as so inherent in divine nature that by attaining to them we apprehend God.

ERNEST F. SCOTT, *The Ethical Teaching of Jesus*, 1924

Most men find in Jesus a reflection of their own ideals.

GRANVILLE HICKS, *Eight Ways of Looking at Christianity*, 1926

If asked what precisely is the distinctive feature in the ethics of Christ, I should be inclined to answer, "The fact that it is not ethics at all." . . . Christ, instead of a code, gives an ideal; instead of rules, a life; instead of a philosophy, an art.

BURNETT H. STREETER, *Adventure*, 1928

Christ is not only the bearer of an eternal message which he repeats to the astonished

ears of successive individuals, but also he in whom humanity finds an unexpected answer to the problem of its organic unity.
EUGENE MASURE, *Bulletin des anciens élèves de Saint-Sulpice,* November 15, 1931

He is unique. He transcends all the known frontiers and boundaries. He shares in many of the ideas and in the outlooks and expectations of the time. But he is always far beyond them.
RUFUS M. JONES, *The Eternal Gospel,* 1938

With all its fidelity to the spirit and style of the Jewish scholars of his time, the teaching of Jesus did nevertheless pass beyond the boundary, to stand in a place of its own. Had it not done so it most probably would not have created a world religion.
SHOLEM ASCH, *What I Believe,* 1941

We need to forget the imaginary Christ who has been ours too long and to rediscover the real Christ, the Christ of the prophets and the martyrs and the confessors, the Christ who is not only the lover of souls but also the master, a monarch with demands to make in industry, in finance, in education, in the arts, in marriage, in the home.
BERNARD IDDINGS BELL, *Still Shine the Stars,* 1941

Only Christ, "on Whose shoulders rests dominion," can, through His succoring omnipotence, elevate mankind, lift it out of the nameless afflictions that torment it in the course of this life, and set it on the road to happiness.
POPE PIUS XII, December 24, 1943

Caesar hoped to reform men by changing institutions and laws; Christ wished to remake institutions, and lessen laws, by changing men.
WILL DURANT, *Caesar and Christ,* 1944

Like a guide to the hill passes, Jesus took short cuts across the untraversable moun-

tains of class pride, intellectual arrogance and professional specialization.
LEWIS MUMFORD, *The Condition of Man,* 1944

Jesus has sometimes been represented as being merely a teacher of morality, but if he had been that and nothing more there would have been no reason for the Pharisees to have feared him.
MARCHETTE CHUTE, *Jesus of Israel,* 1961

See also Jesus Christ; New Testament; Sermon on the Mount.

JESUS CHRIST: HIS MANHOOD

We are persecuted because we say that the Son had a beginning, but that God was without beginning. . . . He is neither part of God, nor of any subjacent matter. For this we are persecuted.
ARIUS, *Letter to Eusebius,* c. 325

The Son was sent from the Father in no other way than as one of the Prophets.
MICHAEL SERVETUS, *De Trinitatis Erroribus,* 1531

Blessed be God that so much manliness has been lived out, and stands there yet, a lasting monument to mark how high the tides of Divine life have risen in the world of man.
THEODORE PARKER, *A Discourse of Matter Pertaining to Religion,* 1845

We may dwell on the person of Christ and mean no more than a perfectly saintly soul reposing in God. . . . Christ's person has its reality in its active relation to other persons—God or men.
PETER T. FORSYTH, *Positive Preaching and the Modern Mind,* 1907

The immanent Spiritual Life of God focalized in a human personality.
SHAILER MATHEWS, *The Gospel and Modern Man,* 1910

He was the personal embodiment of truths which are permanently central for the spiritual life of mankind.

> EUGENE W. LYMAN, *The Journal of Religion*, IX, April, 1929

There met in Jesus Christ all things that can make man lovely and loveable.

> GERARD MANLEY HOPKINS, *Notebooks and Papers of*, 1937

JESUS CHRIST: HIS PASSION AND DEATH

The Son of God was crucified; I am not ashamed because men must needs be ashamed of it. The Son of God died; it is by all means to be believed, because it is absurd. And He was buried and rose again; it is certain, because it is impossible.

> TERTULLIAN, *De Carne Christe*, c. 210

The death on the Cross . . . was the supreme witnessing act in His witnessing to the iniquity of sin against a world in which malice or ignorance would justify sin.

> FATHER CUTHBERT, *God and the Supernatural*, 1920

The death of Christ is the one truly revolutionary event that ever happened in the world.

> W. G. PECK, *The Divine Revolution*, 1927

The Crucified becomes one with the unrecognized and misused and cruelly treated in every age. The nail-pierced Figure on Calvary haunts our race as a symbol of what is forever taking place generation after generation, and of what each of us has his part in.

> HENRY SLOANE COFFIN, *The Meaning of the Cross*, 1931

Jesus Christ, God and man, lies on His face in the Garden of Gethsemane and sees before Him the cross which His friends prepare for Him. They will do it also tomorrow, the days after tomorrow, all the days until the end of the world.

> SIGRID UNDSET, *Christmas and the Twelfth Night*, 1932

To have faith in the crucified one means to permit oneself to be crucified with him, to permit this judgment also to be passed against oneself.

> RUDOLF BULTMANN, "Faith in God the Creator," 1934, in *Existence and Faith*, ed. S. M. Ogden

Poor was his station, laborious his life, bitter his ending; through poverty, through labor, through crucifixion his majesty of nature more shines.

> GERARD MANLEY HOPKINS, *Notebooks and Papers of*, 1937·

The uniqueness of Jesus in the eyes of mankind is derived from a certain absoluteness of contrast between Him and the secular order within which He lived; and that contrast comes to its climax upon the Cross.

> R. ROBERTS, *The Contemporary Christ*, 1938

It was not weakness which made Christ hang on the Cross; it was obedience to the law of sacrifice, of love. For how could He save us if He ever saved Himself?

> FULTON J. SHEEN, *Radio Sermon*, April 6, 1941

When the strong torture the weak, when the poor cry for bread, when the innocent languish in dungeons, when mothers go insane because they see their children die, when the outcasts roam in the wilderness, when the soldiers go to battle, when those who sit in darkness pray for light, the Cross returns, and the head of the Man on the Cross sinks deeper on the tired breast.

> PIERRE VAN PAASEN, *That Day Alone*, 1941

The most remarkable fact in the whole history of religious thought is this: that when the early Christians looked back and pondered on the dreadful thing that had happened, it made them think of the redeeming love of God.

D. M. BAILLIE, *God Was in Christ,* 1948

"Into thy hands." This final word of Jesus brings completion of faith for others, completion of faith for us. Faith in Him leads us at last to trust. We yield our all to Him because we believe what He said about God and life as true.

JAMES W. KENNEDY, *Advance into Light,* 1948

The Christ had to suffer and die, because whenever the Divine appears in all Its depth, It cannot be endured by men. . . . In the picture of the Crucified, we look at the rejection of the Divine by humanity.

PAUL TILLICH, *The Shaking of the Foundations,* 1948

No, we can never think that Jesus died in despair—or "of a broken heart," as some have said. He was dying in victory, not defeat. He foresaw, if anyone ever did, that future which is more real than the present.

FREDERICK C. GRANT, *Christ's Victory and Ours,* 1950

Suffering inflicted on Jesus by others had the appearance at least of being involuntary. The sufferings of Gethsemane, deep in his soul, could touch him only because he willed it, to give us courage in our own fears, to set us an example, to merit for us the grace needed in our own interior conflicts.

RALPH GORMAN, *The Last Hours of Jesus,* 1960

The religious charge against him was that he was a blasphemer; the political charge, that he was a traitor. He was executed by "good" people, representing the best interests of a great religious tradition and an enlightened political power. But in the last

analysis, no religious, political, ethnic, or other group was primarily responsible for Jesus' death. Offended pride; disappointed hopes; evil exposed by love; the need to destroy that which threatens established securities of private and public life—all of these were at work in the execution of Jesus.

JAMES A. MARTIN, JR., *Fact, Fiction and Faith,* 1960

It is a terrible mistake to understand Jesus as having been crucified by some especially bad people in the first century. Jesus was crucified by the highest reach of human religiosity, morality, and political justice.

ALBERT T. MOLLEGEN, *Christianity and Modern Man,* 1961

He who does not himself remember that God redeemed him from sin and death by the life and passion of Jesus of Nazareth ceases to be a Christian.

PAUL RAMSEY, *Nine Modern Moralists,* 1962

See also Atonement; Calvary; Cross; Crucifixion; Easter; Eucharist; Jesus Christ as Saviour; Jesus and Christians; Redemption; Resurrection; Salvation.

JESUS CHRIST: HIS RESURRECTION

We believe and teach that Christ, in the same flesh in which he died, rose from the dead and ascended to the right hand of God in the highest heaven.

HENRY BULLINGER, *The Helvetic Confession,* 1536

The risen Christ, when he shows himself to his friends, takes on the countenance of all races and each can hear him in his own tongue.

HENRI DE LUBAC, *Catholicism,* 1927

What did Resurrection mean but victory over death and therefore victory over sin and therefore the evidence of a new power at work in the world and therefore the opening of the gates of a new life?

> EDWIN LEWIS, *A Philosophy of the Christian Revelation*, 1940

It is an indication, not of what occurs in the lives of other men, but of what does *not* occur in the lives of other men.

> D. E. TRUEBLOOD, *The Logic of Belief*, 1942

Without the Resurrection, Good Friday would only be the triumph of evil.

> MAURICE NÉDONCELLE, *Suffering: The Christian View*, 1943

The resurrection is an incomprehensible event because it represents the inbreak of the eternal world of God into our temporal sphere.

> EMIL BRUNNER, *Eternal Hope*, 1954

Christ's resurrection, being the decisive event in all history, nothing that can ever happen will equal it in importance.

> JEAN DANIELOU, *The Lord of History*, 1958

One item about the ressurection of Jesus has sometimes been overlooked: he showed himself after death only to those who loved him.

> GEORGE A. BUTTRICK, *Sermons Preached in a University Church*, 1959

The entire character of a man's whole life depends on whether he answers "Yes" or "No" to the historic fact of the Resurrection.

> JOHN E. LARGE, *The Small Needle of Doctor Large*, 1962

The Lord's Resurrection is not an isolated fact, it is a fact that concerns the whole of mankind; from Christ it extends to the world; it has a cosmic importance . . . the source of meaning of the human drama, the solution of the problem of evil, the origin of a new form of life, to which we give the name of Christianity.

> POPE PAUL VI, *Easter Sermon*, 1964

It is on the reality of Christ's Resurrection that the religion that takes its name and life from him is founded.

> POPE PAUL VI, *Easter Sermon*, 1964

See also Calvary; Easter; Immortality; Resurrection.

JESUS CHRIST AND CHRISTIANITY

Everything in the Kingdom, every spiritual thing, refers to Christ and centres in him.

> ISAAC PENNINGTON, *Works*, 1681

The religion of Christ is a mystery which subsists by its own force, and proceeds from a mind which is not a human mind.

> NAPOLEON BONAPARTE (1769–1821), *Napoleon's Argument for the Divinity of Christ* (in conversation with General Bertrand at St. Helena), publ. 1842

All doctrines of Christianity, however widely they may otherwise diverge philosophically or mythically, are yet at one in seeking in him [Jesus] and his appearance *the centre of the world's history*.

> WILHELM WINDELBAND, *A History of Philosophy*, 1883

In Jesus and the primitive Church the prophetic spirit rose from the dead.

> WALTER RAUSCHENBUSCH, *Christianity and the Social Crisis*, 1907

Jesus remains the very heart and soul of the Christian movement, still controlling men, still capturing men—against their wills very often—changing men's lives and using them for ends they never dreamed of.

> T. R. GLOVER, *The Jesus of History*, 1925

Where Christ is not the living center of everything the value of the Church has declined, its life has waned. That, to my mind, is the most striking and outstanding fact in history.

> T. R. GLOVER, *The Jesus of History*, 1925

If we try to look away from the name of Jesus Christ even momentarily, the Christian Church loses the substance in virtue of which it can assert itself in and against the State and society as an entity of a special order.

KARL BARTH, *Church Dogmatics,* 1938

Christianity means community through Jesus Christ and in Jesus Christ. No Christian community is more or less than this.

DIETRICH BONHOEFFER, *Life Together,* 1938

The truth of the Christian religion is in fact enclosed in the one name of Jesus Christ and nothing else.

KARL BARTH, *Church Dogmatics,* 1940

The revivals and reforms of the Church have commonly been due to a sudden consciousness that Jesus Christ has been forgotten or undervalued in the very Church which bore His name.

JAMES MOFFAT, *Jesus Christ the Same,* 1940

Since the time of Jesus there have been some advances in religion, . . . but these advances are usually admitted to be nothing more than the explication of what was already implicit in the teaching of Jesus. We are still trying to catch up with Him.

D. E. TRUEBLOOD, *The Logic of Belief,* 1942

We have greater and sounder ground for believing in the continued life of Christ than the disciples had. . . . We have the overwhelming evidence of nineteen centuries of Christian victories over the world, the flesh and the devil in man.

RUFUS M. JONES, *A Call to What Is Vital,* 1949

Christ is the traveller's bread; and the Christian experience is a little of this bread, which he gives to his own, to prevent them from falling by the wayside.

JEAN MOUROUX, *Christian Experience,* 1954

The orthodox Christian world has forgotten and forsaken the real, human Jesus of the Gospels, and has substituted a "Christ" of dogmatism, metaphysics, and pagan philosophy.

KARL M. CHWOROWSKY, "What Is a Unitarian?" *A Guide to the Religions of America,* ed. L. Rosten, 1955

We may say if we wish, that Christ is never found outside the Church, but we must add in the same breath that wherever Christ is, there is the Church.

CHAD WALSH, *Behold the Glory,* 1955

JESUS CHRIST AND THE JEWS

Judaism had hope for a new world; Christ brought a new humanity.

CHRISTOPHER DAWSON, *God and the Supernatural,* 1920

He has become the most fascinating figure in history. In him is combined what is best and most mysterious and most unchanging in Israel—the eternal people whose child he was.

H. G. ENELOW, *A Jewish View of Jesus,* 1921

He both annulled Judaism as the life-force of the Jewish nation, and also the nation as a nation. For a religion which possesses only a certain kind of conception of God and a morality acceptable to all mankind, does not belong to any special nation and consciously or unconsciously breaks down the barriers of nationality.

JOSEPH KLAUSNER, *Jesus of Nazareth,* 1926

If ever . . . his ethical code be stripped of its wrappings of miracles and mysticism, the Book of the Ethics of Jesus will be one of the choicest treasures in the literature of Israel for all time.

JOSEPH KLAUSNER, *Jesus of Nazareth,* 1926

The Jew believes in the religion *of* Jesus; he cannot bring himself to accept the religion *about* Jesus.

C. P. FAGNANI, quoted in Landman, *Christian and Jew,* 1929

We have lost a Prophet. We miss, even to our own day, the golden page of the sayings of Jesus; that, however, was the price we paid in order that the Jewish genius might give the world a redeemer who brought it under the authority of God.

SHOLEM ASCH, *What I Believe,* 1941

I firmly believe that the Jewish community, in the course of its renaissance, will recognize Jesus, and not merely as a great figure in its religious history, but also in the organic context of a Messianic development extending over millennia, whose final goal is the redemption of Israel and the world. But I believe equally firmly that we will never recognize Jesus as the Messiah Come, for this would contradict the deepest meaning of our Messianic passion.

MARTIN BUBER, quoted by Ernest Simon in *Jewish Frontier,* February, 1948

JESUS CHRIST AS SAVIOUR

Was He sent, think you, as any man might suppose, to establish a sovereignty, to inspire fear and terror? Not so. But in gentleness and meekness has He sent Him, as a king might send his son who is a king. He sent Him, as sending God; He sent Him, as a man unto men; He sent Him, as Saviour, as using persuasion, not force.

Epistle to Diognetus, c. 200

For as the devil through pride led man from pride to death, so Christ through lowliness led back man through obedience to life.

ST. AUGUSTINE, *De Trinitate,* Bk. IV, c. 397

Nothing accords better with the nature of man than the philosophy of Christ, of which the sole end is to give back to fallen nature its innocence and integrity.

DESIDERIUS ERASMUS, *Greek Testament, Notes on,* 1516

We could never recognize the Father's grace and mercy except for our Lord Jesus Christ, who is a mirror of His Father's heart.

MARTIN LUTHER, *Cathechism,* 1530

Jesus Christ stoops and lets the sinner jump on His back, and so saves him from death.

MARTIN LUTHER (1483–1546), *Works,* XL

If Christ is born a thousand times in Bethlehem and not in thee, then art thou lost for ever.

ANGELUS SILESIUS (1624–1677), *Cherubic Pilgrim*

The Lord hath opened to me by His invisible power how that every man was enlightened by the divine Light of Christ; and I saw it shine through all; and they that believed in it came out of condemnation and came to the Light of Life, and became the children of it.

GEORGE FOX, *Journal,* p. 33, 1694

See also Atonement; Avatara; Election; Eucharist; Fall, the; Jesus Christ; Jesus Christ: His Passion and Death; Justification; Predestination; Redemption; Salvation.

JEW

The converted Jew remains a Jew no matter how much he objects to it.

MOSES HESS, *Rome and Jerusalem,* 1862

The Jew assumes for himself the historic post of a sentinel and soldier of righteousness.

E. G. HIRSCH, *Reform Advocate,* I, 1891

He who does not himself remember that God led him out of Egypt . . . is no longer a true Jew.

MARTIN BUBER, *Der Jude,* October, 1917

To be a Jew is to be a friend of mankind, to be a proclaimer of liberty and peace.

LUDWIG LEWISOHN, *Israel,* 1925

To be a Jew . . . is to be strong with the strength that has outlived persecutions.

PHYLLIS BOTTOME, *The Mortal Storm,* 1937

There is hardly a charge or libel against the Jew which is not an echo of the accusations made against Christians in the first three centuries of their history.

SOLOMON GOLDMAN, *Crisis and Decision,* 1938

The tragedy of modern Jewish life is not anti-Semitism, but the loss of the sense of the worthwhileness of being a Jew.

TRUDE WEISS-ROSMARIN, *Jewish Survival,* 1949

A Jew has the right to reject Jewish religious attitudes but not until first he has come to comprehend their logical validity and psychological values.

MILTON STEINBERG, *A Believing Jew,* 1951

Deep in the heart of every Jew, in its purest and holiest recesses, there blazes the fire of Israel.

A. I. KOOK, quoted in A. Hertzberg's *The Zionist Idea,* 1959

See also Anti-Semitism; Assimilation; Israel; Jews; Judaism; Old Testament; Torah.

JEWS

The Jews, though living under Christian princes, are in worse plight than were their ancestors under the Pharaohs. They are driven to leave in despair the land in which their fathers have dwelt since the memory of man. . . . Whenever any unjust attacks upon them come under your notice, redress their injuries, and do not suffer them to be visited in the future by similar tribulations.

POPE INNOCENT IV, 1247, quoted in H. Graetz, *History of the Jews,* III

What a shame it is they should be more miserable under Christian princes than their ancestors were under Pharaoh.

POPE INNOCENT IV, *Letter in Defense of the Jews,* 1247

God vouchsafed both the Law and other special boons to that people, on account of the promise made to their fathers that Christ should be born of them. For it was fitting that the people, of whom Christ was to be born, should be signalized by a special sanctification.

ST. THOMAS AQUINAS, *Summa Theologiae* II, I, Q. 98, art. 4, 1272

The preservation of the Jews is really one of the most signal and illustrious acts of divine Providence.

THOMAS NEWTON, *Dissertations on the Prophecies,* 1766

But since God could not or would not reveal himself any longer to each single individual, he chose a single people for special education, the rudest and most uncivilized, in order to train it from the very beginning.

G. E. LESSING, *Education of the Human Race,* 1780

If humility is Christianity, you, Jews, are true Christians!

WILLIAM BLAKE, *Jerusalem,* 1820

The Jews were the only people who, from the very beginning, knew God, the Creator of the heavens and the earth; the only people, consequently, that could be the custodian of the divine secrets, and it preserved them in a religion that is without equal.

SAMUEL T. COLERIDGE (1772–1834), *Table Talk*

As the nation of the future, they [the Jews] are the world-historical nation *par excellence,* the nation among nations, whose education—whenever the Jew has not changed and corrupted his nature through modern culture—is still always patriarchal, hierarchical, and mnemonic.

J. K. ROSENKRANZ, *Philosophy of Education,* 1848

Jews are the people of the spirit, and whenever they return to the spirit they are great and splendid.

HEINRICH HEINE, *Ludwig Boerne,* 1867

Certainly the heroism of the defenders of every other creed fades into insignificance before this martyr people, who for thirteen centuries confronted all the evils that the fiercest fanaticism could devise, enduring obloquy and spoliation and the violation of the dearest ties, and the infliction of the most hideous sufferings, rather than abandon their faith.

WILLIAM H. LECKY, *Spirit of Rationalism,* II, 1870

We are in the bonds of brother with it. The New Testament rests upon the Old. They believe in half of that for which we would give our lives. Let us then acknowledge that we unite in a common sympathy.

HENRY EDWARD MANNING, *Address,* London, February 1, 1882

Jewry, being a spiritual entity, cannot suffer annihilation: the body, the mould, may be destroyed, the spirit is immortal.

S. M. DUBNOW, *Jewish History,* 1903

I think the Jewish Question is neither a social nor a religious one, although it may likewise take these and other forms. It is a national question which can be solved only by making it a world question to be dealt with by the civilized nations of the world in council.

THEODORE HERTZL (1860–1904), *Hertzl Speaks,* 1960

If it is true that on the secular side our intellectual life is rooted in Greece and Rome, on the religious side it is rooted in Israel. So long as men recognize the abiding value of religion as the answer to their deepest needs, they will turn with inexhaustible interest to the story of the first beginnings and the gradual development of the people whose faith conquered the civilized world.

J. R. DUMMELOW, ed. of *One Volume Commentary on the Bible,* 1909

The Jews gave to the world its three greatest religions, reverence for law, and the highest conceptions of morality.

LOUIS D. BRANDEIS, *The Jewish Problem,* 1919

When the mystical Jew dies, the Jew is dead.

WALDO FRANK, *Our America,* 1919

If it be true, as it obviously is, that the Bible is a creation of the Jews, it is also true, though not so obvious, that the Jews are a creation of the Bible.

JOSEPH JACOBS, *Jewish Contributions to Civilization,* 1919

The Jews are the only people in their world who conceived the idea of a universal religion, and labored to realize it by a propaganda often more zealous than discreet.

G. F. MOORE, *Judaism,* 1927

They were one, more one than all the other peoples of the world; it was the Book that sweated them into unity.

LEON FEUCHTWANGER, *Power,* 1928

The plainest historical evidence for the effectiveness of religion as a positive social form lies in the history of the Jews.

JOHN MACMURRAY, *Creative Society,* 1935

Had it not been for the Catholic Church the Jews would not have survived the Middle Ages in Christian Europe.

S. W. BARON, *Social and Religious History of the Jews,* II, 1937

The great contribution of the Hebrew to religion was that he did away with it.

JOHN MACMURRAY, *The Clue to History,* 1938

We Jews are a community based on memory. A common memory has kept us together and enabled us to survive.

MARTIN BUBER, *Israel and the World,* 1948

They must either follow the imperative of their religion, the return to the Promised Land—or recognize that that faith is no longer theirs. To renounce the Jewish faith does not mean to jettison the perennial values of Judaic tradition. Its essential teachings have passed long ago into the mainstream of Judeo-Christian heritage.

ARTHUR KOESTLER, *The Trail of the Dinosaur and Other Essays,* 1955

The Jews [of the Old Testament] were, in spite of their quarrels among themselves, their frequent backslidings into idolatry . . . one of the great *religiously and morally disciplined people of history.*

CRANE BRINTON, *A History of Western Morals,* 1959

There is an essential view, a philosophy of Jewish life. It is a dynamic approach to the universe through a unifying God about Whom the values of life are woven. This enables the Jew to see his world clearly and to see it whole.

CHARLES SCHULMAN, *What It Means to Be a Jew,* 1960

We [Orthodox Jews] do not revolve as a satellite in any orbit. Nor are we related to any other faith community as "brethren" even though "separated."

JOSEPH B. SOLOVEITTCHIK, *Tradition,* September, 1964

See also Anti-Semitism; Assimilation; Chosen People; Ghettoes; Israel; Jesus Christ and the Jews; Jew; Judaism; Messiah; Old Testament; Synagogue; Torah.

JEWS AND CHRISTIANS

If . . . the cornerstone of my house fail . . . shall I shift my effects to the upper story? . . . Christianity is built on Judaism, and if this falls, that becomes one heap of ruins with it.

MOSES MENDELSSOHN, *Jerusalem,* 1783

It is through Christianity that Judaism has really conquered the world. Christianity is the masterpiece of Judaism, its glory and the fulness of its evolution.

ERNEST RENAN, *History of Israel,* 1895

Such an injustice as that inflicted by the Gentile Church on Judaism is almost unprecedented in the annals of history.

ADOLF HARNACK, *The Expansion of Christianity,* 1905

To the Christian the Jew is the incomprehensibly obdurate man who declines to see what has happened; and to the Jew the Christian is the incomprehensibly daring man, who affirms in an unredeemed world that its redemption has been accomplished. This is a gulf which no human power can bridge.

MARTIN BUBER, *Israel and the World,* 1948

Whenever we both, Christian and Jew, care more for God himself than for our images of God, we are united in the feeling that our Father's house is differently constructed than our human models take it to be.

MARTIN BUBER, *Israel and the World,* 1948

Israel's characteristic absorption of the time sequence, looking to the temporal fulfilment of the Messianic age, was so modified by apostolic Christianity as to constitute a world view that is specifically different.

AELRED GRAHAM, *Christian Thought and Action,* 1951

There can be no such entity as "Jewish-Christian faith." Though rooted in Judaism, Christianity from the first overleaped and transcended its source, the new wine of the Gospel bursting the old wineskins of Hebraism.

AELRED GRAHAM, *Christian Thought and Action,* 1951

If Jewish thought had never existed the world would have been without Christianity and Islam.

LEON ROTH, *Jewish Thought as a Factor in Civilization,* 1954

Jews and Christians cannot and must not abandon the absolute claim laid upon them by their separate witnesses to the truth. Therefore, by the revealed will of divine predestination, they go their separate ways through history, parallel to each other. . . . In the supernatural future of the Kingdom of God, the parallels will intersect, and the two ways will be but one way—will be, indeed, no longer a way, but the goal.

HANS JOACHIM SCHOEPS, *The Jewish-Christian Argument,* 1961

In respect to the reality of historical events, the Jewish side recognizes the divine origin of Christianity and its revelation as to the way of salvation for the Gentile world outside of Israel—although the act of recognition is and must be something quite different from an act of faith!

HANS JOACHIM SCHOEPS, *The Jewish-Christian Argument,* 1961

Since the spiritual patrimony common to Christians and Jews is thus so great, this Sacred Synod wants to foster and recommend that mutual understanding and respect which is the fruit, above all, of biblical and theological studies as well as of fraternal dialogues.

Second Vatican Council, *Declaration on the Relation of the Church to Non-Christian Religions,* October, 1965

True, the Jewish authorities and those who followed their lead pressed for the death of Christ; still, what happened in His passion cannot be charged against all the Jews, without distinction, then alive, nor against the Jews of today. Although the Church is the new people of God, the Jews should not be presented as rejected by God or accursed, as if this followed from the Holy Scriptures. . . . The Church, mindful of the patrimony she shares with the Jews and moved not by political reasons but by the Gospel's spiritual love, decries hatred, persecutions, displays of anti-Semitism, directed against Jews at anytime by anyone.

Second Vatican Council, *Declaration on the Relation of the Church to Non-Christian Religions,* October, 1965

See also Anti-Semitism; Christians.

JOB, BOOK OF

I call it one of the grandest things ever written with a pen. . . . It is our first, oldest statement of the never-ending problem—man's destiny, and God's way with him here on earth.

THOMAS CARLYLE, *Heroes and Hero Worship,* 1840

See also Old Testament.

JOY

The true joy of man is in doing that which is most proper to his nature; and the first property of man is to be kindly affected towards them that are of one kind with himself.

MARCUS AURELIUS, *Meditations,* c. 170 A.D.

To bring joy to a single heart is better than to build many shrines for worship.

ABU SA'ID IBN ABI KHAYR (died 1049 A.D.), quoted in M. Smith's *Readings from the Mystics of Islam*

Spiritual joy arises from purity of the heart and perseverance in prayer!

ST. FRANCIS OF ASSISI (1181?–1226), *Little Flowers of*

No man truly has joy unless he lives in love.

ST. THOMAS AQUINAS (1225–1274), *Opusc.* xxxv, *de Duobus Pracceptsis*

Perfectly to will what God wills, to want what He wants, is to have joy.

MEISTER ECKHART (14th century), *Works*

The joy of a good man is the witness of a good conscience; have a good conscience and thou shalt ever have gladness.

THOMAS À KEMPIS, *Imitation of Christ*, 1441

When we serve with joy, we promote His honor and glory; because we show that we do it with affection, and that all we do is nothing compared to what we would wish to do.

ALPHONSUS RODRIGUEZ, *On Christian Perfection*, 1611

God send you joy, for sorrow will come fast enough.

JOHN CLARKE, *Paroemiologia, Anglo-Latina*, 1639

A Delight of the mind, from the consideration of the present or assured approaching possession of a good.

JOHN LOCKE, *Essay Concerning Human Understanding*, 1690

The contemplation of the divine Being, and the exercise of virtue, are in their own nature so far from excluding all gladness of heart, that they are perpetual sources of it.

JOSEPH ADDISON, *The Spectator*, 1714

When I think of God, my heart is so filled with joy that the notes fly off as from a spindle.

JOSEPH HAYDN (1732–1809), when criticized for the "gaiety" of his church music; quoted by H. T. Henry in his *Catholic Customs and Symbols*, 1925

You shall have joy, or you shall have power, said God; you shall not have both.

RALPH WALDO EMERSON, *Journal*, October, 1842

Perfect human joy is also worship, for it is ordered by God.

FRIEDRICH FROEBEL (1782–1852), *Aphorisms*

Cana of Galilee, . . . Ah, that sweet miracle! It was not men's grief, but their joy Christ visited, He worked his first miracle to help men's gladness.

FEODOR DOSTOEVSKY, *The Brothers Karamazov*, 1880

For the people who know the Bible and Tradition and the complete history of humanity, Joy is the most infallible sign of the presence of God.

LEON BLOY, *Letter*, November 3, 1889

Whenever spirits at once lofty and intense have seemed to attain the highest joys, they have envisaged and attained them in religion.

GEORGE SANTAYANA, *Reason in Religion*, 1905

Joy is a constituent of life, a necessity of life; it is an element of life's value and life's power. As every man has need of joy, so too, every man has a right to joy. . . . It is a condition of religious living.

PAUL WILHELM VON KEPPLER, *More Joy*, 1911

Join the whole creation of animate things in a deep, heartfelt joy that you are alive, that you see the sun, that you are in this glorious earth which nature has made so beautiful, and which is yours to conquer and enjoy.

> SIR WILLIAM OSLER, *A Way of Life, Address to Yale Students,* April 20, 1913

Joy is the realization of the truth of oneness, the oneness of our soul with the world and of the world-soul with the supreme love.

> RABINDRANATH TAGORE, *Gitanjali,* 1913

Life is one long joy, because the will of God is always being done in it, and the glory of God always being got from it.

> F. W. FABER, *The Spirit of Father Faber,* 1914

The trouble with many men is that they have got just enough religion to make them miserable. If there is not joy in religion, you have got a leak in your religion.

> WILLIAM A. (BILLY) SUNDAY, *Sermon,* New York, 1914

The Poor and Peacemakers alone have perfect joy, because they possess wisdom and contemplation par excellence, in the silence of creatures and in the voice of Love.

> JACQUES MARITAIN, *The Philosophy of Art,* 1923

There is, above all, the laughter that comes from the eternal joy of creation, the joy of making the world new, the joy of expressing the inner riches of the soul—laughter from triumphs over pain and hardship in the passion for an enduring ideal, the joy of bringing the light of happiness, of truth and beauty into a dark world. This is divine laughter par excellence.

> J. E. BOODIN, *God: A Cosmic Philosophy of Religion,* 1934

God cannot endure that unfestive, mirthless attitude of ours in which we eat our bread in sorrow, with pretentious, busy haste, or even with shame. Through our daily meals He is calling us to rejoice, to keep holiday in the midst of our working day.

> DIETRICH BONHOEFFER, *Life Together,* 1938

A positive thing: in Joy one does not only feel secure, but something goes out from one's self to the universe, a warm, possessive effluence of love.

> JOHN BUCHAN, *Pilgrim's Way,* 1940

I think we all sin by needlessly disobeying the apostolic injunction to "rejoice" as much as by anything else.

> C. S. LEWIS, *The Problem of Pain,* 1944

The word joy is found 164 times in a concordance of the Bible, and the word rejoice is repeated 191 times. Truly the Bible is a book of joy and gladness because it is a record of God's relationships with man and of man's continuous search for communion and fellowship.

> KIRBY PAGE, *Living Joyously,* 1950

Joy is not a substitute for sex; sex is very often a substitute for Joy. I sometimes wonder whether all pleasures are not substitutes for Joy.

> C. S. LEWIS, *Surprised by Joy,* 1955

See also Cheerfulness; Good; Happiness; Heaven; Laughter; Love of God; Melancholy; Peace; Pleasure; Prayer, Methods and Time of; Religion: Its Nature and Function; Sorrow; Spiritual; Troubles.

JUDAISM

Ancient Judaism has no symbolical books, no articles of faith . . . and, according to the spirit of true Judaism, must hold them inadmissible.

> MOSES MENDELSSOHN, *Jerusalem,* 1783

The emancipation of the Jews in its last significance is the emancipation of mankind from Judaism.

> KARL MARX, *On the Jewish Question,* 1844

It is to the Jewish nation that humanity owes the deepest debt of gratitude, and it is on that nation that humanity has inflicted the deepest wrongs.

> F. W. FARRAR, *Speech,* London, February 1, 1882

We reject as ideas not rooted in Judaism, the beliefs both in bodily resurrection and in Gehenna and Eden.

> Central Conference of American Rabbis, 1885

Everything in Christianity which comes in a direct line from Judaism lives, and will live.

> JAMES DARMESTETER, *Selected Essays,* 1895

Judaism is the only religion that has never entered into conflict, and never can, with either science or social progress, and that has witnessed, and still witnesses, all their conquests without a sense of fear.

> JAMES DARMESTETER, *Selected Essays,* 1895

The two great dogmas which, ever since the prophets, constitute the whole of Judaism—the Divine unity and Messianism; unity of law throughout the world, and the terrestrial triumph of justice in humanity.

> JAMES DARMESTETER, *Selected Essays,* 1895

Every house a temple, every heart an altar, every human being a priest.

> M. LAZARUS, *Ethics of Judaism,* 1900

Judaism is the belief that all life should be sanctified and transfigured by religion. . . . Man is to humanize himself by . . . conscious adherence to . . . the moral law.

> C. G. MONTEFIORE, *Liberal Judaism,* 1903

We are helpless spectators of the Jewish soul wasting away before our very eyes.

> SOLOMON SCHECHTER, *Seminary Addresses,* 1915

Judaism is not only religion and it is not only ethics: it is the sum total of all the needs of a nation, placed on a religious basis.

> JOSEPH KLAUSNER, *Jesus of Nazareth,* 1926

Judaism is the funded cultural activity which the Jewish people has transmitted from generation to generation.

> MORDECAI KAPLAN, *Menorah Journal,* 1927, XIII

If I think of my religion I think of it in terms of my people's religion. I share the faith-life of my group. I like to pray as my fathers prayed.

> ABBA HILLEL SILVER, *Religion in a Changing World,* 1930

The attempt to reduce Judaism to a religion is a betrayal of its true nature.

> MILTON STEINBERG, *The Making of the Modern Jew,* 1933

As long as Judaism continues, nobody will be able to say that the soul of man has allowed itself to be subjugated.

> LEO BAECK, *The Essence of Judaism,* 1936

Judaism is rooted forever in the soil, blood, life-experience and memory of a particular folk—the Jewish people.

> SOLOMON GOLDMAN, *Crisis and Decision,* 1938

Hatred for Judaism is at bottom hatred for Christianity.

> SIGMUND FREUD, *Moses and Monotheism,* 1939

Judaism is a way of life which endeavors to transform virtually every human action into a means of communion with God.

> LOUIS FINKELSTEIN, *Religions of Democracy,* 1941

Judaism will never allow itself to reach even in theory the ethical extremeness characteristic of Christianity; this extremeness has no place in the world of reality.

JOSEPH KLAUSNER, *From Jesus to Paul*, 1944

Judaism is a nation and a religion at one and the same time.

JOSEPH KLAUSNER, *From Jesus to Paul*, 1944

Jewish rules of conduct apply not merely to worship, ceremonial and justice between man and man, but also to such matters as philanthropy, personal friendships and kindnesses, intellectual pursuits, artistic creations, courtesy, the preservation of health and the care of the diet.

LOUIS FINKELSTEIN, *The Jews: Their History, Culture and Religion*, 1949

It blends religion, national devotion, cultural aspirations, and the hope for a better future into an inseparable union of purposeful holinesss.

TRUDE WEISS-ROSMARIN, *Jewish Survival*, 1949

Judaism is a *religion of time* aiming at the *sanctification of time*.

A. J. HESCHEL, *The Sabbath*, 1951

The Old Testament witnesses that Judaism did draw into itself the elements of the whole Syriac culture and the whole Syriac past. But the Old Testament witnesses no less clearly that Judaism transformed them all within its own history, as the other partner in a covenant with the "living God."

GREGORY DIX, *Jew and Greek*, 1953

Judaism has a central, unique and tremendous idea that is utterly original—the idea that God and man are partners in the world and that, for the realization of His plan and the complete articulation of this glory upon earth, God needs a committed, dedicated group of men and women.

T. H. GASTER, at American Council for Judaism, April 20, 1954

The Jewish God is no philosopher and his path is tangled with logical contradictions.

L. ROTH, *Jewish Thought as a Factor in Civilization*, 1954

Judaism . . . taught the possibility of transmuting pain into spiritual greatness.

J. B. AGUS, *Judaism*, Fall, 1955

To accept Judaism without accepting the Mosaic Law is a contradiction in terms.

E. BERKOWITZ, *Judaism: Fossil or Ferment?*, 1956

It is nonetheless untrue to maintain that the Jewish religion is a set of legal commandments divorced from faith. Jewish faith is indefinable in Western theological categories, which are alien to its essence, and by nature it permits variation in belief.

ARTHUR HERTZBERG, *Judaism*, 1961

Judaism, the religion of the Bible, is the classical paradigm of a God-made religion. It is the assertion—not the philosophical proof—that God exists and that He has spoken and speaks to man, giving him clues to the road that he must follow.

ARTHUR HERTZBERG, *Judaism*, 1961

Eternal faith and eternal people, a living dialogue between God and the Jew, between the Jew and God, and among the Jew, his fellow Jew, and the world..

LEO TREPP, *Eternal Faith, Eternal People*, 1962

See also Anti-Semitism; Education, Jewish; Ethics; Freedom of Thought and Speech; Israel; Jesus Christ and the Jews; Jew; Jews; Man and God; Messiah; Old Testament; Prophets; Religion, Revealed; Sabbath; Synagogue; Torah; Trinity; Zionism.

JUDGMENT

He that would well and rightwisely judge his own defaults should not so rigorously judge the defaults of his neighbors.
THOMAS À KEMPIS, *Imitation of Christ,* 1441

Alas, to judge a man of even the highest virtue it is necessary to know the time in which he lived.
Inscription on tomb, Church of Santa Maria dell'Anima, Rome, of the last non-Italian Pope, Adrian VI (died 1523), a Dutchman from Utrecht

In matters of faith we can not admit any other judge than God himself, who through His Word tells us what is true and what is false, what is to be followed and what is to be avoided.
HENRY BULLINGER, *The Helvetic Confession,* 1536

The Church never passes judgment on anyone who has not yet come into her by the door of baptism.
Council of Trent, Sessions XIV, 1551

All universal judgments are treacherous and dangerous.
MONTAIGNE, *Essays,* 1580

Forbear to judge, for we are sinners all.
WILLIAM SHAKESPEARE, *Henry VI, Part II,* c. 1591

It is rashness to go about to make our shallow reason judge of the works of God, and to call vain and superfluous whatever thing in the Universe is not of use to us.
GALILEO, *Dialogue on the Great World Systems,* 1632

No man can justly censure or condemn another, because indeed no man truly knows another. . . . No man can judge another, because no man knows himself.
THOMAS BROWNE, *Religio Medici,* 1642

It is not permitted to the most equitable of men to be a judge in his own cause.
BLAISE PASCAL, *Pensées,* 1670

Knowledge is the treasure, but judgment the treasurer of a wise man.
WILLIAM PENN, *Some Fruits of Solitude,* 1693

If it be an evil to judge rashly or untruly any single man, how much a greater sin it is to condemn a whole people.
WILLIAM PENN, *A Key Opening the Way,* 1693

"Let him who is without sin among you cast the first stone." These are the noblest, the greatest words ever uttered by human lips, or heard by human ear.
From Countess Irma's Diary in Berthold Auerbach's *On the Heights,* 1865

Why, for us every day is a day of judgment—every day is a *Dies Irae,* and writes its irrevocable verdict in the flame of its West. Think you that judgment waits till the doors of the graves are opened? It waits at the doors of your houses—it waits at the corners of your streets; we are in the midst of judgment.
JOHN RUSKIN, *Sesame and Lilies,* 1865

The judgment upon Christianity is really judgment upon the betrayal of Christianity, upon its distortion and defilement, and the justice of this is that of judgment upon the fallen world and its sinful history.
JACQUES MARITAIN, *Freedom in the Modern World,* 1936

The *forgiveness* of the world can only be accomplished by the *judgment* of the world.
RALPH W. SOCKMAN, *The Highway of God,* 1941

To judge means to pronounce the verdict in regard to a person, to anticipate, as it were, the punishment that the sinner deserves from God. This is precisely what the self-righteous man does, and what the true Christian always avoids doing.

DIETRICH VON HILDEBRAND, *True Morality and Its Counterfeits*, 1955

If it be maintained that a man's judgments are themselves completely determined, that he cannot help making the judgments he makes, the answer is that this makes nonsense of all knowledge.

MORRIS GINSBERG, *On the Diversity of Morals*, 1957

God alone can penetrate the innermost recesses of our conscience. That is why Jesus commands us not to judge.

JACQUES LECLERCQ, *Back to Jesus*, 1959

We can render judgment concerning ideas, truth, or errors; good or bad actions, character, temperament, and what appears to us of a man's interior disposition. But we are utterly forbidden to judge the inmost heart.

JACQUES MARITAIN, *Truth and Human Fellowship*, 1959

An Indian's Prayer: "Great Spirit, help me never to judge another until I have walked two months in his moccasins."

Quoted in *Way*, August, 1961, attributed to *Notebook of a Printer*

See also Conscience; Determinism; Discriminating; Moral Law; Necessity; Opinions; Private Judgment; Punishment; Truth, Definitions of; Will.

JUDGMENT, GOD'S

We are not judged at the divine tribunal by faith alone, as though we did not have to answer for our conduct, nor on our conduct alone, as though our faith were not under examination.

ORIGEN, *On the Soul*, c. 240 A.D.

The world is judged according to the preponderance of good or evil, and the individual is judged in the same way.

Kiddushin, Mishna, c. 400 A.D.

Indifferent acts are judged by their ends; sins are judged by themselves.

ST. AUGUSTINE, *To Consentius, Against Lying*, c. 400

Man's advocates are repentance and good deeds.

Talmud: Sabbath, 32a, c. 500

At the day of judgment it shall not be asked of us what we have read, but what we have done; not how well we have said, but how religiously we have lived.

THOMAS À KEMPIS, *Imitation of Christ*, 1441

For that which Christ shall say to thy soul then at the last Judgment, *Enter into thy Master's joy*, He says to thy conscience now, *Enter into thy Master's joy*.

JOHN DONNE, *Sermon*, January 29, 1625

Religion turns our whole life into a sacrifice to God, a state of probation from which we must all appear before the Judgment-Seat of Christ, that everyone may receive the things done in his body.

WILLIAM LAW, *Christian Perfection*, 1726

A man seated in a glass cage is not put to such embarrassment as is a man in his transparency before God. . . . Substantially everyone arrives in eternity bringing with him and delivering the most accurate account of every least insignificance which he has committed or left undone.

SÖREN KIERKEGAARD, *The Sickness unto Death*, 1849

On Judgment Day, God will not ask to what sect you belonged, but what manner of life you led.

I. M. KAGAN, *Hafetz Hayyim*, 1873

What else, indeed, is the judgment, as far as we can grasp it, but the naked setting of our soul as it is now at this moment in the sight of God?

BEDE JARRETT, *Meditations for Layfolk*, 1915

The judgment of God shall turn topsy-turvy the judgments of men.

> EDWARD F. GARESCHE, *The Things Immortal,* 1919

God does not judge me that He may punish me but that He may reward me: He is not looking for the evil in me but for the good.

> R. H. J. STEUART, *The Inward Vision,* 1929

The judgment of God is executed not only at the end of history, it is executed periodically in history.

> REINHOLD NIEBUHR, *Beyond Tragedy,* 1937

Human beings judge one another by their external actions. God judges them by their moral choices.

> C. S. LEWIS, *Christian Behavior,* 1943

As there is no other avenue into the world of glory except through death, so there is no entrance into eternal life except through the narrow pass of judgment.

> EMIL BRUNNER, *Eternal Hope,* 1954

While it is true that it is a terrible thing to fall into the hands of the living God in judgment, it is a much more terrible thing to fall out of his hand.

> ALBERT T. MOLLEGEN, *Christianity and Modern Man,* 1961

See also Conduct; Conscience; Damnation; Determinism; Election; End of the World; Free Will; God: His Wrath; Guilt; Heaven; Hell; Heresy; Immortality; Man and God; Mercy; Necessity; Predestination; Prudence; Punishment; Sin; Soul.

JUST MAN

A man is not just if he carries a matter by violence; no, he who distinguishes both right and wrong and guides others, not by violence, but by the same law, being a guardian of the law, he is called just.

> *Dhammapada,* c. 5th century B.C.

If a man is at heart just, then in so far is he God; the safety of God, the immortality of God, the majesty of God, do enter in that man with justice.

> RALPH WALDO EMERSON, *Divinity School Address,* July, 1838

JUSTICE

He used to define justice as "a virtue of the soul distributing that which each person deserved."

> ARISTOTLE (384–322 B.C.), according to Diogenes Laertius in *Lives and Opinions of Eminent Philosophers*

The origin of justice is to be sought in the divine law of eternal and immutable morality.

> CICERO, *The Laws,* 52 B.C.

Holiness toward God and justice toward men usually go together.

> PHILO, *Abraham,* 37 A.D.

True justice is not to be found save in the republic of which Christ is the Founder and Protector.

> ST. AUGUSTINE, *The City of God,* 426

O you Moslems, stand fast to Justice, when you bear witness, though it is against yourself, or your parents, or your kin, rich or poor. God is nearer to you than any. Therefore follow not passion, lest you swerve from the Truth.

> *Koran,* c. 625

Since all justice is rightness, the justice, which brings praise to the one who preserves it, is in nowise in any except rational beings. . . . This justice is not rightness of knowledge, or rightness of action, but rightness of will.

> ST. ANSELM, *Dialogue on Truth,* c. 1080

If God's justice could be recognized as just by human comprehension, it would not be divine.

MARTIN LUTHER, *On the Slave Will,* 1525

Let the tears of the poor find more compassion, but not more justice, from thee than the applications of the wealthy.

MIGUEL DE CERVANTES, *Don Quixote,* 1605

If justice prevails, good faith is found in treaties, truth in transactions, order in government, the earth is at peace, and heaven itself sheds over us its beneficent light and radiates down to us its blessed influence.

J. B. BOSSUET (1627–1704), *Sermon on Justice*

I do, it is true, expect more justice from one who believes in a God than from one who has no such belief.

VOLTAIRE, "Atheist," *Philosophical Dictionary,* 1764

Justice is the sum of all moral duty.

WILLIAM GODWIN, *An Enquiry Concerning Political Justice,* 1793

The unembodied justice is of Heaven; a Spirit and Divinity of Heaven,—invisible to all but the noble and pure of soul.

THOMAS CARLYLE, *Past and Present,* 1843

Justice is truth in action.

BENJAMIN DISRAELI, *Speech,* February 11, 1851

Justice—Truth is its handmaid, freedom is its child, peace is its companion, safety walks in its steps, victory follows in its train; it is the brightest emanation from the gospel; it is the attribute of God.

SYDNEY SMITH, *Lady Holland: Memoir,* 1855

Justice is a name for certain classes of moral rules, which concern the essentials of human well-being more nearly, and are therefore of more absolute obligation, than any other rules for the guidance of life.

JOHN STUART MILL, *Utilitarianism,* 1863

No human actions ever were intended by the Maker of men to be guided by balances of expediency, but by balances of justice.

JOHN RUSKIN, *Sesame and Lilies,* 1865

And though absolute justice be unattainable, as much justice as we need for all practical use is attainable by all those who make it their aim.

JOHN RUSKIN, *Sesame and Lilies,* 1865

It is necessary to cease to be a man in order to do justice to a microbe; it is not necessary to cease to be a man in order to do justice to men.

G. K. CHESTERTON, *Heretics,* 1905

Whoever tramples on the plea for justice temperately made in the name of peace only outrages peace and kills something fine in the heart of man which God put there when we got our manhood.

WILLIAM ALLEN WHITE, *Emporia Gazette,* July 27, 1922

What room is there in the world for justice if we must extend both cheeks to our assailants and give the thief both coat and cloak?

JOSEPH KLAUSNER, *Jesus of Nazareth,* 1929

The human situation is that while I revere schemes of impartial justice in the abstract, I am never impartially just in my actions.

REINHOLD NIEBUHR, *Harper's Magazine,* CLXV, 1932

Whereas in Greek the idea of justice was akin to harmony, in Hebrew it is akin to holiness.

JOSEPH H. HERTZ, *The Pentateuch and Haftorahs,* 1936

If justice be no concern either of nature or of the gods, it is more preeminently ours.

W. MACNEILE DIXON, *Thoughts for the Times,* 1940

Tenderness is total love, whereas justice is only a part of love, though it believes itself, mistakenly, to be the whole.

C. F. RAMUZ, *What Is Man?,* 1948

Justice is that side of love which affirms the independent right of persons within the love relation.

PAUL TILLICH, *Systematic Theology,* 1951

We must make it plain that the Christian demand for justice does not come from Karl Marx. It comes from Jesus Christ and the Hebrew prophets.

G. BROMLEY OXNAM, *Sermon,* World Council of Churches, 1954

The instinct for justice, when equipped with all the resources of technology, is capable of laying waste to the earth itself.

GEORGES BERNANOS, *Last Essays of,* 1955

Only love can transform calculating justice into creative justice. Love makes justice just. Justice without love is always injustice.

PAUL TILLICH, *The New Being,* 1955

See also Almsgiving; Charity; Injustice; Judgment; Judgment, God's; Law; Mercy; Natural Law; Punishment; Right; Right and Wrong; Rights; Tolerance; Truth.

JUSTIFICATION

And we also, having been called in His will in Christ Jesus, are not justified by ourselves, or by our own wisdom or understanding or piety or the works we have done in holiness of heart, but through the faith.

ST. CLEMENT OF ROME, *Epistle to the Corinthians,* c. 100

God's grace accepted is justification.

MARTIN LUTHER (on Ps. IV), *Lecture on the Psalms,* 1513–1515

As the soul needs only the Word of God for its life and righteousness, so it is justified by faith alone and not any works; for if it could be justified by anything else, it would not need the Word, and consequently it would not need faith.

MARTIN LUTHER, *Freedom of a Christian,* 1520

We are justified, . . . when, having been mortified through the law, we are raised by the word of grace, which is promised in Christ, or the gospel of the forgiveness of sins, and cleave to it in faith.

PHILIP MELANCHTHON, *Loci Communes,* 1521

Men cannot be justified in the sight of God by their own strength, merit or works, but that they are justified freely on account of Christ through faith, when they believe that they are received into grace and that their sins are remitted on account of Christ.

PHILIP MELANCHTHON, *Confession of Augsburg,* 1530

The power of justifying, which faith possesses, does not lie in any worth of works. Our justification rests upon God's mercy alone and Christ's merit.

JOHN CALVIN, *Institutes,* III, 1536

To "justify" means nothing else than to acquit of guilt him who was accused as if his own innocence were confirmed.

JOHN CALVIN, *Institutes,* III, 1536

If anyone saith that without the prevenient inspiration of the Holy Ghost and without His help man can believe, hope, love, or be penitent as he ought, so that the grace of justification may be bestowed upon him; let him be anathema.

Council of Trent, Session III, Canon 3, 1551

Faith is the beginning, the basis and the root of all justification.
> *Council of Trent,* Session VI, chap. 8, 1551

That we are justified by Faith only is a most wholesome Doctrine, and very full of comfort. . . . Good Works, which are the fruits of Faith, and follow after Justification . . . do spring out necessarily of a true and lively Faith.
> *The Thirty-Nine Articles of the Church of England,* 1562

If anyone saith, that by faith alone the impious is justified . . . that nothing else is required to cooperate in order to obtain the grace of Justification . . . let him be anathema.
> *Council of Trent,* 1563

If any one saith, that man may be justified before God by his own works, whether done through the teaching of human nature, or that of the law, without the grace of God through Jesus Christ, let him be anathema.
> *Council of Trent,* 1563

We cannot be justified freely through faith alone without at the same time living holily.
> JOHN CALVIN (1509–1564), *Commentary on I Corinthians*

God will not desert the justified, unless He is first deserted by them.
> *Council of Trent,* Session VI, chap. 2, 1566

Those whom God effectually calleth, He also freely justifieth. . . . Although they can never fall from the state of justification, yet they may by their sins fall under God's fatherly displeasure.
> *Westminster Confession of Faith,* Formulary of the Presbyterian Church of Scotland, 1643

Since without faith it is impossible to please God and to attain to the fellowship of His children, therefore without faith no one has ever attained justification; nor will anyone obtain eternal life unless he shall have persevered in faith unto the end.
> Vatican Council, Session III, 1870

Justification is not a mere covering over of sin. . . . It is the communication of a true inward righteousness, of a new love which re-makes the whole man; it is sanctification.
> KARL ADAM, *The Spirit of Catholicism,* 1924

Justification by Faith represents the final renunciation in the heart of Christianity of the human effort to complete life and history, whether with or without divine grace.
> REINHOLD NIEBUHR, *The Nature and Destiny of Man,* II, 1943

Not only he who is in sin but also he who is in doubt is justified by faith.
> PAUL TILLICH, *The Protestant Era,* 1948

We are accounted righteous before God only for the merit of our Lord and Saviour Jesus Christ, by faith, and not for our own works or deservings. Wherefore, that we are justified by faith only is a most wholesome doctrine, and very full of comfort.
> *Doctrine and Discipline of the Methodist Church,* 1952

Faith is said to be the beginning, middle and end of justification. . . . Man cannot prepare himself for God's activity by a deep sorrow, an earnest longing. . . . Man is justified solely by faith.
> F. E. MAYER, *The Religious Bodies of America,* "Lutheranism," 1954

The witness of the Spirit is an inward impression on the soul, whereby the Spirit of God, the heavenly Comforter, immediately convinces the regenerate believer that he has passed from death unto life, that his sins are all forgiven, and that he is a child of God.

> The Discipline of the Evangelical United Brethren, 1955

Justification is the act of God, whereby He forgives our sins and brings us into fellowship with Him.

> WALTER M. HORTON, Christian Theology, 1955

Whenever a man becomes aware of the real meaning of "The just shall live by faith" the Reformation has come alive in his heart.

> Editorial, National Council Outlook, April, 1956

Justification is not only the forgiveness of sins, but the bestowal of a positive righteousness that derives from beyond us, and which we have through union with Christ.

> T. F. TORRANCE, Scottish Journal of Theology, September, 1960

See also Confession; Faith; Forgiveness; Free Will; Grace; Penitence; Predestination; Reward; Righteousness.

KILLING

Only the Supreme Executioner kills. To kill in place of the Supreme Executioner is to hack in place of a great carpenter. Now if one hacks in place of a great carpenter one can scarcely avoid cutting one's own hand.

> LAO-TZU, The Tao Tê Ching, 6th century B.C.

Viler than unbelievers are those cruel ones who make the law that teaches killing.

> Yogashastra, c. 500 B.C.

This is the quintessence of wisdom: not to kill anything. Know this to be the legitimate conclusion from the principle of rec-

iprocity with regard to non-killing . . . i.e. as you do not wish to be killed, so others do not wish to be killed.

> Sutrakritanga I, Gaina Sutras, c. 5th century B.C.

All men tremble at punishment, all men love life. Remember that thou art like them. Do not kill or cause to slaughter.

> Dhammapada, c. 5th century B.C.

He, who, seeking his own happiness punishes or kills beings who also long for happiness, will not find happiness after death.

> Dhammapada, c. 5th century B.C.

I renounce all killing of living beings whether subtle or gross, whether movable or immovable. Nor shall I myself kill living beings (nor cause others to do it, nor consent to it).

> The first vow of a Jaini monk, c. 5th century B.C. in Sacred Books of the East, Vol. 22

The Buddha said: "Let him [the householder] not kill any living being."

> The Kulavagga of the Sutta-Nipata, c. 5th century B.C.

How can I, in battle, shoot with shafts
On Bhishma, or on Drona—oh thou Chief!—
Both worshipful, both honorable men?
Better to live on beggar's bread
With those we love alive
Than taste their blood in rich feasts spread
And guiltily survive.

> The Song Celestial, Sir Edwin Arnold's translation of the Bhagavad-Gita, 5th to 2nd century B.C.

In our doctrine we are given ampler liberty to be killed than to kill.

> TERTULLIAN, Apology, 197 A.D.

When God prohibits killing, He . . . warns us not to do even those things which are regarded as legal among men. . . . No exception at all ought to be made to the rule that it is always wrong to kill a man, whom God has wished to be a sacrosanct creature.

LACTANTIUS, *Divine Institutions,* c. 310

Him who destroys one human life, the Scripture regards as if he had destroyed the whole world.

Talmud, c. 4th century A.D.

Slay no one, except for the requirements of justice.

Koran, c. 625

And thou, man, who by these my labors dost look upon the marvellous works of nature, if thou judgest it to be an atrocious act to destroy the same, reflect that it is an infinitely atrocious act to take away the life of man.

LEONARDO DA VINCI (1452–1519), *Notebooks of*

See also Abortion; Death; Lynching; Martyrs; Murder; Nuclear War; Self-Defense; Soldier; Suicide; Violence; War; War, Condemnation of.

KINGDOM OF GOD

Dear friends, the kingdom of God,—and we are that kingdom—consists not in speech or in words, but in deeds, in works and exercises.

MARTIN LUTHER, *5th Wittenberg Sermon of 1522*

Before the end even the rich shall enter into the kingdom of God. Together with them will enter in the great, the noble, the honourable; . . . the kings of the earth. Last of all, the wise, the learned . . . will be convinced that they are fools . . . and "enter into the kingdom of God."

JOHN WESLEY (1703–1791), *Sermon,* II.14

Christ has brought the kingdom of God nearer to earth; but he has been misunderstood; and in place of God's kingdom the kingdom of the priest has been established among us.

IMMANUEL KANT, *Religion Within the Limits of Pure Reason,* 1793

That which is given to this generation to study and unfold is the Christian doctrine of Christ's kingdom as the reign of righteousness and love over all the earth in the life and civilization of men.

SAMUEL HARRIS, *Kingdom of Christian Earth,* 1870

The only significance of life consists in helping to establish the kingdom of God; and this can be done only by means of the acknowledgment and profession of the truth by each one of us.

LEO TOLSTOY, *The Kingdom of God,* 1893

By the Kingdom of God Jesus meant an ideal (though progressively approximated) social order in which the relation of men to God is that of sons, and therefore to each other, that of brothers.

SHAILER MATTHEWS, *The Social Teaching of Jesus,* 1902

It is for us to see the Kingdom of God as always coming, always pressing in on the present, always big with possibility, and always inviting immediate action.

WALTER RAUSCHENBUSCH, *A Theology for the Social Gospel,* 1917

All that Christ was, all that He taught, did, created, and suffered, is contained· in these words—He has established the Kingdom of God. . . . The Kingdom of God means that God draws His creature to Himself, and makes us capable of receiving His own fullness.

ROMANO GUARDINI, *The Church and the Catholic,* 1935

It is a betrayal at once of man and of God not to understand that history is a movement towards the Kingdom of God. . . .

But it is absurd to think that it will come as a part of history. . . . It will come at the end of history.

> JACQUES MARITAIN, *True Humanism,* 1936

The Kingdom of God is not the work of man and does not emerge by a natural law of progress from the course of human history. It makes a violent irruption into history and confounds the work of man.

> CHRISTOPHER DAWSON, *The Kingdom of God and History,* 1937

Jesus did not say that it would be a great thing if the Kingdom of God existed. He announced that the Kingdom was at hand.

> W. A. VISSER 'T HOOFT, *None Other Gods,* 1937

Here "on earth" the coming of God's kingdom is largely contingent upon human willingness to do God's will.

> WALTER MARSHALL HORTON, *Our Christian Faith,* 1945

To discover the Kingdom of God exclusively within oneself is easier than to discover it, not only there, but also in the outer world of minds and things and living creatures.

> ALDOUS HUXLEY, *The Perennial Philosophy,* 1945

The Kingdom of God is the Kingdom where God is without shadow, without problems and contradictions, where He is All in All; it is the rule of God in the redeemed world. . . . The Kingdom of God is the world dominion of Jesus Christ in honor of the Father, revealed in the clear light of day.

> KARL BARTH, *Community, Church and State,* 1946

The most solitary hermit is not really a Christian if he does not pray for the Kingdom of God to be spread in this world.

> PIE-RAYMOND RÉGAMEY, *Poverty,* 1949

The Kingdom of God is impossible except as comprising both Church and individual personality, each with its well defined and distinctive nature, but essentially related to the other.

> ROMANO GUARDINI, *The Church and the Catholic,* 1953

See also Children; Christianity; Fellowship; History; Kingdom of Heaven; World and God.

KINGDOM OF HEAVEN

The Church even now is the kingdom of Christ and the kingdom of heaven.

> ST. AUGUSTINE, *City of God,* 426

The Kingdom of Heaven is not servants' wages but sons' inheritance, which only they who have been adopted as sons by the Lord shall enjoy, and that for no other reason than this adoption.

> JOHN CALVIN, *Institutes,* III, 1536

A time of great light and knowledge . . . it [the Kingdom of Heaven on Earth] shall be a time of great holiness . . . it will be a time of excellent order in the church of Christ . . . ease, quietness, pleasantness, and cheerfulness of mind, also wealth and a great increase of children . . . temporal prosperity will be promoted by a remarkable blessing from heaven.

> JONATHAN EDWARDS (1703–1758), *Works,* III, 404

The Kingdom of Heaven has not been a prize for those who are unlike their fellows, but for those who will take their stand by them—who will set up no exclusive pretensions of their own.

> FREDERICK D. MAURICE (1805–1870), *Sermons*

There is no opposition between the Kingdom of Heaven and any kingdom of earth, except what is produced by this selfishness which is the enemy of both.

> FREDERICK D. MAURICE (1805–1870), *Sermons*

The kingdom of heaven is of the childlike, of those who are easy to please, who love and give pleasure.

ROBERT LOUIS STEVENSON, *Across the Plains,* 1880

From the Kingdom of Heaven within us, a Kingdom of Heaven unfolds and establishes itself around us. A new fellowship is established, a society whose bond is the Holy Spirit, whose head is the Saviour.

JOHN LANCASTER SPALDING, *Religion, Agnosticism, Education,* 1902

It took a century and a half of evolutionary preachers . . . to convince us that we and our father are one; that as the kingdom of heaven is within us we need not go about looking for it and crying Lo here! and Lo there!

GEORGE BERNARD SHAW, *Preface, Androcles and the Lion,* 1914

This doctrine of the Kingdom of Heaven, which was the main teaching of Jesus . . . is certainly the most revolutionary doctrine that ever stirred and changed human thought . . . no less than a bold and uncompromising demand for a complete change and cleansing of the life of our struggling race.

H. G. WELLS, *The Outline of History,* 1920

The kingdom of heaven is not the isolation of good from evil. It is the overcoming of evil by good.

ALFRED NORTH WHITEHEAD, *Religion in the Making,* 1927

Kingdom of Heaven—essentially a society in which God should govern as well as reign, a community filled with holiness, righteousness, and peace.

W. R. INGE, *Freedom, Love and Truth,* 1936

The Kingdom of Heaven is that social order where nobody retards anyone else, where nobody employs anyone else as a stepping-stone.

WINIFRED KIRKLAND, *The Man of the Hour,* 1942

What is it that Jesus knew, and what is it that he had seen in his own experience, that was hidden from the kings and prophets? It is condensed in a very brief formula —*The kingdom of heaven is in us.*

V. G. SIMKHOVITCH, *Toward the Understanding of Jesus,* 1958

See also Kingdom of God; Nirvana; Redemption.

KINDNESS

God is in every created being or thing: be cruel towards none, neither abuse any by intemperance.

JEREMY TAYLOR, *Holy Living,* 1650

All the kindness which a man puts out into the world works on the heart and thoughts of mankind.

ALBERT SCHWEITZER, *Memoirs of Childhood and Youth,* 1931

See also Charity; Compassion; Goodness; Sympathy.

KINGS

What life would be more wretched or unenviable than theirs if they had even a particle of wisdom?

DESIDERIUS ERASMUS, *Praise of Folly,* 1509

The State of Monarchy is the supremest thing upon earth: for Kings are only GOD's Lieutenants upon earth, and sit upon GOD's throne, but even by GOD himself they are called Gods.

JAMES I OF ENGLAND, *Speech,* 1609

Kings have the sacrosanct right of ecclesiastical rule even over the very lord pontiffs and dominion over them so that they themselves faithfully and piously should rule Holy Church.

ANONYMOUS, *The Honor of the Married Clergy Maintained,* 1651

See also Divine Right of Kings; Government; Government and God; Government and Religion; Royalty; Rulers; State, the; Tyrants.

KNOWLEDGE

Knowing that this body is fragile like a jar, and making his thought firm like a fortress, one should attack Mara, the tempter, with the weapon of knowledge, one should watch him when conquered, and should never rest.

Dhammapda, c. 5th century B.C.

If a man's faith is unstable and his peace of mind troubled, his knowledge will not be perfect.

Dhammapada, c. 5th century B.C.

There is "true" Knowledge. Learn thou it is this:
To see one changeless Life in all the Lives
And in the Separate, One Inseparable.

Bhagavad-Gita, 5th to 2nd century B.C.

The flame of Knowledge wastes work's dross away.
There is no purifier like thereto
In all this world, and he who seeketh it
Shall find it—being grown perfect—in himself.
Believing he receives it when the soul
Masters itself and cleaves to Truth, and comes—
Possessing Knowledge—to the higher peace,
The uttermost repose.

The Song Celestial, Sir Edwin Arnold's translation of *Bhagavad-Gita,* 5th to 2nd century B.C.

Knowledge is the food of the soul.

SOCRATES, "Protagoras," Plato's *Dialogues,* 399 B.C.

We make the nearest approach to knowledge when we have the least possible intercourse or communion with the body . . . but keep ourselves pure until the hour when God himself is pleased to release us.

PLATO, "Phaedo," *Dialogues,* 399 B.C.

For we can only know that we know nothing, and a little knowledge is a dangerous thing.

Chuang-tzu, c. 300 B.C.

In God knowledge is infinite; in others it is only a germ.

PATANJALI (2nd century B.C.), *Yoga Aphorisms,* I

It is not the tree of knowledge that destroys—it is disobedience that proves destructive. . . . For neither can life exist without knowledge, nor is knowledge secure without life. Wherefore both were planted close together.

Epistle to Diognetus, c. 200 A.D.

Knowledge cannot come from the understanding, nor be apprehended by thought; because to have knowledge in oneself as a peculiar property does not belong to man, but to God.

LACTANTIUS, *The Divine Institutes,* c. 310 A.D.

A man has only so much knowledge as he puts to work.

ST. FRANCIS OF ASSISI (1181–1226), *Mirror of Perfection*

It is certain that never, before God is seen face to face, shall a man know anything with final certainty. . . . And since, in comparison with what a man knows, those things of which he is ignorant are infinite, and beyond comparison greater and more beautiful, he is out of his mind who extols himself in regard to his own knowledge.

ROGER BACON, *Opus Maius,* 1267

The meanest thing that one knows in God —for instance, if one could understand a flower as it has its Being in God—this would be a higher thing than the whole world.

MEISTER ECKHART (1260?–1327?), *Mystiche Schriftgen*

Wicked men grow the worse for their knowledge, but the good improve extremely.

PHILLIPE DE COMINES, *Memoirs*, 1491

Knowledge provides more of a help toward godliness than does beauty, or strength of the body, or wealth.

DESIDERIUS ERASMUS, *Enchiridion*, 1501

The greatest part of what we know, is the least part of what we know not; that is, that that which we think to know, is but a parcel, yea and a small particle of our ignorance.

MICHEL DE MONTAIGNE, *Essays*, Bk. 2, ch. 12, 1580

It is more by the means of our ignorance, than of our skill, that we are wise in heavenly knowledge.

MICHEL DE MONTAIGNE, *Essays*, Bk. 2, ch. 12, 1580

Knowledge is the wing whereby we fly to Heaven.

WILLIAM SHAKESPEARE, *Henry VI, Part II*, 1592?

The desire of power in excess caused the angels to fall; the desire of knowledge in excess caused man to fall.

FRANCIS BACON, *Essays*, 1597

Knowledge is a rich storehouse for the glory of the Creator and the relief of man's estate.

FRANCIS BACON, *Advancement of Learning*, 1605

All knowledge is to be limited by religion.

FRANCIS BACON (1561–1626), *Valerius Terminus*

It hath been the common disease of Christians from the beginning . . . out of a

vain desire to know more than is revealed.

JOHN HALES, *A Treatise Concerning Schism and Schismatics*, 1642

True knowledge is modest and wary; 'tis ignorance that is bold and presuming.

JOSEPH GLANVILLE, *Scepsis Scientifica*, 1665

He that has more knowledge than judgment, is made for another man's use more than his own.

WILLIAM PENN, *Some Fruits of Solitude*, 1693

God cannot impart knowledge to creatures, of which he himself has made them incapable by their nature and formation; he cannot instruct a mole in astronomy or an oyster in music, because he has not given them members or faculties necessary for the acquisition of those sciences.

SOAMES JENYNES, *Nature and Origin of Evil*, 1757

Knowledge is the key that first opens the hard heart, enlarges the affections, and opens the way for men into the kingdom of heaven.

JONATHAN EDWARDS (1703–1758), *Works*, V, 151

We shall be as Gods in knowledge, was and must have been the first temptation.

SAMUEL TAYLOR COLERIDGE, *Biographia Literaria*, 1817

God wishes no narrow-hearted souls or empty heads for his children; but those whose spirit is of itself indeed, poor, but rich in the Knowledge of Him; and who regard this knowledge of God as the only valuable possession.

G. W. F. HEGEL (1770–1831), *The Philosophy of History*, publ. posth.

When revealed truth has given the aim and direction to knowledge, knowledge of all kinds will minister to revealed truth.

JOHN HENRY NEWMAN, *Tamworth Reading Room*, 1841

Knowledge is one thing, virtue another; good sense is not conscience, refinement is not humility, nor is largeness and justness of view faith.

JOHN HENRY NEWMAN, *Present Position of Catholics in England,* 1851

In word indeed, and in idea, it is easy enough to divide Knowledge into human and divine, secular and religious, and to lay down that we will address ourselves to the one without interfering with the other; but it is impossible in fact.

JOHN HENRY NEWMAN, *The Idea of a University,* 1852

I am not one of those who deny a future life. I only say, in the words of my Master, "Our knowledge is of life and not of death," and where my knowledge cease my thoughts must cease.

GUNTHER in Berthold Auerbach's *On the Heights,* 1865

In every man there are latent faculties by means of which he can acquire for himself knowledge of the higher worlds.

RUDOLF STEINER, *The Way of Initiation,* 1910

All knowlege must be built on our intuitive beliefs; if they are rejected, nothing is left.

BERTRAND RUSSELL, *The Problems of Philosophy,* 1912

Knowledge is nothing but the continually burning up of error to set free the light of truth.

RABINDRANATH TAGORE, *Sādhāna,* 1913

Religious knowledge is the highest kind of knowledge, the end and coronation of the whole process of man's intellectual development.

CHRISTOPHER DAWSON, *Christianity and the New Age,* 1931

Faith seeps out as knowledge seeps down.

JOHN HAYNES HOLMES, *Religion Today,* ed. A. L. Swift, 1933

Philosophy seeks knowledge for the sake of understanding, while religion seeks knowledge for the sake of worship.

WILLIAM TEMPLE, *Nature, Man and God,* 1934

The fact that people have religious experiences is interesting from the psychological point of view, but it does not in any way imply that there is such a thing as religious knowledge. . . . Unless he can formulate his "knowledge" in propositions that are empirically verifiable, we may be sure that he is deceiving himself.

A. J. AYER, *Language, Truth and Logic,* 1936

Knowledge without religion will no more sanctify than painted fire will burn, or the sight of water cleanse.

JOHN A. O'BRIEN, *Religion—Does It Matter?,* 1944

It is a prejudice to believe that knowledge is always rational, that there is no such thing as irrational knowledge. Actually, we apprehend a great deal more through feeling than by intellection.

NICHOLAS BERDYAEV, *Solitude and Society,* 1947

According to Confucius, "Knowledge is the basic requisite for moral ends, and knowledge depends upon the investigation of things." This is strikingly similar to the modern empirical emphasis [in education].

CHARLES S. BRADEN, *The Scriptures of Mankind,* 1952

We know too much for one man to know much.

J. ROBERT OPPENHEIMER, *Address,* 1954

When scientists . . . claim that what is demonstrated by the scientific method is the only possible knowledge, their claim is foolish, and cannot but lead to protest and antagonism on the part of Christians.

ARTHUR F. SMETHHURST, *Modern Science and Christian Beliefs,* 1955

Unless there is human knowledge, which alone is capable of being in error, and for which man is responsible, the sin and evil of man's doing are God's responsibility rather than man's.

F. S. C. NORTHROP, *Man, Nature and God,* 1962

See also Agnosticism; Agnostics; Belief; Books; Education; Enlightenment; Error; Faith; Faith, Definitions of; Fall, the; God: Knowledge about Him; Ignorance; Intellect; Learning; Light; Meditation; Metaphysical; Metaphysician; Mind; Philosophy; Reality; Reason; Scholars; Science; Science and Religion; Self-Knowledge; Theology, Truth; Understanding; Values; Wisdom.

KORAN

Can they not consider the Koran? Were it from any other than God, they would have found in it many contradictions.

Koran, 7th century A.D.

The Revelation [sending down] of this Book is from the Mighty, the Wise. . . . As for those whom ye invoke beside God, show me what part of the earth it is which they have created? . . . Bring me a Book sent down by *them,* before this Koran.

Koran, 7th century A.D.

It [the Koran] was not the Prophet who spoke under the influence of the Holy Spirit; it was a Divine Message brought by the Holy Spirit or Gabriel, and delivered in words to the Holy Prophet, who delivered it to Mankind.

MUHAMED ALI, *The Religion of Islam,* 1936

Muslims have always deprecated and at times prohibited any attempt to render it in another language. Anyone who has read it in the original is forced to admit that this caution seems justified; no translation, however faithful to the meaning, has ever been successful. . . . The Arabic of the Qur'ān is by turns striking, soaring, vivid, terrible, tender and breathtaking.

JOHN ALDEN WILLIAMS, *Islam,* 1961

See also Islam.

KRISHNA

But thou canst not behold Me with this [human] eye of yours; I will bestow on thee the supernatural eye. Behold my divine power.

LORD KRISHNA speaking in the *Bhagavad-Gita,* 2nd century B.C.

Yea! I have seen! I see!
Lord! all is wrapped in Thee,
The gods are in Thy glorious frame! the creatures
Of earth and heaven and hell
In Thy Divine form dwell
And in Thy countenance show all the features
Of Brahma, sitting lone
Upon His Lotus-throne. . . .
Yea Infinite King, I see.

ARJUNA'S speech, *Bhagavad-Gita,* 5th to 2nd century B.C.

I make and unmake this universe;
Than Me there is no other Master, Prince!
No other maker! All these hang on me
As hangs a row of pearls upon its string.
I am the fresh taste of water; I
The silver moon, the gold o' the sun,
The word of worship in the Vedas, the thrill
That passeth in the ether, and the strength
Of man's shed seed. I am the good sweet smell
Of the moistened earth, I am the fire's red light
The vital moving in all which moves,
The holiness of hallowed souls, the root
Undying, whence hath sprung whatever is,
The wisdom of the wise, the intellect

Of the informed, the greatness of the
great,
The splendor of the splendid. . . .
> Krishna speaking in *The Song Celestial,*
> Sir Edwin Arnold's translation of the
> *Bhagavad-Gita,* 5th to 2nd century B.C.

Krishna rises to the highest point of development, of course, in the *Bhagavad-Gita,* which has become India's most popular scripture, read and loved quite beyond sectarian limits. . . . It is at this level that he stands on a plane where he may be compared to Jesus, the Christ.
> CHARLES S. BRADEN, *Jesus Compared, A Study of Jesus and Other Great Founders of Religion,* 1957

See also Avatara.

LABOR

Unemployment is inimical to spiritual health; and for this reason the brothers ought to occupy themselves for a certain number of hours a day in doing manual work and, for a certain number, in reading works of divinity.
> SAINT BENEDICT, *Rule of,* ch. XLVIII, c. 530

He who labors as he prays lifts his heart to God with his hands.
> ST. BERNARD OF CLAIRVAUX, *Ad Sororem,* c. 1130

Labor, as well as fasting, serves to mortify and subdue the flesh. Provided the labor you undertake contributes to the glory of God and your own welfare, I would prefer that you should suffer the pain of labor rather than that of fasting.
> ST. FRANCIS OF SALES, *Introduction to the Devout Life,* 1609

Labor we all earnestly in the wages of some lawful calling, that we may have our portion of this world by good means.
> JOHN DONNE, *Sermons,* no. 65, 1640

The Author of our nature has written it strongly in that nature, and has promulgated the same law in His written word, that man shall eat his bread by his labor; and I am persuaded that no man, and no combination of men, can, without great impiety, undertake to say that he *shall not* do so—that they have no sort of right either to prevent the labor or to withhold the bread.
> EDMUND BURKE, *Second Letter to Gentlemen in Bristol,* 1777

Manual labor is a blessing and a dignity. . . . If it be glorious as the world fancies to repel a human foe, how much more is he to be honored who stands up when Want comes upon us, like an armed man, and puts him to rout!
> THEODORE PARKER, *Thoughts on Labor,* 1841

To lift up the hands in prayer gives God glory, but a man with a dungfork in his hand, a woman with a sloppail, give him glory too. He is so great that all things give him glory if you mean they should. So then, my brethren, live.
> GERARD MANLEY HOPKINS (1844–1889), *An Address on St. Ignatius*

We have either to translate *laborare est orare* into modern English and mould our civilization upon it, or else acknowledge as pretentious survivals every remaining bastion of the Christian culture.
> J. H. OLDHAM, *The Church and the Disorder of Society,* 1948

See also Capitalism; Economics and Christianity; Employees; Employment; Labor's Rights; Labor Unions; Wages; Work.

LABOR'S RIGHTS

The rights and interests of the laboring man will be protected and cared for, not by labor agitators, but by the Christian men to whom God in His infinite wisdom has given the control of the property interests of the country.

> GEORGE F. BAER (President of the Philadelphia and Reading Railway), *Letter to Rev. W. F. Clark,* July 17, 1902

If democracy in government may be made the object of a crusade, the workers' demand for a voice in the control of their working life cannot be opposed consistently by those who profess a Christian ethical standard.

> FEDERAL COUNCIL OF CHURCHES OF CHRIST IN AMERICA, *Statement,* Labor Day, 1929

Unless a man apply his labor to his own property, an alliance must be formed between his toil and his neighbor's property, for each is helpless without the other. . . . It is flagrantly unjust that either should deny the efficacy of the other and seize all the profits.

> POPE PIUS XI, *Quadragesimo Anno,* 1931

When labor is denied the right of free choice of representatives and when employers refuse to deal with representatives so chosen, the spirit and purpose of justice and democracy are thwarted.

> EXECUTIVE COMMITTEE, FEDERAL COUNCIL OF CHURCHES OF CHRIST IN AMERICA, *Report,* 1934

Christian charity demands the recognition of certain rights due to the workingman, which the Church has explicitly acknowledged.

> PIUS XI, *Atheistic Communism,* 1937

It is not intended that labor should assume responsibility for the direction of business, beyond its own competency or legitimate interest; nor has labor a right to demand dominating control over the distribution of profits. To set up such claims would amount to an infringement of the rights of property.

> BISHOPS OF ADMINISTRATIVE BOARD OF NATIONAL CATHOLIC WELFARE COUNCIL, *The Church and Social Order,* 1940

See also Employees; Employers; Labor; Labor Unions; Wages.

LABOR UNIONS

The strongest bond of human sympathy, outside of the family relation, should be one uniting all working people, of all nations, of all tongues, and kindreds. Nor should this lead to a war upon property, or the owners of property.

> ABRAHAM LINCOLN, to a Committee from the New York Workingmen's Assn., March 2, 1864

It would be a great folly on our part if we kept aloof from this movement merely because it happens at the present time to be promoted chiefly by men who are hostile to Christianity.

> W. E. VON KETTELER, *Christianity and the Labor Question,* 1864

Unionism is not merely legitimate in itself and worthy of our support, but Christianity alone commands the indispensable elements for directing it properly and making it a real and lasting benefit to the working class.

> W. E. VON KETTELER, *Christianity and the Labor Question,* 1864

We may lay it down as a general and lasting law that workmen's associations should be so organized and governed as to furnish the best and most suitable means for attaining what is aimed at, that is to say, for helping each individual member to better his condition to the utmost in body, mind and property.

> POPE LEO XIII, *Rerum Novarum,* 1891

Trade unionism should be accepted not as the church's enemy but as the church's ally.
> F. M. NORTH, *Address,* Philadelphia, Pa., Federal Council of Churches of Christ in America, 1908

The attitude of the church toward trade unionism should not be sympathetic; . . . poverty is a safer moral condition than inordinate wealth.
> CHARLES W. ELIOT (1836–1926), *Letter to C. S. Macfarland,* quoted in Macfarland's *Across the Years*

I have found more genuine love for individuals and people in the labor movement than I have found in the Church itself as an institution.
> ELLIS VAN RIPER, *Man at Work in God's World,* ed. G. E. DeMille, 1955

The labor world has need of and has the right to be penetrated by the Christian spirit.
> POPE PAUL VI, *Address,* April 18, 1964

See also Employees; Employment; Labor; Labor's Rights; Wages.

LAISSEZ-FAIRE

I expect nothing from the advocate of laissez-faire—the pedants whose glory is in the shame of society, who arrogantly talk of economic science so completely perfected, so universal and all important that common humanity and morality, reason and religion must be pooh-poohed down, if they seem to interfere with its infallible conclusions.
> CHARLES KINGSLEY, *Cheap Clothes and Nasty Clothes,* 1850

See also Capitalism; Competition; Profit.

LAITY

Antiquity teaches us that laymen are in a high degree hostile to the clergy.
> POPE BONIFACE VIII, *Clericis Laicos,* 1296

It belongs rather to the laity to manifest the immanence of Christianity by throwing themselves into the business of this world and acting there like Christians.
> JACQUES MARITAIN, *Questions of Conscience,* 1938

The laity must above all have a conviction ever more and more exact, not only of belonging to the Church, but of being the Church.
> POPE PIUS XII, *Address,* February, 1946

The lay apostolate is subordinate to the ecclesiastical hierarchy, which is of divine institution; therefore it cannot be independent of it.
> POPE PIUS XII, *Address,* October 14, 1951

It is by giving the laity wider and wider responsibilities, and by associating them ever more closely with the work of the hierarchy, that the profound transformation indispensable to the Christianization of the modern world will be brought about.
> EMMANUEL SUHARD, *The Church Today,* 1953

By accepting their responsibilities, the laity will cease to provoke the clergy to intervene in a domain where they have no business.
> YVES DE MONTCHEYIL, *For Men of Action,* 1954

The lay apostolate must be truly *lay.* The thinking, the planning, the carrying out of this tremendous task of mediation belongs to the laymen. They must have autonomy in this field, limited surely by the authority of the hierarchical apostolate, but nonetheless real.
> JOHN F. MURPHY, *Sanctity and Success in Marriage,* 1956

The relations between the Church and the world demand the presence of lay apostles. The *consecratio mundi* (consecration of the world) is in its essence the task of laymen.

POPE PIUS XII, *Address,* Second World Congress of the Lay Apostolate, 1957

When lay people are kept in tutelage and treated more or less as children, they become as indifferent to the Church's faith as to her life.

YVES CONGAR, *Laity, Church and World,* 1960

The layman is at the frontier where the church meets the world. It is he primarily who must penetrate the secular order with the Gospel.

ROSWELL P. BARNES, *Under Orders,* 1961

The role of the laity is not merely to support the church as an institution, but to *be* the church—the church in its relation to secular society.

SAMUEL MCCREA CAVERT, *On the Road to Christian Unity,* 1961

Laymen are members of the people of God called to a total ministry of witness and service in the world. This is what in the New Testament sense a laymen is.

GEORGIA HARKNESS, *The Church and Its Laity,* 1962

Not only do lay people, by virtue of their state, have experience and competence which no priest can hope to have, but it is also true that some laymen of the Church can be found to have a greater knowledge and understanding of the mind of the Church, as well as a greater sanctity and closeness to God, than many a priest.

PAUL-EMILE LEGER, *Sign Magazine,* October, 1962.

From the viewpoint of the layman steeped in recent Catholic thought, possessed of the critical faculties which result from a successful university training, zealous to use his talents in the service of the Church, eager to bring his faith to bear on his secular life, much of what he sees in the Church can only be depressing, frustrating and disillusioning.

DANIEL CALLAHAN, *The Mind of the Catholic Layman,* 1963

The layman is urged to be a free man in society; but if he observes how reliant some bishops and priests are upon docile laymen, how alarmed they become when faced with even a respectful challenge to their wisdom, then it is difficult for the layman to believe that much store is set by freedom—within the Church or outside.

DANIEL CALLAHAN, *The Mind of the Catholic Layman,* 1963

The laity, by their very vocation, seek the kingdom of God by engaging in temporal affairs and by ordering them according to the plan of God. . . . They are called there by God that by exercising their proper function and led by the spirit of the Gospel they may work for the sanctification of the world from within as a leaven. . . . As those everywhere who adore in holy activity, the laity consecrate the world itself to God.

Constitution on the Church, SECOND VATICAN COUNCIL, November, 1964

They [the laity] are, by reason of the knowledge, competence or outstanding ability which they may enjoy, permitted and sometimes even obliged to express their opinion on those things which concern the good of the Church. . . . When occasions arise, let this be done through the organs erected by the Church for this purpose. Let it always be done in truth, in courage and in prudence.

Constitution on the Church, SECOND VATICAN COUNCIL, November, 1964

See also Church: Its Membership; Clergy; Clergy, Criticism of; Leadership; Priesthood.

LAPSES

Is it a chance coincidence that adolescence and the second half of the second decade are peak periods for abandoning the practice of religion? Is it not possible to consider these lapses as . . . psychological phenomena linked with the period of rebellion and rejection?

> J. DOMINIAN, *Psychiatry and the Christian,* 1962

LAUGHTER

God is the creator of laughter that is good.
> PHILO, *The Worse Attacks the Better,* 33 A.D.

Laughter does not seem to be a sin, but it leads to sin.
> ST. JOHN CHRYSOSTOM, *Homilies,* c. 388

There is a kind of smiling and joyful laughter, for anything I know, which may stand with sober gravity, and with the best man's piety.
> RICHARD BERNARD, *The Isle of Man,* 1626

He who laughs at everything is as big a fool as he who weeps at everything.
> BALTASAR GRACIÁN, *The Art of Worldly Wisdom,* 1647

Laughter is the hiccup of a fool.
> JOHN RAY, *English Proverbs,* 1670

Laughter is satanic, and, therefore, profoundly human. It is born of Man's conception of his own superiority. . . . It is at once a sign of infinite grandeur and of infinite wretchedness; of infinite wretchedness by comparison with the absolute Being who exists as an idea in Man's mind; of an infinite grandeur by comparison with the animals.
> CHARLES BAUDELAIRE, *The Essence of Laughter,* 1855

If any laughter of ours does make us incapable of weeping, incapable of entering into the sorrow of the world in which we are dwelling, we ought to feel that there is misery and death in that laughter.
> FREDERICK D. MAURICE (1805–1870), *Sermons*

It is the heart that is not yet sure of its God that is afraid to laugh in His presence.
> GEORGE MACDONALD, *Sir Gibbie,* 1879

Jesus pities not all those who laugh, but those who do nothing else but laugh.
> LYMAN ABBOTT, *Christ's Secret of Happiness,* 1907

Weep before God—laugh before people.
> Proverb

See also Amusements; Happiness; Joy; Pleasure; Weeping.

LAW

It maketh things smooth, it checketh inordinate desires, it dimmeth the glare of wanton pride and withereth the budding bloom of wild delusions; it maketh crooked judgments straight and softeneth arrogant behavior. . . . Under the reign of law sanity and wisdom prevail ever among men.
> SOLON (c. 638–558 B.C.), quoted in I. M. Linforth's *Solon the Athenian*

All human laws are fed by the one Divine law; it prevaileth as far as it listeth, and sufficeth for all, and surviveth all.
> HERACLITUS (535–475 B.C.), *Fragments*

True law is right reason in agreement with nature; it is of universal application, unchanging and everlasting.
> CICERO, *De Republica,* c. 50 B.C.

The law of the kingdom is law.
> *Talmud,* between 2nd and 4th century A.D.

Law is the gift of God, the model of equity, a standard of justice, a likeness of the divine will, the guardian of well-being, a bond of union and solidarity between peoples, a rule defining duties, a barrier against vices and the destroyer thereof, a punishment of violence and all wrong-doing.

> JOHN OF SALISBURY, *Policraticus*, 1159

Human law has the true nature of law only in so far as it corresponds to right reason, and therefore is derived from the eternal law. In so far as it falls short of right reason, a law is said to be a wicked law; and so, lacking the true nature of law, it is rather a kind of violence.

> ST. THOMAS AQUINAS, *Summa Theologiae*, Ia–IIae, q. 93, 1272

The application of legal sanctions is one of the acts of God's mercy, so that the ruler . . . have mercy on God's creatures by deterring men from things rejected by God.

> IBN-TAYMĪYA (died 1328 A.D.), *al-Siyasa al-Shar-īya*

There never was any remarkable lawgiver amongst any people who did not resort to divine authority, as otherwise his laws would not have been accepted by the people.

> NICCOLÒ MACHIAVELLI, *The Prince*, 1513

If justice is the end of the law, the law the work of the prince, and the prince the image of God, it follows of necessity that the law of the prince should be modelled on the law of God.

> JEAN BODIN, *The Six Books of the Republic*, 1579

A distinction must be made between right and law. . . . Law is nothing else than the command of the sovereign in the exercise of his sovereign power. But to take the goods of their subjects at will is contrary to the law of God.

> JEAN BODIN, *The Six Books of the Republic*, 1579

Of Law there can be no less acknowledged, than that her seat is in the bosom of God, her voice the harmony of the world; all things in heaven do her homage.

> RICHARD HOOKER, *Laws of Ecclesiastical Polity*, 1585

A penny-weight of love is worth a pound of law.

> JAMES KELLY, *Complete Collection of Scottish Proverbs*, 1721

Where a law is enacted contrary to reason, or to the eternal law, or to some ordinance of God, obedience is unlawful, lest, while obeying man, we become disobedient to God.

> POPE LEO XIII, *Libertas Humana*, 1888

They who are engaged in framing constitutions and in enacting laws should bear in mind the moral and religious nature of man, and take care to help him, but in a right and orderly way, to gain perfection, neither enjoining nor forbidding anything save what is reasonably consistent with evil as well as with religious requirements.

> POPE LEO XIII, *Sapientiae Christianae*, 1890

The law that will work is merely the summing up in legislative form of the moral judgment that the community has already reached.

> WOODROW WILSON, *Address*, December, 1915

No Law, apart from a Lawgiver, is a proper object of reverence. It is mere brute fact.

> WILLIAM TEMPLE, *Nature, Man and God*, 1934

Juridical positivism . . . invests purely human laws with a majesty to which they have no title, opening the way to a fatal dissociation of law from morality.

> POPE PIUS XII, *Christmas Message*, 1942

Law cannot restrain evil; for the freedom of man is such that he can make the keeping of the law the instrument of evil.

REINHOLD NIEBUHR, *The Nature and Destiny of Man,* II, 1943

The obligation of repressing moral and religious offenses cannot be an ultimate norm of action. It must be subordinated to higher and more generous norms which, in certain circumstances, allow and even perhaps make it obvious that it is better not to prevent error in order to bring about a greater good.

POPE PIUS XII, *Address,* December, 1953

The function of civil law is not to teach theology or even the moral views of the legislator. . . . The morality of divorce, birth control, liquor traffic and the like are one thing. Civil legislation about them is quite another.

GUSTAVE WEIGEL, *Catholic Theology in Dialogue,* 1960

Our legal system would be rendered useless and void if men refused to obey the laws, and the axiom "You can't legislate morality" were accepted.

JOSEPH T. LEONARD, *Theology and Race Relations,* 1963

See also Commandments; Conscience; Divine Law; Injustice; Justice; Moral Law; Morality and State; Natural Law; Obedience; Power; Rebellion; Rule; Rulers; Torah.

LEADERS

The would-be leader of men who affirms and proclaims that he pays no heed to the things of the spirit, is not worthy to lead them.

MIGUEL DE UNAMUNO, *Tragic Sense of Life,* 1921

We need men who are sometimes more than cunning manipulators of the political and economic machine, men who stand not for success or material efficiency, but

for the old Christian ideals of faith, hope and charity.

CHRISTOPHER DAWSON, *The Modern Dilemma,* 1932

What really exasperates the modern man (both outside and inside the Church), far more than the sins of her members, is the lack of any openness among the Church's leaders, at every level, towards new problems and insights, new forms and values; their narrowness, their procrastination.

HANS KÜNG, *The Council, Reform and Reunion,* 1961

See also Hierarchy.

LEADERSHIP

The Christian leadership has passed from the hands of the Church to the hands of the active and practical laity . . . the statesman and educator, the columnists and pundits, the scientists and great men of action. And this is another way of saying that there is no true Christian leadership at all.

Editorial, *Fortune,* January, 1940

Whether Christianity can be adequate to the moral leadership of our civilization today and tomorrow depends on whether it can recapture that "first, fine, careless rapture" of its earliest days.

KIRBY PAGE, *Living Joyously,* 1950

See also Laity.

LEARNING

A man not instructed through reason in philosophy and sound learning is a creature lower than a brute.

DESIDERIUS ERASMUS, *On the Education of Children,* 1516

Thou hast studied thyself but into a dark and damnable ignorance, if thou have labored for much learning only to prove that canst not be saved.

JOHN DONNE, *Sermon,* February 29, 1627

A handful of good life is better than a bushel of learning.
> GEORGE HERBERT, *Outlandish Proverbs,* 1641

The end of learning is to repair the ruins of our first parents by regaining to know God aright, and out of that knowledge to love him, to imitate him, to be like him.
> JOHN MILTON, *Of Education,* 1641

The love of learning and the love of money rarely meet.
> GEORGE HERBERT, *Jacula Prudentum,* 1651

Learning makes a good man better, and an ill man worse.
> THOMAS FULLER, *Gnomologia,* 1732

Learning and wisdom without moral purpose are unworthy of their lofty names.
> GEORGE N. SHUSTER, *Education and Moral Wisdom,* 1960

See also Ignorance; Knowledge; Philosophy; Reason; Wisdom.

LIARS AND LIES

Let none of you attend the liar's words and demands. He leads house, clan, district and country into misery and destruction. Resist them, then, with weapons.
> *Zend Avesta, Yasna,* xxxi, 6th century B.C., or earlier

If a man has transgressed one law, and speaks lies, and scoffs at another world, there is no evil he will not do.
> *Dhammapada,* c. 5th century B.C.

They who lie set the Lord at nought, and become defrauders of the Lord. . . . For they received from him a spirit free of lies.
> *Shepherd of Hermas,* c. 148 A.D.

Lying is wrong even to save chastity.
> ST. AUGUSTINE, *On Lying,* c. 395

It is not the lie that passeth through the mind, but the lie that sinketh in, and settleth in it, that doth the hurt.
> FRANCIS BACON, *Essays,* 1597

The most mischievous liars are those who keep sliding on the verge of truth.
> J. C. and A. W. HARE, *Guesses at Truth,* 1827

Every violation of truth is not only a sort of suicide in the liar, but is a stab at the health of human society.
> RALPH WALDO EMERSON, *Prudence,* 1841

Sin has many tools, but a lie is the handle which fits them all.
> O. W. HOLMES, *The Autocrat of the Breakfast Table,* 1858

See also Dishonesty; Hypocrisy; Integrity; Truth.

LIBERALISM

Liberalism may mean something good or something bad. There are no orthodox rationalists; but there may be orthodox liberals.
> VINCENT MCNABB, *From a Friar's Cell,* 1923

Modern liberalism is steeped in a religious optimism which is true to the facts of neither the world of nature nor the world of history.
> REINHOLD NIEBUHR, *Does Civilization Need Religion?,* 1927

As Liberalism did not create moral ideals, so, too, it cannot preserve them. It lives on the spiritual capital that it has inherited from Christian civilization, and as this is exhausted something else must take its place.
> CHRISTOPHER DAWSON, *Religion and the Modern State,* 1935

The Liberal faith, from the realms of science and metaphysics, had evolved two of its cardinal principles: Nature and Reason. In the construction of its social philosophy, both these precepts were applied and a third added: Humanity. These three—Nature, Reason, and Humanity—became the Trinity of the Liberal's world of ideas.

> JOHN EMMET HUGHES, *The Church and the Liberal Society,* 1944

Liberalism embodies an autonomous, self-sustaining conception of man's relationship to his God, his universe, his society. In this sense is Liberalism a faith, and by virtue of this fact it has been forced to fight other faiths.

> JOHN EMMET HUGHES, *The Church and the Liberal Society,* 1944

Humanitarian liberalism . . . owes its good qualities to what it has retained of the Christian ethic and its patent limitations to its religious and philosophic skepticism.

> AELRED GRAHAM, *Christian Thought and Action,* 1951

Our own Liberal States, . . . while professing that they are not the ultimate end of man, refuse to say what the ultimate end actually is.

> ÉTIENNE GILSON, *Ensign,* March, 1952

Since it itself recognizes that it is neither the Way, nor the Truth, nor the Life, the very least that the liberal State can do is not to shut up its future citizens from Him Who is the Way, the Truth and the Life.

> ÉTIENNE GILSON, *Ensign,* March, 1952

The breakdown of morals is a matter of life and death for the liberal State. After heedlessly squandering the Christian heritage on which it has lived so long a time, the day is now come when it has to make a choice: either to draw openly from all the sources of religious life and thus to survive, or else let them dry up and thus itself to perish.

> ÉTIENNE GILSON, *Ensign,* March, 1952

The uncomfortable, merciless and inexorable "No," a self-evident reality to the Christian, has been obliterated from the liberalistic world view.

> JOSEF PIEPER, *Fortitude and Temperance,* 1954

See also Determinism; Humanism; Irreligion; Liberalism and Religion; Liberals; Man, Modern; Materialism; Modernism; Naturalism; Optimism; Positivism; Progress; Rationalism; Secularism; State, the.

LIBERALISM AND RELIGION

Liberalism is the mistake of subjecting to human judgment those revealed doctrines which are in their nature beyond and independent of it.

> JOHN HENRY NEWMAN, *Apologia pro Vita Sua,* 1864

Liberalism . . . in religion is the doctrine that there is no positive truth in religion but that one creed is as good as another. . . . It is inconsistent with any recognition of any religion, as *true*.

> JOHN HENRY NEWMAN, "Biglietto Speech," on being raised to the Cardinalate, 1879

Liberal religion is symbolizing a totality of facts under the term God which orthodoxy, with a truer moral instinct, could comprehend under no less than two terms, God and the devil.

> REINHOLD NIEBUHR, *Christian Century,* April 22, 1926

At the very center of liberalism, as I understand it, is the conviction that nothing fundamentally matters in religion except those things which create private and public goodness.

> HARRY EMERSON FOSDICK, *Adventurous Religion,* 1926

The liberal ministers are a lot of Judases and deserve the fate of Judas. . . . They are a lot of pussyfooting, white-livered, yellow softies.

REV. WILLIAM A. (BILLY) SUNDAY, at Memphis, Tenn., January, 1932

Despite the liberal use of traditional phraseology modern liberalism not only is a different religion from Christianity, but belongs in a totally different class of religions. . . . It is not the Christianity of the New Testament which is in conflict with modern science, but the supposed Christianity of the modern liberal Church.

J. GRAHAM MACHEN, *Christianity and Liberalism*, 1934

Rationalistic liberalism as represented by the Deists in England, the rationalists of France and their few American followers, was as static in its conceptions and as self-righteous in its attitudes as the ecclesiastical orthodoxy it opposed.

H. RICHARD NIEBUHR, *The Kingdom of God in America*, 1937

The true spirit of liberalism cannot crystallize around specific doctrines and affirm them as final. It sees that in every doctrinal position which our finite intelligence can take there are both a Yes and a No—what it is now the fashion to call a dialectic.

Editorial, *Christian Century*, October 26, 1938

Christian liberalism . . . sought to liberate men, not from positive Christian convictions, but from blindly held convictions which would not cohere with the reasoned inquiry of a free mind.

GEORGIA HARKNESS, *The Modern Rival of Christian Faith*, 1953

Unable to make the Cross and the empty tomb theologically intelligible, Liberalism drifts into sentimentalism.

LESTER DE KOSTER, *Communism and Christian Faith*, 1956

Protestant liberalism expresses a deeply rooted conviction that science has some kind of divine mission to cleanse, even to purify Christian thought.

M. HOLMES HARTSHORNE, *The Promise of Science and the Power of Faith*, 1958

It is typical of liberalism that knowledge of God is said to rest on experience rather than on rational argument.

KENNETH CAUTHEN, *The Impact of Religious Liberalism*, 1962

The unexamined traditional faiths of the past are becoming rapidly irrelevant today, and it is our particular opportunity and responsibility as liberals to lead in the formulation of a new approach to faith.

DONALD S. HARRINGTON, *Sermon, New York Times*, March 5, 1962

See also Humanism; Liberalism; Liberals; Modernism; Secularism.

LIBERALITY

Of all the varieties of virtue, liberality is the most beloved.

ARISTOTLE, *The Nicomachean Ethics*, c. 340 B.C.

Liberality consists less in giving much than in giving at the right moment.

JEAN DE LA BRUYÈRE, *Caractères*, 1688

See also Almsgiving; Charity.

LIBERALS

Though there have undoubtedly been bigoted persons who professed to be liberals, a dogmatic self-opinionated liberal is a contradiction in terms.

GEORGIA HARKNESS, *The Modern Rival of Christian Faith*, 1953

The liberal mind turns faith into a philosophic attitude, takes away all its supernatural characteristics, and then divests it of its religious quality.

ALBERT DONDEYNE, *Tolerance and the Catholic,* 1955

The Church is a scandal to the liberals by its pedestrian insistence upon personal holiness, upon inner reform, upon family and neighborhood values.

JOHN LA FARGE, *An American Amen,* 1958

See also Liberalism; Liberalism and Religion.

LIBERATION

And being indifferent he becomes free from passion, by absence of passion is he liberated, and when he is liberated the knowledge "I am liberated" arises. Rebirth is destroyed, a religious life is lived, duty is done, and he knows there is nothing more for him in this state.

Vinaya, Mahavagga, between 5th and 1st century B.C.

The liberation of the individual soul is therefore the keynote of the definite divine action; it is the primary divine necessity.

SRI AUROBINDO, *The Life Divine,* 1949

LIBERTIES

The liberties we talk about defending today were established by men who took their conception of man from the great religious tradition of Western civilization, and the liberties we inherit can almost certainly not survive the abandonment of that tradition.

WALTER LIPPMANN, New York *Herald Tribune,* December 16, 1938

See also Freedom; Rights.

LIBERTY. See FREEDOM

LIBIDO

The psycho-analyst is satisfied with the theory that religious beliefs are produced by disused, displaced and projected libido.

CAVENDISH MOXON, *Freudian Essays on Religion and Science,* 1925

See also Psychoanalysis; Sexual Desire.

LIFE

The evil life is really the *thoughtless* life.

Dhammapada, c. 5th century B.C.

Life is neither a good nor an evil, but simply the scene of good and evil.

SENECA, *Epistulae Morales ad Lucilium,* c. 63 A.D.

Life is warfare, and the sojourn of a stranger in a strange land.

MARCUS AURELIUS, *Meditations,* c. 170

Human life! Its duration is momentary, its substance in perpetual flux, its senses dim, its physical organism perishable, its consciousness a vortex, its destiny dark.

MARCUS AURELIUS, *Meditations,* c. 170

If we survey life on every side, how greatness and beauty have everywhere the prerogative, we shall straightway perceive the end for which we were created.

LONGINUS, *On the Sublime,* c. 250

That life which is ours, that is, the life of our own free will, is only evil, sinning, and full of iniquity; our real life, true life, is from God, not from ourselves.

ST. AUGUSTINE, *In Johann. Evang.,* tract. xxii.6, c. 416

Know that the life of the world is only play, and idle talk, and pageantry, and boasting among you, and rivalry in respect of wealth and children.

Koran, c. 610–632 A.D.

The present life of man, O king, seems to me . . . like to the swift flight of a sparrow through the room wherein you sit at supper in winter. . . . Whilst the storms of rain and snow prevail abroad; the sparrow, I say, flying in at one door, and immediately out at another, whilst he is within, is safe from the wintry storm; but after a short space of fair weather, he immediately vanished out of your sight, into the dark winter from which he had emerged. So this life of man appears for a short space, but of what went before, or what is to follow, we are utterly ignorant.

> One of King Edwin's men, recounted by Venerable Bede in his *Ecclesiastical History of the English Nation,* 731

The life of man here on earth is a warfare; and as long as we do battle in this body, we are absent from the Lord,—i.e., from the light.

> ST. BERNARD OF CLAIRVAUX (1901–1153), *Sermon on Death of Gerard*

One person who has mastered life is better than a thousand persons who have mastered only the contents of books, but no one can get anything out of life without God.

> MEISTER ECKHART (1260?–1322?), *Meister Eckhart,* translated by R. B. Blakney

I love my life supremely because Thou art my life's sweetness.

> NICHOLAS OF CUSA (1401–1464), *The Vision of God*

Life's but a walking shadow, a poor player
That struts and frets his hour upon the stage,
And then is heard no more: it is a tale
Told by an idiot, full of sound and fury,
Signifying nothing.

> WILLIAM SHAKESPEARE, *Macbeth,* c. 1606

Life is a pure flame, and we live by an invisible sun within us.

> THOMAS BROWNE, *Urn Burial,* 1658

Life is an incurable disease.

> ABRAHAM COWLEY (1618–1667), "To Dr. Scarborough," *Poems*

Between us and Hell or Heaven there is nothing but life, which of all things is the frailest.

> BLAISE PASCAL, *Pensées,* 1670

If we reckon up only those days which God hath accepted of our lives, a life of good years will hardly be a span long.

> THOMAS BROWNE (1605–1682), *A Letter to a Friend*

The life of a man is of greater value with God than many pounds, and ought to be so with men.

> JOHN BELLERS, *Essays,* 1699

Life protracted is protracted woe.

> SAMUEL JOHNSON, *The Vanity of Human Wishes,* 1749

Human life is everywhere a state in which much is to be endured, and little to be enjoyed.

> SAMUEL JOHNSON, *Rasselas,* II, 1759

Has creation a final goal? And if so, why was it not reached at once? Why was the consummation not realized from the beginning? To these questions there is not one answer: God is *Life,* and not merely being. All life has a *fate,* and is subject to suffering and to becoming. To this, then, God has of his own free will subjected himself.

> F. W. VON SCHELLING, *Untersuchungen über das Wesen der Menschlichen Freiheit,* 1809

Life is the one universal soul, which by virtue of the enlivening Breath, and the informing Word, all organized bodies have in common, each after its kind.

> SAMUEL TAYLOR COLERIDGE, *Aids to Reflection,* 1825

The mingled, mingling threads of life are woven by warp and woof: calms crossed by storms, a storm for every calm. There is no steady unretracing in this life.

> HERMAN MELVILLE, *Moby Dick,* 1851

The chessboard is the world, the pieces are the phenomena of the universe, the rules of the game are what we call the laws of Nature. The player on the other side is hidden from us. We know that his play is always fair, just and patient. But also we know, to our cost, that he never overlooks a mistake, or makes the smallest allowance for ignorance.

THOMAS H. HUXLEY, *Lay Sermons,* 1870

Life is the continuous adjustment of internal relations to external relations.

HERBERT SPENCER, *Principles of Biology,* 1872

Life in its essence cannot be conceived in physico-chemical terms.

HERBERT SPENCER, *Principles of Biology,* 1872

Life is not a set campaign, but an irregular work, and the main forces in it are not overt resolutions, but latent and half-involuntary promptings.

WALTER BAGEHOT, *Physics and Politics,* 1876

Life itself is *essentially* appropriation, injury, conquest of the strange and weak, suppression, severity, obtrusion of peculiar forms, incorporation, and at the least, putting it mildest, exploitation.

FRIEDRICH NIETZSCHE, *Beyond Good and Evil,* 1886

Be not afraid of life. Believe that life *is* worth living and your belief will help create the fact.

WILLIAM JAMES, *The Will to Believe and Other Essays,* 1896

Not God but life, more life, a larger, richer, more satisfying life, is, in the last analysis, the end of religion. The love of life, at any and every level of development, is the religious impulse.

J. LEUBA, *Monist,* XI, 1901

Life . . . is a combat without grandeur, without happiness, fought in solitude and silence.

ROMAIN ROLLAND, *Beethoven,* 1903

Life is one long process of getting tired.

SAMUEL BUTLER, *Notebooks of,* ed. H. F. Jones, 1912

Life is the art of drawing sufficient conclusions from insufficient premises.

SAMUEL BUTLER, *Notebooks of,* ed. H. F. Jones, 1912

Young and generous souls are, and ought to be, intensely conscious of life. Nothing could convince them, nothing should convince them, that life is not their immediate concern.

JOHN OMAN, *Grace and Personality,* 1919

All real life is meeting.

MARTIN BUBER, *I and Thou,* 1923

Our lives are merely strange dark interludes in the electrical display of God the Father!

EUGENE O'NEILL, *Strange Interlude,* 1928

Life is a battle in which we fall from the wounds we receive in running away.

WILLIAM L. SULLIVAN, *Epigrams and Criticisms in Miniature,* 1936

We may *assume* that the first primitive forms of life *must* have arisen from non-living matter.

R. BEUTNER, *Life's Beginning on Earth,* 1938

Life is as evanescent as autumnal clouds, as the light of an oilless lamp, and as the ripples on the surface of water.

YOGAVASISTHA, in B. L. Atreya's *The Yogavasistha and Its Philosophy,* 1939

Life, even the hardest life, is the most beautiful, wonderful, and miraculous treasure in the world.

PITIRIM A. SOROKIN, *The Ways and Power of Love,* 1954

That it "must" have originated from matter is based on nothing more scientific than personal disinclination to admit the possibility of a nonmaterial source.

FRANZ E. WINKLER, *Man: The Bridge Between Two Worlds,* 1960

See also Christian Life; Creation; Death; Eternal Life; Evolution; Existence; Faith; Fall, the; Immortality; Life: Its Meaning; Life and Death; Modern Life; Nature and God; Religion, Definitions of; Spiritual Life; Suicide.

LIFE, ARTIFICIAL PRODUCTON OF

The artificial production of a life cell . . . will not weaken but will rather strengthen the traditional belief that an Intelligent Being created life. For . . . an intelligent being, a scientist, will deliberately bring the necessary elements together for the purpose of making a living cell. And that is exactly what religious thinkers have always said: that an Intelligent Being purposely synthesized the elements which He created to form living bodies.

SIMON SCANLON, *Way,* September, 1961

LIFE: ITS MEANING

Not life, but a good life, is to be chiefly valued.

PLATO, "Crito," *Dialogues,* 399 B.C.

As the mother's womb holds us for ten months, making us ready, not for the womb itself, but for life, just so, through our lives, we are making ourselves ready for another birth.

SENECA, *Epistulae ad Lucilium, Epis.* c. 11, sec. 23, c. 63 A.D.

The sole purpose of life in time is to gain merit for life in eternity.

ST. AUGUSTINE (354–430), *Letter 130*

Our life in this world is like the ladder which Jacob saw in his dream; in order to reach Heaven it must be planted by the Lord in a humbled heart. We can only mount it by distinct steps of humility and discipline.

ST. BENEDICT, *Rule of,* c. 530

Life is to live in such a way as not to be afraid to die.

ST. TERESA OF ÁVILA, *Foundations,* 1560

O life, enemy of my happiness, wherefore is it forbidden me to escape thee? I suffer thee because God suffers thee; I embrace thee because thou art His.

ST. TERESA OF ÁVILA (1515–1582), *Exclamation,* XVII

God hath made this life a Bridge to Heaven. It is but a giddy, and a vertiginous thing to stand long gazing upon so narrow a bridge, and over so deep and roaring waters, and desperate whirlpools, as this world abounds with.

JOHN DONNE, *Sermon,* February 11, 1627

God hath given to man a short time here upon earth, and yet upon this short time eternity depends.

JEREMY TAYLOR, *Holy Living,* 1650

For if it be true that man is upon his trial, if the trial is for Eternity, if life is but a vapor, what is there that deserves a serious thought but how to get well out of the world, and make it a right passage to our eternal state?

WILLIAM LAW, *Christian Perfection,* 1726

Life is surely given us for higher purposes than to gather what our ancestors have wisely thrown away.

SAMUEL JOHNSON, *The Rambler,* May 14, 1751

Life is given to us on the definite understanding that we boldly defend it to the last.

CHARLES DICKENS, *The Chimes,* 1844

To be what we are, and to become what we are capable of becoming, is the only end of life.

ROBERT LOUIS STEVENSON, *Familiar Studies of Men and Books,* 1881

The question which divides us, to know whether we live in vain, imposes itself upon every conscious being who breathes. That So-and-So never speaks of it, never thinks of it, may be: but their lives answer for them and testify loudly enough.

PAUL DESJARDINS, *The Present Duty,* 1892

Only if we suppose that the present life of human beings has an end which lies in part beyond the limits of the present natural order . . . can we find a rational meaning and explanation for human life as we see it.

HASTINGS RASHDALL, *The Theory of Good and Evil,* II, 1907

The great use of a life is to spend it for something that outlasts it.

WILLIAM JAMES (1842–1910), quoted in *Thought and Character of William James,* by Ralph Barton Perry

Nothing can be meaner than the anxiety to live on, to live on anyhow and in any shape; a spirit without any honor is not willing to live except in its own way, and a spirit with any wisdom is not over-eager to live at all.

GEORGE SANTAYANA, *Winds of Doctrine,* 1913

The grandest thing next to the radiance that flows from the Almighty Throne, is the light of a noble and beautiful life wrapping itself in benediction round the

destinies of men, and finding its home in the bosom of the everlasting God.

JOHN TEMPLE GRAVES (1856–1925), *Selected Orations*

Our life becomes meaningless and our efforts vain unless we can as far as possible live the life of immortals and think of ourselves as actively co-operating in a scheme which is somehow good.

J. A. SPENDER, *The Public Life,* 1925

If we have to play the game of life, we cannot do so with the conviction that the play is a show and all the prizes in it mere blanks.

RADHADRISHNAN, *Indian Philosophy,* II, 463, 1927

The man who regards life . . . as meaningless is not merely unfortunate but almost disqualified for life.

ALBERT EINSTEIN, *The World As I See It,* 1934

The spiritual life, in addition to the enrichment of our personal life, also commits us to the social life of the Kingdom of God.

FULTON J. SHEEN, *The Fullness of Christ,* 1935

To love life is to love the gods, and in obeying the will-to-live we are fulfilling divine orders. Or why else is the instinct to be found in all creatures as they set forth on their great expedition?

WILLIAM MACNEILE DIXON, *The Human Situation,* 1937

If life is an end in itself, then why do all singular lives conclude in a confession of futility?

PAUL ELMER MORE, *Pages from an Oxford Diary,* 1937

Life is meant to be lived from a Center, a divine Center. . . . There is a divine

Abyss within us all, a holy Infinite Center, a Heart, a Life who speaks in us and through us to the world.

THOMAS R. KELLEY, *A Testament of Devotion,* 1941

Life cannot be "a tale told by an idiot, full of sound and fury, signifying nothing." Why? Because God is infinite wisdom and the work of His hands cannot be without meaning or purpose.

JOHN A. O'BRIEN, *The Test of Courage,* 1943

There is no life if man does not know in whose name he ought to live and to whose glory he ought to work.

JOSEPH L. HROMADKA, *Doom and Resurrection,* 1945

We have come from God in the forgotten past, and are on our way back to him in the distant future, so that here and now our life is one of exile and pilgrimage.

ALAN W. WATTS, *Myth and Ritual in Christianity,* 1948

The question of the Good Life—both the question what it is and the question how it can be found, has to do, first of all, not with human institutions, but with the human being himself.

JOSEPH WOOD KRUTCH, *The Desert Year,* 1951

A man has made at least a start on discovering the meaning of human life when he plants shade trees under which he knows full well he will never sit.

D. E. TRUEBLOOD, *The Life We Prize,* 1951

The ultimate meaning of one's own life and of all life, is a matter of faith, even where one's faith is simply that no such meaning whatever is possible.

M. HOLMES HARTSHORNE, *The Promise of Science and the Power of Faith,* 1958

Each of us has a life to live and we shall want to spend it as well as may be . . . as alert, fair, concerned citizens of a complicated human world, aware in some fashion of God's high purpose for this earth of ours, eager to have a part in His plan for it, and to find joy in the process.

NATHAN M. PUSEY, *Baccalaureate Address,* Harvard Class of 1962

If we believe in the goodness of God, the purposefulness of God, the reasonableness of God, we believe that there is a meaningfulness in life.

HYMAN J. SCHACHTEL, *The Shadowed Valley,* 1962

It is to death life owes its seriousness. A life which ended in nothingness would have nothing serious about it . . . would be a game.

JACQUES LECLERCQ, *Christ and the Modern Conscience,* 1963

See also Death; Eternal Life; Immortality; Life; Life and Death; Religion: Its Nature and Function; Spiritual Life.

LIFE AND DEATH

What is life but the flower or the fruit which falls, when ripe, but yet which ever fears the untimely frost?

Dhammapada, c. 5th century B.C.

Life is nothing but a journey to death.

SENECA, *Ad Polybium de consolatione,* c. 44 A.D.

Our religion hath had no surer humane foundation, than the contempt of life. . . . Why should we fear to lose a thing, which being lost, cannot be moaned?

MICHEL DE MONTAIGNE, *Essays,* xix, 1580

Though our natural life were no life, but rather a continual dying, yet we have two lives besides that, an eternal life reserved for heaven, but yet a heavenly life too, a spiritual life, even in this world.

JOHN DONNE, *Sermon,* January 29, 1625

Our critical day is not the very day of our death; but the whole course of our life.

JOHN DONNE, *Sermon,* February 29, 1627

In the midst of life we are in death.
Book of Common Prayer, 1662

When all is done, human life is, at the greatest and the best, but like a forward child that must be played with and humored a little to keep it quiet till it falls asleep, and then the care is over.

WILLIAM TEMPLE, *Essays: Of Poetry,* c. 1690

Life, like a dome of many-coloured glass,
Stains the white radiance of Eternity,
Until Death tramples it to fragments.

PERCY BYSSHE SHELLEY, *Adonais,* 1820

What is this world? A dream within a dream—as we grow older each step is an awakening. The Grave the last sleep?—no; it is the last and final awakening.

WALTER SCOTT (1771–1832), *Journal*

A little gleam of time between two eternities; no second chance to us forever more!

THOMAS CARLYLE, *Heroes and Hero Worship,* 1841

Rejoice in this dark hour that thy life dwells in the midst of a wider and larger life.

JEAN PAUL RICHTER, *Reminiscences of the Best Hours of Life,* 1841

The fate of the poor shepherd, who, blinded and lost in the snowstorm, perishes in a drift within a few feet of the cottage door, is an emblem of the state of man. On the brink of the waters of life and truth, we are miserably dying.

RALPH WALDO EMERSON, *The Poet,* 1844

Life is indeed a flower which a morning withers and the beat of a passing wing breaks down; it is the widow's lamp, which the slightest blast of air extinguishes.

HENRI AMIEL, *Journal,* 1860

Life is a narrow vale between the cold and barren peaks of two eternities. We strive in vain to look beyond the heights. We cry aloud, and the only answer is the echo of our wailing cry.

ROBERT G. INGERSOLL, at his brother's grave, 1879

Human life, regarded from a merely individual point of view, is deeply sad. Glory, power, grandeur, all perish,—playthings of a day, broken at night.

JOSEPH MAZZINI, *Essays,* 1887

To live a good life; to die a holy death— that is everything.

ST. THÉRÈSE OF LISIEUX (1873–1897), *Autobiography,* publ. posth.

Dying is easy work compared with living. Dying is a moment's transition; living a transaction of years.

MALTBIE D. BABCOCK, *Thoughts for Everyday Living,* 1901

Let us so live that when we come to die even the undertaker will be sorry.

MARK TWAIN (1835–1910), *Notebook,* publ. 1935

Nothing seems so tragic to one who is old as the death of one who is young, and this alone proves that life is a good thing.

ZOE AKINS, *The Portrait of Tiero,* 1920

Live as though every day was your last— and someday you will be right.

ANONYMOUS, c. 1960

See also Creation; Death; Eternal Life; Immortality; Life; Life: Its Meaning; Spiritual Life.

LIGHT

Lead me from the unreal to the real!
Lead me from darkness to light! Lead me
from death to immortality.

> Ancient Hindu prayer found in the *Bri-hadaranyaka Upanishad,* quoted from the much older *Yajur-Veda,* 1000 B.C. or earlier

While the fire of passion, and hatred, and
ignorance is always burning, ye, surrounded by darkness, why seek ye not a
light?

> *Dhammapada,* c. 5th century B.C.

Unite the light within you with the light of
Brahman. Thus will the source of ignorance be destroyed, and you will rise above
karma.

> *The Svetasvatara Upanishad,* before 400
> B.C.

Praise thou the hidden light by means of
the gleaming from Him: hard is it for the
eye of the soul to look at the secret Light.
By means of the shining from Him it is
able to go to meet Him.

> EPHRAIM THE SYRIAN (306–373 A.D.),
> MARGARET SMITH'S *Studies in Early
> Mysticism in the Near and Middle East*

Light gives testimony of itself . . . and is
a witness itself that the light may be
known. Likewise Wisdom, the word of
God.

> ST. AUGUSTINE, *In Joan.,* 8, c. 416

The Divine Gloom is the unapproachable
Light in which God is said to dwell. And
in this gloom, invisible indeed, on account
of the surpassing brightness, and unapproachable on account of the excess of the
superessential.

> DIONYSIUS THE PSEUDO-AREOPAGITE, c.
> 5th century A.D.

For the Lord is light; and so far as any
one is not in Him, so far he is in darkness.

> ST. BERNARD OF CLAIRVAUX (1091–
> 1153), *Sermon on Death of Gerard*

The essence of the First Absolute Light,
God, gives constant illumination . . . and
brings all things into existence. . . .
Everything in the world is derived from
the Light of His Essence. . . . To obtain
fully to this illumination is salvation.

> SUHRAWARDI HALABE (fl. 1191 A.D.),
> quoted in MARGARET SMITH'S *Readings
> From the Mystics of Islam*

He who is imbued with or illuminated by
the Eternal or Divine Light and inflamed
or consumed with Eternal or Divine Love,
he is a deified man and a partaker of the
Divine Nature.

> *Theologia Germanica,* c. 1350

O Everlasting Light, surpassing all created
luminaries: dart the beams of Thy brightness from above and penetrate all the
corners of my heart. Purify, beautify and
vivify my spirit with all its powers: that I
may cleave unto Thee with transports of
jubilation.

> THOMAS À KEMPIS, *Imitation of Christ,*
> 1441

But if God did once put away that Duski-
ness, which moves about the Light, and
that thy Eyes were opened, then in that
very place where thou standest, sittest, or
liest, thou shouldst see the glorious Countenance or Face of God and the whole
heavenly Gate.

> JAKOB BOEHME, *Aurora,* 1612

Light is God's eldest daughter.

> THOMAS FULLER, *Holy and Profane
> State,* 1642

The light we have gained, was given us,
not to be ever staring on, but by it to
discover outward things more remote from
our knowledge.

> JOHN MILTON, *Aeropagitica,* 1644

One beam in a dark place hath exceeding
much refreshment in it. Blessed be His
name for shining upon so dark a heart as
mine.

> OLIVER CROMWELL (1599–1658),
> *Letters and Speeches,* ed. Carlyle

If thou wouldst be a child of God, and a believer in Christ, thou must be a child of light.

WILLIAM PENN, *No Cross, No Crown,* 1669

The Light strives and wrestles with all in order to save them; he that resists its strivings is the cause of his own condemnation; he that resists it not, it becomes his salvation.

ISAAC PENNINGTON (1616–1679), *Works,* II, 148

Universal Light! It is through thee alone that we see anything. Sun of the soul, who dost shine more brightly than the material sun! seeing nothing except through thee, we see not thee thyself.

FRANÇOIS DE FÉNELON (1651–1715), *Selections from,* ed. Fellen

As light increases, we see ourselves to be worse than we thought.

FRANÇOIS FÉNELON (1651–1715), *Spiritual Letters of*

Light which gives illumination from the examining of intelligible truths is the light of philosophic knowledge. It is accordingly called inward because it searches into the inward and hidden causes and does this through the principles and disciplines of natural truth which are implanted naturally in man.

ST. BONAVENTURE (1638–1715), *De Reductione Artium ad Theologiam*

When a man contemplates inwardly the eternal light, the mind is pure, and has in [it] no sensuous images.

ST. SERAPHIM OF SAROV (1759–1833), quoted in A. F. Dobbie-Bateman's biography of St. Seraphim

A man should learn to detect and watch that gleam of light which flashes across his mind from within, more than the lustre of the firmament of bards and sages.

RALPH WALDO EMERSON, "Self-Reliance," *Essays,* 1841

If there is anything more poignant than a body agonizing for want of bread it is a soul which is dying of hunger for light.

VICTOR HUGO, *Les Miserables,* 1862

He who says light does not necessarily say joy. There is suffering in the light; in excess it burns. Flame is hostile to the wing. To burn and yet to fly, this is the miracle of genius.

VICTOR HUGO, *Les Miserables,* 1862

From within or from behind, a light shines through us upon things, and makes us aware that we are nothing, but the light is all.

RALPH WALDO EMERSON, *Lecture on the Times,* 1876

It is because they have mistaken the dawn for a conflagration that theologians have so often been foes of light.

F. W. FARRAR, *History of Interpretation,* 1885

In the moral world we are ourselves the lightbearers, and the cosmic process is in us made flesh. For a brief space it is granted to us, if we will, to enlighten the darkness that surrounds our path.

HAVELOCK ELLIS, *The New Spirit,* 1891

A poor, meager, starved, bruised life, if only it keeps the true human quality, and does not become inhuman, and if it is obedient to God in its blind, dull half-conscious way becomes a light.

PHILLIPS BROOKS, *The Candle of the Lord and Other Sermons,* 1899

We are not left without light in the world; even in our own dulled and clouded hearts, when the radiance of God beats upon them, we see sometimes an answering gleam within, like the secret fire that sleeps in the uncut gem.

ARTHUR CHRISTOPHER BENSON, *The Gate of Death,* 1906

I said to the man who stood at the gate of the year, "Give me a light that I may tread safely into the unknown," and he replied, "Go out into the darkness and put your hand into the hand of God. That shall be to you a better light and safer than a known way."

M. L. HOSKINS, *The Gate of the Year,* 1908

In proportion as we can reach out towards that larger knowledge of God, is not the light of that other world breaking upon the hilltops of this life with its morning splendor?

CHARLES E. GARMAN, *Letters, Lectures, Addresses,* 1909

The business of a Christian, by the means of which he attains all his purposes, . . . is everywhere and always one: to increase one's fire and let it give light to men.

LEO N. TOLSTOY (1828–1910), *Letters of*

Whether in the intellectual pursuits of science or in the mystical pursuits of the spirit, the light beckons ahead and the purpose surging in our natures responds.

ARTHUR EDDINGTON, *The Nature of the Physical World,* 1928

By whatever road we travel, if we walk always by the light that is given us, like the Wise Men, to Christ in the end we shall come, for all the noblest aspirations of the human heart find their satisfaction in Him and nowhere else.

R. J. H. STEUART, *The Inward Vision,* 1929

The lights of great cities go out, and there is a howling darkness to all appearance. But always since men began, the light of the pure God-knowing human consciousness has kept alight.

D. H. LAWRENCE, "On Human Destiny, *Assorted Articles,* 1930

The one essential thing is that we strive to have light in ourselves. Our strivings will be recognized by others, and when people have light in themselves, it will shine out from them.

ALBERT SCHWEITZER, *Memories of Childhood and Youth,* 1931

The light which shines from the Crucified is a light shining in the darkness. It is this light which both illuminates the obscurity of being and overcomes the darkness of non-being.

NICHOLAS BERDYAEV, *Freedom and the Spirit,* 1935

The duty of being faithful to the light, and of always following it to the extent that one sees it, is a duty which cannot be evaded.

JACQUES MARITAIN, *Ransoming the Time,* 1941

Like the athletes in the old Athenian torch race of Pan, let us not run so fast that we put out the Light! For without God everything is darkness in human society.

ROBERT I. GANNON, *God in Education,* 1943

The Christian life is a journey. . . . Do not wait for great strength before setting out, for immobility will weaken you further. Do not wait to see very clearly before starting; one has to walk toward the light.

PHILIPPE VERNIER, *With the Master,* 1943

The illumination given us by Christ is like the dawn; it is light by which to walk, not arbitrary command that would rob us of our manhood. We can close our eyes against it . . . but He is still the light and life without which we die.

GEORGE A. BUTTRICK, *Christ and Man's Dilemma,* 1946

It must not be forgotten that the first Christmas song was sung in the night. . . . That is a comforting fact. When the world is dark, the light shines, not from among men but from heaven.

CLELAND B. MCAFEE, *Near to the Heart of God,* 1954

The Light within is not to be identified with conscience, which is the human faculty, imperfect because human, through which the Light shines.

Faith and Practice of the Philadelphia Yearly Meeting, 1955

Every religion has in itself sparks of light that must be neither despised nor extinguished, even though they be insufficient to give man that clarity that he needs or to achieve the miracle of the light of Christianity which makes truth coincide with life.

POPE PAUL VI, *Easter Sermon, 1964*

See also Beatific Vision; Conscience; Darkness; Enlightenment; Gloom; God: Finding Him; Grace, Definitions of; Holy Spirit; Inspiration; Intuition; Knowledge; Pentecost; Poems and Poets; Poetry; Prophets; Quakers; Reality; Religion; Religion, Revealed; Revelation; Vision; Wisdom.

LIMITATIONS

That which makes things the things they are, is not limited to such things. The limits of things are their own limits in so far as they are things.

CHUANG-TZU (4th century B.C.), *Texts of Taoism,* ed. J. Legge

LITERATURE

Just as in plucking the blooms from a rosebed we avoid the thorns, so also in garnering from such writings whatever is useful, let us guard ourselves against what is harmful.

ST. BASIL THE GREAT (330–379), *Address to Young Men*

Satan receives a wound in every word written by him who makes fresh texts of the ancient law of the Lord. Though, indeed, the scribe must sit in one place, yet by scattering of his labor he walks through divers provinces.

CASSIODORUS, *On the Arts and Disciplines of Liberal Letters,* c. 550 A.D.

Happy is the aim, praiseworthy is the eagerness, to reveal tongues with the fingers, silently to give salvation to men, to fight with pen and ink against the attacks of the devil.

CASSIODORUS, *On the Arts and Disciplines of Liberal Letters,* c. 550 A.D.

There is in every word set down by the imaginative mind an awful undercurrent of meaning, and evidence and shadow upon it of the deep place out of which it has come.

JOHN RUSKIN, *Modern Painters,* Vol. 2, 1846

On the whole I think it will be found, and ever found, as a matter of course, that Literature, as such, no matter of what nation, is the science or history, partly and at best of the natural man, partly of man in rebellion.

JOHN HENRY NEWMAN, *The Idea of a University,* 1852

If Literature is to be made a study of human nature, you cannot have a Christian Literature. It is a contradiction in terms to attempt a sinless literature of sinful man.

JOHN HENRY NEWMAN, *The Idea of a University,* 1852

Man will never continue in a mere state of innocence; he is sure to sin, and his literature will be the expression of his sin, and this whether he be heathen or Christian.

JOHN HENRY NEWMAN, *Idea of a University,* 1852

Literature does its duty . . . in raising our fancy to the height of what may be noble, honest, and felicitous in actual life; in giving us, though we may ourselves be poor and unknown, the companionship of the wisest fellow-spirits of every age and country.

JOHN RUSKIN, *The Eagle's Nest,* 1872

The spirit of romance, the glorification of personal honor and passionate love, was not in truth compatible with Christian ethics. . . . The Church had no place in its scheme of life for secular literature.

H. J. C. GRIERSON, *Background of English Literature,* 1915

Literature is the expression, through the aesthetic medium of words, of the dogmas of the Catholic Church, and that which is in any way out of harmony with these dogmas is not literature . . . unless you have assimilated the final dogmas . . . the eternal truths, you can never write literature.

ARTHUR MACHEN, *Hieroglyphics,* 1923

The whole of modern literature is corrupted by what I call Secularism . . . it is simply unaware of, simply cannot understand the meaning of, the primacy of the supernatural over the natural life.

T. S. ELIOT, "Religion and Literature," 1935, in *Selected Prose*

The "greatness" of literature cannot be determined solely by literary standards; though we must remember that whether it is literature or not can be determined only by literary standards.

T. S. ELIOT, "Religion and Literature," 1935, in *Selected Prose*

If there is warrant for recognizing among the corrupt myths of paganism certain remnants and survivals of revealed truth, then we cannot but discern in the literature of antiquity a fragmentary utterance of that truth, the shadow and figure of a greater utterance to come.

BLANCHE MARY KELLY, *The Well of English,* 1936

It is not going too far to suggest that every individual who pursues his search for spiritual illumination with sufficient persistence finally finds himself obliged to leave secular literature behind him.

DOUGLAS V. STEERE, *Prayer and Worship,* 1938

The danger of bad literature, is, indeed, under certain aspects, more fatal than that of bad company, because it can render itself more treacherously familiar.

POPE PIUS XII, *Address,* July 1, 1940

A good part of current literature is positively possessed. In it could be verified some of the signs used by priests to detect possession: the horror of holy things, pseudo-prophecy, the use of unknown tongues.

JACQUES MARITAIN, *Art and Poetry,* 1943

Sin may never be so treated, whether explicity or by suggestion, as to be a source of temptation to the normally discriminating reader.

HAROLD C. GARDINER, *Tenets for Readers and Reviewers,* 1944

The author of any piece of literature is *in* his work and in judging his work I will necessarily have to judge him. . . . to judge him through his work, and not his work through him.

HAROLD C. GARDINER, *Tenets for Readers and Reviewers,* 1944

When Ernest Psichari proclaims that one must write with fear and trembling under the eye of the Trinity, he is being the mouthpiece of all those who believe in the immortality of each individual soul, and therefore believe in the extreme importance of their writings as effecting each immortal destiny.

FRANÇOIS MAURIAC, *God and Mammon,* 1946

The laws of expression do not change because the subject becomes religious.

NEIL KEVIN, *Irish Ecclesiastical Record,* December, 1947

There are leaders of the Church who regard literature as a means to one end, edification. That end may be of the highest value, of far higher value than literature, but it belongs to a different world. Literature has nothing to do with edification.

GRAHAM GREENE, *The Lost Childhood and Other Essays,* 1951

The subject of the imaginative writer is necessarily men as they are behaving, not as they ought to behave.

ALLEN TATE, *The New Republic,* January 5, 1953

Literature is a generation and an incarnation, an earthly likeness of the eternal utterance and its manifestation in time.

PETER J. R. DEMPSEY, *Freud, Psychoanalysis, Catholicism,* 1956

If we ask what literature is about, we have to answer that it is about the mystery of the human heart and its passage through time.

HUGH DINWIDDY, *The Springs of Morality,* ed. J. M. Todd, 1956

Our chief problem, of course, is not literary censorship, but literary creation. This is true in the Church. She has no trouble in finding censors; but she prays continually that God may give her men of learning who can write books that need to be written.

JOHN COURTNEY MURRAY, *The Critic,* 1956

Novelists seldom write for a believing public; they take for granted that their readers will be as themselves, that is, human beings without a definite standard of morals, without preconceived conceptions of truth.

MARTIN C. D'ARCY, *The Nature of Belief,* 1958

The religious dimension is something intrinsic to and constitutive of the nature of literature as such.

NATHAN A. SCOTT, JR., *Modern Literature and the Religious Frontier,* 1958

Faith has its own rhetoric, and spiritual things are not only spiritually discerned but are reported in a spiritual tongue.

AMOS N. WILDER, *Theology and Modern Literature,* 1958

The work of a Christian writer is bound to be colored by his beliefs and we are entitled to call it Christian literature.

JOSEPH R. FOSTER, *Contemporary Christian Writers,* 1963

If a writer's Christianity does not affect his work decisively, it must be that his acceptance of Christianity is something less than whole-hearted.

JOSEPH R. FOSTER, *Contemporary Christian Writers,* 1963

See also Art and Religion; Author; Bible; Bible as Literature; Books; Censorship; Criticism; Culture and Christianity; Culture and Religion; Freedom of Thought and Speech; Imagination; Obscenity; Old Testament; Poems and Poets; Poetry; Reading; Word, the; Words.

LITURGY

The prayers of the liturgy alone can be uttered with impunity by any man, for it is the peculiarity of these inspirations that they adapt themselves in all ages to every state of the mind and every phase of life.

J. K. HUYSMANS, *The Cathedral,* 1898

The people are better instructed in the truths of the Faith by the annual celebration of our sacred mysteries than by even the weightest pronouncements of the teachings of the Church.

POPE PIUS XI, December 11, 1925

The liturgical art of the services of the church, like the architectural art of the cathedrals, rouses a response in me which cannot be awakened by any modern service or by any modern building.

KIRSOPP LAKE, *The Religion of Yesterday and Tomorrow,* 1925

The practice of the liturgy means that by the help of grace, under the guidance of the Church, we grow into living works of art before God, with no other aim or purpose than that of living and existing in His sight.

> ROMANO GUARDINI, *The Spirit of the Liturgy,* 1935

The liturgy does not say "I" but "We," . . . The liturgy is not celebrated by the individual, but by the body of the faithful.

> ROMANO GUARDINI, *The Spirit of the Liturgy,* 1935

The faithful cannot truly take part in the liturgical worship of the Church without to some extent participating actively in the priestly sacrifice from which all further life flows.

> VIRGIL MICHEL, *Life of Christ,* 1935

Great liturgies cannot be manufactured; they grow.

> ARNOLD LUNN, *Within That City,* 1936

This then is the sublime function of the liturgy of the Church: to assimilate us unto Christ, to make us partakers of the Christlife, of the eternal life of God.

> VIRGIL MICHEL, *The Liturgy of the Church,* 1937

It is by means of the liturgy that theology . . . infuses into mind and heart the effective inspirations for a Christian life of virtue and produces the great fruits of Christian piety.

> VIRGIL MICHEL, *The Liturgy of the Church,* 1937

Liturgy is . . . not merely something which the individual man or men united in the Church give to God. Liturgy is also the instrument or organ, through which God gives His grace to men.

> PIUS PARSCH, *Orate Frates,* XXI, 1946–1947

Although public liturgical prayer has a greater excellence than private prayer, yet through the latter the faithful become properly disposed to receive the sanctifying action of the liturgical rites.

> POPE PIUS XII, *Mediator Dei,* 1947

Without the worship of the heart liturgical prayer becomes a matter of formal routine; its technically finished performance may give aesthetic pleasure, but the spirit has gone out from it.

> AELRED GRAHAM, *Catholicism and the World Today,* 1952

"Liturgy" turns into "contemplation" as soon as our prayer ceases to be a search for God and turns into a celebration, by interior experience, of the fact that we have found Him.

> THOMAS MERTON, *Bread in the Wilderness,* 1953

Christianity is a liturgical religion. The Church is first of all a worshipping community. Worship comes first, doctrine and discipline second.

> GEORGES FLOROVSKY, *One Church,* 1959

The liturgy carried out to perfection . . . even with the knowledge and spiritual disposition striven after by the best liturgists, will be a tinkling cymbal in the ears of God unless the ones who celebrate it continue to glorify the same Lord in the economic, social, political, and cultural fields.

> H. A. REINHOLD, *The Dynamics of Liturgy,* 1961

The great danger is that liturgy creates a world of things over against the secular, instead of a vision of the sacredness of the secular.

> ERIC JAMES, *The Roots of the Liturgy,* 1962

A liturgical movement unaccompanied by a contemplative movement is a kind of romanticism, an escape from time.

> HANS URS VON BALTHASAR, *Prayer,* 1962

The liturgy cannot simply be restored, as Williamsburg was restored. The liturgy must be re-inserted into the center of Christian life in the twentieth century. It is not a question of making that life relevant to liturgy; the liturgy must be made relevant to that life.

> PHILIP SCHARPER, *The Critic,* August–September, 1962

The liturgy is the summit toward which the activity of the Church is directed; at the same time it is the fount from which all her power flows.

> *Constitution on Sacred Liturgy,* Second Vatican Council, Rome, December 4, 1963

The liturgy, "through which the work of our redemption is accomplished," most of all in the divine sacrifice of the eucharist, is the outstanding means whereby the faithful may express in their lives, and manifest to others, the mystery of Christ and the real nature of the true Church.

> *Constitution on the Sacred Liturgy,* Second Vatican Council, Rome, December 4, 1963

The brethren divided from us also use many liturgical actions of the Christian religion. These most certainly can truly engender a life of grace in ways that vary according to the condition of each church or community. These liturgical actions must be regarded as capable of giving access to the community of salvation.

> *Decree on Ecumenism,* Second Vatican Council, November, 1965

See also Art and Christianity; Art and Religion; Bible and Prayer; Church: Its Authority; Contemplation; Devotion; Eucharist; Grace; Mass, the; Music; Ritual; Sacraments; Unity; Worship.

LOGICAL POSITIVISM. See POSITIVISM

LOGOS

Christ is the Logos in whom the whole human race participates; and all who lived in accord with this Logos were Christians, even if they were considered to be atheists as were Socrates and Heraclitus.

> ST. JUSTIN MARTYR, *Apologia I, 46,* c. 150

The Logos is God's expression, His utterance of Himself, His Word. Logos is wisdom, intelligence, mind, thought, will-purpose. . . . He is the divine Agent, the Image of God, the first born Son of God.

> RUFUS M. JONES, *The Church's Debt to Heretics,* 1924

The Greek philosophers used the word Logos (Word) in a cosmic sense, to mean something like the Divine Reason breathing through the world. It was a way of expressing their sense of the immanent Divine.

> JAMES BISSETT PRATT, *Religious Liberals Reply,* 1947

See also Jesus Christ; Revelation and Reason; Truth and Religion; Word, the; World and God.

LONELINESS

No soul is desolate as long as there is a human being for whom it can feel trust and reverence.

> GEORGE ELIOT, *Romola,* 1863

The human spirit has fashioned its prayers out of its loneliness, its persuasion of being something other than earth-dust or star-dust.

> GAIUS GLENN ATKINS, *Religion in our Times,* 1932

All religion, all life, all expression comes down to this: to the effort of the human soul to break through its barrier of loneliness, of intolerable loneliness, and make some contact with another seeking soul, or with what all souls seek, which is (by any name) God.

> DON MARQUIS, *Chapters for the Orthodox,* 1934

Our present economic, social and international arrangements are based, in large measure, upon organized lovelessness.

> ALDOUS HUXLEY, *The Perennial Philosophy,* 1944

Loneliness is the stuff of hell; it is a big price to pay for power and glory.

> GERALD VANN, *The Heart of Man,* 1945

The soul hardly ever realizes it, but whether he is a believer or not, his loneliness is really a homesickness for God.

> HUBERT VAN ZELLER, *We Die Standing Up,* 1949

Loneliness is a game of pretense; for the essential loneliness is an escape from an inescapable God.

> WALTER FARRELL, *The Looking Glass,* 1951

See also Brotherhood; Community; Existentialism; Fellowship; Hell; Isolation; Religion, Necessity of; Sin: Its Consequences; Solitude.

LORD'S PRAYER

I would have all good Christians, to say the *Pater noster,* and if no other prayer, at least not to omit that. . . . It is the only prayer I use in every place, at all times, and upon every accident.

> MICHEL DE MONTAIGNE, *Essays,* lvi, 1580

See also Prayer.

LOVE

He who defends with love will be secure; Heaven will save him, and protect him with love.

> LAO-TZU, *The Tao Tê Ching,* 6th century B.C.

Fau Chih asked about benevolence. The Master said: "To love all men."

> CONFUCIUS, *The Analects of,* 5th century B.C.

Let, therefore, no man love anything; loss of the beloved is evil. Those who love nothing, and hate nothing, have no fetters.

> *Dhammapada,* ch. XVI, c. 5th century B.C.

"Then," she said, "the conclusion of the whole matter is that men love the good." "Yes," I said. . . . "And not only the possession, but the everlasting possession of the good?" "That may be added, too." "Then love," she said, "may be described generally as the love of the everlasting possession of the good?" "That is most true," I said.

> Socrates' speech, "The Symposium," PLATO, *Dialogues,* 4th century B.C.

Love is the high nobility of heaven, the peaceful home of man. To lack love, when nothing hinders us, is to lack wisdom.

> *Mencius,* c. 300 B.C.

In this life two loves are striving in every trial for mastery—love of the world and love of God. The conquering love, whichever it be, puts force upon the lover and draws him after itself.

> ST. AUGUSTINE (354–430), *Sermo.* xxxiv

He who is not loving to God's creatures and to his own children, God will not be loving to him.

> MOHAMMED, *Speeches and Table-Talk of,* 7th century A.D.

Keep Hatred from you; let nothing tempt Your mind to violence;—hold on to love.
Gatha Spenta, Yasna, 7th century B.C.

Love means that the attributes of the lover are changed into those of the Beloved.
JUNAYD OF BAGDAD (died 910 A.D.), quoted in AL MARGHINĀNI, *al-Hidāya*

Love is of two natures, the love that is tranquil, which is found among both the elect and the common folk, and the love which is rapture, which is found only among the elect; this is the road which leads direct to God; therein is found no vision of the self or the creaturely; nor any vision of motives or states, but the lover is absorbed in the vision of God and what is from him.
ABU BAKR AL-KALABADHI (born 995 A.D.), *Readings from the Mystics of Islam,* ed. Margaret Smith

Love is ghostly wine freshening and fortifying the minds of its chosen, and raising them beyond thought or care of worldly allurements.
RICHARD ROLLE (c. 1300–1349), *Incendium Amoris*

Love is the fairest and most profitable guest that a reasonable creature can enter-'>in. To God it is the most acceptable and pleasing of all things.
RICHARD ROLLE (c. 1300–1349), *Incendium Amoris*

The well of life is love, and he who dwelleth not in love is dead.
JOHN TAULER (1300–1361), *Sermon for Thursday in Easter Week*

Never was there war in this world nor wretchedness so bitter
That love,, if he liked, might not bring it to laughing.
WILLIAM LANGLAND, *Piers Plowman,* 1362

I love, but love what I would not love, what I would that I might hate.
PETRARCH (1304–1374), *Letter to San Sepolcro*

Love is the abridgment of all theology.
ST. FRANCIS OF SALES, *Treatise on the Love of God,* 1607

Let the burden be never so heavy, love makes it light.
ROBERT BURTON, *Anatomy of Melancholy,* III, 1621

Love and Bacchus are so violent gods, so furiously rage in our minds, that they make us forget all honesty, shame, and common civility.
ROBERT BURTON, *Anatomy of Melancholy,* III, 1621

Love, being the highest principle, is the virtue of all virtues, from whence they flow forth. Love, being the greatest majesty, is the power of all powers, from whence they severally operate.
JAKOB BOEHME (1575–1624), *A Dialogue between a Scholar and His Master*

All bodies together and all minds together and all their products are not equal to the least motion of love; that belongs to an order higher by infinity.
BLAISE PASCAL, *Pensées,* 1670

What is love? . . . It is the sweetness of life; it is the sweet, tender, melting nature of God, flowing up through his seed of life into the creature, and of all things making the creature most like unto himself, both in nature and operation.
ISAAC PENNINGTON, *Works,* 1681

Love is the noblest frailty of the mind.
JOHN DRYDEN (1631–1700), *The Indian Emperor*

Love is a malady without a cure.
JOHN DRYDEN (1631–1700), *Palamon and Arcite*

Call your love often to account at the bar of reason and scripture, to enquire whether the object of it be proper, and the degree of it reasonable.

ISAAC WATTS (1674–1748), *The Doctrine of the Passions*

Love is a desire of the whole being to be united to some thing, or some being, felt necessary to its completeness, by the most perfect means that nature permits, and reason dictates.

SAMUEL TAYLOR COLERIDGE, *Lectures on Shakespeare and Milton*, 1808

There is nothing holier, in this life of ours, than the first consciousness of love—the first fluttering of its silken wings.

HENRY WADSWORTH LONGFELLOW, *Hyperion*, 1839

Love is our highest word, and the synonym of God.

RALPH WALDO EMERSON, "Love," *Essays*, 1841

God has given us love that the weary soul may give and receive support upon the way of life. It is the flower springing up on the path of duty; but it cannot change its course.

GIUSEPPE MAZZINI, *Speech*, 1848

It is to the credit of human nature, that, except where its selfishness is brought into play, it loves more readily than it hates.

NATHANIEL HAWTHORNE, *The Scarlet Letter*, 1850

Love at its highest point—love, sublime, unique, invincible—leads us straight to the brink of the great abyss, for it speaks to us directly of the infinite and of eternity. It is eminently religious.

HENRI AMIEL, *Journal*, September 2, 1862

Love has no middle term; either it destroys or it saves.

VICTOR HUGO, *Les Miserables*, 1862

Love all God's creation, both the whole and every grain of sand. Love every leaf, every ray of light. Love the animals, love the plants, love each separate thing. If thou love each thing thou wilt perceive the mystery of God in all.

FEODOR DOSTOEVSKY, *The Brothers Karamazov*, 1880

Love is a portion of the soul itself, and it is of the same nature as it. . . . Love is the celestial breathing of the atmosphere of paradise.

VICTOR HUGO (1802–1885), *Treasure Bits From*, ed. Porter

There is no soul that does not respond to love, for the soul of man is a guest that has gone hungry these centuries back.

MAURICE MAETERLINCK, *The Treasures of the Humble*, 1896

So long as we love we serve; so long as we are loved by others, I would almost say we are indispensable; and no man is useless while he has a friend.

ROBERT LOUIS STEVENSON, *Lay Morals and Other Papers*, 1898

It is only the souls that do not love that go empty in this world.

ROBERT HUGH BENSON, *The History of Richard Raynal Solitary*, 1906

Love is a brilliant illustration of a principle everywhere discoverable: namely, that human reason lives by turning the friction of material forces into the light of ideal goods.

GEORGE SANTAYANA, *Reason in Society*, 1906

The love we give away is the only love we keep.

ELBERT HUBBARD (1859–1915), *Notebook*

Let us have *love* and more love; a love that melts all opposition, a love that conquers all foes, a love that sweeps away all barriers, a love that aboundeth in charity, a large-heartedness, tolerance, forgiveness and noble striving, a love that triumphs over all obstacles.

ABDUL BAHA (1844–1921), *I Heard Him Say*

In love we find a joy which is ultimate because it is the ultimate truth.

RABINDRANATH TAGORE, *Creative Unity*, 1922

In the dark love, you turn from God's sunlight and clean flowers and chaste trees into a hot evil place, because of some evil you have invited into yourself.

DONN BYRNE, *Brother Saul*, 1927

There is a land of the living and a land of the dead and the bridge is love, the only survival, the only meaning.

THORNTON WILDER, *The Bridge of San Luis Rey*, 1927

Outside of Christianity, at any rate, there is no other religion which has put so much stress upon love as has Buddhism. Universal pity, sympathy for all suffering beings, good will to every form of sentient life, these things characterized the Tathagata [the Buddha] as they have few others of the sons of men.

J. B. PRATT, *The Pilgrimage of Buddhism*, 1928

The very angels themselves cannot persuade the wretched and blundering children on earth as can one being broken on the wheel of living. In Love's service only the wounded soldiers can serve.

THORNTON WILDER, *The Angel That Troubled the Waters*, 1928

Love is an evident part of the divine plan and therefore can only be regarded as normal.

ERNEST DIMNET, *What We Live By*, 1932

Never was anything in the world loved too much, but many things have been loved in a false way. . . . We do not love that too much, but other things too little.

ALDOUS HUXLEY, *Ends and Means*, 1937

Love is immortality struggling within a mortal frame, and all the mortal pains that flesh is heir to become golden with immortal life as they are touched by love.

A. VICTOR MURRAY, *Personal Experience and the Historic Faith*, 1939

Creative love flowing freely among all persons and organizing their common life— this I take to be the meaning of God in history.

F. ERNEST JOHNSON, *The Social Gospel Re-examined*, 1940

Every creature, being a more or less remote derivation of infinite love, is therefore the fruit of love and does not move except through love.

POPE PIUS XII, *Address*, October 23, 1940

He who practices the law without loving does not practice the law, because the first commandment is love. And he who loves while scorning the law does not love, because the law is the first will of Him Who loves us, and Whom we love.

JACQUES MARITAIN, *Art and Poetry*, 1943

Love is the most freely willed of any activity of which we are able to think.

EMIL BRUNNER, *The Divine-Human Encounter*, 1944

The happy man is he who lives the life of love, not for the honors it may bring, but for the life itself.

R. J. BAUGHAN, *Undiscovered Country*, 1946

The theologian is right. Why not admit it? More than anything else the world needs love.

SEBASTIAN DE GRAZIA, *The Political Community,* 1948

Love is the strongest force the world possesses, and yet it is the humblest imaginable.

MAHATAMA GANDHI, *Selections From,* ed. by N. K. Bose, 1948

Christ utterly believed and proved with His life that love is more potent than any possible array of mere physical force.

FRANCIS B. SAYRE, *Reader's Digest,* July, 1948

He who loves brings God and the world together.

MARTIN BUBER, *At the Turning,* 1952

Of all the worn, smudged, dog-eared words in our vocabulary, "love" is surely the grubbiest, smelliest, slimiest. . . . And yet it has to be pronounced, for, after all, Love is the last word.

ALDOUS HUXLEY, *Tomorrow and Tomorrow and Tomorrow,* 1952

Love is the supreme value around which all moral values can be integrated into one ethical system valid for the whole of humanity.

PITIRIM A. SOROKIN, *The Ways and Power of Love,* 1954

In all conflict with evil, the method to be used is love and not force. When we use evil methods to defeat evil, it is evil that wins.

SRI RADHAKRISHNAN, *East and West,* 1955

Love in all its subtleties is nothing more and nothing less, than the more or less direct trace marked on the heart of the elements by the psychical convergence of the universe upon itself.

PIERRE TEILHARD DE CHARDIN, *The Phenomenon of Man,* 1955

Between the past and the future, between the perfect love of the cross and the fulfilled love of everlasting life, stands the present demand of love now.

WILLIAM HAMILTON, *Interpretation,* October, 1957

There is an ideal surging through our Judeo-Christian heritage that in the happiest of circumstances could catch ethics up to science in time to lift man's hand from the ultimate button. . . . It is the ancient, simple, and virtually inoperative idea that love can conquer hate.

LEONARD GROSS, *God and Freud,* 1959

The only place outside Heaven where you can be perfectly safe from all the dangers and perturbations of love is Hell.

C. S. LEWIS, *The Four Loves,* 1960

Not many men may be willing to die for love these days. But you can't escape the fact that millions are dying daily for the very *lack* of it.

JOHN E. LARGE, *The Small Needle of Doctor Large,* 1962

See also Beautiful, the; Beauty; Brotherhood; Charity; Creation; Desires; Faith; Friendship; Happiness; Hatred; Humanity; Jesus Christ; Justice; Love, Divine; Love, Human; Love, Physical; Love, Spiritual; Love of God; Lust; Malice; Marriage; Modesty; Morals; Neighbor; Pacifism; Pacifists; Passions; Psychoanalysis; Purity; Religion: Its Nature and Function; Romance; Sex; Sexual Attraction; Sexual Desire; Sexual Intercourse; Soul; Tolerance; Unity; War.

LOVE, DIVINE

And unto those—thus serving well, thus
    loving ceaselessly—
I give a mind of perfect mood, whereby
    they draw to Me [Krishna];
And, all for love of them, within their
    darkened souls I dwell.

And with bright rays of wisdom's lamp, their ignorance dispel.
The Song Celestial, Sir Edwin Arnold's translation of the *Bhagavad-Gita,* 5th to 2nd century B.C.

God loves these three: the person who does not get angry; the one who does not get drunk, and the one who does not insist upon his privileges.
Pesahim, Talmud, c. 500 A.D.

In order that we might receive that love whereby we should love, we were ourselves loved, while as yet we had it not.
ST. AUGUSTINE, *De gratia Christi,* 426

I never give thanks to God for loving me, because He cannot help it; whether He would or not it is His nature to.
MEISTER ECKHART (1260?–1327?), *Meister Eckhart*

The sun does not look less upon one rose in the midst of a thousand millions of other flowers than if he looked down upon it alone. And God does not shed His love less upon one soul while He loves an infinity of others than if He loved it alone.
ST. FRANCIS OF SALES (1567–1622), *Consoling Thoughts of,* ed. Huguet

Love is the greatest thing that God can give us; for Himself is love; and it is the greatest thing we can give to God.
JEREMY TAYLOR, *Holy Living,* 1650

God, in so far as He loves Himself, loves men, and consequently the love of God for men and the Mind's intellectual love towards God is one and the same thing.
BARUCH SPINOZA, *Ethics,* 1677

Let him who would know the love of the maker become sorely athirst, and drink of the brook by the way—then lift up his heart—not at that moment to the maker of oxygen and hydrogen, but to the inventor and mediator of thirst and water, that man may foresee a little of what his soul finds in God.
GEORGE MACDONALD, *Unspoken Sermons,* Third Series, 1889

Love is God's essence; Power but his attribute; therefore is his love greater than his power.
RICHARD GARNETT, Preface, *De Flagello Myrteo,* 1897

Nobody is worthy to be loved. The fact that God loves man shows us that in the divine order of ideal things it is written that eternal love is to be given to what is eternally unworthy.
OSCAR WILDE, *De Profundis,* 1905

Every frailest creature, every little wild flower on the veldt has a certain link with that which abides—with the eternal Love of God.
GEORGE CONGREVE, *The Spiritual Order,* 1905

Divine Love always has met and always will every human need.
MARY BAKER EDDY, *Science and Health,* 1908

If divine love is the author of all existence, it follows that nothing can exist wherein love cannot find expression.
A. C. TURNER, *Concerning Prayer,* 1916

God not only loves us more and better than we can ever love ourselves—but God loved us before we loved, or could love, Him. God's love of us rendered possible and actual our love of God.
FRIEDRICH VON HÜGEL, *Essays and Addresses* (2nd Series), 1924

God's love for us is a mystery and a joy, balanced by the mystery and sorrow of our coldness toward Him.
JAMES J. DALY, *The Road to Peace,* 1936

God's love is primarily not a response to man's love, but an appeal to it.

> EDWIN LEWIS, *A Philosophy of the Christian Revelation,* 1940

The divine love hovers over the life of man with the vivacious persistence of April calling earth to life.

> WALTER FARRELL, *The Looking Glass,* 1951

When it is said that God loves man this is not a judgment on what man is like, but on what God is like.

> ANDERS NYGREN, *Agape and Eros,* 1953

As the artist creates patterns in a vain effort to catch a beauty which escapes him, because it is behind his thought and never realized in what he sees, so the love of God beckons and draws the soul of man, though he has never heard the sacred Name.

> MARTIN C. D'ARCY, *The Nature of Belief,* 1958

No sooner do we believe that God loves us than there is an impulse to believe that He does so, not because He is Love, but because we are intrinsically lovable.

> C. S. LEWIS, *The Four Loves,* 1960

The Father who pities his children is the superlatively appropriate symbol of God, not because the worshipper, being one of the children, may hope to profit by paternal indulgence, but because all-reaching and infinitely patient love is the one thing supremely worshipful.

> RALPH BARTON PERRY (born 1876), quoted in *Contemporary American Philosophy,* II, ed. G. P. Adams and W. P. Montague

See also Charity; Creation; God, Fatherhood of; God: His Wrath; Immortality; Jesus Christ; Love; Love, Spiritual; Love of God; Man and God; Passions; Providence; Soul; Worship.

LOVE, HUMAN

Yet because we are of the flesh and begotten through the concupiscence of the flesh, our yearning love must begin from the flesh; yet if rightly directed, advancing under the leadership of grace, it will be consummated in spirit.

> ST. BERNARD OF CLAIRVAUX (1091–1153), *Ep.* ii *ad. Guigonem*

Against thy lover bear it not in mind
If once, or twice, in life he proves unkind.

> SHAIKH SAADI, *Gulistan,* c. 1265

Love is the true means by which the world is enjoyed: our love to others, and others' love to us.

> THOMAS TRAHERNE (1636–1674), *Centuries of Meditation*

Love is sure to be something less than human if it is not something more.

> COVENTRY PATMORE, *The Rod, the Root, and the Flower,* 1895

Were there left but one rock with two loving souls upon it, that rock would have as thoroughly moral a constitution as any possible world which the eternities and immensities could harbor.

> WILLIAM JAMES, *The Will To Believe,* 1896

Mysterious is the fusion of two loving spirits: each takes the best from the other, but only to give it back again enriched with love.

> ROMAIN ROLLAND, *Jean Christophe,* 1912

Love is the expansion of two natures in such fashion that each includes the other, each is enriched by the other.

> FELIX ADLER, *Life and Destiny,* 1913

Human love and the delights of friendship, out of which are built the memories that endure, are also to be treasured up as hints of what shall be hereafter.

BEDE JARRETT, *Meditations for Layfolk,* 1915

Human love, which is as distinct from desire by as much as it transcends it, can be regarded as an intervention of Christ.

JACQUES RIVIÈRE, *Études,* 1924

If the higher companionship which love should be does not make men and women nobler, more generous, more ready to sacrifice even their beautiful life for a lofty purpose, there is a suspicion that their love is not love but a combination of egoisms.

ERNEST DIMNET, *What We Live By,* 1932

When love is real love, when people's souls go out to their beloved, when they lose their hearts to them, when they act in the unselfish way in which these exquisite Old English phrases denote, a miracle is produced.

ERNEST DIMNET, *What We Live By,* 1932

If you love a person you love him or her in their stark reality, and refuse to shut your eyes to their defects and errors.

JOHN MACMURRAY, *Reason and Emotion,* 1936

Through the love of women men have learned redemption, for it is in that experience that the super-natural world swims into our ken and the world that now is has least hold upon us.

A. VICTOR MURRAY, *Personal Experience and the Historic Faith,* 1939

The love which we bestow upon our fellow man may be said to be the completion of the homage which we render to God when we love Him directly and immediately.

JOHN A. O'BRIEN, *Religion—Does It Matter?,* 1944

How terrible when people are led to believe, or left to believe, that once they are in love they have nothing to do but live happily ever after, they have nothing further to learn.

GERALD VANN, *The Heart of Man,* 1945

Human love, which can carry so strong a charge of animal instinct, would never have the power, the infinity, one might almost say the divinity it has, were it not rooted in a spirit capable of the infinite and an express image of God.

JEAN MOUROUX, *The Meaning of Man,* 1948

Love between man and woman, a mother's love for her child, are necessities of human nature. They are strong and beautiful, but at their source they are blind. Christian love is seeing. It is bound with knowledge.

C. F. VON WEIZSÄCKER, *The History of Nature,* 1949

Love is a mutual self-giving which ends in self-recovery.

FULTON J. SHEEN, *Three to Get Married,* 1951

Love is union under the condition of preserving one's integrity.

ERICH FROMM, *The Art of Loving,* 1956

I believe that the most lawless and inordinate loves are less contrary to God's will than a self-invited and self-protective lovelessness.

C. S. LEWIS, *The Four Loves,* 1960

See also Affections; Agape; Bereavement; Brotherhood; Charity; Chastity; Children; Christian Life; Church: Its Work; Community; Eros; Erotic; Family; Fellowship; Friendship; Hatred; Love; Love, Physical; Love of God; Love of Mankind; Lust; Marriage; Passions; Romance; Sex; Sexual Attraction; Sexual Desire; Sexual Intercourse; Virginity; Woman.

LOVE, PHYSICAL

Love is too strong to be overcome by anything except flight, nor ought mortal creature to be so presumptuous as to stand the encounter, since there is need of something more than human, and indeed heavenly, powers to vanquish human passion.

MIGUEL DE CERVANTES, *Don Quixote,* 1615

Some boldly apply the name of "love" to a caprice of a few days, a connection without attachment, passion without affection, the affection of cicisbeism, a cold usage, a romantic fancy, a taste speedily followed by a distaste. They apply the name of a thousand chimeras.

VOLTAIRE, *Philosophical Dictionary,* II, 1764

In the conducting medium of Fantasy, flames-forth that fire-development of the universal Spiritual Electricity, which, as unfolded between man and woman, we first emphatically denominate LOVE.

THOMAS CARLYLE, *Sartor Resartus,* 1836

Nuptial love bears the clearest marks of being nothing other than the rehearsal of a communion of a higher nature.

COVENTRY PATMORE, *Principles in Art,* 1889

Love, to the lover, is a noble and immense inspiration; to the naturalist it is a thin veil and prelude to the self-assertion of lust.

GEORGE SANTAYANA, *Reason in Society,* 1906

The great enrichment and deepening of sexual love which has taken place since the time of the Ancient World is the direct result of the self-forgetful love, the immense spiritual elevation above the sensuous sphere and the passionate inner life which have sprung from the religious feeling.

F. W. FOERSTER, *Marriage and the Sex Problem,* 1912

If love has come to be less often a sin, it has come also to be less often a supreme privilege.

JOSEPH WOOD KRUTCH, *Atlantic Monthly,* August, 1928

Love has ceased to be the rather fearful, mysterious thing it was, and become a perfectly normal, almost commonplace, activity—an activity, for many young people especially in America, of the same nature as dancing or tennis, a sport, a recreation, a pastime.

ALDOUS HUXLEY, *Do What You Will,* 1929

Physical love is the token of total intimacy. It is the sign that the lovers have nothing to refuse each other; that they belong wholly to each other.

JACQUES LECLERCQ, *Marriage and the Family,* 1941

Sex-love is set into the world not as an apology for the miseries of existence . . . but as a symbol of the nature of things.

WILLIAM ERNEST HOCKING, *Science and the Idea of God,* 1945

If they love each other with all the violence of a human passion, it is because it is their calling; and their calling is to desire God's love, and is God's choice; therefore they only love each other because God has loved them first—and they love each other with the same love.

A. CARRÉ, *Companions for Eternity,* 1947

The attraction of one creature for another, even when condemned by reason for its passionate origin, is always worthy of respect, because it reveals to us something of the order of creation.

A. CARRÉ, *Companions for Eternity,* 1947

If we love a thing or a fair face as if it could give us God, then the poor thing we have chosen ends by crumbling beneath our eyes, and leaves nothing behind in the fingers but a little pinch of dust.

JEAN MOUROUX, *The Meaning of Man,* 1948

Sex is biological and physiological and has its definite zones of satisfaction. Love, on the contrary, includes all of these but is directed to the *totality* of the person loved, i.e., as a creature composed of body and soul and made to the image and likeness of God.

FULTON J. SHEEN, *Three to Get Married,* 1951

In true Christian love, the husband and wife see God coming *through* their love.

FULTON J. SHEEN, *Three to Get Married,* 1951

Love is the complete abandonment of self to another. It is not only unitive (unites the lovers in heart and soul), it is also benevolent (wishes the greatest good to another). This unitive and benevolent love is expressed and completed when married love becomes a complete donation of self through sexual union.

IGNATIUS W. COX, *The Divine Romance of Marriage,* 1951

Sexual love, or any other form of human love, cannot be the source of its own salvation.

REUL L. HOWE, *Sex and Religion Today,* ed. S. Doniger, 1953

Genuine romantic love is much more than mere stupefying and intoxicating sex haze. . . . True romantic love *is* real love. The characteristic mark of the experience, as in the case of all loving, is the blinding revelation that some other being can be more important to the lover than he is to himself.

J. V. L. CASSERLEY, *The Bent World,* 1955

This romantic love might be defined as a total intoxication of the human being by sexual desire taking the loftiest forms and disguised as pure and absolutely disinterested, pure and eternal love of the other.

JACQUES MARITAIN, *Reflections on America,* 1958

There has grown up a folklore which passes as Christian sexual ethics, which is no more than a conglomeration of inflated fallacies. The valid expression of physical love in its manifold manifestations is suffocated by irrelevant prohibitions.

J. DOMINIAN, *Psychiatry and the Christian,* 1962

Nowhere but in this realm of love do we perceive so distinctly that man is neither angel nor beast; nowhere else do we find a clearer revelation that man's toilsome greatness resides precisely within the narrow and precarious margin that separates in him the beast from the angel.

HENRI GIBERT, *Love in Marriage,* 1964

Human love, through human sex, must use the body in the service of the partner's spiritual welfare.

HENRI GIBERT, *Love in Marriage,* 1964

See also Adultery; Birth Control; Chastity; Courtship; Eros; Erotic; Husband and Wife; Love; Love, Human; Lust; Marriage; Romance; Sex; Sexual Attraction; Sexual Desire; Sexual Intercourse; Sexual Sin; Virginity; Woman.

LOVE, SPIRITUAL

If a man lives a hundred years, and engages the whole of his time and attention in religious offerings to the gods, sacrificing elephants and horses and other things, all this is not equal to one act of pure love in saving life.

Dhammapada, c. 5th century B.C.

To render, spontaneously, good for evil, such disposition to do good to those who hate us belongs to a perfect spiritual love.

ST. MAXIMUS THE CONFESSOR, *Centuries on Charity*, c. 626

Tell me, fool: which is the greatest and truest love to be found in a creature?— The Fool of Love replied: that which is one with the Creator, for the Creator has nothing further from which to make a creature more noble.

RAMÓN LULL, *Book of the Lover and the Beloved*, c. 1280

Love of friends, nuptial, heroical, profitable, pleasant, honest, all these loves put together, are little worth, if they proceed not from a true Christian illuminated soul, if it not be done for God's sake.

ROBERT BURTON, *Anatomy of Melancholy*, II 1621

I like that love which, by a soft ascension, by degrees possesses itself of the soul.

OWEN FELLTHAM, *Resolves, Divine, Moral and Political*, 1626

The soul is not where it lives but where it loves.

THOMAS FULLER, *Gnomologia*, 1732

Perfect love is a kind of self-dereliction, a wandering out of ourselves, it is a kind of voluntary death, wherein the lover dies to himself and all his own interests.

HENRY SCOUGAL, *The Life of God in the Soul of Man*, c. 1760

True love for the things of this earth, and for God, the final cause of all, does not ask for love in return. We love the divine spark that dwells in creatures themselves unconscious of it.

GUNTHER in Berthold Auerbach's *On the Heights*, 1865

With love our soul expands, and is enlarged with the greater life that attracts our affections, and is purified with its purity, and the soul goes forth out of herself, to live in the object of her love.

W. BERNARD ULLATHORNE, *Endowment of Man*, 1889

What love does in transfiguring life, that religion does in transfiguring love.

COVENTRY PATMORE, *The Rod, the Root, and the Flower*, 1895

On the wings of Christianity came the great truth that Love is of the soul, and with the soul coeval.

FRANCIS THOMPSON, *Essays*, 1910

Love is the fruitful mother of fortitude, undying fidelity, absolute self-forgetfulness. It is on the wings of this love that human nature soars above lower self and curbs it in the interest of higher love.

IGNATIUS W. COX, *The Divine Romance of Marriage*, 1951

The whole spiritual drama is contained in this cry of anguish from St. Francis of Assisi: "The beloved is not loved!"

NICOLAS CORTE, *Who Is the Devil?*, 1958

See also Contemplation; Love; Love, Divine; Love, Physical; Love of God; Man's Quest of God; Prayer.

LOVE OF GOD

He that loves God will soar aloft and take him wings; and, leaving the earth, fly up to heaven, wander with the sun and moon, stars, and that heavenly troop, God himself being his guide.

PHILO JUDAEUS (c. 20 B.C.–40? A.D.), *Lib de victimis*

The love of God in its essence, is really the illumination of the heart by joy, because of its nearness to the Beloved.

AL MUHASIBI (died 857 A.D.), quoted in Margaret Smith's *An Early Mystic of Bagdad*

Love for God is the furthest reach of all stations, the sun of the highest degrees, and there is no station after that of love, except its fruit and its consequences.

AL-GHAZALI (died 1111 A.D.), quoted in M. Watt's *Faith and Practice of al-Ghazali*

You asked me why we should love God and how much we should love him. I reply that we should love God because He is God and that the measure of our love should be to love him without measure.

ST. BERNARD OF CLAIRVAUX, *The Love of God*, c. 1127

Man's love of God is identical with his knowledge of Him.

MAIMONIDES, *Guide for the Perplexed*, 1190

Love of God is in fact more meritorious than love of our neighbor.

ST. THOMAS AQUINAS (1225–1274), *Summa Theologiae*, IIa-IIae, q. 181

To serve God with fear is good; to serve Him out of love is better; but to fear and love Him together is best of all.

MEISTER ECKHART (1260?–1327?), *Sermons*

Perfect love maketh God and the soul to be as if they both together were but one thing.

WALTER HILTON (died 1396), *Treatise to a Devout Man*

When the mind is defiled by sin it is cleansed by the love of the Name [God, in Sikh is "the Name"].

Attributed to Nanak (1469–1538), *Japji*

Whosoever performeth [pilgrimages, austerities, etc.] may obtain some little honor;
But he who heareth and obeyeth and loveth God in his heart,

Shall wash off his impurity in the place of pilgrimage within him.

Attributed to Nanak (1469–1538), *Japji*

Let them seek God in all things, putting off as far as possible all love of creatures to place all their love in the Creator, loving Him in all creatures, and all creatures in Him.

ST. IGNATIUS LOYOLA (1491–1556), *Epistolae*, III

Let him be content with the knowledge of Him that he has through faith, and apply his will and his love, since with love alone can he embrace Him.

ST. PETER OF ALCÁNTARA (1499–1562), quoted in *The Mystics of Spain*, by Allison Peers

Did we believe in him, I say not through faith, but with a simple belief, yea (I speak it to our confusion) did we but believe and know him, as we do another story, or as one of our companions, we should then love him above all other things, by reason of the infinite goodness, and unspeakable beauty that is, and shines in him.

MICHEL DE MONTAIGNE, *Essays*, Bk. 2, ch. 12, 1580

A soul that loveth God despiseth all things that be inferior unto God.

GERTRUDE MORE, *A Lover's Confessions*, 1658

As the love of God is man's highest happiness and blessedness, and the ultimate end and aim of all human actions, it follows that he alone lives by the Divine law who loves God not from fear of punishment, or from love of any other object, . . . but solely because he has knowledge of God.

BARUCH SPINOZA, *Theologico-Political Treatise*, 1670

They that love beyond the world cannot be separated by it.

THOMAS TRAHERNE (1636–1674), *Centuries of Meditation*

That same love, for which God created and beautified the world, is the only means for us to return unto Him, who is the fountain of our being.

ALGERNON SIDNEY (1622–1683), *Of Love*

On the roaring billows of Time, thou art not engulfed, but borne aloft into the azure of Eternity. Love not Pleasure; love God. This is the Everlasting Yea.

THOMAS CARLYLE, *Sartor Resartus,* 1836

Love is the gentle, tranquil, satisfied acquiescence and adherence of the soul in the contemplation of God; . . . delight in Him because He is God, and because His commandments are good.

JOHN HENRY NEWMAN, *Parochial and Plain Sermons,* IV, 1843

As all forms of human love, the love of God is subject to excess and distortion. But if it be the truest of all forms of love, then there is all the more reason to pardon its excesses.

C. A. SAINTE-BEUVE, *Port-Royal,* 1848

Love being the supreme act of the soul, and the masterpiece of man, what we owe God is to love Him.

JEAN BAPTISTE LACORDAIRE, *Thoughts and Teachings of,* 1902

Souls loving God in His Infinite Individuality will necessarily love Him beyond their intellectual comprehension of Him.

FRIEDRICH VON HÜGEL, *The Mystical Element of Religion,* 1908

Mystic love is a total dedication of the will; the deep-seated desire and tendency of the soul towards its Source.

EVELYN UNDERHILL, *Mysticism,* 1911

For God to be loved He must be thought of as worthy of love, and it is difficult to believe that He is worthy of love if He wills such a world as ours except as a

means to some better one, for those at least of his creatures who are worthy of it.

E. S. BRIGHTMAN, *Religious Values,* 1925

To love God here is to have eternal life, without the bounds and bands of time.

VINCENT MCNABB, *Joy in Believing,* 1939

Love is a union of wills. The perfect love of God is a perfect union of wills with God: that means the inability to will anything that God does not will.

THOMAS MERTON, *The Waters of Siloe,* 1949

There are many who love God, but not so many who love His will.

HUBERT VAN ZELLER, *We Die Standing Up,* 1949

What gives faith its movement towards God, makes it vital and infectious, and carries people away, is love.

ADRIENNE VON SPEYR, *Meditations on the Gospel of St. John,* 1961

See also Contemplation; Detachment; God, Praise of; Joy; Love; Love, Divine; Love, Spiritual; Man and God; Man's Quest of God; Mysticism; Obedience; Prayer; Selflessness.

LOVE OF MANKIND

No one who is a lover of money, a lover of pleasure, or a lover of glory, is likewise a lover of mankind; but only he who is a lover of virtue.

EPICTETUS (1st century A.D.), *Enchiridion*

Be as large-hearted as we may, we shall never be able to contribute such love toward man as we stand in need of at the hand of a God that loveth man.

ST. JOHN CHRYSOSTOM (345?–407), *Homilies on the Epistle of St. Paul the Apostle to the Romans*

No sinner should be loved in that he is a sinner, and every man should be loved for the sake of God, and God should be loved for His own sake. And if God is to be loved more than any man, everyone should love God more than himself.

ST. AUGUSTINE, *On Christian Doctrine*, 427

And let no men's sins dishearten thee: love a man even in his sin, for that love is a likeness of the divine love, and is the summit of love on earth.

FATHER ZOSSIMA'S Discourse, Feodor Dostoyevsky, *The Brothers Karamazov*, 1880

Love is *between I* and *Thou*. The man who does not know this . . . does not know love. . . . In the eyes of him who takes his stand in love, and gazes out of it, men are cut free from their entanglement in bustling activity.

MARTIN BUBER, *I and Thou*, 1923

There is no other God than Truth. . . . To see the universal and all-pervading Spirit of Truth face to face one must be able to love the meanest of creation as oneself.

MOHANDAS K. GANDHI, *Autobiography*, 1927

Love is the result of an identification—the identifying of our wills with the will of God, and our fate with that of all men, however obscure, fallen and needy.

ROSE TERLIN, *Christian Faith and Social Action*, 1940

Love for one person implies love for man as such.

ERICH FROMM, *Escape from Freedom*, 1941

To love, if we study the revelation of Jesus' behavior, means to desire for any individual, at any cost to himself or us, his release to growth.

WINIFRED KIRKLAND, *The Man of the Hour*, 1942

I know no one in any time who has succeeded in loving every man he met.

MARTIN BUBER, *Between Man and Men*, 1947

Christian love is growing interest in, appreciation of, and responsibility for every person as a member of one family of God.

PAUL E. JOHNSON, *Christian Love*, 1951

The most prevalent failure of Christian love is the failure to express it.

PAUL E. JOHNSON, *Christian Love*, 1951

If matter and energy and chance are all there is, it takes a man of most unusual courage to build an unselfish love for humanity on such foundations.

EDMUND W. SINNOTT, *Two Roads to Truth*, 1953

Christian love is not the motion we feel towards those who are dear to us; it consists in wishing our fellow men well and in taking a genuine and active interest in their spiritual and material welfare.

Joint Pastoral Letter of the Hierarchy of Northern Rhodesia, January 6, 1958

If I am asked to love all mankind from China to Peru, I can only confess that *I* do not feel equal to it.

F. L. LUCAS, *The Greatest Problem*, 1960

A Zaddick once cried from the depth of his heart: "Would I could love the best of men as tenderly as God loves the worst."

The Hasidic Anthology, ed. L. I. Newman, 1963

Love of men leads to the love of God.

Hindustani Proverb

See also Brotherhood; Charity; Community; Fellowship; Love; Love, Human; Mankind; Neighbor; Sinners.

LOYALTY

If I had served my God as diligently as I have done the King, He would not have given me over in my grey hairs.

> THOMAS WOLSEY, on his deathbed, November 29, 1530

I am a Jew and will remain a Jew. I would not become a Christian even if I could become an emperor. Changing one's religion is a matter for consideration by a free man; it is an evil thing for a prisoner.

> SUSS OPPENHEIMER, before his execution, to Pastor Rieger, in 1738, quoted by Stern in *The Court Jew*

Loyalty is the Will to Believe in something eternal, and to express that belief in the practical life of a human being. . . . And all lesser loyalties . . . are but fragmentary forms of the service of the cause of universal loyalty.

> JOSIAH ROYCE, *The Philosophy of Loyalty*, 1908

More's words are the most weighty and the most haughty ever spoken on the scaffold. Dante could not have bettered them. "The King's good servant, but God's first."

> R. W. CHAMBERS, *Thomas More*, 1935

He who sings the song of loyalty to his earthly country must not become a deserter and traitor in disloyalty to his God, his Church and his heavenly country.

> POPE PIUS XI, *Mit Brennender Sorg*, March 14, 1937

I am a disciple of Jesus Christ, I am not a Judas.

> ARCHBISHOP STANISLAU GALL, in Warsaw when confronted with a proposal to collaborate with the Nazi governor, 1939

Loyalty to Christ safeguards the lesser loyalties.

> RALPH W. SOCKMAN, *The Highway of God*, 1941

We definitely and firmly refuse the demand that we should show our loyalty to our country by being faithless to Christ and our Church.

> Catholic Bishops of Germany at the Tomb of St. Boniface in Fulda, 1942

Loyalty to the heritage of Christian civilization and the courageous defense of it against all atheistic or anti-Christian movements is the keystone that may not be sacrificed to any temporary advantage.

> POPE PIUS X, *Broadcast Message*, September 1, 1944

Loyalty to God in and through the life of the Church takes precedence of any possible loyalty to state and nation.

> J. V. L. CASSERLEY, *The Bent World*, 1955

I've been accused of being disloyal to the King. I don't know about that. What I do know, however, is that I am loyal to Jesus Christ. If that isn't the same thing as being loyal to the King, then that's something for the King to worry about, not Studdert Kennedy.

> STUDDERT KENNEDY, British Army chaplain during World War One, quoted in J. E. Large's *The Small Needle of Doctor Large*, 1962

See also Belief; Conscience; Patriotism; Rebellion; Sedition; State, the; Treason; War.

LUST

As rain breaks through an ill-thatched roof, so lust breaks through an ill-trained mind.

> *Dhammapada*, c. 5th century B.C.

From lust comes grief, from lust comes fear; he that is free from lust knows neither grief nor fear.

> *Dhammapada*, 5th century B.C.

Those who indulge in pleasure and give way to lust hand their souls over to their

body and condemn it to death; inasmuch as they make themselves their body's slaves, and over the body death has power.
LACTANTIUS, *The Divine Institutes,* c. 310 A.D.

Lust is an appetite by which temporal goods are preferred to eternal goods.
ST. AUGUSTINE, *On Lying,* c. 395

Sinful lust is not nature, but a disease of nature.
ST. AUGUSTINE, *Of Continence,* c. 425

Deliver yourself from the fetters of lust and passion . . . for God did not create you to be their captive, but that they should be your thralls, under your control, for the journey which is before you.
AL-GHAZALI (fl. 1100 A.D.), quoted in Margaret Smith's *Al-Ghazali, the Mystic*

The expense of spirit in a waste of shame
Is lust in action; and till action, lust
Is perjured, murderous, bloody, full of
    blame,
Savage, extreme, rude, cruel, not to trust;
Enjoy'd no sooner but despised straight.
. . .
A bliss in proof,—and proved, a very
    woe;
Before, a joy proposed; behind, a dream;
All this the world well knows; yet none
    knows well
To shun the heaven that leads men to this
    hell.
WILLIAM SHAKESPEARE, *Sonnet 129,* c. 1600

Love grows, Lust wastes by Enjoyment, and the Reason is, that one springs from an Union of Souls, and the other from an Union of Sense.
WILLIAM PENN, *Some Fruits of Solitude,* 1718

In all enjoyment there is a choice between enjoying the other and enjoying yourself through the instrumentality of the other. The first is the enjoyment of love, the second is the enjoyment of lust. When people enjoy themselves through each other, that is merely mutual lust.
JOHN MACMURRAY, *Reason and Emotion,* 1936

Poverty and lust seek each other out and call to each other in the darkness like two famished beasts.
GEORGES BERNANOS, *The Diary of a Country Priest,* 1937

Lust is a mysterious wound in the side of humanity; or rather at the very source of its life! To confound this lust in man with that desire which unites the sexes is like confusing a tumor with the very organ which it devours.
GEORGES BERNANOS, *The Diary of a Country Priest,* 1937

When a man is enjoying the gratification of sexual passion or the pleasure of eating he ought to feel the presence of poison and be reminded of original sin. That is the nature of every enjoyment connected with lust.
NICHOLAS BERDYAEV, *The Destiny of Man,* 1937

Too often the saint has agreed with the debauchee that the only difference between married love and lust is that one is allowed and the other is not.
SYDNEY CAVE, *The Christian Way,* 1949

Lust . . . is both prevalent and reprehensible; but it may be doubted whether it does as much harm in the world day by day as the less socially disreputable misdemeanors of anger and envy.
AELRED GRAHAM, *Christian Thought and Action,* 1951

What is essentially wrong with lust is not that the body is used carnally but that the situation is such, the human relations are such, that this particular use of the body is the implementation of a wrong spirit.

> JAMES A. PIKE, *Beyond Anxiety*, 1952

See also Adultery; Anger; Desires; Discipline; Dissipation; Evil; Gluttony; Greed; Hedonism; Immorality; Impurity; Love; Love, Human; Love, Physical; Marriage; Passions; Pleasure; Purity; Renunciation; Sensuality; Sex; Sexual Attraction; Sexual Desire; Sexual Intercourse; Sexuality; Vice; Worldliness.

LUTHER, MARTIN

To suppose that Luther's gospel of the free, forgiving love of God in Christ was unknown in the ancient and medieval Church is a great mistake.

> A. C. MCGIFFERT, *Protestant Thought Before Kant*, 1911

The difference between Luther and the early Fathers was at bottom as great as between him and the schoolmen. It did not lie in the sphere of theology—there was much in common among them all—but in their respective conceptions of the nature of the Christian life.

> A. C. MCGIFFERT, *Protestant Thought Before Kant*, 1911

Luther, taking into account nothing but his own violent and personal experience, projected it into an abstract and universal theological doctrine.

> YVES CONGAR, *Divided Christendom*, 1939

A meeting between Catholicism and Protestantism will only be possible when *its point of departure is taken with Luther. Forward from Luther* must the bridges be constructed which will span the chasm between the Christian confessions. . . . Only a determined return of our divided brethren to Luther will make possible the return home to the Mother Church.

> KARL ADAM, *Una sancta in Katholischer Sicht*, 1948

The experience which drove Luther to his world-shaking action stemmed from his own failure to achieve the life of perfection in imitation of Christ in the monastery.

> ALBERT T. MOLLEGEN, *Christianity and Modern Man*, 1961

Anyone who refuses to believe that Luther was fundamentally one of those individuals for whom life and belief are serious matters is guilty of traducing history and psychological truth.

> HENRI DANIEL-ROPS, *The Protestant Reformation*, 1962

See also Ecumenism; Protestantism; Reformation, the; Repression; Unity.

LUXURY

The Superior Man rests in this—that he will indulge in no luxurious ease.

> *The Shu Ching*, 6th century B.C.

Luxury is a criminal affection for pleasures opposed to Christian chastity.

> ST. JOHN BAPTISTE DE LA SALLE, *Les devoirs du chrétien*, 1703

Every degree of luxury hath some connection with evil.

> JOHN WOOLMAN, *Journal*, 1774

Most of the luxuries, and many of the so-called comforts, of life are not only not indispensable, but positive hindrances to the elevation of mankind.

> HENRY DAVID THOREAU, *Walden*, 1854

See also Comfort; Ease; Pleasure; Possessions; Wealth; Worldliness.

LYNCHING

All who actively cooperate in the lynching are in some degree guilty of the same sin. . . . Not only the man who fires the shot or who holds the rope, but all who deliberately assist the action in any way;

those who by their presence encourage others to action.

FRANCIS J. GILLIGAN, *The Morality of the Color Line,* 1929

See also Capital Punishment; Killing; Murder.

MACHINES

To worship the Machine, to worship the Thing it produces, is to worship a Fetish. . . . The Machine-believer proudly flaunts the fact that he has rid himself of God.

JOHN COURNOS, *Autobiography,* 1935

Man, desiring no longer to be the image of God, becomes the image of the machine.

NICHOLAS BERDYAEV, *The Fate of Man in the Modern World,* 1935

The machine is one of the most compellingly rational of human discoveries. The madness is in those who would use a rational thing to further the irrational ends of exploitation and domination.

GREGORY VLASTOS, *Christian Faith and Democracy,* 1939

The great tragedy of our time is that mechanization can no longer be prevented; we become more mechanical as the machine eats into our lives.

ROBERT PAYNE, *Saturday Review,* April 15, 1950

If the Day of Judgment came tomorrow, and God asked us what we had made of His revelation, of His grace and our freedom, . . . we would be hard put to it to explain the advantages of a machine civilization whose highest efficiency is used for murder and slavery.

R. L. BRUCKBERGER, *One Sky to Share,* 1952

It is . . . a clear sign of modern man's profound degradation that the idea of annihilating his precious machines, his adored machines, is so shocking to him,

whereas he considers with such coldness the massacre of millions of people by the same machines.

GEORGES BERNANOS, *Last Essays of,* 1955

Man made the machine and the machine became man, by a kind of diabolical inversion of the mystery of the Incarnation.

GEORGE BERNANOS, *Last Essays of,* 1955

The real cause for dread is not a machine turned human, but a human turned machine.

FRANZ E. WINKLER, *Man: The Bridge Between Two Worlds,* 1960

See also Industrialism; Nuclear Energy; Power; Science; Technology.

MALICE

Malice drinketh up the greater part of its own poison.

THOMAS FULLER, *Gnomologia,* 1732

The malicious have a dark happiness.

VICTOR HUGO, *Les Miserables,* 1862

See also Charity; Enemy; Evil; Hatred; Love; Mercy; Revenge.

MAMMON

Mammon is a serpent which twineth herself round the world. She devoureth him at last who waiteth upon her.

AMAR DAS (c. 1565), *The Sikh Religion,* M. A. Macauliffe, I

Oh, if you could dethrone that Brute-god Mammon, and put a Spirit-god in his place!

THOMAS CARLYLE, *Past and Present,* 1843

Mammon, n. The god of the world's leading religion. His chief temple is in the holy city of New York.

AMBROSE BIERCE, *Devil's Dictionary,* 1906

The only rival of God is Mammon, and it is only when his sacred name is blasphemed that men throw the Christians to the lions.

WALTER RAUSCHENBUSCH, *Christianity and the Social Crisis,* 1907

See also Money; Possessions; Renunciation; Riches; Success.

MAN

Wonders are many, and none is more wonderful than man.

SOPHOCLES, *Antigone,* c. 470 B.C.

Of all the treasures which the universe has in its store there is none more sacred and godlike than man, the glorious cast of a glorious image.

PHILO JUDAEUS, *De Specialibus Legibus,* c. 12 A.D.

Why was man created on the sixth day, after the creation of all the other creatures? So that, should he become overbearing, he can be told "The gnat was created before you were."

Sanhedrin, Mishnah, c. 400 A.D.

Drest in a little brief authority,
Most ignorant of what he's most assured,
His glassy essence,
Like an angry ape,
Plays such fantastic tricks before high
   heaven
As make the angels weep.

WILLIAM SHAKESPEARE, *Measure for Measure,* c. 1604

Every man is as Heaven made him, and sometimes a great deal worse.

MIGUEL DE CERVANTES, *Don Quixote,* 1605

For as every man is a world in himself, so every man is a Church in himself, too.

JOHN DONNE, *Sermon,* February 29, 1627

It is easier to know mankind than any man.

LA ROCHEFOUCAULD, *Maxims,* 1665

It is certain that God attaches more importance to a man than to a lion, but I do not know that we can be sure that he prefers one man to the entire species of lions.

G. W. VON LEIBNIZ, *Théodicé,* 8, 118, 1710

What is the difference between man and ape, based on natural history? Most definitely I see no difference. I wish some one could show me one distinction.

CAROLUS LINNAEUS, *Letter to J. G. Gmelin,* February 14, 1747

Man is the cruelest enemy of man.

J. G. FICHTE (1762–1814), *The Vocation of Man*

Half dust, half duty, unfit alike to sink or
   soar.

LORD BYRON, *Manfred,* Act I, sc. 2, 1820

Man passes away; his name perishes from record and recollection; his history is as a tale that is told, and his very monument becomes a ruin.

WASHINGTON IRVING, *The Sketch-Book,* 1820

If man is not rising upwards to be an angel, depend upon it, he is sinking downwards to be a devil. He cannot stop at the beast.

SAMUEL TAYLOR COLERIDGE, *Table Talk,* August 30, 1833

Oh God! that man should be a thing for immortal souls to sieve through!

HERMAN MELVILLE, *Moby Dick,* 1851

Ah, if man were wholly made in heaven, why catch we hell-glimpses? Why, in the noblest marble pillar that stands beneath the all comprising vault, ever should we descry the sinister vein?

HERMAN MELVILLE, *Pierre: or, The Ambiguities,* 1852

Man rises to fall; he tends to dissolution from the moment he begins to be; he lives on, indeed, in his children, he lives on in his name, he lives not on in his own person. He is, as regards the manifestations of his nature here below, as a bubble that breaks, and as water poured out upon the earth.

JOHN HENRY NEWMAN, *The Second Spring,* 1852

The first condition under which we can know a man at all is, that he be in essentials something like ourselves.

J. A. FROUDE, *The Dissolution of the Monasteries,* 1857

Among the works of man, which human life is rightly employed in perfecting and beautifying, the first in importance is surely man himself.

JOHN STUART MILL, *On Liberty,* 1859

Under all the false, overloaded and glittering masquerade, there is in every man a noble nature beneath.

B. AUERBACH, *On the Heights,* 1865

The animals wait for man to name them. . . . The forest waits to catch the color of his light; the beasts hesitate in fear or anger until he shall tame them to his service, or bid them depart. The earth under his feet holds its fertility at his command and answers the summons of his grain and flower seeds. The very sky over his head regards him, and what he does upon the earth is echoed in the changes of the climate and the haste or slowness of the storms.

PHILLIPS BROOKS, *National Needs and Remedies,* 1890

Man is the only animal that blushes. Or needs to.

MARK TWAIN, *Following the Equator,* 1897

The natural man has but two primal passions, to get and to beget.

WILLIAM OSLER, *Science and Immortality,* 1904

In every concrete individual, there is a uniqueness that defies formulation. We can feel the touch of it and recognize its taste, so to speak, relishing or disliking, as the case may be, but we can give no ultimate account of it, and we have in the end simply to admire the Creator.

WILLIAM JAMES, *Memories and Studies,* 1911

Man is the only creature in the animal kingdom that sits in judgment on the work of the Creator and finds it bad—including himself and Nature.

ELBERT HUBBARD (1859–1915), *Notebook*

If it is "good" for him to be here, then necessarily God is "good." It cannot be an accident that man, with his peculiar powers—mental, moral, spiritual, and physical—should occupy his present position among living creatures.

KIRTLY F. MATHER, *The Forum,* January, 1929

The life of each man enlarges itself infinitely into the life of others, the *communio sanctorum,* and each man *is* humanity.

SERGIUS BULGAKOV, *The Orthodox Church,* 1935

What happens to a man is less significant than what happens *within* him.

THOMAS MANN, *In Quest of the Bluebird,* 1938

Every man has a kingdom. Your kingdom is your own inner being, the kingdom of mind and soul.

WINIFRED RHOADES, *The Self You Have to Live With,* 1938

Man as such is the highest value of Judaism. The degradation of any man to the level of "an animated machine" is unthinkable in the Jewish setting.

TRUDE WEISS-ROSMARIN, *Jewish Survival,* 1949

It is the emancipation from the security of Paradise which is the basis for man's truly human development.

ERICH FROMM, *Psychoanalysis and Religion,* 1950

I believe that man will not merely endure: he will prevail. He is immortal, not because he alone among creatures has an inexhaustible voice, but because he has a soul, a spirit capable of compassion and sacrifice and endurance.

WILLIAM FAULKNER, *Speech* accepting Nobel Prize, January, 1951

Everything originates with man himself and that includes all thoughts and feelings concerning God.

PETER MOEN, *Diary,* 1951

If, indeed, man came to possess the key to the universe, he would become God, able to create and annihilate; and no one in his senses can think such a thing.

FRANCESCO SEVERI, *The World Crisis and the Catholic,* 1958

We cannot acclaim the sacredness of any man until we acknowledge the sacredness of all men.

KYLE HASELDEN, *The Racial Problem in Christian Perspective,* 1959

"There is nothing new under the sun," says the despairing. But what about you, O thinking man? Unless you repudiate reflection, you must admit that you have climbed a step higher than the animals.

PIERRE TEILHARD DE CHARDIN, *The Phenomenon of Man,* 1959

We human beings are capable of greater nobility than other species, but we are also potentially much more vicious. No other animal can be persuaded to fear and to hate multitudes of its own kind whom he has never seen.

BENJAMIN P. SPOCK, *Fellowship,* November, 1965

See also Adam; Believing; Common Man; Creation; Dialectical Man; Evolution; Humanity; Immortality; Individual; Individual Responsibility; Individualism; the various rubrics under Man; Mankind; Nature and Man; Person; Personality; Religious; Soul; Spirit, Human; Wonder; World and Man.

MAN: DEFINED AND INTERPRETED

The Good of man is the active exercise of his soul's faculties in conformity with excellence or virtue, or, if there be several human excellences or virtues, in conformity with the best and most perfect of them.

ARISTOTLE, *Nicomachean Ethics,* I, c. 340 B.C.

Man is a social animal.

SENECA, *De Beneficis,* c. 63 A.D.

The man who was made in God's image is the inner man, the incorporeal, incorruptible, immortal one.

ORIGEN (185–254), *Homily on Genesis*

A rational soul using a mortal and earthly body.

ST. AUGUSTINE, *De Moribus Eccl.* I.27, 368

Man is a gentle animal.

ST. JOHN CHRYSOSTOM, *Homilies,* c. 388

The man that was manifested at the first creation of the world, and he that shall be after the consummation of all, are alike: they equally bear in themselves the Divine image.

ST. GREGORY OF NYSSA (c. 335–c. 395), *On the Making of Man*

An earthly animal, but worthy of Heaven.

ST. AUGUSTINE, *The City of God,* XXII, 426

Man is a little world, in which we may discern a body mingled of earthly elements, and a heavenly spirit and the vegetable soul of plants, and the senses of the lower animals, and reason, and the mind of angels, and the likeness of God.

PICO DELLA MIRANDOLA, *On the Dignity of Man,* 1486

What a piece of work is man! how noble in reason! how infinite in faculty! in form and moving how express and admirable! in action how like an angel! in apprehension how like a god! the beauty of the world!

WILLIAM SHAKESPEARE, *Hamlet,* c. 1601

Man, if we look to final causes, may be regarded as the center of the world; insomuch that if man were taken away from the world, the rest would seem to be all astray, without aim or purpose.

FRANCIS BACON, *De Sapientia Veterum, Works,* VI. 747, 1609

We are only that amphibious piece between a corporeal and spiritual Essence, the middle form that links those two together, and makes good the Method of GOD and Nature.

THOMAS BROWNE, *Religio Medici,* 1635

Man is a noble animal, splendid in ashes and pompous in the grave.

THOMAS BROWNE, *Urn Burial,* 1658

What a chimera, then, is man! what a novelty, what a monster, what a chaos, what a subject of contradiction, what a prodigy! A judge of all things, feeble worm of the earth, depositary of the truth, cloaca of uncertainty and error, the glory and the shame of the universe!

BLAISE PASCAL, *Pensées,* 1670

What is man in nature? A nothing when compared to infinity; a whole when compared to nothing; a middle point between nothing and whole.

BLAISE PASCAL, *Pensées,* 1670

Man is but a reed, the most feeble thing in nature; but he is a thinking reed. . . . If would still be more noble than that which the universe were to crush him, man killed him, because he knows that he dies and the advantage which the universe has over him; the universe knows nothing of this.

BLAISE PASCAL, *Pensées,* 1670

There are only two kinds of men: the righteous who believe themselves sinners; the rest, sinners, who believe themselves righteous.

BLAISE PASCAL, *Pensées,* 1670

A certain intellectual idea formed eternally in the divine Mind.

JOHANNES SCOTUS ERIGENA, *On the Division of Nature,* 1681

Men are children of a larger growth.

JOHN DRYDEN (1631–1700), *All for Love*

Man is naturally good . . . it is by our institutions alone that men became wicked.

JEAN JACQUES ROUSSEAU, *Autobiography,* 1749

Man is a being purely physical.

P. H. D. HOLBACH, *The System of Nature,* 1770

At every moment of his life man is only a passive instrument in the hands of necessity.

P. H. D. HOLBACH, *The System of Nature,* 1770

Man is like a precious stone: cut and polished by morals, adorned by wisdom.

ISAAC F. SATANOV, *Mishle Asaf,* 1789

Man is a digestive tube.

PIERRE CABANIS, *Rapports du physique et du moral de l'homme,* 1796

Man is simply a bulb with thousands of roots. It is his nerves alone that feel.

G. C. LICHTENBERG, *Reflections,* 1799

Man is the only animal that laughs and weeps; for he is the only animal that is struck with the difference between what things are, and what they ought to be.

> WILLIAM HAZLITT, *Lectures on the English Comic Writers,* 1819

He is by nature no more inclined or disposed to vice than to virtue, and is equally capable . . . of either.

> HENRY WARES, *Letters addressed to Trinitarians and Calvinists,* 1820

Man is an embodied paradox, a bundle of contradictions.

> COLTON, *Lacon,* 1822

Man is a fallen god who remembers the heavens.

> ALPHONSE DE LAMARTINE, *Nouvelles méditations poétiques,* 1823

Just because he knows himself to be an animal, he ceases in virtue of such knowledge to be an animal, and, through such self-knowledge only, can characterize himself as mind or spirit.

> G. W. F. HEGEL (1770–1831), *The Philosophy of Art,* publ. posth.

To the eye of Pure Reason what is he? A Soul, a Spirit, and divine Apparition. Round his mysterious Me, there lies under all those wool-rags, a Garment of Flesh (or of Senses) contextured in the Loom of Heaven.

> THOMAS CARLYLE, *Sartor Resartus,* 1836

Man is a god in ruins.

> RALPH WALDO EMERSON, *Nature,* 1836

Of the universal mind each individual man is one more incarnation.

> RALPH WALDO EMERSON, "History," *Essays,* 1841

Every man is a divinity in disguise, a god playing the fool. It seems as if heaven sent its insane angels into our world as to an asylum.

> RALPH WALDO EMERSON, "History," *Essays,* 1841

Never forget . . . that the individuality of man lasts out the greatest suffering and the most entrancing joy alike unscathed, while the body crumbles away in the pains and pleasures of the flesh.

> JEAN PAUL RICHTER, *Reminiscences of the Best Hours of Life,* 1841

A man . . . but who is he? Some clod the truth has snatched from the ground, and with fire has fashioned to a momentary man. Without the truth, he is a clod again.

> RALPH WALDO EMERSON, *North American Review,* May, 1878

To touch the heart of his mystery, we find in him one thought, strange to the point of lunacy; the thought of duty; the thought of something owing to himself, to his neighbour, to his God.

> ROBERT LOUIS STEVENSON, *Across the Plains,* 1880

Man, physical, intellectual, and moral, is as much a part of nature, as purely a product of the cosmic process, as the humblest weed.

> THOMAS HENRY HUXLEY, *Evolution and Ethics,* 1893

Man himself is but a tiny grain of protoplasm in the perishable framework of organic nature.

> ERNEST HAECKEL, *The Riddle of the Universe,* 1899

Man, n. An animal so lost in rapturous contemplation of what he thinks he is as to overlook what he indubitably ought to be.

> AMBROSE BIERCE, *Devil's Dictionary,* 1906

The compound idea of infinite Spirit; the spiritual image and likeness of God; the full representation of Mind.

> MARY BAKER EDDY, *Science and Health,* 1908

Man is the revelation of the Infinite, and it does not become finite in him. It remains the Infinite.

MARK RUTHERFORD, *More Pages from a Journal,* 1910

The essence of man lies in this, in his marvelous faculty for seeking truth, seeing it, loving it, and sacrificing himself to it.

GIUSEPPE PREZZOLINI, *La Voce,* April 13, 1911

Man is a kind of miscarriage of the ape.

I. I. METCHNIKOFF, *Nature of Man,* 1916

Man is not a being different from the animals, or superior to them.

SIGMUND FREUD, *Introductory Lectures on Psychoanalysis,* 1917

A little child of God . . . God's last, best and so far as we know, final expression of Himself.

W. S. RAINSFORD, *The Story of a Varied Life,* 1922

Man is not the creature of a drawing room or the Stock Exchange, but a lonely soul confronted by the Source of all souls.

ARTHUR MACHEN, *Hieroglyphics,* 1923

We are like God inasmuch as we have an intellect; we are like beasts inasmuch as we have flesh.

FULTON J. SHEEN, *God and Intelligence,* 1925

For we each of us already form, at our best, one particular link in but one great chain from earth to heaven; yet, each little link is also, severally, already linked directly to Heaven itself.

FRIEDRICH VON HÜGEL, *Essays and Addresses, Second Series,* 1926

We regard him as little more than a chance deposit on the surface of the world, carelessly thrown up between two ice ages

by the same forces that rust iron and ripen corn.

CARL L. BECKER, *Heavenly City of the 18th Century Philosophers,* 1932

Man is but a foundling in the cosmos, abandoned by the forces that created him.

CARL L. BECKER, *Heavenly City of the 18th Century Philosophers,* 1932

If you remove from the word "human" all that belief in the supernatural has given to man, you can view him finally as no more than an extremely clever, adaptable and mischievous little animal.

T. S. ELIOT, *Selected Essays,* 1932

The Christian religion, having the example of its Master before it, assures man that he must begin with littleness if he is to reach infinity, and that the best illustration of littleness is himself.

MARTIN C. D'ARCY, *Mirage and Truth,* 1935

Man is created and destined to be different from the world, to be holy. As the image of God he belongs to that other, the higher life; he is "a child of the world to come."

LEO BAECK, *The Essence of Judaism,* 1936

He is a being out of joint and wounded—wounded by the devil with the wound of concupiscence and by God's wound of love.

JACQUES MARITAIN, *True Humanism,* 1936

The astonishing and least comprehensible thing about him is his range of vision; his gaze into the infinite distance; his lonely passion for ideas and ideals.

W. MACNEILE DIXON, *The Human Situation,* 1937

Man occupies a unique position in the universe precisely because he is the lowest of all spiritual natures. He is the point at which the world of spirit touches the world of sense, and it is through him and in him that the material creation attains to intelligibility and becomes enlightened and spiritualized.

CHRISTOPHER DAWSON, *Progress and Religion,* 1938

Just an aggregate of trillions of cells, each of them a collection of diverse molecules.

JEAN ROSTAND, *Pensées d'un biologiste,* 1939

The essential truth. . . . is that man is under absolute mandate to express divinity in his own life and his whole nature.

F. ERNEST JOHNSON, *The Social Gospel Re-examined,* 1940

We can define man as the being that is aware of the world as a whole. Man is therefore a metaphysical or a religious being. He is religious not accidentally but essentially.

RICHARD KRONER, *The Religious Function of Imagination,* 1941

A spirit who stands outside of nature, life, himself, his reason and the world.

REINHOLD NIEBUHR, *Human Nature,* 1941

On the topmost rung of living, God placed man, endowed with a spiritual soul, to be the prince and sovereign of the animal kingdom.

POPE PIUS XII, *Allocution,* November 30, 1941

Man is . . . a walking argument of God's existence, a moving advertisement of God's power, an articulate herald of God's intelligence. As man is the crowning work of God, so we affirm man is the supreme argument and the blinding evidence of God's existence.

JOHN A. O'BRIEN, *God: Can We Find Him?,* 1942

It is man who must be restored to his place among men. It is man that is the essence of our culture. Man the keystone in the arch of the community. Man, the seed from whence springs our victory.

ANTOINE DE SAINT-EXUPÉRY, *Flight to Arras,* 1942

All monistic systems of psychology break down before the simple and paradoxical fact that man is free as a spirit, and at the same time determined as a body. . . . He lives at the same time in the spiritual and in the physical atmosphere. . . . Every action being one and indivisible expresses itself, as it were, in two different languages. Something happens in the spiritual world; a decision is made, responsibility is established. . . . And something happens in the physical world, too. A letter is written, or a car is driven, or a house is built. But the action is one.

FRITZ KUNKEL, *In Search of Maturity,* 1943

Man is not alone and neither his mind nor his conscience nor his creative powers can be truly understood if they are regarded as orphans without some universal Parent.

JOSHUA LOTH LIEBMAN, *How Can I Believe in God Now?,* 1943

To say that a man is a person is to say that in the depths of his being he is more a whole than a part and more independent than servile. It is this mystery of our nature which religious thought designates when it says that the person is the image of God.

JACQUES MARITAIN, *Education at the Crossroads,* 1943

To say that a man is made up of certain chemical elements is a satisfactory description only for those who intend to use him as a fertilizer.

HERBERT J. MULLER, *Science and Criticism,* 1943

Modern man is Christian man in revolt.

MICHAEL FOSTER, *Christian News Letter,* November 26, 1947

Man is the medium between spirit and matter; he is between the visible and the invisible world. He sums them up in his person, as in a universal center.
> ADRIEN-EMANUEL ROQUETTE, *Chata-Ima* (Life of Roquette), D. R. Lebreton, 1947

Man is a self-compulsive bundle of 126 instincts, whose end is his becoming. This is the meaning of the instinctive psychology of Freud, of the behavioristic psychology of Watson, of the laissez-faire sociology of William Graham Sumner, of *The Gospel of Wealth* of Andrew Carnegie, of the pragmatism of William James, of the subjective legalism of Oliver Wendell Holmes, Jr., the terrifying historical naturalism of J. H. Robinson, of the mechanistic philosophy of history of Brooks Adams, of Thorstein Veblen's ironic principle of conspicuous consumption in his *Theory of the Leisure Class*. None of these allows man an end outside himself.
> WILLIAM T. COSTELLO, *Address*, August 24, 1948

Science gives us the low view of man—man as matter, man as animal, at best, man as one of the mass.
> F. SHERWOOD TAYLOR, *Man and Matter*, 1951

For this is man, without God a reed, without reason a poor animal, but with God a rising flame of truth and liberty upon the earth.
> ANTON C. PEGIS, *Disputed Questions in Education*, 1954

Man . . . is so different from the beasts that he is another sort of being.
> EDMUND W. SINNOTT, *Matter, Mind and Man*, 1957

Man is described by science not as being "a little lower than the angels" but rather as being a bit higher than the apes.
> PAUL E. SABINE, *Science Ponders Religion*, ed. H. Shapley, 1960

The philosophical presupposition that man is a biological animal and that human laws should get right in line with biological nature is not a hair-breadth away from the philosophy of Adolf Hitler.
> ALBERT T. MOLLEGEN, *Christianity and Modern Man*, 1961

Man is ever a contingent being in search of necessity.
> GEORGE BRANTL, *Catholicism*, 1962

Post-modern man is more profoundly perplexed about the nature of man than his ancestors were. He is on the verge of spiritual and moral insanity. He does not know who he is.
> F. S. C. NORTHROP, *Man, Nature and God*, 1962

Man is the only significant link between the physical order and the spiritual one. Without man the universe is a howling wasteland contemplated by an unseen Deity.
> POPE KIRIL I, in Morris West's novel *The Shoes of the Fisherman*, 1963

See also Creation; Humanity; Individual; the various rubrics under Man; Mankind; Person; Personality; Spirit; Spirit, Human.

MAN: HIS DESTINY AND GOAL

Man is made for the contemplation of heaven, and is in truth a heavenly plant, to come to the knowledge of God.
> ST. CLEMENT OF ALEXANDRIA, *Exhortation to the Greeks*, c. 200

Nature never intended man to be a low, groveling creature. From the moment of his birth she implants in him an inextinguishable love for the noble and the good.
> LONGINUS, *On the Sublime*, c. 250

Can it be that handicraftsmen have some end in view in their work, but that there is no goal for the life of man?
> ST. BASIL THE GREAT (330–379), *Address to Young Men*

Man is created to praise, honor and serve God, his Lord, and by so doing to save his soul. Whatever else there is on earth is created for man's sake: it is there to help him reach his goal. It follows that man must use it in so far as it helps him to attain his goal, and abstain from it so far as it hinders him.

> ST. IGNATIUS LOYOLA, *Spiritual Exercises,* 1548

Every man is born for heaven.

> EMMANUEL SWEDENBORG, *Heaven and Hell,* 1758

Each man is meant to represent humanity in his own way, continuing its elements uniquely so that it may reveal itself in every mode, and all that can issue from its womb would be made actual in the fullness of unending space and time.

> F. SCHLEIERMACHER, *The Monologen,* 1810

What is man born for but to be a Reformer, a Remaker of what man has made; a renouncer of lies; a restorer of truth and good.

> RALPH WALDO EMERSON, *Man, the Reformer,* 1841

Man, a being endued with reason, cannot on that very account live altogether at random; he is obliged in some sense to live on principle, to live by rule, to profess a view of life, to have an aim, to set up a standard.

> JOHN HENRY NEWMAN, *Discourses to Mixed Congregations,* 1849

While by no manner of vivisection you can learn what a *Beast* is, by only looking into your own hearts you may know what a *Man* is,—and know that his only true happiness is to live in hope of something to be won by him, in Reverence of something to be worshipped by him, and in Love of something to be cherished by him, and cherished—for ever.

> JOHN RUSKIN, *Sesame and Lilies,* 1865

A religious man is guided in his activity not by the consequence of his action, but by the consciousness of the destination of his life.

> LEO TOLSTOI, *Confessions,* 1879

In the light of the eternal we are manifest, and even this very passing instant pulsates with a life that all the worlds are needed to express. In vain would we wander in the darkness; we are eternally at home in God.

> JOSIAH ROYCE, *The World and the Individual,* 1900

We and God have business with each other; and in opening ourselves to his influence our deepest destiny is fulfilled.

> WILLIAM JAMES, *Varieties of Religious Experience,* 1902

Uniqueness is the essential property of man, and it is given to him in order that he may unfold it.

> MARTIN BUBER, *Jewish Mysticism and the Legends of Baalshem,* 1916

Our business on earth is to be colonizers of heaven, to redeem the world and set up in it an order of life which will incarnate the spirit and principles of Jesus.

> HALFORD E. LUCCOCK, *Preaching Values in the New Translation of the New Testament,* 1928

I think it not improbable that man, like the grub that prepares a chamber for the winged things it never has seen but is to be—that man may have cosmic destinies that he does not understand.

> OLIVER WENDELL HOLMES, JR. (1841–1935), quoted in *An Autobiography of the Supreme Court,* ed. A. F. Westin

Man . . . is destined to realize his potentialities in eternity, in conditions far more real than those which have so far hemmed his efforts.

> NICHOLAS BERDYAEV, *The Meaning of History,* 1936

Man, as a reasonable being, is a great good, and that not only in himself but also on account of the whole destiny that awaits him, and, above all, of the beatitude of which he is capable.

ÉTIENNE GILSON, *The Spirit of Medieval Philosophy*, 1936

The career of mankind, since it reflects the creative design of God, is no mere groping from one futility to another, but represents the march of the human spirit onward toward the achievement of God's Kingdom on earth.

ISRAEL GOLDSTEIN, *Book of Jewish Thoughts*, ed. Hertz, 1943

The destiny of Man is not limited to his existence on earth and he must never forget that fact. He exists less by the actions performed during his life than by the wake he leaves behind him like a shooting star.

LECOMTE DU NOÜY, *Human Destiny*, 1947

I do not have to win the world, even for Christ. I have to save my soul. That is what I must always remember, against the temptation of success in the apostolate.

HENRI DE LUBAC, *Paradoxes*, 1948

What a man does here and now with holy intent is no less important, no less true—being a . . . link with divine being—than the life in the world to come.

MARTIN BUBER, *The Way of Man*, 1950

We are put here not merely to go to heaven, but to go there with all the fullness of the riches and beauty which our Lord offers us from His grace.

FRANCIS DEVAS, *The Law of Love*, ed. by Caraman, 1954

His inborn instinct is to try to make the Universe revolve around himself; his spiritual task in life is to overcome his self-centredness in order to put himself in harmony with the absolute spiritual Reality that is the true center of everything in the phenomenal world. This "flight of the alone to the alone" is the goal of Man's endeavors.

A. J. TOYNBEE, *Study of History*, Vol. XII, *Reconsiderations*, 1961

See also Creation; Destiny; Determinism; Election; Evolution; Fatalism; Fate; Immortality; Man, and the various other rubrics under Man; Mankind; Perfection; Predestination; Progress; Religion, Necessity of.

MAN: HIS POTENTIAL

This is the culminating gift of God, this is the supreme and marvelous felicity of man . . . that he can be that which he wills to be. . . . God the Father endowed man, from birth, with the seeds of every possibility and every life.

PICO DELLA MIRANDOLA, *On the Dignity of Man*, 1486

There is no limit set to the perfecting of the powers of man; human perfectibility is in reality indefinite.

MARQUIS DE CONDORCET, *History of the Progress of the Human Spirit*, 1796

Each man is a new power in nature. He holds the keys of the world in his hands.

RALPH WALDO EMERSON, *Natural History of Intellect*, 1883

If man as the existentialist sees him is not definable, it is because to begin with he is nothing. He will not be anything until later, and then he will be what he makes himself. Thus, there is no human nature, because there is no God to have a conception of it. Man simply is.

JEAN PAUL SARTRE, *Existentialism and Humanism*, 1948

The central conception of Man in the Gospels is that he is an unfinished creation capable of reaching a higher level by a definite evolution which must begin by his own efforts.

MAURICE NICOLL, *The New Man*, 1950

See also Evolution; Immortality; the various rubrics under Man; Mankind; Perfection; Progress.

MAN: HIS SELF-DEIFICATION

Is it possible to imagine anything so ridiculous, as this miserable and wretched creature, which is not so much as master of himself, exposed and subject to offenses of all things, and yet dareth to call himself Master and Emperor of this Universe?

> MICHEL DE MONTAIGNE, *Essays*, Bk. 2, ch. 12, 1580

Man is strong when he contents himself with being what he is: he is weak when he desires to raise himself above humanity.

> JEAN JACQUES ROUSSEAU, *Émile*, 1762

When God saw that Adam had eaten of the tree, he said, "Behold, Adam is become as one of us, knowing Good and Evil." . . . Implicitly and explicitly, then, we have the truth that man through Spirit— through cognition of the Universal and the Particular—comprehends God Himself.

> G. W. F. HEGEL (1770–1831), *The Philosophy of History*, publ. posth.

Religion progresses as it suppresses relationship with God, and develops into a religion under a new form, a superior form, the cult of man.

> LUDWIG FEUERBACH, *The Essence of Christianity*, 1841

Man feels nothing towards God which he does not feel towards man. *Homo homini deus est.* Man is god to man.

> LUDWIG FEUERBACH, *The Essence of Christianity*, 1841

What was formerly contemplated and worshipped as God is now perceived to be something *human.*

> LUDWIG FEUERBACH, *The Essence of Christianity*, 1841

The substance and object of religion is altogether human. . . . Divine wisdom is human wisdom. . . . The secret of theology is anthropology. . . . The absolute mind is the so-called finite subjective mind.

> LUDWIG FEUERBACH, *The Essence of Christianity*, 1841

There is a universal religion, made for the alchemists of thought, a religion that emerges from man himself, man regarded as a divine memento.

> CHARLES BAUDELAIRE (1821–1867), *Journals and Notebook*

The dim and shadowy outline of the superhuman deity fades slowly away from us; . . . we perceive with greater and greater clearness the shape of a yet grander and nobler figure. . . . From the dim dawn of history, and from the inmost depth of every soul, the face of our father Man looks out upon us with the fire of eternal youth in his eyes, and says, "Before Jehovah was, I am."

> W. K. CLIFFORD, *Lectures and Essays*, Vol. II, 1879

I do not see why the very existence of an invisible world may not in part depend on the personal response which any one of us make to the religious appeal. God himself, in short, may draw vital strength and increase of being from our fidelity.

> WILLIAM JAMES, *The Will to Believe and Other Essays*, 1896

Glory to Man in the Highest! for Man is the master of things.

> ALGERNON CHARLES SWINBURNE (1837–1909), "Hymn of Man," *Poems*

Society, democratic from end to end, can brook no such radical class distinction as that between a supreme being favored with eternal and absolute perfection and the man of beings doomed to the lower ways of imperfect struggle.

> HARRY A. OVERSTREET, *Hibbert Journal*, Vol. XI, 1913

God is ourselves.

> HARRY A. OVERSTREET, *Hibbert Journal*, Vol. XI, 1913

Those thinkers who cannot believe in any gods often assert that the love of humanity would be in itself sufficient for them; and so, perhaps, it would, if they had it.

> G. K. CHESTERTON, *Tremendous Trifles,* 1915

We also help to maintain and sustain the nature of God and are not merely his subjects. . . . Not only does he matter to us, but we matter to him. . . . He is in the strictest sense not a creator but a creature.

> S. ALEXANDER, *Space, Time and Deity,* II, 1922

In all things it is well to exalt the dignity of Man, by freeing him as far as possible from the tyranny of the non-human Power.

> BERTRAND RUSSELL, *Mysticism and Logic* 1925

One cannot speak of God simply by speaking of man in a loud voice.

> KARL BARTH, *The Word of God and the Word of Man,* 1928

Between God and man there is an impassable barrier, which man from his side can never cross. Every effort of man to exalt himself to the Divine is regarded as an act of presumption. . . . The gulf between God and man can only be bridged by God himself.

> ANDERS NYGREN, *Agapé and Eros,* I, 1932

If one is not clear about God, one will always tend to shy away toward something more accessible, like one's own conscious state.

> GREGORY VLASTOS, *The Religious Way,* 1934

The modern savage—the twentieth century savage—understands the most intimate secrets of nature. . . . He is so ingenious that he thinks he is God.

> DOROTHY THOMPSON, *Ladies Home Journal,* September, 1945

Man's claim to be like God has been rejected once more; not one foundation of the life of our civilization has remained unshaken.

> PAUL TILLICH, *The Shaking of the Foundations,* 1948

If he doesn't believe in God he doesn't believe that God decides and that means that he has to decide everything for himself. And *that* means he's God himself.

> ANISETTA in Aubrey Menen's *The Backward Bride,* 1950

Even among the most hardened the longing for God betrays its presence under another guise. So as to get along without God more painlessly, they look for the equivalent of God in themselves.

> FRANÇOIS MAURIAC, *Words of Faith,* 1955

What rubbish has been written about being masters of our fate and captains of our souls and creators of an ideal commonwealth! Such talk bowed God out of His universe, and put men on the throne.

> HENRY SLOANE COFFIN, *Joy in Believing,* 1956

Man creates God just as he creates himself, and he creates God in his own image, often as he aspires to be, often as he in reality is.

> M. F. ASHLEY MONTAGU, *This Is My Faith,* ed. S. G. Cole, 1956

See also Adam; Evolution; Humanism; Humanity; Idolatry; the various rubrics under Man; Perfection; Progress; Secularism; Self-Will; Vanity.

MAN: HIS WICKEDNESS

Of all the creatures that creep and breathe on earth there is none more wretched than man.

> HOMER, *Iliad,* c. 800 B.C.

Man, of himself and his own, is nothing, has nothing, can do and is capable of nothing, but only infirmity, evil, and wickedness.

Theologica Germanica, 14th century A.D.

Sin is that inborn corruption of man, derived and propagated from our first parents, whereby we are immersed in depraved lusts, averse to goodness and prone to all evil, and unable of ourselves to do or think anything that is good. . . . We are all by nature under the Wrath of God, and subject to just punishment.

HENRY BULLINGER, *The Helvetic Confession,* 1536

His heart is so thoroughly infected by the poison of sin that it cannot produce anything but what is corrupt.

JOHN CALVIN, *Institutes,* II, 1536

Whatever is in man, from intellect to will, from the soul to the flesh, is all defiled and crammed with concupiscence.

JOHN CALVIN, *Institutes,* 1536

As we are all vitiated by sin, we cannot but be hateful to God, and that not from tyrannical cruelty, but the strictest justice.

JOHN CALVIN, *Institutes,* 1536

We have altogether a confounded, corrupt, and poisoned nature, both in body and soul; throughout the whole man is nothing that is good.

MARTIN LUTHER (1483–1546), *Table Talk*

If anyone says that it is not within man's power to turn from his evil ways, and that evil works, like good works, come from God, . . . let him be anathema.

Council of Trent, 1563

We are utterly indisposed, disabled, and made opposite to all good, and wholly inclined to all evil.

Westminster Confession of Faith, Formulary of the Presbyterian Church of Scotland, 1643

A little wretched, despicable creature; a worm, a mere nothing, and less than nothing; a vile insect that has risen up in contempt against the majesty of Heaven and earth.

JONATHAN EDWARDS, *The Justice of God in the Damnation of Sinners,* 1734

I believe, and hold it as the fundamental article of Christianity, that I am a fallen creature; that I am of myself capable of moral evil, but not of myself capable of moral good, and that an evil ground existed in my will, previously to any given act, or assignable moment of time, in my consciousness. I am born a child of wrath.

SAMUEL TAYLOR COLERIDGE, *Aids to Reflections,* 1825

The very birth of a human being is an event which involves the certainty of entire moral depravity, without the supernatural interposition of God to prevent it.

NATHANIEL TAYLOR, *Concio ad Clerum,* 1828

Depravity of will and corruption of nature are transmitted wherever life itself is transmitted. . . . Evil does flow down the generations through the channels of biological coherence.

WALTER RAUSCHENBUSCH, *A Theology for the Social Gospel,* 1917

Luther's insistence . . . upon man's total depravity is hardly tenable either on Christian, moral, or reasonably considered grounds. . . . To propound the *utter* worthlessness of man implies the curious paradox in which salvation is conceived to be effected upon a worthless object.

VERGILIUS FERM, *What Is Lutheranism?,* 1930

Man is one who has fallen away from God, one who is separated from God, a sinner, whose divinely created nature and connection with God has been perverted by his sin.

EMIL BRUNNER, *The Divine Imperative,* 1937

If our depravity were total we should not know ourselves to be depraved.

C. S. Lewis, *The Problem of Pain,* 1940

One of the great ironies of our time is the fact that just as the theologians, assisted by the educational theorists, had succeeded in ridding theology of the alleged incubus of "natural depravity," the psychologists began to bring it back . . . with lurid descriptiveness.

Edwin Lewis, *A Philosophy of the Christian Revelation,* 1940

We must have faith in man. But we cannot. . . . The present world of man has been for us a revelation of evil; it has shattered our confidence. . . . Our vision of man has been covered over by the unforgettable image of the bloody ghosts in extermination camps.

Jacques Maritain, *The Range of Reason,* 1952

Man's radical self-assertion then blinds him to the fact of sin, and this is the clearest proof that he is a fallen being. Hence it is no good telling man that he is a sinner.

Rudolf Bultmann, *Kerygma and Myth,* 1954

His basic trouble is that his freedom is infected with a mysterious bias toward evil which universally results in a prideful rebellion against God which issues in moral disobedience.

Kenneth Cauthen, *The Impact of American Religious Liberalism,* 1962

Man has always been a wolf—a wolf with his own refinement who often enjoys befouling those whom he tortures—one could say that goodness is spread very wide and that it manifests itself among the harshest if only the wolf within them is asleep. But what a light sleeper he is!

François Mauriac, *Cain, Where Is Your Brother?,* 1962

See also Election; Evil; Fall, the; God: His Wrath; Hell; Man, and the various rubrics under Man; Original Sin; Predestination; Punishment; Sin; Sinners; Wicked, the.

MAN, MODERN

Modern emancipated man . . . does not believe the words of the Gospel but he believes the best-advertised notion. . . . The modern man has ceased to believe, without ceasing to be credulous, hangs, as it were, between heaven and earth, and is at rest nowhere.

Walter Lippmann, *A Preface to Morals,* 1929

Rationalism has robbed them of faith in God and the spiritual love-life of union with Him. Being men, not calculating-machines or vegetables, they must have life, concrete, intense, passionate. They therefore turn to sex . . . not for what it really can give and has given in all ages, but for the content of that other and supreme love-life which it reflects.

E. I. Watkin, *The Bow in the Clouds,* 1931

He functions as a distracted atom in a growing chaos made poor by his wealth, made empty by his fulness, reduced to monotony by his very opportunities for variety.

Lewis Mumford, *The Condition of Man,* 1944

The modern soul has definitely limited its horizons; having negated the eternal destinies, it has even lost its trust in nature, for nature without God is traitorous.

Fulton J. Sheen, *Peace of Soul,* 1949

Modern man is master of his fate. What he suffers he suffers because he is stupid or wicked, not because it is nature's decree.

Bertrand Russell, *New York Times Magazine,* September 3, 1950

Modern man . . . has so long believed that right and wrong were only differences in point of view, that now when evil works itself out in practice he is paralyzed to do anything against it.

FULTON J. SHEEN, *Way to Happiness,* 1953

Modern man is earthed; materially environed. His devotions are transmuted. There is no advance in all this. We are enmeshed in this materialism.

GEORGE MACLEOD, *Only One Way Left,* 1956

There is a deep sickness which infects the soul of modern man. Among rationalists its name is positivism. Among the romantics, its name is existentialism. Both are afraid of life. Both . . . are afraid of reason. Both . . . are afraid of emotion. Neither one has a belief, a hope.

ROBERT E. FITCH, *New Republic,* June 17, 1957

Modern man wouldn't live with God; now he can't live with himself.

STANLEY JONES, *Conversion,* 1959

See also Agnosticism; Atheism; Determinism; Dialectical Man; Liberalism; Man and the various rubrics under Man; Materialism; Modernism; Naturalism; Positivism; Rationalism.

MAN AND GOD

To him who sees Me in everything and everything in Me, I am never lost, and he is not lost to me.

Bhagavad-Gita, c. 800 B.C.

Man proposes, God disposes.

PLAUTUS, *Bacchides,* 200 B.C.

If God be my friend I cannot be wretched.

OVID, *Tristia,* c. 10 A.D.

Live with men as if God saw you; converse with God as if men heard you.

SENECA, *Epistolae ad Lucilium,* c. 63 A.D.

Our service of God does not afford God anything, nor has he need of human obedience; but he has granted, to those who follow him and serve him, life and incorruption and eternal glory.

ST. IRENAEUS, *Adversus Haereses,* c. 175

The Almighty Creator of the Universe, the Invisible God Himself from heaven planted among men the truth and the holy teaching which surpasseth the wit of man, and fixed it firmly in their hearts.

Epistle to Diognetus, c. 200

There is an enmity between what is of God and what is of man.

TERTULLIAN, *The Christian's Defense,* c. 215

In every just man . . . there is a statue which is an image of God. The man carves it himself, keeping his eye fixed on God.

ORIGEN, *Contra Celsum,* 246

The voice of God is heard as it were through sleep when with tranquil mind we withdraw from the activity of this world and ponder upon the divine precepts.

POPE ST. GREGORY THE GREAT, *Moralium Lib.,* 584

We belong to God, and to Him we return.

Koran, c. 625

If we desire to . . . be truly men of God, we must wake from our sleep and bear in mind that the great King is over us.

MAIMONIDES, *Guide for the Perplexed,* 1190

All that He has, all that He is, He gives: all that we have, all that we are, He takes.

JOHN RUYSBROECK (1293–1381), *Speculum Aeternae Salutis,* cap. vii

For as the body is clad in cloth, and the flesh in skin and the bones in the flesh and the heart in the whole, so are we, soul and body, clad in the Goodness of God and enclosed.

> JULIANA OF NORWICH, *Revelations of Divine Love,* 1397

All men of right judgment will testify that there is engraved on human minds a sense of the divine which can never be expunged.

> JOHN CALVIN, *Institutes,* I, 1536

Let your *desire* be to see God; your *fear* lest you lose Him; your *grief* that you do not enjoy Him; and let your *joy* be for what may lead you to Him.

> ST. TERESA OF ÁVILA (1515–1582), *Maxim,* 69

Man is of kin to the beasts by his body, and if he is not kin to God by his spirit, he is a base and ignoble creature.

> FRANCIS BACON, *Essays,* 1597

Man appoints, and God disappoints.

> MIGUEL DE CERVANTES, *Don Quixote,* 1605

As the Sun does not set to any Nation, but withdraw it self, and return again; God, in the exercise of his mercy, does not set to thy soul, though he benight it, with an affliction.

> JOHN DONNE, *Sermon,* 1624

God wisheth none should wreck on a
> strange shelf:
To him man's dearer than to himself.

> BEN JONSON (1572–1637), *The Forest*

It is not necessary for being with GOD to be always at church. We may make an oratory of our heart wherein to retire from time to time to converse with Him in meekness, humility, and love.

> NICHOLAS HERMAN OF LORRAINE, Brother Lawrence, *Practice of the Presence of God,* c. 1666

If you say that man is too little for God to speak to him, you must be very big to be able to judge.

> BLAISE PASCAL, *Pensées,* 1670

The power of man, in so far as it is manifested by his actual essence, is part of the infinite power of God or Nature, that is to say, part of His essence.

> BARUCH SPINOZA, *Ethics,* 1677

As for myself, I am content with the conviction that God's eyes are ever upon me, and that His providence and justice will follow me into the future life as it has protected me in this.

> MOSES MENDELSSOHN, *Phaedon,* 1767

There never was a time when God had not spoken to man and told him to a certain extent his duty.

> JOHN HENRY NEWMAN, *The Arians of the Fourth Century,* 1833

Whence come my conceptions of the intelligence, and justice, and goodness, and power of God? It is because my own spirit contains the germs of these attributes.

> WILLIAM ELLERY CHANNING (1780–1842), *Works*

We begin by degrees to perceive that there are but two beings in the whole universe, our own soul, and the God who made it.

> JOHN HENRY NEWMAN, *Parochial and Plain Sermons,* 1843

There is but one thing needful—to possess God. All our senses, all our powers of mind and soul . . . are so many ways of approaching the divinity, so many modes of tasting and adoring God.

> HENRI AMIEL, *Journal,* July 16, 1848

Has God made faces beautiful and limbs strong, and created these strange, fiery, fantastic energies, and created the splendor of substance and the love of it . . . only that these things may lead His creatures away from Him?

> JOHN RUSKIN, 1858, *Works,* VII

There is but one way in which man can ever help God—that is, by letting God help him; and there is no way in which His name is more guiltily taken in vain, than by calling the abandonment of our work the performance of His.

JOHN RUSKIN, *The Ethics of the Dust,* 1866

The magnetic needle always points towards the north, and hence it is that the sailing vessel does not lose its course. So long as the heart of man is directed towards God, he cannot be lost in the ocean of Worldliness.

SRI RAMAKRISHNA (1836–1886), *His Life and Sayings,* ed. F. M. Muller, 1899

If man is naturally a servant of God, by grace he becomes a child of God; if originally he was only above the nature of the brute, he now rises above his own nature.

M. JOSEPH SCHEEBEN, *Glories of Divine Grace,* 1886

Man is the cornerstone; and from the true conception of man have the Jewish thinkers risen to the noblest conception of the Deity.

E. G. HIRSCH, *Reform Advocate,* V. 244, 1893

Man is to become divine by realizing the divine. Idols or temples, or churches or books are only the supports, the help of his spiritual childhood.

SWAMI VIVEKANANDA, *Address,* Parliament of World Religions, 1893

Whoever has in him the human quality, whoever has the spirit of man, has the candle of the Lord.

PHILLIPS BROOKS, *The Candle of the Lord and Other Sermons,* 1899

God's life . . . sees the plan fulfilled through all the manifold lives.

JOSIAH ROYCE, *The World and the Individual,* 1900

To Christ himself the truth that man was God's child by nature was the great fact of man's existence; and the desire that man might be God's child in reality was the motive of His own life and work.

PHILLIPS BROOKS, *The Influence of Jesus,* 1903

As soon as I believed there was a God, I understood I could not do otherwise than live for Him alone.

CHARLES DE FOUCAULD (1858–1910), *Letters to Henry de Castries*

God, no more than man, can help us except through our own purpose, guided by our own insight, dealing with our own world; and, only as grace works in that personal way through ourselves, is it God's dealing with us as His children.

JOHN OMAN, *Grace and Personality,* 1919

Every particular Thou is a glimpse through to the eternal Thou; by means of every particular Thou the primary word addresses the eternal Thou.

MARTIN BUBER, *I and Thou,* 1923

There is no relation to God which is not in practice a relation to man, and therefore we cannot come to a true understanding of life's purpose apart from knowledge of one another in the deepest place of our being.

Statement by Friends [Quakers] of Great Britain, 1925

The greatest question of our time is not communism vs. individualism, not Europe vs. America, not even the East vs. the West; it is whether men can bear to live without God.

WILL DURANT, *On the Meaning of Life,* 1932

In the Church man becomes a universal being: his life in God unites him to the life of all creation by the bonds of cosmic love.

SERGIUS BULGAKOV, *The Orthodox Church,* 1935

It is imperative to understand once more that the rediscovery of man will also be the rediscovery of God. That is the essential theme of Christianity.

　　NICOLAS BERDYAEV, *Solitude and Society,* 1938

This is the fundamental view of the Bible—man gains his distinctiveness, his truly human nature, by the fact that God speaks to him and that man in faith receives this Word and answers it with the "yes" of faith.

　　EMIL BRUNNER, *The Christian Understanding of Man,* 1938

The conception of a God so constituted that we are, as individuals, of direct concern to Him appears both presumptuous—considering our individual insignificance in the scheme as a whole—and unnecessary for that feeling of helpless reverence in face of the universal order which is the essence of religious experience.

　　HANS ZINSSER, *As I Remember Him,* 1940

Though God reigns and the arguments for His existence stand irrefutable, yet it is, it seems, a part of the penalty that we must pay in our fallen exile that there are moods in which we feel ourselves deserted by Him.

　　CHRISTOPHER HOLLIS, *The Noble Castle,* 1941

Wherever we found a false idea about men its origin lay in a false idea of God.

　　LORD HALIFAX, Speech, *New York Times,* May 31, 1943

Remove God and you strip from man every vestige of that reflected glory wherein his unique dignity lies.

　　JOHN A. O'BRIEN, *Religion—Does it Matter?,* 1944

The same Voice which spoke long ago and said, "Let there be light," spoke again, and said, "Let there be a human soul." You were, and are, as much God's individual creature as much the object of his unique regard, as if he had never made anything else.

　　RONALD A. KNOX, *Retreat for Priests,* 1946

It is one of the oldest mistakes in the world, and one of the most fatal, to suppose that you or anybody else is necessary to God's purposes.

　　RONALD A. KNOX, *Retreat for Priests,* 1946

Man is to be filled with eternity. But for that he must walk as a child with God, he must be able to receive His life, he must know and love and serve Him.

　　GERALD VANN, *The Divine Pity,* 1946

The greatest moral catastrophe of our age is the growing number of Christians who lack a sense of sin because personal responsibility to God is not a moving force in their lives.

　　Roman Catholic Bishops of the U.S., 1947

The pious man of the Old Testament, the mystical saint of the Middle Ages, the reformer in the Christian Church, and the prophet of atheism are all united through that tremendous human experience: man cannot stand the God Who is really God.

　　PAUL TILLICH, *The Shaking of the Foundations,* 1948

God meant it, too, when He said in the first commandment that He was jealous and would have no others before Him. He wants you—all of you.

　　FULTON OURSLER, *Why I Know There Is a God,* 1949

In basic structure, God's experience does not differ from ours. There is form and content in God's mind, and there is challenge, enjoyment and struggle in his life.

　　PETER A. BERTOCCI, *Introduction to the Philosophy of Religion,* 1951

There is in the Christian life man's part and God's part; but what we cannot be persuaded of is that man never finds strength for his own part if he is preoccupied with it, but only when his eyes are on God's part.

WILLIAM RUSSELL MALTBY, *Obiter Scripta,* ed. F. B. James, 1952

Man has thought to do without God. In those terrible words of Nietzsche's he has proclaimed: "God is dead"; now he is discovering that it is he himself who is the first victim of this negation. It is he who is cast helpless into that abyss of nothingness into which he had designed to cast God.

HENRI DANIEL-ROPS, *Christianity and Freedom,* 1952

Is not man in chronic rebellion against the very idea of a God who might make claims upon him?

JAMES HASTINGS NICHOLS, *Religion in America,* ed. John Cogley, 1958

At the level of life, only the experience of God can resist the experience of evil; at the level of intellect, only the progressive discovery of God can resist the progressive discovery of evil.

CHARLES JOURNET, *The Meaning of Evil,* 1961

A God who confronted men simply as exalted, distant and strange would be a God men would have to avoid because they would not be able to meet His demands.

KARL BARTH, Lecture, University of Chicago, quoted in *New York Times,* April 24, 1962

God does not die on the day when we cease to believe in a personal deity, but we die on the day when our lives cease to be illuminated by the steady radiance, renewed daily, of a wonder, the source of which is beyond all reason.

DAG HAMMARSKJOLD, *Markings,* 1964

Man proposes, and God laughs.
Yiddish Proverb

See also All; Beatific Vision; Bible; Buddhism; Call; Christianity; Church, Definitions of; Church: Its Nature; Communion; Conscience; Creation; Eucharist; Experience, Religious; Forgiveness; Genius; God: Finding Him; God: His Omnipotence; Grace; Happiness; Heart; Heaven; Holy Spirit; Humanity; Ideal; Immortality; Incarnation; Islam; Jesus Christ; Judaism; Judgment, God's; Love, Divine; Love of God; Man and the various rubrics under Man; Mystical Experience; Mysticism; One; Perfection; Prayer; Prayer: Defined and Explained; Providence; Reason and God; Religion; Religion: Its Nature and Function; Religion, Necessity of; Soul; Soul and God; Spirit, Human; Spiritual Life; Virtue; Vision.

MAN INDWELT BY GOD

He, the eternal, dwells concealed in the heart of all beings. Though himself devoid of all senses, he is the illuminator of all the senses, the source of their powers.

The Mahanirvana Tantra, prior to 6th century B.C.

He is the one God hidden in all beings, all-pervading, the self within all beings, watching over all worlds, dwelling in all beings, the witness, the perceiver.

Svetasvatara Upanishad, prior to 400 B.C.

There is a God within us, and we glow when He stirs us.

OVID, *Fasti,* c. 5 A.D.

Bear in mind, then, when you eat, who you are that eat and whom you are nourishing; when you cohabit with women, who you are that do this. . . . You are bearing God with you, you poor wretch, and know it not!

EPICTETUS, *Discourses,* c. 110 A.D.

God is not external to anyone, but is present with all things, though they are ignorant that He is so.

> PLOTINUS (205–270), *Ennead,* vi, 9

His kingdom dwelleth in thee; lo! the riches of heaven are within thy soul, if thou be willing.

> EPHRAIM THE SYRIAN (306–373), quoted in Margaret Smith's *Early Mysticism in the Near and Middle East*

I was wandering like a lost sheep, searching outside of myself for that which was within. I ran through all the streets and squares of this great city, the world, searching for Thee, O God, and I found Thee not, because I sought Thee wrongly. Thou wert within me and I sought Thee without.

> ST. AUGUSTINE, *Soliloquies,* 387

And we must dare affirm that the Creator, by reason of love, is drawn from his transcendent throne above all things to dwell within the heart of all things, while he yet stays within himself.

> DIONYSIUS THE AREOPAGITE, *The Divine Names,* c. 500

If men wish to draw near to God, they must seek Him in the hearts of men.

> ABÚ SA'ÍD IBN ABI KHAYR (died 1049 A.D.), quoted in M. Smith's *Readings from the Mystics of Islam*

God is near us, but we are far from Him, God is within, we are without, God is at home, we are in the far country.

> MEISTER ECKHART (1260?–1327?), *Sermons*

As soon as He finds you ready, God is bound to act, bound to pour Himself into your being, just as, when the air is pure and clear, the sun must pour into it without holding back.

> MEISTER ECKHART (1260?–1327?), *Meister Eckhart*

In those limpid souls where God can see the reflection of himself, God is reposing in the soul and the soul is reposing in God.

> MEISTER ECKHART (1260?–1327?), *Meister Eckhart*

The image of God is found essentially and personally in all mankind. Each possesses it whole, entire and undivided, and all together not more than one alone.

> JAN VON RUYSBROECK (1293–1381), *The Adornment of the Spiritual Marriage*

God dwells in a secret and hidden way in all souls, in their very substance, for if He did not, they could not exist at all.

> ST. JOHN OF THE CROSS (1542–1591), *Living Flame of Love*

God is in thy heart, yet thou searchest for Him in the wilderness.

> ARJAN (died 1606), *The Sikh Religion,* M. A. Macauliffe, III

If a drop of water, thrown into an ocean of some priceless essence, were alive, and could speak and declare its condition, would it not cry out with great joy: O mortals! I live indeed, but I live not myself, but this ocean lives in me, and my life is hidden in this abyss?

> ST. FRANCIS OF SALES, *Treatise on the Love of God,* 1607

Ah! how little it matters if everything dies in us, provided God reigns and lives there!

> ST. FRANCIS OF SALES (1567–1622), *Consoling Thoughts of,* ed. Huguet

The Son of God, the Eternal Word in the Father, who is the glance, or brightness, and the power of the light of eternity, must become man and be born in you, if you will know God: otherwise you are in the dark stable and go about groping.

> JAKOB BOEHME (1575–1624), *The Threefold Life of Man*

Whatever is, is in God, and nothing can exist or be conceived without God. . . . God is the indwelling and not the transient cause of all things.

BARUCH SPINOZA, *Ethics,* 1677

God, through Christ, hath placed his Spirit in every man, to inform him of his duty, and to enable him to do it; and those who live up to this, are the people of God, and those that live in disobedience are not God's people.

WILLIAM PENN, *Primitive Christianity Revived,* 1696

Now as God is infinite and omnipresent in all places, he consequently is within the bodies of men, as well as without them. . . . He penetrates all beings and spirits more thoroughly than the visible light at noonday doth the air.

JOHN BELLERS, *Essays,* 1699

Reason as well as revelation assures us, that he cannot be absent from us, notwithstanding he is undiscovered by us.

JOSEPH ADDISON, *The Spectator,* 1714

Inwardly, he has a seed of the Divine Life given into the birth of his soul, a seed that has all the riches of eternity in it, and is always wanting to come to birth in him, and be alive in God.

WILLIAM LAW, *The Spirit of Prayer,* 1749

Can it be that thousands are made for one? all the generations that have passed away, merely for the last? . . . The All-wise sports not in this manner: he invents no fine-spun shadowy dreams; he lives and feels in each of his children with paternal affection, as though it were the only creature in the world.

JOHANN G. HERDER, *Philosophy of the History of Man,* 1791

All spiritual being is in man. A wise old proverb says, "God comes to see us without bell": that is, as there is no screen or ceiling between our heads and the infinite heavens, so is there no bar or wall in the soul where man, the effect, ceases, and God, the cause, begins.

RALPH WALDO EMERSON, "The Over-Soul," *Essays,* 1841

The only God whom our thoughts can rest on, our hearts cling to, and our conscience can recognize, is the God whose image dwells in our own souls.

WILLIAM ELLERY CHANNING (1780–1842), *Works*

I have come to the stage of realization in which I see that God is walking in every human form and manifesting himself alike in the sage and in the sinner.

SRI RAMAKRISHNA (1834–1886), quoted in Romain Rolland, *Prophet of the New India*

The individual man is partly the animal from which he has come, and partly the God who is coming into him; but God is steadily displacing the animal.

LYMAN ABBOTT, *Evolution of Christianity,* 1892

We are thus not only the sons of God; so far as we are wise our lives are hid in God, we are in Him, of Him.

JOSIAH ROYCE, *The Spirit of Modern Philosophy,* 1892

It is the experience of myriads of trustful souls, that this sense of God's unfailing presence with them in their going out and in their coming in, and by night and day, is a source of absolute repose and confident calmness.

CHARLES VOYSEY, *The Mystery and Pain of Death,* 1892

The great central fact in human life, in your life and in mine, is the coming into a conscious, vital realization of our oneness with this Infinite Life and the opening of ourselves fully to this divine inflow.

RALPH WALDO TRINE, *In Tune with the Infinite,* 1897

To believe in the God over us and around us and not in the God within us—that would be a powerless and fruitless faith.

PHILLIPS BROOKS, *Sermons for Principal Festivals,* 1901

The highest truth is this: God is present in all beings. They are his multiple forms. There is no other God to seek. He alone serves God who serves all other beings.

VIVEKANANDA (1863–1902), quoted in Romain Rolland, *Prophet of the New India*

The simplest view is that which regards the Spirit as a term expressive of God's activity in the soul of man, as distinct from his outward manifestation in nature and history.

W. A. BROWN, *Christian Theology in Outline,* 1906

The Divine Life, which each of us in person is called to live, is within us. Faith, hope, charity, the moral virtues and the gifts of the Holy Ghost are all so many centres from which light and heat radiate unceasingly.

DÉSIRÉ JOSEPH MERCIER, *Conferences of,* 1907

Even while we little suspect it, He breathes forth in the depths of our souls yearnings that no human words could render.

DÉSIRÉ JOSEPH MERCIER, *Conferences of,* 1907

How is it, then, that the voice of God is not more distinctly heard by men? The answer to this question is: To be heard it must be listened for.

DÉSIRÉ JOSEPH MERCIER, *Conferences of,* 1907

God is always with us, why should we not always be with God?

W. B. ULLATHORNE, *Humility and Patience,* 1909

We cannot get away from God, though we can ignore Him. When Him we fly, He is the wings.

RICHARD C. CABOT, *What Men Live By,* 1915

I seemed alone with immensity, and there came at last that melting of the divine darkness into the life within me for which I prayed. Yes, I still belonged, however humbly, to the heavenly household.

GEORGE W. RUSSELL (Æ), *The Candle of Visions,* 1918

Men talk of "finding God," but no wonder it is difficult; He is hidden in that darkest of hiding-places, your own heart. *You* yourself are a part of Him.

CHRISTOPHER MORLEY, *Religio Journalistici,* 1924

The ocean of Divinity in which we float is not affected by what our shrunken personality may do.

ERNEST DIMNET, *What We Live By,* 1932

We affirm that man is the embodiment of the Divine, and that every human being containing within himself something of God, is of infinite moral worth, too sacred to be exploited or oppressed.

ISRAEL GOLDSTEIN, *A Book of Jewish Thoughts,* ed. Hertz, 1943

The last end of man, the ultimate reason for human existence, is unitive knowledge of the divine Ground—the knowledge that can come only to those who are prepared to "die to self" and so make room, as it were, for God.

ALDOUS HUXLEY, *The Perennial Philosophy,* 1944

By giving man liberty and conscience God abdicated a part of his omnipotence in favor of his creature and this represents the spark of God in man.

LECOMTE DU NOÜY, *Human Destiny,* 1947

Not before a man can say I in perfect reality—that is, finding himself—can he in perfect reality say Thou—that is, to God.

MARTIN BUBER, *Between Man and Man,* 1947

In the partial possession of God in this life, we catch glimmerings of that supreme ecstasy which the soul will experience when it shall be in intimate union with infinite Beauty, Truth and Love.

JOHN A. O'BRIEN, *Truths Men Live By,* 1947

I believe in the absolute oneness of God and therefore of humanity. What though we have many bodies? We have but one soul. . . . I know God is neither in heaven nor down below, but in everyone.

M. K. (MAHATMA) GANDHI (1869–1948), *The Essential Gandhi,* ed. L. Fischer

The divine Nature, free and perfect and blissful, must be manifested in the individual in order that it may manifest in the world.

SIR AUROBINDO, *Synthesis of Yoga,* 1950

If we believe that God speaks to real persons in guidance and learning, we must believe that the Christian conscience is the voice of God, determining my duty here and now.

W. R. FORRESTER, *Christian Vocation,* 1951

It would be rather more accurate to say that God contains us than that we have God within us.

WALTER FARRELL, *My Way of Life,* 1952

The very existence of spiritual qualities in man suggests that they are manifestation in him of something like them in the universe outside. . . . Man's spirit, rooted in life, may actually be a part of the Universal Spirit, emerging from and returning to it again.

EDMUND W. SINNOTT, *Biology of the Spirit,* 1955

The modern philosophical atheist who asks man to free himself from God doesn't understand that God is man's element. To ask him to rid himself of God is like asking the fish to free itself from the sea, the bird from the air.

JAMES M. GILLIS, *This Mysterious Human Nature,* 1956

He whose power is at work in us is powerful enough to carry out His purpose beyond all our hopes and dreams.

VINCENT P. McCORRY, *America,* September 29, 1962

Search yourself and you will find God.

Kurdish Proverb

I like to think that we are never really alone, because I can take God with me and leave Him there with you.

Letter from a soldier in camp to his wife, no date or author given

See also Conscience; Consciousness; Divinity; Experience, Religious; Holy Spirit; Jesus Christ; Love, Divine; the various rubrics under Man; Mystical Experience; Mysticism; One; Pantheism; Soul; Spirit; Word, the.

MAN'S QUEST OF GOD

He who in truth seeketh after God with all his heart will remove his mind far away from every earthly thing and he will direct the gaze of his understanding towards God.

PALLADIUS OF EGYPT, *Paradise of the Fathers,* c. 300 A.D.

We do not walk to God with the feet of our body, nor would wings, if we had them, carry us to Him, but we go to Him by the affections of our soul.

> St. Augustine (354–430), *Serm.* XXXLIV

Every mortal is troubled with many and various anxieties, and yet all desire, through various paths . . . by different means to attain one happiness: in a word, God.

> Boethius, *Consolations of Philosophy,* c. 525

With a pure mind and will, you can approach God anywhere.

> Judah Halevi, *Cuzari,* c. 1135

All things, by desiring their own perfection, desire God Himself; inasmuch as the perfection of all things are so many similitudes of the divine essence.

> St. Thomas Aquinas, *Summa Theologiae,* I q. 6 a.l, ad 2, 1272

Nobody hath found God by walking his own way.

> Ram Das (c. 1580), *The Sikh Religion,* M. A. Macauliffe, III

My greatest desire is that I may perceive the God whom I find everywhere in the external world, in like manner also within and inside myself.

> Johannes Kepler (1571–1630), quoted by J. W. von Goethe in his *Maxims and Reflections*

To come to God there is a straight line for every man everywhere.

> John Donne, *Sermons,* no. 67, 1640

The place where man vitally finds God . . . is within his own experience of goodness, truth, and beauty, and the truest images of God are therefore to be found in man's spiritual life.

> Harry Emerson Fosdick, *Adventurous Religion,* 1926

There are innumerable definitions of God because his manifestations are innumerable. They overwhelm me with wonder and awe and for a moment stun me. But I worship God as Truth only. I have not found him, but I am seeking after Him. I am prepared to sacrifice the things dearest to me in pursuit of this quest.

> Mahatma Gandhi, *My Experiment with Truth,* 1927

Only as one consorts with the seers and prophets and poets of the faith shall he discover the secret of the Highest, shall he enter His inner courts.

> Henry Burke Robins, *The Colgate-Rochester Bulletin,* June, 1930

We think we must climb to a certain height of goodness before we can reach God. But . . . if we are in a hole the Way begins in the hole. The moment we set our face in the same direction as His, we are walking with God.

> Helen Wodehouse, *Inner Light,* I, 1931

The search for God is, indeed, an entirely personal undertaking. By the exercise of the normal activities of his consciousness, man may endeavor to reach an invisible reality both immanent in and transcending the material world. Thus, he throws himself into the most audacious adventure that one can dare.

> Alexis Carrel, *Man, the Unknown,* 1935

Whoever seeks the Truth or loves the Good or strives in prose or in verse, in bronze, in marble, on canvas, or through the insubstantial, ethereal, elusive, evanescent medium of melody and harmony, to express the Beautiful, is really, though he know it not, striving for God.

> James M. Gillis, *If Not Christianity, What?,* 1935

I cannot feel that God would give the intimations of His presence by giving His gifts, but withhold Himself.

> E. Stanley Jones, *Victorious Living,* 1936

The deepest need of man is not food and clothing and shelter, important as they are. It is God.

THOMAS R. KELLEY, *A Testament of Devotion,* 1941

The quest of man for God which becomes in the end the most ardent and enthralling of all his quests, begins with the first vague questioning of Nature and a sense of something unseen both in himself and her.

SRI AUROBINDO, *The Life Divine,* 1949

Many souls fail to find God because they want a religion which will remake society without remaking themselves.

FULTON J. SHEEN, *Peace of Soul,* 1949

Ever since the days of Adam, man has been hiding from God and saying, "God is hard to find."

FULTON J. SHEEN, *Peace of Soul,* 1949

God only comes to those who ask him to come; and he cannot refuse to come to those who implore him long, often and ardently.

SIMONE WEIL, *Waiting for God,* 1951

Because man was made for God, God has built man with certain powers by which he is to take hold of God, and certain needs by which he is moved to the exercise of these powers.

FRANK J. SHEED, *Society and Sanity,* 1953

The man who does not need God will not find God.

GEORGE BRANTL, *Catholicism,* 1962

See also Church: Its Nature; Contemplation; Detachment; Experience, Religious; Man and God; Man's Unity with God; Meditation; Mysticism; Nature; Prayer; Religion; Religion, Necessity of; Spiritual Life.

MAN'S UNITY WITH GOD

Know God, and all fetters will be loosed. Ignorance will vanish. Birth, death, and rebirth will be no more. Meditate upon him and transcend physical consciousness. Thus will you reach union with the lord of the universe.

Svetsavatara Upanishad, prior to 400 B.C.

The wise in heart cleave to Me [Krishna]
  into my Being brought;
Hearts fixed on Me, breaths breathed on
  Me; praising Me, each to each,
So have they happiness and peace.

The Song Celestial, SIR EDWIN ARNOLD'S translation of the *Bhagavad-Gita,* 5th to 2nd century B.C.

Whither shall anyone go away, or where shall anyone run away from him who embraces the whole universe.

ST. CLEMENT OF ROME, *Epistle to the Corinthians,* c. 100

A spirit united to God, in a habitual manner by prayer and charity, acquires wisdom, goodness, strength, benevolence, liberality, greatness of soul.

ST. MAXIMUS THE CONFESSOR, *Centuries of Charity,* c. 626

Let him who wishes to be near to God abandon all that alienates him from God.

HARITH IBN ASAD AL-MUHĀSIBI (died 857 A.D.), *Al-Ahkām al-Sultanīya*

He [Man] is to God as the pupil of the eye; through him God sees His creation and has mercy on it. . . . He is the King's viceroy, who bears His seal and safeguards His treasure, and the world shall not cease to be safeguarded so long as the Perfect Man remains in it.

MUHYĪ AL-DIN IBN AL-ARABĪ (died 1240 A.D.), *Fusūs al-Hikam*

God can as little do without us, as we without Him.

MEISTER ECKHART (1260?–1327?), *Sermons*

All our life as it is in God is immersed in blessedness: all our life as it is in ourselves is immersed in active love. And though we live wholly in ourselves and wholly in God, it is but one life.

JOHN RUYSBROECK (1293–1381), *De Calculo,* cap. ix

As soon as a man turneth himself in spirit, and with his whole heart and mind entereth into the mind of God which is above time, all that ever he hath lost is restored in a moment.

Theologica Germanica, 14th century

God does not demand the impossible, but He tells us to do what we can and to ask for what we cannot do, then He helps us to be able.

Council of Trent, 1563

When both thy intellect and will are quiet and passive to the expressions of the eternal Word and Spirit, and when thy soul is winged up above that which is temporal . . . *then* the eternal Hearing, Seeing and Speaking will be revealed in thee.

JAKOB BOEHME (1575–1624), *Three Dialogues of the Supersensual Life*

We are all strings in the concert of His joy; the spirit from His mouth strikes the note and tune of our strings.

JAKOB BOEHME (1575–1624), *The Threefold Life of Man*

All things flow constantly from God as water flows from a spring, and tends ever to return to Him as water tends ever to return to its level.

JOHANNES SCOTUS ERIGENA, *The Division of Nature,* 1681

As men's will and affections come to be subdued to the will of God, he discovers to the souls of men what is to be known of him, the pure in heart only seeing God.

JOHN BELLERS, *Essays,* 1699

Follow the path God opens to you without hesitation; do not desire a higher kind of prayer in order to be more united to God, but desire a higher and closer union with Him, that He may fill and absorb you more and more.

JACQUES-BENIGNE BOSSUET (1627–1704), *Letters of*

We are nothing in ourselves; we are only what God has made us to be; and that only while it pleases him. He has only to withdraw the hand which supports us in order to replunge us into the abyss of our nothingness.

FRANÇOIS FÉNELON (1651–1715), *Selections from,* ed. by Fellen

If your will is with God you work with God; God is then the life of your soul, and you will have your life with God to all eternity.

WILLIAM LAW (1686–1761), *The Way to Divine Knowledge*

We are attached to the Supreme Being by a supple chain which restrains without enslaving us. What is most admirable in the universal order of things is the action of free men under the divine hand.

JOSEPH DE MAISTRE, *Considérations sur la France,* 1796

By withdrawing into intimate dialogue with God, man can attain the complete abandonment of his passions and evil habits, i.e. he can free himself from the claims of his flesh and return to his Source.

RABBI NAHMAN OF BRATSLAV (1772–1811), quoted in *Judaism,* ed. A. Hertzberg, 1961

All our life is His life. We are in His hand, and abide therein, and no one can pluck us out of His hand. We are eternal, because He is eternal.

J. G. FICHTE (1762–1814), *The Vocation of Man*

Man lives and is from God. He is, as it were, the fast-flitting pulse of the Divinity.

BRONSON ALCOTT January 2, 1835, *Journal of,* ed. O. Shepard, 1938

Ineffable is the union of man and God in every act of the soul. The simplest person who in his integrity worships God, becomes God; yet forever and ever the influx of this better and universal self is new and unsearchable.

    RALPH WALDO EMERSON, "The Over-Soul," *Essays,* 1841

Only be at peace with self, live in the presence of God, in communion with Him, and leave the guidance of existence to those universal powers against whom thou canst do nothing.

    HENRI AMIEL, *Journal,* July 16, 1848

But if the great sun move not of himself; but is as an errand-boy in heaven; nor one single star can revolve, but by some invisible power; how then can this one small heart beat; this one small brain think thoughts; unless God does that beating, does that thinking, does that living, and not I.

    HERMAN MELVILLE, *Moby Dick,* 1851

To conceive one's self as separate from God is an error; yet only when one sees oneself as separate from God, can one reach out to God.

    E. H. PALMER, quoting Sufis teaching, *Oriental Mysticism,* 1867

The soul of God is poured into the world through the thoughts of men.

    RALPH WALDO EMERSON, "Perpetual Forces," *Lectures,* 1877

Much on earth is hidden from us, but there is given us in recompense the secret conviction of our living bond with another world, a celestial and loftier world: and the very roots of our thoughts and sensations are not less but there, in other worlds.

    FATHER ZOSSIMA'S Discourse in Feodor Dostoevsky, *The Brothers Karamazov,* 1880

When a soul becomes perfect and absolute, it must become one with Brahman.

. . . To gain this universal individuality this miserable little prisoner individuality must go. Then alone can death cease, when I am one with Life; then alone can misery cease when I am one with Happiness; then alone can all errors cease when I am one with Knowledge.

    SWAMI VIVEKANANDA, *Address,* World Parliament of Religions, 1893

Put God underneath all your life, and your life must rest upon the everlasting arms.

    PHILLIPS BROOKS (1835–1893), *Perennials from*

In essence the life of God and the life of man are identically the same, and so are one. They differ not in essence, in quality; they differ in degree.

    RALPH WALDO TRINE, *In Tune with the Infinite,* 1897

The conscious communion of man with God and with nature, as it is transformed by the soul, is the vital source of religion.

    JOHN LANCASTER SPALDING, *Religion, Agnosticism and Education,* 1902

Man is the center of a great web and network of Divine influence. Spiritual forces play upon him, moulding and communicating with him.

    W. J. DAWSON, *The Evangelistic Note,* 1905

To those who obey Him, whether they be wise or simple, He will reveal Himself in the toils, the conflicts, the sufferings which they shall pass through in His fellowship, and, as an ineffable mystery, they shall learn in their own experience Who He is.

    ALBERT SCHWEITZER, *The Quest of the Historical Jesus,* 1906

You are always nearer the divine and true source of your power than you think.

    JOHN BURROUGHS, *The Divine Soil,* 1908

Whether God stands above the things or lives in the things themselves, whether there is one God or many, remains a consideration of secondary importance.

HUGO MUNSTERBERG, *Eternal Values,* 1909

Thought pure and simple is as near to God as we can get; it is through this that we are linked to God.

SAMUEL BUTLER, *Notebooks,* 1912

The relations between man and God have, in the course of religious history, become more deeply personal and passionate, with the deepening sense of evil and spiritual distress. The soul finds at length its divine companion.

WILLIAM E. HOCKING, *The Meaning of God in Human Experience,* 1912

There is a native, elemental homing instinct in our souls which turns us to God as naturally as the flower turns to the sun.

RUFUS M. JONES, *The Inner Life,* 1916

We feel God less as a superhuman consciousness than as the actual consciousness of the whole human race, past, present, and future, as the collective consciousness of the whole race, and still more, as the total and infinite consciousness which embraces and sustains all consciousness.

MIGUEL DE UNAMUNO, *Tragic Sense of Life,* 1921

The normal relation between the human will and the divine is one of subordination, cooperation, and fellowship in the pursuit of the moral ends for which the world exists.

E. GRIFFITH-JONES, *Providence Divine and Human,* Vol. 1, Bk. 1, 1925

The turning away from the world, sorrow over one's life hitherto, is the first approach to the Being of God, the first unconscious prayer, which opens the first way for the Holy Spirit to our hearts.

JOANNES JORGENSEN, *Autobiography,* 1928

All the length of our conscious life, God . . . in Whom alone we can find what we want and understand what we mean, presents Himself to the apprehension of our soul, tempts our desire, pursues our will.

R. H. J. STUART, *The Inward Vision,* 1929

I believe it will come to be seen that the fullest view of human nature and life is that which predicates conscious vitality in the powers behind the things we see and which perceives that Man is morally related to these powers and under obligation to them.

G. A. JOHNSTON ROSS, *Behavior and Destiny,* 1931

Man without God is no longer man.

NICHOLAS BERDYAEV, *The End of Our Time,* 1933

God is a secret audible only when self is silent.

MAURICE ZUNDEL, *The Splendour of the Liturgy,* 1934

Religion . . . regards God, above all, as a Being who can hold communication with us: now this is just what the God of Aristotle . . . is incapable of doing.

HENRI BERGSON, *Two Sources of Morality and Religion,* 1935

We are always in touch with God; everything that happens is His arrangement, His Providence, and a means of grace, a push on to heaven, only most people try to go their own way, and thus put obstacles to God's action.

JOHN CHAPMAN, *Spiritual Letters of,* 1935

A Christian on earth could not become one of the blessed in heaven unless he had already received divine life.

REGINALD GARRIGOU-LAGRANGE, *Christian Perfection and Contemplation,* 1937

It is the simple truth that in every event of a man's life God is knocking at his door . . . and if you let Him in, the event is transfigured. . . . As one event comes after another, your soul takes a momentary flight towards God in an unspoken prayer; and so the events become the altar-stairs by which you draw nearer to the Holiest.

> RICHARD ROBERTS, *The Contemporary Christ,* 1938

God designed the human machine to run on Himself. He Himself is the fuel our spirits were designed to burn, or the food our spirits were designed to feed on. There isn't any other. That's why it's no good asking God to make us happy in our own way without bothering about religion.

> C. S. LEWIS, *The Case for Christianity,* 1943

There is a sort of infinity in man, because of his power not only to become in a manner of all things, but even, by the gift of God, to become one with the Maker of all things.

> GERALD VANN, *The Divine Pity,* 1946

There is something in man's inmost being that can be kindled and struck into flame by God and as we feed the flame with our lives we can become revealing places for God, a flame of God's life.

> RUFUS M. JONES, *The Luminous Trail,* 1947

It is something to know that God is a transcendent and sovereign Self, but it is something else again to enter oneself and with all one's baggage—one's own existence and flesh and blood—into the vital relationship.

> JACQUES MARITAIN, *Existence and the Existent,* 1948

The basic and original phenomenon of religious life is the meeting and mutual interaction between God and man, the movement of God towards man and of man towards God.

> NICHOLAS BERDYAEV, *The Divine and the Human,* 1949

God expresses Himself in the visible and recognizes Himself in us. Our striving after the visible is God seeking Himself.

> ANTONIN SERTILLANGES, *Recollections,* 1950

An instant of separation from God would be instant annihilation, for every moment of our life is nourished from the very life of God.

> WALTER FARRELL, *My Way of Life,* 1952

God is the terminal point of reference at which the life-lines of all His creatures intersect, and in Him all the walls which create interior separation between His creatures will be thrown down.

> KARL HEIM, *Transformation of the Scientific World View,* 1953

Too many are waiting for God to do things *for* them rather than *with* them.

> RALPH W. SOCKMAN, *How to Believe,* 1953

The religious person enjoys a great advantage when it comes to answering the crucial question that hangs over our times like a threat: he has a clear idea of the way his subjective existence is grounded in his relation to "God."

> C. G. JUNG, *The Undiscovered Self,* 1957

God created the heavens and the earth. And then He created man. He did not create society. . . . God looks upon man and continues to address man as His creature. In other words, God addresses man as man and as nothing else.

> PETER L. BERGER, *The Precarious Vision,* 1961

Whosoever walks towards God one cubit, God runs towards him twain.

Hebrew Proverb

See Also Abandonment; Beatific Vision; Church: Its Nature; Contemplation; Creation; Detachment; Experience, Religious; Grace; Holy Spirit; Immortality; Love, Divine; Love of God; Man and God; Man's Quest of God; Meditation; Mysticism; Prayer; Religion, Necessity of; Selflessness; Spiritual Life.

MANKIND

We are like men who, knowing little of painting, blame the artist because the colors in his picture are not all beautiful— not seeing that he has given to each part what was appropriate to it.

PLOTINUS (205–270 A.D.), *Enneads*, III, 2, 11

All mankind is of one Author, and in one volume; when one Man dies, one chapter is not torn out of the book, but translated into a better language; and every Chapter must be so translated.

JOHN DONNE (1573–1631), *Devotions upon Emergent Occasions*

To worship mankind as it is would be to deprive it of what alone makes it akin to the divine—its aspirations. For this human dust lives; this misery and crime are dark in contrast to an imagined excellence, they are lighted up by a prospect of good.

HENRY MORE, *The Life of*, by R. Ward, 1710

Yes, truly, if Nature is one, and a living indivisible whole, much more is Mankind, the Image that reflects and creates Nature, without which Nature were not.

THOMAS CARLYLE, *Sartor Resartus*, 1836

Mankind are earthen jugs with spirits in them.

NATHANIEL HAWTHORNE, *American Notebooks*, 1842

Seat thyself sultanically among the moons of Saturn, and take high abstracted man alone; and he seems a wonder, a grandeur, and a woe. But from the same point, take mankind in mass, and for the most part, they seem a mob of unnecessary duplicates.

HERMAN MELVILLE, *Moby Dick*, 1851

Those who desire to worship their Creator must worship him through mankind. Such it is plain is the scheme of Nature.

WINWOOD READE, *The Martyrdom of Man*, 1872

We are no aliens in a stranger universe governed by an outside God; we are parts of a developing whole, all enfolded in an embracing and interpenetrating love.

SIR OLIVER LODGE, *Hibbert Journal*, Vol. II, p. 475, July, 1904

We are only cave men who have lost their cave.

CHRISTOPHER MORLEY, *The Man Who Made Friends with Himself*, 1949

The proper study of mankind is God and man-before-God in their interrelation.

H. R. NIEBUHR, *The Purpose of the Church and Its Ministry*, 1956

Hitherto man had to live with the idea of his death as an individual; from now onward mankind will have to live with the idea of its death as a species.

ARTHUR KOESTLER, *New York Times Magazine*, March 20, 1960

See also Brotherhood; Democracy; Fall, the; Humanity; Internationalism; Love of Mankind; Man; Man: Defined and Interpreted; Man Indwelt by God; Society; Unity of Mankind; Wonder.

MARKET PLACE

When He found legalized robbery in the Temple of God He did not propose arbitration nor resort to the orderly process of diplomacy but drove the robbers out by the terror of His presence.

LYMAN ABBOTT, *Outlook,* July, 1898

Conscientious persons in church pews are baffled by the discrepancy between the beautiful ideals of the Master and the brute facts of the market place.

RALPH W. SOCKMAN, *The Highway of God,* 1941

I . . . argue that the Cross be raised . . . at the centre of the market-place as well as in the steeple of the church. . . . Jesus was not crucified in a cathedral between two candles, but on a cross between two thieves; on the town garbage-heap; at a crossroad so cosmopolitan that they had to write his title in Hebrew and in Latin and in Greek; . . . at the kind of place where cynics talk smut, and thieves curse, and soldiers gamble. Because that is where he dies. And that is what he dies about. And that is where churchmen should be and what churchmanship should be about.

GEORGE MACLEOD, *Only One Way Left,* 1959

See also Capitalism; Competition; Economics and Christianity; Money; Trade; Traders.

MARRIAGE

The man who has a wife is far above him who lives in continence; he who keeps a house is far above him who has none: he who has children is far above him who has none.

Zend-Avesta, 6th century B.C.

It is fitting for those who marry—both the men and the women—to accomplish their union with the consent of the Bishop, that their marriage may be according to God, and not according to lust.

ST. IGNATIUS OF ANTIOCH, *Ad Polycarp,* c. 109

Where the flesh is one, one also is the spirit. Together husband and wife pray, together perform their fasts, mutually teaching, exhorting, sustaining. Equally they are found in the church of God, equally at the banquet of God, equally in persecutions and in refreshments.

TERTULLIAN, *To His Wife,* c. 206

How can we find words to describe the happiness of that marriage which the Church joins together; which offering confirms; which the blessing seals; which the angels report; which the Father ratifies.

TERTULLIAN, *To His Wife,* c. 206

We do not give up marriage because of the possibility of lust any more than we give up clothes because of the possibility of luxury.

TERTULLIAN, *Against Marcion,* c. 207

When thou makest a marriage, go not round from house to house borrowing mirrors and dresses; for the matter is not one of display, nor dost thou lead thy daughter to a pageant. . . . As many as thou knowest to be of good character, those invite, and bid them be content with what there is. Let no one from the orchestra be present, for such expense is superfluous, and unbecoming. Before all the rest, invite Christ.

ST. JOHN CHRYSOSTOM, *Homilies on Colossians,* c. 388

If any persons have been hindered by the marriage state, let them know that marriage is not the hindrance but their purpose which made an ill use of marriage. . . . It is not wine which makes drunkenness, but the evil purpose, and the using it beyond measure.

ST. JOHN CHRYSOSTOM, *Homilies on Hebrews,* c. 388

If a man and wife prove deserving, the *Shekhinah* dwells among them. If not, a fire consumes them.

Sotah, Mishnah, c. 400 A.D.

When a divorced man marries a divorced woman, there are four minds in the bed.
Talmud: Pesahim, c. 500

And marry not idolatresses until they believe; for assuredly a slave who believeth is better than an idolatress, though she please you more.
Koran, c. 625

The essential nature of marriage consists in a certain indivisible union of minds by which each one of the consorts is bound to keep inviolably his faith with the other.
ST. THOMAS AQUINAS, *Summa Theologicae* III, q. 29, art. 2, 1272

Just as I may eat, drink, sleep, walk . . . and do business with a heathen, a Jew, a Turk, or a heretic, so also may I marry any of them. Do not give heed to the fool's law which forbids this.
MARTIN LUTHER, *The Babylonian Captivity,* 1520

We are all made for marriage, as our bodies show and as the Scriptures state.
MARTIN LUTHER, *Letter,* March 27, 1525

It is God who arrangeth marriages. . . . Those whom he hath once joined he joineth for ever.
GURU NANAK (1496–1538), *The Sikh Religion,* M. A. Macauliffe, I

The state of matrimony is the chief in the world after religion; but people shun it because of its inconveniences, like one who, running out of the rain, falls into the river.
MARTIN LUTHER (1483–1546), *Table Talk*

No man is so virtuous as to marry a wife only to have children.
MARTIN LUTHER (1483–1546), *Table Talk*

On account of the loss of original innocence the passions begin to rise in rebellion against right reason; and man, conscious of his own frailty and unwilling to fight the battles of the flesh, is supplied by marriage with an antidote by which to avoid sins of lust.
Council of Trent, 1563

Whoever said that marriage is to be put above virginity or celibacy, and that it is not more blessed to remain chaste than to marry, let him be anathema.
Decree of Council of Trent, 1564

It is the nursery of Christianty, which supplies the earth with faithful souls, to complete the number of the elect in heaven.
ST. FRANCIS OF SALES, *Introduction to a Devout Life,* 1608

The holy liberty of marriage has a particular force to extinguish the fire of concupiscence; but the frailty of them that enjoy this liberty passes easily from permission to dissolution.
ST. FRANCIS OF SALES, *Introduction to the Devout Life,* 1608

It may be bad, it may be good, as it is a cross and calamity on the one side, so 'tis a sweet delight, an incomparable happiness, a blessed estate, a most unspeakable benefit, a sole content, on the other, 'tis all in the proof.
ROBERT BURTON, *Anatomy of Melancholy,* III, 1621

To contract before that they will have no children, makes it no marriage, but an adultery; to deny themselves to one another, is as much against marriage as to give themselves to another.
JOHN DONNE, *Sermon,* May 30, 1621

Some married persons, even in their marriage, do better please God than some virgins in their state of virginity: they by giving great example of conjugal affection, by preserving their faith unbroken, by educating children in the fear of God . . . do not only please God, but do so in a higher degree than those virgins whose piety is not answerable to their great opportunities and advantages.

JEREMY TAYLOR, *Holy Living,* 1650

To have and to hold from this day forward, for better, for worse, for richer, for poorer, in sickness and in health, to love and to cherish, till death do us part.

The Book of Common Prayer, 1662

Between a man and his wife nothing ought to rule but love.

WILLIAM PENN, *Some Fruits of Solitude,* 1693

Never marry but for Love; but see that thou Lov'st what is lovely.

WILLIAM PENN, *Some Fruits of Solitude,* 1718

More belongs to Marriage than four bare Legs in a Bed.

THOMAS FULLER, *Gnomologia,* 1732

Marriage is the best state for man in general; and every man is a worse man in proportion as he is unfit for the married state.

SAMUEL JOHNSON, *Boswell's Life of,* March, 1776

It has its foundation in nature, and is the only lawful relation by which Providence has permitted the continuance of the race.

JAMES KENT, *Kent's Commentary,* 1830

It may be, as Don Juan says to Zerline, that only in the soft arms of a blameless wife does true felicity reside, . . . but the question is whether there is not also something else one can only too easily forget in these soft arms—namely, what Christianity is.

SÖREN KIERKEGAARD, *Attack upon Christendom,* 1854

Sacred union of souls beneath the immortal yoke of love freely promised, pleasures and duties for ever in common, misfortunes borne together, joys of paternity tempered by the anxieties of the future, indescribable mingling of good and evil, virtue ever present to sustain the feebleness of the heart against the chafings and trials of life.

JEAN BAPTISTE LACORDAIRE (1802–1861), *Thoughts and Teachings of*

Marriage is the most inviolable and irrevocable of all contracts that were ever formed. Every human compact may be lawfully dissolved but this.

JAMES GIBBONS, *Faith of Our Fathers,* 1876

Marriage has God for its Author, and was from the very beginning a kind of foreshadowing of the Incarnation of His Son; and therefore there abides in it a something holy and religious; not extraneous but innate; not derived from men, but implanted by nature.

POPE LEO XIII, *Arcanum,* February, 1880

In Christian marriage the contract is inseparable from the sacrament, and . . . for this reason the contract cannot be true without being a sacrament as well. . . . Hence it is clear that among Christians every marriage is, in itself and by itself, a sacrament.

POPE LEO XIII, *Arcanum,* February, 1880

Inasmuch as laws have been enacted by Congress, which laws have been pronounced constitutional by the court of last resort. . . . I publicly declare that my advice to the Latter-Day Saints is to refrain from contracting any marriage forbidden by the law of the land.

WILFORD WOODRUFF, President of the Mormon Church, 1890

As a church in general conference assembled we accept his [Wilford Woodruff] declaration concerning plural marriages as authoritative and binding.

> General Council of Mormon Church, 1890

One of the happiest sights in the world . . . is the appealing, attractive picture of the young Christian man with the young Christian woman of his choice, kneeling at the foot of the altar and receiving humbly from the hand of God the blessing of their union.

> F. A. P. DUPLANLOUP (19th century, France), *Christian Marriage*

Marriage is not regarded by Christianity as a mere accident of life, . . . but it is taken as a recognized vocation essential to the building up of the Church on earth, and thereby entering into the scheme of the world's salvation.

> FATHER CUTHBERT, *Catholic Ideals in Social Life,* 1904

Adam could not be happy even in Paradise without Eve.

> JOHN LUBBOCK, *Peace and Happiness,* 1909

We steadfastly uphold what must always be regarded as the governing considerations of Christian marriage. One is the primary purpose for which marriage exists, namely, the continuance of the race through the gift and heritage of children; the other is the paramount importance in married life of deliberate and thoughtful self-control.

> Lambeth Conference (of Anglican Bishops), 1920

Marriage was not instituted for their happiness, nor sexual instinct implanted for its own sake alone. Rather Nature baits the trap with a romantic allurement to induce men and women to fulfil the purpose it has in view—the continuation of life on earth, the preservation of the species.

> P. J. GANNON, *Holy Matrimony,* 1923

The system of law and custom which upheld the old theological conception of marriage is today a crumbling, motheaten, dangerously toppling ruin which has served its purpose and now needs to be junked.

> BENJAMIN LINDSEY, *The Companionate Marriage,* 1927

I say the Devil never invented anything worse than this piece of "sacramental" poppycock that has been "sanctifed" by the Christian Church. . . . I say that such absurdities are on an intellectual level with devil worship.

> BENJAMIN LINDSEY, *The Companionate Marriage,* 1927

State and the law should take no notice of sexual relations apart from children. . . . No marriage ceremony should be valid unless accompanied by a medical certificate of the woman's pregnancy.

> BERTRAND RUSSELL, *Letter to Judge B. J. Lindsey,* quoted in latter's *The Companionate Marriage,* 1927

The union is organic; and it is God who unites them, which means that it is a profound biological-spiritual experience which comes out of the depths of life. The union is for life.

> Committee on Marriage and Home, Federal Council of the Churches of Christ in America, 1929

To love means to decide independently to live with an equal partner, and to subordinate oneself to the formation of a new subject, a "we."

> FRITZ KUNKEL, *Let's Be Normal,* 1929

Marriage, before being a union of bodies, is first and more intimately a union and harmony of minds, brought about not by any passing affection of sense or heart but by a deliberate and resolute decision of the will; and from this cementing of minds, by God's decree, there arises a sacred and inviolable bond.

POPE PIUS XI, *Casti Connubi,* December 31, 1930

The Christian ideal of love and marriage is based upon the love of one man for one woman and one woman for one man, and it is incompatible with the subordination of either.

Federal Council of Churches of Christ in America, *Report,* 1932

Marriage is that relation between man and woman in which the independence is equal, the dependence mutual, and the obligation reciprocal.

LOUIS K. ANSPACHER, *Address,* December 30, 1934

Before marriage man hovers above life, observes it from without; only in marriage does he plunge into it, entering it through the personality of another.

ALEXANDER YELCHANINOV (1881–1934), *Fragments of a Diary*

Success in marriage requires continence as well as potency. In other words, character is indispensable in well-ordered sexual life.

ALEXIS CARREL, *Reader's Digest,* July, 1939

Only supernatural charity, a bond of friendship between God and man, can tie knots strong enough to resist all shocks, all the vicissitudes, all the inevitable trials of a long life spent together; only divine grace can make you rise superior to all the little daily miseries, all the nascent contrasts and disparities of tastes or of ideas.

POPE PIUS XII, *Address,* January 29, 1941

The institution of marriage has a threefold significance: religiously it is a Sacrament; sociologically it is the corner-stone of the family and therefore the foundation of organized society; legally it is a contract.

WENZEL, J., *Shea v. Shea,* 46 N.Y.S. 2nd 141, 1943

The true meaning of marriage is a sublimation of physical passion, in which the intensity and warmth of natural appetite is retained on the higher level of domestic life, and there enriched with the values of parentage, companionship, and fidelity.

RALPH BARTON PERRY, *Puritanism and Democracy,* 1944

The fundamental mystery of Christianity, the nuptial relationship between Christ and His Church, the fact that Christ and His Church are one sole Body, is realized anew in every Christian marriage.

KARL ADAM, *Orate Frates,* 1949

The Christian ideal of marriage is that of indissoluble unity. . . . It is difficult to see on what ground failure in marriage should be treated as if it was the one failure for which the penitent cannot be forgiven.

SYDNEY CAVE, *The Christian Way,* 1949

That there is something intrinsically sacred in the marriage contract is evidenced by the fact that all religions, even the most corrupt, always have regarded it as such and surrounded it with religious rites and ceremonies.

K. J. I. HOCHBAN, *Canadian Messenger of the Sacred Heart,* August, 1950

It is nature's way, the gentle trickery of nature, to lead man and woman in virtue of the psychical need they have of each other to form that close relationship of marriage by which those who are already one in mind and heart become one physical principle for the propagation of the human race.

IGNATIUS W. COX, *The Divine Romance of Marriage,* 1951

To wed is to bring not only our worldly goods but every potential capacity to create more values in living together. . . . In becoming one these two create a new world that had never existed before.

PAUL E. JOHNSON, *Christian Love,* 1951

Marriage is the only sacrament which transforms a human action into an instrument of the divine action, using a human act which up to then had been used for a natural end.

JACQUES LECLERCQ, *Marriage a Great Sacrament,* 1951

It is a fusion of two hearts—the union of two lives—the coming together of two tributaries, which after being joined in marriage, will flow in the same channel in the same direction . . . carrying the same burdens of responsibility and obligation.

PETER MARSHALL, quoted by Catherine Marshall, in her *A Man Called Peter,* 1951

Marriage, as a natural institution, by virtue of the will of the Creator, has not as a primary and intimate end of personal perfecting of the couple but the procreation and education of a new life.

POPE PIUS XII, *Address,* October 29, 1951

Too many married people expect their partner to give that which only God can give, namely, an eternal ecstasy.

FULTON J. SHEEN, *Three to Get Married,* 1951

Marriage is a requirement to all who are not prevented by physical or other disability from assuming the sacred responsibilities of the wedded state.

JAMES E. TALMAGE, *Articles of Faith* (of Church of Jesus Christ of Latter-Day Saints), 1952

The ideal marriage is a marriage in which everything of one participates in every-thing of another, and basic to it all is the receiving and giving through full sexual relationships.

JOHN H. VRUWUNK, *The Lively Tradition,* 1952

Much marriage difficulty and unhappiness are due to the failure of the partners to accept the fact of their finiteness and its meaning. Instead, they hold themselves up to ideals of performance possible only to God.

REUL L. HOWE, *Sex and Religion Today,* ed. S: Doniger, 1953

In marriage reverence is more important even than love. . . . A steady awareness in each that the other has a kinship with the eternal.

F. J. SHEED, *Society and Sanity,* 1953

Love God and laugh at the devil. Assuming that a husband and wife obey these twin commandments, and thereby keep their love for each other this side of idolatry, what can Christian marriage do but bring them nearer to God?

CHAD WALSH, *Behold the Glory,* 1955

What makes a marriage is the consent of the partners, their serious intention to live together in some sense, however dimly perceived, as "one flesh," a union of their two separate existences into still a third existence, the marriage itself. . . . The question of external status is entirely and altogether unnecessary.

WILLIAM G. COLE, *Sex in Christianity and Psychoanalysis,* 1955

Marriage itself is not solely an institution for the propagation of children, but is also for the fruition of that richer fellowship God intended when he saw that it was not good for man to live alone.

GEORGE G. HOCKMAN, *Religion in Modern Life,* 1957

It has to *transmute* romantic love, or what existed of it at the beginning, into real and indestructible *human* love.

> JACQUES MARITAIN, *Reflections on America,* 1958

The goal in marriage is not to think alike, but to think together.

> ROBERT C. DODDS, *Two Together,* 1959

There would be more marriages made in heaven if there were more young people who with the thought of their future children, were prayerfully willing to give God a voice in their final decision.

> LEO TRESE, *Parent and Child,* 1962

Being united in one flesh means being united in one life. . . . This community of life is human; while it is primarily of the spirit and must not play the part of the beast, neither must it try impossibly to be angelic.

> HENRI GIBERT, *Love in Marriage,* 1964

Islam requires every Muslim to marry provided he can afford to do so. Celibacy is strictly prohibited in Islam.

> "Islam Laws of Marriage and Divorce," in *The Review of Religions* (a Moslem publication), July, 1965

See also Adultery; Artificial Insemination; Birth Control; Celibacy; Chastity; Children; Divorce; Eros; Family; Father; Home; Husband; Husband and Wife; Love; Love, Human; Love, Physical; Lust; Miscegnation; Mother; Parents; Passions; Reproduction; Romance; Sacraments; Separation; Sex; Sexual Attraction; Sexual Desire; Sexual Intercourse; Sterilization; Virginity; Wife; Woman.

MARTHA

She did not fail to give Jesus food. Thank God there are Marthas! Where would the world be if everyone sat at the feet of Jesus and nobody cooked?

> VINCENT MCNABB, *The Craft of Prayer,* 1951

MARTYRDOM

We call martyrdom perfection, not because the man comes to the end of his life as others, but because he has exhibited the perfect work of love.

> ST. CLEMENT OF ALEXANDRIA, *In Praise of Martyrdom,* c. 200

Martyrdom is the perfection and crown of Christian sanctity and Christian life.

> ST. JEAN EUDES (1601–1680), *The Reign of Christ*

It is a mistake to regard martyrdom as a merit, when from their own point of view it was in reality a privilege.

> JOHN LUBBOCK, *The Pleasures of Life,* 1887

The annals of Christian martyrdom are not confined to the hour of death. There are souls who have been courageous enough to *live* gloriously.

> GEORGE MATHESON, *Studies in the Portrait of Christ,* 1902

The championship of social justice is almost the only way left open to a Christian nowadays to gain the crown of martyrdom.

> WALTER RAUSCHENBUSCH, *Christianity and the Social Crisis,* 1907

Love makes the whole difference between an execution and a martyrdom.

> EVELYN UNDERHILL, *The Fruits of the Spirit,* 1942

Fathers of the ancient Church, from St. Cyprian to St. Gregory of Nazianz and St. Ambrose, actually assumed that God would most readily withdraw the strength of endurance from those who, arrogantly trusting their own resolve, thrust themselves into martyrdom.

> JOSEF PIEPER, *Fortitude and Temperance,* 1954

Martyrdom is . . . the archetypal form of conflict with evil, the summit of Christian sanctity through conformation to Christ, and . . . the official proclamation of the Gospel to the accredited representatives of the earthly city.

> JEAN DANIELOU, *The Lord of History,* 1958

See also Capital Punishment; Martyrs; Murder; Persecution; Saints; Sanctity; Self-Giving; Selflessness; Self-Sacrifice; Suffering.

MARTYRS

The Proconsul [at Smyrna] continued insisting and saying, "Swear, and I release you; curse Christ." And Polycarp said, "Eighty-six years I have served Him, and He has done me no wrong; how then can I blaspheme my King who saved me?"

> *The Martyrdom of Polycarp* (probable date of his martyrdom, February 22, 156)

Polycarp said: "You threaten the fire that burns for an hour, and after a little while it is quenched; for you are ignorant of the fire of the judgment to come, and everlasting punishment reserved for the ungodly. But why delay? Do what you wish."

> *The Martyrdom of Polycarp* (probable date of martyrdom, February 22, 156)

The blood of the martyrs is the seed of the Church.

> A saying adapted from a passage in Tertullian's *Apologeticus,* 197

That person cannot be a martyr who has not held fast the charity of brotherhood.

> ST. CYPRIAN, *De Unitate Ecclesiae,* XIV, 251

He that dies a martyr proves that he was not a knave, but by no means that he was not a fool.

> C. C. COLTON, *Lacon,* 1820

One with God is always a majority, but many a martyr has been burned at the stake while the votes were being counted.

> THOMAS B. REED, *Speech,* Congress, 1880

Martyr, n. One who moves along the line of least reluctance to a desired death.

> AMBROSE BIERCE, *Devil's Dictionary,* 1906

"I have power to kill you," said a Roman judge to a martyr, who replied, "But I have power to be killed."

> E. STANLEY JONES, *Victorious Living,* 1936

The Church had martyrs throughout the entire Roman Empire before a single book of the New Testament was written.

> FULTON J. SHEEN, *The Woman,* 1951

O my Lord, if not for those few who lived and died for Your glory, this were a world of jackals and serpents. It is Your favored ones who lend substance to this life; they give it meaning and purpose and the sweet scent of holiness.

> DAGOBERT D. RUNES, *Letters to My God,* 1958

See also Death; Killing; Martyrdom; Murder; Persecution; Saints; Sanctity; Self-Giving; Selflessness; Self-Sacrifice.

MARXISM

Marxism is a revolt against capitalism, but it has been bred by it and carries the fatal mark of its materialistic spirit.

> NICHOLAS BERDYAEV, *Christianity and Class War,* 1933

Marx is right in emphasizing the material reproduction of mankind as the foundation of the whole historical process. But the distortion of this insight into a mechanistic economics or into a metaphysical materialism must be rejected.

> PAUL TILLICH, *Christianity and Society,* VII, no. 2, 1942

Its materialism is, on the whole, a justified reaction to pietistic religions which do not understand the social character of life and to "spiritual" versions of Christianity which do not understand the unity of individual and collective man in the material and spiritual dimensions of his life.

REINHOLD NIEBUHR, *Faith and History,* 1949

As a religion, Marxism is a secularized form of the idea of predestination.

NICHOLAS BERDYAEV, *The Realm of Spirit and the Realm of Caesar,* 1952

Theologians, whether of the Social Gospel or of more traditional persuasion, are justified in finding facets of Marxism helpful in their interpretation of human nature and sin.

ROGER L. SHINN, *Christianity and the Problem of History,* 1953

The deepest point of opposition between Marxism and Christianity comes from the fact that both are finally religious.

ROGER L. SHINN, *Christianity and the Problem of History,* 1953

There would be very little temptation to believe in Marxism if modern men and women could only be delivered from the misleading . . . prejudices and attitudes that make it impossible for them to believe in Christianity.

J. V. L. CASSERLEY, *The Bent World,* 1955

Marx, in many ways, seems to have played the "sedulous ape" to Christian doctrine, in each instance substituting the natural for the supernatural, the material for the spiritual, and the human for the Divine.

LESTER DE KOSTER, *Communism and Christian Faith,* 1956

The Christian case against Marxism is both more pentrating and more humble

than the conventional capitalist opposition.

ROGER L. SHINN, *The Ethics of Power,* ed. Lasswell and Cleveland, 1962

The Church as a whole must take the challenge of Marxism seriously. Marxist materialism is a strong reminder of the social dimension of life and of the fact that human existence is conditioned by history, to a Church which has spiritualized the gospel, overemphasized the value of the individual to the neglect of society.

ELIZABETH ADLER, *Unity in Mid-Career,* 1963

See also Atheism; Capitalism; Communism; Dictatorship; Materialism; Religion, Caustic Comments about; Socialism; Soviet Russia; Totalitarianism.

MARY, THE MOTHER OF JESUS

Mary the Virgin is found obedient, saying, "Behold the handmaid of the Lord". . . . But Eve was disobedient. . . . The knot of Eve's disobedience was loosed by the obedience of Mary. For what the virgin Eve bound fast through unbelief, this did the Virgin Mary set free through faith.

ST. IRENAEUS, *Adv. haer.* 3, 22–24, c. 175

If anyone does not believe that holy Mary is the mother of God, he is severed from the Godhead.

ST. GREGORY OF NAZIANZUS, *Ep.* ci, 380

Such was Mary that her life alone is a lesson for all. . . . Let the virginity and the life of Mary be portrayed before us as in a picture, from which as from a mirror is reflected the beauty of chastity and the loveliness of virtue.

ST. AMBROSE, *De Virginibus,* c. 390

And since the holy Virgin brought forth corporally God made one with flesh according to nature, for this reason we also call her Mother of God, not as if the nature of the Word has the beginning of its existence from the flesh.

ST. CYRIL OF ALEXANDRIA, *Epistle to Bishop Nestorius,* 430

From the Virgin Mary, Life was born in Person, and thus did Mary become the mother of all living.

ST. EPIPHANIUS (died 535), *Panarion III*

We recognize that things have crept into the cult of Mary which disfigure it, and they may do so again. . . . There are some fanatics who have grown crazy enough to practice superstition and idolatry instead of the true cult.

PETER CANISIUS (1521–1597), quoted by Henry Fries in his *Answer to Asmussen*

They hurt Religion as much, that ascribe too little to the Blessed Virgin, as they who ascribe too much.

JOHN DONNE, *Sermon,* 1624

Ordered: That all such pictures as have the representation of the Virgin Mary upon them shall be forthwith burned.

Order of the House of Commons, 1645

If we take a survey at least of Europe, we shall find that it is not those religious communions which are characterized by devotion towards the Blessed Virgin that have ceased to adore her Eternal Son, but those very bodies which have renounced devotion to her.

JOHN HENRY NEWMAN, *Development of Christian Doctrine,* 1845

It was altogether becoming that as the Only Begotten had a Father in Heaven whom the seraphim extol as thrice holy, so he should have a Mother on earth who should never lack the splendor of holiness.

POPE PIUS IX, *Ineffabilis Deus,* December 8, 1854

The world is governed by ideals; and seldom or never has there been one which has exercised a more profound and, on the whole, a more salutary influence than the medieval conception of the Virgin.

W. H. LECKY, *History of the Rise and Influence of the Spirit of Rationalism in Europe,* 1868

God gave us Mary for a support in our weakness, a consolation in our sufferings, a help in our dangers, and a refuge in our sinfulness.

EDOUARD DE LEHEN, *The Way of Interior Peace,* 1888

It is impossible to think of any individual who has ever contributed or ever will contribute as much service toward the reconciliation of men with God as Mary.

POPE LEO XIII, *Fidentem Pumque,* 1896

To comprehend the greatness of the dignity to which Mary was thus raised, it would be necessary to measure the greatness of God Himself. It was the closest union that could subsist between the uncreated and a creature.

P. A. SHEEHAN, *Mary, the Mother of God,* 1902

We cannot by any possibility conceive how God can exalt a creature more than He exalted Mary, by making her His mother. She occupies a sphere peculiarly her own.

P. A. SHEEHAN, *Mary, the Mother of God,* 1902

I would give very little, indeed, for the Christianity of the man, who, looking upon a picture of the Madonna and Child, could realize to himself the fact that the Infant is God, and yet gaze with cold indifference on the face of the Mother who holds Him.

P. A. SHEEHAN, *Mary, the Mother of God,* 1902

Just as Eve was the mother of all living in the physical order, so Mary is the Mother of all the living in the supernatural order; as Eve was the mother of all unto death, so Mary is the Mother of all unto life.

Dominic J. Unger, footnote to his 1948 translation of POPE PIUS X, *Ad Diem Illium*, February, 1904

If Mary is the Mother of Christ, and surely she is His mother, then she is also our mother.

POPE PIUS X, *Ad Diem Illium*, February, 1904

After Christ we find in Mary the end of the Law and the fulfillment of the figures and oracles.

POPE PIUS X, *Ad Diem Illium*, February, 1904

We are very far from attributing to the Virgin the power of producing supernatural grace, which belongs to God alone.

POPE PIUS X, *Ad Diem Illium*, February, 1904

Since she surpasses all creatures in sanctity, and in union with Christ, and since she was chosen by Christ to be His associate in the work of human salvation . . . she is the principal minister of the graces to be distributed.

POPE PIUS X, *Ad Diem Illium*, February, 1904

[From the Council of Ephesus in 431 A.D.] the devotion [to Mary] became increasingly fervent throughout the whole Church with each succeeding century. The veneration of the martyrs had already spread to such an extent that it was a simple completion to place Mary at their head as queen of the heavenly hosts. Prayer to her became a universal custom . . . when . . . the humanity of Christ had been in the popular mind swallowed up in the divinity; the need was felt of further human mediation through which the Divine Majesty might be approached and the severity of the awful Judge miti-

gated. From the lowly recipient of grace, she became a source and giver of grace.

SCHAFF and HERZOG in *Encyclopedia of Religious Knowledge*, VII, 1910

The Church does not rest only on Christ, on divine grace, but also on the Virgin Mary, the Mother of God . . . which, having achieved purity and chastity, conceived in the spirit instead of through sinful nature.

NICHOLAS BERDYAEV, *Freedom and the Spirit*, 1935

In her, creation is utterly and completely divinized, conceives, bears and fosters God.

S. N. BULGAKOV, *The Wisdom of God*, 1937

She is always, in her relations with Him and her relations with us, the Mother of Jesus. . . . Her influence is wherever the Saviour is come to dwell. . . . She is not the Source but the "aqueduct" through which the Source flows to us.

MAURICE ZUNDEL, *Our Lady of Wisdom*, 1940

To the cult of the Virgin Mother of God the epoch of the Middle Ages owed in great part its power. From this cult it drew the singular beauty of its art, the rare lucidity of its thought, the glow of its compassion.

ALGERNON CECIL, *A House in Bryanston Square*, 1944

The worship of Mary transformed Catholicism from a religion of terror—perhaps necessary in the Dark Ages—into a religion of mercy and love.

WILL DURANT, *The Age of Faith*, 1950

What then of the Virgin? Let Mary continue to be "blessed among women," the greatest and most honored woman who ever lived. But let us not do her wrong. That she was honored to bring Christ the Saviour into the world is no basis for believing that she should now be Christ's substitute in the world. Today, alas, the blessed Virgin, whom Protestants, too, love devotedly, is being given a religious status for which there is no Biblical authority, and a redemptive role for which there is no spiritual necessity.

JOHN A. MACKAY, in *Foreword* to *The Virgin Mary* by Giovanni Miegge, 1955

When the effort has been made to sympathize and appreciate [the cult of Mary], misgivings and reservations yet remain. This devotion to Mary appears to carry men away from strict responsibility to the basic truths of Christianity that God is a father of infinite love and compassion and understanding; that Jesus is still one with both. The devotion to Mary carries Men away from the Scriptural standards of the Christian Church; the rational faculty is suspended and the devout imagination is undisciplined.

WALDO SMITH in *Preface* to his translation of Giovanni Miegge's *The Virgin Mary*, 1955

Because of our union with Christ through faith and graces we feel a spiritual kinship with His Mother. We pay her great honor and give her great love, but we do not worship her. Worship is for God alone. We do not deify her and make her a goddess, but we believe that God made her the purest and loveliest of His creatures.

JOHN J. DOUGHERTY, *Chosen Vessels*, 1955

What a world of difference lies between the reverent love for the Mother of Christ which we find in early Christianity and the in many ways intolerable exaggerations of the Madonna cult . . . fantasy run riot and by an emotionally extravagant popular sentimental attachment, with a corresponding lack of any theocentric or Christocentric orientation of life!

OTTO KARRER (born 1888), quoted by Henry Fries in his *Answer to Asmussen*, 1958

Every step the Lord took towards His divine destiny Mary took with Him—not in the way of understanding, but in the way of faith.

ROMANO GUARDINI, *Jesus Christus*, 1959

This most holy synod . . . admonishes all the sons of the Church that the cult, especially the liturgical cult, of the Blessed Virgin, be generously fostered. . . . But it exhorts theologians and preachers of the divine word to abstain zealously both from false exaggerations as well as from a too great narrowness of mind in considering the singular dignity of the Mother of God. . . . True devotion consists neither in sterile or transitory affection, nor in a certain vain credulity, but proceeds from true faith, by which we are led to know the excellence of the Mother of God, and we are moved to a filial love toward our mother and to the imitation of her virtues.

Constitution on the Church, Second Vatican Council, November, 1964

See also Assumption of Mary; Immaculate Conception; Nestorianism; Virgin Birth.

MASKS

Ever since Adam donned the fig leaf, men have been mask-makers. Man knows that the profound colloqualism "you can't take it with you" includes these masks.

JAMES A. PIKE, *Beyond Anxiety*, 1953

MASS, THE

And on the day called of the Sun an assembly in one place is made of all who live in the town and in the country; and the commentaries of the apostles or the writings of the prophets are read . . . bread is brought up and wine and water, and the president sends up prayers in the same way and a thanksgiving, so far as he has the power, and all the people cry out saying, "Amen," and each one receives a distribution of the share of the Eucharist and it is taken to those not present by the deacons.

St. Justin Martyr, *First apology,* c. 150

When we offer this Sacrifice, when we sacrifice Jesus Christ, the Lord's Victim, when we say, "Let us pray," then be assured that Heaven descends to earth, and the angels come amongst us.

St. John Chrysostom, *Ep. ad Eph. c. 1, Hom. iii,* c. 388

By the daily sacrifice, the Church, which is the Body of Christ, learns to offer herself through Him Who is her head.

St. Augustine, *The City of God,* X, 20, 426

I gladly agree that the prayers, which we pour out before God as soon as we assemble to partake of the mass, are good works and appropriate acts. In them we confess to one another, utter our own desires, pray for the common weal, and for each other. . . . Yet the prayers are not the mass, but the works of the mass.

Martin Luther, *The Babylonian Captivity,* 1520

Let this then stand as a first and infallible truth, that the mass or Sacrament of the Altar is the testament of Christ, which He left behind Him at His death, distributing an inheritance to those who believe in Him.

Martin Luther (1483–1546), *First Principles of the Reformation*

If anyone saith that the sacrifice of the mass . . . ought not to be offered for the living and for the dead for sins, pains, satisfactions, and other necessities; let him be anathema.

Council of Trent, 1562

To me nothing is so consoling, so piercing, so thrilling, so overcoming, as the Mass said as it is amongst us. I could attend Masses for ever and not be tired.

John Henry Newman, *Discourses to Mixed Congregations,* 1849

Our Lord not only offered Himself as a Sacrifice on the Cross, but He makes Himself a perpetual, a daily sacrifice to the end of Time. In the Holy Mass the one Sacrifice on the Cross once offered is renewed, continued, applied to our benefit.

John Henry Newman, *Meditations and Devotions,* 1893

The Mass is the Sacrifice of the Mystical Body of Christ, and is one with Calvary, which was the sacrifice of the physical body of Christ. The Mass, in other words, is a supra-temporal reality, by which the glorified Christ in Heaven prolongs His sacrifice on the Cross by and through us.

Fulton J. Sheen, *The Fullness of Christ,* 1935

The Mass is a true and real Sacrifice. It is identical with the Sacrifice of the Cross. Of course our Lord does not suffer any more, But the *giving,* the rendering of homage to God the Father, the Sacrifice, is exactly the same.

Paul Bussard, *The Sacrifice,* 1939

Was ever another command so obeyed? For century after century, spreading slowly to every continent and country and among every race on earth, this action has been done, in every conceivable circumstance, for every conceivable human need . . . from the pinnacles of earthly greatness to the refuge of fugitives in the caves and dens of the earth.

Gregory Dix, *The Shape of the Liturgy,* 1945

The Mass is the chief act of divine worship; it should also be the source and center of Christian piety.

Pope Pius XII, *Mediator Dei,* November, 1947

Yesterday, today and for ever—cast your mind forward to the last Mass that will ever be said on earth. That Mass will be the World's Viaticum.

Ronald A. Knox, *The Window in the Wall,* 1956

See also Calvary; Communion; Eucharist; Liturgy; Music; Prayer; Sacraments; Sacrifice; Transubstantiation; Worship.

MATERIALISM

I understand the main tenet of materialism to be that there is nothing in the universe but matter and force; and that all the phenomena of nature are explicable by deduction from the properties assignable to these two primitive factors.

THOMAS HENRY HUXLEY, *Science and Morals*, 1886

The simplest use of the term is an implication *that there is nothing else in existence* except the material universe which we know so well.

JOHN COWPER POWYS, *Psychoanalysis and Morality*, 1923

Materialism is as dead as a dodo. . . . Matter is discovered not to be dead, but to be very much alive, if energy be life. "The nature of all reality (quoting Sir Arthur Eddington) is spiritual, not material."

GEORGE CRAIG STEWART, in *Varieties of American Religion*, edited by Charles S. Braden, 1936

Like a pestiferous breath, materialism pervades more and more the entire life and produces its evil fruits in matrimony, in the family, and in the youth.

POPE PIUS XII, *Address*, July 24, 1949

The doctrine that nothing exists except matter and its movements and modifications: also that the phenomena of consciousness and will are wholly due to the operation of material agencies.

Oxford Dictionary, 1951

But beneath the crude shell of materialism there lies in most men an innate longing for the spiritual and the eternal.

JOHN LA FARGE, *An American Amen*, 1958

Our worship of consumer goods, the covetousness and hedonism so prevalent in the West, are not substantially different from the materialism of the Communists.

FRANZ MUELLER, *Social Justice Review*, October, 1961

Materialism is the denial that there is a higher and a lower in existence and that the higher is completely independent of the lower and can never be reduced to it. . . . When the whole—any whole—is looked upon as only the sum total of its parts—that is materialism.

CHARLES MALIK, *The Freeman*, January, 1962

Reaction against materialism may, please God, result in a renewed commitment to spiritual values, turning our search for wealth into a vocation of service.

Roman Catholic Bishops of U.S., *Bonds of Union*, November, 1963

See also Civilization and Christianity; Existence; Humanism; Irreligion; Liberalism and Religion; Marxism; Matter; Matter and Spirit; Modernism; Philosophy; Positivism; Possessions; Religion, Caustic Comments about; Unbelief; Worldliness.

MATERIALIST

The materialist is a Calvinist without a God.

E. BERNSTEIN, *Evolutionary Socialism*, 1899

See also Materialism.

MATERNITY

Maternity, with its cares, its sufferings, and its risks, calls for and exacts courage; the wife, in the field of honor and of conjugal duty, must be no less heroic than her husband in the field of honor of civil duty, where he makes the gift of his life to his country.

POPE PIUS XII, *Address*, October 21, 1942

See also Mother; Motherhood; Poverty; Woman.

MATRIMONY. See MARRIAGE

MATTER

Matter is such as God would have formed it.
> ORIGEN, *De Principiis*, Bk. 2, ch. i, Vol. IV, c. 254

For in Matter we have no mere absence of means of strength; it is utter destitution—of sense, of virtue, of beauty, of pattern, of Ideal principle, of quality. This is surely ugliness, utter disgracefulness, unredeemed evil.
> PLOTINUS (c. 203–262 A.D.), *Enneads*, II

I have no reason for believing the existence of matter. I have no immediate intuition thereof; neither can I immediately, from my sensations, ideas, notions, actions, or passions, infer an unthinking, unperceiving, inactive substance—either by probable deductions or necessary consequence.
> GEORGE BERKELEY, *Dialogues Between Hylas and Philonous*, 1713

You, who know that matter does not perish, will dispute whether God has the power to preserve in that matter the noblest quality with which He has endowed it.
> VOLTAIRE, "Soul," *Philosophical Dictionary*, 1764

If, therefore it be asked, whence came matter? it is a very reasonable reply to say, it has always existed.
> P. H. d'HOLBACH, *The System of Nature*, 1770

Matter acts, because it exists, and exists to act. If it be inquired how, or for why, matter exists? we answer, we know not.

But . . . we should be of opinion, it exists necessarily, or because it contains within itself a sufficient reason for its existence.
> P. H. d'HOLBACH, *The System of Nature*, 1770

The immediate unity of existence with itself.
> G. W. F. HEGEL, *The Doctrine of Essence*, c. 1818

The annihilation of matter is unthinkable for the same reason that the creation of matter is unthinkable.
> HERBERT SPENCER, *First Principles*, 1862

Sensation in the sensationless; mind originating in matter; the opposite of truth; the opposite of Spirit; the opposite of God; that of which immortal Mind takes no cognizance; that which mortal mind sees, feels, hears, tastes and smells only in belief.
> MARY BAKER EDDY, *Science and Health*, 1908

We reach through the veil of what we call matter and are in a higher World which is kin to our minds and to which, as great amphibians, we really belong.
> RUFUS M. JONES, *Spirit in Man*, 1941

Matter is itself a kind of non-being, a mere potency or ability to receive forms and undergo substantial mutations; in short, an avidity for being.
> JACQUES MARITAIN, *The Person and the Common Good*, 1947

Matter is not evil or indifferent; it is good, and it has a role to play in the drama of salvation. The duty of the Christian is to spiritualize it and to bring it to the peak of perfection God wants it to have.
> JAMES F. MULLIGAN, *America*, October 10, 1959

Matter is not just weight that drags us down, the mire that sucks us in, the bramble that bars our way. . . . It is simply the slope on which we can go up as well as go down, the medium that can uphold just as well as give way.

PIERRE TEILHARD DE CHARDIN, *The Divine Milieu,* 1960

See also Cause; Creation; Evolution; Existence; Materialism; Matter and Spirit; Mind; Reality; Science and Religion; Spirit.

MATTER AND SPIRIT

For Matter, were it never so despicable, is Spirit, the manifestation of Spirit, were it never so honorable, can it be more?

THOMAS CARLYLE, *Sartor Resartus,* 1836

Materialism and spiritualism are opposite poles of the same absurdity—the absurdity of imagining that we know anything about either spirit or matter.

THOMAS HUXLEY to Charles Kingsley, May 22, 1863, in *Life and Letters of Thomas Henry Huxley,* by Leonard Huxley, 1901, Vol. 1

There is a point at which the world of spirit comes in conscious contact with the world of matter.

CHRISTOPHER DAWSON, *God and the Supernatural,* 1920

Christianity, based as it is on the Incarnation, regards matter as destined to be the vehicle and instrument of spirit, and spirit as fully actual so far as it controls and directs matter.

WILLIAM TEMPLE, *Readings in St. John's Gospel,* First Series, 1939

See also Materialism; Matter; Spirit.

MATURITY

Maturity may be recognized in the slowness with which a man believes.

BALTASAR GRACIÁN, *Art of Worldly Wisdom,* 1653

MEALS

It is meet before we partake of food to bless the Maker of all things, and to sing when we drink.

ST. CLEMENT OF ALEXANDRIA, *Paedagogus,* c. 220

MEANS

A good end cannot sanctify evil means; nor must we ever do evil, that good may come of it.

WILLIAM PENN, *Some Fruits of Solitude,* 1793

MECHANISM

We eat, drink, and reproduce not because mankind has reached an agreement that this is desirable, but because machinelike, we are compelled to do so.

JACQUES LOEB, *The Mechanistic Conception of Life,* 1912

A scientific realism based on mechanism, is conjoined with an unwavering belief in the world of men and of the higher animals as being composed of self-determining organisms. This radical inconsistency at the basis of modern thought accounts for much that is half-hearted and wavering in our civilization.

ALFRED NORTH WHITEHEAD, *Science and the Modern World,* 1925

See also Determinism; Free Will; Necessity; Will.

MECHANIZATION. See MACHINES

MEDIOCRITY

The most dangerous shortsightedness consists in underestimating the mediocre; mediocrity is a colorless and odorless gas; allow it to accumulate undisturbed, and suddenly it explodes with a force beyond all belief. . . . The dire omen for all of us is . . . not that Christians would be less numerous but that the number of mediocre Christians should increase.

GEORGES BERNANOS, *Plea for Liberty*, 1946

MEDITATION

That happiness which belongs to a mind which by deep meditation has been washed clear of all impurity and has entered within the Self, cannot be described by words; it can be felt by the inward power only.

Maitranyana Brahmana Upanishad, c. 1000 B.C.

Thou art Divine, I know, O Lord Supreme,
Since God found entrance to my heart through Love.
This taught me that for steady inner growth
Quick and silent meditation's best.

Zend-Avesta (attributed to Zoroaster), 6th century B.C.

Without knowledge there is no meditation, without meditation there is no knowledge. He who has knowledge and meditation is near to *Nirvana*.

Dhammapada c. 5th century B.C.

Meditation is no other thing than an attentive thought, voluntarily reiterated and entertained in the mind, to excite the will to holy and salutary affections and resolutions.

ST. FRANCIS OF SALES, *Treatise on the Love of God*, 1607

A free man thinks of death least of all things; and his wisdom is a meditation not of death but of life.

BARUCH SPINOZA, *Ethics*, 1670

Meditation is like a needle after which comes a thread of gold, composed of affections, prayers and resolutions.

ST. ALPHONSUS (1696–1787), *Veritable Épouse de J.C.*

It is meditation that leads us in spirit into the hallowed solitudes wherein we find God alone—in peace, in calm, in silence, in recollection.

J. CRASSET, *A Key to Meditation*, 1907

It is of primary importance that a certain space of time be allotted daily to meditation on eternal things. No priest can omit this without a serious manifestation of negligence and without a grave loss to his soul.

POPE PIUS X, *Haerent animo*, August 4, 1908

If our Faith is to be made vivid, it must be by meditation.

JOHN CHAPMAN, *Spiritual Letters of*, 1935

But a saint, whether Buddhist or Christian, who knows his business as a saint is rightly meditative and in proportion to the rightness of his meditations is the depth of his peace.

IRVING BABBITT, *Dhammapada*, 1936

Meditation, because it is free of dogma, of historical commitments and narrow prejudices, because it is practiced for the most part silently and therefore secretly, and because it is practiced by some members of all religions—meditation is a channel for seekers of all faiths or no faith, a river into which many streams can freely flow.

BRADFORD SMITH, *Meditation: The Inward Art*, 1963

See also Action; Acts; Bible; Bible and Prayer; Brahma; Brahman; Contemplation; Experience, Religious; Man's Unity with God; Prayer; Silence; Worship.

MEEKNESS

Why art thou angry? Be not angry, Tusa, Meekness is best for thee, and to restrain Anger, conceit, hypocrisy is best.
It is for this we live the righteous life.

Sutta Nipata (attributed to Buddha), 6th century B.C.

Meekness in itself is nought else but a true knowing and feeling of man's self as he is.
The Cloud of Unknowing, 14th century

Meekness takes injuries like pills, not chewing, but swallowing them down.
Sir Thomas Browne, *Christian Morals,* c. 1680

See also Humility.

MEETING

We judge it the duty of all to be diligent in the assembling of themselves together . . . and when assembled, the great work of one and all ought to be to wait upon God: and returning out of their own thoughts and imaginations, to feel the Lord's presence.
Robert Barclay, *Apology,* 1678

See also Community; Congregation.

MELANCHOLY

The devil asks only for sadness and melancholy; and as he is sad and melancholy himself, and will be so eternally, he wishes that every one else should become like him.
St. Francis of Sales (1567–1622), *Consoling Thoughts of,* ed. Huguet

He who has overcome passion has overcome also melancholy.
St. Seraphim of Sarov (1759–1833), quoted in A. F. Dobbie-Bateman's biography of St. Seraphim

The chronic melancholy which is taking hold of the civilized races with the decline of belief in a beneficent power.
Thomas Hardy, *Tess of the D'Urbervilles,* 1891

The Christian whose life is all sadness, and whose only hopes lie beyond the grave, may then be sure that there is something amiss in his life or in his method.
John Cuthbert Hedley, *The Christian Inheritance,* 1896

Save us from the deadly melancholy of our triumphant civilization.
Nicholas Berdyaev, *Colosseum,* March, 1934

See also Cheerfulness; Despair; Fear; Hope; Joy; Sadness; Sorrow; Suicide.

MELODIES

Heard melodies are sweet, but those unheard
Are sweeter.
John Keats, *Ode on a Grecian Urn,* 1819

See also Music; Song.

MEN. See MAN

MENTAL ILLNESS

A high percentage of mental illness is caused by disease in our morals.
George C. Anderson, *Man's Right to Be Human,* 1959

See also Mind; Neurosis; Psychiatrists; Psychiatry; Psychoanalysis; Psychology; Psychotherapy; Sterilization.

MERCY

Pray to God for mercy until the last shovelful of earth is cast upon thy grave.
Talmud (Ta'anit), c. 200 A.D.

Whoever is able to plead God's mercy for his fellow man and does not do so is a sinner.
Talmud, Berakot, 12b., c. 200 A.D.

Mercy imitates God, and disappoints Satan.
St. John Chrysostom, *Homilies,* c. 388

Dost wish to receive mercy? Show mercy to thy neighbor.
St. John Chrysostom, *Homilies,* c. 388

Thy malice may be measured, but God's mercy cannot be defined; thy malice is circumscribed, his mercies infinite.

> ST. JOHN CHRYSOSTOM, *Homilies,* 3, c. 388

Mercy is not ordinarily held to consist in pronouncing judgment on another man's deserts, but in relieving his necessities; in giving aid to the poor, not in inquiring how good they are.

> ST. AMBROSE, *De Nabuthe,* VIII, 40, 395

And what is more unworthy of mercy than the unhappy man who is proud—too proud to accept mercy.

> ST. AUGUSTINE, *De Libero Arbitri,* c. 400

The mercy of God is never to be despaired of by men who truly repent, each according to the measure of his sin.

> ST. AUGUSTINE, *Enchiridion,* 421

The simple expression of the publican, "God be merciful to me a sinner," was sufficient to open the floodgates of the Divine compassion.

> ST. JOHN CLIMACUS (525–600), *Climax*

The mercy which GOD shall freely bestow on mankind, *there is* none who can withhold; and what he shall withhold, *there is* none who can bestow, besides him.

> *Koran,* c. 625

If mercy were a sin, I believe I could not keep from committing it.

> ST. BERNARD OF CLAIRVAUX (1091–1153), *Life and Works of,* ed. J. Mabillson

The work of divine justice always presupposes the work of mercy; and is founded thereon.

> ST. THOMAS AQUINAS, *Summa Theologiae,* I, 214, 1272

God is the God of the humble, the miserable, the oppressed, and the desperate, and of those who are brought even to nothing; and his nature is to give sight to the blind, to comfort the broken-hearted, to justify sinners, to save the very desperate and damned.

> MARTIN LUTHER, *Commentary on Galatians,* 1531

God has decreed that those who show no mercy should also perish without mercy.

> MARTIN LUTHER, *Letter,* July 21, 1535

Mercy to human beings is more acceptable than bathing at the sixty-eight places of pilgrimage, and than all alms offered there.

> ARJAN (died 1606), *The Sikh Religion,* M. A. Macauliffe

We should feel exceeding joy when we observe how God disperses His mercy with a beneficent hand among men and angels, in heaven and upon earth.

> ST. FRANCIS OF SALES, *Treatise on the Love of God,* 1607

The mercy of God has been more salutary for the redemption of men than the wretchedness of Adam has been poisonous for its destruction.

> ST. FRANCIS OF SALES, *Treatise on the Love of God,* 1607

His mercy hath no relation to time, no limitation in time, it is not first, nor last, but eternal, everlasting.

> JOHN DONNE, *Sermon,* St. Paul's Cathedral, London, 1621

Let the Devil make me so far desperate as to conceive a time when there was no mercy, and he hath made me so far an Atheist, as to conceive a time when there was no God.

> JOHN DONNE, *Sermon,* 1624

A man wakes at midnight full of unclean thoughts, and he hears a passing Bell; this is an occasional mercy, if he call that his own knell, and consider how unfit he was to be called out of the world then.

> JOHN DONNE, *Sermon,* 1624

God made Sun and Moon to distinguish seasons, and day and night, and we cannot have the fruits of the earth but in their seasons: But God hath made no decree to distinguish the seasons of His mercies. . . . In Heaven it is always Autumn, his mercies are ever in their maturity.

JOHN DONNE, LXXX *Sermons*, Sermon II, 1624

When I survey the occurrences of my life, and call into account the Finger of GOD, I can perceive nothing but an abyss and mass of mercies, either in general to mankind, or in particular to myself.

THOMAS BROWNE, *Religio Medici*, 1635

When thou fallest into a fault, in what matter soever it be, do not trouble nor afflict thyself for it. For they are effects of our frail Nature, stained by Original Sin. . . . If thou seest thyself fallen once and a thousand times, thou oughtest to make use of the remedy which I have given thee, that is, of a loving confidence in the divine mercy.

MIGUEL DE MOLINOS, *Spiritual Guide*, II, 1675

There is but one sin which makes us unworthy of that Mercy, and that is if we harden ourselves against it and refuse to hope for it.

FRANÇOIS FÉNELON (1651–1715), *Spiritual Letters*

The more merciful Acts thou dost, the more Mercy thou wilt receive.

WILLIAM PENN, *Some Fruits of Solitude*, 1718

God seeth different abilities and frailties of men, which may move His goodness to be merciful to their different improvements in virtue.

WILLIAM LAW, *Christian Perfection*, 1726

God's mercy is over all his works, but divines of all sort lessen that mercy too much.

JONATHAN SWIFT, *Thoughts on Religion*, 1728

A God all mercy is a God unjust.

EDWARD YOUNG, *Night Thoughts*, 1742

The essential and unbounded mercy of my Creator is the foundation of my hope, and a broader and surer the universe cannot give me.

WILLIAM ELLERY CHANNING (1780–1842) *Works*

The French scholar and Christian, Frederick Ozanam, once said that if God has, as of course He has, some mysteries yet unrevealed to us, no doubt they are secrets of mercy.

SUSAN L. EMERY, *The Inner Life of the Soul*, 1903

In the last ebb of consciousness who knows what mercies God has in store?

BEDE JARRETT, *Meditations for Layfolk*, 1915

If we can see reasons for mercy that are true reasons and not unjust excuses, God sees many more.

C. C. MARTINDALE, *God and the Supernatural*, 1920

Every Christian must reject with detestation that covert propaganda for cruelty which tries to drive mercy out of the world by calling it names such as "Humanitarianism" and "sentimentality."

C. S. LEWIS, *The Problem of Pain*, 1940

The good news of the gospel is that there is a resource of divine mercy which is able to overcome a contradiction within our own souls, which we cannot overcome ourselves.

REINHOLD NIEBUHR, *Christianity and Power Politics*, 1940

Once we recognize we are under Divine Wrath, we become eligible for Divine Mercy.

FULTON J. SHEEN, *Communism and the Conscience of the West,* 1948

The appeal to God's mercy is really honest and sincere only if a man has the basic will to follow the paths of the Lord, if he hates sin, and ardently strives to avoid it.

DIETRICH VON HILDEBRAND, *True Morality and Its Counterfeits,* 1955

Ultimately, this is what you go before God for: You've had bad luck and good luck and all you really want in the end is mercy.

ROBERT FROST, on the radio, quoted in *Collier's,* April 27, 1956

Unless we learn the meaning of mercy by exercising it towards others, we will never have any real knowledge of what it means to love Christ.

THOMAS MERTON, *Life and Holiness,* 1963

God tempers the wind to the shorn lamb.
English Proverb

See also Almsgiving; Charity; Compassion; Damnation; Election; Forgiveness; God, Fatherhood of; God: His Wrath; Grace; Hope; Judgment; Judgment, God's; Justice; Malice; Penitence; Pity; Predestination; Providence; Punishment; Repentance; Sinners.

MERIT

Reward is what you receive, merit is what you do.

ST. THOMAS AQUINAS, *Disputations Concerning Truth,* 13th century

The sufficiency of merit is to know that my merit is not sufficient.

FRANCIS QUARLES, *Emblems,* 1635

The more merit, the less affectation.

BALTASAR GRACIÁN, *The Art of Wordly Wisdom,* 1647

Where has the Scripture made merit the rule or measure of charity?

WILLIAM LAW, *A Serious Call to the Devout and Holy Life,* 1728

The merits of each one depends not directly on what sort of soil God has given him to cultivate, but on what use he makes of what God has given.

EDWARD F. GARESCHÉ, *Ever Timely Thoughts,* 1925

See also Charity; Determinism; Election; Free Will; Martyrdom; Predestination.

MESSIAH

Jews have no Messiah to expect, for they already had him at the time of Hezekiah.

HILLEL b. GAMALIEL III, *Talmud: Sanhedrin,* 99a, c. 500 A.D.

These religions [Christianity and Islam] are the preparation and preface to the Messiah we expect.

JUDAH HALEVI, *Cuzari,* c. 1135

Jesus was Himself convinced that He was the Christ, the Messiah for whose coming the prophets had for centuries been looking. The fact has been questioned by a few, a very few, competent scholars.

BURNETT H. STREETER, *Adventure,* 1928

When the Messiah ceases to be a leader, a fulfiller, and a herald, and moved by exaggerated egoism aims at being an example and a reformer, his office falls to pieces in his hands. This constituted the tragedy of Jesus, and the turning point in his career.

JULIUS KATZENSTEIN, *History and Destiny of the Jews,* 1933

He [Jesus] confessed himself to be the Messiah in a very special sense, that is to say, he was a Messiah who had given up all idea of gratifying the longings of his people, but came forward with claims of his own.

JULIUS KATZENSTEIN, *History and Destiny of the Jews,* 1933

Today we do not believe in a personal Messiah, or a Messiah people, but in mankind, acting as its own Messiah.

LOUIS I. NEWMAN, *Religion Today*, ed. A. L. Swift, 1933

The thought underlying the Messianic conception is that the soul must not allow itself to be subjugated to anyone but God.

LEO BAECK, *Essence of Judaism*, 1936

The deeds of Jesus of Nazareth acquire their religious value and become factors of high importance in the new faith, through the proclamation that he holds in his hand the authority of God—as the Messiah.

SHOLEM ASCH, *What I Believe*, 1941

Only upon the interpretation of that judicial murder on Calvary as the *deliberate offering of the Messianic Sacrifice by the Messianic High-priest* was any proclamation of Jesus as Messiah by or to the Jews possible at all.

GREGORY DIX, *The Apostolic Ministry*, 1946

The Messianic idea is the most glistening jewel in the glorious crown of Judaism!

JOSEPH KLAUSNER, *Messianic Idea in Israel*, 1955

The Jewish Messianic world . . . is idealistic and exalted, but it remains terrestrial. The Kingdom of Heaven of the Jewish Messiah is not only within the soul of man, but also upon the earth.

JOSEPH KLAUSNER, *The Messianic Idea in Israel*, 1955

See also Israel; Jesus Christ; Jews; Judaism

METAPHYSICAL

I will call metaphysical all those propositions which claim to represent knowledge about something which is over or beyond all experience.

RUDOLF CARNAP, *Philosophy and Logical Syntax*, 1935

See also Knowledge; Metaphysician; Metaphysics; Philosophy; Reason; Religion.

METAPHYSICIAN

Metaphysician: A man who excels in writing with black ink on a black ground.

TALLEYRAND (1754–1838), quoted in H. S. Leigh's *Jeux d'Esprit*

He has spent all his life in letting down empty buckets into empty wells, and he is frittering away his age in trying to draw them up again.

SYDNEY SMITH, *A Memoir of Rev. Sydney Smith*, by his daughter Lady Holland, 1855

A metaphysician is a man who goes into a dark cellar at midnight without a light looking for a black cat that is not there.

Ascribed to Baron Bowen of Colwood (1835–1894)

See also Metaphysical; Metaphysics; Philosophers; Theologians.

METAPHYSICS

The principles of knowledge, among which is the explication of the principal attributes of God, of the immaterality of the soul, and of all the clear and simple notions that are in us.

RENÉ DESCARTES, *Principles of Philosophy*, 1644

Metaphysics begins and ends with God.

JOHANNES SCOTUS ERIGENA, *The Division of Nature*, 1681

Metaphysics consists of two parts, first, that which all men of sense already know, and second, that which they can never know.

VOLTAIRE, *Letter to Frederick the Great*, April 17, 1737

A man may be a metaphysician without being a geometrician. Metaphysics is more entertaining; it constitutes often the romance of the mind.

> VOLTAIRE, *Philosophical Dictionary,* II, 1764

It is in reality nothing but an inventory of all our possessions acquired through Pure Reason, systematically arranged.

> IMMANUEL KANT, *Critique of Pure Reason,* 1781

Metaphysics has for the real object of its investigation three ideas only: *God, Freedom,* and *Immortality.*

> IMMANUEL KANT, *Critique of Pure Reason,* 1781

Considered as a whole, the Christian religion of late ages has been continually dissipating itself into Metaphysics; and threatens now to disappear, as some rivers do, in deserts of barren sand.

> THOMAS CARLYLE, *London and Westminster Review,* 1838

I hate metaphysics worse than physics.

> W. S. LANDOR, *Letter to Robert Browning,* 1860

The culmination and fruit of literary artistic expression, and its final fields of pleasure for the human soul, are in metaphysics, including the mysteries of the spiritual world, the soul itself, and the question of immortal continuation of our identity.

> WALT WHITMAN, footnote to *Democratic Vistas,* 1871

If there be anything with which metaphysics have nothing to do, and where a plain man, without skill to walk in the arduous paths of abstruse reasoning, may yet find himself at home, it is religion.

> MATTHEW ARNOLD, *Literature and Dogma,* 1873

Metaphysics is the finding of bad reasons for what we believe upon instinct, but to find these reasons is no less an instinct.

> F. H. BRADLEY, *Appearance and Reality,* 1893

An attempt to learn matters of fact by means of logical or moral or rhetorical constructions.

> GEORGE SANTAYANA, *Scepticism and Animal Faith,* 1923

Metaphysics is merely our human attempt to decipher the meaning of things.

> J. E. BOODIN, *God and Creation,* 1934

Metaphysics evaporates into thin air, or it leads us to religion.

> CHARLES HARTSHORNE, *Man's Vision of God,* 1941

Whether in the Orient or in the Occident, philosophy has been concerned about metaphysics. Even the current positivistic attempt to refute all metaphysics is a concern about metaphysics, and a tribute to its persistence. In whatever guise it appears, metaphysics is an attempt to define what is truly and completely real.

> EDGAR S. BRIGHTMAN, *Radhakrishnan: Comparative Studies in Philosophy,* 1948

Metaphysics is valid knowledge of both sensible and suprasensible being. Metaphysics is able to demonstrate the existence of suprasensible being, for it can demonstrate the existence of God, by appealing to the evidence of the senses and the principles of reason, and without any reliance upon articles of religious faith.

> MORTIMER ADLER, *Vital Speeches,* December, 1949

See also Knowledge; Metaphysician; Metaphysics; Philosophy; Reason; Religion; Theology.

MIDDLE PATH

This middle path . . . is the noble path, namely: right views, right intent, right speech, right conduct, right means of livelihood, right endeavor, right mindfulness, right meditation. . . . Which leads to insights, leads to wisdom, which conduces to

calm, to knowledge, to perfect enlightenment, to Nirvana.

The Mahavagga of the Vinya Texts,
between 5th and 1st century B.C.

See also Nirvana.

MIGHTY

Who is mighty? He who subdues his [evil]
inclination. . . . He that ruleth his spirit
is better than he that taketh a city.

Pirke Aboth, Talmud, between 2nd and
4th century A.D.

MILITARISM

The rise of militarism and the Gospel of
Force in the modern world is a result of
the vacuum created by the abandonment
of the Cross.

FULTON J. SHEEN, *Radio Sermon,* April
6, 1941

See also Armaments; Force; Military Service; Pacifism; War.

MILITARY SERVICE

Do not think that it is impossible for
anyone to please God while engaged in
active military service. Among such persons was the holy David, to whom God
gave so great a testimony.

ST. AUGUSTINE, *To Publicola,* 398

The drillmaster will teach to every young
man at his most impressionable age absolute unquestioning obedience to human
command, even though such command
leads to actions wholly contrary to the
teachings of home, of school and of
church.

Pendle Hill [Quaker] *Bulletin,* No. 60,
1945

See also Armaments; Conscience; Conscientious Objector; Conscription; Militarism; Pacifism; War.

MILLENNIUM

The Christian of the nineteenth century
has been stationed by Providence on a
sublime eminence, from which he can behold the fulfillment of illustrious prophecies and look backwards upon nearly the
whole train of events leading to the millennium.

ALEXANDER CAMPBELL, *The Millennial
Harbinger,* 1830

Millennium, n. The period of a thousand
years when the lid is to be screwed down,
with all reformers on the under side.

AMBROSE BIERCE, *Devil's Dictionary,*
1906

MIND

It is good to tame the mind, which is
difficult to hold in and flighty, rushing
wherever it listeth; a tamed mind brings
happiness.

Dhammapada, c. 5th century B.C.

The way in which a man loses his proper
goodness of mind is like the way in which
the trees are denuded by axes and bills.
Hewn down day after day, can it—the
mind—retain its beauty?

CONFUCIUS (4th century B.C.), *The
Works of Mencius*

Mind seems to be an independent substance implanted within the soul and to be
incapable of being destroyed.

ARISTOTLE (384–322 B.C.), *De Anima,*
I, 4, 408b

Mind is held to be of all phenomena the
most supernatural.

ARISTOTLE, *Metaphysics,* XII, ix, I, c.
322 B.C.

Only the mind cannot be sent into exile.

OVID, *Epistulae ex Ponto,* c. 5 A.D.

If a person had delivered up your body to
some passer-by, you would certainly be

angry. And do you feel no shame in delivering up your own mind to any reviler, to be disconcerted and confounded?

> EPICTETUS (1st century A.D.), *Echiridion*

The final joy of man consists in the superlative activity of his supreme power, namely the activity of mind engaged with incomparable truth.

> ST. THOMAS AQUINAS (1225–1274), *Opusc. X, de Causis,* Lect. 1

To know and to think, to see the truth with the eye of the mind, is always a joy. . . . As love is the life of the heart, so is the endeavor after knowledge and truth the life of the mind.

> NICHOLAS OF CUSA, *Dialogue on Peace,* 1452

All the bodies that exist, the firmament, the stars, the earth and its kingdoms, are of less value than the least of minds; for it is aware of them, and of itself—while they are aware of nothing.

> BLAISE PASCAL, *Pensées,* 1670

The man who does not lift his mind above himself does not deserve to be a man.

> ANGELUS SILESIUS (1624–1677), *Cherubic Pilgrim*

Minds are conquered not by arms but by greatness of soul.

> BARUCH SPINOZA, *Ethics,* IV, 1677

The human mind cannot be absolutely destroyed with the human body, but there is some part of it which remains eternal.

> BARUCH SPINOZA, *Ethics,* V, 1677

All the choir of Heaven and furniture of earth . . . have not any substance without a mind.

> GEORGE BERKELEY, *The Principles of Human Knowledge,* 1710

The human mind must be subject to the general law. . . . Its destiny can be noth-

ing other than to exercise imagination, to invent, and to perfect. No; Men were not made to wander in the forests after the manner of bears and tigers.

> J. B. R. ROBINET, *De la Nature,* III, 1766

My own mind is my own church.

> THOMAS PAINE, *The Age of Reason,* 1795

The mind is like a sheet of white paper in this: that the impressions it receives the oftenest, and retains the longest, are black ones.

> J. C. and A. W. HARE, *Guesses at Truth,* 1827

There is an unseemly exposure of the mind as well as of the body.

> WILLIAM HAZLITT, *Sketches and Essays,* 1839

On earth there is nothing great but man; in man there is nothing great but mind.

> WILLIAM HAMILTON, *Lectures on Metaphysics,* c. 1850

The moral cause of the world lies behind all else in the mind.

> RALPH WALDO EMERSON, *North American Review,* April, 1866

The *mind* of man has to be accounted for, as well as his body; and if the unforeseen actions of atoms could not have produced a human body, with its wonderful marks of design, still less could they have produced a human mind able to know and argue about them.

> W. H. TURTON, *The Truth of Christianity,* 1905

Mortal mind and body are one. Neither exists without the other, and both must be destroyed by immortal Mind.

> MARY BAKER EDDY, *Science and Health,* 1908

Mind no longer appears as an accidental intruder into the realm of matter; we are beginning to suspect that we ought rather to hail it as the creator and governor of the realm of matter—not of course our individual minds, but the mind in which the atoms out of which our individual minds have grown exist as thought.

JAMES JEANS, *The Mysterious Universe,* 1930

The only way to truth that lies open to us at all is the way through our own minds. If we cannot find a clue here in our own human reason, we can find it nowhere.

RUFUS M. JONES, *Pathways to the Reality of God,* 1931

The mind coupled to religion, is a stronger mind for it, a mind not so readily swayed by the passions that parade as reason under an enlarged vocabulary.

HENRY C. LINK, *The Return to Religion,* 1936

There is no such thing as your mind, my mind, and God's Mind. There's only Mind, in which we all "live and move and have our being."

ERNEST HOLMES, *The Science of Mind,* 1938

When we reach the mind of man, we reach the pinnacle of all creation. It is the apex in the pyramid of values to be found in the universe. It is this which constitutes the dignity of man as a moral personality, and makes him a being of surpassing worth.

JOHN A. O'BRIEN, *God: Can We Find Him?,* 1942

Man's mind belongs to a category of being essentially different from matter and superior to it, however limitless the dimensions of matter may be.

POPE PIUS XII, *Allocution,* September 7, 1952

Physical theory in its present stage strongly suggests the indestructibility of Mind in Time.

ERWIN SCHRÖDINGER, *Mind and Matter,* 1958

See also Christian Science; Education; Freedom of Thought and Speech; Genius; God: His Intervention in the World; God: His Nature; Heart; Imagination; Inspiration; Intellect; Intuition; Knowledge; Man: Defined and Interpreted; Man and God; Mind and God; Nature and Mind; Peace of Mind; Psychiatry; Psychoanalysis; Psychology; Reason; Reason and God; Spirit, Human; Thinking; Thought; Truth; Universe; Universe and God; Wisdom.

MIND, SHALLOW

It is a shallow mind which can see to the bottom of its own beliefs, and is conscious of nothing but what it can measure in evidence and state in words.

JAMES MARTINEAU, *Hours of Thought on Sacred Things,* 1879

MIND AND GOD

It is in the mind that God has made man to His image and likeness. . . . If the mind is not to be fathomed even by itself that is because it is the image of God.

ST. AUGUSTINE, *De Symbols,* I, 2, c. 395

There is one Mind. It is absolutely omnipresent, giving mentality to all things.

GIORDANO BRUNO, *De monade numero et figura,* 1591

I had rather believe all the fables in the [Golden] Legend, and the Talmud, and the Alcoran, than that this universal frame is without a mind.

FRANCIS BACON, "Of Atheism," *Essays,* 1597

When I consider how many and how great mysteries men have understood, discovered, and contrived, I very plainly know and understand the mind of man to be one of the works of God, yea, one of the most excellent.

GALILEO, *Dialogue on the Great World Systems,* 1632

The eternal wisdom of God . . . has shown itself forth in all things, but chiefly in the mind of man, and most of all in Jesus Christ.
> BARUCH SPINOZA, *Tractatus Theologico-Politicus*, 1670

The mind's highest good is the knowledge of God, and the mind's highest virtue is to know God.
> BARUCH SPINOZA, *Ethics*, IV, 1677

The Divine Mind imparts itself to the single person: his whole duty is to this rule and teaching.
> RALPH WALDO EMERSON, *North American Review*, April, 1866

See also Genius; Intellect; Mind; Reason.

MINISTER

A proud minister is a devil; but the gift of Christ that comes through him is not contaminated, it runs pure.
> ST. AUGUSTINE, *In Evang. Joannis*, Tract 5, c. 416

Whenever any are true ministers of Jesus Christ, it is from the operation of His Spirit upon their hearts, first purifying them, and thus giving them a just sense of the conditions of others.
> JOHN WOOLMAN, *The Journal of*, 1774

The dramas of his people's lives are all replayed on the stage of his sympathies. . . . Their temptations and victories are his.
> PHILLIPS BROOKS, *Sermon on the Christian Ministry*, 1893

Minister, n. An agent of a higher power with a lower responsibility.
> AMBROSE BIERCE, *Devil's Dictionary*, 1906

We speak of a minister being called to "serve a congregation." We seldom, if ever, speak of a minister being called to "save a congregation."
> RALPH W. SOCKMAN, *The Highway of God*, 1941

The minister's task is to lead men from what they want to what they need.
> RALPH W. SOCKMAN, *The Highway of God*, 1941

You cannot ordain a minister as you appoint a professional at a golf club, or an errand boy in a shop. . . . He is a minister of the Word and Sacraments, a minister of the Gospel, a minister of Christ.
> B. L. MANNING, *A Layman in the Ministry*, 1944

See also Call; Clergy; Ministry; Ordination; Pastor; Preachers; Preaching; Priesthood; Priests; Sermons; Vocation.

MINISTRY

He uses the ministry of men whom He employs as His delegates, not to transfer His right and honor to them, but only that He may Himself do His work by their lips.
> JOHN CALVIN, *Institutes*, II, 1536

The ministry of men, which God employs in his government of the church, is the principal bond which holds the faithful together in one body.
> JOHN CALVIN, *Institutes*, II, 1536

"Come you," this wistful race says to the preacher, "and we will set you free from other toil. You shall study the Book. You shall listen in Silence. You shall toil in the fields of the Spirit. Week by week you shall bring us the harvest of the Unseen."
> GEORGE A. BUTTRICK, *Jesus Came Preaching*, 1931

It is divine because it arose in harmony with the divine will and does a divine work.
> A. C. KNUDSON, *The Doctrine of Redemption*, 1933

The ministry is divinely ordained, but only in the sense as everything wise, appropriate, morally necessary can be said to have divine sanction, not in the sense that an express divine command for the establishment of the public ministry can be shown.

FRANCIS PIEPER, *Christian Dogmatics,* III, 1953

See also Call; Celibacy; Clergy; Clergy, Criticism of; Hierarchy; Minister; Ordination; Preachers; Preaching; Priesthood; Priests; Psychoanalysis; Sermons; Theologians; Vocation.

MINORITIES

National minorities have a right to maintain their language, customs, sense of unity and all their other national characteristics, so long as these possessions are not clearly and gravely detrimental to the welfare of the majority, or of the state as a whole.

Report, Catholic Association for International Peace, *International Ethics,* 1942

Justice is seriously violated by whatever is done to limit the strength and numerical increase of these minority peoples.

POPE JOHN XXII, *Pacem in Terris,* April, 1963

See also Christians.

MINUTES

He that hopes hereafter to look back with satisfaction upon past years, must learn to know the present value of single minutes.

SAMUEL JOHNSON (1696–1772), *The Rambler*

MIRACLES

That the dead really were raised and that those who penned the Gospels did not invent this, is very apparent from the fact that if it were a figment they would have told us many more were so raised and would have made out that they had remained much longer in the tomb.

ORIGEN, *Contra Celsum,* 246

God acts against the wonted course of nature, but by no means does He act against the supreme law; because He does not act against Himself.

ST. AUGUSTINE, *Contra Faust,* XXVI, c. 400

Miracles were performed for our ancestors, because they sacrificed their lives for the sanctification of the Name.

ABAYÉ, *Talmud, Berakot,* c. 500

All men wondered to see the water turned into wine. Every day the earth's moisture being drawn into the root of a vine, is turned by the grape into wine, and no man wonders. Full of wonder then are all the things, which men never think to wonder at.

POPE ST. GREGORY THE GREAT, *Morals on the Book of Job,* 584

A miracle cannot prove what is impossible; it is useful only to confirm what is possible.

MAIMONIDES, *Guide for the Perplexed,* 1190

That miracles have been, I do believe; that they may yet be wrought by the living, I do not deny; but I have no confidence in those which are fathered on the dead.

THOMAS BROWNE, *Religio Medici,* 1642

A miracle is an effect which exceeds the natural force of the means employed for it.

BLAISE PASCAL, *Pensées,* 1670

Had it not been for the miracles, there would have been no sin in not believing in Jesus Christ.

BLAISE PASCAL, *Pensées,* 1670

Signifies nothing more than an event, a phenomenon, the cause of which cannot be explained by another familiar instance, or in any case, which the narrator is unable to explain.

BARUCH SPINOZA, *Tractatus Theologico-Politicus,* 1670

Miracles are the principal external proof and confirmation of the divinity of a doctrine.

JOHN TILLOTSON (1630–1694), *Works,* Vol. III

Many of the miracles of Jesus as recorded by the Evangelist . . . either in whole or in part were never wrought as they are commonly believed nowadays, but are only related as prophetical and parabolical narratives of what would be mysteriously and more wonderfully done by Him.

THOMAS WOOLSTON, *The Old Apology for the Truth of the Christian Religion Against the Jews and Gentiles Revived,* 1727

A course of plain undeniable miracles attesting the truth of a revelation is the highest and utmost evidence of its coming from God.

WILLIAM LAW, *The Case of Reason or Natural Religion Fairly and Fully Stated,* 1731

Miracle is a transgression of a law of nature by a particular volition of the Deity, or by the interposition of some invisible agent.

DAVID HUME, *On Miracles,* 1748

No testimony is sufficient to establish a miracle. Unless the testimony be of such a kind, that its falsehood would be more miraculous, than the fact, which it endeavors to establish. . . . A miracle can never be proved, so as to be the foundation of a system of religion.

DAVID HUME, *On Miracles,* 1748

All is miracle. The stupendous order of nature, the revolution of a hundred mil-

lions of worlds around a million of suns, the activity of light, the life of animals, all are grand and perpetual miracles.

VOLTAIRE, *Philosophical Dictionary,* II, 1764

In what way can a revelation be made but by miracles? In none which we are able to conceive.

WILLIAM PALEY, *Evidences of Christianity,* 1794

Many a man who is now willing to be shot down for the sake of his belief in a miracle would have doubted, if he had been present, the miracle itself.

G. C. LICHTENBERG, *Reflections,* 1799

Miracles are not the proofs, but the necessary results, of revelation.

SAMUEL TAYLOR COLERIDGE, *Omniana,* 1812

If there are no miracles, there is no religion. No proof of divine commission could be afforded but through the miraculous displays of God's power. Nothing is left that can be called Christianity, if its miraculous character be denied. Its essence is gone.

ANDREWS NORTON, *Discourse on the Latest Form of Infidelity,* 1838

The word miracle, as pronounced by Christian churches, gives a false impression; it is a monster. It is not one with the blowing clover and the failling rain.

RALPH WALDO EMERSON, *Divinity School Address,* Cambridge, Mass., July 15, 1838

Christianity is not only confirmed by miracles, but is in itself, in its very essence, a miraculous religion.

WILLIAM ELLERY CHANNING (1780–1842), *Works*

Christian Miracles are attested by evidence even stronger than can be produced for any of those historical facts which we most firmly believe.

> JOHN HENRY NEWMAN, *Two Essays on Biblical and on Ecclesiastical Miracles,* 1842

Depend upon it, it is not the want of greater miracles but of the soul to perceive such as are allowed us still, that makes us push all the sanctities into the far spaces we cannot reach. The devout feel that wherever God's hand is, *there* is miracle.

> JAMES MARTINEAU, *Endeavours After a Christian Life,* 1847

To me every hour of the light and dark is a miracle,
Every cubic inch of space is a miracle.

> WALT WHITMAN, "Miracles," *Leaves of Grass,* 1856

No miracle has ever taken place under conditions which science can accept.

> ERNEST RENAN, *Life of Jesus,* 1863

The establishment of Christianity in the world does not rest on any miracle but the miracle of being the broadest and most humane doctrine.

> RALPH WALDO EMERSON, *North American Review,* April, 1866

However skillfully the modern ingenuity of semibelief may have tampered with supernatural interpositions, it is clear to every honest and unsophisticated mind, that, if miracles be incredible, Christianity is false.

> F. W. FARRAR, *The Witness of History to Christ,* 1870

The more we know of the fixed laws of nature the more incredible do miracles become.

> CHARLES DARWIN (1809–1882), *Autobiography of*

It is absolutely chimerical to expect of science the establishment of any miracle whatsoever.

> AUGUSTE SABATIER, *Outlines of a Philosophy of Religion,* 1899

Miracles are propitious accidents, the natural causes of which are too complicated to be readily understood.

> GEORGE SANTAYANA, *Introduction to the Ethics of Spinoza,* 1910

Belief is not dependent on evidence and reason. There is as much evidence that the miracles occurred as that the Battle of Waterloo occurred.

> GEORGE BERNARD SHAW, Preface, *Androcles and the Lion,* 1914

The Miracles of the Church seem to me to rest not so much upon faces or voices or healing power coming suddenly near to us from afar off, but upon our perceptions being made finer, so that for a moment our eyes can see and our ears can hear what is there about us always.

> WILLA S. CATHER, *Death Comes for the Archbishop,* 1927

Miracles are God's signature, appended to His masterpiece of creation; not because they ought to be needed, but because they are needed.

> RONALD A. KNOX, *Miracles,* 1928

The same power which sent the stars rolling on their courses gives sudden health to some poor cripple at Lourdes, and we say, "Impossible!" The feeding of the five thousand, *that* taxes our powers of belief to the utmost. And yet . . . what is the feeding of the five thousand compared with that patient process by which vast plains of wheat shoot up and bud and mature, under God's hand, to make the slices of bread which you forgot to say prayers over yesterday?

> RONALD A. KNOX, *Miracles,* 1928

The idea of a Being who interferes with the sequence of events in the world is absolutely impossible.

> ALBERT EINSTEIN, *Has Science Discovered God?,* ed. E. H. Cotton, 1931

No kind of miracle is related in Scripture the counterpart of which cannot be found and found repeatedly in the records of other religions.

HARRY EMERSON FOSDICK, *The Modern Use of the Bible*, 1934

If miracles had happened in the Bible and had not happened since, then God has changed his way of running the world.

HARRY EMERSON FOSDICK, *The Modern Use of the Bible*, 1934

Miracles—whether prophetical or of other sorts—always occur in connection with some message from heaven, and are intended by God as a seal, or endorsement of the messenger and his words.

ALOYSIUS MCDONOUGH, *Jesus Christ— The Divine Bridge-Builder*, 1937

If the world is really the medium of God's personal action, miracle is wholly normal.

D. E. TRUEBLOOD, *The Logic of Belief*, 1942

The great messages of Jesus are by Him deliberately built upon an immediately preceding miracle in an integration so complete that separation is impossible without destruction of the lesson's point.

ERIC MONTIZAMBERT, *Christianity in Crisis*, 1945

To the reverent scientist . . . the simplest features of the world about us are in themselves so awe-inspiring that there seems no need to seek new and greater miracles as evidences of God's care.

CARL WALLACE MILLER, *A Scientist's Approach to Religion*, 1947

In the case of miracles, we do not imply that the laws of nature are destoyed or rendered inoperative: we simply affirm that a greater force has been introduced. . . . To deny God the power to apply a force necessary to attain a desired end is to deny the existence of God as a personal, free agent.

JOHN A. O'BRIEN, *Why a Divine Revelation?*, 1949

I would define a miracle as follows: A miracle is a law-abiding event by which God accomplishes His redemptive purposes through the release of energies which belong to a plane of being higher than any with which we are normally familiar.

LESLIE D. WEATHERHEAD, *Psychology, Religion and Healing*, 1951

The miracles are as much, nay more, manifestations of God's love than demonstrations of his power.

AELRED GRAHAM, *A Catholic Commentary on Holy Scripture*, 1952

The miracles are a particular case of the immanence of the divine in matter and we have, therefore, no right to *expect* them to be intelligible.

C. E. M. JOAD, *Recovery of Belief*, 1952

Miracles are signs pointing to the presence of a divine power in nature and history; they are in no way negations of natural law.

PAUL TILLICH, *The New Being*, 1955

The capacity to reveal Himself through miracles, i.e., by interfering with his own order, is an inherent attribute of God, and all miracles were foreseen by Him.

ZSOLT ARADI, *The Book of Miracles*, 1956

The gospel story is full of miracle and miracles; yet not one bit of that "evidence" would have been visible to a newsreel camera or the observation of a scientifically trained reporter. A miracle is visible only to the heart it touches.

M. HOLMES HARTSHORNE, *The Promise of Science and the Power of Faith*, 1958

What seems the greatest miracle of all, namely, the lack of interruption of the natural order.

HENRY MARGENAU, *Science Ponders Religion*, 1960

Miracles are related not as documentary accounts of the deeds of Christ but as terse action shots of the messianic mercy which He is ready to renew in the here and now.

BARNABAS M. AHERN, *The Critic,* August–September, 1962

See also Belief; Creation; God; His Intervention in the World; God: His Omnipotence; Healing; Jesus Christ; Nature; Phenomena; Revelation; Science.

MISCEGENATION

Marriages between whites and Negroes . . . are valid by ecclesiastical law so long as the impediment of servile condition does not occur. If some wish to enter such a marriage, they cannot be forbidden the sacraments. . . . They are exercising a natural right which the Church in no way prohibits.

FRANCIS P. KENRICK, *Theologiae Moralis,* 1843

MISERY

It remains a fact and the fixed and necessary constitution of being, that all of its constituents are misery.

BUDDHA, *Anguttara-Nikaya,* 6th Century B.C.

Only when men shall roll up the sky like a hide, will there be an end to misery, unless God has first been known.

Svetasvatara Upanishad, before 400 B.C.

Knowledge only on the surface: love bought for money: food at the expense of another: these are three miseries of men.

Hitopadesa, 13th century A.D.

If in this world there is one misery having no relief, it is the pressure on the heart from the Incommunicable.

THOMAS DE QUINCEY, *Confessions of an English Opium Eater,* 1821

See also Adversity; Affliction; Anxiety; Hell; Hope; Peace of Mind; Self-Pity; Sickness; Sorrow; Suffering; Tribulations; Wicked, the.

MISFORTUNE

It is the most unhappy kind of misfortune to have been happy.

BOETHIUS, *Consolations of Philosophy,* c. 523 A.D.

Everyone is the artificer of his own misfortune.

MIGUEL DE CERVANTES, *Don Quixote,* 1615

Ill Fortune never crush't that man whom good Fortune deceived not.

BEN JONSON, *Discoveries,* 1641

See also Adversity; Affliction; Anxiety; Temporal; Tribulations; Troubles.

MISSION

Mission is not the kindness of the lucky to the unlucky; it is mutual, united obedience to the one God Whose mission it is.

Anglican Manifesto, Toronto, August 17, 1963

MISSIONARIES

Go ye forth, brethren, on your journey, for the profit of many, for the bliss of many, out of compassion for the world, for the welfare and profit of *devas* and mankind. . . . Both in the spirit and the letter do ye make known the all-perfected, utterly pure, religious life. There are beings—perishing through not hearing the Norm. There will be some who will understand.

Vinaya, in *Some Sayings of the Buddha,* ed. by F. L. Woodward, 1927

As a result of its missionary task, Christianity had to disguise the "spiritual process" in the garments of paganism . . . so that the latter might recognize it as a demand arising from its own life.

SALOMON FORMSTECHER, *Religion des Geistes,* 1841

He [the missionary] will never cease to reflect that, being in no sense the missionary of his country but the missionary of Christ, he must so behave that whoever meets him will have no hesitation in recognizing him as the minister of a religion that is not foreign in any nation because she includes all men who worship God in spirit and in truth.

POPE BENEDICT XV, *Maximum Illud.,* 1919

The wind is now beginning to blow from East to West. Whereas formerly Christian missionaries used to come to the East to make these simple-minded people yield to the doctrine of the Trinity, the disciples of Ahmad [founder of the Ahmadiyya Movement in Islam] now are leaving their homes, their wives and children to carry the teachings of Islam to the sons of the cross in their own lands.

MIRZA MUBARAK AHMAD, *Our Foreign Missions,* 1951

MISSIONARY—A person sent by the ruling church (in the majority of cases with the support of the government) for religious propaganda among backward peoples (for example, in colonial or semicolonial countries); he is usually an advance espionage agent of the imperialist usurpers.

Slovar Inostrannjkh Slov (*Dictionary of Foreign Words*), published by Soviet government, Moscow, Russia, 1951

The missionary movement of the Church is confronted by the contagion and the power of rival and revolutionary faiths.

NORMAN GOODALL, *Missions Under the Cross,* 1953

At the moment when dark and forbidding curtains have abruptly altered missionary manoeuvre-ability and advance, the missionary movement is being judged for its failures and called to repent. At the same time, the opportunities which open out

before the Christian mission are gifts of God which call for fresh obedience.

NORMAN GOODALL, *Missions Under the Cross,* 1953

It is the Will of the Almighty to establish Islam as the only sound basis for achieving the cherished goal of mankind, and for establishing peace among nations. Islam shall go forth as the greatest spiritual power, and it shall free the world of the perpetual anxiety and fear which has been its lot so long. This will be accomplished through a teaching which is in accord with human nature, and which satisfies all its needs.

The Review of Religion (an Islam periodical), May, 1958

Above all, the Christian today must have a profound sense of mission, which will cause him to bear witness to his religious faith and his moral convictions as the early Christians did—by deed and affirmation, even by death.

Catholic Bishops of the U. S., 1961

The contemporary reactions abroad in favor of political self-determination and modern Western, tolerative, free democratic legal and political institutions are, in considerable part, the result of the influence of Christian missionaries.

F. S. C. NORTHROP, *Man, Nature and God,* 1962

The nationalist with an eye on his own country's history cannot altogether believe that the Cross which was brought by a Western missionary into his country has nothing to do with the colonial flag which arrived around the same time in the wake of European traders.

U. KYAW THAN, *Unity in Mid-Career,* 1963

The Ramakrishna movement in Hinduism has missionaries in the West, frequently called Vedanta Societies. Even the lesser

religions of India, Sikhism and Jainism, have sought to win followers in the West.
CHARLES S. BRADEN, *A Journal of Church and State,* Autumn, 1965

Foreign missionaries will be more successful when they can show civilization to the heathens and not merely tell them about it.
ANONYMOUS

See also Church: Its Work; Evangelism; Witness.

MISTAKES

There is nothing final about a mistake, except its being taken as final.
PHYLLIS BOTTOME, *Strange Fruit,* 1928

MOBILIZATION

When entire nations are mobilized, it becomes impossible to distinguish the legitimate objectives from those which morality forbids one to touch.
R. RAYMOND ARON, *The Ethics of Power,* ed. Lasswell and Cleveland, 1962

See also Armaments; War.

MODEL

Praise and imitate that man to whom, while life is pleasing, death is not grievous.
SENECA (4 B.C.–65 A.D.), *Ep. LIV*

MODERATION

Of eight things a little is good and much is evil: travel, mating, wealth, work, wine, sleep, spiced drinks, medicine.
Gittin, Talmud, c. 500 A.D.

Moderation is the silken-string running through the pearl-chain of all virtues.
THOMAS FULLER, *The Holy State and the Profane State,* 1642

See also Abstinence; Asceticism; Discipline; Pleasure; Self-Denial; Sobriety; Temperance; Wine.

MODERN LIFE

Under the spell of agnostic or atheistic teachings, modern life has become largely a technique for the evasion of moral responsibility.
WILLIAM AYLOTT ORTON, *The Challenge of Christian Liberalism,* 1946

See also Man, Modern; Modernism.

MODERNISM

Take away the supernatural order and the history of Church origins must rest upon quite a different foundation, and so these innovators [Modernists] rearrange the monuments of history according to their own whims.
POPE PIUS X, *Encyclical Honoring Gregory the Great,* 1904

The use of the methods of modern science to find, state and use the permanent and central values of inherited orthodoxy in meeting the needs of a modern world.
SHAILER MATHEWS, *The Faith of Modernism,* 1924

The God of Modernism, who is variously pictured as the *élan vital* within the evolutionary process, or as the sum total of the laws of nature, is really a kind of constitutionalism deified.
WALTER LIPPMANN, *A Preface to Morals,* 1929

It is a nice question whether the use of God's name is not misleading when applied by modernists to ideas so remote from the God men have worshipped.
WALTER LIPPMANN, *A Preface to Morals,* 1929

Often the modernist movement, adjusting itself to a man-centered culture, has encouraged this mood, watered down the thought of the Divine and . . . left souls standing like the ancient Athenians, before an altar to an Unknown God.

HARRY EMERSON FOSDICK, sermon quoted in *Christian Century*, December, 1935

See also Humanism; Liberalism; Liberalism and Religion; Materialism; Naturalism; Orthodoxy; Rationalism; Secularism.

MODERNIZATION

The Christian, Catholic and apostolic spirit of the whole world expects a step forward toward a doctrinal penetration and a formation in consciences in faithful and perfect conformity to the authentic doctrine which, however, should be studied and expounded through the methods of research and through the literary forms of modern thought.

POPE JOHN XXIII, October 18, 1962

MODESTY

Modest and grave, with manhood nobly mixed
With patience, fortitude and purity,
An unrevengeful spirit never given
To rate itself too high;—such be the signs of him whose feet are set
On that fair path which leads to heavenly birth.

The Song Celestial, Sir Edwin Arnold's translation of the *Bhagavad-Gita*, c. 5th century B.C.

It is a kind of quick and delicate feeling in the soul, which makes her shrink and withdraw herself from every thing that has danger in it.

JOSEPH ADDISON, *The Spectator*, 1714

If you banish modesty out of the world, she carries away with her half the virtue that is in it.

JOSEPH ADDISON, *The Spectator*, 1714

What is modesty but hypocritical humility, by means of which, in a world swelling with envy, a man seeks to obtain pardon for excellences and merits from those who have none?

ARTHUR SCHOPENHAUER, *The World as Will and Idea*, I, 1818

Christian modesty is the tabernacle we build around the natural sacrament of love because, since the Fall, there are thieves in the house.

DEMETRIUS MANOUSOS, *Address*, March 14, 1950

See also Chastity; Humility; Primness; Purity; Self-Knowledge; Smugness; Virginity.

MOHAMMED

Be not extravagant in praising me, as the Christians are in praising Jesus, Mary's Son, by calling him God and the Son of God; I am only the Lord's servant; then call me the servant of God, and his messenger.

MOHAMMED, *Speeches and Table-Talk of*, 7th century A.D.

MOMENT

One moment of a man's life is a fact so stupendous as to take the lustre out of all fiction.

RALPH WALDO EMERSON, *Demonology*, 1877

Terrible and sublime thought, that every moment is supreme for some man or woman, every hour the apotheosis of some passion.

WILLIAM McFEE, *Casuals of the Sea*, 1916

See also Present, the.

MONARCHY

Monarchy is the true pattern of Divinity.

JAMES I OF ENGLAND, *The True Law of Free Monarchies*, 1598

MONASTERY

In a [Trappist] monastery through which there circulate powerful currents of spiritual life, the soul of the monk, ever carried onward by the stream from which no instant, no occasion ever withdraws him, finds itself lifted up without realizing how.
FRANÇOIS DE SALES POLLIEN, *La Vie Contemplative,* 1900

The monastery is a society of men campaigning under one Rule and under the leadership of an Abbott, with the object of rendering to God a perfect act of homage: the sacrifice of obedience.
COLUMBA MARMION, *Christ the Ideal of the Monk,* 1922

See also Monasticism; Religious Orders.

MONASTICISM

Monasticism is not godliness, but a kind of life, either useful or useless to anyone, depending on one's habit of body and temperament.
DESIDERIUS ERASMUS, *Enchiridion,* 1501

Monasticism represented something more positive than a protest against the world. We believe it to have been the realization of the infinite loveliness and beauty of personal purity.
J. A. FROUDE, *The Lives of the Saints,* 1852

See also Monastery; Priesthood; Religious Orders.

MONEY

Money is life to us wretched mortals.
HESIOD, *Work and Days,* c. 700 B.C.

The image of Caesar is money, the image of God is man. Give money to Caesar, and give thyself to God.
TERTULLIAN, *De Idol.* 15, c. 211 A.D.

Nothing that is God's is obtainable by money.
TERTULLIAN, *The Christian's Defense,* c. 215

The wealth he bade his questioner renounce must be taken in a spiritual sense; it was a wealth of passions, a brood of sins in the soul, not money itself, but the love of money.
ST. CLEMENT OF ALEXANDRIA (died c. 215), *The Rich Man's Salvation*

Love of money is the disease which makes men most groveling and pitiful.
LONGINUS, *On the Sublime,* c. 250

Silly people think that money commands the bodily goods most worth having.
ST. THOMAS AQUINAS, *Summa Theologiae,* la-2ae, ii.I, ad I, 1272

Men mad with the mounting up of money move the Lover of God to be mad with love.
RAMÓN LULL, *Book of the Lover and the Beloved,* c. 1280

Those who seek money as a great thing, with immense solicitude, and upon it establish the especial defense of life . . . have fashioned for themselves too many gods.
DESIDERIUS ERASMUS, *Enchiridion,* 1501

Let him live in his poverty and not sin. For money is a sterile thing.
MARTIN LUTHER, *Table Talk,* June 14, 1542

He that serves God for money will serve the Devil for better wages.
ROGER L'ESTRANGE, 1692

The love of money has been in all ages, one of the passions that have given great disturbances to the tranquillity of the world.
SAMUEL JOHNSON, *Rambler,* October 6, 1750

He that is of opinion money will do everything may well be suspected of doing everything for money.

BENJAMIN FRANKLIN, *Poor Richard's Almanac*, 1753

The only money of God is God. He pays never with anything less or anything else.

RALPH WALDO EMERSON, "Friendship," *Essays*, 1844

Superfluous wealth can buy superfluities only. Money is not required to buy one necessary of the soul.

HENRY DAVID THOREAU, *Walden*, 1854

We do great injustice to Iscariot, in thinking him wicked above all common wickedness. He was only a common money-lover, and like all money-lovers, did not understand Christ.

JOHN RUSKIN, *The Crown of Wild Olives*, 1865

But it is not the rich man only who is under the domination of things; they too are slaves who, having no money, are unhappy from the lack of it.

GEORGE MACDONALD, *Unspoken Sermons, 1st Series*, 1869

The crying need of the nation is not for better morals, cheaper bread, temperance, liberty, culture, redemption of fallen sisters and erring brothers, nor the grace, love and fellowship of the Trinity, but simply for enough money.

GEORGE BERNARD SHAW, Preface, *Major Barbara*, 1905

Money, n. A blessing that is of no advantage to us excepting when we part with it.

AMBROSE BIERCE, *Devil's Dictionary*, 1906

Love is the grandest thing on God's earth, but fortunate the lover who has plenty of money.

RUSSELL H. CONWELL, *What You Can Do With Your Will Power*, 1917

Money, material though it be, does lie at the base of the most useful work you do. In itself nothing, it is the basis of much of the best effort which can be made for spiritual purposes.

A. J. BALFOUR, *The Mind of*, ed. W. F. Short, 1918

You ought to have money. If you can honestly attain unto riches in Philadelphia, it is your Christian and godly duty to do so. It is an awful mistake of those pious people to think you must be awfully poor in order to be pious.

RUSSELL H. CONWELL, *Sermon*, Philadelphia, 1925

The great curse of our modern society is not so much the lack of money as the fact that the lack of money condemns a man to a squalid and incomplete existence.

CHRISTOPHER DAWSON, *The Modern Dilemma*, 1932

The moral problem of our age is concerned with the love of money, with the habitual appeal to the money motive in nine-tenths of the activities of life, with the universal striving after individual economic security as the prime object of endeavor, with the social approbation of money as the measure of constructive success.

J. M. KEYNES, *The General Theory of Employment, Interest and Money*, 1936

The love of money is a form of infantilism. The man who loves money is the man who has never grown up. He has never passed from the world of fairy tales into the world of philosophy.

ROBERT LYND, *Searchlights and Nightingales*, 1939

The dispute between Marx and the capitalist is merely concerned with the question who shall have money.

EMIL BRUNNER, *Christianity and Civilization*, 1943

An American journalist in China watched a Sister cleaning the gangrenous sores of wounded soldiers. "I wouldn't do that for a million dollars!" the visitor remarked.

Without pause in her work, the Sister replied, "Neither would I."

Maryknoll, the Field Afar, 1947

You cannot love money and your brethren at the same time.

     EMMANUEL SUHARD, *The Church Today,* 1953

We ought to change the legend on our money from "In God We Trust" to "In Money We Trust." Because, as a nation, we've got far more faith in money these days than we do in God.

     ARTHUR HOPPE, *Way,* June, 1963

Money is a dream. It is a piece of paper on which is imprinted in invisible ink the dream of all the things it will buy, all the trinkets and all the power over others. A kind of institutionalized dream which, along with its companion dream-institution of Success, constitutes the main fantasy on which our way of life has been built.

     DAVID T. BAZELON, *The Paper Economy,* 1963

Money is a good servant but a bad master.

     Proverb

When money speaks the truth is silent.

     Russian Proverb

The love of evil is the root of all money.

     ANONYMOUS

If you want to know what God thinks of money, look at the people he gives it to.

     American Proverb

Shrouds have no pockets.

     Proverb

See also Avarice; Business; Capitalism; Charity; Covetousness; Desires; Economics and Christianity; Gold; Greed; Honor; Idolatry; Mammon; Market Place; Possessions; Poverty; Profit; Property; Riches; Selfishness; Success; Trade; Usury; Wealth; Worldliness.

MONOPOLY

The holder of a monopoly is a sinner and offender.

     MOHAMMED (570–632), *Speeches and Table-Talk of,* ed. S. P. Lane

See also Bigness.

MONOTHEISM

And if monotheism displaces polytheism it does so because it is found by experience to be the more faithful interpretation of that idea of God which even the polytheist has in his soul.

     F. B. JEVONS, *The Idea of God in Early Religions,* 1910

MORAL

An Englishman thinks he is moral when he is only uncomfortable.

     GEORGE BERNARD SHAW, *Man and Superman,* 1903

MORAL ATMOSPHERE

The moral atmosphere of the present century is charged with three distinct disturbances,—the waning of religious belief, the insatiable demand for intense sensations, and the increasing number of those who live uncompanied, and walk abroad in solitude.

     EDGAR E. SALTUS, *Philosophy of Disenchantment,* 1885

MORAL BEAUTY

What strikes us at once in superior lives is their magnetism: moral beauty has only to show itself immediately to gather a following.

     ERNEST DIMNET, *What We Live By,* 1932

See also Beauty; Good; Goodness; Virtue.

MORAL CODE

I never . . . believed there was one code of morality for a public, and another for a private man.

THOMAS JEFFERSON, *Letter to Don Valentine de Feronda,* 1809

In reference to our moral conduct, there is not a single principle now known to the most cultivated Europeans which was not likewise known to the ancients.

H. T. BUCKLE, *History of Civilization in England,* 1861

The nation, being in effect a licensed predatory concern, is not bound by the decencies of that code of law and morals that governs private conduct.

THORSTEIN VEBLEN, *Absentee Ownership,* 1923

For a justification of our moral code, we need no longer have recourse to theological revelation or to a metaphysical Absolute. Freud in combination with Darwin suffice to give us our philosophic vision.

JULIAN HUXLEY, *Hibbert Journal,* April, 1943

See also Conduct; Moral Law; Moral Order; Moral Standards; Morality; Natural Law; Psychoanalysis.

MORAL DIGNITY

The moral dignity of a society is measured by what it does to educate and form the personality of its members; the moral dignity of an individual, by what he does for his brothers and for the social body to which he belongs.

AUGUSTE SABATIER, *Religions of Authority and Religion of the Spirit,* 1903

MORAL DISORDER

Call it materialism, call it atheism, call it secularism, call it nationalism, call it greed, call it hate, call it injustice—the evil stalking the modern world is a deadly epidemic of all these moral disorders. Essentially that is what it is: . . . a deep-seated moral disorder throughout the whole wide world.

ROBERT C. HARTNETT, *Broadcast,* January 20, 1952

See also Immorality; Sin.

MORAL EDUCATION

There is only one sound method of moral education. It is in teaching people to think.

EVERETT DEAN MARTIN, *The Meaning of a Liberal Education,* 1926

See also Education, Catholic; Education, Parochial; Education, Religious.

MORAL EXCELLENCE

If I were to choose the three virtues that summarize moral excellence—my first choice would be social conscience, or sense of moral responsibility. My second would be courage, the courage of one's convictions, the courage to nonconform. The third would be truth, or honesty, or faith in the triumph of virtue.

ADLAI STEVENSON, *Ladies Home Journal,* December, 1961

MORAL EVIL

Moral evil is just as impossible to explain by materialism as by God.

VOLTAIRE, *Traité de la métaphysique,* 1738

Moral evil does not float through the air. It walks the world on the two feet of an individual—directed by an evil mind and motivated by an evil heart.

Catholic Herald Citizen (Milwaukee), March 18, 1964

See also Evil.

MORAL FORCE

Moral force is, unhappily, no substitute for armed force, but it is a very great reinforcement.

WINSTON S. CHURCHILL, *Speech,* House of Commons, December 21, 1937

MORAL HEROISM

Fearlessness, singleness of soul, the will
Always to strive for wisdom. . . .
Such be the signs of him whose feet are set
On that fair path which leads to heavenly birth

The Song Celestial, Sir Edwin Arnold's translation of *Bhagavad-Gita,* 5th to 2nd century B.C.

The men of moral grandeur, particularly those whose inventive and simple heroism has opened new paths to virtue, are revealers of metaphysical truth.

HENRI BERGSON, *Mind-Energy,* 1919

See also Heroism.

MORAL INSTINCT

I sincerely believe . . . in the general existence of a moral instinct. I think it the brightest gem with which human character is studded, and the want of it as more degrading than the most hideous of the bodily deformities.

THOMAS JEFFERSON, *Letter to Thomas Law,* June 13, 1814

MORAL LAW

The law of God, which we call the moral law, must alone be the scope, and rule, and end, of all laws.

JOHN CALVIN, *Institutes,* 1536

Two things fill me with constantly increasing admiration and awe, the longer and more earnestly I reflect on them: *the starry heavens without and the moral law within.*

IMMANUEL KANT, *Critique of Practical Reason,* 1788

Opinions alter, manners change, creeds rise and fall, but the moral law is written on the tablets of eternity.

J. A. FROUDE, *The Science of History,* 1864

All morals laws are merely statements that certain kinds of actions will have good effects.

G. E. MOORE, *Principia Ethica,* 1903

It is a law written in the intellect after the manner of knowledge, and communicated to the will as a moral obligation.

BERNARD J. OTTEN, *The Reason Why,* 1912

When the notions of right, of duty, and of justice . . . come into conflict with other passions whose impulse would carry man elsewhere, the moral law makes itself heard.

CHARLES RENOUVIER, *Psychologie Rationelle,* Vol. II, 1912

The moral law is the law which reigns throughout the infinite spiritual universe applied within the narrow confines of human society. It is applied within those confines, it is spiritual, universal in its jurisdiction.

FELIX ADLER, *An Ethical Philosophy of Life,* 1918

The moral laws are deeply imbedded in the constitution of things—we do not break them, we break ourselves upon them.

E. STANLEY JONES, *Victorious Living,* 1936

God, eternally real, estimates the nations of the earth by one standard: obedience or non-obedience to the moral law. . . . What else is the meaning of our present chaos, of a world at war, humanity in sorrow, but this—that contemporary man is tried before the bar of the Eternal, and found wanting?

BERNARD IDDINGS BELL, *Still Shine the Stars,* 1941

Every person who engages in moral judgment . . . implies by his judgment the existence of an objective moral order.

D. E. TRUEBLOOD, *The Logic of Belief,* 1942

If all events, including the events in human lives, are inevitable results of a mechanical process, what is the point in making moral judgments at all.

D. E. TRUEBLOOD, *The Logic of Belief,* 1942

If this be God's world it must be based upon moral law, and God's inexorable moral law can no more be evaded or outwitted than can His physical law. Whatever forces violate moral law contain the seeds of their own destruction.

FRANCIS B. SAYRE, *Reader's Digest,* July, 1948

To deny as the sanction of ethical principles the moral law proceeding from God is to reject the very cornerstone upon which the founders of our nation established their daring experiment in democracy.

ALLAN P. FARRELL, *Whither American Education?,* 1949

Moral law within, which commands and can be obeyed or disobeyed, has value greater than the natural laws which describe necessary processes.

WALTER M. HORTON, *Christian Theology,* 1955

Order between the political communities must be built upon the unshakable and unchangeable rock of the moral law, made manifest in the order of nature by the Creator Himself and by Him engraved on the hearts of men with letters that may never be effaced.

POPE JOHN XXIII, *Pacem in Terris,* April, 1963

See also Church and State; Divine Law; Ethics; Law; Moral Code; Moral Standards; Moral Theology; Morality and God; Morality and Religion; Morality and State; Natural Law; Rights.

MORAL OBLIGATION

Moral obligation is the necessity of doing or avoiding certain actions in view of the well-being we seek in social life.

P. H. D'HOLBACH, *La Morale Universelle,* I, 1820

A moral obligation is no less compelling because it may end in failure.

HAROLD J. LASKI, *The State in Theory and Practice,* 1935

MORAL ORDER

Granted that wherever intelligence exists, there is a certain moral order; but the difference is that the just man subjects himself to the whole moral order, whilst the unjust man subordinates the whole moral order to himself, and constitutes himself the center of all things.

JEAN JACQUES ROUSSEAU, *Émile,* 1762

It is not doubtful, but the most certain of all certainties—nay, the foundation of all certainties—the one absolutely valid objective truth—that there is a moral order in the world.

J. G. FICHTE (1762–1814), *A Divine Government in the World*

The recognition of the moral order and of its relation to nature and man, involves the acknowledgement of the Supreme Mind or God as the ground of all reality.

W. R. SORLEY, *Moral Values and the Idea of God,* 1915

No known race is so low in the scale of civilization that it has not attributed a moral order to the World, because no known race is so little human as not to suppose a moral order so innately desirable as to have an inevitable existence.

JOSEPH WOOD KRUTCH, *The Modern Temper,* 1929

See also Authority; Ethics; Moral Code; Morality; Natural Law.

MORAL PARALYSIS

The awful problem of our time is not so much the dreams, the monsters, which may take shape and consume us, but the moral paralysis in our own souls which leaves us immobile, inert, passive, tongue-tied, ready and even willing to succumb.

THOMAS MERTON, *Way,* June, 1963

MORAL PHILOSOPHY

There is, indeed, in every science a practical side. . . . But only of moral philosophy can it be said that it is . . . essentially practical, for it deals with human conduct, with virtue and vice, with happiness and misery. . . . The science of morality is the mistress of every department of philosophy.

ROGER BACON, *Opus Maius,* 1267

See also Philosophy.

MORAL PROGRESS

Moral progress in history lies not so much in the improvement of the moral code as in the enlargement of the area within which it is applied.

WILL DURANT, *Our Oriental Heritage,* 1935

See also Evolution; Perfection; Progress.

MORAL SENSE

Moral sense is almost completely ignored by modern society. We have, in fact, sup-

pressed its manifestations. All are imbued with irresponsibility. Those who discern good and evil, who are industrious and provident, remain poor and are looked upon as morons.

ALEXIS CARREL, *Man, the Unknown,* 1935

MORAL STANDARDS

Reading, reflection and time have convinced me that the interests of society require the observation of those moral precepts only in which all religions agree (for all forbid us to murder, steal, plunder, or bear false witness) and that we should not intermeddle with the particular dogmas in which all religions differ, which are totally unconnected with morality.

THOMAS JEFFERSON, *Letters to James Fishback,* September 27, 1809

It can be plausibly argued that our religion in its later phases has little in common with the original gospel. But its moral standards have always been those of Jesus as found in the New Testament. They have been maintained, with no essential change, in all ages and by all sections of the Church.

ERNEST F. SCOTT, *The Evolution of Ethics,* ed. E. Sneath, 1927

Men who assert that all moral standards are relative, still believe that it is right to speak the truth about the relativity of moral standards.

H. R. NIEBUHR, *Intercollegian and Far Horizons,* October, 1939

The radical and ultimate cause of the evils which we deplore in modern society is the denial and rejection of a universal norm of morality as well for the individual and social life as for international relations.

POPE PIUS XII, *Summi Pontificatus,* October, 1939

If no set of moral ideas were truer or better than any other there would be no sense in preferring civilized morality to savage morality, or Christian morality to Nazi morality.

C. S. LEWIS, *The Case for Christianity,* 1943

If we are content to accept as morally inoffensive all that is legally unpunishable, we have lowered greatly our moral standards.

ROMAN CATHOLIC BISHOPS OF THE U. S., 1957

The central error of the New Morality lies in its subordination of all objective moral principles, to the overriding claims of vague "personality-values."

Editorial, *America,* October 17, 1959

Our national ideal no longer rests upon a foundation of popular morality. Ignorance of moral principles and the rejection of the very notion of morality are on the rise today and threaten to undermine our nation and its most sacred traditions.

CATHOLIC BISHOPS OF THE U. S., November, 1961

The sophomore who once told me seriously that before he adopted a moral code as his own he intended to try several and then decide which he would accept probably spoke for a number of his young intellectual contemporaries.

HAROLD W. DODDS, *Ladies Home Journal,* December, 1961

There is a difference between a society that recognizes differences among people, and a society, such as we are getting into, where "anything goes"—that is to say, where there is no common moral ground.

ROBERT E. FITCH, *Ladies Home Journal,* December, 1961

Generally speaking, all great societies have come into being and have been maintained through the people's acceptance of certain objective moral standards. Such standards

aren't created; they exist and cannot be displaced. They are stronger, indeed, than we are.

ADLAI STEVENSON, *Ladies Home Journal,* December, 1961

See also Ethics; Moral Code; Moral Law; Natural Law; Society.

MORAL THEOLOGY

The more moral theology in this [Roman Catholic] tradition lays claim to clear and certain knowledge of the natural law, the more charity is ruled out of any influence upon moral decisions.

PAUL RAMSEY, *Nine Modern Moralists,* 1962

When we make a vice of the rigidity and inflexibility of moral theology in the Roman Church we may be in danger of making a virtue of the lack of rigor and substance in our own thinking about the moral life.

PAUL RAMSEY, *Nine Modern Moralists,* 1962

See also Moral Law; Natural Law; Theology.

MORAL TRUTH

The Church . . . has never maintained that outside her fold and apart from her teaching, man cannot arrive at any moral truth. . . . She does however say, has said, and will ever say, . . . she alone possesses what she has immediately from God and can never lose, the whole of moral truth.

POPE PIUS XI, *Christian Education of Youth,* 1929

See also Truth.

MORAL VALUES

The process of determining moral values by the consent of the majority is false in principle and sanction. Morality has its source in God and it binds all men.

CATHOLIC BISHOPS OF THE U. S., November, 1951

See also Moral Code; Moral Law; Values; Values, Spiritual.

MORALISM

Bases politics upon non-political foundations. It takes its stand outside the state in ethical principles of right or good, and then appraises the state thereby. . . . Moralism concludes that the state is indispensable not only to life, but to virtue and to the good life.

RALPH BARTON PERRY, *Puritanism and Democracy,* 1944

"Moralism" is the tone of voice of a religious body which has stood still in its thinking while a society shifts from monochromatic to polychromatic religious patterns. It is the tone of voice of resolutions which once had authority and are now empty of significance.

FRANKLIN H. LITTELL, *From State Church to Pluralism,* 1962

MORALITY

It is certain that the mortality or immortality of the soul must make an entire difference to morality.

BLAISE PASCAL, *Pensées,* 1670

The greater part of morality is of a fixed eternal nature, and will endure when faith shall fail.

JOSEPH ADDISON, *The Spectator,* August 12, 1712

A person may be qualified to do greater good to mankind, and become more beneficial to the world, by morality without faith than by faith without morality.

JOSEPH ADDISON, *The Spectator,* August 16, 1712

Morality is eternal and immutable.

RICHARD PRICE, *The Principal Questions in Morals,* 1758

The fundamental principle of all morality is that man is a being naturally good, loving justice and order; that there is not any original perversity in the human heart, and that the first movements of nature are always right.

J. J. ROUSSEAU, *Reply to Archbishop de Beaumont's Condemnation* of the book *Émile,* 1763

There is no morality in superstition, it exists not in ceremonies, and has nothing to do with dogmas. . . . Morality is the same among all men who make use of their reason. Morality proceeds from God, like light; our superstitions are only darkness.

VOLTAIRE, *Philosophical Dictionary,* II, 1764

To enjoy and give enjoyment, without injury to yourself or others: this is true morality.

NICHOLAS CHAMFORT, *Maxims et pensées,* 1785

Morality is not properly the doctrine how we make ourselves happy, but how we make ourselves worthy of happiness.

IMMANUEL KANT, *Critique of Practical Reason,* 1788

Of all the systems of morality, ancient or modern, which have come under my observation, none appear to me so pure as that of Jesus. He who follows this steadily need not, I think, be uneasy.

THOMAS JEFFERSON, *Letter to William Canby,* September 18, 1813

In New Christianity all morality will be derived directly from the principle that "Men should treat each other as brothers." . . . This principle, regenerated, will be proclaimed as follows: religion should guide the community towards the great aim of improving as quickly as possible the condition of the poorest class.

C. H. DE SAINT-SIMON, *The New Christianity*, 1825

We know no spectacle so ridiculous as the British public in one of its periodical fits of morality.

THOMAS BABINGTON MACAULAY, *On Moore's Life of Byron*, 1831

Morality: Keeping up appearances in this world, or becoming suddenly devout when we imagine that we may be shortly summoned to appear in the next.

HORACE SMITH (1779–1849), *The Tin Trumpet*

Morality is character and conduct such as is required by the circle or community in which the man's life happens to be passed. It shows how much good men require of us.

HENRY WARD BEECHER, *Life Thoughts*, 1858

The Gospel always refers to a pre-existing morality, and confines its precepts to the particulars in which that morality was to be corrected, or superseded by a wider and higher; expressing itself, moreover, in terms most general, often impossible to be interpreted literally.

JOHN STUART MILL, *Of Liberty of Thought and Discussion*, 1859

The moral feelings are not innate, but acquired.

JOHN STUART MILL, *Utilitarianism*, 1863

Neither the individuals nor the ages most distinguished for intellectual achievements have been most distinguished for moral excellence.

W. E. H. LECKY, *History of European Morals*, 1869

Man . . . derives his moral sense from the social feelings which are instinctive or innate in the lower animals.

CHARLES DARWIN, *The Descent of Man*, 1871

Morality is primarily a means of preserving the community and saving it from destruction. Next it is a means of maintaining the community on a certain plane and in a certain degree of benevolence.

FRIEDRICH NIETZSCHE, *Human, All Too Human*, 1878

Christian morality is the safe road from childhood to manhood, and the qualities enjoined by Jesus are indispensable to success in life.

HENRY WARD BEECHER, *North American Review*, August, 1882

The safety of morality lies neither in the adoption of this or that philosophical speculation, or this or that theological creed, but in a real and living belief in that fixed order of nature which sends social disorganization upon the track of immorality, as surely as it sends physical disease after physical trespasses.

THOMAS HENRY HUXLEY, *Science and Morals*, 1886

There is a master-morality and a slave-morality.

FRIEDRICH NIETZSCHE, *Beyond Good and Evil*, 1886

The foundation of morality is to . . . give up pretending to believe that for which there is no evidence, and repeating unintelligible propositions about things beyond the possibilities of knowledge.

THOMAS HENRY HUXLEY, *Essays upon Controversial Questions*, 1889

An endeavor to find for the manifestation of impulse in special situations an office of refreshment and renewal.

JOHN DEWEY, *Psychology*, 1891

Morality (modern) is the act of defining your principles to oppose your practices.

> FRANCIS THOMPSON, *Paganism Old and New,* 1910

Morality is a means for the satisfaction of human wants. In other words, morality must justify itself at the bar of life, not life at the bar of morality.

> MAX C. OTTO, *Things and Ideals,* 1924

Morality, if it is not fixed by custom and authority, becomes a mere matter of taste determined by the idiosyncracies of the moralist.

> WALTER LIPPMANN, *A Preface to Morals,* 1929

When people talk of the "new morality" they are merely committing a new immorality and looking for a way of introducing contraband goods.

> JOSÉ ORTEGA Y GASSET, *Revolt of the Masses,* 1930

Morality is not an imposition removed from life and reason; it is a compendium of the minimum of sacrifices necessary for man to live in company with other men, without suffering too much or causing others to suffer.

> GINA LOMBROSO, *The Tragedies of Progress,* 1931

Morality is not static but a set of experiments, being gradually worked out by mankind, a dynamic, progressive instrument which we can help ourselves to forge.

> DURANT DRAKE, *Problems of Conduct,* 1935

Most of our so-called "Christian" morality, particularly in the field of sex, has little fundamental relationship to the outlook and spirit of the founder of Christianity.

> JOHN MACMURRAY, *Reason and Emotion,* 1935

The order of human existence is too imperiled by chaos, the goodness of man too corrupted by sin, and the possibilities of man too obscured by natural handicaps, to make human order and human possibilities solid bases of the moral imperative.

> REINHOLD NIEBUHR, *An Interpretation of Christian Ethics,* 1935

To justify Christian morality because it provides a foundation of morality, instead of showing the necessity of Christian morality from the truth of Christianity, is a very dangerous inversion.

> T. S. ELIOT, *The Idea of a Christian Society,* 1940

If I had to write a book on morality, it would have a hundred pages and ninety-nine would be blank. On the last page I should write: "I recognize only one duty, and that is to love." And, as far as everything else is concerned, I say *no.*

> ALBERT CAMUS, *Notebooks,* 1935–1942

The morality of modern civilized man has turned out to be a terribly thin covering of ice over a sea of primitive barbarity.

> KARL BARTH, *Community, Church and State,* 1946

The same marvelous faculty that drives us along the road to morality often acts as a sadistic slave driver, a self-accusing fury, and a tireless jobber in guilt.

> JOSHUA LOTH LIEBMAN, *Peace of Mind,* 1946

The dogma of the clergy, the pedanticism of professors, the close adherence to the letter of the law or contract by legal men, often run counter to simple moral laws.

> WILLIAM SEIFRIZ, *Perspectives on a Troubled Decade,* ed. Bryson, Finkelstein, and MacIver, 1950

We do not need the laws of Church and State, nor the findings of science and psychiatry, to tell us the simple rules of ethics and morality.

> WILLIAM SEIFRIZ, *Perspectives on a Troubled Decade,* ed. Bryson, Finklestein, and MacIver, 1950

For those who adopt the scientific view of man there is no foundation for morality, except present expediency.

F. SHERWOOD TAYLOR, *Man and Matter,* 1951

There is a basic morality to which we owe a supreme loyalty, a morality derived from our common humanity, a morality greatly affected by the conditions under which men work and live.

NORMAN THOMAS, *A Socialist's Faith,* 1951

Morality involves the correct and careful regulation of three relationships: man to God, man to himself, and man to his fellow men.

ROMAN CATHOLIC BISHOPS OF THE U. S., November, 1951

Whereas the old morality saw things as so simple that moral judgment was always easy, the new morality sees things as so complicated that moral judgment becomes practically impossible.

JOHN COURTNEY MURRAY, *We Hold These Truths,* 1960

What we have tried to do, in the academies and out of them, is to sustain a Christian morality based on a non-Christian, even anti-Christian philosophy of life. Morally, we have tried to be Christians; intellectually, we have been Freudians, behaviorists, pragmatists, materialists of one variety or another, determinists—and sometimes all at the same time.

JOHN COGLEY, *Commonweal,* March, 1960

Morality, including political morality, has to do with the definition of right *conduct,* and this not simply by way of the ends of action. *How* we do *what* we do is as important as our goals.

PAUL RAMSEY, *War and the Christian Conscience,* 1961

See also Armaments; Art and Morality; Atheism; Atomic Bomb; Beauty; Behavior; Bible and Morality; Communist Morality;

Conduct; Conscience; Determinism; Duties; Election; Ethics; Evil; Expediency; Faith; Fear; Free Will; God, Nonexistence of; Goodness; Immortality; Moral Code; Moral Law; Moral Order; Moral Standards; Morals; Necessity; Politics; Prosperity; Religion, Definitions of; Science; Sin; Virtue.

MORALITY, POSITIVE

The first principle of Positive morality is the preponderance of social sympathy.

AUGUSTE COMTE, *Positive Polity,* 1820

Positive Morality is the body of laws (the ethical code) accepted by an age or community as correct principles for determining the true worth of actions.

REGINALD A. P. ROGERS, *A Short History of Ethics,* 1911

All moral theories are the product in the last analysis of the economic stage which society has reached at that particular epoch.

FRIEDRICH ENGELS, *Anti-Dühring,* 1878

MORALITY AND ECONOMICS

I hold that not even the Church itself is more dependent upon fundamental moralities than is the whole commercial structure of the world.

HENRY WARD BEECHER, *Address,* May 8, 1883

Insistence upon the impracticability of the morality of Jesus is in effect the assertion of the supremacy of the economic appetites over the rest of life.

HARRY F. WARD, *Our Economic Morality and the Ethic of Jesus,* 1929

We now know that anything which is economically right is also morally right; there can be no conflict between good economics and good morals.

HENRY FORD (1863–1937), quoted by C. E. Hudson, *Christian Morals*

See also Economics and Christianity.

MORALITY AND FREEDOM

Where there is no free agency, there can be no morality.
WILLIAM H. PRESCOTT, *The Conquest of Peru,* 1847

The possibility of morality thus depends on the possibility of liberty; for if man be not a free agent, he is not the author of his actions, and has, therefore, no responsibility,—no moral personality at all.
WILLIAM HAMILTON, *Lectures on Metaphysics,* II, 1870

Morality cannot exist one minute without freedom. . . . Only a free man can possibly be moral. Unless a good deed is voluntary, it has no moral significance.
EVERETT DEAN MARTIN, *Liberty,* 1930

The highest law of morality may be expressed in the form of the norm: Be free; negatively: Do not be a slave to forces which tend to compel you to act as they command.
HENRY LANZ, *In Quest of Morals,* 1941

Moral liberty is the basis of ethics and the indispensable condition of morality. Without it, there can be neither duty, obligation, responsibility, nor merit.
JOHN A. O'BRIEN, *Is the Will Free?,* 1946

See also Ethics; Free Will; Freedom; Morality.

MORALITY AND GOD

It is God's will, not merely that we should *be* happy, but that we should make ourselves happy. This is true morality.
IMMANUEL KANT, *Lecture at Königsberg,* 1775

There is only one view of morality which reconciles the trampling on self with ultimate happiness; that is the mystery of God's judgment.
JOHN CUTHBERT HEDLEY, *The Christian Inheritance,* 1896

It is in God that morality has its foundation and guarantee.
LEO BAECK, *Essence of Judaism,* 1836

Ethical monotheism . . . the sublime idea that morality is something Divine, spiritual in its inmost essence—that is the distinctive teaching of the Hebrew Scriptures.
JOSEPH H. HERTZ, *The Pentateuch and Haftorahs,* 1936

A morality without God is as weak as a traffic law when the policeman is on foot.
WILL DURANT, *On the Meaning of Life,* 1937

Universal tradition makes it plain that without a higher aid the moral life neither endures nor uplifts itself.
MARTIN J. O'MALLEY, *The Peace of Christ,* 1939

Apart from God there is no moral code of universal and lasting application. The rule of right, the standard of truth and the norm of good is determined by the nature of God.
JAMES M. GILLIS, *God in Government,* 1943

Morality, concerned with bringing human activity into conformity with God's will, has a bearing on everything that touches human rights and duties.
CATHOLIC BISHOPS OF THE U. S., November, 1951

Mankind has lost its morality because it has lost its God.
JOSEPH KLAUSNER, *Judaism,* January, 1953

The backbone of all moral attitudes is the love of God, through Christ, with Christ, and in Christ.
DIETRICH VON HILDEBRAND, *Christian Ethics,* 1953

The splendor and metaphysical reality of morality flashes forth only when the absolute *goodness* is seen not merely as the platonic idea, but as the living God.

DIETRICH VON HILDEBRAND, *True Morality and Its Counterfeits,* 1955

One cannot appeal to God's universal law against what goes on in communist Russia, without at the same time inviting judgment of the same moral law on our own attitude to, say, the colored peoples, or to the undernourished and the ill-cared for two-thirds of the world's population.

AELRED GRAHAM, *Address,* Pittsburgh, Pa., April, 1961

In a world in which "God is dead," there is only room for a "morality without sin."

PAUL ACIAUX, *The Sacrament of Penance,* 1962

See also Good; Goodness; Moral Law; Natural Law.

MORALITY AND RELIGION

Attempts have been made to constitute reason the basis of virtue, but I find that religion is the only solid basis for morality.

JEAN JACQUES ROUSSEAU, *Émile,* 1762

There is no religion which dispenses one from the duties of morality.

JEAN JACQUES ROUSSEAU, *Émile,* 1762

Reason and experience both forbid us to expect that national morality can prevail in exclusion of religious principles.

GEORGE WASHINGTON, *Farewell Address,* September 19, 1796

Morality without religion is only a kind of dead reckoning—an endeavor to find our place on a cloudy sea by measuring the distance we have run, but without any observation of the heavenly bodies.

HENRY WADSWORTH LONGFELLOW, *Kavanagh,* 1849

Religions, considered as moral teachers, are realized and effective only when their moral teaching is in conformity with the teaching of their age.

W. E. H. LECKY, *History of European Morals,* I, 1869

There are many religions, but there is only one morality.

JOHN RUSKIN, *Lectures on Art,* 1884

Religious morality is a morality of sacrifice, which is dear to the weak and degenerate, but to all other people is a species of slavery.

BENITO MUSSOLINI, *Speech,* July, 1904

The precepts of morality unsupported by faith in God and the verities of religion are incapable of producing the highest attainments of character.

COMMISSION ON CHURCH AND RELIGIOUS EDUCATION, FEDERAL COUNCIL OF CHURCHES OF CHRIST IN AMERICA, *Report,* 1912

Certainly one of the most dangerous errors of our age is the claim to separate morality from religion, thus removing all solid basis for any legislation.

POPE PIUS XI, *Caritate Christi Compulsi,* 1932

Morals is its own religion, exercises its own authority, and reveals its own necessity.

JOHN HAYNES HOLMES, *Religion Today,* ed. A. L. Swift, 1933

The morality code that remains after the religion that produced it is rejected is like the perfume that lingers in an empty bottle.

SIGRID UNDSET, *Stages on the Road,* 1934

It is . . . by the superiority of its morality that a religion wins over souls and reveals to them a certain conception of things.

HENRI BERGSON, *The Two Sources of Morality and Religion,* 1935

Without religion morality becomes simply a matter of individual taste, of public opinion or majority vote.
CATHOLIC BISHOPS OF THE U. S., November, 1952

The progressive recession of belief in Christianity's traditional doctrines has been accompanied by a progressive advance in the practice of Christianity's moral precepts.
A. J. TOYNBEE, *A Study of History,* Vol. XII, *Reconsiderations,* 1961

See also Christianity; Moral Law; Natural Law; Religion.

MORALITY AND STATE

If the moral and physical fiber of its manhood and its womanhood is not a state concern, the question is, what is?
BENJAMIN CARDOZO, *Adler vs. Deegan,* 1929, 251 *N. Y. Reports,* 467

The legal code can never be identified with the code of morals. It is no more the function of government to impose a moral code than to impose a religious code. And for the same reason.
R. M. MACIVER, *The Web of Government,* 1947

A State is not morally free to allow anarchy and license instead of lawful liberty, even if the majority should so desire; and the majority are not morally free to become a tyranny and destroy the rights of minorities.
CATHOLIC ASSOCIATION FOR INTERNATIONAL PEACE, *Timeless Rights,* 1948

See also Government and Religion; Law; Moral Law; Natural Law.

MORALS

The highest and most perfect [science] which, presupposing an entire knowledge of the other sciences, is the last degree of wisdom.
RENÉ DESCARTES, *The Principles of Philosophy,* 1644

The notion of morals implies some sentiment common to all mankind which recommends the same objects to general approbation and makes every man, or most men, agree in the same opinion or decision concerning it.
DAVID HUME, *Enquiry Concerning the Principles of Morals,* 1751

There are two springs of established acceptance in morals; first, that self-interest is the mainspring of all our actions, and secondly, that utility is the test of their value.
C. C. COLTON, *Lacon,* 1820

The great secret of morals is love; or a going out of our own nature, and an identification with the beautiful which exists in thought, action, or person, not our own.
PERCY BYSSHE SHELLEY, *A Defense of Poetry,* 1821

Morals is the direction of the will on universal ends. He is immoral who is acting to any private end.
RALPH WALDO EMERSON, *North American Review,* April, 1866

The morals of men are more governed by their pursuits than by their opinions.
W. E. H. LECKY, *History of European Morals,* 1869

If your morals make you dreary, depend upon it they are wrong.
ROBERT LOUIS STEVENSON, *Across the Plains and Other Essays,* 1880

Our system of morals is a body of imperfect social generalizations expressed in terms of emotion.
OLIVER WENDELL HOLMES, *Collected Legal Papers,* 1920

The sum of taboos and prescriptions in the folkways by which right conduct is defined. Right conduct is what the group approves of, wrong conduct what the group disapproves of.
Encyclopedia of Social Sciences, "Morals," X, 643, 1937

True morals must start from a consideration of man's true destiny which is supernatural.

MARTIN J. O'MALLEY, *The Peace of Christ,* 1939

Morals embrace not only the way in which we behave towards our neighbors, but also the way in which we cling to the integrity of our own thinking.

J. V. L. CASSERLEY, *Retreat from Christianity in the Modern World,* 1952

See also Behavior; Conduct; Immorality; Love; Morality.

MORTGAGE

The mortgage that the peasant has on heavenly blessings guarantees the mortgage that the bourgeois has on peasant lands.

KARL MARX, *The Class Struggles in France,* 1848–1850

MOSES

Moses with his law is most terrible; there never was any equal to him in perplexing, affrighting, tyrannizing, threatening, preaching and thundering.

MARTIN LUTHER, *Table Talk,* 1569

In his artlessness, Moses strikes a note so sublime and majestic that nothing can equal it.

JACQUES BÉNIGNE BOSSUET, *Discourse on Universal History,* c. 1675

See also Old Testament.

MOTHER

Mother is the name of God in the lips and hearts of little children.

WILLIAM MAKEPEACE THACKERAY, *Vanity Fair,* 1848

To the mother alone it has been given, that her soul during the nine months should

touch the soul of the child, and impose upon it predispositions to truth, gentleness, goodness, the culture of which precious germs she should complete in the light of day, after having sown them in the mysterious mysteries of her maternity.

JEAN BAPTISTE LACORDAIRE, *Conferences of,* 1850

The mother's heart is the child's schoolroom.

HENRY WARD BEECHER, *Life Thoughts,* 1858

The mother's face and voice are the first conscious objects as the infant soul unfolds, and she soon comes to stand in the very place of God to her child.

G. STANLEY HALL, *Pedagogical Seminary,* June, 1891

The mother is indeed a gardener of God doing a veritable priestly work in the Christian care of her children.

VIRGIL MICHEL, *Catholic Mind,* Vol. 37, 1940

The working class mother with a large family is the real heroine . . . of our civilization.

WILLIAM TEMPLE, *Speech,* House of Lords, 1942

See also Children; Daughters; Family; Marriage; Mary, the Mother of Jesus; Maternity; Motherhood; Parents; Son.

MOTHER AND CHILD, LIFE OF

Only God is the lord of the life of a man not guilty of a crime punishable by death! The physician does not have the right to dispose of the life of either a child or its mother; and no one in the world, no private person, no human authority, may authorize him to proceed to its direct destruction.

POPE PIUS XII, *Address,* November 12, 1943

Never and in no case has the Church taught that the child's life must be preferred to that of the mother. It is a mistake to formulate the question with this alternative: either the child's life or the mother's. No; neither the mother's life nor the child's may be submitted to an act of direct suppression. For the one and for the other the requirement can be only this: to make every effort to save the life of both the mother and the child.

POPE PIUS XII, *Address,* November 27, 1951

See also Abortion; Pregnancy, Termination of.

MOTHERHOOD

Motherhood is the keystone of the arch of matrimonial happiness.

THOMAS JEFFERSON, *Letter to Martha Jefferson Randolph,* 1791

The heroism of motherhood is the exaltation and glory of the Christian bride: in the desolation of her home, if it is without the joy of an infant.

POPE PIUS XII, *Address,* October 26, 1941

See also Children; Family; Marriage; Maternity; Mother; Parents; Woman.

MOTHER-IN-LAW

Christ's first public miracle of healing was wrought upon a mother-in-law—the mother of Peter's wife (Mark I: 30). Certainly that was no mere accident.

JOHN ELLIS LARGE, *The Small Needle of Doctor Large,* 1962

MOTION PICTURES

The sanctity of the institution of marriage and the home shall be upheld. No film shall infer that casual or promiscuous sex relationships are the common thing. . . . These [seduction and rape] should never

be more than suggested, and then only when essential to the plot. They should never be shown explicitly. . . . Crime shall never be presented in such a way as to throw sympathy with the crime. . . . Brutal killings are not to be presented in detail. . . . Revenge, in modern times, shall not be justified. . . . Mercy killing shall never be made to seem right or permissible. . . . Dances suggesting or representing sexual actions or emphasizing indecent movements are to be regarded as obscene. . . . Laws—divine, natural or human—shall not be ridiculed.

Motion Picture Production Code, adopted 1930, relaxed in 1961 to permit the depiction of dope addiction and a lessening of the regulation concerning homosexuality.

Catholics are called by God, the Pope, the bishops and priests to a united and vigorous campaign for the purification of the cinema, which has become a deadly menace to morals.

AMLETO GIOVANNI CICOGNANI, Statement to the press, 1933

In deciding the ratings of the films, no consideration is given to artistic, technical or dramatic values. Only moral content is weighed.

Legion of Decency, 1933

So great is the power of the motion picture to impress the youth of the land that one hour spent in the darkness of a cinema palace, intent on the unfolding of the wrong kind of story, can and frequently does nullify years of careful training on the part of the Church, the school, the home.

JOHN J. CANTWELL, *Ecclesiastical Review,* February, 1934

It is one of the privileges of adulthood in a free country to expose oneself to picturization of life and make one's own interpretations. The task of the church is not to spare adults this experience, but rather to provide them with the right canons of interpretation and to furnish them with answers in depth to questions asked in depth.

JAMES A. PIKE, Sermon, in *New York Times,* December, 1956

Those who do not want the sexual aspect of life included in the portrayal of real-life situations had better burn their Bibles as well as abstain from the movies.

JAMES A. PIKE, Sermon, in *New York Times,* December, 1956

Our big pictures this year have had some intriguing themes—sex, perversion, adultery and cannibalism. We'll get those kids away from their TV sets yet.

BOB HOPE, 1960

The churches are under the mandate of Christ to bring the judgment of the Gospel to bear upon the policies and practices of organizations which operate the mass media, as well as upon the total use which men make of the media.

NATIONAL COUNCIL OF CHURCHES, 1960

The commission of sin in movies is vivid and dramatic. But repentance is purely internal. How often can you show someone kneeling in church? . . . To create sympathy for a sinner is not to sympathize with sin.

GEOFFREY M. SHURLOCK (Administrator of the Motion Picture Code), quoted in Murray Schumach's *The Face on the Cutting-Room Floor,* 1964

Motion pictures should never embarrass a man when he brings his family to the theatre. Public morality is a very important factor on the screen. . . . I seriously object to seeing on the screen what belongs in the bedroom.

SAMUEL GOLDWYN, quoted in Murray Schumach's *The Face on the Cutting-Room Floor,* 1964

In its fight against self-classification [of motion pictures so that they would be labeled as fit or not for younger people], the American movie industry, with its extraordinary history of chicanery, is trying to perpetrate a hoax on the American public that would be hilarious if it were not so serious. It has tried to create the impression that it is fighting censorship. Actually, it is perverting freedom of the cinema art in its lust for cash.

MURRAY SCHUMACH, *The Face on the Cutting-Room Floor,* 1964

Motion pictures have ruined a lot more evenings than they have morals.

ANONYMOUS

See also Censorship; Obscenity.

MOUNTAINS

These, the great Alps, seen thus, link one in some way to one's immortality. . . . I saw, as it were, my religion. I mean, humility, the fear of death, the terror of height and of distance, the glory of God, the infinite potentiality of reception whence springs that divine thirst of soul; my aspiration also toward completion, and my confidence in the dual destiny.

HILAIRE BELLOC, *The Path to Rome,* 1900

MOURNING

The wise in heart mourn not for those who live, nor for those who die.

Bhagavad-Gita, Mahabarata, c. 2nd century B.C.

The house of mourning teaches charity and wisdom.

ST. JOHN CHRYSOSTOM, *Homilies,* c. 388

See also Bereavement; Death; Grief; Sorrow.

MURDER

Murder is a crime if one person commits it; but it is acclaimed as virtuous and brave if many commit it! So it is no longer innocence, but the enormity of the crime that assures exemption from punishment!
St. Cyprian (200–258), *Ad. Don.*

The first judgment that God will pass on man at the Day of Resurrection will be for murder.
Mohammed (570–632), *Speeches and Table Talk of*, ed. S. P. Lane

Unless we think of man's life in terms of his worth to God, we have already in principle justified his possible murder for the sake of the "greatest happiness of the greatest number" or some other quite reasonable earthly goal.
Paul Ramsey, *Nine Modern Moralists*, 1962

See also Abortion; Bloodshed; Capital Punishment; Conquest; Euthanasia; Genocide; Impurity; Killing; Lynching; Martyrs; Suicide; Violence; War.

MUSIC

Let my song go forth like the path of the sun!
May all the sons of the Immortal listen—
They who have reached their heavenly homes!
Svetesvara Upanishad, c. 1000 B.C.

Our fathers have broken even the strong fortresses by their hymns, the rock by their shouting. They have opened to us the path of the great heaven.
Rig-Veda, c. 1000 B.C.

Fashion a hymn in the mouth. Expand like the cloud. Sing a song of praise.
Rig-Veda, c. 1000 B.C.

For changing peoples' manners and altering their customs there is nothing better than music.
Shu Ching, 6th century B.C.

It must be banned, this artificial music which injures souls and draws them into various states of feelings, snivelling, impure, and sensual, even a bacchic frenzy and madness.
St. Clement of Alexandria (150–220), quoted in Alec Robertson's *Christian Music,* 1961

Let us leave colored [chromatic] harmonies to banquets where no one even blushes at music crowned with flowers and harlotry.
St. Clement of Alexandria (150–220), quoted in Alec Robertson's *Christian Music,* 1961

I wept at the beauty of your hymns and canticles, and was powerfully moved at the sweet sound of your Church singing. These sounds flowed into my ears, and the truth streamed into my heart.
St. Augustine, *Confessions,* IX, 397

It must be submitted to severe control: and everything must be banished which recalls the cult of pagan gods and the songs of actors.
St. John Chrysostom (c. 347–407), quoted in Alec Robertson's *Christian Music,* 1961

Music doth extenuate fears, furies, appeaseth cruelty, abateth heaviness, and to such as are wakeful it causeth quiet rest; it cures all irksomeness and heaviness of soul.
Cassiodorus, *The Divine Letters,* c. 550

Let the chant be full of gravity; let it be neither worldly, nor too rude and poor. . . . Let it be sweet, yet without levity, and, while it pleases the ear, let it move the heart.
St. Bernard of Clairvaux (1091–1153), quoted in Alec Robertson's *Christian Music,* 1961

When natural music is sharpened and polished by art, then one begins to see with amazement the great and perfect wisdom of God in His wonderful work of music. . . . He who does not find this an inexpressible miracle of the Lord is truly a clod, and is not worthy to be considered a man.

MARTIN LUTHER, 1538, quoted by R. Bainton in *Here I Stand*

I have no pleasure in any man who despises music. It is no invention of ours; it is the gift of God. I place it next to theology.

MARTIN LUTHER (1483–1546), *Sayings of*

Exclude from churches all such music as . . . introduces anything of the impure or lascivious, in order that the house of God may truly be seen to be . . . the house of prayer.

Council of Trent, 1562

Music is a tonic for the saddened soul, a Roaring Meg [cannon] against melancholy, to rear and revive the languishing soul.

ROBERT BURTON, *The Anatomy of Melancholy*, 1621

What a pleasure it will be to hear a splendid High Mass, in which all kinds of instruments are employed to make music —organ, drums, trombones, horns, strings and voices.

FRIEDRICH VON SPEE (1591–1635), *The Golden Book of Virtue*

Music is the greatest good that mortals know,
And all of heaven we have below.

JOSEPH ADDISON (1672–1719), *Song for St. Cecilia's Day*

What is to reach the heart must come from above, if it does not come thence, it will be nothing but notes—body without spirit.

BEETHOVEN to J. A. Stumpff, 1824, quoted by Marion Scott in *Beethoven*

It is the only cheap and unpunished rapture upon earth.

SYDNEY SMITH, *Letter to Countess of Carlisle*, August, 1844

The musician who would follow religion in all her relations is obliged to learn the art of imitating the harmonies of solitude. He ought to be acquainted with the melancholy notes of the waters and the trees; he ought to study the sound of the winds in the cloister and those murmurs that pervade the Gothic temple, the grass of the cemetery and the vaults of death.

VISCOUNT DE CHATEAUBRIAND, *The Genius of Christianity*, 1856

Music is well said to be the speech of angels.

THOMAS CARLYLE, *Essays: The Opera*, 1857

Music is love in search of a word.

SIDNEY LANIER, *The Symphony*, 1875

The organ, the master instrument, is the voice of the Christian Church, "the seraph-haunted queen of harmony," sounding like an echo from a mystic and hidden world.

JOHN LANCASTER SPALDING, *Essays and Reviews*, 1877

Sacred music, being a complementary part of the solemn liturgy, participates in the general scope of liturgy, which is the glory of God and the sanctification and edification of the faithful.

POPE PIUS X, *Motu Proprio* (on Sacred Music), November 22, 1903

Gregorian Chant has always been looked upon as the supreme model of Church music. . . . The more closely a Church composition approaches plain chant in movement, inspiration, and feeling, the more holy and liturgical it becomes; and the more out of harmony it is with this supreme model, the less worthy is it of the temple.

POPE PIUS X, *Motu Proprio* (on Sacred Music), 1903

Music is the Lost Chord that has strayed hither from heaven.

> P. A. SHEEHAN, *Under the Cedars and the Stars,* 1903

Music being the universal expression of the mysterious and supernatural, the best that man has ever attained to, is capable of uniting in common devotion minds that are only separated by creeds, and it comforts our hope with a brighter promise of unity than any logic offers.

> ROBERT BRIDGES, *Collected Essays,* 1935

The Masses and motets so earnestly hailed as "modern liturgical music" are rarely modern, liturgical or music. . . . They are full of musical legerdemain, including painless inversions of common chords to produce sounds, trite, trivial and tuneful, but not too much so for church use.

> JOSEPH J. BLY, *Orate Frates,* XXII, 1947–1948

Music and religion are as intimately related as poetry and love; the deepest emotions require for their civilized expression the most emotional of arts.

> WILL DURANT, *The Age of Faith,* 1950

Music was as vital as the church edifice itself, more deeply stirring than all the glory of glass or stone. Many a stoic soul, doubtful of the creed, was melted by the music, and fell on his knees before the mystery that no words could speak.

> WILL DURANT, *The Age of Faith,* 1950

Music is as well or better able to praise [God] than the building of the church and all its decorations: it is the Church's greatest ornament . . . religious music without religion is almost always vulgar.

> IGOR STRAVINSKY, *Conversations with Igor Stravinsky,* By Stravinsky and R. Craft, 1959

Though the Church went singing into the world from her foundation, music is to her

not an absolute necessity but a most beautiful and desirable embellishment.

> ALEC ROBERTSON, *Christian Music,* 1961

Sacred music is to be considered the more holy in proportion as it is more closely connected with the liturgical action, whether it adds delight to prayer, fosters unity of minds, or confers greater solemnity upon the sacred rites.

> *Constitution on Sacred Liturgy,* Ecumenical Council, Rome, December 4, 1963

See also Art; Art and Religion; Liturgy; Melodies; Pleasure; Prayer; Ritual; Song; Worship.

MYSTERIES

The mysteries which were hidden until the apostles' time and were handed down by them as they received them from the Lord, and were hidden under the Old Covenant and revealed to the saints, were one thing; but the ordinary revelation to the faithful was another matter.

> ST. CLEMENT OF ALEXANDRIA, *Stromateis,* c. 193

What was visible in the life of Christ has passed over into the mysteries.

> ST. LEO THE GREAT (390?–461), *Sermo* 74, 2

The simple, absolute, and unchangeable mysteries of heavenly Truth lie hidden in the dazzling obscurity of the secret Silence, outshining all brilliance with the intensity of their darkness.

> DIONYSIUS THE AREOPAGITE, *On the Divine Names,* c. 500

The greatest and most profound mysteries of God, hidden from those who go about in the world, however wise they may be, have been revealed to the small and humble in the faith of Jesus.

> NICHOLAS OF CUSA, *De Docta Ignorantia,* c. 1433

It is Faith alone that vividly and with certainty embraces the sublime mysteries of our religion.

MICHEL DE MONTAIGNE, *Essays,* 1588

The heavenly powers are to be reverenced, and not searched into; and their mercies rather by prayers to be sought, than their hidden counsels by curiosity.

PHILIP SIDNEY, *Arcadia,* 1590

As for those wingy Mysteries in Divinity, and airy subtleties in Religion, which have unhing'd the brains of better heads, they never stretched the *Pia Mater* of mine.

THOMAS BROWNE, *Religio Medici,* 1635

We all walk in mysteries. We do not know what is stirring in the atmosphere that surrounds us, nor how it is connected with our own spirit.

J. W. VON GOETHE, *Conversations with Eckermann,* 1848

The divine mysteries by their very nature so far transcend the created mind, that even when they are delivered by revelation and received by faith, they remain covered by the veil of faith itself.

Vatican Council, 1870

The joy of all mysteries is the certainty which comes from their contemplation, that there are many doors yet for the soul to open on her upward and inward way.

ARTHUR CHRISTOPHER BENSON, *From a College Window,* 1906

There are people who say that they cannot accept religion because they cannot believe in mysteries. They have no business trying to know anything about science then, because science is full of mysteries.

JAMES J. WALSH, *Address,* January 23, 1929

The deepest and strangest mysteries, the weirdest and most wonderful, the most shocking and most sublime, are those that even after all these aeons lie concealed in the dark and tortuous depths of the mind of man.

JAMES M. GILLIS, *The Church and Modern Thought,* 1935

Those who concede that we are literally surrounded by mysteries in the natural order are most inconsistent in their refusal to admit mysteries in the supernatural order.

J. F. NOLL, *The Christian Faith Before the Bar of Reason,* 1948

See also Bible; Bible: Its Interpretation; Faith; Mystery; Religion; Revelation; Science.

MYSTERY

There is nothing beautiful or sweet or great in life that is not mysterious.

FRANÇOIS RÉNE DE CHATEAUBRIAND, *Beauties of the Christian Religion,* 1802

Willingly I too say, Hail! to the unknown awful powers which transcend the ken of the understanding.

RALPH WALDO EMERSON, "Demonology," *Lectures,* 1839

What is mysterious, secret, unknown, cannot at the same time be known as an object of faith.

WILLIAM ELLERY CHANNING (1780–1842), *Works*

Mystery is in reality only a theological term for religious allegory. All religions have their mysteries. Properly speaking, a mystery is a dogma which is plainly absurd, but which, nevertheless conceals in itself a lofty truth.

ARTHUR SCHOPENHAUER, "A Dialogue," *Essays,* 1851

The huge concentric waves of universal life are shoreless. The starry sky that we study is but a partial appearance. We grasp but a few meshes of the vast network of existence.

VICTOR HUGO, *William Shakespeare,* 1864

The deepest mystery of all lies in the conviction, which seems to be inextricably rooted in the human spirit, namely, the instinct to distinguish between the impulses which we believe emanate from God, and the impulses which we believe emanate from ourselves.

ARTHUR CHRISTOPHER BENSON, *From a College Window,* 1906

The man who prides himself on the complete absence of mystery in his view of the world is not only not representing the scientific outlook but will speedily become quite unable to understand it.

J. W. N. SULLIVAN, *Aspects of Science,* 1925

The great evil today is no longer materialism and scientism; it is an unbridled spirituality. But the true supernatural is none the more recognized. "Mystery" envelops everything, and is installed in the sombre regions of the ego it ravages, at the centre of the reason it drives away from its domain.

HENRI MASSIS, *Defense of the West,* 1927

The most beautiful thing we can experience is the mysterious. It is the source of all true art and science. He to whom this emotion is a stranger, who can no longer pause to wonder and stand rapt in awe, is as good as dead; his eyes are closed.

ALBERT EINSTEIN, *The Forum,* October, 1930

It is enough for me to contemplate the mystery of conscious life perpetuating itself through all eternity, which we dimly perceive, and to try humbly to comprehend even an infinitesimal part of the intelligence manifested in nature.

ALBERT EINSTEIN, *Living Philosophies,* 1931

In this domain [sex] man is faced at every turn by mystery. He surrenders himself after a unique fashion—encounters either the mystery of wedded love or the mystery of terrible sin.

DIETRICH VON HILDEBRAND, *In Defense of Purity,* 1933

A religion without the element of mystery would not be a religion at all.

EDWIN LEWIS, *A Philosophy of the Christian Revelation,* 1940

Perhaps some day, the modern man will learn that mystery is not the prison of the mind of man, it is his home.

WALTER FARRELL, *A Companion to the Summa,* 1941

Even in natural science, now, the known is dissolved into the unknown, and the static view is replaced by the dynamic view, and once more the familiar things become weird and incomprehensible, just as they were ten thousand years ago, when religion began.

FRITZ KUNKEL, *In Search of Maturity,* 1943

If you know the love that can lead you near to heartbreak, if you know not only the heights of ecstasy but the depths of pain, then you will know you stand before a mystery and you will be silenced.

GERALD VANN, *The Heart of Man,* 1945

The standard device for getting around a logical contradiction by elevating it to the status of a truth beyond logic.

MAX C. OTTO, *Religious Liberals Reply,* 1947

Real faith . . . means holding ourselves open to the unconditional mystery which we encounter in every sphere of our life and which cannot be comprised in any formula. . . . Real faith means the ability to endure life in the face of this mystery.

MARTIN BUBER, *Israel and the World,* 1948

There are many theological questions which can be asked—even interesting ones, for which the truest answer this side of the grave is, "I don't know."

JAMES A. PIKE, *Beyond Anxiety,* 1953

Both the man of science and the man of action live always at the edge of mystery, surrounded by it.

J. ROBERT OPPENHEIMER, *Address,* 1954

When the park-keeper, mistaking Schopenhauer for a tramp, asked him in the Tiergarten at Frankfurt, "Who are you?" Schopenhauer replied bitterly: "I wish to God I knew."

W. E. SANGSTER, *The Pure in Heart,* 1954

Each mystery affirms the final mystery that is at once the ground and illumination of all lesser mysteries, the goad and goal of our searching.

CHAD WALSH, *Behold the Glory,* 1955

Religion has no monopoly of mystery. The whole universe is crammed with mystery. . . . If a scientist declares that he will not accept religion because he refuses to recognize mystery, you may also put him down as a charlatan.

JAMES M. GILLIS, *This Mysterious Human Nature,* 1956

If the Christian faith cannot enable a man to face the unknown without blinding himself to the fact that the mystery is there; to follow, in the unknown, the traces of meaning accessible to his mind; to live with his face to the existential winds that blow across the great void which modern science has opened up before us in many spheres: then it cannot really be Christian faith.

THOMAS F. O'DEA, *An American Catholic Dilemma,* 1958

See also Eucharist; Evil; Evil: Its Nature; Evil, Problem of; Existence; Faith; Mysteries; Religion, Definitions of; Religion: Its Nature and Function; Revelation; Science; Understanding; Unknown.

MYSTIC

His spirit is as if it were sunk and lost in the Abyss of Deity, and loses the consciousness of all creature-distinctions. All things are gathered together in one with the divine sweetness, and the man's being is so penetrated with the divine substance that he loses himself therein.

JOHN TAULER (1300–1361), *Sermon for Septuagesima Sunday*

They [mystics] desire to know, only that they may love; and their desire for union with the principle of things in God, who is the sum of them all, is founded on a feeling which is neither curiosity nor self-interest.

E. RECÉJAC, *Essay on the Basis of the Mystical Knowledge,* 1899

One of the marks of the true mystic is the tenacious and heroic energy with which he pursues a definite moral idea.

J. H. LEUBA, *Revue Philosophique,* July, 1902

Each mystic brings back confirmation of his own creed. . . . The mystic brings his theological beliefs to the mystical experience; he does not derive them from it.

GEORGE A. COE, *The Hibbert Journal,* Vol. VI (1907–1908)

To be a mystic is simply to participate here and now in that real and eternal life.

EVELYN UNDERHILL, *Mysticism,* 1912

A mystic is not one who sees God in nature, but one for whom God and nature fit into one plane.

BEDE JARRETT, *Meditations for Layfolk,* 1915

The visions of the mystics are determined in content by their belief, and are due to the dream imagination working upon the mass of theological material which fills the mind.

> J. B. PRATT, *The Religious Consciousness,* 1921

True mystics simply open their souls to the oncoming wave. . . . That which they have allowed to flow into them is a stream flowing down and seeking through them to reach their fellow-men; the necessity to spread around them what they have received affects them like an onslaught of love.

> HENRI BERGSON, *Two Sources of Morality and Religion,* 1935

All great mystics declare that they have the impression of a current passing from their soul to God, and flowing back again from God to mankind.

> HENRI BERGSON, *The Two Sources of Morality and Religion,* 1935

The perfect mystic would be as such the perfect Christian, and we mean a Christian whom the highest of divine favors does not withdraw from solidarity in the sufferings and the triumphs of the Church militant.

> JOSEPH L. MARÉCHAL, *Studies in the Psychology of the Mystics,* 1937

The mystics all teach that no soul can have this direct experience of God, except by purification of self; the cleansing of the soul from self-love and sensuality is essential for those who would attain to Divine Wisdom and the Vision of God, for the perfection of Eternal Life, which they hold can be attained to here and now, is to see God in His Essence. Self can only be conquered by means of a greater love than self-love, and so the mystics have been the lovers of God, seeking the consummation of their love in Union with the Beloved.

> MARGARET SMITH, *Readings from the Mystics of Islam,* 1950

See also Absolute, the; Adoration; Experience, Religious; Mystical Experience; Mysticism; Saints.

MYSTICAL BODY OF CHRIST

The Holy Scriptures declare the body of Christ, animated by the Son of God, to be the whole Church of God, and the members of this body—considered as a whole —to consist of those who are believers.

> ORIGEN, *Against Celsus,* Bk. VI, ch. 48, 246

Of one and all Christ makes a single body. Thus he who lives in Rome may look on the Indians as his own members. Is there any union that may be likened to this? Christ is the head of all.

> ST. JOHN CHRYSOSTOM, *Homilies,* 65, c. 388

I am not offended if you call this river of life—this immortal core of Godhead—the mystical body of Christ, so long as you leave it there nakedly in the universe and do not try to clap a cover on it or claim it for your sect.

> JOHN JAY CHAPMAN, *Notes on Religion,* 1915

There is no state in life great or small that has not its part in the thanksgiving, praise, supplication, and reparation of the common prayer of the Mystical Body of Christ, which is the Church.

> POPE PIUS XI, *Caritate Christi Compulsi,* 1932

A lasting world unity is only to be realized when all mankind is incorporated into the Mystical Body of Christ. This is the ideal and ultimate solution to the problem of human unity, for which in all ages the Church prays and strives.

> JOHN LA FARGE, *The Race Question and the Negro,* 1943

It is owing to the Savior's infinite mercy that place is allowed in His mystical body here below for those whom, of old, He did not exclude from the banquet. For not every sin, however grave it may be, is such as of its own nature to sever a man from the body of the Church, as does schism or heresy or apostasy.

POPE PIUS XII, *Mystici Corporis Christi,* June, 1943

All the faithful, without exception, are members of the mystical body of Jesus Christ. . . . All are therefore held, and today quite especially, to think, in prayer and sacrifice, not only of their own private needs, but also about the great intentions of the Kingdom of God in the world.

POPE PIUS XII, *Address,* October 14, 1951

The Soul of the Mystical Body is the Holy Ghost. It is the Holy Spirit Who unites each of us individual cells with each other, and with Christ our Head.

LEO J. TRESE, *Many Are One,* 1952

The peaceful embrace of the children of the same heavenly Father, equally coheirs of the same reign of glory, will mark the celebration of the triumph of the Mystical Body of Christ.

POPE JOHN XXIII, *Encyclical,* November 11, 1961

See also Atomic Bomb; Catholicism; Christianity; Church, Definitions of; Church: Its Membership; Communion of Saints; Fellowship; Universality; War, Condemnation of.

MYSTICAL EXPERIENCE

The estate of Divine union consists in the total transformation of the will into the will of God, in such a way that every movement of the will shall be always the movement of the will of God only.

ST. JOHN OF THE CROSS (1542–1591), *Ascent of Mt. Carmel*

It seems to me that the only alternatives are either to count all such surrender to the mystical contact of Nature as mischievous and ethically wrong, or to admit

that in these moods we catch something of the true relation of the world to ourselves.

A. S. EDDINGTON, *The Nature of the Physical World,* 1929

The most beautiful and most profound emotion we can experience is the sensation of the mystical. It is the dower of all true science. . . . To know what is impenetrable to us really exists, manifesting itself as the highest wisdom and the most radiant beauty which our dull faculties can comprehend only in their most primitive forms—this knowledge, this feeling is at the centre of true religiousness.

ALBERT EINSTEIN, *Out of My Later Years,* 1950

The mystic vision of God, or ecstasy of felt union with Him, is, to those who attain it, an affair of ravishing emotional intensity, of vivid intellectual illumination, and on both of these counts of supreme value.

EDWIN A. BURTT, *Types of Christian Philosophy,* 1957

Mystical experience appears to be no less a product of the nervous system than is the reflex action to a pinprick or the appreciation of a Beethoven symphony.

HUDSON HOAGLAND, *Science Ponders Religion,* H. Shapley, 1960

If we strip the mystical experience of all intellectual interpretation such as that which identifies it with God, or with the Absolute, or with the soul of the world, what is left is simply the undifferentiated unity.

WALTER T. STACE, *The Teachings of the Mystics,* 1960

See also Abandonment; Consciousness; Contemplation; Detachment; Experience, Religious; God: Finding Him; God: His Existence; Man and God; Mystic; Mysticism; Prayer; Reality; Selflessness.

MYSTICISM

By mysticism we mean, not the extravagance of erring fancy, but the concentration of reason in feeling, the enthusiastic love of the good, the true, the one, the sense of the infinity of knowledge and of the marvel of the human faculties.

> BENJAMIN JOWETT, his *Introduction* to his translation of Plato's *Phaedrus*, 1871

Much on earth is hidden from us, but to make up for that we have been given a precious mystic sense of our living bond with the other world, and with the higher heavenly world.

> FEODOR DOSTOEVSKY, *The Brothers Karamazov*, 1880

The "sea of the Talmud" has also its gulf stream of mysticism.

> SOLOMAN SCHECHTER, *Studies in Judaism*, 1, xxiii, 1896

What the world, which truly knows *nothing,* calls "mysticism" is the science of ultimates . . . the science of self-evident Reality, which cannot be "reasoned about," because it is the object of pure reason or perception.

> COVENTRY PATMORE, *The Rod, the Root, and the Flower*, 1907

Broadly speaking, I understand it to be the expression of the innate tendency of the human spirit towards complete harmony with the transcendental order.

> EVELYN UNDERHILL, *Mysticism*, 1911

Christian mysticism, whether of the quasi or the mixed type, is connected with a craving for intensity of experience at the cost of clarity and sanity.

> PAUL ELMER MORE, *The Catholic Faith*, 1931

Mysticism is essentially . . . leading to immediate contact with God.

> THOMAS HUGHES, *The Philosophic Basis of Mysticism*, 1937

Mysticism postulates an absolute Unity behind the duality of the relational form.

> W. R. INGE, *Christian Mysticism*, 1948

A consciousness of the beyond.

> W. R. INGE, *Christian Mysticism*, 1948

Communion with God, contact with reality.

> W. R. INGE, *Mysticism in Religion*, 1948

The rationalistic mysticism in which so many intellectuals seek refuge in their ivory towers from everyday realities, has little that is genuinely religious about it.

> AELRED GRAHAM, *Christian Thought and Action*, 1951

One common trait that links all the philosophical and literary extremes in vogue today . . . is the fact that they are mysticisms from which God is missing.

> FRANÇOIS MAURIAC, *Words of Faith*, 1955

See also Asceticism; Ecstasy; Emotion; Enlightenment; Experience, Religious; Love of God; Man and God; Man Indwelt by God; Man's Quest of God; Man's Unity with God; Meditation; Mystic; Mystical Experience; Piety; Poems and Poets; Poetry; Prayer; Prayer: Defined and Explained; Reality; Religion, Definitions of; Religion: Its Nature and Function; Selflessness; Soul and God; Spiritual; Spiritual Life.

MYTH

Myth is expression, it is not prophecy. . . . Myth is something on which the mind rests; it is an ideal interpretation in which the phenomena are digested and transmuted into human energy, into imaginative tissue.

> GEORGE SANTAYANA, *Reason in Religion*, 1905

A myth contains the story that is preserved in popular memory and that helps bring to life some deep stratum buried in the depths of the human spirit.

NICHOLAS BERDYAEV, *The Meaning of History,* 1936

By myths we mean the value-impregnated beliefs and notions that men hold, that they live by or live for. . . . We imply nothing concerning the grounds of belief, so far as belief claims to interpret reality.

R. M. MACIVER, *The Web of Government,* 1947

The real purpose of myth is not to present an objective picture of the world as it is, but to express man's understanding of himself in the world in which he lives.

RUDOLF BULTMANN, *Kerygma and Myth,* 1953

The use of imagery to express the otherwordly in terms of this world, and the divine in terms of human life, the other side in terms of this side.

RUDOLF BULTMANN, *Kerygma and Myth,* 1953

The myth is mostly invented, but the faith at the back of it has at least a good deal of probability about it.

GILBERT MURRAY, *Letter to Lord Russell,* July 26, 1954

See also Belief; Symbolism.

NATION

All people are a single nation.

Koran, c. 625

A nation cannot be really good so long as it feels malice or hostility against other nations, and fails to recognize them as neighbors and to love them as itself.

VLADIMIR SOLOVIEV (1853–1900), *The Justification of the Good*

See also Country; State, the.

NATIONAL HONOR

The high moral ideal of national honor is a factor handed down from one generation to another, enshrining something positively sacred, and compelling the individual to sacrifice himself to it.

HEINRICH VON TREITSCHKE, *Politics,* 1895

See also Nationalism; Patriotism.

NATIONAL RELIGION. See RELIGION, NATIONAL

NATIONALISM

There is scarcely any folly or vice more epidemical among the sons of men than that ridiculous and hurtful vanity, by which the people of each country are apt to prefer themselves to those of every other.

HENRY ST. JOHN, LORD BOLINGBROKE, *Letters on the Study and Use of History,* 1735

The dogma of nationalism. . . . That was Christianity's most dangerous competing religion, the most dangerous rival of Christian principles on earth.

HARRY EMERSON FOSDICK, *Introduction to Kirby Page's War: Its Causes, Consequences and Cure,* 1923

Born in iniquity and conceived in sin, the spirit of nationalism has never ceased to bend human institutions to the service of dissension and distress.

THORSTEIN VEBLEN, *Absentee Ownership,* 1923

Nationalism is simply one of the effective ways in which the modern man escapes life's ethical problems. Delegating his vices to larger and larger groups, he imagines himself virtuous.

REINHOLD NIEBUHR, *Christian Century,* April 22, 1926

The modern emergence of nationalism as both a religion and a theory of state-absolutism is the proper logic of a naturalism which has abandoned all belief in a creative God.

EDWIN LEWIS, *A Philosophy of the Christian Revelation,* 1940

With the decline of the spiritual authority of the Church in national affairs, however badly that authority may have been exercised, the way was open to the rise of nationalism as a false and pernicious religion.

ERNEST JOHNSON, *Religion and World Order,* 1944

Nationalism is a heretical religion based on the erroneous doctrine that nations have a soul and that this soul is more permanent, more "eternal," so to speak, than the soul of an individual.

FRANZ WERFEL, *Between Heaven and Earth,* 1944

The nation has its own place in God's purpose for mankind, but national egotism is sin against the Creator of all people, great and small alike.

Provisional Committee of the World Council of Churches, Geneva, February, 1946

See also National Honor; Nuclear War; Patriotism.

NATURAL AND SUPERNATURAL

The true Christian does not renounce the activities of this life, he does not stunt his natural faculties; but he develops and perfects them, by coordinating them with the supernatural.

POPE PIUS XI, *Christian Education of Youth,* 1929

NATURAL GOODNESS. See GOODNESS

NATURAL LAW

No man can override the unwritten and undying laws of the gods.

SOPHOCLES, *Antigone,* 4th century B.C.

There is not one law at Rome and another at Athens, nor one now and another hereafter, but for all time one eternal unchangeable law will bind all peoples, and there will be one common master and commander of all, God, who drew up, spoke for, and put forward this law.

CICERO, *De Republica,* III, 22–33, c. 50 B.C.

If you are looking for the law of God, you have it in that common one prevailing throughout the world, inscribed on tables of nature, to which the Apostle was wont to appeal, as when, speaking of the veiling of women, he says, "Does not nature teach you?"

TERTULLIAN, *De Corona,* c. 200 A.D.

I contend that before the law written by Moses on tablets of stone, there was an unwritten law which was known naturally and was habitually kept by the fathers.

TERTULLIAN, *Adversus Judaeas,* c. 216

Thy law is written in the hearts of men which ingenuity itself effaces not.

ST. AUGUSTINE, *Confessions,* ii, 397

Natural law is natural reasoning, keeping control over sense appetite and eliminating that irrational behavior which is the disruption of what is naturally coherent.

ST. MAXIMUS THE CONFESSOR (580–662), *Questions to Thalassios*

We must say that the natural law, as to general principles, is the same for all, both as to rectitude and as to knowledge. . . . The written law is said to be given for the correction of the natural law, either because it supplies what was wanting in the natural law; or because the natural law was perverted in the hearts of some men, as to certain matters, so that they esteemed those things good which are naturally evil, which perversion stood in need of correction. . . . The natural law dates from the creation of the rational creature. It does not vary according to time, but remains unchangeable.

> St. Thomas Aquinas, *Summa Theologiae,* 1–2, 94.4–94.5, 1272

Every law depends upon the law of nature; and if it contradicts this it cannot be a valid law.

> Nicholas of Cusa, *De Concordantia Catholica,* 1433

The general and perpetual voice of men is as a sentence of God himself. For that which all men have at all times learned, Nature herself must needs have taught; and God being the author of Nature, her voice is but his instrument.

> Richard Hooker, *Law of Ecclesiastical Polity,* 1594

The law of nature is so unalterable that it cannot be changed by God Himself.

> Hugo Grotius, *De Jure Belli et Pacis,* 1625

The law of nature is that which God at the time of creation of the nature of man infused into his heart, for his preservation and direction; and this is *Lex aeterna,* the moral law, called also the law of nature.

> Sir Edward Coke (1552–1634), *The Reports of Sir Edward Coke,* ed. by J. H. Thomas and J. F. Fraser, IV, 1826

The law of nature is the only law of laws truly and properly to all mankind fundamental; the beginning and the end of all government.

> John Milton, *The Ready and Easy Way to Establish a Free Commonwealth,* 1660

The tables of natural law are so obvious that no man who is able to read the plainest character can mistake them, and therefore no political society ever framed a system of law in direct and avowed contradiction of them.

> H. St. J. Bolingbroke (1678–1751), *Fragment,* or *Minutes of Essays,* Vol. IV of *Works*

Natural Law is the instinct by which we feel justice.

> Voltaire, *Philosophical Dictionary,* II, 1764

Man, considered as a creature, must necessarily be subject to the laws of his Creator. . . . This law of nature, being co-eval with mankind, and dictated by God Himself, is of course superior in obligation to any other. It is binding all over the globe, in all countries, and at all times.

> William Blackstone, *Commentaries,* 1765

The laws of nature are the laws of God, Whose authority can be superseded by no power on earth.

> George Mason, before the Virginia General Court, 1772, *Jefferson's Va. Reports* 109

Good and wise men . . . have supposed that the Deity, from the relations we stand in to Himself and to each other, has constituted an eternal and immutable law, which is indispensably obligatory upon all mankind, prior to any human institution whatsoever.

> Alexander Hamilton, *The Farmer Refuted,* 1775

There are laws larger than any Russian legislation—the laws of humanity and of God, which are the foundation of all other laws, and if in any legislation they be violated, all the nations of Christian Europe, the whole commonwealth of civilized and Christian men would instantly acquire a right to speak out loud.

HENRY EDWARD MANNING, *Address,* London, February 1, 1882

The Natural Laws originate nothing, sustain nothing, they are merely responsible for uniformity in sustaining what has been originated and what is being sustained. . . . They are great lines running not only through the world, but through the universe, reducing it like parallels of latitude to intelligent order.

HENRY DRUMMOND, *Natural Law in the Spiritual World,* 1883

The Supreme and all-pervading law of nature . . . is . . . the law of substance. . . . Under the name of "law of substance" we embrace the two supreme laws of different origin and age—the older is the chemical law of the "conservation of matter," and the younger is the physical law of the "conservation of energy." . . . The great cosmic law applies throughout the whole of nature. . . . It definitely rules out the three central dogmas of metaphysics—God, freedom, and immortality.

ERNEST HAECKEL, *The Riddle of the Universe,* 1899

What men call "natural law," by which they mean the law of greed and strife . . . is not a natural law; it is unnatural; it is a crime against nature; the law of brotherhood is the only natural law. The law of nature is the law of sympathy, of fellowship, of mutual help and service.

WASHINGTON GLADDEN, *Social Facts and Forces,* 1899

That naive state of mind that accepts what has been familiar and accepted by them [jurists who believe in natural law] and their neighbors as something that must be accepted by all men everywhere.

OLIVER WENDELL HOLMES, *Collected Legal Papers of,* 1918

The laws of nature are objectively nothing else than the forces with which God has endowed His creatures, and by reason of which they must, when left to themselves, always act the same way if placed under the same circumstances.

B. J. OTTEN, *The Reason Why,* 1921

Those human laws which are irreconcilably opposed to natural law have an innate defect.

POPE PIUS XI, *Mit Brenneder Sorg,* March 14, 1937

The natural law is only part of the divine moral law. God has called us to something far greater than human nature is of itself fitted for: to the supernatural life of heaven.

ROBERT H. LORD, *Pilot* (Boston, Mass.), May 7, 1938

The natural law may be described briefly as a force working in history which tends to keep human beings human.

J. V. L. CASSERLEY, *The Fate of Modern Culture,* 1940

The only practical knowledge all men have naturally and infallibly in common is that we must do good and avoid evil. This is the preamble and the principle of natural law; it is not the law itself. Natural law is the ensemble of things to do and not to do which follow therefrom in necessary fashion, and from the simple fact that man is man, nothing else being taken into account.

JACQUES MARITAIN, *The Rights of Man and Natural Law,* 1943

The rule of human conduct that is called natural law is deduced from the nature of man as it reveals itself in the basic inclinations of that nature under the control of reason, independently of any formal intervention of any legislator whatsoever, divine or human.

JEAN DABIN, *General Theory of Law,* 1944

The opposition to the law of nature has not only prepared the way for the totalitarian State but made it possible.

EMIL BRUNNER, *Justice and the Social Order,* 1945

This thing which I have called for convenience the Tao, and which others may call Natural Law or Traditional Morality or the First Principles of Practical Reason or the First Platitudes, is not one among a series of possible systems of value. It is the sole source of all value judgments. If it is rejected, all value is rejected.

C. S. LEWIS, *The Abolition of Man,* 1947

There are no natural laws. There are only temporary habits of nature.

ALFRED NORTH WHITEHEAD, November, 1947, *Dialogues of,* as recorded by L. Price

The moral law of God made clear to us through the judgments of human reason and the dictates of conscience.

ROMAN CATHOLIC BISHOPS OF THE U. S., November 20, 1948

The law of nature is that which God at the time of creation of the nature of man infused into his heart for his preservation and direction; and this is the eternal law, the moral law, also the law of nature.

CLARENCE E. MANION, *The Founding Fathers and the Natural Law,* 1950

The principles of the natural law, absolute, stable and unchangeable are applicable to all the changing conditions and circumstances in which man finds himself.

CATHOLIC BISHOPS OF THE U. S., November, 1951

Natural law for man is *moral* law, because man obeys or disobeys it freely, not necessarily, and because human behavior pertains to a particular, privileged order which is irreducible to the natural order of

the cosmos and tends to a final end superior to the immanent common good of the cosmos.

JACQUES MARITAIN, *Man and the State,* 1951

Only when the Gospel has penetrated to very depth of human substance will natural law appear in its flower and its perfection.

JACQUES MARITAIN, *Man and the State,* 1951

The public philosophy is known as natural law. . . . This philosophy is the premise of the institutions of the Western society, and they are, I believe, unworkable in communities that do not adhere to it. Except on the premises of this philosophy, it is impossible to reach intelligible and workable conceptions of popular election, majority rule, representative assemblies, free speech, loyalty, property, corporations and voluntary associations.

WALTER LIPPMANN, *The Public Philosophy,* 1954

The ancient tradition of natural law is beginning to climb out of the footnotes of the learned books into the very text of our time, as the conviction dawns that there are resources in the idea that might possibly make the next page of the text sound less like a tale told by an idiot.

JOHN COURTNEY MURRAY, *We Hold These Truth,* 1960

If the full reach of the natural law were exactly known, it seems obvious that the Church would hardly need vast and deep channels for exploration of theology and ethics.

JOHN ROCK, *The Time Has Come,* 1963

See also Communism; Conduct; Divine Law; Ethics; Evolution; Freedom; Freedom and God; Justice; Moral Law; Moral Order; Moral Standards; Morality and State; Obedience; Religion, Natural; Rights; Society; State, the; Tao; Totalitarianism.

NATURAL PHILOSOPHY. See PHILOSOPHY

NATURAL RELIGION. See RELIGION, NATURAL; and DEISM

NATURAL RIGHTS. See RIGHTS

NATURAL SELECTION

The principle of natural selection is absolutely incompatible with the word of God . . . contradicts the revealed relations of creation to its Creator . . . inconsistent with the fullness of his glory . . . a dishonoring view of nature.

> SAMUEL WILBERFORCE, *Quarterly Review*, July, 1860

Not only is natural selection not the instrument of a god's sublime purpose, it is not even the best mechanism for achieving evolutionary progress.

> JULIAN HUXLEY, *Evolution, the Modern Synthesis*, 1942

See also Creation; Evolution.

NATURAL THEOLOGY. See THEOLOGY, NATURAL

NATURALISM

The integrity of Catholic faith cannot be reconciled with opinions verging on Naturalism or Rationalism, the essence of which is utterly to sterilize Christianity, and to install in society the supremacy of man to the exclusion of God.

> POPE LEO XIII, *The Christian Constitution of States*, 1885

Who would pay the slightest attention to Naturalism, if it did not force itself into the retinue of science, assume her livery, and claim, as a kind of poor relation, in some sort to represent her authority and to speak with her voice?

> A. J. BALFOUR, *The Foundations of Belief*, 1895

The chief elements of this naturalistic creed are: renunciation of the contact between the natural and the supernatural. . . . Belief that the essential order of the world is mechanical. . . . All actions are determined by prior conditions. . . . All values are purely subjective.

> D. E. TRUEBLOOD, *The Logic of Belief*, 1942

That people . . . try to keep what they admire in a system inconsistent with naturalism, even while they suppose themselves to be adherents of the naturalistic creed, is a damning piece of evidence against the tenability of that creed.

> D. E. TRUEBLOOD, *The Logic of Belief*, 1942

The least common denominator of all historic naturalism . . . is not so much a set of specific doctrines, as the methods of scientific or rational empiricism.

> SIDNEY HOOK, *Naturalism and the Human Spirit*, 1944

An innocent name for an appalling affliction. . . . Teaches that there is nothing Supernatural, nothing spiritual, nothing to hope for. . . . In the last analysis a kind of perverted religion. . . . The spirit of Naturalism [is] the spirit of despair.

> ROBERT I. GANNON, *Address, Herald Tribune* Youth Forum, March 6, 1949

There is no doubt that naturalism, with its corollary of the futility of human life, has brought despair into the world. It is the root-cause of the modern spiritual malaise.

> W. T. STACE, *Religion and the Modern Mind*, 1952

The "Natural" man is not the care-free, life-affirming pagan that secularism has painted him. He is, in fact, a frightened creature, conscious of his own weakness and terrified of the massive powers and fates that determine his life.

> LANGDON GILKEY, *Maker of Heaven and Earth*, 1959

NATURE

All things in nature work silently. They come into being and possess nothing. They fulfill their function and make no claim. All things alike do their work, and then we see them subside. When they have reached their bloom, each returns to its origin. . . . This reversion is an eternal law. To know that law is wisdom.

> LAO-TZE (6th century B.C.), *Sayings of,* Translated by Giles

Whatever befalls in the course of nature should be considered good.

> CICERO, *De Senectute,* c. 78 B.C.

Nature resolves everything into its component elements, but annihilates nothing.

> LUCRETIUS, *De Rerum Natura,* 57 B.C.

Nature is the nature of all things that are; things that are have a union with all things from the beginning.

> MARCUS AURELIUS, *Meditations,* c. 170 A.D.

Material nature is the principle of becoming and is so evil that it fills with evil any being which is not yet in it and which does no more than look at it.

> PLOTINUS (203–262), *1st Ennead*

All nature is good.

> ST. AUGUSTINE, *Of Continence,* c. 425

Believe one who has tried, you shall find a fuller satisfaction in the woods than in books. The trees and the rocks will teach you that which you cannot hear from masters.

> ST. BERNARD OF CLAIRVAUX (1091–1153), *Life and Works of,* ed. J. Mabillon

Follow the order of nature, for God's sake! Follow it! It will lead who follows; and those who will not, it will drag along anyway.

> MICHEL DE MONTAIGNE, *Essays,* 1588

Nature is not governed except by obeying her.

> FRANCIS BACON, *De Augmentis Scientiarum,* 1623

The book of nature is a fine and large piece of tapestry rolled up, which we are not able to see all at once, but must be content to wait for the discovery of its beauty and symmetry little by little, as it gradually comes to be more unfolded.

> ROBERT BOYLE, *The Christian Virtuoso,* 1690

The visible series of effects or sensations imprinted on our minds according to certain fixed and general laws.

> GEORGE BERKELEY, *Principles of Human Knowledge,* 1710

Wolves may lose their Teeth, but not their Nature.

> THOMAS FULLER, *Gnomologia,* 1732

Everything in temporal nature is descended out of that which is eternal, and stands as a palpable visible outbirth of it.

> WILLIAM LAW, *An Appeal to All Who Doubt,* 1740

Everything in nature is in continual motion. . . . But it will be asked, from whence did she receive her motion? Our reply is, from herself, since she is the great whole, out of which consequently, nothing can exist.

> P. H. D'HOLBACH, *The System of Nature,* 1770

O Nature, sovereign of all beings! and ye, her adorable daughters, Virtue, Reason, and Truth! remain forever our revered

protectors! it is to you that belong the praises of the human race; to you appertains the homage of the earth.
P. H. D'HOLBACH, *System of Nature,* ch. 14, 1770

Art, glory, freedom fail, but nature still is fair.
LORD BYRON, *Childe Harolde,* 1818

Nature is the term in which we comprehend all things that are representable in the forms of Time and Space.
SAMUEL TAYLOR COLERIDGE, *Aids to Reflection,* 1825

The forces of nature move in numbered squadrons, with measured step, and on a predetermined plan, as if under the command of a presiding intelligence.
JAMES MCCOSH, *The Method of Divine Government,* 1850

The wild goats that leap along those rocks have as much passion of joy in all that fair work of God as the men that toil among them.
JOHN RUSKIN, *Modern Painters,* IV, 1856

Nature says to me all that I am capable of understanding—gives all that I can receive.
ROBERT G. INGERSOLL (1833–1899), *Selections from*

A structure of evolving processes. The reality is the process.
ALFRED NORTH WHITEHEAD, *Science and the Modern World,* 1925

Seen from within, nature is a war of living powers of will.
KARL HEIM, *Transformation of the Scientific World View,* 1953

The basic tenets of all great religions, the distilled spiritual wisdom of humanity, coincide closely with what science reveals in nature. The universe is based on order, not on chaos and chance.
GEORGE RUSSELL HARRISON, *What Man May Be,* 1956

See also Art and Nature; Creation; Death; Deism; Evolution; God: Considered as Impersonal; God: His Existence; God: His Goodness; God: His Omnipresence; Man: Defined and Interpreted; Naturalism; Nature and God; Nature and Man; Nature and Mind; Necessity; Providence; Religion, Natural; Science and God; Science and Religion; Supernatural; Truth, Definitions of; Universe; World; World, Praise of.

NATURE AND GOD

God made the beauties of nature like a child playing in the sand.
Ascribed to Appolonius of Tyana, c. 50 B.C.

Nature herself has imprinted on the minds of all the idea of God.
CICERO, *De Natura Deorum,* 45 B.C.

Nature is school-mistress, the soul the pupil; and whatever one has taught or the other learned has come from God—the Teacher of the teacher.
TERTULLIAN, *De Testimonio Animae,* c. 199 A.D.

If there be any man who is not enlightened by this sublime magnificence of created things, he is blind. If there be any man who is not aroused by the clamor of nature, he is deaf. If there be any one who, seeing all these works of God, does not praise him, he is dumb; if there be any one who, from so many signs, cannot perceive the First Principle, that man is foolish.
ST. BONAVENTURE, *Intinerarium Mentis in Deum,* 1259

Nature is the art of God Eternal.
DANTE, *De Monarchia,* c. 1320

Nature is the vicar of th' Almightie Lord.
GEOFFREY CHAUCER, *The Parlement of Foules,* c. 1380

God being the author of nature, her voice is but His instrument.
RICHARD HOOKER, *Laws of Ecclesiastical Polity,* I, 1585

I do account it, not the meanest, but an impiety monstrous to confound God and nature, be it but in terms.
WALTER RALEIGH, *History of the World,* 1614

They should admire not the ingenuity of nature but the wisdom of the Creator, for He made nature and discovered the way to accomplish all these wonders.
ST. ROBERT BELLARMINE, *On the Ascent of the Mind to God,* 1615

God does not interfere directly with the natural order, where secondary causes suffice to produce the intended effect.
FRANCIS SUAREZ (1548–1617), *De Opere Sex Dierum,* II, C. X., p. 13

It is impossible to make any profound inquiry into natural causes, without being inclined thereby to believe there is one God eternal.
THOMAS HOBBES, *Leviathan,* 1651

I have a hundred times wished that if a God maintains nature, she should testify to Him unequivocally, and that, if the signs she gives are deceptive, she should suppress them altogether.
BLAISE PASCAL, *Pensées,* 1670

Nature has some perfections to show that she is the image of God, and some defects, to show that she is only His image.
BLAISE PASCAL, *Pensées,* 1670

Nature does nothing for the sake of an end, for that eternal and infinite Being whom we call God or Nature acts by the same necessity by which He exists.
BARUCH SPINOZA, *Ethics,* 1677

All are but parts of one stupendous whole, Whose body nature is, and God the soul.
ALEXANDER POPE, *An Essay on Man,* 1732

As far as we understand nature, we are become acquainted with the character of God; for the knowledge of nature is the revelation of God.
ETHAN ALLEN, *Reason the Only Oracle of Man,* 1744

If there be a God, He is the Author of nature as well as of revelation. He gave us the one to explain the other, and reason to make them agree.
J. O. DE LA METTRIE, *L'Homme machine,* 1748

The fruitfulness of Nature is without limits, since it is nothing but the exercise of the divine omnipotence.
IMMANUEL KANT, *Allgemeine Naturgeschichte,* 1755

The system of law established by the Creator for the existence of things and the succession of beings.
G. L. L. BUFFON, *Natural History,* 1788

Nature . . . is a great organ, on which our Lord God plays, and the Devil blows the bellows.
J. W. VON GOETHE, *Faust,* 1790

Nature is a name for an effect, whose cause is God.
WILLIAM COWPER (1731–1800), "The Winter Morning Walk," *The Task*

Why should we not recognize in the lightning, the thunder, and the stormwind, the approach of an overwhelming Power, and in the scent of flowers and the gently rustling zephyr the presence of a Being full of love?
J. W. VON GOETHE (1749–1832), *Maxims and Reflections*

Nature, which is the time-vesture of God and reveals Him to the wise, hides Him from the foolish.

THOMAS CARLYLE, *Sartor Resartus,* 1836

Nature . . . is a Volume written in celestial hieroglyphs, in a true Sacred-writing; of which even Prophets are happy that they can read here a line and there a line.

THOMAS CARLYLE, *Sartor Resartus,* 1836

From each object of nature and of life, there goes a path toward God.

FRIEDRICH FROEBEL (1782–1852), *Aphorisms*

Nature is incessantly chanting the praises of the Creator, and nothing can be more religious than the hymns chanted in concert with the winds by the oaks of the forest and the reeds of the desert.

VISCOUNT DE CHATEAUBRIAND, *Genius of Christianity,* 1856

If there be a divine Spirit of the universe, nature, such as we know her, cannot possibly be its *ultimate word* to man. Either there is no Spirit revealed in nature, or else it is inadequately revealed there.

WILLIAM JAMES, *The Will to Believe and Other Essays,* 1896

The anthropomorphic notion of a deliberate architect and ruler of the world has gone forever from this field; the "eternal iron laws of nature" have taken its place.

ERNEST HAECKEL, *The Riddle of the Universe,* 1901

If we do not find God in nature we may conclude, either that we do not understand the expression of nature, or have mistaken ideas or poor feelings about him.

GEORGE MACDONALD (1824–1905), *Selections from,* ed. Dewey

Nature has no heart. . . . Absolute nature lives not in our life, nor yet is lifeless, but lives in the life of God: and in so far, and so far merely, as man himself lives in that life, does he come into sympathy with Nature.

FRANCIS THOMPSON, *Nature's Immortality,* 1910

Nature . . . is God's daughter.

FRANCIS THOMPSON, *Nature's Immortality,* 1910

If we can find God only as he is revealed in nature we have no moral God.

REINHOLD NIEBUHR, *Christian Century,* April 22, 1926

The scientist who recognizes God . . . feels that . . . the orderly ways in which nature works are themselves the manifestations of God's will and purpose.

ARTHUR HOLLY COMPTON, *The Religion of a Scientist,* 1938

In Nature we best see God under a disguise so heavy that it allows us to discern little more than that someone is there; within our own moral life we see Him with the mask, so to say, half fallen off.

A. E. TAYLOR, *Essays Catholic and Critical,* 1938

To regard Nature as the symbol of God's glory is not at all strange or unnatural. It is very human. It is, perhaps, the thing we are ultimately led to do when, thoroughly sophisticated, disillusioned, and disenchanted, we take ourselves seriously in hand and ask what is our business here. Then we stand confronted by the Ancient of Days.

FREDERICK J. E. WOODBRIDGE, *An Essay on Nature,* 1940

Nature is one grand cosmic book describing the power and the majesty of God and bearing on its title-page those memorable words of Genesis which express so beautiful and so sublime a truth: "In the beginning God created heaven and earth. . . . And God created man to His own image."

JOHN A. O'BRIEN, *The Origin of Man,* 1947

The deity which the religious person seeks to bring closer to himself by his palpable symbols, is consubstantial with the power acting in accordance with natural laws for which the sense data of the scientist provides a certain degree of evidence.

> MAX PLANCK, Lecture delivered in 1937, reprinted in *Scientific Autobiography and Other Papers,* 1949

Broadly speaking, all nature, since it has no claim to existence, manifests the grace of God.

> AELRED GRAHAM, *Christian Thought and Action,* 1951

"Nature" has silently displaced God as the ultimate basis to which all other things are referred.

> WALTER MOBERLY, *The Crisis in the University,* 1951

Nature, as a whole and in all its elements, enunciates something that may be regarded as an indirect self-communication of God to all those ready to receive it.

> MARTIN BUBER, *At the Turning,* 1952

One may point to nature and say, "There *is* a God," but one cannot point to nature and say *"There* God is."

> CARL MICHALSON, *Faith and Ethics,* ed. P. Ramsey, 1957

Does morality bid man live according to nature? Hardly, nature is neither kind nor cruel, neither benevolent or malevolent. Nature is blind, irrational, capricious. This is why it is blasphemous to identify God and nature.

> FREDERICK E. FLYNN, *Address* to Catholic Physicians' Guild of Southern California, 1960

Advance in understanding of nature or even in control of nature does not diminish God. God is not the sum total of what man does not know about nature or what man cannot control in nature.

> WALTER J. ONG, Letter, *New York Times,* March 8, 1962

See also Cause; Creation; Design; Genesis; Glory of God; God: Finding Him; Life; Miracles; Natural Law; Nature; Nature and Man; Nature and Mind; Pantheism; Religion, Natural; Revelation; Universe.

NATURE AND MAN

Man is the servant and interpreter of Nature.

> FRANCIS BACON, *Aphorisms* 1620

Nature is perfect, wherever we look, but man always deforms it.

> J. C. F. VON SCHILLER, *Die Braut von Messina,* 1803

The duty of man is the same in respect to his own nature as in respect to the nature of all other things, namely not to follow but to amend it.

> JOHN STUART MILL (1806–1873), *Nature,* publ. posth.

The scheme of Nature regarded in its whole extent, cannot have had, for its sole or even principal object, the good of human or other sentient beings. What good it brings them, is mostly the result of their own exertions.

> JOHN STUART MILL (1806–1873), *Nature,* publ. posth.

I still incline to believe that nature is the virtuality of mind—that the soul is the fruit of life, and liberty the flower of necessity—that all is bound together, and that nothing can be done without.

> HENRI AMIEL, *Journal,* 1874

After you have exhausted what there is in business, politics, conviviality, love, and so on—what remains? Nature remains.

> WALT WHITMAN, *Specimen Days,* 1877

The more men know about nature, and the more they rely upon nature, the more agnostic and hopeless they become.

> O. A. CURTIS, *The Christian Faith,* 1905

The mastery of nature is vainly believed to be an adequate substitute for self-mastery.

REINHOLD NIEBUHR, *Christian Century*, April 22, 1926

Nature, by reason of Adam's sin, is deprived and wounded, but not depraved; that deprivation is made up for us by a restoration through the second Adam.

WILLIAM J. McGUCKEN, *The Philosophy of Catholic Education*, 1951

Nature is not his [man's] home; it is the sphere of his deciding. He lives in it, but his spirit is not of it. The meaning of his life can never consist in any relationship with nature.

M. HOLMES HARTSHORNE, *The Promise of Science and the Power of Faith*, 1958

Man has always frustrated nature, from the time he invented the first tool, and will continue to do so until on his last day on earth he lays down his latest invention.

FREDERICK E. FLYNN, *Address* to Catholic Physicians' Guild of Southern California, 1960

The more our knowledge of the natural has grown, the more we have lost our former capacity to respond to supernatural reality transcendent to nature.

WILLIAM G. POLLARD, *Space Age Christianity*, 1963

See also Fall, the; Man; Nature; Nature and God; Nature and Mind; Original Sin.

NATURE AND MIND

The more completely we include Mind within Nature, the more inexplicable must Nature become except by reference to Mind.

WILLIAM TEMPLE, *Nature, Man and God*, 1934

See also Mind; Nature; Nature and God; Nature and Man.

NECESSITY

For if we are all possessed of free will, some spiritual powers may very likely be able to urge us on to sin and others to assist us to salvation; we are not, however, compelled by necessity to act either rightly or wrongly.

ORIGEN, *De Principiis*, c. 254 A.D.

Life, sense perception, appetite, memory, thought and anything else there may be are subject to necessity, except in so far as they are subject to free will.

ST. BERNARD OF CLAIRVAUX, *Concerning Grace and Free Will*, c. 1128

We do everything of necessity, and nothing by "free-will"; for the power of "free-will" is nil, and does no good, nor can do, without grace.

MARTIN LUTHER, *Bondage of the Will*, 1525

Because every act of man's will, and every desire and inclination proceedeth from some cause, and that from another cause, in a continual chain, whose first link is in the hand of God the first of all causes, proceed from *necessity*.

THOMAS HOBBES, *Leviathan*, 1651

Those creatures which are endued with understanding, and consequently with a will, may not only be necessitated in their actions by a greater power, but also as necessarily be determined by the proposal of an infinite good.

JOHN PEARSON, *Exposition of the Creed*, 1659

Whatever comes to pass, comes to pass by the will and eternal decree of God; that is, whatever comes to pass comes to pass according to laws and rules which involve eternal necessity and truth; nature, therefore, always observes laws and rules which involve eternal necessity and truth.

BARUCH SPINOZA (1632–1677), *Letters*, I, 83

Wicked men are not less to be feared, and not less harmful, when they are wicked from necessity.

> BARUCH SPINOZA (1632–1677), *Chief Works*, II

We might in point of justice, insist upon it, that if men are ty'd to Sin, and do it by Necessity, and cannot otherwise act, there is both Pardon and Commiseration due unto them.

> HENRY MORE, *On Account of Virtue*, 1690

Necessity is not only all-powerful in the physical world; it also controls and regulates the moral world.

> P. H. D'HOLBACH, *The System of Nature*, 1770

No event could have been otherwise than as it *has been, is,* or *is* to *be.*

> JOSEPH PRIESTLEY, *Doctrine of Philosophical Necessity*, 1779

All that I am and shall be I am and shall be of necessity, and it is impossible that I should be otherwise.

> J. C. FICHTE, *Die Bestimmung des Menschen*, 1800

If we adopt the system of necessity, the terms *moral obligation* and *accountableness, praise* and *blame . . . wisdom* and *folly, virtue* and *vice,* ought to be disused, or to have new meanings given them when they are used in religion, in morals, or in civil government.

> THOMAS REID, *Essays on the Active Powers of the Human Mind*, 1822

Every man . . . can absolutely never do anything else than just what at that moment he does do. . . . The whole course of a man's life, in all its incidents great and small, is as necessarily pre-determined as the course of a clock.

> ARTHUR SCHOPENHAUER, "Free Will and Fatalism," *Complete Essays of Schopenhauer*, 1841

Given the motives which are present to an individual's mind, and given likewise the character and disposition of the individual, the manner in which he will act may be unerringly inferred.

> JOHN STUART MILL, *A System of Logic*, 1856

The assertion of absolute necessity . . . is virtually the negation of a moral universe.

> WILLIAM HAMILTON, *Lectures on Metaphysics*, 1870

Every individual, with no exception whatever, is but an involuntary product of natural and social environment.

> FRIEDRICH NIETZSCHE, *Human, All Too Human*, 1878

Everything is necessity, all is guiltlessness, and knowledge is the way of insight into this guiltlessness.

> FRIEDRICH NIETZSCHE, *Human, All Too Human*, 1878

Whoever accepts the existence of an omniscient Deity as a dogma of theology, affirms that the order of things is fixed from eternity to eternity; for the foreknowledge of an occurrence means that the occurrence will certainly happen.

> THOMAS HENRY HUXLEY, *Science and Morals*, 1886

A man could in no case have acted differently from the manner in which he did act, supposing the state of his mind, and the circumstances in which he was placed to be the same; which is merely saying, that the same causes would always produce the same effects.

> CHARLES BRAY, *The Philosophy of Necessity*, 1889

The three eldest children of Necessity: God, the World, and Love.

> RICHARD GARNETT, *Preface, De Flagello Myrteo*, 1897

It is just as impossible for the impartial and critical observer to detect a "wise providence" in the fate of individual human beings as a moral order in the history of people. Both are determined with iron necessity by a mechanical causality which connects every single phenomenon with one or more antecedent causes.

ERNEST HAECKEL, *The Riddle of the Universe,* 1899

See also Cause; Chance; Choice; Determinism; Election; Fatalism; Fate; Foreknowledge; Free Will; Freedom; God: His Intervention in the World; God: His Omnipotence; God: His Omniscience; Grace; Guilt; Judgment, God's; Mechanism; Predestination; Philosophy; Progress; Providence; Sin; Will.

NEEDS

He who needs less, let him thank God and not be dismayed; but he who needs more, let him be humiliated on account of his infirmity, and not exalted on account of the mercy that is shown him.

ST. BENEDICT OF NURSIA (c. 480–c. 553), *Rule of*

NEGATIVISM

We are gone a little mad following this flight of proud human intelligence into turmoil, strife, and deepening trouble under the banner of the Great Against.

ROBERT RAYNOLDS, *In Praise of Gratitude,* 1961

NEGROES

The familiar unbalanced hatred of the Negro race and its individual members is sinful. The failure to repress or attempt to control prejudice and antipathy against the Negro is just as wrong as the neglect to attempt the repression of the passion of anger or of sloth.

FRANCIS J. GILLIGAN, *The Morality of the Color Line,* 1929

We owe to these fellow citizens, who have contributed so largely to the development of our country, and for whose welfare history imposes on us a special obligation of justice, to see that they have in fact the rights which are given them in our Constitution.

ROMAN CATHOLIC BISHOPS OF U.S., 1943

When the Negro Christian does not follow the logic of white thought, when he does what he thinks we think that he as a Christian should do, when he seeks his full rights, . . . then we are quick to say, not that the Gospel has borne its fruits in him, but rather that he has fallen under the subverting influence of some doctrine alien to American life.

KYLE HASELDEN, *The Racial Problem in Christian Perspective,* 1959

What does the Christian owe to man as man? When we have answered that question we shall know automatically what the Christian owes to that man who has the subtitle Negro.

KYLE HASELDEN, *The Racial Problem in Christian Perspective,* 1959

The Magna Charta of the Negro is the declaration: "I am a man whom God made and loves; nothing God intends for man must be denied to me."

KYLE HASELDEN, *The Racial Problem in Christian Perspective,* 1959

The Negro church stands as the symbol of the white Christian's shame; yet it is a tribute to the power of the Gospel and to the faith of the Negro.

KYLE HASELDEN, *The Racial Problem in Christian Perspective,* 1959

Christianity has been profaned in the relationship of the white Christian church and white Christians to the Negro.

KYLE HASELDEN, *The Racial Problem in Christian Perspective,* 1959

The [black] ghetto houses the most dissident and disinherited, the people who wake up to society's kick in the teeth each morning, and fall exhausted with a parting kick each night. These are the people who are ready for revolution—any kind of revolution.

C. ERIC LINCOLN, *The Black Muslims,* 1961

The faith of Negro Christians has a biblical scope and grandeur sadly lacking in the white churches of North and South in the half-century following the Emancipation.

FRANKLIN H. LITTELL, *From State Church to Pluralism,* 1962

The issue is not whether the Negroes want to come; it is whether they are welcome.

JAMES SELLERS, *The South and Christian Ethics,* 1962

Our present suffering and our nonviolent struggle to be free may well offer to Western civilization the kind of spiritual dynamic so desperately needed for survival.

MARTIN LUTHER KING, *Strength to Love,* 1963

One day we shall win freedom, but not for ourselves. We shall so appeal to your heart and conscience that we shall win you in the process, and our victory will be a double victory.

MARTIN LUTHER KING, *Strength to Love,* 1963

Only Christian charity which recognizes the Negro as a fellow creature of God, who is working and striving, like ourselves, toward his ultimate goal, which sees him as beloved by God, and redeemed by the sacrifice of Christ, and sees Christ in the individual Negro, can permanently extinguish the fires of prejudices, injustice, and hatred.

JOSEPH T. LEONARD, *Theology and Race Relations,* 1963

Catholics are obliged by the law of charity to show the common signs of friendship to Negroes, and this is *per se* a serious and grave obligation.

JOSEPH T. LEONARD, *Theology and Race Relations,* 1963

Often the treatment meted out to members of the Mystical Body because they are Negroes is a denial of that unity.

JOSEPH T. LEONARD, *Theology and Race Relations,* 1963

The decisive weapon in the civil rights struggle was the very complex that the white Southerner most insistently pressed upon the Negro slave—Christianity and the Bible.

HARRY GOLDEN, *Mr. Kennedy and the Negroes,* 1964

If Christianity is saving the Negro, so is he saving Christianity. It is the twentieth-century Negro in America who rediscovered Christianity's ethic and upon rediscovery, made that ethic an effective ethic. . . . The Negro . . . uses Christianity to discipline himself, to give himself order and cohesion and a rationale.

HARRY GOLDEN, *Mr. Kennedy and the Negroes,* 1964

See also Discrimination; Intolerance; Race; Racial Conflict; Racial Equality; Racial Injustice; Racial Prejudice; Rights.

NEIGHBOR

The love of our neighbor hath its bounds in each man's love of himself.

ST. AUGUSTINE, *On Lying,* c. 395

As the prudent vintager eats only ripe grapes, and gathers not those which are green, so the eyes of a wise man rests only upon the virtue in others; whereas the eye of the fool seeks only to discover in his neighbor vices and defects.

ST. JOHN CLIMACUS (525–600), *Climax*

In order that to love one's neighbor may be a matter of perfect justice, it is imperative that it be referred to God as its cause. Otherwise how can he love his neighbor without alloy?

ST. BERNARD OF CLAIRVAUX, *On the Necessity of Loving God*, 1126

No one may forsake his neighbor when he is in trouble. Everybody is under obligation to help and support his neighbor as he would himself like to be helped.

MARTIN LUTHER, *Letter*, November, 1527

The love towards our neighbor must be like the pure and chaste love between bride and bridegroom, where all faults are connived at and borne with, and only the virtues regarded.

MARTIN LUTHER (1483–1546), *Table Talk*

We never love our neighbor so truly, as when our love for him is prompted by the love of God.

FRANÇOIS FÉNELON (1651–1715), *Selections from*, ed. Fellen

I have but one word to say to you concerning love for your neighbor, namely, that nothing save humility can mould you to it; nothing but the consciousness of your own weakness can make you indulgent and pitiful to that of others.

FRANÇOIS FÉNELON (1651–1715), *Spiritual Letters of*

We are made for one another, and each is to be a supply to his neighbor.

BENJAMIN WHICHCOTE, *Moral and Religious Aphorisms*, 1753

"Thou shalt love thy neighbor as thyself." Why? Because every human being has a root in the Unity, and to reject the minutest particle of the Unity is to reject it all.

Baal-Shem, (Rabbi Israel ben Eliezer Baal Shem Tov, 1700–1760)

The love of our neighbour is the only door out of the dungeon of self.

GEORGE MACDONALD, *Unspoken Sermons*, 1st Series, 1869

A man must not choose his neighbour; he must take the neighbour that God sends him. The neighbour is just the man who is next to you at the moment, the man with whom any business has brought you into contact.

GEORGE MACDONALD, *Unspoken Sermons*, 1st Series, 1869

There is an idea abroad among moral people that they should make their neighbors good. One person I have to make good: myself. But my duty to my neighbor is much more nearly expressed by saying that I have to make him happy—if I may.

ROBERT LOUIS STEVENSON, *Across the Plains and Other Essays*, 1880

We have to love our neighbor because he is there. . . . He is the sample of humanity that is actually given us. Precisely because he may be anybody he is everybody.

G. K. CHESTERTON, *Heretics*, 1905

If you have Christian love for your neighbor, then all heaven will love you; if you have union of spirit with your fellow-creatures, then you shall have union with God and all the dwellers of heaven; if you are merciful to your neighbor, then God and all the angels and saints will be merciful to you; if you pray for others, then all heaven will intercede for you.

JOHN SERGIEFF OF CRONSTADT (1829–1908), *My Life in Christ*

No one can love his neighbor on an empty stomach.

WOODROW WILSON, *Speech*, New York City, May 23, 1912

Everything that is unconscious in ourselves we discover in our neighbor, and treat him accordingly. . . . What we combat in him is usually our inferior side.

> C. G. JUNG, *Modern Man in Search of a Soul,* 1932

Service of God consists in what we do to our neighbor.

> LEO BAECK, *Essence of Judaism,* 1936

It is discouraging to try to be a good neighbor in a bad neighborhood.

> WILLIAM R. CASTLE, *Dragon's Teeth in South America,* 1939

Jesus was a neighbor to the thief on the cross. That is, He was conscious of his need and did something about it. Imagine, even with His last breath of life almost gone, He gave to the dying thief.

> JAMES W. KENNEDY, *Advance into Light,* 1948

You are asked to love your neighbour as yourself. You are not called upon to share his opinions. He may be a Pharisee.

> AUBREY MENEN, *Dead Man in the Silver Market,* 1953

It is not enough, according to the New Testament, for men simply to treat each other justly. They are also under the seemingly impossible requirement to love each other. . . . This is the biblical call for neighborliness, which is a great deal more than mere justice.

> JAMES SELLERS, *The South and Christian Ethics,* 1962

In our times a special obligation binds us to make ourselves the neighbor of every person without exception, and of actively helping him when he comes across our path.

> SECOND VATICAN COUNCIL, *The Church in the Modern World,* December, 1965

See also Agape; Almsgiving; Brotherhood; Charity; Cheating; Community; Compassion; Fellowship; Humility; Isolation; Love; Love of Mankind; Unity.

NEO-ORTHODOXY

Neo-Orthodoxy is Fundamentalism in a new spring dress. . . . She is a pleasant little Protestant Jesuit.

> JAY WILLIAM HUDSON, *Religious Liberals Reply,* 1947

The neo-orthodox have the disconcerting habit of posturing as the listed subscribers to a private line to headquarters.

> PETER L. BERGER, *The Precarious Vision,* 1961

See also Orthodoxy.

NESTORIANISM

I have learned from Scripture that God passed through the Virgin Mother of Christ; that God was born of her I have never learned.

> NESTORIUS, *Reply to Proclus,* 429

NEUROSIS

From the point of view of cure, the advice to go and "express your instincts" is only one degree more foolish than the antiquated advice which used to be given every neurotic girl: "All you need is to get married." In actual experience I have never known a true neurosis cured by marriage, still less by sexual libertinism.

> J. A. HADFIELD, *Psychology and Morals,* 1923

Neurosis is an inner cleavage—the state of being at war with oneself.

> C. G. JUNG, *Modern Man in Search of a Soul,* 1933

Side by side with the decline of religious life, the neuroses grow noticeably more frequent.

> CARL JUNG, *Modern Man in Search of a Soul,* 1933

At the bottom of every neurosis there is a metaphysical problem.

> RUDOLF ALLERS, *The Psychology of Character,* 1943

The only person that can be entirely free from neurosis is the man whose life is spent in genuine devotion to the natural and supernatural obligations of life, and who has steadfastly accepted and affirmed his position as creature, and his place in the order of creation: beyond the neurotic there stands only the saint.

RUDOLPH ALLERS, *The Psychology of Character,* 1943

In a neurosis the whole of the personality is involved and therefore moral and spiritual problems cannot be excluded.

FRANZ B. ELKISCH, *Springs of Morality,* ed. J. M. Todd, 1956

Severe psychoneurosis adulterates religious experience, reducing it to exceedingly immature and neurotic forms.

H. GUNTRIP, *Mental Pain and the Cure of Souls,* 1956

See also Mental Illness; Neurotic; Psychiatrists; Psychiatry; Psychoanalysis; Psychology; Psychotherapy.

NEUROTIC

A saint minus his saintliness is a neurotic.

ALEXANDER YELCHANINOV (1881–1934), *Fragments of a Diary*

Sanctity requires a certain integrity in the psychic order. This does not mean neurotics cannot have utmost confidence in God and an intense love of God, but they still lack that integrity which is required for sanctity.

JORDAN AUMANN, *Faith, Reason and Psychiatry,* ed. Braceland, 1955

See also Neurosis; Psychiatry; Psychology; Psychotherapy; Sanctity.

NEW RELIGIONS

The New Religions are in many ways suited to the new conditions; but they are only suited to the new conditions.

G. K. CHESTERTON, *The Catholic Church and Conversion,* 1926

NEW TESTAMENT

The gospels and the rest of the New Testament, Mani says, were given as lessons from the good principle, and he asserts that not even these are quite free from the element that is contrary to God. Thus he takes upon himself the correction of the Scriptures . . . he dares to suppose that he is the Holy Ghost.

TITUS OF BOSTRA, *Adv. Manich.,* c. 363

There is nought in the Gospels which does not shine and illumine the world by its splendor, so that even things that seem trifling and unimportant shine with the majesty of the Holy Spirit.

ST. JEROME, *In Ezech,* 382

I should not believe the Gospel except as moved by the authority of the Catholic Church.

ST. AUGUSTINE, *Against the Epistle of Manichaeus Called Fundamental,* 397

You who believe what you like of the gospels and believe not what you like, believe yourselves rather than the gospel.

ST. AUGUSTINE, *Contra Faustum Manichaeum,* 400

For the grace of the Law which hath passed away we have received the abiding grace of the Gospel; for the shadows and the figures of the Old Testament we have the Truth of Jesus Christ.

ST. JEROME (340–420), *Adv. Pelag.* I.31, P.L. XXIII

Christian men and women, old and young, should study fast in the New Testament, for it is of full authority, and open to understanding of simple men, as to the points that be most needful to salvation.

JOHN WYCLIFF, Preface to his translation of *The Bible,* c. 1383

Would that men were content to let Christ rule by the laws of the Gospel, and that they would no longer seek to strengthen their obscurant tyranny by human decrees!

DESIDERIUS ERASMUS, *Greek Testament,* notes on, 1516

If the footprints of Christ be anywhere shown to us, we kneel down and adore. Why do we not rather venerate the living and breathing picture of Him in these books?

DESIDERIUS ERASMUS, Introduction to *Novum Instrumentum,* 1516

These sacred words give you the very image of Christ speaking, healing, dying, rising again, and make him so present, that were he before your very eyes you would not more truly see him.

DESIDERIUS ERASMUS, Preface to his translation of the *New Testament,* 1516

The gospel is the promise of grace or the forgiveness of sins through Christ.

PHILIP MELANCHTHON, *Loci Communes,* 1521

The true kernel and marrow of all the books, those which should rightly be ranked first, are the gospel of St. John and St. Paul's epistles, especially that to the Romans, together with St. Peter's first epistle.

MARTIN LUTHER, *Preface to the New Testament,* 1522

No poor fellow chained in sin, dead, and bound for hell can ever hear anything more comforting and encouraging than this precious and lovely message about Christ.

MARTIN LUTHER, *Preface to the New Testament,* 1522

When the doctrine of the Gospel becomes the reason of our mind, it will become the principle of our life.

BENJAMIN WHICHCOTE, *Religious Aphorisms,* 1753

Consider the gentleness of Jesus, the purity of His morals, the persuasiveness of His teaching. How lofty His principles! What wisdom in His words! How opportune, frank and direct His answers! How can the Gospel history be an invention?

JEAN JACQUES ROUSSEAU, *Émile,* Bk. 4, 1762

The gospel contains marks of truth so great, so striking, so perfectly inimitable, that the inventor of them would be more extraordinary than the hero.

JEAN JACQUES ROUSSEAU, *Émile,* 1762

What are all the Gifts of the Gospel; are they not all mental Gifts? . . . And are not the Gifts of the Spirit Everything to Man?

WILLIAM BLAKE, *Jerusalem,* 1820

It is the glory of the Gospel charter and the Christian constitution, that its author and head is the Spirit of truth, essential reason as well as absolute and incomprehensible Will.

SAMUEL TAYLOR COLERIDGE, *Aids to Reflection,* 1825

Is there any reason that we, who have not heard Christ speak, should have a clearer apprehension of the meaning of His recorded discourses on a given point, than the Apostles who did?

JOHN HENRY NEWMAN, *Essays and Sketches,* I, 1838

He who cultivates only one precept of the Gospel to the exclusion of the rest in reality attends to no part at all.

JOHN HENRY NEWMAN, *Parochial and Plain Sermons,* I, 1843

My heart has always assured me that the gospel of Jesus Christ must be Divine Reality.

DANIEL WEBSTER, from his epitaph, dictated the day before he died, 1852

Christianity does not rest on the infallible authority of the New Testament. It depends on this collection of books for the historical statement of its facts.

THEODORE PARKER, *Views of Religion,* 1855

It was not till the Faith had been everywhere preached, believed, defined in creeds, recorded in the mind of the universal Church, embodied in sacraments, and manifested in perpetual worship, that the New Testament was formed.

HENRY EDWARD MANNING, *The Temporal Mission of the Holy Ghost,* 1865

It is the best book that ever was or ever will be known in the world, and because it teaches you the best lessons by which any human creature who tries to be truthful and faithful to duty can possibly be guided.

CHARLES DICKENS, *Letter to his son,* September, 1868

The more we convince ourselves of the liability of the New Testament writers to mistake, the more we really bring out the greatness and worth of the New Testament. . . . The New Testament exists to reveal Jesus Christ, not to establish the immunity of its writers from error.

MATTHEW ARNOLD, *Literature and Dogma,* 1873

The spirit of the gospel is democratic. The tendency of the gospel is leveling; leveling up, not down. It is carrying the poor and the multitude onward and upward.

HENRY WARD BEECHER (1813–1887), *Sermon*

The Gospel is a social message, solemn and over-powering in its force; it is the proclamation of solidarity and brotherliness, in favor of the poor.

ADOLF VON HARNACK, *What Is Christianity?,* 1901

It is the holiness of our Lord's heart that fills the New Testament full and makes it

the unparalleled and unapproachable Book that it is.

ALEXANDER WHYTE, *Walk, Conversation and Character of Jesus Christ,* 1905

The New Testament is the history of the life and the testimony of common men who rallied to the fellowship of Jesus Christ and who by their faith and preaching remade a world that was under the thrall of a Roman army.

WOODROW WILSON, *Address,* May, 1911

The New Testament is the most joyful book in the world. It opens with joy over the birth of Jesus, and it ends with a superb picture of a multitude which no man could number, singing Hallelujah Choruses.

HARRY EMERSON FOSDICK, *The Manhood of the Master,* 1913

Without the proper clues the gospels are, to a modern educated person, nonsensical and incredible, whilst the apostles are unreadable. But with the clues, they are fairly plain sailing.

GEORGE BERNARD SHAW, Preface, *Androcles and the Lion,* 1914

The Gospel is so welded together in truth, that if one part or article is renounced, the rest is at once deprived of meaning.

BEDE JARRETT, *Meditations for Layfolk,* 1915

The religion of the New Testament is too rich and many-sided to be reduced to one single type. It is profoundly inward and mystical, but it is at the same time outreaching and social.

RUFUS M. JONES, *The World Within,* 1918

The Kingdom of the Gospel was not simply the restoration of Israel; it was internal and spiritual, as well as external and cosmic. . . . The conception of the new world living in germ in the bosom of the present order.

CHRISTOPHER DAWSON, *God and the Supernatural*, 1920

I do not dare read the N. T. for fear of its awakening a storm of anxiety and self-reproach and doubt and dread for having taken the wrong path, of having been traitor to the plain and simple God.

GAMALIEL BRADFORD, *Journal*, September 8, 1921

The Gospels rank among the best attested works of the Graeco-Roman world. They are better attested than the works of Pindar, or Xenophon, or Horace; of Pliny, Polybius, or Suetonius; of Terence or Plautus, Sophocles or Euripedes, or of a score of others, the genuineness and authenticity of whose writings are cheerfully accepted by every classical scholar in the world.

J. P. ARENDZEN, *The Gospels—Fact, Myth or Legend?*, 1923

Our very assurance as to what the New Testament contains rests historically on the teaching authority of the bishops of the fifth century, and the successors of the Apostles commissioned and guaranteed by Christ.

E. R. HULL, *What the Catholic Church Is*, 1925

There appears nowhere in the New Testament a consciousness that its writers were thereby supplying Christendom with the one sole and adequate Rule of Faith.

E. R. HULL, *What the Catholic Church Is*, 1925

The Gospel, because it was the message of God to humanity, could only reveal itself in the simplest of garments.

ADOLPH DEISSMANN, *The New Testament in the Light of Modern Research*, 1929

When I open and turn over with reverent joy the leaves of the Gospels, I feel that here is enshrined the highest achievement of Man the Artist, a creation to which nothing can be added, from which nothing can be taken away.

HAVELOCK ELLIS, *The Fountain of Life*, 1930

The Federal Council has no message to utter in behalf of any other gospel than that which deals with the renewal of individual life by the power of God.

Federal Council of Churches of Christ in America, *Report*, 1932

The New Testament, and to a very large extent the Old, is the soul of man. You cannot criticize it. It criticizes you.

JOHN JAY CHAPMAN (1862–1933), quoted in C. Hurd's *Treasury of Great American Quotations*

I recite the creeds, and wonder and doubt. And then I read in the Gospels, and out of some sentence or some act . . . springs a flash of light, comes a sudden lifting of the curtain, which compels me to say: This thing is of man and more than man.

PAUL ELMER MORE, *Pages from an Oxford Diary*, 1937

It is from other Faiths that we learn how great is the gulf between our Christianity and the Gospel.

HEINRICH FRICK, *The Gospel, Christianity and Other Faiths*, 1938

I have read the most important so-called biographies of Jesus; in none of them do I find so much religious life as in the Gospels. The Gospels have the very smell of reality.

THOMAS G. MASARYK, *Thought and Life*, 1938

What the Christian religion is has been laid down once and for all by the founder of that religion in words that can be read by all in a translation of singular beauty.

VIRGINIA WOOLF, *Three Guineas*, 1938

We could not possibly base a Christian philosophy on the Gospel alone, for even where it does not cite the Old Testament it everywhere presupposes it.

ÉTIENNE GILSON, *The Spirit of Medieval Philosophy,* 1940

If what the New Testament says about Jesus Christ is true, it can be true only on the ground that God by the Holy Spirit led men to this truth.

EDWIN LEWIS, *A Philosophy of the Christian Revelation,* 1940

The whole of the New Testament seemed to me covered, explained and held together by the saying, "If Christ be not risen from the dead, then is our preaching vain."

L. P. JACKS, *Confessions of an Octogenarian,* 1942

If we had ancient sources like those in the Gospels for the history of Alexander the Great we should not cast any doubt upon them whatsoever.

JOSEPH KLAUSNER, *From Jesus to Paul,* 1943

The primary task of the historical Church is the proclamation of the Gospel. To proclaim the Gospel means inevitably to pass a judgment upon the world. The Gospel itself is a judgment and a condemnation.

Man's Disorder and God's Design (Amsterdam Assembly Series), I, 1948

The New Testament knows nothing of a "simple teaching of Jesus" which has only to be systematized to provide the solution of all our problems. Many of our problems receive in the New Testament not only no solution but no attention.

SYDNEY CAVE, *The Christian Way,* 1949

The Christian message was not Good Advice; it was News, Good News of God.

SYDNEY CAVE, *The Christian Way,* 1949

No one, I venture, reading the Gospels attentively, but must feel, "If God ever spoke to man, this is what He would say."

JOHN A. CASS, *Quest for Certainty,* 1950

As the Gospel reached to the very source of thought and feeling, and modified it, the change it produced was one that once accomplished, could never be reversed, without the suppression of Christianity itself.

JOSEPH HUBY, *God, Man and the Universe,* 1950

When we move from the Gospels to the Epistles we pass from the inauguration of the Kingdom to the erection of the Church.

JOHN T. MCNEILL, *History of the Cure of Souls,* 1951

When finally the Gospels were written, they did not prove what the Christian believed; they confirmed it.

FULTON J. SHEEN, *The Woman,* 1951

The authority of the New Testament is absolute in so far as it brings us the Word of God and His grace. This message is found by the guidance of the Spirit and normally within the fellowship of the Church.

R. NEWTON FLEW, *The Nature of the Church,* 1952

The reception of "the Gospel" is neither a static nor a mechanical process. There is an organic advance, generation by generation, in its meaning, without any deviation from orthodoxy.

GREGORY DIX, *Jew and Greek,* 1953

The whole Gospel story is a missionary story.

EMMANUEL SUHARD, *The Church Today,* 1953

If life is pleasant for you and you have no hunger you cannot satisfy, you do not need to read the New Testament. For you will not know what it is talking about.

F. O. STOCKWELL, *With God in Red China,* 1954

Actually, there is power in the Gospel for those who know how to receive it. The three letters TNT, abbreviation for The New Testament, on the back of some small editions of this book, cryptically suggest this fact!

G. RAY JORDAN, *Beyond Despair,* 1955

From the beginning we are presented with a dilemma by the Gospels: Such a Person never could have lived; Such a Person never could have been invented! Which horn will you choose?

NATHANIEL MICKLEM, *Ultimate Questions,* 1955

Reading the New Testament is the discovery of a new path of human understanding by the flares that burned on the heights of Golgotha. . . . Out of the New Testament came a definition of divine love that has lit the tapers of faith and hope in the hearts of the world.

A. M. SULLIVAN, *The Three-Dimensional Man,* 1956

The fact that the Christians called their collection of first-century literature The New Testament indicates that they thought of it as being continuous with, but somehow fulfilling, the literature and history of the Jews.

JAMES A. MARTIN, JR., *Fact, Fiction and Faith,* 1960

It is only if we as Christians can view ourselves as the sort of people who crucified Christ that the New Testament can have any saving effect upon us.

JAMES A. PIKE, *Look,* March 14, 1961

It is the crown and completion of the Old Testament teaching which, because so much of it is concerned with promises not yet redeemed and expectations not yet fulfilled, cries out for some such completion.

JOHN BAILLIE, *The Sense of the Presence of God,* 1962

See also Apostles; Bible; Bible: Its Inspiration; Bible: Its Interpretation; Bible and the Church; Bible and Civilization; Bible and Doctrine; Bible and History; Bible as Literature; Buddhism and Christianity; Chosen People; Christian; Christianity; Christians; Church, Definitions of; Church: Its Nature; Church: Its Work; Doctrine; Ethics; God, Word of; Immortality; Jesus Christ; Miracles; Old Testament; Preachers; Preaching the Bible; Private Judgment; Religion; Religion, Revealed; Revelation; Sermon on the Mount; Tradition; Unity; War, Just; Word, the; Works.

NEW THOUGHT

If we simmer all the modernistic and New Thought concoction down to its base, we find there nothing more than the simple idea that man is not the Worm that the old theology said he was.

CHARLES W. FERGUSON, *The Confusion of Tongues,* 1928

NIHILISM

The moral breakdown in our civilization . . . discloses itself in a cult of nihilism, a cult which denies the fundamental discriminations between good and bad, between higher and lower . . . the debasement of justice and the disregard of law.

LEWIS MUMFORD, *Saturday Review,* January 15, 1950

NINETEENTH CENTURY

Never before in a period of equal length had Christianity or any other religion penetrated for the first time as large an area as it had in the nineteenth century. . . . Never before . . . had Christians come so near the goal of reaching all men with their message. . . . Never had the faith won adherents among so many peoples and in so many countries.

KENNETH SCOTT LATOURETTE, *A History of the Expansion of Christianity,* IV, V, VI, VII, 1938

The history of the last century has at times the look of a morality play, with the individual conscience buttressed by the ethical and religious inheritance from the past contending with the dogma of inevitability; the inevitability of progress on the one hand, the inevitability of doom on the other hand.

MARQUIS W. CHILDS and DOULASS CATER, *Ethics in a Business Society,* 1954

See also Missionaries.

NIRVANA

Just as all rivers lose themselves in the great ocean, and all the waters of the air pour into it, yet the great ocean thereby knows neither increase nor diminution; so when many Arahants [Saints] become extinguished in the pure realm of Nirvana, the Nirvana realm knows neither increase nor diminution. . . . There water, earth, fire, air are not. . . . When the enlightened has attained in stillness to insight, then is he free from form and formlessness, from pleasure and from pain.

Udana, V (Sayings of the Buddha), 6th century B.C.

All thy rafters are broken, thy ridge-pole is sundered; thy mind, approaching Nirvana, has attained to extinction of all desires.

Dhammapada, c. 5th century B.C.

Nirvana is where the thinking-mind with all its discriminations, attachments, aversions and egoism is forever put away; is where logical measures, as they are seen to be inert, are no longer seized upon; is

where even the notion of truth is treated with indifference because of its causing bewilderment; is where, getting rid of the four propositions, there is insight into the abode of reality.

Surangama Sutra, c. 1st century A.D.

Nirvana is where there is no birth, no extinction; it is seeing into the state of suchness, absolutely trancending all the categories constructed by mind; for it is the Tathagata's [Buddha's] inner consciousness.

Lankavatara Sutra, prior to 400 A.D.

Those who, afraid of the sufferings arising from the discrimination of birth-and-death, seek for Nirvana, do not know that birth-and-death and Nirvana are not to be separated from one another.

Lankavatara Sutra, prior to 400 A.D.

Nirvana represents the entrance of the soul into rest, a subduing of all wishes and desires, indifference to joy and pain, to good and evil; and absorption of the soul in itself, and a freedom from the circles of existence from birth to death, and from death to a new birth.

MAX MÜLLER, *Historic Magazine, and Notes and Queries,* II, 1882

It is only conceptually that "Nirvana" is a negation; it is felt in consciousness as in the strongest degree positive; it exercises a "fascination" by which its votaries are as much carried away as are the Hindu or the Christian by the corresponding objects of their worship.

WINSTON L. KING, *Buddhism and Christianity,* 1962

Nirvana is like a world in which nothing exists save a completely transparent atmosphere, yet with nothing at all to see in its transparency, and no sense of being one who is beholding this transparency, but of somehow being the transparency itself.

WINSTON L. KING, *Buddhism and Christianity,* 1962

Nirvāna, or self-extinction in Brahman, clearly implies extinction of the ego, the false self, in the higher Self—the source of all knowledge, of all existence, and of all happiness. One who experiences it . . . unites himself in consciousness with Brahman, the all-pervading and divine Being. This consciousness is the transcendental consciousness; it is the samādhi of the yogis, the nirvāna of the Buddhists, and the kingdom of heaven of the Christians.

SWAMI PRABHAVANANDA, *The Spiritual Heritage of India,* 1963

See also Brahman· Immortality; Immortality, Belief in; Middle Path; Vision.

NOBILITY

Virtue is the truest nobility.

MIGUEL DE CERVANTES, *Don Quixote,* 1605

Send your noble blood to market and see what it will bring.

THOMAS FULLER, *Gnomologia,* 1732

Those who think nobly are noble.

ISAAC BICKERSTAFF, *The Maid of the Mill,* 1765

If you mean to act nobly and seek to know the best things God has put within reach of men, you must learn to fix your mind on that end, and not on what will happen to you because of it.

GEORGE ELIOT, *Romola,* 1863

We elevate to the only nobility we have, the nobility of moral greatness, only those men who are governed by love.

WOODROW WILSON, *Address,* October, 1904

Inner superiority to world fortune is the essence of genuine nobility, spirituality, or . . . the truly philosophic life.

M. R. COHEN, *A Dreamer's Journey,* 1949

See also Class Distinctions; Royalty.

NONATTACHMENT

The ideal man is the non-attached man. Non-attached to his bodily sensations and lusts. Non-attached to his cravings for power and possessions. Non-attached even to science and speculation and philanthropy.

ALDOUS HUXLEY, *Ends and Means,* 1937

NONCOMBATANT

War hath no fury like a non-combatant.

C. E. MONTAGUE, *Disenchantment,* 1922

NONCONFORMITY

I give thanks to my God that I am worthy to be one whom the world hates.

ST. JEROME (c. 340–420), *Epist. 99.* .

Whoso would be a man must be a nonconformist. He who would gather immortal palms must not be hindered by the name of goodness, but must explore if it be goodness.

RALPH WALDO EMERSON, "Self-Reliance," *Essays,* 1844

Nonconformity to the mere customs of a local tradition has no moral significance whatever.

DIETRICH VON HILDEBRAND, *True Morality and Its Counterfeits,* 1955

See also Complacency; Conformity; Criticism; Custom; Opinions; Rebellion.

NONEXISTENCE

The Portal of God is Non-Existence. All things sprang from Non-Existence. Existence could not make existence existence. It must have proceeded from Non-Existence. And Non-Existence and Nothing are one.

Chuang-tzu, c. 300 B.C.

The utility of the house depends on the empty spaces. Thus, while the existence of things may be good, it is the nonexistent in them which makes them serviceable.

Tao Tê Ching, between 6th and 3rd century B.C.

See also Existence.

NONRESISTANCE

The one who from weakness does not resist commits a sin, and therefore cannot receive any benefit from his nonresistance; while the other would commit a sin by offering resistance.

VIVEKANANDA (1863–1902), *Complete Works of,* I, 36

This nonresistance is the highest manifestation of power in actual possession, and what is called the resisting of evil is but a step on the way towards it.

VIVEKANANDA (1863–1902), *Complete Works of,* I, 37

See also Force; Nonviolence; Nonviolent Resistance; Nuclear War; Pacifism; Peace; Power; Violence; War.

NONVIOLENCE

The essence of right conduct is not to injure anyone; one should know only this, that non-injury is religion.

Naladiyar, c. 500 B.C.

Let us therefore blush when we ourselves perversely become wolves to our foes. While we remain sheep we have the victory. . . . As soon as we become wolves we are beaten. The Shepherd leaves us. He feeds sheep, not wolves.

ST. JOHN CHRYSOSTOM, *Homilies* 33, c. 388

I wanted to avoid violence. I want to avoid violence. Non-violence is the first article of

my faith. It is also the last article of my creed.

MOHANDAS K. GANDHI, to the judge in South Africa, when sentenced to jail, March, 1921

Non-violence is the greatest force at the disposal of mankind. It is mightier than the mightiest weapon of destruction devised by the ingenuity of man.

MOHANDAS K. GANDHI, *My Experiment with Truth,* 1927

I object to violence because when it appears to do good, the good is only temporary; the evil it does is permanent.

MOHANDAS K. GANDHI, *Selections from Gandhi,* ed. by Nirmal Kumar Bose, 1945

At the center of non-violence stands the principle of love.

MARTIN LUTHER KING, *Stride Toward Freedom,* 1958

Nonviolence means that we will match your capacity to inflict pain with our capacity to endure it. . . . We have the choice in this world today between nonviolence and nonexistence.

MARTIN LUTHER KING, *Address,* Drew University, February, 1964

See also Coercion; Force; Nonresistance; Nonviolent Resistance; Nuclear War; Pacifism; Peace; Racial Conflict; Violence.

NONVIOLENT RESISTANCE

We urge upon our fellow-Christians and upon governmental agencies and educational leaders serious study of the possibilities of nonviolent resistance to possible aggression and injustice.

Statement, signed by five hundred ministers and laymen, issued by the Church Peace Mission, New York City, April, 1962

See also Force; Nonresistance; Nonviolence; Pacifism; Peace; Violence; War.

NOW

The splendor of the momentary "now" points always toward an eternal "now" which is not broken, not fleeting, not a small coral reef washed on every side by destructive time.

CHAD WALSH, *Behold the Glory,* 1955

NUCLEAR ENERGY

A little "splitting" of the rays of religion and a little "releasing of the energy" of the Bible seems in order. If we would only spend sums like the two billion dollars spent on our atomic bombs to harness the forces of God's teachings, what a blessing it would be for the human race.

RICHARD J. CUSHING, *Permanent Industrial Peace,* 1946

Ours is a world of nuclear giants and ethical infants.

OMAR BRADLEY, *Address,* Armistice Day, 1948

I have stood within nine miles, not of our biggest, but one of our sizeable nuclear explosions. I stood riveted, dumbfounded, awe-stricken. I had a feeling that I was looking into eternity.

THOMAS E. MURRAY, *Address,* December 4, 1951

If men will not live by virtue, they may have to die by power!

THOMAS E. MURRAY, *Address,* December 4, 1951

By grace of the new sacrament, the sacrament of Bikini, man really becomes spirit —but in another way than he had dreamed.

GEORGES BERNANOS, *Last Essays of,* 1955

Ethics alone will decide whether atomic energy will be an earthly blessing or the source of mankind's utter destruction.

WERNER VON BRAUN, *This Week,* January 24, 1960

No scientific development has ever brought man face to face with the problem of good and evil more starkly than the achievement whereby he summoned atomic energy forth from the deep recesses of the universe.

THOMAS E. MURRAY, *Nuclear Policy for War and Peace,* 1960

In an age in which mankind's collective power has suddenly been increased, for good or evil, a thousandfold through the tapping of atomic energy, the standard of conduct demanded from ordinary human beings can be no lower than the standard attained in times past by rare saints.

A. J. TOYNBEE, *A Study of History,* Vol. XII, *Reconsiderations,* 1961

See also Armaments; Atomic Bomb; End; Machines; Nuclear War; Science; Technology; War.

NUCLEAR WAR

A choice must be made and cannot be evaded: the way of atomic war or the way of Jesus.

A. J. MUSTE, *Fellowship,* October, 1945

The policy of obliteration bombing as actually practiced in World War II, culminating in the use of atomic bombs against Japan, is not defensible on Christian premises.

Atomic Warfare and the Christian Faith, Commission on the Relation of the Church and the War in the Light of the Christian Faith, Federal Council of Churches, 1946

To lay down in advance that a statesman, responsible for the defense of his nation and confronted by naked aggression, must, for moral or Christian reasons, refrain in all circumstances from recourse to atomic warfare would reduce to futility the argument that the use of the bomb as a deterrent may be the sole means of preventing war.

The Era of Atomic Power, Commission of British Council of Churches, 1946

The question has to be asked afresh whether the destruction of an entire population, including the aged and the young, is not an act so absolutely wrong in itself that no Christian can assent to it or share in it.

> The Era of Atomic Power, Commission of British Council of Churches, 1946

Today, when humanity is threatened with complete destruction by the liberation of atomic forces, people begin to realize that the only efficient protection lies in a greater and higher moral development.

> LECOMTE DU NOÜY, Human Destiny, 1947

Since any war that is started in the future will very probably begin with a large shower of atomic bombs and without warning, it is to be doubted that in the future any war at all will be a moral one.

> WILFRED PARSONS, The Ethics of Atomic War, pamphlet of Catholic Association for International Peace, 1947

The atomic bomb is inadmissible as a means of attack upon objectives in inhabited cities.

> The Church and the Atom: A Study of Moral and Theological Aspects, Report of Church of England Commission, 1948

There is no objection to the use of the H-bomb in a just war, as far as God's law is concerned, if it is launched directly against a military target.

> FRANCIS J. CONNELL, The Sign, March, 1950

Should the evil consequences of adopting this method of warfare ever become so extensive as to pass utterly beyond the control of man, then indeed its use must be rejected as immoral.

> POPE PIUS XII, Address to World Medical Association, 1954

Granted a sufficiently important military target which could not be safely eliminated by any less drastic means, nuclear bombing would be morally justified, even if it involved the resultant loss of a large segment of the civilian population.

> JOHN R. CONNERY, Theology Digest, Winter, 1957

Civil and military leaders who would plan and execute the dropping of a series of high megaton H-bombs on an area like Moscow or New York: (1) would not in practice avoid the direct intention of violence to the innocent; (2) could not, if they would; . . . and would have no proportionate justifying reason for permitting the evils which this type of all-out nuclear warfare would let loose.

> JOHN C. FORD, Theology Digest, Winter, 1957

The justly warring state may use these weapons against the enemy's stockpile of similar weapons when it is clear that he intends to use them; and especially when this aggressor is atheistic and amoral.

> PELAYO ZAMAYON, Theology Digest, Winter, 1957

The use of weapons to slaughter civilian populations, recklessness in regard to future generations, and the destruction of the fabric of national community and of civilized life are opposed to all that the churches have taught in the past.

> JOHN BENNETT, "Background paper" prepared for the Fifth World Order Study Conference of the National Council of Churches, Cleveland, 1958

The killings and . . . the mutilation of whole populations by all-out war, could mean worse suffering and might be less justifiable than even the acceptance of defeat under the conditions imposed by a tyrannic victor.

> Christians and the Prevention of War in an Atomic Age, World Council of Churches, August, 1958

The use of the H-Bomb constitutes an atrocity not to be justified in a belligerent even if the enemy is guilty of it.

Christians and the Prevention of War in an Atomic Age, World Council of Churches, August, 1958

It is *never* possible that no world would be preferable to some worlds, and there are in truth *no* circumstances in which the destruction of human life presents itself as a reasonable alternative.

Worldview (editorial), May, 1958

The nation which . . . uses massive retaliation as a threat, and Christians who condone or justify this policy are now morally committed to massive retaliation. . . . They are involved in the hopeless contradiction of saying that they will under certain circumstances use the diabolical weapons which they must not use because God forbids it!

A Christian Approach to Nuclear War, Published by Church Peace Mission, 1959

Since no theoretical limits can be placed upon the invoking of destructive atomic power, those who employ or plan to employ such power come dangerously close to usurping the sole prerogative of the Creator.

A Christian Approach to Nuclear War, published by Church Peace Mission, 1959

Atomic war so offends against the doctrine of creation that a Christian rationale for war is no longer tenable.

A Christian Approach to Nuclear War, published by Church Peace Mission, 1959

Here our main concern must be to see that man, whose own folly once drove him from the Garden of Eden, does not now commit the blasphemous act of destroying, whether in fear or in greed, the great and lovely world in which, even in his fallen state, he has been permitted by the grace of God to live.

GEORGE F. KENNAN, *Atlantic Monthly,* May, 1959

The existence of man on earth is at stake. Christians are supposed to know God's purpose for man's existence on earth and to be concerned that God's will be done. The God we know through Christ intends the salvation of man; that purpose surely would be defeated by the extermination of man.

HAROLD E. FEY, *The Christian Century,* 1960

Fifteen years of suspension over the fires of nuclear hell is long enough. It is time for a change. Let us say straight out that we are not going to destroy our enemies and menace our friends by nuclear war.

HAROLD E. FEY, *The Christian Century,* 1960

Previously the Christian statesman could threaten the use of force available to him —and mean it. Now he can mean it only if he believes that God delegates to him the right to wield apocalyptic destructive powers.

NORMAN K. GOTTWALD, *The Christian Century,* 1960

If a Christian believes that political and social orders are possible only through threatening an act which dissolves all recognizable human order, what is left of his belief in God the Creator?

NORMAN K. GOTTWALD, *The Christian Century,* 1960

An atomic war waged within the limits of military necessity may be not only something we are morally permitted to do; it may be something we are *morally obliged to do.*

THOMAS E. MURRAY, *Nuclear Policy for War and Peace,* 1960

There is a definite limit to *the number* of large thermonuclear weapons we could employ under any conceivable circumstances with military and moral justification.

THOMAS E. MURRAY, *Nuclear Policy for War and Peace,* 1960

There can be no good sufficiently great, or evil repelled sufficiently grave, to warrant the destruction of mankind by mankind's own action.

PAUL RAMSEY, *War and the Christian Conscience,* 1961

There is no achievement in human experience, no record, no thing of beauty that cannot now be rescinded and all its benefits and traces swept into void. . . . Earlier generations have had the power merely to affect history; ours is the power to expunge it.

NORMAN COUSINS, *In Place of Folly,* 1961

It is better to accept the darkness, to surrender ourselves to the all-holy justice and mercy of God, than to take part in mass murder only because the other side commits it.

FRANZISKUS STRATMANN, *God and the H-Bomb,* ed. D. Keys, 1962

The debate of the last few years on nuclear policy is simply a continuation of the long debate, at every level of our civilization, between absolute and relative moralities.

WALTER STEIN, *Nuclear Weapons,* 1962

The incentive to wipe out Bolshevism may well be one of the apocalyptic temptations of 20th-century Christendom.

THOMAS MERTON, *Commonweal,* February 9, 1962

See also Aggression; Armaments; Atomic Bomb; Conscientious Objector; Creation; End; End of the World; Internationalism; Killing; Nationalism; Nonresistance; Non-

violence; Nonviolent Resistance; Nuclear Energy; Pacifism; Pacifists; Peace; Science; War; War, Condemnation of.

NUDISM

This so-called "return to nature," which presupposes an abandonment of all spiritual control and a complete contempt for modesty, is nothing either more or less than a religion of the body.

JEAN MOUROUX, *The Meaning of Man,* 1948

NUPTIAL LOVE. See LOVE, PHYSICAL

OATHS

The abolishing of oaths is more useful than any fasting; it is more profitable than any austerity.

ST. JOHN CHRYSOSTOM, *Homilies,* c. 388

Many public officials are required to take an oath of office. . . . If a man who has taken such an oath is deliberately neglectful or dishonest in the performance of his duties, he is guilty of a sin of irreligion against the citizens of his country.

FRANCIS J. CONNELL, *Morality and Government,* 1949

A man's word should be as good as his sworn statement.

Faith and Practice of the Philadelphia Yearly Meeting, 1955

See also Perjury

OBEDIENCE

Wise people, after they have listened to the laws, become serene, like a deep, smooth, and still lake. . . . Those who, when the Law has been well preached to them, follow the Law, will pass across the dominion of death, however difficult to overcome.

Dhammapada, c. 5th century B.C.

You will give us joy and gladness if you obey what we have written through the Holy Spirit.

ST. CLEMENT OF ROME, *Epistle to the Corinthians,* c. 100

Avoid divisions, as the beginning of evil. Follow, all of you, the bishop, as Jesus Christ followed the Father; and follow the presbytery as the Apostles. Moreover, reverence the deacons as the commandment of God.

ST. IGNATIUS OF ANTIOCH, *To the Smyrnaeans,* VIII, c. 108

He that strives to draw himself from obedience, withdraws himself from grace.

THOMAS À KEMPIS, *Imitation of Christ,* 1441

Whenever it be clearly seen that the commands of superiors are contrary to God's commandments, and especially when contrary to the precepts of charity, no one is in such case bound to obedience.

GIROLAMO SAVONAROLA, *Sermon,* 1496, quoted in *Cambridge Modern History,* I

Christians must necessarily obey their magistrates and laws, save only when they command any sin; for then they must rather obey God than men.

PHILIP MELANCHTHON, *Augsburg Confession,* 1530

All citizens owe reverence and obedience to the magistrate as the minister of God in all righteous commands, and even their lives when the public safety and welfare require it.

HENRY BULLINGER, *The Helvetic Confession,* 1536

Simple minds, less curious, less well instructed, are made good Christians, and through reverence and obedience hold their simple belief and abide by the laws.

MICHAEL DE MONTAIGNE, *Essays,* I, 1580

Obedience to the spirit of God, rather than to the fair seeming pretense of men, is the best and most dutiful order that a Christian can observe.

JOHN MILTON, *An Apology Against a Pamphlet,* 1642

The observances of the Church concerning feasts and fasts are tolerably well kept upon the whole, since the rich keep the feasts and the poor the fasts.

SYDNEY SMITH (1771–1845), *Wit and Wisdom of*

All the things that God would have us do are hard for us to do—remember that—and hence, He oftener commands us than endeavors to persuade. And if we obey God, we must disobey ourselves, wherein the hardness of obeying God consists.

HERMAN MELVILLE, *Moby Dick,* 1851

It is not enough for Catholic scholars to accept and venerate the dogmas of the Church, they ought further to submit themselves both to doctrinal decisions of the pontifical congregations, and to points of doctrine which by common and constant consent are held in the Church to be truths and theological conclusions so certain that the contrary opinions, although they cannot be qualified as heretical, yet deserve some other note of theological censure.

POPE PIUS IX, Apostolic letter *Tuas Libenter,* to the Archbishop of Munich, December 21, 1863

Man being wholly dependent upon God, as upon His Creator and Lord, and created reason being absolutely subject to uncreated truth, we are bound to yield to God, by faith in His revelation, the full obedience of our will and intelligence.

The Vatican Council, Session III, 1870

The one only reason which men have for not obeying is when anything is demanded of them which is openly repugnant to the natural or divine law.

POPE LEO XIII, *On Civil Government,* 1881

The Catholic priesthood must have the spirit of discipline, or, to use a more deeply Christian word, obedience. It is obedience which binds together all ranks into the harmony of the Church's Hierarchy.

POPE PIUS XI, *The Catholic Priesthood,* 1935

Duty and genuine goodness are mutually exclusive. . . . The sense of "ought" shows me the Good at an infinite impassable distance from my will. Willing obedience is never the fruit of an "ought" but only of love.

EMIL BRUNNER, *The Divine Imperative,* 1937

If ye love me ye will keep my commandments. (John XIV, 15) If we don't, we shan't. Let no one deceive himself about that. There is no possibility of meeting His claim upon us, unless we truly love Him. So devotion is prior to obedience itself.

WILLIAM TEMPLE, *Readings in St. John's Gospel,* 1939

Obedience is the "virtue-making virtue."

GEORGE J. HAYE, *Obedience,* 1944

It is only as free obedience that obedience is a moral act, not as the purely external fulfilment of some external order.

H. HIRSCHMANN, *Stimmen der Zeit,* Vol. 161, 1957–1958

See also Authority; Commandments; Conscience; Discipline; Doctrine; Dogma; Free Will; Government; Mary, the Mother of Jesus; Natural Law; Private Judgment; Pope, the; Rebellion; Religion: Its Nature and Function; Resignation; Submission; Worship.

OBLIGATION

Whoever says "ought" at all, must mean that at least when the requisite conditions are fulfilled the obligation is absolute.

A. E. TAYLOR, *Essays Catholic and Critical,* 1938

See also Duties, Moral Obligation.

OBLIVION

Oblivion is not to be hired: the greater part must be content to be as though they had not been, to be found in the Register of GOD, not in the record of man.

THOMAS BROWNE, *Urn Burial,* 1658

Oblivion, n. Fame's eternal dumping ground. Cold storage for high hopes.

AMBROSE BIERCE, *Devil's Dictionary,* 1906

See also Anonymity; Death; Fame; Reputation.

OBSCENITY

There is a deep in Gehenna for the user of obscenity, and for the man who hears it willingly.

Talmud (Sabbath), c. 200 A.D.

Obscenity in any company is a rustic, uncreditable talent.

JEREMY COLLIER, *A Short View of the Immorality and Profaneness of the English Stage,* 1698

The test of obscenity is this: whether the tendency of the matter charged as obscenity is to deprave and corrupt those whose minds are open to such immoral influences, and into whose hands a publication of this sort may fall.

CHIEF JUSTICE COCKBURN, Judgment in *Regina vs. Hicklin,* 1868

A book is said to be obscene when it is offensive to decency or chastity, which is immodest, which is indelicate, impure, causing lewd thoughts of an immoral tendency.

JUDGE CLARKE of Federal District Court at Boston, Charge to jury in *U.S. vs. Heywood,* 1877

Every obscene, lewd, or lascivious, and every filthy book, pamphlet, picture, paper, letter, writing, print or other publication of an indecent character . . . is hereby declared to be nonmailable matter, and shall not be conveyed in the mails or delivered from any postoffice by any letter carrier.

U.S. Criminal Code, March 4, 1909

The meaning of the word "obscene" as legally defined by the Courts is: tending to stir the sex impulses or to lead to sexually impure and lustful thoughts. . . . Whether a particular book would tend to excite such impulses and thoughts must be tested by the Court's opinion as to its effect on a person with average sex instincts. . . . It is only with normal persons that the law is concerned.

JUDGE JOHN M. WOOLSEY, U.S. vs. One Book called "Ulysses," December 6, 1933

Where a book is claimed to be obscene it must first be determined, whether the intent with which it was written was what is called, according to the usual phrase, pornographic—that is, written for the purpose of exploiting obscenity. If the conclusion is that the book is pornographic that is the end of the inquiry and forfeiture must follow.

JUDGE JOHN M. WOOLSEY, U.S. vs. One Book called "Ulysses," December 6, 1933

Obscenity is not protected by the freedoms of speech and press. . . . The unconditional phrasing of the First Amendment was not intended to protect every utterance. . . . Implicit in the history of the First Amendment is the rejection of obscenity as utterly without redeeming social importance. . . . Sex and obscenity are not synonymous. . . . It is therefore vital that the standards for judging obscenity safeguard the protection of freedom of speech and press for material which does not treat sex in a manner appealing to prurient interest.

JUSTICE WILLIAM J. BRENNAN, majority opinion, U.S. Supreme Court, Roth v. U.S. and Albert v. U.S., 1957

By these standards punishment is inflicted for thoughts provoked, not for overt acts nor anti-social conduct. . . . This issue cannot be avoided by saying that obscenity is not protected by the First Amendment. The question remains, what is the constitutional test of obscenity?

Dissenting opinion, JUSTICES DOUGLAS and BLACK, Roth v. U.S. and Albert v. U.S., 1957

If a work is to be called obscene it must, of its nature, be such as actually to arouse or calculated to arouse in the viewer or reader such veneral pleasure. If the work is not of such a kind, it may, indeed, be vulgar, disgusting, crude, unpleasant, what you will—but it will not be, in the strict sense which Canon Law obliges us to apply, obscene.

HAROLD C. GARDINER, Catholic Viewpoint on Censorship, 1957

Erotic realism is a historical movement in art and literature, representing in part the artist or writer's rebellion against social pressures to deny and falsify life by forcing him to exclude, minimize and distort the sexual element in his artistic creation. . . . Its only goal is to depict life as it is.

EBERHARD and PHYLLIS KRONHAUSEN, Pornography and the Law, 1959

If we want our obscenity laws tidied up, we had better first tidy up our life.

ROGER J. KILLY, The Critic, October-November, 1963

See also Books; Censorship; Impurity; Literature; Motion Pictures.

OBSTINACY

Obstinacy is the result of the will forcing itself into the place of the intellect.

ARTHUR SCHOPENHAUER, "Psychological Observations," Essays, 1851

See also Perseverance.

OCCUPATION. See VOCATION

OFFICE

Office does not make a holy man, as is proved by the apostle Judas and by the bishops and priests who murdered Christ. The saints affirm that the worthier the office the greater the damnation of the incumbent if he be sinful.
JOHN HUS, *Of Simony*, 1413

See also Equality; Fame; Glory; Honor; Religious Test for Office; Reputation.

OLD AGE

He who greets and constantly reveres the aged, four things will increase to him, namely life, beauty, happiness and power.
Dhammapada, c. 5th century B.C.

Old age consoles itself by giving good precepts for being unable to give bad examples.
LA ROCHEFOUCAULD, *Maxims*, 1665

Piety is the only proper and adequate relief of decaying man. He that grows old without religious hopes, as he declines into imbecility, and feels pains and sorrows incessantly crowding upon him, falls into a gulf of bottomless misery, in which every reflection must plunge him deeper, and where he finds only new gradations of anguish and precipices of horror.
SAMUEL JOHNSON, *Rambler*, November 13, 1750

Grow old along with me!
The best is yet to be,
The last of life for which the first was made.
Our times are in His hand
Who saith: "A whole I planned,
Youth shows but half; trust God: see all nor be afraid."
ROBERT BROWNING (1812–1889), "Rabbi Ben Ezra," in *Poems*

To walk with God takes courage, and in old age God asks us to walk with Him.
JOHN LA FARGE, *Reflections on Growing Old*, 1963

OLD TESTAMENT

The Old Testament given by Moses was a promise, not of remission of sins, nor of eternal blessings, but of temporal ones, namely, those of the land of Canaan; and by it no one could be renewed in spirit and fitted to receive a heavenly inheritance.
MARTIN LUTHER (1483–1546), *First Principles of the Reformation*

Israel's Sacred Books stand so happily combined together, that, even out of the most diverse elements, the feeling of a whole still rises before us. They are complete enough to satisfy, fragmentary enough to excite, barbarous enough to rouse, tender enough to appease.
J. W. VON GOETHE, *Wilhelm Meister's Travels*, 1821

When we consider the Old Testament as written by divine inspiration, and preserved, beyond the time of its own Dispensation, for us Christians . . . we ought not surely to read any portion of it with indifference, nay without great and anxious interest. . . . Christ and His Apostles cannot have put the Law and the Prophets into our hands for nothing.
JOHN HENRY NEWMAN, *Parochial and Plain Sermons*, 1843

Our Jewish Bible has implanted itself in the table-talk and household life of every man and woman in the European and American nations.
RALPH WALDO EMERSON, *Representative Men: Plato*, 1845

The discipline of the Old Testament may be summed up as a discipline teaching us to abhor and flee from sin.
MATTHEW ARNOLD, *Culture and Anarchy*, 1869

I had gradually come, by this time, to see that the Old Testament from its manifestly false history of the world and from its attributing to God the feelings of a revengeful tyrant, was no more to be trusted than the sacred books of the Hindoos, or the beliefs of any barbarian.

CHARLES DARWIN (1809–1882), *Autobiography of*

In the Old Testament of the Jews, the book of Divine righteousness, there are men, events and words so great that there is nothing in Greek or Indian literature to compare with it.

FRIEDRICH NIETZSCHE, *Beyond Good and Evil,* 1885

It is precisely in the Old Testament that is reached the highest ethical note ever yet sounded . . . by man.

ISRAEL ZANGWILL, *Menorah Journal,* 1918

The early Hebrews had created the Bible out of their lives; their descendants created their lives out of the Bible.

ABRAHAM LEON SACHAR, *A History of the Jews,* 1930

The Old Testament cannot be understood without the New, which comes to fulfill, to justify and explain.

PAUL CLAUDEL, *Introduction au Livre de Ruth,* 1938

Old Testament religion is clearly about this world, and about nothing else.

JOHN MACMURRAY, *Clue to History,* 1939

To say that the Old Testament in its totality is inspired is to create almost insuperable difficulties for our mind.

EDWIN LEWIS, *A Philosophy of the Christian Revelation,* 1940

The books of the Old Testament, in their entirety, provide the most final and pro-

found literature of human loneliness that the world has known.

THOMAS WOLFE, *The Hills Beyond,* 1941

The sublimest working of God reaches so deeply that the two domains of the sublime and the everyday are not only not in fact separated but are fundamentally inseparable.

ERICH AUERBACH, *Mimesis,* 1946

The Old Testament differs from the Scriptures of other religions in that it proclaims a God whose righteous will is the norm of history and of individual lives.

SYDNEY CAVE, *The Christian Way,* 1949

The Old Testament is the story of how God educated mankind to be able to receive the gifts He destined for them.

JEAN DANIELOU, *Advent,* 1950

The Scriptures of the Old Israel remained the Scriptures of the "New," for they contained the Revelation of God which He had vindicated and fulfilled. They "testified" of Him.

GREGORY DIX, *Jew and Greek,* 1953

It is not a pretty picture of a hope and an ideal, a dream and a delusion. It is the factual, concrete record of what God has done to save men.

LEONARD JOHNSTON, *Witnesses to God,* 1961

The verdict from within Judaism must agree with that of Paul: to this day the veil of Moses hangs over the understanding of the Old Testament.

HANS JOACHIM SCHOPES, *The Jewish-Christian Argument,* 1963

See also Adam; Bible; Bible: Its Inspiration; Bible: Its Interpretation; Bible and the Church; Bible and Civilization; Bible and Doctrine; Bible and History; Bible as Literature; Chosen People; Commandments; Community; Genesis; God: His Intervention in the World; God, Word of; Israel; Jews; Job, Book of; Judaism; Miracles; Moses; New Testament; Preaching and the Bible; Private Judgment; Prophets; Psalms; Religion; Religion, Revealed; Revelation; Torah; Tradition; Word, the.

OM

The sacred syllable Om is explained in the scriptures as a combination of the sounds A, U, M, representing creation, preservation, and dissolution respectively. I compare the sound of Om to the sound of a bell that dissolves in silence. The relative universe dissolves in the imperishable absolute—the great silence.

SRI RAMAKRISHNA (1836–1886), *Kathamrta,* I

OMENS

Omen? . . . If the gods think to speak outright to man, they will honorably speak outright; not shake their heads, and give an old wives' darkling hint.

HERMAN MELVILLE, *Moby Dick,* 1851

OMNIPOTENCE

The moral sentiment alone is omnipotent.

RALPH WALDO EMERSON, *North American Review,* April, 1866

See also God: His Omnipotence.

ONE

We always move round the One—if we did not, we should dissolve and cease to exist —but we do not always look towards the One.

PLOTINUS (205–270 A.D.), *Enneads,* vi, 9

The One is perfect because it seeks for nothing, and possesses nothing, and has need of nothing; and being perfect, it overflows, and this its superabundance produces an Other.

PLOTINUS (205–270 A.D.), *Enneads,* V.2, 1

When a man is at one, God is One.

Zohar c. 1290, quoted in *The Life of Moses,* by E. Fleg, 1928

We live in succession, in division, in part, in particles. Meantime within man is the soul of the whole; the wise silence; the universal beauty, to which every part and particle is equally related; the eternal ONE.

RALPH WALDO EMERSON, "The Over-Soul," *Essays,* 1841

See also All; the various rubrics under God; Joy: Man and God; Man Indwelt by God; Soul, Definitions of; Soul and God.

ONE WORLD

All states should put aside mutual suspicion and unite in one sole society or rather family of peoples, both to guarantee their own independence and safeguard order in the civil concert of peoples.

POPE BENEDICT XV, *International Reconciliation,* 1920

A time may come when the local heritages of the different historical nations, civilizations and religions will have coalesced into a common heritage of the whole human family. . . . The missions of the higher religion are not competitive; they are complementary.

A. J. TOYNBEE, *A Historian's Approach to Religion,* 1956

See also Internationalism; Unity; Unity of Mankind.

OPEN MIND

We confess that we know but in part, and that we are ignorant of many things which we desire and seek to know; and if any shall do us that friendly part to show us from the word of God that we see not, we shall have cause to be thankful to God and them.

Particular Baptist Confession, 1646

OPINIONS

Men are disturbed not by events which happen, but by the opinion they have of these events. Thus death is nothing terrible . . . but the opinion we have about death is that it is terrible, this is the terrifying thing.

> EPICTETUS, *Enchiridion*, V, c. 110

As the thoughts of man are altogether unfettered, reasoning which disregards the holy texts and rests on individual opinion only has no proper foundation.

> SAMKARA (c. 750 A.D.), *Sacred Books of the East*, XXXIV

Men are tormented by the opinions they have of things, not by the things themselves.

> MICHEL DE MONTAIGNE, *Essays*, I, 1580

After all, it is setting a high value on our opinions to roast people alive on account of them.

> MICHEL DE MONTAIGNE, *Essays*, III, 1588

Difference of opinion is advantageous in religion. The several sects perform the office of *censor morum* over each other.

> THOMAS JEFFERSON, *Notes on Virginia*, 1779

Reward and punish no doctrine; hold out no allurement or bribe for the adoption of theological opinions. . . . Suffer no one to be a searcher of hearts and a judge of opinions . . . to assume the right which the Omniscient has reserved to Himself.

> MOSES MENDELSSOHN, *Jerusalem*, 1783

Error of opinion may be tolerated where reason is left free to combat it.

> THOMAS JEFFERSON, *Inaugural Address*, March 4, 1801

If thinking men would have the courage to think for themselves, and to speak what they think, it would be found they do not differ in religious opinions as much as is supposed.

> THOMAS JEFFERSON, *Letter to John Adams*, 1813

Men are never so good or so bad as their opinions.

> JAMES MACKINTOSH, *Progress of Ethical Philosophy*, 1830

It is easy in the world to live after the world's opinion; it is easy in solitude to live after our own; but the great man is he who in the midst of the crowd keeps with perfect sweetness the independence of solitude.

> RALPH WALDO EMERSON, "Self-Reliance," *Essays*, 1841

We can never be sure that the opinion we are endeavoring to stifle is a false opinion; and even if we were sure, it would be an evil still.

> J. S. MILL, *On Liberty*, 1859

The only sin which we never forgive in each other is a difference of opinion.

> RALPH WALDO EMERSON, *Clubs*, 1877

Truth generally lies in the coordination of antagonistic opinions.

> HERBERT SPENCER, *Autobiography*, 1904

Wide differences of opinion in matters of religious, political and social belief must exist if conscience and intellect alike are not to be stunted.

> THEODORE ROOSEVELT, *Speech*, April 23, 1910

Now we do not care to ascertain whether an opinion is true or false, but only whether it is life-furthering, life-preserving. We start with a certain view of life, think of a few things as necessary to it, and conclude that they are true and objective.

> RADHAKRISHNAN, *The Reign of Religion in Contemporary Philosophy*, 1922

The religious opinions of the unreligious are no more valuable than are the scientific opinions of the unscientific.

> DAVID E. TRUEBLOOD, *The Logic of Belief,* 1942

The notion that one opinion is as good as another will not work in any other area of human experience, why should it work in the area of faith?

> DAVID E. TRUEBLOOD, *Philosophy of Religion,* 1957

See also Bigots; Conformity; Division; Fear; Freedom; Intolerance; Nonconformity; Pluralism; Reason; Tolerance; Unity.

OPPONENTS

The writers against religion, whilst they oppose every system, are wisely careful never to set up any of their own.

> EDMUND BURKE, *Preface, Vindication of Natural Society,* 1756

OPPRESSORS

It is too common a sort of oppression for the rich in all places to domineer too insolently over the poor, and force them to follow their wills and to serve their interests, be it right or wrong. . . . An oppressor is an Anti-Christ and an Anti-God . . . not only an agent of the Devil, but his image.

> RICHARD BAXTER, *The Christian Directory,* 1673

God does not always punish a nation by sending it adversity. More often He gives the oppressors their hearts' desire, and sends leanness withal into their soul.

> W. R. INGE, *Personal Religion and the Life of Devotion,* 1924

See also Persecution.

OPTIMISM

We are not to take hold of the worse, but rather to be glad we may find hope that mankind has not grown monstrous.

> PHILIP SIDNEY, *Arcadia,* 1590

Optimism is the madness of maintaining that everything is right when it is wrong.

> VOLTAIRE, *Candide,* 1739

Optimism, n. The doctrine, or belief that everything is beautiful, including what is ugly, everything good, especially the bad, and everything right that is wrong. . . . An intellectual disorder, yielding to no treatment but death.

> AMBROSE BIERCE, *Devil's Dictionary,* 1906

The fact of the religious vision, and its history of persistent expansion, is our one ground for optimism. Apart from it, human life is a flash of occasional enjoyments lighting up a mass of pain and misery, a bagatelle of transient experience.

> ALFRED NORTH WHITEHEAD, *Science and the Modern World,* 1925

Nothing is too great or too good to be true. Do not believe that we can imagine things better than they are. In the long run, in the ultimate outlook, in the eye of the Creator, the possibilities of existence, the possibilities open to us, are beyond our imagination.

> OLIVER LODGE, *Science and Human Progress,* 1926

The scientific optimism of which Huxley may be taken as a typical exponent was merely a new variety of faith, resting upon certain premises which are no more unassailable than those which have supported other vanished religions of the past.

> JOSEPH WOOD KRUTCH, *The Modern Temper,* 1929

All the slippery optimism which has so devitalized the democratic peoples has sprung not from accidental misjudgments about particular events; it has sprung from an essential defect, which is best seen in its intellectual nakedness, in the philosophy of pragmatic liberalism.

> LEWIS MUMFORD, *Faith for Living,* 1940

The theological vacuum left by revivalism was already being filled, well before the nineties, by an emphasis that was quite in keeping with the popular mood of complacent and self-confident optimism.

> W. S. HUDSON, *The Great Tradition of the American Churches,* 1953

Optimism believes that the indefinite progress of the universe by technical achievement due to an inherent law of dialectics will result in absolute happiness for humanity. The first duty is thus to believe in the future, to advance, to dedicate oneself unreservedly to the possession of the world.

> EMMANUEL SUHARD, *The Church Today,* 1953

Nine times out of ten, optimism is a sly form of selfishness, a method of isolating oneself from the unhappiness of others.

> GEORGES BERNANOS, *Last Essays of,* 1955

Christianity did not come into the world with a fixed, silly grin on its face and vapid Cheerio on its lips. At its center was a cross. That heritage must be saved from being perverted by the Bright-side boys, whether in the pulpit or out of it.

> HALFORD E. LUCCOCK, *Living Without Gloves,* 1957

All sunshine makes a desert.

> Arab Proverb

See also Confidence; Cross; Evolution; Faith; Hope; Liberalism; Optimist; Perfection; Pessimism; Pragmatism; Progress; Security; Self-Reliance; Vision.

OPTIMIST

An optimist is a believer in the best, and any man who believes that anything less than the best is the ultimate purpose of God, and so the ultimate possibility of God's children, has no business to live upon the earth.

> PHILLIPS BROOKS, *National Needs and Remedies,* 1890

See also Optimism.

ORATOR

Here comes the orator, with his flood of words, and his drop of reason.

> BENJAMIN FRANKLIN, *Poor Richard's Almanac,* 1735

See also Eloquence; Preachers; Preaching; Rhetoric; Speech; Words.

ORDER

Original Sin brought into the world concupiscence, ignorance and spiritual infirmity, from which spread confusion and discord. So that man from the beginning has been looking for a lost happiness, an inner peace, a peace that can come only with order.

> ROBERT I. GANNON, *God in Education,* 1943

If we as Christians are to do our part in restoring order to a chaotic world, Christ must be the Master in our classrooms and lecture halls and the Director of our research projects.

> Catholic Bishops of the U.S., 1948

See also Chaos; Discord; Moral Law; Moral Order; Peace; Serenity; Social Order.

ORDERS. See ORDINATION

ORDINATION

God commanded a priest to be appointed before all the congregation; that is, He instructs and shows us that the ordination of priests ought only to be solemnized with the knowledge of the people standing by.

> ST. CYPRIAN, *Ep. LXVII,* 254

Impose not hands after the first trial, nor after the second, nor yet the third, but only after frequent and careful observation and searching examination.

> ST. JOHN CHRYSOSTOM, *Hom.* 16 *in Tim.,* c. 388

If ordination is interpreted in relation to the ministry of the Word, we have no objection to calling ordination a sacrament. . . . If ordination is interpreted in this way, we shall not object to calling the laying on of hands a sacrament.

PHILIP MELANCHTHON, *Apology to the Augsburg Confession,* 1531

It is not enough that the Bishop know nothing evil of the ordinand; he must have positive evidence of his uprightness.

ST. ALPHONSUS DE LIGUORI, *Theol. mor., de Sacram. Ordin.,* 1753

If the sacrament of Orders is administered without the intention of ordaining priests to offer sacrifice, the persons ordained are not priests at all.

E. A. KNOX, *National Review,* September, 1925

Ordination we account as nothing else but the solemn putting a man into his place and office in the church.

G. G. ATKINS and F. L. FAGLEY, *History of American Congregationalism,* 1941

It is absurd, when a man takes Holy Orders to say, as we usually do, that he is "going into the church." He cannot do that, because he is there already; all baptized people are "in" the church; they are the church.

DOROTHY L. SAYERS, *Begin Here,* 1941

Every ordination means the creation of a fresh unit of spiritual force. And as God chose your soul, chose that it should exist, so he chose, before the foundation of the world, your priesthood; determined that you and not some other should stand at his altar and minister to his people.

R. A. KNOX, *Retreat for Priests,* 1946

The repudiation of ordination as a sacrament demolished the caste system of clericalism and provided a sound basis for the priesthood of believers.

ROLAND H. BAINTON, *Here I Stand,* 1950

Methodism teaches that ordination by any established evangelical Church is valid. A letter from any Christian Church may be accepted as the only condition of membership.

C. C. SELECMAN, *The Methodist Primer,* 1953

The layman's new assurance has been gained at the expense of the parish minister. . . . Sooner or later the theologians of the Reformation traditions will have to face the question whether ordination means anything at all in their theology, and if so, what?

ROBERT PAUL, *Unity in Mid-Career,* 1963

[The bishop] should not confer holy orders on anyone, unless from positive signs he is morally certain of canonical fitness; otherwise he not only sins grievously, but also places himself in danger of sharing in the sins of others.

Roman Catholic Code of Canon Law, Can. 973

See also Call; Clergy; Minister· Ministry; Preachers; Priesthood; Priests; Sacraments; Vocation.

ORIGINAL SIN

Nothing good and nothing evil, on account of which we are deemed either laudable or blameworthy, is born with us, but is done by us; for we are born not fully developed, but with a capacity for either conduct; we are formed without either vice or virtue.

PELAGIUS (c. 370–c. 440), quoted in *The Anti-Pelagin Works of St. Augustine*

Every human being who is conceived by the coition of a man with a woman is born with original sin, subject to impiety and death, and therefore a child of wrath.

GRATIAN, *Decretum,* c. 1150

Death and all bodily miseries are among the pains of original sin.

ST. THOMAS AQUINAS, *Summa Theologiae* Ia, IIae, q. 85, 1272

Original sin seems to be a hereditary depravity and corruption of our nature, diffused into all parts of the soul, which first makes us liable to God's wrath.

JOHN CALVIN, *Institutes*, II, 1536

Original sin remains in Christians until they die, yet itself is mortified and continually dying. Its head is crushed in pieces, so that it cannot condemn us.

MARTIN LUTHER (1483–1546), *Table Talk*

If anyone asserts that the sin of Adam injured him alone and not his descendants, or that only in regard to himself alone did he lose the holiness and justice which he had from God and did not lose it for us as well; or that stained as he was by the sin of disobedience Adam transmitted death and affliction of body to all the human race but did not also transmit sin which is the death of the soul, let him be anathema.

Council of Trent, Session V, 1550

By which transgression, commonly called Original Sin, was the image of God utterly defiled in man; and he and his posterity of nature became enemies to God, slaves to Satan, and servants to sin.

Confession of Faith, Presbyterian Church of Scotland, August 1, 1560

If we come into the World infected and depraved with sinful Disposition, then Sin must be natural to us; and if natural, then necessary; and if necessary, then no Sin.

JOHN TAYLOR, *The Scripture—Doctrine of Original Sin*, 1746

The guilt a man has upon his soul at first existence, is one and simple, viz., the guilt of the original apostasy, the guilt by which the species first rebelled against God.

JONATHAN EDWARDS, *The Great Christian Doctrine of Original Sin Defended*, 1758

Wherever the Science of Ethics is acknowledged and taught, there the Article of Original Sin will be an Axiom of Faith in all classes . . . a fact acknowledged in all ages, and recognized, but not originating, in the Christian Scriptures.

SAMUEL TAYLOR COLERIDGE, *Aids to Reflections*, 1825

Each soul as it enters on existence, receives its nature from Him· and to affirm that this "nature is *itself* sinful," and that every cause partakes of the character of its effect, is not only to make God the author of sin, but to make Him *sinful* to boot!

CHAUNCEY GOODRICH, *Quarterly Christian Spectator*, June, 1829

Original sin is the effect of Adam's sin upon the constitution of his race, in consequence of his being their federal head and representative by a divine appointment or covenant.

LYMAN BEECHER, *Views on Theology*, 1836

The doctrine of original sin (assertion of the will) and of salvation (denial of the will) is the great truth which constitutes the essence of Christianity.

ARTHUR SCHOPENHAUER, "Religion," *Essays*, 1841

Original sin with us cannot be called sin, in the more ordinary sense of the word sin; it is a term denoting Adam's sin as transferred to us or the state to which Adam reduces his children.

JOHN HENRY NEWMAN, *Difficulties of Anglicans*, Vol. II, 1850

If there be a God, *since* there is a God, the human race is implicated in some terrible aboriginal calamity. It is out of joint with the purposes of its Creator. . . . Thus the doctrine of . . . original sin becomes to me almost as certain as that the world exists, and as the existence of God.

JOHN HENRY NEWMAN, *Apologia pro Vita Sua*, 1864

Original sin is at work everywhere.

KARL MARX, *Das Kapital,* I, 649, 1867

Original Sin . . . is no positive taint or corruption inherent in our nature, but a negative fact, the deprivation of an un-owed super-human gift intended by God for us—namely, *Ultimate Redemption.*

C. C. MARTINDALE, *God and the Super-natural,* 1920

What is the dogma of original sin but a means of making the things of the flesh enter a spiritual system?

JACQUES RIVIÈRE, *Études,* 1924

Original sin . . . has so totally corrupted human nature that man is incapable of any spiritual good and inclined to all evil.

W. H. T. DAU, *What Is Lutheranism?,* ed. by V. Ferm, 1930

We are all . . . tainted from birth with a tendency towards what we know as evil. But the dogma of original sin so extended as to embrace inherited guilt is a pure fabrication of occidental theology.

PAUL ELMER MORE, *The Catholic Faith,* 1931

The faithful priest accounts for man's in-born tendency to sin by tracing his descent from Adam. The modern biologist regards "original sin" as man's inheritance from the jungle.

ARTHUR KEITH, *Living Philosophies,* 1931

Original sin is not an inherited corruption, but it is an inevitable fact of human exis-tence, the inevitability of which is given by the nature of man's spirituality.

REINHOLD NIEBUHR, *An Interpretation of Christian Ethics,* 1935

The doctrine of original sin, and the con-quest of the natural man, so important in religion, is profoundly true from a psycho-logical point of view.

HENRY C. LINK, *The Return to Religion* 1936

Each of us takes his place in the center of his own world. But I am not the center of the world, or the standard of reference as between good and bad; I am not, and God is. In other words, from the beginning I put myself in God's place. This is my original sin.

WILLIAM TEMPLE, *Christianity and the Social Order,* 1942

The despair that lies in the Christian doc-trine of original sin is rooted in experience.

C. F. VON WEIZSÄCKER, *The History of Nature,* 1949

A concept of original sin is typical of a view of life which makes the past an authority over the present.

DAVID RIESMAN, *Psychiatry,* Vol. 13, no. 2, 1950

To reject the doctrine of original sin . . . was to fall victim to a shallow optimism . . . which led men to think that the mil-lennium was just around the corner wait-ing to be introduced by a society of ade-quately psycho-analyzed, prosperous Socialists.

C. E. M. JOAD, *The Recovery of Belief,* 1952

It has required the public atrocities com-mitted by the children of our Western civilization in our lifetime to extort from us the recognition that Original Sin is still alive in Western Man.

A. J. TOYNBEE, *An Historian's Ap-proach to Religion,* 1956

Judaism does not attribute man's constant backsliding to original sin. Every child is born completely untainted.

SIMON GREENBERG, *Patterns of Faith in America Today,* ed. F. E. Johnson, 1957

Sin is original in the sense of a permanent human tendency, and the Fall of man happened not once but is perpetual falling away from the life of loving obedience which God requires of us.

GEORGIA HARKNESS, *The Providence of God,* 1960

However we look at it, the mystery of original sin . . . indeed appears as the really massive and primordial fact of all human history. Without accepting it in faith, it seems neither possible to explain in any final sense the experimental postulates of modern psychology nor to give them any meaning.

MARC ORAISON, *Sin,* 1962

See also Adam; Antichrist; Baptism; Birth; Corruption; Death; Despair; Election; Fall, the; Foreknowledge; Free Will; Guilt; Human Nature; Intellectual Pride; Man: His Wickedness; Nature and Man; Pain; Predestination; Redemption; Salvation; Sin; Soul; Will.

ORTHODOX

And prove their doctrine orthodox,
By apostolic blows and knocks.

SAMUEL BUTLER, *Hudibras,* 1663

Every church is orthodox to itself; to others, erroneous or heretical.

JOHN LOCKE, *A Letter Concerning Toleration,* 1685

If we were all before the gates of Heaven and the question were put, "Which of you is orthodox?," the Jew, the Turk and the Christian would answer in unison, "I am."

IMMANUEL KANT, *Lecture at Königsberg,* 1775

Orthodox, n. An ox wearing the popular religious yoke.

AMBROSE BIERCE, *Devil's Dictionary,* 1906

See also Belief; Doctrine; Dogma; Faith; Fundamentalism; Heresy; Modernism; Neo-Orthodoxy; Orthodoxy; Religion.

ORTHODOXY

We may observe the behavior of some of the most zealous for orthodoxy, who have often great friendships and intimacies with vicious immoral men, provided they do but agree with them in the same scheme of belief.

JOSEPH ADDISON, *The Spectator,* 1714

Orthodoxy is my doxy—heterodoxy is another man's doxy.

WILLIAM WARBURTON (1698–1779) quoted by Joseph Priestley in *Memoirs*

Even the heretics and atheists, if they have had profundity, turn out after a while to be forerunners of some new orthodoxy. . . . .They yearn mightily in their own souls after the religious acceptance of a world interpreted in their own fashion.

GEORGE SANTAYANA, *Reason in Religion,* 1905

Strict orthodoxy . . . encourages a certain type of character structure. The "believer" is rated as sincere and wholehearted to the extent that he takes things on faith and exempts certain areas of experience from critical examination. . . . Thus . . . he is invited to remain immature.

H. A. OVERSTREET, *The Mature Mind,* 1949

Orthodoxy is characterized by a spirit, and a very proper one, of reverent agnosticism towards the central mysteries of the faith.

J. V. L. CASSERLEY, *Retreat from Christianity in the Modern World,* 1952

It was heresy that made orthodoxy necessary.

JAMES A. MARTIN, JR., *Fact, Fiction and Faith,* 1960

In Protestantism no system of orthodoxy can determine a man's faith. The faith is organically related to man's free spirit and thus is forever being forced to test the creeds and confessions which are worked out.

J. LESLIE DUNSTAN, *Protestantism,* 1962

OSTENTATION

Our moralism, name-in-print charity, is getting us nowhere. The "decent, godless" people have returned to God with no less of decency. The showily moral path is part of the organizational climb.

MARTIN E. MARTY, *The New Shape of American Religion,* 1958

OTHER

The other is infinitely distant from me, more distant than the farthest stars. I can wander through all the ways of space that are geometrically possible, traverse land and sea and fly in the upper air, without coming one pace nearer to where the other dwells. Nevertheless the other is infinitely near me.

KARL HEIM, *The Certitude of Faith,* 1923

OTHER WORLDS

For it is probable that different worlds have existed and will exist, some in the past and some in the future.

ORIGEN, *De Principiis,* c. 254

And to think that there may be more Worlds than one, is neither against Reason, or Scripture. If God glorify'd Himself in making one World, the more Worlds He made the greater must be His Glory.

B. L. B. FONTENELLE, *Plurality of Worlds,* 1686

Heaven has connection with other worlds. Its inhabitants are God's messengers through the creation. They have great trusts. In the progress of their endless being, they may have the care of other worlds.

WILLIAM ELLERY CHANNING (1780–1842), *Works*

It would not seem opposed to our faith to theorize that life may arise in many parts of the cosmos, in the course of God's ordinary providence and so develop through evolution that, when it is sufficiently organized, God infuses in it an immortal soul and makes it into a creature called man.

L. C. McHUGH, *Sign,* December, 1961

OTHER WORLDLINESS

The evil bred by the traditional conception of God may be called by the general name of "otherworldliness." It would be difficult to evaluate the harm done to humanity in the past by the conviction that the real destination of man is the World to Come.

J. H. LEUBA, *Psychology of Religious Mysticism,* 1925

OWNERSHIP

The Christian conscience cannot admit as just a social order which either denies, in the main, or renders practically impossible or vain the natural right of possession, both over consumer goods and over the means of production.

POPE PIUS XII, *Broadcast,* September 1, 1943

No more proletarians; all property owners; this must be the slogan of those striving to restore society to a true human and Christian basis.

EMMANUEL SUHARD, *The Church Today,* 1953

See also Capitalism; Possessions; Property; Wealth.

PACIFISM

It is not good . . . nought of good
Can spring from mutual slaughter. Lo, I hate
Triumph and domination, wealth and ease
Thus sadly won. . . .
Shall I deal death on these

Even though they seek to slay us?
. . . Killing these
Must breed anguish. . . .
Better I deem it, if my kinsmen strike,
To face them weaponless and bare my
breast
To shaft and spear, than answer blow with
blow.
> *The Song Celestial*, Sir Edwin Arnold's translation of *Bhagavad-Gita*, 5th to 2nd century B.C.

We utterly deny all outward wars and strife, and fightings with outward weapons, for any end, or under any pretense whatever; this is our testimony to the whole world. The Spirit of Christ by which we are guided is not changeable.
> *Declaration from the Quakers to King Charles the Second of England*, 1660

What, then, are the duties of a subject who believes that all war is incompatible with his religion, but whose governors engage in a war and demand his service? We answer explicitly, *It is his duty mildly and temperately, yet firmly, to refuse to serve.*
> JONATHAN DYMOND, *Essay on War*, 1823

Let the preachers repentantly resolve that they will never again put Christ in khaki or serve as recruiting officers.
> *Christian Century*, January 31, 1924

A mystical pacifism, which does not demand at least as much courage and as many risks as the religion of war, is simply a mask for weakness and fear.
> GUSTAVE THIBON, *War and Love*, 1946

The Church seeks to maintain a fellowship of all who sincerely follow the guidance of conscience. It does, however, recommend that as a matter of Christian conviction and practice, its membership support the historic position of the Church, namely non-participation in military training and service and the war system in general.
> *Statement*, Church of the Brethren, 1948

When all considerations except those of ultimate religious obedience are eliminated, it seems that the ultimate principle of love would demand the pacifist position.
> EDWARD LEROY LONG, JR., *The Christian Response to the Atomic Crisis*, 1950

True Christian pacifism is based on the recognition that the distinctive and typical Christian attitude to evil is not resistance, but suffering, willingly undergone on behalf of others.
> W. R. FORRESTER, *Christian Vocation*, 1951

We therefore reject the concept of vocational pacifism. . . . We must maintain firmly that to put pacifism aside as a special "calling" for a few to keep the conscience of Christendom alive is a misinterpretation of the Gospel ethic.
> *Peace Is the Will of God: A Testimony to the World Council of Churches*, statement prepared by the Historic Peace Churches and International Fellowship for Reconciliation, October, 1953

See also Armaments; Conscience; Conscientious Objector; Conscription; Force; Freedom, Religious; Military Service; Nonresistance; Nonviolence; Nonviolent Resistance; Nuclear War; Peace; Soldier; Violence; War.

PACIFISTS

And we, who were filled full of war, and slaughter of one another, and every kind of evil, have from out of the whole earth each changed our weapons of war, our swords into ploughshares and our pikes into farming tools, and we farm piety, righteousness, the love of man, faith, and hope.
> ST. JUSTIN MARTYR, *Dialogue with Trypho*, c. 135

Pacifist Christians have not faced sufficiently the charge that they make an absolute of peace at the expense of justice.

The Christian Hope and the Task of the Churches (survey brochure for the Evanston Assembly of World Conference of Churches), 1954

See also Conscience; Conscientious Objector; Pacifism.

PAGAN

The pagan who concerns himself with the teaching of God is like to the High Priest.
Sanhedrin, Talmud, c. 500

See also Paganism; Pantheism.

PAGANISM

Paganism hides itself in the uniform of the Church. Paganism has only taken the oath of allegiance, taken the cross, but is Paganism still, outvotes the true men by millions of majority, carries the bag, spends the treasure, writes the tracts, elects the minister, and persecutes the true believer.
RALPH WALDO EMERSON, *North American Review,* April, 1866

Paganism is better than pantheism, for paganism is free to imagine divinities, while pantheism is forced to pretend, in a priggish way, that all things are equally divine.
G. K. CHESTERTON, *The Catholic Church and Conversion,* 1926

Men do not live long without gods; but when the gods of the New Paganism come they will not be merely insufficient . . . nor merely false; they will be evil. . . . The New Paganism, foolishly expecting satisfaction, will fall, before it knows where it is, into Satanism.
HILAIRE BELLOC, *Essays of a Catholic,* 1931

The new Paganism is the resultant of two forces which have converged to produce it: appetite and the sense of doom.
HILAIRE BELLOC, *Essays of a Catholic,* 1931

The idolatrous worship of organized human power is the fatal error which is common to all the varieties of our postwar paganism. The error is so profound that the triumph of this paganism could spell nothing but disaster for mankind.
A. J. TOYNBEE, *Christian Century,* March 10, 1937

See also Pagan; Religion.

PAIN

For after all, evil and pain are identical; it is those unable to see pain as the natural result of doing evil that continue to do evil.
Dhammapda, c. 5th century B.C.

Certain pains are bad in an absolute manner, others are bad only in so far as they deprive us of some good.
ARISTOTLE, *Nicomachean Ethics,* c. 340 B.C.

Pain is either an evil for the body—and if so, let the body state its case—or for the soul; but the soul can maintain its own unclouded calm, and refuse to view it as an evil.
MARCUS AURELIUS, *Meditations,* c. 170 A.D.

Considered in themselves, painful things can never be loved, but considered in the light of their source—as ordained by Providence and the will of God—they are infinitely delightful.
ST. FRANCIS OF SALES, *Treatise on the Love of God,* 1607

No pain, no palm; no thorns, no throne; no gall, no glory; no cross, no crown.

WILLIAM PENN, *No Cross, No Crown,* 1669

The problems that vex us here will be fully solved hereafter; eternity will explain this brief life. This is the wondrous music which we wring from the jarring notes of the world's pain and sin.

MORRIS JOSEPH, *Judaism as Creed and Life,* 1903

Man has ever risen near to God by the altar-stairs of pain and sorrow.

S. A. ADLER, *The Discipline of Sorrow,* 1906

There is a kind and quality of pain that is creative, curative, redemptive, and . . . this is a kind of pain which man is privileged to share with God.

B. H. STREETER, *Reality,* 1926

Pain and death have become the means of redemption and sanctification for every man who does not deny Christ.

POPE PIUS XII, *Address,* November 12, 1943

Pain at a certain intensity is transmuted to the highest joy and all the great tragic poets of the Occident know it.

ROMAIN ROLLAND (1866–1944), *Letter to D. K. Roy,* quoted in D. K. Roy's *Among the Great*

Pain in the human world is the birth of personality, its fight for its own nature.

NICHOLAS BERDYAEV, *Slavery and Freedom,* 1944

In the garden of humanity, ever since it ceased to be called the earthly paradise, there has ripened, and will always ripen one of the bitter fruits of original sin: pain.

POPE PIUS XII, *Address,* July 14, 1950

Pain and death always have the last word in this world of ours. . . . There is enough pain in one alley of a big city slum or in one hospital ward to convince even the dreamiest optimist that life is not naturally good.

OSWALD C. J. HOFFMANN, *Life Crucified,* 1959

The pearl of great price always begins as a pain in the oyster's stomach!

JOHN E. LARGE, *The Small Needle of Doctor Large,* 1962

The greatest pain is the one you can't tell others about.

Proverb

See also Adversity; Affliction; Behavior; Euthanasia; Evil; Hell; Serenity; Sin; Sorrow; Suffering.

PANTHEISM

The religion of beauty, imagination, and philosophy, without constraint moral or intellectual, a religion speculative and self-indulgent. Pantheism, indeed, is the great deceit which awaits the Age to come.

JOHN HENRY NEWMAN, *Difficulties of Anglicans,* 1850

Aspirants to a philosophic religion turn, as a rule, more hopefully nowadays towards idealistic pantheism than towards the older dualistic theism.

WILLIAM JAMES, *Pragmatism,* 1907

Pantheism inevitably strengthens those forces in religion which tend to sanctify the real rather than to inspire the ideal.

REINHOLD NIEBUHR, *Christian Century,* April 22, 1926

Confronted with a cancer or a slum the Pantheist can say, "If you could only see it from the divine point of view, you would realize that this also is God." The Christian replies, "Don't talk damned nonsense."

C. S. LEWIS, *The Case for Christianity,* 1943

There is the fact of the nearness of God, what the books call his *immanence*. Push it too far and you have *pantheism*—a God lost in the world to which he is near.

CLELAND B. MCAFEE, *Near to the Heart of God,* 1954

If I am part of God, if the Self at its core is God, then I cannot deny Him, nor He deny me, and there is no relationship, for He is constrained by His being as I, and He is not the only necessary being, for I am necessary too, and He exists by my will as much as I do by His.

ANNE FREEMANTLE, *The Age of Belief,* 1955

If pantheism is true, God will die when the world dies.

DAVID E. TRUEBLOOD, *Philosophy of Religion,* 1957

Brahmanism moved finally into a thoroughgoing pantheism and prepared the way for Buddhism by developing a philosophy which denied that the Vedas were in themselves sufficient for salvation.

MARTIN A. LARSON, *The Religion of the Occident,* 1959

See also God: Considered as Impersonal; God: His Omnipotence; God: His Omnipresence; God, Unorthodox Comments About; Idolatry; Man Indwelt by God; Nature; Nature and God; Paganism; Religion, Natural; Soul and God.

PARABLES

From Creation to Revelation all is parable.

ABBA MARI, *Minat Kenaot,* c. 1300 A.D.

Religious knowledge is obliged to express the invisible by the visible, the eternal by the temporal, spiritual realities by sensible images. It can speak only in parables.

AUGUSTE SABATIER, *Outlines of a Philosophy of Religion,* 1879

Statements about God . . . are in effect parables, which are referred, by means of the proper name "God," out of our experience in a certain direction.

IAN CROMBIE, *New Essays in Philosophical Theology,* ed. Flew and MacIntyre, 1955

PARACLETE. See
HOLY SPIRIT

PARADISE

But joyous on that day shall be the inmates of Paradise, in their employ. In shades, on bridal couches reclining, they and their spouses: Therein shall they have fruit and shall have whatever they require. Peace! shall be the word on the part of a merciful Lord.

Koran, 7th century A.D.

The legend of Paradise appears in almost all folklore—in Egypt, Tibet, Babylonia, Persia, Greece, Polynesia, Mexico, etc. Most of these Edens had forbidden trees, and were supplied with serpents or dragons that stole immortality from men, or otherwise poisoned Paradise.

WILL DURANT, *Our Oriental Heritage,* 1935

See also Heaven.

PARADOXES

The Christian religion has deposited upon the altar of wisdom the most profound and most beautiful set of paradoxes ever laid there: Defeat with lips to the Bugle of Victory; Hopelessness burning with Expectation; Sadness radiant with Love; Darkness dazzled with Morning; Death shaken with the song of immortal Life!

WILLIAM L. SULLIVAN, *Epigrams and Criticisms in Miniature,* 1936

It is the great paradox, so it seems, of Christianity that it urges us to attain to completest self-development yet to endure the total loss of ourselves.

GUSTAVE THIBON, *Christianity and Freedom,* 1952

PARDON. See
FORGIVENESS

PARENTS

The joys of parents are secret; and so are their griefs and fears; they cannot utter the one; nor they will not utter the other. Children sweeten labors; but they make misfortunes more bitter.
FRANCIS BACON, *Essays,* 1597

Every noble youth looks back, as to the chiefest joy which this world's honor ever gave him, to the moment when first he saw his father's eyes flash with pride, and his mother turn away her head, lest he should take her tears for tears of sorrow.
JOHN RUSKIN, *A Joy Forever,* 1857

Parents hold from nature their right of training the children to whom they have given birth, with the obligation superadded of shaping and training the education of their little ones to the end for which God vouchsafed the privilege of transmitting life.
POPE LEO XIII, *Sapientiae Christianae,* 1890

An ounce of parent is worth a pound of the clergy.
Spanish Proverb

See also Children; Daughters; Education, Parents' Rights in; Family; Father; Home; Husband; Marriage; Maternity; Mother; Son.

PAROCHIAL SCHOOL. See
EDUCATION, PAROCHIAL

PASSIONS

As rain does not break through a well-thatched house, passion will not break through a well-reflecting mind.
Dhammapada, c. 5th century B.C.

The passion of a heedless man grows like a creeper, and he runs from life to life, like a monkey seeking fruit in the forest.
Dhammapada, c. 5th century B.C.

If men's passions are deep, their divinity is shallow.
Chuang-tzu, c. 300 B.C.

Chastise your passions, that they may not chastise you.
EPICTETUS, *Enchiridion,* c. 110

Passion is an unnatural movement of the soul that is the result of a love without reason, or of an irrational aversion for some concrete object.
ST. MAXIMUS THE CONFESSOR, *Centuries of Charity,* c. 626

The passions that produce war and battles and the beginnings of all quarrels, are due without doubt to the fraudulent wiles of the devil.
POPE NICHOLAS I to the Bulgarians in his *Responsa,* 866

The pious man . . . subdues his passions, keeping them in bonds, but giving them their share in order to satisfy them as regards food, drink, cleanliness, etc.
JUDAH HALEVI, *Cuzari,* II, c. 1135

There are some passions so close to virtues that there is danger lest we be deceived by the doubtful distinction between them.
DESIDERIUS ERASMUS, *Enchiridion,* 1501

Pure prayer directed to heaven subdues passion, for it is a citadel inaccessible to the enemy.
DESIDERIUS ERASMUS, *Enchiridion,* 1501

There is no passion in the mind of man so weak but it mates and masters the fear of death.
FRANCIS BACON, *Essays,* 1625

We are ne'er like angels till our passion dies.
THOMAS DEKKER, *The Honest Whore,* 1630

Passions are spiritual Rebels, and raise sedition against the understanding.
BEN JONSON, *Discoveries,* 1641

Passion is a sort of Fever in the Mind, which ever leaves us weaker than it found us. . . . It may not unfitly be termed, the Mob of the Man, that commits a Riot upon his Reason.
WILLIAM PENN, *Some Fruits of Solitude,* 1693

Passion, joined with power, produceth thunder and ruin.
THOMAS FULLER, *Gnomologia,* 1732

A man in a passion rides a wild horse.
BENJAMIN FRANKLIN, *Poor Richard's Almanac,* 1749

No passion or affection, with which we are born, can be in itself sinful: it becomes so, only by wilful or careless indulgence.
JONATHAN MAYHEW, *Sermons,* 1755

Truth needs not the service of passion; yea, nothing so disserves it, as passion when set to serve it. The *Spirit of Truth* is the *Spirit of Meekness.*
SAMUEL TAYLOR COLERIDGE, *Aids to Reflection,* 1825

Nothing great in the world has been accomplished without passion.
G. W. F. HEGEL (1770–1831), *Philosophy of History,* publ. posth.

We are not indebted to the Reason of man for any of the great achievements which are the landmarks of human action and human progress. . . . Man is only truly great when he acts from the passions; never irresistible but when he appeals to the imagination.
BENJAMIN DISRAELI, *Coningsby,* 1844

Even he who is lost through passion has not lost so much as he who has lost passion, for the former had the possibility.
SÖREN KIERKEGAARD, *Postscript,* 1846

The power of the soul for good is in proportion to the strength of its passions.
COVENTRY PATMORE, *The Rod, the Root, and the Flower,* 1895

It is by their passions that men know they belong to the same race. They all slip in the same direction; they roll down the same slope.
FRANÇOIS MAURIAC, *Holy Thursday,* 1944

When passion breaks away from the deep life of a man it can never enlarge him, it has nothing to say to the heart; it can never be a marriage of gods, only an animal mauling its prey.
GERALD VANN, *The Heart of Man,* 1945

Today—psychologists write with the frankness of Freud or Kinsey on the sexual passions of mankind, but blush and grow silent when the religious passions come in view.
G. W. ALLPORT, *The Individual and His Religion,* 1951

Theologians have always recognized that passions may overwhelm the person suddenly and completely to the point where freedom of choice does not exist and responsibility is not present.
J. DOMINIAN, *Psychiatry and the Christian,* 1962

See also Anger; Body; Fanaticism; Feelings; Love, Physical; Lust; Marriage; Reason; Repentance; Servitude; Sex; Sexual Desire; Sexual Intercourse; Sexuality; Temperance; Vice.

PASTOR

As great as is the difference between the rational and irrational part of creation, should be the superiority of the pastor over the flock.

> St. John Chrysostom, *On the Priest-hood*, c. 385

The pastors are to be fervidly zealous about the inner wants of their subjects, without neglecting the care of their outer wants.

> Pope St. Gregory the Great, *Pastoral Care*, 590

A pastor is the deputy of Christ for the reduction of man to the obedience of God.

> George Herbert, *A Priest to the Temple*, 1632

Pastor: One employed by the wicked to prove to them by his example that virtue doesn't pay.

> H. L. Mencken, *A Little Book in C Major*, 1916

The pastor . . . much more than the psychiatrist, holds the key to a patient's confidence; he, in a much deeper sense than can ever be applied to the physician, is a physician of the soul.

> John Rathobone Oliver, *Psychiatry and Mental Health*, 1936

The pastor who rules his parish with a rod of iron is still with us. By such a pastor I mean one who uses social pressures and *ad hoc* sanctions to enforce his rulings, arbitrary and otherwise. One who takes advantage of the immunity of his pulpit to beat down opposition and advantage of respect for the cloth to enforce his own opinions.

> George W. Casey, *Boston Pilot*, August 5, 1961

Let pastors recognize and promote the dignity as well as the responsibility of the laity in the Church. Let them willingly employ their prudent advice. Let them confidently assign duties to them in the service of the Church, allowing them freedom and room for action. . . . Let them consider with fatherly love the projects,

suggestions and desires proposed by the laity. . . . Let pastors respectfully acknowledge that just freedom which belongs to everyone in the earthly city.

> *Constitution on the Church*, Second Vatican Council, November, 1965

See also Clergy; Clergy, Criticism of; Ministry; Preachers; Priesthood; Priests; Theologians.

PATHS

Let us not be uneasy that the different roads we may pursue, as believing them the shortest, to that of our last abode; but, following the guidance of a good conscience, let us be happy in the hope that by these different paths we shall all meet in the end.

> Thomas Jefferson, *Letter to Miles King*, September 26, 1814

So many religions, so many paths to reach the same goal. I have practiced Hinduism, Islam, Christianity, and in Hinduism again, the ways of the different sects. I have found that it is the same God towards whom all are directing their steps, though along different paths.

> Sri Ramakrishna (1836–1886), *Gospel of Sri Ramakrishna*

As one can ascend to the top of a house by means of a ladder or a bamboo or a staircase or a rope, so divers are the ways and means to approach God, and every religion in the world shows one of these ways.

> Sri Ramakrishna, *His Life and Sayings*, ed. F. M. Müller, 1899

How often do we hear it said: "It doesn't matter what we believe. By different roads we are all heading for the same goal." What assurance have we that all the different roads, mapped out by mere human beings, lead to the same goal?

> John J. Wade, *Conquering with Christ*, 1942

As different streams having different sources and with wanderings crooked or straight, all reach the sea, so Lord, the different paths which men take, guided by their different tendencies, all lead to Thee.

> From a Hindu Prayer, said daily by millions, quoted in J. James' *The Way of Mysticism,* 1950

Let a Christian follow the precepts of his own faith, let a Hindu and a Jew follow theirs. If they strive long enough, they will ultimately discover God, Who runs like a seam under the crusts of rituals and forms.

> SWAMI NIKHILANANDA, *Perspectives on a Troubled Decade,* ed. Bryson, Finklestein and MacIver, 1950

Go Godward: thou wilt find a road.
> Russian Proverb

See also Belief; Denominationalism; Division; Pluralism; Religious Conflict; Rivalry; Salvation; Sects and Sectarianism; Tao; Tolerance; Truths, Conflict of; Unity.

PATIENCE

Patience is the companion of wisdom.
> ST. AUGUSTINE, *On Patience,* c. 425

Rail not at fickle Fortune! Those who eat
The fruit of bitter Patience find it sweet.
> SHAIKH SAADI, *Gulistan,* c. 1265

Study to be patient in bearing the defects of others and their infirmities be they what they may: for thou hast many things which he must bear withal.
> THOMAS À KEMPIS, *Imitation of Christ,* 1441

All men commend patience, although few be willing to practice it.
> THOMAS À KEMPIS, *Imitation of Christ,* 1441

Be patient with everyone, but above all with thyself. I mean, do not be disheart-ened by your imperfections, but always rise up with fresh courage.
> ST. FRANCIS OF SALES (1567–1622), quoted in *The Spirit of St. Francis de Sales,* ed. J. P. Camus

Patience, the beggar's virtue.
> PHILIP MASSINGER, *A New Way to Pay Old Debts,* 1633

They also serve who only stand and wait.
> JOHN MILTON, *Sonnet on His Blindness,* c. 1650

If God has taken away all means of seeking remedy, there is nothing left but patience.
> JOHN LOCKE, *Treatise on Government,* 1690

Patience is sorrow's salve.
> CHARLES CHURCHILL, *The Prophecy of Famine,* 1763

It is an easy thing to talk of patience to the afflicted.
> WILLIAM BLAKE, *The Four Zoas,* 1797

Faith, Love, and Hope once felt, in a peaceful, sociable hour, a plastic impulse in their nature; together they set to work and created a lovely image, a Pandora in the higher sense, namely Patience.
> J. W. VON GOETHE (1749–1832), *Maxims and Reflections*

Patience, n. A minor form of despair, disguised as a virtue.
> AMBROSE BIERCE, *Devil's Dictionary,* 1906

He preacheth patience that never knew pain.
> Proverb

See also Charity; Peace; Resignation; Serenity; Suffering.

PATRIOTISM

Next to the love of God, the love of country is the best preventive of crime. He who is proud of his country will be particularly cautious not to do anything which is calculated to disgrace it.

GEORGE BORROW, *The Bible in Spain,* 1843

Your Country should be your Temple. God at the summit, a People of equals at the base.

GIUSEPPE MAZZINI, *The Duties of Man,* 1858

As religion is imitated and mocked by hypocrisy, so public duty is parodied by patriotism.

J. E. THOROLD ROGERS, *Six Centuries of Work and Wages,* 1885

Let every man honor and love the land of his birth and the race from which he springs and keep their memory green. It is a pious and honorable duty.

THEODORE ROOSEVELT, *Speech,* 1888

Patriotism is . . . to most men, a moral necessity. It meets and satisfies that desire for a strong, disinterested enthusiasm in life which is deeply implanted in our nature.

W. E. H. LECKY, *Democracy and Liberty,* 1896

Standing as I do in view of God and eternity, I realize that patriotism is not enough. I must have no hatred or bitterness toward anyone.

EDITH CAVELL, to the English chaplain just before her execution at Brussels by the Germans for spying, October 11, 1915

The religion of Christ has made of patriotism a law. A perfect Christian must perforce be a perfect patriot.

DESIRÉ MERCIER, *Voix de la Guerre,* ed. Thone, 1937

Patriotism is classified under the virtue of piety. Filial piety makes us respect and love our parents; patriotic piety makes us

true, loyal citizens, loving our country as our parent.

JOHN T. MCNICHOLAS, *No Wall Between God and the Child,* 1947

It is when patriotism assumes the "supernatural sanction" of religion that an explosive mixture appears leading almost inevitably to war.

W. R. FORRESTER, *Christian Vocation,* 1951

I believe that love of country, for its full, true flowering, must be seen in the context of our country's relation to the universal good of humanity.

JOHN LA FARGE, *An American Amen,* 1958

Patriotism, once the last refuge of the scoundrel, now has become the first refuge of the fool.

JOHN COURTNEY MURRAY, *We Hold These Truths,* 1960

See also Allegiance; Conscientious Objector; Loyalty; Nationalism; Rebellion; Sedition; State, the; Treason; War; War, Defense of.

PEACE

Ask not that events should happen as you will, but let your will be that events should happen as they do, and you shall have peace.

EPICTETUS, *Manual of,* c. 110 A.D.

It is one thing to see the land of peace from a wooded ridge . . . and another to tread the road that leads to it.

ST. AUGUSTINE, *Confessions,* vii, XXI, 397

Even in waging war, cherish the spirit of a peace-maker; that, by conquering those whom you attack, you may lead them back to the advantages of peace.

ST. AUGUSTINE, *To Publicola,* 598

Amidst the calm and tranquillity of peace the human race accomplishes most freely and easily its given work. . . . Whence it is manifest that universal peace is the best of those things that are ordained for our beatitude.
DANTE, *De Monarchia*, Bk. I, ch. 4, c. 1300

His will is our peace.
DANTE, "Paradise," *Divine Comedy*, c. 1310

All men desire peace, but few desire the things that make for peace.
THOMAS À KEMPIS, *Imitation of Christ*, 1441

No man may live here without some trouble. Therefore he that can best suffer shall have most peace.
THOMAS À KEMPIS, *Imitation of Christ*, 1441

The most disadvantageous peace is better than the most just war.
DESIDERIUS ERASMUS, *Adagia*, 1508

Let human prudence say what it likes and reason as it pleases, it is impossible to produce true temporal peace and tranquillity by things repugnant or opposed to the peace and happiness of eternity.
SILVIO ANTONIANO (1540–1603), *The Christian Education of Youth*

The fewer desires, the more peace.
THOMAS WILSON, *Maxims of Piety and Christianity*, c. 1755

It is absurd to seek peace while rejecting God. For where God is left out, justice is left out, and where justice is lacking there can be no hope of peace.
PIUS X, *Supremi apostolatus*, October 4, 1903

The most solid and satisfying peace is that which comes from this constant spiritual warfare.
WOODROW WILSON, *Address*, May, 1911

Peace at any price can be the abnegation of morality entirely, the refusal of even a negative contribution to righteouness.
P. T. FORSYTH, *The Christian Ethic of War*, 1916

The world can be at peace only if life is stable, and there can be no stability where the will is in rebellion, where there is not tranquillity of spirit and a sense of justice, of freedom, and of right.
WOODROW WILSON, *Address*, to U.S. Senate, January 22, 1917

Peace is self-control at its widest,—at the width where the "self" has been lost, and interest has been transferred to coordinations wider than personality
ALFRED NORTH WHITEHEAD, *Adventures of Ideas*, 1933

Without repentance those who have created peace through their power imagine that they have created pure peace; and suffer from the delusion that the enemies of their peace are God's enemies.
REINHOLD NIEBUHR, *Beyond Tragedy*, 1937

Peace is that state in which fear of any kind is unknown.
JOHN BUCHAN, *Pilgrim's Way*, 1940

Only when we feel that through all our vicissitudes some unfathomable purpose runs, and that by meeting life nobly and courageously we can co-operate in the fulfillment of that purpose, do we find peace.
ALICE HEGAN RICE, *Happiness Road*, 1942

Peace is essentially a moral fact, and only subordinately a political fact as a means to the end; peace is above all an act of reconciliation.
LUIGI STURZO, *Address to Liturgical Conference*, Chicago, October, 1943

Either for God or against God . . . Upon that choice hangs the fate of the world. In

every department of life, in politics and economics, in the sciences and arts, in the State and in domestic life we follow God's laws to peace or bypass them into chaos.
RICHARD J. CUSHING, *Permanent Industrial Peace,* 1946

Since wars begin in the minds of men, it is in the minds of men that the defenses of peace must be constructed.
Preamble to UNESCO Charter, 1946

The world will believe in peace only when the Churches will demonstrate that it can exist.
LECOMTE DU NOÜY, *Human Destiny,* 1947

The Assembly believes that an international order conformed to the will of God and established in His peace can be achieved only through the reconciliation which Christ makes possible.
The Evanston Report, ed. W. A. Visser 't Hooft, 1955

No more war, war never again! Peace, it is peace which must guide the destinies of people and of all mankind.
POPE PAUL VI, *Address to the United Nations,* October, 1965

See also Anxiety; Armaments; Buddhism and Christianity; Concord; Fear; Force; Happiness; Harmony; Heaven; Hope; Internationalism; Jesus Christ; Joy; Nonresistance; Nonviolence; Nonviolent Resistance; Nuclear War; Order; Pacifism; Pacifists; Patience; Peace of Mind; Rebellion; Serenity; Silence; Soldier; Tranquillity; Troubles; Victory; War, Condemnation of; War, Defense of; War, Just.

PEACE OF MIND

For nowhere can a mind find a retreat more full of peace or more free from care than his own soul.
MARCUS AURELIUS, *Meditations, c.* 170

As for our proper peace, we have it double with God; here below by faith, and hereafter above by sight. But all peace we have here, be it public or peculiar, is rather a solace to our misery, than any assurance of our felicity.
ST. AUGUSTINE, *The City of God,* 426

Let no temporal things be the cause of thy peace; for then wilt thou be as worthless and fragile as they. You would have such a peace in common with the brutes; let thine be that of the angels, which proceeds from truth.
GUIGES DU CHASTEL (1084–1137), *Meditations*

The Christian has a deep, silent, hidden peace, which the world sees not, like some well in a retired and shady place. . . . What he is when left to himself and to his God, that is his true life.
JOHN HENRY NEWMAN, *Parochial and Plain Sermons,* Vol. 5, 1843

Nothing can bring you peace but yourself.
RALPH WALDO EMERSON, "Self-Reliance," *Essays,* 1844

Get but that "peace of God which passeth understanding," and the questions of the understanding will cease from puzzling and pedantic scruples be at rest.
WILLIAM JAMES, *The Will to Believe and Other Essays,* 1896

No one can get inner peace by pouncing on it, by vigorously willing to have it. Peace is a margin of power around our daily need. Peace is a consciousness of springs too deep for earthly droughts to dry up. Peace is the gift not of volitional struggle but of spiritual hospitality.
HARRY EMERSON FOSDICK, *Radio Address,* January 6, 1946

Lasting peace of mind is impossible apart from peace with God; yet enduring peace with God comes only when a man is ready to surrender his own peace of mind.
A. ROY ECKARDT, *Christian Century,* November 17, 1954

The peace-of-mind cult readily turns into religious narcissism. . . . Here is piety concentrating on its own navel.

A. ROY ECKARDT, *Christian Century,* November 17, 1954

The Bible nowhere calls upon men to go out in search of peace of mind. It does call upon men to go out in search of God and the things of God.

ABBA HILLEL SILVER, *Where Judaism Differed,* 1957

Giving oneself to God, even in the contemplative life, is no way to get peace of mind, but rather to get into the thick of the fighting.

JEAN DANIELOU, *The Lord of History,* 1958

See also Affliction; Blessedness; Mind; Misery; Peace; Serenity; Suffering; Tranquillity; Troubles.

PENITENCE

Before God created the world, he created Penitence and said to him: "I am going to create a man in the world, on condition that every time he turns to you you are ready to forgive him his sins."

Zohar, c. 1290

The time will come when thou wilt wish for one day or hour to amend, and I know not whither thou shalt obtain it.

THOMAS À KEMPIS, *Imitation of Christ,* 1441

Concerning penitence or penance we teach that it consists in the acknowledgement of sins and genuine trust in God, who forgives them all for Christ's sake.

MARTIN LUTHER, *Sermon,* 1528

We seek sensible consolations impatiently, out of fear of lacking penitence. Why not let our penitence take the shape of renouncing the consolation we so eagerly seek?

FRANÇOIS FÉNELON (1651–1715), *Spiritual Letters*

There is no virtue in penance and fasting, which waste the body; they are only fanatical and monkish.

IMMANUEL KANT, *Lecture at Königsberg,* 1775

The notion of the need of penance and expiation is lost in proportion as belief in God is weakened, and the idea of an original sin and of a first rebellion of man against God becomes confused and disappears.

POPE PIUS XI, *Caritate Christi Compulsi,* 1932

If penance is being practiced as it should be, it is an act of prayer—positively uniting us with the Passion, positively expressing love, positively surrendering self.

HUBERT VAN ZELLER, *We Die Standing Up,* 1949

See also Compassion; Confession; Forgiveness; Grace; Guilt; Jesus Christ as Saviour; Justification; Mercy; Punishment; Repentance; Sin.

PENTECOST

If God can communicate His Power to a human nature made one with His Divine Person in the Incarnation, why can not He continue to communicate it through other human natures made one with Him by the unifying spirit of Pentecost?

FULTON J. SHEEN, *The Fullness of Christ,* 1935

Pentecost marks not only the beginning of the church as an organized society, but also the recognition of its unity. . . . That there is a basic oneness of the Christian community is a reality which Pentecost never allows us to forget.

SAMUEL MCCREA CAVERT, *National Council Outlook,* May, 1959

See also Catholicism; Holy Spirit; Light; Spirit; Unity.

PENTECOSTAL FIRES

The pentecostal fires have been stolen from the altar of God, and now burn as tongues of fire in those who grind the altars into dust.

> FULTON J. SHEEN, *Radio Sermon*, April 6, 1941

PEOPLE

The voice of the people is the voice of God.

> ALCUIN, *Epistles*, c. 800 A.D.

The people comprise the patient thrust of the activities of the human intellect and human labor multiplying in individual lives at the ground level of civilized existence.

> JACQUES MARITAIN, *Christianity and Existence*, 1944

PEOPLE OF GOD

Becoming a people of God means rather that the attributes of God revealed to it, justice and love, are to be made effective in its own life, in the lives of its members with one another.

> MARTIN BUBER, *At the Turning*, 1952

PERFECTION

Man reacheth perfection by each being intent on his own duty.

> *Bhagavad-Gita*, c. 500 B.C. or later

A man will reach perfection if he does his duty as an act of worship to the Lord.

> *Bhagavad-Gita*, between 5th and 2nd centuries B.C.

The creature, by the very fact of its creation, can only be imperfect. God will bring it gradually to perfection.

> ST. IRENAEUS, *Adversus Haereses*, c. 175

I know of no one man perfect in all things at once but still human . . . except Him alone who for us clothed Himself with humanity.

> ST. CLEMENT OF ALEXANDRIA, *The Miscellanies*, c. 200

When the soul has passed through all the virtues and reached the summit of perfection, it leaves the world and goes away.

> ORIGEN (185–254), *In Numeros Hom.*, XXVII

True perfection consists not in surrendering vice out of slavish fear of punishment, nor in practicing virtue like merchants who traffic in a business-like hope of reward and in a bargained-for asceticism of life, but . . . in having but one fear, the loss of God's friendship.

> ST. GREGORY OF NYSSA (c. 335–395), *De Vita Moysis*

Since all the faithful together and separately constitute the one and the same temple of God, it is necessary that it be perfect in each one as it must be perfect in the whole; because, even if the beauty is not equal in all the members, nor the merits equal in such a great diversity of parts, the bond of charity produces the communion in beauty.

> POPE ST. LEO THE GREAT (440–461), quoted by Pope John XXIII

Man's perfection is to be like God . . . in unity of spirit, whereby man not only becomes one with God in the sense that he wills the same things as God, but in the sense that he is unable to will what God does not will.

> WILLIAM OF ST. THIERRY (1085–1148), *Epistola ad Fratres de Monte Dei*, no. 16

It is not enough to serve God in the hope of future reward; a man must do right and avoid wrong because he is a man, and owes it to his manhood to seek perfection.

> MAIMONIDES, *Siraj*, 1168

The service of God is not intended for God's perfection; it is intended for our perfection.

MAIMONIDES, *Guide for the Perplexed,* 1190

If thou desire to mount up to the height of perfection, thou must begin manly and set the axe to the root, that thou mayest root up and destroy all inordinate inclination to thyself and to all private and material good.

THOMAS À KEMPIS, *Imitation of Christ,* 1441

Many, mistaking *devotions* for *devotion,* imagine perfection to consist in reciting a great number of prayers, in joining sundry religious societies.

ADOLPHE TANQUERAY, *The Spiritual Life,* 1490

If thou wilt be perfect, sell thy will, and give to the poor in spirit; come to Christ through meekness and follow Him to Calvary and the grave.

ST. JOHN OF THE CROSS (1542–1591), *Maxims of*

Generally speaking, in order to reach perfection, it is necessary that a certain space of time be regularly devoted to mental prayer.

ST. FRANCIS OF SALES, *Introduction to the Devout Life,* 1609

Perfection and imperfection are really only modes of thought; that is to say, notions which we are in the habit of forming from the comparison with one another of individuals of the same species or genus.

BARUCH SPINOZA, *Ethics,* 1677

To love truth for truth's sake is the principal part of human perfection in this world, and the seed-plot of all other virtues.

JOHN LOCKE, *Letter to Anthony Collins,* October, 1703

The love of God never looks for perfection in created beings. It knows that it dwells with Him alone. As it never expects perfection, it is never disappointed.

FRANÇOIS FÉNELON (1651–1715), *Selections from,* ed. Fellen

Perfection does not consists in any singular state or condition of life, or in any particular set of duties, but in holy and religious conduct of ourselves in every state of Life.

WILLIAM LAW, *Christian Perfection,* 1726

Christianity is the highest perfection of humanity.

SAMUEL JOHNSON, *Letter to William Drummond,* August 13, 1766

God's perfections are marvelous but not lovable.

IMMANUEL KANT, *Lecture at Königsberg,* 1775

What is Christian perfection? The loving God with all our heart, mind, soul, and strength. This implies that no wrong temper, none contrary to love, remains in the soul; and that all the thoughts, words, and actions are governed by pure love.

JOHN WESLEY (1703–1791), *Plain Account of Christian Perfection*

The moral goodness of man, the necessary consequence of his constitution, is capable of indefinite perfection like all his other faculties, and nature has linked together in an unbreakable chain truth, happiness and virtue.

A. N. DE CONDORCET, *Progress of the Human Mind,* 1794

The ultimate development of the ideal man is logically certain—as certain as any conclusion in which we place the most implicit faith; for instance, that all men will die.

HERBERT SPENCER, *Social Statics,* 1851

The pursuit of perfection, then, is the pursuit of sweetness and light. He who

works for sweetness and light, works to make reason and the will of God prevail.
MATTHEW ARNOLD, *Culture and Anarchy,* 1869

There is no one in the world who cannot arrive without difficulty at the most eminent perfection by fulfilling with love obscure and common duties.
J. P. DE CASSAUDE, *Abandonment,* 1887

The law of duty demands moral perfection or holiness. But this is impossible in our present life, therefore it can only be attained by an indefinite progress, and this progress is only possible under the hypothesis of an existence and a personality that are indefinitely prolonged.
P. A. R. JANET and G. SÉAILLES, *A History of the Problems of Philosophy,* II, 1902

If we knew everything and could feel everything we should see and feel what finiteness, pain and evil mean, and how they play a part in perfection itself.
B. BOSANQUET, *The Principle of Individuality and Value,* 1912

For frail mortals, perfection is achieved not by never falling, but by rising every time we fall.
JOHN A. O'BRIEN, *Religion, Does It Matter?,* 1944

The Creation of man whom God in His foreknowledge knew doomed to sin was the awful index of God's omnipotence. For it would have been a thing of trifling and contemptible ease for Perfection to create mere perfection. To do so would, to speak truth, be not creation but extension.
ROBERT PENN WARREN, Jack Burden in *All the King's Men,* 1946

Perfection is being, not doing; it is not to effect an act but to achieve a character.
FULTON J. SHEEN, *Way to Happiness,* 1953

See also Buddhism; Evolution; Goodness; Holiness; Man: His Destiny and Goal; Man: His Potential; Man: His Self-Deification; Man and God; Martyrdom; Moral Progress; Optimism; Optimist; Priety; Progress; Sanctity; Spiritual Progress; Suffering: Its Value.

PERFORMANCE

God is the master of the scenes; we must not choose which part we shall act; it concerns us only to be careful that we do it well.
JEREMY TAYLOR, *Holy Living,* 1650

PERJURY

It is beyond all doubt, worse to swear falsely by the true God than to swear truly by the false gods; for the greater the holiness of that by which we swear, the greater is the sin of perjury.
ST. AUGUSTINE, *To Publicola,* 398

See also Liars and Lies; Oaths; Truth.

PERSECUTION

This is the course I have taken with those who were accused before me as Christians. I asked them whether they were Christians, and if they confessed, I asked them a second and third time with threats and punishment. If they kept to it, I ordered them for execution.
PLINY THE YOUNGER (Writing to Trajan, from the province of Bithynia), *Epp. X,* c. 112

For in the Jewish war which lately raged [132–135], Barcochba, the leader of the revolt of the Jews, gave orders that Christians alone should be led to cruel punishments, unless they would deny Jesus Christ and utter blasphemy.
ST. JUSTIN MARTYR, *Apology,* c. 150

If the Tiber cometh up to the walls, if the Nile cometh not up to the fields, if the heaven hath stood still, if the earth hath been moved, if there be any famine, if any pestilence, "The Christians to the lions," is forthwith the word.

TERTULLIAN, *Apologetic and Practical Treatises*, 197

When ye encounter the unbelievers, strike off their heads, until ye have made a great slaughter among them. Verily, if God pleased, He could take vengeance on them without your assistance, but He commandeth you to fight His battles.

Koran, c. 625

Those even who persecuted Christ or His followers, whom they considered it their duty to persecute, are said to have sinned in action; but they would have committed a graver fault if, contrary to their conscience, they had spared them.

PETER ABELARD, *Scito te Ipsum*, c. 1138

The instances cannot be found in the history of mankind, in which an anti-Christian power could long abstain from persecution.

JOHN HENRY NEWMAN, *Oxford University Sermons*, 1843

We are engaged in a great, a joyful work, but in proportion to God's grace is the fury of His enemies. They have welcomed us as the lion greets his prey.

JOHN HENRY NEWMAN, *The Second Spring*, 1852

We hear much of martyrs and confessors . . . but we know little of that still larger number who by the mere threat of persecution have been driven into an outward abandonment of their real opinions; and who . . . have passed the remainder of their lives in the practice of a constant and humiliating hypocrisy. It is this which is the real curse of religious persecution.

HENRY THOMAS BUCKLE, *History of Civilization in England*, 1861

It is an undoubted fact that an overwhelming majority of religious persecutors have been men of the purest intentions, of the most admirable and unsullied morals. . . . Such men as these are not bad, they are only ignorant; ignorant of the nature of truth, ignorant of the consequences of their own acts.

HENRY THOMAS BUCKLE, *History of Civilization in England*, 1861

If you can impress any man with an absorbing conviction of the supreme importance of some moral or religious doctrine; if you can make him believe that those who reject that doctrine are doomed to eternal perdition; if you then give that man power, and by means of his ignorance blind him to the ulterior consequences of his own act,—he will infallibly persecute those who deny his doctrine.

HENRY THOMAS BUCKLE, *History of Civilization in England*, 1861

Opposition may become sweet to a man when he has christened it persecution.

GEORGE ELIOT, *Janet's Repentance*, 1877

It is not worldly ecclesiastics that kindle the fires of persecution, but mystics who think they hear the voice of God.

GEORGE SANTAYANA, *New Republic*, January 15, 1916

Cruel persecution and intolerance are not accidents, but grow out of the very essence of religion, namely, its absolute claims.

MORRIS R. COHEN, *Religion Today*, ed. A. L. Swift, 1933

A man who is possessed by fear always begins to persecute.

NICHOLAS BERDYAEV, *Slavery and Freedom*, 1941

It is God, in silence and wisdom, who uses the Church's enemies to perfect His saints and purify His religion.

THOMAS MERTON, *The Waters of Siloe*, 1949

So long as a church is proscribed, it can build up a new society at its own peril without being implicated in the old society's weaknesses and sins.

A. J. TOYNBEE, *An Historian's Approach to Religion,* 1956

In the past religion was often persecutor of men: today it is nonreligion. The forces of opposition to all religion possess power such as no religious leader of the ages gone by ever dreamed of.

JEROME G. KERWIN, *Catholic Viewpoint on Church and State,* 1960

See also Anti-Semitism; Bigots; Christianity, Criticism of; Christians; Fanaticism; Genocide; Intolerance; Martyrdom; Martyrs; Opinions; Oppressors.

PERSEVERANCE

He ne'er was so good as he should be, that doth strive to be better than he is: He never will be better than he is, that doth not fear to be worse than he was.

ARTHUR WARWICK, *Spare Minutes,* 1637

See also Obstinacy.

PERSON

Person is the individual substance of a rational nature.

BOETHIUS, *5th Theological Treatise,* c. 523 A.D.

The person is that which is most noble and most perfect in all nature. . . . A subsistent individual of a rational nature.

ST. THOMAS AQUINAS, *Summa Theologiae* I, 29, 3, 1272

A thinking intelligent being, that has reason and reflection, and can consider itself as itself.

JOHN LOCKE, *Essay Concerning Human Understanding,* 1690

See also Individual; Man; Man: Defined and Interpreted; Man: His Destiny and Goal; Personality.

PERSONALITY

There is one approach to an infinite realm where God *might be.* There is one door that opens into the holy of holies. The true path is through personality. The search must *begin* in your own bosom.

RUFUS M. JONES, *Social Law in the Spiritual World,* 1904

When it comes to the deepest secrets of personality, the methods of science break down, and the last word must always be spoken by the human spirit.

WILLIAM ADAMS BROWN, *An Outline of Christian Theology,* 1906

The essential meaning of personality is selfhood, self-consciousness, self-control, and the power to know. These elements have no corporeal significance.

BORDEN P. BOWNE, *Personalism,* 1908

Our notions of knowledge and its nature, our conception of reality and causality, our thoughts respecting space and time— the two great intimidating phantoms— these are the things that decide our general way of thinking and give direction to our thought even in morals and religion.

BORDEN P. BOWNE, *Personalism,* 1908

Its [Christianity's] originality consists not so much in its single doctrines, or even its teaching as a whole . . . as in its revelation, through the person and example of its Founder, of the altogether unsuspected depths and inexhaustibleness of human Personality, and of this Personality's source and analogue in God.

FRIEDRICK VON HÜGEL, *The Mystical Element of Religion,* I, 1908

Every man who begets a free act projects his personality into the infinite.

LEON BLOY, *Pilgrim of the Absolute— Selections from Writings of,* 1909

Human personality and individuality written and signed by God on each human countenance . . . is something altogether sacred, something for the Resurrection, for eternal Life, for the beatific union.

> LEON BLOY, *Pilgrim of the Absolute—Selections from Writings of*, 1909

Our personality is what we are able to realize of the infinite wealth which our divine-human nature contains hidden in its depths.

> W. R. INGE, *The Philosophy of Plotinus*, 1918

Personality, the most valuable thing in the universe, revealing the real nature of the Creative Power and the ultimate meaning of creation, the only eternal element in a world of change, the one thing worth investing everything in . . . that is the essential Christian creed.

> HARRY EMERSON FOSDICK, *As I See Religion*, 1932

We have reason to assert without mitigation the full Personality of that ultimate Reality in which the *whole universe* is grounded.

> WILLIAM TEMPLE, *Nature, Man and God*, 1934

The best definition of a "personality" known to me is a human being in whom all the different aspects of man's nature, mind and spirit, intellect and emotion, impulse and desire, tastes and sentiments are dovetailed into an harmonious whole, with the result that the whole force of the man is behind his every act, thought and wish. Such a man is a "personality."

> C. E. M. JOAD, *Return to Philosophy*, 1936

First with Descartes, then with Rousseau and Kant, rationalism has set up a proud and splendid image of the *personality* of man, inviolable, jealous of his immanence and his autonomy, and finally good in essence. . . . Yet in a little more than a century, this proud anthropocentric personality has perished.

> JACQUES MARITAIN, *True Humanism* 1936

The ramifications of sexual interest are broad enough and deep enough in any life without the need to exaggerate their place by making the sexual history of certain typical neurotics the prototype for personality in general.

> GORDON W. ALLPORT, *Personality*, 1937

Where personality is developed for its own sake, and not in order that it may be transcended, there tends to be a raising of the barriers of separateness.

> ALDOUS HUXLEY, *Ends and Means*, 1937

The entire world is nothing in comparison with human personality, with the unique person of a man, with his unique destiny.

> NICHOLAS BERDYAEV, *Slavery and Freedom*, 1944

Personality is . . . the aggregate of the spirit's self-consciousness and of the liberty which rests thereon.

> M. J. SCHEEBEN, *The Mysteries of Christianity*, 1946.

Personality is the subsistence of the spiritual soul communicated to the human composite.

> JACQUES MARITAIN, *The Person and the Common Good*, 1947

God Himself I may declare to be the supreme expression of personality, a necessary and final value *required* to explain and to conserve all other values of selfhood.

> GORDON W. ALLPORT, *The Individual and His Religion*, 1951

Theology tells us that each child is of ultimate value in the sight of God, and is to be treated as such. Modern idealism talks of respect for personality, which leads to the same results for the wrong reasons.

R. C. MILLER, *Pastoral Psychology*, January, 1952

The summons of faith is neither to an integrated personality nor to the laying by of all questions, but to the dedication of personality—with all its fears and questions—to its duty and destiny under God.

JOHN BRIGHT, *The Kingdom of God*, 1953

The primacy of human personality has been . . . a postulate both of Christianity and of liberal democracy; but it is a *fact* of evolution.

JULIAN HUXLEY, *Evolution in Action*, 1953

If man's spirit is always expressed in human personalities, why may we not expect the greater Spirit, as well, to be manifest as a Person?

EDMUND W. SINNOTT, *The Biology of Spirit*, 1955

The whole dignity of man, the whole much-boasted "value of human personality," resides in man's awareness of being thus under obligation to something greater than himself.

PAUL TILLICH, *Biblical Religion and the Search for Ultimate Reality*, 1955

Man's intellectual and spiritual life on earth is not a circle, rounded and complete, but a parabola that runs out into infinity. To suppose that any conceivable God creates such personality only to destroy it, and . . . is content with the destruction of all personalities, is to me incredible.

HARRY EMERSON FOSDICK, *Dear Mrs. Brown*, 1961

See also Communism; Democracy; God: Considered as Personal; Immortality; Individual; Individualism; Man; Man: Defined and Interpreted; Man: His Destiny and Goal; Self; Soul; Soul, Definitions of; Soul and God; Spirit, Human; Universe and God.

PERSPECTIVE

We have our nose to the ground to ferret out the scent of the adversary; we have our ears to the ground to hear the distant rumbling; before we know it, something decisive has happened to us. We are no longer upright. Our gaze is no longer fixed on God and man in charity.

KARL STERN, *The Third Revolution*, 1954

Two men look out through the same bars; One sees mud, and one the stars.

FREDERICK LANGBRIDGE (1849–1923), "A Cluster of Quiet Thoughts"

PERSUASION

We are more easily persuaded, in general, by the reasons we ourselves discover than by those which are given to us by others.

BLAISE PASCAL, *Pensées*, 1670

Let any man speak long enough, he will get believers.

ROBERT LOUIS STEVENSON, *The Master of Ballantrae*, 1889

PERVERSION

The common characteristic of all perversions . . . is that it has renounced the aim of reproduction and follows the pursuit of pleasure as an independent goal. . . . Everything that serves the pursuit of pleasure alone must carry the term "perverse" and as such be regarded with contempt.

SIGMUND FREUD, *A General Introduction to Psychoanalysis*, 1917

See also Evil: Its Nature; Hedonism; Homosexuality; Pleasure; Sexual Sin.

PESSIMISM

The power by virtue of which Christianity was able to overcome first Judaism, and then the heathenism of Greece and Rome, lies solely in its pessimism, in the confession that our state is both exceedingly wretched and sinful, while Judaism and heathenism were both optimistic.

    ARTHUR SCHOPENHAUER, *Essays*, II, 1841

The modern pessimist is a Buddhist who has strayed from the Orient, and who in his exodus has left behind him all his fantastic shackles, and has brought with him, together with ethical laws, only the cardinal tenet, "Life is evil."

    EDGAR E. SALTUS, *Philosophy of Disenchantment*, 1885

As a philosophy, Pessimism is self-destructive. The mind which conceives the good and the ideal is made in the same breath to deny their value.

    MARTIN C. D'ARCY, *The Problem of Evil*, 1928

Christianity has never shut its eyes to the reality of the burden of inherited evils that weigh down human history, and for that reason it has been condemned as pessimistic.

    CHRISTOPHER DAWSON, *Listener*, August, 1933

The romantic pessimism which culminates in Freud may be regarded as symbolic of the despair which modern man faces when his optimistic illusions are dispelled; for under the perpetual smile of modernity, there is a grimace of disillusion and cynicism.

    REINHOLD NIEBUHR, *Nature and Destiny of Man*, I, 1941

Some people like to describe the Christian attitude as one of active pessimism. This is indeed our philosophy for the evil days.

But I think it is better defined as a tragic optimism.

    EMMANUEL MOUNIER, *Be Not Afraid: A Denunciation of Despair*, 1963

See also Fear; Gloom; Sadness; Self-Pity.

PETER, SAINT

We are apt to speak depreciatively of Peter's denial, and appreciatively of his later life. But there is one thing we do not sufficiently mark—that a glance was enough for him.

    SÖREN KIERKEGAARD (1813–1855), *Meditations from*, ed. T. H. Croxall

Nothing was conferred on the apostles apart from Peter, but . . . several things were conferred on Peter apart from the apostles.

    POPE LEO XIII, *Satis Cognitum*, 1896

It is the human wobbly Peter, not the mystic Philip seeking the vision of the Father, who becomes the pillar of the Church.

    EVELYN UNDERHILL, *The Fruits of the Spirit*, 1942

See also Church: Its Authority; Pope, the.

PHARISAISM

Pharisaism does not mean wearing a cloak of righteousness; it means sincerely believing that one is more rightous than one really is.

    RALPH BARTON PERRY, *Puritanism and Democracy*, 1944

The central conception of Pharisaism is Torah, the divine Teaching, the full and inexhaustible revelation which God had made.

    R. TRAVERS HERFORD, Introduction to his translation of *Pirke Aboth*, 1945

Pharisaism in the mitigated form of self-righteousness . . . is a specifically great danger because, unlike other forms of pride, it does not present itself to one's mind as a rebellion against morality.

DIETRICH VON HILDEBRAND, *True Morality and Its Counterfeits*, 1955

See also Hypocrisy; Pharisee; Righteousness; Self-Righteousness.

PHARISEE

The satanically proud man . . . hates God and wants to dethrone Him. The pharisee, on the contrary, seeks the satisfaction of his pride by adorning himself with "moral perfection." . . . Yet he hates true morality and substitutes for it a merely legalistic and ritualistic morality. He wants to relish his piety and goodness, to glorify himself before a merely formal God.

DIETRICH VON HILDEBRAND, *True Morality and Its Counterfeits*, 1955

To me a lay pharisee is the person who pretends to believe that Christianity is an easy thing and asks of the Christian, on the basis of an external view of Christianity, more than he asks of himself.

ALBERT CAMUS, *Resistance, Rebellion and Death*, 1960

See also Hypocrisy; Pride; Righteousness; Self-Righteousness.

PHENOMENA

God does nothing out of order. Thus what passes for extraordinary is so only with regard to a particular order established among created things; as regards the universal order, everything conforms to it.

G. W. VON LEIBNIZ, *Discourse on Metaphysics*, 1685

Space and time, and with them all phenomena, are not things by themselves, but representations, and cannot exist outside the mind.

IMMANUEL KANT, *The Critique of Pure Reason*, 1781

The expression of religious phenomena in purely psychological terms is absolutely irrelevant to the question of the validity of religious experience.

E. J. PRICE, *Hibbert Journal*, XXII, 1924

Religious phenomena are to be understood only on the model of the neurotic symptoms of the individual—as a return of long-forgotten happenings in the primeval history of the race.

SIGMUND FREUD, *Moses and Monotheism*, 1939

See also Experience, Religious; Miracles.

PHILISTINES

Philistine must have originally meant, in the minds of those who invented the nickname, a strong, dogged, unenlightened opponent of the chosen people, of the children of light.

MATTHEW ARNOLD, *Function of Criticism at the Present Time*, 1865

The people who believe most that our greatness and welfare are proved by our being very rich, and who most give their lives and thoughts to becoming rich, are just the very people whom we call Philistines.

MATTHEW ARNOLD, *Culture and Anarchy*, 1869

PHILOSOPHERS

There is no statement so absurd that no philosopher will make it.

CICERO, *De divinatione*, 78 B.C.

Nature laughs uproariously at them all the time. The fact that they can never explain why they constantly disagree with each other is sufficient proof that they do not know the truth about anything.

DESIDERIUS ERASMUS, *Praise of Folly*, 1509

The deepest philosopher that ever was (saving the reverence of the schools) is but an ignorant sot to the simplest Christian.

> JOSEPH HALL, *Meditations and Vows,* 1606

To ridicule philosophy, that is to be a real philosopher.

> BLAISE PASCAL, *Pensées,* 1670

Many talk like philosophers and live like fools.

> THOMAS FULLER, *Gnomologia,* 1732

A philosopher is a fool who torments himself while he is alive, to be talked about after he is dead.

> JEAN LE ROND D'ALEMBERT, *Elements of Philosophy,* 1759

O philosophers, proud rulers of the human mind, where are your flocks, where are the souls you love with a filial love, . . . Where are the tears dried up, the confessions heard, the amelioration of existence, the consolations which have gone forth from you?

> JEAN BAPTISTE LACORDAIRE, *Thoughts and Teachings of,* c. 1850

No one has taken the name of the Lord his God in vain so frequently and so unconcernedly as the philosopher.

> RALPH BARTON PERRY, *Present Philosophical Tendencies,* 1912

It would be . . . interesting to know why, even in our own days, so many philosophers seem to turn to Christianity for a more satisfying solution of philosophic problems than they find in philosophy itself.

> ÉTIENNE GILSON, *The Spirit of Medieval Philosophy,* 1936

As we well know, the imbecility of "profound" philosophers is so immense that it is exceeded only by the infinite mercy of God.

> GIOVANNI PAPINI, *The Devil,* 1955

See also Intellectuals; Metaphysician; Philosophy; Theologians.

PHILOSOPHY

The acquisition of knowledge; . . . knowledge which will do us good.

> PLATO, "Euthydemus," *Dialogues,* 4th century B.C.

By philosophy I do not mean the Stoic, nor the Platonic, nor the Epicurean and Aristotelic, but all good doctrine in every one of the schools, all precepts of holiness combined with religious knowledge.

> ST. CLEMENT OF ALEXANDRIA, *Stromateis,* c. 200

Philosophy then before the coming of the Lord was necessary to the Greeks to bring them to righteousness, but now it is profitable to bring them to piety.

> ST. CLEMENT OF ALEXANDRIA, *Stromateis,* c. 200

For philosophy it is which is the material of the world's wisdom, the rash interpreter of the nature and dispensation of God. Indeed heresies are themselves instigated by philosophy.

> TERTULLIAN, *On Prescription Against Heretics,* c. 206

In earnestly investigating and attempting to discover the reason of all things, every means of attaining to a pious and perfect doctrine lies in that science and discipline which the Greeks call philosophy.

> JOHANNES SCOTUS ERIGENA, *De Divina Praedestinatione,* c. 851

A natural interpretation of the universe, a general view of things taken from the point of view of reason.

> ST. THOMAS AQUINAS (1225–1274), *The Philosophy of St. Thomas Aquinas,* translated by Edward Bullough

Philosophy has gradually crept into Christianity, and the impious dogma of Free

Will has been received and the beneficence of Christ has been obscured by that profane and animal wisdom of human reason.
PHILIP MELANCHTHON, *Common Topics,* 1521

A little philosophy inclineth man's mind to atheism, but depth in philosophy bringeth men's minds about to religion.
FRANCIS BACON, *Essays,* 1597

In theology the weight of Authority, but in philosophy the weight of Reason is valid.
JOHANNES KEPLER, *The New Astronomy,* 1608

In every age Natural Philosophy has had a troublesome adversary and hard to deal with; namely, superstition, and the blind and immoderate zeal of religion.
FRANCIS BACON, first book of Aphorisms of *Novum Organum,* 1620

Philosophy is written in that vast book which stands forever open before our eyes. I mean the universe.
GALILEO, *Il Saggiatore,* 1622

Philosophy triumphs easily over past evils and future evils; but present evils triumph over it.
LA ROCHEFOUCAULD, *Maxims,* 1665

Nothing else but the study of Wisdom and Truth.
GEORGE BERKELEY, *Principles of Human Knowledge,* 1710

The wisdom to discern what is essentially and actually right and reasonable in the real world.
G. W. F. HEGEL, *The Philosophy of Mind,* c. 1818

Philosophy is the account which the human mind gives to itself of the constitution of the world.
RALPH WALDO EMERSON, *Representative Men,* 1850

By the unity of doctrine or faith the Church has taken up all philosophies, and consolidated them into one.
HENRY EDWARD MANNING, *Temporal Mission of the Holy Ghost,* 1866

Philosophy does not seek to overthrow revelation; it seeks rather to defend it against assailants.
POPE LEO XIII, *Inscrutabili,* April 21, 1878

Philosophy, if rightly made use of by the wise, in a certain way tends to smooth and fortify the road to true faith, and to prepare the souls of its disciples for the fit reception of revelation.
POPE LEO XIII, *Scholastic Philosophy,* 1879

Those who to the study of philosophy unite obedience to the Christian faith are philosophers indeed.
POPE LEO XIII, *Scholastic Philosophy,* 1879

Philosophy . . . is not a presumptuous effort to explain the mysteries of the world by means of any superhuman insight or extraordinary cunning, but has its origin and value in an attempt to give a reasonable account of our own personal attitude toward the more serious business of life.
JOSIAH ROYCE, *The Spirit of Modern Philosophy,* 1892

If writers on physics travel outside the boundaries of their own branch, and carry their erroneous teaching into the domain of philosophy, let them be handed over to philosophers for refutation.
POPE LEO XIII, *Holy Scripture,* 1893

We think for a landlady considering a lodger it is important to know his income, but still more important to know his philosophy.
G. K. CHESTERTON, *Heretics,* 1905

Philosophy, n. route of many roads leading from nowhere to nothing.
> AMBROSE BIERCE, *Devil's Dictionary*, 1906

Our individual way of just seeing and feeling the total push of and pressure of the cosmos.
> WILLIAM JAMES, *Pragmatism*, 1907

Philosophy is only a matter of passionate vision rather than of logic—logic only finding reasons for the vision afterwards.
> WILLIAM JAMES, *Pluralistic Universe*, 1909

A steady contemplation of all things in their order and worth.
> GEORGE SANTAYANA, *Three Philosophical Poets*, 1910

Men are suffering from the fever of violent emotion, and so they make a philosophy of it.
> S. RADHAKRISHNAN, *The Reign of Religion in Contemporary Philosophy*, 1922

It is a great advantage for a system of philosophy to be substantially true.
> GEORGE SANTAYANA, *The Unknowable*, 1923

Unified knowledge unifying life.
> WILL DURANT, *Address*, Harvard University, 1926

All genuine philosophy is, in the end if not consciously in the beginning, a quest of God.
> ANDRÉ BREMOND, *Philosophy in the Making*, 1930

Philosophy in interpreting the world cannot leave out, without loss of adequacy, God as ultimate cause, final purpose, and directive presence.
> ALFRED E. GARVIE, *The Christian Faith*, 1936

I call Christian, every philosophy which although keeping the two orders [the natural and supernatural] formally distinct, nevertheless considers the Christian revelation as an indispensable auxiliary to reason.
> ÉTIENNE GILSON, *The Spirit of Medieval Philosophy*, 1936

Religion is the search for a value underlying *all* things, and as such is the most comprehensive of all the possible philosophies of life.
> GORDON W. ALLPORT, *Personality*, 1937

Philosophy loses its influence when it turns revivalist.
> HENRY S. HOSKINS, *Meditations in Wall Street*, 1940

Philosophy has the task and the opportunity of helping banish the concept that human destiny here and now is of slight importance in comparison with some supernatural destiny.
> JOHN DEWEY, *Fortune*, August, 1944

Philosophy has become either the errand boy of the natural sciences or the playboy of linguistic shell-games whose name at present is logical positivism.
> ALLEN TATE, *New York Times Book Review*, March, 1952

Why should those who profess the Christian faith and its doctrines see themselves excluded from philosophy simply because they prefer to philosophize about what they believe?
> ÉTIENNE GILSON, *The Philosopher and Theology*, 1962

See also Absolutism; Christian Philosophy; Determinism; Existentialism; Hegelianism; Knowledge; Learning; Materialism; Metaphysical; Metaphysics; Moral Philosophy; Naturalism; Necessity; Pantheism; Philosophers; Positivism; Pragmatism; Rationalism; Reason; Science and Religion; Theology; Thomism; Truth; Truths, Conflict of; Utilitarianism; Wisdom.

PHYSICAL LAW

Physical law is merely a statement of the way God's mind works when it does a certain kind of work.

CHARLES E. GARMAN, *Letters, Lectures, Addresses,* 1909

PHYSICIANS

In nothing does one more nearly approach the gods than in giving health to men.

CICERO, *De Oratore,* c. 80 B.C.

I have nothing but praise for the physicians who adhere closely to their principles. But they should not take amiss if I cannot always agree with them, for they wish to make a fixed star out of me when I am a roving planet. . . . A physician must be humble—that is, he must be God-fearing, and unless he practices with the fear of God, he is a murderer.

MARTIN LUTHER, *Table Talk,* July, 1538

The art of medicine is rooted in the heart. If your heart is just, you will be a true physician.

PARACELSUS (1493?–1541) *Selected Writings of,* ed. J. Jacobi, 1951

God heals, and the physician hath the thanks.

GEORGE HERBERT, *Outlandish Proverbs,* 1640

To preserve a man alive in the midst of so many chances and hostilities, is as great a miracle as to create him.

JEREMY TAYLOR, *Holy Dying,* 1650

Physicians must not meddle with desperate diseases, and known to be incurable, without declaring their sense before hand.

JEREMY TAYLOR, *Holy Living,* 1650

I remember an ingenious physician, who told me, in the fanatic times, he found most of his patients so disturbed by troubles of conscience that he was forced to play the divine with them, before he could begin the physician.

SIR WILLIAM TEMPLE (1629–1699), *Discourse of Health and Long Life*

A physician can sometimes parry the scythe of death, but has no power over the sand in the hourglass.

HESTER LYNCH PIOZZI, *Letter* to Fanny Burney, 1781

The person of the physician and all his activities move constantly in the sphere of moral order and under the dominion of its laws. In no statement, in no action, in no intervention may the physician keep outside the sphere of morals, free and independent from the fundamental principles of ethics and religion.

POPE PIUS XII, *Address,* November 12, 1943

It would be a sad thing if in showing more appreciation for God's healing power through the mind, we should show less wonder at His healing by means of the medical profession's science.

GERALD KENNEDY, *A Reader's Notebook,* 1953

One of the great creations of God is the family physician. . . . Physicians are truly God's agents of healing, whether or not they acknowledge this fact.

JOHN SUTHERLAND BONNELL, *No Escape from Life,* 1958

See also Healing; Health.

PIETY

Visible worship is not condemned, but God is pleased only by invisible piety.

DESIDERIUS ERASMUS, *Enchiridion,* 1501

To carry piety as far as superstition is to destroy it.

BLAISE PASCAL, *Pensées,* 1670

Piety requires us to renounce no ways of life where we can act reasonably, and offers what we do to the glory of God.
WILLIAM LAW, *A Serious Call to the Devout and Holy Life,* 1728

There is no trusting to . . . crazy piety.
SAMUEL JOHNSON, *Boswell's Life,* March 25, 1776

The common element in all howsoever diverse expressions of piety . . . is this: the consciousness of being absolutely dependent, or, which is the same thing, of being in relation with God.
F. SCHLIERMACHER, *The Christian Faith,* 1822

Piety is not an end, but a means: a means of attaining the highest culture through the purest tranquillity of soul.
J. W. VON GOETHE (1749–1832), *Maxims and Reflections*

Volumes might be written upon the impiety of the pious.
HERBERT SPENCER, *First Principles,* 1862

Piety in its nobler and Roman sense, may be said to mean man's reverent attachment to the sources of his being and the steadying of his life by that attachment. . . . Piety is the spirit's acknowledgment of its incarnation.
GEORGE SANTAYANA, *Reason in Religion,* 1905

Piety, n. Reverence for the Supreme Being, based on His supposed resemblance to man.
AMBROSE BIERCE, *Devil's Dictionary,* 1906

Christian piety all too often has seemed to be the withdrawal from the world and from men, a sort of transcendent egoism, the unwillingness to share the suffering of the world and man.
JACQUES MARITAIN, *Freedom in the Modern World,* 1936

See also Detachment; Goodness; Holiness; Mysticism; Perfection; Prayer; Prudence; Reunion; Reverence; Sanctity; Virtue; Worship.

PILGRIMS

The pious ones of Plymouth, who, reaching the Rock, first fell upon their own knees and then upon the aborigines.
WILLIAM M. EVARTS, quoted by Henry Watterson in *Louisville Courier,* July 4, 1913

The Pilgrimage [to Mecca] is obligatory on every adult only once in his life, and its performance oftener is voluntary. . . . But the obligation is subject to the condition that one is able to take a journey to Mecca.
MUHAMMAD ALI, *The Religion of Islam,* 1936

PITY

Pity is a mental illness induced by the spectacle of other people's miseries. . . . The sage does not succumb to mental diseases of that sort.
SENECA (4 B.C.–65 A.D.), *De Clementia,* II

Now when a man suffers himself, it is called misery; when he suffers in the suffering of another, it is called pity.
ST. AUGUSTINE, *Confessions,* 397

If, perchance, the scales of justice be not correctly balanced, let the error be imputable to pity, not to gold.
MIGUEL DE CERVANTES, *Don Quixote,* 1605

Pity is sworn servant unto love.
SAMUEL DANIEL (1562–1619), "The Queen's Arcadia," *Poems*

He that pities another remembers himself.
GEORGE HERBERT, *Outlandish Proverbs,* 1640

To pity the unhappy is not contrary to selfish desire; on the other hand, we are glad of the occasion to thus testify friendship and attract to ourselves the reputation of tenderness, without giving anything.
BLAISE PASCAL, *Pensées*, 1670

We pity in others only those evils that we have ourselves experienced.
JEAN JACQUES ROUSSEAU, *Émile*, 1762

More helpful than all wisdom is one draught of simple human pity that will not forsake us.
GEORGE ELIOT, *The Mill on the Floss*, 1860

The corrupt and shifty pity that permeates our laws, disarms our governors, and exposes us to our successors is the soul of our dying society.
DONAT O'DONNELL, *Maria Cross*, 1953

Christ told men to love: the most they could manage was pity; it was something.
DONAT O'DONNELL, *Maria Cross*, 1953

See also Brotherhood; Charity; Compassion; Forgiveness; Mercy; Sympathy.

PLATITUDES

What is all wisdom save a collection of platitudes? . . . They embody the concentrated experience of the race, and the man who orders his life according to their teaching cannot go far wrong.
NORMAN DOUGLAS, *South Wind*, 1917

PLEASURE

From pleasure comes grief, from pleasure comes fear; he who is free from pleasure knows neither grief nor fear.
Dhammapada, c. 5th century B.C.

The individual soul, forgetful of the Lord, attaches itself to pleasure and thus is bound. When it comes to the Lord, it is freed from all its fetters.
Svetasvatara Upanishad, before 400 B.C.

Death spoke, and said: ". . . There is no future for the fool who seeks pleasure, who is befooled by love of wealth. 'This is the world, there is no other.' If one thinks thus, he comes again and again into my power."
Katha Upanishad, before 400 B.C.

Love of pleasure is the disease which makes men most despicable.
LONGINUS, *On the Sublime*, c. 250 A.D.

Purification of the soul . . . consists in scorning the pleasures that arise through the senses, in not feasting the eyes on the silly exhibitions of jugglers or on the sight of bodies which give the spur to sensual pleasures, in not permitting licentious songs to enter through the ears and drench the soul.
ST. BASIL THE GREAT, *Address to Young Men*, c. 370

The man of this world, whenever he feels secure in any pleasure thereof, the world drives over into some unpleasantness, and whenever he attains any part of it and squats him down in it, the world turns him upside down.
AL-HASAN AL-BASRI (died 728 A.D.), quoted in *Sūfism*, translated by A. J. Arberry

There is nothing pleasurable save what is uniform with the most inmost depths of the divine nature.
HENRY SUSO (1300–1366), *Life of Blessed Henry Suso by Himself*

To have pleasure in sins is of the devil, but participation in proper and honorable pleasures with good and God-fearing people is pleasing to God.
MARTIN LUTHER, *Letter*, May 23, 1534

We have never been forbidden to laugh, or to be filled, or to join new possessions to old or ancestral ones, or to delight in musical harmony, or to drink wine.
JOHN CALVIN, *Institutes*, III, 1536

There is pleasure in gold, pleasure in silver and in women, pleasure in the perfume of sandal; there is pleasure in horses, pleasure in couches and in palaces, pleasure in sweets, and pleasure in meats. When such are the pleasures of the body, how shall God's name obtain a dwelling therein?

GURU NANAK (1496–1538), *The Sikh Religion*, M. A. Macauliffe, I

Our loving God wills that we eat, drink, and be merry.

MARTIN LUTHER (1483–1546), *Table Talk*

God might grant us riches, honors, long life and health, but many times to our own hurt: for whatsoever is pleasing to us, is not always healthful for us.

MICHEL DE MONTAIGNE, *Essays*, Bk. 2, ch. 12, 1580

That thou mayest have pleasure in everything, seek pleasure in nothing.

ST. JOHN OF THE CROSS, *The Ascent of Mount Carmel*, c. 1584

No pleasure is comparable to the standing upon the vantage-ground of truth.

FRANCIS BACON, *Essays*, 1597

Pleasures are but shadows, which hold no longer than the sunshine of my fortunes.

ARTHUR WARWICK, *Spare Minutes*, 1637

A longing after sensual pleasures is a dissolution of the spirit of a man.

JEREMY TAYLOR, *Holy Living*, 1650

The ridiculous chase after imaginary pleasures cannot be sufficiently exposed, as it is the greatest source of those evils which generally undo a nation.

JOSEPH ADDISON (1672–1719), *The Spectator, Selections from*

The present disciples of Jesus Christ are to have no more to do with worldly enjoyments than those that He chose whilst He Himself was on earth.

WILLIAM LAW, *Christian Perfection*, 1726

Every wise man will consider this life only as it may induce to the happiness of the other, and cheerfully sacrifice the pleasures of a few years to those of an eternity.

JOSEPH ADDISON, *Evidences of the Christian Religion*, 1730

The liberty of using harmless pleasure will not be disputed but it is still to be examined what pleasures are harmless.

SAMUEL JOHNSON, *Rasselas*, 1759

Pleasure is in itself a good; nay, even setting aside immunity from pain the only good.

JEREMY BENTHAM, *The Principles of Morals and Legislation*, 1789

There are only three pleasures in life pure and lasting, and all derived from inanimate things—books, pictures, and the face of nature.

WILLIAM HAZLITT, *Criticisms of Art*, 1843

Pleasure and freedom from pain are the only things desirable as ends.

JOHN STUART MILL, *Utilitarianism*, 1863

In youth the absence of pleasure is pain; in old age the absence of pain is pleasure.

Old Farmer's Almanac, 1892

I took pleasure where it pleased me, and passed on. I forgot that every little action of the common day makes or unmakes character. . . . I allowed pleasure to dominate me. I ended in horrible disgrace.

OSCAR WILDE, *De Profundis*, 1896

No school can avoid taking for the ultimate moral aim a desirable state of feeling called by whatever name, gratification, pleasure, happiness.

HERBERT SPENCER, *The Data of Ethics*, 1898

Is not the modern world seeking in its despair, distractions from inevitable evil? Most of its pleasures are distractions from inevitable death.

VINCENT MCNABB, *God's Way of Mercy,* 1928

The pleasure of sin is of short duration. . . . It operates on a law of diminishing returns. The more often it is repeated, the more familiar with its face, the less pleasure sin gives.

IGNATIUS SMITH, *Christ Today,* 1932

A man is to give account in the hereafter for permissible pleasures from which he abstained.

ISIDORE EPSTEIN, *Judaism,* 1939

Only the prig and the fool refuse their affection to the happy paganism of Theleme, to "laughter and the love of friends"; yet such things are a recreation, not a philosophy. Man cannot rest content with them for a faith.

CHRISTOPHER HOLLIS, *The Noble Castle,* 1941

There is wisdom in knowing how to play, to touch lightly, uninvolved and uncommitted, on what is pleasurable.

AELRED GRAHAM, *Christian Thought and Action,* 1951

Incessant waves of the pleasure principle are invading the world and threaten to submerge in the growing tide of its thoughts, desires, and acts, the whole of married life.

POPE PIUS XII, *Address,* October 29, 1951

Pleasure is the death and failure of desire.

JEAN PAUL SARTRE, *Being and Nothingness,* 1956

See also Alcohol; Amusements; Delight; Desires; Dissipation; Drunkenness; Evil; Gluttony; Happiness; Hedonism; Idolatry; Impurity; Joy; Laughter; Lust; Luxury; Moderation; Music; Perversion; Remorse; Self-Interest; Sensuality; Sex; Sexual Intercourse; Sexuality; Sobriety; Temporal; Utilitarianism; Wine; Worldliness.

PLURALISM

Were there but one religion in England, its despotism would be fearful; were there but two, they would cut each other's throats; but there are thirty, and they live in peace and happiness.

VOLTAIRE, *Lettres Philosophiques,* Letter 6, 1734

Brother, you say there is but one way to worship and serve the Great Spirit. If there is but one religion, why do you white people differ so much about it? Why do not all agree, as you can all read the Book?

RED JACKET, Chief of the Seneca Indian tribe, *to Christian missionaries,* 1805

I . . . find the multiplicity of religions to be grounded in the nature of religion . . . This multiplicity is necessary for the complete manifestation of religion. It must seek for distinctive character, not only in the individual but in society.

FRIEDRICH SCHLEIERMACHER (1768–1834), *Reden über die Religion,* V

There is a place for both the conservative and the liberal, the facing seat of the Friends and the altar of St. Peter's. There is room in the imperial enterprise of Christianity for the authority of the congregation and the authority of the bishop, with all that lies between.

GAIUS GLENN ATKINS, *Religion in Our Times,* 1932

A skeptical, pagan world has almost ceased to pay attention to the Church because it has been more impressed by our differences and by the fact that we are custodians of our denominational traditions than by our challenging Gospel.

> W. STANLEY RYCROFT, *Toward World-Wide Christianity*, ed. O. F. Nolde, 1946

The Church has usually been most serviceable to God and most faithful in its witness to truth and righteousness and freedom as a broken Body. It may be that there is a fundamental mystical reason and necessity in this, involved in the genius of our faith.

> W. R. FORRESTER, *Christian Vocation*, 1951

There are in the United States of America some 255 Christian denominations and sects. . . . The Protestant method, moreover, invites the faithful to follow the Spirit speaking in and through Scripture.

> ÉMILE CAILLIET, *The Christian Approach to Culture*, 1953

Within the Western nations . . . there is "a plurality of incompatible faiths": there is also a multitude of secularized and agnostic people.

> WALTER LIPPMANN, *The Public Philosophy*, 1954

It is both dangerous and absurd for our world to be a group of communions mutually excommunicate.

> ALAN W. WATTS, Preface, *The Way of Zen*, 1957

Commitment to the religion clauses of the Constitution is a moral commitment to them as articles of peace in a pluralistic society.

> JOHN COURTNEY MURRAY, *We Hold These Truths*, 1960

It used to be assumed that pluralism represented "progress." But now the question has arisen, whether its proliferation may not be causatively related to certain observable decadences within the area of intellectual life.

> JOHN COURTNEY MURRAY, *We Hold These Truths*, 1960

Religious pluralism is against the will of God. But it is the human condition; it is written into the script of history. It will not somehow cease to trouble the City.

> JOHN COURTNEY MURRAY, *We Hold These Truths*, 1960

The ecumenical movement is rather convincing testimony that other Christian confessions do not regard pluralism as a fitting witness to Christ.

> JOSEPH CARDINAL RITTER, *The Advocate* (organ of Newark, N.J., Roman Catholic archdiocese), October 31, 1963

There is no contradiction between coordinating our cultural activities with all men and at the same time confronting them as members of another faith community.

> JOSEPH B. SOLOVEITCHIK, *Tradition*, September, 1964

The idea of total conversion [of all non-Christians as held by numerous Christians] means of course ultimately that there will be only one world religion, namely Christianity. But which Christianity? Roman Catholic, Orthodox Catholic, Protestantism? The answer would have to be, one supposes, a pluralism of organized forms of Christianity, but to the exclusion of all so-called non-Christian religions.

> CHARLES S. BRADEN, *A Journal of Religion and State*, Autumn, 1965

A pluralism of religions coexisting side by side seems to me the inevitable state of things for the forseeable future, as it has been through the ages until now. The relationship may be one of envy, of jealousy, of disrespect, or of open hostility, or it may be one of continuingly better understanding and appreciation of the values represented in each by the other.

> CHARLES S. BRADEN, *A Journal of Religion and State*, Autumn, 1965

POEMS and POETS

We shall not praise the poets when they revile or mock, or when they depict men engaged in amours or drunken, or when they define happiness in terms of an overabundant table or dissolute songs.

ST. BASIL THE GREAT, *Address to Young Men,* c. 370

A poem is the very image of life expressed in its eternal truth.

PERCY BYSSHE SHELLEY, *Defense of Poetry,* 1821

A poet participates in the eternal, the infinite, and the one. . . . defeats the curse which binds us . . . redeems from decay the visitations of the divinity in man.

PERCY BYSSHE SHELLEY, *Defense of Poetry,* 1821

A man who keeps no secrets from God in his heart, and who, in singing his griefs, his fears, his hopes, and his memories, purifies and purges them all from falsehood. . . . The poet is he whose flesh emerges from the shell, whose soul oozes forth.

MIGUEL DE UNAMUNO, *Essays and Soliloquies,* 1925

The poet in the last resort is but an evanescent mystic whose mysticism breaks down.

HENRI BREMOND, *Prayer and Poetry,* 1927

POETRY

More and more mankind will discover that we have to turn to poetry to interpret life for us, to console us, to sustain us. Without poetry, our science will appear incomplete and most of what now passes with us for religion and philosophy will be replaced by poetry.

MATTHEW ARNOLD, *The Study of Poetry,* 1865

Poetry transcends logic as the spiritual transcends the physical and the intellectual. It reveals life eternally and the instruments of time are too mean to record its mystery.

HUGH I'ANSON FAUSSET, *Studies in Idealism,* 1923

The psychological mechanism used by grace to raise us to prayer is the same that puts in movement the poetic experience.

HENRI BREMOND, *Prayer and Poetry,* 1927

The greater poetry is a flowing in of light from the source of all light, from that King from whom comes our knowledge of the kingly, in whose wisdom we advance, under whose majesty we move, and in whose beauty, if we have cared for beauty, we may come to dwell.

JOHN MASEFIELD, *Address,* London, 1931

The capacity for writing poetry is rare; the capacity for religious emotion of the first intensity is rare; and it is to be expected that the existence of both capacities in the same individual should be rarer still.

T. S. ELIOT, *After Strange Gods,* 1934

The expression of the hunger for elsewhere.

BENJAMIN DE CASSERES, *The Muse of Lies,* 1936

Poetry and mysticism have . . . this in common, that both alike belong to the field of contemplation rather than of action.

> HELEN C. WHITE, *The Metaphysical Poets,* 1936

Poetry will not save the world. But poetry can force the soul into the precincts of its last evasion.

> STANLEY HOPPER, *The Crisis of Faith,* 1944

To ask poetry to save us is to impose a burden upon poetry that it cannot sustain. The danger is that we shall merely get an ersatz religion and an ersatz poetry.

> CLEANTH BROOKS, *Sewanee Review,* Winter, 1953

That intercommunication between the inner being of things and the inner being of the human Self which is a kind of divination.

> JACQUES MARITAIN, *Creative Intuition in Art and Poetry,* 1953

Poetry even at its purest is not prayer; but it rises from the same depths as the need to pray.

> ÉTIENNE GILSON, *Choir of Muses,* 1954

There is a certain sense in which religion is the only theme of important poetry.

> WILLIAM K. WIMSATT, JR., *New Scholasticism,* January, 1958

See also Art; Art and Religion; Bible as Literature; Imagination; Inspiration; Light; Literature; Poems and Poets.

POLITICAL IDEAS

Political ideas acquire operative force in human affairs when . . . they acquire legitimacy, when they have the title of being right which binds men's consciences.

> WALTER LIPPMANN, *The Public Philosophy,* 1954

POLITICAL ORGANIZATION

When political organization is made an end in itself, whether as nationalism, democracy, progress or what not, it represents the city of Satan over against the city of God.

> JEAN DANIELOU, *The Lord of History,* 1958

POLITICAL POWER

Such power as I possess for working in the political field derived from my experiments in the spiritual field.

> MAHATMA GANDHI, *Autobiography,* 1948

POLITICIANS

A politican . . . one that would circumvent God.

> WILLIAM SHAKESPEARE, *Hamlet,* c. 1602

Among politicians, the esteem of religion is profitable, the principles of it are troublesome.

> BENJAMIN WHICHCOTE (1609–1683), quoted in *Duckett's Register,* (May, 1957)

Men say I am a saint losing myself in politics. The fact is that I am a politician trying my hardest to be a saint.

> MAHATMA GANDHI (1869–1948), quoted in Louis Fischer, *The Life of Mahatma Gandhi*

In the quiet study, the good politician sees a hovering ideal: it is the City of God. In the smoke-filled room he learns how far the city of man is from that ideal. He must begin with the earthly city as it is. He does not despair: he has seen the vision. . . . In the majority of politicians I now discern, to a varying degree, an awareness of the hovering ideal, and some recognition of the city of man as groping toward the City of God.

CHAD WALSH, *Behold the Glory,* 1955

POLITICS

If religious excitement be in its decline, and political excitement just beginning, the latter passion will extinguish the former.

ALEXIS DE TOCQUEVILLE (1805–1859), *Letters and Remains,* I

Those who would treat politics and morality apart will never understand one or the other.

JOHN VISCOUNT MORLEY, *Address on Aphorisms,* 1891

It would not be permissible for Catholic Action to become an organization of party politics.

POPE PIUS XII, *Address,* May 3, 1951

The Christian in politics should be judged by the standard of whether through his decisions and actions he has advanced the cause of justice and helped, at least, to achieve the highest degree of perfection possible in the temporal order.

EUGENE J. MCCARTHY, *Frontiers in American Democracy*

If any man is hungry, this is both a religious and a political concern, and out of a religious concern for one created in God's image, political means must be devised for ensuring that everyone gets enough bread—which is a suitable enough definition of the art of politics.

ROBERT MCAFEE BROWN, *The Spirit of Protestantism,* 1961

The level of politics can be little higher than the level of the morality and sense of responsibility of the people.

ADLAI STEVENSON, *Ladies Home Journal,* December, 1961

I will never admit, and no one in the world will ever make me admit, that the Christian is free in his political choices, that he is free to choose the methods he adopts in order to make them triumph.

FRANÇOIS MAURIAC, *What I Believe,* 1962

Christian political action does not mean waiting for the orders of the Bishop or campaigning under the banner of the Church; rather, it means bringing to politics a sense of Christian responsibility.

FRANZISKUS KOENIG, *Statement* to the National Catholic Welfare Council, July, 1964

See also Clericalism; Government; Honor; Office; Preaching; Religious Test for Office; Rulers.

POOR, THE

It is not the man who has little, but he who desires more, that is poor.

SENECA, *Epistulae Morales ad Lucilium,* c. 63 A.D.

Take heed, O poor man, that if your flesh is mortal, your soul is precious and everlasting. If you lack money, you do not lack grace; and if you have no spacious house nor wide acres, the heavens spread above you, the earth is free.

ST. AMBROSE, *Hexameron,* c. 389

Quit thine oppressions of earth's feeble poor,
That to the sky their curses mount no more.

SHAIKH SAADI, *Gulistan,* c. 1265

Every town should provide for its own poor.

MARTIN LUTHER, *To the Christian Nobility,* 1520

The poor man hath title to the rich man's goods; so that the rich man ought to let

the poor man have part of his riches to help and comfort him withal.
HUGH LATIMER (1485–1555), *Fifth Sermon on the Lord's Prayer*

No man is poor who does not think himself so; but if, in a full fortune, with impatience he desires more, he proclaims his wants and his beggarly condition.
JEREMY TAYLOR, *Holy Living*, 1650

There none poor but such as God hates.
JAMES HOWELL, *Proverbs*, 1659

Every one but an idiot knows that the lower classes must be kept poor, or they would never be industrious.
ARTHUR YOUNG, *Eastern Tour*, 1771

Their more lowly paths have been allotted to them by the hand of God; . . . it is their part faithfully to discharge its duties, and contentedly to bear its inconveniences.
WILLIAM WILBERFORCE, *Practical View of the System of Christianity*, 1797

The peace of mind which Religion offers indiscriminately to all ranks afford more true satisfaction than all the expensive pleasures which are beyond the poor man's reach; . . . in this view the poor have the advantage.
WILLIAM WILBERFORCE, *Practical View of the System of Christianity*, 1797

If we know that some are poor only through their own idleness and laziness, with such we are not obliged to share the abundance earned by our labor.
JOHN SERGIEFF OF CRONSTADT (1829–1908), *My Life in Christ*

While we should sympathize with God's poor—that is, those who cannot help themselves—let us remember there is not a poor person in the United States who was not made poor by his own shortcomings, or by the shortcomings of someone else.
RUSSELL H. CONWELL, *Sermon*, Philadelphia, 1925

If we are one body bound to one Head—to Christ—then how shall we tolerate the presence amongst us of poor, hungry brothers?
ALEXANDER YELCHANINOV (1881–1934), *Fragments of a Diary*

Why, damn it all, after twenty centuries of Christianity, to be poor ought not still to be a disgrace. Or else you have gone and betrayed that Christ of yours!
GEORGES BERNANOS, *The Diary of a Country Priest*, 1937

The poor in Jewish thought have a claim to support from the more fortunate as a matter of right, the "haves" being regarded as mere trustees appointed by Providence on behalf of the "have-nots."
ISIDORE EPSTEIN, *Judaism*, 1939

See also Adversity; Affliction; Beggars; Charity; Civilization; Compassion; Desires; Generosity; Greed; Possessions; Poverty; Rich, the; Rights; Sympathy; Wealth Worldliness.

POPE, THE

We commit to thee, as the chief ruler of the universal Church standing on the firm rock of the Faith, what is to be done.
Council of Constantinople to Pope Agatho, 680

The successor of the Apostles was commissioned to lead the Lord's sheep to pasture, not to fleece them.
EDWARD III OF ENGLAND, to Pope Clement VI, c. 1350, quoted in L. Pastor's *History of the Popes*, I

The power of jurisdiction of the Roman Pontiff claims the obedience of the faithful in matters not only of *faith and morals* but also of discipline.
The Vatican Council, 1870

The Orthodox Church does not accept the doctrine of Papal authority . . . but at the same time Orthodoxy does not deny to the Holy and Apostolic See of Rome a *primacy of honour,* together with the right (under certain conditions) to hear appeals from all parts of Christendom. . . . [The] Orthodox regard the Pope as the bishop "who presides in love."

TIMOTHY WARE, *The Orthodox Church,* 1963

Without the Pope the Catholic Church would no longer be catholic. . . . the unity of the Church would utterly collapse.

POPE PAUL VI, *Ecclesiam Suam,* August, 1964

See also Authority; Bishops; Catholicism; Church: Its Authority; Infallibility; Obedience; Peter, St.; Unity.

POPULARITY

Popularity? It is glory's small change.
VICTOR HUGO, *Ruy Blas,* 1838

POPULATION EXPLOSION

The recent explosive growth of the world's population could be a greater threat to world peace and prosperity than the atomic bomb.

KARL SAX, *The Population Explosion,* 1956

The world population problem forms the first world problem in history . . . the implications of which are of direct importance to the welfare of universal humanity.

GEORGE H. L. ZEEGERS, *Cross Currents,* Winter, 1958

Where overpopulation exists, there is a human evil. . . . If reason and medicine bid us to take off excess weight, surely reason and humanity bid us reduce overpopulation.

FREDERICK E. FLYNN, *Lecture* before the Catholic Physicians' Guild of Southern California, May 25, 1960

See also Birth Control.

PORNOGRAPHY. *See* OBSCENITY

POSITIVISM

Each of our leading conceptions passes through three different theoretical conditions: the Theological, or fictitious; the Metaphysical, or abstract; and the Scientific, or positive.

AUGUSTE COMTE, *Positive Philosophy,* 1848

Positivists more truly than theological believers of whatever creed, regard life as a continuous and earnest act of worship; . . . Positivism becomes, in the true sense of the word, a Religion; the only religion which is real and complete; destined therefore to replace all imperfect and provisional systems resting on the primitive basis of theology.

AUGUSTE COMTE, *A General View of Positivism,* 1851

Positivism, that vision of the world in which the supernatural has no place, is destroyed by the scientists, who, after having overthrown the dogmas of faith, are overthrowing their own dogmas. The scientific universe is once more full of mystery.

HENRI MASSIS, *Defense of the West,* 1927

They [Positivists] canalize thought and observation within predetermined limits, based upon inadequate metaphysical assumptions dogmatically assumed.

ALFRED NORTH WHITEHEAD, *Adventures of Ideas,* 1936

The basic doctrine of positivism . . . is itself obviously neither a principle of logic nor the conclusion of any empirical science; it is, therefore, by its own criterion, nonsense.

WILL HERBERG, *Judaism and Modern Man,* 1951

The majority of positivists are . . . for the most part professional philosophers trying to jump on to the scientific bandwagon as it pursues its triumphal march amidst the plaudits of the assembled multitude.

    J. V. L. CASSERLEY, *Retreat from Christianity in the Modern World,* 1952

As surrealism seemed to provide a method of producing works of art without imagination, so logical positivism seems to provide a method of philosophizing without insight and wisdom.

    T. S. ELIOT, Introduction to Josef Pieper's *Leisure, the Basis of Culture,* 1952

One serious consequence of the spread of logical positivism has been to widen the gap between those who accept a natural law basis for moral action and those who reject it.

    JAMES COLLINS, *America,* November 9, 1957

See also Liberalism; Man, Modern; Materialism; Morality; Naturalism; Philosophy; Progress; Rationalism; Science; Science and Religion; Unbelief.

POSSESSIONS

The Lord admits the use of outward things, bidding us put away, not the means of living, but the things that use these badly; and these are, as we have seen, the infirmities and passions of the soul.

    ST. CLEMENT OF ALEXANDRIA (died c 215), *The Rich Man's Salvation*

It is easier to renounce worldly possessions than it is to renounce the love of them.

    WALTER HYLTON (died c. 1396), *The Scale of Perfection*

If there is anything that is mine, then is there nothing that is Divine.

    MICHEL DE MONTAIGNE, *Essays,* Bk. 2, ch. 12, 1580

What God takes away is His own, and not ours, and who shall say: Why hast Thou done this?

    FRANÇOIS FÉNELON (1651–1715), *Spiritual Letters*

See also Desires; Greed; Luxury; Mammon; Materialism; Money; Ownership; Poor, the; Property; Renunciation; Rich, the; Self-Interest; Success; Temporal; World, the; Worldliness.

POSSIBILITIES

To believe only possibilities is not faith, but mere philosophy.

    THOMAS BROWNE, *Religio Medici,* 1642

POSTHUMOUS ECHOES

Like footsteps in a gallery, our lightest movements are heard along the ages.

    S. ALEXANDER, *Moral Order and Progress,* 1889

POVERTY

Poverty which is through honesty is better than opulence which is from the treasure of others.

    Zend-Avesta, 6th century B.C.

Poverty urges us to do and suffer anything that we may escape from it, and so leads us away from virtue.

    HORACE, *Carmina,* c. 20 B.C.

No one should commend poverty but the poor.

    ST. BERNARD, *Sermon,* c. 1150

Poverty is not a shame, but the being ashamed of it.

    THOMAS FULLER, *Gnomologia,* 1732

Poverty often deprives a man of all spirit and virtue.

    BENJAMIN FRANKLIN, *Poor Richard's Almanac,* 1757

Poverty seduces and withdraws men from Heaven as much as wealth.

EMMANUEL SWEDENBORG, *Heaven and Hell*, 1758

All the arguments which are brought to represent poverty as no evil show it to be evidently a great evil. You never find people laboring to convince you that you may live very happily with a plentiful fortune.

SAMUEL JOHNSON, *Boswell's Life*, July 20, 1763

Poverty is the open-mouthed, relentless hell which yawns beneath civilized society. And it is hell enough.

HENRY GEORGE, *Progress and Poverty*, 1879

Although moral conditions are not the sole causes, they are principal causes, of the poverty of the working classes throughout the world.

HENRY WARD BEECHER (1813–1887), *Sermon*

Spiritual poverty consists in esteeming oneself as though not existing, and God alone as existing . . . in considering God's will in everything, both for ourselves and others, entirely renouncing our own will.

JOHN SERGIEFF OF CRONSTADT (1829–1908), *My Life in Christ*

Voluntary poverty turns us toward poverty in spirit, just as does enforced poverty.

PIE-RAYMOND REGAMY, *Poverty*, 1949

See also Adversity; Affliction; Almsgiving; Beggars; Capitalism; Charity; Desires; Detachment; Evil: Its Nature; Greed; Money; Perfection; Politics; Poor, the; Possessions; Property; Riches; Social Conscience; Wealth; Worldliness.

POWER

For all power is from the Lord God, and has been with Him always, and is from everlasting. The power which the prince has is therefore from God, for the power of God is never lost, nor severed from Him.

JOHN OF SALISBURY, *Policraticus*, 1159

Absolute power only implies freedom in relation to positive laws, and not in relation to the law of God.

JEAN BODIN, *The Six Books of the Republic*, 1579

Let all the world learn to give mortal men no greater power than they are content they shall use, for use it they will. . . . It is necessary . . . that all power that is on earth be limited, church-power or other.

JOHN COTTON, *An Exposition of the Thirteenth Chapter of the Revelation*, 1656

Royal power . . . controls the kingdom as God controls the world.

JACQUES BOSSUET, *La Politique Tirée*, 1679

A power over a man's subsistence amounts to a power over his will.

ALEXANDER HAMILTON, *The Federalist*, 1788

To suppose that man has a power independent of God, is to suppose that God's power does not extend to all things, i.e., is not infinite.

DAVID HARTLEY, *Observations on Men*, 1834

The highest proof of virtue is to possess boundless power without abusing it.

T. B. MACAULAY, *Edinburgh Review*, July, 1843

There is no power of which man has ever dreamed that can regenerate human character except religion.

PHILLIPS BROOKS, *Essays and Addresses*, 1894

To have what we want is riches; but to be able to do without is power.

GEORGE MACDONALD (1824–1905), *Selections from,* ed. Dewey

God possesses all the power there is.

HASTING RASHDALL, *Philosophy and Religion,* 1909

If Power is bad, as it seems to be, let us reject it, from our hearts. In this lies man's freedom: in determination to worship only the God created by our own love of the good, to respect only the heaven which inspires the insight of our last moments.

BERTRAND RUSSELL, *Mysticism and Logic,* 1918

Pentecost, the healing miracles of the Apostolic Age, the triumphant progress of the religion through the Roman Empire, the heroic deeds of saints and martyrs,— all these point to the sense of a power newly discovered.

J. A. HADFIELD, *The Spirit,* ed. B. H. Streeter, 1919

All power wherever found is power for evil as well as for good; and the greater the power, the greater the evil.

VINCENT MCNABB, *From a Friar's Cell,* 1923

Unbridled ambition for domination has succeeded the desire for gain; the whole economic life has become hard, cruel and relentless in a ghastly measure.

POPE PIUS XI, *Quadragesimo Anno,* 1931

The power of man has grown so great that it has denied and shut out the power of the Spirit and consequently it is destroying the world.

CHRISTOPHER DAWSON, *Dublin Review,* July, 1942

I am very doubtful whether history shows us one example of a man who, having stepped outside traditional morality and attained power, has used that power benevolently.

C. S. LEWIS, *The Abolition of Man,* 1947

Power is a dangerous thing to handle, even in religion.

JOSEPH R. SIZOO, *Preaching Unashamed,* 1949

One of the paradoxes of our time is that we have more power at our disposal than ever before, and yet we seem more powerless than ever.

RALPH W. SOCKMAN, *How to Believe,* 1953

The love of power is oppressive in every sphere, but in the religious most of all.

ROMANO GUARDINI, *The Church and the Catholic,* 1953

Power can be invested with a sense of direction only by moral principles. It is the function of morality to command the use of power, to forbid it, to limit it.

JOHN COURTNEY MURRAY, *We Hold These Truths,* 1960

See also Ambition; Church and State; Dictatorship; Equality; Fame; Freedom; God: His Omnipotence; Government; Law; Machines; Nonresistance; Nuclear Energy; Paganism; Political Power; Property; State, the; Technology.

PRACTICE

Like a beautiful flower full of color but without scent are the fair words of him who himself does not act accordingly.

Dhammapada, c. 5th century B.C.

Every one of us, whatever our speculative opinions, knows better than he practices, and recognizes a better law than he obeys.

J. A. FROUDE, *On Progress,* 1882

When it was over I had time to take stock of the congregation: they would have been equally horrified at hearing the Christian religion doubted and at seeing it practiced.

SAMUEL BUTLER, *The Way of All Flesh*, 1884

Disbelief in Christianity is not so much to be dreaded as its acceptance with a complete denial of it in society and politics.

MARK RUTHERFORD, *More Pages from a Journal*, 1910

Anyone who concluded that the behavior of the Christians showed that they did not really believe in God but only thought they believed, might then equally conclude that the Communists really believed in God and only thought they did not.

JOHN MACMURRAY, *Creative Society*, 1935

If we speak the truth without *doing* it, we run the risk of leading men to regard truth as an imposture.

JACQUES MARITAIN, *Ransoming the Time*, 1941

If we are to be realistic, we must face these two facts: the uncompromising principle of our Christian profession and the unprincipled practice of our daily living.

A. K. CHALMERS, *High Wind at Noon*, 1948

The threat to the religious attitude lies not in science but in the predominant practices of daily life.

ERICH FROMM, *Psychoanalysis and Religion*, 1950

Faith and practice must go together; the doing of the works is a condition of the learning of the doctrine.

CHARLES E. RAVEN, *Theological Basis of Christian Pacifism*, 1952

Monday religion is better than Sunday profession.

ANONYMOUS

See also Acts; Apathy; Behavior; Belief; Believing; Clergy, Criticism of; Commitment; Conduct; Deeds; Duties; Faith; Hypocrisy; Inaction; Individual Responsibility; Preachers; Preaching.

PRAGMATISM

The part of wisdom as well as of courage is *to believe what is in the line of your needs,* for only by such belief is the need fulfilled.

WILLIAM JAMES, *The Will to Believe and Other Essays*, 1896

If the hypothesis of God works satisfactorily in the widest sense of the word—experience shows that it certainly does work—it is true.

WILLIAM JAMES, *Pragmatism*, 1907

The true is the name of whatever proves itself to be good in the way of belief.

WILLIAM JAMES, *Pragmatism*, 1907

The mind of today is intensely practical, if not pragmatic. It insists that for it, at least, a valid Christianity is to be known not by its *roots*, but by its *fruits*.

CHARLES D. WILLIAMS, *A Valid Christianity for Today*, 1909

The pragmatist is bound by his own theory that the time may come when it will no longer be found adequate to the requirements of a wider experience to say that truth is relative.

C. F. RUSSELL, *Religion and the Natural Law*, 1924

See also Absolutes; Belief; Expediency; Optimism; Philosophy; Relativity; Skepticism; Truth.

PRAISE

He has the soundest perception who recognizes that even the love of praise is a vice.

ST. AUGUSTINE, *The City of God*, 426

In the morning, when the sun rises, all men ought to praise God, who created it for our use, for all things are made visible by it. But in the evening, when it is night, all men ought to praise God for Brother Fire, which gives our eyes light at night.
> ST. FRANCIS OF ASSISI (1181?–1226), *Little Flowers of*

He who loves praise, loves temptation.
> THOMAS WILSON, *Maxims of Piety and Christianity,* 1755

We pour out our painful *misereres* in the ear of Heaven. Why should not an exultant *Magnificat* occasionally rise above them.
> P. A. SHEEHAN, *Under the Cedars and the Stars,* 1903

It is impossible not to praise God when you remember that you were predestined from the foundation of the world for eternal blessedness, quite without cause, not in accordance with your merits—when you remember what grace God has bestowed upon you for your salvation during all your lifetime.
> JOHN SERGIEFF OF CRONSTADT (1828–1908), *My Life in Christ*

See also Adoration; Flattery; God, Praise of; Prayer; Self-Praise; Worship.

PRAYER

Pray, for all men need the aid of the gods.
> HOMER, *Odyssey,* c. 800 B.C.

Prayer is the greatest of spells, the best healing of all spells. . . . Amongst all remedies this one is the healing one that heals with the Holy Word.
> *Yasht, Zend-Avesta,* c. 700 B.C.

Prayer smites down the strength of all the creatures of Ahriman [the Zoroastrian "devil"]. It is the greatest, the best of all spells.
> *Zend-Avesta,* 6th century B.C.

He who offends against heaven has none to whom he can pray.
> CONFUCIUS, *Analects of,* c. 5th century B.C.

An angel collects all the prayers offered in the synagogues, weaves them into garlands, and puts them on God's head.
> MEIR. *Exod. R.,* 21.4, *Zohar, Gen.,* c. 150 A.D.

If Apostles and martyrs, while still in the body, can pray for others, when they ought still to be anxious for themselves, how much more must they do so after they have their crowns and victories and triumphs?
> ST. JEROME, *Attack on Vigilantius,* c. 396

He prays in the temple of God who prays in the peace of the Church, in the unity of Christ's body; which body of Christ consists of the many in the whole world who believe.
> ST. AUGUSTINE, *Ennaration on Psalm CXXX,* c. 415

What time is so holy and fit for sanctification and the receiving of gifts as the time of prayer, in which man speaks with God?
> ST. ISAAC OF NINEVEH, c. 700, *The Apostolic Fathers,* ed. Lightfoot

And why pierceth it heaven, this little short prayer of one syllable [God]? for it is prayed with a full spirit, in the height and in the depth, in the length and in the breadth of his spirit that prayeth it.
> *The Cloud of Unknowing,* 14th century

The Goodness of God is the highest prayer.
> JULIANA OF NORWICH, *Revelations of Divine Love,* 15th century

Accursed the life of him in this world who breatheth without uttering the Name.
> GURU NANAK (1496–1538), *The Sikh Religion,* M. A. Macauliffe

Granting that we are always in the presence of God, yet it seems to me that those who pray are in His presence in a very different sense; for they, as it were, see that He is looking upon them.

ST. TERESA OF ÁVILA, *Autobiography,* 1565

Let him never cease from prayer who has once begun it, be his life ever so wicked; for prayer is the way to amend it, and without prayer such amendment will be much more difficult.

ST. TERESA OF ÁVILA, *Autobiography,* 1565

To pray alone, and reject ordinary means, is to do like him in Aesop, that when his car was stalled, lay flat on his back and cried aloud, help Hercules!

ROBERT BURTON, *Anatomy of Melancholy,* II, 1621

A good prayer, though often used, is still fresh and fair in the eyes and ears of Heaven.

THOMAS FULLER, *Good Thoughts in Bad Times,* 1645

There is not in the world a kind of life more sweet and delightful than that of a continual conversation with GOD.

NICHOLAS HERMAN OF LORRAINE, Brother Lawrence, *Practice of the Presence of God,* c. 1666

Prayer is the world in tune.

HENRY VAUGHAN (1622–1695), *The Morning Watch*

He who has learned to pray has learned the greatest secret of a holy and happy life.

WILLIAM LAW, *Christian Perfection,* 1726

There is nothing that makes us love a man so much as praying for him. . . . By considering yourself as an advocate with God for your neighbors and acquaint-ances, you would never find it hard to be at peace with them yourself.

WILLIAM LAW, *A Serious Call,* 1728

Each prayer has its own proper meaning and it is therefore the specific key to a door in the Divine Palace, but a broken heart is an axe which opens all the gates.

RABBI ISRAEL BAAL-SHEM TOB (1700–1760), quoted in *Judaism,* ed. A. Hertzberg

The wish to talk to God is absurd. We cannot talk to one we cannot comprehend —and we cannot comprehend God; we can only believe in Him. The uses of prayer are thus only subjective.

IMMANUEL KANT, *Lecture at Königsberg,* 1775

The prayers of an old man are the only contributions left in his power.

THOMAS JEFFERSON, *Letter to Mrs. K. D. Morgan,* 1822

Prayer is always possible for everyone, rich and poor, noble and simple, strong and weak, healthy and suffering, righteous and sinful. Great is the power of prayer; most of all does it bring the Spirit of God and easiest of all it is to exercise.

ST. SERAPHIM OF SAROV (1759–1833), *Conversation with Nicholas Motovilov*

No man ever prayed heartily without learning something.

RALPH WALDO EMERSON, *Nature,* 1836

The enthusiasm of prayer is likewise a mystery between man and God; like modesty it casts a veil over thought and hides from men what is meant for heaven.

ALPHONSE DE LAMARTINE, *Travels in the East,* 1839

The shorter our allotted time is, the easier it perhaps is to decide to pray for one's enemies.

SÖREN KIERKEGAARD (1813–1855), *Meditations from,* ed. T. H. Croxall

It is not well for a man to pray cream, and live skim milk.

HENRY WARD BEECHER, *Life Thoughts*, 1858

I knew that defeat in a great battle on Northern soil involved loss of Washington. . . . I went to my room and got down on my knees in prayer. Never before had I prayed with as much earnestness.

ABRAHAM LINCOLN, to General Daniel G. Sickles shortly after the Battle of Gettysburg, 1863

Be not forgetful of prayer. Every time you pray, if your prayer is sincere, there will be new feeling and new meaning in it, which will give you fresh courage, and you will understand that prayer is an education.

FEODOR DOSTOEVSKY, *The Brothers Karamazov*, 1880

Failure in prayer is the loss of religion itself in its inward and dynamic aspect of fellowship with the Eternal.

HARRY EMERSON FOSDICK, *The Meaning of Prayer*, 1915

Only a theoretical deity is left to any man who has ceased to commune with God, and a theoretical deity saves no man from sin and disheartenment.

HARRY EMERSON FOSDICK, *The Meaning of Prayer*, 1915

Greater than prayer is the spirit in which it is uttered.

GLENN CLARK, *The Soul's Sincere Desire*, 1925

There is no going out of sin into Grace without prayer, some sort of desire for Almighty God; some sort of Hope.

VINCENT MCNABB, *God's Way of Mercy*, 1928

The prayer that we find hardest to comprehend, namely, the intercessory, Jesus took most easily and naturally for granted.

FRANCIS J. MCCONNELL, *The Christlike God*, 1929

We can prove the reality of prayer only by praying.

SHERWOOD EDDY, *We Believe in Prayer*, 1930

In his moments of prayer, when he and God tried to commune with each other, it wasn't his own shortcomings that were brought on the carpet, but God's.

CLARENCE DAY, *God and My Father*, 1932

What a spectacle for heaven and earth is not the Church in prayer! For centuries without interruption, from midnight to midnight, is repeated on earth the divine psalmody of the inspired canticles; there is no hour of the day that is not hallowed by its special liturgy.

POPE PIUS XI, *Caritate Christi Compulsi*, 1932

The wish to pray is a prayer in itself.

GEORGES BERNANOS, *The Diary of a Country Priest*, 1937

When has any man of prayer told us that prayer has failed him?

GEORGES BERNANOS, *The Diary of a Country Priest*, 1937

It is prayer that brings home to a man the right and claims of God, and the duty of man towards Him.

ALBAN GOODIER, *Ascetical and Mystical Theology*, 1938

It is more natural to pray to a finite God, who may be moved by our infirmities.

E. S. BRIGHTMAN, *A Philosophy of Religion*, 1940

For whatever high reasons, men of prayer must knock and knock—sometimes with bleeding knuckles in the dark.

GEORGE A. BUTTRICK, *Prayer*, 1942

For a man to argue, "I do not go to church; I pray alone," is no wiser than if

he should say, "I have no use for symphonies; I believe only in solo music."
GEORGE A. BUTTRICK, *Prayer*, 1942

Eloquent prayers are apt to be addressed, not to God, but to the congregation.
L. P. JACKS, *Confession of an Octogenarian*, 1942

Men have been urged to pray, when they would have done better to think, observe and act.
H. G. WOODS, *Christianity and Civilization*, 1943

Of all the things the world now desperately needs, none is more needed than an upsurge of vital, God-centered, intelligently grounded prayer.
GEORGIA HARKNESS, *Prayer and the Common Life*, 1948

When we dispute over dogmas we are divided. But when we take to the religious life of prayer and contemplation, we are brought together. The deeper the prayers, the more is the individual lost in the apprehension of the Supreme.
S. RADHAKRISHNAN, *Religion and Society*, 1948

You have to have darkness to find a picture on the sensitive plate, and you have to have prayer to bring out the invisible presence of God.
FULTON OURSLER, *Why I Know There Is a God*, 1949

Prayer is the one human activity where any inner suggestion of triumph, any shy satisfaction is most likely to be false.
JOHN W. LYNCH, *Hourglass*, 1952

What debilitates our prayer life . . . is our presupposition that the pressures of life are on one side while God is on some other side.
GEORGE MACLEOD, *Only One Way Left*, 1956

What is the use of praying if at the very moment of prayer we have so little confidence in God that we are busy planning our own kind of answer to our prayer?
THOMAS MERTON, *Thoughts in Solitude*, 1958

Our Lord's first public act was prayer. "As he prayed the heavens were opened." The last act of the Crucified before giving up His life in atonement for the world's sin was prayer.
OSWALD C. J. HOFFMANN, *Life Crucified*, 1959

Your influence for Christ will depend, beyond all your knowing and beyond anybody else's knowing, on your having one foot set on the ladder of prayer.
R. A. KNOX, *University and Anglican Sermons*, 1963

The most pious prayer can become a blasphemy if he who offers it tolerates or helps to further conditions which are fatal to mankind, which render him unacceptable to God, or weaken his spiritual, moral or religious sense.
ALFRED DELP, *Prison Meditations of Father Alfred Delp*, 1963

He that prays much by night, his face is fair by day.
Traditional Moslem saying

If your knees are knocking, kneel on them. Sign outside London Air Raid Post, World War II

Kneeling will keep you in good standing.
ANONYMOUS

See also Action and Prayer; Adoration; Blessings; Brotherhood; Church and State; Community; Confidence; Contemplation; Desire and Prayer; Devotion; Emotion, Experience, Religious; Faith and Prayer; God: Finding Him; God, Praise of: Grace; Heart; Holiness; Hope; Labor; Liturgy;

Lord's Prayer; Love of God; Man and God; Man's Quest of God; Man's Unity with God; Meditation; Music; Mystical Experience; Mysticism; Perfection; Poems and Poets; Poetry; Praise; other rubrics under Prayer; Religion, Definitions of; Rosary; Silence; Solitude; Song; Spiritual; Spiritual Life; Spiritual Progress; Sunday; Temptation; Thanksgiving; Words; Worship.

PRAYER: DEFINED AND EXPLAINED

He who has no prayer free from his thoughts has no weapon for battle. By prayer I mean the prayer which is constantly active in the innermost secret places of the soul.

> HESYCHIUS OF JERUSALEM, *On Sobriety,* c. 425 A.D.

Prayer is the service of the heart.
> *Talmud: Taanit,* 2a., c. 500

The highest state of prayer, they say, is when the spirit leaves the body and the world, and, in the act of prayer, loses all matter and all form.

> ST. MAXIMUS THE CONFESSOR, *Centuries of Charity,* c. 626

The unfolding of one's will to God that He may fulfill it.

> ST. THOMAS AQUINAS, *Summa Theologiae,* III, 21, i, 1272

Prayer is the drowning and unconsciousness of the soul.

> JALA AL-DIN RUMINI (died 1273 A.D.), quoted in *Rumi: Poet and Mystic,* translated by R. A. Nicholson

He that truly devoutly prays has not his heart wavering in earthly things but raised to God in heavens.

> RICHARD ROLLE (1290?–1349), *The Fire of Love*

Prayer is nought but a rising desire of the heart into God by withdrawing of the heart from all earthly thoughts.

> WALTER HYLTON, *The Scale of Perfection,* 1494

And to make a Prayer a right Prayer, there go so many essential circumstances, as that the best man may justly suspect his best Prayer; for, since Prayer must be of faith, Prayer can be but so perfect, as the faith is perfect.

> JOHN DONNE, *Sermon,* Funeral of Sir William Cockayne, December 26, 1626

Prayer is an actuation of an intellective soul towards God, expressing, or at least implying, an entire dependence on Him as the author and fountain of all good, a will and readiness to give Him his due, which is no less than all love, all obedience, all adoration, glory and worship.

> AUGUSTINE BAKER, *Holy Wisdom,* 1657

Prayer is the peace of our spirit, the stillness of our thoughts, the evenness of recollection, the seat of meditation, the rest of our cares, and the calm of our tempest; prayer is the issue of a quiet mind, of untroubled thoughts.

> JEREMY TAYLOR (1613–1667), "The Return of Prayers," *Sermons*

True prayer, and that which is best, lies in whatever unites us to God, whatever enables us to enjoy Him, to appreciate Him, to rejoice in His Glory, and to love Him as one's very own.

> JACQUES BÉNIGNE BOSSUET (1627–1704), *Letters of*

The Spirit of Prayer is a pressing forth of the soul out this earthly life. It is a stretching with all its desire after the life of God.

> WILLIAM LAW, *The Spirit of Prayer,* 1749

755

Prayer is an act of daring. Otherwise it is impossible to stand in prayer before God.

> RABBI ISRAEL BAAL-SHEM TOB (1700–1760), quoted in *Judaism*, ed. A. Hertzberg

Prayer that craves a particular commodity, anything less than all good, is vicious. Prayer is the contemplation of the facts of life from the highest point of view. It is the soliloquy of a beholding and jubilant soul. It is the spirit of God pronouncing His works good.

> RALPH WALDO EMERSON, "Self-Reliance," *Essays*, 1841

Christianity would teach us that prayer, blessed as it is in itself, reaches toward something more blessed, and is not in itself the height of blessedness.

> SÖREN KIERKEGAARD (1813–1855), *Meditations from*, ed. T. H. Croxall

Anything large enough for a wish to light upon, is large enough to hang a prayer upon.

> GEORGE MACDONALD, *Unspoken Sermons*, 1st Series, 1869

Prayer is and remains always a native and deepest impulse of the soul of man.

> THOMAS CARLYLE, *Letter to G. A. Duncan*, June 9, 1870

All good and beneficial prayer is . . . at bottom nothing else than an energy of aspiration towards the eternal *not ourselves* that makes for righteousness, of aspiration towards it, and of cooperation with it.

> MATTHEW ARNOLD, *Literature and Dogma*, 1873

By prayer I do not mean a request preferred to a deity; I mean . . . intense aspiration.

> RICHARD JEFFERIES, *Story of My Heart*, 1883

The very act of prayer justifies God, honors God, and gives glory to God; for it confesses that God is what He is, a good God.

> CHARLES KINGSLEY, *Westminster Sermons*, 1890

Prayer is religion in act; that is, prayer is real religion. It is prayer that distinguishes the religious phenomenon from such similar or neighboring phenomena as purely moral or aesthetic sentiment.

> AUGUSTE SABATIER, *Esquisse d'une Philosophie de la Religion*, 1891

Prayer is the constant feeling (the recognition) of our infirmity or spiritual poverty, the sanctification of the soul, the foretaste of future blessedness, the angelic bliss, the heavenly rain, refreshing, watering, and fertilizing the ground of the soul, the power and strength of the soul and body, the purifying and freshening of the mental air, the enlightenment of the countenance, the joy of the spirit, the golden link, uniting the creature to the Creator.

> JOHN SERGIEFF OF CRONSTADT, *My Life in Christ*, 1897

With me prayer is a lifting up of the heart, a look towards Heaven, a cry of gratitude and love uttered equally in sorrow and in joy; in a word, something noble, supernatural, which enlarges my soul and unites it to God.

> ST. THÉRÈSE OF LISIEUX (1873–1897), *Autobiography*, publ. posth.

The very movement itself of the soul, putting itself into a personal relation of contact with the mysterious power—of which it feels the presence.

> WILLIAM JAMES, *Varieties of Religious Experience*, 1902

In rational prayer the soul may be said to accomplish three things important to its welfare: it withdraws within itself and defines its good, it accommodates itself to destiny, and it grows like the ideal which it conceives.

> GEORGE SANTAYANA, *Reason in Religion*, 1905

Prayer is not a substitute for work; it is a desperate effort to work further and to be efficient beyond the range of one's powers.

GEORGE SANTAYANA, *Reason in Religion,* 1905

Prayer winds in and out through the manifold actions, moral and otherwise, that forever are springing up in our field of life; it gathers them together in sheaves, and bears them into the granaries of the Divine Reaper.

DESIRÉ JOSEPH MERCIER, *Conferences of,* 1907

Prayer, rightly understood, prepares the soul for action, sustains her on life's road when weary and worn, and arms her for the fight when the foe assails her.

DESIRÉ JOSEPH MERCIER, *Conferences of,* 1907

To pray means to relive one's heart, to bid care begone, to breathe out misery and distress, to breathe in the pure mountain air and the energy of another world.

PAUL WILHELM VON KEPPLER, *More Joy,* 1911

The whole function is expressed in a word, it is simply this—the child at his father's knee, his words stumbling over each other from very earnestness, and his wistful face pleading better than his hardly intelligible prayer.

FREDERICK W. FABER, *The Spirit of,* 1914

Prayer is a gift and sacrifice *we* make; sacrament is a gift and sacrifice that God makes . . . in prayer we go to God, in Sacrament He comes to us.

P. T. FORSYTH, *The Church and the Sacraments,* 1917

The Christian who prays, recollects himself, that is to say he discovers himself, gathers himself together, frees himself from all useless masters, from all unknown hands, from all fast-holding desires which

tear him to pieces and so prevent him from being himself.

PIERRE CHARLES, *Prayer for All Times,* 1925

Each stage of a progressive prayer-life is a stage in the putting to death of the self that God may work and reign.

E. HERMAN, *Creative Prayer,* 1925

Why is poetry incapable of apprehending God as prayer apprehends Him? Because not only contemplation, but the humblest prayer worthy of the name is a supernatural gift of God.

HENRI BREMOND, *Prayer and Poetry,* 1927

It is a direct approach to the throbbing heart of the universe.

ISRAEL BETTAN, *Post-Biblical Judaism: Its Spiritual Note,* 1930

The passionate yearning which is poured forth in prayer does not spring from man's narrow heart, but from God's eternal love to allure and draw man upward toward Himself.

FRIEDRICH HEILER, *Prayer,* 1932

Prayer wells up from the subconscious life of the soul.

FRIEDRICH HEILER, *Prayer,* 1932

Prayer is not a vain attempt to change God's will; it is a filial desire to learn God's will and to share it.

GEORGE A. BUTTRICK, *The Christian Fact and Modern Doubt,* 1934

Prayer should be understood, not as a mere mechanical recitation of formulas, but as a mystical elevation, an absorption of consciousness in the contemplation of a principle both permeating and transcending our world.

ALEXIS CARREL, *Man, the Unknown,* 1935

Prayer, in the sense of union with God, is the most crucifying thing there is. One must do it for God's sake, but one will not get any satisfaction out of it, in the sense of feeling "I am good at prayer."

JOHN CHAPMAN, *Spiritual Letters,* 1935

He who prays must commit himself and his wants to the transforming power of God. He must seek what is genuinely the greatest good and not merely the specific things which will satisfy his present wants.

HENRY N. WIEMAN, *Normative Psychology of Religion,* 1935

The purpose of prayer is to leave us alone with God.

LEO BAECK, *Essence of Judaism,* 1936

When we pray it is not a question of persuading God, of inclining Him, of changing His providential dispositions; it is simply a question of raising our will to the level of His will so as to will with Him what He has decided to give us.

REGINALD GARRIGOU-LAGRANGE, *Christian Perfection and Contemplation,* 1937

Prayer is not asking for things—not even for the best things; it is going where they are.

GERALD HEARD, *The Third Morality,* 1937

A great deal of prayer is instinctive and proceeds primarily from self-love. This type of prayer is supernatural, but it is natural as well, since it is promoted by self-interest.

OTTOKAR PROHASZKA, *Meditations on the Gospels,* 1937

The agony of prayer is giving up ourselves and our own wills, and accepting blindly all that seems to go much against our prospects.

WILLIAM OF GLASSHAMPTON (1862–1937), quoted in Geoffrey Curtis, *William of Glasshampton*

Strictly speaking there is really only one legitimate object in prayer, and that is the desire for communion with God.

A. VICTOR MURRAY, *Personal Experience and the Historic Faith,* 1939

Prayer is the effort of man to reach God, to commune with an invisible being.

ALEXIS CARREL, *Reader's Digest,* March, 1941

When we pray, we link ourselves with the inexhaustible power that spins the universe. We ask that a part of this power be apportioned to our needs. Even in asking, our human deficiencies are filled and we arise strengthened and repaired.

ALEXIS CARREL, *Reader's Digest,* March, 1941

To pray is to expose oneself to the promptings of God; and, by the same token, to become less suggestible to the low persuasions of the world.

GEORGE A. BUTTRICK, *Prayer,* 1942

Prayer is not bending to my will, but it is a bringing of my will into conformity with God's will, so that His work may work in and through me.

E. STANLEY JONES, *How to Pray,* 1943

Prayer . . . is . . . a technique for contacting and learning to know Reality . . . the exploration of Reality by exploring the Beyond, which is within.

GERALD HEARD, *A Preface to Prayer,* 1944

The impulse to pray, the ultimate impulse, is the inrush of the divine waters, waters that must return to the ocean of the Godhead and in their return bear along with them the soul of man.

JAMES EDWARD O'MAHONY, *The Music of Life,* 1944

Praying is identifying oneself with the divine Will by the studied renunciation of one's own, not by curbing one's desire but by acquiescing in a stronger Will.

PAUL CLAUDEL, *Lord, Teach Us to Pray,* 1948

The act of praying centers attention on the higher emotion, unifies the spirit, crystallizes emotions, clarifies the judgments, releases latent powers, reinforces confidence that what needs to be done can be done.

GEORGIA HARKNESS, *Prayer and the Common Life,* 1948

Systematized prayer is a sort of mental crutch—something to lean upon when the limbs have not sufficient strength to propel the body on their own.

HUBERT VAN ZELLER, *We Die Standing Up,* 1949

A lot of the trouble about prayer would disappear if we only realized—*really* realized, and not just supposed that it was so—that we go to pray not because we love prayer but because we love God.

HUBERT VAN ZELLER, *We Die Standing Up,* 1949

Prayer enables us to disregard self, and it allows us to become disentangled from the trammels of egotism. In prayer as in nothing else we can find refuge from the degradation of self-love.

WILLIAM L. SULLIVAN, *Worry! Fear! Loneliness!,* 1950

If prayer were a cringing, whining, coaxing of a whimsical God, it would debase a man; where, in fact, it is the shouldering of the burden of his own destiny, a doing of his part in winning heaven.

WALTER FARRELL, *My Way of Life,* 1952

A voluntary dedication, a daily assignment of all work and play and activity for the glory of God can make anything genuine prayer, whether it is digging ditches, doing the dishes, selling insurance, or even playing golf, which is often the same as digging ditches.

JOHN W. LYNCH, *Hourglass,* 1952

In prayer we open the gates of our larger self . . . God comes in to us and claims his own.

J. J. WEINSTEIN, *Gentle Rain,* 1953

To pray is to become a ladder on which thoughts mount to God to join the movement toward Him which surges unnoticed throughout the entire universe.

ABRAHAM J. HESCHEL, *Man's Quest for God,* 1954

In prayer we shift the center of living from self-consciousness to self-surrender.

ABRAHAM J. HESCHEL, *Man's Quest for God,* 1954

Prayer is our humble answer to the inconceivable surprise of living.

ABRAHAM J. HESCHEL, *Man's Quest for God,* 1954

It is God Himself who prays through us, when we pray to Him. . . . We cannot bridge the gap between God and ourselves even through the most intensive and frequent prayers; the gap between God and ourselves can only be bridged by God.

PAUL TILLICH, *The New Being,* 1955

When we pray for another, it is not an attempt to alter God's mind toward him. In prayer we add our wills to God's good will . . . that in fellowship with Him He and we may minister to those whom both He and we love.

HENRY SLOANE COFFIN, *Joy in Believing,* 1956

Prayer is God's own psychotherapy for His sinful children. It is His method of uncovering unconscious motivations and of recalling to consciousness those things which have been excluded as painful and humiliating.

RAPHAEL SIMON, *Hammer and Fire,* 1959

See also Abandonment; Aspiration; Detachment; Mysticism; other rubrics under Prayer; Reality; Self-Giving; Selflessness.

PRAYER: ITS EFFICACY

The only thing which binds God is prayer.
TERTULLIAN, *De Oratione*, c. 200

Prayer altogether blots out very little and daily sins.
ST. AUGUSTINE, *On Faith, Hope and Charity*, c. 421

Prayer is . . . the source and origin of every upward progress that has God for goal.
ST. BONAVENTURE, *The Journey of the Mind to God*, 1259

If prayer do not aid me first,
That riseth up from heart which lives in grace,
What other kind avails, not heard in heaven?
DANTE, "Purgatory," *Divine Comedy,* c. 1310

God hears us not the sooner for our many words, but much the sooner for an earnest desire.
JEREMY TAYLOR, *Holy Living,* 1650

He that would pray with effect must live with care and piety.
JEREMY TAYLOR, *Holy Living,* 1650

As a coal is revived by incense, prayer revives the hope of the heart.
G. W. VON GOETHE (1749–1832), *Maxims and Reflections of,* ed. B. Saunders

Prayer is the queen of the world. Clothed in humble garments, with bowed head, with outstretched hands, it protects the universe by its supplicant majesty.
JEAN BAPTISTE LACORDAIRE (1802–1861), *Thoughts and Teaching of*

When the gods wish to punish us they answer our prayers.
OSCAR WILDE, *An Ideal Husband,* 1895

The prayer that reforms the sinner and heals the sick is an absolute faith that all things are possible to God,—a spiritual understanding of Him, an unselfed love.
MARY BAKER EDDY, *Science and Health,* 1908

On all my expeditions, prayer made me stronger, morally and mentally, than any of my non-praying companions.
HENRY M. STANLEY, *Autobiography of,* 1909

From the purely scientific point of view we may be bound to regard the efficacy of prayer as due to suggestion. . . . The mechanism of suggestion in prayer may be regarded as God's way of reinforcing our energies through the subconscious.
E. J. PRICE, *Hibbert Journal,* XXII, 1924

The heavens are as brass toward any petition that asks for what is against the laws of nature. There is a law of prayer and its answer.
DOUGLAS CLYDE MACINTOSH, *The Reasonableness of Christianity,* 1925

God rules the world; the laws of Nature are His laws and in no way constrain His freedom. Thus there is no reason to believe that God cannot grant favorable answers to the crudest petitionary prayers.
E. W. BARNES, *Scientific Theory and Religion,* 1933

True prayer, by which we ask for ourselves with humility, confidence, and perseverance, the gifts necessary for our sanctification, is infallibly efficacious.
REGINALD GARRIGOU-LAGRANGE, *Christian Perfection and Contemplation,* 1937

It seems to us that the will of God bends when our prayer is heard and granted; yet it is our will alone that ascends. We begin to will in time what God has willed us from all eternity.
REGINALD GARRIGOU-LAGRANGE, *Christian Perfection and Contemplation,* 1937

We derive most power from prayer when we use it, not as a petition, but as a supplication that we may become more like Him.

ALEXIS CARREL, *Reader's Digest*, March, 1941

It is the only power in the world that seems to overcome the so-called "laws of nature."

ALEXIS CARREL, *Reader's Digest*, March, 1941

The real tragedy of our prayers is not that God so often refuses to grant them. The tragedy is we so often ask for the wrong thing.

R. A. KNOX, *Retreat for Priests*, 1946

The efficacy of prayer is not to be judged by whether it fulfills a specific request, but by the power of God which it brings to the person who commits himself to its method.

E. LEROY LONG, JR., *Science and Christian Faith*, 1950

It is not very good for people to know how well they pray! To try to find out whether we are standing well with God is rather a perilous thing.

VINCENT MCNABB, *The Craft of Prayer*, 1951

When we succeed in mastering the act of prayer, we can face the twilight of life, its tragedy and trials, and yet look hopefully for the dawn.

ROBERT GORDIS, *The Ladder of Prayer*, 1956

Believe that you are receiving answers to your prayers. Belief tends to create that which is held in the mind by faith.

NORMAN VINCENT PEALE, *Try Prayer Power*, 1959

When in prayer you clasp your hands, God opens his.

German proverb

See also God: His Intervention in the World; God: His Omnipotence; Will.

PRAYER: ITS NECESSITY

We never need to pray so earnestly as when we cannot lay hold of any pleasure in prayer.

FRANÇOIS FÉNELON (1651–1715), *Spiritual Letters*

For this is the necessity of our nature, pray we must, as sure as our heart is alive, and therefore when the state of the heart is not a Spirit of Prayer to God, we pray without ceasing to some other part of the Creation.

WILLIAM LAW, *the Spirit of Prayer*, 1749

Prayer is the most perfect and most divine action that a rational soul is capable of. It is of all actions and duties the most indispensably necessary.

AUGUSTINE BAKER, *Holy Wisdom*, 1876

Though God knows all our needs, prayer is necessary for the cleansing and enlightenment of the soul.

JOHN SERGIEFF OF CRONSTADT, *My Life in Christ*, 1897

We hear in these days of scientific enlightenment a great deal of discussion about the efficacy of *Prayer*. . . . Very little is said of the reason we do pray. The reason is simple: We pray because we cannot help praying.

WILLIAM JAMES, *The Varieties of Religious Experience*, 1902

What can a man do but pray. He is here—helpless—and his origin, the breath of his soul, his God must be somewhere. And what else should he pray about but the thing that troubles him?

GEORGE MACDONALD (1824–1905), *Selections from*, ed. Dewey

No one can find out except by trying whether he needs prayer once an hour, once a week, or less often.

RICHARD C. CABOT, *What Men Live By,* 1915

The more moral a man is the more desperately he needs the techniques of prayer . . . which . . . alone can humble him in his own eyes.

J. V. L. CASSERLEY, *Retreat from Christianity in the Modern World,* 1952

See also other rubrics under Prayer.

PRAYER, METHODS AND TIME OF

The only prayer which a well-meaning man can pray is, O ye gods, give me whate'er is fitting unto me!

APOLLONIUS OF TYANA, c. 50 B.C.

We should have fixed hours for praying, so that if we happen to be engaged in some business, the time itself will remind us our duty. Everyone knows that the third, sixth, and ninth hours, dawn, too, and evening, are the right times.

ST. JEROME, *To Eustochium,* c. 405

To use much speaking in prayer is to employ a superfluity of words in asking a necessary thing; but to prolong prayer is to have the heart throbbing with continued pious emotion towards Him to whom we pray. For in most cases prayer consists more in groaning than in speaking, in tears rather than in words.

ST. AUGUSTINE, *To Proba,* 412

It is neither wrong nor unprofitable to spend much time in praying, if there be leisure for this without hindering other good and necessary works to which duty calls us.

ST. AUGUSTINE, *To Proba,* 412

Do you wish to pray in the temple? Pray in your own heart. But begin by being

God's temple, for He will listen to those who invoke Him in His temple.

ST. AUGUSTINE, *In Johann. Evang.,* tract. XV.6, c. 416

We should pray frequently, it is true, but our prayer should be brief lest, while we linger, the deceitful enemy find an opportunity of invading our hearts.

JOHN CASSIAN, *Conferences,* IX, 36, c. 420

Our prayer ought to be short and pure, unless it happens to be prolonged by inspiration of divine grace. In community, however, let prayer be very short.

ST. BENEDICT, *Rule of,* c. 530

The earth is a mosque for thee; therefore wherever the time of prayer reaches thee, there pray.

Koran, c. 625 A.D.

O true believers, when ye prepare yourselves to pray, wash your faces, and your hands unto the elbows; and rub your heads, and your feet unto the ankles; and if ye be polluted by having lain with a woman, wash yourselves all over.

Koran, c. 625 A.D.

Do not pray when you are drunk, until you know what you utter.

Koran, c. 625 A.D.

Who sincerely loves God also prays absolutely undistracted, and who prays absolutely undistracted also sincerely loves God.

ST. MAXIMUS THE CONFESSOR, *Centuries on Charity,* c. 626

The quieter it is the more powerful, the worthier, the deeper, the more telling and more perfect the prayer is.

MEISTER ECKHART (1260?–1327?), *Meister Eckhart*

No one prays to God aright but he that prays to God for God without a thought of aught but God.
MEISTER ECKHART (1260?–1327?), *Meister Eckhart*

He that can inwardly lift his mind up to God and can little regard outward things, needeth not to seek for time or place to go to prayers, or to do other good deeds or virtuous works.
THOMAS À KEMPIS, *Imitation of Christ,* 1441

Mental prayer is nothing else . . . but being on terms of friendship with God, frequently conversing in secret with Him.
ST. TERESA OF ÁVILA, *Life of St. Teresa,* 1565

Do not as some ungracious pastors do,
Show me the steep and thorny way to heaven,
While, like a puff'd and reckless libertine,
Himself the primrose path of dalliance treads.
WILLIAM SHAKESPEARE, *Hamlet,* c. 1602

He who prays fervently knows not whether he prays or not, for he is not thinking of the prayer which he makes, but of God, to whom he makes it.
ST. FRANCIS OF SALES, *Treatise on the Love of God,* 1607

Prayer should be the key of the morning and the lock of the night.
OWEN FELLTHAM, *Resolves,* c. 1620

If we can speak to Our Lord, let us speak to Him, praise Him, beseech Him, listen to Him; if we cannot, because we are hoarse, let us remain in His chamber, and pay Him reverence; He will observe us there, regard our patience, be pleased with our silence.
ST. FRANCIS OF SALES (1567–1622), *Consoling Thoughts of,* ed. Huguet

We ask our daily bread, and God never says you should have come yesterday, he never says you must again go tomorrow, but today if you will hear his voice, today he will hear you.
JOHN DONNE, *Sermon,* 1624

Use prayer to be assisted in prayer; pray for the spirit of supplication, for a sober, fixed, and recollected spirit.
JEREMY TAYLOR, *Holy Living,* 1650

Every time that is not seized upon by some other duty is seasonable enough for prayer.
JEREMY TAYLOR, *Holy Living,* 1650

All prayer must be made with faith and hope; that is, we must certainly believe we shall receive the grace which God hath commanded us to ask.
JEREMY TAYLOR, *Holy Living,* 1650

The soul, by its fidelity to mortification and recollection, usually receives a purer and more interior form of prayer which may be called the prayer of simplicity. This consists in a simple interior view, regard or loving attention towards some divine object.
J. B. BOSSUET, *Instructions sur les états d'oraison,* Bk. VII, 1652

We have never made a better prayer than when, after having made it, we do not know how it was made, since that is a sure sign that our soul was so attached to God as not to have had enough attention left to reflect upon itself.
PERE HAYNEUVE (1588–1663), *Solid Virtue*

I have quitted all forms of devotion and set prayers but those to which my state obliges me, and I make it my business only to persevere in His holy presence, . . . an habitual, silent, and secret conversation of the soul with God.
NICHOLAS HERMAN OF LORRAINE, Brother Lawrence, *Practice of the Presence of God,* c. 1666

Prayer should be short, without giving God Almighty reasons why He should grant this, or that; He knows best what is good for us.

 JOHN SELDEN, *Table Talk*, 1689

None can pray well but he that lives well.

 THOMAS FULLER, *Gnomologia*, 1732

Work as if you were to live 100 years. Pray as if you were to die tomorrow.

 BENJAMIN FRANKLIN, *Poor Richard's Almanac*, 1758

Pray only for the suppression of evil, and never for one's material well-being, for a separating veil arises if one admit the material into the spiritual.

 Baal-Shem, Rabbi Israel ben Eliezer Baal Shem Tov (1700–1760)

A single grateful thought toward Heaven is the most perfect prayer.

 G. E. LESSING, *Minna von Barnhelm*, 1767

He prayeth well, who loveth well
Both man and bird and beast.
He prayeth best, who loveth best
All things both great and small;
For the dear God that loveth us,
He made and loveth all.

 SAMUEL TAYLOR COLERIDGE, *The Ancient Mariner*, 1798

Our motive for prayer must be the divine will, not our own.

 D. LAURENCE SCUPOLI, *The Spiritual Combat*, 1843

Do not usually pray, extempore, above eight or ten minutes (at most) without intermission.

 The Doctrines and Discipline of the Methodist Episcopal Church, South, 1846

A man of prayer does not pore over learned books, for he is the wise man

"whose eyes are opened"—when he kneels down.

 SÖREN KIERKEGAARD, *Purity of Heart*, 1847

He . . . folded his large brown hands across his chest, uplifted his closed eyes, and offered a prayer so deeply devout that he seemed kneeling and praying at the bottom of the sea.

 HERMAN MELVILLE, *Moby Dick*, 1851

There is no prayer so blessed as the prayer which asks for nothing.

 O. J. SIMON, *Faith and Experience*, 1895

During prayer represent to yourself vividly all men as forming one body with yourself, and each separately as a member of the Body of Christ and your own member.

 JOHN SERGIEFF OF CRONSTADT, *My Life in Christ*, 1897

I have not the courage to search through books for beautiful prayers. . . . Unable either to say them all or choose between them, I do as a child would do who cannot read—I say just what I want to say to God, quite simply, and He never fails to understand.

 St. Thérèse de Lisieux (1873–1897), *Autobiography*, ed. T. N. Taylor

Do not pray for easy lives; pray to be stronger men. Do not pray for tasks equal to your powers; pray for power equal to your tasks.

 PHILLIPS BROOKS, *Perennials*, 1898

All the saints have loved the night-prayer. There is no hour so dear to them as the matin-hour, which is in deepest darkness, as it precedes the dawn.

 P. A. SHEEHAN, *Under the Cedars and the Stars*, 1903

Prayer is not to be used as a confessional, to cancel sin. Such an error would impede true religion. Sin is forgiven only as it is destroyed by Christ—Truth and Light.

MARY BAKER EDDY, *Science and Health*, 1908

I must get my faith quite clear, or at least as clear as I can, before I settle down to pray. . . . If I leave faith aside, no wonder my prayers are dull, monotonous, a bore to me.

BEDE JARRETT, *Meditations for Layfolk*, 1915

You pray in your distress and in your need; would that you might pray also in the fullness of your joy and in your days of abundance.

KAHLIL GIBRAN, *The Prophet*, 1923

The actual technique of prayer—the kneeling, the hiding of the face in the hands, the uttering of words in an audible voice, the words being addressed into empty space—helps by its mere dissimilarity from ordinary actions of everyday life to put one into a devout frame of mind.

ALDOUS HUXLEY, *Those Barren Leaves*, 1925

Now there is no doubt that the prayer of quiet, that a certain formless recollection and loving feeding upon the sense and presence of God, of God, as here and now, is a most legitimate prayer.

FRIEDRICH VON HÜGEL, *Life of Prayer*, 1929

Since it is to him who prays in solitude that God reveals His nature and will, every new creation in the sphere of religion has its origin in solitary prayer.

FRIEDRICH HEILER, *Prayer*, 1932

One should wish for no prayer, except precisely that prayer that God gives us,— the only way to pray is to pray, and the way to pray well is to pray much.

JOHN CHAPMAN, *Spiritual Letters*, 1935

The kind of prayer that puts into action the Christian virtues is of more value and

merit than that which consists in study about God and His revelation of Himself.

S. C. HUGHSON, *Contemplative Prayer*, 1935

I have often been told by a man whose spirit I honor, that it is best to pray before dawn and after sunset . . . when the clutch of unredeemed matter is less heavy upon us.

LLEWELYN POWYS, *Earth Memories*, 1938

In entering prayer we have a perfect right to choose from this random mass of heterosuggestions some that we regard as more significant than others, and to dwell upon them. Autosuggestion is no more than this act of dwelling upon selected aspects of experience.

DOUGLAS V. STEERE, *Prayer and Worship*, 1938

Those who pray as Christ taught us to pray are never praying against each other; for they do not pray that their own will may be done, but God's.

WILLIAM TEMPLE, *The Hope of a New World*, 1940

We ought always to pray is the same as saying: we must always desire eternal things, the temporal things which serve the eternal, our daily bread of every kind and for every need, in all its fulness, earthly and heavenly.

ANTONIN SERTILLANGES, *The Intellectual Life*, 1946

Our prayer for others ought never to be: "God, give them the light Thou hast given to me!" but: "God! Give to them all the light and truth they need for their highest development!"

MOHANDAS K. GANDHI (1869–1948), quoted by J. Nehru in his *The Discovery of India*

If you have nothing to say, say so.

HUBERT VAN ZELLER, *We Live with Our Eyes Open*, 1949

Prayer is a form of physical worship assigned to the Muslim five times a day at specified times. . . . He can perform them anywhere—at the mosque, at home, in the fields, at the factory, in the office, when the time falls due for prayer.

> KENNETH W. MORGAN, *Islam—The Straight Path,* 1958

It is not the thing believed in that brings an answer to prayer; the answer to prayer results when the individual's subconscious mind responds to the mental picture or thought in his mind. This law of belief is operating in all the religions of the world, and is the reason why they are psychologically true.

> JOSEPH MURPHY, *The Power of Your Subconscious Mind,* 1963

Pray as though no work could help, and work as though no prayer could help.

> German Proverb

See also other rubrics under Prayer.

PREACHERS

If the Lord Jesus Christ sent the Apostles to preach, others than those whom Christ appointed ought not to be received as preachers.

> TERTULLIAN, *The Rule of Faith,* c. 205

The life of the speaker has greater weight in determining whether he is obediently heard than any grandness of eloquence.

> ST. AUGUSTINE, *On Christian Doctrine,* 397

Vainly does the preacher utter the Word of God exteriorly unless he listens to it interiorly.

> ST. AUGUSTINE (354–430), *Serm.* CLXXIX

The Redeemer of mankind in the day-time exhibits His miracles in cities, and spends the night in devotion to prayer upon the mountain, namely, that He may teach all perfect preachers, that they should neither entirely leave the active life, from love of the speculative, nor wholly slight the joys of contemplation.

> POPE ST. GREGORY THE GREAT, *Morals on the Book of Job,* 584

The priest must preach the law of the Gospel; but for that preaching to be effective, the most persuasive argument, is to see the actual practice of the law in him who preaches it.

> POPE ST. GREGORY THE GREAT (540–604), *Epist.,* lib. I, ep. 25

The first duty of a preacher of the gospel is to declare God's law and describe the nature of sin.

> MARTIN LUTHER, *Preface to Romans,* 1522

A preacher conducts the household of God by virtue and on the strength of his commission and office, and he dare not say anything different from what God says and commands.

> MARTIN LUTHER, *Sermon,* 1528

The test of a preacher is that his congregation goes away saying, not What a lovely sermon, but I will do something!

> ST. FRANCIS OF SALES, *Introduction to the Devout Life,* 1609

Were I a preacher, I should, above all other things, preach the practice of *the presence of* GOD.

> NICHOLAS HERMAN OF LORRAINE, Brother Lawrence, *Practice of the Presence of God,* c. 1666

An advantage itinerant preachers have over those who are stationary, the latter cannot well improve their delivery of a sermon by so many rehearsals.

> BENJAMIN FRANKLIN, *Autobiography,* 1790

If I had to counsel a young preacher, I should say: When there is any difference felt between the foot-board of the pulpit and the floor of the parlor, you have not yet said that which you should say.

RALPH WALDO EMERSON, *Address,* May 25, 1879

Those preachers are foolish and improvident who, in speaking of religion and proclaiming the things of God, use no words but those of human science and human prudence, trusting to their own reasonings rather than to those of God.

POPE LEO XIII, *Providentissimus Deus,* 1893

As a career, the business of an orthodox preacher is about as successful as that of a celluloid dog chasing an asbestos cat through Hell.

ELBERT HUBBARD (1859–1915), quoted in C. Hurd's *Treasury of Great American Quotations*

Why, being an ordinary man, should he thunder and declaim as though he were an archangel trumpeting the oracles of heaven?

GEORGE A. BUTTRICK, *Jesus Came Preaching,* 1931

The task of the preacher is to lift men above the low view of their times, to give them the elevation and outlook which enables them to distinguish currents from eddies.

RALPH W. SOCKMAN, *The Highway of God,* 1941

The preacher is a messenger, not an actor.

RALPH W. SOCKMAN, *The Highway of God,* 1941

The preacher's task is to bring the longing Heavenly Father and His seeking bewildered children together.

RALPH W. SOCKMAN, *The Highway of God,* 1941

One of the men of the French court once said to a famous court preacher, "Sire,

your sermons terrify me, but your life reassures me."

CLARENCE E. MACARTNEY, *Preaching Without Notes,* 1946

It should not be forgotten that no true preacher of the Gospel can ever conceivably practice what he preaches.

AELRED GRAHAM, *Christian Thought and Action,* 1951

The preacher of the Gospel must be ready to afflict the comfortable as well as comfort the afflicted.

AELRED GRAHAM, *Christian Thought and Action,* 1951

The most inspired misprint, or at least one of them, that ever appeared was one in which a newspaper story recorded that the preacher's text was "Though I speak with the tongues of men and of angels and have not *clarity,* it profiteth me not."

FREDERICK M. MEEK, *Monday to Friday Is Not Enough,* 1951

If the requirement for preaching were that one be an example of the Sermon on the Mount, then we would have no preachers.

JAMES A. PIKE, *Beyond Anxiety,* 1953

The paradox of the pulpit is that its occupant is a sinner whose chief right to be there is his perpetual sense that he has no right to be there, and is there only by grace and always under a spotlight of divine judgment.

A. C. CRAIG, *Preaching in a Scientific Age,* 1954

If he is to be a preacher he must first be a pastor. All good preaching arises out of the lives of the people.

JOHN B. COBURN, *Minister,* 1963

Some unidentified wit has described the kind of preacher not to become:

I humbly feel that my success, my power of attraction, is mainly due to following out this golden rule of action: See all from all men's point of view; use others' eyes to see with; and never preach what anyone could ever disagree with.

JOHN B. COBURN, *Minister,* 1963

Preacher's silent prayer before speaking:
   Lord, fill my mouth with worthwhile stuff,
   And nudge me when I've said enough.

ANONYMOUS

See also Celibacy; Clergy; Clergy, Criticism of; Congregation; Eloquence; Minister; Ministry; Orator; Pastor; Preaching; Preaching and the Bible; Priesthood; Priests; Sermons; Speech; Theologians; Word, the.

PREACHING

What they should preach . . . can . . . properly be proved in no other way than by those very churches which the Apostles themselves founded by preaching to them.

TERTULLIAN, *The Rule of Faith,* c. 205

When a debater's point is not impressive, he brings forth many arguments.

Talmud Jerushalmi Birakot, c. 400 A.D.

Preaching the Word of God is as great as hearing it.

JOHN WYCLIF, *The Pastoral Office,* 1378

Among all the duties of the pastor after justice of life, holy preaching is most to be praised.

JOHN WYCLIF, *The Pastoral Office,* 1378

If what is delivered from the pulpit be a grave, solid, rational discourse, all the congregation grow weary, and fall asleep . . . whereas if the preacher be zealous, in his thumps of the cushion, antic gestures, and spend his glass in telling of pleasant stories, his beloved shall then stand up, tuck their hair behind their ears, and be very devoutly attentive.

DESIDERIUS ERASMUS, *In Praise of Folly,* 1511

If anybody wants to preach, let him suppress his own words and let them prevail in worldly and domestic affairs; here in the church he should speak nothing but the Word of this rich Householder, otherwise it is not the true church.

MARTIN LUTHER, *Sermon,* 1528

The second thing to be performed by him that preacheth, is a reverent gravity; this is considered first in the style, phrase, and manner of speech, that it be spiritual, pure, proper, simple, and applied to the capacity of the people.

WALTER TRAVERS, *A Directory of Church Government,* 1585

It is very morning in an orator when the soul seems to speak as well as the tongue.

OWEN FELLTHAM, *Resolves, Divine, Moral and Political,* 1626

The preaching of divines helps to preserve well-inclined men in the course of virtue, but seldom or never reclaims the vicious.

JONATHAN SWIFT, *Thoughts on Various Subjects,* 1706

A Preacher has no Occasion to shove and to heave as tho' he was tugging at an Oar in a Boat. He has no need to clap his Hands, to set his Arms a Kimbo, nor to bounce or spring, nor to giggle and laugh, nor any Reason for Howlings and hideous Lamentations.

PETER THE GREAT (of Russia), *Spiritual Regulation,* 1721

Such preaching of others hath most commanded my heart which hath most illuminated my head.

BENJAMIN WHICHCOTE, *Aphorisms,* 1753

Sir, a woman preaching is like a dog's walking on his hind legs. It is not done well; but you are surprised to find it done at all.

SAMUEL JOHNSON, *Boswell's Life of,* 1772

Preach faith till you have it; and then, because you have it, you will preach faith.

JOHN WESLEY (1703–1791), *The Heart of Wesley's Journal*

The object of preaching is constantly to remind mankind of what mankind are constantly forgetting; not to supply the defects of human intelligence, but to fortify the feebleness of human resolutions.

SYDNEY SMITH, *Six Sermons*, 1800

The preacher, who naturally uses eloquence, the first of the arts, should make his audience tremble by depicting the miserable state of the man, who, in this life, deserves the condemnation of the people.

C. H. SAINT-SIMON, *The New Christianity*, 1825

When we preach unworthily it is not always in vain. There is poetic truth concealed in all the commonplaces of prayer and of sermons, and though foolishly spoken, they may be wisely heard.

RALPH WALDO EMERSON, *Divinity School Address*, July 15, 1838

In the sanctuary, as well as on the hustings, we hear *vox populi est vox Dei*. The pulpit is thus forced, instead of proclaiming . . . the word of God . . . to echo popular convictions and prejudices, popular passions and errors, and to vary its tone with the varying moods of the congregation.

ORESTES BROWNSON, *Address*, Dartmouth College, July 26, 1843

It is no part of the duty of a clergyman to preach upon subjects purely political, but it is not therefore his duty to avoid religious subjects which have been distorted into political subjects.

SYDNEY SMITH, *Lady Holland's Memoirs, I*, 1855

There is no such thing as preaching patience into people, unless the sermon is so long that they have to practice it while they hear.

HENRY WARD BEECHER, *Life Thoughts*, 1858

Condense some daily experience into a glowing symbol, and an audience is electrified.

RALPH WALDO EMERSON, *Address*, May 1877

I do not love sensation[al] preaching,— the personalities for spite, the hurrah for our side, the review of our appearances and what others say of us!

RALPH WALDO EMERSON, *Address*, May 5, 1879

Most preachers handle sin as they would handle snakes, at arm's length and with no greater intimacy and for no longer time than is absolutely necessary.

S. M. SHOEMAKER, *Realizing Religion*, 1921

The best preaching is always the natural overflow of a ripe mind.

JAMES BLACK, *The Mystery of Preaching*, 1924

A congregation except in the rarest instances, does not dismiss its minister because of what he preaches, but because of what he does not preach.

RAYMOND CALKINS, *The Eloquence of the Christian Experience*, 1927

Preaching needs no *ex cathedra* attitude. It is killed by pontifical tones. It is doubly killed by a martyred voice, as though the preacher were the sole defender of the faith.

GEORGE A. BUTTRICK, *Jesus Came Preaching*, 1931

People are driven from the church not so much by stern truth that makes them uneasy, as by weak nothings that make them contemptuous.

GEORGE A. BUTTRICK, *Jesus Came Preaching*, 1931

That we should practice what we preach is generally admitted; but anyone who preaches what he and his hearers practice must incur the gravest moral disapprobation.

LOGAN PEARSALL SMITH, *Afterthoughts*, 1931

When the Lord has drawn from me some word for the good of souls, I know, because of the pain of it.

GEORGES BERNANOS, *The Diary of a Country Priest*, 1937

The priest who descends from the pulpit of Truth, with a mouth like a hen's vent, a little hot but pleased with himself, he's not been preaching: at best he's been purring like a tabby-cat.

GEORGES BERNANOS, *The Diary of a Country Priest*, 1937

Let any preacher honestly probe into the great causes of human misfortune and misery, and nothing will keep people from his church.

FREDERICK K. STAMM, *Country Home Magazine*, December, 1939

There is ever the danger of tempering the wind to the shorn lambs—in fur coats!

RALPH W. SOCKMAN, *The Highway of God*, 1941

The pulpit is in more danger of selling its freedom through catering to the public than of losing its liberty through governmental pressure.

RALPH W. SOCKMAN, *The Highway of God*, 1941

Preaching is inherent and central in the Protestant conception of Christianity. The Reformation is inconceivable without a strong emphasis on preaching.

HALFORD E. LUCCOCK, *Protestantism; a Symposium*, ed. W. K. Anderson, 1944

The great renewal of Christianity, its recurring springtimes which make the most stirring chapters of history, have been accompanied, often started, by preaching.

HALFORD E. LUCCOCK, *Protestantism; a Symposium*, ed. W. K. Anderson, 1944

Pictorial preaching is the most effective because it is easier to get at the average mind by a picture than by an idea.

PETER MARSHALL, quoted by Catherine Marshall in her *A Man Called Peter*, 1951

Preaching is an art, and in this, as in all other arts, the bad performers far outnumber the good.

ALDOUS HUXLEY, *The Devils of Loudon*, 1952

Christ meets us in the preaching as one crucified and risen. He meets us in the word of preaching and nowhere else. The faith of Easter is just this—in the word of preaching.

RUDOLF BULTMANN, *Kerygma and Myth*, 1954

To the end of time preaching can only be an embarrassed stammering. Do not call it difficult, therefore; call it impossible.

A. C. CRAIG, *Preaching in a Scientific Age*, 1954

Dust thumped out of the pulpit-cushion is more likely to hide the Gospel from our contemporaries than commend it to them.

A. C. CRAIG, *Preaching in a Scientific Age*, 1954

The modern pulpit is so often simply the platform for the subjective feelings of the preacher, or of his world view, or of his most recent reading.

WILLIAM J. WOLF, *Man's Knowledge of God*, 1955

My preaching at its best has itself been personal counseling on a group scale.

H. E. FOSDICK, *The Living of These Days*, 1956

Good preaching sounds reveille, not taps.

JAMES M. GILLIS, *This Mysterious Human Nature*, 1956

The churches force frustrations upon the New Americans when they preach individualistic and autonomous activism in little pulpit moralisms: men cannot carry them out in the new society.

MARTIN E. MARTY, *The New Shape of American Religion,* 1958

True Christian preaching is . . . a proclamation which claims to be the call of God through the mouth of man and, as the word of authority, demands belief.

RUDOLF BULTMANN, *Religion and Culture,* ed. W. Liebrecht, 1959

Popular preaching today is sluggish, its popularity based on words which are familiar and images that had content in the agrarian society but are irrelevant to the complex society of industrial civilization.

FRANKLIN H. LITTELL, *From State Church to Pluralism,* 1962

The priest who has not kept near the fires of the tabernacle can strike no sparks from the pulpit.

FULTON J. SHEEN, *The Priest Is Not His Own,* 1963

The freedom of the pulpit is freedom to be responsible to the revelation of God in Christ and not to any national or socially dominant ideas concerning what is good.

JOHN C. BENNETT, *Christian Century,* January 6, 1954

If the beard were all, goats could preach.

Danish Proverb

Preach about God and about twenty minutes, said the bishop to the young clergyman when asked for advice.

ANONYMOUS

He is the best speaker who can turn the ear into an eye.

Arab Proverb

See also Church, Definitions of; Church: Its Work; Congregation; Minister; Min-istry; Orator; Practice; Preachers; Preaching and the Bible; Priesthood; Priests; Revivalism; Rhetoric; Sermons; Speech; Word, the.

PREACHING AND THE BIBLE

A man speaks more or less wisely in proportion as he has made more or less progress in Holy Scriptures.

ST. AUGUSTINE, *Do Doctrina Christiana,* 397

One would almost fancy that instead of being a degraded species of oratory, it must be a fine thing to pervert the meaning of the text and compel that reluctant Scripture to yield the meaning one wants!

ST. JEROME, *Epistle LIII,* c. 400

Often read the divine Scriptures; yea, let holy reading be always in thy hand; study that which thou thyself must preach.

ST. JEROME (340–420), *Epistle to Nepotian*

God preaches to us in the Scripture, and by his secret assistances and by spiritual thoughts and holy motions.

JEREMY TAYLOR, *Holy Living,* 1650

The Holy Ghost is certainly the best preacher in the world, and the words of Scripture the best sermons.

JEREMY TAYLOR, *Holy Living,* 1650

But what is the use of preaching the Gospel to men whose whole attention is concentrated upon a mad, desperate struggle to keep themselves alive?

WILLIAM BOOTH, *In Darkest England and the Way Out,* 1890

The best preachers of all ages . . . have gratefully acknowledged that they owed their repute chiefly to the assiduous use of the Bible, and to devout meditation on its pages.

POPE LEO XIII, *Holy Scripture,* 1893

The Word of God in the Book is a dead letter. . . . In the preacher that Word becomes again as it was when first spoken by prophet, priest, or apostle. It springs up in him as if it were first kindled in his heart.

> EDGAR DE WITT JONES, *The Royalty of the Pulpit,* 1951

Whenever we hear the Word of God in the human word, the message of the Bible becomes no longer a message out of the past, but an event in the present.

> ALAN RICHARDSON and W. SCHWEITZER, *Biblical Authority for Today,* 1951

Preaching is the word of the Bible addressed to people who live in the concrete decisions and difficulties of the world.

> GUSTAVE WINGREN, *Theology in Conflict,* 1958

The Gospel as the Word of God is properly spoken to the ear and not written for the eye.

> AMOS N. WILDER, *Theology and Modern Literature,* 1958

The preaching office is always concerned to hold together people and the Gospel. It is the Word of God directed to the lives of people together with the response of people to God and to one another.

> JOHN B. COBURN, *Minister,* 1963

All the preaching of the Church must be nourished and regulated by sacred Scripture.

> Second Vatican Council, *Constitution on Divine Revelation,* November, 1965

See also Bible; Eloquence; Holy Spirit; Orator; Preachers; Preaching; Revivalism; Sermons; Word, the.

PREDESTINATION

Enveloped in darkness, creatures are not masters of their own weal or woe. They go to heaven or hell urged by God Himself.

> *Mahabharata,* c. 800 B.C.

Nothing has ever happened which has not been predestinated, and nothing will ever occur.

> CICERO, *De Divinatione,* c. 78 B.C.

In his eternity and co-eternal word, He predeterminated what was in time to be manifested.

> ST. AUGUSTINE, *City of God,* XI, 16, 426

By divine predestination the elect are chosen for eternal happiness, the rest are left graceless and damned to everlasting hell.

> MARTIN LUTHER, *De Servo Arbitrio,* 1525

God has from eternity predestinated or freely chosen, of his mere grace, without any respect of men, the saints and whom he will save in Christ.

> HENRY BULLINGER, *The Helvetic Confession,* 1536

By an eternal and immutable counsel God has once for all determined both whom He would admit to salvation, and whom He would condemn to destruction. . . . To those whom He devotes to condemnation, the gate of life is closed by a just and irreprehensible, but incomprehensible, judgment.

> JOHN CALVIN, *Institutes,* III, 1536

All those whom God hath predestinated unto life . . . and those only—He is pleased, in His appointed and accepted time, effectually to call by His Word and Spirit.

> *Westminster Confession of Faith,* Formulary of the Presbyterian Church of Scotland, 1643

That God has foreordained everything is self-evident.

> RENÉ DESCARTES, *Principles of Philosophy,* 1644

God hath, before the foundation of the world, foreordained some men to eternal life through Jesus Christ, to the praise and

glory of His grace; leaving the rest in their sin, to their just condemnation, to the praise of His justice.
Baptist Confession of Faith, 1646

Whatever comes about, since it is made by God, must therefore be necessarily predetermined by him, because otherwise he would be changing, which in him would be a great imperfection. . . . We therefore deny that God can omit to do what he actually does.
BARUCH SPINOZA, *Short Treatise,* 1665

If Providence is omnipotent, Providence intends whatever happens, and the fact of its happening proves that Providence intended it. If so, everything which a human being can do, is predestined by Providence and is a fulfilment of its designs.
JOHN STUART MILL (1806–1873), *Nature,* publ. posth.

It has hitherto seemed that physics comes down heavily on the side of predestination. The quantum theory has entirely removed this bias. Whatever view we may take of free will on philosophical grounds we cannot appeal to physics against it.
A. S. EDDINGTON, *Nature,* February 26, 1927

By the decree of God, for the manifestation of His glory, some men and angels are predestined unto everlasting life, and others foreordained to everlasting death.
Constitution of the Presbyterian Church in U.S.A., 1930

The rest of mankind, God was pleased, according to the unsearchable counsel of his own will . . . to ordain them to dishonor and wrath for their sin, to the praise of his glorious justice.
Constitution of the Presbyterian Church in U.S.A., 1930

If everything happens according to the eternal foreknowledge and act of the Creator, the responsibility for evil recoils upon God.
J. E. BOODIN, *God and Creation,* 1934

The idea of personal predestination could hardly survive amidst the evangelists' earnest entreaties to "come to Jesus."
TIMOTHY L. SMITH, *Revivalism and Social Reform in Mid-19th Century America,* 1957

God predestines every man to be saved. The Devil predestines every man to be damned. Man has the casting vote.
Attributed by William Lyon Phelps to an anonymous Negro preacher

See also Chance; Choice; Commitment; Damnation; Death; Determinism; Destiny; Duties; Election; Fall, the; Fatalism; Fate; Foreknowledge· Free Will; Freedom; God: His Intervention in the World; God: His Omniscience; God: His Wrath; Guilt; Hell; Individual Responsibility; Judgment, God's; Justice; Justification; Man: His Wickedness; Mercy; Merit; Necessity; Original Sin; Providence; Punishment; Redemption; Salvation; Sin; Wicked, the; Will.

PREGNANCY, TERMINATION OF

If, in spite of all the progress of science, there still remain in future, cases in which the mother's death must be reckoned with, when she wants to carry to birth the life she bears within her and not to destroy it in violation of God's commandment: "Thou shalt not kill!" man, while endeavoring up to the last moment to help and to save, has no alternative but to bow in awe to the laws of nature, and the dispositions of divine Providence.
POPE PIUS XII, *Address,* November 27, 1951

See also Abortion; Mother and Child, Life of.

PREJUDICE

An opinion without judgment.
VOLTAIRE, *Philosophical Dictionary,* II, 1764

Prejudice does not mean false ideas, but only . . . opinions adopted before examination.

JOSEPH DE MAISTRE (1753–1821), *Étude sur la Souveraineté*

Any prejudice whatever will be insurmountable if those who do not share it themselves, truckle to it, and flatter it, and accept it as a law of nature.

JOHN STUART MILL, *Representative Government*, 1861

It is impossible to see why Plato, Aristotle, Leibnitz and Kant, and why again Phidias and Michelangelo, Raphael and Rembrandt, Bach and Beethoven, Homer and Shakespeare, are to be held in deepest gratitude, as revealers, respectively of various kinds of reality and truth if Amos and Isaiah, Paul, Augustine and Aquinas, Francis of Assisi and Joan of Arc are to be treated as pure illusionists, in precisely what constitutes their specific greatness.

FRIEDRICH VON HÜGEL, *Essays and Addresses on the Philosophy of Religion*, 1924

Our method of transferring our own sickness to others. It is our ruse for disliking others rather than ourselves.

BEN HECHT, *A Guide for the Bedeviled*, 1944

Prejudice, put theologically, is one of man's several neurotic and perverted expressions of his will to be God.

KYLE HASELDEN, *The Racial Problem in Christian Perspective*, 1959

See also Anti-Semitism; Bigots; Class Distinctions; Discrimination; Equality; Hatred; Intolerance; Race; Racial Conflict; Racial Injustice; Racial Prejudice; Tolerance.

PREMARITAL SEX

Many young people in seeking freedom to love as they wish and to express themselves unrestrainedly, launched out like pioneers seeking an El Dorado. Some have won through to a new land. But many who started forth so gallantly were not equipped to be pioneers. The ocean is strewn with frail barks which have not reached the shore of the promised land. Some are nearly swamped, some are hopelessly shipwrecked, and others are drifting aimlessly.

M. ESTHER HARDING, *The Way of All Women*, 1945

If she refuses to have intercourse with one whom she dearly loves, not out of coyness, but through allegiance to a moral value, which is a real value to her, the potential of their love will mount behind the barrier she interposes.

M. ESTHER HARDING, *The Way of All Women*, 1945

We don't *urge* couples to fully explore. But when they come in for premarital counseling and in the course of the interview we ask, "Well, what sort of sexual experience have you had together?" and they say they've had relations, we don't say "Bad," we say "Good."

FREDERICK C. KEUTHER, Director, American Foundation of Religion and Psychiatry, interviewed by Leonard Gross, reported in his *God and Freud*, 1959

I believe that the real issue about premarital sex is the risk of producing illegitimate children who from the start are denied the protection every human society has found it necessary to give.

MARGARET MEAD, *Redbook*, October, 1962

By accepting this new morality, parents, teachers, guidance authorities and preachers have abdicated their responsibility to young people. Instead of encouraging them to realize the opportunity to remain single and abstinent during their developing student years, the college has turned into a place where pregnancy—if it ends in marriage—is not penalized but rewarded.

MARGARET MEAD, *Redbook*, October, 1962

Sex experience *before* confidentiality, empathy and trust have been established can hinder, and may actually destroy, the possibility of a solid, permanent relationship.

MARY STEICHEN CALDERONE, *Redbook*, February, 1964

If the [college-bound] girl is unmoved by ethical or religious injunctions against premarital sex—and she should be made to face that issue—then the parents must help her to see the fraudulence of boys' pleading . . . a young man's craving for ego-nurture.

JENNIE LOITMAN BARRON, *Ladies' Home Journal*, January–February, 1964

Haunted by ill-digested Freudian strictures against parental repression, bedeviled by the "progressive" cult of self-expression, urged toward permissiveness and beguiled by false doctrines of family democracy, parents have too often abdicated their responsibility for setting standards of behavior and limitations on their children's freedom of action.

JOHN A. LOGAN, JR., *Commencement Address*, Hollins College, June, 1964

No case can be made on the basis of conservation of health for requiring sexual relations for men or women before marriage or outside it. Psychologically and morally such relations offer no incontestable advantage; quite the reverse, they present a number of drawbacks, chiefly that of distorting from the very first a young man's concept of womanhood.

HENRI GIBERT, *Love in Marriage*, 1964

We grant the Freudian thesis that the repression of primitive instincts leads to neurosis; but the repression of moral aspirations often produces an identical effect.

IGNACE LEPP, *The Authentic Morality*, 1965

Sex is just about the most powerful and explosive force that is built into us. Every instinct and every bit of counseling experience I have had tells me that it is too dangerous a commodity to be handed over to people with no strings attached.

NORMAN VINCENT PEALE, *Man, Morals and Maturity*, 1965

I believe that the sexual restraints devised by society are an unconscious manifestation of the wisdom of the human race. They deepen erotic power by controlling and focusing it, and the resulting energy is used to drive mankind upward along the path of civilization.

NORMAN VINCENT PEALE, *Man, Morals and Maturity*, 1965

Present self-denial in order to gain greater benefits in the future is the hallmark of a rational human being.

NORMAN VINCENT PEALE, *Man, Morals and Maturity*, 1965

See also Fornication; Sex; Sexual Sin.

PRESENT, THE

We are today more exercised about life with God on earth than on what will happen to us after . . . death.

C. G. MONTEFIORE, *Liberal Judaism*, 1903

Present, n. That part of eternity dividing the domain of disappointment from the realm of hope.

AMBROSE BIERCE, *Devil's Dictionary*, 1906

If we are ever to realize our great destiny, then we must learn to appreciate the insignificance of the present, except as the symbol and vehicle of the future.

JOSEPH MCSORELY, *Be of Good Heart*, 1924

See also Moment.

PRESIDENCY, UNITED STATES

I do not speak for my church on public matters—and the church does not speak for me.

> JOHN F. KENNEDY, *Speech,* September 12, 1960

I believe in a President whose religious views are his own private affair, neither imposed by him upon the nation, or imposed by the nation upon him as a condition to holding that office.

> JOHN F. KENNEDY, *Speech,* September 12, 1960

But if the time should ever come—and I do not concede any conflict to be even remotely possible—when my office would require me to violate my conscience or violate the national interest, then I would resign the office, and I hope any conscientious public servant would do the same.

> JOHN F. KENNEDY, *Speech,* September 12, 1960

See also Church and State.

PRESS

This is the true apostolate of the press—to dare to be involved, to dare to direct, to dare to be heard, to dare even to be wrong and, at that point, to dare to acknowledge it.

> RICHARD CUSHING, *Sermon,* New York City, April 5, 1959

It cannot be lawful for the press, under the pretext that it must be free, to make daily and systematic attempts on the moral and religious health of mankind.

> POPE JOHN XXIII, *Address,* December 8, 1959

PRESUMPTION

Presumption is less a sin than despair, for it is more characteristic of God to pity and spare than to punish.

> ST. THOMAS AQUINAS, *Summa Theologiae,* a 2a–2ae.xx.2, 1272

Presumption is our natural and original infirmity. Of all creatures man is the most miserable and frail, and therewithal the proudest and disdainfulest.

> MICHEL DE MONTAIGNE, *Essays,* Bk. 2, ch. 12, 1580

PRETENSE

Do not try to seem very devout or more humble than necessary. It is possible to seek glory by despising it.

> ST. JEROME, *To Eustochium,* c. 405

See also Hypocrisy; Sincerity.

PRIDE

Holding himself good, one loses his goodness.

> *Shu Ching,* c. 490 B.C.

If ever a man becomes proud, let him remember that a mosquito preceded him in the divine order of creation!

> *Tosefta: Sanhedrin,* prior to 3rd century A.D.

Pride thinks its own happiness shines the brighter, by comparing it with the misfortunes of other persons. . . . This is that infernal serpent that creeps into the breasts of mortals.

> ST. THOMAS MORE, *Utopia,* 1516

The pride of those shall be punished who, not content with the will of God revealed, delight to mount and fly above the skies, there to ask the secret will of God.

> JOHN KNOX (1505?–1572), quoted in E. Muir's *John Knox*

God deliver us from anybody who wishes to serve Him and thinks about her own dignity, and fears to be disgraced.

> ST. TERESA OF ÁVILA, *The Interior Castle,* 1577

This acceptable disease, which so sweetly sets upon us, ravishing our senses, lulls our

souls asleep, puffs up our hearts as so many bladders.
> ROBERT BURTON, *The Anatomy of Melancholy*, I, 1621

They are proud in humility; proud in that they are not proud.
> ROBERT BURTON, *The Anatomy of Melancholy*, I, 1621

I thank God, amongst those millions of Vices I do inherit and hold from Adam, I have escaped one, and that a mortal enemy to Charity, the first and father-sin, not only of man, but of the devil, Pride.
> THOMAS BROWNE, *Religio Medici*, 1635

Pride is a kind of pleasure produced by a man thinking too well of himself.
> BARUCH SPINOZA, *Ethics*, 1677

Pride is a sin that sticks close to nature, and is one of the final follies wherein it shows itself to be polluted.
> JOHN BUNYAN, *The Life and Death of Mr. Badman*, 1680

Pride may be allowed to this or that degree, else a man cannot keep up his dignity.
> JOHN SELDEN, *Table Talk*, 1689

The first peer and president of Hell.
> DANIEL DEFOE, *The True-Born Englishman*, 1701

To be proud of virtue is to poison yourself with the antidote.
> BENJAMIN FRANKLIN, *Poor Richard's Almanac*, 1756

There is perhaps no one of our natural passions so hard to subdue as *pride*. Disguise it, struggle with it, beat it down, stifle it, mortify it as much as one pleases, it is still alive, and will every now and then peep out and show itself.
> BENJAMIN FRANKLIN, *Autobiography*, 1790

The principal cause of our troubles when we do fall is a secret pride which makes us vexed and irritated at being obliged to acknowledge our fall even to ourselves.
> JEAN GROU, *Meditations in the Form of a Retreat*, c. 1795

There is a certain noble pride through which merits shine brighter than through modesty.
> JEAN PAUL RICHTER, *Titan*, 1803

Of all the marvellous works of the Deity perhaps there is nothing that the angels behold with such supreme astonishment as a proud man.
> C. C. COLTON, *Lacon*, 1820

Pride and self-opinion kindled the flaming sword which waves us off from Paradise.
> WALTER SCOTT, *The Abbot*, 1820

The prouder a man is, the more he thinks he deserves; and the more he thinks he deserves, the less he really does deserve.
> HENRY WARD BEECHER, *Royal Truths*, 1862

Pride helps us; and pride is not a bad thing when it urges to hide our own hurts—not to hurt others.
> GEORGE ELIOT, *Middlemarch*, 1872

As soon as God touches you, you shall burn with a light so truly your own that you shall reverence your own mysterious life, and yet so truly His that pride shall be impossible.
> PHILLIPS BROOKS, *Perennials*, 1898

Every generous person [will] agree that the one kind of pride which is wholly damnable is the pride of the man who has something to be proud of. . . . And it does him most harm of all to value himself for the most valuable thing on earth—goodness.
> G. K. CHESTERTON, *Heretics*, 1905

There was one who thought he was above me, and he was above me until he had that thought.

ELBERT HUBBARD, *Dictionary and Book of Epigrams*, 1923

The final sin is always a religious sin, for it expresses the unconscious pride of the human heart in an almost unconscious pretension of divinity.

REINHOLD NIEBUHR, *The Christian Faith and the Common Life*, ed. N. S. Ehrenström, 1938

Man falls into pride when he seeks to raise his contingent existence to unconditional significance.

REINHOLD NIEBUHR, *The Nature and Destiny of Men*, I, 1941

When man remembers that he is *dust raised up by God* and made tremendously important, then he has Lawful Pride. He knows then that he is "sanctified dust."

GEORGE J. HAYE, *Obedience*, 1944

Wherever we find the secular and civic morality flourishing, . . . we find also pride . . . disconcertingly enthroned among the virtues.

J. V. L. CASSERLEY, *Retreat from Christianity in the Modern World*, 1952

The satanically proud man rejoices at immoral actions of other persons. . . . He sees in them a triumph of evil, a victory in war waged against God.

DIETRICH VON HILDEBRAND, *True Morality and Its Counterfeits*, 1955

What we now call the lust for power, and tend to regard as a fairly modern phenomenon, is in fact almost identical with what our ancestors called the sin of pride, the first of the Seven Deadly Sins.

COLIN CLARK, *The Springs of Morality*, ed. J. M. Todd, 1956

Pride is man's malady, and because it is man's malady, man cannot save himself.

A. T. MOLLEGEN, *Christianity and Modern Man*, 1961

Nothing stands nearer to the centre of the Christian gospel than the lowliness of Christ, his humility and humiliation. This it is that robs us of the last shred of justification of that human pride which is the very root of the disease from which we need to be made whole.

JOHN BAILLIE, *The Sense of the Presence of God*, 1962

God does not listen to the prayers of the proud.

Hebrew Proverb

See also Conceit; Despair; Falsehood; Humility; Intellectual Pride; Intellectuals; Office; Pharisee; Self-Contempt; Self-Deception; Self-Knowledge; Self-Love; Self-Praise; Self-Respect; Self-Will; Superstition; Vainglory; Vanity.

PRIESTHOOD

When it becomes necessary to appoint someone over the church, and to put in trust the care of so many souls, the nature of the female, and indeed of the majority of the male sex, must be deemed inferior to the weight of such a charge.

ST. JOHN CHRYSOSTOM, *On the Priesthood*, c. 385

Every divine law is held in the bosom of the Two Testaments. In which bosom I cannot find that anxiety or care concerning temporal things was commended to the priesthood.

DANTE, *De Monarchia*, c. 1300

If a man who is morally perverse or ignorant or otherwise deficient is promoted to the priesthood . . . the peril of eternal death and of many civil disadvantages thereby threatens the people. . . . And the Christian people has, and reasonably ought to have, the power of discretion or caution, for otherwise it could not avoid this evil.

MARSIGLIO OF PADUA (1280–1343), *Defensor Pacis*

It is sweet, it is beautiful, it is glorious to belong to that holy phalanx enlisted in the eternal cause.

ADRIEND-EMANUEL ROQUETTE, *Propagateur Catholique,* March 30, 1883

You will be tempted to believe that your sacred office is not a mission and vocation, but a mere profession. . . . If you harbor that temptation for a moment, in that moment you have bartered and forfeited your birthright; you have cancelled the character of your nobility; you have revoked your oath of ordination.

P. A. SHEEHAN, *The Literary Life and Other Essays,* 1921

The general priesthood conferred on the faithful in baptism gives them the right and duty to do what is necessary for their life as members of Christ.

VIRGIL MICHEL, *Life of Christ,* 1935

The human race has always felt the need of a priesthood; of men, that is, who have the official charge to be mediators between God and humanity, men who should consecrate themselves entirely to this mediation, as to the very purpose of their lives, men set aside to offer sacrifices in the name of human society.

POPE PIUS XI, *The Catholic Priesthood,* 1935

All Protestants agree that there is a universal priesthood of believers. . . . The Christian is not dependent on priest or ecclesiastical rites, but may exercise the right and duty of private judgment.

SAMUEL McCREA CAVERT, *Protestantism: A Symposium,* ed. W. K. Anderson, 1944

The true meaning of the Reformation phrase, "the priesthood of the laity" is not that everybody is his priest, so that no community is necessary, but rather that everybody must be a priest to everybody else, so that community is a necessity.

ROBERT McAFFEE BROWN, *Patterns of Faith in America Today,* ed. F. E. Johnson, 1957

Our priesthood is best illumined in the fires of victimhood. We become significant to our fellowmen not by being a regular guy, but by being another Christ.

FULTON J. SHEEN, *The Priest Is Not His Own,* 1963

Though they differ from one another in essence and not only in degree, the common priesthood of the faithful and the ministerial or heirarchical priesthood are nonetheless interrelated: each of them in its own special way is a participation in the one priesthood of Christ.

Constitution on the Church, Second Vatican Council, November, 1964

See also Apostolic Succession; Call; Celibacy; Clergy; Clericalism; Eucharist; Laity; Minister; Ministry; Obedience; Ordination; Pastor; Preachers; Preaching; Priests; Vocation.

PRIESTS

Wherefore a people, which obeys the precepts of the Lord, and fears God, ought to separate itself from a prelate who is a sinner, nor mingle itself with the sacrifices of a sacrilegious priest.

ST. CYPRIAN, *Ep. LXVII,* 254

He who is entrusted with the care of men, the rational flock of Christ, subjects himself, for any injury sustained by the flock, not to the loss of temporal possessions, but to the loss of his own soul.

ST. JOHN CHRYSOSTOM, *On the Priesthood,* c. 385

The priest must be so pure that, if he were to be lifted up and placed in the heavens themselves, he might take a place in the midst of the Angels.

ST. JOHN CHRYSOSTOM, *De Sacerdotio,* III, 4, c. 385

The priest should be a man above human weaknesses. He should be a stranger to every diversion. . . . All eyes keep watch upon him to see that he fulfils his mission.

He is of little use or none, unless he has made himself austere, unyielding to any form of pleasure.

SYNESIUS, *To His Brother*, c. 400

If you meet a bad Christian, accuse neither his faith nor his priesthood, but him who turns so great a thing to such ill account.

ST. JOHN CHRYSOSTOM (347–407), *In I Cor. Homil. IV*

There are two powers by which this world is ruled, namely, the sacred authority of the priests and the royal power. Of these, that of the priests is the more weighty, since they have to render an account for even kings in the divine judgment.

POPE GELASIUS I, *Letter to Emperor Anastasius*, c. 493

The priest is the same as the people, when he does the same as they do, and has the same aspirations as they.

POPE ST. GREGORY THE GREAT, *Pastoral Care*, 590

How can we presume to undertake the office of mediator between God and other men, who is not sure of being himself intimate with God through the merits of his life. . . . Let him not desire to intercede for the sins of others who is disgraced with his own.

POPE ST. GREGORY THE GREAT, *Pastoral Care*, 590

He, beyond all others, should make it his special duty to read the Scriptures, to study the canons, to imitate the examples of the saints, to give himself up to watching, fasting and prayer, to preserve peace with his brethren, to despise no member of the Church, to condemn no one without proof, to excommunicate no one without consideration.

ST. ISIDORE OF SEVILLE (560–636), *The Perfection of the Clergy*

God never abandons His Church; and so the number of priests will be always suffi-

cient for the needs of the faithful, provided the worthy are advanced and the unworthy sent away.

ST. THOMAS AQUINAS, *Summa Theologiae, Supplem.* q. 36, a. 4, 1272

To fulfil the duties of holy Orders, common goodness does not suffice; but excelling goodness is required; that they who receive Orders and are thereby higher in rank than the people, may also be higher in holiness.

ST. THOMAS AQUINAS, *Summa Theologiae, Supplem.* q. 35, a. 1, ad 3m, 1272

Let lords and kings mend them . . . constrain priests to hold to the poverty that Christ ordained.

JOHN WYCLIF (c. 1320–1384), *English Works*

It is far better to have fewer and good priests than to have many and bad priests, for these last call down the anger of God upon the cities and the peoples.

GIROLAMO SAVONAROLA, *Sermon Against Tyrants*, 1497

Priests are said in Scripture to devour the sins of the people; and they find sins so hard to digest that they must have the best of wine to wash them down.

DESIDERIUS ERASMUS, *Collectanea Adagiorum*, 1500

Since we are all priests alike no man may put himself forward, or take upon himself, without our consent or election, to do that which we all alike have power to do.

MARTIN LUTHER, *Address to the Christian Nobility of the German Nation*, 1520

Placed high in the eyes of men they must also be lifted up to the peak of virtue before the eyes of Him Who seeth all; otherwise their elevation will be not to their merit but to their damnation.

ST. LAURENCE JUSTINIAN, *De Inst. Prael.*, 1606

It is the duty of priests to bark not only at ordinary people, but also at nobles and princes, and to wake them from sleep, when a danger arises in the night.

> FRIEDRICH VON SPEE (1591–1635), *Cautio Criminalis*

Consequently every baptized Christian is a priest already, not by appointment or ordination from the pope or any other man, but because Christ himself has begotten him as a priest and has given birth to him in baptism.

> MARTIN LUTHER (1483–1546), *What Luther Says*, III, p. 1139; 1959

Christ was made a Priest for ever: He was initiated or consecrated on the cross, and there began His priesthood. . . . It began on earth, but was to last and be officiated in heaven.

> JEREMY TAYLOR, *Holy Living*, 1650

Christ's priests have no priesthood but His. They are merely His shadows and organs, they are His outward signs; and what they do, He does.

> JOHN HENRY NEWMAN, *Parochial and Plain Sermons*, VI, 1843

He who would drive the priest out of the Church must first of all drive the miracle out of religion.

> D. F. STRAUSS, Preface, *Life of Jesus*, 1860

Judaism demands no mediation . . . every one shall be his own priest, his own mediator between himself and God.

> A. GEIGER, *Judaism and Its History*, 1865

Every man is a priest, even involuntarily; his conduct is an unspoken sermon, which is for ever preaching to others;—but there are priests of Baal, of Moloch, and of all the false gods.

> HENRI AMIEL, *Journal of*, 1882

The priest is still, and will, we think, remain one of the necessary types of humanity. . . . It is his triumph to achieve as much faith as possible in an age of negation.

> WALTER PATER, *London Guardian*, March, 1888

The essence of the priest is that he should believe himself, however humbly and secretly, to be set in a certain sense between humanity and God.

> ARTHUR CHRISTOPHER BENSON, *From a College Window*, 1906

The ordinary Christian cannot be a priest in the strict sense, for he can offer, not a real sacrifice, but only the figurative sacrifice of prayer.

> JOSEPH POHLE, "Priesthood," *The Catholic Encyclopedia*, XII, 1911

Fortunately for India, the Brahmin priest is not really representative of her religious life. Much more genuinely typical as well as more deeply religious, is that characteristically Indian figure, the "sannyasi," the renouncer.

> J. B. PRATT, *India and Its Faiths*, 1915

I could never take seriously the fear of the priest, as of something unnatural and unholy; a dangerous man in the home. Why should a man who wanted to be wicked encumber himself with special and elaborate promises to be good?

> G. K. CHESTERTON, *The Catholic Church and Conversion*, 1926

Priests are no more necessary to religion than politicians to patriotism.

> JOHN HAYNES HOLMES, *Sensible Man's View of Religion*, 1933

The priest is the minister of Christ, an instrument, that is to say, in the hands of the Divine Redeemer.

> POPE PIUS XI, *The Catholic Priesthood*, 1935

Even the most lamentable downfall, which, through human frailty, is possible to a priest, can never blot out from his soul the priestly character.

POPE PIUS XI, *The Catholic Priesthood*, 1935

He is not indeed forbidden to receive fitting sustenance. . . . A priest must expect no other recompense than that promised by Christ to His Apostles: "Your reward is very great in Heaven." Woe to the priest who, forgetful of these divine promises should become "greedy of filthy lucre."

POPE PIUS XI, *The Catholic Priesthood*, 1935

Earthly priests do nothing but lend their hands and their lips, and however unworthy they are, the grace which comes through them is neither less pure nor less august. Someone else, the Priest, acts through them.

P. MERSCH, *Morale est Corps mystique*, 1937

All men are priests in virtue of their vocation to be "Christ" among their brethren. Though it is not for all to perform the sacramental rite which restores to the mystical body the presence of its Head.

MAURICE ZUNDEL, *The Splendor of the Liturgy*, 1939

The twelve apostles are the first twelve priests; Judas is the first bad priest.

FRANÇOIS MAURIAC, *The Eucharist*, 1944

Priests [Hindu] believe that there is a God (or god), but that this God can be approached and known only through them. People can enter the holy of holies only with the permission of priests. . . . If you want to thrive in this life and go to heaven after death, you have to pass through their hands.

SWAMI VIVEKANANDA, Address delivered in 1900, in *Yoga and Other Works*, 1953

The Second Commandment of the Decalogue is always directed to him: "Thou shalt not take the name of the Lord Thy God in vain." In modern terms this means that the priest will never invoke his priesthood to establish a despotic clericalism or to lay claims to honors and gifts meant for God.

EMMANUEL SUHARD, *The Church Today*, 1953

The priest, like Christ, brings to humanity a gift without compare, that of disquietude. He must be the minister of disquietude, the dispenser of a new hunger and thirst.

EMMANUEL SUHARD, *The Church Today*, 1953

The power of "the priests" today is not there to *supplant* the supreme mediation of Jesus, but to *make it present*. He alone is *the* perfect Priest. They are *His* priests.

CHARLES JOURNET, *The Church of the Word Incarnate*, Vol. 1, 1955

See also Call; Celibacy; Clergy, Criticism of; Clericalism; Eucharist; Hierarchy; Minister; Ministry; Ordination; Pastor; Preachers; Preaching; Priesthood; Psychoanalysis; Theologians; Vocation.

PRIMNESS

An element of conscientious primness in a Christian act may make it more detestable than a healthy animal outbreak.

WILLIAM TEMPLE, *Christian Faith and the Common Life*, ed. N. Ehrenström, 1938

See also Modesty, Smugness.

PRINCIPLES

No principles but those of religion are sufficient to make a great man.

RICHARD STEELE, *Christian Hero*, 1701

Rendering unto Caesar only comes after rendering unto God, and a prince is nothing by the side of a principle.

> VICTOR HUGO (1802–1885), *Treasure Bits from*, ed. P. Rose

Certainly, there are explicit principles; and these are true exactly as we know them. But it is not as we know them that they are eternal. They are eternal as God knows them.

> WALTER J. ONG, *The Barbarian Within*, 1962

PRIVATE JUDGMENT

Besides that, we are all priests, as I have said, and have all one faith, one Gospel, one Sacrament; how then should we not have the power of discerning and judging what is right or wrong in matters of faith.

> MARTIN LUTHER, *The Appeal to the German Nobility*, 1520

Whosoever thru his private judgment, willingly and purposely, doth openly break the traditions and ceremonies of the Church, which be not repugnant to the Word of God, and be ordained and approved by common authority, ought to be rebuked openly.

> *Thirty-nine Articles of Religion* (Church of England), 1563

Our full persuasion and assurance of the infallible truth and divine authority is from the inward work of the Holy Spirit, bearing witness, by and with the Word, in our hearts.

> *Westminster Confession of Faith*, formulary of the Presbyterian Church of Scotland, 1643

God and nature and the gospel of Christ enjoin it upon us as a duty to maintain the right of private judgment.

> JONATHAN MAYHEW, *Seven Sermons*, 1746

I must still insist on the right of private judgment. I dare call no man Rabbi. I

cannot yield either implicit faith or obedience to any man or number of men under heaven.

> JOHN WESLEY, *Journal*, July 6, 1746

A federation of Christians is inconceivable in which each member retains his own opinions and private judgment in matters of faith.

> POPE PIUS XI, *Mortalium Animos*, January 6, 1928

Once it is allowed that each man may select from the Bible as he sees fit, judging each passage by his own notions of what is "abiding," you have stripped the Scriptures of their authority to command men's confidence and to compel their obedience.

> WALTER LIPPMANN, *A Preface to Morals*, 1929

The whole idea of private judgment . . . implies an obligation on the part of the individual Christian to know the facts upon which his judgment rests, to avoid actions and decisions which rest merely upon prejudice and partial or misleading information, and to grow in critical intelligence.

> Federal Council of Churches of Christ in America, *Information Service*, October 7, 1933

The "good theological reasons" which led to the adoption of the voluntary principle in religion were reasons drawn from the common treasury of Reformation faith.

> W. S. HUDSON, *The Great Tradition of the American Churches*, 1953

See also Bible; Bible: Its Interpretation; Bible and the Church; Conscience: Experience, Religious; Faith; Holy Spirit; Individualism; Light; New Testament; Obedience; Reformation, The.

PRIVILEGE

One privilege only is lawful—the privilege of Genius when Genius reveals itself in brotherhood with Virtue; but it is a privilege conceded by God and not by men.

Giuseppe Mazzini, *The Duties of Man*, 1858

Lamentably, it is an historical fact that privileged groups seldom give up their privileges voluntarily. Individuals may see the light and give up their unjust posture; but as Reinhold Niebuhr has reminded us (*Moral Man—Immoral Society*), groups tend to be more immoral than individuals.

Martin Luther King, *Why We Can't Wait*, 1964

PRIZE FIGHTING

It is difficult to reconcile prizefighting, as we have it today, with Catholic principles of morality.

Francis Connell, *American Ecclesiastical Review*, January, 1950

Today the cumulative weight of theological and medical opinion has become so great that the immorality of prize fighting is rapidly becoming common theological teaching.

Joseph T. Leonard, *Theology and Race Relations*, 1963

PROBLEM OF EVIL. See EVIL, PROBLEM OF

PROCRASTINATION

By day I think "To-night I'll pray,"
All night I plot to meet the day.
Shaikh Saadi, *Gulistan*, c. 1265

PROCREATION. See SEXUAL INTERCOURSE

PROFIT

Neither the Church of Christ, nor a Christian Commonwealth, ought to tolerate such as prefer private gain to the public weal, or seek it to the hurt of their neighbors.

Martin Bucer, *De Regno Christi*, 1557

If God show you a way in which you may lawfully get more than in another way (without wrong to your soul, or to any other) if you refuse this, and choose the less gainful way . . . you refuse to be God's steward.

Richard Baxter, *A Christian Directory*, 1673

To make one's profit out of the need of another is condemned by all laws, human and divine. To defraud any one of wages that are his due is a crime which cries to the avenging anger of Heaven.

Pope Leo XIII, *Encyclical*, May, 1891

We rebel against God and repudiate his will when we set our profit and ambition above the welfare of our fellows and above the Kingdom of God which binds them together.

Walter Rauschenbusch, *A Theology for the Social Gospel*, 1917

The Christian conscience can be satisfied with nothing less than the complete substitution of motives of mutual helpfulness and good will for the motive of private gain.

Federal Council of Churches of Christ in America, *Report*, 1933

Private profit as the cornerstone of the economic order appeals to men to be selfish when the Christian gospel bids them to be unselfish and seek the common good.

Federal Council of Churches of Christ in America, *Report*, 1933

Profit is the real God, which is competing today with Jesus' concept of a Father God.

Jerome Davis, *Harper's Magazine*, January, 1937

The profit motive has so far extinguished any other more worthy motive that the legitimate emotions of men are debased to the point of animalism.

Roland Simonitsch, *Sanctity and Success in Marriage*, 1956

See also Business; Capitalism; Competition; Economics and Christianity; Industrialism; Money; Property; Riches; Trade; Traders; Wealth.

PROGRESS

Progress requires that the subject be enlarged in itself, alteration, that it be transformed into something else.
ST. VINCENT OF LÉRINS, *A Commonitory,* 434

The perfectibility of man is absolutely indefinite. . . . Everything tells us that we are approaching one of the grand revolutions of the human race.
MARQUIS DE CONDORCET, *Progress of the Human Mind,* 1796

Progress is not . . . a thing within human control, but a beneficent necessity.
HERBERT SPENCER, *First Principles,* 1880

The vice of the modern notion of mental progress is that it is always something concerned with the breaking of bonds, the effacing of boundaries, the casting away of dogmas.
G. K. CHESTERTON, *Heretics,* 1905

Practically all the progress that man has made is due to the fact that he is mortal. . . . If there were no death, life would become a thing stagnant, monotonous, and unspeakably burdensome.
ROBERT W. MACKENNA, *The Adventure of Death,* 1917

We cannot leave behind what has once been true, for progress is an advance into truth, a deeper appreciation and love of what is familiar, be it a birthright, or a gift such as Revelation.
MARTIN C. D'ARCY, *God and the Supernatural,* 1920

The belief in progress, not as an ideal but as an indisputable fact, not as a task for humanity but as a law of Nature, has been the working faith of the West for about a hundred and fifty years.
W. R. INGE, *The Idea of Progress,* 1920

The real religious problem of our society is to secure the general acceptance of a religion adapted to the requirements of continuous progress towards an ideal, consisting of all humanity.
CHARLES A. ELLWOOD, *The Reconstruction of Religion,* 1922

This generation's deepest need is not these dithyrambic songs about inevitable progress, but a fresh sense of personal and social sin.
HARRY EMERSON FOSDICK, *Christianity and Progress,* 1922

If there were good cause for believing that the earth would be uninhabitable in A.D. 2000 or 2100 the doctrine of Progress would lose its meaning and would automatically disappear.
J. B. BURY, *The Idea of Progress,* 1932

Real human progress depends upon a good conscience.
ALBERT EINSTEIN, *Avukah Journal,* 1932

A historian without any theological bias whatever . . . cannot portray the progress of humanity honestly without giving a foremost place to a penniless teacher from Nazareth.
H. G. WELLS, *Reader's Digest,* May, 1935

There is no such thing in history as simple progress in human happiness. There is only progress in the tragic sense of the inner principles of being . . . of good and evil in collaboration.
NICHOLAS BERDYAEV, *The Meaning of History,* 1936

It is undeniable that much of the true progress in social history is due to the open or indirect action of Christianity upon the human spirit.

JACQUES MARITAIN, *Freedom in the Modern World,* 1936

We can exist only in progress toward another world; we are not fixed in a permanent position within a crude and self-sufficient universe; we dwell in the midst of mystery.

NICHOLAS BERDYAEV, *Dream and Reality,* 1939

The idea of progress is the underlying presupposition of what may be broadly defined as "liberal" culture. If that assumption is challenged the whole structure of meaning in the liberal world is imperiled.

REINHOLD NIEBUHR, *The Nature and Destiny of Man,* II, 1943

It is clearly untrue that we are automatically progressing and that the Churches and religion ought to hasten to adjust themselves to all the novelties of the age.

KARL MANNHEIM, *Diagnosis of Our Time,* 1944

There is no significance for man in terms of progress. . . . Man must and can be saved from futility only by the intervention of God.

B. I. BELL, *Atlantic Monthly,* January, 1946

In the later nineteenth century the idea of progress became almost an article of faith. This conception was a piece of sheer metaphysics derived from evolutionary naturalism and foisted upon history by the temper of the age.

R. G. COLLINGWOOD, *The Idea of History,* 1946

The belief in progress has played out its fatally dazzling role, and Western humanity, which had staked all hope on this one card, found itself facing the nothingness of despair.

EMIL BRUNNER, *Christianity and Civilization,* 1948

The Supreme Judge, who awaits us at the end of our earthly life on the threshold of eternity, admonishes everyone, high and low, to make conscientious use of the gifts received from God, to avoid all injustice, and to seize every opportunity for doing works of love and kindness. Such is the only measure of real progress.

POPE PIUS XII, *Address,* October 31, 1948

The aim, and test, of progress under a truly Christian dispensation on Earth would not lie in the field of mundane social life; the field would be the spiritual life of individual souls in their passage through this earthly life from birth into this world to death out of it.

A. J. TOYNBEE, *Civilization on Trial,* 1948

Closely connected with the doctrine of progress is the Utopia of terrestrial paradise and beatitude, which is nothing more than a perversion and distortion of the religious faith in the coming of the Kingdom of God on earth.

NICHOLAS BERDYAEV, *The Realm of Spirit and the Realm of Caesar,* 1952

Progress is what happens when inevitability yields to necessity. And it is an article of the democratic faith that progress is a basic law of life.

ADLAI STEVENSON, *Radio Address,* October 2, 1952

Perhaps . . . the main effect of progress in history is to heighten the possibilities both for achievement and for disaster.

R. L. SHINN, *Christianity and the Problem of History,* 1953

The morality of devoted and convinced protagonists of progress demands a resolute and irreconcilable struggle against all kinds of religious survival and superstitions which spiritually cripple and abase mankind.

Pravda, August 11, 1954

Life must progress in part by the imprudence of those who undertake the impossible, not knowing what they do.

> WILLIAM E. HOCKING, *The Meaning of Immortality*, 1957

No progress can ever bring about for us what we have already got in Christ; that which is beyond all progress is here and now in him; the last state exists already in the Christian mysteries.

> JEAN DANIELOU, *The Lord of History*, 1958

The religion of progress and the dogma of "salvation of mankind through man," so far from being a rudimentary form of real faith, is on the contrary the real sin of our contemporary world.

> JEAN DANIELOU, *The Lord of History*, 1958

When a nation makes progress in science, technology, economic life, and the prosperity of its citizens, a great contribution is made to civilization. But all should realize that these things are not the highest good, but only instruments for pursuing such goods.

> POPE JOHN XXIII, *Mater et Magistra*, May 15, 1961

Only Rover Boy fiction could picture the last fifty years as man climbing by his own power upward and onward to emancipated mind and the fraternal society.

> GEORGE A. BUTTRICK, *Christ and History*, 1963

See also Despair; End; Evolution; Liberalism; Man: His Destiny and Goal; Man: His Potential; Man: His Self-Deification; Moral Progress; Necessity; Optimism; Perfection; Positivism; Spiritual Progress; Vision.

PROMISE

A Christian cannot promise to do or not to do a given thing at a given moment, for he cannot know what the law of love, of which is the rule of his life, may require of him at that moment.

> LEO TOLSTOY, *The Kingdom of God Is Within You*, 1893

See also Vows.

PROOF

Probable proofs, by being added, not only increase the evidence, but multiply it.

> JOSEPH BUTLER, *The Analogy of Religion*, II, 1736

PROPERTY

Faith is in this world the best property for a man.

> *Sutta-Nipata*, 6th century B.C.

The whole country is called God's property and it is against piety to have anything that is God's property registered under other masters.

> PHILO JUDAEUS, *De Specialibus Legibus*, c. 35 A.D.

My lord, if we possessed property we should need arms to defend it.

> ST. FRANCIS OF ASSISI (1181–1226), *Tres Socii*

God has declared explicitly in His Law that it is not just to take, or even to covet, the goods of another. . . . The prince . . . cannot take his subjects' property without just and reasonable cause, that is to say by purchase, exchange, legitimate confiscation, or to secure peace with the enemy.

> JEAN BODIN, *The Six Books of the Republic*, 1579

It is plainly the intention of Providence that certain things should be owned— should be held as property.

> WILLIAM ELLERY CHANNING (1780– 1842), *Works*

The right to possess private property is derived from nature, not from man; and the state has by no means the right to abolish it, but only to control its use and bring it into harmony with the interests of the public good.

POPE LEO XIII, *Rerum Novarum*, 1891

The force of the religious spirit should be bent toward asserting the supremacy of life over property. Property exists to maintain and develop life. It is unchristian to regard human life as a mere instrument for the production of wealth.

WALTER RAUSCHENBUSCH, *Christianity and the Social Crisis*, 1907

Provided that the natural and divine law be observed, the public authority, in view of the common good, may specify more accurately what is licit and what is illicit for property owners in the use of their possessions.

POPE PIUS XI, *Quadragesimo Anno*, 1931

The riches and goods of Christians are not common, as touching the right, title and possession of same, as some do falsely boast.

Doctrines and Discipline of the Methodist Episcopal Church, 1932

All property which represents social power stands in special need of moral scrutiny, since power to determine the lives of others is the crucial point in any scheme of justice.

Oxford Conference, 1937, in *The Churches Survey Their Tasks*, ed. J. H. Oldham

The starving person has a natural right to the food he needs to preserve his life; the property owner has a natural right to property. The conflict is solved by the fact that the right of the starving man to preserve his life is a more important, more necessary means for carrying out God's plan than the right of the property holder, who is not starving, to maintain his property.

Catholic Association for International Peace, *Timeless Rights*, 1948

One of the great problems which appears when we distinguish between property for use and property for power is that there is a limit to the good we can consume, but there is no limit to the power men can express.

WALTER G. MUELDER, *Religion and Economic Responsibility*, 1953

Property, personal and family, and some tools of production are indispensable to the human person. Each person has this right, and the right is rooted in man's nature, i.e., it comes from God the Creator. To cease having this right, man would cease to be man.

EMMANUEL SUHARD, *The Church Today*, 1953

If it can be maintained that the dignity of man, his freedom, and his development, require some form of . . . private property as well as common property—and if it is true that Christianity demands such freedom as an aspect of the soul's dignity, . . . then we must say that there is *something within the law* of property for which Christianity stands, and will always stand.

WILLIAM E. HOCKING, *The Coming World Civilization*, 1956

There is a social duty essentially inherent in the right of private property.

POPE JOHN XXIII, *Pacem in Terris*, April, 1963

See also Business; Capitalism; Economics and Christianity; Ownership; Possessions; Profit; Riches; Rights; Wages; Wealth.

PROPHECY

Prophecy consists in the most perfect development of the imaginative faculty . . . an emanation from the Divine Being.

MAIMONIDES, *Guide for the Perplexed*, 1190

Prophecy implies a certain obscurity and remoteness from intelligible truth; hence they are more strictly termed "prophets" who see through some vision in the imagination.

St. Thomas Aquinas, *Summa Theologiae*, 2da., 2dae., cl., XXIV, 1272

The task of prophecy has been to "discern the signs of the times," to see what God is bringing to pass as the history of peoples and societies unfolds, to point to the judgment he brings upon all institutions.

John B. Coburn, *Minister*, 1963

See also Prophets.

PROPHETS

The prophets are the interpreters of God.

Philo, *Special Laws*, C. 10 A.D.

There were long ago men more ancient than any of the philosophers now in repute, men who were happy, upright, and beloved of God, who spoke by the divine Spirit and gave oracles of the future which are now coming to pass. These men are called prophets.

St. Justin Martyr, *Dialogue with Trypho*, c. 135

Prophets . . . lifted in ecstasy above the natural operation of their minds by the impulses of the Divine Spirit, were inspired to utterance, the Spirit making use of them as a flute-player breathes into his flute.

Athenagoras, *Apology*, ch. ix, c. 177

The men of God were spirit-borne and became prophets; being breathed upon by God Himself and made wise, they were taught of God, holy and just.

Theophilus of Antioch, *Letter to Autolycus*, c. 180

And every prophet that teaches the truth if he does not what he teaches is a false prophet. . . . But whosoever shall say in the spirit: Give me money, or any other thing, ye shall not listen to him: but, if he

bid you give for others that are in need, let no man judge him.

Didache, The Doctrine of the Twelve Apostles (discovered at Constantinople in 1875), attributed to 2nd century

To believe in the prophet is to admit that there is above reason a sphere in which there are revealed to the inner visions truths beyond the grasp of reason.

al-Ghazali (1058–1111), *The Religious Life and Attitude in Islam*

The prophets are the physicians of the diseases of the soul.

al-Ghazali (1058–1111), *The Religious Life and Attitude in Islam*

Through prophecy Israel became the prophet of mankind.

Carl Heinrich Cornill, *Prophets of Israel*, 1894

The noble characters in each generation are the prophets of God.

Hamilton Wright Mabie, *The Life of the Spirit*, 1898

The prophets . . . are the beating hearts of the Old Testament.

Walter Rauschenbusch, *Christianity and the Social Crisis*, 1907

The fundamental conviction of the prophets . . . was the conviction that God demands righteousness and demands nothing but righteousness.

Walter Rauschenbusch, *Christianity and the Social Crisis*, 1907

The true prophet is a social worker who is absolutely independent, and neither fears nor submits to, anything external.

V. Soloviev, *Justification of the Good*, 1918

The prophet who dares to speak out against public opinion is indispensable to the church.

Francis J. McConnell, *Religion Today*, ed. A. L. Swift, 1933

They [Old Testament prophets] offered to the unfortunate of the earth a vision of brotherhood that became the precious and unforgotten heritage of many generations.

WILL DURANT, *Our Oriental Heritage,* 1935

The ancient prophets walk through the world of Judaism, like living geniuses reawaking from generation to generation.

LEO BAECK, *Essence of Judaism,* 1936

The prophet is the man of God *par excellence.* . . . Before being called, the majority of the prophets led a life of obedience and even intimacy with God; the moment of their call is that when communion with God takes on such a constraining aspect that in the form of a vision it imposes itself as a new reality.

EDMOND JACOB, *Theology of the Old Testament,* 1955

See also Bible; Bible: Its Inspiration; False Prophets; God: His Intervention in the World; Jesus Christ; Old Testament; Prophecy.

PROSPERITY

Learn . . . not to say in your heart, "Things go well with me because I serve God." For you will see men who do not serve God doing well according to your notion of prosperity, and your steps will be moved.

ST. AUGUSTINE (354–430), *Sermon* XIX, 4

I utterly disavow a common custom among us, which is to ground and establish our religion upon the prosperity of our enterprises. Our belief hath other sufficient foundations, and need not be authorized by events.

MICHEL DE MONTAIGNE, *Essays,* XXXI, 1580

If adversity hath killed his thousand, prosperity hath killed his ten thousand.

ROBERT BURTON, *The Anatomy of Melancholy,* II, 1621

Generally, the proposition is true, that where you find the most religion, there you will find the most wordly prosperity—in communities, I mean; not in single persons.

HENRY WARD BEECHER, in 1877, quoted in H. F. May, *Protestant Churches and Industrial America*

The country that has got the least religion is the most prosperous, and the country that has got the most religious is in the worst condition.

ROBERT C. INGERSOLL, *Speech,* Boston, April 23, 1880

The Church and the Store have a common business before them, to lay the foundation of sound morality, as a ground of temporal prosperity, to say nothing of any other direction.

HENRY WARD BEECHER, *Address,* May 8, 1883

In the long run, it is only to the man of morality that wealth comes. We believe in that harmony of God's universe. . . . Godliness is in league with riches. . . . Material prosperity is helping to make the national character sweeter, more joyous, more unselfish, more Christlike.

RUSSELL H. CONWELL, *Russell H. Conwell,* by Albert H. Smith, 1899

Liberalism, Protestantism, Judaism, positivism all have the same ultimate aim and standard. It is prosperity, or as Lutheran theologians put it, union with God at our level, not at God's level.

GEORGE SANTAYANA, *Persons and Places,* 1942

Prosperity really means that we are able to appreciate and use God's spiritual ideas of abundance. These ideas include not only infinite spiritual goodness, but manifest goodness, intelligence, harmony, peace, and substance. . . . Our Father has created substance and goodness enough to supply all of His children's needs forever.

LOWELL FILLMORE, *The Prayer Way to Health, Wealth and Happiness,* 1964

See also Adversity.

PROTESTANTISM

A real Protestant is a person who has examined the evidences of religion for himself, and who accepts them because, after examination, he is satisfied of their genuineness and sufficiency.

P. G. HAMERTON, *French and English*, 1889

Protestantism stiffened into its classical forms under intellectual influences long antedating our modern world, and the chaos and turmoil in Christian thought today are the consequences.

HARRY EMERSON FOSDICK, *Adventurous Religion*, 1926

A positive affirmation of the Christian gospel rather than an anti-Catholic movement. Insofar as it was a dynamic manifestation of the Christian faith it was in opposition to the static form which faith had assumed in the church; insofar as it became static in turn it had little if any advantage over its Catholic rival.

H. RICHARD NIEBUHR, *The Kingdom of God in America*, 1937

The Protestantism which stems from Luther has continued to concentrate its energies upon maintaining the freedom of the Word and has been inclined to yield to political and economic forces in what seem to be purely temporal matters.

H. RICHARD NIEBUHR, *The Kingdom of God in America*, 1937

Protestantism always leaves room for free criticism of the church in the light of God's revelation of His will in Christ, but at the same time struggles for the realization of the Christian community as one Body of Christ throughout the world.

SAMUEL MCCREA CAVERT, *Protestantism: A Symposium*, ed. W. K. Anderson, 1944

The temptation of Protestantism has always been to magnify freedom at the expense of unity. The temptation of Roman Catholicism, on the other hand, has been to magnify unity at the expense of freedom.

SAMUEL MCCREA CAVERT, *Protestantism: A Symposium*, ed. W. K. Anderson, 1944

Protestant philosophers of religion have been concerned above all with the "meaning of God in human experience," "religious values," and "the source of human good." Their thinking has been value-centered rather than God-centered.

ARNOLD S. NASH, *Protestant Thought in the Twentieth Century*, 1951

The official protest has become the only thing that all the multifarious institutions and cultural manifestations known as Protestant have in common. This is the opposition to the Catholic Church and all Catholic thought as expressed in literature, art, science, and culture in general: an opposition in the name of individual responsibility before God.

GERHARD RITTER, "Protestantism," *Twentieth Century Encyclopedia of Religious Knowledge*, II, 1955

Protestantism belonged to the same genus of thought as medieval Catholicism.

FRANKLIN LEV. BAUMER, *Main Currents of Western Thought*, 1956

Today we realize better than ever before that, while rejecting many Catholic notions, Protestantism has still kept many authentic Christian values.

GERARD PHILIPS, *The Role of the Laity in the Church*, 1956

Far from being the fulfilment of the Reformers' aims, modern Protestantism is in a state of anarchy exceeding even the anarchy that made possible . . . the movements in the sixteenth century to which the name Reformation is commonly given.

GEDDES MACGREGOR, *The Hemlock and the Cross*, 1963

See also Catholic and Non-Catholic; Catholicism; Church: Its Authority; Church: Its Nature; Communism; Denominationalism; Division; Luther, Martin; Private Judgment; Rationalism; Reformation, the; Unity.

PROVIDENCE

Any one thing in the creation is sufficient to demonstrate a Providence to an humble and grateful mind.
　　EPICTETUS, *Discourses of,* c. 110 A.D.

Divine Providence is God's will from which all existing things receive fitting ends.
　　ST. GREGORY OF NYSSA (c. 335–c. 395), *Memesius, De. Nat.,* Hom. XLIII

If nothing in the world is without a share in the Good, and evil is the deficiency of Good and no thing in the world is utterly destitute of Good, then the Divine Providence is in all things, and nothing that exists can be without it.
　　DIONYSIUS THE AREOPAGITE, *The Divine Names,* c. 5th century

Providence embraces all things equally, however different they may be, even however infinite; when they are assigned to their own places, forms and times, Fate sets them in an orderly motion; so that this development of the temporal order, unified in the intelligence of the mind of God, is Providence.
　　BOETHIUS, *Consolations of Philosophy,* c. 525

Providence is the care God takes of all existing things. And again, Providence is the will of God through which all existing things receive their fitting issue.
　　ST. JOHN DAMASCENE (700?–754?), *Exposition of the Orthodox Faith*

Events depend principally on Divine Providence which is superior to nature and alone knows the predetermined times of events.
　　LOUIS LEROY, *On the Vicissitudes or Variety of the Things in the Universe,* 1577

A watchful and continual care (yet without cark [worry or anxiety]) whereby he holdeth, searcheth, and knoweth all things: And knowing them, disposeth and ordereth the same by an immutable course to us unknown. And this is it which here I call PROVIDENCE.
　　JUSTUS LIPSIUS, *Two Books of Constancie,* I, 1593

We ought to repose on Divine Providence, not only for what concerns temporal things, but much more for what relates to our spiritual life and perfection.
　　ST. FRANCIS OF SALES (1567–1622), *Consoling Thoughts of,* ed. Huguet

Nothing is omitted by Divine Providence of what concerns the government of human affairs; but that there may not be other things in the Universe that depend upon the same infinite wisdom, I cannot . . . bring myself to believe.
　　GALILEO, *Dialogue on the Great World Systems,* 1632

If you leap into a Well, Providence is not bound to fetch you out.
　　THOMAS FULLER, *Gnomologia,* 1732

I believe in a general Providence, dear sister, which has laid down from all eternity the law which governs all things, like light from the sun; but I believe not that a particular Providence changes the economy of the world for your sparrow or cat.
　　VOLTAIRE, "Providence," *Philosophical Dictionary,* 1764

A firm persuasion of the superintendence of Providence over all our concerns is absolutely necessary to our happiness.
　　WILLIAM COWPER, *Letter to Lady Hesketh,* 1765

Providence is . . . the real, effective, redeeming power of God in history, restoring lost freedom to the individual man and to the whole human race and, with that freedom, the effectual power to do good.

FRIEDRICH SCHLEGEL, *Philosophy of History,* 1829

Divine Providence is Wisdom, endowed with an infinite Power, which realizes its aim, viz., the absolute rational design of the world.

G. W. F. HEGEL (1770–1831), *The Philosophy of History,* publ. posth.

As there is a particular Providence, so of necessity that Providence is secretly concurring and co-operating with that system which meets the eye, and which is commonly recognized among men as existing.

JOHN HENRY NEWMAN, *Difficulties of Anglicans,* 1850

If, as is the more religious theory, Providence intends not all which happens, but only what is good, then indeed man has it in his power, by his voluntary actions, to aid the intentions of Providence.

JOHN STUART MILL (1806–1873), *Nature,* publ. posth.

There is a radical absurdity in all these attempts to discover, in detail, what are the designs of Providence, in order when they are discovered to help Providence in bringing them about.

JOHN STUART MILL (1806–1873), *Nature,* publ. posth.

The belief in free-will is not in the least incompatible with the belief in Providence, provided you do not restrict the Providence to fulminating nothing but fatal decrees.

WILLIAM JAMES, *The Will to Believe and Other Essays,* 1896

Man learns to see providence in the great universal forces of nature, in the wind and the rain, in the soil underfoot and in the cloud overhead.

JOHN BURROUGHS, *The Divine Soil,* 1908

There are many scapegoats for our blunders, but the most popular one is Providence.

MARK TWAIN (1835–1910), *Notebook*

It means that there is significance in everything that happens in the world, and a heart, a concern, and a power stronger than all the powers of the world which is able to fulfill the purpose of its care for man.

ROMANO GUARDINI, *The Loving God,* 1947

It is not the depth of our suffering, but the depth of our separation from God, which destroys our faith in Providence.

PAUL TILLICH, *The Shaking of the Foundations,* 1948

Faith in providence is faith altogether. It is the courage to say yes to one's own life and life in general, in spite of the driving forces of fate, in spite of the catastrophes of existence and the breakdown of meaning.

PAUL TILLICH, *The New Being,* 1955

The Christian cause is not well served by assuming that whatever happens is God's will. . . . Neither liberal faith nor Christian experience substantiate this conclusion.

GEORGIA HARKNESS, *The Providence of God,* 1960

Belief in Providence in the most general sense, implies the goodness as well as the power of God in the creation, ordering and maintaining of this world, embracing the entire world of physical nature, biological life, and human persons.

GEORGIA HARKNESS, *The Providence of God,* 1960

See also Call; Creation; Destiny; Determinism; Election; Evolution; Faith; Fatalism; Fate; Foreknowledge; Forgiveness; Free Will; God, Fatherhood of; God: His Existence; God: His Goodness; God: His Intervention in the World; God: His Omnipotence; God: His Omnipresence; God: His Omniscience; History; Love, Divine; Man and God; Mercy; Necessity; Predestination; Redemption; Salvation; Security; Trust; World and God.

PRUDENCE

Prudence scorns the things of the world for the contemplation of divine things; it directs all the thoughts of the soul toward God.

> ST. THOMAS AQUINAS, *Summa Theologiae*, Ia, IIae, q. 61, 1272

Prudence consists in a certain judgment how to choose Good.

> BALDASSARE CASTIGLIONE, *The Courtier*, 1528

Prudence, my lord, is the virtue of those who command, not of those who obey.

> ST. IGNATIUS LOYOLA, responding to a query as to his obedience of the Pope (1491–1556), quoted by Francis Thompson, *St. Ignatius Loyola*

Prudence and Piety were always very good friends. . . . You may gain enough of both worlds if you would mind each in its place.

> RICHARD STEELE, *The Tradesman's Calling*, 1684

Prudence: a rich, ugly, old maid courted by Incapacity.

> WILLIAM BLAKE, *Proverbs of Hell*, 1790

Though prudence in itself is neither virtue nor spiritual holiness, yet without prudence, or in opposition to it, neither virtue nor holiness can exist.

> SAMUEL TAYLOR COLERIDGE, *Aids to Reflection*, 1825

Prudence is the final imprudence when by slow degrees it prepares the mind to do without God.

> GEORGES BERNANOS, *The Diary of a Country Priest*, 1937

No dictum in traditional Christian doctrine strikes such a note of strangeness to the ears of contemporaries, even contemporary Christians, as this one: that the virtue of prudence is the mold and "mother" of all the other cardinal virtues.

> JOSEPH PIEPER, *Prudence*, 1959

Prudence aims primarily at achieving an end, and not at standing about in a paralyzing timidity.

> THEODORE L. WESTOW, *The Variety of Catholic Attitudes*, 1963

PSALMS

Psalmody is the rewarding work of the night, the grateful relaxation of the busy day, the good beginning and the fortifying conclusion of all work. It is the ministry of angels, the strength of the heavenly host, the spiritual sacrifice.

> ST. AMBROSE (c. 333–397), *Commentary on Psalm I*

It could well be called a "little Bible" since it contains, set out in the briefest and most beautiful form, all that is to be found in the whole Bible.

> MARTIN LUTHER, *Preface to the Psalms*, 1528

The Book of Psalms contains the whole music of the heart of man, swept by the hand of his Maker . . . a mirror in which each man sees the motions of his own soul. They express in exquisite words the kinship which every thoughtful human heart craves to find with a supreme, unchanging, loving God.

> ROWLAND E. PROTHERO, *The Psalms in Human Life*, 1904

The Psalms are our Bread of Heaven in the wilderness of our Exodus.

THOMAS MERTON, *Bread in the Wilderness,* 1953

They lament and cry out in despair; they curse, and pray for vengeance; they wonder at the good fortunes of bad men; they hate sickness and fear death. . . . Yet they are more overwhelmed by the greatness and goodness of God.

MARY ELLEN CHASE, *The Psalms for the Common Reader,* 1963

See also Bible; Bible: Its Inspiration; Music; Old Testament; Song.

PSEUDO RELIGION

After mankind has done away with the pseudo-religion of race and blood, it is faced with the even greater danger of a technocratical pseudo-religion.

EMIL BRUNNER, *The Scandal of Christianity,* 1951

PSYCHE

The soul is a theological concept, hence only understandable in theological and ontological terms, whereas the psyche is a psychological construct.

VICTOR WHITE, *Soul and Psyche,* 1960

See also Soul.

PSYCHIATRISTS

And sometimes those who are to be physicians of the mind, although they cannot understand anything of the spiritual precepts, are not ashamed of taking upon themselves to be physicians of the mind.

POPE ST. GEGORY I, *Pastoral Care,* 590

A wise minister will work with a psychiatrist, not without one, but if the churches substitute any other kind of success for the successful handling of the spiritual aspects

of individual problems, they will be vacating their most obvious functions.

HARRY EMERSON FOSDICK, *Literary Digest,* December 17, 1927

Only a priestly man can be a complete psychiatrist. For with him the relation to the patient and the inner activities of the patient have been lifted out of the realm of the subjectivity of the finite into the inclusive life of the eternal.

PAUL TILLICH, *The Religious Situation,* 1932

It is doubtless true that religion has been the world's psychiatrist throughout the centuries.

K. M. MENNINGER, *Man Against Himself,* 1938

The sick soul and the psychiatrist are twin features, peculiar features of this end of the modern era. The psychiatrist is the embodiment of applied science, attempting to deal with the ravages of the mistakes of science. What he finds is, that more science is not enough.

WILLIAM ERNEST HOCKING, *What Man Can Make of Man,* 1942

Gazing steadily, unflinchingly, at our inward selves, we learn under the psychiatrist's guidance to draw the picture of our own soul.

JOSHUA LOTH LIEBMAN, *Peace of Mind,* 1946

Whenever Freud or other analysts, psychiatrists, or psychologists have tried to deduce philosophical and religious attitudes solely from their scientific data, the results have generally been naive and palpably untenable.

ROLLO MAY, *Liberal Learning and Religion,* ed. A. N. Wilder, 1951

The psychiatrist, even though he may be a religious man, does not have the task of preaching good tidings; but to him it is given to "prepare the ways of the Lord and make straight His paths."

RUDOLF ALLERS, *Faith, Reason and Modern Psychiatry,* ed. F. Braceland, 1955

The oaths of the religious leader and the psychiatrist often meet, sometimes converge, but they are never identical.

LOUIS LINN and LEO W. SCHWARZ, *Psychiatry and Religious Experience,* 1958

Divine power is the most wonderful therapeutic gift of all, once psychiatrists understand and reverence it.

GEORGE C. ANDERSON, *Man's Right to Be Human,* 1959

The integrity of the majority of practicing psychiatrists, whatever their beliefs, is beyond criticism. Even if they do not share an identical outlook with their Christian patients, they are unlikely to advise any conduct likely to clash with the dictates of the patient's conscience.

J. DOMINIAN, *Psychiatry and the Christian,* 1962

See also Confession; Freud; Freudianism; Mental Illness; Neurosis; Neurotic; Psychiatry; Psychoanalysis; Psychologists; Psychology; Psychotherapy.

PSYCHIATRY

Love—incomparably the greatest pyschotherapeutic agent—is something that professional psychiatry cannot of itself create, focus, nor release.

GORDON W. ALLPORT, *The Individual and His Religion,* 1950

Psychiatry is just waking up to the fact that . . . it must exercise practical and religious functions which put it on the side of "sound religion" instead of "no religion."

DAVID E. ROBERTS, *The Church and Mental Health,* 1950

A sound philosophy or a sincere religious belief does not obviate the need for psychiatric assistance with emotional disorders.

FRANCIS J. BRACELAND, *Faith, Reason and Modern Psychiatry,* 1955

A mental illness, no matter how serious and profound, never takes from the patient his status as a man, and therein lies the basis of Christian psychiatric help.

KARL STERN, *Faith, Reason and Modern Psychiatry,* ed. F. Braceland, 1955

Psychiatry is now prepared to recognize that normal psychological development cannot occur except on a firm moral basis.

LOUIS LINN and LEO W. SCHWARZ, *Psychiatry and Religious Experience,* 1958

Religion and psychiatry meet on common ground in their ministry to the soul; the task of the psychotherapist is to keep the soul well, and that of the priest to save the soul.

GEORGE C. ANDERSON, *Man's Right to Be Human,* 1959

Psychiatry can give us added strength of mind, but we shall need religion to give us spiritual strength to preserve our minds.

GEORGE C. ANDERSON, *Man's Right to Be Human,* 1959

It always fascinates me to realize—despite the jargon of even *pagan* psychiatrists— that the terminology of psychiatry is simply a roundabout and veiled corroboration of Christian doctrine.

JOHN E. LARGE, *The Small Needle of Doctor Large,* 1962

Any system of psychiatry which totally ignores man's obligations and aspirations in the spiritual order cannot but diminish his stature and be incomplete.

J. DOMINIAN, *Psychiatry and the Christian,* 1962

Psychiatry offers no support or any acceptable foundation for the disruption of accepted sexual ethics.

J. DOMINIAN, *Psychiatry and the Christian,* 1962

See also Confession; Conscience; Dreams; Freud; Freudianism; Mental Illness; Mind; Neurosis; Neurotic; Psychiatrists; Psychoanalysis; Psychologists; Psychology; Psychotherapy; Science and Religion; Unconscious Mind.

PSYCHIC PHENOMENA

There exists in that Eternal World the permanent realities of every thing, which we see reflected in this vegetable glass of nature.

WILLIAM BLAKE, *Vision of the Last Judgment,* 1790

The world of psychical phenomena appears to me to be as much a part of "Nature" as the world of physical phenomena; and I am unable to perceive any justification for cutting the Universe into two halves, one natural and one supernatural.

THOMAS HENRY HUXLEY, *Collected Essays,* 1872

The existence all about us of thousands and tens of thousands of persons, not perceptibly hysteric or unhealthy, who are mediumistic . . . is a phenomenon of human life. . . . Add the fact that the mediumship often gives supernormal information, and it becomes evident that the phenomenon cannot consist of pure eccentricity and isolation.

WILLIAM JAMES, *Proceedings of Society for Psychical Research,* 1903

We have no warrant for the assumption that the phantom seen, even though it be somehow *caused* by a deceased person, *is* that deceased person, in any ordinary sense of the word. . . . We shall find for the ghost a much closer parallel in those hallucinatory figures or phantasms which living persons can sometimes project at a distance. . . . It may bear such a relation to the deceased that it can reflect or represent his presumed wish to communicate, or it may not. . . . So let us describe a "ghost" as *a manifestation of persistent personal energy,* or an indication that some kind of force is being exercised after death which is in some way connected with a person previously known on earth. . . . It is theoretically possible that this force or influence . . . may indicate no continuing action on his part, but may be some kind of residue of the force or energy which he generated while yet alive.

F. W. H. MYERS, *Human Personality,* 1903

Telepathy looks like a law prevailing in the spiritual as well as in the material world. And that it does so prevail . . . is proved by the fact that those who communicated with us telepathically in this world communicate with us telepathically from the other.

F. W. H. MYERS, *Human Personality,* 1903

The old conception of the *ghost*—a conception which seemed to belong only to primitive animism and to modern folklore —has received a new meaning from observations of phenomena occurring between living men. . . . Wraiths of this kind correspond with death too often to leave the correspondence attributable to chance alone. . . . There is evidence that the self-same living spirit is still operating, and it may be in the self-same way.

F. W. H. MYERS, *Human Personality,* 1903

In the question of spirit survival scientific method has both a problem and something real to attack, and parapsychology has a mandate.

J. B. RHINE, *Journal* of the American Society for Psychical Research, April, 1949

There is something operative in man that transcends the laws of matter and, therefore, by definition, a nonphysical or spiritual law is made manifest. . . . This new world of the mind, represented and perhaps only suggested by the psi operations already identified, may very well, through further exploration, expand into an order of significance for a spiritual universe beyond the dreams of religion's own prophets and mystics.

J. B. RHINE, *New World of the Mind*, 1953

If parapsychology deals with all the personality manifestations that are beyond explanation by physics, then by definition it should claim the entire spiritual order of reality.

J. B. RHINE, *New World of the Mind*, 1953

If there are daemons that are actually experienced, and such experiences "show not only the danger of being devoured by the Unconscious," then there are also the spiritual and cosmic hierarchies and angelic powers. Why should they too not be experienced, in appropriate form, by the spiritual man?

GEBHARD FREI, *Beyond the Five Senses*, ed. Eileen J. Garrett, 1957

The importance of parapsychology lies mainly in the well-founded expectation that it will considerably enrich, even beyond the sign-posts which dynamic psychology has so much displaced, our vistas and conceptions about human personality.

EMILIO SERVADIO, *Beyond the Five Senses*, ed. Eileen J. Garrett, 1957

No Christian, nor indeed many theists of any sort, can allow for a moment that any psychic experience, which must of its nature be something finite and is, *ex hypothesi*, an observable phenomenon, can possibly *be* God.

VICTOR WHITE, *Soul and Psyche*, 1960

Does some part of man live on after death? Certain psi experiences suggest that the answer is "yes." Indeed, the idea of an afterlife has surely been strengthened by "psychic" occurrences that suggest the agency of persons deceased.

LOUISA E. RHINE, *Hidden Channels of the Mind*, 1961

PSYCHOANALYSIS

In itself psychoanalysis is neither religious or nonreligious, but an impartial tool both priest and layman can use in the service of the sufferer.

SIGMUND FREUD, to Oskar Pfister, 1909, quoted in *Psychoanalysis and Faith*, ed. H. Meng and E. L. Freud

No idea is comparable with that of God for enabling the mind to reconstruct itself, and would that we heard so much of psycho-synthesis as we do of psycho-analysis.

C. C. MARTINDALE, *Faith of the Roman Church*, 1927

Freudian psychoanalysis is limited to the task of making conscious the shadow-side and the evil within us. It simply brings into action the civil war that was latent, and lets it go at that.

C. G. JUNG, *Modern Man in Search of a Soul*, 1932

Sure you can psychoanalyze, but, as Baehr used to say, why bother to sort garbage?

MARTIN H. FISCHER, *Fischerisms*, 1943

Analysis requires that the psychiatrist be the recipient of unreserved self-avowal. . . . If science is a partial judge of life, if science is omitting the moral ingredient, omits an essential part of true judgment, then confession to the scientist must by its own logic be incomplete.

WILLIAM ERNEST HOCKING, *Science and the Idea of God*, 1944

Psycho-analysis leaves the fundamental problems of the human soul where it found them.

> ROLAND DALBIEZ, *Psycho-Analytical Methods and the Doctrine of Freud,* Vol. II, 1945

Psycho-analytical investigation does not explain the philosophical aspect of philosophy, the artistic aspect of art, the scientific aspect of science, the moral aspect of morality, or the religious aspect of religion.

> ROLAND DALBIEZ, *Psycho-Analytical Methods and the Doctrine of Freud,* Vol II, 1945

Psycho-analysis has in truth done much to undermine religion; by its own methods it has continued the work in this direction that the physical and biological sciences had begun. But it has no more "disproved" religion than have these other sciences.

> J. C. FLUGEL, *Man, Morals and Society,* 1945

Psychoanalysis may be said to be but the confessional technique developed by the psychiatrist in the probing of psychic disturbances and in effecting their removal.

> JOHN A. O'BRIEN, *Psychiatry and Confession,* 1948

There are thousands of patients on their backs who would be made better if they were on their knees instead.

> FULTON J. SHEEN, *Peace of Soul,* 1949

"Psychoanalysis" becomes very wrong indeed when it ceases to be a method of treatment and pretends to be a philosophy.

> FULTON J. SHEEN, *Peace of Soul,* 1949

The analyst . . . as a physician of the soul . . . is concerned with the very same problems as philosophy and theology; the soul of man and its cure.

> ERICH FROMM, *Psychoanalysis and Religion,* 1950

While psychological analysis is not ordained to forgive sin, it may do much to free the patient from those compulsions which make both sin and repentance from sin—and even any clear-eyed self-examination—impossible.

> VICTOR WHITE, *The Commonweal Reader,* ed. E. S. Skillin, 1950

The analyst who plays the confessor will be as bad an analyst as the confessor who plays the analyst will be a bad confessor.

> VICTOR WHITE, *The Commonweal Reader,* ed. E. S. Skillin, 1950

There need be no opposition between the Catholic religion and analytical psychiatry, so long as the latter avoids smuggling into either its psychological theories or its therapy any philosophical principles that are unacceptable to the former.

> JAMES H. VANDERVELDT and ROBERT P. ODENWALD, *Psychiatry and Catholicism,* 1952

World peace may not be finally realized, till the Westerners will outgrow Christianity, and Easterners the Buddhism by means of psychoanalysis.

> KENYI OTSUKI, *Tokyo Journal of Psychoanalysis,* March, 1954

Many Christian critics of psychoanalysis are evidently handicapped by the thought that one has to accept all the tenets.

> KARL STERN, *The Third Revolution,* 1954

Psychoanalysis is beginning to recognize that, in its suspicion of legalism, moralism, and rationalism its powerful ally is religion.

> SEWARD HILTNER, *Pastoral Psychology,* November, 1956

The approach is a technique, not a substitute for a moral code, and to confuse the two is to invite catastrophe.

> LOUIS LINN and LEO W. SCHWARZ, *Psychiatry and Religious Experience,* 1958

The psychoanalyst is the high priest of our secular culture.

A. T. MOLLEGEN, *Christianity and Modern Men*, 1961

The material with which the analysts are primarily concerned is the irrational, unacknowledged compulsive content of the unconscious, which has a bearing on the present conscious conduct.

J. DOMINIAN, *Psychiatry and the Christian*, 1962

Both religion and psychoanalysis seek . . . the path that would lead to serenity. . . . Both give the principle the same name—love. One sees in love the means for ultimate salvation, the other, the means for ultimate health.

GREGORY ZILBOORG, *Psychoanalysis and Religion*, 1962

Its basic recognition is the radical imperfectibility of man, a concept it derives not from the Christian Fall, but from the Darwinian Descent.

STANLEY EDGAR HYMAN, *The Promised End*, 1963

See also Confession; Conscience; Dreams; Freud; Freudianism; Libido; Mental Illness; Mind; Neurosis; Neurotic; Psychiatrists; Psychiatry; Psychologists; Psychology; Psychotherapy; Unconscious Mind.

PSYCHOLOGISTS

Every psychotherapist should be able to point, as John the Baptist pointed to Jesus, to One who is greater than the psychologist.

HOWARD E. COLLIER, *The Place of Worship in Modern Medicine*, 1944

Psychologists crying down Christian morality, arrived at their conclusions from the travesty of Christian morality presented to them by neurotic patients.

FRANZ B. ELKISCH, *The Springs of Morality*, ed. J. M. Todd, 1956

See also Psychiatrists; Psychiatry; Psychoanalysis; Psychology; Psychotherapy.

PSYCHOLOGY

The business of psychology is to tell us what actually goes on in the mind. It cannot possibly tell us whether the beliefs are true or false.

HASTINGS RASHDALL, *Philosophy and Religion*, 1909

Psychology must supply us with the facts about the human mind and its experiences. . . . It is then the task of the theologian to explain what kind of universe it is in which such experiences occur, i.e., in the end to ask what God is like.

F. R. BARRY, *Christianity and Psychology*, 1923

The idea of religion which is merely based upon psychology and involves nothing else is a delusion.

H. THOULESS, *Introduction to the Psychology of Religion*, 1923

God can no more become an object for psychological science than for chemical and physical science. In investigating the experience of the communion of the soul with God, the psychology of religion can deal only with the mental factors involved.

E. J. PRICE, *The Hibbert Journal*, XXII, 1924

A form of myth making, whereby men supply the place of knowledge by converting their conjectures into dogma, and then do battle on behalf of the dogmas.

C. E. M. JOAD, *Return to Philosophy*, 1936

Most psychological problems are intertwined with religious, and religious problems have in most cases a very clear psychological aspect.

ROLLO MAY, *Springs of Creative Living*, 1940

Psychology alone is never enough for man's great adventure—life. Like all other sciences, it formulates no moral goal; it is not a philosophy of life, nor did its pioneers ever intend it to be. It is a *key* to the temple, not the temple itself.

JOSHUA LOTH LIEBMAN, *Peace of Mind,* 1946

I believe that it [psychology] must be supplemented by religion, and that only the blended light of these two great beacons will guide individuals and nations through the hazardous channels ahead.

JOSHUA LOTH LIEBMAN, *Peace of Mind,* 1946

There is inherent absurdity in supposing that psychology and religion, both dealing with the outward reaching of man's mind, must be permanently and hopelessly at odds.

GORDON W. ALLPORT, *The Individual and His Religion,* 1950

We should certainly not find fault with depth psychology, if it deals with the psychic aspects of religious phenomena and endeavors to analyze and reduce it to a scientific system, even if this research and its terminology was not in use in times past.

POPE PIUS XII, *Address,* 1953

Modern psychology is afraid of the concept of the soul because it seems to establish a reality which is unapproachable by scientific methods and may interfere with their results. The fear is not unfounded.

PAUL TILLICH, *Dynamics of Faith,* 1957

The crucial conflict is not between Christianity and physics, or even between Christianity and biology; it is between religion and psychology. . . . The focus of both of these disciplines is the same, namely, the nature and transformation of human feelings, evaluations, needs, beliefs, purposes and actions.

HENRY A. MURRAY, *Science Ponders Religion,* ed. H. Shapley, 1960

To the religious thinker it may appear almost sacrilegious to approach the highest content of religion—God—with the "dissecting knife" of psychology.

VICTOR WHITE, *Soul and Psyche,* 1960

The growth of religion as a psychological phenomenon with its vulnerable periods is one of the most urgent tasks for investigation facing the Christian psychologists.

J. DOMINIAN, *Psychiatry and the Christian,* 1962

See also Freud; Freudianism; Mental Illness: Mind; Neurosis; Neurotic; Psyche; Psychiatrists; Psychiatry; Psychoanalysis; Psychologists; Psychotherapy; Science and Religion.

PSYCHOTHERAPY

Speaking as a student of psychotherapy, who, as such, has no concern with theology, I am convinced that the Christian religion is one of the most valuable and potent influences that we possess for producing that harmony and peace of mind and that confidence of soul which is needed to bring health and power to a large proportion of nervous patients.

J. A. HADFIELD, *The Psychology of Power,* 1923

My own experience convinces me that religious group psychotherapy in right hands and under proper conditions has a great contribution to make to neurotic healing.

HOWARD E. COLLIER, *The Place of Worship in Modern Medicine,* 1944

Psychotherapy knows the healing power of love, but finds itself unable to do anything about it.

GORDON W. ALLPORT, *The Individual and His Religion,* 1950

See also Healing; Mental Illness; Neurosis; Neurotic; Psychiatrists; Psychiatry; Psychoanalysis; Psychologists, Psychology.

PUBLIC SCHOOL. See
EDUCATION, SECULARIZED;
EDUCATION, STATE

PUBLIC WELFARE

It is the duty of the individual to bear hardships, even to suffer martyrdom, for the common welfare.

JUDAH HALEVI, *Cuzari*, c. 1135

Ultimate public welfare becomes actual in the private joys of single individuals. The common welfare is the well-being of individual men.

RALPH W. SOCKMAN, *The Highway of God*, 1941

See also Social Action; Social Cause; Social Conscience; Social Cooperation; Social Gospel; Social Order; Social Welfare; Socialism; Wages; Welfare State.

PULPIT. See
PREACHING

PUNISHMENT

The whole world is kept in order by punishment, for a guiltless man is hard to find; through fear of punishment the whole world yields the enjoyments which it owes.

Code of Manu, between 1200 and 500 B.C.

Men suffer individually for the deeds they themselves have done.

Sutra-Krit-Anga, between 600 and 200 B.C.

And it often happens that a man with fifty murders on his head loses it but once. Where, then, will he pay the penalty for forty-nine of them? You must charge God with lack of justice, if there be not judgment and recompense after this world.

ST. CYRIL OF JERUSALEM, *Catechetical Lectures*, 350

When the bad are punished, others become better.

ST. JOHN CHRYSOSTOM, *Homilies*, c. 388

Sin is a suppurating wound; punishment is the surgeon's knife.

ST. JOHN CHRYSOSTOM, *Homilies*, c. 388

Sins that are easiest to amend bring the greatest punishment.

ST. JOHN CHRYSOSTOM, *Homilies*, c. 388

When God punishes sinners, He does not inflict His evil on them, but leaves them to their own evil.

ST. AUGUSTINE, *Enarrationes in Psalms*, V, 10, c. 415

To be gone from the kingdom of God, to be an exile from God's city, to be cut off from the divine life, to be without the manifold sweetness of God—is so mighty a punishment that no torments that we know can be compared with it.

ST. AUGUSTINE, *Enchiridion*, 421

If, moreover, God should chastise men according to their deserts, He would not leave even a reptile on the back of the earth!

Koran, c. 625

It was not for punishment that He formed us, but to share His goodness, inasmuch as He is a good God. But inasmuch as He is a just God, His will is that sinners should suffer punishment.

ST. JOHN DAMASCENE (700?–754?), *Exposition of the Orthodox Faith*

The punishment of the wicked is that they will not merit such life [in the world to come] but will be utterly cut off in their death. Whoever does not merit such life is a dead thing who will never live but is cut off in his wickedness and perishes like an animal.

MAIMONIDES, *Mishneh Torah*, 1170

Man punishes the action, but God the intention.

THOMAS FULLER, *Gnomologia*, 1732

The object of punishment is prevention from evil; it never can be made impulsive to good.

HORACE MANN, *Lectures on Education*, 1840

The sin they do by two and two they must pay for one by one.

RUDYARD KIPLING, *Tomlinson*, 1891

Every person that does any evil, that gratifies any passion, is sufficiently punished by the evil he has committed, by the passion he serves, but chiefly by the fact that he withdraws himself from God, and God withdraws Himself from him.

JOHN SERGIEFF OF CRONSTADT (1829–1908), *My Life in Christ*

See also Capital Punishment; Compassion; Condemnation; Damnation; Death; Deeds; Election; Evil; Force; Free Will; God: His Wrath; Guilt; Hell; Immortality; Judgment; Judgment, God's; Justice; Man: His Wickedness; Mercy; Predestination; Purgatory; Reward; Reward and Punishment; Salvation; Sin; Sin: Its Consequences; Soul.

PURGATORY

A man will not be able to participate in divinity until the cleansing fire will have purged him of every fault which has found its way into his soul.

ST. GREGORY OF NYSSA (c. 335–c. 395), *Oratio de Mortuis*

This fire will be more severe than anything which a man can suffer in this life.

ST. AUGUSTINE, *In Psalm 37 Enarratio*, c. 415

I know that at the end of this life some will do penance by purgatorial flames.

POPE ST. GREGORY THE GREAT (540–604), *Ps.* III *Poenit*, i

Fear [in purgatory] is cast out because of the strengthening of the will by which the soul knows that it cannot sin.

ST. BONAVENTURE (1221–1274), *Lib.* IV, d 20, a i, q. 4

The soul in purgatory feels great happiness and great sorrow, and the one does not hinder the other.

ST. CATHERINE OF GENOA, *Treatise on Purgatory*, c. 1480

When the soul finds itself on the road back to its first state, its need to be transformed in God kindles a fire so great that this is its Purgatory . . . its instinct to God, aflame and thwarted, makes a Purgatory.

ST. CATHERINE OF GENOA, *Treatise on Purgatory*, c. 1480

Rust, which is sin, covers the soul, and in Purgatory is burnt away by fire; the more it is consumed, the more do souls respond to God, the true sun.

ST. CATHERINE OF GENOA, *Treatise on Purgatory*, c. 1480

Defective piety or love in a dying person is necessarily accompanied by great fear, which is greatest where the piety or love is least. This fear or horror is sufficient in itself, whatever else might be said, to constitute the pain of purgatory.

MARTIN LUTHER, *The Ninety-Five Theses* (No. 14 and 15), 1517

There seems to be the same difference between hell, purgatory, and heaven as between despair, uncertainty, and assurance.

MARTIN LUTHER, *The Ninety-Five Theses* (No. 16), 1517

Once could for a time perhaps in a way conceal that it was devised apart from God's word in a curious and bold rashness; that men believed in it by some sort of "revelations" forged by Satan's craft; and that some passages of Scripture were ignorantly distorted to confirm it.

JOHN CALVIN, *Institutes* III, 1536

It is perfectly clear . . . that the blood of Christ is the sole satisfaction for the sins of believers, the sole expiation, the sole purgation. . . . Purgatory is simply a dreadful blasphemy against Christ.

JOHN CALVIN, *Institutes* III, 1536

If the fire is not real, it will be something more terrible, such as God can prepare in order to show His power in this respect.

ST. ROBERT BELLARMINE, *De Purgatorio* II, 1601

Why sir, it is a very harmless doctrine. They are of opinion that the generality of mankind are neither so obstinately wicked as to deserve everlasting punishment, nor so good as to merit being admitted into the society of blessed spirits; and therefore that God is graciously pleased to allow of a middle state, where they may be purified by certain degrees of suffering.

SAMUEL JOHNSON, *Boswell's Life of Johnson*, 1772

To deny Purgatory was to set an alternative between Heaven and Hell, so sharp as to be too painful for faith and hope and love.

BEDE JARRETT, *Meditations for Layfolk*, 1915

Purgatory is only a thoroughfare to the Father, toilsome indeed and painful, but yet a throughfare, in which there is no standing still and which is illuminated by glad hope.

KARL ADAM, *The Spirit of Catholicism*, 1924

As the soul has passed beyond the time of merit it must suffer in Purgatory till the dross of sin is removed. It can do nothing but suffer.

GERALD C. TREACY, *After Death—What?*, 1927

In no state is there so paradoxical a combination of suffering and joy. For the soul will sufficiently "see" God to realize its own unlikeness to Him, His beauty and its ugliness. . . . But also, it knows that it is becoming more and more like to God, and in *that* is a joy far greater than any we experience here.

C. C. MARTINDALE, *The Catholic Bedside Book*, 1953

See also Death; Immortality; Immortality, Belief in; Penitence; Punishment; Sin; Sin: Its Consequences; Soul; Suffering; Violence.

PURITAN

The Puritan was intensely human; but you will remember that he apologized to God as many as three times a day for the fact.

WOODROW WILSON, *Address*, December, 1900

The Puritan flings himself into practical activities with the demonic energy of one, who, all doubts allayed, is conscious that he is a sealed and chosen vessel.

R. H. TAWNEY, *Religion and the Rise of Capitalism*, 1926

Across the empty seas they came with no intention of permitting political or religious freedom. They did not come to pioneer a new democracy. They came to set up a Bible State, . . . and they came because they could not have their way in England.

ROBERT C. WHITTEMORE, *Makers of the American Mind*, 1964

PURITANISM

Puritanism . . . has no intellectual basis; no internal idea, no principle of unity, no theology. . . . It has no straightforward view on any one point, on which it professes to teach, and to hide its poverty it has dressed itself out in a maze of words.

JOHN HENRY NEWMAN, *British Critic*, April, 1839

What the Puritans gave the world was not thought, but action.

WENDELL PHILLIPS, *Speech,* December, 1855

Puritanism, believing itself quick with the seed of religious liberty, laid, without knowing it, the egg of democracy.

JAMES RUSSELL LOWELL, *Among My Books,* 1870

Puritanism was a Protestant Renaissance of the Old Testament and a reversion to biblical precedents for the regulation of the minutest details of daily life.

OSCAR L. STRAUSS, *Origin of Republican Form of Government,* 1885

A determined and varied effort to erect the holy community.

A. S. P. WOODHOUSE, *Puritanism and Liberty,* 1938

Puritanism was a cutting edge which hewed liberty, democracy, humanitarianism, and universal education out of the black forest of feudal Europe and the American wilderness. Puritan doctrine taught each person to consider himself a significant if sinful unit to whom God had given a particular place and duty, and that he must help his fellow men. Puritanism therefore is an American heritage to be grateful for and not to be sneered at because it required everyone to attend divine worship and maintained a strict code of moral ethics.

SAMUEL ELIOT MORISON, *The Oxford History of the American People,* 1965

Puritanism was essentially and primarily a religious movement; attempts to prove it to have been a mask for politics or money-making are false as well as unhistorical. In the broadest sense Puritanism was a passion for righteousness; the desire to know and do God's will.

SAMUEL ELIOT MORISON, *The Oxford History of the American People,* 1965

See also Capitalism; Economics and Christianity; Enterprise; Work.

PURITY

Purity is for man, next to life, the greatest good, that purity that is procured by the law of Mazda to him who cleanses his own self with good thoughts, words, and deeds.

Vendidad, Zend-Avesta, c. 700 B.C.

Purity and stillness are the correct principles for mankind.

LAO-TZU (6th century B.C.), *Sayings of,* translated by Lionel Giles

The pure and impure stand and fall by their own deeds; no one can purify another.

Dhammapada, c. 5th century B.C.

All created things perish, he who knows and sees this becomes passive in pain; this is the way to purity.

Dhammapada, c. 5th century B.C.

To the virtuous all is pure.

Tripitaka, 80 B.C.

When a man reproached Diogenes for going into unclean places he said, "The sun too penetrates into privies, but it is not polluted by them."

DIOGENES LAERTIUS, 2nd or 3rd century A.D.

Purity of soul cannot be lost without consent.

ST. AUGUSTINE, *On Lying,* c. 395

Fortunate indeed is that man who was able to maintain control of his carnal senses in the time of his youth.

Bhartrihari: The Springa Sataka, c. 625

By purity God is made captive in me, purity makes me God-conscious and conscious of naught beside God, purity begets detachment. The pure soul has a light-

birth as it were, purity is satisfied with God alone.
> MEISTER ECKHART (1260?–1327?), *Meister Eckhart*

Abide pure amidst impurities of the world; thus shalt thou find the way of religion.
> GURU NANAK (1496–1538), *The Sikh Religion*, M. A. Macauliffe

The Sun is never the worse for shining on a Dunghill.
> THOMAS FULLER, *Gnomologia*, 1732

Man flows at once to God when the channel of purity is opened.
> H. D. THOREAU, *Walden*, 1854

Who knows what sort of life would result if we had attained to purity? If I knew so wise a man as could teach me purity I would go seek him forthwith.
> H. D. THOREAU, *Walden*, 1854

Purity is the sum of all loveliness, as whiteness is the sum of all colors.
> FRANCIS THOMPSON (1859–1907), *Works*, III

Purity. Of this word itself an impure use has been made. It has become an equivocal word, dragged about everywhere.
> JACQUES MARITAIN, *Art and Poetry*, 1943

It is not an inactive virtue; it does not merely consist in not committing certain sins. It means using your life in the way God wants, exercising constant restraint.
> FRANCIS DEVAS, *The Law of Love*, 1954

Purity is the condition for a higher love— for a possession superior to all possessions: that of God.
> FRANÇOIS MAURIAC, *What I Believe*, 1962

See also Celibacy; Chastity; Good; Goodness; Impurity; Infidelity; Love; Lust; Modesty; Sex; Virginity; Virtue.

PURPOSE

Although the word *purpose* has been carefully removed from the scientist's official vocabulary, it is a far more difficult matter to eliminate the *idea* of purpose from his mind.
> KENNETH WALKER, *Meaning and Purpose*, 1942

See also Creation; Creator; Design; God: His Intervention in the World, Universe.

PURSUIT

In pursuit of those far mysteries we dream of, or in tormented chase of that demon phantom that, some time or other, swims before all human hearts; while chasing such over his round globe, they either lead us on in barren mazes or midway leave us whelmed.
> HERMAN MELVILLE, *Moby Dick*, 1851

QUAKERS

The sect of Quakers in their best representatives appear to me to have come nearer the sublime history and genius of Christ than any other of the sects.
> RALPH WALDO EMERSON, *Lecture*, Boston, April, 1869

The main differences between ourselves and most other bodies of Christians arise from the emphasis we place on the Light of God's Holy Spirit in the human soul. . . . This direct contact between the Spirit of Christ and the human spirit we are prepared to trust to, as the basis of our individual and corporate life.
> *Faith and Practice of the Philadelphia Yearly Meeting*, 1955

QUALITIES

Qualities are nothing else but *sensations* or *ideas*, which exist only in a mind perceiving them.
> GEORGE BERKELEY, *Principles of Human Knowledge*, 1710

QUARRELS

'Tis by our quarrels that we spoil our prayers.
COTTON MATHER, *The Wonders of the Invisible World,* 1693

Subtleties of which not a trace can be found in the Gospels are the source of the bloody quarrels of Christian history.
VOLTAIRE, *Treatise on Toleration,* 1766

See also Discord; Disputation; Religious Conflict.

RACE

An honorable race is what? The race of men! The race that fears God. A despicable race is what? The race of men! The race that transgresses the commandments.
Apochrypha: Ben Sira, 10.19, c. 300–190 B.C.

God will not ask man of what race he is. He will ask what he has done.
Adi Gronath, c. 1600 A.D.

Whoever exalts race, or the people, or the State, or a particular form of State . . . whoever raises these notions above their standard value and divinizes them to an idolatrous level, distorts and perverts an order of the world planned and created by God.
POPE PIUS XI, *Mit Brennender Sorge,* March, 1937

The capital sin of pride includes as well the false race pride which commits whole segments of our population to a role of inferiority.
JULIAN J. REISS, *Address,* October 11, 1946

It was for the human race in its entirety—Caucasoid, Mongoloid, and Negroid—that He died, rose from the dead, and estab-

lished His Church. And we may not forget that He prayed that the human race be one with Him.
FRANCIS J. HAAS, *Catholics, Race and Law,* 1947

Racism is a way of thinking that has dogmatized the notion that one ethnic group is condemned by the laws of nature to hereditary inferiority and another group is marked off as hereditarily superior.
JOSEPH F. DOHERTY, *Moral Problems of Interracial Marriage,* 1949

One thing we can be grateful for—it is getting very hard indeed for a Christian to think that God likes his race better than other races.
ALAN PATON, *Christian Century,* March 31, 1954

See also Anti-Semitism; Apartheid; Brotherhood; Class Distinctions; Community; Discrimination; Equality; Fellowship; Genocide; Ghettoes; Hatred; Miscegnation; Negroes; Neighbor; Prejudice; Pride; Pseudo Religion; Racial Conflict; Racial Equality; Racial Injustice; Racial Prejudice; Righteousness; Rights; Tolerance; Unity of Mankind.

RACIAL CONFLICT

To demonstrate that Christian ideals are sufficient to solve the difficult problems of race relations in America is one of the most challenging tasks before the Church today.
FEDERAL COUNCIL OF CHURCHES OF CHRIST IN AMERICA, *Report,* 1924

The violent forces of race prejudice and hatred . . . make inter-racial brotherhood and fellowship of supreme concern to every Christian.
FEDERAL COUNCIL OF CHURCHES OF CHRIST IN AMERICA, *Report,* 1940

Charity is friendship of men for God, and for fellowmen on account of God. . . .

The divine life through charity is the common ground on which all men meet. . . . Such teaching leaves no room for race conflicts or class warfare.

A. J. MUENCH, "Social Charity," *Summa of St. Thomas Aquinas*, III, 1948

Few of us realize that racism is man's gravest threat to man, the maximum of hatred for a minimum of reason, the maximum of cruelty for a minimum of thinking.

ABRAHAM J. HESCHEL, *Address*, Chicago, January, 1963

See also Anti-Semitism; Apartheid; Charity; Community; Discrimination; Equality; Fellowship; Ghettoes; Hatred; Intolerance; Love; Negroes; Neighbor; Nonviolence; Prejudice; Race; Racial Equality; Racial Injustice; Racial Prejudice; Unity of Mankind.

RACIAL EQUALITY

Catholicity in principle, the natural disposition to admit all men of all races, was an integral part of the Church's teaching from the very beginning.

ANDRÉ RÉTIF, *The Catholic Spirit*, 1959

The Christian Church should lead, not follow. But everywhere it has left it to secular and lay persons to make the initial fight [for racial equality].

RALPH MCGILL, quoted in *Newsweek*, June 25, 1962

The victory of the law only raises a further and more profound issue for the social conscience of our country.

When the limits of law have been reached, as they have been reached, the whole issue [of racial equality] in all its subtlety of reach, is inescapably presented to the higher tribunal of conscience.

JOHN COURTNEY MURRAY, *Address*, New York City, May 20, 1963

Even though human beings differ from one another by virtue of their ethnic peculiarities, they all possess certain common elements and are inclined by nature to meet each other in the world of spiritual values.

POPE JOHN XXIII, *Pacem in Terris*, April, 1963

This is not a legal or legislative issue alone. . . . We are confronted primarily with a moral issue. It is as old as the Scriptures and is as clear as the American Constitution. The heart of the question is whether all Americans are to be afforded equal rights and equal opportunities. . . . We face, therefore, a moral crisis as a country and as a people.

JOHN F. KENNEDY, June, 1963

The first step in meeting any racial problem is to treat all men and women as persons, without reference to patterns of difference. But forgetfulness of God (which is the defect of secularism) and preoccupation with the physical (which is the effect of materialism) prevents this first step. They cause us to lose the view of man as God sees him.

ROMAN CATHOLIC BISHOPS OF U.S., *Bonds of Union*, November, 1963

See also Anti-Semitism; Apartheid; Brotherhood; Charity; Class Distinctions; Community; Discrimination; Equality; Fellowship; Ghettoes; Love; Negroes; Neighbor; Prejudice; Race; Racial Conflict; Racial Injustice; Racial Prejudice; Rights; Tolerance; Unity of Mankind.

RACIAL INJUSTICE

No slave, free negro, or mulatto shall preach, or hold any meeting for religious purposes either day or night.

Virginia Legislature, 1831

The members of the executive and legislative branches of state governments are guilty of an objective sin of injustice; positively, if they encourage segregation, negatively, if they remain inactive. Their primary obligations are the protection of *natural rights* and the promotion of the common good.

FRANCIS J. GILLIGAN, *The Morality of the Color Line,* 1929

The Fifth Commandment, which forbids injuries to our neighbors, forbids as well the appalling injuries which our prejudices and acts of discrimination cause whole groups of our neighbors.

JULIAN J. REISS, *Address,* October 11, 1946

The restoration of the Negro to the plane of equal opportunity is one of the primary obligations on the collective conscience of American society.

WILLIAM J. SMITH, *What Is the Catholic Attitude?,* 1946

The worker's right to a job and his right to self-improvement are *his* rights because God gave them to him. To the Christian all the links of the chain fit together. To him the Negro or the member of any "minority" is just as precious as any one else in the sight of God, and therefore no one else has the right to exclude him from exercising his God-given rights.

FRANCIS J. HAAS, *Catholics, Race and Law,* 1947

Any Catholic college which refuses to supply [educational] opportunity because of racial considerations, takes part in a general denial of rights possessed under distributive justice.

RICHARD J. ROCHE, *Catholic Colleges and the Negro Student,* 1948

Unless we make haste rapidly, by word but especially by example, in bringing complete justice to the American Negro . . . we shall be facing up to the totalitarians with one arm tied behind our back and . . . we shall be risking the vengeance of Almighty God.

JAMES E. MURRAY, *Address,* March 31, 1948

It is not just negative inertia and caution which lie behind racial discrimination, but the positive counterfaiths which produce them. The "conflicting valuations" turn out to be a warfare of the gods in the soul of man. Ultimately the racial problem is not one of hypocrisy but idolatry.

WALDO BEACH, *Faith and Ethics: The Theology of H. R. Niebuhr,* ed. P. Ramsey, 1957

The Christian response is not trust in racial integration, or any other human arrangement as final, but a radical obedience to the God and Father of our Lord Jesus Christ who gives and requires the love of the neighbor in and for himself.

WALDO BEACH, *Faith and Ethics: The Theology of H. R. Niebuhr,* ed. P Ramsey, 1957

Unless America can rather quickly make her racial practices express good conscience before the conscience of the world, she is not likely to retain the leadership so largely entrusted to her now, or even to retain her own self-respect.

LISTON POPE, *The Kingdom Beyond Caste,* 1957

White supremacy is an absolute. It overrides justice. It transcends the teaching of Christ. It is a purpose dwarfing every other purpose, an end justifying any means.

CATHOLIC BISHOPS OF UNION OF SOUTH AFRICA, July, 1957

We warn all Catholics that they cannot reconcile with their Catholic conscience any tendency to introduce legislation which would secure the rights of one section of the community by curtailing the rights of others.

HIERARCHY OF NORTHERN RHODESIA, *Pastoral Letter,* January, 1958

When the white Christian church looks at itself in the mirror of race, the reflection which comes back to it is clearly and

unmistakably the countenance of a sinner.
KYLE HASELDEN, *The Racial Problem in Christian Perspective*, 1959

White Christians who employ Christianity to tame the protesting Negro, to keep him a partial man, to perpetuate his servile role in American society, are justifying, however unwittingly, the Marxist contention that religion is the opiate by which the exploited are appeased.
KYLE HASELDEN, *The Racial Problem in Christian Perspective*, 1959

No man has a moral right to use his property, a creature of God, against the children of God. Racial discrimination even in the use of purely private property, is immoral at least as transgressing the supreme law of charity.
WILLIAM J. KENEALY, *The New Negro*, ed. M. H. Ahmann, 1961

There can never be a good prudential or pastoral reason for the Church in the United States to remain silent on interracial justice or to permit its practice to reflect the patterns of segregation.
JOHN L. MCKENZIE, *The Critic*, August–September, 1961

Going along with measures of justice does not reach the real point of the matter, which is that the Negro, as a son of God has more than legal standing alongside other men.
JAMES SELLERS, *The South and Christian Ethics*, 1962

By negligence and silence we have all become accessory before the God of mercy to the injustice committed against the Negroes by men of our nation.
ABRAHAM J. HESCHEL, *Address*, Chicago, January, 1963

The plague of racial injustice is not contained within geographical limits. It is not a regional issue. It is a national issue and a national disgrace.
PAUL J. HALLINAN, *Address*, Chicago, January, 1963

How can a Christian be at ease in Zion when he sees a man's racial background leads his fellow countrymen to treat him as a second class citizen?
HARRY EMERSON FOSDICK, *The Meaning of Being a Christian*, 1964

If and when the means of legal recourse have been exhausted . . . Christians may then choose to serve the cause of racial justice by disobeying a law that clearly involves the violation of their obligations as Christians.
Resolution adopted by 700 delegates to biennial convention of the Lutheran Church in America, July, 1964

The white Christian in the developing American culture confused Christianity with morality, morality with gentility, and gentility with aloofness from the Negro.
KYLE HASELDEN, *New York Times Magazine*, August 2, 1964

Not the extremists but the great, white midstream America—i.e. Christian America—produces and preserves the racial chasm in American society.
KYLE HASELDEN, *New York Times Magazine*, August 2, 1964

See also Anti-Semitism; Apartheid; Brotherhood; Charity; Class Distinctions; Community; Discrimination; Equality; Fellowship; Genocide; Ghettoes; Hatred; Intolerance; Love; Negroes; Neighbor; Prejudice; Race; Racial Conflict; Racial Equality; Racial Prejudice; Tolerance; Unity of Mankind.

RACIAL PREJUDICE

The color line has been drawn so incisively by the church itself that its proclamation of the gospel of brotherhood has sometimes the sad sound of irony, and sometimes falls upon the ear as unconscious hypocrisy—but sometimes there is in it the bitter cry of repentance.
H. RICHARD NIEBUHR, *Social Sources of Denominationalism*, 1929

Race prejudice, in its gravest and most typical form, is the passing judgment of criminality or of essential inferiority upon all the members of a racial or ethnic group, with no sufficient intellectual motive for such a judgment.

JOHN LA FARGE, *Interracial Justice,* 1937

It were a sham Christianity were we to try to exclude from the embrace of justice any man, or to make our charity narrower than the outstretched arms of Christ on Calvary.

SAMUEL A. STRITCH and EMMET E. WALSH, in name of Roman Catholic hierarchy of the U.S., *Letter to President T. W. Turner* of Hampton Institute, November, 1939

Segregation is the sin. Both in principle and practical procedure it is the sin. . . . We are lost if racial segregation continues. The important issue is not whether you or I may like it.

A. K. CHALMERS, *High Wind at Noon,* 1948

The only form of segregation that might conceivably be morally justifiable is segregation by mutual agreement and with equal rights. Even this, it seems to me, is *per se* contrary to the bond of union that should exist between peoples of the same nation and contrary to the common good of the nation itself.

GERALD KELLEY, *Theological Studies,* XIII, 1952

There is no segregation of races to be tolerated in the diocese of Raleigh, N.C. . . . All special churches for Negroes shall be abolished immediately as lending weight to the false notion that the Catholic Church, the Mystical Body of Christ, is divided.

VINCENT S. WATERS, *Pastoral Letter,* June 12, 1953

When we are given Christian insight the whole pattern of racial discrimination is seen as an unutterable offense against God, to be endured no longer, so that the very stones cry out.

WORLD COUNCIL OF CHURCHES, statement, 1954

The chief sin of segregation is the distortion of human personality. It damages the soul of both the segregator and the segregated.

BENJAMIN E. MAYS, *The Segregation Decisions,* 1956

The "racial" rejection of the Jew was unknown in the Middle Ages. It was all a matter of belief. The Churchmen were eager to win souls the conversion of the Jews was an ideal.

MAURICE SAMUEL, *The Professor and the Fossil,* 1956

Out of comfort, fear, and blindness the churches have for the most part capitulated to the segregation and prejudices of the world, and have become salt without savor.

WALDO BEACH, *Faith and Ethics: The Theology of H. R. Niebuhr,* ed. P. Ramsey, 1957

The thrashings of the troubled conscience caught on the hook of God's judgment are nowhere more easily seen than in the clichés and phrases which are commonly made to justify segregation and the status quo.

WALDO BEACH, *Faith and Ethics: The Theology of H. R. Niebuhr,* ed. P. Ramsey, 1957

Nor may a person refuse to associate with other persons of equal educational standing solely on the grounds of color, for such a refusal is a denial of human dignity and man's essential unity.

Statement of Catholic Bishops of South Africa, July, 1957

Segregation of the races had its beginning in the church quite as early as its emergence in secular society. . . . Jim Crowism had some of its first expressions in the church.

KYLE HASELDEN, *The Racial Problem in Christian Perspective*, 1959

Segregation in the church violates something that is basic in the nature of the church. How can a church exclude from "the church of God" those who are children of God? How can it, as "the body of Christ," withhold the privilege of worship from those who have been brought into union with Christ?

T. B. MASTON, *Segregation and Desegregation: A Christian Approach*, 1959

A Church which preserves itself by accepting segregation is not preserving itself as the Catholic Church.

JOHN L. MCKENZIE, *The Critic*, August–September, 1961

Legal segregation or any form of compulsory segregation, in itself and by its very nature imposes a stigma upon the segregated people. . . . We cannot reconcile such a judgment with the Christian view of man's nature and rights.

EUGENE MCMANUS, *Studies in Race Relations*, 1961

It is disgraceful that people are being barred from neighborhoods and clubs on a basis that would have barred Jesus Himself.

JAMES A. PIKE, *Look*, March 14, 1961

We must insist that the white man who refuses to cross the racial line . . . is free in the sense that he can do as he pleases; yet it is also true that he is not free of the "unrepentant Kingdom" so long as his acceptance of desegregation is at the purely public or compulsory level.

JAMES SELLERS, *The South and Christian Ethics*, 1962

Segregation must be discussed for what it is: a religion, a theology. It is in fact the

unrepentant Southern kingdom of God, offering the same comfortable false piety to white Southerners today that the institution of slavery did a hundred years ago.

JAMES SELLERS, *The South and Christian Ethics*, 1962

Deprivation of the right of association with his fellow-men is the basic and fundamental reason for the immorality of racial segregation.

JOSEPH T. LEONARD, *Theology and Race Relations*, 1963

We repeat with all the conviction at our command, what the assembly [of the World Council of Churches] said in 1954, that "any form of segregation based on race, color or ethnic origin is contrary to the Gospel, and is incompatible with the Christian doctrine of man and with the nature of the Church of Christ."

WORLD COUNCIL OF CHURCHES, August 31, 1963

This blasphemy [Racial Segregation] attributes to God that which is of the devil. To co-operate passively with an unjust system makes the oppressed as evil as the oppressor.

MARTIN LUTHER KING, *Strength to Love*, 1963

The essential corruption of racial segregation is not that it is supported by lies but that people believe the lies.

HARRY GOLDEN, *Mr. Kennedy and the Negroes*, 1964

The straitjackets of race prejudice and discrimination do not wear only Southern labels. The subtle psychological technique of the North has approached in its ugliness and victimization of the Negro the outright terror and open brutality of the South.

MARTIN LUTHER KING, *Why We Can't Wait*, 1964

See also Anti-Semitism; Apartheid; Brotherhood; Charity; Class Distinctions;

Community; Discrimination; Equality; Fellowship; Ghettoes; Hatred; Intolerance; Love; Negroes; Neighbor; Prejudice; Race; Racial Conflict; Racial Equality; Racial Injustice; Tolerance; Unity of Mankind.

RADICALS

A society without its radicals is a dead society; just as a church without its saints is a blighted church. They—the nonconformists of every age—do not need us; we need them to remind us of uncomfortable truths.

EDITORIAL, *Commonweal,* July 1, 1955

RASHNESS

Christianity badly needs rash men who will not flinch from the crispness of religion, nor fear the result of stirring up wasps' nests.

H. R. L. SHEPPARD, *The Impatience of a Parson,* 1929

RATIONALISM

Rationalism is the exercise of reason instead of faith in matters of faith.

JOHN HENRY NEWMAN, *An Essay on the Development of Christian Doctrine,* 1845

[Rationalism] is the growth and gradual diffusion through all religious thinking of the supremacy of reason.

MARK PATTISON, *Essays and Reviews,* 1860

The Rationalist makes himself his own center, not his Maker; he does not go to God, but he implies that God must come to him.

JOHN HENRY NEWMAN, *Essays Critical and Historical,* I, 1871

It is Rationalism to accept the Revelation, and then to explain it away; to speak of it as the Word of God, and to treat it as the word of man, to refuse to let it speak for itself . . . to put aside what is obscure, as if it had not been said at all; to accept one half of what has been told us, and not the other half.

JOHN HENRY NEWMAN, *Essays Critical and Historical,* I, 1871

Every attempt to tell the story of Jesus Christ from the standpoint of appreciative rationalism fails to commend itself to a candid mind. We are as it were driven by the investigation of the Human Christ to acknowledge that He must be also Divine.

HENRY B. SWETE, *Essays on Theological Questions,* 1905

Rationalism ultimately made its home in Protestantism . . . because the divisions within the Protestant ranks made greater toleration necessary.

A. C. MCGIFFERT, *Protestant Thought Before Kant,* 1911

It cannot be too strongly emphasized that rationalism was at bottom as much of a break with Protestantism as with Catholicism.

A. C. MCGIFFERT, *Protestant Thought Before Kant,* 1911

The [rationalist] is one who rejects the claims of "revelation," the idea of a personal God, the belief in personal immortality, and in general the conceptions logically accruing to the practices of prayer and worship.

J. M. ROBERTSON, *Rationalism,* 1912

The error of modern rationalism consists exactly in the attempt to establish a system of human rights and a general theory of law in the light of the nature of man as a being standing by himself, with no necessary reference whatever to a superior Being.

POPE PIUS XII, *Address,* November 6, 1949

The attempt to live on Christian ethical capital without Christ has been disastrous;

another generation has squandered what rationalism has no power to keep.

RALPH RUSSELL, *The Springs of Morality*, ed. J. M. Todd, 1956

The rationalism of the medieval philosophers was contained by the mysteries of faith and dogma, which were altogether beyond the grasp of human reason. . . . Hence, this rationalism of the medieval philosophers does not end with the attenuated, bleak or grim picture of man we find in the modern rationalists.

WILLIAM BARRETT, *Irrational Man*, 1958

An insidious rationalism has wanted more ultimates than God Himself.

WALTER J. ONG, *The Barbarian Within*, 1962

See also Humanism; Intellectuals; Irreligion; Liberalism; Man, Modern; Modernism; Naturalism; Philosophy; Positivism; Reason; Religion.

RATIONALIZATION

In the prevailing popular culture all philosophies are the instruments of some man's purpose, all truths are self-centered and self-regarding, and all principles are the rationalizations of some special interest. There is no public criterion of the true and the false, of the right and the wrong.

WALTER LIPPMAN, *The Public Philosophy*, 1954

READING

Ambrose . . . records in a letter to Origen from Athens that they never sat down to a meal together without something being read aloud to them, and that they never went to bed without one of the brethren to read the Scriptures aloud. Thus it was both day and night, prayer followed reading, and reading, prayer.

ST. JEROME, *Letter to Marcella*, c. 400

See also Author; Bible; Bible as Literature; Books; Literature; New Testament; Obscenity.

REAL PRESENCE

The temples of those who deny the real Presence are like corpses. The Lord was taken away and we do not know where they have laid Him. We can feel the gloominess of those churches.

FRANÇOIS MAURIAC, *Holy Thursday*, 1944

What the sun is to the material world, the Real Presence is to the Church.

JAMES EDWARD O'MAHONY, *As in a Mirror*, 1948

See also Church: Its Nature; Eucharist.

REALITY

That finest essence which you do not perceive—verily from that finest essence this great tree thus arises. . . . That which is the finest essence—this whole world has that as its soul. That is Reality. That is *Atman*.

Chandogya Upanishad, between 700–400 B.C.

That alone is truly real which abides unchanged.

ST. AUGUSTINE, *Confessions*, 397

The nature of one Reality must be known by one's own clear spiritual perception; it cannot be known through a pandit [learned man].

SHANKARA (9th century A.D.), *Viveka-Chudamani*.

Pure, absolute and eternal Reality—such is Brahman, and thou are that! Meditate upon this truth within your consciousness.

SHANKARA (9th century A.D.), quoted in Aldous Huxley's *The Perennial Philosophy*

Reality is the pure concept of the understanding, that which corresponds to a sensation in general.

IMMANUEL KANT, *Critique of Pure Reason*, 1781

Spirit is the only Reality. It is the inner being of the world, that which essentially is, and is *per se.*

G. W. F. HEGEL, *Phenomenology of Mind*, 1807

God himself culminates in the present moment, and will never be more divine in the lapse of all the ages. And we are able to apprehend at all what is sublime and noble only by the perpetual instilling and drenching of the reality that surrounds us.

HENRY DAVID THOREAU, *Walden*, 1854

Since in ultimate Reality all existence, and all thought and feeling, become one, we may even say that every feature in the universe is the absolutely good.

F. H. BRADLEY, *Appearance and Reality*, 1894

The man who seeks a reality more solid than that of the religious consciousness seeks he does not know what.

F. H. BRADLEY, *Appearance and Reality*, 1894

There is in the human consciousness a sense of reality, a feeling of objective presence, a perception of what we may call "something there," more deep and more general than any of the special and particular senses, by which the current psychology supposes existent realities to be originally revealed.

WILLIAM JAMES, *The Varieties of Religious Experience*, 1902

God or Spirit is the only independent reality, and any other being or event is but a dependent "phase" or "state" or "product" of this activity.

CHARLES E. GARMAN, *Letters, Lectures, Addresses*, 1909

Reality is in general what truths have to take account of.

A. E. TAYLOR, *Elements of Metaphysics*, 1912

I think it more likely than not that in religious and mystical experience man comes into contact with some Reality or aspect of Reality which they do not come into contact with in any other way.

C. D. BROAD, *Hibbert Journal*, 1926

If we make the assumption . . . that the fundamental element in Reality is of the nature of Life, it follows that Reality can only be partially understood by the methods of pure science.

B. H. STREETER, *Reality*, 1926

If man's quest for some satisfying reality be baffled by the bleak stretches of interstellar space and the aimless whirling of blazing suns it is but natural that he should turn his gaze inward to find such reality within his own mind.

CLIFFORD KILPATRICK, *Religion in Human Affairs*, 1929

It may well be possible that it is in our periods of spiritual activity that we come as close as we ever can to reality, that unmovable something which lies, we are sure, behind the changing show of facts on which our minds feed.

JOSEPH S. NEEDHAM, *The Skeptical Biologist*, 1930

Were the whole human race to be blotted out, God would still, as from all eternity, be the only reality, and in His existence what is real in us would continue to live.

J. B. S. HALDANE, *Science and Religion*, 1931

Reality is just itself, and it is nonsense to ask whether it be true or false.

ALFRED NORTH WHITEHEAD, *Adventures in Ideas*, 1933

The Church is always confronting man with the Reality which creates in him the right attitude of mind; namely, the Absolute.

ROMANO GUARDINI, *The Church and the Catholic*, 1935

Under many names, names which are not that of God, in ways known only to God, the interior act of a soul's thought can be directed towards a reality which in fact truly may be God.

JACQUES MARITAIN, *True Humanism*, 1936

The supreme reality is incomprehensible in the sense that it cannot be expressed in logical propositions but it is increasingly apprehensible by the purified mind.

RADHAKRISHNAN, *Eastern Religion and Western Thought*, 1939

Ultimate Reality is not clearly and immediately apprehended except by those who have made themselves loving, pure in heart and poor in spirit.

ALDOUS HUXLEY, *The Perennial Philosophy*, 1945

As the Holy One, God is the Wholly Other, the Incomparable, the Sole Reality, who in His incomparable uniqueness wills to be known and recognized.

H. E. BRUNNER, *Revelation and Reason*, 1946

Spiritual reality is a matter of perception, not of proof.

PETER MARSHALL, quoted by Catherine Marshall in her *A Man Called Peter*, 1951

Certainly for most of the Bible . . . God is simply not the kind of reality concerning which doubt can be seriously entertained.

JOHN HUTCHINSON, *Faith, Reason and Existence*, 1956

Man is confronted by something spiritually greater than himself which, in contrast to Human Nature and to all other phenomena, is Absolute Reality. And this Absolute Reality of which Man is aware is also an Absolute Good for which he is athirst.

A. J. TOYNBEE, *An Historian's Approach to Religion*, 1956

Knowledge of reality has never the certainty of complete evidence. . . . Every knowledge of reality by the human mind has the character of higher or lower probability.

PAUL TILLICH, *Dynamics of Faith*, 1957

Given the one concept, God, and the whole of reality bursts into lucidity, the rationality of the universe, its uniformity, the emergence of life, of consciousness, and conscience, all become intelligible.

MILTON STEINBERG, *Anatomy of Faith*, 1960

Reality is what I "come up against," what takes me by surprise, the other-than-myself which pulls me up and obliges me to reckon with it and adjust myself to it because it will not consent simply to adjust itself to me.

JOHN BAILLIE, *The Sense of the Presence of God*, 1962

Where I find myself in most assured contact with reality is in the relation with God that is mediated to me through my relation with my fellows, and in the relation with my fellows that is mediated to me through my relations with God.

JOHN BAILLIE, *The Sense of the Presence of God*, 1962

God is the Reality undergirding and penetrating through the whole derived creation.

NORMAN PITTENGER, *Theology*, LXV, February, 1962

God is, by definition, ultimate reality. And one cannot argue whether ultimate reality really exists. One can only ask what ultimate reality is like.

J. A. T. ROBINSON, *Honest to God*, 1963

See also Absolute, the; Actuality; Being; Consciousness; Existence; Experience, Religious; God: Considered as Impersonal; God: His Existence; God: His Omnipresence; Infinite; Knowledge; Light; Matter; Mystical Experience; Mysticism; Personality; Prayer: Defined and Explained; Religion: Its Nature and Function; Science; Science and Religion; Self; Spirit, Human; Spiritual; Spiritual Life; Symbols: Truth; Truth, Definitions of; Universe; Vision.

REALIZATION

Realization is real religion; all the rest is only preparation.
SWAMI VIVEKANANDA (1863–1902), *Complete Works of,* I, 232, 1950

REASON

Reason is that by which the soul thinks and judges.
ARISTOTLE, *De Anima, c.* 330 B.C.

What the good man ought to do he does; for reason in each of its possessors chooses what is best for itself, and the good man obeys his reason.
ARISTOTLE (384–322 B.C.), *Politics*

My reason is not framed to bend or stoop; my knees are.
MICHEL DE MONTAIGNE, *Essays,* III, 1588

There cannot any one moral reason be proposed whereof a man may not justly demand a reason; which would be perfectly ridiculous if they were innate, or so much as self-evident.
JOHN LOCKE, *Essay Concerning Human Understanding,* 1690

Our Reason is capable of nothing but the creation of a universal confusion and universal doubt.
PIERRE BAYLE, *Dictionary,* 1697

The supreme tribunal which is the court of last resort from which there is no further appeal is reason speaking by the axioms of the light of nature.
PIERRE BAYLE (1647–1706), "Commentaire Philosophique sur les Paroles de Jesus Christ," *Works,* II

Passion and prejudice govern the world; only under the name of reason.
JOHN WESLEY, *Letter,* October 5, 1770

Reason is the constant condition of all free actions by which man takes his place in the phenomenal world. . . . Reason therefore acts freely, without being determined dynamically, in the chain of natural causes, by external or internal conditions, anterior in time.
IMMANUEL KANT, *Critique of Pure Reason,* 1781

My question is, what can we hope to achieve with reason, when all the material and assistance of experience are taken away.
IMMANUEL KANT, *Critique of Pure Reason,* 1781

I am immortal, imperishable, eternal, as soon as I form the resolution to obey the laws of reason.
J. G. FICHTE (1762–1814), *The Vocation of Man*

On the one hand, Reason is the substance of the Universe; viz. that by which and in which all reality has its being and subsistence. On the other hand, it is the *Infinite Energy* of the Universe. . . . It is the *Infinite complex* of things, their entire Essence and Truth. . . . Reason is Thought conditioning itself with perfect freedom.
G. W. F. HEGEL (1770–1831), *The Philosophy of History,* publ. posth.

If there is no higher reason—and there is not—then my own reason must be the supreme judge of my life.
LEO TOLSTOY, *My Confession,* 1879

The life of reason is no fair reproduction of the universe, but the expression of man alone.

GEORGE SANTAYANA, *The Life of Reason*, 1905

Reason requires the fusion of two types of life . . . one a life of impulse expressed in affairs and social passions, the other a life of reflection expressed in religion, science, and the imitative arts.

GEORGE SANTAYANA, *Reason in Common Sense*, 1906

Reason inspired by love of truth is the only eye with which man can see the spiritual heavens above us.

CHARLES E. GARMAN, *Letters, Lectures, Addresses*, 1909

Reason is man's imitation of divinity.

GEORGE SANTAYANA, *Scepticism and Animal Faith*, 1923

If the determinist is right, reasoning can prove nothing: it is merely an ingenious method for providing us with apparently rational excuses for believing what in any case we cannot help believing. But if all reasoning is a "pathetic fallacy," then the reasons for believing in Determinism itself are fallacious. . . . Unless reason is that which can *discriminate*, there is no criterion of truth and falsehood, all knowledge collapses; one hypothesis is as good as another, and Science itself is a fairy tale.

BURNETT H. STREETER, *Reality*, 1926

A free activity of the mind, reaching conclusions under no compulsion save that of evidence.

C. E. M. JOAD, *Return to Philosophy*, 1936

Reason in my philosophy is only a harmony among irrational impulses.

GEORGE SANTAYANA, *The Middle Span*, 1945

The breach of communion between the spiritual and rational order is the most formidable problem that confronts the modern world.

CHRISTOPHER DAWSON, *Religion and Culture*, 1947

The enthronement of reason means the enthronement of man who becomes his own lawgiver.

W. A. VISSER 'T HOOFT, *The Kingship of Christ*, 1948

It is doubtful if a truly good world, a better and a fuller life for man, can ever be established through reason alone.

EDMUND W. SINNOTT, *Two Roads to Truth*, 1953

I do not believe man possesses an avenue to truth which is superior to his reason.

ROLAND B. GITTELSOHN, *Man's Best Hope*, 1961

See also Anger; Authority; Belief; Conscience; Experience, Religious; Faith; Faith and Reason; Intellect; Knowledge; Learning; Metaphysical; Metaphysics; Mind; Opinions; Passions; Philosophy; Rationalism; Reason and God; Reason and Religion; Revelation and Reason; Superstition; Theologians; Thinking; Thought; Universe.

REASON AND FAITH
See FAITH AND REASON

REASON AND GOD

Those whom God wishes to destroy, he first deprives of their senses.

EURIPIDES, *Fragment*, 5th century B.C.

The Almighty does nothing without reason, though the frail mind of man cannot explain the reason.

ST. AUGUSTINE, *City of God*, XXI, 426

Human reason is the norm of the human will, according to which its goodness is measured, because reason derives from the eternal law which is the divine reason itself.

St. Thomas Aquinas, *Summa Theologiae,* Ia–IIae, q. 19, 1272

We should rather marvel greatly if at any time the process by which the eternal counsels are fulfilled is so manifest as to be discerned by our reason.

Dante, *Conivivio,* c. 1310

The first dictate of reason is the kindling in us a love and reverence for the Divine Majesty, to whom we owe both all we have, and all that we can ever hope for.

St. Thomas More, *Utopia,* 1516

I do not feel obliged to believe that the same God who has endowed us with sense, reason, and intellect has intended us to forgo their use.

Galileo, *Letter to Grand Duchess of Tuscany,* 1615

Reason is natural revelation, whereby the eternal Father of light . . . communicates to mankind that portion of truth which he has laid within the reach of their natural faculties.

John Locke, *Essay on Human Understanding,* Bk. IV, 1690

The existence of one God is according to reason; the existence of more than one God, contrary to reason; the resurrection of the dead, above reason.

John Locke, *Essay Concerning Human Understanding,* 1690

No man serves God with a good conscience, who serves him against his reason.

Samuel Taylor Coleridge, *Aids to Reflection,* 1825

Is it a sign of highest reason to deny God until I see Him, and blind myself to the life eternal till I am born into its surprise?

James Martineau, *Hours of Thought on Sacred Things,* 1879

We must hold that reason and the works of reason have their source in God: that from Him they draw their inspiration: and that if they repudiate their origins by this very act they proclaim their own insufficiency.

A. J. Balfour, *Theism and Humanism,* 1915

The revolters against reason have asserted that . . . when human reason conceives of the deity to be worshipped and rules that the evidence is favorable to the worshipping of such a deity, man is creating his own God.

L. Harold De Wolf, *Religious Revolt Against Reason,* 1949

Reason will find God, but reason will find, too, the need to transcend reason, the promise of more than reason can offer.

George Brantle, *Catholicism,* 1962

See also Belief; Faith; Faith and Reason; Reason; Reason and Religion.

REASON AND RELIGION

Where the Scripture is silent, the Church is my text; where that speaks, 'tis but my Comment; where there is a joint silence of both, I borrow not the rules of my Religion from Rome or Geneva, but the dictates of my own reason.

Thomas Browne, *Religio Medici,* 1635

If we submit everything to reason, our religion will have nothing in it mysterious or supernatural. If we violate the principles of reason, our religion will be absurd and ridiculous.

Blaise Pascal, *Pensées,* 1670

If each man relies on his individual reason for his religious beliefs, the result will be anarchy of belief or the annihilation of religious sovereignty.

Joseph de Maistre (1753–1821), *Étude sur la Souveraineté*

I feel myself bound to sacrifice to Christianity property, reputation, life; but I ought not to sacrifice to any religion that reason which lifts me above the brute and constitutes me a man.

> WILLIAM ELLERY CHANNING (1780–1842), *Works*

Reason cannot injure true Religion, for true Religion is reason.

> M. JOSEPH, *The Ideal in Judaism*, 1893

Religion, in its intent, is a more conscious and direct pursuit of the Life of Reason than is society, science, or art.

> GEORGE SANTAYANA, *Reason in Religion*, 1905

Reason retains its dignity only if it does not yield to the temptation of competing with religious imagination—if it does not transgress its own limitations.

> RICHARD KRONER, *Perspectives on a Troubled Decade*, ed. Bryson, Finklestein and MacIver, 1950

Is it really too much to ask and hope for a religion whose content is perennial but not archaic, which provides ethical guidance, teaches the lost art of contemplation, and restores contact with the supernatural without requiring reason to abdicate?

> ARTHUR KOESTLER, *The Trial of the Dinosaur and Other Essays*, 1951

See also Belief; Faith; Faith and Reason; Reason; Reason and God; Religion; Sin.

REBELLION

What greater rebellion, impiety, or insult to God, can there be, than not to believe His promises?

> MARTIN LUTHER, *On Christian Liberty*, 1520

The religion that sets men to rebel and fight against their Government, because, as they think, that Government does not sufficiently help some men to eat their bread in the sweat of other men's faces, is not the sort of religion upon which people can get to heaven.

> ABRAHAM LINCOLN, Reply to two women who pleaded for release of their husbands, *Washington Chronicle*, March 4, 1865

The Church, guardian of the truest and highest notion of political sovereignty, since she attributes its origin to God, has always reproved the doctrines and condemned the men that rebel against the legitimate authority.

> POPE LEO XII, *Encyclical to the French Cardinals*, May 3, 1892

There is endless room for rebellion against ourselves.

> GEORGE MACDONALD (1824–1905), *George MacDonald, an Anthology*, ed. C. S. Lewis

In life as in art the mood of rebellion closes up the channels of the soul, and shuts out the airs of heaven.

> OSCAR WILDE, *De Profundis*, 1909

The history of revolt from the Church is at the same time a history of the progressive decomposition of the primitive faith in Christ.

> KARL ADAM, *The Spirit of Catholicism*, 1924

The only true revolt is creation—the revolt against nothingness. Lucifer is the patron saint of mere negativistic revolt.

> JOSÉ ORTEGA Y GASSET, *Mission of the University*, 1930

As the first sin of man was revolt against God, the second sin was revolt of brother against brother. Apostasy of man from God led the way to apostasy of man from his brother-man. That has been the history of human kind ever since.

> IGNATIUS W. COX, *God, Man and Redemption*, 1933

Salvation is not to be found in revolution. To aspire . . . to a revolution which is to proceed from injustice and civil insubordination, and to render oneself responsible for shedding the blood of one's fellow countrymen and the destruction of common wealth, is contrary to the genuine and sincere profession of Christianity.

POPE PIUS XII, *Address,* January 13, 1943

If the men of our time had their way, God would be on the carpet all the time offering soothing explanations to angry questions.

WALTER FARRELL, *The Looking Glass,* 1951

The human being who denies his nature as a created being, ends up by claiming for himself attributes which are a sort of caricature of those that belong to the Uncreated.

GABRIEL MARCEL, *Man Against Mass Society,* 1952

Revolution within the soul is the Christian adventure. . . . The sword it carries is not turned against our neighbor, but against our absurd over-valuation of the self. . . . It is the only revolution that ever issues in true peace.

FULTON J. SHEEN, *Way to Happiness,* 1953

The Christian faith . . . perceives the only real revolution to be one which works from within outwards . . . sees true revolution to consist in the fact that man surrenders his claim to freedom and received his true freedom from dependence upon God.

EMIL BRUNNER, *Eternal Hope,* 1954

If God lived on earth, people would break His windows.

Proverb

See also Allegiance; Authority; God, Blasphemous Statements about; Government; Heresy; Law; Loyalty; Man: His Self-

Deification; Nonconformity; Obedience; Patriotism; Peace; Reform; Sedition; Sin; State, the; Treason.

REBIRTH. See REINCARNATION

RECOMPENSE

Recompense injury with justice and recompense kindness with kindness.

CONFUCIUS, *Analects of,* c. 5th century B.C.

RECONCILIATION

He can never therefore be reconciled to your sin, because sin itself is incapable of being altered: but He may be reconciled to your person, because that may be restored.

THOMAS TRAHERNE (1634?–1704), *Centuries of Meditation*

When Jesus prayed for those who had done Him to death, we reach the critical point in revelation—that God was in Christ reconciling the world to Himself, and that that reconciliation must express itself in the reconciliation of man to man.

R. ROBERTS, *The Contemporary Christ,* 1938

Oh may the Lord grant that the blessed day of universal reconciliation may soon dawn, when an immense chorus of jubilant love will rise from the one and only family of the redeemed and when they, praising the divine mercy, will sing with the Psalmist: "Behold how good and how pleasant it is for brethren to dwell together in unity."

POPE JOHN XXIII, *Encyclical,* November 11, 1961

See also Reunion; Unity.

RECREATION. See PLEASURE

REDEMPTION

It was necessary that Adam should be summed up in Christ that mortality might be swallowed up and overwhelmed by immortality, and Eve summed up in Mary, that a virgin should be a virgin's intercessor, and by a virgin's obedience undo and put away that disobedience of a virgin.

ST. IRENAEUS (130–c. 200), *The Demonstration of the Apostolic Preaching*

The sole key to the Bible is the Redemption by Christ and applied to all subsequent generations by the Church which, as the Bible clearly teaches, Christ instituted for that purpose.

HUGE POPE, *The Catholic Church and the Bible,* 1929

Redemption is continuous. . . . The spirit of Israel is attuned to the hum of the redemptive process, to the sound of the waves of its labors which will end only with the coming of the days of the Messiah.

A. I. KOOK (1864–1936), quoted in *The Zionist Idea,* ed. A. Hertzberg

The spiritual history of man, as seen by God, is not one of progress but of recovery, or redemption.

AELRED GRAHAM, *Christian Thought and Action,* 1951

Perhaps the deepest mystery of redemption and divine love is precisely that we can be redeemed not only *from* our squalors but in a sense *in* our squalors.

GERALD VANN, *The Water and the Fire,* 1954

Israel does not need to be redeemed by an atoning sacrifice, because it has already been elected by God.

HANS JOACHIM SCHOEPS, *The Jewish-Christian Argument,* 1961

See also Atonement; Calvary; Fall, the; God: His Goodness; Immortality; Incarnation; Jesus Christ: His Passion and Death; Jesus Christ as Saviour; Original Sin; Pain; Providence; Salvation; Sin; Suffering.

REFLECTION

Reflection is the path of immortality, thoughtlessness the path of death. Those who reflect do not die, those who are thoughtless are as if dead already.

Dhammapada, c. 5th cenutury B.C.

REFORM

Be not angry that you cannot make others as you wish them to be, since you cannot make yourself as you wish to be.

THOMAS À KEMPIS, *Imitation of Christ,* 1441

Every reform, however necessary, will by weak minds be carried to an excess which will itself need reforming.

SAMUEL TAYLOR COLERIDGE, *Biographia Literaria,* 1817

If there exists an actual necessity for a great reform amongst a people, God is with it, and it prospers.

J. W. VON GOETHE, *Conversations with Eckermann,* 1824

The church is not susceptible of being reformed in her doctrines. The church is the work of an Incarnate God. Like all God's works, it is perfect. It is, therefore, incapable of reform.

JAMES GIBBONS, *The Faith of Our Fathers,* 1876

Reform must come from within, not from without. You cannot legislate for virtue.

JAMES GIBBONS, *Address,* Baltimore, September 13, 1909

All true and permanent reform has in the last resort originated in sanctity, from men who were inflamed with the love of God and their neighbor, who by their great generosity in answering every appeal from God . . . have enlightened and renewed the times in which they lived.

POPE PIUS XI, *Mit Brennender Sorge,* March, 1937

Lord reform thy world, beginning with me.

> Prayer of a Chinese Christian, quoted by President Roosevelt at press conference, December 17, 1941

Self-reform is the answer to world-reform.

> SEBASTIAN MIKLAS, *Sanctify Your Emotions*, 1955

Someone has said that though the aisles of any church are dirty, only a man on his knees can clean them.

> GEORGE A. BUTTRICK, *Sermons Preached in a University Church*, 1959

Catholic reform is *not revolution:* it does not aim at the violent overthrow either of values or of authority. . . . Catholic reform is intent upon preserving the continuity of historical development, and hence is not innovation but *renewal*.

> HANS KÜNG, *The Council, Reform and Reunion*, 1962

There are no irreformable areas of the Church.

> HANS KÜNG, *The Council, Reform, and Reunion*, 1962

The important thing to remember with regard to reform is that it is done within the Church, within the framework of ecclesiastical authority, within the visible Body—it is the work of the Spirit sanctifying the Body. When it takes place outside this framework, it is not reform but a wounding action on the Body of Christ.

> RICHARD CUSHING, *Lenten Pastoral Letter*, 1962

The reform at which the Council aims is not a turning upside down of the church's present way of life or a breaking with what is essential and worthy of veneration in her tradition, but it is rather an honoring of tradition by stripping it of what is unworthy or defective so that it may be rendered firm and fruitful.

> POPE PAUL VI, *Homily*, September 29, 1963

A man who reforms himself has contributed his full share toward the reformation of his neighborhood.

> ANONYMOUS

See also Church, Criticism of; Jesus Christ and Christianity; Rebellion; Reformation, the; Reformers; Renewal; Unity; Zealots.

REFORMATION, THE

It cannot be denied that corruption of morals prevailed in the sixteenth century to such an extent as to call for a sweeping reformation, and that laxity of discipline invaded even the sanctuary.

> JAMES GIBBONS, *The Faith of Our Fathers*, 1876

The period of the Reformation was a judgment day for Europe, when all the nations were presented with an open Bible and all the emancipation of heart and intellect which an open Bible involves.

> THOMAS CARLYLE (1795–1881), quoted by Ernest Sutherland Bates in his *The Bible Designed to Be Used as Living Literature*

The Protestant Reformation was not exclusively nor even chiefly a religious movement. It involved a break with the historical ecclesiastical institution and the organization of new churches independent of Rome, but the break itself was as much political as religious, both in its causes and in its results.

> A. C. McGIFFERT, *Protestant Thought Before Kant*, 1911

The Reformation destroyed the unity of faith and ecclesiastical organization of the Christian peoples of Europe, cut many millions off from the true Catholic Church and robbed them of the greatest portion of the salutary means of the cultivation and maintenance of the supernatural life. Incalculable harm was thereby wrought from the religious standpoint.

> *The Catholic Encyclopedia*, art. "Reformation," XII, 1913

If it is true that the Reformation released forces which were to act as a solvent of the traditional attitude of religious thought to social and economic issues, it did so without design, and against the intention of most reformers.

R. H. TAWNEY, *Religion and the Rise of Capitalism,* 1926

The Reformation in England was a parliamentary transaction. All the important changes were made under statutes, and the actions of the King as supreme head of the Church were done under a title and in virtue of powers given him by statute.

MAURICE POWICKE, *The Reformation in England,* 1936

Such negative terms as "Protestant" and "Reformation" are unhappy designations for a movement that in essence was not protest but affirmation, not reform but conservation, not reaction, but propulsion. Its best name is "evangelical."

A. R. MENTZ, *Protestantism: a Symposium,* ed. W. K. Anderson, 1944

The Reformation, as the religious phase of the Renaissance, invited man to become just independent enough to take the step from one orthodoxy into another.

H. A. OVERSTREET, *The Mature Mind,* 1949

The Reformation was . . . a time when prophetic voices spoke but to reaffirm for their own time those great and original Christian convictions which are the wellspring of our Christian life.

JAMES A. PIKE, *Advance,* October 19, 1953

The Reformation . . . by shifting its emphasis from the universal Church . . . to the local churches so apparently smaller than the nations that contain them, prepared the way for a new application of Hebrew messianic ideas to the nations themselves.

J. V. L. CASSERLEY, *The Bent World,* 1955

It is a perversion of the Reformers' intent . . . to charge them with trying to invent a new religion, or to do away with the need for authority, or to inaugurate an "era of private judgment." Their concern . . . was to purify and revitalize an "old" religion, the old but ever living and ever new gospel which they discovered at the heart of the New Testament.

ROBERT MCAFEE BROWN, *Patterns of Faith in America Today,* ed. F. E. Johnson, 1957

Contemporary theology must consider the fact that the Reformation was not only a religious gain but also a religious loss.

PAUL TILLICH, *Systematic Theology,* III, 1964

See also Catholicism; Church, Criticism of; Luther, Martin; Private Judgment; Protestantism; Rebellion; Reform; Reformers; Schisms; Unity.

REFORMERS

In efforts to soar above our nature we invariably fall below it. Your reformist demigods are merely devils turned inside out.

EDGAR ALLAN POE, *Marginalia,* 1849

Reformers are those who educate people to appreciate the things they need.

ELBERT HUBBARD (1859–1915), *Notebook*

We may say that the successful reformers are those who are seeking not so much to "make people good" as to share an enthusiasm.

CHARLES A. BENNETT, *Philosophical Study of Mysticism,* 1923

The great moral reformers have usually found the greatest opposition not in the "immoral" and impulsive individual, but in the regularly constituted organs of social authority and law.

CHRISTOPHER DAWSON, *Sociological Review,* July, 1925

A reformer is a guy who rides through a sewer in a glass-bottomed boat.

JAMES J. WALKER, *Speech*, 1928

One of the marks of a certain type of bad man is that he can't give up a thing without wanting everyone else to give it up. That isn't the Christian way.

C. S. LEWIS, *Christian Behavior*, 1944

One of the besetting fallacies of reformers is the delusion that their plans will be carried out by people who think precisely as they do.

JOHN MAURICE CLARK, *Guideposts in a Time of Change*, 1949

See also Reform; Zealots.

REINCARNATION

I brethren when I so desire it can call to mind my various states of birth . . . one birth, two—a hundred thousand births . . . in all their specific details . . . my previous states of existence.

Attributed to Buddha (6th century B.C.), *Sutta Nipata*

The Worlds, Arjuna!—even Brahma's world—
Roll back again from Death to Life's unrest;
But they, O Kunti's son! that reach to me [Krishna]
Taste birth no more.

The Song Celestial, Sir Edwin Arnold's translation of the *Bhagavad-Gita*, c. 5th century B.C.

Krishna the god speaking:
Manifold the renewal of my birth. . . .
I come, and go, and come. When Righteousness
Declines, O Bhavata! When wickedness
Is strong, I rise, from age to age, and take
Visible shape, and move, a man with men
Succoring the good, thrusting the evil back,

And setting Virtue on her seat again.

The Song Celestial, Sir Edwin Arnold's translation of the *Bhagavad-Gita*, 5th to 2nd century B.C.

All things return eternally, and ourselves with them: We have already existed in times without number, and all things with us.

FRIEDRICH NIETZSCHE, *Thus Spake Zarathustra*, 1885

The doctrine of *reincarnation*, or of successive lives spent by each soul on this planet . . . was probably the opinion both of Plato and Virgil. . . . There is nothing here which is alien to the best reason or to the highest instincts of men. Nor, indeed, is it easy to realize any theory of the *direct creation* of spirits at such different stages of advancement as those which enter upon the earth in the guise of mortal man. There must, one feels, be some kind of continuity—some form of spiritual Past. Yet for reincarnation there is at present no valid evidence.

F. W. H. MYERS, *Human Personality*, 1903

The spiritual perfection which opens before man is the crown of long patient, millennial outflowering of the Spirit in life and nature. This belief in a gradual spiritual progress and evolution is the secret of the almost universal Indian acceptance of the truth of reincarnation.

SRI AUROBINDO, *Silver Jubilee Commemorative Volume of the Indian Philosophical Congress*, 1950

Belief in rebirth is common to several ancient religions of the world, and the distinctive contribution of Hinduism to the doctrine of transmigration is that it has attempted to give a metaphysical and ethical interpretation of that belief.

KENNETH W. MORGAN, *The Religion of the Hindus*, 1953

Vishnu is not worshipped directly as much as in his reincarnations, of which there are ten, according to tradition . . . [including] Rama, Krishna, Buddha and one to come. Some Vishnuites are inclined to consider Christ as the tenth, thus incorporating Christianity, as they have Buddhism, into Hinduism.

> CHARLES S. BRADEN, *The World's Religions,* 1954

If survival occurs, then reincarnation may be one form it could take, for all, for many, or only for some human beings. Survival could occur without reincarnation. On the other hand, reincarnation by definition, cannot occur without some preceding survival of a physical death.

> IAN STEVENSON, *The Evidence for Survival from Claimed Memories,* 1961

We believe that the dissolution of the spirit, soul and body caused by death, is annulled by rebirth of the same Spirit and soul in another body here on earth, . . . that the repeated incarnations of man to be a merciful provision of our loving Father, to the end that all may have opportunity to attain immortality through regeneration, as did Jesus.

> *Statement of Faith,* Unity School of Christianity, contemporary U.S.A.

REJECTION

He who both rejects the blessed Peter's confession, and gainsays Christ's Gospel, is far removed from union with this building; for he shows himself never to have had any zeal for understanding the Truth.

> POPE ST. LEO I, *To the Synod of Ephesus,* 449

Shallow understanding from people of good will is more frustrating than absolute misunderstanding from people of ill will. Lukewarm acceptance is much more bewildering than outright rejection.

> MARTIN LUTHER KING, JR., *Why We Can't Wait,* 1964

RELATIVITY

This so-called doctrine of the "relativity of truth" is nothing more and nothing less

than the admission that a complex state of affairs cannot be described in over-simplified language. . . . The most ardent advocates of "absolute truth" avail themselves of the doctrine of the "relativists" whenever they have to face a real human issue.

> PHILIP FRANK, *Perspectives on a Troubled Decade,* ed. Bryson, Finklestein and MacIver, 1950

See also Absolutes; Certainty; Doubt; Pragmatism; Right; Right and Wrong; Sin; Truth.

RELICS

We do not worship the relics of the martyrs, but honor them in our worship of Him whose martyrs they are. We honor the servants in order that the respect paid to them may be reflected back to the Lord.

> ST. JEROME, *Reply to Vigilantius,* c. 396

RELIGION

Religion is a disease, but it is a noble disease.

> HERACLITUS, *Fragments,* c. 500 B.C.

We are tied to God and bound to Him (*religati*) by the bond of piety, and it is from this, and not as Cicero holds from careful consideration (*relegendo*) that religion has received its name.

> LACTANTIUS, *Divine Institutes,* c. 310

In religion, as in human learning, we need a gradual introduction, beginning by the more easily learned matters and the first elements. The Creator comes to our aid so that our eyes, accustomed to darkness, may be gradually opened to the full light of truth.

> ST. GREGORY OF NYSSA (c. 335–395), *On the Holy Spirit*

Those who adulterate pure religion, as all must necessarily do who put forward opinions of their own devising, make a departure from the one true God.

> JOHN CALVIN, *Institutes,* I, 1536

For where there is no certain knowledge of God, there is no religion.

JOHN CALVIN (1509–1564), *Opera,* in *Corpus Reformatorum*

The truth of religion lies in its very obscurity, in the little light we have on it, and in our indifference to that light.

BLAISE PASCAL, *Pensées,* 1670

Men hate and despise religion, and fear it may be true.

BLAISE PASCAL, *Pensées,* 1670

You must also own religion in rags, as well as when in silver slippers; and stand by him, too, when bound in irons, as well as when he walketh the streets with applause.

JOHN BUNYAN, *Pilgrim's Progress,* 1678

Religion consists not in knowing many things but in practicing the few plain things we know.

JOSEPH GLANVILL, *An Essay Concerning Preaching,* 1678

Religion is a profound humility, a universal charity.

BENJAMIN WHICHCOTE (1609–1683), *Sermons*

A man is quickly convinced of the truth of religion, who finds it not against his interests that it should be true.

JOSEPH ADDISON, *The Spectator,* August 23, 1712

Religion is the best Armour in the World, but the worst Cloak.

THOMAS FULLER, *Gnomologia,* 1732

A good life is the only religion.

THOMAS FULLER, *Gnomologia,* 1732

When I say religion I m an the Christian religion, and not just the Christian religion but the Protestant religion, and not just the Protestant religion but the Church of England.

PARSON THWACKUM in Fielding's *Tom Jones,* 1749

Every man who has interest enough to hire a conventicle may set up for himself and sell off a new religion.

OLIVER GOLDSMITH, *Citizen of the World,* 1762

The religion of man . . . has neither temples, nor altars, nor rites, and is confined to the purely internal cult of the supreme God and the eternal obligations of morality.

JEAN JACQUES ROUSSEAU, *Social Contract,* Bk. IV, 1762

Worship God and practice justice—this is the sole religion of the Chinese *literati*—O Thomas Aquinas, Scotus, Bonaventure, Francis, Dominic, Luther, Calvin, canon of Westminster, have you anything better?

VOLTAIRE, *Dieu est les homines,* 1769

If men are so wicked as we now see them with religion, what would they be if without it?

BENJAMIN FRANKLIN, *Letter,* c. 1786

Religion is the basis of civil society, and the source of all good and of all comfort.

EDMUND BURKE, *Reflections on the Revolution in France,* 1790

The moral capacity of man is the foundation and interpreter of all religion.

IMMANUEL KANT, *Religion Within the Limits of Pure Reason,* 1793

Man must and will have some Religion; if he has not the Religion of Jesus, he will have the Religion of Satan, and will erect the synagogue of Satan, calling the Prince of this world, God.

WILLIAM BLAKE, *Jerusalem,* 1820

Men will wrangle for religion; fight for it; die for it, anything but—live for it.

C. C. COLTON, *Lacon,* 1820

The first and last lesson of religion is, "The things that are seen are temporal; the things that are unseen are eternal."

RALPH WALDO EMERSON, *Nature,* 1836

While the law permits the Americans to do what they please, religion prevents them from conceiving, and forbids them to commit, what is rash or unjust.

ALEXIS DE TOCQUEVILLE, *Democracy in America,* 1839

Religion is the dream of the human mind.

LUDWIG FEUERBACH, *The Essence of Christianity,* 1841

The one end, essence, and use of all religion, past, present, and to come, was this only: To keep the same Moral Conscience, or Inner Light of ours, alive and shining.

THOMAS CARLYLE, *Past and Present,* 1843

In every age of Christianity since it was first preached, there has been what may be called a religion of the world, which so far imitates the one true religion as to deceive the unstable and unwary.

JOHN HENRY NEWMAN, *Parochial and Plain Sermons,* I, 1843

What is the world's religion now? It has taken the brighter side of the Gospel,—its tidings of comfort, its precepts of love; all the darker, deeper views of man's condition and prospects being comparatively forgotten. This is the religion natural to a civilized age, and well has Satan dressed and completed it into an idol of the Truth.

JOHN HENRY NEWMAN, *Parochial and Plain Sermons,* 1843

The religions of men are the ejaculations of a few imaginative men.

RALPH WALDO EMERSON, "The Poet," *Essays, Second Series,* 1844

Religion is the metaphysics of the masses.

ARTHUR SCHOPENHAUER, "A Dialogue," *Essays,* 1851

Anything which makes religion a second object, makes religion no object. . . . He who makes religion his first object, makes it his whole object.

JOHN RUSKIN, *Lectures on Architecture and Painting,* 1853

Religion, as a mere sentiment, is to me a dream and a mockery.

JOHN HENRY NEWMAN, *Apologia pro Vita Sua,* 1864

The religions we call false were once true. They also were affirmations of the conscience correcting the evil customs of their times.

RALPH WALDO EMERSON, *North American Review,* April, 1866

No religion yet has been a religion of physics or philosophy.

JOHN HENRY NEWMAN, *Grammar of Assent,* 1870

Religions, as they grow by natural laws out of man's life, are modified by whatever modifies life.

WALTER PATER, *The Renaissance,* 1873

If religion be other than Personal and one with the purest friendship, I must affirm that it is yet a stranger in my breast and I am without a God to love, reverence and experience.

BRONSON ALCOTT (1799–1888), *The Journal of*

The worst kind of religion is no religion at all.

JAMES RUSSELL LOWELL, *Review of Reviews,* October, 1891

Life, more life, a larger, richer, more satisfying life, is in the last analysis the end of religion.

JAMES LEUBA, *The Monist,* July, 1901

But for religion, in its strong and fully developed manifestations, the service of the highest never is felt as a yoke.

WILLIAM JAMES, *The Varieties of Religious Experience,* 1902

The goal of all religions is the same, but the language of the teachers differs. The goal is to kill the false "I" so that the real "I," the Lord, will reign.

> SWAMI VIVEKANANDA (1863–1902), *The Yoga and Other Works*

There are said to be ten thousand definitions of religion.

> JOHN MORLEY, *Nineteenth Century*, April, 1905

The attempt to speak without speaking any particular language is not more hopeless than the attempt to have a religion that shall be no religion in particular.

> GEORGE SANTAYANA, *Reason in Religion*, 1905

Religion has the same original relation to life that poetry has. . . . Like poetry, it improves the world only by imagining it improved.

> GEORGE SANTAYANA, *Reason in Religion*, 1905

Each religion, so dear to those whose life it sanctifies, and fulfilling so necessary a function in the society that has adopted it, necessarily contradicts every other religion, and probably contradicts itself.

> GEORGE SANTAYANA, *Reason in Religion*, 1905

We live and die its wise servants, or its blind slaves, or in futile impoverishing revolt against it; we never for good or for evil really get beyond its reach.

> FRIEDRICH VON HÜGEL, *Mystical Elements*, I, 1908

As far as our present knowledge goes, religion appears to be universal among men. There is no community of which we can say with certainty that it is without religion.

> C. H. TOY, *Introduction to the History of Religions*, 1913

Religion must be separated from the otherworldly pull of the traditional theologies and be sanely grounded in the outlook of modern knowledge.

> R. W. SELLARS, *The Next Step in Religion*, 1918

Religion is an experience which no definition exhausts.

> RUFUS M. JONES, *Spiritual Energies in Daily Life*, 1922

A religion which does not tie the soul of man up with some permanent reality beyond the show of sense is no religion.

> J. A. LEIGHTON, *Man and the Cosmos*, 1922

Religion is a word whose right meaning has long since been definitely fixed. Self-deception is in fact the most innocent name one can give to attempts at the transference of a creditable name to secular activities however meritorious.

> ROBERT SHAFER, *Progress and Science*, 1922

Religion is primarily emotional and therefore is in the broadest sense of sex-origin.

> S. SWISHER, *Religion and the New Psychology*, 1923

There is something odd about the weakness which irreligious men feel for religion. Almost invariably it becomes their favorite topic.

> PHILIP GUEDELLA, *A Gallery*, 1924

At last religion has come to reckon with the fact that its highest quest is not for a supernatural order but just for natural goodness in the largest and fullest measure.

> E. S. AMES, *The New Orthodoxy*, 1925

Religion has its origin and its support in *dissatisfaction* with life, resulting from reflection on the failure of life to satisfy the primary desires of man.

> K. DUNLAP, *Social Psychology*, 1925

Religion is not an intelligence test, but a faith.

E. W. Howe, *Sinner Sermons,* 1926

Religion is something that only secondarily can be taught. It must primarily be absorbed.

Harry Emerson Fosdick, *World's Work,* February, 1929

Religion is the mother of dreams. Over the gray world, ruined by deluge and death, it has sought ever, and found the arching window of hope.

A. E. Haydon, *The Quest of the Ages,* 1929

The march of religions moves toward the Great Society in which all individuals will have a fair chance for the joy of living, and personal satisfactions will blend with social responsibility and creative powers.

A. E. Haydon, *The Quest of the Ages,* 1929

As for starting a new religion, as some suggest, you might as well try to build a tree.

W. R. Inge, *Living Philosophies,* 1931

To most people religion is just a matter of loyalty to the accepted ways hallowed by our ancestors.

Morris R. Cohen, *Religion Today,* ed. A. L. Swift, 1933

No religion in the world is without some elements of truth. No religion is without its profound error.

Emil Brunner, *The Mediator,* 1934

The divine is revealed in pagan religions as well as in Christianity, and it is manifested through nature in natural religions.

Nicholas Berdyaev, *Freedom and Spirit,* 1935

Through religion all men get a little of what a few privileged souls possessed in full.

Henri Bergson, *The Two Sources of Morality and Religion,* 1935

All religion is an attempt to express . . . what is essentially inexpressible. Every new religion has to create its own language.

Leo Baeck, *Essence of Judaism,* 1936

The perpetual danger which besets religion is that it may substitute gentility and aestheticism for prophetic insight and power.

Georgia Harkness, *The Resources of Religion,* 1936

A man must put his mind into his religion if he will keep his heart in it.

Thomas A. Carney, *The "Lost" Radiance of the Religion of Jesus,* 1937

Religion, according to the Hindu, is not compounded of dogmas and creeds. Religion is a way of life in consonance with rationality and Truth. Truth is not and cannot be revealed once and for all—it must ever be a progressive revelation.

Harold F. Mazumdar, Preface, *The Bibles of Mankind,* ed. M. A. Sobrab, 1939

We miss the true spirit of religion if we recommend it on account of its secular advantages.

Sarvepalli Radhakrishnan, *Eastern Religions and Western Thought,* 1939

Religion, as an enduring aspect of human life, and God, as the object of man's aspirations and vision, cannot but remain amidst all changing forms so long as human nature itself is unaltered.

J. H. Randall, *The Making of the Modern Mind,* 1940

Religion indeed wishes to be useful and beautiful, but it also means to be true.

James Bissett Pratt, *Can We Keep the Faith?,* 1941

People prefer a religion which makes them feel safe and good rather than right and real.

Ralph W. Sockman, *The Highway of God,* 1941

Religion does not always make life *better,* but not often does it fail to make life *different.*

D. E. TRUEBLOOD, *The Logic of Belief,* 1942

The final religion is as absurd a dream as the final poem or the final symphony. The religious quest must forever remain a piece of "unfinished business" for open-minded and sensitive men.

STERLING P. LAMPRECHT, *Naturalism and the Human Spirit,* ed. Y. H. Krikorian, 1944

Primitive societies without religion have never been found.

WILLIAM HOWELLS, *The Heathens,* 1948

No word in either Greek or Latin corresponds exactly to English "religion," "religious."

Oxford Classical Dictionary, 1949

An individual religion can be as misleading and uninformed as an individual astronomy or an individual mathematics.

FULTON J. SHEEN, *Peace of Soul,* 1949

In many respects religion is the most interesting of man's ways, for it is his ultimate commentary on life and his only defense against death.

WILL DURANT, *The Age of Faith,* 1950

Religion has become an elective in the university of life.

Saying, U.S.A., 1950

If the student is to develop a respect for religion . . . he must have evidence, as tough and challenging as anything he meets in the laboratory, that in religion there is something to be discovered, and that its discovery is worth the effort.

ROBERT MACLEOD, *Religious Perspectives in College Teaching,* ed. H. N. Fairchild, 1951

By positing God it inhibits man from laying claim to being God. It prevents his becoming less than man through the arrogance of claiming to be more.

MILTON STEINBERG, *A Believing Jew,* 1951

When the American poor turn to religion, as most of them do, they turn not to faith in revolution, but to a more radical revolt against faith in their fellow man.

HERBERT WALLACE SCHNEIDER, *Religion in the 20th Century,* 1952

The modern hatred of religion is hatred of the truth, hatred of all sublimity, hatred of the laughter of the gods. It is puerile human vanity trying to justify itself by a lie.

GEORGE SANTAYANA, *My Host the World,* 1953

Religion is the natural reaction of the imagination when confronted by the difficulties of a truculent world.

GEORGE SANTAYANA, *Atlantic Monthly,* Vol. CXCL, no. 4 (1953)

There is nothing in the Bible to support the view that religion is necessarily a good thing. . . . On the contrary, it is highly suspicious of much that passes for religion.

A. ROY ECKARDT, *Christian Century,* November 17, 1954

Many people are turning to religion as they would to a benign sedative, to soothe their nerves and to settle their minds.

P. A. O'BOYLE, *McCall's,* June 19, 1955

Religion is not an opiate, for religion does not help people to forget, but to remember. It does not dull people. It does not say *Take,* but *Give.*

BEDE JARRETT, *The Catholic Mother,* 1956

The practical test of a religion, always and everywhere, is its success or failure in helping human souls to respond to the challenges of Suffering and Sin.

A. J. TOYNBEE, *An Historian's Approach to Religion,* 1956

From what I have seen, I am driven to the conclusion that religion is only for good people. . . . Only good people can afford to be religious. For the others, it is too great a temptation—a temptation to the deadly sins of pride and anger, chiefly, but one might also add sloth.

MARY MCCARTHY, *Memories of a Catholic Girlhood,* 1957

Religion is the supreme art of humanity.

ABBA HILLEL SILVER, *Where Judaism Differed,* 1957

A literalistic religion may not reveal so much faith as it does disrespect, for it makes God into a "great big being up there," and turns religion into a space-travel agency, with the sole task of getting people from this low place to that high place.

LANGDON GILKEY, *Maker of Heaven and Earth,* 1959

One cannot invent a religion.

CHARLES P. SNOW, *The Two Cultures and the Scientific Revolution,* 1961

A religion would not be worth my adherence if I could live up to it perfectly.

GEDDES MACGREGOR, *The Hemlock and the Cross,* 1963

(Since everything in this volume either refers to or is relevant to Religion, the cross-referencing here must necessarily be limited to those categories which embrace a specific religious or antireligious concept, which link Religion with another activity, and to categories each of which embrace various aspects of Religion.) *See also* Agnosticism; Art and Religion; Atheism; Belief; Buddhism; Catholicism; Christian Science; Christianity; Civilization and Reli-

gion; Communism; Congregationalism; Culture and Religion; Deism; Democracy, Religion of; Division; Doctrine; Dogma; Ecumenism; Education and Religion; False Religions; Government and Religion; Humanism; Islam; Judaism; Materialism; Morality and Religion; Naturalism; Paganism; Pantheism; Paths; Positivism; Protestantism; Pseudo Religion; Quakers; Reason and Religion; various rubrics under Religion; Revelation and Reason; Science and Religion; Secularism; Society and Religion; Theism; Truth and Religion; Unitarians; Unity.

RELIGION: CAUSTIC COMMENTS ABOUT

We have just enough religion to make us hate, but not enough to make us love one another.

JONATHAN SWIFT, *Thoughts on Various Subjects,* 1706

Religion is the sigh of the oppressed creature, the feeling of a heartless world, just as it is the spirit of unspiritual conditions. It is the opium of the people.

KARL MARX, *Critique of Hegelian Philosophy,* 1844

God has allowed all who have variously sought Him in the most earnest way, to be blinded. . . . Puritan—monk—Brahmin —churchman—Turk—all are merely names for different madnesses and ignorances.

JOHN RUSKIN, *Letters From Venice,* 1851–1852, ed. J. L. Bradley

Religion is a mounumental chapter in the history of human egotism.

WILLIAM JAMES, *The Varieties of Religious Experience,* 1902

Religion is a species of mental disease. It has always had a pathological reaction on mankind.

BENITO MUSSOLINI, *Speech,* July, 1904

Religion is a clumsy sort of spiritual whiskey in which the slaves of capital drown their human being and their revenge for an existence little worthy of man.

NIKOLAI LENIN, *New Life,* December 16, 1905

Religion, n. A daughter of Hope and Fear, explaining to Ignorance the nature of the Unknowable.

AMBROSE BIERCE, *Devil's Dictionary,* 1906

The struggle against religion must not be confined to an abstract preaching of ideals. The struggle must be firmly bound to the concrete action of class action, even aiming at the total disappearance of the social roots from which religion takes its source.

NIKOLAI LENIN, *The Proletariat,* May, 1909

[Religion is] the sum of the superstitious beliefs which hinder the legitimate working of man's faculties.

SOLOMON REINACH, *Orpheus,* 1909

What the religious interest strives to do is to preserve intact an infantile image of the ideal father, perfect and "pure" and sinless.

E. D. MARTIN, *The Mystery of Religion,* 1924

Religion is comparable to a childhood neurosis.

SIGMUND FREUD, *Future of an Illusion,* 1928

Religion is revealed as the unchangeable foe of Christianity.

J. F. RUTHERFORD, *Religion Reaps the Whirlwind,* 1944

Theoretically, religion wishes to make men serene and inwardly peaceful by reaching a loving and forgiving God. But in practice, there is too much undissolved wrath and punishment in most religions.

JOSHUA LOTH LIEBMAN, *Peace of Mind,* 1946

Religion is but a desperate attempt to find an escape from the truly dreadful situation in which we find ourselves. Here we are in this wholly fantastic Universe with scarcely a clue as to whether our existence has any real significance. No wonder then that many people feel the need for some belief that gives them a sense of security, and no wonder that they become very angry with people like me who say that this is illusory.

FRED HOYLE, *The Nature of the Universe,* 1950

As a set of *cognitive* beliefs, religion is a speculative hypothesis of an extremely low order of probability.

SIDNEY HOOK, *The Partisan Review,* March, 1950

I think all the great religions of the world . . . both untrue and harmful.

BERTRAND RUSSELL, *Why I Am Not a Christian,* 1957

As a social and as a personal force, religion has become a dependent variable. It does not originate; it reacts. It does not denounce; it adapts. It does not set forth new models of conduct and sensibility; it imitates. Its rhetoric is without deep appeal; the worship it organizes is without piety. It has become less a revitalization of the spirit in permanent tension with the world than a respectable distraction from the sourness of life.

C. WRIGHT MILLS, *The Nation,* March 8, 1958

Religion declined not because it was refuted, but because it became irrelevant, dull, oppressive, insipid.

ABRAHAM JOSHUA HESCHEL, *Religion in America,* ed. John Cogley, 1958

A very large proportion of what passes for religion in our society is exactly the sort of neurotic illness that Freud describes.

JOHN WREN-LEWIS, *They Became Anglicans,* 1959

A good bit of religion today seems hollow; it does not seem to matter except behind stained-glass windows on a Sunday morning. It is not dishonest religion so much as restricted religion—a way of thinking for a special time and a special place.

SAMUEL H. MILLER, *Look,* December 19, 1961

Religion sanctifies the ground upon which men live their social roles. . . . Religion is an excellent investment for fuller, more satisfying life. The Christian faith is not.

PETER L. BERGER, *The Precarious Vision,* 1962

Religion is a fantastic, distorted reflection of the world in the human mind. . . . From the moment of its first appearance on the scene and right down to our days, religion has played and still plays a reactionary role.

Social Science, textbook used in schools of Soviet Russia, 1963

See also Agnosticism; Atheism; Communism; God, Blasphemous Statements about; God: Nonexistence of; God: Unorthodox Comments about; Godlessness; Humanism; Irreligion; Marxism; Materialism; Naturalism; Positivism· Religion; Unbelief.

RELIGION, DEFINITIONS OF

Wherein does religion consist? It consists in doing as little harm as possible, in doing good in abundance, in the practice of love, of compassion, of truthfulness and purity, in all the walks of life.

Asoka's Edicts, c. 260 B.C.

The holy service of God.

WILLIAM CAMDEN, *Remains Concerning Britain,* 1667

Religion is nothing else but love of God and man.

WILLIAM PENN, *Some Fruits of Solitude,* 1693

By Religion I mean, such a sense of divine Truth, as enters into a Man, and becomes a Spring of a new Nature within him; reforming his Thoughts and Designs, purifying his Heart, and sanctifying him, and governing his whole Deportment.

GILBERT BURNET, *A History of My Own Times,* 1734

Morals in reference to God as legislator. . . . The recognition of our duties as divine commands.

IMMANUEL KANT, *Critique of Judgment,* 1790

And so religion is life in the endless nature of the whole, in one and all, in God; having and possessing all in God and God in all.

F. SCHLEIERMACHER, *Reden über die Religion,* 1799

Religion is moral life rising to think, i.e. becoming aware of the free universality of its concrete essence . . . the consciousness of "absolute" truth.

G. W. F. HEGEL, *Philosophy of Mind,* c. 1818

The Trinity is the Idea: The Incarnation, which implies the Fall, is the Fact; the redemption is the mesothesis of the two— that is—the Religion.

SAMUEL TAYLOR COLERIDGE, *Table Talk,* October 15, 1833

Religion is neither a theology nor a theosophy; it is more than that, it is a discipline, a law, a yoke, and indissoluble engagement.

JOSEPH JOUBERT, *Pensées,* 1838

A religion is not a proposition, but a system; it is a rite, a creed, a philosophy, a rule of duty, all at once.

JOHN HENRY NEWMAN, *A Grammar of Assent,* 1870

The true meaning of religion is this, not simply morality, but *morality touched by emotion.*

MATTHEW ARNOLD, *Literature and Dogma,* 1873

Religion is . . . the emotion of reverence which the presence of the universal mind ever excites in the individual.

RALPH WALDO EMERSON, *North American Review,* May, 1878

Religion is an intercourse, a conscious and voluntary relation, entered into by a soul in distress with the mysterious power upon which it feels itself to depend, and upon which its fate is contingent.

AUGUSTE SABATIER, *Esquisse d'une Philosophie de la Religion,* 1891

A sort of sentiment, or obscure perception, a deep recognition of a something in the circumambient ALL.

C. S. PEIRCE, *The Marriage of Religion and Science,* 1893

A fixed feeling of fear, resignation, admiration or approval, no matter what the object, provided only that this feeling reaches a certain strength, and is qualified by a certain degree of reflection.

F. H. BRADLEY, *Appearance and Reality,* 1894

Religion is human experience interpreted by human imagination.

GEORGE SANTAYANA, *The Sense of Beauty,* 1896

Religion is the life of God in the soul of man.

LYMAN ABBOTT, *An Evolutionist's Theology,* 1897

Religion . . . shall mean for us, the feelings, acts, and experiences of individual men in their solitude, so far as they apprehend themselves to stand in relation to whatever they may consider the divine.

WILLIAM JAMES, *The Varieties of Religious Experience,* 1902

True religion is the establishment by man of such a relation to the Infinite Life around him, as, while connecting his life with this Infinitude and directing his conduct, is also in agreement with his reason and with human knowledge.

LEO TOLSTOY, *What Is Religion?,* 1902

Religion is a perception of the Divine existence, issuing in duty.

MORRIS JOSEPH, *Judaism as Creed and Life,* 1903

Religion consists of conscious ideas, hopes, enthusiasms, and objects of worship; it operates by grace and flourishes by prayer.

GEORGE SANTAYANA, *Reason in Religion,* 1905

By religion I mean the power, whatever it be, which makes a man choose what is hard rather than what is easy, what is lofty and noble rather than what is mean and selfish; that puts courage into timorous hearts, and gladness into clouded spirits; that consoles men in grief, misfortune, and disappointment; that makes them joyfully accept a heavy burden; that, in a word, uplifts men out of the dominion of material things.

ARTHUR CHRISTOPHER BENSON, *From a College Window,* 1906

Religion is an emotion resting on a conviction of a harmony between ourselves and the universe at large.

T. MCTAGGART, *Some Dogmas of Religion,* 1906

Religion is man's sense of the disposition of the universe to himself.

RALPH BARTON PERRY, *The Approach to Philosophy,* 1908

[Religion] in its highest historical forms is the interpretation both of the eternal and of the spirit of loyalty through emotion, and through a fitting activity of the imagination.

JOSIAH ROYCE, *The Philosophy of Loyalty,* 1908

Religion is the consciousness of the highest social values.

E. S. AMES, *The Psychology of Religious Experience,* 1910

An experience of securing spiritual integrity, whether arrived at by growth, maintained against disruptive forces, or regained by human faith and divine grace.

EUGENE W. LYMAN, *The Meaning and Truth of Religion,* 1910

Religion may be defined as the natural belief in a Power or Powers beyond our control, and upon whom we feel ourselves dependent.

M. JASTROW, *The Study of Religion,* 1911

Religion should be looked upon as a functional part of life, as that mode of behavior in the struggle for life in which use is made of powers characterized here as psychic, superhuman, and usually personal.

J. A. LEUBA, *A Psychological Study of Religion,* 1912

Religion is the mind and will of God, existing as God exists, objectively outside of men and of peoples, superior to all men, exacting from man the obedience due by the creature to the Creator.

JOHN IRELAND, *Address,* August 11, 1913

Religion is a *feeling adjustment* to the deeper things of life, and to the larger reality that encompasses the personal life.

EDWIN STARBUCK, *American Journal of Religious Psychology,* 7, 1915

Nobody is anything except as he joins himself to something. You cannot be a whole unless you join a whole. This, I believe, is religion.

BERNARD BOSANQUET, *What Religion Is,* 1920

The sense of outgoing to the whole universe in its process towards the quality of deity.

S. ALEXANDER, *Space, Time and Deity,* II, 1922

Religion means the consecration of individual life, at first for love and spiritual ends, but finally for humanitarian ends.

CHARLES A. ELLWOOD, *Reconstruction of Religion,* 1922

By religion, then, I understand a propitiation or conciliation of powers superior to man which are believed to direct and control the course of nature and of human life.

JAMES G. FRAZER, *The Golden Bough,* 1922

A sense of something transcending the expected or natural, a sense of the Extraordinary, Mysterious, or Supernatural.

R. LOWIE, *Primitive Religion,* 1924

Religion is the serious and social attitude of individuals or communities toward the power or powers which they conceive as having ultimate control over their interests and destinies.

JAMES B. PRATT, *The Religious Consciousness,* 1924

The reaction of mankind to something apprehended but not comprehended.

J. SHOTWELL, *The Religious Revolution of Today,* 1924

Religion is the vision of something which stands beyond, behind, and within, the passing flux of immediate things; something which is real, and yet waiting to be realized . . . something that gives meaning to all that passes, and yet eludes apprehension.

ALFRED NORTH WHITEHEAD, *Science and the Modern World,* 1925

Religion is not mere conformity to moral law, it is an espousal of moral ideals, a dedication of the heart, a loyal devotion, the perpetual renewal of a right spirit within us.

DURANT DRAKE, *Journal of Religion,* March, 1927

Religion is the glorious challenge of human life for the mastery of the planet; the loyal pursuit of the vision of the complete life through the ages.

A. E. HAYDON, *Journal of Religion,* March, 1927

Religion is force of belief cleansing the inward parts.

ALFRED NORTH WHITEHEAD, *Religion in the Making,* 1927

Religion is what the individual does with his own solitariness.

ALFRED NORTH WHITEHEAD, *Religion in the Making,* 1927

Religion . . . is the acceptance neither of a primitive absurdity nor of a sophisticated truism, but of a momentous possibility— the possibility namely that what is highest in spirit is deepest in nature.

W. P. MONTAGUE, *Belief Unbound,* 1930

The essence of religion is belief in a relation to God involving duties superior to those arising from any human relation. . . . duty to a moral power higher than the state.

CHIEF JUSTICE HUGHES, *U.S. v. Macintosh,* 283, U.S. 633, 1931

Religion is primarily and at heart the personal meeting of the soul with God and conscious communion with Him.

RUFUS M. JONES, *Pathways to the Reality of God,* 1931

It is a technique by which the human being gains more personal value from personal adjustment with responsive cosmic activities.

SHAILER MATHEWS, *The Growth of the Ideal God,* 1931

Religion etymologically means a bond or a connection. It is in fact a bridge between the visible and the invisible and should primarily be regarded as the key to a riddle, the explanation of a mystery.

ERNEST DIMNET, *What We Live By,* 1932

A consciously accepted system of make-believe.

ALDOUS HUXLEY, *Texts and Pretexts,* 1932

Religion consists of those actions, purposes, and experiences which are humanly significant. Nothing human is alien to the religious. It includes labor, art, science, philosophy, love, friendship, recreation. . . . The distinction between the sacred and the secular can no longer be maintained.

A Humanist Manifesto, 1933

Religion is a strictly collective term and the collection it stands for is not even of the kind illustrated in text books of logic. It has not the unity of a regiment or assembly but that of any miscellaneous aggregate. . . . Any activity pursued in behalf of an ideal end against obstacles and in spite of threats of personal loss because of conviction of its general enduring value is religious in quality.

JOHN DEWEY, *A Common Faith,* 1934

The heart of Religion is not an opinion about God, such as Philosophy might reach as the conclusion of its argument; it is a personal relation with God.

WILLIAM TEMPLE, *Nature, Man, and God,* 1934

Religion is the search for a value underlying all things, and as such is the most comprehensive of all the possible philosophies of life.

GORDON W. ALLPORT, *Personality, a Psychological Interpretation,* 1937

Religion . . . is the process whose distinguishing feature is to seek in the deepest part of the soul an increasing participation in the primal energy of things, to ask love to identify us with the supreme generosity of the spirit.

R. L. LE SENNE, *Introduction à la Philosophie*, 1939

Religion is a phase of a people's total interaction with the objective world of nature, organized society and the accumulated tradition of an historic past.

WILLIAM CLAYTON BOWER, *Church and State in Education*, 1944

Religion is the everlasting dialogue between humanity and God.

FRANZ WERFEL, *Between Heaven and Earth*, 1944

Personal cooperation with a trusted Creator of Values.

PAUL E. JOHNSON, *Psychology of Religion*, 1945

Religion is devoted and loyal commitment to the best that reason and insight can discover. The liberal understands what loyalty to the best means as the authoritarian never can.

JULIUS S. BIXLER, *Conversations with an Unrepentant Liberal*, 1946

Religion is the way we react to what we cannot evade.

NELS F. S. FERRÉ, *Faith and Reason*, 1946

By religion I mean the accumulated spiritual wisdom and ethical precepts dating from the time of the earliest Prophets and gradually formulated into a body of tested truth for man's moral guidance and spiritual at-homeness in the universe.

JOSHUA LOTH LIEBMAN, *Peace of Mind*, 1946

An adequate definition of religion is unattainable. It remains the supreme symbol of what is perhaps its most fundamental quality, which is mystery.

HERSCHEL BAKER, *The Image of Man*, 1947

A man's religion is what he thinks about his relation to the universe, or rather, is what he feels about this relation; or better, it is what he *does* about this relation; or best it is *how* he acts.

R. H. BLYTH, *Zen in English Literature*, 1948

A religion is the organized quest of a people for salvation, for helping those who live by the civilization of that people to achieve their destiny as human beings.

MORDECAI KAPLAN, *The Future of the American Jew*, 1948

[Religion is] the way we set our personalities for the purpose of meeting the whole stream of events.

HERBERT BUTTERFIELD, *Christianity and History*, 1949

Religion—The one perfect definition of religion is *The Life of God in the Soul of Man*.

JOSEPH FORT NEWTON, *Publisher's Weekly*, February 26, 1949

A man's religion is the audacious bid he makes to bind himself to creation and to the Creator.

GORDON W. ALLPORT, *The Individual and His Religion*, 1950

Religion is a man's search . . . for strength and courage to be gained from the heart of spiritual reality greater than matter, greater than an individual man, greater than the more or less human race.

B. I. BELL, *Life*, October 16, 1950

I understand by religion any system of thought and action shared by a group which gives the individual a frame of orientation and an object of devotion.

ERICH FROMM, *Psychoanalysis and Religion*, 1950

Religion is the hunger of the soul for the impossible, the unattainable, the inconceivable. . . . This is its essence and this is its glory. This is what religion *means*. Anything which is less than this is not religion.

W. T. STACE, *Time and Eternity*, 1952

A religion is a doctrine which resolves the problem of the afterlife and, based on this doctrine, a discipline which establishes relationship between man and the powers which rule over him.

JACQUES LECLERCQ, *Back to Jesus*, 1959

Religion is Man's attempt to get into touch with an absolute spiritual Reality behind the phenomena of the Universe, and, having made contact with It, to live in harmony with It.

A. J. TOYNBEE, *A Study of History*, Vol. XII, *Reconsiderations*, 1961

Religion is the divinity within us reaching up to the divinity above.

Bahá'í Sayings

See also Belief; Experience, Religious; Faith; Mysticism; Religion; Religion: Its Nature and Function; Religion, National; Religion, Natural; Religion, Organized; Religion, Revealed; Theology.

RELIGION: ITS DECLINE

In politics, religion is now a name; in art, a hypocrisy or affectation.

JOHN RUSKIN, *Modern Painters*, III, 1856

Religion, whatever destinies may be in store for it, is at least for the present hardly any longer an organic power.

JOHN VISCOUNT MORLEY, *On Compromise*, 1874

Little by little the barrier grows, and "religion" becomes a *rule* of life, not life itself.

MICHAEL FAIRLESS, *The Roadmender*, 1895

Religion and art have had their day.

GEORGE SANTAYANA, *Reason in Science*, 1906

Religion, which was once an omnipotent power, has become, for the modern man, a thing of quite secondary importance, nay, a mere illusion, and the world of immediate experience has more and more completely absorbed his whole thought and feeling.

RUDOLF EUCKEN, *Main Currents of Modern Thought*, 1912

The crisis in the religious world has been brought about by the failure of existing religion to adapt itself to two outstanding facts in our civilization—science and democracy.

CHARLES A. ELLWOOD, *The Reconstruction of Religion*, 1922

Religion is tending to degenerate into a decent formula wherewith to embellish a comfortable life.

ALFRED NORTH WHITEHEAD, *Science and the Modern World*, 1925

Like a river dammed by its own ice, religion is held back by its congealed formulations.

HARRY EMERSON FOSDICK, *Adventurous Religion*, 1926

The theological mould which shaped political theory from the Middle Ages to the seventeenth century is broken. . . . Religion, ceasing to be the master-interest of mankind, dwindles into a department of life with boundaries which it is extravagant to overstep.

R. H. TAWNEY, *Religion and the Rise of Capitalism*, 1926

The great characteristic of our age is not its love of religion, but its love of talking about religion.

FULTON J. SHEEN, *The Eternal Galilean*, 1934

Modern religion has become merely a department of culture, with a special place reserved for it—a very small one. It must again become *all*, the force which transfigures and irradiates the whole of life from within.

NICHOLAS BERDYAEV, *The Fate of Man in the Modern World*, 1935

If religion were a light in the physical sense, the inhabitants of other worlds would have seen our planet, luminous since the ice age, suddenly extinguished.

DMITRI MEREJKOWSKI, *Yale Review*, XXIV, 1935

The formulas and instruments of all our inherited religions were shaped in accordance with a world-outlook and a world-order which we have outgrown and to which we can never return.

MAX C. OTTO, *Religious Liberals Reply*, 1947

The decline of religion in modern times means simply that religion is no longer the uncontested center and ruler of man's life, and that the church is no longer the final and unquestioned home and asylum of his being.

WILLIAM BARRETT, *Irrational Man*, 1958

Religion has become an impersonal affair, an institutional loyalty. It survives on the level of activities rather than in the stillness of commitment.

ABRAHAM JOSHUA HESCHEL, *Religion in America*, ed. John Cogley, 1958

See also Agnosticism; Atheism; Godlessness; Humanism; Irreligion; Religion; Science; Secularism.

RELIGION: ITS NATURE AND FUNCTION

The way of religion is to lead the things which are lower to the things which are higher through the things which are intermediate.

POPE BONIFACE VIII, the bull *Unam Sanctam*, 1302

True religion . . . rears the dejected soul of man, and amidst so many cares, miseries, persecutions, which this world affords, it is a sole ease, an unspeakable comfort, a sweet reposal, a light yoke, an anchor and a haven.

ROBERT BURTON, *Anatomy of Melancholy*, III, 1621

Religion, in a large sense, doth signify the whole duty of man, comprehending in it justice, charity, and sobriety. . . . In a more restrained sense, it is taken for that part of duty which particularly relates to God in our worshipping and adoration of Him.

JEREMY TAYLOR, *Holy Living*, 1650

Religion does not consist in the anxious observance of petty formalities, but in the virtue proper to the condition of each individual.

FRANÇOIS FÉNELON, To the Duke of Burgundy, *Spiritual Letters*

True religion, in great part, consists in holy affections . . . the more vigorous and sensible exercises of the inclination and will of the soul.

JONATHAN EDWARDS, *Religious Affections*, 1746

There is and can be but *one true* Religion for the fallen soul, and that is, the Dying to *Self*, to *Nature* and *Creature;* and a turning with all the *Will*, the *Desire*, and *Delight* of the Soul to God.

WILLIAM LAW, *The Spirit of Prayer*, 1749

The proper office of religion is to regulate the heart of men, humanize their conduct, infuse the spirit of temperance, order, and obedience.

DAVID HUME, *Concerning Natural Religion*, 1779

The body of all true religion consists in obedience to the will of the Sovereign of the World, in a confidence in His declarations, and an imitation of His perfections.

EDMUND BURKE, *Reflections on the Revolution in France*, 1790

Religion elevates him who is devoted to her service above time as such, above the transient and the perishable, and puts him in immediate possession of eternity.

J. G. FICHTE, *Characteristics of the Present Age*, 1804

The content of religion is absolute truth, and consequently the religious is the most sublime of all dispositions. As intuition, feeling, representative knowledge, its task is concentrated upon God as the unrestricted principle and cause on which everything hangs.

G. W. F. HEGEL, *The Philosophy of Right*, 1821

The great office of religion is to call forth, elevate, and purify the spirit of man, and thus to conform it to its divine original.

WILLIAM ELLERY CHANNING (1780–1842), *Works*

Inborn religious faculty is the basis and cause of all religion. . . . If man have not a religious element in his nature, miraculous or other "revelations" can no more render him religious than fragments of sermons and leaves of the Bible can make a lamb religious when mixed and eaten with its daily food.

THEODORE PARKER, *Views of Religion*, 1855

The antithesis between *ethical* and *religious* is thus quite a false one. . . . Religion . . . is ethics heightened, enkindled, lit up by feeling.

MATTHEW ARNOLD, *Literature and Dogma*, 1873

The union of the soul with God, through faith, hope, and love is the first and highest aim of religion.

JOHN LANCASTER SPALDING, *Essays and Reviews*, 1877

Instead of leaving man in an interminable pursuit of a vanishing ideal, it makes him the actual partaker of a divine or infinite life.

JOHN CAIRD, *Introduction to the Philosophy of Religion*, 1880

Religion—that is, the life of God in the soul of man—is better comprehended, and will be better promoted, by the philosophy which regards all life as divine, and God's way of doing things as the way of continuous, progressive change.

LYMAN ABBOTT, *Theology of an Evolutionist*, 1897

Religion has in it all there is in mental therapeutics, and has it in the best form. Living up to our [religious] ideas will do anything for us that can be done.

H. H. GODDARD, *American Journal of Psychology*, X, 1899

The practical need and experiences of religion seem to me sufficiently met by the belief that beyond each man and in a fashion continuous with him there exists a larger power which is friendly to him and to his ideals.

WILLIAM JAMES, *The Varieties of Religious Experience*, 1902

Religion should not be conceived as having taken the place of anything better, but rather as having come to relieve situations, which, but for its presence, would have been infinitely worse.

GEORGE SANTAYANA, *Reason in Religion*, 1905

Religion pursues rationality through the imagination. When it explains events or assigns causes, it is an imaginative substitute for science. When it gives precepts, insinuates ideals, or remoulds aspiration, it is an imaginative substitute for wisdom.

GEORGE SANTAYANA, *Reason in Religion*, 1905

In Man, the positive content of religion is the instinctive sense—whether conscious or subconscious—of an inner unity and continuity with the world around. This is the stuff out of which religion is made.

EDWARD CARPENTER, *Pagan and Christian Creeds*, 1920

Instead of hiding the great crises, . . . religion reveals them, makes us aware of them, sharpens our consciousness of their presence; but at the same time reveals us to ourselves as beings who are capable of overcoming them.

L. P. JACKS, *Religious Perplexities*, 1922

In its simplified element religion is thus found to be the expression of man's mental attitude toward the unknown which is not capable of being known by any method of investigation available at the time.

G. M. IRVINE, *Churches, Religion and Progress*, 1924

Because it is a process of projection and pursuit, religion is an ever moving process in the direction of complete personal adjustment and control in man's total environment.

EDWIN E. AUBREY, *Journal of Religion*, 1925

No interpretation of religion can be worthy of its great object . . . which does not exhibit it as a thing born of, and nourished by, the fullest daylight of human intelligence.

JOHN BAILLIE, *The Roots of Religion in the Human Soul*, 1926

Religion at its best furnishes a noble aesthetic interpretation of the meaning of life . . . brings poetry and music and pageantry and adoration into the life of men.

GERALD BINNEY SMITH, *Religious Education*, XXIII, 1927

Religion is both individual and social. It is an inward mystical experience, but if it is wholesome it overflows in cooperative fellowship. No man can be completely religious alone.

HARRY EMERSON FOSDICK, *World's Work*, February, 1929

Religion though it begins in a seminal individual inspiration, only comes to great flower in a great church coextensive with a civilization.

C. S. PEIRCE, *Collected Papers*, ed. Hartshorne and Weiss, VI, 1931

Religion begins with a full affirmation of a Reality, of a Reality other than and more than all mankind. . . . It is a gift from above downwards. . . . It is not like Science, a coral-reef, it is more like a golden shower from above.

FRIEDRICH VON HÜGEL, *Selected Letters*, 1933

The heart of Religion is not an opinion about God, such as philosophy might reach as the conclusion of an argument; it is a personal relation with God.

WILLIAM TEMPLE, *Nature, Man and God*, 1934

Religion is a function in man's struggle for existence. . . . The struggle for existence is the primary thing, and religion is one of the tools man has forged whereby he can attain in this struggle a satisfactory and if possible a delightful existence. . . . Religion is of human, not divine origin, existing because of the role it plays in human life and not because of its divine source.

JOHN H. DIETRICH, "Humanism," ch. 12, *Varieties of American Religion*, ed. Charles S. Braden, 1936

Religion is about fellowship and community. . . . The task of religion is the maintenance and extension of human community.

JOHN MACMURRAY, *The Structure of Religious Experience*, 1936

Religion is born when we accept the ultimate frustration of mere human effort, and at the same time realize the strength which comes from union with superhuman reality.

JOHN BUCHAN, *Pilgrims Way*, 1940

Religion, like everything great and noble and demanding within us, increases the tension in mankind; and together with the tension, suffering; and with the suffering, spiritual effort; and with the spiritual effort, joy.

JACQUES MARITAIN, *Ransoming the Time*, 1941

Sometimes the strange notion becomes current that religion encourages men to feel "good." As a matter of fact it does quite the opposite.

D. E. TRUEBLOOD, *The Logic of Belief*, 1942

Religion floods our darkness with a divine light. . . . Religion brings into the focus of attention the two supreme values—God and the human soul.

JOHN A. O'BRIEN, *Religion—Does It Matter?*, 1944

Religion has its origin in the depths of the soul and it can be understood only by those who are prepared to take the plunge.

CHRISTOPHER DAWSON, *Religion and Culture*, 1947

Religion is proposed not as a transcendent revelation of the nature of man and the world, but as a means of weathering the storms of life, or of deepening one's spiritual experience, or of preserving the social order, or of warding off anxiety.

LEO LOWENTHAL and N. GUTERMAN, *Prophets of Deceit*, 1949

The function of religion is to confront the paradoxes and contradictions and the ultimate mysteries of man and the cosmos; to make sense and reason of what lies beneath the irreducible irrationalities of man's life; to pierce the surrounding dark-

ness with pinpoints of life, or occasionally to rip away for a startling moment the cosmic shroud.

LEWIS MUMFORD, *The Conduct of Life*, 1951

Religion makes the adventurous leap from the spirit of man to the Universal Spirit it calls God.

EDMUND W. SINNOTT, *The Biology of the Spirit*, 1955

Religion begins in the anguish of a man who faces the abyss of nothingness and who wanders through a broken world made desolate in the absence of God.

GEORGE BRANTL, *Catholicism*, 1962

Whatever else it is—let us be clear about that from the outset—religion is something we belong to, not something which belongs to us; something that has got hold of us, not something we have got hold of.

RONALD A. KNOX, *University and Anglican Sermons*, 1964

Religion is a journey, not a destination.
Author Unknown

See also Brotherhood; Community; Fellowship; Man and God; Mysticism; Religion; Religion, Definitions of.

RELIGION, NATIONAL

None but superficial minds could stumble into concepts of a national God, of a national religion; or attempt to lock within the frontiers of a single people, within the narrow limits of a single race, God, the Creator of the universe.

POPE PIUS XI, *Mit Brennender Sorge*, March, 1937

It is ironic that a national religion should have developed in a nation which had not intended to have one. . . . The attitude which has been raised to religious ultimacy is the advocacy of support of official religion, an overarching nationalization of that religion-in-general which is the product of the erosion of particularity and which makes religious distinctions irrelevant.

MARTIN E. MARTY, *The New Shape of American Religion*, 1958

See also Church and State; Government and Religion; Religion; Religion, State; State, the.

RELIGION, NATURAL

Natural religion is the foundation of all revealed religion, and revelation is designed simply to establish its duties.

JOHN TILLOTSON (1639–1694), *Works*, Bk. II

There is a religion of nature written in the hearts of everyone of us from the first creation; by which all mankind must judge of the truth of any instituted religion whatever.

MATTHEW TINDALE, *Christianity as Old as the Creation*, 1730

I understand by natural religion the principle of morality common to the human race.

VOLTAIRE, *Elements of the Philosophy of Newton*, 1745

One of the most important effects of Natural Religion on the mind, in preparation for Revealed, is the anticipation which it creates, that a Revelation will be given.

JOHN HENRY NEWMAN, *A Grammar of Assent*, 1870

Natural religion . . . finds a God who is majestic, but not majestic enough to threaten human self-esteem.

REINHOLD NIEBUHR, *Do the State and Nation Belong to God or Man?*, 1937

It is the worship of God as prescribed by reason unaided by revelation.

JOHN A. O'BRIEN, *Religion—Does it Matter?*, 1944

If religion is the state of being grasped by an ultimate concern, "natural religion" can only mean that the ultimate concern is experienced in an encounter with nature.

PAUL TILLICH, *Journal of Religion*, January, 1947

Even natural religion raises us to the transcendent level of that being without whom there is no sufficient reason for existing, for thinking, for working, nor any basis for hopes that is free from deception.

POPE PAUL VI, *Easter Sermon*, 1964

See also Nature; Nature and God; Pantheism; Religion; Religion, Revealed.

RELIGION, NECESSITY OF

A man without some sort of religion is at best, a poor reprobate, the football of destiny, with no tie linking him to infinity, and the wondrous eternity that is begun with him; but woman without it is even worse—a flame without heat, a rainbow without color, a flower without perfume!

DONALD G. MITCHELL ("Ike Marvel"), *Reveries of a Bachelor*, 1851

Religion is necessary, not because it is useful or consoling, but because it is involved in the nature of man and in the nature of things.

JOHN LANCASTER SPALDING, *Religion, Agnosticism and Education*, 1902

Among my patients in the second half of life—that is to say over thirty-five—there has not been one whose problem in the last resort was not that of finding a religious outlook on life. None of them had been really healed who did not regain this religious outlook.

C. G. JUNG, *Modern Man in Search of a Soul*, 1932

One of the greatest griefs of my life is that so few people seem to realize that religion is something that they need, and cannot get on without.

LOUIS HOLLAND, *Autobiography of a Cathedral*, 1937

Man needs religion to give him that sense of responsibility which prevents human existence from becoming a wilderness of warring passions and aimless strivings. He needs religion because, apart from God, man is lonely and he can never find in himself or in the institutions which bear his image the means to fill up that void of loneliness which is in the human heart.
Catholic Bishops of the U.S., 1952

See also Belief; Damnation; Ethics; Godlessness; Grace; Irreligion; Loneliness; Man: His Destiny and Goal; Man: His Potential; Man and God; Man's Quest of God; Man's Unity with God; Religion; Religion, Definitions of.

RELIGION, ORGANIZED

The main weakness of organized Christianity has been the tendency to settle into a "sacred" form and system.
RUFUS M. JONES, *Studies in Mystical Religion,* 1909

Hardly any problem of exegesis is more difficult than to discover in the gospels an administrative or organizing or ecclesiastical Christ.
F. G. PEABODY, *Jesus Christ and the Social Question,* 1915

Organized, institutionalized, creedalized, ritualized—religion has become for multitudes a stuffy and uninteresting affair.
HARRY EMERSON FOSDICK, *Adventurous Religion,* 1926

A religious organization is a somewhat idle affair unless it be sworn in as a regiment of that great army that takes life in hand . . . in grimmest fight to put down the principle of self-seeking, and to make the principle of love triumphant.
C. S. PEIRCE, *Collected Papers,* ed. Hartshorne and Weiss, VI, 1931

When organized religion is completely accepted by the mass as no more than a pleasing and fashionable facet of culture, then it falls prey to the mass-produced platitude.
STANLEY ROWLAND, JR., *The Nation,* July 28, 1956

Organized religion is too respectable, too much at home in America, and so too much inclined to abdicate its responsibility as a judge of society.
HERBERT J. MULLER, *Religion and Freedom in the Modern World,* 1963

See also Christianity; Church, Criticism of; Institutionalism; Religion.

RELIGION, REVEALED

He who today would retain at once his faith as a Christian and his integrity of mind can do so only . . . by arguing for the probability of a revelation which is authoritative without being absolute, and reasonable without being rationalistic.
Fourth Lateran Council, 1215

For our faith rests upon the revelation made to the Apostles and the prophets who wrote the canonical books, but not on the revelations eventually made to other Doctors.
ST. THOMAS AQUINAS, *Summa Theologiae,* I. q. 1 a. 8. ad 2, 1272

There is something true and divinely revealed in every religion all over the earth, overloaded, as it may be, and at times even stifled by the impieties which the corrupt will and understanding of man have incorporated with it.
JOHN HENRY NEWMAN, *The Arians of the Fourth Century,* 1833

Revealed religion . . . is the doctrine taught in the Mosaic and Christian dispensations, and contained in the Holy Scriptures, and is from God in a sense in which no other doctrine can be said to be from Him.
JOHN HENRY NEWMAN, *The Arians of the Fourth Century,* 1833

The unity of God, the freedom of man, and the creation of the world. Upon these three pillars, and upon them alone, rests and must rest every revealed religion, including the religion of Christ, if it is to retain the name of revealed religion.

S. L. STEINHEIM, *Offenbarungslehre,* 1856

Religion springing out of an experience of the power, the grandeur, the necessity of righteousness, . . . whether we find it in Sophocles or in Isaiah . . . revealed religion is properly so named, just in proportion as it is in a pre-eminent degree natural.

MATTHEW ARNOLD, *Literature and Dogma,* 1873

The ahderents of every religion . . . always claimed that their beliefs about God were due to God.

A. J. BALFOUR, *The Foundations of Belief,* 1895

Religions are not revealed; they are evolved. If a religion were revealed by God, that religion would be perfect in whole and in part, and would be as perfect at the first moment of its revelation as after ten thousand years of practice.

ROBERT BLATCHFORD, *God and My Neighbor,* 1903

We who believe that Christ came to inaugurate the religion of the Spirit—are content with a progressive dynamic revelation, always true to "the mind of Christ."

W. R. INGE, *Speculum Animae,* 1911

If, indeed, Christianity is a divinely revealed religion, as it professes to be, it follows that Christians are not at liberty to bargain and barter amongst themselves as to how much, or how little, of that revelation they shall accept.

RICHARD DOWNEY, *Critical and Constructive Essays,* 1934

Every religion in which we can see a measure of divine illumination is a revealed religion. Where the divine is manifested, there is revelation.

NICHOLAS BERDYAEV, *Freedom and Spirit,* 1935

Supernatural religion is the sum of man's duties to God as known by divine revelation.

JOHN A. O'BRIEN, *Religion—Does It Matter?,* 1944

Divine assistance, intended to preserve revelation from errors and distortions, was promised to the Church and not to individuals.

POPE PIUS XII, *Broadcast,* March 24, 1952

The living essence of religion is revealed once and for all, in its sole perfect manifestation, in the Christian revelation and in the relation with God which that revelation makes possible for men.

HERBERT FARMER, *Revelation and Religion,* 1954

See also Bible; Bible: Its Inspiration; Church: Its Nature; Judaism; Light; New Testament; Old Testament; Revelation; Religion; Religion, Natural.

RELIGION, STATE

The consecration of the state, by a state religious establishment, is necessary also to operate with a wholesome awe upon free citizens.

EDMUND BURKE, *Reflections on the Revolution in France,* 1790

It is necessary that there be a religion of the state as there is a politics of the state. . . . Religious and political dogmas, mixed and blended, together form a rather strong universal or national reason in order to repress the aberrations of individual reason.

JOSEPH DE MAISTRE (1753–1821), *Étude sur la Souveraineté*

Religion cannot sink lower than when somehow it is raised to a state religion . . . it becomes then an avowed mistress.

HEINRICH HEINE, *Letter from Berlin,* March 16, 1822

See also Church and State; Government and Religion; Religion, National; State, the.

RELIGIOSITY

Our religiosity seems to have as little to do with the Christian faith as the religiosity of the Athenians. The "unknown god" in America seems to be faith itself.

REINHOLD NIEBUHR, *Christianity and Crisis,* January 24, 1955

RELIGIOUS

Any influence is religious which fills the mind with gratitude and peace, which makes a man humble and patient and wise, which teaches him that the only happiness possible is to attune and harmonize his mind with the gracious purpose of God.

ARTHUR CHRISTOPHER BENSON, *From a College Window,* 1906

The religious life represents a dramatization on a cosmic plane of the emotions, fears and longing which arise in the child's relation to his parents.

E. JONES, *Journal of Medical Psychology,* Vol. VI, 1927

If we should venture to name this deep-set desire which we call religious it might be represented as an ultimate demand for self-preservation; it is man's leap for eternal life in some form, in presence of an awakened fear of fate.

WILLIAM E. HOCKING, *The Meaning of God in Human Experience,* 1928

To know that what is impenetrable to us really exists, manifesting itself as the highest wisdom and the most radiant beauty which our dull faculties can only comprehend in their most primitive forms—this knowledge, this feeling is the center of true religiousness.

ALBERT EINSTEIN, *Living Philosophies,* 1931

The religious man is not the attractive personality. He does not draw men to himself. He is the transparent personality: a window to something beyond himself.

GREGORY VLASTOS, *The Religious Person in the World Today,* 1934

Any activity pursued in behalf of an ideal and against obstacles and in spite of threats of personal loss because of conviction of its general and enduring value is religious in quality.

JOHN DEWEY, *A Common Faith,* 1937

It is the spiritual power of religion that he who is religious can fearlessly look at the vanity of religion.

PAUL TILLICH, *The New Being,* 1955

This is the first feature of religious life: a willing and joyful farewell to the things of the world, in order to belong to the Lord in perfect purity of heart.

POPE JOHN XXIII, *Address,* January 29, 1960

See also Emotion; Experience, Religious; Feelings; Science and Religion; Vision.

RELIGIOUS CONFLICT

I swear by God in whose hand is my life that marching about morning and evening to fight for religion is better than the world and everything that is in it; and verily the standing of one of you in the line of battle is better than supererogatory prayers performed in your house in sixty years.

MOHAMMED, *Speeches and Table Talk of,* 7th century A.D.

Religious conflict is not just a nuisance but is a sin. It is sinful because it arouses the wild beast in Human Nature . . . is sinful because no one has a right to stand between another human soul and God.

A. J. TOYNBEE, *An Historian's Approach to Religion,* 1956

The primary source of religious tension has its origin, it would seem, in the fact that the religions are not content to restrict their authority to their own members.

ARTHUR COHEN, *Religion and the Free Society,* 1958

See also Concord; Conflict; Controversy; Denominationalism; Discord; Disputation; Division; Harmony; Intolerance; Paths.

RELIGIOUS ORDERS

The greatest enemy of religious Orders is not the persecutor who closes monasteries and dispels communities and imprisons monks and nuns; it is the noonday demon who persuades them to go in for enterprises that have nothing whatever to do with the ideals of their founders.

THOMAS MERTON, *The Waters of Siloe,* 1949

See also Monastery; Monasticism.

RELIGIOUS TEST FOR OFFICE

The prescribing any citizen as unworthy the public confidence by laying upon him an incapacity of being called to offices of trust and emolument, unless he profess or renounce this or that religious opinion, is depriving him injuriously of those privileges and advantages to which in common with his fellow citizens he has a natural right.

THOMAS JEFFERSON, *An Act for Establishing Religious Freedom,* Assembly, Virginia, 1786

See also Church and State; Freedom, Religious; Office.

REMORSE

Remorse is the fatal egg by pleasure laid.
WILLIAM COWPER (1731–1800), *Progress of Error*

See also Penitence; Repentance.

RENEWAL

The great forces running through the Church, the waves surging up from the depths and uplifting her, are not the signs of death. They show the rising of the sap, the thrust of spring.

EMMANUEL SUHARD, *The Church Today,* 1953

See also Reform.

RENUNCIATION

Fools! give up thy thirst for wealth, banish all desires from thy heart. Let thy mind be satisfied with what is gained by thy *Karma.*

Mohamudgara (c. 800 A.D.), quoted by Max Muller, *Six Systems* (sometimes attributed to Shankara)

O God! Give to Thine enemies whatever Thou hast assigned to me of this world's goods, and to Thy friends whatever Thou hast assigned to me in the life to come; for Thou Thyself art sufficient for me.

RABIA A-ADAWIYYA (717–801), quoted in P. K. Hitti's *History of the Arabs*

God asks only one thing of you: that you dethrone the creaturely self and let Him be God in you.

MEISTER ECKHART (1260?–1327?), *Meister Eckhart,* R. B. Blakney

If thou wilt be a spiritual pilgrim, thou shalt strip thyself naked of all that thou hast.

WALTER HILTON, *Scale of Perfection,* c. 1390

Now that my heart is closed against all desire for earthly things, now that I have no longer any sense for the transitory and perishable, the universe appears before my eyes clothed in a more glorious form.

J. G. FICHTE (1762–1814), *The Vocation of Man*

See also Abandonment; Desires; Detachment; Greed; Lust; Mammon; Possessions; Sacrifice; Self-Denial; Self-Giving; Selflessness; Self-Sacrifice; Submission; Wealth; Worldliness.

REPENTANCE

He who has committed a sin and has repented, is freed from that sin, but he is purified only by the resolution of ceasing to sin and thinking "I will do so no more."

Code of Manu, between 1200 and 500 B.C.

O Lord, do not cast aside thy servant;
He is cast unto the mire; take his hand!
The sin which I have sinned, turn to mercy!
The iniquity which I have committed, let the wind carry away!
My many transgressions tear off like a garment!
Babylonian Hymn (c. 6th century B.C.), quoted in R. F. Harper's *Assyrian and Babylonian Literature*

This alone will turn a wolf into a sheep, make a publican a preacher, turn a thorn into an olive, make a debauchee a religious fellow.

ST. JOHN CHRYSOSTOM, *Hom.* 5, c. 388

In the place where repentant sinners stand perfect saints cannot stand.

Berakot, Talmud, c. 400 A.D.

He who says "I will sin and repent, and sin again and repent again" will be given no chance to repent.

Yoma, Mishnah, c. 400 A.D.

A sincere repenter of faults is like him who hath committed none.

MOHAMMED (7th century A.D.), *Sayings of, Wisdom of East Series*

Let not a repentant sinner imagine that he is remote from the estate of the righteous because of the sins and misdeeds that he has done. This is not true, for he is beloved and precious to God as if he had never sinned.

MAIMONIDES, *Mishneh Torah,* 1170

Repentance is a change of heart produced in a sinner by the word of the gospel and the Holy Spirit, and includes a knowledge of native and actual depravity, a godly sorrow and hatred of sin, and a determination to live hereafter in virtue and holiness.

HENRY BULLINGER, *The Helvetic Confession,* 1536

Reason effaces other griefs and sorrows, but engenders those of repentance.

MICHEL DE MONTAIGNE, *Essays,* Bk. 3, ch. 2, 1580

The end of passion is the beginning of repentance.

OWEN FELLTHAM, *Resolves,* c. 1620

Christ saved one thief at the last gasp, to show that there may be late repentance.

JOHN DONNE, *Sermon,* May 30, 1621

Repentance is a sovereign remedy for all sins, a spiritual wing to rear us, a charm for our miseries, a protecting amulet to expel sin's venom, an attractive lodestone to draw God's mercy and graces unto us.

ROBERT BURTON, *The Anatomy of Melancholy,* III, 1621

Repentance, of all things in the world, makes the greatest change; it changes things in heaven and earth; for it changes the whole man from sin to grace.

JEREMY TAYLOR, *Holy Living,* 1650

Our repentance is not so much regret for the ill we have done as fear of the ill that may happen to us in consequence.

LA ROCHEFOUCAULD, *Maxims,* 1665

He that feels himself alarmed by his conscience, anxious for the attainment of a better state and afflicted by the memory of his past faults, may justly conclude that the great work of repentance has begun.

SAMUEL JOHNSON, *The Rambler,* April 6, 1751

What is repentance but a kind of leave-taking, looking backward indeed, but yet in such a way as precisely to quicken the steps toward that which lies before.

SÖREN KIERKEGAARD, *Philosophical Fragments,* 1844

Repentance . . . is recoil, recoil not from the bad act and its painful consequences, but from the principle underlying the act.

FELIX ADLER, *An Ethical Philosophy of Life,* 1918

There is in repentance this beautiful mystery—that we may fly fastest home on broken wing.

WILLIAM L. SULLIVAN, *Epigrams and Criticisms in Miniature,* 1936

Collective sinning is a dire reality, but collective repentance is usually too diluted to be curative.

RALPH W. SOCKMAN, *The Highway of God,* 1941

Repentance was perhaps best defined by a small girl: It's to be sorry enough to quit."

C. H. KILMER, *The New Illustrator,* 1945

Repentance is . . . not only a realization of failure, not only a burst of contrition for having failed the good, not only a readiness to admit this failure freely . . . but also a determination not to fail the good again.

DOUGLAS V. STEERE, *Door into Life,* 1948

Repentance is not self-regarding, but God-regarding. It is not self-loathing, but God-loving.

FULTON J. SHEEN, *Peace of Soul,* 1949

We need to repent of the sins of others with which we find ourselves identified . . . by sharing in their economic or other advantages, by our loyal self-identification with groups that have sinned.

HAROLD DE WOLF, *Theology of the Living Church,* 1953

The real God is the relentless One who pursues us and gives us no peace until our religiosity is transformed by repentance.

A. ROY ECKARDT, *Christian Century,* November 17, 1954

See also Communion; Compassion; Confession; Conscience; Contrition; Forgiveness; Grace; Mercy; Penitence; Sin; Sinners.

REPOSE

God offers to every mind its choice between truth and repose. Take which you please,—you can never have both.

RALPH WALDO EMERSON, "Intellect," *Essays, First Series,* 1841

See also Rest; Sleep.

REPRESSION

The popular idea that the restraint of basic emotional drives is in itself unhealthy is nonsense. Such restraint is compelled by the emotional drives themselves.

HARRY EMERSON FOSDICK, *On Being a Real Person,* 1943

With few exceptions Western religion has insisted that men and women can become good only through the stern repression of sensual thoughts and impulses. This mechanism of repression by which we mute the horrid voice of "sin" is responsible for much of the grief, illness, and anxiety that lash the soul of modern men.

JOSHUA LOTH LIEBMAN, *Peace of Mind,* 1946

Our Christian education, our asceticism and striving for perfection tend all too much to repress and eliminate the natural soul. There is still no affirmation of our total human nature; the deeper levels of the soul are still excluded from Christian penetrations.

JOSEF GOLDBRUNNER, *Holiness Is Wholeness,* 1955

See also Celibacy; Chastity; Continence; Desires; Discipline; Lust; Sensuality; Sexual Desire; Virginity.

REPRODUCTION

Our genital organs were given us, as their name implies, in order that we might beget the next generation. This divine law we must devoutly obey.

LACTANTIUS, *The Divine Institutes,* c. 310 A.D.

Reproduction . . . depletes; it is an expense of spirit, a drag on physical and mental life; it entangles rather than liberates; it fuses the soul again into the impersonal, blind flux.

GEORGE SANTAYANA, *Reason in Society,* 1906

Reproduction seems to be the only field where private enterprise always triumphs. Historically, governments and churches have had remarkably little success in influencing breeding habits.

Time, January 11, 1961

See also Birth Control; Marriage; Sexual Intercourse.

REPUTATION

Good name in man and woman, dear my lord,

Is the immediate jewel of their souls:
Who steals my purse steals trash; 'tis something, nothing;
'Twas mine, 'tis his, and has been slave to thousands;
But he that filches from me my good name
Robs me of that which not enriches him,
And makes me poor indeed.

WILLIAM SHAKESPEARE, *Othello,* c. 1604

In vain we compute our felicities by the advantage of our good names, since both have equal duration.

THOMAS BROWNE, *Urn Burial,* 1658

Do you wish people to believe good of you? Don't speak.

BLAISE PASCAL, *Pensées,* 1670

See also Calumnies; Fame; Gossip; Honor; Oblivion; Office.

RESEARCH

The only deeply religious people of our largely materialistic age are the earnest men of research.

ALBERT EINSTEIN, *Cosmic Religion,* 1931

There is less difference than people think between research and adoration. . . . However far knowledge pushes its discovery of the "essential fire" and however capable it becomes some day of remodelling and perfecting the human element, it will always find itself in the end facing the same problem—how to give each and every element its final value by grouping them in the unity of an organized whole.

PIERRE TEILHARD DE CHARDIN, *The Phenomenon of Man,* 1959

RESIGNATION

To serve one's own heart so as to permit neither joy nor sorrow within, but to cultivate resignation to the inevitable,—this is the climax of Virtue.

CHUANG TZU, c. 300 B.C.

He who has calmly reconciled his life to fate, and set proud death beneath his feet, can look fortune in the face, unbending both to good and bad; his countenance unconquered he can show.

BOETHIUS, *Consolations of Philosophy,* c. 525 A.D.

God will work out His purification in us, as long as we freely give our consent by means of resignation.

M. MOLINOS, *Spiritual Guide,* I, vii, 1675

The great thing is to resign all your interests and pleasures and comfort and fame to God. He who unreservedly accepts whatever God may give him in this world —humiliation, trouble, and trial from within or from without—has made a great step towards self-victory.

FRANÇOIS FÉNELON (1651–1715), *Letters to Women*

Resignation is confirmed desperation.

HENRY DAVID THOREAU, *Walden,* 1854

Resignation is a virtue which religion and philosophy alike inculcate; but there is need of watchfulness lest it degenerate into indifference, sloth, negligence, and insensibility; and this danger hides also in humility, obedience, and patience.

JOHN LANCASTER SPALDING, *Glimpses of Truth,* 1903

The attitude of resignation which the disinherited have imbibed with mother's milk is the difficult achievement of the middle-class man.

H. RICHARD NIEBUHR, *Social Sources of Denominationalism,* 1929

The readiness to meet the supreme test by dying in patient endurance so that the good may be realized does not exclude the willingness to fight and to attack.

JOSEF PIEPER, *Fortitude and Temperance,* 1954

Centuries ago Christian resignation everywhere went toward the scaffold and the stake with head held high, burning eyes, and hands soberly crossed over the heart. Today it sits by the corner of a fire which does not even warm it, with hanging hands and vacant eyes.

GEORGES BERNANOS, *Last Essays of,* 1966

See also Abandonment; Acceptance; Detachment; Humility; Obedience; Patience; Self-Giving; Selflessness; Serenity; Submission; Suffering.

RESPECT

Tolerance is in itself a vicious word; the term "respect" would be much better. Respect for the sacred personality and natural rights of all men, even while rejecting their errors of mind or life, serves to eradicate vicious antagonisms without surrendering of beliefs or principles.

IGNATIUS SMITH, *Perspectives on a Troubled Decade,* ed. Bryson, Finklestein and MacIver, 1950

See also Reverence; Self-Respect; Tolerance.

RESPECTABILITY

An envious, stingy, dishonest man does not become respectable by means of much talking only, or by the beauty of his complexion.

Dhammapada, c. 5th century B.C.

In its great hours, Christianity has never been "respectable." It was one of the deadly charges against Jesus that he was the friend of sinners and ate with publicans and other riffraff.

HALFORD E. LUCCOCK, *Living Without Gloves,* 1957

The trouble with modern civilization is that we so often mistake respectability for character.

ANONYMOUS

RESPONSIBILITY

No good is served by a long inquiry as to who are the causes of these evils, seeing that we cannot even name any other causes but ourselves.

REGINALD POLE, *Address,* Second Session, Council of Trent, January, 1546

Before the tribunal of God's mercy, we, the shepherds, should make ourselves responsible for all the evils now burdening the flock of Christ.

REGINALD POLE, *Address,* Second Session, Council of Trent, January, 1546

See also Choice; Duties; Free Will; Freedom; Guilt; Individual Responsibility.

REST

Why dost thou look to have rest here since this is not thy resting place? Thy full rest must be in heavenly things.

THOMAS À KEMPIS, *Imitation of Christ,* 1441

See also Repose; Sleep.

RESTITUTION

Restitution: The founding or endowing of universities and public libraries by gift or bequest.

AMBROSE BIERCE, *Devil's Dictionary,* 1906

RESTLESS

Thou hast made us for Thyself, O Lord, and our hearts are restless until they rest in Thee.

ST. AUGUSTINE, *Confessions of,* 397

RESULTS

Reverence the simple, the prosaic, the natural, the real, but demand of every common thing of life, whether it be your body or your money or your daily experience, that it shall bloom into fine results in your own soul and in your influence upon the world.

PHILLIPS BROOKS, *Perennials,* 1898

See also Pragmatism.

RESURRECTION

The dead shall rise, life shall return to the bodies, and they shall breathe again. . . . The whole physical world shall become free from old age and death, from corruption and decay, forever and ever.

Zend-Avesta, 6th century B.C.

Let us consider, beloved, how the Lord is continually revealing to us the resurrection that is to be. Of this He has constituted the Lord Jesus Christ the first-fruits, by raising Him from the dead.

ST. CLEMENT OF ROME, *Letter to the Corinthians,* c. 100

Let none of you say that this flesh is not judged and does not rise again . . . for as you were called in the flesh, you shall also come in the flesh.

ST. CLEMENT OF ROME, *Second Epistle to the Corinthians,* c. 100

He who maintains that the resurrection is not a biblical doctrine has no share in the world to come.

Mishna: Sanhedrin, 10.1, c. 200 A.D.

At the day of Resurrection the glory of the Holy Spirit *comes out from within,* decking and covering the bodies of the saints— the glory which they had before, but hidden within their souls.

Attributed to St. Macarius (300–390), but possibly as late as the fifth century *Homilies of Macarius*

Yet that bodies of all men—both those who have been born and those who shall be born, both those who have died and those who shall die—shall be raised again, no Christian ought to have the shadow of a doubt.

St. Augustine, *Enchiridion,* 421

The life and spirit of all our actions is the resurrection, and a stable apprehension that our ashes shall enjoy the fruits of our pious endeavors; without this, all religion is a fallacy.

Thomas Browne, *Religio Medici,* 1635

What reason have atheists for saying that we cannot rise again? Which is the more difficult, to be born, or to rise again? That what has never been, should be, or that what has been, should be again? Is it more difficult to come into being than to return to it?

Blaise Pascal, *Pensées,* 1670

Earth to earth, ashes to ashes, dust to dust, in sure and certain hope of the Resurrection unto eternal life.

Book of Common Prayer (American version), first published 1876

The whole history of the Christian life is a series of resurrections. . . . Every time a man finds his heart is troubled, that he is not rejoicing in God, a resurrection must follow; a resurrection out of the night of troubled thought into the gladness of the truth.

George MacDonald (1824–1905), *Selections from,* ed. Dewey

There is a monastic order today called "The Community of the Resurrection." It would be a good name for the whole church.

Robert McAfee Brown, *The Significance of the Church,* 1958

It is not belief in some vague intangible essence, but the re-establishment of personal life on the farther side of the grave, the conviction that the total personality, invested by God with a perfect organism, lives on.

Robert J. McCracken, *Sermon,* March 29, 1964

See also Body; Body and Soul; Death; Easter; Immortality; Immortality; Belief in; Incarnation; Jesus Christ: His Passion and Death; Jesus Christ: His Resurrection; Salvation; Unitarians.

RETIREMENT

When your work is done and fame has been achieved, then retire into the background; for this is the Way of Heaven.

Lao-tzu, *The Sayings of,* c. 500 B.C.

REUNION

There can be no fulfillment of the divine purpose in any scheme of reunion which does not ultimately include the great Latin Church of the West.

Lambeth Conference of Anglican Bishops, 1908 (and repeated in 1920, 1930 and 1948)

With persevering prayer to the Spirit of love and truth We wait for them with open arms to return not to a stranger's house, but to their own, their Father's house.

Pope Pius XII, *Mystici Corporis,* 1943

This excellent work of "reunion" of all Christians in the one true Faith and Church should become daily more integrated as a distinguished part of the universal pastoral charge and be made an object of concern which the whole Catholic people take to heart and recommend to God in fervent supplication.

Instruction of the Sacred Congregation of the Holy Office to Local Ordinaries, December 20, 1949

We can speak of the reunion of Christendom, but we cannot with theological accuracy speak of the reunion of the Church. If the Church of Christ does not now exist in the world, then there is nothing we can do to bring it into being.

Aelred Graham, *Christian Thought and Action,* 1951

Often it is not theology but popular piety (on both sides) which stands in the way of reunion.

> HANS KÜNG, *The Council, Reform and Reunion,* 1961

We ask of our separated brothers only that which we set before ourselves as our objective, namely that every step toward reunion and interchange of views should be inspired by love of Christ and the Church.

> POPE PAUL VI, *Address,* Holy Land, January 6, 1964

The thorniest item—as it always is, in reunion plans, the issue of bishops. When everything else has been worked out, this is the area in which Protestant plans of reunion almost invariably founder and finally sink.

> ROBERT MCAFEE BROWN, *Commonweal,* June 11, 1965

See also Ecumenism; Reconciliation; Unity.

REVELATION

Those who deny Revelation shall not enter Paradise until the camel goes through the eye of a needle.

> *Koran,* c. 625 A.D.

If the adversary do but grant any portion of the divine revelation, we have an argument against him; thus, against a heretic we can employ Scripture authority, and against those who deny one article we can use another. But if our opponent reject divine revelation entirely, there is no way left to prove the Article of Faith by reasoning.

> ST. THOMAS AQUINAS, *Summa Theologiae,* p. I, q. 1, a. 8, 1272

Even as regards those truths about God which human reason could have discovered, it was necessary that man should be taught by a divine revelation; because the truth about God such as reason could discover would only be known by a few, and that after a long time, and with the admixture of many errors.

> ST. THOMAS AQUINAS, *Summa Theologiae,* I, q. 1, a. 2, 1272

Private revelations . . . do not form a part of Catholic faith. . . . Hence, there is no obligation for the faithful to believe them. Even when the Church approves them, she does not make them the object of Catholic faith.

> ADOLPH TANQUERAY, *Spiritual Life,* 1490

There was plainly wanting a divine revelation to recover mankind out of their universal corruption and degeneracy, and without such a revelation it was not possible that the world should ever be effectually reformed.

> SAMUEL CLARKE, *Discourse Concerning the Unchangeable Obligations of Natural Religion,* 1705

A revelation is to be received as coming from God, not because of its internal excellence, or because we judge it to be worthy of God; but because God has declared it to be His in as plain and undeniable a manner as He has declared creation and providence to be His.

> WILLIAM LAW, *The Case of Reason or Natural Religion Fairly and Fully Stated,* 1731

If you say you have a revelation from God, I must have a revelation from God too before I can believe you.

> BENJAMIN WHICHCOTE, *Aphorisms,* 1753

What education is to the individual, revelation is to the whole human race.

> G. E. LESSING, *Education of the Human Race,* 1780

No revelation can be complete and systematic, from the weakness of the human intellect; *so far as* it is not such, it is mysterious. . . . A Revelation is religious doctrine viewed on its illuminated side; a Mystery is the selfsame doctrine viewed on the side unilluminated.

JOHN HENRY NEWMAN, *Essays and Sketches,* Vol. I, 1838

Revelation consists in the manifestation of the Invisible Divine Power, or in the substitution of the voice of a Lawgiver for the voice of conscience.

JOHN HENRY NEWMAN, *An Essay on the Development of Christian Doctrine,* 1845

Revelation is all in all in doctrine; the Apostles its sole depository, the inferential method its sole instrument, and ecclesiastical authority its sole sanction. The Divine Voice has spoken once and for all, and the only question is about its meaning.

JOHN HENRY NEWMAN, *The Idea of a University,* 1852

The Book of God is not closed. The coming generations are not disinherited. . . . Revelation, which is, as Lessing says, the education of the human race, descends continuously from God to man.

GIUSEPPE MAZZINI, *The Duties of Man and Other Essays,* 1858

If we believe in the revelation, we believe in what is revealed, in all that is revealed, however it may be brought home to us, by reasoning or in any other way.

JOHN HENRY NEWMAN, *Grammar of Assent,* 1870

In order that the obedience of our faith might be in harmony with reason, God willed that to the interior help of the Holy Spirit, there should be joined exterior facts, and especially miracles and prophecies.

Vatican Council, Session III, 1870

The Rule of Faith once lost, souls wander and perish. The effect of this is that men have come to state, as scientifically certain, that there is no definite doctrine in revelation.

HENRY EDWARD MANNING, *Lectures of,* 1872

I gradually came to disbelieve in Christianity as a divine revelation . . . and have never since doubted even for a single second that my conclusion was correct.

CHARLES DARWIN (1809–1882), *Autobiography of*

Revelation is not so much *from* God as *of* God.

THEODORE T. MUNGER, *The Freedom of Faith,* 1883

He who does not believe that revelation is continuous does not believe in revelation at all.

GEORGE BERNARD SHAW, *The Quintessence of Ibsenism,* 1890

The works I have written in Christian Science contain absolute Truth, and my necessity was to tell it. . . . I was a scribe under orders; and who can refrain from inscribing what God indites?

MARY BAKER EDDY, writing in 1894, *Miscellaneous Writings of*

The revelation in the first century is the supreme warrant for our faith that God is essentially self-revealing and that man can find Him and know Him and become His organ of manifestation.

RUFUS M. JONES, *Social Law in the Spiritual World,* 1904

Current revelation is equally plain with that of former days in predicting the yet future manifestations of God through His appointed channels. The canon of scripture is still open; many lines, many precepts, are yet to be added.

JAMES E. TALMAGE, *Articles of Faith,* 1920

Religion . . . is God revealed by man and not man by God. Our revelation today is from earth to heaven, from clod to God—not vice versa as in the old days.

JOHN HAYNES HOLMES, *Essays Toward Truth*, 1924

Revelation is concerned primarily with conduct and supernatural life and not with speculative answers to speculative questions.

MARTIN C. D'ARCY, *Problem of Evil*, 1928

When God gave us His revelation, with all the terrible responsibility it involved for human souls, He would not leave its genuineness in doubt. He put His seal upon it, and that seal was miracle.

RONALD A. KNOX, *Miracles*, 1928

Revelation is such knowledge of the divine will as cannot be found through submersion in myself or in the secret of the world, but . . . an act of personal self-impartation from outside our own range, in which God gives us himself.

EMIL BRUNNER, *The Word and the World*, 1931

At best God can only reveal Himself to us in terms of our experience in our historic setting. And the revelation that comes to us is to cooperate with God to bring form and order into the world as it is.

J. E. BOODIN, *God and Creation*, 1934

The main claim of revelation is not that the human recipient is made aware by a special method, of a set of truths about God, but the far more exciting claim that he is made aware of *God Himself.*

WILLIAM TEMPLE, *Nature, Man and God*, 1934

To talk of meanings, and hence of symbols and signs, is to talk of revelation, and to talk of revelation is to talk of the conveyance of truth.

EDWIN LEWIS, *A Philosophy of the Christian Revelation*, 1940

Revelation means the moment in our history through which we know ourselves to be known from beginning to end, in which we are apprehended by the knower.

H. RICHARD NIEBUHR, *The Meaning of Revelation*, 1941

It took the first four centuries of the Christian era to prove that without revelation neither the pagan Greek passion for logic and truth nor the pagan Roman genius for law and order could provide mankind with a satisfying culture or a stable civilization.

GERALD G. WALSH, *Thought*, March, 1943

Revelation when genuine is simply the record of the immediate experience of those who are pure enough in heart and poor enough in spirit to be able to see God.

ALDOUS HUXLEY, *The Perennial Philosophy*, 1945

When one has sought long for the clue to a secret of nature, and is rewarded by grasping some part of the answer, it comes as a blinding flash of revelation. . . . This conviction is of something revealed, and not something imagined.

LAWRENCE BRAGG, *Science and the Adventure of Living*, 1950

Theologians must always go back to the sources of divine revelation.

POPE PIUS XII, *Humani Generis*, August, 1950

Revelation is an act whereby God speaks to men through Himself or through His messenger, making a statement the truth of which He guarantees. It is not an interior emotional experience.

WILLIAM J. MCGUCKEN, *The Philosophy of Catholic Education*, 1951

Before reaching us, divine revelation has passed through social contexts whose coloring it tended to assume; and to catch its spirit it is often necessary to relive the past and breathe its atmosphere.

FERDINAND PRAT, *Jesus Christ, Preface,* 1951

The stumbling block of revelation is the belief in God in time, God in history. But this is exactly what theology must affirm: God's revelation is the event of Jesus Christ.

ROGER L. SHINN, *Christianity and the Problems of History,* 1953

In the Scriptures we have the accumulated revelation of the mystery of God, the result of centuries during which God has been revealing Himself and His Word to man.

E. S. WILLIAMS, *Systematic Theology,* 1954

While we recognize the Scriptures as God's revelation, the unfolding of God's Word and will may also be considered revelation.

E. S. WILLIAMS, *Systematic Theology,* 1954

All revelation is given, not in the form of directly communicated knowledge, but through events occurring in the historical experience of mankind, events which are apprehended by faith as the "mighty acts" of God.

JOHN BAILLIE, *The Idea of Revelation in Recent Thought,* 1956

The scientist bridles at the word "revelation," but he could not discover anything, if it were not there already waiting to be found, free gift before it could be discovery.

GEORGE A. BUTTRICK, *Sermons Preached in a University Church,* 1959

The Bible contains revelation, it is the medium by which revelation is made known, but it is not revelation itself.

BRUCE VAWATER, *The Bible in the Church,* 1959

Without prior revelation there could have been no Christian revelation at all. . . . The early Church fathers thought of Christians as the "third people." Revelation, they said, had come in three stages—pagan, Jewish, Christian—each succeeding stage being made possible by the one before.

ALBERT T. MOLLEGEN, *Christianity and Modern Man,* 1961

Revelation is not a series of propositions about God; it is the record of God's acts in time, His often violent intrusions into human history.

PHILIP SCHARPER, *The Critic,* August–September, 1962

See also Belief; Bible; Bible: Its Inspiration; Church: Its Authority; Doctrine; Exclusiveness; Experience, Religious; Faith; God: Finding Him; God: His Intervention in the World; History; Holy Spirit; Immortality; Infallibility; Inspiration; Jesus Christ; Jesus Christ: His Divinity; Man and God; Miracles; Mysteries; Mystery; Nature and God; New Testament; Old Testament; Rationalism; Reason and God; Reason and Religion; Religion; Religion, Natural; Religion, Revealed; Revelation and Reason; Science and Religion; Truth and Religion; Truths, Conflict of; Unbelief; World, the.

REVELATION AND REASON

Revealed truths are above our intelligence, and I would not dare submit them to the feebleness of my reason.

RENÉ DESCARTES, *Discourses,* 1637

Whatever God hath revealed is certainly true: no doubt can be made of it. This is the proper object of faith: but whether it be a *divine* revelation or no, reason must judge.

JOHN LOCKE, *Essay Concerning Human Understanding,* 1690

Revelation is natural reason enlarged by a new set of discoveries communicated by God immediately, which reason vouches the truth of, by the testimony and proof it gives, that they come from God.

JOHN LOCKE, *Essay Concerning Human Understanding,* 1690

He that takes away reason, to make way for revelation, puts out the light of both.

JOHN LOCKE, *Essay on Human Understanding,* Bk. IV, 1690

All our reasonings about revelation are necessarily gathered by our natural notions about religion, and therefore he who sincerely desires to do the will of God is not apt to be imposed on by vain pretenses of divine revelation.

JOHN TILLOTSON (1630–1694), *Sermons*

It is universally acknowledged that revelation itself is to stand or fall by the test of reason.

EDMUND GIBSON, *Second Pastoral Letter,* 1780

A Revelation that will not suffer us to judge for its Dictates by our Reason, is so far from improving Reason, that it forbids the use of it.

MATTHEW TINDAL, *Christianity as Old as Creation,* 1730

The greater stress you lay on Reason, the more you extol Revelation; which being design'd to exalt and perfect our rational Nature, must be itself highly reasonable.

MATTHEW TINDAL, *Christianity as Old as Creation,* 1730

Reason is the only faculty we have wherewith to judge concerning anything, even revelation itself.

JOSEPH BUTLER, *The Analogy of Religion,* 1736

Any person seasoned with a just sense of the imperfections of natural reason, will fly to revealed truth with the greatest avidity.

DAVID HUME, *Dialogues Concerning Natural Religion,* 1779

Revelation does not give anything to the human race which human reason, if left to itself, would not attain; but it has given and still gives the most important of these things earlier.

G. E. LESSING, *Education of the Human Race,* 1780

The transition to a new order of things ought rather to be effected by the principle of a pure religion according to reason, considered as a Divine revelation constantly being made to all men through their reason only.

IMMANUEL KANT, *Religion Within the Limits of Pure Reason,* 1793

Human reasoning, sound as it may be, is still human, while Revelation is the Logos of God, the Eternal speaking in time.

MARTIN C. D'ARCY, *God and the Supernatural,* 1920

Reason and revelation cannot be in conflict because they are on different sides of the gap: revelation is part of that to which we react while reason is part of our reaction.

NELS F. S. FERRÉ, *Faith and Reason,* 1946

If reason were able to find out the truth about God, revelation would not be necessary.

RICHARD KRONER, *Perspectives on a Troubled Decade,* ed. Bryson, Finklestein and MacIver, 1950

The Koran purports to be nothing less than the very word of the all-wise, all-powerful God to humanity, as given (by revelation) through Mohammed—given first "in visions," later in the form of regulations for community living—laws of inheritance, responsibilities in marriage, care of orphans and the helpless.

> CHARLES S. BRADEN, *The Scriptures of Mankind,* 1952

Sacred literatures (of most religions, though not all) are as a usual rule regarded as in some sense the word of God or the gods, revealed to man. In other words they are . . . regarded as inspired books. The degree of inspiration, or the nature of it, varies among the religions, and within any given faith.

> CHARLES S. BRADEN, *The Scriptures of Mankind,* 1952

See also Reason; Reason and Religion; Revelation.

REVENGE

Revenge is the poor delight of little minds.
> JUVENAL, *Satires,* 128 A.D.

The precept "Resist not evil," was given to prevent us from taking pleasure in revenge, in which the mind is gratified by the sufferings of others, but not to make us neglect the duty of restraining men from sin.
> ST. AUGUSTINE, *To Publicola,* 398

O true believers, the law of retaliation is ordained you for the slain: the free shall die for the free, and the servant for the servant, and a woman for a woman.
> *Koran,* c. 625 A.D.

A man that studieth revenge keeps his own wound green.
> FRANCIS BACON, *Essays,* 1597

Revenge is a kind of wild justice, which, the more man's nature runs to, the more ought law to weed it out.
> FRANCIS BACON, *Essays,* 1597

He who wishes to revenge injuries by reciprocated hatred will live in misery.
> BARUCH SPINOZA, *Ethics,* IV, 1677

In taking revenge a man is but even with his enemy; but in passing it over, he is superior.
> THOMAS FULLER, *Gnomologia,* 1732

Revenge is barren. It feeds on its own dreadful self.
> J. C. F. VON SCHILLER, *Wilhelm Tell,* 1804

Ah, God! what trances of torments does that man endure who is consumed with one unachieved revengeful desire.
> HERMAN MELVILLE, *Moby Dick,* 1851

See also Capital Punishment; Forgiveness; Golden Rule; Hatred; Malice.

REVERENCE

I should not say that where fear is there is also reverence. . . . but where reverence is, there is fear.
> SOCRATES, Plato's *Euthyphro,* Vol. III, c. 380 B.C.

Pigs eat acorns, but neither consider the sun that gave them life, nor the influence of the heavens by which they were nourished, nor the very root of the tree from whence they came.
> THOMAS TRAHERNE (1634?–1704), *Centuries of Meditation*

The Jews would not willingly tread upon the smallest scrap of paper in their way, but took it up; for possibly, said they, the name of God may be on it.
> SAMUEL TAYLOR COLERIDGE, *Aids to Reflection,* 1825

The name of God may be written upon that soul thou treadest on.
> SAMUEL TAYLOR COLERIDGE, *Aids to Reflection,* 1825

All real joy and power of progress in humanity depend on finding something to reverence, and all the baseness and misery of humanity begin in a habit of disdain.
> JOHN RUSKIN, *The Crown of Wild Olives,* 1866

There is much in the world that cannot be explained without knowing what came before life and what is to come after it, and of that we know nothing, for faith is not knowledge. All that we can do is to take refuge, in reverence and submission.

EDWARD GREY, *Letter to Margot Asquith,* published in her *Autobiography,* 1922

A man is ethical only when life, as such, is sacred to him, that of plants and animals as that of his fellowman, and when he devotes himself helpfully to all life that is in need of help.

ALBERT SCHWEITZER, *Out of My Life and Thoughts,* 1933

See also Piety; Respect; Wonder.

REVIVALISM

The successful revivalist has learned the art of controlling a congregation as a whole. The unit which he deals with is the crowd, not the individual soul.

Editorial, *Christian Century,* July 1, 1909

Every religious revival is a return to the realization of a direct communion between the human spirit and the Divine.

G. K. HIBBERT, *The Inner Light and Modern Thought,* 1924

The passing of the religious revival from the American scene has deprived our churches . . . of what has been for at least a century the one most familiar means of recruiting the ranks of members.

WILLIARD L. SPERRY, *Religion in America,* 1946

The tendency of the revivalist was to oversimplify theological issues and the ultimate result was to render the faith devoid of content.

W. S. HUDSON, *The Great Tradition of the American Churches,* 1953

A century of revivalism with its progressive simplification of the faith and its tendency to move in a Pelagian direction has largely dismantled the intellectual defenses of historic Protestantism.

W. S. HUDSON, *The Great Tradition of the American Churches,* 1953

Inherent in revivalism is the temptation to stress results and to justify whatever produces them.

W. S. HUDSON, *The Great Tradition of the American Churches,* 1953

See also Communism; Emotion; Evangelism; Evangelists; Preachers; Preaching; Rhetoric; Sermons; Witness.

REVOLT. See REBELLION

REVOLUTION. See REBELLION

REWARD

Verily God does not reward man for what he does, but for what he is.

Chuang-Tzu, c. 300 B.C.

This is our highest reward that we should fully enjoy God, and that all who enjoy Him should enjoy one another in Him.

ST. AUGUSTINE, *De Moribus Ecclesiae,* 368

Since every reward is sought for the reason that it is held to be good, who shall say that the man, that possesses goodness, does not receive his reward?

BOETHIUS, *Consolations of Philosophy,* c. 524

Those who have faith and do good works are the rightful owners of the Garden [of Eden] and will dwell in it.

Koran, c. 625

What reward can there be for one that has passed his whole life, not only without

pleasure, but in pain, if there is nothing to be expected after death.
ST. THOMAS MORE, *Utopia,* 1516

All religions promise a reward . . . for excellences of the *will* or heart, but none for excellences of the head or understanding.
ARTHUR SCHOPENHAUER, *The World as Will and Idea,* II, 1818

Great is the conduct of a man who lets rewards take care of themselves—come if they will or fail to come—but goes on his way, true to the truth simply because it is true, strongly loyal to the right for its pure righteousness.
PHILLIPS BROOKS, *Perennials,* 1898

To demand the good of victory without the existence of an antagonist, is to demand something with no meaning.
WILLIAM TEMPLE, *Mens Creatrix,* 1917

See also Heaven; Immortality; Punishment; Reward and Punishment.

REWARD AND PUNISHMENT

All of us, Greeks and Jews, heretics and Christians acknowledge that God is just. Now many who have sinned passed away without being punished, while many others who led virtuous lives did not die until they had suffered innumerable tribulations. If God is just how will He reward the latter and punish the former unless there be a Hell and a Resurrection?
ST. JOHN CHRYSOSTOM, *Homily on Eph. ad. Phil.,* c. 388

They that have done good shall go into everlasting happiness, and they that have done evil into everlasting fire.
General Council of Constantinople (of Roman Catholic Church), 543

Since it is most certain and undeniable that the happiness of the blessed shall continue forever without mixture of mis-

ery, so likewise shall the unhappiness of the damned continue forever without mixture of comfort.
ROBERT BELLARMINE, *On the Ascent to God,* 1616

A fundamental, and as many believe, the most essential part of Christianity, is its doctrine of reward and punishment in the world beyond; and a religion which has nothing at all to say about this great enigma we should hardly feel to be a religion at all.
G. LOWES DICKINSON, *The Greek View of Life,* 1896

See also Heaven; Hell; Immortality; Immortality, Arguments for; Punishment; Reward.

RHETORIC

We do not set great store by rhetoric or clever argument. The mere gaining of debating points is found to be unhelpful and alien to the spirit of worship which should govern the rightly ordered Meeting.
Statement London Yearly Meeting [of Quakers], 1925

See also Eloquence; Sermons; Speech; Words.

RHYTHM METHOD

The moral licitness of such conduct on the part of the couple would have to be approved or denied according to whether or not the intention of observing those periods constantly was based on sufficient and secure moral grounds.
POPE PIUS XII, *Address to Italian Midwives,* October, 1946

We affirm the legitimacy and, at the same time, the limits—in truth very wide—of a regulation of offspring which, unlike the so-called "birth control," is compatible with the law of God. One may even hope that science will succeed in providing this licit [rhythm] method with a sufficiently secure basis.

POPE PIUS XII, *Address,* November 21, 1951

See also Birth Control; Marriage; Sexual Intercourse.

RICH, THE

Better is a beggar who is in the hand of God, than the rich who are safely housed in a comfortable dwelling.

The Teaching of Amen, c. 1000 B.C., ed. E. A. W. Budge

There are people it is necessary to consider as rich:—one is he who is perfect in wisdom; the second whose body is healthy, and he lives fearlessly; the third, who is content with that which has come; the fourth, he whose destiny is a helper in virtue; the fifth, who is well-famed in the eyes of the sacred beings, and by the tongues of the good; the sixth, whose trust is on this one pure, good religion of the Mazda-worshippers; and the seventh, whose wealth is from honesty.

Menog-i Khrad, Zend-Avesta, c. 700 B.C.

The rich man is not one who is in possession of much, but one who gives much.

ST. JOHN CHRYSOSTOM, *Homilies,* c. 388

How great a judgment, O rich man, do you draw down upon yourself! The people go hungry, and you close your granaries; the people weep, and you turn your finger-ring about. Unhappy man, who have the power but not the will to save so many souls from death.

ST. AMBROSE, *De Nabuthe,* 395

A man is rich in proportion to the number of things he can afford to let alone.

HENRY DAVID THOREAU, *Walden,* 1854

In this world it is not what we take up, but what we give up, that makes us rich.

HENRY WARD BEECHER, *Life Thoughts,* 1858

The man who dies rich dies disgraced.

ANDREW CARNEGIE, 1889, quoted by Dwight Macdonald in *The Ford Foundation*

The rich should tremble at the threatenings of Jesus Christ.

POPE LEO XIII, *Rerum Novarum,* May 15, 1891

If we assume the words of Christ to have meant the very least that they could mean, His words must at the very least mean this—that rich men are not very likely to be morally trustworthy.

G. K. CHESTERTON, *Orthodoxy,* 1908

Heaven must be populated at this moment with the generous rich of every century who gave of their wealth, of their service and even their lives to prove their love of God in the service of their neighbors.

IGNATIUS SMITH, *Christ Today,* 1932

It is impossible for the truly religious man to become rich if what constitutes wealth must in any sense be subtracted from others.

CHRISTIAN GAUSS, *A Primer for Tomorrow,* 1934

There are two kinds of rich men: firstly, rich atheists, who, being rich, understand nothing of religion . . . secondly, the pious rich men, who, being rich, understand nothing of Christianism. So they profess it.

CHARLES PEGUY, *Basic Verities,* 1943

No one has the right to despise the rich until, like Our Lord, he has proven himself free from the passion to possess . . . and then he will not wish to despise any one.

FULTON J. SHEEN, *Way to Happiness,* 1953

See also Almsgiving; Charity; Greed; Poor, the, Possessions; Poverty; Riches; Wealth.

RICHES

As to worldly riches, if you do not possess them, let them not be sought after on earth by doing evil; and if you possess them, let them by good works be paid up in heaven.
　　ST. AUGUSTINE, *To Publicola*, 398

Riches are not from an abundance of worldy goods, but from a contented mind. It is difficult for a man laden with riches to climb the steep path that leadeth to bliss.
　　MOHAMMED (7th century A.D.), *Sayings of, Wisdom of East Series*

We forget that godliness is great riches, and that if we first seek the Kingdom of God all other things will be given unto us. . . . Lasting riches do wait upon them thah are zealous for the advancement of the Kingdom of Christ.
　　RICHARD HAKLUYT, *Divers Voyages Touching the Discovery of America,* 1582

We need greater virtues to sustain good than evil fortune.
　　LA ROCHEFOUCAULD, *Maxims,* 1665

It is not a sin to have riches, but it is a sin to fix our hearts upon them.
　　ST. JOHN BAPTIST DE LA SALLE, *Les devoirs du chrétien,* 1710

If Heaven had looked upon riches to be a valuable thing, it would not have given them to such a scoundrel.
　　JONATHAN SWIFT, *Letter to Miss Vanhomrigh,* August 12, 1720

If your riches are yours, why don't you take them with you to t'other world.
　　BENJAMIN FRANKLIN, *Poor Richard's Almanac,* 1758

Riches ennoble a man's circumstances, but not himself.
　　IMMANUEL KANT, *Lecture at Königsberg,* 1775

Man is the only animal which esteems itself rich in proportion to the number and voracity of its parasites.
　　GEORGE BERNARD SHAW, *The Socialism of,* ed. J. Fuchs, 1926

Genuine Christianity teaches men not so much how to make and save riches as to how to get rid of them with the greatest possible advantage to their eternal salvation.
　　IGNATIUS SMITH, *Christ Today,* 1932

It is not a crime to be rich, nor a virtue to be poor. . . . The sin lies in hoarding wealth and keeping it from circulating freely to all who need it.
　　CHARLES FILLMORE, *Prosperity,* 1940

Not a single outstanding teacher of moral wisdom has failed to warn that riches tend to isolate their owners, make them petty, vulnerable, a little ridiculous.
　　BERNARD IDDINGS BELL, *A Man Can Live,* 1947

See also Almsgiving; Charity; Covetousness; Desires; Gold; Greed; Mammon; Money; Ownership; Poor, the; Possessions; Poverty; Profit; Property; Rich, the; Success; Usury.

RIGHT

Better than one who knows what is right is one who is fond of what is right; and better than one who is fond of what is right is one who delights in what is right.
　　CONFUCIUS, *Analects of,* c. 5th century B.C.

Extremity of right is wrong.
　　JOHN CLARKE, *Paroemiologia Anglo-Latina,* 1639

One truth is clear: whatever is, is right.
　　ALEXANDER POPE, *An Essay on Man,* 1732

Nothing else but whatever reason certainly acknowledges as a sure and concise means of attaining happiness, and approves as such.

> JEAN J. BURLAMAQUI, *Works of,* I, 1763

Nature in an absolute manner wills that right should at length obtain the victory.

> IMMANUEL KANT, *Perpetual Peace,* 1795

Let us have faith that right makes might; and in that faith let us dare to do our duty as we understand it.

> ABRAHAM LINCOLN, *Speech,* New York City, February 21, 1859

See also Absolutes; Certainty; Evil; Goodness; Injustice; Justice; Relativity; Right and Wrong; Righteousness; Sin; Virtue.

RIGHT AND WRONG

Right and wrong are the same for all in the same circumstances.

> RICHARD PRICE, *The Principal Questions in Morals,* 1758

So far there has been no known human society in which the distinction between right and wrong, and the obligation to do right, have been denied.

> A. J. TOYNBEE, *A Study of History,* Vol. XII, *Reconsiderations,* 1961

See also Absolutes; Conscience; Determinism; Evil; Goodness; Injustice; Justice; Relativity; Right; Sin.

RIGHTEOUS, THE

In a region bright with golden lustre—center of light and immortality—the righteous after death shall dwell in bliss.

> *Mahabharata,* 800 B.C. to 400 A.D.

If a grain of wheat, buried naked, sprouts forth in many robes, how much more so the righteous!

> MEIR. T. *Sanhedrin,* 90b., c. 150 A.D.

Righteousness is this: whosoever believeth in God, and the Last Day, and the angels, and the Book, and the Prophets; and whosoever, for the love of God, giveth of his wealth unto his kindred, unto orphans, and the poor, and the wayfarer, and to the beggar, and for the release of captives . . . and who are patient in adversity . . . these are the righteous.

> *Koran,* ii, c. 625

The question is, not how we can be righteous, but how, though unrighteous and unworthy, we can be considered as righteous.

> JOHN CALVIN, *Institutes,* II, 1536

See also Righteousness; Self-Righteous.

RIGHTEOUSNESS

Let not the nation count wealth as wealth; let it count righteousness as wealth.

> CONFUCIUS, *Great Learning,* 5th century B.C.

I like life, and I also like righteousness. If I cannot keep the two together, I will let life go and choose righteousness.

> *Works of Mencius,* c. 300 B.C.

The angel of righteousness is delicate and meek and gentle.

> *Shephard of Hermas,* c. 148

Nothing will do except righteousness; and no other conception of righteousness will do, except Christ's conception of it.

> MATTHEW ARNOLD, *Literature and Dogma,* 1873

The humblest citizen of all the land, when clad in the armor of a righteous cause, is stronger than all the hosts of Error.

> WILLIAM JENNINGS BRYAN, *Speech,* 1896

The saint is able to suffer for the sins of a man as though they were his own. To live in the life of others, this alone is righteousness.

MARTIN BUBER, *Jewish Mysticism and the Legends of Baalshem,* 1916

When men look for the victory of righteousness to come without their own bitter sacrifice and the shedding of their own heart's blood, righteousness is always beaten.

W. G. PECK, *The Divine Revolution,* 1927

The righteousness of God means the righteousness that God imparts by his word, the acquittal that frees man of his sin.

RUDOLF BULTMANN, "The Concept of Revelation," 1929, in *Existence and Faith,* ed. S. M. Ogden

See also Dhamma; Forgiveness; Good; Goodness; Justification; Pharisee; Prophets; Selflessness; Self-Righteousness; Vanity.

RIGHTS

Should anyone turn aside the right of the stranger, it is as though he were to turn aside the right of the most high God.

Hagigah, Talmud, c. 500

Natural rights simply mean interests which we think ought to be satisfied. It is perfectly true that neither law nor state creates them. But it is fatal to all sound thinking to treat them as legal conceptions.

ROSCOE POUND, *The Spirit of the Common Law,* 1921

A natural right is a claim justified in the absence of government and positive law.

RALPH BARTON PERRY, *Puritanism and Democracy,* 1944

[Natural rights are] moral claims to those spheres of action which are necessary for the welfare of the individual and the development of his personality.

M. S. BATES, *Religious Liberty: An Inquiry,* 1945

The unity of the human race under God is not broken by geographical distance or by diversity of civilization, culture and economy, and the adequate use of the world's resources by all peoples is not to be denied because of these factors.

Declaration of Rights, Committee Appointed by National Catholic Welfare Council, February, 1947

The right to serve God or fulfill the moral law is the most basic of all rights and includes in it all the other rights. It could also be called the right to the pursuit of happiness.

CATHOLIC ASSOCIATION FOR INTERNATIONAL PEACE, *Timeless Rights,* 1948

[Natural rights are] the conception of the nature of a man—his needs, reactions, and capacities—and of the arrangements he needs in order to fulfill his individual nature and to do his job in society.

JOHN MAURICE CLARK, *Alternative to Serfdom,* 1948

Only if we believe that men have been endowed by their Creator, by nature and nature's God, with an inalienable core within their being which defies trespass or human dominion over them, is there basic assurance of human rights.

PAUL RAMSEY, *Nine Modern Moralists,* 1962

The Declaration of Independence affirms that all men have been endowed by their Creator with certain inalienable rights. . . . The Charter of Human Rights of the United Nations is content with the statement that these rights have simply been endowed upon man—presumably by nothing and no one at all! Derived from the fullness of nonentity, suspended from vacancy, grounded in the grandeur of nothing, it is no wonder that human rights are fast running out.

PAUL RAMSEY, *Nine Modern Moralists,* 1962

A major element of our heritage has been the translation of the rights of man, conferred by God, into civil rights, guaranteed by the state.

ROMAN CATHOLIC BISHOPS OF U.S., *Bonds of Union,* November, 1963

Your neighbor's right is God's right.
Turkish Proverb

See also Coercion; Conscience; Conscience and Law; Conscience and State; Education, Catholic; Education, Parochial; Education, Parents' Rights in; Freedom, Religious; Freedom of Thought and Speech; Individualism; Justice; Liberties; Moral Law; Natural Law; Negroes; Poor, the; Property; Race; Racial Equality; Totalitarianism; War, Just; War, Unjust.

RIGIDITY

We can imagine fewer illusions of more potential danger to the Church than the notion that what was successful at one moment in Church history must be, for that reason, institutionalized in a permanent and unchanging fashion.

RICHARD J. CUSHING, *Statement to the Catholic Laity,* June, 1963

See also Institutionalism.

RISK

For without risk there is no faith, and the greater the risk, the greater the faith.

SÖREN KIERKEGAARD, *Postscript* to *Philosophical Fragments,* 1846

There is an element of venture or risk in every statement of the truth. Yet we can take this risk in the certainty that this is the only way in which truth can reveal itself to finite and historical beings.

PAUL TILLICH, *The Protestant Era,* I, 1948

See also Belief; Calculation; Doubt; Safety.

RITUAL

We ought to do in due order all things which the Lord hath commanded us to perform at appointed times. The offerings and services he has commanded to be performed carefully, and not to be done in a haphazard or disorderly way, but at fixed times and season.

ST. CLEMENT OF ROME, *First Epistle to the Corinthians,* c. 100

When Christianity turned its deepest interest from ethical conduct to sacramental ritual, it thereby paralyzed its power of moral transformation.

WALTER RAUSCHENBUSCH, *Christianity and the Social Crisis,* 1907

Marvelous service! It was the voice of the Church itself, waking at last from its contemplation and turning to tell us what it had learned. There was the ring of eternity in it. But there was also the pulse of time and the human accent.

ZEPHRINE HUMPHREY, *The Edge of the Woods and Other Papers,* 1913

The foundations and institutes, just as once the new Christian chapels and congregations stood side by side with pagan temples and heathen shrines, may oust their rivals, and assume the monopoly of ritual.

LOUIS BERMAN, *The Glands and Human Personality,* 1921

Any religion . . . is for ever in danger of petrifaction into mere ritual and habit, though ritual and habit be essential to religion.

T. S. ELIOT, 1927, *Selected Essays, 1917–1932*

Granted that ritual in any realm from courtesy to worship can become formal, empty, and stiff. Nevertheless, with all its dangers it is an absolute necessity. We cannot . . . train children in the spirit of religion if the appropriate activities of worship and devotion are forgotten.

HARRY EMERSON FOSDICK, *World's Work,* February, 1929

Difference of rite ought not to involve differences of faith.

CHRISTOPHER DAWSON, *The Judgment of the Nations,* 1942

It needs to be emphasized that ritual is not religion, but only a recognition of the importance of religion, and an aid to the formal observance of it,—a technique of organized religion.

HAROLD SCOTT, *Theological Terms in the Light of Modern Scholarship,* 1944

When the ritual has ceased to be a routine ritual for the priest, it will cease to be a mumbo-jumbo formula for the laity. Love will beget love.

LEE J. TRESE, *Commonweal,* June 4, 1947

Ritual may be man-made in the sense that human hands fashioned it. But what inspired those hands to do their work is the Divine Influence.

BEN ZION BOKSAR, *Perspectives on a Troubled Decade,* ed. Bryson, Finklestein and MacIver, 1950

It is not necessary that rites and ceremonies in all places be the same, or exactly alike; for they have always been different, and may be changed according to the diversity of countries, times and men's manners.

Doctrines and Discipline of the Methodist Church, 1952

The Jewish ritual is the expression of the history of a people that, when faithful to Judaism, sees history as a manifestation of God's will.

MAURICE SAMUEL, *The Professor and the Fossil,* 1956

Brahmanism thus sagely resolves the Western dispute as to the necessity or advisability of ritual. It affirms it for those who have not attained the end of all ritual. It lessens and refines ritual as spiritual progress is made upwards; it dispenses with it altogether when there is no longer need for it.

JOHN WOODROFFE, *Sakiti and Säkta,* 1959

The fact, however, that Christian ritual and its accompanying theology is a *living* culture pattern gives it a functional value as a rallying point of the emotions, hopes and fears of mankind through two thousand years of religious experience.

E. O. JAMES, *Christian Faith and Ritual: A Historical Study,* 1965

The most obvious "change" in the Constitution on the Sacred Liturgy [of the Roman Catholic Church] is the switch from Latin to the vernacular. It may be argued, and rightly, that this is merely the restoration of an ancient tradition, but, given the continuity of the Latin Mass for seven or eight centuries, the switch to the vernacular is at least a vivid psychological change.

ALBERT C. DUTLER, *Address,* January 26, 1966

See also Church: Its Authority; Devotion; Eucharist; Liturgy; Music; Ritualism; Sacraments; Unity.

RITUALISM

Ritualism, n. A Dutch Garden of God where He may walk in rectilinear freedom, keeping off the grass.

AMBROSE BIERCE, *Devil's Dictionary,* 1906

See also Ritual.

RIVALRY

How can the church call men to the worship of one God, if it calls them to rival shrines?

WILLIAM TEMPLE, *Address,* Conference of Faith and Order, August, 1937

See also Denominationalism; Division; Ecumenism; Paths; Sects and Sectarianism; Unity.

ROGUES

Men who are rogues in detail are very honest taken together; they love morality.
CHARLES DE MONTESQUIEU, *The Spirit of the Laws,* 1748

ROMAN CATHOLIC CHURCH

The Roman Church, as the mother and mistress of all the faithful, obtains primacy of jurisdiction over all other Churches.
Fourth Council of Lateran, 1215

The history of the Church joins together the two great ages of human civilization. No other institution is left standing which carries the mind back to the times when the smokes of sacrifice rose from the Pantheon, and when camelopards and tigers bounded in the Flavian amphitheatre. The proudest royal houses are but of yesterday, when compared with the line of the supreme Pontiffs.
THOMAS BABINGTON MACAULAY, *Essay on Ranke's "History of the Popes,"* 1839

She saw the commencement of all the governments and of all the ecclesiastical establishments that now exist in the world; and we feel no assurance that she is not destined to see the end of them all.
THOMAS BABINGTON MACAULAY, *Essay on Ranke's "History of the Popes,"* 1839

She may still exist in undiminished vigor when some traveler from New Zealand shall, in the midst of a vast solitude, take his stand on a broken arch of London Bridge to sketch the ruins of St. Paul's.
THOMAS BABINGTON MACAULAY, *Essay on Ranke's "History of the Popes,"* 1839

See also Catholicism.

ROMANCE

And it is this will that stirs in us to have the creatures of earth and the affairs of earth, not as they are, but "as they ought to be," which we call romance. But when we note how visibly it sways all life we perceive that we are talking about God.
JAMES BRANCH CABELL, *Beyond Life,* 1919

See also Love; Love, Human; Love, Physical; Marriage; Sex.

ROOTLESSNESS

The individual simply drifts, anxiously awaiting the shock of events which will determine his tomorrow. Having kicked over, first Christianity, and then the bourgeois code, he lives without benefit of a standard of values to which these events might be referred.
FRANKLIN LEV. BAUMER, *Main Currents of Western Thought,* 1956

See also Godlessness; Irreligion.

ROSARY

The length of time during which mind and heart shall rest on God is measured . . . by the circling of the beads through hands that pray and the wreathing of Paters and Aves by lips that love.
VINCENT McNABB, *The Wayside: A Priest's Gleanings,* 1916

See also Prayer.

ROYALTY

We have established by the Scriptures that royalty has its origin in divinity itself.
JACQUES BOSSUET, *La Politique Tirée,* 1679

See also Class Distinctions; Divine Right of Kings; Kings; Nobility.

RUIN

All men that are ruined are ruined on the side of their natural propensities.

EDMUND BURKE, *Letters on a Regicide Peace,* 1797

The road to ruin is always kept in good repair.

ANONYMOUS

RULE

Rule by love.

Mencius, c. 300 B.C.

The right to rule is not necessarily bound up with any special mode of government. It may become this or that form provided only that it be of a nature to ensure the general welfare.

POPE LEO XIII, *The Christian Constitution of States,* 1885

See also Authority; Government; Kings; Law; Rulers; State, the.

RULERS

Ye rulers on Earth, fear the rulers in Heaven.

AESCHYLUS (525–456 B.C.), *Cheophoras*

Though a prince need not possess all the virtues, to seem to have them is useful.

NICCOLÒ MACHIAVELLI, *The Prince,* 1513

A prince cannot observe all those things which are considered good in men, being often obliged, in order to maintain the state, to act against faith, against charity, against humanity, and against religion.

NICCOLÒ MACHIAVELLI, *The Prince,* 1513

It is far otherwise with divine and natural laws. All the princes of the earth are subject to them, and cannot contravene them without treason and rebellion against God. His yoke is upon them, and they must bow their heads in fear and reverence before His divine majesty.

JEAN BODIN, *The Six Books of the Republic,* 1579

If those who are in authority rule unjustly, if they govern overbearingly or arrogantly, and if their measures prove hurtful to the people, they must remember that the Almighty will one day bring them to account, the more strictly in proportion to the sacredness of their office and preeminence of their dignity.

POPE LEO XIII, *The Christian Constitution of States,* 1885

See also Allegiance; Authority; Church and State; Dictatorship; Disobedience; Divine Right of Kings; Freedom, Religious; Government; Government and God; Government and Religion; Kings; Law; Natural Law; Obedience; Royalty; Rule; Tyrants.

RUSSIA. See SOVIET RUSSIA

SABBATH

He who observes the Sabbath because the work of creation was finished on it acknowledges the creation itself. He who believes in creation believes in the Creator.

JUDAH HALEVI, *Cuzari,* II, c. 1135

The Sabbath is the choicest fruit and flower of the week, the Queen whose coming changes the humblest home into a palace.

JUDAH HALEVI, *Cuzari,* c. 1135

The Sabbath has been instituted as an opportunity for fellowship with God, and for glad, not austere, service of Him.

JUDAH HALEVI, *Cuzari,* c. 1135

The Sabbath is the great organ of the divine administration—the only means provided by God to give ubiquity and power to his moral government.

LYMAN BEECHER (1775–1863), *Works,* I, 332

Has it ever struck you that the trouts bite best on the Sabbath? God's critters tempting decent men.

JAMES M. BARRIE, *The Little Minister,* 1891

The Sabbath, which a critical age might justify on hygienic grounds, is inconceivable without a religious sanction.

GEORGE SANTAYANA, *The Life of Reason, Reason in Religion,* 1905

All the moral doctrines of Judaism may be grouped around the idea of Sabbath.

JUDAH L. MAGNES, *Gleanings,* 1911

This is the meaning of the Jewish Sabbath, to give to man peaceful hours, hours completely diverted from everyday life, seclusion from the world in the midst of the world.

LEO BAECK, *Essence of Judaism,* 1936

"And God blessed the seventh day and made it holy" (Gen. 2:3). There is no reference in the record of creation to any object in space that would be endowed with the quality of holiness. . . . It seems as if to the Bible it is *holiness in time,* the Sabbath, which comes first.

A. J. HESCHEL, *The Sabbath,* 1951

The Sabbaths are our great cathedrals.

A. J. HESCHEL, *The Sabbath,* 1951

The Sabbath is the visible sign of the insufficiency of the material and the need for its re-integration with the spiritual.

L. ROTH, *Jewish Thought,* 1954

See also Day; Days; Sunday; Weekdays.

SACRAMENTS

The spiritual virtue of a sacrament is like light,—although it passes among the impure, it is not polluted.

ST. AUGUSTINE, *Tract on St. John,* c. 416

I must deny the existence of seven sacraments, and must for the time being assert three only, baptism, penance, and the bread.

MARTIN LUTHER, *The Babylonian Captivity,* 1520

An outward and visible sign of an inward and spiritual grace.

The Book of Common Prayer, 1662

The sacraments are the highest feature of religion—the sensuous symbols of an extraordinary divine grace and favor. In holy communion the earthly lips are to receive a divine essence embodied in earthly form. This is its meaning in all Christian churches.

J. W. VON GOETHE, *Autobiography,* II, 1812

The sacraments are nought else than a visible guarantee, authenticated by the word of Jesus and the usage of the apostles, that Jesus is working in the midst of us.

KARL ADAM, *The Spirit of Catholicism,* 1924

In the broad sense of the term everything in the world is a sacrament inasmuch as it is a material thing used as a means of spiritual sanctification.

FULTON J. SHEEN, *The Life of All Living,* 1929

Holy signs and seals of the covenant of grace.

Constitution of the Presbyterian Church in the U.S.A., 1930

The unworthiness of the minister does not make void the Sacraments he administers; since the Sacraments derive their efficacy from the Blood of Christ, independently of the sanctity of the instrument.

Pope Pius XI, *The Catholic Priesthood,* 1935

In Christianity the sacrament between God and man represents a relationship. In Judaism it is only the word, the word of the prayer, or the word of the Bible and tradition that establish a relationship between God and man.

I. Maybaum, *Synagogue and Society,* 1944

We delight to recognize in all the great civilizations their particular foreshadowings for each of our sacraments.

Jean Danielou, *Advent,* 1950

If man's mind and will do not respond to what is presented by the senses, as an occasion for imaginative reminiscence, the Christian sacraments are being abused.

Aelred Graham, *Christian Thought and Action,* 1951

Rites which have the command of God and to which the promise of grace has been added.

Arthur C. Piepkorn, *What the Symbolical Books of the Lutheran Church Have to Say About Worship and the Sacraments,* 1952

Baptism, the Lord's Supper, and Absolution, which is the Sacrament of Repentance, are truly Sacraments.

Arthur C. Piepkorn, *What the Symbolical Books of the Lutheran Church Have to Say About Worship and the Sacraments,* 1952

The Sacraments were not ordained of Christ to be gazed upon, or to be carried about; but that we should duly use them.

Doctrines and Discipline of the Methodist Church, 1952

Sacraments are sometimes a hindrance to spiritual life, in that many people rely upon them rather than upon Christ.

The Salvation Army Handbook of Doctrine, 1955

The sacramental life is the life in which the individual accepts the offering of God's own self through God-chosen means. . . . A life opened up to God and transformed by him is called the sacramental life.

Dora Chaplin, *Living Thankfully,* ed. H. R. Landon, 1961

The purpose of the sacraments is to sanctify men, to build up the body of Christ, and, finally, to give worship to God; because they are signs they also instruct. They not only presuppose faith, but by words and objects they also nourish, strengthen and express it.

Constitution on Sacred Liturgy, Ecumenical Council, Rome, December 4, 1963

See also Baptism; Church, Definitions of; Confession; Confirmation; Eucharist; Grace; Liturgy; Marriage; Mass, the; Ordination; Ritual; Unity.

SACRED, THE

It is precisely the loss of all sacral features in our civilization which has occasioned the resurgence among many today of a primitive sense of the sacred.

P. R. Regamey, *L Art Sacre au xxᵉ Siècle,* 1952

SACRIFICE

For me not personally to be present at a sacrifice, is as if I did not sacrifice.

Confucius, *Analects,* 5th century B.C.

In bringing themselves, worshippers offer the best of sacrifices, the full and truly perfect oblation of noble living.

Philo, *Special Laws,* c. 10 A.D.

The sacrifice most acceptable to God is complete renunciation of the body and its passions. This is the only real piety.
> ST. CLEMENT OF ALEXANDRIA, *De Spectaculis*, c. 200

In so far as man himself, consecrated by God's name and dedicated to God, dies to the world that he may live for God, he is a sacrifice.
> ST. AUGUSTINE, *The City of God*, X, 426

We must offer the Lord whatever interior sacrifice we are able to give Him, and His Majesty will unite it to that which He offered to the Father upon the Cross, so that it will have the value won for it by our will, even though our actions may be in themselves trivial.
> ST. TERESA OF ÁVILA, *The Interior Castle*, 1577

There is no Christian truth so clearly revealed as this, that the spirit of every Christian must be a spirit of sacrifice.
> P. A. SHEEHAN, *Mary, The Mother of God*, 1902

Sacrifice signifies neither amputation nor repentance. It is, in essence, an act. It is the gift of oneself to the being of which one forms a part.
> ANTOINE DE SAINT-EXUPÉRY, *Flight to Arras*, 1942

Nothing that we consider evil can be offered to God in sacrifice. Therefore, to renounce life in disgust is no sacrifice. . . . One of the chief tasks of Christian asceticism is to make our life and our body valuable enough to be offered to God in sacrifice.
> THOMAS MERTON, *No Man Is an Island*, 1955

See also Abandonment; Asceticism; Detachment; Eucharist; Fasting; Mass, the; Renunciation; Self-Denial; Selflessness; Self-Sacrifice; Worship.

SADISM

Sadism is evident even in Christian doctrine, for instance in that of endless punishment in hell.
> NICHOLAS BERDYAEV, *The Fate of Man in the Modern World*, 1935

See also Bloodshed.

SADNESS

Sadness obstructs communion with God.
> BAAL SHEM, *Tzavaat HaBesht*, 1797

Sadness lies at the heart of every merely positivistic, agnostic, or naturalistic scheme of philosophy.
> WILLIAM JAMES, *Varieties of Religious Experience*, 1902

So much pleasure, and so little joy; so much learning, and so little wisdom; . . . the one divine thing left to us is sadness. . . . Without sadness where were brotherliness? . . . She is the Spartan sauce which gives gusto to the remainder-viands of life, the broken meats of love. . . . All things take on beauty which pass through the hueless flame of *her* aureole.
> FRANCIS THOMPSON, *Moestitiae Encomium*, 1910

The great enemy of the soul is not trial but sadness, which is the bleeding wound of self-love.
> F. X. LASANCE, *Remember-Thoughts*, 1936

See also Affliction; Bereavement; Gloom; Grief; Melancholy; Pessimism; Self-Pity; Sorrow; Tears; Tribulations.

SAFETY

A man who is good for anything ought not to calculate the chance of living or dying; he ought only to consider whether in doing anything he is doing right or wrong—acting the part of a good man or a bad.

PLATO, "Apology," *Dialogues,* 399 B.C.

A man who really thought of nothing but getting safe to heaven would be as bad as a man in a shipwreck who thought of nothing but getting himself safe into a boat.

BERNARD BOSANQUET, *Address,* Ethical Society, 1886

There is no temper of the soul more antithetic to New Testament religion than that which plays for safety.

A. VICTOR MURRAY, *Personal Experience and the Historic Faith,* 1939

The consciousness of abiding safety in the bosom of the Church is one of the most serious obstacles to an honest confrontation with the Christian faith.

PETER L. BERGER, *The Precarious Vision,* 1961

See also Calculation; Certainty; Risk.

SAINTS

I contemplate the saints more pleasantly when I envisage them as the teeth of the Church cutting off men from their errors and transferring them to her body after their hardness has been softened as if by being bitten and chewed.

ST. AUGUSTINE, *On Christian Doctrine,* 397

The saints in each generation, joined to those who have gone before, and filled like them with light, become a golden chain, in which each saint is a separate link, united to the next by faith, works, and love.

SYMEON THE NEW THEOLOGIAN (949–1022), *Apophthegmata*

The true saint goes in and out amongst the people, eats and sleeps with them, buys and sells in the market, marries and takes

part in social intercourse, and never forgets God for a single moment.

ABU SAID (died 1049), quoted in T. W. Arnold and A. Guillaume's *The Legacy of Islam*

If, having God, for other goods I faint, Call me what thing you will—but not a saint.

SHAIKH SAADI, *Gulistan,* c. 1265

Saintliness does not come from occupation; it depends upon what one *is.*

MEISTER ECKHART (1260?–1327?), *Meister Eckhart,* R. B. Blakney

The true way to worship the saints is to imitate their virtues.

DESIDERIUS ERASMUS, *Handbook of the Christian Knight,* 1503

For where there are baptism and the gospel no one should doubt that there are saints.

MARTIN LUTHER (1483–1546), *Works,* XXVII, 108

The saints, who reign together with Christ, offer up their own prayers to God for men; . . . it is good and useful suppliantly to invoke them, and to have recourse to their prayers, aid, and help for obtaining benefits from God.

Council of Trent, 1563

To make a saint, it must indeed be by grace; and whoever doubts this does not know what a saint is, or a man.

BLAISE PASCAL, *Pensées,* 1670

The worst of madmen is a saint run mad.

ALEXANDER POPE, *First Epistle of the First Book of Horace,* 1735

One should be fearful of being wrong in religion when one thinks differently from the saints.

JOSEPH JOUBERT, *Pensées,* 1842

If you would in fact have a literature of saints, first of all have a nation of them.

JOHN HENRY NEWMAN, *The Idea of a University*, 1852

When the Spirit of God speaks so plainly to each soul, it were an impiety to be listening to one or another saint.

RALPH WALDO EMERSON, *North American Review*, May, 1878

They are choice patterns of the theological virtues; they all are blessed with a rare and special union with their Maker and Lord. . . . They have the thoughts, feelings, frames of mind, attractions, sympathies, antipathies of other men, so far as these are not sinful, only they have these properties of human nature purified, sanctified, and exalted.

JOHN HENRY NEWMAN, *Sermons on Various Occasions*, 1881

To honor the saints is to honor sanctity; the Church which teaches man to love the holy, helps him to love holiness.

A. M. FAIRBAIRN, *Catholicism, Roman and Anglican*, 1899

In the life of saints, technically so called, the spiritual faculties are strong, but what gives the impression of extravagance proves usually on examination to be a relative deficiency of intellect.

WILLIAM JAMES, *The Varieties of Religious Experience*, 1902

The world is not yet with them, so they often seem in the midst of the world's affairs to be preposterous. Yet they are impregnators of the world, vivifiers and animators of potentialities of goodness which but for them would lie forever dormant.

WILLIAM JAMES, *The Varieties of Religious Experience*, 1902

The history of the saints is mainly the history of insane people.

BENITO MUSSOLINI, *Speech*, July, 1904

Each stands alone, letting his life flow forth in a reckless torrent that is apparently controlled only by the uncontrollable passion of love to God and love to man.

B. W. MATURIN, *The Laws of the Spiritual Life*, 1907

The saints in the spiritual world are like rays of the sun in the material world. God is the eternal, life-giving Sun, and the saints are the rays of this wise Sun.

JOHN SERGIEFF OF CRONSTADT (1829–1908), *My Life in Christ*

It is far more dangerous to be a saint than to be a conqueror.

GEORGE BERNARD SHAW, Preface to *Saint Joan*, 1923

The saints are neither special creations nor spiritual freaks, but those who have learned St. Augustine's aspiration: "My life shall be a real life, being wholly full of Thee."

EVELYN UNDERHILL, *Concerning the Inner Life*, 1926

Saints and mystics are the great teachers of the loving-kindness and fascination of God.

EVELYN UNDERHILL, *Man and the Supernatural*, 1927

"Would you like to be a saint?" I once asked a girl. . . . "yes," was the answer, "only my parents would not like it." The girl did not know that if she had been a saint her parents . . . would have been spell-bound by her saintliness.

ERNEST DIMNET, *What We Live By*, 1932

"It is easy," said Marx, "to be a saint if you have no wish to be human." Then, in fact, you are neither human nor a saint; it is the ancient lie of pharisaism.

JACQUES MARITAIN, *True Humanism*, 1936

The difference between ordinary people and saints is not that saints fulfill the plain duties which ordinary men neglect. The things saints do have not usually occurred to ordinary people at all.

A. D. LINDSAY, *Two Moralities,* 1940

It is remarkable that in the New Testament the name "saint" is almost exclusively used in the plural, saintliness being social in its intrinsic meaning. For the name refers not to any human achievement, but to a gift, to sanctification or consecration.

Man's Disorder and God's Design (Amsterdam Assembly Series), I, 1948

The saint . . . is one who succeeds in giving us at least a glimpse of eternity, despite the thick opacity of time.

HENRI DE LUBAC, *Parodoxes,* 1948

The succession of saints is one of the major evidences that the Eternal Spirit is a continuing and present reality in this strange world.

RUFUS M. JONES, *A Call to What Is Vital,* 1949

The saints were like magnifying glasses, bringing to light the subtle loveliness of whatever came along, whether of nature, of grace, or of art. They were God's showmen.

HUBERT VAN ZELLER, *We Die Standing Up,* 1949

It is a sheer invention of religiosity to depict a saint as a human being who does deeds of spiritual derring-do of which no mere mortal is capable.

CLARE BOOTHE LUCE, *Saints for Now,* 1952

It is never an idle criticism of any account of Christian history to ask "Where are the saints?"

THOMAS J. HIGGINS, *Perfection Is for You,* 1953

A cardinal is recognizable from so far away by his beautiful scarlet cape, while a saint is not in his lifetime distinguishable by the slightest detail of his clothing.

GEORGES BERNANOS, *Last Essays of,* 1955

A hero gives the illusion of surpassing humanity. The saint doesn't surpass it, he assumes it, he strives to realize it in the best possible way.

GEORGES BERNANOS, *Last Essays of,* 1955

Only God knows how many married saints there have been. Perhaps when and if we get to heaven we may find that some of the brightest jewels in His crown are obscure husbands and wives, fathers and mothers, that nobody paid any attention to here on earth.

JOHN C. CORT, *The Grail,* August, 1957

If the first step on Man's road toward sainthood is the renunciation of Man's traditional role of being his brother's murderer, the second step would be an acceptance of Man's new role of being his brother's keeper.

A. J. TOYNBEE, *A Study of History,* Vol. XII, *Reconsiderations,* 1961

One of the chief functions of the saints is to provide us other Christians with proximate living examples of how Christ would apply His thought and action to the specific circumstances of our own vocations.

JOHN J. WRIGHT, *Way,* October, 1962

The saint . . . wants himself to be simply a window through which God's mercy shines on the world. And for this he strives to be holy . . . in order that the goodness of God may never be obscured by any selfish act of his.

THOMAS MERTON, *Life and Holiness,* 1963

It is great to live with the saints in Heaven, but it is hell to live with them on earth.

RICHARD J. CUSHING, *Speech,* Boston, Mass., February, 1964

The authentic cult of the saints consists not so much in the multiplying of external acts, but rather in the greater intensity of our love, whereby for our own greater good and that of the whole Church, we seek from the saints "example in their way of life, fellowship in their communion, and aid by their intercession."

SECOND VATICAN COUNCIL, *Constitution on the Church*, November, 1964

See also America; Blessedness; Christianity; Church, Definitions of; Communion of Saints; Devil; Heretics; Holiness; Martyrdom; Martyrs; Meditation; Saints and Sinners; Sanctity; Sin; Sinners.

SAINTS AND SINNERS

The word *saint* means a man called out from among sinners, and in this sense all good men are saints.

FRANÇOIS FÉNELON (1651–1715), *Spiritual Letters*

A minor saint is capable of loving minor sinners. A great saint loves great sinners.

RABBI ISRAEL BAAL-SHEM TOV (1700–1760), quoted in *Judaism*, ed. A. Hertzberg

God creates out of *nothing*—wonderful, you say; yes, to be sure, but he does what is still more wonderful; he makes saints out of sinners.

SÖREN KIERKEGAARD, *Journal*, July 7, 1838

A saint is a dead sinner, revised and edited.

AMBROSE BIERCE, *The Devil's Dictionary*, 1906

There is no man who is not potentially a saint, and sin or sins, even the blackest, are but accidents that in no way alter the substance.

LEON BLOY, *The Pilgrim of the Absolute*, 1909

Let the saints say what they will, they have a sly liking for strong sinners.

HARRY EMERSON FOSDICK, *On Being a Real Person*, 1943

The sinner holds out a hand to the saint, gives a hand to the saint, since the saint gives a hand to the sinner. And all together, one by means of the other, one pulling up the other, they ascend to Jesus.

CHARLES PEGUY, *Basic Verities*, 1943

Fancy believing in sinners and not believing in saints.

ANISETTA in Aubrey Menen's *The Backward Bride*, 1950

A saint is a sinner who kept on trying.

ANONYMOUS

See also Sanctity; Saints; Sinners.

SALVATION

The process of salvation must come from within.

Dhammapada, c. 5th century B.C.

But they that once professed and recognized that this is the Christ, and for some cause or other passed over into the life under the Law, denying that this is the Christ, and do not repent before death, cannot, I declare, in any wise be saved.

ST. JUSTIN MARTYR, *Dialogue With Trypho*, c. 135

It was, thanks no doubt to heavenly power and aid, that the doctrine of salvation like the rays of the sun, suddenly lighted up the whole world.

EUSEBIUS, *Ecclesiastical History*, c. 192

For the greatest and most regal work of God is the salvation of humanity.

ST. CLEMENT OF ALEXANDRIA, *Paedagogus*, c. 220

If we wish to be saved, let us not, clinging to faith, neglect our conduct, nor, on the other hand, do not let us be too sure of our conduct: it is by both—let us know this, understand this, believe this—that we shall receive acquittal or beatitude, or the contrary.

ORIGEN, *On the Soul,* c. 240

Whosoever parts company with the Church, and joins himself to an adulteress, is estranged from the promises of the Church. He who leaves the Church of Christ, attains not to Christ's rewards. He is an alien, an outcast, an enemy. He can no longer have God for a Father, who has not the Church for a mother.

ST. CYPRIAN, *On the Unity of the Catholic Church,* to the Council at Carthage, 251

Let no one then mistake, let no one deceive himself: . . . outside the Church, no one is saved; he who leaves it is himself responsible for his own death.

ORIGEN (185–254), *Hom.* III, no. 5

There is no inconsistency between creation and salvation; for the one Father has employed the same agent for both works, effecting the salvation of the world through the same Word who made it in the beginning.

ST. ATHANASIUS, *Incarnation of the Word of God,* sec. 1, c. 319

God never draws anyone to Himself by force and violence. He wishes all men to be saved, but forces no one.

ST. JOHN CHRYSOSTOM, *Sermon,* c. 388

The kingdom of death so reigned over men, that the deserved penalty of sin would have hurled all headlong even into the second death, of which there is no end, had not the undeserved grace of God saved some therefrom.

ST. AUGUSTINE, *The City of God,* XIV, 426

Whosoever wishes to be saved, before all things it is necessary that he hold the Catholic faith. And if a man do not keep this faith inviolate and intact, without doubt he will perish.

Athanasian Creed, 5th century

If a man born among infidels and barbarians does what lies in his power God will reveal to him what is necessary for salvation, either in inward inspiration or by sending him a preacher of the faith.

ST. THOMAS AQUINAS, *Summa Theologiae,* 1272

The Church is like the ark of Noah, outside of which nobody can be saved.

ST. THOMAS AQUINAS (1225–1274), *Exposition of the Apostles' Creed*

Every consideration of a man that does not belong to his salvation is full of blindness, and leads down to the darkness of hell.

ROGER BACON (c. 1212–1292), *Opus Majus*

We declare, affirm, define and pronounce that it is altogether necessary for salvation for every creature to be subject to the Roman pontiff.

POPE BONIFACE VIII, *Unam Sanctam,* 1302

That there is one holy catholic and apostolic Church we are compelled to believe and to hold, . . . outside of which there can be no salvation, or remission of sins.

POPE BONIFACE VIII, *Unam Sanctam,* 1302

He desires that all men should be saved . . . and the fault is in the will which does not receive Him. . . . But why the Majesty does not remove or change this fault of will in every man (for it is not in the power of man to do it), or why He lays this fault to the charge of the will, when man cannot avoid it, it is not lawful to ask.

MARTIN LUTHER, *Bondage of the Will,* 1525

God has taken my salvation out of the control of my own will, and put it under the control of His, and promised to save me. . . . I have the comfortable certainty that He is faithful and will not lie to me.

> MARTIN LUTHER, *Bondage of the Will,* 1525

For outside of the Christian Church is no truth, no Christ, no salvation.

> MARTIN LUTHER (1483–1546), *Works,* Vol. X, p. 162

The stars move still, time runs, the clock will strike,
The Devil will come, and Faustus must be damned.
O, I'll leap up to my God! Who pulls me down?
See, see where Christ's blood streams in the firmament!
One drop would save my soul—half a drop; ah, my Christ!

> CHRISTOPHER MARLOWE, *Faustus,* 1601

They whom God hath accepted . . . can neither totally nor finally fall away from the state of grace.

> *Westminster Confession of Faith,* Formulary of the Presbyterian Church of Scotland, 1643

God gives light sufficient for its salvation, to every soul that attains to the use of reason in this life.

> JUAN DE LUGO (1583–1660), *De Fide,* XIX

From all evil and mischief; from sin; from the crafts and assaults of the Devil; from Thy wrath, and from everlasting damnation, Good Lord, deliver us.

> *The Book of Common Prayer,* 1662

No man can fail of the benefits of Christ's salvation, but through an unwillingness to have it.

> WILLIAM LAW, *The Spirit of Prayer,* 1749

Whoever dares to say "Outside the Church is no salvation," ought to be driven from the State.

> JEAN JACQUES ROUSSEAU, *The Social Contract,* 1762

If the degree of enlightenment of a people admits, all truths necessary to the salvation of the human race ultimately can be constructed upon knowledge gained by reason.

> MOSES MENDELSSOHN, *Gegenbetrachtungen,* 1770

No man has the right to abandon the care of his salvation to another.

> THOMAS JEFFERSON, *Notes on Religion,* 1776

By salvation I mean . . . a present deliverance from sin, a restoration of the soul to its primitive health, its original purity, a recovery of the divine nature.

> JOHN WESLEY (1703–1791), *A Further Appeal to Men of Reason and Religion,* in *Works,* XII

True salvation, deliverance from life and suffering, cannot be imagined without complete denial of the will.

> ARTHUR SCHOPENHAUER, *The World as Will and Idea,* 1819

I can never believe that a man may not be saved by that religion, which doth but bring him to the true love of God and to heavenly mind and life; nor that God will ever cast a soul into hell that truly loveth Him.

> SAMUEL TAYLOR COLERIDGE, *Aids to Reflection,* 1825

Salvation and Christian obedience are one and the same. Nor, indeed, can salvation be anything else.

> WILLIAM ELLERY CHANNING (1780–1842), *Works*

Outside the Church, no salvation: *that is to say in the last analysis, outside the congregation of the just,* outside of good faith responding to grace, outside of the quest for truth in a sincere and pure heart.

H. L. PERREYVE, *Entretiens sur l'Église Catholique*, II, 1865

If our assurance of salvation were made to depend upon our knowledge that every word of the Bible was of divine origin, our hopes of eternal life would be altogether obscure.

WASHINGTON GLADDEN, *Who Wrote the Bible*, 1891

When any one of us falls, he falls alone; but no one is saved alone. He is saved in the Church, as a member of it, and in union with all its other members.

ALEKSEI KHOMYAKOV, "The Church Is One," quoted by Birkbeck in *Russia and the English Church*, 1895

Salvation is not putting a man into Heaven, but putting Heaven into man.

MALTBIE D. BABCOCK, *Thoughts for Everyday Living*, 1901

In no single act or passion can salvation stand: far hence, beyond Orion and Andromeda, the cosmic process works and shall work forever through unbegotten souls.

FREDERIC W. H. MYERS, *Human Personality*, 1906

The mysterious bonds that unite the earthly Church with the rest of mankind are not revealed to us; therefore we have neither the right nor the inclination to suppose that all who remain outside the visible Church will be severely condemned, especially as such a supposition would contradict the Divine mercy.

ALEKSEI KHOMYAKOV, *Satchineniya*, 1911

The Church is the true and ordinary institute of the grace and truth of Jesus. But that does not prevent there being, alongside this ordinary institute, extraordinary ways of salvation, or hinder the grace of Christ from visiting particular men without the mediation of the Church.

KARL ADAM, *The Spirit of Catholicism*, 1924

The declaration that there is no salvation outside the Church is not aimed at individual non-Catholics, at any person or persons, but at non-Catholic churches and communions, in so far as they are non-Catholic communions.

KARL ADAM, *The Spirit of Catholicism*, 1924

To save one's soul is not an instantaneous deed, but a life-long adventure. . . . The creation of a type of personality through loyalty to concrete values as these are at issue in everyday experience.

MAX C. OTTO, *Things and Ideals*, 1924

The Buddha came to save the world, and his method for the accomplishment of this end is the destruction of ignorance and the dissemination of knowledge as to the true values of life and the wise way to live. The Buddha indeed cannot save us; we must do that for ourselves . . . in large part through the attainment and application of his knowledge or insight.

J. B. PRATT, *The Pilgrimage of Buddhism*, 1928

This is the way Jesus saves us: by revealing the nature of God and by creating within us the desire for fellowship with Him; by exhibiting life as it ought to be and may be and thus inspiring us to nobler conduct.

KIRBY PAGE, *Jesus or Christianity?*, 1929

God desires not the death of any sinner, but has provided in Christ a. salvation sufficient for all. . . . Men are fully responsible for their treatment of God's gracious offer. . . . His decree hinders no man from accepting that offer. . . . No man is condemned except on the ground of his sin.

Constitution of the Presbyterian Church in the U.S.A., 1930

The Holy Scriptures contain all things necessary to salvation; so that whatsoever is not read therein, nor may be proved thereby, is not to be required requisite or necessary to salvation.

The Doctrines and Discipline of the Methodist Episcopal Church, 1932

Only in Divine-humanity, in the Body of Christ, can man be saved. Otherwise he will be torn to pieces by demonic forces, by the demons of hatred and malice.

JACQUES MARITAIN, *Freedom in the Modern World, 1936*

Salvation is actualized in history whenever a demonic power in social or individual existence is overcome by the divine power which has become visible in Christ.

PAUL TILLICH, *The Kingdom of God and History, 1937*

Heavens and Hells play a prominent part in motivating human conduct in Buddhist teaching (particularly the late popular Mahayana sects). But heavens do not constitute salvation; they are only steps on the way to final salvation or release.

CHARLES S. BRADEN, *Man's Quest for Salvation, 1941*

Every great religion has some term descriptive of its ultimate goal. In Christianity it is *salvation*, in Hinduism it is *Moksha*. Each religion defines it differently, and employs different methods in its achievement, but in the end the quest in all religions seems to be for supremely enduring satisfaction either in this life or beyond.

CHARLES S. BRADEN, *Man's Quest for Salvation, 1941*

There is one thing we most of us forget. Christ taught it. The Church teaches it

. . . though you wouldn't think so to hear a great many of us today. No one in good faith can ever be lost.

A. J. CRONIN, *The Keys of the Kingdom, 1941*

If Catholics hold there is no salvation outside the Church, you can see that this maxim can shock only those who understand it wrongly and who are ignorant of what is commonly taught concerning the "soul of the Church." All it means is that there is no salvation outside the Truth, which, explicitly or implicitly, is freely offered to all.

JACQUES MARITAIN, *Ransoming the Time, 1941*

Man is saved, not from the world but with the world, because he is its guardian and master; he is saved, not apart from others, but with the rest of the Christian family, as one of its members.

NICHOLAS ZERNOV, *The Church of the Eastern Christians, 1944*

The essence of religion is the human quest for salvation.

MORDECAI KAPLAN, *Future of the American Jew, 1948*

That one may obtain eternal salvation, it is not always required that he be incorporated into the Church actually as a member, but it is necessary that at least he be united to her by desire and longing.

Congregation of the Holy Office, *Decree*, July 28, 1949

When a person is involved in invincible ignorance God accepts also an implicit desire, so called because it is included in that good disposition of soul whereby a person wishes his soul to be conformed to the will of God.

Congregation of the Holy Office, *Decree*, July 28, 1949

No one will be saved who, knowing the Church to have been divinely established by Christ, nevertheless refuses to submit to the Church or withholds obedience from the Roman Pontiff, the Vicar of Christ on earth.

Congregation of the Holy Office, *Decree,* July 28, 1949

There is no such thing as a single scheme of salvation. Salvation is not the monopoly of any church. All paths lead to the hilltop of one and the same God-consciousness. The different religions are suited to the different aspirants in their various stages of progress.

SWAMI NIKHILANANDA, *Perspectives on a Troubled Decade,* ed. Bryson, Finkelstein and MacIver, 1950

When will you recognize that you cannot save Christian man without Christ?

R. L. BRUCKBERGER, *One Sky to Share,* 1951

Even in the dark hour after he has become guilty against his brother, man is not abandoned to the forces of chaos. God Himself seeks him out, and even when He comes to call him to account, His coming is salvation.

MARTIN BUBER, *At the Turning,* 1952

The ultimate aim of man [in Hinduism] is liberation; liberation not only from the bondage of the flesh, but also from the limitation of a finite being. In other words, *moksha* means becoming a perfect spirit like the Supreme Spirit. . . . But the law of *Karma* postulates that every individual has to pass through a series of lives either on earth or somewhere else before he attains *moksha* or liberation.

D. S. SARMA, *The Religion of the Hindus,* ed. K. W. Morgan, 1953

If mankind, united in sin, faces a universal need for salvation, then the answer to that need is universal.

ROGER L. SHINN, *Christianity and the Problem of History,* 1953

Persons who are truly saved may backslide entirely and be eternally lost.

The Salvation Army Handbook of Doctrine, 1955

Infidels are saved in so far as they are among the faithful, pagan and heretics by that in them which is neither heretical nor pagan.

CHARLES JOURNET, *The Church of the Word Incarnate,* Vol. I, 1955

A child cannot "save his soul" in a vacuum—salvation must be effected in a social environment in which love of God and man must be in constant operation.

ROLAND SIMONITSCH, *Sanctity and Success in Marriage,* 1956

In the Christian tradition, the history of salvation begins, not with the choosing of Abraham, but with the creation of the world.

JEAN DANIELOU, *The Lord of History,* 1958

The Church's own littleness is the key to its greatness. God wishes to show that man's salvation is His work, and not man's.

JOHN LA FARGE, *An American Amen,* 1958

The emphatic direction of Jewish tradition would seem to be that salvation may be wrought by human initiative in disjunction, indeed even without, divine grace.

MILTON STEINBERG, *Anatomy of Faith,* 1960

There is no free creature who does not owe his salvation to the divine goodness.

CHARLES JOURNET, *The Meaning of Evil,* 1961

The Church, now sojourning on earth as an exile, is necessary for salvation. Christ, present to us in His body, which is the Church, is the one Mediator and the unique way of salvation. . . . Whosoever, therefore, knowing that the Catholic

Church was made necessary by Christ, would refuse to enter it or to remain in it, could not be saved. . . . He is not saved, however, who, though part of the body of the Church, does not persevere in charity.

Constitution on the Church, Second Vatican Council, November, 1964

Nor is God far distant from those who in shadows and images seek the unknown God. . . . Those also can attain to salvation who through no fault of their own do not know the Gospel of Christ or His Church, yet sincerely seek God and moved by grace strive by their deeds to do His will as it is known to them through the dictates of conscience. Nor does Divine Providence deny the help necessary for salvation to those who, without blame on their part, have not yet arrived at an explicit knowledge of God and with His grace strive to live a good life. Whatever good or truth is found amongst them is looked upon by the Church as a preparation for the Gospel.

Constitution on the Church, Second Vatican Council, November, 1964

See also Atonement; Baptism; Bible; Bible and Doctrine; Bible and History; Calvary; Chastity; Church, Definitions of; Church: Its Work; Cross; Damnation; Death; Election; End of the World; Eternal Life; Faith; Fall, the; Free Will; God: His Goodness; Grace; Immortality; Incarnation; Jesus Christ: His Passion and Death; Jesus Christ as Saviour; Justification; Original Sin; Paths; Predestination; Providence; Punishment; Redemption; Religion, Necessity of; Sin; Sinners; Social Order; Soul.

SAMĀDHI

When one attains samādhi, then alone comes the knowledge of Brahman, and one attains the vision of God. In that ecstatic realization, all thoughts cease, and one becomes perfectly silent.

SRI RAMAKRISHNA (1836–1886), *Kathāmrta,* III, 9

SANCTIFICATION

Sanctification is the work of God, whereby through the Holy Spirit He continually renews us and the whole Church, delivering us from the power of sin, giving us increase in holiness.

WALTER M. HORTON, *Christian Theology,* 1955

See also Sacraments.

SANCTIMONIOUSNESS. See HYPOCRISY

SANCTITY

The principal sanctity is that of the virgin, because it is free from affinity to fornication.

TERTULLIAN, *On Exhortation to Chastity,* px ix, c. 209

Hither and thither goes the man whom God drives from His gate,
But those He calls for guests and friends at no door need to wait.

SHAIKH SAADI, *Gulistan,* c. 1265

Sanctity consists in but one thing—fidelity to the order of God.

J. J. DE CAUSSADE, *Abandonment,* 1880

There is sanctity in pure knowledge, as there is in pure beauty, and the disinterested quest of truth is perhaps the greatest purification.

GEORGE SARTON, *History of Science,* 1927

The whole history of religious enthusiasm bears witness that the highest sanctity often runs on the very borderlines of sanity.

RONALD A. KNOX, *Miracles,* 1928

Sanctity of life is not a peculiar benefit which is offered to some and denied to others, but it is the common lot and duty of all.

POPE PIUS XI, *Casti Connubi,* December 31, 1930

Some folk who would be horrified to think themselves saintly live in an almost continuous consciousness of God.

JOHN W. LYNCH, *Hourglass,* 1952

We can never begin to be saints, until we realize that all sanctity consists in the replacing of ourselves and our lives by Christ and His life.

M. EUGENE BOYLAN, *The Priest's Way to God,* 1962

See also Beatific Vision; Blessedness; Goodness; Grace, Definitions of; Heaven; Holiness; Martyrdom; Martyrs; Neurotic; Perfection; Piety; Reform; Saints; Saints and Sinners; Sin; Suffering.

SATAN. See DEVIL

SATANISM

A history of Satanism would be a history of the whole human race; it would be a history of errors and crimes, of idolatry and false religions, of hatred and war, of the reign of sin and death, of the road leading to hell.

NICOLAS CORTE, *Who Is the Devil?,* 1958

SAVIOUR

But in the popular [Buddhist] sects there is clear dependence upon a gracious saviour Buddha or Boddhisattva, Amitabha, Awalokitesvara, or others through whose accumulated merits and grace, they may by faith, love, devotion and repetition of the name or some other *bhakti* practice, be born into Paradise.

CHARLES S. BRADEN, *Man's Quest of Salvation,* 1941

Only when the kingdom of God on earth is merged into the kingdom of God in heaven will Jesus be able to say of his role of Saviour, "It is consummated."

RALPH GORMAN, *The Last Hours of Jesus,* 1961

See also Avatara; Cross; Jesus Christ as Saviour.

SCANDAL

If scandal is taken at the truth, then it is better to allow scandal to arise than to abandon the truth.

POPE ST. GREGORY THE GREAT (c. 540–604), *In Ezech.,* Hom. 7

Scandal in the theological sense is not mere surprise or shock at the action of others, nor is it uncharitable talk. . . . The main feature of scandal, as the term is used in Catholic theology, is that it furnishes a bad example to someone, furnishing him with an occasion of sin.

FRANCIS CONNELL, *Outlines of Moral Theology,* 1953

Theologically, scandal is an occasion of spiritual harm to the neighbor. Scandal is very seriously involved when white Catholics practice segregation and discrimination.

GERALD KELLEY, *Guidance for Religious,* 1957

See also Calumnies; Gossip.

SCARE

A good scare is worth more to a man than good advice.

E. W. HOWE, *Country Town Sayings,* 1911

See also Fear.

SCHISMS

Have we not one God, and one Christ, and one Spirit of grace poured out upon us?

And is there not one calling in Christ? Why do we divide and tear asunder the members of Christ, and raise up strife against our own body, and reach such a pitch of madness as to forget that we are members of one another?

St. Clement of Rome, *Letter to the Corinthians,* c. 100

If anyone follow a man who causes a schism he "does not inherit the kingdom of God." And any man who goes in for strange doctrine dissociates himself from the Passion.

St. Ignatius of Antioch, *To the Philadelphians,* c. 109

Jealousy of the bishop's position begets schisms.

Tertullian, *On Baptism,* c. 206

How can two or three be gathered together in Christ's name if they are manifestly separated from Christ and His Gospel? For we did not go out from them, but they from us.

St. Cyprian, *De Unitate,* 251

I say and protest that it is as wrong to divide the Church as to fall into heresy.

St. John Chrysostom, *Hom.* ix, *in Epist. ad Ephes.,* c. 388

There is nothing more grievous than the sacrilege of schism . . . there can be no just necessity for destroying the unity of the Church.

St. Augustine, *Contra Epistolam Parmeniani,* 400

There can be no contradiction or schism where God is. His truth cannot be otherwise than one truth, one life, one love.

Karl Adam, *The Spirit of Catholicism,* 1924

Most of the great schisms and heresies have their roots in social or national antipathies.

Christopher Dawson, *Science for a New World,* ed. Thompson and Crowther, 1934

At the origin of the great secessions there was as a rule a genuine spiritual impetus which, in so far as it was positive and disinterested, was truly Catholic.

Yves Congar, *Divided Christendom,* 1939

See also Disputation; Division; Heresy; Reformation, the; Unity.

SCHOLARS

A bastard who is a scholar [of the Law] takes precedence of an ignorant high priest.

Maimonides, *Mishneh Torah,* 1171

The scholar's mission is to instruct and inspire the race in reference to the general end,—progress,—for which God has made and placed us here.

Orestes Brownson, *Address,* Dartmouth College, July 26, 1843

The world is full of scholars who speak about extending the frontiers of knowledge . . . who love to knock at the door of truth but would drop dead if that door ever opened to them.

Fulton J. Sheen, *Peace of Soul,* 1949

A man can accept anything to do with God until scholars begin to go into the details and the implications.

Pierre Morin in Graham Greene's "Visit to Morin," *Harper's Bazaar,* January, 1957

Through the Church the scholar apprehends those truths which no scholarship ever attains and on which a way of life is founded.

John L. McKenzie, *The Critic,* August-September, 1961

See also Education; Genius; Intellectuals.

SCIENCE

Science without conscience is but the ruin of the soul.

Rabelais, *Gargantua and Pantagruel,* II, viii, 1551

Science is the great antidote to the poison of enthusiasm and superstition.

> ADAM SMITH, *The Wealth of Nations,* 1776

If science produces no better fruits than tyranny, murder, rapine and destitution of national morality, I would rather wish our country to be ignorant, honest and estimable, as our neighboring savages are.

> THOMAS JEFFERSON, *Letter to John Adams,* 1812

Man is born not to solve the problems of the universe, but to find out where the problem begins, and then to restrain himself within the limits of the comprehensible.

> J. W. VON GOETHE, *Conversations with Eckermann,* June 11, 1825

Thou canst not tell where one drop of water or one grain of sand will be tomorrow noon; and yet with thy impotence thou insultest the sun! Science! Curse thee, thou vain toy.

> HERMAN MELVILLE, *Moby Dick,* 1851

If Physical Science be dangerous, as I have said, it is dangerous because it necessarily ignores the idea of moral evil.

> JOHN HENRY NEWMAN, *The Idea of a University,* 1852

With all your science, can you tell me how and whence it is that light comes into the soul?

> HENRY DAVID THOREAU (1817–1862), *Journal*

Science may prove the insignificance of this globe in the scale of creation, but it cannot prove the insignificance of man.

> BENJAMIN DISRAELI, *Lothair,* 1870

Physical science makes no investigation at all into things that are absolutely inaccessible to exact investigation or as yet inaccessible to it.

> ERNEST MACH, *The Science of Mechanics,* IV, 1883

Human science is but the backward undoing of the tapestry web of God's science.

> GEORGE MACDONALD, *Unspoken Sermons,* 3rd Series, 1887

Science must constantly be reminded that her purposes are not the only purposes and that the order of uniform causation which she has use for, and is therefore right in postulating, may be enveloped in a wider order, on which she has no claim at all.

> WILLIAM JAMES, *Principles of Psychology,* Vol. 2, 1890

Modern science, in substituting a new heaven and a new earth for the old—the reign of law for the reign of caprice, and the idea of evolution for that of creation—has added, and is steadily adding a new revelation divinely inspired.

> ANDREW D. WHITE, *History of Warfare of Science with Theology,* 1896

Its [science's] short way of killing any opinion that it disbelieves is to call it "unscientific."

> WILLIAM JAMES, *The Will to Believe and Other Essays,* 1896

Science has become too complex to affirm the existence of universal truths, but it strives for nothing else.

> HENRY ADAMS, *The Education of Henry Adams,* 1906

Science has given us back something strangely like a World-Soul.

> JANE HARRISON, *Ancient Art and Ritual,* 1913

The greatest of all modern ideas, in its originality, in its widespread adoption, and in its far-reaching importance, is the idea that man can make his way through all the difficulties and dangers that beset him, by means of applied science or technology.

> RALPH BARTON PERRY, *The Present Conflict of Ideas,* 1922

Science knows nothing about the first cause of things.

SIR OLIVER LODGE, *Literary Review,* February 23, 1924

The history of science is the same wayward chronicle of human effort and human mistakes as is that of philosophy and religion.

LOUIS T. MORE, *The Dogma of Evolution,* 1925

Science confers power, not purpose. It is a blessing, therefore, if the purpose which it serves is good; it is a curse, if the purpose is bad.

WILLIAM LOUIS POTEAT, *Can a Man Be a Christian Today?,* 1926

It was once believed that science forced us into rationalism; it is now almost believed that it forces us into irrationalism.

HENRY MASSIS, *Defense of the West,* 1927

No science is an illusion; but it would be an illusion to suppose that we could get anywhere else what science cannot give us.

SIGMUND FREUD, *The Future of an Illusion,* 1928

Science has always promised two things not necessarily related—an increase first in our powers, second in our happiness or wisdom, and we have come to realize that it is the first and less important of the two promises which it has kept most abundantly.

JOSEPH WOOD KRUTCH, *The Modern Temper,* 1929

Science has not only helped to destroy popular traditions that might have nourished a modern spirit of admiration, but has fostered a wintry scepticism, making man appear not an imperfect angel, but a super-educated monkey.

A. R. THOMPSON, *Humanism and America,* ed. R. Forester, 1930

It is rather pedantic to say that science never *explains* anything, but it is true to say that its explanations are never in terms of purpose, or deep-down meaning.

ARTHUR THOMPSON, *Science and Religion,* 1931

Science has not closed, and will never close the soul's east window of surprise.

RUFUS M. JONES, *A Preface to Christian Faith in a New Age,* 1932

Science in the making, science as an end to be pursued, is as subjective and psychologically conditioned as any other branch of human endeavour.

ALBERT EINSTEIN, *The World as I See It,* 1934

The modern man, finding that Humanism and Sex both fail to satisfy, seeks his happiness in Science. . . . But Science fails too, for it is something more than a knowledge of matter the soul craves.

FULTON J. SHEEN, *The Eternal Galilean,* 1934

Our lives would be exceedingly narrow if we based our thoughts and actions solely on facts that can be subjected to scientific tests.

ARTHUR H. COMPTON, *The Freedom of Man,* 1935

Whatever knowledge is attainable must be attainable by scientific methods; and what science cannot discover, mankind cannot know.

BERTRAND RUSSELL, *Religion and Science,* 1935

Science burrows its insulted head in the filth of slaughterous inventions.

WINSTON S. CHURCHILL, Article, *Evening Standard,* September, 1936

The readiness with which the public will now believe almost anything if it be called scientific is making this age, in which

887

science most prevails, the most unscientific age of all.

T. E. JESSOP, *The Christian Understanding of Man,* 1938

Our science tells us how to do an infinitely greater number of things, it picks apart the cog-wheels of nature; but it is not wise, it does not discriminate what is worth doing, and before the greatest problem of all, what meaning can man give to his life in this vast world, it gives a despairing "Nescio," if not an "I don't care."

J. H. RANDALL, *The Making of the Modern Mind,* 1940

At the present time only science has the vigor, and the authority of achievement, which is necessary to give them that fresh vivacious *joie de vivre* which captivates men's hearts and mind.

C. H. WADDINGTON, *The Scientific Attitude,* 1941

The most amazing fact about scientific knowledge is the evidence it provides that there is an actual correlation between the mind and the natural order which it apprehends. The most stupendous conclusion to which science leads is the conclusion that ours is the kind of world in which science is possible.

D. E. TRUEBLOOD, *The Logic of Belief,* 1942

Science can only deal with what is, and nothing about what ought to be, which is the concern of ethics; science can tell us means to ends, but not about what the ends should be.

LEONARD HODGSON, *Theology in an Age of Science,* 1944

When civilized man, with his science, his technique, his power, loses his soul, he becomes the most terrible monster the world has ever seen.

DOROTHY THOMPSON, *Ladies' Home Journal,* September, 1945

If we want to heal humanity, science can tell us how; if we want to destroy humanity, science can tell us how; but on what grounds can it tell us which of the two to do ?

GERALD VANN, *The Heart of Man,* 1945

Science can be and is being made into an escapist philosophy—into a dodge of moral disciplines and spiritual responsibilities.

NELS F. S. FERRÉ, *Faith and Reason,* 1946

Created by life, in definite circumstances, to act on definite things, how can it [science] embrace life, of which it is merely an emanation or aspect?

RUTH N. ANSHEN, *Our Emergent Civilization,* 1947

The emphasis today is no longer on Western ideas but rather on the Western scientific techniques.

CHRISTOPHER DAWSON, *Religion and Culture,* 1947

Science does not exclude faith . . . science does not teach a harsh materialism. It does not teach anything beyond its boundaries, and those boundaries have been severely limited by science itself.

VANNEVAR BUSH, *Modern Arms and Free Men,* 1949

Science points the way to survival and happiness for all mankind through love and cooperation.

ASHLEY MONTAGU, *Saturday Review,* 1949

Science deals with but a partial aspect of reality and . . . there is no faintest reason for supposing that everything science ignores is less real than what it accepts.

J. W. N. SULLIVAN, *The Limitations of Science,* 1949

The theist is persuaded that while nothing that contradicts science is likely to be true, still nothing that stops with science can be the whole truth.

GORDON W. ALLPORT, *The Individual and His Religion,* 1950

Science can only ascertain what *is,* but not what *should be,* and outside of its domain value judgments of all kinds remain necessary.

ALBERT EINSTEIN, *Out of My Later Years,* 1950

The statement "Science can embrace all truth," is not a statement of scientific fact.

E. LEROY LONG, JR., *Science and Christian Faith,* 1950

The tendency of science is to make men indifferent or sceptics, merely by being exclusively pursued.

ROGER J. MCHUGH, *Christianity and the Sceptic,* 1950

Science has done everything it could to make us feel at home on earth. Suddenly it produces something which could make us all homeless.

FULTON J. SHEEN, *The Woman,* 1951

Scientific research has opened up the possibility of unprecedented good or unlimited harm for mankind, but the use that is made of it depends in the end on moral judgments of the whole community of men.

A. V. HILL, *Presidential Address,* British Association, September, 1952

We can be assured of neither peace, nor liberty, nor dignity in the world of tomorrow so long as . . . science and wisdom are not reconciled.

JACQUES MARITAIN, *The Range of Reason,* 1952

Unless we are blind idiots or self-satisfied morons, we will know that scientific organization is not the fulfillment of the spirit of man.

SARVEPALLI RADHAKRISHNAN, *The Philosophy of,* 1952

Science is an imaginative adventure of the mind seeking truth in a world of mystery.

CYRIL HINSHELWOOD, *Address,* Science Masters Association, Oxford, England, 1953

Our western science is a child of moral virtues; and it must now become the father of further moral virtues if its extraordinary material triumphs in our time are not to bring human history to an abrupt, unpleasant and discreditable end.

A. J. TOYNBEE, *New York Times Magazine,* December 26, 1954

We realize the absurdity of applying science to artistic or moral subjects if we try to speak of half a pound of beauty or two inches of courage.

ARTHUR F. SMETHURST, *Modern Science and Christian Beliefs,* 1955

What is needed in the present plight of mankind is not more science but a change of heart that shall move mankind to devote to constructive and peaceful purposes what science there is.

RALPH BARTON PERRY, *The Humanity of Man,* 1956

Existing scientific concepts cover always only a very limited part of reality.

WERNER HEISENBERG, *Physics and Philosophy,* 1958

Science at best can only ward off the threats of fate, through engineering and medicine; and at worst, only increase the deadliness of the threats to our life through nuclear weapons.

LANGDON GILKEY, *Maker of Heaven and Earth,* 1959

Science tends to develop natural virtues which are basically Christian—humility, patience, perseverance, honesty and integrity.

JOSEPH F. MULLIGAN, *America,* October 10, 1959

The Word of God freely limited Himself by assuming our condition. . . . The scientist who looks upon nature and sees in it the imprint of this same Word cannot fail to realize that his commitment to truth must involve an equal commitment to love, and that the discovery of truth must lead man to humility, not to pride.

> ERNAN MCMULLIN, *America,* December 12, 1959

A man entrusted with the tremendous power and responsibility of science requires more than intellect to bring true blessings to the world.

> FRANZ E. WINKLER, *Man: The Bridge Between Two Worlds,* 1960

There is a moral component right in the grain of science itself.

> CHARLES P. SNOW, *The Two Cultures and the Scientific Revolution,* 1961

See also Astronomy; Bible; Cause; Christian Science; Creation; Darwinism; Design; Evolution; Genesis; Knowledge; Machines; Miracles; Mysteries; Nuclear Energy; Nuclear War; Positivism; Psychiatry; Psychology; Reality; Religion: Its Decline; Science, Religion of; Science and Creation; Science and God; Science and Religion; Scientists; Technology; Unconscious Mind; Universe; War.

SCIENCE, RELIGION OF

The faith, ideals, and ethics of science constitute a form of natural religion.

> EDWIN GRANT CONKLIN, *Science,* December 31, 1837

In our church—if I may be permitted to use for a moment an expression which I so detest— . . . we have a chief, an invisible Christ, science.

> M. A. BAKUNIN, *God and the State,* 1882

The day I believe will come when its [science's] evangelists will spread through the country, be heard in every house, and be seen on every street preaching and teaching the only faith which is consonant with the reason, with the dignity of man.

> KARL PEARSON, *The Ethic of Freethought,* 1888

Science is a religion, science alone will henceforth make the creeds, science alone can solve for men the eternal problems.

> ERNEST RENAN, *The Future of Science,* 1891

Science is daily more and more personified and anthropomorphized into a god.

> SAMUEL BUTLER, *Notebooks of,* ed. H. F. Jones, 1912

The religion of science. Science also as a religion, as a faith to bind men together, as a substitute for the moribund old mythologies and theologies which kept them sundered, is commencing to be talked of in a more serious tone.

> LOUIS BERMAN, *The Glands and Human Personality,* 1921

The religion of science will play the great part of the Liberator of mankind from the whole system of torments that have made the way of all flesh a path of rocks along which a manacled prisoner crawls to his doom.

> LOUIS BERMAN, *The Glands and Human Personality,* 1921

The relation of intelligent man to the world of nature, and the social possibilities that grow out of such a relation, are the elements which might be made the basis of "a new religion," the religion of science, and the religion of humanity.

> I. W. HOWERTH, *Science Monthly* Vol. XVII, November, 1923

The marriage of science to a philosophy of naturalism . . . and the result is an enlightened paganism whose god is science.

> GEORGIA HARKNESS, *The Resources of Religion,* 1936

Science is supposed by many to have banished every realm of the sacred; and behold, science becomes the sacred cow!

NELS F. S. FERRÉ, *Faith and Reason,* 1946

Today science has almost unconsciously developed a philosophy or religion of its own, by which the great masses of people in the western world live.

MARY B. HESSE, *Science and the Human Imagination,* 1955

See also Positivism; Science; Science and Creation; Science and God; Science and Religion; Scientists.

SCIENCE AND CREATION

It [science] brings before us phenomena, and it leaves us, if we will, to call them works of design, wisdom or benevolence; and further still, if we will, to proceed to confess an Intelligent Creator.

JOHN HENRY NEWMAN, *Grammar of Assent,* 1870

Science is at least as much as Theology compelled to postulate a Rational Ground or Cause of the world, . . . who made it intelligible and *us* in some faint degree able to understand it.

A. J. BALFOUR, *The Foundations of Belief,* 1895

The idea of creation by divine will without natural processes is just as contrary to the facts as revealed by science, as is the opposite materialistic view of creation by natural processes without divine will.

HENRY HIGGINSON LANE, *Evolution and Christian Faith,* 1923

The doctrine of special creation . . . appeals to the spiritual faculties, and also to the logical. Every fact of natural science is explainable logically from the viewpoint of special creation.

FRANK L. MARSH, *Evolution, Creation and Science,* 1944

An interpretation which embodies the essential truth of Genesis and the conclusions logically deduced from the findings of science would seem to make for greater peace, serenity and integrity of mind than one which goes contrary to the overwhelming mass of scientific evidence.

JOHN A. O'BRIEN, *The Origin of Man,* 1947

The age of the earth and of life upon it, no matter what antiquity be imputed to both, does not disturb any principle of the Christian faith or of the Biblical revelation when the latter is properly understood.

JOHN A. O'BRIEN, *The Origin of Man,* 1947

Creation, of its very nature, must have taken place at the beginning of the world's existence; but science contemplates the world as it is *now,* namely already created.

ANTONIO ROMANA, *God, Man and Universe,* ed. J. Bivort de la Saudée, 1950

The scientist is by no means renouncing his true function when he makes way for the philosopher and respects the philosopher's arguments that the world was created by God.

ANTONIO ROMANA, *God, Man and Universe,* ed. J. Bivort de la Saudée, 1950

It would indeed seem that present-day science, going back in an instant over millions of years, has managed to witness this original *Fiat lux,* this moment when out of nothing there arose, with matter, an ocean of light and radiations, while the particles of the chemical elements separated and reformed in millions of galaxies.

POPE PIUS XII, *Address* to Pontifical Academy of Sciences, October 22, 1951

Why do we suppose that the order that science observes is the order God created, for is it not certain that finite man could perceive but an aspect of the whole order that is known by the infinite God?

F. SHERWOOD TAYLOR, *Man and Matter,* 1951

The question of cosmic origins does not cease to be a religious question because it has become a scientific question.

JOHN L. MCKENZIE, *The Two-Edged Sword*, 1959

If we are to prepare for eternal life by the development, both natural and supernatural, of our faculties of intellect and will, it would seem that scientific understanding is among the highest of natural activities, one that every Christian should hold in the most profound esteem.

ERNAN MCMULLIN, *America*, December 12, 1959

See also Adam; Bible; Creation; Evolution; Genesis; Science, Religion of; Science; Science and God; Science and Religion; Scientists.

SCIENCE AND GOD

All these facts proclaim aloud the One God, whom man may know, adore, and love; and Natural History must, in good time, become the analysis of the thoughts of the Creator of the Universe, as manifested in the animal and vegetable kingdoms.

LOUIS AGASSIZ, *Essay on Classifications*, 1857

Nothing has afforded me so convincing a proof of the Deity as these purely mental conceptions of numerical and mathematical science . . . all of which must have existed in that sublimely omniscient mind from eternity.

MARY SOMERVILLE, *Personal Recollections*, 1874

Throughout the whole of astronomy, geology, physics, and chemistry there is no question today of a "moral order" or a personal God.

ERNEST HAECKEL, *The Riddle of the Universe*, 1901

Science is thinking God's thoughts after Him just as truly as when we read the scripture.

CHARLES E. GARMAN, *Letters, Lectures, Addresses*, 1909

It is a sublime conception of God which is furnished by science, and one wholly consonant with the highest ideals of religion, when it represents Him as revealing Himself through inbreathing of life into its constituent matter, culminating in man with his spiritual nature and all His Godlike powers.

Joint Statement upon the Relations of Science and Religion, signed by eminent scientists, 1923

Scientists generally speak of *religion* rather than of God. Their belief in God, in so far as it persists at all, is a rather vague emotional inheritance.

GERALD B. SMITH, *Journal of Religion*, July, 1925

What modern science is doing for multitudes of people, as anybody who watches American life can see, is not to disprove God's theoretical existence, but to make him "progressively less essential."

HARRY EMERSON FOSDICK, *Adventurous Religion*, 1926

The scientific interpretation of natural phenomena has made the interest in God more remote, God's existence more problematical, and even the idea of God unnecessary.

H. W. CARR, *Changing Backgrounds in Religion and Ethics*, 1927

Mathematics and physics are making it increasingly difficult to assign a place for God in our co-ordinations and constructions of the universe.

H. W. CARR, *Changing Backgrounds in Religion and Ethics*, 1927

My religion as a scientist does not contradict a single element of the religion which my mother and the people of my native village held when I was a boy. Science has simply brought me to a higher, broader view of the Creator.

MICHAEL PUPIN, *The American Magazine,* September, 1927

If the laws of psychology are not applicable to astronomy, and the laws of music not transferable to law, and the predicates of an amoeba not applicable to a Pantheon, why should the categories of physics, psychology and sociology be applicable to God?

FULTON J. SHEEN, *Religion Without God,* 1928

Science recognizes no personal powers in the universe responsive to the prayers and needs of men.

CLIFFORD KILPATRICK, *Religion in Human Affairs,* 1929

Science has not yet proceeded far in its search for God. But there is no reason for discouragement. No great gulf divides the natural from the supernatural.

KIRTLEY F. MATHER, *The Forum,* January, 1929

Without the presupposition of God, Science is fragmentary and baseless. He is the antecedent condition of all being, the unitary ground of existence.

GEORGE HERBERT PALMER, *The Autobiography of a Philosopher,* 1930

The fact that scientific method seems to reduce God to something like an ethical code may throw some light on the nature of scientific method; I doubt if it throws much light on the nature of God.

ARTHUR S. EDDINGTON, *Science and Religion,* 1931

The progress of science may greatly clarify our ideas about the kind of God we have a right to expect to find in the universe.

RUFUS M. JONES, *Pathways to the Reality of God,* 1931

The method of natural science depends upon the presuppositions which are held about nature, and the presuppositions about nature in turn upon the doctrine of God.

M. B. FOSTER, *Mind,* Vol. 43, no. 172, 1934

Nothing stands in our way—and our instinctive intellectual striving for a unified world picture demands it—from identifying with each other the two everywhere active and yet mysterious forces: the world order of natural science and the God of religion.

MAX PLANCK, Lecture delivered in 1937, reprinted in *Scientific Autobiography and Other Papers,* 1949

Science is seen to be just one of those great flights of altar stairs that lead through darkness up to God.

EDGAR J. GOODSPEED, *Four Pillars of Democracy,* 1940

The role of God in the material world has been reduced stage by stage with the advance of science, so much so that He only survives in the vaguest mathematical form in the minds of older physicists and biologists.

J. D. BERNAL, *Science and Ethics,* ed. C. H. Waddington, 1942

Because science shows the world to be intelligible, at least to a considerable degree, science becomes a witness to intelligent Purpose in nature and consequently: it bears testimony to the credibility of theism.

D. E. TRUEBLOOD, *The Logic of Belief,* 1942

Science, which had denied the spiritual life, while it vainly thought to have acquired full freedom and autonomy by disowning God, sees itself punished today through the most humiliating bondage, having become the slave and the practically automatic fulfiller of policies and orders that take into no account whatever the rights of truth and of the human person.

POPE PIUS XII, *Broadcast,* December 24, 1943

Modern scientific leaders like Eddington and Jeans talk about God in a way that would have scandalized most scientists of fifty years ago.

R. G. COLLINGWOOD, *The Idea of Nature,* 1945

And so far as traditional Christianity is concerned, "God" has not made one single contribution to science, nor one single scientific revelation.

JAY WILLIAM HUDSON, *Religious Liberals Reply,* 1947

Any man who believes in God must realize that no scientific fact, as long as it is true, can contradict God. Otherwise, it would not be true. Therefore, any man who is afraid of science does not possess a strong faith.

LECOMTE DU NOÜY, *Human Destiny,* 1947

It ought to be part of the job of the scientist to show us what he sees of the nature of God. . . . But the scientist sees only his discoveries as revealing the work of God when he is prepared for something of that kind.

C. A. COULSON, *God, the Creator,* 1951

We will have bought our conquest of matter at too high a price if it robs us of that humility which enables us to detect in every majestic scientific discovery the pathways and the laws marked out by the Divine Architect.

THOMAS E. MURRAY, *Address,* December 4, 1951

The more true science advances, the more it discovers God, almost, as though He

were standing, vigilant behind every door which science opens.

POPE PIUS XII, *Address,* November 22, 1951

The idea of the universe formed by a person acquainted with modern science gives a far worthier and more credible picture of God than was gathered from the unreliable science of the Middle Ages or in the crudely mechanistic science of the Victorian era.

F. SHERWOOD TAYLOR, *Man and Matter,* 1951

All sciences . . . will tend to exclude the thought of God if they are not cultivated with reference to Him.

HENRY P. VAN DUSEN, *God in Education,* 1951

No scientific argument—by which I mean an argument drawn from the phenomena of nature—can ever have the slightest tendency either to prove or disprove the existence of God. . . . Science is irrelevant to religion.

W. T. STACE, *Religion and the Modern Mind,* 1952

Has science discovered God? must always be answered negatively if it is answered honestly. Yet every new discovery within every science brings to light data giving support and corroboration to the religious faith God made the world.

GEORGIA HARKNESS, *The Modern Rival of Christian Faith,* 1953

However little its followers may recognize this, it is still true that science is "helping to put a face on God": it is one of the ways in which He is revealed.

C. A. COULSON, *Science and Christian Belief,* 1955

There is no "God of the gaps" to take over at those strategic places where science fails; and the reason is that gaps of this sort have the unpreventable habit of shrinking.

C. A. COULSON, *Science and Christian Belief*, 1955

If God exists He must be manifest somehow in matter, and His ways there are what science is discovering.

EDMUND W. SINNOTT, *The Biology of the Spirit*, 1955

It is not difficult for a scientist to see the hand of God in the patterns which protons, neutrons and electrons take in forming atoms, and those which the atom take to form molecules, molecules to form cells, cells to form tissues, organs, and bodies, and bodies to form social aggregates.

GEORGE RUSSELL HARRISON, *What Man May Be*, 1956

The God who called Israel out of Egypt into his service and calls the Christian out of his sin into newness of life cannot be discovered by science, for He is not in the world of nature.

M. HOLMES HARTSHORNE, *The Promise of Science and the Power of Faith*, 1958

Religious truth, then, is different from scientific truth because its object, God, is not one of the many creatures of the world with which science is concerned.

LANGDON GILKEY, *Maker of Heaven and Earth*, 1959

What the scientists find is what God Himself has put there, the intelligible structures which are the proper objects of man's God-given intellect.

ERNAN MCMULLIN, *America*, December 12, 1959

Scientific knowledge is cumulative; the breaches between natural events become fewer and narrower. This diminishes a God who stands apart from the created world; not so the God who includes the Creation in His divine being.

THEODOSIUS DOBZHANSKY, *Science Ponders Religion*, ed. H. Shapley, 1960

The theologian who truly believes that God is spirit and not a material entity will find a significant similarity between his "God of Law" and the scientists' "administration of the universe."

KIRTLEY F. MATHER, *Science Ponders Religion*, ed. H. Shapley, 1960

While the light of the science of nature is increasing, darkness is spreading over the science of God and in consequence over man's true science.

POPE PAUL VI, *Homily*, September 29, 1963

Intelligence is the daughter of God. And the true man of science is easily carried towards the base of religion: adoration of the God-Creator and Sovereign Master of all things.

POPE PAUL VI, *Address*, December 16, 1963

See also Bible; God: His Omnipotence; God: His Omniscience; Science; Science, Religion of; Science and Creation; Science and Religion; Scientists.

SCIENCE AND RELIGION

The gospels do not tell us that our Lord said, "I will send you the Holy Ghost to teach you the course of the sun and the moon"; we should endeavor to become Christians and not astronomers.

ST. AUGUSTINE (354–430), *De Genesi ad litteram*

What do I care if the heavens are a circumambient sphere and not a sort of dish-cover?

ST. AUGUSTINE (354–430), *P.L.*, XXXIV

People give ear to an upstart astrologer who strove to show that the earth revolves, not the heavens or the firmament, the sun and the moon. . . . This fool wishes to reverse the entire scheme of astronomy; but sacred Scripture tells us that Joshua commanded the sun to stand still, not the earth.

> MARTIN LUTHER, about 1530, in *Table Talk*

The view that the sun stands motionless at the center of the universe is foolish, philosophically false, and utterly heretical, because contrary to Holy Scripture. The view that the earth is not the center of the universe and even has a daily rotation is philosophically false, and at least an erroneous belief.

> Holy Office, Roman Catholic Church, *Edict* of March 5, 1616

Methinks that in the discussion of natural problems we ought not to begin at the authority of places in Scripture; but at sensible experiments and necessary demonstrations.

> GALILEO, *Dialogue on the Two Chief Systems of the World*, 1632

Natural science is subservient to purposes of a higher kind, and is chiefly to be valued as it lays a sure foundation for Natural Religion and Moral Philosophy.

> COLIN MACLAURIN, *An Account of Sir Isaac Newton's Philosophical Discoveries*, 1748

He who made us would have been a pitiful bungler, if he had made the rules of our moral conduct a matter of science. For one man of science, there are thousands who are not.

> THOMAS JEFFERSON, *Letter to Peter Carr*, August 10, 1787

If persons would . . . but apply something of the same temper and calm judgment to religion which they do not refuse to science, there would be but few objections to the truths of the Bible.

> JOHN HENRY NEWMAN, *The Christian Observer*, 1821

Science has nothing to do with Christ, except in so far as the habit of scientific research makes a man cautious in admitting evidence.

> CHARLES R. DARWIN (1809–1882), *Life and Letters*, publ. posth.

I confidently expect that in the future even more than in the past, faith in an order, which is the basis of science, will not be dissevered from faith in an Ordainer, which is the basis of religion.

> ASA GRAY (1810–1888), inscribed beneath his bust in Hall of Fame, New York

To suppose that a Christian must either renounce his confidence in the achievements of scientific research or abandon his faith in Scripture is a monstrous perversion of Christian freedom.

> HERBERT EDWARD RYLE, *The Early Narratives of Genesis*, 1892

If we could frame a satisfying philosophy of Science and a satisfying philosophy of Religion, we should, I imagine, have little difficulty in framing a philosophy which should embrace them both.

> A. J. BALFOUR, *The Foundations of Belief*, 1895

Unless it borrows something from Theology, a philosophy of Science is impossible.

> A. J. BALFOUR, *The Foundations of Belief*, 1895

Science seems to me to teach in the highest and strongest manner the great truth which is embodied in the Christian conception of entire surrender to the will of God. Sit down before fact as a little child, be prepared to give up every preconceived notion, follow humbly wherever and to whatever abyss nature leads.

> THOMAS HUXLEY (1825–1895), *Life and Letters of,* Leonard Huxley, I, 316

The scientist, so-called, is, during his scientific hours at least, so materialistic that one may well say that on the whole the influence of science goes against the notion that religion should be recognized at all.

> WILLIAM JAMES, *The Varieties of Religious Experience,* 1902

Though the scientist may individually nourish a religion, and be a theist in his irresponsible hours, the days are over when it could be said that for Science herself the heavens declare the glory of God and the firmament showeth his handiwork.

> WILLIAM JAMES, *The Varieties of Religious Experience,* 1902

It is not the object of the writers of Scripture to impart physical instruction or to enlarge the bounds of scientific knowledge. But if any one wishes to know what connection the world has with God, if he seeks to trace back all that now is to the very fountain-head of life, if he desires to discover some unifying principle, some illuminating purpose in the history of this earth, then we confidently refer him to the Scriptures as his safest, and indeed only guide to the information he seeks.

> MARCUS DODS, *The Expositors Bible,* 1908

These [science and religion] are reconciled in amiable and sensible people but nowhere else.

> SAMUEL BUTLER, *Notebooks of,* ed. H. F. Jones, 1912

If the latent religious significance of scientifically directed effort be clearly brought out by Christianity, the territory of Christian aspiration and activity will be so expanded as to create boundless enthusiasm.

> GERALD BINNEY SMITH, *Social Idealism and the Changing Theology,* 1913

The purpose of science is to develop, without prejudice or preconceptions of any kind, a knowledge of the facts, the laws, and the processes of nature. The even more important task of religion, on the other hand, is to develop the consciences, the ideals, and the aspirations of mankind. Each of these two activities represent a deep and vital function of the soul of man, and both are necesary for the life, the progress, and the happiness of the human race.

> Joint Statement upon the Relation of Science and Religion, by thirty-five clergymen and scientists, 1924, reprinted in R. A. Millikan's *Science and Life,* 1924

Some people say that religion and science are opposed; so they are, but only in the same sense as that in which the thumb and forefinger are opposed—and between the two one can grasp everything.

> SIR WILLIAM BRAGG, Lecture in 1925 at Royal Institution, heard by Arthur F. Smethhurst and reported in his *Modern Science and Christian Beliefs,* 1955

Why have we not the right to bar science if it comes from the four corners of the earth to tear the vitals of our religion? . . . Who says we can't bar science that deprives us of all hope of the future life to come?

> TOM STEWART, public prosecutor, Scopes Trial, Dayton, Tenn., as reported in *New York Herald-Tribune,* July 26, 1925

The faith in the possibility of science, generated antecedently to the development of modern scientific theory, is an unconscious derivative from medieval theology.

> ALFRED NORTH WHITEHEAD, *Science in the Modern World,* 1925

There are wider truths and finer perspectives within which a reconciliation of a deeper religion and a more subtle science will be found.

> ALFRED NORTH WHITEHEAD, *Science in the Modern World,* 1925

The general tendency of scientific discovery has been to weaken not only religious but ethical values.

> REINHOLD NIEBUHR, *Christian Century,* April 22, 1926

The Communist party cannot be neutral toward religion. It stands for science, and all religion is opposed to science.

> JOSEPH STALIN, to the first American labor delegation to Russia, September 9, 1927

If you want God to give you an opportunity to make the most of your own life, to provide you with resources with which to meet your responsibilities, in short, to play the role of executive partner in the firm of "God and Man," then you may welcome the contribution which modern science makes to your faith.

> KIRTLEY F. MATHER, *The Forum,* January, 1929

How could science be any enemy of religion when God commanded man to be a scientist the day He told him to rule the earth and subject it?

> FULTON J. SHEEN, *The Life of All Living,* 1929

To say that a great mass of hundreds of millions can dispense with the old ethics and rule themselves according to science is, if I may say so, the sheerest drivel.

> JAMES TRUSLOW ADAMS, *Living Philosophies,* 1931

The cosmic religious experience is the strongest and noblest force behind the driving force of scientific research.

> ALBERT EINSTEIN, *Cosmic Religion,* 1931

It [science] cannot destroy religion, because that is the outcome of the religious spirit, and the religious spirit is just as much a property of human nature as is the scientific spirit.

> JULIAN HUXLEY, *Science and Religion,* 1931

While the practical task of science is to provide man with new knowledge and increased powers of control, the practical task of religion is to help man to decide how he shall use that knowledge and those powers.

> JULIAN HUXLEY, *Science and Religion,* 1931

There is nothing unscientific in following the experts, the explorers of the high places of the spiritual life, when they tell us what they have found.

> W. R. INGE, *Science and Religion,* 1931

It [science] has nothing to say, and can have nothing to say, on the question of ultimate realities of an eternal order which are essential to a spiritual religion.

> RUFUS M. JONES, *A Preface to Christian Faith in a New Age,* 1932

Religion belongs to that realm that is inviolable before the law of causation and therefore closed to science.

> MAX PLANCK, *Where Is Science Going?,* 1932

The scientist is possessed by the sense of universal causation. . . . His religious feeling takes the form of a rapturous amazement at the harmony of natural law, which reveals an intelligence of such superiority that, compared with it, all the systematic thinking and acting of human beings is an utterly insignificant reflection.

> ALBERT EINSTEIN, *The World as I See It,* 1935

The world is replete with mystery because it is filled with God. God is mystery. When we unveil a corner of the mystery we are nearer to seeing God. . . . When science awakens to that fact, science will become a partner . . . with theology.

> JAMES M. GILLIS, *The Church and Modern Thought,* 1935

The question whether science or religion shall predominate will determine the future structure of our social life, and lies at the root of every other problem.

JOHN MACMURRAY, *Reason and Emotion,* 1935

The discovery of radioactivity in 1896 revealed an entirely new property of matter. . . . It forced us . . . to begin to think in terms of a universe which is changing, living, growing . . . a dynamic instead of a static universe. . . . It is at this point that one of the great contributions to religion is now being made.

ROBERT A. MILLIKAN, *Evolution in Science and Religion,* 1935

Religion welcomes with eager hospitality every new finding which science can tease from the tangled skein of nature. She knows in advance that if it is really true, it will not only harmonize with spiritual truth, but will aid us in securing a better vision of God and a deeper insight into the Divine Administration of the universe.

JOHN A. O'BRIEN, *The New Knowledge and the Old Faith,* 1935

It was not modern science, that grand uniter of minds, that destroyed Christian philosophy. When modern science was born there was no longer any living Christian philosophy there to welcome and assimilate it.

ÉTIENNE GILSON, *The Spirit of Medieval Philosophy,* 1936

Religion and natural science . . . are in agreement, first of all, on the point that there exists a rational world order independent from man, and secondly, on the view that the character of this world order can never be directly known but can only be indirectly recognized or suspected. Religion employs in this connection its own characteristic symbols, while natural science uses measurements founded on sense experiences.

MAX PLANCK, Lecture delivered in 1937, reprinted in *Scientific Autobiography and Other Papers,* 1949

What is false in science cannot be true in religion. Truth is one and indivisible. God is bound by His own laws.

H. M. LOEWE, *A Rabbinic Anthology,* 1938

The presuppositions that go back to make up this Catholic Faith, preserved for many centuries by the religious institutions of Christendom, have as a matter of historical fact been the main or fundamental presuppositions of natural science ever since.

R. G. COLLINGWOOD, *Essay on Metaphysics,* 1940

Religion needs science, to protect it from religion's greatest danger, superstition.

EDGAR J. GOODSPEED, *Four Pillars of Democracy,* 1940

Science needs religion, to prevent it from becoming a curse to mankind instead of a blessing.

EDGAR J. GOODSPEED, *Four Pillars of Democracy,* 1940

True science neither lowers nor humiliates man in his origin. Rather, it elevates and exalts him because it perceives, recognizes, and admires in every member of the human family greater or lesser traces of the divine image and likeness stamped upon him.

POPE PIUS XII, *Allocution,* November 30, 1941

The beginning of the modern adventure in both science and religion was the revival of the essential Christian conception of the infinity of God and the consequent realization that God had given man an infinite task in understanding and doing His Will and Knowing His world.

A. D. LINDSAY, *Religion, Science and Society,* 1943

To mention Science and Religion in the same sentence is . . . to affirm an antithesis and suggest a conflict.

CHARLES E. RAVEN, *Science, Religion and the Future,* 1943

The necessary condition for the reforming of our civilization involves the reintegration of science into a unity with philosophy and religion.

HUGH S. TAYLOR, *Commonweal*, April 30, 1943

The scientific scrap-heap is one of the biggest scrap-heaps in the world. But great religious principles, once discovered and verified in universal human experience, have remained unshaken through the centuries.

RUFUS M. JONES, *The Radiant Life*, 1944

The new scientific culture is devoid of all positive spiritual content. It is an immense complex of techniques and specialisms without a guiding spirit, with no basis of common moral values, with no unifying spiritual aim.

CHRISTOPHER DAWSON, *Religion and Culture*, 1947

While the sacred writers communicate great spiritual and religious truths, they reflect merely the views on natural science prevalent in their day.

JOHN A. O'BRIEN, *The Origin of Man*, 1947

Each time that scientific thought has undergone revolution there has been a widespread collapse of religious faith on the part of those who have accepted the newly discovered facts, but have too little help from the Church to fit the new facts into a religious faith that could satisfy enlightened minds.

RUFUS M. JONES, *A Call to What Is Vital*, 1949

Science and philosophy are not bound to square their observations and conclusions with any current ideas of religious dogma. . . . If left free in their action, they will find the unity of Truth with Good and Beauty and God, and give these a greater meaning than any dogmatic religion.

AUROBINDO, *The Human Cycle*, 1950

Science without religion is lame, religion without science is blind.

ALBERT EINSTEIN, *Out of My Later Years*, 1950

Not science, but wisdom, is the real content, ground and goal of Scripture.

RICHARD KRONER, *Perspectives on a Troubled Decade*, ed. Bryson, Finklestein and MacIver, 1950

Religion and natural science are fighting a joint battle in an incessant, never relaxing crusade against skepticism and against dogmatism, against disbelief and against superstition, and the rallying cry in this crusade has always been, and always will be, "On to God."

MAX PLANCK, *Scientific Autobiography*, 1950

The Christian is free to reject belief concerning the facts of the natural order which find expression in the Bible, but which are contrary to the established and tested findings of competent scientific research.

The Interpreter's Bible, I, 1952

If . . . while faith humbly subjects itself to the discipline of scientific instruction, science at the same time subjects itself to the overriding claims of a devout spiritual life, then perhaps the two can be so agreed as to walk together in peace.

JOHN BAILLIE, *Natural Science and the Spiritual Life*, 1952

I believe that the illicit extension of the categories of natural science to the inner life of the spirit presages the final betrayal of our human birthright.

JOHN BAILLIE, *Natural Science and the Spiritual Life*, 1952

The pursuit of science in itself is never materialistic. It is a search for the principles of law and order in the universe, and as such essentially religious endeavor.

ARTHUR KOESTLER, *Arrow in the Blue*, 1952

To pursue science is not to disparage the things of the spirit. In fact, to pursue science rightly is to furnish a framework on which the spirit may rise.

VANNEVAR BUSH, *Address,* Massachusetts Institute of Technology, October 5, 1953

The difference between Science and Religion is that Science is material and Religion is immaterial.

L. M. HEYWOOD, *Education and Spirit,* 1954

Before the close of the seventeenth century our forefathers consciously took their treasure out of religion and reinvested it in natural science.

A. J. TOYNBEE, *New York Times Magazine,* December 26, 1954

Science is one aspect of God's presence, and scientists therefore part of the company of His heralds.

C. A. COULSON, *Science and Christian Belief,* 1955

Today almost all the positive logical reasons based on science for the rejection of the Christian faith have been shown to be without foundation . . . but suspicion of religion has penetrated so deeply into men's minds that the mere removal of logical difficulties is no longer enough.

MARY B. HESSE, *Science and the Human Imagination,* 1955

There is no satisfying snythesis of Science and Christianity this side of the Kingdom of God.

MARY B. HESSE, *Science and the Human Imagination,* 1955

Advances of science ultimately lead to the recognition on purely scientific grounds of truths long known to Christians through their faith and through revelation.

ARTHUR F. SMETHURST, *Modern Science and Christian Beliefs,* 1955

Religion and science are the two conjugated faces or phases of one and the same act of complete knowledge—the only one which can embrace the past and future of evolution so as to contemplate, measure and fulfill them.

PIERRE TEILHARD DE CHARDIN, *The Phenomenon of Man,* 1955

There is more than a mere suspicion that the scientist who comes to ask metaphysical questions and turns away from metaphysical answers may be afraid of those answers.

GREGORY ZILBOORG, *Faith, Reason and Modern Psychiatry,* 1955

Science does not contradict the truth of religion; it never deals with it. . . . Faith implies an absolute judgment, not a provisional criticism: it is judged by God, not men.

M. HOLMES HARTSHORNE, *The Promise of Science and the Power of Faith,* 1958

In religion especially, scientific objectivity is not merely misleading; it is meaningless. A man does not take upon himself a cross and follow Christ in a spirit of experimentation.

M. HOLMES HARTSHORNE, *The Promise of Science and the Power of Faith,* 1958

Within its own limited field, the secular cosmology of natural science is as impregnable to theological criticism as it is irrelevant to religious problems.

WALTER MARSHALL HORTON, *Christian Theology,* 1958

The new age of science, using telescopes instead of microscopes, and gazing out into God's clear space instead of back into our own murky psychological depths, may let fresh air into modern thought. In such air it may be easier for the Spirit, moving where It will, to evoke more ready response.

JOHN J. WRIGHT, *Ave Maria,* April 5, 1958

It is no longer possible to maintain that science and religion must operate in thought-tight compartments or concern separate sectors of life; they are both relevant to the whole of human existence.
JULIAN HUXLEY, *Introduction* to Teilhard de Chardin's *The Phenomenon of Man,* 1959

The Galileo affair was an isolated, and in fact quite untypical, episode in the history of the relations between science and theology, almost as untypical as the Dayton monkey trial was. But its dramatic circumstances, magnified out of all proportion, created a popular belief that science stood for freedom, the Church for oppression of thought.
ARTHUR KOESTLER, *The Sleepwalkers,* 1959

Happily we have survived into a day when science and theology no longer speak to each other in the language of fishmongers.
JOHN L. MCKENZIE, *The Two-Edged Sword,* 1959

In uncovering the secrets of nature the scientist is cooperating in a form of natural revelation which gives insights into God's universe that cannot be gotten from any other source.
JOSEPH F. MULLIGAN, *America,* October 10, 1959

While the enemies of religion and morality have attempted to make science the principal weapon of their attack, actually science itself has no part in this warfare.
Catholic Bishops of the U.S., November, 1961

The rising gale of scientific discovery has blown away the chaff of traditional religion, and in doing this it has done mankind a service; but it has blown so hard that it has blown away the grain with the husk; and this has been a disservice, since

neither science nor the ideologies have a grain of their own to offer as a substitute.
A. J. TOYNBEE, *Study of History,* Vol. XII, *Reconsiderations,* 1961

The mathematical genius of an Einstein is no qualification for handing down decisions about an afterlife.
F. X. CANFIELD, *The Catholic Bookman's Guide,* ed. Sr. M. Regis, I.H.M., 1962

The reality that scientific research and theological revelation seek to understand is the same reality. There is in scientific research something equivalent to revelation.
DONALD S. HARRINGTON, *Sermon, New York Times,* March 5, 1962

It is true . . . that it is not always science that speaks when scientists talk. Unfortunately, it is not always Divine revelation that has been defended when religious spokesmen have gone forth to do battle with the scientists.
ALFRED S. HORRIGAN, *Science and Religion,* ed. J. C. Monsma, 1962

One of the oldest and most harmful blunders associated on both sides with religion-science conflict is the insistence that the only valid method for arriving at truth is that proper to one's own craft.
ALFRED F. HORRIGAN, *Science and Religion,* ed. J. C. Monsma, 1962

Science itself gives us an understanding of the mechanism of nature, but faith discloses the Spirit behind the mechanism and its regularity.
ERIC CHARLES RUST, *Science and Religion,* ed. J. C. Monsma, 1962

In the minds of the young religious values should be cultivated and moral conscience refined in a manner to keep pace with the continuous and ever more abundant assimilation of scientific and technical knowledge.
POPE JOHN XXIII, *Pacem in Terris,* April, 1963

Science raises and solves immense problems in its order, but it stops at the sacred threshold of the soul and of the conscience in their relationship to the divine.

POPE PAUL VI, *Address,* December 16, 1963

See also Bible; Evolution; Positivism; Religion; Revelation; Science; Science, Religion of; Science and Creation; Science and God; Scientists.

SCIENTISM. See HUMANISM

SCIENTISTS

Scientists animated by the purpose of proving that they are purposeless constitute an interesting subject for study.

ALFRED NORTH WHITEHEAD, *The Function of Reason,* 1929

I wonder that scientists, at work in their laboratories or their observatories, do not fall on their knees, and bow their heads in silent adoration of the vast Unseen. Perhaps they do.

JAMES M. GILLIS, *So Near Is God,* 1935

They [scientists] stand with the great idealists of other ages. However unaware or reluctant they may be about it, this selfless devotion of theirs to an ideal is one of the great spiritual assets of our time.

EDGAR J. GOODSPEED, *Four Pillars of Democracy,* 1940

He [the scientist] either knows or he does not know. If he knows, there is no room for faith or belief. If he does not know, he has no right to faith or belief.

A. J. CARLSON, *Scientific Monthly,* August, 1944

See also Astronomers; Atomic Bomb; Dogmatism; Nuclear Energy; Nuclear War; Positivism; Religion of Science; Science; Science, Religion of; Science and

Creation; Science and God; Science and Religion.

SCRIPTURES

See Bible and other rubrics beginning with Bible; also Creation; Genesis; Inspiration; Job, Book of; Koran; New Testament; Old Testament; Psalms; Revelation; Science and Creation.

SECLUSION

Every pious man should seek retirement and seclusion, and should only in case of necessity associate with others.

MAIMONIDES, *Guide for the Perplexed,* 1190

SECOND COMING

We preach not one advent only of Christ, but a second also, far more glorious than the former. For the former gave to view His patience but the latter brings with it the Crown of the divine kingdom.

ST. CYRIL OF JERUSALEM, *Catechetical Lectures,* 350

See also End of the World; Jesus Christ.

SECTS AND SECTARIANISM

As to those who split up their religions and become sects, have thou nothing to do with them: their affair is with God only.

Koran, 7th century A.D.

There must be sects, and the Word of God must face battle. . . . Let us leave in His hands the combat and free encounter of minds.

MARTIN LUTHER, *Letter to Elector Frederick,* April 21, 1524

Sectarianism is part of original sin.

WALTER RAUSCHENBUSCH, *The American Journal of Theology,* XI, 1907

When we come to believe that we are in possession of our God because we belong to some particular sect it gives us such a complete sense of comfort, that God is needed no longer except for quarreling with others whose idea of God differs from ours in theoretical details.

RABINDRANATH TAGORE, *Thought Relics,* 1909

Theology may be the Queen of the Sciences, but she has no right to compel any of her subjects to call themselves by a doctrinal name and to go about with it stamped on their foreheads.

L. P. JACKS, *Confession of an Octogenarian,* 1942

Most sects represent something real—the satisfaction of some fundamental need of the human spirit which, for one reason or another, is not being met in the groups from which the sects spring.

CHARLES S. BRADEN, *Protestantism: a Symposium,* ed. W. K. Anderson, 1944

Sectarianism is not a peculiarly Christian vice. It is found in every religion that had developed far beyond the tribal stage. There are more than fifty sects of Hinduism in India. Buddhism is divided into two major schools and a great many sects and sub-sects. The same is true of Islam, of Judaism and of Shintoism.

CHARLES S. BRADEN, *Protestantism: a Symposium,* ed. W. K. Anderson, 1944

If the church is to play a reconciling or prophetic role in a community issue, those involved must feel that this is Christ's Church at work and not some fragmentary, sectarian body.

WILLIAM B. CATE, *Unity in Mid-Career,* 1963

See also Disputation; Division; Paths; Pluralism; Religion; Rivalry; Unity; Universality.

SECULARISM

Once society is launched on the path of secularization it cannot stop in the halfway house of Liberalism, it must go on to the bitter end, whether that end be Communism or some alternative type of totalitarian secularism.

CHRISTOPHER DAWSON, *Religion and the Modern State,* 1935

The church must either surrender in the face of a secularist order which makes a mockery of its ideals or set about changing that order.

F. ERNEST JOHNSON, *Church and Society,* 1935

The secularism of the twentieth century is due partly to the fact that we do not find all our richest values in the church, as the medievalist or Puritan did. He had nowhere else to go. But we have. Science, art, literature, and the drama all give us the sense of significant depth in life—a function performed in the past by religion alone.

R. A. SCHERMERHORN, *Journal of Religion,* XV, 1935

The disintegration of society has one root cause. Human life is falling to pieces because it has tried to organize itself into unity on a secularistic and humanistic basis without any reference to the divine will.

"Report on Church and Community," Oxford Conference, 1937

The secularization of society is a final achievement in the evolution of mankind.

HAROLD J. LASKI, *Reflections on the Revolution of Our Time,* 1943

Secularism is not normal, because it is the product of an abnormal condition, the disruption of the spiritual unity of Christianity.

JOHN LA FARGE, *Secularism's Attack on World Order,* 1944

Cooperation between peoples is the necessary condition for any cooperation between states and governments. But secularism has no basis for cooperation between peoples as such.

> JOHN LA FARGE, *Secularism's Attack on World Order,* 1944

A concomitant of the fragmentizing of Christendom was the divorcement of large areas of life from effective religious and moral sanctions—in other words, the rise of secularism.

> F. ERNEST JOHNSON, *Religion and World Order,* 1944

What is implied by secularism is that man's religious life is conceived as an inner and private affair, having no necessary relevance to his business or political activities and incapable of furnishing him with sanctions to guide his organized social relationships.

> F. ERNEST JOHNSON, *Religion and the World Order,* 1944

Secularism has inundated American culture like a tidal wave and Protestantism has not been able to resist it. That is what I mean when I say that we have been losing our religion. We have been losing it to secularism.

> CHARLES CLAYTON MORRISON, *Bulletin* of America's Town Meeting of the Air, February 14, 1946

It [secularism] is the view of life that limits itself not to the material in exclusion of the spiritual, but to the human here and now in exclusion of man's relation to God here and hereafter.

> Catholic Bishops of the U.S., 1947

The atmosphere of Secularism is perfect for breeding un-Christian and anti-Christian social philosophies, and the amazing thing is not that there have been great tragedies, but that there have not been greater tragedies.

> JOHN D. FEE, *Secularism,* 1947

There can be no such thing as neutrality toward God, and whether they be secularists or atheists who recommend patterns for social life without God, by this very fact they enter upon the field of Theology.

> JOHN D. FEE, *Secularism,* 1947

Modern man has become, through Secularism, like the Roman who showed a readiness to provide a niche in the Pantheon for Christ, side by side with the pagan god.

> JOHN D. FEE, *Secularism,* 1947

To combat secularism the individual Christian must get the full vision of Christian truth. It is not divisible. One cannot pick and choose from it. Either it is accepted as a whole or it counts for little in real life.

> Catholic Bishops of the U.S., 1948

Something is smothering our lives, coarsening us and our homes. The demoralization of personal and family life is the fruit of present-day secularism.

> HAZEN G. WERNER, *The Christian Faith and Secularism: a Symposium,* ed. J. Richard Spann, 1948

Secularism is the stance of mind assumed by those who decide that they can have what they desire without departing from any "sensible" code of morals; that, as a matter of fact, it is possible subtly to revamp standards of conduct without losing the right to a Christian coat of varnish.

> GEORGE N. SHUSTER, *The Christian Faith and Secularism: a Symposium,* ed. J. Richard Spann, 1948

In the main, secularism is to be charged with exteriorizing our values, glorifying the physical, dissolving our checks and restraints, inflating the ego, robbing us of our moral sensibilities, atrophying our sense of meaning.

> HAZEN G. WERNER, *The Christian Faith and Secularism: a Symposium,* ed. J. Richard Spann, 1948

Secularism is practical atheism. . . . Its nature is neither to affirm nor to deny religious faith, but to live indifferently to it.

LEROY E. LOEMKER, *The Christian Faith and Secularism: a Symposium,* ed. J. Richard Spann, 1948

Secularism produces animals who are schooled in social relationships, are filled with pride and position, are clever, skilled, finished in inter-personal contacts, taught to value economic security above all things, whose god is their belly.

WILLIAM T. COSTELLO, *Address,* December, 1948

To the secularist, society is an amorphous mass, compulsively and obsessively in pursuit of nothing. Secularism is hell-bent for nowhere.

WILLIAM T. COSTELLO, *Address,* December, 1948

The greatest question of our time is not communism vs. individualism, not Europe vs. America, not even the East vs. the West; it is whether man can bear to live without God.

PAUL SCHERER, *The Plight of Freedom,* 1948

Secularism pours into the private and public life of our time like the salt water of the North Sea pouring in through the breached dikes on the island of Walcheren, sterilizing the soil that seven centuries of the costliest labor had succeeded in reclaiming.

DOUGLAS V. STEERE, *Door into Life,* 1948

Secularism has fashioned our idea of the Church. We still think and talk of it as a bureau, as an organization. We see its strength in numbers and in Catholics in high place—political and economic—rather than in the Holy Spirit molding individuals and institutions.

DANIEL M. CANTWELL, *The Commonweal Reader,* ed. E. S. Skillin, 1950

Secularism is the practice of the absence of God.

ANONYMOUS, c. 1950

The most remarkable feature with regard to the situation of the Christian heritage today is that its custody has to a considerable degree passed over into the keeping of secularized groups and forces.

AMOS WILDER, *Modern Poetry and the Christian Tradition,* 1952

Secularism has almost wholly engulfed our culture and is on the way to swallowing up our churches and our souls.

GEORGIA HARKNESS, *The Modern Rival of Christian Faith,* 1953

Secularism is "This-ageism," "This-is-all-there-is-ism," "There-isn't-any-more-ism."

JAMES A. PIKE, *Beyond Anxiety,* 1953

When secularists accused Christians of "living in the past," Christians ought to have retaliated by pointing out that secularists were "living off the past."

GEDDES MACGREGOR, *From a Christian Ghetto,* 1954

What can justly be called the unifying mission of secularism has a sanctity all its own. Rightly understood and valued, secularism will accelerate its Christian democratic mission to make us all brothers of one another.

AGNES MYER, *Speech to American Unitarian Association,* 1954

Men who affirm that nothing can separate us from the love of God must renounce the practical atheism that lies in the affirmation that God is not relevant to all the activities of men.

G. BROMLEY OXNAM, *Sermon,* Assembly World Council of Churches, 1954

In a world . . . which has largely returned to its condition of original secularism, the church . . . best fulfills her mission, the more purely . . . she is given over to her spiritual work of spreading the Gospel and confines herself to her strictly sacred activities.

YVES M. J. CONGAR, *Tolerance and the Catholic*, 1955

Secularism is the sawdust of the mills of science, and minds that feed on its synthetic fare soon suffer from anemia.

A. M. SULLIVAN, *The Three-Dimensional Man*, 1956

Many of the battles that now rage over "Church-State" issues tell more about the growth of dogmatic secularism in our society than they do about the Constitution.

WILLIAM CLANCY, *Religion and the Free Society*, 1958

The secularist . . . has converted the secular from the neutral into the *de facto* opponent of religion. Being unwilling to allow religion free entry into the secular order, he has transformed what is essentially open to all currents of doctrine—religious and non-religious—into the ideological opponent of religion. He has converted the secular into secularism.

ARTHUR COHEN, *Religion and the Free Society*, 1958

The insights of contemporary secularism hardly extend beyond the reach of the scientific spirit, except for a romantic tendency to deify nature, the dangers of which were apparent in Hitler's doctrines of Aryan blood and soil.

M. HOLMES HARTSHORNE, *The Promise of Science and the Power of Faith*, 1958

The nerve and center of secularism is this: the conviction that man has power of control over his world and can exercise it without sin—without corruption, disaster, and despair.

M. HOLMES HARTSHORNE, *The Promise of Science and the Power of Faith*, 1958

This determination of the modern secularist, either to confine the Church to the sacristy or to use it as the obedient servant of the totalitarian state, threatens the freedom of Christian life to a degree in which it has never been threatened before.

CHRISTOPHER DAWSON, *The Movement of World Revolution*, 1959

Secularism is the form in which the fallen world demonically seeks to replace God, from whom it receives its being in each moment of its existence.

KARL HEIM, *Religion and Culture*, ed. W. Leibrecht, 1959

What alarms him [the secularist] is religion as a thing, visible, corporate, organized, a community of thought that presumes to sit, superior to it, and in judgment on, the "community of democratic thought," and that is furnished somehow with an armature of power to make its thought and judgment publicly prevail.

JOHN COURTNEY MURRAY, *We Hold These Truths*, 1961

The present "wall of separation" has served to turn the welfare state into a secularized theocracy. In the United States the Supreme Court has become the *ex cathedra* spokesman for social-political morality.

STANLEY PARR, *The Ethics of Power*, ed. Lasswell and Cleveland, 1962

[Secularism is] a perspective on life and reality taken on faith which includes men and things, but not God; time and history, but not eternity.

JAMES A. PIKE, *New York Times*, July 13, 1962

As secularism has steadily grown in American legal philosophy, our moral values have revealed an increased materialism.

Roman Catholic Bishops of the U.S., *Bonds of Union*, November, 1963

Secularization represents an authentic consequence of Biblical faith. Rather than oppose it, the task of Christians should be to support and nourish it.

HARVEY COX, *The Secular City,* 1964

Secularization . . . places the responsibility for the forging of human values, like the fashioning of political systems, in man's own hands.

HARVEY COX, *The Secular City,* 1964

See also America; American People; Capitalism; Church and State; Civilization; Communism; Democracy; Democracy, Religion of; Education; Education, Catholic; Education, Parochial; Education, Secularized; Education and Religion; Godlessness; Government and Religion; Humanism; Irreligion; Liberalism and Religion; Man: His Self-Deification; Modernism; Naturalism; Religion; Religion: Its Decline; Social Atheism; Society and Religion; Unbelief.

SECURITY

A recognition of truth and the practice of virtue is the title to security for both the individuals, and the whole of mankind.

JOHN OF SALISBURY, *Politcratius,* 1159

The real security of Christianity is to be found in its benevolent morality, in its exquisite adaptation to the human heart, in the facility with which its scheme accommodates itself to the capacity of every human intellect, in the consolation which it bears to the house of mourning, in the light with which it brightens the great mystery of the grave.

THOMAS BABINGTON MACAULAY, *Southey's Colloquies,* 1830

Security is a feeling that there is a larger and more enduring life surrounding, appreciating, upholding the individual, and guaranteeing that his efforts and sacrifice will not be in vain.

CHARLES H. COOLEY, *Social Progress,* 1908

Security of the workingman as against uenmployment, old age, sickness, accident and death, must be frankly accepted as a special responsibility of industry jointly with society.

Bishops of Administrative Board of National Catholic Welfare Council, *The Church and Social Order,* 1940

Life wants to secure itself against the void that is raging within. The risk of eternal void is to be met by the premium of temporal insurance . . . social security, old age pensions, etc. It springs no less from metaphysical despair than from material misery.

FRANZ WERFEL, *Between Heaven and Earth,* 1947

This is the Hartford heresy. Economic, material security, life insurance, endowments, annuities take the place of a providential destiny, so that ultimate values are not built upon a rock whose name is Peter, but upon a rock whose name is Prudential.

WILLIAM T. COSTELLO, *Address,* December, 1948

An overemphasis on temporal security is a compensation for a loss of the sense of eternal security.

FULTON J. SHEEN, *Peace of Soul,* 1949

The only security that man has ever had has been in the warm enfoldment of the natural and social environment.

A. EUSTACE HAYDON, *This Is My Faith,* ed. S. G. Cole, 1956

Social security depends on *personal* security. And *personal* security depends on *spiritual* security. Spiritual security is primary, in the sense that every other kind of security stems from it. Without spiritual security, there just can't be any other kind of lasting security.

JOHN E. LARGE, *The Small Needle of Doctor Large,* 1962

SEDITION

A tyrannical government is not just. . . . Consequently there is no sedition in disturbing a government of this kind, unless indeed the tyrant's rule be disturbed so inordinately, that his subjects suffer greater harm from the subsequent disturbance than from the tyrant's government.

THOMAS AQUINAS, *Summa Theologiae*, II-I., Q. 42, 1272

If anything pass in a religious meeting seditiously and contrary to the public peace let it be punished in the same manner and no otherwise than as if it had happened in a fair or market.

THOMAS JEFFERSON, *Notes on Religion*, 1776

SEGREGATION

See Race, and also rubrics beginning with Racial.

SELF

Self is the lord of self.

Dhammapada, c. 5th century B.C.

Self is the one invincible foe when acting with the four cardinal passions: anger, pride, deceitfulness, and greed.

Uttaradhyayana-sutra, c. 500 B.C.

He who dwelling in the earth is other than the earth, whom the earth knows not, whose body the earth is, who inwardly rules the earth, is thy Self (Atman) the Inward Ruler, the deathless. He who, dwelling in all beings, is other than all beings, whom all beings know not, whose body all beings are, who inwardly rules all beings, is thy Self, the Inward Ruler, the deathless.

Brihadaranayaka Upanishad, III, prior to 400 B.C.

The Self is to be described as not *this,* not *that.* It is incomprehensible, for it cannot be comprehended.

Brihadaranayaka Upanishad, before 400 B.C.

The Self, deep-hidden in all beings, is not revealed to all; but to the seers, pure in heart, concentrated in mind—to them is he revealed.

Katha Upanishad, prior to 400 B.C.

Soundless, formless, intangible, undying, tasteless, odorless, eternal, immutable, beyond Nature, is the Self.

Katha Upanishad, prior to 400 B.C.

This [Self] is never born, nor does It die, nor after once having been, does It go into non-being. This [Self] is unborn, eternal, changeless, ancient. It is never destroyed even when the body is destroyed.

Bhagavad-Gita, c. 2nd century B.C.

Thou wilt never escape from thy self until thou slay it. Thy self, which is keeping thee far from God, and saying "So-and-so has treated me ill . . . such a one has done well by me"—all this is polytheism; nothing depends upon the creatures, all upon the Creator.

ABU SAID (died 1049), R. A. Nicholson's *Translations of Eastern Poetry and Prose*

The Kingdom of Self is the Fall of Man, or the great apostasy from the life of God in the soul, and everyone wherever he be, that lives unto self is still under the fall and great apostasy from God.

WILLIAM LAW, *The Spirit of Prayer,* 1749

If there is but one and the same final Self for each and all; then, with a literalness indeed appalling, He is we, and we are He; nay, He is I, and I am He.

GEORGE H. HOWISON, *The Conception of God,* 1898

It is part of man's very nature to think of his real self as soul, and to think of that soul as imperishable.

MORRIS JOSEPH, *Judaism As Creed and Life,* 1903

To "lose self" in a Society of some kind is the only means of saving self.

R. H. BENSON, *The Friendship of Christ,* 1912

Self is the only prison that can ever bind the soul.

HENRY VAN DYKE (1852–1933), "The Prison and the Angel"

When we come to know that our whole environment and everything that happens is God's hand upon us . . . every detail of life is a means arranged by Him to lead us to Himself; then we find that our great trouble is self.

JOHN CHAPMAN, *Spiritual Letters of,* 1944

Where religion goes wrong it is because, in one form or another, men have made the mistake of trying to turn to God without turning away from self.

AELRED GRAHAM, *Christian Thought and Action,* 1951

See also Individual; Individual Responsibility; Person; Personality; Self-Conquest; Self-Knowledge; Self-Will; Soul.

SELF-CONQUEST

The first and last step is the conquest of self. . . . For self is the lord of self, self is the refuge of self; therefore curb thyself as the merchant curbs a noble horse.

Dhammapada, c. 5th century B.C.

If one man conquers in battle a thousand times a thousand men, and if another

conquers himself, he is the greatest of conquerors.

Dhammapada, c. 5th century B.C.

He . . . got the better of himself, and that's the best kind of victory one can wish for.

MIGUEL DE CERVANTES, *Don Quixote,* 1605

There are such things as internal earthquakes; the penetration of a desperate certainty into a man is not effected without removing and breaking certain profound elements which are at times the man himself.

VICTOR HUGO (1802–1885), *Treasure Bits from,* ed. P. Rose

See also Asceticism; Discipline; Self; Self-Denial; Self-Knowledge; Spiritual Progress; Temptation.

SELF-CONTEMPT

We cannot think of ourselves as we ought to think without utterly despising everything that may be supposed as excellence in us. This humility is unfeigned submission of a mind overwhelmed with a weighty sense of its own misery and poverty.

JOHN CALVIN, *Institutes,* III, 1559

One who despises himself is the nearest to a proud man.

BARUCH SPINOSA, *Ethics,* IV, 1677

See also Humility; Pride; Spiritual Struggle; Vanity.

SELF-DECEPTION

Great care must be taken, lest the mind, believing what it does not see, fashion for itself what does not exist, and hope and love what is false.

ST. AUGUSTINE, *De Trinitate,* Lib. VIII, c. 397

Men are deceived by the long-suffering of the laws of nature; and mistake, in a nation, the reward of the virtue of its sires for the issue of its own sins.

JOHN RUSKIN, *Sesame and Lilies,* 1865

See also Humility; Pride; Self-Knowledge; Self-Love; Self-Pity; Self-Righteousness; Vainglory; Vanity.

SELF-DEFENSE

And one who attacks you, attack him in like manner. . . . Whoso defendeth himself after he hath suffered wrong, there is no way against them.

Koran, ii and xlii, c. 625 A.D.

Nor is it necessary for salvation that a man omit the act of self-defense in order to avoid killing the other man, since one is bound to take more care of one's own life than of another's.

ST. THOMAS AQUINAS, *Summa Theologiae,* II-II, Q. 64, 1272

The natural law . . . clearly authorizes the individual to defend himself by force against unjust aggression. The unjust aggressor has forfeited his right to physical integrity. . . . All the arguments that justify force in the vindiction of individual rights are fully applicable to the political groups known as nations.

Report, Catholic Association for International Peace, *International Ethics,* 1942

As long as the danger of war remains and there is no competent and sufficiently powerful authority at the international level, governments cannot be denied the right to legitimate defense once every means of peaceful settlement has been exhausted.

Second Vatican Council, *The Church in the Modern World,* December, 1965

See also Aggression; Armaments; Killing; Self-Interest; Self-Love; Self-Preservation; Self-Respect; War; War, Defense of; War, Just.

SELF-DENIAL

Since all Christians are to offer up their bodies at death, as a sacrifice or suffering for sin, this plainly teaches us that a state of self-denial and suffering is the proper state of this life.

WILLIAM LAW, *Christian Perfection,* 1726

There is a great deal of self-denial and manliness in poor and middle-class houses, in town and country, that has not got into literature, and never will, but that keeps the earth sweet.

RALPH WALDO EMERSON, *The Conduct of Life,* 1860

See also Abstinence; Asceticism; Charity; Desires; Discipline; Fasting; Moderation; Renunciation; Sacrifice; Self-Conquest; Self-Discipline; Self-Sacrifice; Virginity.

SELF-DISCIPLINE

One's own self is the most difficult to subdue.

Dhammapada, c. 5th century B.C.

When strict with oneself one rarely fails.

CONFUCIUS, *Sayings of,* 5th century B.C.

I have indeed no other business in life than to go about persuading you all, young and old, to care less for your bodies and your possessions and to make the protection of your souls your chief concern.

SOCRATES, "Apology," PLATO, *Dialogues,* 399 B.C.

Self-discipline must necessarily be in proportion to the misuse of any sense or power, but it is the true use of it we aim at in every act of self-discipline.

B. W. MATURIN, *Self-Knowledge and Self-Discipline,* 1939

Self-discipline never means giving up anything—for giving up is a loss. Our Lord did not ask us to give up the things of earth, but to exchange them for better things.

> FULTON J. SHEEN, *Lift Up Your Hearts,* 1950

See also Conquest; Discipline; Moderation; Self-Conquest; Self-Denial.

SELF-GIVING

You give but little when you give your possessions.

It is when you give of yourself that you truly give.

> KAHLIL GIBRAN, *The Prophet,* 1923

See also Abandonment; Detachment; Martyrs; Martyrdom; Prayer: Defined and Explained; Sacrifice; Selflessness; Self-Sacrifice; Spiritual Progress; Worship.

SELF-HELP

Verily the best things which ye eat are those which ye earn yourselves, or which your children earn.

> MOHAMMED, *Speeches and Table Talk of,* 7th century A.D.

Divine providence is doubtless to be acknowledged, but it is highly desirable to supplement Divine providence by self-help.

> EDWARD DOWDEN, *Puritan and Anglican,* 1900

SELF-INTEREST

There is not any of us that will be so much offended to see himself compared to God, as he will deem himself wronged to be depressed in the rank of other creatures. So much are we more jealous of our own interest, than of our Creator's.

> MICHEL DE MONTAIGNE, *Essays,* Bk. 2, ch. 12, 1580

I conceive that when a man deliberates whether he shall do a thing or not do it, he does nothing else but consider whether it is better for himself to do it or not to do it.

> THOMAS HOBBES, *Questions Concerning Liberty,* 1656

The modern trouble is in a low capacity to believe in precepts which restrict and restrain private interests and desire.

> WALTER LIPPMANN, *The Public Philosophy,* 1954

See also Covetousness; Desires; Greed; Jealousy; Pleasure; Possessions; Self-Defense; Selfishness; Self-Love; Self-Preservation; Self-Respect.

SELFISHNESS

Our subtle, disguised selfishness takes refuge behind such a sheaf of checks and loveless generosity that we almost forget how hard our hearts really are.

> S. M. SHOEMAKER, *Realizing Religion,* 1921

I lose God, I lose the world, I lose myself, if I want only to clutch at things and use them only for my own pleasure or profit.

> GERALD VANN, *The Divine Pity,* 1946

See also Almsgiving; Charity; Covetousness; Desires; Greed; Happiness; Money; Self-Interest; Self-Love; Self-Will; Social Conscience; Worldliness.

SELF-KNOWLEDGE

He who knows others is clever, but he who knows himself is enlightened.

> LAO-TZU, *Sayings of,* c. 500 B.C.

When you see a good man think of emulating him; when you see a bad man, examine your own heart.

> CONFUCIUS, *Analects of,* c. 5th century, B.C.

Holy men, the higher they raise themselves, approaching to God, the more clearly do they perceive their own unworthiness, because, being encompassed with a purer light, they discover in themselves those defects which before they could not see.

POPE ST. GREGORY THE GREAT, *Morals of the Book of Job*, I. 27, 584

It is a great grace of God to practice self-examination; but too much is as bad as too little.

ST. TERESA OF ÁVILA, *The Interior Castle*, 1577

Make it thy business to know thyself, which is the most difficult lesson in the world.

MIGUEL DE CERVANTES, *Don Quixote*, 1605

Who hath sailed about the world of his own heart, sounded each creek, surveyed each corner, but that there still remains therein much terra incognita to himself?

THOMAS FULLER, *The Holy State and the Profane State*, 1642

One must know oneself. If this does not serve to discover truth, it at least serves as a rule of life, and there is nothing better.

BLAISE PASCAL, *Pensées*, 1670

Man must be lenient with his soul in her weaknesses and imperfections and suffer her failings as he suffers those of others, but he must not become idle, and must encourage himself to better things.

ST. SERAPHIM OF SAROV (1759–1833), quoted in A. F. Dobbie-Bateman's biography of St. Seraphim

An imaginative man recognizes at once a portion of himself in his fellow man and speaks to that. . . . The imaginative man is sensitive and merciful to others out of merest mercy to himself.

ALEXANDER SMITH, *Dreamthorp*, 1863

The struggle against the evil that is in mankind we have to carry on not by judging others, but by judging ourselves.

ALBERT SCHWEITZER, *Civilization and Ethics*, 1923

Radical self-criticism is one of its [Christianity's] chief characteristics, because the revelation of Christ to which it testifies erects the absolute authority of God's holy will and judgment over all life, historical Christianity included.

HENDRIK KRAEMER, *The Christian Message in a Non-Christian World*, 1938

True self-revelation has always as its counterpart a growth in knowledge of God. For it is only in the light of God that we see ourselves for what we are.

EDWARD LEEN, *Progress Through Mental Prayer*, 1940

The only fruitful self-knowledge, and the only true one, is that which grows out of man's self-confrontation with God.

DIETRICH VON HILDEBRAND, *Transformation in Christ*, 1948

See also Faults; Humility; Hypocrisy; Modesty; Pride; Self; Self-Contempt; Self-Deception; Self-Love; Self-Pity; Self-Praise; Self-Respect; Self-Righteousness; Spiritual Progress; Vainglory; Vanity.

SELFLESSNESS

As flowing rivers disappear into the sea, losing their name and form, thus a wise man, freed from name and form, goes to the divine person who is beyond all.

Mundaka Upanishad, between 700 and 400 B.C.

Cast your slough. Spit forth intelligence. Ignore all differences. Become one with the infinite. Release your mind. Free your soul. Be vacuous. Be Nothing! Let all things revert to their original consititution.

Chuang-tzu, c. 300 B.C.

By the unceasing and absolute renunciation of thyself and all things, thou shalt in pureness cast all things aside, and be released from all, and so shalt be led upwards to the Ray of that Divine Darkness which exceedeth all existence.

DIONYSIUS THE AREOPAGITE, *De Mystica Theologia*, c. 500 A.D.

Forsake thyself, resign thyself, and thou shalt enjoy great inward peace.

> THOMAS À KEMPIS, *Imitation of Christ,* 1441

When we empty ourselves of all that is creature and rid ourselves of it for the love of God, that same Lord will fill our souls with Himself.

> ST. TERESA OF ÁVILA, *The Interior Castle,* 1577

The more we address and commit ourselves to God, and reject ourselves, the better it is for us.

> MICHEL DE MONTAIGNE, *Essays,* Bk. 2, ch. 12, 1580

Man can become part of God's unity, which is eternal, only by forgetfulness of self.

> RABBI NAHMAN OF BRATSLAV (1772–1811), quoted in *Judaism,* ed. A. Hertzberg

My "little way" is the way of spiritual childhood, the way of trust and absolute self-surrender.

> ST. THÉRÈSE OF LISIEUX (1873–1897), *Autobiography,* publ. posth.

As the soul ceases to be "self-regarding" in its activities, it becomes "God-regarding."

> EDWARD LEEN, *Progress Through Mental Prayer,* 1940

Our Lady said yes for the human race. Each one of us must echo that yes for our own lives. We are all asked if we will surrender what we are, our humanity, our flesh and blood, to the Holy Spirit and allow Christ to fill the emptiness by the particular shape of our life.

> CARYLL HOUSELANDER, *The Reed of God,* 1944

When man is capable of forgetting himself for another, then he is a man.

> ROBERT W. GLEASON, *To Live in Christ,* 1961

See also Abandonment; Asceticism; Contemplation; Detachment; Freedom; Ideals; Love; Love of God; Man's Unity with God; Martyrdom; Martyrs; Mystical Experience; Prayer: Defined and Explained; Religion: Its Nature and Function; Renunciation; Resignation; Sacrifice; Self-Giving; Self-Sacrifice; Spiritual; Submission; Suffering; Virtue; Worship.

SELF-LOVE

The good man should be a lover of self (for he will both profit himself by doing noble acts, and will benefit his fellows), but the wicked man should not.

> ARISTOTLE (384–322 B.C.), *Politics*

Our self-love endures more impatiently the condemnation of our tastes than of our opinions.

> LA ROCHEFOUCAULD, *Maxims,* 1665

None loves himself too little.

> BENJAMIN WHICHCOTE, *Moral and Religious Aphorisms,* 1753

Self-love, in the true sense, is the love of one's real good—of truth, of virtue, of beauty, of God. It is the strongest in those who are most alive in their higher nature. It is the opposite of selfish love.

> JOHN LANCASTER SPALDING, *Glimpses of Truth,* 1903

Self-love is the great enemy which must be overcome. Self-love separates man from God, it blocks the channels of self-spending and self-offering, both toward God and toward man.

> ANDERS NYGREN, *Agape and Eros,* I, 1932

Concentration on self—auto-eroticism—is the beginning of all sin.

> ALEXANDER YELCHANINOV (1881–1934), *Fragments of a Diary*

Only a love that comes to us from without and gives our lives a new centre in the One

who loves us can break the fetters of our
self-love.
> W. A. VISSER 'T HOOFT and J. H. OLD-
> HAM, *The Church and Its Function in
> Society,* 1937

Sin is a tree with a great many branches,
but it has only one root, namely, the
inordinate love of self.
> KIRBY PAGE, *Living Joyously,* 1950

See also Falsehood; Pride; Self-Deception;
Self-Defense; Self-Interest; Selfishness; Self
Knowledge; Self-Praise; Self-Respect; Self-
Will; Vainglory; Vanity.

SELF-PITY

I wept because I had no shoes, then I met
a man who had no feet.
> Saying derived from Sa'di (1193–1292)

See also Gloom; Misery; Pessimism; Melancholy; Pessimism; Sadness; Self-Deception, Self-Knowledge.

SELF-PRAISE

Do not say things. What you are stands
over you the while, and thunders so that I
cannot hear what you say to the contrary.
> RALPH WALDO EMERSON, *Letters and
> Social Aims,* 1876

See also Conceit; Falsehood; Humility;
Man: His Self-Deification; Praise; Pride;
Self-Knowledge; Self-Love; Vainglory;
Vanity.

SELF-PRESERVATION

The more a man can preserve his being
and seek what is useful to him, the greater
is his virtue.
> BARUCH SPINOZA, *Ethics,* IV, 1677

See also Health; Self-Defense; Self-Interest; Self-Love, War, Just.

SELF-RELIANCE

Whosoever . . . shall be a lamp unto
themselves, and a refuge unto themselves,
. . . holding fast to the Truth as their
lamp . . . shall not look for refuge to any
one besides themselves—it is they . . .
who shall reach the very topmost height.
> BUDDHA (563–483 B.C.), *Dialogues of
> Buddha,* ed. T. W. R. Davids

Trust thyself: every heat vibrates to that
iron string. Accept the place the divine
Providence has found for you; the society
of your contemporaries, the connection of
events.
> RALPH WALDO EMERSON, "Self-Reli-
> ance," *Essays,* 1841

See also Confidence; Optimism; Security;
Self-Respect.

SELF-RESPECT

If a person could be persuaded . . . that
we are all originally descended from God,
and that he is the Father of gods and men,
I conceive he never would think meanly or
degenerately concerning himself.
> EPICTETUS, *Discourses of,* c. 110 A.D.

See also Self-Defense; Self-Interest; Self-
Knowledge; Self-Love; Self-Reliance.

SELF-RIGHTEOUSNESS

A cold, self-righteous prig who goes regularly to Church, may be far nearer to hell
than a prostitute. But, of course, it is
better to be neither.
> C. S. LEWIS, *Christian Behavior,* 1943

In the kind of world that I see in history
there is one sin that locks people up in all
their other sins . . . the sin of self-righteousness.
> HERBERT BUTTERFIELD, *Christianity
> and History,* 1950

Beware of the man of complete unquestionable virtue, the upstanding self-righ-

teous citizen, who for all creatures of weakness has one general attitude: "Give them hell."

DAVID ABRAHAMSEN, *Who Are the Guilty?*, 1958

See also Pharisee; Righteousness; Self-Deception; Self-Knowledge; Self-Love; Self-Praise; Zealots.

SELF-SACRIFICE

Self-sacrifice is the most conspicuous element of a virtuous and religious character; and it is certainly far less common among men than among women, whose whole lives are usually spent in yielding to the will and consulting the pleasure of another.

W. E. H. LECKY, *History of European Morals*, 1869

Self-sacrifice is the real miracle out of which all the reported miracles grew.

RALPH WALDO EMERSON, *Courage*, 1877

The Christian duty of self-sacrifice for something higher has no existence whatever for the State, because there is nothing whatever beyond it in world-history; consequently it cannot sacrifice itself for anything higher.

HEINRICH TREITSCHKE (1834–1896), *Selections from Politics*

We need not surely hesitate to count among the "blessed dead," all those to whom death came in answer to the offer of the best which they could give, in a supreme endeavor to fulfill life's highest purpose.

JOHN MAUD, *Our Comradeship with the Blessed Dead*, 1915

It is only through the mystery of self-sacrifice that a man may find himself anew.

CARL G. JUNG, *Two Essays on Analytical Psychology*, 1928

As an arranged scheme of self-deliverance from evil, self-sacrifice is apt to be only an arranged scheme of self-exaltation.

JOHN OMAN, *The Natural and the Supernatural*, 1931

He who sacrifices his life to achieve any purpose for an individual or for humanity is practicing life-affirmation.

ALBERT SCHWEITZER, *Indian Thoughts*, 1936

See also Abandonment; Abstinence; Asceticism; Celibacy; Detachment; Discipline; Fasting; Martyrdom; Martyrs; Renunciation; Resignation; Sacrifice; Self-Denial; Self-Discipline; Self-Giving; Selflessness; Submission; Virginity.

SELF-WILL

Hell is nothing but self-will, and if there were no self-will there would be no Devil and no hell. . . . When we say self-will, we mean: To will otherwise than as the One and Eternal Will of God wills.

Theologica Germanica, 14th century

Be not under the dominion of thine own will; it is the vice of the ignorant, who vainly presume on their own understanding.

MIGUEL DE CERVANTES, *Don Quixote*, 1605

I have no higher idea than disbelief in God. . . . to recognize that there is no God and not to recognize at the same instant that one is God oneself is an absurdity. . . . The attribute of my godhead is self-will!

KIRILLOV, in Feodor Dostoevsky's *The Possessed*, 1871

If there is no God, then I am God. . . . If God exists, all is His will and from His will I cannot escape. If not, it's all my will and I am bound to show self-will. . . . I want to manifest my self-will . . . I am bound to shoot myself because the highest point of my self-will is to kill myself with my own hands.

KIRILLOV, in Feodor Dostoevsky's *The Possessed,* 1871

See also Free Will; Man: His Self-Deification; Pride; Self; Selfishness; Self-Love; Vainglory; Vanity.

SEMINARIES

The seminary puts emphasis on the instincts of passivity and submission.

SERGIUS WROBLEWSKI, *Proceedings* of 5th Annual National Catholic Education Association Convention, April, 1962

A pervasive seriousness of purpose, and a disciplined approach of a Seminary to its task; a manifest enthusiasm on the part of faculty and students in a deep mutuality of interest to discover Christian truth and to relate it to the needs of the contemporary world; an openness to the insights and findings of secular disciplines and movements as these offer illumination to the Seminary in its work . . . a recognition by the Seminary of the value of honest differences in enriching the Christian fellowship; and a steady resolve to maintain, against further fragmentation, the integrity of the Christian witness before the world.

From Statement of Requirements for membership in the American Association of Theological Schools, *Bulletin,* June, 1962

Given the universal nature of the Christian Gospel, no purist attitude toward the academic life can justify the withdrawal of the seminary community from the more inclusive community of Christ. The sight of seminarians being educated in denominational isolation on their respective holy hills is not a happy one.

WALTER D. WAGONER, *Unity in Mid-Career,* 1963

What a bland and sterile clergy will be produced if seminaries are expected to be only the assembly lines for properly molded churchmen of this or that lineage!

WALTER D. WAGONER, *Unity in Mid-Career,* 1963

See also Education, Religious; Theology.

SENSES. See SENSUALITY

SENSUALITY

He who lives looking for pleasures only, his senses uncontrolled, immoderate in his enjoyments, idle and weak. Mara [the tempter] will certainly overcome him, as the wind blows down a weak tree.

Dhammapada, c. 5th century B.C.

For the mind that yields to the uncontrolled and wandering senses, carries away his wisdom just as a boat on water is carried away by wind.

Bhagavad-Gita, c. 2nd century B.C.

When the soul is troubled, lonely and darkened, then it turns easily to the outer comfort and to the empty enjoyment of the world.

ST. FRANCIS OF ASSISI (1181?–1226), *Little Flowers of*

The soul that has been created for no other end than to love God, and to live in union with Him, will never be able to find peace or happiness in sensual enjoyments; God alone can make it perfectly content.

ST. ALPHONSUS DE LIGUORI, *Preface for Death,* c. 1760

Sensuality is the vice of young men and of old nations.

W. E. H. LECKY, *History of European Morals,* 1869

A religion which neglects the senses is doomed to failure for the simple reason that men and women in all the major concerns of life, whether it be love-making or the formation of city and community life, are stirred by what they can see and feel and touch.

> MARTIN C. D'ARCY, *Mirage and Truth,* 1935

As Christians, we do not have to renounce everything that gives pleasure to the senses. But we do have to moderate our use of sense pleasures. Original sin has left us easy marks for the allurements of sense.

> JOHN C. FORD, *Sanctity and Success in Marriage,* 1956

See also Alcohol; Gluttony; Lust; Pleasure; Repression; Sex; Sexual Intercourse; Sexuality; Vice; Worldliness.

SENTIMENTALISM

We know immediately what "Dick" Sheppard meant when he told the Church that it had reduced Christ's whole message to the motto "Be kind to granny and the cat."

> F. B. SPEAKMAN, *The Salty Tang,* 1954

See also Emotion.

SEPARATED BRETHREN

We may be separated brethren; but we are "brethren" notwithstanding.

> AELRED GRAHAM, *Christian Thought and Action,* 1951

If we are in any way to blame for this separation [between the Church of Rome and non-Roman Catholic Christians] we humbly beg God's pardon and ask our separated brothers also to forgive us for whatever we have done that injured them. For our part we willingly forgive the injuries the Catholic Church [Roman] has suffered and forget the grief caused during the long period of dissension and separation.

> POPE PAUL VI, *Address,* opening of the Second Session of Vatican Council II, 1963

SEPARATION

He who sends his wife away is a hateful person.

> JOHANN., *Talmud: Gittin,* c. 500 A.D.

Husbands and wives should never separate if there is no Christian demand for it. It is better to await the logic of events than for a wife precipitately to leave her husband, or for a husband to leave his wife.

> MARY BAKER EDDY, *Science and Health,* 1908

See also Divorce; Marriage.

SERENITY

He who discerns all creatures in his Self, and his Self in all creatures, has no disquiet thence. What delusion, what grief can be with him?

> *Isavasya Upanishad,* between 700 and 400 B.C.

A serene spirit accepts pleasure and pain with an even mind, and is unmoved by either. He alone is worthy of immortality.

> *Bhagavad-Gita,* between 500 and 200 B.C.

Undisturbed calmness of mind is attained by cultivating friendliness toward the happy, compassion for the unhappy, delight in the virtuous, and indifference toward the wicked.

> PATANJALI (2nd century B.C.), *Yoga Aphorisms*

Seek not to have that everything should happen as you wish, but wish for everything to happen as it actually does happen, and you will be serene.

> EPICTETUS, *Enchiridion,* VIII, c. 110 A.D.

There's naught so much the spirit calms as rum and true religion.

> LORD BYRON, *Don Juan,* 1819

Serenity comes not alone by removing the outward causes and occasions of fear, but by the discovery of inward reservoirs to draw upon.

RUFUS M. JONES, *The Testimony of the Soul,* 1936

The final wisdom of life requires not the annulment of incongruity but the achievement of serenity within and above it.

REINHOLD NIEBUHR, *The Irony of American History,* 1952

See also Abandonment; Acceptance; Anxiety; Detachment; Fear; Grief; Nirvana; Optimism; Order; Pain; Patience; Peace; Peace of Mind; Resignation; Selflessness; Silence; Suffering; Tranquillity.

SERMON ON THE MOUNT

The Sermon on the Mount was and is seditious. It finally put Jesus on the cross, and it will do the same for his followers who follow it in modern life.

E. STANLEY JONES, *The Christ of the Mount,* 1931

The sheer genius of the Sermon on the Mount lies in the fact that within its short compass the great Master Teacher has told us the inner truth about our own lives in such a manner that it continually, age after age, searches out our weaknesses, our blind spots, our hidden secrets, which we hardly like to lay bare even to ourselves.

C. F. ANDREWS, *The Sermon on the Mount,* 1942

There is a hard wall of separation between the sublime and non-violent ethics of the Sermon on the Mount and their application in everyday life. It is as though it were more important to belong than it is to believe.

NORMAN COUSINS, *In Place of Folly,* 1961

SERMONS

He that has but one word of God before him, and out of that word cannot make a sermon, can never be a preacher.

MARTIN LUTHER (1483–1546), *Table Talk*

The great object of modern sermons is to hazard nothing; their characteristic is decent debility.

SYDNEY SMITH, *Edinburgh Review,* 1802

Every attempt in a sermon to cause emotion, except as the consequence of an impression made on the reason, or the understanding, or the will, I hold to be fanatical and sectarian.

SAMUEL TAYLOR COLERIDGE, *Table Talk,* January 7, 1833

The making and delivery of an effective sermon is not only the most conspicuous, but the most influential single service the minister is privileged to render in the whole round of the week's activity.

CHARLES R. BROWN, *The Art of Preaching,* 1922

We are not called upon to produce great sermons, or to become "great preachers," as the saying of some is,—we are commissioned to produce by our work as preachers some great Christians.

CHARLES R. BROWN, *The Art of Preaching,* 1922

The best sermon is that preached in such human understanding that a hearer can say: "It was preached for me as though I had been alone."

GEORGE A. BUTTRICK, *Jesus Came Preaching,* 1931

When the congregation becomes the norm by which sermons are measured, a minister has put a mortgage on his soul.

RALPH W. SOCKMAN, *The Highway of God,* 1941

No sermon lands effectively on the field of a sinful heart unless at some point it opposes the trend of that heart's earthly desire.

> RALPH W. SOCKMAN, *The Highway of God,* 1941

A near-hit bolt of lightning can create a lot more Christian thinking than a long-winded sermon.

> DUANE DEWEL, *Kossuth County Advance,* Iowa, quoted in *A Little Treasury of Main Street, U.S.A.,* 1952

The devil's favorite Sunday-morning entertainment is the sermon which does not cause a ripple of disturbance, intellectual, moral or emotional, to man, woman, or beadle.

> A. C. CRAIG, *Preaching in a Scientific Age,* 1954

Ministers have learned nice people don't like ugly sermons.

> WALDO BEACH, *News and Observer,* Raleigh, N.C., July 26, 1959

Though a true sermon may be in a measure true anywhere, it is most centrally and sharply true in the congregation for whom it is prepared.

> GEORGE A. BUTTRICK, *Sermons Preached in a University Church,* 1959

I'd rather see a sermon than hear one any day;
I'd rather one should walk with me than merely tell the way.

> EDGAR A. GUEST (1881–1959), "Sermons We See"

The church bell sometimes does better work than the sermon.

> American Proverb

See also Congregation; Eloquence; Minister; Ministry; Orator; Preachers; Preaching; Preaching and the Bible; Revivalism; Rhetoric; Speech; Word, the; Words.

SERVANTS

It is a bad servant who serves God from fear and terror or from the desire of a reward.

> RĀBI'A AL-'ADAWĪYA (died 801 A.D.), *al-Hidāya*

Ladies and gentlemen are permitted to have friends in the kennel, but not in the kitchen.

> GEORGE BERNARD SHAW, *Socialism of,* ed. J. Fuchs, 1926

SERVICE

In this life no man reaches the point at which he can be excused from practical service.

> MEISTER ECKHART (1260?–1327?), *Meister Eckhart,* R. P. Blakney

Christianity . . . makes a man's greatness consist in the amount of service he renders to the world.

> THEODORE PARKER, *Thoughts on Labor,* 1841

The vocation of every man and woman is to serve other people.

> LEO TOLSTOY, *What Is To Be Done?,* 1886

You must act in your friend's interest whether it pleases him or not; the object of love is to serve, not to win.

> WOODROW WILSON, *Address,* Princeton, May 9, 1907

Take that gift that God has entrusted to you no matter how humble it may seem to be, and use it in the service of Christ and your fellow men. He will make it glow and shine like the very stars of heaven.

> JOHN SUTHERLAND BONNELL, *What Are You Living For?,* 1950

See also Call; Humanity; Vocation; Work.

SERVITUDE

A man's inability to moderate and control his passions I call servitude.
> BARUCH SPINOZA, *Ethics*, 1677

SEX

Christianity places the sexual instinct under a spiritual law, and permits its gratification only for the definite purpose of creating a Christian home.
> FATHER CUTHBERT, *Catholic Ideals in Social Life*, 1904

We have two tyrannous physical passions: concupiscence and chastity. We become mad in pursuit of sex: we become equally mad in the persecution of that pursuit. Unless we gratify our desire the race is lost; unless we restrain it we destroy ourselves.
> GEORGE BERNARD SHAW, Preface, *Androcles and the Lion*, 1914

The judgment of sex in its modern idolatry becomes a testimony to man's need of the life and love which God alone can bestow, a witness to the reality it prefigures and reflects.
> E. I. WATKIN, *The Bow in the Clouds*, 1931

The most powerful stimulant of sex is the effort to suppress it. There is only one cure—to take it up simply, frankly and naturally into the circle of our activities.
> JOHN MACMURRAY, *Reason and Emotion*, 1936

Sex which is not integrated and transfigured by spirit is always evidence of man's subjugation to the genus.
> NICHOLAS BERDYAEV, *Dream and Reality*, 1939

To use the word "sex" intelligently, means to connote by it more than a specific sensory excitement. It involves the whole affectional life of man, and a major part of his motive power in every realm of creativity.
> HARRY EMERSON FOSDICK, *On Being a Real Person*, 1943

There are people who want to keep our sex instinct inflamed in order to make money out of us. Because, of course, a man with an obsession is a man who has very little sales-resistance.
> C. S. LEWIS, *Christian Behavior*, 1943

The person is in search of the absolute, i.e., perfect happiness. To use sex as a substitute for the absolute is a vain attempt to turn the copy into the original.
> FULTON J. SHEEN, *Peace of Soul*, 1949

We pray that the young men and women of today and tomorrow will grow up with the realization that sex is a beautiful flame they carry in the lantern of their bodies.
> DEMETRIUS MANOUSOS, *Address*, March 14, 1950

In the history of theology specific discussions of sex have fallen prevailingly under the topic of "sin" and have received scant positive attention under "salvation."
> DAVID E. ROBERTS, *Psychotherapy and a Christian View of Man*, 1950

When it comes to denouncing sexual license, it is safe for all of us to mount the bandwagon. Still more profitably, perhaps, we may keep in mind the occasions when Christ our Lord refused to mount it.
> AELRED GRAHAM, *Christian Thought and Action*, 1951

When sex is divided from love there is a feeling that one has been stopped at the vestibule of the castle of pleasure; that the heart has been denied the city after crossing the bridge.
> FULTON J. SHEEN, *Three to Get Married*, 1951

If sex does not mount to heaven it descends into hell. There is no such thing as giving the body without giving the soul. Those who think they can be faithful in soul to one another, but unfaithful in body, forget that the two are inseparable.

FULTON J. SHEEN, *Three to Get Married*, 1951

Our sex standards in an era of medical technology and urban anonymity depend for their sanction upon devotion rather than dread.

JOSEPH FLETCHER, *Sex and Religion Today*, ed. Simon Doniger, 1953

Because of the fact of human freedom, sex is certainly an aspect of the doctrine of sin. But if we understand its nature, and attempt to have it include the sacramental, the romantic, and the interpersonal, it can also be a vital aspect of the doctrine of salvation.

SEWARD HILTNER, *Sex and Religion Today*, ed. Simon Doniger, 1953

Creation is the work of omnipotence. But procreation is pro-creation, a kind of deputy creation. So that sex in its essential nature is man's greatest glory in the physical order.

F. J. SHEED, *Society & Sanity*, 1953

There is a tendency to think of sex as something degrading; it is not, it is magnificent, an enormous privilege, but, because of that, the rules are tremendously strict and severe. . . . It is easy to serve God in most other ways, but it is not so easy here.

FRANCIS DEVAS, *The Law of Love*, 1954

For the very reason that sexual power is so noble and necessary a good, it needs the preserving and defending order of reason.

JOSEF PIEPER, *Fortitude and Temperance*, 1954

Human sexuality is too noble and beautiful a thing, too profound a form of experience, to turn into a mere technique of physical relief, or a foolish and irrelevant pastime.

J. V. L. CASSERLEY, *The Bent World*, 1955

Our tawdry doting on sex—quick to the soonest bed!—is an erotic rotting of gratitude that makes a travesty of love, a travesty of the wonder and joy of love that waits only upon our gratitude to be born in the great antiphonal song of man and woman, which no other creature on earth knows and sings.

ROBERT RAYNOLDS, *In Praise of Gratitude*, 1961

Christian teaching about sex is by no means clear in detail, but what shines with pellucid clarity throughout the Christian tradition is that sex is a very holy subject.

GEDDES MACGREGOR, *The Hemlock and the Cross*, 1963

Allowing for its crudities, the sexual revolution has been one of the few blessings in the life of this century.

V. S. PRITCHETT, quoted in *Time*, March 22, 1963

Sex is not a moral question. For answers you don't turn to a body of absolutes. The criterion should not be, "Is it morally right or wrong?" but "Is it socially feasible, is it personally healthy and rewarding, will it enrich life?"

GRANCOLLE FISHER, quoted in *Time*, January 24, 1964

See also Birth Control; Chastity; Courtship; Desires; Discipline; Dissipation; Eros; Erotic; Flesh; Fornication; Freud; Harmony; Hedonism; Homosexuality; Immorality; Love; Love, Human; Love, Physical; Lust; Marriage; Obscenity; Passions; Pleasure; Premarital Sex; Purity; Sensuality; Sex Education; Sexual Attraction; Sexual Desire; Sexual Intercourse; Sexual Love; Sexual Sin; Sexuality; Unchastity; Vice.

SEX EDUCATION

Far too common is the error of those who with dangerous assurance . . . propagate a so-called sex-education, falsely imagining

they can forearm youth against the dangers of sensuality by means purely natural.
POPE PIUS XI, *Christian Education of Youth,* 1929

It is a privilege to help children and youth effect the transition from sexual ignorance, superstition, and immaturity to an enlightened, wholesome maturity and adulthood.
ALEXANDER A. SCHNEIDERS, *The Child and Problems of Today,* 1952

There is nothing more damaging to adequate sex instruction than timidity, shame, embarrassment, or a general hyper-emotionalism regarding matters of sex. The attitude that sex is shameful, disgusting, immoral, and so on, makes it *impossible* for anyone to deal adequately with the problem.
ALEXANDER A. SCHNEIDERS, *The Child and Problems of Today,* 1952

Sexual information without relation to values is intellectually irresponsible.
PETER A. BERTOCCI, *Sex and Religion Today,* ed. Simon Doniger, 1953

It is simpler to treat sex morally than reasonably. Moreover, believing in sin is a kind of tactful armor. A girl might find, in a given situation, that it was better to tell a young man that he was doing wrong than that he was being a social dunce. His self-esteem would suffer less.
PHYLLIS MCGINLEY, *Good Housekeeping,* August, 1954

Knowing that children are healthfully curious—about sex as well as trucks and motors and planes—you can be active in helping them. . . . Children want and need to learn a great deal; sex has a niche in this learning but it is not the whole show. . . . One of the surprises is that sex barely holds it own with young children in competition with the million and one other ideas they also do not understand.
JAMES L. HYMES, JR., *How to Tell Your Child About Sex,* pamphlet, 1959

Wherever social life has become more urban, mobile and complex, the school has had to bridge this gap in learning that once was absorbed at the hearth.
ARON KRICH, Preface to *Facts of Love and Marriage for Young People,* ed. Aron Krich, 1962

No growth of understanding, which has not love as its centre, can ever claim to fulfill adequately the spiritual, psychological and physical requirements of this subject.
J. DOMINIAN, *Psychiatry and the Christian,* 1962

See also Premarital Sex.

SEXUAL ATTRACTION

A mutual sexual attraction is no proper basis for a human relationship between a man and a woman. It is an organic thing, not personal.
JOHN MACMURRAY, *Reason and Emotion,* 1936

The greatest illusion of lovers is to believe that the intensity of their sexual attraction is the guarantee of the perpetuity of their love. It is because of this failure to distinguish between the glandular and the spiritual . . . that marriages are so full of deception.
FULTON J. SHEEN, *Three to Get Married,* 1951

See also Courtship; Love, Human; Love, Physical; Lust; Marriage; Sex; Sexual Desire; Sexual Intercourse; Sexuality; Woman.

SEXUAL DESIRE

Whoever cannot bridle his carnal affections, let him keep them within the bounds of lawful wedlock.
Lactantius. *The Divine Institutes,* c. 310

The question is not whether we have sex-desire, but whether sex-desire has us.

E. STANLEY JONES, *Victorious Living,* 1936

A man and a woman may want one another passionately without either loving the other.

JOHN MACMURRAY, *Reason and Emotion,* 1936

Love may or may not include sexual attraction. It may express itself in sexual desire. But sexual desire is not love. Desire is quite compatible with personal hatred, or contempt, or indifference.

JOHN MACMURRAY, *Reason and Emotion,* 1936

See also Courtship; Desires; Libido; Love; Love, Human; Love, Physical; Lust; Marriage; Passions; Repression; Sex; Sexual Attraction; Sexual Intercourse; Sexuality; Woman.

SEXUAL ETHICS

Perhaps when we know more we shall be able to say that the best sexual ethic will be quite different in one climate from what it would be in another, different again with one kind of diet than from what it would be with another.

BERTAND RUSSELL, *Marriage and Morals,* 1929

See also Adultery; Fornication; Marriage; Sex; Sexual Intercourse; Sexual Sin.

SEXUAL INTERCOURSE

Now in this usual function of the sexes which brings male and female together—I mean, in ordinary intercourse—we know that the soul and the body both take part; the soul through the desire, the body through its realization, the soul through the impulse, the body through the act.

TERTULLIAN, *De Anima,* c. 209 A.D.

Nature is to be reverenced, not blushed at. It is lust, not the act itself, that makes sexual union shameful; it is excess, not the [marital] state as such, that is unchaste.

TERTULLIAN, *De Anima,* c. 209

The union of the two sexes is meant only for the purpose of procreation in a man's lifetime, and the carnal affections are rendered legitimate by the production of children.

LACTANTIUS, *The Divine Institutes,* c. 310

Where it is possible at once to be true to the diviner love, and to embrace wedlock, there is no reason for setting aside this dispensation of nature and misrepresenting as abominable that which is honorable.

ST. GREGORY OF NYSSA (c. 335–c. 395), *On Virginity*

Rabbi Joshua ben Levi said: "A man who knows that his wife fears heaven and does not fulfill his marital duty of cohabitation is to be called a sinner."

Yebamot, Mishnah, c. 400 A.D.

But I am aware of some that murmur: if all men should abstain from intercourse, how will the human race exist? Would that all would abstain; much more speedily would the City of God be filled, and the end of the world hastened.

ST. AUGUSTINE, *On the Good of Marriage,* c. 401

An advance beyond moderation in demanding the due of either sex . . . is allowed to married persons as a matter of pardon.

ST. AUGUSTINE, *On the Good of Marriage,* c. 401

The union of male and female for the purpose of procreation is the natural good of marriage. But he makes a bad use of this good who uses it bestially, so that his intention is on the gratification of lust, instead of the desire of offspring.

ST. AUGUSTINE, *On Marriage and Concupiscence,* c. 425

Let not the fear of bad offspring deter you. . . . You do your duty and the Holy One will do what pleases Him.

HAMMUNA, *Talmud: Berakot,* c. 500

Although connubial intercourse with one's wife is always permitted, this relation should be invested by the scholar with sanctity. He should not always be with his spouse, like a rooster.

MAIMONIDES, *Mishneh Torah,* 1170

As long as the sexual act itself corresponds to the rational order, the abundance of pleasure does not conflict with the proper mean of virtue. . . . And even the fact that reason is unable to make a free act of cognition of spiritual things simultaneously with that pleasure does not prove that the sexual act conflicts with virtue.

ST. THOMAS AQUINAS, *Summa Theologicae,* II, II, 153, oly. 2, ad. 2, 1272

The marriage act is always sinful or meritorious in one who is in a state of grace. For if the motive for the marriage act be virtue, whether of justice that they may render the debt or of religion, that they may beget children for the worship of God, it is meritorious. But if the motive be lust . . . it is a venial sin.

ST. THOMAS AQUINAS, *Summa Theologicae,* Q. 41, art. 4, *Suppl.* III, 1272

When God at first institution of marriage, had this first use of marriage in contemplation, that it should be a remedy against burning, God gave man that remedy, before he had the disease; for marriage was instituted in the state of innocency, when there was no inordinateness in the affections of man, and no burning.

JOHN DONNE, *Sermon,* May 30, 1621

In truth all experiences of the Divine Unity and Holiness depend on the union between man and woman, for the ultimate meaning of this act is very lofty.

RABBI NAHMAN OF BRATSLAV (1772–1811), quoted in *Judaism,* ed. A. Hertzberg

The whole world depends on the holiness of the union between man and woman, for the world was created for the sake of God's glory and the essential revelation of His glory comes through the increase of mankind.

RABBI NAHMAN OF BRATSLAV (1772–1811), quoted in *Judaism,* ed. A. Hertzberg

The beauty of love . . . vanishes if its mere physical expression be consciously sought as a means of sensual gratification, without the spiritual and aesthetic accompaniments that alone give it human value.

HARRY ROBERTS, Letter, *New Statesman and Nation,* August 29, 1931

It is not true that the relations between the sexes are of the same order with the rest of man's instincts. They have social consequences which place them in a class apart.

ERNEST DIMNET, *What We Live By,* 1932

Sexual culmination of biological union with natural life and consequent procreation of that life, is the best reflection on the natural plane of that spiritual union and fecundity in which the spiritual life culminates.

E. I. WATKINS, *The Bow in the Clouds,* 1932

Either the mysterious union of two human beings takes place in the sight of God or man flings himself away, surrenders his secret, delivers himself over to the flesh, desecrates and violates the secret of another, severs himself in a mysterious fashion from God.

DIETRICH VON HILDEBRAND, *In Defense of Purity,* 1933

Real personal love is the basis in the absence of which sexual relations are unchaste and immoral.

JOHN MACMURRAY, *Reason and Emotion,* 1936

Between two human beings who love one another, the sexual relationship is one of the possible expressions of love. . . . It is neither something high and holy, something to venerate and be proud of, nor is it something low and contemptible, to be ashamed of. It is a simple organic function to be used like all the others, for the expression of personality in the service of love.

JOHN MACMURRAY, *Reason and Emotion,* 1936

Married love is a creative enterprise. It is not achieved by accident or instinct. Perfunctory coitus is a confession of lack of intelligence and character. There is a profound beauty and even holiness in the act of fecundation.

ALEXIS CARREL, *Reader's Digest,* July, 1939

To reduce cohabitation and the conjugal act to a simple organic function for the transmission of seed would be converting the home, the sanctuary of the family, into a mere biological laboratory.

POPE PIUS XII, *Address to Italian Midwives,* October, 1946

If the union of man and woman is the fruit of a love that is given in purity, generosity and fidelity, then the body itself is spiritualized in the service of a love that ennobles it, and, with God's blessing, sanctifies.

JEAN MOUROUX, *The Meaning of Man,* 1948

The union between the partners is transcendental. God has bound them together. Each party should love the Christ in the other. Every time intercourse occurs they do something holy.

ALLEN KEENAN, *Neuroses and Sacraments,* 1950

The fact of human experience seems to be that persons enjoy deeper, more lasting, and more profound satisfaction when normal experience of sex lust is not primarily an end in itself but a symbolic expression of other values.

PETER A. BERTOCCI, *The Human Venture in Sex, Love and Marriage,* 1951

The gravity and sanctity of the Christian moral law do not permit an unrestrained satisfaction of the sexual instinct, which tends only to pleasure and enjoyment; they do not allow rational man to let himself be dominated up to that point, as to either the substance or the circumstances of the act.

POPE PIUS XII, *Address to Newlyweds,* October 29, 1951

Vital ecstasy is self-surrender not to the other being as such but to the other being as far as it is the other side of the love-unity.

PAUL TILLICH, *Moral Principles of Action,* ed. Ruth N. Anshen, 1952

The sexual act takes on qualitative significance and value which transcends the other meanings the sexual act can have, when lovers use the act purposely to become parents. For now the two lovers express their faith in love itself, in the possibilities open to their children within the social order and in this world.

PETER A. BERTOCCI, *Sex and Religion Today,* ed. Simon Doniger, 1953

A *holy* sexual relationship is one in which the interrelatedness and wholeness of *function* and *being* are preserved and honored in thought and act.

Reuel L. Howe, *Sex and Religion Today,* ed. Simon Doniger, 1953

A union of bodies is not the fulness of sexual union. It is valid only as an expression of the union of two personalities.

F. J. SHEED, *Society and Sanity,* 1953

In marriage and the consummation of marriage you get, where it is done perfectly by perfect lovers and perfect lovers of God, the very final culmination of love, a complete man and complete woman, body, soul, imagination, emotion,—all united in subservience to God.

FRANCIS DEVAS, *The Law of Love,* 1954

The creation of one flesh in the biblical sense involves the joining of two total existences, economically, spiritually, and psychologically, and not just the union of two bodies. To attempt the one without the other is dangerous to the entire relationship.

WILLIAM G. COLE, *Sex in Christianity and Psychoanalysis,* 1955

The marriage act ought not to be something roughly demanded or taken but something tenderly sought and mutually given, with each party realizing his or her obligation in justice to cooperate.

CHARLES HUGO DOYLE, *The Grail,* September, 1957

Only when husband and wife unite naturally is the union of sperm and ovum possible. Therefore the primary purpose of the marital act is in conception of human life.

GEORGE A. KELLEY, *The Catholic Marriage Manual,* 1958

The Biblical revelation . . . does not limit the function of sexuality and the family to the reproductive purpose. Equally deeply rooted in Genesis is the reflection of a second factor—the need of man and woman for each other, to complement and fulfill each other and to establish a durable partnership against the loneliness and rigor of life.

Lambeth Conference (of Anglican Bishops), 1958

This act, done under the influence of a soaring and iridescent Eros, which reduces the role of the senses to a minor consideration, may yet be plain adultery, may involve breaking a wife's heart, deceiving a husband. . . . It has not pleased God that the distinction between a sin and a duty should turn on fine feelings.

C. S. LEWIS, *The Four Loves,* 1960

Judaism does not regard sexual union as a concession to the flesh but as a proper and sacred act.

ARTHUR HERTZBERG, *Judaism,* 1961

The sexual act has no resemblance to any other act: its demands are frenzied and participate in infinity. It is a tidal wave able to cover everything and bear away everything.

FRANÇOIS MAURIAC, *What I Believe,* 1962

The popular morality is now a wasteland. It is littered with the debris of broken convictions. A new concept is emerging, of sexual relationships as a source of pleasure, but also as a mutual encountering of personalities in which each explores the other and at the same time discovers new depths in himself or herself.

GEORGE MORRISON CARSTAIRS, BBC lecture, quoted in *Time,* March 22, 1963

Grandeur and beauty come to the moment of sexual union from the total of what a man and a woman have been able to express in all the rest of their life together. Sexual union will then be the culmination of past love, and the sustenance of love to come.

HENRI GIBERT, *Love in Marriage,* 1964

Because the human self is a person (not just a body), marital intercourse must be a communion of *persons,* a loving *personal* exchange. To the extent that actual sexual intimacy recedes from the personal, to that extent it ceases to be an act of love and approximates more closely to the mating of mere animals.

RICHARD A. McCORMICK, *America,* January 11, 1964

Outside marriage, sexual intercourse is a self-giving without self-commitment, and hence is meaningless.

RICHARD A. McCORMICK, *America,* January 11, 1964

See also Abortion; Adultery; Artificial Insemination; Birth Control; Celibacy; Chastity; Continence; Desires; Eros; Erotic; Fornication; Hedonism; Husband and Wife; Immorality; Impurity; Love; Love, Human; Love, Physical; Lust; Marriage; Passions; Pleasure; Reproduction, Rhythm Method; Sensuality; Sex; Sexual Attraction; Sexual Desire; Sexual Ethics; Sexual Sin; Sexuality; Sterilization; Virginity; Woman.

SEXUAL LOVE. See
LOVE, HUMAN;
LOVE, PHYSICAL;
SEXUAL INTERCOURSE

SEXUAL SIN

In Catholic sex morality, the deliberate arousal of sexual thoughts that are of their nature destined to be preparatory to sexual stimulation and the complete act is of itself a serious sin.

> HAROLD C. GARDINER, *Catholic Viewpoint of Censorship,* 1957

Sexual incontinence . . . is not the gravest of sins. Compared to the spiritual pride of the Pharisees, Our Lord seems to have viewed it almost with mildness. But there can be no doubt that control by the faith-enlightened reason of the most imperious of human instincts is a condition, a *sine qua non,* of any sustained devotion to religion.

> AELRED GRAHAM, *Christian Thought and Action,* 1951

Penal sanctions are not justified for the purpose of attempting to restrain sins against sexual morality committed in private by responsible adults.

> J. DOMINIAN, *Psychiatry and the Christian,* 1962

See also Adultery; Dissipation; Fornication; Homosexuality; Impurity; Perversion; Premarital Sex; Sexual Ethics; Unchastity.

SEXUALITY

What has been encouraged as healthy sexuality is but an expression of the brutal, fiendish rationalism (not reason) that harries love, and the relationship between man and woman has become one of the saddest commentaries of our time.

> RUTH N. ANSHEN, *Our Emergent Civilization,* 1947

We must know how to give sexuality the high and exact place that belongs to it when it serves to express the gesture of an open-handed giver and not the grasping move of a selfish hoarder.

> HENRI GIBERT, *Love in Marriage,* 1964

It is not human "to act the beast," to deify sexuality and set it up as an absolute. Raw sexual appetite is no more a sign of love than violence and brutality are signs of strength.

> HENRI GIBERT, *Love in Marriage,* 1964

See also Desires; Eros; Lust; Pleasure; Passions; Sensuality; Sex; Sexual Attraction; Sexual Desire; Sexual Intercourse.

SHADOW

Always there is a black spot in our sunshine—the shadow of ourselves.

> THOMAS CARLYLE, *Sartor Resartus,* 1836

SHAME

Shame is the mark of a base man, and belongs to a character capable of shameful acts.

> ARISTOTLE, *The Nicomachean Ethics,* c. 340 B.C.

In shame there is no comfort, but to be beyond all bounds of shame.

> PHILIP SIDNEY, *Arcadia,* 1590

I never wonder to see men wicked, but I often wonder to see them not ashamed.

> JONATHAN SWIFT, *Thoughts on Various Subjects,* 1706

Where there's no shame before men, there's no fear of God.

> Yiddish Proverb

SICKNESS

To be born and in a mortal body is to begin to be sick.

> ST. AUGUSTINE, *Ennart. in Ps.*, c. 415

Both sin and sickness are error, and Truth is their remedy.

> MARY BAKER EDDY, *Science and Health,* 1908

Man is never sick, for Mind is not sick and matter cannot be. . . . Sickness is not real. . . . Truth can destroy its seeming reality.

> MARY BAKER EDDY, *Science and Health,* 1908

Illness is often a blessing. By ravaging the body it frees the soul and purifies it. . . . No man who has never been ill can have a thorough knowledge of himself.

> ROMAIN ROLLAND, *Jean Christophe,* 1912

See also Adversity; Affliction; Christian Science; Healing; Health; Misery; Pain; Suffering.

SILENCE

All my days I grew up among the sages, and I have found nothing better for a person than silence.

> *Pirke Aboth, Talmud,* between 2nd and 4th century A.D.

When one of the flock sins mortally through his own fault, then he who is set above, because he kept silent, is responsible.

> POPE ST. GREGORY THE GREAT (540–604), *In Ezech.*

Cautious silence is the holy of holies of worldly wisdom.

> BALTASAR GRACIÁN, *The Art of Worldly Wisdom,* 1647

Silence is the greatest persecution.

> BLAISE PASCAL, *Pensées,* 1670

That soul is not idle which, holding itself in the presence of God, keeps interior silence. . . . For the will to keep silence is an act of veneration.

> F. MALAVA (fl. 1671), *A Simple Method*

The world would be happier if men had the same capacity to be silent that they have to speak.

> BARUCH SPINOZA, *Ethics,* 1677

Think not silence the wisdom of fools; but, if rightly timed, the honor of wise men, who have not the infirmity, but the virtue of taciturnity.

> THOMAS BROWNE, *Christian Morals,* 1680

How can you expect God to speak in that gentle and inward voice which melts the soul, when you are making so much noise with your rapid reflections? Be silent and God will speak again.

> FRANÇOIS FÉNELON (1651–1715), *Spiritual Letters,* no. XXII

Silence is golden only to those who have power to hear divine melodies—songs of angels and symphonies of heaven.

> JOHN LANCASTER SPALDING, *Essays and Reviews,* 1877

The cruelest lies are often told in silence.

> ROBERT LOUIS STEVENSON, *Virginibus Puerisque,* 1881

Among all nations there should be vast temples raised where people might worship Silence and listen to it, for it is the voice of God.

> JEROME K. JEROME, *Diary of a Pilgrimage,* 1891

No sooner are the lips still than the soul awakes, and sets forth on its labors.

> MAURICE MAETERLINCK, *The Treasure of the Humble,* 1897

The voices that speak to us out of the silence are silent voices, though they are by no means voices that cannot be heard. . . . The voice of God can be heard only in and through the silence.

> GLENN CLARK, *The Soul's Sincere Desire*, 1925

"Be still and know that I am God" is not an arbitrary command; it is a psychological necessity.

> A. MAUDE ROYDEN, *Federal Council Bulletin*, January, 1931

All speech and reasoning, all eloquence and science, all methods and all psychologies, all slogans and suggestions, are not worth a minute's silence, in which the soul, completely open, yields itself to the embrace of the Spirit.

> MAURICE ZUNDEL, *The Splendor of the Liturgy*, 1939

Prayer begins by *talking* to God, but it ends by listening to Him. In the face of Absolute Truth, silence is the soul's language.

> FULTON J. SHEEN, *The Woman*, 1951

Silence is needed that man may be whole. If a man has within himself the substance of silence, he need not always be watching the movements of his heart or ordering them by his will.

> MAX PICARD, *The World of Silence*, 1952

Listen or thy tongue will keep thee deaf.
> American Indian Saying

Silence is the fence around wisdom.
> Proverb

See also Contemplation; Futility; Meditation; Peace; Prayer; Serenity; Solitude; Speech; Tranquillity.

SIMONY

Manifest simoniacs should be rejected by the faithful as the first and pre-eminent heretics; and if after admonition they re-fuse to desist, they should be suppressed by the secular power.

> POPE PASCHAL (817–824), quoted by John Hus in *On Simony*, 1413

SIMPLICITY

Real simplicity lies in a *juste milieu*, equally free from thoughtlessness and affectation.

> FRANÇOIS FÉNELON (1651–1715), *Letters to Women*

Christian simplicity is the very perfection of the interior life—God, His Will and pleasure as its sole object.

> JEAN NICOLAS GROU (1731–1803), *The Hidden Life of the Soul*

It is no good asking for a simple religion. After all, real things *aren't* simple. They *look* simple, but they're not.

> C. S. LEWIS, *The Case for Christianity*, 1943

See also Sincerity.

SIN

If a man commits a sin, let him not do it again; let him not delight in it, for the accumulation of evil is painful.

> *Dhammapada*, c. 5th century B.C.

Fight thine own sins, not the sins of others.

> CONFUCIUS, *Analects of*, c. 5th century B.C.

No city hath he who for his rashness, dwells with sin.

> SOPHOCLES, *Antigone*, c. 470 B.C.

Other men's sins are before our eyes; our own are behind our back.

> SENECA, *De Ira.*, c. 43 A.D.

The soul which does not live in God is the author of its own evil; that is why it sins.

> ST. AMBROSE, *De Isaac et Anima*, c. 387

When we sin we are all ashamed at the presence of our inferiors.

ST. JOHN CHRYSOSTOM, *Homilies,* c. 388

But however much you may advance in the love of God and of your neighbor, and in true piety, do not imagine as long as you are in this life, that you are without sin.

ST. AUGUSTINE, *To Publicola,* 398

No one sins by an act he cannot avoid.

ST. AUGUSTINE, *De Libero Arbitro,* c. 400

You are asked to get rid of your sins, not to show that others have committed the like.

ST. JOHN CHRYSOSTOM (347–407), *In 1 Cor. Homil. XIV*

We may not sin in order to prevent another's sinning.

ST. AUGUSTINE, *On Faith, Hope and Charity,* c. 421

It is not unfitly said that every sin is a lie. For we never sin except with a desire to do ourselves good, or to prevent our hurt. Therefore, it is a lie when that which we think will do us good turns to our hurt; or that which we think will improve us, makes us worse.

ST. AUGUSTINE, *The City of God,* Bk. 14, 426

Who doesn't attempt to prevent sin is answerable for the sin.

Talmud: Sabbath, 54b., c. 500

We presume none sins unless he stands to profit by it.

Talmud: Baba Metzia, 5b. *Shebuot,* 42.b., c. 500

Tremble before a minor sin, lest it lead you to a major one.

Talmud: Derek Eretz, 1.26, c. 500

The soul accustomed to light transgressions has no horror of more serious ones.

POPE ST. GREGORY THE GREAT, *Liber Pastoralis,* Part IV, 590

Think not of the smallness of your sin, but of the greatness of Him against whom you have sinned!

BAHYA (JOSEPH IBN PAKUDA), *Hobot HaLebabot,* 1040

Excellence of the person never diminishes sin; but on the contrary increases it. Therefore a sin is not less grievous in a believer than an unbeliever, but much more so. For the sins of an unbeliever are more deserving of forgiveness on account of their ignorance.

ST. THOMAS AQUINAS, *Summa Theologiae,* Pt. Ia IIae. Q. 89, 1272

When thou attackest the roots of sin, fix thy thought more upon the God who thou desirest than upon the sin which thou abhorrest.

WALTER HYLTON (died c. 1396), *The Scale of Perfection*

Whoever excuses a sin on the ground of custom could by that same argument excuse any sin.

JOHN HUS, *Of Simony,* 1413

A private sin is not so prejudicial in this world as a public indecency.

MIGUEL DE CERVANTES, *Don Quixote,* 1605

The least trifle of a distraction cannot withdraw your soul from God, since nothing withdraws us from God but sin.

ST. FRANCIS OF SALES (1567–1622), *Consoling Thoughts of,* ed. Huguet

Thy merry sins, thy laughing sins, shall grow to be crying sins even in the ears of God.

JOHN DONNE (1572–1631), *Sermon to the Lords of Council*

Every sin, the oftener it is committed, the more it acquireth in the quality of evil; as it succeeds in time, so it proceeds in degrees of badness.

THOMAS BROWNE, *Religio Medici,* 1635

He that falls into sin is a man; that grieves at it, is a saint; that boasteth of it, is a devil.

THOMAS FULLER, *The Holy State and the Profane State,* 1642

That God by an immediate agency of his own, creates the sinful volitions of mankind, is a doctrine not warranted, in my view, either by Reason, or Revelation.

TIMOTHY DWIGHT, *Theology Explained and Defended,* 1818

It is one thing to perceive this or that particular deed to be sinful . . . and another thing to feel sin within us independent of particular actions.

SAMUEL TAYLOR COLERIDGE, *Aids to Reflections,* 1825

That which we call sin in others is experiment for us.

RALPH WALDO EMERSON, "Experience," *Essays, Second Series,* 1844

Suffering and taking sin upon himself might have been right for that preacher of small people. But I rejoice in great sin as my great solace.

FRIEDRICH NIETZSCHE, *Thus Spake Zarathustra,* 1883

Instead of telling men they are sinners Vedanta takes the opposite position and says "You are pure and perfect, and what you call sin does not belong to you." Sins are very low degrees of Self-manifestation; manifest the Self in a high degree. That is the one thing to remember.

SWAMI VIVEKANANDA (in 1896), *Yoga and Other Works,* 1953

We need a deeper and more tormenting sense of sin, a profounder consciousness of the eternal truth that a sin whether of indifference or intent against our brother or our sister is an offense against an outraged and indignant God.

C. S. MACFARLAND, *Christian Service in the Modern World,* 1912

Gross sin has this one great advantage: you can't tog it up in hypocrisy and make it pass for righteousness.

S. M. SHOEMAKER, *Realizing Religion,* 1921

Sin always comes openly and can at once be grasped by means of the senses. It walks on its roots and does not have to be torn out.

FRANZ KAFKA (1883–1924), *Reflections*

It would be well if the intelligent classes could forget the word sin and think less of being good.

O. W. HOLMES, to Pollock, 1926, *Holmes-Pollock Letters*

The historical Jesus has a different category of sins from that of the Old Testament or of Paul or of ecclesiastical writers after him. The sins which occupied the attention of Jesus were hypocrisy, worldliness, intolerance, and selfishness. The sins which occupy the principal attention of the Church . . . are impurity, murder, the drinking of alcohol, swearing, the neglect of the Church's services and ordinances.

ROBERT KEABLE, *Atlantic Monthly,* December, 1928

Sin is disappointing. Whoever got out of sin half as much pleasure as he expected?

IGNATIUS SMITH, *Christ Today,* 1932

Our sinful status is in our very creatureliness, not in our specific deeds.

C. S. LEWIS, *A Christian Manifesto,* 1934

God is against sin. God is against the sinful status which is every man's heritage.

. . . If you say, "How could God be holy *and* continue to create us inevitably foredoomed to be sinners?" the answer can only be *that is just what he does.*

C. S. LEWIS, *A Christian Manifesto,* 1934

We cannot doubt that God foresaw the issues of conferring selfhood upon finite beings, so that sin falls within His purpose, and is even part of it, though it cannot be said that He directly willed or wills it.

WILLIAM TEMPLE, *Nature, Man and God,* 1934

Sin is to be regarded as neither a necessity of man's nature nor yet as a pure caprice of his will.

REINHOLD NIEBUHR, *Human Nature,* 1941

If anyone thinks that Christians regard unchastity as *the* great vice, he is quite wrong. The sins of the flesh are bad, but they are the least bad of all sins. All the worst pleasures are purely spiritual: the pleasure of putting other people in the wrong, of bossing and patronizing and spoiling sport, and back-biting; the pleasures of power, of hatred.

C. S. LEWIS, *Christian Behavior,* 1943

Those of us who were brought up as Christians and have lost our faith have retained the sense of sin without the saving belief in redemption.

CYRIL CONNOLLY, *The Unquiet Grave,* 1944

The greatest of all sins is the philosophizing of sin out of existence.

HAROLD C. GARDINER, *Tenets for Readers and Reviewers,* 1944

The basic formula of all sin is: frustrated or neglected love.

FRANZ WERFEL, *Between Heaven and Earth,* 1944

In the sin itself of the creature abides a mystery which is sacred to us; this wound at least belongs to him, it is his miserable good for which he engages his eternal life, and in the folds of which are hidden God's justice and compassion.

JACQUES MARITAIN, *Art and Poetry,* 1945

Only a fool could deny the fact of sin, though we may choose to call it by another name.

GERALD VANN, *The Heart of Man,* 1945

The core of sin is in the heart of him who wills it, not in any physical action by which he makes it manifest. Its external completion is but the husk and shell, adding little more than intensity as a rule to its wickedness.

JOHN B. HARNEY, *Sin,* 1949

Sins which are against the Creator, i.e. against Faith, Hope, Charity and the virtue of Religion, are the most grievous of all.

CHRISTOPHER J. WILMOT, *Lift Up Your Hearts,* 1949

The big moment is not when a man sins but when a man surrenders to the direction of his sin.

HUBERT VAN ZELLER, *We Die Standing Up,* 1949

The real trouble with our times is not the multiplication of sinners, it is the disappearance of sin.

ÉTIENNE GILSON, *Ensign,* March, 1952

We are not yet convinced that we have outwitted sin by changing its name to "complex" or that we have discarded our devilishness by treating our glands.

RALPH W. SOCKMAN, *How To Believe,* 1953

The idea of sin is not an arbitrary insertion into developing religion, but a necessary consequence of man's occupation with an absolute ideal . . . with requirements of the impossible, such as the call for perfection.

WILLIAM E. HOCKING, *The Coming World Civilization*, 1956

The sins that we should hate most are not those of our neighbor but our own. These are the only sins over which God has given us immediate power.

RAPHAEL SIMON, *Hammer and Fire*, 1959

Talk about sin will not be intelligible to one who has no sense of lack, no sense of life's being at cross-purposes, no sense of self-defeat.

JAMES A. MARTIN, JR., *Fact, Fiction and Faith*, 1960

Sin is the disease. Christ the cure. The result is a miracle.

FRANK BUCHMAN, *Frank Buchman's Secret*, Peter Howard, 1962

One man's sin may be another man's duty and a third man's bliss. . . . A democratic community cannot recognize the category of sin, legislate against it and punish those for whom the proscribed action is not sinful.

SIDNEY HOOK, *Address*, National Institute on Religious Freedom and Public Affairs, Washington, D.C., reported in *New York Times*, November 21, 1962

The heart and the eye are the agents of sin.

Proverb

No matter how many new translations of the Bible come out, the people still sin the same way.

ANONYMOUS

See also Absolutes; Adam; Atomic Bomb; Baptism; Birth Control; Christianity; Communism; Confession; Conscience; Cross; Damnation; Death; Despair; Determinism; Devil; Election; Evil; Evil: Its Nature; Evil, Problem of; Fall, the; For-giveness; Free Will; Grace; Heart; Hell; Holy Spirit; Immortality; Justification; Man and God; Man: His Wickedness; Morality; Necessity; Original Sin; Pain; Pleasure; Preaching; Predestination; Punishment; Purgatory; Rebellion; Relativity; Repentance; Right and Wrong; Saints; Saints and Sinners; Sex; Sexual Sin; Sin, Definitions of; Sin: Its Consequences; Sin: Its Prevalence; Sinners; Soul; Suffering; Unbelief; Vice; Virtue; War, Condemnation of; Wicked, the; Will.

SIN, DEFINITIONS OF

Sin is disease, deformity, weakness.

PLATO, *The Republic*, c. 370 B.C.

The word SIN in the Bible means something more than the external works done by our bodily action. It means all the circumstances that act together and excite or incite us to what is done; in particular, the impulses operating in the depths of our hearts.

MARTIN LUTHER, *Preface to Romans*, 1522

Sin is an Attempt to *control* the immutable and unalterable Laws of everlasting Righteousness, Goodness and Truth, upon which the Universe depends.

BENJAMIN WHICHCOTE, *Moral and Religious Aphorisms*, 1753

Sin is rebellion against God; it is a traitor's act who aims at the overthrow and death of His sovereign. . . . Sin is the mortal enemy of the All-holy, so that He and it cannot be together.

JOHN HENRY NEWMAN, *Parochial and Plain Sermons*, V, 1843

A natural principle in man lowering him, deadening him, pulling him down by inches to the mere animal plane, blinding reason, searing conscience, paralyzing will.

HENRY DRUMMOND, *Natural Law in the Spiritual World*, 1883

Sin is not an offense against God, but against our humanity.
> E. G. HIRSCH, *Reform Advocate*, 1894, VII

Sin is the refusal of the creature to his God who invites him to union with Him.
> COLUMBA MARMION, *The Spiritual Doctrine of*, ed. M. M. Phillipson, 1901

Three elements combine to complete the idea of sin; first, that the deed was one that ought not to have been done, . . . because it was opposed to what is intrinsically right. . . . Secondly, the idea of sin implies that the sinner himself is the doer of the deed. . . . Thirdly, it is characteristic of sin that the fuller knowledge that the harmful deed is sinful *comes after the act.*
> FELIX ADLER, *An Ethical Philosophy of Life*, 1918

Failure to make that adaptation to God which the growing life requires.
> HENRY NELSON WIEMAN, *The Wrestle of Religion with Truth*, 1927

Sin in his [Buddha's] opinion is essentially irrational conduct; conduct that tends to destroy more values than it creates, either for the actor or other sentient beings whom it affects.
> J. B. PRATT, *The Pilgrimage of Buddhism*, 1928

By the use of this word the Christian always intends to convey that moral evil, as he understands it, entering a created universe by the act of free will, directly bears upon the fundamental relation of dependence which unites the creature to God.
> ÉTIENNE GILSON, *Spirit of Medieval Philosophy*, 1936

The evil of sin consists in its being the fully wilful rejection of God; it is, as it were, an attempt to annihilate God, and, were this possible, it would do so. . . . It is only in so far as we realize that God is

one supreme Reality that we can realize that sin is the one supreme evil.
> BRUNO WEBB, *Why Does God Permit Evil?*, 1941

When man says "Yes" to the forbidden fruit, he says "No" to the prohibiting God. . . . He estranges himself from God and divine will: aversion to God and the intimate essence of grave sin consist in this.
> POPE PIUS XII, *Allocution*, February 23, 1944

Sin, like freedom, is by hypothesis inexplicable, since moral action presupposes freedom in the sense of real choices. . . . If sin, universal as it is, is to be treated as a moral fact and not as a natural fact . . . it must remain inexplicable.
> J. S. WHALE, *Christian Doctrine*, 1946

The higher and nobler the virtue to which it is opposed the more grievous is the sin. . . . The most terrible and grievous of all sins are the hatred of God, despair, unbelief, formal heresy, blasphemy, and the like.
> CHRISTOPHER J. WILMOT, *Lift Up Your Hearts*, 1949

Thanks to those gifts which the Creator has given him, man can emancipate himself from his Creator and make himself his own lord. That is what the Bible calls sin.
> EMIL BRUNNER, *The Scandal of Christianity*, 1951

Sin is the infidelity of man to the image of what he ought to be in his eternal vocation as an adopted son of God.
> FULTON J. SHEEN, *Three to Get Married*, 1951

I am often struck by the word Jesus used for sin. It comes from archery practice; to sin (in the thought of Jesus) means to miss the mark: miss the target. To miss the target at least implies you are aiming at something.
> G. F. MACLEOD (contemporary U.S.A.) quoted by V. Gollancz, *From Darkness to Light*, 1956

Sin is not exhausted in describing individual acts which aren't very nice. "Sin" is fundamentally a description of our entire situation, one of separation from God, alienation from him, arising out of our rebellion, our refusal to do his will, our insistence upon following our own wills.

ROBERT MCAFEE BROWN, *Patterns of Faith in America Today*, ed. F. E. Johnson, 1957

See also Sin.

SIN: ITS CONSEQUENCES

As long as the sin bears no fruit, the fool, he thinks it honey; but when the sin ripens, then, indeed, he goes down in sorrow.

Dhammapada, c. 5th century B.C.

Sin is nothing, and men become nothing when they sin.

ST. AUGUSTINE, *In Joan, Evang.*, c. 416

Every sin is more injury to him who does it than him who suffers it.

ST. AUGUSTINE, *On Faith, Hope and Charity*, c. 421

He who sins is still worse if he rejoices in his loss of righteousness.

ST. AUGUSTINE, *The City of God*, 426

The sinner wills a good, an advantage, and to obtain it he freely consents to turn away from his final end: this is the evil of sin.

ST. THOMAS AQUINAS, *Summa Theologiae*, Ia IIae, 75, a.1, 1272

Man is by nature rational. When, therefore, he acts according to reason, he acts of himself and according to his free will; and this is liberty. . . . When he sins, he acts in opposition to reason, is moved by another, and is the victim of foreign misapprehensions. Therefore, *Whosoever committeth sin is the slave of sin.*

ST. THOMAS AQUINAS (1225?–1274), quoted by Pope Leo XIII, *Libertas Humana*, 1888

It is obvious from faith in Holy Scripture that no one can sin without weakening or disturbing peace with God and in consequence with every creature.

JOHN WYCLIFF, *De Officio Regis*, 1378

Sin, the sad fearful winter of the soul, kills the holy works which it finds there.

ST. FRANCIS OF SALES (1567–1622), *Consoling Thoughts of*, ed. Huguet

With the first sin came sin into the world. Exactly in the same way is this true of every subsequent first sin of man, that with it sin comes into the world.

SÖREN KIERKEGAARD, *The Concept of Dread*, 1844

Sin would be only an evil for him who commits it, were it not a crime towards the weak brethren, whom it corrupts.

HENRI AMIEL, *Journal of*, 1882

Every person that does any evil, that gratifies any passion, is sufficiently punished by the evil he has committed, by the passions he serves, but chiefly by the fact that he withdraws himself from God, and God withdraws Himself from him.

JOHN OF CRONSTADT, *My Life in Christ*, 1897

Grievous sin is death and life in a monstrous union.

WALTER ELLIOTT, *The Spiritual Life*, 1914

Sin penetrates the soul as a needle does the body; for this will work its way for years, slowly and surely, till it pierces an intestine, or even the heart itself.

WALTER ELLIOTT, *The Spiritual Life*, 1914

Its effect on the soul is to be measured neither by the guilt nor by the temporal punishment inexorably fixed, but by that deep sense of loneliness it brings with it.

BEDE JARRETT, *Meditations for Layfolk*, 1915

A sin vibrates to the extremes of the spiritual universe and, if there be no end to that, sin, unless rectified, itself has no end. The consequences abide, in the sinner who has spoiled himself, and in the world, that he has helped to mar and to unmake.

C. C. Martindale, *Faith of the Roman Church*, 1927

We are not punished for our sins, but by them.

Leon Harrison, *The Religion of a Modern Liberal*, 1931

Sin leaves behind it a sting that must be endured as a payment; remorse of conscience; terrors of soul; an army of skeletons of past misdeeds haunt and taunt and mock.

Ignatius Smith, *Christ Today*, 1932

Sin is a tyrant. It exiles a man from himself and from his conscience and sends him elsewhere, anywhere, everywhere in his search for peace and rest.

Ignatius Smith, *Christ Today*, 1932

Sin has done injury, I, to God, II: to oneself, III: to other men, IV: to the Mystical Body, i.e., to the human race, of which the sinner is an integral member.

Alban Goodier, *Ascetical and Mystical Theology*, 1938

It does not matter how small the sins are provided their cumulative effect is to edge the man away from the Light and out into the Nothing. Murder is no better than cards if cards can do the trick.

C. S. Lewis, *The Screwtape Letters*, 1942

Sin repented can still leave a crushing weight upon the soul, even one sin.

Frank J. Sheed, *Theology and Sanity*, 1946

To sin is to poison the public reservoir.

Leslie D. Weatherhead, *Psychology, Religion and Healing*, 1951

Sin is poison poured into the stream of time.

George A. Buttrick, *Sermons Preached in a University Church*, 1959

See also Conscience; Fall, the; Damnation; Death; Guilt; Hell; Punishment; Purgatory; Sin; Sin, Definitions of.

SIN: ITS PREVALENCE

We do not need artificially to conjure up a sense of sin. All we need to do is to open our eyes to facts. Take one swift glance at the social state of the world today. . . . That should be sufficient to indicate that this is no fool-proof universe automatically progressive but that moral evil is still the central problem of mankind.

Harry Emerson Fosdick, *Christianity and Progress*, 1922

Most newspaper headlines are more effective examples of man's sin writ large than any book on theology can ever hope to be.

Robert McAfee Brown, *Patterns of Faith in America Today*, ed. F. E. Johnson, 1957

SIN, ORIGINAL. See ORIGINAL SIN

SINCERITY

I do not see how a man without sincerity can be good for anything. How can a cart or carriage be made to go without yoke or crossbar?

Confucius, *Sayings of,* 5th century B.C.

Sincerity is the way to Heaven.

Mencius, c. 300 B.C.

In the visible temple you fall down on the knees of your body, but nothing is accomplished thereby if in the temple of the breast you stand up against God.

Desiderius Erasmus, *Enchiridion*, 1501

The sincerity which is not charitable proceeds from a charity which is not sincere.
> Ascribed to St. Francis of Sales, in Camus's *The Spirit of St. Francis of Sales,* 1641

Seek much after this, to speak nothing with God, but what is the sense of a single unfeigned heart.
> SAMUEL TAYLOR COLERIDGE, *Aids to Reflection,* 1825

Who can tell where sincerity merges into humility, and where it folds itself over and becomes hypocrisy, and where it touches self-righteousness.
> SALVADOR DE MADARIAGA, *Englishmen, Frenchmen, Spaniards,* 1931

See also Heart; Prayer; Pretense; Simplicity.

SINNERS

Most people are angry with the sinner, not with the sin.
> SENECA, *De Ira,* c. 43 A.D.

Thou shalt love the man, be he never so sinful, and thou shalt hate sin in ilk a man what that he be.
> WALTER HYLTON (died c. 1396), *The Scale of Perfection*

Many sinners would not have been saved if they had not committed some greater sin at last, than before; for the punishment of that sin, hath brought them to a greater remorse of all their other sins formerly neglected.
> JOHN DONNE, *Sermon,* LXXXX, 1640

There is in truth a sort of reverence due to sinners, when we look at them not as in their sins, but simply as having sinned, and being the objects of a Divine yearning.
> FREDERICK W. FABER, *The Spirit of,* 1914

He who separates himself from sinners walks in their guilt.
> MARTIN BUBER, *Jewish Mysticism and the Legends of Baalshem,* 1916

When Jesus juxtaposes the repentant publican to the self-satisfied Pharisee, or the "prodigal" son to the correct elder son, he makes clear who the real sinner is— namely, the one who . . . supposes that he is able to stand in God's presence because of his correctness and accomplishments, and does not understand that God demands the *entire* man.
> RUDOLF BULTMANN, "The Meaning of Christian Faith in Creation," 1936, in *Existence and Faith,* ed. S. M. Ogden

There is not only a communion of saints; there is also a communion of sinners. In their hatred of one another, their contempt, sinners unite, embrace, intermingle, become as one.
> GEORGES BERNANOS, *The Diary of a Country Priest,* 1937

Man is a sinner not because he is finite but because he refuses to admit that he is.
> REINHOLD NIEBUHR, *Christianity and Power Politics,* 1940

When thinking of sinners we shall never go wrong to include ourselves.
> AELRED GRAHAM, *Christian Thought and Action,* 1951

There are no incorrigible sinners; God has no permanent problem children.
> NELS F. S. FERRÉ, *The Christian Understanding of God,* 1951

There is a type of person who doesn't go to church because he has sinned. In Christ's estimation that is the person who has one added reason for being in church.
> SEBASTIAN MIKLAS, *Sanctify Your Emotions,* 1955

See also Church, Definitions of; Compassion; Damnation; Devil; Forgiveness; Free

Will; Grace; Guilt; Hell; Love of Mankind; Man: His Wickedness; Mercy; Punishment; Saints; Saints and Sinners.

SINNERS AND SAINTS. See SAINTS AND SINNERS

SKEPTIC

Skeptic always rhymes with septic; the spirit died of intellectual poisoning.
> FRANZ WERFEL, *Realism and Inwardness,* 1930

See also Agnostics; Skepticism.

SKEPTICISM

Skepticism is less reprehensible in inquiring years, and no crime in juvenile exercitation.
> JOSEPH GLANVILLE, *The Vanity of Dogmatizing,* 1661

The deepest, the only theme of human history, compared to which all others are of subordinate importance, is the conflict of scepticism with faith.
> J. W. VON GOETHE (1749–1832), *Wisdom and Experience*

Scepticism means, not intellectual doubt alone, but moral doubt.
> THOMAS CARLYLE, *Heroes and Hero-Worship,* 1840

If a man have a strong faith he can indulge in the luxury of sceptisism.
> FRIEDRICH NIETZSCHE, *The Twilight of the Idols,* 1889

Religious minds prefer scepticism. The true saint is a profound sceptic; a total disbeliever in human reason, who has more than once joined hands on this ground with some who were at best sinners.
> HENRY ADAMS, *Education of Henry Adams,* 1906

Scepticism, riddling the faith of yesterday, prepares the way for the faith of tomorrow.
> ROMAIN ROLLAND, *Jean Christophe,* 1912

Scepticism is the chastity of the intellect.
> GEORGE SANTAYANA, *Scepticism and Animal Faith,* 1923

Scepticism is an exercise, not a life; it is a discipline fit to purify the mind of prejudice and render it all the more apt, when the time comes, to believe and to act wisely.
> GEORGE SANTAYANA, *Scepticism and Animal Faith,* 1923

Through his scepticism the modern man is thrown back upon himself; his energies flow towards their source and wash to the surface those psychic contents which are at all times there, but lie hidden in the silt as long as the stream flows smoothly in its course.
> C. G. JUNG, *Modern Man in Search of a Soul,* 1932

Skepticism often makes big calls on our faith.
> MAURICE SAMUEL, *Prince of the Ghetto,* 1948

A sound belief is always accompanied by a sane skepticism. It is only by disbelieving in some things that we can ever believe in other things. Faith does not mean credulity.
> SAMUEL H. MILLER, *The Great Realities,* 1955

Faith without skepticism is not faith. It is superstition.
> SAMUEL H. MILLER, *The Great Realities,* 1955

See also Absolutes; Agnosticism; Belief; Cynicism; Doubt; Faith; Intellect; Intellectuals; Pragmatism; Relativity; Skeptic; Unbelief.

SLAVERY

If you put chains around the neck of a slave, the other end fastens itself around your own.

RALPH WALDO EMERSON, "Compensation," *Essays, First Series,* 1841

The Hebrew language has about thirty words to express justice and humanity, but not a single one for slave.

J. S. BLOCH, *My Reminiscences,* 1882

If man remains a material and economic being and his spiritual nature is regarded as an illusion of consciousness, then man remains a slave.

NICHOLAS BERDYAEV, *Slavery and Freedom,* 1944

When you know what it is to be loved by free men, all the low bowing of slaves no longer has meaning for you.

CHARLES PEGUY, *Mysteries of the Holy Innocents,* 1958

See also Conformity; Equality; Freedom; Individual; Personality; Servitude.

SLEEP

The long sleep of death cures our scars and the short sleep of life our wounds.

JEAN PAUL RICHTER, *Hesperus,* 1795

To sleep is to strain and purify our emotions, to deposit the mud of life, to calm the fever of the soul, to return into the bosom of maternal nature, thence to reissue, healed and strong. Sleep is a sort of innocence and purification.

H. F. AMIEL, *Journal,* March 20, 1853

See also Dreams; Repose; Rest.

SMUGNESS

Surely within the church there must be a definite attempt to . . . oppose the use of the Christian religion as a means of commending ourselves, our policies and our institutions to ourselves and to the world.

JOHN C. BENNETT, *Christian Century,* January 6, 1954

Smugness is by any reckoning a first class ticket to hell.

GEDDES MACGREGOR, *The Hemlock and the Cross,* 1963

See also Apathy; Complacency; Modesty; Primness.

SOBRIETY

Be sober, as God's athlete. The prize is incorruption and life eternal.

ST. IGNATIUS OF ANTIOCH, *Letter to Polycarp,* c. 109

Christian sobriety is all that duty that concerns ourselves in the matter of meat and drink, and pleasures and thoughts.

JEREMY TAYLOR, *Holy Living,* 1650

See also Abstinence; Alcohol; Drunkenness; Moderation; Pleasure; Wine.

SOCIAL ACTION

If the power of God through Christ is to be made a regenerating influence in the world, it must be applied through united witness and in united action to the social and industrial order in which men live.

Pastoral Letter, Protestant Episcopal Church, 1922

In Judaism social action is religiousness, and religiousness implies social action.

LEO BAECK, *Essence of Judaism,* 1936

The strength of religious social action lies precisely in its being religious, with the limitations and the powers that such a sphere implies.

JOHN LA FARGE, *Secularism's Attack on World Order,* 1945

See also Social Conscience; Social Cooperation; Social Gospel; Social Order; Social Welfare; Unity.

SOCIAL ATHEISM

Much of the outer life of Christendom has ceased to be Christian except in name, and has become in effect a society without God. And this social atheism is pushing society to its own destruction.

JOHN D. FEE, *Secularism,* 1947

See also Agnosticism; Atheism; Godlessness; Humanism; Secularism.

SOCIAL CAUSE

Our hope in Christ enables us to know that there are limitations set upon every human ideal and achievement, so that we never make an idol out of any social cause.

W. A. VISSER 'T HOOFT, *The Evanston Report,* 1955

See also Public Welfare; Security; Social Action; Social Conscience; Social Cooperation; Social Gospel; Social Order; Social Welfare.

SOCIAL CONSCIENCE

If any man be so addicted to his private, that he neglect the common state, he is void of the sense of piety and wisheth peace and happiness to himself in vain.

WILLIAM LAUD (1573–1645), *Works,* I

We cannot be interested in the salvation of individual personalities without being at once concerned about the slums that damn them or the unemployment that works havoc to the spirit of man no less than to his body.

Federal Council of Churches of Christ in America, *Report,* 1933

The problem is to get a conscience about what we do in groups that is as strong as the conscience we have as individuals. This

is called a "social conscience." . . . It means that in those parts of life where the individual must go along with the group, we must make the group responsible to God.

MARSHALL L. SCOTT, *The Christian and Social Action,* 1948

To have social conscience is to be unwilling to make a separate peace with the giant social evils of Want, Despair, Squalor, Ignorance, Idleness, escaping into personal prosperity oneself, while leaving one's fellows in their clutches.

LORD BEVERIDGE, *Voluntary Action,* 1949

See also Conscience; Poverty; Public Welfare; Security; Selfishness; Social Action; Social Cooperation; Social Gospel; Social Order; Social Welfare; Socialism; Wages.

SOCIAL COOPERATION

This gradual assimilation of religious casuistry, scientific psychiatry, and secular ethics to each other, their willingness to meet each other in saving human lives and spirits in spite of their theoretical incompatibilities, is one of the major moral creations of the 20th century.

HERBERT WALLACE SCHNEIDER, *Religion in the 20th Century,* 1952

See also Public Welfare; Security; Social Action; Social Cause; Social Conscience; Social Gospel; Social Order; Social Welfare.

SOCIAL ETHICS

By dividing the teachings of Jesus into commands (meant for everyday living) and counsels of perfection (meant for monastics and saints), by incorporating the common sense of Aristotle and the Stoics, by its system of penance, the Roman church worked out a social ethic that led Europe from tribalism to high civilization.

ROGER L. SHINN, *The Ethics of Power,* ed. Lasswell and Cleveland, 1962

SOCIAL FAITH

Ever since man has been man his existence has centered about a social faith. . . . What passed for religion was socially created. The Gods were the Gods of the people. Religion was a social faith before it became the more transcendent or universal faith we now call religion. . . . And we may conjecture that even the more universal religions would not have developed were it not for the dawning of the larger "consciousness of kind."

R. M. MacIver, *The Ramparts We Guard,* 1950

See also Brotherhood; Christianity; Church, Definitions of; Community; Fellowship; Religion.

SOCIAL GOSPEL

Now that God has smitten slavery unto death, he has opened the way for the redemption and sanctification of our whole social system.

Edwin Beecher, *Bibliotheca Sacra,* 1865

The Church's judgment of social processes, institutions, problems, and reforms is part of a comprehensive spiritual view of life.

William J. Kerby, *Encyclopedia of Social Reform,* ed. W. D. P. Bliss, 1908

If our theology is silent on social salvation, we compel college men and women, working men, and theological students, to choose between an unsocial system of theology and an irreligious system of social salvation.

Walter Rauschenbusch, *A Theology for the Social Gospel,* 1917

Social teaching alone will not usually convert people to the Christian gospel. But the impression that Christianity is socially irrelevant can keep them away.

John C. Bennett, *Union Seminary Quarterly Review,* June, 1951

The central idea [of social gospel] is that the redemption or salvation of mankind collectively, the regeneration of the social order, is the ultimate goal of religion.

Herbert Wallace Schneider, *Religion in the 20th Century,* 1952

See also Poverty; Public Welfare; Security; Social Action; Social Cause; Social Conscience; Social Cooperation; Social Order; Social Welfare; Socialism.

SOCIAL IMMORTALITY

Modern men have talked so much about "social immortality" or about finding the meaning of life in identification with on-going society . . . that at last tyrants have caught on to the idea and given "social immortality" to millions of people who somehow stood in their way.

Paul Ramsey, *Nine Modern Moralists,* 1962

SOCIAL ORDER

If a man does accept in any sincerity a faith in Jesus and Jesus' God, . . . it is impossible to see how he can be at peace with the present social order whose God is profit and whose largest loyalty is the inadequate and divisive loyalty of nationalism.

Norman Thomas, *As I See It,* 1932

While man does not live by bread alone, an unjust social order can place many obstacles in the way of virtue. Destitution and oppression stimulate a spirit of revolt against society.

John F. Cronin, *Communism,* 1947

Grace builds upon nature. . . . Without a good social order, man finds it increasingly difficult to save his soul.

John F. Murphy, *Sanctity and Success in Marriage,* 1956

There is no social order without violence. There can, therefore, be no social order which is ratified in the sign of the cross.

Peter L. Berger, *The Precarious Vision,* 1962

See also Order; Public Welfare; Salvation; Social Action; Social Conscience; Social Gospel; Society.

SOCIAL WELFARE

New Christianity is called upon to pronounce anathema upon theology, and to condemn as unholy any doctrine trying to teach men that there is any other way of obtaining eternal life, except that of working with all their might for the improvement of the conditions of life of their fellow men.
C. H. SAINT-SIMON, *The New Christianity,* 1825

When two or three are gathered together, cooperating for social good, there is the Divine Spirit in the midst of them.
BERNARD BOSANQUET, *Address,* Ethical Society, 1886

The church has no authoritative message concerning trusts or labor unions, lockouts or strikes, capital or wages, or taxation, currency or colonies. It is neither appointed nor fitted to dictate social or economic laws.
Methodist Episcopal Church, *Journal of the General Conference,* 1900

The full responsibility for the promotion of moral and social welfare in any real sense remains upon the Church. . . . If we are to secure social welfare we must effect the spiritual regeneration and the moral renovation and sanctification of the individuals.
Minutes of the United Lutheran Church, 1922

It is not possible to be a saint and invoke the gospel we preach without doing all we can to assure for all men conditions of work, housing, food, rest and human culture without which life ceases to be human.
EMMANUEL SUHARD, *The Church Today,* 1953

See also Public Welfare; Social Action; Social Conscience; Social Cooperation; Social Gospel; Social Order.

SOCIALISM

Christian Socialism is but the holy water with which the priest consecrates the heartburnings of the aristocrat.
KARL MARX, *Manifesto of the Communist Party,* 1848

What is socialism?—It is the Gospel in action. How so?—Socialism has as its goal to realize among men the four fundamental maxims of the Gospel: Love one another; Do not unto others what you would not have that they should do unto you; The first amongst ye shall be the servant of the rest; Peace to all men of good will.
LOUIS BLANC, *Socialist Catechism,* 1849

The main tenet of *Socialism,* the community of goods, must be utterly rejected; for it would injure those whom it is intended to benefit, it would be contrary to natural rights of mankind.
POPE LEO XIII, Encyclical, May, 1891

The combination of religious sentimentality, industrial insanity, and moral obliquity.
F. J. C. HEARNSHAW, *A Survey of Socialism,* 1928

Whether Socialism be considered as a doctrine, or as a historical fact, or as a movement, if it really remain Socialism, it cannot be brought into harmony with the dogmas of the Catholic Church . . . the reason being that it conceives human society in a way utterly alien to Christian truth.
POPE PIUS XI, *Quadragesimo Anno,* 1931

The clearest line of demarcation between Christian and Marxist socialism lies in the fact that the Christian takes sin seriously.
GEORGIA HARKNESS, *The Resources of Religion,* 1936

See also Communism; Marxism; Public Welfare; Social Conscience; Social Gospel; Social Welfare; Welfare State.

SOCIETY

Civil society doth more to content the nature of man than any private kind or solitary kind of living.

RICHARD HOOKER, *The Laws of Ecclesiastical Polity*, 1594

It is as manifest that we were made for society, and to promote the happiness of it, as that we were intended to take care of our own life, and health, and private good.

JOSEPH BUTLER, *Sermons upon Human Nature*, 1726

Society, from which we have everything, is a new master, a new spook, a new supreme being, which takes us into its service and allegiance.

MAX STIRNER, *The Ego and Its Own*, 1845

Upon the lapsing of Christian institutions and morality, the main foundation of human society must necessarily be uprooted. Force alone will remain to preserve public tranquillity and order.

POPE LEO XIII, *Sapientiae Christianae*, 1890

The moment that a society claims the complete allegiance of its members, it assumes a quasi-religious authority. For since man is essentially spiritual, any power that claims to control the whole man is forced to transcend relative and particular aims and to enter the sphere of absolute values, which is the realm of religion.

CHRISTOPHER DAWSON, *The Modern Dilemma: The Problem of European Unity*, 1932

In the Creator's plan, society is a natural means which man can and must use to reach his destined end. Society exists for man and not man for society.

POPE PIUS XI, *Divini Redemptoris*, March 19, 1937

Three alternatives confront society today —the collapse of civilization, the acceptance of a new pagan faith like fascism or communism or the revival of Christianity on a scale and at an intensity beyond anything our day is visualizing.

Federal Council of Churches of Christ in America, *Report*, 1938

Society can never be greatly improved, until such time as most of its members choose to become theocentric saints.

ALDOUS HUXLEY, *Grey Eminence*, 1941

My own advice to anyone starting out in the world would be the same as Ruskin's to his nephew: "Fit yourself for the best society; and then don't enter it."

PATRICK MAHONY, *You Can Find a Way*, 1950

Human existence cannot derive its ultimate meaning from society, because society itself is in need of meaning.

ABRAHAM JOSHUA HESCHEL, *Man Is Not Alone: A Philosophy of Religion*, 1951

Human society . . . ought to be regarded above all as a spiritual reality in which men communicate knowledge to each other in the light of truth, in which they can enjoy their rights and fulfill their duties, and are inspired to strive for moral good.

POPE JOHN XXIII, *Pacem in Terris*, April, 1963

See also Brotherhood; Christian Society; Christians; Church, Definitions of; Civilization; Communism; Community; Culture and Christianity; Culture and Religion; Democracy, Religion of; Family; Fellowship; Humanism; Humanity; Individual;

Individualism; Man: His Potential; Mankind; Moral Standards; Natural Law; Public Welfare; Social Atheism; Social Order; Social Welfare; Socialism; Society and Religion; Unity; Words.

SOCIETY AND RELIGION

Religion is the basis of civil society, and the source of all good and of all comfort.
EDMUND BURKE, *Reflections on the Revolution in France,* 1790

Civil society must acknowledge God as its Founder and Parent, and must obey and reverence His power and authority. Justice therefore forbids, and reason itself forbids, the State to be godless; or to adopt a line of action which would end in godlessness.
POPE LEO XIII, *Libertas Humana,* 1888

It is the religious impulse which supplies the cohesive force which unifies society and a culture. The great civilizations of the world do not produce the great religions as a kind of cultural by-product; in a very real sense, the great religions are the foundations on which the great civilizations rest.
CHRISTOPHER DAWSON, *The Quarterly Review,* January, 1925

The Church can fully serve men only as it helps them to see the whole of their life and all their activities in relation to the purpose of God. The Church has a responsibility to the community or nation as well as to the individual.
W. A. VISSER 'T HOOFT and J. H. OLDHAM, *The Church and Its Function in Society,* 1937

An ordering of society which relegates religion, democracy and good faith among nations to the background can find no place within it for the ideals of the Prince of Peace. The United States rejects such an ordering, and retains its ancient faith.
FRANKLIN D. ROOSEVELT, *Address to Congress,* January, 1939

The Christian can be satisfied with nothing less than a Christian organization of society—which is not the same thing as a society consisting exclusively of devout Christians.
T. S. ELIOT, *The Idea of a Christian Society,* 1940

The Christian finds himself in an almost alien world, where Christ the Eternal must surreptitiously gain a hearing in the counsels of society which is called Christian.
JOHN D. FEE, *Secularism,* 1947

Unless religion with its binding force in justice and charity supplies the foundation of law and authority, there remains only human convention or brute force as the unifying element in society.
Catholic Bishops of the U.S., November, 1952

Our contemporaries are dreaming of a society which is human. . . . They think, for fear of losing it, they must dream of it without God. They have closed man and nature and history within a dark island of time, and they have torn time from eternity, in order to cling to man with determination and, yes, with desperation.
ANTON C. PEGIS, *Disputed Questions in Education,* 1954

No matter how religion is reconstructed there will always be a difference between the secular and rational approach to the problems of man and society and the approach of religion.
SIDNEY HOOK, *Religious Experience and Truth,* 1962

See also Christianity; Church and State; Ethics; Humanism; Religion; Secularism; Society.

SOCIOLOGY

Sociology is of the mind of the angel who bore a torch in one hand and a vase of water in the other, with one to burn

Heaven, and with the other to quench Hell, that man might be influenced neither by the hope of the one and the fear of the other.

> CHARLES W. ELIOT, *Theology at the Dawn of the 20th Century*, ed. J. V. Morgan, 1901.

Ever since the time of Comte, there has been a constant succession of theological sociologies which aim . . . at the reformation of society on the basis of a new religious ideal. . . . They try to produce a synthesis between religion and sociology, and they succeed only in creating a hybrid monstrosity that is equally obnoxious to scientific sociology and to genuine religious thought.

> CHRISTOPHER DAWSON, *Science for a New Work*, ed. Thompson and Crowther, 1934

SOLDIER

A soldier is a man whose business it is to kill those who never offended him, and who are the innocent martyrs of other men's iniquities. Whatever may become of the abstract question of the justifiableness of war, it seems impossible that the soldier should not be a depraved and unnatural thing.

> WILLIAM GODWIN, *The Enquirer*, 1797

A soldier's vow to his country is that he will die for the guardianship of her domestic virtue, of her righteous laws, and of her anyway challenged or endangered honor. A state without virtue, without laws, and without honor, he is bound not to defend.

> JOHN RUSKIN, *The Crown of Wild Olives*, 1866

Must one believe that God exacts of a brave soldier engaged in raging combat the methodological logic of the moralist or the theologian? We admire the heroism of the soldier. Who can doubt that God looks upon it with affection?

> DESIRÉ MERCIER, *Voix de la Guerre*, ed. Thone, 1937

A soldier may not participate in a particular military operation which he is convinced is against the law of God.

> FRANCIS J. CONNELL, *The Sign*, March, 1950

See also Conscientious Objector; Conscription; Killing; Pacifism; Pacifists; Peace; War.

SOLEMNITY

Solemnity is a device of the body to hide the faults of the mind.

> LA ROCHEFOUCAULD, *Maxims*, 1665

SOLITARY

Solitary we must be in life's great hours of moral decision: solitary in pain and sorrow; solitary in old age and in going forth to death.

> WILLIAM L. SULLIVAN, *Under Orders*, 1944

There is no such a being as a solitary Christian.

> RALPH W. SOCKMAN, *How to Believe*, 1953

See also Alone; Brotherhood; Community Fellowship; Isolation; Loneliness; Solitude

SOLITUDE

He who has tasted the sweetness of solitude and tranquillity, is free from fear and free from sin.

> *Dhammapada*, c. 5th century B.C.

He who lives in solitude and no longer communicates with men, is either a beast or a god.

> ARISTOTLE, *Politics*, c. 330 B.C.

No one in solitude recognizes his own defects, since he has no one to correct him and in gentleness and mercy direct him on his way.

> ST. BASIL, *Rule of*, c. 360

By all means flee solitude, for the devil watches and lies in wait for you most of all when you are alone.

MARTIN LUTHER, *Letter,* July, 1530

Now solitude is not estimated by the number of people who live together, but by the retirement from bad passions. . . . Where such solitude is present there is indeed the closest companionship. He is happily solitary who is corrupted by no wicked company, who has in his heart no tumultuous passions striving with each other out of harmony with God.

DESIDERIUS ERASMUS, Preface to *Psalms of Hayno,* 1534

I do not only acknowledge but admire solitude. . . . It is requisite to the growth of piety, and I reverence the virtue that seeks and uses it.

WILLIAM PENN, *Some Fruits of Solitude,* 1693

An hour of solitude passed in sincere and earnest prayer, or the conflicts with, and conquest over, a single passion or "subtle bosom sin," will teach us more of thought, will more effectually awaken the faculty, and form the habit, than a year's study in the Schools without them.

SAMUEL TAYLOR COLERIDGE, *Aids to Reflection,* 1825

Unlovely, nay, frightful, is the solitude of the soul which is without God in the world.

RALPH WALDO EMERSON, *Address,* May 5, 1879

It is only in solitude, when it has broken the thick crust of shame that separates us from one another and separates us all from God, that we have no secrets from God; only in solitude do we raise our heart to the Heart of the Universe.

MIGUEL DE UNAMUNO, *Essays and Soliloquies,* 1925

A discipline of solitude and silence is essential for those who would acquaint themselves with God and be at peace.

E. HERMAN, *Creative Prayer,* 1934

The cultivation of individual solitude is a first step to the solution of our social problems.

RALPH W. SOCKMAN, *The Highway to God,* 1941

Solitude is full of God.

Serbian Proverb

See also Alone; Brotherhood; Community; Contemplation; Fellowship; Isolation; Loneliness; Prayer; Silence.

SON

Build me a son, O Lord, who will be strong enough to know when he is weak and brave enough to face himself when he is afraid . . . whose wishes will not take the place of deeds; a son who will know Thee . . . whose heart will be clear, whose goal will be high, a son who will master himself before he seeks to master other men.

DOUGLAS MACARTHUR, quoted in *New York Times,* April 5, 1964

SONG

The command to sing psalms in the name of the Lord was obeyed by everyone in every place. . . . In the whole Church the people of Christ, who are gathered from all nations sing hymns with a loud voice.

EUSEBIUS (260?–340?), *Ecclesiastical History*

Each man does his utmost in singing what will be a blessing to all. Psalms are sung in the home and rehearsed on the streets. A psalm is learnt without labor and remembered with delight. Psalmody unites those who disagree, makes friends of those at odds, brings together those who are out of charity with one another.

ST. AMBROSE (c. 333–397), *Commentary on Psalm I*

The fineness which a hymn or psalm affords
Is, when the soul unto the lines accords.
> GEORGE HERBERT (1593–1633), *A True Hymn*

Song is the daughter of prayer, and prayer is the companion of religion.
> VISCOUNT DE CHATEAUBRIAND, *Genius of Christianity*, 1856

True devotion produces as of itself a song; song, in turn excites devotion, and this reciprocal action augments the value of both, like two mirrors, which, facing each other, multiply the same image even to the profundity, so to speak, of the infinite.
> JOSEPH POTHIER, *Les Mélodies Grégoriennes*, 1880

See also Melodies; Music; Psalms; Worship.

SORROW

All men are attached to children, wives and kind; they sink down in the slimy sea of sorrows, like age-worn forest-elephants.
> *Mahabharata*, xii, c. 800 B.C.

There is no greater sorrow than to recall happiness in times of misery.
> DANTE, *Inferno*, c. 1320

Earth has no sorrow that Heaven cannot heal.
> ST. THOMAS MORE, *Come, Ye Disconsolate*, 1535

Sorrow is uneasiness in the mind, upon the thought of a good lost, which might have been enjoyed longer; or the sense of a present evil.
> JOHN LOCKE, *Essay Concerning Human Understanding*, 1690

Every man has a rainy corner in his life.
> JEAN PAUL RICHTER, *Titan*, 1803

The sorrow for the dead is the only sorrow from which we refuse to be divorced. . . . The love which survives the tomb is one of the noblest attributes of the soul.
> WASHINGTON IRVING, *The Sketch Book*, 1819

Every man has his secret sorrows which the world knows not; and oftentimes we call a man cold when he is only sad.
> HENRY WADSWORTH LONGFELLOW, *Hyperion*, 1839

Sorrow draws towards great souls as thunder-storms do to mountains, but the storms also break upon them; and they become the clearing point in the skies for plains beneath them.
> JEAN PAUL RICHTER, *Death of an Angel and Other Writings*, 1844

If sorrow devours me, and I lose what is dearest to me; if I feel no comfort, and no prayer of mine is heard, it can only lead me to Thee; so be welcome, flame and sword!
> ANNETTE VON DROSTE-HÜLSHOFF (1797–1848), *The Spiritual Year*

That mortal man who hath more of joy than of sorrow in him, that mortal man cannot be true. . . . The truest of all men was the Man of Sorrows.
> HERMAN MELVILLE, *Moby Dick*, 1851

Let us rather be thankful that our sorrow lives in us as an indestructible force, only changing its form, as forces do, and passing from pain into sympathy—the one poor word which includes all our best insight and our best love.
> GEORGE ELIOT, *Adam Bede*, 1859

It is sorrow. . . . Sorrow and failure, which forces me to believe that there is One who heareth prayer, forces them to lift up their eyes to One from whom cometh their help.
> CHARLES KINGSLEY, *Westminster Sermons*, 1890

God, pitying our weakness, makes the future dark to us, and so the sorrows of life come to us in installments, one by one, and we easily glide over them by His assistance and go our ways cheerfully.

P. A. SHEEHAN, *Mary, The Mother of God,* 1902

If the world has indeed been built of sorrow, it has been built by the hands of love, because in no other way could the soul of man, for whom the world was made, reach the full stature of its perfection. Pleasure for the beautiful body, but pain for the beautiful soul.

OSCAR WILDE, *De Profundis,* 1905

Where there is sorrow there is holy ground.

OSCAR WILDE, *De Profundis,* 1905

The man who has never wept over the sorrows of his people is blind to the taller peaks of life.

KIRBY PAGE, *Living Creatively,* 1932

Sorrow is an invitation to go to God. It is a sign of vocation. And, if love has a part, it is at the same time an initiation into that future.

ANTONIN SERTILLANGES, *Recollections,* 1950

Where sorrow is concerned, not repression but expression is the wholesome discipline.

SIDNEY GREENBERG, *Treasury of Comfort,* 1954

You cannot prevent the birds of sorrow from flying over your head, but you can prevent them from building nests in your hair.

Chinese Proverb

When the heart weeps for what it has lost, the spirit laughs for what it has found.

ANONYMOUS

See also Adversity; Affliction; Bereavement; Cross; Death; Gloom; Grief; Joy; Melancholy; Misery; Mourning; Pain; Prayer; Sadness; Suffering; Tears; Tragedy.

SOUL

Smaller than the hundredth part of a tip of hair, the Soul of the living being is capable of infinity. Male is he not nor female nor neuter, but is joined with whatever body he takes as his own.

Svetavatara Upanishad, c. 600 B.C.

The bounds of the soul thou shalt not find, though you travel every way.

HERACLITUS (535–475 B.C.), *Fragments*

And I say let a man be of good cheer about his soul. When the soul has been arrayed in her own proper jewels—temperance, and justice, and courage, and nobility and truth—she is ready to go on her journey when the hour comes.

SOCRATES, minutes before his execution, PLATO, "Phaedo," *Dialogues,* 399 B.C.

Of all things which a man has, next to the gods, his soul is the most divine and most truly his own.

PLATO, *Laws,* Bk. IV, 4th century B.C.

The soul which is not moved,
The soul that with a strong and constant calm
Takes sorrow and takes joy indifferently,
Lives in the life undying!

Bhagavad-Gita, c. 2nd century B.C.

When I reflect on the nature of the soul, it seems to me by far more difficult and obscure to determine its character while it is in the body, a strange domicile, than to imagine what it is when it leaves it, and has arrived in the empyreal regions, in its own and proper home.

CICERO, *Tusculanarum Disputationum,* Bk. I, 44 B.C.

The soul is master of every kind of fortune: itself acts in both ways, being the cause of its own happiness and misery.
SENECA, *Epistolae*, 98, c. 63 A.D.

The rational soul wanders round the whole world and through the encompassing void, and gazes into infinite time, and considers the periodic destructions and rebirths of the universe, and reflects that our posterity will see nothing new, and that our ancestors saw nothing greater than we have seen.
MARCUS AURELIUS, *Meditations*, c. 170

The soul is naturally Christian.
TERTULLIAN, *Apology*, xvii, 197

There are souls in all living things, even in those which live in the waters.
ORIGEN, *De Principiis*, c. 254

Never did eye see the sun unless it had first become sunlike, and never can the soul have vision of the First Beauty unless itself be beautiful.
PLOTINUS (203–262 A.D.), *The Ennaeds*

No soul shall bear the burden of another.
Koran, c. 625

The soul is a stranger in this world.
BAHYA (Joseph Ibn Pakuda), *Hobot HaLebabot*, 1040

The soul is the primary principle of our nourishment, sensation, movement, and understanding.
ST. THOMAS AQUINAS, *Summa Theologiae*, 1272

The feet carry the body as affection carries the soul.
ST. CATHERINE OF SIENA, *Dialogo*, cap. xxvi, c. 1378

The soul, mindful of its ethereal nature, presses upward with exceedingly great force, and struggles with its weight. It

distrusts things seen. . . . It seeks those things which truly and everlastingly are.
DESIDERIUS ERASMUS, *Enchiridion*, 1501

Soul is the greatest thing in the least continent.
ELIZABETH GRYMESTON, *Miscellanea— Meditation*, 1604

The soul of man (whose life or motion is perpetual contemplation or thought) is the mistress of two potent rivals, the one reason, the other passion, that are in continual suit.
JAMES HARRINGTON, *The Commonwealth of Oceana*, 1656

I should suppose that souls which will some day become human have, like those of the other species, been in the seed, and in the ancestors, up to Adam, and have consequently existed since the beginning of things, always in a sort of organized body.
G. W. VON LEIBNIZ, *Philos. Schriften*, VI, 1714

We call "soul" that which animates. Owing to our limited intelligence we know scarcely anything more of the matter. . . . No one has found it, or ever will find it.
VOLTAIRE, *Philosophical Dictionary*, II, 1764

Four thousand volumes of metaphysics will not teach us what the soul is.
VOLTAIRE, "Soul," *Philosophical Dictionary*, 1764

Diseases of the body destroy the body, diseases of the soul do not destroy the soul. It remains the soul no matter how ignorant or vicious it is.
VOLTAIRE (1694–1778), *Scribbling Books*, publ. posth.

Everywhere the human soul stands between a hemisphere of light and another of darkness on the confines of two everlasting hostile empires,—Necessity and Free Will.

THOMAS CARLYLE, *Essays: Goethe's Works,* 1832

Nothing is more difficult than to realize that every man has a distinct soul, that every one of all the millions who live or have lived, is as whole and independent a being in himself, as if there were no one else in the whole world but he.

JOHN HENRY NEWMAN, *Parochial and Plain Sermons,* 1843

We need not fear that we can lose anything by the progress of the soul. The soul may be trusted to the end. That which is so beautiful and attractive must be succeeded and supplanted only by what is more beautiful and so on forever.

RALPH WALDO EMERSON, "Love," *Essays,* 1845

Nothing can be greater than it. . . . It is wider than space, older than time, wide as hope, rich as love.

RALPH WALDO EMERSON, *The Method of Nature,* 1849

Our souls are like those orphans whose unwedded mothers die in bearing them: the secret of our paternity lies in their grave, and we must there learn it.

HERMAN MELVILLE, *Moby Dick,* 1851

As this appalling ocean surrounds the verdant land, so in the soul of man there lies one insular Tahiti, full of peace and joy, but encompassed by all the horrors of the half known life. God keep thee! Push not off from that isle, thou canst never return!

HERMAN MELVILLE, *Moby Dick,* 1851

Souls are not saved in bundles. The Spirit saith to man, "How is it with thee? thee personally? is it well, is it ill?"

RALPH WALDO EMERSON, *Worship,* 1860

Close by the rights of man, side by side with them, are the rights of the soul.

VICTOR HUGO, *Les Miserables,* 1862

The man who in this world can keep the whiteness of his soul, is not likely to lose it in any other.

ALEXANDER SMITH, *Dreamthorp,* 1863

Were our heaven never overcast, yet we meet the brightest morning only in escape from recent night; and the atmosphere of our souls, never passing from ebb and flow of love into a motionless constancy, must always break the white eternal beams into a colored and tearful glory.

JAMES MARTINEAU, *Hours of Thought on Sacred Things,* 1879

On this earth of ours there are but few souls that can withstand the dominion of the soul that has suffered itself to become beautiful.

MAURICE MAETERLINCK, *The Treasure of the Humble,* 1895

There is only one such Self, and that one self is you. Standing behind this little nature is what we call the Soul. . . . He is the Soul of your soul. . . . You are one with Him.

SWAMI VIVEKANANDA (1862–1902), *The Yoga and Other Works,* 1953

The soul has aspirations toward a truth in which it can repose.

BERNARD BOSANQUET, *Address,* 1903

The greater number of men pass through life with souls asleep.

PAUL SABATIER, *The Life of St. Francis of Assisi,* 1920

In the laboratory there can be found no trace of the soul except certain rather undignified phenomena which give rise to the illusion that we have one.

JOSEPH WOOD KRUTCH, *The Modern Temper,* 1929

It is no use saying that modern scientists have totally given up the use of the word "soul." They may have given up the word. They cannot help making use of the thing.

JOHN COWPER POWYS, *A Philosophy of Solitude,* 1933

The fact of our being able to form abstract or universal ideas is, in itself, a proof of the immateriality, or, as it is technically called, the spirituality of the soul, a proof that the soul is, in its essence, independent of matter.

RICHARD DOWNEY, *Critical and Constructive Essays,* 1934

Spirit unites itself inwardly to soul and transfigures it. The distinction between spirit and soul does not imply their separation.

NICHOLAS BERDYAEV, *Freedom and the Spirit,* 1935

As the least beautiful of our kind is human, and humanity the most beautiful thing in our world, everyone is capable of transfiguration when the comely soul shines through.

LANE COOPER, *Evolution and Repentance,* 1935

The soul needs a physical body here . . . but when . . . the body is no longer an adequate instrument through which the soul may function, it lays the present body aside and continues to function through a more subtle one.

ERNEST HOLMES, *The Science of Mind,* 1938

Deep within us all there is an amazing inner sanctuary of the soul, a holy place, a Divine Center, a speaking Voice. . . . Life from the Center is a life of unhurried peace and power. It is simple. It is serene. It is amazing. It is radiant.

T. R. KELLY, *A Testament of Devotion,* 1941

The individual soul is a thing created in the fullness of time to have just those characteristics which the time requires if God's purpose is to be fulfilled.

R. G. COLLINGWOOD, *The Idea of History* 1946

However far back we go in the history of the race, we can never find a time or place where man was not conscious of the soul and of a divine power on which his life depended.

CHRISTOPHER DAWSON, *Religion and Culture,* 1947

Our whole being subsists in virtue of the subsistence of the spiritual soul which is in us a principle of creative unity, independence and liberty.

JACQUES MARITAIN, *The Person and the Common Good,* 1947

The soul in action is nothing but thought transforming itself into works.

ANTONIN SERTILLANGES, *Recollections,* 1950

There is plenty of evidence for an Original Virtue underlying Original Sin. . . . The knowledge that there is a central chamber of the soul, blazing with the light of divine love and wisdom, has come, in the course of history, to multitudes of human beings.

ALDOUS HUXLEY, *The Devils of Loudon,* 1952

The human soul is no more than a spark of the divine in us, which upon death returns to reunite with God as the original source of its being, than is the body.

SIMON GREENBERG, *Patterns of Faith in America Today,* ed. F. E. Johnson, 1957

Science's horizon is limited by the bounds of Nature, the ideologies by the bounds of human social life, but the human soul's range cannot be confined within either of these limits.

A. J. TOYNBEE, *Study of History,* Vol. xii, *Reconsiderations,* 1961

See also Beacons; Beauty; Birth; Body and Soul; Community; Creation; Damnation;

Death; Evolution; Grace; Heaven; Immortality; Immortality, Belief in; Judgment, God's; Justification; Love; Man; Man, Defined and Interpreted; Man Indwelt by God; Man's Quest of God; Mind; Original Sin; Personality; Psyche; Punishment; Purgatory; Religion: Its Nature and Function; Salvation; Science; Self; Sin: Its Consequences; Soul, Definitions of; Soul and God; Spirit; Spirit, Human; Virtue.

SOUL, DEFINITIONS OF

Soul is actuality in the sense in which knowledge is so, for the presence of the soul is compatible both with sleep and with waking, and waking is analogous to the exercise of knowledge . . . the soul is the first actualization of a natural body potentially having life.

ARISTOTLE (384–322 B.C.), *De Anima*

These are the properties of the rational soul: it seeth itself: it analyseth itself, and maketh itself such as it will; and all things that happen unto it appear such as it will: the fruit which it beareth it enjoyeth in itself . . . and it attaineth its own end wheresoever the limit of life may be fixed.

MARCUS AURELIUS, *Meditations,* xi, i and vi, c. 170 A.D.

The life whereby we are joined into the body is called the soul.

ST. AUGUSTINE, *Of the Faith and of the Creed,* c. 393

Although united to the whole body, it has, nevertheless, its principal seat in the brain, where alone it not only understands and imagines, but also perceives; and this by the medium of the nerves, which are extended like threads from the brain to all the other members.

RENÉ DESCARTES, *The Principles of Philosophy,* 1644

The soul is the mirror of an indestructible universe.

G. W. VON LEIBNIZ, *The Monadology,* 1714

We live in succession, in division, in parts, in particles. Meantime within man is the soul of the whole; the wise silence; the universal beauty, to which every part and particle is equally related; the eternal ONE.

R. W. EMERSON, *Heroism,* 1841

By the word soul, or psyche, I mean the inner consciousness which aspires.

RICHARD JEFFERIES, *The Story of My Heart,* 1883

It is . . . a purely phenomenal existence, an appearance incomplete and inconsistent, and with no power to maintain itself as an independent "thing." . . . The soul is a finite centre of immediate experience, . . . a particular group of psychical events, so far as these events are to be taken merely as happening in time.

F. H. BRADLEY, *Appearance and Reality,* 1894

My soul is myself; the well-spring or point of consciousness, or center of inner activity . . . the most real thing in the universe to me; the start for all other knowing, the test by which I judge all other data.

UPTON SINCLAIR, *What God Means to Me,* 1935

The soul is the aspect of ourselves that is specific of our nature and distinguishes man from all other animals. We are not capable of defining this familiar and profoundly mysterious entity.

ALEXIS CARREL, *Man, the Unknown,* 1935

Whether or not the philosophers care to admit that we have a soul, it seems obvious that we are equipped with something or other which generates dreams and ideals, and which sets up values.

JOHN ERSKINE, *On the Meaning of Life,* ed. W. Durant, 1937

A dramatic centre of action and passion . . . utterly unlike what in modern philosophy we call consciousness. The soul causes the body to grow, to assume its ancestral shape, to develop all its ancestral instincts, to wake and to sleep by turns . . . and at the same time determines the responses that the living body shall make to the world.

> GEORGE SANTAYANA, *The Realm of Truth,* 1938

That unified being which, in our case as in every other, is evident only to itself; luminous to itself, to every other eye obscure.

> GUSTAV T. FECHNER, *Religion of a Scientist, Selections from Fechner,* ed. Walter Lowrie, 1946

See also Body and Soul; Soul; Soul and God; Spirit.

SOUL AND GOD

The soul should not attribute to itself but to God, its toil for virtue.

> PHILO, *Allegories,* c. 10 A.D.

The soul alone renders us noble . . . Do you ask where the Supreme Good dwells? In the soul. And unless the soul be pure and holy, there is no room in it for God.

> SENECA, *Epistulae ad Lucilium, Epis.* 44.5, c. 63 A.D.

God is not only the Creator, but the Country of the soul.

> ST. AUGUSTINE, *Confessions of,* c. 397

As it must be confessed that the human soul is not that which God is, so it must be presumed that among all the things which He created, nothing is nearer to God than it.

> ST. AUGUSTINE (354–430), *De Quantitate Animae*

God first purifies the souls in which He dwells, then He illumines them, and finally leads them to divine union.

> DIONYSIUS, *The Ecclesiastical Hierarchy,* c. 500 A.D.

Since the human soul cannot be produced by the transmutation of matter, it cannot but be produced immediately by God.

> ST. THOMAS AQUINAS, *Summa Theologiae,* la, xc, 1272

I affirm that there is a power in the Soul which is unmoved by time or the flesh: this power floweth from the Spirit, yet abideth therein. Yea, it is all spirit.

> MEISTER ECKHART (1260?–1327?), *Meister Eckhart*

We should mark and know of a very truth that all manner of virtue and goodness, and even the Eternal Good, which is God Himself, can never make a man virtuous, good or happy so long as it is outside the soul.

> *Theologica Germanica,* c. 1350

Our soul is *made* to be God's dwelling-place; and the dwelling place of the soul is God, which is *unmade.*

> JULIANA OF NORWICH, *Revelations of Divine Love,* 15th century

If the soul of man be an emanation from the essence of God, it will follow that the Divine nature is not only mutable and subject to passions, but also to ignorance, desires and vices of every kind. . . . Who would not dread such a monstrous tenet?

> JOHN CALVIN, *Institutes,* I, 1536

Each of us possesses a soul, but we do not prize our souls as creatures made in God's image deserve, and so we do not understand the great secrets which they contain.

> ST. TERESA OF ÁVILA, *The Interior Castle,* 1577

The soul can perform no acts, but it is the Holy Spirit that moves it to perform them. . . . God is the agent, and . . . He is secretly speaking to the solitary soul while the soul keeps silent.

> ST. JOHN OF THE CROSS, *Living Flame,* Vol. 3, c. 1584

954

The soul, when it shall have driven away from itself all that is contrary to the divine will, becomes transformed in God by love.

    St. John of the Cross, *The Ascent of Mount Carmel*, c. 1584

Every soul is as a world apart, independent of everything else except God.

    G. W. von Leibniz, *Discourse on Metaphysics*, 1685

God's design for the soul is that it should be lost in himself, in a manner unknown to ordinary Christians.

    Madame Guyon, *Spiritual Torrents*, c. 1690

The essences of our soul were a breath in God before they became a living soul, they lived in God before they lived in the created soul, and therefore the soul is a partaker of the eternity of God and can never cease to be.

    William Law, *Appeal to All That Doubt*, 1740

The human soul is a silent harp in God's quire, whose strings need only to be swept by the divine breath to chime in with the harmonies of creation.

    Henry David Thoreau, *Journal*, August 10, 1838

It [the soul] is truly an image of the infinity of God, and no words can do justice to its grandeur.

    William Ellery Channing (1780–1842), *Works*

We cannot describe the natural history of the soul, but we know that it is divine.

    Ralph Waldo Emerson, *The Method of Nature*, 1849

The whole sum of God that there is on earth, within all men, concentrates itself in a single cry to affirm the soul.

    Victor Hugo, *William Shakespeare*, 1864

In its highest sense [the soul is] a vast capacity for God. . . . A chamber with elastic and contractile walls, which can be expanded, with God as its guest, illimitably, but which without God shrinks and shrinks until every vestige of the Divine is gone, and God's image is kept without God's Spirit.

    Henry Drummond, *Natural Law in the Spiritual World*, 1883

There is no separation between your soul and the soul of the universe. In the deepest sense you are the great universal soul. Man is God incarnate.

    Ralph Waldo Trine, *What All the World's A-Seeking*, 1896

The terms *souls* or spirits is as improper as the term *gods*. Soul or Spirit signifies Deity and nothing else. There is no finite soul nor spirit. Soul or Spirit means only one Mind, and cannot be rendered in the plural.

    Mary Baker Eddy, *Science and Health*, 1908

Is there, as the medieval mystics taught, a "spark" at the core of the Soul, which never consents to evil, a Divine nucleus in the heart of the personality, which can take no stain?

    W. R. Inge, *The Philosophy of Plotinus*, 1918

The human soul, in so far as science can penetrate, is the last chapter of cosmic history as far as it has been written. It is in the soul that Divinity resides.

    Michael Pupin, *The American Magazine*, September, 1927

A star like Betelguese . . . is enormous, nearly three hundred million miles in diameter. Our whole solar system could swing around inside it. But what is Betelguese. Nothing but a big gas bag—that's all. With all its size, it has no soul. It cannot hear the call which I heard as an ignorant boy, to worship at the altar of Almighty God.

> MICHAEL PUPIN, *The American Magazine,* September, 1927

In the mystic sense of the creation around us, in the expression of art, in a yearning towards God, the soul grows upward and finds fulfilment of something implanted in its nature.

> ARTHUR EDDINGTON, *The Nature of the Physical World,* 1928

It was in the recognition that there is in each man a final essence, that is to say an immortal soul, which only God can judge, that a limit was set upon the dominion of men over men.

> WALTER LIPPMANN, *The Good Society,* 1937

Christianity teaches that the human soul is directly related to God. Such immediacy is the hallmark of the Divinity of the soul and the center of our freedom.

> HELMUT KUHN, *Freedom Forgotten and Remembered,* 1943

There is no emptiness of soul ever for those whose life is devoted to God.

> WILLIAM LAWSON, *For Goodness Sake,* 1951

Every soul is valuable in God's sight, and the story of every soul is the story of self-definition for good or evil, salvation or damnation. Every soul is valuable in God's sight. Or, with the secularization of things, we may say: every soul is valuable in man's sight.

> ROBERT PENN WARREN, *Address,* Columbia University, 1954

In each soul, God loves and partly saves the whole world which that soul sums up in an incommunicable and particular way.

> PIERRE TEILHARD DE CHARDIN, *The Divine Milieu,* 1960

The soul of man is the lamp of God.

> ANONYMOUS

See also All; Beatific Vision; Creation; Damnation; Evolution; Grace; Holy Spirit; Immortality; Man and God; Mysticism; One; Pantheism; Soul, Spirit.

SOUL AND IMMORTALITY. See IMMORTALITY

SOURCE

All things come from that one source, from the ruling Reason of the Universe, either under a primary impulse from it or by way of consequence.

> MARCUS AURELIUS, *Meditations,* c. 170 A.D.

SOVIET RUSSIA

In order to insure to citizens freedom of conscience, the church in the U.S.S.R. is separated from the state, and the school from the church. Freedom of religious worship and freedom of anti-religious-worship propaganda is recognized for all citizens.

> *Constitution of the U.S.S.R.,* January 31, 1924

Several visitors to the U.S.S.R. . . . have recently estimated that about ten per cent of the population go to church on any given Sunday—that is, between twenty and thirty million people. . . . In proportion to the total population, Church attendance in Russia after forty years of Communism is higher than in many countries of western Europe.

> TIMOTHY WARE, *The Orthodox Church,* 1963

See also Communism; Marxism.

SPACE MAN

The difficulty is that the space man with all his intelligence still has the soul of a chimpanzee. He is handling vast forces with great intelligence, but he is morally and spiritually unfit to handle those forces.

> E. STANLEY JONES, *Conversion,* 1959

See also Other Worlds.

SPEECH

The truly good man is slow of speech.
CONFUCIUS, *Sayings of,* 5th century B.C.

Does not the difficulty of deciding what is right to *do* necessarily imply slowness to *speak?*
CONFUCIUS, *Saying of,* 5th century B.C.

This manner of speech in a Christian, is full of indiscretion and irreverence: God cannot die, God cannot gainsay himself, God cannot do this or that. I cannot allow a man should so bound God's heavenly power under the Laws of our word.
MICHEL DE MONTAIGNE, *Essays,* Bk. 2, ch. 12, 1580

O God! that men should put an enemy in their mouths to steal away their brains!
WILLIAM SHAKESPEARE, *Othello,* c. 1604

Speak the truth and shame the devil.
MIGUEL DE CERVANTES, *Don Quixote,* 1605

We can examine what goes into our mouths, and why not what comes out of them as well? . . . More have repented themselves of their speaking than of their silence.
JOHN BONA, *Guide to Eternity,* 1672

A tongue without a guard upon it is like a city without a wall. . . . It is not for nothing that nature herself thought fit to enclose the tongue with a double fence, both of teeth and lips.
JOHN BONA, *Guide to Eternity,* 1672

Speak the truth, and all things alive or brute are vouchers, and the very roots of the grass underground there do seem to stir and move to bear your witness.
RALPH WALDO EMERSON, *Divinity School Address,* July, 1838

He who does not bellow the truth when he knows the truth makes himself the accomplice of liars and forgers.
CHARLES PEGUY, *Basic Verities,* 1943

See also Eloquence; Freedom of Thought and Speech; Orator; Preachers; Preaching; Rhetoric; Sermons; Silence; Truth.

SPEED

Sober speed is wisdom's leisure.
ROBERT SOUTHWELL, *Loss in Delay,* c. 1595

SPIRIT

There is no certain form given to the spirit conceived with the body. Once dead it is again born—the connection of sin and of merit cannot be overreached.
Dhammapada, c. 5th century B.C.

Know, beloved, that we cannot understand the future world until we know what death is: and we cannot know what death is until we know what life is; nor can we understand what life is until we know what the spirit is—the seat of the knowledge of God.
AL-GHAZZALI (born 1058 A.D.), *Alchemy of Happiness*

The life of the spirit is not our life, but the life of God within us.
ST. TERESA OF ÁVILA, *Life Written by Herself,* 1565

It is a riddle to me . . . how so many learned heads should so far forget their metaphysics, and destroy the ladder and scale of creatures, as to question the existence of spirits.
THOMAS BROWNE, *Religio Medici,* 1635

One simple, undivided, active being—as it perceives ideas it is called the *understanding,* and as it produces or otherwise operates about them it is called the will.
GEORGE BERKELEY, *Principles of Human Knowledge,* 1710

Matter has its essence out of itself; Spirit is *self-contained existence*.

    G. W. F. HEGEL (1770–1831), *The Philosophy of History,* publ. posth.

The substance, the essence, of Spirit is Freedom.

    G. W. F. HEGEL (1770–1831), *The Philosophy of History,* publ. posth.

You and I may never see it, but ultimately nothing is so certain as the triumph of the things of the spirit over the gross material forces of American civilization.

    BLISS PERRY, *A Study of Prose Fiction,* 1902

There is not a tissue in the human body wholly removed from the influence of the spirit.

    British Medical Journal, June 18, 1910

The heights of the spirit can only be climbed by passing through the portals of humanity.

    RUDOLF STEINER, *Knowledge of the Higher Worlds,* 1910

Either spirit is the supreme fact, supreme over all changes of process and lasting through them all; or life is to be defined as a mechanical process suffering from the illusion that it is not mechanical.

    A. CLUTTON-BROCK, *Immortality,* ed. B. H. Streeter, 1917

Even in the limited field of experience open to our minds, the power of spirit is out of all proportion to that of other forces of nature.

    CHRISTOPHER DAWSON, *God and the Supernatural,* 1920

Spirit is a fountain of clearness, decidedly wind-blown and spasmodic, and possessing at each moment the natural and historical actuality of an event.

    GEORGE SANTAYANA, *Scepticism and Animal Faith,* 1923

Spirit is awareness, intelligence, recollection. It requires no dogmas.

    GEORGE SANTAYANA, *Platonism and the Spiritual Life,* 1927

Spirit itself is not human; it may spring up in any life . . . it may exist in all animals, and who knows in how many undreamt-of beings, or in the midst of what worlds?

    GEORGE SANTAYANA, *Platonism and the Spiritual Life,* 1927

It is easy enough to drive the spirit out of the door, but when we have done so the salt of life grows flat—it loses its savor.

    CARL G. JUNG, *Modern Man in Search of a Soul,* 1932

It was not the body that made the spirit sin, it was the spirit that brought death to the body.

    ÉTIENNE GILSON, *The Spirit of Medieval Philosophy,* 1936

I find an Eternal Gospel of the Spirit dimly breaking through the time-stream in many ways.

    RUFUS M. JONES, *The Eternal Gospel,* 1938

Spirit is the principle of Unity back of all things. Spirit is all Life, Truth, Love, Being, Cause and Effect, and is the only Power in the Universe that knows Itself.

    ERNEST HOLMES, *The Science of Mind,* 1938

The heathen spirit is wingless. It cannot lift itself to heights from which the totality of being is visible.

    SHOLEM ASCH, *What I Believe,* 1941

Spirit. It is in the flesh itself that modern heresy seeks the spirit. It plants therein all the sins of the spirit, pride, the disdain of God.

    JACQUES MARITAIN, *Art and Poetry,* 1943

The problems that divide the world most deeply are centered not in matter but in spirit. Whether spirit is reality or illusion is the greatest question that confronts mankind.

EDMUND W. SINNOTT, *The Biology of the Spirit,* 1955

The spirit inherent in religions is found to be one spirit when we truly put ourselves in the other person's place.

MARCUS BACH, *Rotarian Magazine,* December, 1962

See also Angels; Body; Body and Soul; Demons; God: Considered as Personal; God: His Nature; Holy Spirit; Immortality, Belief in; Man, Defined and Interpreted; Man and God; Man Indwelt by God; Matter; Matter and Spirit; Pentecost; Personality; Reality; Soul; Soul and God; Spirit, Human; Supernatural; Universe and God; Word, the.

SPIRIT, HOLY. See HOLY SPIRIT

SPIRIT, HUMAN

Our spirit is a being of a nature quite indestructible and its activity continues from eternity to eternity. It is like the sun, which seems to set only to our earthly eyes, but which, in reality, never sets, but shines on unceasingly.

J. W. VON GOETHE, *Conversations with Eckermann,* I, 1848

The spirit can for the time pervade and control every member and function of the body, and transmute what in form is the grossest sensuality into purity and devotion.

HENRY DAVID THOREAU, *Walden,* 1854

If I try to think of the "spirit" which a man . . . carries about under his hat, as something devoid of relation to space, and as something indivisible, even in thought, while it is, at the same time, supposed to be in that place and to be possessed of half a dozen different faculties, I confess I get quite lost.

THOMAS HENRY HUXLEY, *Science and Morals,* 1886

In direct proportion as a man recognizes himself as spirit, and lives accordingly, is he able to transcend in power the man who recognizes himself merely as material.

RALPH WALDO TRINE, *In Tune with the Infinite,* 1897

The spirit of man is an inward flame; a lamp the world blows upon but never puts out.

MARGOT ASQUITH, *Autobiography,* Vol. 2, 1922

Man cannot live without a permanent trust in something indestructible in himself, though both the indestructible element and the trust may remain permanently hidden from him.

FRANZ KAFKA (1883–1924), *Reflections*

Man has spirit only in that it is addressed by God. . . . Therefore the human self is nothing that exists in its own right.

EMIL BRUNNER, *God and Man,* 1936

Spirit is at first a new force, a new impetus in man. By its increasing activity it develops into a perfected faculty of the human being.

ERICH KAHLER, *Man the Measure,* 1943

As we grow older, in fact, we discover that the lives of most human beings are worthless except in so far as they contribute to the enrichment and emancipation of the spirit.

CYRIL CONNOLLY, *The Unquiet Grave,* 1944

Although the universe dwarfs man by its size and power, yet he can rest secure in the unique gift of spirit wherewith he can observe and discuss it all.

JOHN A. CASS, *Quest for Certainty,* 1950

The revolution of the individual can never become the status quo, because the human spirit, as revealed in Palestine by the founder of Christianity, is limitless.

> RUSSELL W. DAVENPORT, and editors of *Fortune, U.S.A.: The Permanent Revolution*, 1951

The human spirit is a glass through which we can peer more deeply into reality than by purely rational instruments alone.

> EDMUND W. SINNOTT, *The Biology of Spirit*, 1955

Mysteriously though man's spirit may seem to move, and high as its destiny may sometimes prove to be, it is *born* in living matter, and the biologist can therefore legitimately claim it as part of his domain.

> EDMUND W. SINNOTT, *The Biology of the Spirit*, 1955

See also Body and Soul; Death; Immortality; Intellect; Man; Man and God; Mind; Personality; Spirit; Trinity.

SPIRITS, EVIL

It is not more strange that there should be evil spirits than evil men—evil unembodied spirits than evil embodied spirits.

> SAMUEL JOHNSON, *Boswell's Tour of the Hebrides*, August 16, 1773

See also Angels; Devil; Evil; Guardian Angel; Spirit.

SPIRITUAL

Do you know when people really become spiritual? It is when they become the slaves of God and are branded with His sign, which is the sign of the Cross, in token that they have given Him their freedom.

> ST. TERESA OF ÁVILA, *The Interior Castle*, 1577

If ever you would be Divine, you must admit this principle: That spiritual things

are the greatest, and that spiritual strength is the most excellent, useful, and delightful.

> THOMAS TRAHERNE (1634–1674), *Centuries of Meditation*

Spirituality lies in regarding existence merely as a vehicle for contemplation, and contemplation merely as a vehicle for joy.

> GEORGE SANTAYANA, *Soliloquies in England*, 1922

See also Abandonment; Aspiration; Contemplation; Detachment; Joy; Mysticism; Prayer; Reality; Selflessness; Spiritual Life; Supernatural.

SPIRITUAL BLINDNESS

A man was amazed at how easily he went along the road to eternity; the fact was he was rushing along it downhill.

> FRANZ KAFKA (1883–1924), *Reflections*

See also Spiritual Lethargy.

SPIRITUAL CONFLICT

We are faced with a spiritual conflict of the most acute kind, a sort of social schizophrenia which divides the soul of society between a non-moral will to power served by inhuman techniques and a religious faith and a moral idealism which have no power to influence human life.

> CHRISTOPHER DAWSON, *Religion and Culture*, 1947

Mere freedom from spiritual conflict is one of the most wretched ideals ever to lull a congregation into complacency.

> L. HAROLD DE WOLF, *Religious Revolt Against Reason*, 1949

We are challenged to a knightly combat ending in life or death. The hero exclaims: "How splendid!" the coward clenches his teeth; the soul, conscious of her weakness, leans trustingly.

> ANTONIN SERTILLANGES, *Recollections*, 1950

The present world crisis . . . is a crisis of man's spirit. It is a great religious and moral upheaval of the human race, and we do not really know half the causes of this upheaval.

THOMAS MERTON, *Way,* June, 1963

See also Doubt; Spiritual Struggle.

SPIRITUAL FORMATION

We blanch cotton, and strengthen steel, and refine sugar, and shape pottery; but to brighten, to strengthen, to refine, or to form a single living spirit, never enters into our estimate of advantages.

JOHN RUSKIN, *Stones of Venice,* 1853

SPIRITUAL LETHARGY

The root of modern evils and of their baneful consequences is not, as in pre-Christian times or in regions yet pagan, invincible ignorance of the eternal destiny of man and of the principal means of attaining it; rather it is lethargy of the spirit, weakness of the will, and coldness of heart.

POPE PIUS XII, *Address,* February 10, 1952

See also Apathy; Complacency; Inaction.

SPIRITUAL LIFE

The great error of the doctrines on the spirit has been the idea that by isolating the spiritual life from all the rest, by suspending it in space as high as possible above the earth, they were placing it beyond attack, as if they were not thereby simply exposing it to be taken as an effect of mirage!

HENRI BERGSON, *Creative Evolution,* 1911

The spiritual life . . . means the ever more perfect and willing association of the invisible human spirit with the invisible Divine Spirit for all purposes; for the glory of God, for the growth and culture of the praying soul.

EVELYN UNDERHILL, *Man and the Supernatural,* 1927

In the spiritual life there is nothing obligatory. Those who have spirit in them will live in the spirit, or will suffer horribly in the flesh.

GEORGE SANTAYANA, *The Realm of Essence,* 1928

See also Contemplation; Eternal Life; Immortality; Life; Life: Its Meaning; Life and Death; Man and God; Man's Quest of God; Man's Unity with God; Mysticism; Prayer; Reality.

SPIRITUAL PROGRESS

The first step that the soul of the faithful man made, placed him in the Good-Thought Paradise; the second step . . . in the Good-Word Paradise; the third step . . . in the Good-Deed Paradise; the fourth step . . . in the Endless Lights.

Yasht, Zend-Avesta, c. 700 B.C.

Notice carefully, O pilgrim, the law of thy progress: after thou hast buried and done to death the concupiscences, thou wilt come to the wide open spaces of beatitude.

ORIGEN (185–254 A.D.), *In Numeros Hom.,* XXVII

Let each one remember that he will make progress in all spiritual things only insofar as he rids himself of self-love, self-will and self-interest.

ST. IGNATIUS LOYOLA, *Spiritual Exercises,* 1548

See also Abandonment; Detachment; Evolution; Holiness; Humility; Perfection; Prayer; Sanctity; Self-Conquest; Self-Knowledge; Selflessness; Self-Sacrifice.

SPIRITUAL STRUGGLE

We do not advance through fixed gradations, and at the last one pause:—through
infancy's unconscious spell, boyhood's
thoughtless faith, adolescence's doubt (the
common doom), then scepticism, then disbelief, resting at last in manhood's pondering repose of If. But once gone through,
we trace the round again: and are infants,
boys, and men, and If eternally.
  HERMAN MELVILLE, *Moby Dick*, 1851

See also Belief; Doubt; Faith; Self-Conquest; Self-Knowledge; Spiritual Conflict;
Spiritual Progress; Temptation.

SPIRITUAL WORLD

There is nothing besides a spiritual world;
what we call the world of the senses is Evil
in the spiritual world, and what we call
Evil is only the necessity of a moment in
our eternal evolution.
  FRANZ KAFKA (1883–1924), *Reflections*

SPIRITUALISM

We believe in Infinite Intelligence; and
that the phenomena of nature, both physical and spiritual, are the expression of
Infinite Intelligence . . . and that communication with the so-called dead is a
fact scientifically proved by the phenomena of Spiritualism.
  National Spiritualist Association, *Religious Bodies, Census of*, II, Pt. 2, p.
  1600; 1946

See also Immortality; Spirit; Psychic Phenomena.

STAR

Among all the strange things that men
have forgotten, the most universal and
catastrophic lapse of memory is that by
which they have forgotten that they are
living on a star.
  G. K. CHESTERTON, *Defendant*, 1901

STARS

The light of the stars is a part of the life-
giving breath of God.
  MICHAEL PUPIN, *The New Reformation*, 1927

STATE, THE

If God presides not over the establishment
of a State; if it has only a human foundation, it cannot escape calamity.
  PLATO, *The Republic*, c. 370 B.C.

The State . . . is the ethical spirit as revealed, self-conscious, substantial will.
. . . The State is the march of God
through the world. . . . The State is the
world which the spirit has made for itself.
  G. W. F. HEGEL, *The Philosophy of
  Law*, 1821

The state is the divine will, in the sense
that it is mind present on earth, unfolding
itself to be the actual shape and organization of a world.
  G. W. F. HEGEL, *The Philosophy of
  Right*, 1821

States or bodies politic are to be considered as moral persons having a public will,
capable and free to do right and wrong,
inasmuch as they are collections of individuals, each of whom carries with him
into the service of the community the
same binding law of morality and religion
which ought to control his conduct in
private life.
  JAMES KENT, *Kent's Commentaries*, I,
  p. 2, 1830

The State is the Divine Idea as it exists on
Earth. . . . The State is the Idea of Spirit

in the external manifestation of human Will and its Freedom.

G. W. F. HEGEL (1770–1831), *The Philosophy of History*, publ. posth.

All the worth which the human being possesses—all spiritual reality, he possesses only through the state.

G. W. F. HEGEL (1770–1831), *The Philosophy of History*, publ. posth.

Christianity, with its doctrine of humility, of forgiveness, of love, is incompatible with the state, with its haughtiness, its violence, its punishments, its wars.

LEO TOLSTOY, *The Kingdom of God Is Within You*, 1893

Every State represents human sin on the large scale. . . . In the State we human beings see our sin magnified a thousand times. The State is the product of collective sin.

MAX HUBER, *Staatenpolitik und Evangelium*, 1923

The authority of the state is subordinate authority. It has no claim to moral infallibility. In such event we should submit cheerfully to pay any penalty of the law, knowing that by conscientious disobedience to human laws we are not only obeying God, but are also best serving our nation.

Faith and Practice of the Religious Society of Friends of Philadelphia and Vicinity, 1935

In the State we human beings see our own sin magnified a thousand times.

EMIL BRUNNER, *The Divine Imperative*, 1937

The Church should remind its members that the principle of the unconditional supremacy of the state or nation, advanced either in time of peace or of war, is incompatible with the Church's faith in Jesus Christ as its only Lord and therefore unacceptable as the final word of judgment or action.

Report on the Universal Church and the World of Nations, Oxford Conference, 1937

Since the state is a community of human beings it is as truly subject to the moral law as any private society.

Report, Catholic Association for International Peace, *International Ethics*, 1942

Only those states are to be tolerated which take as their symbol the value of man, and not the majesty of the state.

NICHOLAS BERDYAEV, *Slavery and Freedom*, 1944

There is only one limit to the sovereignty of the state; it is the knowledge of the sovereignty of God. . . . Where this is lacking there is no limit to the *superbia* of the state, for there is only one remedy for *superbia*—fear of God.

EMIL BRUNNER, *Justice and the Social Order*, 1945

The greater the decline in the moral vigor of society, the more tasks the State must take upon itself.

EMIL BRUNNER, *Justice and the Social Order*, 1945

However much human error and human tyranny may be involved in it, the State is not a product of sin but one of the constants of the divine Providence and government of the world in its action against sin. It is therefore an instrument of divine grace.

KARL BARTH, *The Christian Community and the Civic Community*, 1946

The State that undermines the authority of God and rejects the supremacy of the moral order is thereby destroying the strongest supports of its own authority and is on the way to ruin.

JOHN T. McNICHOLAS, *No Wall Between God and the Child*, 1947

The day when Christians assert that the State—any State—can do no wrong, that day marks the end of the Christian era in that country where it is affirmed.
DOROTHY THOMPSON, *Look,* 1948

In the measure the State has excluded religion, it has shown a tendency to become an instrument of tyranny. The irreligious state sets itself up in the place of God, substituting its own arbitrary dictates for the decrees of eternal Wisdom.
CATHOLIC BISHOPS OF THE U.S., November, 1952

The state has won ascendancy over religious and philosophical trends not because of the state's desire to, but because of the lack of vitality in both religious and philosophical traditions.
STANLEY PARR, *The Ethics of Power,* ed. Lasswell and Cleveland, 1962

See also Authoritarianism; Authority; Church and State; Colonialism; Communism; Conscience and State; Country; Democracy; Dictatorship; Divine Right of Kings; Education, Catholic; Education, Parents' Rights in; Education, Parochial; Education and Religion; Freedom, Religious; Freedom and God; Freedom of Thought and Speech; Government, Government and God; Government and Religion; Idolatry; Law; Liberalism; Loyalty; Morality and State; Natural Law; Patriotism; Power; Rebellion; Religion, National; Religion, State; Rule; Rulers; Sin; Statism; Totalitarianism; Treason; Tyrants; War, Defense of.

STATE MONOPOLIES

It is rightly contended that certain forms of property must be reserved to the state, since they carry with them an opportunity of domination too great to be left to private individuals without injury to the community at large.
POPE LEO XIII, *Rerum Novarum,* 1891

STATISM

Modern statism . . . is . . . the State, in one form or another, deified and made an object of worship.
Declaration, Oxford Conference, 1937

See also Communism; Dictatorship; Loyalty; State, the; Totalitarianism.

STERILIZATION

Wilful sterility is, from the standpoint of the human race, the one sin for which the penalty is national death, race death; a sin for which there is no atonement.
THEODORE ROOSEVELT, *Message to Congress,* December 3, 1906

Christian doctrine establishes, and the light of human reason makes it most clear, that private individuals have no other power over the members of their bodies than that which pertains to their natural ends; and they are not free to destroy or mutilate their members, or in any other way render themselves unfit for their natural functions, except when no other provisions can be made for the good of the whole body.
POPE PIUS XI, *Casti Connubi,* December 31, 1930

Society has the right to protect itself adequately against the danger resulting from the presence and the increase of the mentally diseased. If sterilization can be proved to be the only sufficient means by which this purpose can be accomplished and national degeneration staved off, public authority cannot be denied the right to use it for the protection of the common good.
BERTRAND L. CONWAY, *The Church and Eugenics,* 1951

See also Abortion; Marriage; Sexual Intercourse.

STICKLER

A Devout Man is one thing, a Stickler quite another.
> WILLIAM PENN, *Some Fruits of Solitude*, 1718

STILLNESS

There is nothing in all creation so like God as stillness.
> MEISTER ECKHART (1260?–1327?), *Meister Eckhart*

STRONG

He is strong whom God defends.
> AESCHYLUS (525–456 B.C.), *Seven Against Thebes*

SUBLIME

The sublime, introduced at the right moment, carries all before it with the rapidity of lightning, and reveals at a glance the mighty power of genius.
> LONGINUS, *On the Sublime*, c. 250 A.D.

The feeling of the sublime is the root of the religious sentiment.
> F. ADLER, *Creed and Deed*, 1877

SUBMISSION

Without thee, Lord, what could there be
For the king thou lovest, and dost call his name?
. . . I, the prince obeying thee,
Am what thy hands have made.
> NEBUCHADNEZZAR (605–562 B.C.), quoted in *Cambridge Ancient History*

I have no hope at all but in thy great mercy. Grant what thou commandest and command what thou wilt.
> ST. AUGUSTINE, *Confessions of*, 397

If by God's decree I shall be made into a clay pot that serves for ablutions, I am thankful and content.
> ABU'L-'ALA AL-MA'ARRI (973–1057), R. A. Nicholson's *Translation of Eastern Poetry and Prose*

As he who sails on board a ship does not advance by his own motion, but by the motion of the vessel, so the heart embarked on board the divine good-pleasure should have no other wish than that of being carried by the will of God.
> ST. FRANCIS OF SALES (1567–1622), *Consoling Thoughts of*, ed. Huguet

Remember then thy station as a being sacred to God. . . . Doth he claim my body as his temple, and graciously require that I may be sacred to him? O that I may prize this favor, and that my whole life may be conformable to this character!
> JOHN WOOLMAN, *A Word of Remembrance and Caution to the Rich*, 1793

The final state which we are to contemplate with hope, and to seek by discipline, is that in which our will shall be one with the will of God.
> WILLIAM EVART GLADSTONE, *Letter to his wife*, January, 1844

In every request, heart and soul and mind ought to supply the low accompaniment, "Thy will be done."
> GEORGE MACDONALD, *Unspoken Sermons*, 1st Series, 1869

It is the prerogative of man's spiritual nature that he can yield himself up to a thought and will that are infinitely larger than his own.
> JOHN CAIRD, *Introduction to the Philosophy of Religion*, 1880

If we trust, and if we relinquish our will, and yield to the Divine will, then we find that we are afloat on a buoyant sea of peace and under us are the everlasting arms.

HELEN KELLER, *Story of My Life*, 1905

It is easy to submit to the Will of God when it sends us joy and peace, when it makes us courageous, high-hearted, and just. The difficulty is to acquiesce when He sends us adversity, ill-health, suffering.

ARTHUR CHRISTOPHER BENSON, *From a College Window*, 1906

Subordinate your every wish to the holy will of God and you will be a king. "To serve God is to reign."

DÉSIRÉ JOSEPH MERCIER, *Conferences of* 1907

In the foothills of the Himalayas, among the Khonds of North India, one hears the prayer: "Oh Lord, we know not what is good for us. Thou knowest what it is. For it we pray."

HARRY EMERSON FOSDICK, *The Meaning of Prayer*, 1915

If a man will link himself to the will of God and the reign of God over all human affairs; if he lives for it, dies for it, life and death are merged in the life and purpose of God and therefore he is indestructible.

JOHN GARDNER, *Letters to Bill on Faith and Prayer*, 1918

If a man says with Pascal, "Lord, I give You everything," and in a tone that really commits him, his friends can expect or fear anything from him save that he will turn his life into a farce.

FRANÇOIS MAURIAC, *God and Mammon*, 1946

The considerable success of A. A. is not in the least surprising to any Christian, who sees the submission of the human will to the divine plan as the ennobling enhancement of his life on earth and the means of fulfilling his eternal destiny.

J. DOMINIAN, *Psychiatry and the Christian*, 1962

See also Abandonment; Acceptance; Obedience; Renunciation; Resignation; Self-Giving; Selflessness.

SUBURBIA

"Salvation" and "redemption" are disturbing to suburbia. These words disturb everyone, of course, but suburbia sees them as representing sticky, nonactive, old-fashioned Christianity.

GIBSON WINTER, *Christian Century*, September 28, 1955

Suburbia is the prime representative of individualistic thinking. The church's captivity to it is the death blow to recovery of the biblical view of corporate life, corporate sin and corporate salvation.

GIBSON WINTER, *Christian Century*, September 28, 1955

Nestled down among the ranch-type houses, deep in the forest of TV aerials, the new suburban churches find their members all birds of about the same native, white, middle-class feather, terribly self-conscious of their own kind.

WALDO BEACH, *Christianity and Crisis*, April 2, 1956

The suburban church tends to baptize existing values and to sanction existing complacency. According to standard criticisms, suburbanites like their gospel—unlike their martinis—diluted, and the peddlers of dilution are legion.

MARTIN E. MARTY, *The New Shape of American Religion*, 1958

American churches are indeed vulnerable for their adaptation to, and identification with, the nonreligious values of suburbia which, after they acquire a thin veneer of religious terminology, are made to look Christian.

MARTIN E. MARTY, *The New Shape of American Religion*, 1958

Religion in suburbia . . . provides an easy ratification of the various escape routes that converge in the suburban way of life.

PETER L. BERGER, *The Precarious Vision*, 1961

The suburban church is long on verbalised "values" and short on involvement.

FRANKLIN H. LITTELL, *From State Church to Pluralism*, 1962

The suburb is a parasitical growth, and the religion which serves it tries artificially to recollect the vision of a simple rural and village life which no longer exists.

FRANKLIN H. LITTELL, *From State Church to Pluralism*, 1962

See also City.

SUCCESS

A good sermon of Mr. Gifford's at our church. . . . He showed, like a wise man, that righteousness is a surer moral way of being rich, than sin and villainy.

SAMUEL PEPYS, *Diary*, August 23, 1668

Why should we be in such desperate haste to succeed, and in such desperate enterprises? If a man does not keep pace with his companions, perhaps it is because he hears a different drummer.

HENRY DAVID THOREAU, *Walden*, 1854

How a man is to fare in this world is something which the gospel (in contrast with novels, romances, lies, and other time-wasting) does not waste its time by considering.

SÖREN KIERKEGAARD (1813–1855), *Meditations from*, ed. T. H. Croxall

When a man has done all he can do, still there is a mighty, mysterious agency over which he needs influence to secure success. The only way he can reach it is by prayer.

RUSSELL H. CONWELL, *What You Can Do with Your Will Power*, 1917

What definition did Jesus give of "success"? He said that true success is to complete one's life. It is to attain to eternal life; all else is failure.

TOYOHIKO KAGAWA, *The Religion of Jesus*, 1931

While we fight among ourselves about doctrine we are united in the common worship of money and material success.

ERIC GILL, *Autobiography*, 1941

The compulsion of success in business has tended to make a man neglectful of his Christian faith. He finds he must somehow try to reconcile what one observer has described as the impersonal imperative of profit and efficiency with the personal imperative of Christian ethics.

MARQUIS W. CHILDS and DOUGLASS CATER, *Ethics in a Business Society*, 1954

See also Economics and Christianity; Failure; Greed; Mammon; Money; Possessions; Riches; Wealth.

SUFFERING

No suffering befalls the man who calls nothing his own.

Dhammapada, c. 5th century B.C.

This, monks, is the noble truth concerning the origin of suffering: verily it originates in craving for pleasures, craving for becoming, craving for not becoming.

The Mahavagga of the Vinya Texts, between 5th and 1st century B.C.

What thou avoidest suffering thyself seek not to impose on others.

EPICTETUS, *Enchiridion*, c. 100 A.D.

Whosoever grows wrathful for any reason against his sufferings has therein departed from the way of the just, because he may not doubt that these things have happened to him by divine dispensation.

PETER ABELARD, *The Story of My Misfortunes*, 1135

If thou can be still and suffer awhile thou shalt without doubt see the help of God come in thy need.

THOMAS À KEMPIS, *Imitation of Christ*, 1441

The more Christian a man is, the more evils, sufferings, and deaths he must endure.

MARTIN LUTHER, *Freedom of a Christian*, 1520

Suffering out of love of God is better than working miracles.

ST. JOHN OF THE CROSS, *Steps to Perfection*, c. 1584

God's suffering for man was the Nadir, the lowest point in God's humiliation; man's suffering for God is the Zenith, the highest point of man's exaltation.

JOHN DONNE, *Sermon*, February 29, 1627

Suffering is only sent to lead us on. When God purposes to accomplish a great work in a short time, He sends many crosses, and His blows fall heavily; but, oh, how full of love they are, even when they seem to crush us pitilessly.

FRANÇOIS FÉNELON (1651–1715), *Spiritual Letters*

It would be strange to suppose that mankind were redeemed by the sufferings of their Saviour, to live in ease and softness themselves; that suffering should be necessary atonement for sin and yet that sinners should be excused from sufferings.

WILLIAM LAW, *Christian Perfection*, 1726

What is the greatest evil of suffering? Not the suffering itself but our rebellion against it, the state of interior revolt which so often accompanies it.

JEAN GROU, *Meditations in the Form of a Retreat*, c. 1795

Nine-tenths of our suffering is caused by others not thinking so much of us as we think they ought.

MARY LYON (1797–1849), quoted by Gamaliel Bradford in his *Journal*

Clergymen and people who use phrases without wisdom sometimes talk of suffering as a mystery. It is really a revelation. One discerns things one never discerned before.

OSCAR WILDE, *De Profundis*, 1896

Any one that suffers is God's representative.

VIVEKANANDA (1863–1902), *Works of*

It is the language of imperfection.

RABINDRANATH TAGORE, *Personality*, 1917

Perfect souls—who realize that Jesus is greatly concerned about their perishing; so greatly concerned that He died for them— are very much afraid of suffering, of the Cross. But they are afraid of being afraid; afraid of getting down from the Cross.

VINCENT MCNABB, *God's Way of Mercy*, 1928

Christ came and He did not really explain it [suffering]: He did far more, He met it, willed it, transformed it, and He taught us how to do all this, or rather He Himself does it within us, if we do not hinder His all-healing hands.

FRIEDRICH VON HÜGEL, *Selected Letters*, 1933

There may be some profound ethical necessity in the nature of God Himself which exacts a price in suffering from God Himself if the wrong is to be righted without annulling the freedom of His creatures. He may win them, but not compel them.

ALFRED NOYES, *The Unknown God*, 1934

Anything that the Christian thinks of suffering has to be shot through with what he thinks of Christ.

C. C. MARTINDALE, *Christianity Is Christ*, 1935

It is in suffering that we are withdrawn from the bright superficial film of existence, from the sway of time and mere things, and find ourselves in the presence of a profounder truth.

YVES M. CONGAR, *God, Man and the Universe*, 1950

Just as there are many people who shrink from the sight of the suffering face of Christ on the Veil of Veronica and on the Holy Shroud, there are many today who shrink from the sight or the knowledge of the suffering on the face of humanity in general.

CARYLL HOUSELANDER, *The Messenger of the Sacred Heart*, August, 1952

The modern view is that suffering has no purpose because nothing that happens has any purpose. The world is run by causes, not by purposes.

W. T. STACE, *Religion and the Modern Mind*, 1952

Suffering is of the essence of life, because it is the inevitable product of an unresolvable tension between a living creature's essential impulse to try to make itself into the centre of the Universe and its essential dependence on the rest of Creation and on the Absolute Reality.

A. J. TOYNBEE, *An Historian's Approach to Religion*, 1956

Those who suffer, in a Christian view of the world, are not merely parasites. They have their work to do. Their function is no longer productive, from the human point of view. But they have a purpose—a divine purpose. All man's hours have a present and a future.

ROBERT W. GLEASON, *Sign*, January, 1962

One of the tendencies of our age is to use children's suffering to discredit the goodness of God. . . . In this popular pity, we mark our gain in sensibility and our loss in vision. If other ages felt less, they saw more.

FLANNERY O'CONNOR, *A Memoir of Mary Ann*, 1962

See also Acceptance; Adversity; Affliction; Anxiety; Atonement; Calvary; Cross; Evil, Problem of; Hell; Martyrdom; Pain; Patience; Redemption; Resignation; Serenity; Soul; Tragedy.

SUFFERING: ITS VALUE

When sufferings come upon him man must utter thanks to God, for suffering draws man near unto the Holy One, blessed be He.

RABBI ELEAZAR BEN JACOB, *Talmud*, c. 4th century A.D.

To suffer is almost the only good we can do in this world; for rarely do we perform any good without mixing up some evil along with it.

ST. FRANCIS OF SALES (1567–1622), *Consoling Thoughts of*, ed. Huguet

Those who accept what they suffer have no suffering of the will, and thus they are in peace.

FRANÇOIS FÉNELON, *Spiritual Letters of*, c. 1700

There is no remembrance more blessed, and nothing more blessed to remember, than suffering overcome in solidarity with God; this is the mystery of suffering.

SÖREN KIERKEGAARD, *Christian Discourses*, 1847

If Christ has to be made perfect by suffering, much more must we. If He needed to learn obedience by sorrow, much more must we. If He needed in the days of His flesh, to make supplications to God His

Father with strong crying and tears, so do we.

CHARLES KINGSLEY, *The Good News of God,* 1859

Suffering was a curse from which man fled, now it becomes a purification of the soul, a sacred trial sent by Eternal Love, a divine dispensation meant to sanctify and ennoble us, an acceptable aid to faith, a strange initiation into happiness.

HENRI AMIEL, *Journal,* 1882

It is one of the many things in God's dealing with us, that seems so very mysterious, that He should have made suffering a condition of sanctity.

P. A. SHEEHAN, *Mary, the Mother of God,* 1902

Suffering is the substance of life and the root of personality, for it is only suffering that makes us persons.

MIGUEL DE UNAMUNO, *The Tragic Sense of Life,* 1913

No dogma of religion is surer than this: if one would be close to God he must suffer.

WALTER ELLIOTT, *The Spiritual Life,* 1914

The pangs of pain, of failure, in this mortal lot, are the birth-throes of transition to better things.

JOHN ELOF BOODIN, *Cosmic Evolution,* 1925

Suffering which produces the kind of character we admire and love is not only not regrettable but precious.

MARTIN C. D'ARCY, *Problem of Evil,* 1928

God is more living and real than all suffering and all sin; and . . . He can and will, and does give concomitant opportunities and graces and growths to the sufferer, if and when the latter is humble, watchful and prayerful in such utilizations.

FRIEDRICH VON HÜGEL, *Selected Letters,* 1933

The saint's willingness to suffer results in an integrated, balanced personality; it liberates the capacity for love.

CARYLL HOUSELANDER, *Guilt,* 1941

Suffering is a test of faith. . . . If God's love calls you in suffering, respond by self-surrender, and you will learn the mystery of love.

J. MESSNER, *Man's Suffering and God's Love,* 1941

See also Euthanasia; Hell; Misery; Pain; Peace of Mind; Perfection; Sanctity; Sorrow; Suffering.

SUICIDE

Parricide is more wicked than homicide, but suicide is the most wicked of all.

ST. AUGUSTINE, *On Patience,* c. 425

Ony He who gave the soul may take it back!

HANINA B. TERADION, *Talmud: Aboda Zara,* c. 500

Everything naturally loves itself, the result being that everything naturally keeps itself in *being,* and resists corruption as far as it can. Wherefore suicide is contrary to the inclination of nature, and to charity whereby every man should love himself.

ST. THOMAS AQUINAS, *Summa Theologiae,* II-II, qu. 64, art. 5, 1272

It is very certain that, as to all persons who have killed themselves, the Devil put the cord round their necks, or the knife to their throats.

MARTIN LUTHER (1483–1546), *Table Talk*

He that stabs another can kill his body; but he that stabs himself, kills his own soul.

ROBERT BURTON, *The Anatomy of Melancholy,* II, 1621

Those who commit suicide are powerless souls, and allow themselves to be conquered by external causes repugnant to their nature.

BARUCH SPINOZA, *Ethics,* 1677

Suicide is not abominable because God forbids it; God forbids it because it is abominable.

IMMANUEL KANT, *Lecture at Königsberg,* 1775

There is no refuge from confession but suicide; and suicide is confession.

DANIEL WEBSTER, *Argument* at trial of Captain White for murder, April 6, 1830

Suicide thwarts the attainment of the highest moral aim by the fact that, for a real release from this world of misery, it substitutes one that is merely apparent.

ARTHUR SCHOPENHAUER, *Studies in Pessimism,* 1851

I am killing myself to prove my independence and my new terrible freedom.

KIRILLOV in Feodor Dostoevsky's *The Possessed,* 1871

Those books are prohibited which defend suicide as lawful.

POPE LEO XIII, *General Decree Concerning the Prohibition and Censorship of Books,* January 25, 1897

It is the suicide who dares to rebel against the plans of an all-wise God, who tries, though in vain, to force his way through to escape what he fears, who is blind to the whisperings of the graces of God in his heart and who is materialistic enough to see only the things of the earth, disregarding the things eternal.

ADOLPH DOMINIC FRENAY, *Is Life Worth Living?,* 1933

Some of the destruction that curses the earth is *self-destruction;* the extraordinary propensity of the human being to join hands with external forces in an attack

upon his own existence is one of the most remarkable of biological phenomena.

KARL MENNINGER, *Man Against Himself,* 1938

There is only one philosophical problem that is really serious, and that is suicide. To decide whether life is worth living or not is to answer the fundamental question in philosophy.

ALBERT CAMUS, *Le Mythe de Sisyphe,* 1942

In Christian thought, the supreme fact in the life of the individual was death. In the life of the Liberal state, the climactic experience was suicide.

JOHN EMMET HUGHES, *The Church and the Liberal Society,* 1944

God has reserved to Himself the right to determine the end of life, because He alone knows the goal to which it is His will to lead it. It is for Him alone to justify a life or to cast it away.

DIETRICH BONHOEFFER, *Ethics,* 1955

Suicide is man's attempt to give a final human meaning to a life which has become humanly meaningless.

DIETRICH BONHOEFFER, *Ethics,* 1955

See also Atomic Bomb; Death; Euthanasia; Existence; Independence; Life.

SUNDAY

But Sunday is the day on which we all hold our common assembly, because it is the first day on which God, when He changed the darkness and matter, made the world; and Jesus Christ our Savior, on the same, rose from the dead.

ST. JUSTIN MARTYR, *First Apology,* c. 150

All judges and city people and the craftsmen shall rest upon the venerable day of the Sun. But countrymen may without hindrance attend to agriculture, since it often happens that this is the most suitable day for sowing grain or planting vines, so that the advantage given by providence may not . . . perish.

> EMPEROR CONSTANTINE to Elpidus, March 7, 321, *Cod. Justinunus*

It is less of a crime to cut the throats of a thousand men than to set a stitch on a poor man's shoe on the Lord's day.

> DESIDERIUS ERASMUS, *The Praise of Folly,* 1511

Resolved: Never to utter anything that is sportive or matter of laughter, on a Lord's day.

> JONATHAN EDWARDS, *Resolutions,* 1722

The importance of regular attendance upon the duties of the Christian Sabbath in social communion has impressed itself more deeply on my mind in proportion as I have advanced in years.

> JOHN QUINCY ADAMS, *Diary,* 1843

The Sunday is the core of our civilization, dedicated to thought and reverence. It invites to the noblest solitude and the noblest society, to whatever means and aids of spiritual refreshment.

> RALPH WALDO EMERSON, *North American Review,* April, 1866

What hope is there of guarding the moral beauty of the day when the authority which set it apart is no longer recognized?

> GEORGE GISSING, *The Private Papers of Henry Ryecroft,* 1903

You can tell Mr. and Mrs. John Q. Citizen that it is important to be decent and honest; you can't tell them it's wrong to go swimming on Sunday. They know it doesn't matter to God whether they swim or not; they don't stop swimming, they stop going to church.

> CHANNING POLLOCK, *American Mercury,* October, 1940

Sunday is a continual proclamation of the message of Easter: Christ is risen.

> GUSTAVE WINGREN, *Theology in Conflict,* 1958

See also Sabbath; Worship.

SUNDAY SCHOOL

Sunday School: A prison in which children do penance for the evil consciences of their parents.

> H. L. MENCKEN, *A Little Book in C Major,* 1916

See also Education, Religious.

SUPERLATIVES

The best preacher is the heart; the best teacher is time; the best book is the world; the best friend is God.

> *Talmud,* 4th century A.D.

SUPERMAN

Dead are all Gods; now we will that superman live. . . . I teach you superman. Man is a something that shall be surpassed.

> FRIEDRICH NIETZSCHE, *Thus Spake Zarathustra,* 1883

SUPERNATURAL

Nature expresses the law in process, the supernatural the end to which it tends.

> DAVID HUME, *Dialogues Concerning Natural Religion,* 1779

Faith in the supernatural is a desperate wager made by man at the lowest ebb of his fortunes.

> GEORGE SANTAYANA, *Reason in Science,* 1906

The supernatural . . . is the state of the created and finite spiritual being, into which it is raised by a direct act of God,

. . . making the spirit inherently capable of seeing God face to face.

ANSCAR VONIER, *The Human Soul,* 1913

Every human creature is the object of some particular Providence that enables it to receive the supernatural. How, where, and when, is the mystery of God.

ANSCAR VONIER, *The Human Soul,* 1913

There are few among our ecclesiastics and theologians who would spend five minutes in investigating alleged supernatural occurrences in our own time. It would be assumed that if true it must be ascribed to some obscure natural cause.

W. R. INGE, *Outspoken Essays,* 1919

There is nothing impossible in the existence of the supernatural. Its existence seems to me decidedly probable.

GEORGE SANTAYANA, *The Genteel Tradition at Bay,* 1931

To the successive abandonment of the Supernatural we have added the rebellion against humanity.

JOHN D. FEE, *Secularism,* 1947

Nothing is more irritating to the modern than this dogma of the supernatural, a dogma that cannot . . . be demonstrated by human reason; it requires God's revelation to bring to our knowledge this fact that man is supernaturalized.

WILLIAM J. McGUCKEN, *The Philosophy of Catholic Education,* 1951

See also Naturalism; Spirit; Spiritual.

SUPERSTITION

Religion is not removed by removing superstition.

CICERO, *De Divinatione,* c. 78 B.C.

There are none more silly, or nearer their wits end, than those who are too superstitiously religious.

DESIDERIUS ERASMUS, *The Praise of Folly,* 1511

Superstition obeys pride as a father.

MICHEL DE MONTAIGNE, *Essays,* Bk. 2, ch. 12, 1580

It were better to have no opinion of God at all, than such an opinion as is unworthy of him: for the one is unbelief, the other is contumely: and certainly superstition is the reproach of the Deity.

FRANCIS BACON, *On Superstition,* 1597

How blest would our age be if it could witness a religion freed from all the trammels of superstition!

BARUCH SPINOZA, *Theologico-Political Treatise,* 1670

Conscience without judgment is superstition.

BENJAMIN WHICHCOTE, *Moral and Religious Aphorisms,* 1753

This is the cruelest enemy of the pure worship due to the Supreme Being. Let us detest this monster which has always torn the bosom of its mother; those who combat it are the benefactors of the human race; it is a serpent which chokes religion in its embrace; we must crush its head without wounding the mother whom it devours.

VOLTAIRE, "God," *Philosophical Dictionary,* 1764

Superstition is to religion what astrology is to astronomy—the mad daughter of a wise mother.

VOLTAIRE, *Essay on Toleration,* 1766

Superstition is the religion of feeble minds.

EDMUND BURKE, *Reflections on the Revolution in France,* 1790

Superstition may be defined as constructive religion which has grown incongruous with intelligence.

> JOHN TYNDALL, *Fragments of Science,* II, 1896

Superstition is the serpent that crawls and hisses in every Eden and fastens its poisonous fangs in the hearts of men.

> ROBERT INGERSOLL (1833–1899), *The Truth*

Because we can commit ourselves only to such truth as is capable of verification by approved methods, . . . we are therefore under necessity of regarding Christianity, at least in certain alleged factual and conceptual features of it, as a quite . . . indefensible superstition.

> JOHN DEWEY, *A Common Faith,* 1934

On the grave of faith there blooms the flower of superstition.

> GUSTAVE THIBON, *Christianity and Freedom,* 1952

Superstition may easily creep into the religion of Christians if that religion be allowed to express itself solely by exercises and ceremonies without regard to the inner worship of the spirit, which is faith, hope, and charity.

> R. L. BRUCKBERGER, *Toward the Summit,* 1956

Even Christians who in practice dislike superstition as much as I do still often treat it as a minor aberration to be hushed up rather than a radical perversion to be denounced.

> JOHN WREN-LEWIS, *They Became Anglicans,* 1959

Religions are born and may die, but superstition is immortal.

> WILL DURANT, *The Age of Reason Begins,* 1961

See also Faith; Fanaticism; Reason; Religion; Science and Religion; Soul; Truth; Witchcraft.

SUPPRESSION

Never since the Thirty Year War has the Church oppressed freedom of thought and expression to an extent comparable to the terror based on the "scientific" ideologies of Nazi Germany or Soviet Russia.

> ARTHUR KOESTLER, *The Sleepwalkers,* 1959

There's been so much suppression of real, deep thought and intellectual alertness and integrity in the Church.

> ALEC VIDLER, *Radio Address,* B.B.C., November 4, 1962

SUPREME COURT, UNITED STATES

The Supreme Court has just deconsecrated the nation.

> JAMES A. PIKE, *New York Times,* July 13, 1962, referring to New York School prayer decision.

The Supreme Court . . . little by little . . . is discarding religious traditions hallowed by a century and a half of American practice.

> PATRICK A. O'BOYLE, quoted in *New York Times,* June 18, 1963

See also Education; Religion.

SURGERY

I dressed him; God cured him.

> AMBROSE PARÉ, French surgeon, concluded many of his surgical reports with this, 1552–1573

SURVIVAL

The recovery of moral control and the return to spiritual order have now become the indispensable condition of human survival. But they can be achieved only by a profound change in the spirit of modern civilization.

> CHRISTOPHER DAWSON, *Religion and Culture,* 1947

SUSPICION

Many religious people are deeply suspicious. They seem—for purely religious reasons, of course—to know more about iniquity than the Unregenerate.

> RUDYARD KIPLING, *Plain Tales,* 1887

Most of our suspicions of others are aroused by what we know about ourselves.

> HENRY S. HASKINS, *Meditations in Wall Street,* 1940

SWEETNESS

There is a kind of sweetness of character that stinks.

> BENJAMIN DECASSERES, *Fantasia Impromptu,* 1933

SYMBOLISM

Symbolism is not sober judgment; it is a simplification and subordination of the concrete complexity in order to point a moral.

> RALPH BARTON PERRY, *Puritanism and Democracy,* 1944

A complete abandonment of all symbolism, or attempt at its abandonment, could only result in a sort of bizarre rationalism.

> JOHN LA FARGE, *Religious Symbolism,* ed. F. E. Johnson

What it accomplishes is to reduce beliefs to make-believes, observance to ceremony, prophecy to literature, theology to esthetics.

> ABRAHAM JOSHUA HESCHEL, *Religious Symbolism,* ed. F. E. Johnson, 1955

See also Myth; Rationalism; Symbols.

SYMBOLS

Symbols are deeper than words; speak when words become silent; gain where words lose in meaning; and so in hours of holiest worship the Church teaches, by symbols, truths language may not utter.

> A. M. FAIRBAIRN, *Catholicism, Roman and Anglican,* 1899

Whoever has the symbol has thereby the beginning of the spiritual idea; symbol and reality together furnish the whole.

> ODO CASEL, *Mysterium,* 1926

Most mistakes in philosophy and logic occur because the human mind is apt to take the symbol for the reality.

> ALBERT EINSTEIN, *Cosmic Religion,* 1931

The symbol or significant image, is not . . . a substitute for spiritual truth. It is rather the point where the physical and metaphysical meet—a half-way house where the world of things and the world of spirit unite.

> EVELYN UNDERHILL, *Worship,* 1937

The reason why the religious symbol, even in its most developed forms, never loses the character of poetry is that religious language must be lyrical and dramatic or it is nothing.

> WILBUR M. URBAN, *Language and Reality,* 1939

A religious symbol leads to communion rather than to communication.

> WILBUR M. URBAN, *Language and Reality,* 1939

The thoughtless, conventional use of religious symbols may be not only dishonest but deadening.

> JAMES BISSETT PRATT, *Can We Keep the Faith?,* 1941

Symbols are directed toward the infinite which they symbolize and toward the finite

through which they symbolize it. They force the infinite down to finitude and the finite up to infinity. They open the divine for the human and the human for the divine.
> PAUL TILLICH, *Systematic Theology*, I, 1951

What is necessary is not *to have a symbol, but to be a symbol.*
> ABRAHAM JOSHUA HESCHEL, *Religious Symbolism*, ed. F. E. Johnson, 1955

Symbols are the primary mode of our becoming aware of things. They are the way we register meanings in our depths.
> GAIL C. RICHARDSON, *Religious Symbolism*, ed. F. E. Johnson, 1955

One of the things I always forbid my students to say is "only a symbol." . . . Symbols participate in the power of what they symbolize.
> PAUL TILLICH, *Gregorianum*, January, 1956

Man's ultimate concern must be expressed symbolically, because symbolic language alone is able to express the ultimate.
> PAUL TILLICH, *The Dynamics of Faith*, 1957

See also Cross; Images; Sacraments; Symbolism.

SYMPATHY

Thou who unmoved canst others' sorrows scan:
May be a monarch, but nowise a man.
> SHAIKH SAADI, *Gulistan*, c. 1265

Sympathy is your pain in my heart.
> ANONYMOUS, quoted by Halford E. Luccock in *365 Windows*, 1960

See also Compassion; Kindness; Mercy; Pity.

SYNAGOGUE

The Synagogue service is essentially the expression of the soul of collective Israel.
> MORRIS JOSEPH, *Judaism as Creed and Life*, 1903

The synagogue alone speaks of the common striving of a group of Jews to establish a conscious relationship between themselves and God.
> SIMON GREENBERG, *Address to United Synagogue Convention*, 1950

See also Israel; Jew; Jews; Judaism.

TALK

He who talks too much commits a sin.
> *Talmud (Pirke Aboth)*, c. 200

TAO

He who attains Tao is everlasting. Though his body may decay he never perishes.
> *Tao Tê Ching*, c. 500 B.C.

The perfecting of self implies virtue; the perfecting of others, wisdom. These two, virtue and wisdom, are the moral qualities of the hsing, or nature, embodying the Tao, or Right Way.
> CONFUCIUS, *Doctrine of the Mean*, 5th century B.C.

That which Heaven has conferred is called the Nature; accordance with this nature is called the Tao (Way or Path), the regulation of this way is called Instruction.
> CONFUCIUS, *Doctrine of the Mean*, 5th century B.C.

What there was before the universe, was Tao; Tao makes things what they are, but is not itself a thing. Nothing can produce Tao; yet everything has Tao within it, and continues to produce it without end.
> CHUANG-TZU (4th century B.C.), *Texts of Taoism*, ed. J. Legge

Tao though possessed of feeling and power of expression is passive and formless. It can be transmitted yet not received, apprehended yet not seen. Its root is in itself, having continued from of old before heaven and earth existed.

> CHUANG-TZU (4th century B.C.), *Texts of Taoism,* ed. J. Legge

Before Heaven and Earth existed, from the beginning Tao was there. It is Tao that gave ghosts their holy power, that gave holy power to Dead Kings. It gave life to Heaven, gave life to Earth. . . . It . . . has no duration; its age is greater than that of the Longest Age, yet it does not grow old.

> CHUANG-TZU (4th century B.C.), *Three Ways of Thought in Ancient China*

There was something undefined and coming into existence before Heaven and Earth. How still it was and formless, standing alone and undergoing no change; reaching everywhere and in no danger of being exhausted! I do not know its name, and I give it the designation of the Tao. It may be regarded as the Mother of all things! . . . Man takes his law from Earth, the Earth takes its law from Heaven; Heaven takes its law from Tao. The law of the Tao is its being what it is.

> *Tao Tê-Ching,* variously dated to 3rd century B.C.

The perfect Way [Tao] is without difficulty
Save that it avoids picking and choosing.
Only when you stop liking and disliking
Will all be clearly understood.

> SENG-TS'AN, *Hsin-hsin Ming,* c. 593 A.D.

See also Natural Law; Way, the.

TASTE
See CHOICE; VALUES; VALUES, SPIRITUAL

TEACHERS

Truly, when a weak and ignorant man departs in any vicious way, to serve the Devil against God, yet he carries away but a Single Man, and serves but a common Soldier; but he that hath good parts, and good education, carries a Regiment in his person, and Armies and munitions for a thousand in himself.

> JOHN DONNE, *Sermon,* February 29, 1627

A teacher affects eternity; he can never tell where his influence stops.

> HENRY ADAMS, *The Education of Henry Adams,* 1906

The great task of the teacher of morality today is to free his fellows from their obsession with their modernity.

> W. G. CHANTER, *A Self Worth Having,* 1938

Too many have brought to their tasks spiritual ignorance, spiritual confusion, spiritual revolt. Too many have been poisoned by drinking at poisoned wells. They have renounced their allegiance to God and have substituted a dedication to civil society.

> ROBERT I. GANNON, *God in Education,* 1943

Here is the Christian teacher's problem; to study and to teach science so as to include —or at least not to exclude—the Christian view of nature.

> F. SHERWOOD TAYLOR, *Man and Matter,* 1951

The educator becomes God's mind at work to help grow the best possible plants in God's garden. He exists to prepare the soil, to sow the good seed, to weed, to water, and to harvest.

> NELS F. S. FERRÉ, *Christian Faith and Higher Education,* 1954

See also Education; Theologians.

TEARS

Tears are the silent language of grief.

> VOLTAIRE, *Philosophical Dictionary,* II, 1764

Heaven knows we need never be ashamed of our tears, for they are rain upon the blinding dust of earth, overlying our hard hearts.

CHARLES DICKENS, *Hunted Down,* 1867

Jewish tears are the heaviest. They have the weight of many centuries.

LEON BLOY, *Pilgrim of the Absolute,* 1909

The Lord gave to us lachrymal glands that we may use them, and the flow of tears is healing to the spirit.

JOHN SUTHERLAND BONNELL, *No Escape from Life,* 1958

See also Bereavement; Gloom; Grief; Sadness; Sorrow; Unbelief.

TECHNOLOGY

The hope that technology will save us or will miraculously effect our moral improvement is a kind of modern idolatry.

RUDOLF DIESEL, *Theory and Construction of a Rational Heatmotor,* 1894

Modern technology unfolds before contemporary man a vision so vast as to be confused by many with the infinite itself. As a consequence, one attributes to it an impossible autonomy, which in turn is transformed in the minds of some into an erroneous conception of life and of the world.

POPE PIUS XII, *Allocution,* December 24, 1953

The danger of the cult of technological progress lies in its tendency to restrict and confine mankind within the adoring contemplation of his own creative power.

JEAN DANIELOU, *The Lord of History,* 1958

Uncontrolled technology can certainly bring down disaster, perhaps irreparable, on our race. The only protection against t

is a growth in man's spiritual and moral maturity proportionate to his growth in technical skill and power.

W. NORRIS CLARKE, *America,* September 26, 1959

Technology has wiped out the frontiers that formerly separated men, countries and peoples. Man has become a citizen of the world. Thus, modern man finds himself in an environment without spiritual unity or religious homogeneity.

ALBERT DONDEYNE, *Faith and the World,* 1962

The technological society has relegated religion, the arts and all other elements of high culture to a limbo from which they may still return to revenge themselves.

PHILIP RIEFF, at an international symposium on the technological society, quoted by P. N. Noth in North American Newspaper Alliance feature article, June, 1966

See also Industrialism; Machines; Nuclear Energy; Power; Science.

TEMPERANCE

Intemperance is the pestilence which killeth pleasure; temperance is not the flail of pleasure, it is the seasoning thereof.

MICHEL DE MONTAIGNE, *Essays,* III, 1588

Temperance is not the absence of passion, but is the transfiguring of passion into wholeness. Without it . . . you will have the senses usurping sovereignty and excluding the spirit; you will have them deciding good and evil and excluding God.

GERALD VANN, *The Heart of Man,* 1945

See also Abstinence; Alcohol; Drunkenness; Moderation; Passions; Wine.

TEMPORAL

It is lawful to desire temporal blessings, not putting them in the first place, as though setting up our rest in them, but regarding them as aids to blessedness, inasmuch as they support our corporal life and serve as instruments for acts of virtue.

St. Thomas Aquinas, *Summa Theologiae*, 2a-2ae, Q. lxxxiii, 1272

Behold heavenly goods and thou shalt see that all these temporal goods be as none but that they shall be full uncertain, and more grieving than easing; for they are never had without business and dread.

Thomas à Kempis, *Imitation of Christ*, 1441

Few things are more impressive . . . in the Scriptures, . . . than the light and casual way in which temporal misfortunes or achievements are spoken of . . . and the immense importance that is attached even to the smallest . . . moral goods and or evils.

Edward F. Garesche, *The Things Immortal*, 1919

To put the temporal in the place of God, when done with full deliberation, is the sin of pride in all its gravity.

Jean Mouroux, *The Meaning of Man*, 1948

We are sometimes in danger of looking on the temporal as something profane, as if God were only active in the spiritual. The temporal is not foreign to God.

Anders Nygren, *Ecumenical Review*, I, 3, 1949

See also Achievement; Misfortune; Passions; Pleasure; Possessions; World, the; Worldliness.

TEMPT

The desire to please by outward charms, which we know naturally invites lust, does not spring from a sound conscience. Why should you rouse an evil passion?

Tertullian, *Women's Dress*, c. 220

See also Temptation.

TEMPTATION

He who knows that his body is like froth, and as unsubstantial as a mirage, will break the flower-tipped arrow of the Great Tempter and never see the King of Death.

Dhammapada, c. 5th century B.C.

An expert seaman is tried in a tempest, a runner in a race, a captain in a battle, a valiant man in adversity, a Christian in temptation and misery.

St. Basil (330–379), *Hom. 8*

There is no attack of the enemy so violent, that is, no temptation so formidable, that an eager study of the Scriptures will not easily beat off.

Desiderius Erasmus, *Enchiridion*, 1501

And let us fence us in with faith and comfort us with hope and smite the devil in the face with the firebrand of charity. . . . That fire of charity, thrown in his face, striketh the devil suddenly so blind that he cannot see where to fasten a stroke on us.

St. Thomas More, *Dialogue of Comfort*, 1535

God delights in our temptations, and yet hates them; He delights in them when they drive us to prayer; He hates them when they drive us to despair.

Martin Luther (1483–1546), *Table Talk*

The cunning livery of hell.

William Shakespeare, *Measure for Measure*, c. 1604

Every temptation, every tribulation is not deadly. But their multiplicity disorders us, discomposes us, unsettles us, and so hazards us.

John Donne, *Sermon*, Spring, 1618

When we expose ourselves to temptations, temptations hit us, that were not expressly directed, nor meant to us. And even then, when we begin to fly from temptations, the arrow overtakes us.

> JOHN DONNE, *Sermon,* Spring, 1618

All the temptations of hell cannot sully a soul which is displeased with them.

> ST. FRANCIS OF SALES (1567–1622), *Consoling Thoughts of,* ed. Huguet

He that can apprehend and consider vice with all her baits and seeming pleasures, and yet abstain, and yet distinguish, and yet prefer that which is truly better, he is the true warfaring Christian.

> JOHN MILTON, *Aeropagitica,* 1644

When we resist temptation it is usually because temptation is weak, not because we are strong.

> LA ROCHEFOUCAULD, *Maxims,* 1665

God is better served in resisting a Temptation to Evil, than in many formal Prayers.

> WILLIAM PENN, *Some Fruits of Solitude,* 1718

The evil inclination is to be compared to a conjurer who runs around among people with a closed hand daring them to guess what is in it. . . . Everyone therefore runs after him. Once the conjurer stops for a moment and opens his hand, it becomes clear to everyone that it is completely empty.

> MOSES LUZZATO (1707–1747), *Mesillat Yesharim*

No virtue is ever so strong that it is beyond temptation.

> IMMANUEL KANT, *Lecture at Königsberg,* 1775

Some day, in years to come, you will be wrestling with the great temptation, or trembling under the great sorrow of your life. But the real struggle is here, now in these quiet weeks.

> PHILLIPS BROOKS (1835–1893), *Perennials from*

What augments our spiritual forces?—a temptation which has been overcome.

> ALEXANDER YELCHANINOV (1881–1934), *Fragments of a Diary*

The last temptation is the greatest treason: To do the right deed for the wrong reason.

> T. S. ELIOT, *Murder in the Cathedral,* 1935

As we go up the scale of spiritual excellence, temptation follows us all the way, becoming more refined as our lives are more refined, more subtle as our spiritual sensitiveness is keener.

> A. VICTOR MURRAY, *Personal Experience and the Historic Faith,* 1939

"Oh, Lawd, prop us up in all ouah leanin' places."

> Prayer of a Negro preacher, quoted by Archibald Rutledge, *Reader's Digest,* October, 1940

The whole effort—the object—of temptation is to induce us to substitute something else for God. To obscure God.

> R. H. J. STEWART, *Spiritual Conferences of,* 1952

In the hour of grievous temptation reason is a slender reed on which to lean. As Adam found to his sorrow, eating of the tree of the *knowledge* of good and evil by no means guarantees that one will choose the good.

> EDMUND W. SINNOTT, *The Biology of the Spirit,* 1955

Temptation is not an effect of original sin; it made its appearance in the earthly paradise. But since then it has gained in power.

> CHARLES JOURNET, *The Meaning of Evil,* 1961

See also Affliction; Conscience; Demons; Desires; Devil; Self-Conquest; Spiritual Struggle; Tempt, Virtue.

TEN COMMANDMENTS. *See* COMMANDMENTS

TERROR

Terror, which is a sudden madness and paralysis of the soul, that I say is from hell, and not to be played with or considered or put in pictures or described in stories.

HILAIRE BELLOC, *The Path to Rome*, 1900

THANKSGIVING

Everyone is to practice thanksgiving continually, and it is requisite that he maintain it through good and bad.

Sad Dar, Zend-Avesta, c. 700 B.C.

No duty is more urgent than that of returning thanks.

ST. AMBROSE, *On the Passing of His Brother Satyrus*, Bk. 1, c. 380

To stand on one's legs and prove God's existence is a very different thing from going on one's knees and thanking him.

SÖREN KIERKEGAARD, *The Present Age*, 1846

For three things I thank God every day of my life: thanks that he has vouchsafed me knowledge of His Works; deep thanks that He has set in my darkness the lamp of faith; deep, deepest thanks that I have another life to look forward to—a life joyous with light and flowers and heavenly song.

HELEN KELLER, *Story of My Life*, 1905

See also Gratitude.

THEFT

If any one steal cattle or sheep . . . if it belong to a god or to the court, the thief shall pay thirtyfold therefor; if they belonged to a freedman of the king he shall pay tenfold; if the thief have nothing with which to pay he shall be put to death.

Code of Hammurabi, c. 2000 B.C.

Who is the more heinous sinner? He who consumes anything which is received into his custody, and becomes an embezzler. . . . He who commits theft or abets theft.

Zend-Avesta, 6th century B.C.

If there is no other remedy it is lawful to a man to succor his own needs by means of another's property, by taking it either openly or secretly.

ST. THOMAS AQUINAS, *Summa Theologiae*, 1272

THEISM

Theism is good sense not yet instructed by revelation.

VOLTAIRE, *Philosophical Dictionary*, II, 1764

The great body of our beliefs, scientific, ethical, aesthetic and theological, form a more coherent and satisfactory whole in a Theistic than in a Naturalistic setting.

A. J. BALFOUR, *The Foundations of Belief*, 1895

If theism is true there is only one world. "In Him we live and move, and have our being." There is no outside to God. The universe is his mental creation, as truly as our dreams are the products of our thoughts.

CHARLES E. GARMAN, *Letters, Lectures, Addresses*, 1909

Theism is the only metaphysical position that has any consistent answer to the problem of life. It affirms that there is one law of being for the entire universe.

CHARLES E. GARMAN, *Letters, Lectures, Addresses*, 1909

See also Atheism; Belief; God: His Existence; Immortality, Arguments for; Theist.

THEIST

The theist is a man firmly persuaded of the existence of a supreme being as good as he is powerful, who has formed all things . . . ; who punishes, without cruelty, all crimes, and recompenses with goodness all virtuous actions. . . . His religion is the most ancient and the most widespread; for the simple worship of a God preceded all the systems of the world.

> VOLTAIRE, "Theist," *Philosophical Dictionary,* 1764

A theist needs to have so much confidence in God that he can believe that God's goodness can prevail even in a society where there are many non-Christians and atheists.

> EDGAR S. BRIGHTMAN, *Perspectives on a Troubled Decade,* ed. Bryson, Finklestein and MacIver, 1950

A theistic believer cannot explain how he knows the divine presence to be mediated through his human experience. He just finds himself interpreting his experience in this way.

> JOHN HICKS, *Faith and Knowledge,* 1957

See also Belief; God: His Existence; Theism.

THEOCRACY

The theory of "theocracy" suggests the absolute rule of God, or a polity of passive obedience. From God's will itself there is no appeal.

> RALPH BARTON PERRY, *Puritanism and Democracy,* 1944

THEOLOGIANS

There is no wild beast like an angry theologian.

> JULIAN THE APOSTATE (332–363), quoted in E. Carpenter's *Pagan and Christian Creeds*

Their opinion of themselves is so great that they behave as if they were already in heaven.

> DESIDERIUS ERASMUS, *Praise of Folly,* 1509

They may attack me with an army of six hundred syllogisms; and if I do not recant, they will proclaim me a heretic. With this thunderbolt they terrify the people they don't like.

> DESIDERIUS ERASMUS, *Praise of Folly,* 1509

They are protected by a wall of scholastic definitions, arguments, corollaries, implicit and explicit propositions; they have so many hideaways that they could not be caught even by the net of Vulcan.

> DESIDERIUS ERASMUS, *Praise of Folly,* 1509

Reason, however sound, has little weight with ordinary theologians.

> BARUCH SPINOZA, *Theologico-Political Treatise,* 1670

It is the speculations of crazy theologists which have made a Babel of a religion the most moral and sublime ever preached to man, and calculated to heal, and not to create differences.

> THOMAS JEFFERSON, *Letter to Ezra Stiles,* June 25, 1819

Divinity is necessarily the first of the professions, because it is necessary for all times.

> SAMUEL TAYLOR COLERIDGE, *Table Talk,* March 14, 1833

Every religious man is to a certain extent a theologian.

> JOHN HENRY NEWMAN, *Grammar of Assent,* 1870

Every man is his own doctor of divinity, in the last resort.

> ROBERT LOUIS STEVENSON, *An Inland Voyage,* 1878

You say that an ordinary man would think it his duty to listen to any great mechanical philosopher who should bring reasons for even so great a paradox as the possibility of perpetual motion; why should such personal reverence be reserved for mechanicians alone? why not for theologians?

> JOHN HENRY NEWMAN, *Letter to William Froude*, 1879, in *Newman-Froude Correspondence*, ed. G. H. Harper

The theologian seems to be less a philosopher and more a social engineer and, one had almost said, a social psychoanalyst.

> SHAILER MATTHEWS, *Contemporary American Theology*, ed. V. Ferm, 1933

To be a theologian and not merely a devotee means to take up the burden of rational analysis, exposition, and argument without which *theologica* is a misnomer.

> ROBERT L. CALHOUN, *God and the Common Life*, 1935

It has always seemed to me a little impudent when a theologian tells God why He does things.

> WILLIAM SEIFRIZ, *Perspectives on a Troubled Decade*, ed. Bryson, Finklestein and MacIver, 1950

Every creative philosopher is a hidden theologian.

> PAUL TILLICH, *Systematic Theology*, I, 1951

Theologians have a gentle habit of playing by themselves in a walled garden shut off from public view and using a language which nobody else understands.

> A. VICTOR MURRAY, *Natural Religion and Christian Theology*, 1956

Perhaps the theologian's most important role today is to be precisely what his name indicates—a man who thinks, and then gives us the fruit of this thought, about God.

> AELRED GRAHAM, *Address*, Pittsburgh, Pa., April, 1960

A theologian who unconsciously tends to equate his own thoughts with the divine reality is not a theologian at all.

> PETER FRANSEN, *Cross Currents*, Spring, 1963

There is something comic about our theologians going right on discussing just what rights—of worship, of propaganda—we should concede to non-Catholics, when practically everywhere the question is how much freedom to function we ourselves can manage to hold on to.

> FRANK J. SHEED, *Sheed and Ward Trumpet*, Spring, 1964

See also Hell; Metaphysician; Philosophers; Teachers; Theology; War, Just.

THEOLOGY

It illuminates our spirit with a transforming fire, and brings it into contact with those spirits who verily serve the Lord.

> DIODICUS, *Spiritual Perfection*, 5th century

The chief aim of this science is to impart a knowledge of God, not only as existing in Himself, but also as the origin and end of all things, and especially of rational creatures.

> ST. THOMAS AQUINAS, Prologue, *Summa Theologiae*, 1272

To be still searching what we know not, by what we know, still closing up truth to truth as we find it, this is the golden rule in *Theology* as well as in *Arithmetic*, and makes up the best harmony in a Church.

> JOHN MILTON, *Areopagitica*, 1644

Now I maintain that all attempts of reason to establish a theology by the aid of speculation alone are fruitless, that the principles of reason as applied to nature do not conduct us to any theological truths, and consequently, that a rational theology can have no existence, unless founded upon the laws of morality.

> IMMANUEL KANT, *Critique of Pure Reason*, 1781

A professorship of theology should have no place in our institution.

THOMAS JEFFERSON, *Letter to Thomas Cooper,* 1814, referring to University of Virginia.

Theology is the fundamental and regulating principle of the whole Church system.

JOHN HENRY NEWMAN, *Via Media,* 1837

The theological problems of original sin, origin of evil, predestination, and the like are the soul's mumps, and measles, and whooping-coughs.

RALPH WALDO EMERSON, "Spiritual Laws," *Essays, First Series,* 1841

Theology is nothing else than anthropology. . . . The knowledge of God is nothing else than a knowledge of man.

LUDWIG FEUERBACH, *The Essence of Christianity,* 1841

University education without theology is simply unphilosophical. Theology has at least as good a right to claim a place there as astronomy.

JOHN HENRY NEWMAN, *On the Scope and Nature of University Education,* 1852

I consider theology to be the rhetoric of morals.

RALPH WALDO EMERSON, *North American Review,* April, 1866

Dogmatic theology is an attempt at both literary and scientific criticism of the highest order; and the age which developed dogma had neither the resources nor the faculty for such a criticism.

MATTHEW ARNOLD, *Literature and Dogma,* 1873

Theology . . . is the most noble of studies.

POPE LEO XIII, *Aeterni Patris,* August 4, 1879

Theology itself, that is not based on the profoundest morality, is an empty cloud that sails through the summer air, leaving as much drought as it found.

HENRY WARD BEECHER, *Address,* May 8, 1883

Over all the theories of theology, I think that education will lead more men to heaven than any high Church theology, or any other kind that leaves that out.

HENRY WARD BEECHER, *Address,* May 8, 1883

Theology does not receive her first principles from any other science, but immediately from God by revelation.

POPE LEO XIII, *Holy Scripture,* 1893

The divine test of a man's worth is not his theology but his life.

MORRIS JOSEPH, *Judaism as Creed and Life,* 1903

Theologies are judged, in the long run, not by their symmetry or elaborateness, but by their contribution to the solution of human problems.

EUGENE W. LYMAN, *Theology and Human Problems,* 1910

Certainly we love Jesus Christ, but nothing in the world will make us love moral theology.

PAUL CLAUDEL, *Feuilles des Saints,* 1926

Christianity is a stirring and costly adventure in personal character and social relationships. Theological theories can help. . . . But they do not come first; they come last.

HARRY EMERSON FOSDICK, *Adventurous Religion,* 1926

Because it has turned away from theology . . . not only has the West no truth to give to the world, but the world throws back at it its own follies.

HENRI MASSIS, *Defense of the West,* 1927

Theology, or something that goes under that name, is still kept alive by the faithful, but only by artificial respiration.

CARL L. BECKER, *Heavenly City of the 18th Century Philosophers,* 1932

I consider Christian theology to be one of the great disasters of the human race.

ALFRED NORTH WHITEHEAD, *Dialogues of,* August, 1941, as recorded by L. Price

We have had our last chance. . . . The problem is basically theological. It must be of the spirit if we are to save the flesh.

GENERAL DOUGLAS MACARTHUR, when the Japanese surrendered at Tokyo, 1945

In no circumstances can the study of theology or the mind's assent to theological propositions take the place of what William Law calls "the birth of God within."

ALDOUS HUXLEY, *The Perennial Philosophy,* 1945

It is difficult to see how a Christian theologian, especially if he be a sociologist and an historian to boot, could find rest in anything but in an ecumenically oriented theology.

JOACHIM WACH, *Church, Denomination and Sect,* 1946

Natural Theology says not only look up and look out—it also says look down and look in, and you will find the proofs of the reality of God in the depth of your own nature.

CHRISTOPHER DAWSON, *Religion and Culture,* 1947

Theology is a rational superstructure erected on the foundations of the Christian theology of revelation.

CHRISTOPHER DAWSON, *Religion and Culture,* 1947

The term "theo-logy" implies, as such, a mediation, namely, between the mystery,

which is *theos,* and the understanding, which is *logos.*

PAUL TILLICH, *The Protestant Era,* 1948

Sacred theology is superior to philosophy, both theoretically and practically; theoretically, because it is more perfect knowledge of God and His creatures; practically, because moral philosophy is insufficient to direct man to God as his last end.

MORTIMER ADLER, *Vital Speeches,* December, 1949

So significant you are, so universally relevant. But how, and by what right? Beware of asking; that way lies theology.

RONALD A. KNOX, *Stimuli,* 1951

Apologetic theology is "answering theology."

PAUL TILLICH, *Systematic Theology,* 1951

Religion belongs to the sphere of the unsayable, so it is not to be wondered at that in theology there is much nonsense.

THOMAS MCPHERSON, *New Essays in Philosophical Theology,* ed. Flew and MacIntyre, 1955

The fact that astronomies change while the stars abide is a true analogy of every realm of human life and thought, religion not least of all. No existent theology can be a final formulation of spiritual truth.

HARRY EMERSON FOSDICK, *The Living of These Days,* 1956

What is known and knowable in theology is God in relation to self and to neighbor, and self and neighbor is relation to God. This complex of related beings is the object of theology.

H. RICHARD NIEBUHR, *The Purpose of the Church and Its Ministry,* 1956

A truly ecumenical theology would be one in which various schools of Catholic and Protestant theology would confront each other systematically, and strive toward an ultimate reconciliation, in view of their common concern to interpret the same Christian faith to "all the world" and "every creature." . . . Ecumenical theology is . . . interconfessional.

> WALTER MARSHALL HORTON, *Christian Theology, An Ecumenical Approach,* 1958

While theology is bound to respect the neutrality of natural science, it cannot escape its duty to challenge and expose destructive cosmic philosophies masquerading as "scientific."

> WALTER MARSHALL HORTON, *Christian Theology,* 1958

The churches would do well to shore up their resources of constructive theology. They will have to be ready to take a stand, to speak for truth or to deny that there is such a thing!

> MARTIN E. MARTY, *The New Shape of American Religion,* 1958

As a common core of religious affirmation, the "fatherhood of God and the brotherhood of man" reduces theology to triviality.

> JAMES HASTINGS NICHOLS, *Religion in America,* ed. John Cogley, 1958

Theology is reflection upon the reality of worship and an explication of it. As such it is a rational affair. . . faith seeking to understand.

> ALBERT C. OUTLER, *Christian Century,* February 3, 1960

More often than not, attacks upon theology come from uncritical use on the part of theologians themselves of *devotional* language in a context where *theological* language is called for.

> JOHN E. SMITH, *Reason and God,* 1961

Theology is an incubus that a humanist can never shake off. He may seek refuge from theism in atheism or from animism in materialism. But after each desperate twist and turn he will find himself committed to some theological position or other. Theology is inescapable, and it is dynamite.

> A. J. TOYNBEE, *A Study of History,* Vol. XII, *Reconsiderations,* 1961

Any theology which attempts to speak to an age in its own language runs the danger of compromising the eternal message of the Gospel with the temporarily plausible conviction of the time.

> KENNETH CAUTHEN, *The Impact of American Religious Liberalism,* 1962

We cannot have an authentic theology in our time without dialogue with contemporary men.

> BERNARD HARING, *The Johannine Council,* 1963

The death of God, obedience to Jesus, and a new optimism—these are three of the themes I see emerging in the new radical movement in theology today.

> WILLIAM HAMILTON, quoted in New York *Herald Tribune,* November 7, 1965

Sacred theology rests on the written word of God, together with sacred tradition, as its primary and perpetual foundation.

> Second Vatican Council, *Constitution on Divine Revelation,* November, 1965

The old theology starts with the divinity of Christ and tries to explain how God became man. The new theology starts with the only indisputable fact—that Christ was man—and tries to show how God acted through Him uniquely.

> HUGH MONTEFIORE, interview with Christopher S. Wren, *Look,* February 22, 1966

A blind man in a dark room searching for a black cat which isn't there—and finding it.

> ANONYMOUS

THINKER

Beware when the great God lets loose a thinker on this planet.
RALPH WALDO EMERSON, "Circles," *Essays, First Series,* 1841

THINKING

Thinking is another attribute of the soul; and here I discover what properly belongs to myself. This alone is inseparable from me. I am—I exist: this is certain; but how often? as often as I think.
RENÉ DESCARTES, *Meditations,* 1641

Everything proves the solidarity of individuals, and no one can think at all except by means of the general store of thought, accumulated and refined by centuries of cultivation and experience.
HENRI AMIEL, *Journal,* 1882

Thinking is not worship, but if it is initiated by a wrench of sorrow which banishes the half-gods of our superficial existence, God may appear.
RICHARD C. CABOT, *What Men Live By,* 1914

Thinking *plus* agonized questioning of the scheme of things which has rolled me in the dust, has not the confident appeal of the believer to his God; but if it is serious it will probably come to that.
RICHARD C. CABOT, *What Men Live By,* 1914

One of the hardest things for the student to learn . . . is just the simple fact that *brain-power is no guarantee for the rightness of thinking,* that . . . a restlessly outreaching mind, unchecked by the humility of common sense, is more than likely to lead its owner into bogs of duplicity.
PAUL ELMER MORE, *Humanism and America,* ed. R. Forester, 1930

All thinking is not prayer. But thinking can be prayer, just as walking and talking and washing the floor can be prayer.
VINCENT McNABB, *The Craft of Prayer,* 1951

Some of the finest exponents of Christian faith have fallen victim to . . . hardening of the arteries of Christian thinking.
C. A. COULSON, *Science and Christian Belief,* 1955

THOMISM

Neo-Thomist Philosophy . . . is the intellectual front of the incurable passion for temporal power—whether deliberately so or not is the secret of the strategists.
MAX C. OTTO, *Religious Liberals Reply,* 1947

THOUGHT

All that we are is the result of what we have thought.
Dhammapada, c. 5th century B.C.

By virtue of space I am comprehended and engulfed in a universe as a mere point; but by virtue of thought I comprehend it.
BLAISE PASCAL, *Pensées,* 1670

Man is but a reed, the most feeble thing in nature; but he is a thinking reed. . . . All our dignity consists, then, in thought.

BLAISE PASCAL, *Pensées,* 1670

The rise of thought beyond the world of sense, its passage from the finite to the infinite, the leap into the super-sensible which it takes when it snaps asunder the links of the chain of sense, all this transition is thought and nothing but thought.

G. W. F. HEGEL, *Logic,* 1816

Beautiful it is to understand that a Thought did never yet die; that as thou, the originator thereof, hast gathered and created it from the whole Past, so thou wilt transmit it to the whole Future.

THOMAS CARLYLE, *Sartor Resartus,* 1836

We may be as base as we please in thought, and yet walk through human courts with proud eye, and head erect.

FREDERICK W. FABER, *Growth in Holiness,* 1855

A vivid thought brings the power to paint it; and in proportion to the depth of its source is the force of its projection.

RALPH WALDO EMERSON, *Address,* May 5, 1879

It would be as wise and reasonable to say that it does not matter which way the rudder swings as the ship moves, as to say that it does not matter what a man thinks.

W. J. DAWSON, *The Making of Manhood,* 1895

If you would live a high life, you must begin by encouraging the growth of high thoughts. If you would voyage Godward, you must see to it that the rudder of thought is right.

W. J. DAWSON, *The Making of Manhood,* 1895

Thought pure and simple is as near to God as we can get; it is through that we are linked with God.

SAMUEL BUTLER, *Notebooks of,* ed. H. F. Jones, 1912

This then is the final triumph of thought— that it disintegrates all societies, and at last destroys the thinker himself.

WILL DURANT, *On the Meaning of Life,* 1932

We are thought. Thought leads us. Therefore, the secret of our destiny lies here: in regulating our thoughts.

ANTONIN SERTILLANGES, *Recollections,* 1950

It is in the last analysis not freedom of thought which endangers Jewish values, but the freedom which some people arrogate to themselves not to think at all.

MILTON STEINBERG, *A Believing Jew,* 1951

The first apostolate, at the crossroads where we stand, is the Apostolate of Thought. The Church is at a turning-point such that she can lose everything or gain everything, according to the spirituality she asks humanity to adopt.

EMMANUEL SUHARD, *The Church Today,* 1953

See also Contemplation; Freedom of Thought and Speech; God: Considered as Personal; Ideals; Imagination; Inspiration; Intuition; Knowledge; Meditation; Mind; Reason; Thinker; Thinking; Thoughts; Universe; Universe and God; Wisdom; Words.

THOUGHTS

Let the wise man guard his thoughts, for they are difficult to perceive, very artful, and they rush wherever they list; thoughts well guarded bring happiness.

Dhammapada, c. 5th century B.C.

He whose heart has been set on the love of learning and true wisdom, and has exercised this part of himself, *that* man *must* without fail have thoughts that are immortal and divine, if *he lay hold on truth.*
PLATO, "Timaeus," 90, *Dialogues,* c. 370 B.C.

In truth we should be aware above all that our thoughts have three possible sources—God, the devil and ourselves.
JOHN CASSIAN, *Conferences,* I, ch. 19, c. 420 A.D.

They are never alone that are accompanied with noble thoughts.
PHILIP SIDNEY, *Arcadia,* 1590

God intends even our thoughts to set forward the sanctification of our souls, and it rests with ourselves whether they do so or not.
FRANÇOIS FÉNELON (1651–1715), *Spiritual Letters of*

For all our penny-wise wisdom, for all our soul-destroying slavery to habit, it is not to be doubted that all men have sublime thoughts.
RALPH WALDO EMERSON, *Divinity School Address,* July 15, 1838

Carry thy thoughts forward through eternity toward that universal sun; thou shalt not arrive at darkness nor emptiness; what is empty dwells only between the worlds, not around the world.
JEAN PAUL RICHTER, *Reminiscences,* 1841

Thoughts invite us, more than words and deeds, to continue in sin, for thoughts can be concealed, while words and deeds cannot.
SÖREN KIERKEGAARD (1813–1855), *Meditations from,* ed. T. H. Croxall

The highest possible stage in moral culture is when we recognise that we ought to control our thoughts.
CHARLES DARWIN, *The Descent of Man,* 1871

None of us know . . . what fairy palaces we may build of beautiful thoughts—proof against all adversity . . .—houses built without hands, for our souls to live in.
JOHN RUSKIN, *The Eagle's Nest,* 1872

If you accept your thoughts as inspirations from the Supreme Intelligence, obey them when they prescribe difficult duties, because they come only so long as they are used.
RALPH WALDO EMERSON, *Courage,* 1877

The soul is dyed with the color of its leisure thoughts.
W. R. INGE, *Recreation,* quoted in *Reader's Digest,* April, 1936

The Dean of Humanities spoke with awe "of an approaching scientific ability to control man's thoughts with precision."—I shall be very content to be dead before that happens.
WINSTON S. CHURCHILL, *Address,* Massachusetts Institute of Technology, March 30, 1949

See also Freedom of Thought and Speech; Inspiration; Thinker; Thinking; Thought.

TIME

The moving image of eternity.
PLATO, "Timaeus," *Dialogues,* c. 380 B.C.

Pythagoras, when he was asked what time was, answered that it was the soul of this world.
PLUTARCH, *Platonic Questions,* c. 66 A.D.

What then is time? If no one asks me, I know; if I want to explain it to a questioner, I do not know.
ST. AUGUSTINE, *Confessions of,* XI, 397

Time is nothing else than protraction, but of what I know not; and I marvel, if it be not of the mind itself.
ST. AUGUSTINE, *Confessions of,* XI, 33, 397

Time is the chariot of all ages to carry men away.
> FRANCESCO PETRARCH, *View of Human Life*, c. 1346

Time is the herald of Truth.
> ELIZABETH GRYMESTON, *Miscellanea—Meditations*, 1604

Time is the author of authors.
> FRANCIS BACON, *The Advancement of Learning*, 1605

Let time flow by, with which we flow on to be transformed into the glory of the children of God.
> ST. FRANCIS OF SALES (1567–1622), *Consoling Thoughts of*, ed. Huguet

Time is the rider that breaks youth.
> GEORGE HERBERT, *Jacula Prudentum*, 1640

All that really belongs to us is time; even he who has nothing else has that.
> BALTASAR GRACIÁN, *The Art of Worldly Wisdom*, 1647

Time cures sorrows and squabbles because we all change and are no longer the same persons. Neither the offender nor the offended is the same.
> BLAISE PASCAL, *Pensées*, 1670

Ask what Time is, it is nothing else but something of eternal duration become finite, measureable and transitory.
> WILLIAM LAW, *Appeal to All that Doubt*, 1740

The slow, the silent power of time.
> J. C. F. VON SCHILLER, *Wallenstein's Death*, 1799

Time, a maniac scattering dust.
> ALFRED TENNYSON, *In Memoriam*, 1850

Time is that which in all things passes away; it is the form under which the will to live has revealed to it that its efforts are in vain; it is the agent by which at every moment all things in our hands become as nothing, and lose all value.
> ARTHUR SCHOPENHAUER, *The Vanity of Existence*, 1851

As if you could kill time without injuring eternity.
> HENRY DAVID THOREAU, *Walden*, 1854

Time is a file that wears and makes no noise.
> H. C. BOHN, *Handbook of Proverbs*, 1855

Time is precious, but truth is more precious than time.
> BENJAMIN DISRAELI, *Speech*, September 21, 1865

Time, whose tooth gnaws away everything else, is powerless against truth.
> THOMAS HENRY HUXLEY, *Administrative Nihilism*, 1871

Time is the great physician.
> BENJAMIN DISRAELI, *Endymion*, 1880

As is well known, the Devil is the Prince of Time, and God is the King of Eternity. Time without end, that is Hell. Perfect presence, that is Eternity.
> DENIS DE ROUGEMONT, *The Devil's Share*, 1944

Time exists because there is activity. . . . Time is the product of *changing* realities, beings, existences.
> NICHOLAS BERDYAEV, *Solitude and Society*, 1947

To understand the teaching of the Bible, one must accept its premise that time has a meaning which is at least equal to that of space; that time has a significance and sovereignty of its own.
> A. J. HESCHEL, *The Sabbath*, 1951

Time, although the philosophers declare it to be completely distinct from eternity, is certainly an available instrument for reaching the Eternal.

JOHN W. LYNCH, *Hourglass,* 1952

The here-and-now is no mere filling of time, but a filling of time with God.

JOHN FOSTER, *Requiem for a Parish,* 1962

See also End; End of the World; Eternal; Eternal Life; Future; Infinite; Reality.

TOLERANCE

Like the bee gathering honey from different flowers, the wise man accepts the essence of different Scriptures and sees only the good in all religions.

Srimad Bhagavatam, between 1200 and 500 B.C.

It is forbidden to decry other sects; the true believer gives honor to whatever in them is worthy of honor.

Decree of Asoka, Buddhist Emperor of India (264–228 B.C.)

Think on this doctrine,—that reasoning beings were created for one another's sake; that to be patient is a branch of justice, and that men sin without intending it.

MARCUS AURELIUS, *Mediations of,* c. 170 A.D.

Since each virtue shines by its own proper light, the merit of tolerance is resplendent with a very special glory.

JOHN OF SALISBURY, *Policraticus,* 1159

Do not despise others because, as it seems to you, they do not possess the virtues you thought they had; they may be pleasing to God for other reasons which you cannot discover.

ST. JOHN OF THE CROSS (1542–1591), *The Living Flame of Love*

He that is willing to tolerate any religion, or discrepant way of religion, besides his own, unless it be in matters merely in-different, either doubts of his own, or is not sincere in it.

NATHANIEL WARD, *The Simple Cobbler of Aggawan,* 1646

Whatsoever is against the foundation of faith, or contrary to good life, or the laws of obedience, or destructive to human society and the public and just interests of bodies politic, is out of the limits of my question and does not pretend to compliance or toleration.

JEREMY COLLIER, *A Discourse on the Liberty of Prophesying,* 1649

And O, how sweet and pleasant it is to the truly spiritual eye to see several sorts of believers, several forms of Christians in the school of Christ, every one learning their own lesson, loving one another in their several places and different performances to their Master.

ISAAC PENNINGTON, *Works,* 1681

Those are not at all to be tolerated who deny the being of God. Promises, covenants, and oaths, which are the bonds of human society, can have no hold upon an atheist. The taking away of God, though but even in thought, dissolves all.

JOHN LOCKE, *A Letter Concerning Toleration,* 1685

All religions must be tolerated, and the sole concern of the authorities should be to see that one does not molest another, for here every man must be saved in his own way.

FREDERICK THE GREAT, *Order,* June 22, 1740

The longer I live, the larger allowances I make for human infirmities.

JOHN WESLEY, *Letter to Samuel Furley,* February 21, 1756

Now that there is and can be no longer an exclusive national religion, tolerance should be given to all religions that tolerate others, so long as their dogmas contain nothing contrary to the duties of citizenship.

JEAN JACQUES ROUSSEAU, *The Social Contract,* 1762

Of all religions, the Christian is without doubt the one which should inspire tolerance most, although up to now Christians have been the most intolerant of men.

VOLTAIRE, "Tolerance," *Philosophical Dictionary,* 1764

What is toleration? It is the appurtenance of humanity. We are all full of weakness and errors; let us mutually pardon each other our follies—it is the first law of nature.

VOLTAIRE, "Toleration," *Philosophical Dictionary,* 1764

Toleration is good for all, or it is good for none.

EDMUND BURKE, *Speech,* House of Commons, 1773

Toleration is not the *opposite* of Intolerance, but is the *counterfeit* of it. Both are despotisms. The one assumes itself the right of withholding liberty of conscience, and the other of granting it.

THOMAS PAINE, *Rights of Man,* 1792

I have seen gross intolerance shown in support of toleration.

SAMUEL TAYLOR COLERIDGE, *Biographia Literaria,* 1817

I write with freedom, because, while I claim to believe in one God, or so my reason tells me, I yield as freely to others that of believing in three. Both religions, I find, make honest men, and that is the only point society has any right to look to.

THOMAS JEFFERSON, *Letter to James Smith,* December 8, 1822

Toleration is a herb of spontaneous growth in the soil of indifference.

SAMUEL TAYLOR COLERIDGE, *Aids to Reflection,* 1825

Toleration ought in reality to be merely a transitory mood. It must lead to recognition. To tolerate is to affront.

J. W. VON GOETHE (1749–1832), *Maxims and Reflections*

We are not here altogether to tolerate. We are here to resist, to control and vanquish withal.

THOMAS CARLYLE, *Heroes and Hero Worship,* 1840

It [toleration] implies a confession that there are insoluble problems upon which even revelation throws but little light.

FREDERIC TEMPLE, *Essays and Reviews,* 1860

While not conceding any right to anything save what is true and honest, she [the Church] does not forbid public authority to tolerate what is at variance with truth and justice, for the sake of avoiding some greater evil, or of obtaining or preserving some greater good.

POPE LEO XIII, *Libertas Humana,* 1888

It is well that the stately synagog should lift its walls by the side of the aspiring cathedral, a perpetual reminder that there are many mansions of the Father's earthly house as well as in the heavenly one; that civilized humanity . . . is mightier than any one institution.

OLIVER WENDELL HOLMES, *Over the Teacups,* 1891

Is there any religion whose followers can be pointed to as distinctly more amiable and trustworthy than those of any other?

SAMUEL BUTLER, *Notebooks,* 1912

Nothing was further from the minds of the leading Reformers than the toleration of doctrines differing from their own. . . . They set up the authority of the Bible instead of the Church, but it was the Bible according to Luther, or the Bible according to Calvin.

J. B. BURY, *A History of Freedom of Thought,* 1913

Religious toleration, to a certain extent, has been won because people have ceased to consider religion so important as it was once thought to be.

BERTRAND RUSSELL, *Free Thought and Official Propaganda,* Lecture, March 24, 1922

It is rather ridiculous to ask a man just about to be boiled in a pot and eaten, at a purely religious feast, why he does not regard all religions as equally friendly and fraternal.

G. K. CHESTERTON, *The Everlasting Man,* 1925

Tolerance is a better guarantee of freedom than brotherly love; for a man may love his brother so much that he feels himself thereby appointed his brother's keeper.

EVERETT DEAN MARTIN, *Liberty,* 1930

The modern theory that you should always treat the religious convictions of other people with profound respect finds no support in the Gospels. Mutual tolerance of religious views is the product not of faith, but of doubt.

ARNOLD LUNN, *Now I See,* 1937

Tolerance in the sense of moderation or superior knowledge or scepticism is actually the worst form of intolerance.

KARL BARTH, *Church Dogmatics,* 2nd half-vol., 1940

Tolerance . . . is the lowest form of human cooperation. It is the drab, uncomfortable, halfway house between hate and charity.

ROBERT I. GANNON, *Address,* Boston, April 23, 1942

Tolerance means that we shall give our enemies a chance.

MORRIS R. COHEN, *The Faith of a Liberal,* 1946

The tolerance of the skeptic . . . accepts the most diverse and indeed the most con-tradictory opinions, and keeps all his suspicions for the "dogmatist."

JEAN GUITTON, *Difficultés de croire,* 1948

Toleration . . . is not true liberty when it is only a gracious concession by the state to the individual. Gracious concessions are incompatible with liberty of religion which is not something that a state, or an absolutist church offers, but that which the citizen claims and the law protects.

CECIL NORTHCOTT, *Religious Liberty,* 1948

Tolerance grows only when faith loses certainty; certainty is murderous.

WILL DURANT, *The Age of Faith,* 1950

Apocalyptic religion has its merits, but tolerance is not one of them.

W. R. FORRESTER, *Christian Vocation,* 1951

Tolerance does not . . . do anything, embrace anyone, champion any issue. It wipes the notes off the score of life and replaces them with one long bar of rest. It does not attack error, it does not champion truth, it does not hate evil, it does not love good.

WALTER FARRELL, *The Looking Glass,* 1951

Our attitude to other religions should be defined in the spirit of that great saying in a play of Sophocles, where Antigone says, "I was not born to share men's hatred, but their love."

SARVEPALLI RADHAKRISHNAN, *The Philosophy of,* 1952

Tolerance implies a respect for another person, not because he is wrong or even because he is right, but because he is human.

JOHN COGLEY, *Commonweal,* April 24, 1959

Religious toleration results from the erosion of religious conviction under the accumulating pressure of Humanist ideology.

BARBARA WOOTTON, *The Humanist Frame,* ed. J. Huxley, 1961

The full circle of spiritual truth will be completed only when we realize that, but for a destiny not fully understood, we might actually have been born in the other person's faith.

MARCUS BACH, *Rotarian Magazine,* December, 1962

See also Anti-Semitism; Bigots; Brotherhood; Charity; Community; Disputation; Division; Dogmatism; Ecumenism; Fellowship; Freedom, Religious; Hatred; Indifference; Intolerance; Love; Negroes; Paths; Prejudice; Race; Racial Equality; Respect; Rights; Unity; Zeal; Zealots.

TORAH

Moses received Torah from Sinai and delivered it to Joshua, and Joshua to the Elders, and the Elders to the Prophets, and the Prophets delivered it to the Men of the Great Synagogue.

Pirke Aboth, I, c. 20 A.D.

The Torah cannot prevent us from considering to be true that which our reason urges us to believe.

LEVI BEN GERSON, *Battles of the Lord,* 1329

Its content and connotations embrace more than "religion" or "creed" alone. . . . It is a mystic, almost cosmic, conception. The Torah is the tool of the Creator; with it and for it He created the universe. The Torah is older than creation. It is the highest idea and the living soul of the world.

HAYIM NAHMAN BIALIK, *Address,* Jerusalem, 1925, quoted in *The Zionist Idea,* ed. A. Hertzberg, 1959

Torah is not law. It is an expression for the aggregate of Jewish teachings.

LOUIS GINZBERG, *Students, Scholars, and Saints,* 1928

The study of Torah . . . means much more than the study of the Pentateuch, or even of the whole of Scripture, regarded as mere literature, written documents. It means the study of the revelation made through those documents, the divine teaching therein imparted, the divine thought therein disclosed.

R. TRAVERS HERFORD, Introduction to his translation of *Pirke Aboth,* 1945

The real Torah is not merely the written texts of the Five Books of Moses; the real Torah is the meaning enshrined in that text, as expounded . . . and unfolded by successive generations of Sages and Teachers in Israel.

JOSEPH H. HERTZ, *Daily Prayer Book,* 1948

It is not the Jews that are unique, but the Torah as the Word of God and the Jews as the bearers of the Torah.

J. B. AGUS, *Judaism,* Fall, 1955

The Torah is commandment, but it is much more. . . . It is the whole of the sacred tradition, especially as expressed in all the writings of the faith, from the Bible to the present.

ARTHUR HERTZBERG, *Judaism,* 1961

See also Belief; Bible; God, Word of; Israel; Jew; Jews; Judaism; Law; Old Testament.

TOTALITARIANISM

A totalitarian state is the kingdom of Satan.

NICHOLAS BERDYAEV, *Slavery and Freedom,* 1944

It is the terrifying Absolute State, which recognizes only individuals, which counts its citizens like heads of cattle, which tramples personality and makes zoos out of its universities. This challenge to Christian Humanism and objective science must be met at any cost, unless we want to see the end of everything worth living for.

ROBERT I. GANNON, *After Black Coffee,* 1946

A totalitarian government must deny the existence of God, if it would be consistent with its own philosophy, for if it admitted a Supreme Being, it would have to recognize limits to its authority.

FRANCIS J. CONNELL, *Morality and Government,* 1949

Totalitarianism is wrong because it is a violation of the personal rights which man's very nature gives him; and consequently it is an insult to God, the Creator of man's nature.

FRANCIS J. CONNELL, *Morality and Government,* 1949

The dehumanized type that gradually takes shape in the crucible of our modern technocracies and totalitarianisms is at the very opposite pole to the Christian man.

GUSTAVE THIBON, *Christianity and Freedom,* 1952

The observer who regards history from the viewpoint of the Apocalypse "recognizes" the totalitarian State, without surprise and with accurate understanding of its innermost tendencies and structures as a milder preliminary form of the State of Antichrist.

JOSEF PIEPER, *The End of Time,* 1954

Totalitarian man will die of thirst while crossing a spiritual desert where there will be nothing to quench his thirst except the blood of his fellow-men.

GEORGES BERNANOS, *Last Essays of,* 1955

See also Anti-God Totalitarians; Communism; Dictatorship; Divine Right of Kings; Government; Humanism; Marxism.

TRADE

The man who buys it in order that he may gain by selling it again unchanged and as he bought it; that man is of the buyers and sellers who are cast forth from God's temple.

GRATIAN, *Decretum Gratiani,* c. 1140

The rule that a man may sell his goods as dear as he will is false and unchristian.

MARTIN LUTHER, *On Trading and Usury,* 1524

You may buy as cheap ordinarily, as you can; and sell as dear as you can . . . when you contract on equal terms with persons in all senses (as to the matter and skill of bargaining) equal to yourself . . . when there is no deceit, and no necessity and no monopoly.

JEREMY TAYLOR, *Holy Living,* 1650

See also Business; Clergy; Competition; Economics and Christianity; Enterprise; Industrialism; Market Place; Money.

TRADE UNIONS. *See* LABOR UNIONS

TRADERS

I never cease wondering at the number of novel inflexions which, in this new language of avarice, have been added to the usual forms in the conjugation of that ill-omened verb "to rob."

ST. FRANCIS XAVIER (a reference to European traders in the Orient), *Letter to King John of Portugal,* 1545

See also Business; Economics and Christianity; Market Place; Profit; Trade.

TRADITION

Whoever would know the truth, may see the tradition of the Apostles. . . manifest in all the Churches. . . . We confute all who assemble together unlawfully . . . by pointing out to them the tradition received from the Apostles, and preached to men, and handed down by the succession of Bishops to our own day, in that

Church, the greatest, the most ancient, and known to everyone, founded and established at Rome by the two most glorious Apostles Peter and Paul.

ST. IRENAEUS, *Against the Heresies,* c. 175

Like a man turned into a brute . . . as were the victims of Circe—he who repudiates the ecclesiastical traditions embraces the human heresies, ceases to be a man of God and becomes unfaithful to the Lord.

ST. CLEMENT OF ALEXANDRIA, *Stromata,* lib. vii, cap. xvl, c. 193

For how can anything come into use, if it has not first been handed down?

TERTULLIAN, *On the Soldier's Crown,* c. 211

We have some articles of faith from the Holy Scriptures and others we have received BY THE TRADITION OF THE APOSTLES, which the Apostles preached and the Fathers believed, and the Martyrs confirmed with their blood.

ST. BASIL, *Treatise on the Holy Ghost,* II, c. 375

I have left you two things and you will not stray as long as you hold them fast. The one is the book of God [the Koran], and the other the Tradition of His Prophet.

MOHAMMED (7th century A.D.), *Dictionary of Islam,* ed. Hughes, 1885

Human traditions, instituted to propitiate God, to merit grace, and to make satisfaction for sins, are opposed to the Gospel and the doctrine of faith.

PHILIP MELANCHTHON, *Augsburg Confession,* 1530

Tradition is everywhere the mother of religion; it precedes and engenders sacred books, as language precedes and engenders scripture; its existence is rendered immovable in the sacred books, as the existence of the Word is rendered immovable in Scripture.

JEAN BAPTISTE LACORDAIRE, *Conferences of,* c. 1850

If the sacred books have taken possession of the world, it is because the world bears in its bosom sacred traditions of which those books are but the expression more or less pure, more or less corrupted. Every sacred book is a traditional book, it was venerated before it existed, it existed before it appeared.

JEAN BAPTISTE LACORDAIRE, *Conferences of,* c. 1850

By "Tradition" I mean that body of revealed truths, received by the Apostles from the lips of Christ Himself or told them by the Holy Ghost, that has come down to us, delivered as it were by hand, and preserved in the Catholic Church by unbroken succession.

PIETRO GASPARRI, *The Catholic Catechism for Adults,* 1932

Tradition is the witness of the Spirit; the Spirit's unceasing revelation and preaching of good tidings. . . . It is, primarily, the principle of growth and regeneration.

GEORGES FLOROVSKY, *The Church of God,* ed. F. L. Mascall, 1934

Tradition means that instinctive mind of the Church, that inspired sense of hers, which enables her to handle the Word of God.

R. KEHOE, *Eastern Churches Quarterly,* October, 1946

This handing on is known as tradition, and through it, and through it alone, was the Christian faith spread until the formation of the collection of apostolic writings known as the Canon of the New Testament. Even then the New Testament did not become a substitute for tradition.

H. E. SYMONDS, *The Eastern Churches Quarterly,* October, 1946

Large strata and movements in the western world are outside the church. But the religious tradition operates in them still in an indirect and disguised way. The river has gone underground; it has not ceased to flow.

AMOS WILDER, *Modern Poetry and the Christian Tradition,* 1952

There is a growing recognition that tradition is not simply a thing of the past, but a living reality.

Ways of Worship, Faith and Order, Commission Paper, no. 6, 1952

We know tradition as a living social process constantly changing, constantly in need of criticism, but constant also as the continuing memory, value system and habit structure of a society.

H. RICHARD NIEBUHR, *The Purpose of the Church and Its Ministry,* 1956

The very principle of *sola Scriptura* is itself a tradition.

JAROSLAV PELIKAN, *Pulpit Digest,* November, 1959

To an Orthodox Christian, Tradition means . . . the books of the Bible; it means the Creed; it means the decrees of the Ecumenical Councils and the writings of the Fathers; it means the Canons, the Service Books, the Holy Icons—in fact, the whole system of doctrine, Church government, worship, and art which Orthodoxy has articulated over the ages.

TIMOTHY WARE, *The Orthodox Church,* 1963

Tradition is not only kept by the Church— it lives in the Church, it is the life of the Holy Spirit in the Church.

TIMOTHY WARE, *The Orthodox Church,* 1963

Every attempt of a given tradition in Protestantism to be faithful to its own best insights and to submit them to fresh scrutiny in the light of the gospel will finally draw us the [Church] closer together.

ROBERT MCAFEE BROWN, *Commonweal,* September 24, 1965

Sacred Scripture is the word of God inasmuch as it is consigned to writing under the divine Spirit, while sacred tradition takes the word of God entrusted by Christ the Lord and the Holy Spirit to the Apostles, and hands it on to their successors in its full purity. . . . Therefore both sacred tradition and sacred Scripture are to be accepted and venerated with the same sense of loyalty and reverence. Sacred tradition and sacred Scripture form one sacred deposit of the word of God. . . . Sacred tradition, sacred Scripture, and the teaching authority of the Church . . . are so linked and joined together that one cannot stand without the others.

SECOND VATICAN COUNCIL, *Constitution on Divine Revelation,* November, 1965

Tradition should be deabsolutized, but not scrapped. We're in a two thousand year continuity, and that which expresses continuity is valuable. In a state of flux on doctrine, continuity of tradition has even more value.

JAMES A. PIKE, interviewed by Christopher S. Wren, *Look,* February 22, 1966

See also Apostles; Apostolic Succession; Authority; Bible; Bible: Its Interpretation; Bible and the Church; Chaos; Church, Criticism of; Church: Its Authority; Doctrine; Heresy; New Testament; Reform; Truth and Religion; Unity.

TRAGEDY

And every life, no matter if its hour is rich with love and every moment jeweled with joy, will, at its close, become a tragedy as sad and deep and dark as can be woven of the warp and woof of mystery and death.

ROBERT G. INGERSOLL, at his brother's grave, 1879

There is nothing more tragic in life than the utter impossibility of changing what you have done.

JOHN GALSWORTHY, *Justice,* 1910

It appears that when life is broken by tragedy God shines through the breach.
GEORGE A. BUTTRICK, *Prayer,* 1942

The ancient Hebrews, by virtue of inner resources . . . turned their tragedy . . . into one of the half-dozen creative moments in world history.
HERBERT BUTTERFIELD, *Christianity and History,* 1950

The tragedy of life is not death but in what dies inside a man while he lives—the death of genuine feeling, the death of inspired response, the death of the awareness that makes it possible to feel the pain or the glory of other men in oneself.
NORMAN COUSINS, *Saturday Review,* October 2, 1954

Tragedy strips a secular view of life of its only possible ground of meaning.
LANGDON GILKEY, *Maker of Heaven and Earth,* 1959

See also Affliction; Bereavement; Death; Sorrow; Trials; Tribulations.

TRANQUILLITY

I consider tranquillity of soul to be nothing else than heaven at the core of one's soul which henceforth looks on all the wiles of the evil one as so many nothings.
ST. JOHN CLIMACUS (525–600), *Scala Paradisi*

A wise man will always be a Christian, because the perfection of wisdom is to know where lies tranquillity of mind, and how to attain it, which Christianity teaches.
W. S. LANDOR, *Imaginary Conversations,* 1824

See also Abandonment; Acceptance; Detachment; Nirvana; Patience; Peace; Peace of Mind; Rebellion; Resignation; Selflessness; Serenity; Silence.

TRANSCENDENCE

It is highly important . . . for religious thinking—and for philosophic thinking also—to rid itself of a transcendence which seeks to magnify God's greatness by separating Him from the world, placing Him at a distance from it and making Him self-sufficient and complete without it.
HENRY JONES, *A Faith That Inquires,* 1921

The old doctrine of transcendence is nothing more than an assertion of an outmoded view of the world.
R. GREGOR SMITH, *The New Man,* 1956

See also Experience, Religious; Transcendent; Transcendentalism.

TRANSCENDENT

Perpetual absorption in the transcendent is a human impossibility, and the effort to achieve it is both unsocial and silly.
EVELYN UNDERHILL, *Practical Mysticism,* 1914

See also Transcendence; Transcendentalism.

TRANSCENDENTALISM

It was the glowing expression of philosophic Utopianism, the flaring up of the old fires of idealism, before the scientific and materialistic reactions destroyed its romantic dreams.
VERNON L. PARRINGTON, *Main Currents in American Thought,* 1930

Transcendentalism was never a religion. It was the rhapsody with which some New Englanders rebelled against the ferocity of Calvinism.
BROOKS ATKINSON, *New York Times,* April 24, 1962

See also Transcendence; Transcendent.

TRANSFIGURATION

As the least beautiful of our kind is human and humanity [is] the most beautiful thing in our world, everyone is capable of transfiguration when the comely soul shines through.

LANE COOPER, *Evolution and Repentance,* 1925

TRANSITION

Out of the ashes of past religions may arise the truth that cannot be destroyed. Out of an age of transition like this can come at least a new synthesis of faith and reason, deep enough to command life as a whole, and intelligent enough to compel the mind.

NELS F. S. FERRÉ, *Learning and World Peace,* 1948

TRANSITORY

All transient things are permanent in God.

THOMAS TRAHERNE (1634?–1704), *Centuries of Meditation*

TRANSUBSTANTIATION

Transubstantiation must be considered as an invention of human reason, since it is based neither on Scripture nor sound reasoning.

MARTIN LUTHER, *The Babylonian Captivity,* 1520

When we reflect that Sir Thomas More was ready to die for the doctrine of transubstantiation, we cannot but feel some doubt whether the doctrine of transubstantiation may not triumph over all opposition.

T. B. MACAULAY, *Edinburgh Review,* October, 1840

For myself, I cannot indeed prove it, I cannot tell *how* it is; but I say, "Why should it not be? What's to hinder it? What do I know of substance and matter? Just as much as the greatest philosophers, and that is nothing at all."

JOHN HENRY NEWMAN, *Apologia pro Vita Sua,* 1864

See also Eucharist; Mass, the.

TREASON

Christians can expect at times to be regarded by some people as taking positions which are treasonable. Ever since the first apostles said "We must obey God rather than men" this has been a possibility.

JOHN C. BENNETT, *Christian Century,* January 6, 1954

See also Authority; Loyalty; Patriotism; Rebellion; State, the.

TRIALS

We always find that those who walked closest to Christ Our Lord were those who had to bear the greatest trials.

ST. TERESA OF ÁVILA, *The Interior Castle,* 1577

Ah, when that dark day seems coming on us, and bringing some misery which looks to us beforehand quite unbearable—then how our lip belief and book-faith is tried and burnt up in the fire of God, in the fire of our own proud, angry hearts, too!

CHARLES KINGSLEY, *The Good News of God,* 1859

Wherever souls are being tried and ripened, in whatever commonplace and homely ways:—there God is hewing out the pillars for His temple.

PHILLIPS BROOKS (1835–1893), *Perennials*

See also Adversity; Affliction; Anxiety; Cross; Misfortune; Suffering; Tribulations.

TRIBULATIONS

Corn is not separated but by threshing, nor men from worldly impediments but by tribulation.

> ST. JOHN CHRYSOSTOM, *Hom. 2 in 3 Matt.*, c. 388

With whatever kind of tribulation we may be afflicted, we should always keep this end in view, to habituate ourselves to a contempt of the present life that we may thereby be excited to meditation on that which is to come.

> JOHN CALVIN, *Institutes*, III, 1536

See also Adversity; Affliction; Anxiety; Bereavement; Cross; Misery; Misfortune; Peace of Mind; Sadness; Sorrow; Suffering; Tragedy; Trials; Troubles.

TRINITY

The Trinity is One God, not so that the Father be the same Person, who is also the Son and the Holy Ghost; but that the Father be the Father, and the Son be the Son, and the Holy Ghost be the Holy Ghost, and this Trinity One God.

> ST. AUGUSTINE, *Of the Faith and of the Creed*, c. 393

The operations of the Trinity are indivisible, even as the essence of the Trinity is indivisible.

> ST. AUGUSTINE, *De. Trin.*, c. 397

We worship one God in Trinity, and Trinity in Unity, neither confounding the Persons, nor dividing the substance, for there is one Person of the Father, another of the Son, and another of the Holy Ghost; but the godhead of the Father, of the Son, and of the Holy Ghost is one, the glory equal, the majesty co-eternal.

> *Athanasian Creed*, c. 500

For we recognize one God, but only in the attributes of Fatherhood, Sonship, and

Procession, both in respect of cause and effect and perfection of subsistence, that is, manner of existence, do we perceive difference.

> ST. JOHN OF DAMASCUS (675–749), *Exposition of the Orthodox Faith*

God, considered not in Himself but as the cause of all things, has three aspects: He is, He is wise, and He lives. His being is called the Father, His wisdom the Son, His life is called the Holy Ghost, words which denote not the three aspects themselves, but their relation to each other.

> JOHANNES SCOTUS ERIGENA, *The Division of Nature*, 867

Although the Son and the Holy Ghost are in a certain sense derived from the Father, so that only the Father is without any source, they are in no wise created by Him, but are coeternal and coessential with Him.

> JOHANNES SCOTUS ERIGENA, *The Division of Nature*, 867

How can plurality consist with unity, or unity with plurality? To examine the fact closely is rashness, to believe it is piety, to know it is life, and life eternal.

> ST. BERNARD, *De Consideratione*, c. 1150

The Persons themselves are nothing else than one God, one divine Substance, one divine Nature, one divine and supreme Majesty.

> ST. BERNARD, *De Consideratione*, c. 1150

When we speak of the Trinity, we must do so with caution and modesty, for, as St. Augustine saith, nowhere else are more dangerous errors made, or is research more difficult, or discovery more fruitful.

> ST. THOMAS AQUINAS, *Summa Theologiae*, ia q. xxxi, 1272

What doth it profit thee to discuss the deep mystery of the Trinity, if thou art lacking

in humility and so displeasing to the Trinity. . . . I would rather choose to feel compunction than to know its definition.
THOMAS À KEMPIS, *Imitation of Christ*, 1441

All those who believe in a Trinity in the essence of God are tritheists . . . true atheists.
MICHAEL SERVETUS, *De Trinitatis Erroribus*, 1531

If there be three distinct and separate Persons, then three distinct and separate Substances. . . . And since the Father is God, the Son is God, and the Spirit is God . . . then unless the Father, Son and Spirit are three distinct Nothings, they must be three distinct Substances, and consequently three distinct Gods.
WILLIAM PENN, *Sandy Foundation Shaken*, 1667

There is one divine essence which is called and is God, eternal without body, indivisible, of infinite power and goodness, the Creator and Preserver of all Things Visible and Invisible Alike. Yet there are three persons of essence and power who are also co-eternal.
Augsburg Confession, 1630

The three persons in the Godhead are three in one sense and one in another. We cannot tell how—and that is the mystery.
SAMUEL JOHNSON, *Boswell's Life*, August 22, 1773

God is recognized as *Spirit* only when known as the Triune. This new principle is the axis on which the History of the World turns. "When the fullness of the time was come, God sent his Son," is the statement of the Bible. This means nothing else than that *self-consciousness* has reached the phase of development whose resultant constitutes the Idea of Spirit.
G. W. F. HEGEL (1770–1831), *The Philosophy of History*

Power, Love, Wisdom—there you have a real trinity which makes up the Jewish God.
ISRAEL ZANGWILL, *Children of the Ghetto*, 1892

The Church is accustomed most fittingly to attribute to the Father those works of the divinity in which power excels, to the Son those in which wisdom excels, and those in which love excels to the Holy Ghost.
POPE LEO XIII, *The Holy Spirit*, 1904

Theoretically it [the Trinity] is the affirmation of a full rich life in God as distinct from all abstract and barren conceptions of his being. Practically, it is the affirmation that the true nature of God must be learned from his historic revelation in Christ, and from the experience which Christ creates.
WILLIAM ADAMS BROWN, *Christian Theology in Outline*, 1906

The existence in Three Persons of the one Godhead is the foundation of the supernatural order; that is, of the communication by God to His free and intelligent creatures of His own life and happiness.
VALENTIN-M. BRETON, *The Blessed Trinity*, 1934

In the liturgical life of [Russian] Orthodoxy . . . the name of the Holy Trinity predominates over the name of Jesus, which shows that the knowledge of Christ is inseparably connected with that of the Holy Trinity.
SERGIUS BULGAKOV, *The Orthodox Church*, 1935

The doctrine of the Trinity . . . is more satisfactory than all the ancient and modern pantheons wherein we ascend beyond the many gods or values to someone who is limited by them.
H. RICHARD NIEBUHR, *The Meaning of Revelation*, 1941

In the mystery of the Trinity . . . lies the chief infraction against the faith of Israel, which rests on the certainty of a free and direct communication between Creator and Creation.

> FRANZ WERFEL, *Between Heaven and Earth*, 1944

Why do you complain that the proposition God is three in one is obscure and mystical and yet acquiesce meekly in the physicist's fundamental formula "two P minus PQ equals IH over two Pi where I equals the square root of minus I" when you know quite well that the square root of I is paradoxical and Pi is incalculable?

> DOROTHY L. SAYERS, *Current Religious Thought*, 1947

It is the presence of the Triune God, Whose glory is veiled from us in the darkness of our faith, which is the tremendous fact, the mystery of grace underlying all man's experience of Divinity.

> AELRED GRAHAM, *Catholicism and the World Today*, 1952

Between the Trinity and Hell there lies no other choice.

> V. LOSSKY, *The Mystical Theology of the Eastern Church*, 1957

It affirms that the mystery of God is to be defined by means of the character of Jesus Christ. . . . It asserts that the love which we see is Jesus Christ, and experience in the Holy Spirit, is one with the eternal power and being of Almighty God.

> LANGDON GILKEY, *Maker of Heaven and Earth*, 1959

The Trinity is not necessary. . . . Our Lord never heard of it. The apostles knew nothing of it.

> JAMES A. PIKE, *Sermon*, New York City, August 30, 1964

See also God: Considered as Personal; God: Fatherhood of; God: His Nature; other rubrics under God; Holy Spirit; Incarnation; Jesus Christ; Mystery; Spirit.

TROUBLES

As the earth is but a point in respect of the heavens, so are earthly troubles compared to heavenly joys.

> GEORGE HERBERT, *Letter to his mother*, May 29, 1622

There are many troubles which you cannot cure by the Bible and the Hymn Book, but which you can cure by a good perspiration and a breath of fresh air.

> HENRY WARD BEECHER, *Life Thoughts*, 1858

To suffer and endure is the lot of humankind. Let them strive as they may, they will never summon up enough strength and cunning to throw off the ills and troubles which beset them.

> POPE LEO XIII, *Rerum Novarum*, May 15, 1891

Man's freedom is never in being saved troubles, but it is the freedom to take trouble for his own good, and to make the trouble an element in his joy.

> RABINDRANATH TAGORE, *Sādhanā*, 1913

See also Adversity; Affliction; Anxiety; Calamity; Cross; Misfortune; Peace; Trials; Tribulations.

TRUE

The true is Godlike; we do not see it itself; we guess at it through its manifestations.

> J. W. VON GOETHE (1749–1832), *Maxims and Reflections*, ed. B. Saunders

See also Truth.

TRUST

Delay not the health of thy soul through trust in friends or in neighbors; for men will forget sooner than thou thinkest; it is better to make provision betimes and send before thee some good than to trust in other men's help.

THOMAS À KEMPIS, *Imitation of Christ,* 1441

Put thy full trust in God. Let him be thy love and dread above all things, and he will answer for thee and will do for thee in all things as shall be most needful and most expedient for thee.

THOMAS À KEMPIS, *Imitation of Christ,* 1441

The more miserable we know ourselves to be, the more occasion we have to confide in God, since we have nothing in ourselves in which to confide.

ST. FRANCIS OF SALES (1561–1622), *Consoling Thoughts of,* ed. Huguet

A man who should act, for one day, on the supposition that all the people about him were influenced by the religion which they professed, would find himself ruined before night.

T. B. MACAULAY, *Edinburgh Review,* January, 1831

Things infinite and divine . . . are given not so much for definition as for trust; are less the objects we think of than the very tone and color of our thought, the tension of our love, the unappeasable thirst of grief and reverence.

JAMES MARTINEAU, *Hours of Thought on Sacred Things,* 1879

Every relationship of trust between two men has its roots in a faith which extends far beyond their relation to one another, the faith that there exists an obligation valid for all subjects, all places and all times.

KARL HEIM, *The Certitudes of Faith,* 1923

When we grow afraid of life and death, let us have the sense of the trustworthiness of the universe, of its encompassing embrace and its sustaining care.

JOSHUA LOTH LIEBMAN, *Peace of Mind,* 1946

Can anyone think of believing in God without trusting Him? Is it possible to trust in God for the big things like forgiveness and eternal life, and then refuse to trust Him for the little things like clothing and food?

OSWALD C. J. HOFFMANN, *Life Crucified,* 1959

Sin arises out of mistrust. Man is afraid to trust the divine destiny and to accept his limits. The rebellion that follows is a decisive act of repudiation, a trusting of self over against God.

JAMES I. McCORD, *The Nature of Man,* ed. S. Doniger, 1962

See also Confidence; Faith; Optimism; Providence.

TRUTH

Those who know the truth are not equal to those who love it.

CONFUCIUS, *Analects,* c. 500 B.C.

To be absolutely sure of the truth of matters concerning which there are many opinions is an attribute of God not given to man.

PLATO, *Laws,* c. 360 B.C.

Truth is the beginning of every good thing, both in Heaven and on earth; and he who would be blessed and happy should be from the first a partaker of the truth, for then he can be trusted.

PLATO, *Laws,* c. 360 B.C.

The high-minded man must care more for the truth than for what people think.

ARISTOTLE, *Nicomachean Ethics,* c. 240 B.C.

This alone truth sometimes craves, that it be not condemned unheard.

TERTULLIAN, *Apolog.,* 197 A.D.

All truth wherever it is found belongs to us as Christians.

> St. Justin Martyr, *Second Apology,* 2nd century

We believe that there is no body of philosophers however wrong, no individual however stupid, who has not had at least a glimpse of the truth.

> Lactantius, *Inst. Div. VII,* c. 310

Turn not to the outside world! Into thine own self go back! In the inner man alone resides truth.

> St. Augustine, *On True Religion,* 390

The sweetness of truth is eternal.

> St. Augustine (354–430), *De Verb. Dom. Serm.*

Becoming, as it were, a ladder between earth and heaven, Truth repaired God's original ladder smashed in Adam.

> St. Bonaventure, *The Journey of the Mind to God,* 1259

If God were able to backslide from truth I would fain cling to truth and let God go.

> Meister Eckhart (1260?–1327?), *Meister Eckhart*

When all treasures are tried . . . truth is the fairest.

> William Langland, *Piers Plowman,* c. 1400

Truth, which only doth judge itself, teacheth, that the inquiry of Truth, which is the love-making, or wooing of it; the knowledge of Truth, which is the presence of it; and the belief of Truth, which is the enjoyment of it; is the sovereign good of human nature.

> Francis Bacon, *Essays,* 1597

Although it may not be always advisable to say all that is true, yet it is never allowable to speak against the truth.

> St. Francis of Sales, *Introduction to the Devout Life,* 1609

Truth is as impossible to be soiled by any outward touch as the sunbeam.

> John Milton, *Doctrine and Discipline of Divorce,* 1633

For who knows not that truth is strong, next to the Almighty; she needs no policies, nor stratagems, nor licensings to make her victorious, those are the shifts and the defenses that error uses against her power: give her but room, and do not bind her when she sleeps, for then she speaks not true.

> John Milton, *Aeropagitica,* 1644

Truth is more ancient than error, for error is nothing else but deviation and swerving from truth.

> John Hales (1584–1666), *Private Judgment in Religion*

'Tis incredible what a vast good a little truth might do, spoken in such seasons.

> Alexander Pope, *Letter to William Wycherley,* June 23, 1705

For tho' every Truth is One, yet our Sight is so feeble, that we cannot (always) come to it Directly, but by many Inferences, and laying of things together.

> Charles Leslie, *Certainty of the Christian Religion,* 1719

Truth makes the Devil blush.

> Thomas Fuller, *Gnomologia,* 1732

The credibility, or the certain truth of a matter of fact does not immediately prove anything concerning the wisdom or goodness of it.

> Joseph Butler, *The Analogy of Religion,* 1736

Deal ingenuously with truth, and love all [of] it for itself.

> Benjamin Whichcote, *Moral and Religious Aphorisms,* 1753

Not the truth which a man possesses or thinks he possesses, but the steadfast task to which he has applied himself of striving after truth, is the true worth of man.

> G. E. LESSING, *Duplik in Werke,* XIII, 23, 1778

If God had all truth shut in his right hand, and in his left nothing but the ever-restless search after truth, although with the condition of for ever and ever erring, and should say to me, "Choose!" I should bow humbly to his left hand and say, "Father, give! pure truth is for Thee alone!"

> G. E. LESSING, *Eine Duplik,* 1780

Such is the irresistible nature of truth that all it asks, and all it wants, is the liberty of appearing. The sun needs no inscription to distinguish him from darkness.

> THOMAS PAINE, *The Rights of Man,* 1791

To hate truth as truth . . . is the same as to hate goodness for its own sake.

> ETHAN ALLEN, *Reason the Only Oracle of Man,* 1794

Truth is the golden girdle of the world.

> WILLIAM COWPER (1731–1808), "Charity," *Poems*

It is one thing to wish to have truth on our side, and another to wish sincerely to be on the side of truth.

> RICHARD WHATELEY, *On the Love of Truth,* 1825

Man passes away; generations are but shadows; there is nothing stable but truth.

> JOSIAH QUINCY, *Speech,* September 17, 1830

It is not always needful for truth to take a definite shape: it is enough if it hovers about us like a spirit and produces harmony: if it is wafted through the air like the sound of a bell, grave and kindly.

> J. W. VON GOETHE (1749–1832), *Maxisms and Reflections,* translated by B. Saunders

Love of truth shows itself in this, that a man knows how to find and value the good in everything.

> J. W. VON GOETHE (1749–1832), *Maxims and Reflections,* ed. B. Saunders

He in whom love of truth predominates will keep himself aloof from all moorings, and afloat.

> RALPH WALDO EMERSON, "Intellect," *Essays, First Series,* 1841

He that speaks the truth executes no private function of an individual will, but the world utters a sound by his lips.

> RALPH WALDO EMERSON, "Character," *Essays, Second Series,* 1844

Nothing is mightier than we, when we are vehicle of a truth before which the State and the individual are alike ephemeral.

> RALPH WALDO EMERSON, *The Young American,* 1844

Truth never yet fell dead in the streets; it has such affinity with the soul of man, the seed however broadcast will catch somewhere, and produce its hundred fold.

> THEODORE PARKER, *A Discourse of Matter Pertaining to Religion,* 1845

A sincere attachment to truth, moral and scientific, is a habit which cures a thousand little infirmities of mind.

> SYDNEY SMITH (1771–1845), *Wit and Wisdom of*

Ethical truth is as exact and peremptory as physical truth.

> HERBERT SPENCER, *Social Statics,* 1851

Men esteem truth remote, in the outskirts of the system, behind the farthest star, before Adam and after the last man. In eternity there is indeed something true and sublime. But all these times and places and occasions are now and here.

> HENRY DAVID THOREAU, *Walden,* 1854

Truths and roses have thorns about them.
HENRY DAVID THOREAU, *Walden*, 1854

The simplest and most necessary truths are always the last believed.
JOHN RUSKIN, *Modern Painters*, 1856

Truths are first clouds; then rain, then harvest and food.
HENRY WARD BEECHER, *Life Thoughts*, 1858

You can pass your hand under the largest mob, a nation in revolution even. . . . But an individual standing on truth you cannot pass your hand under, for his foundations reach to the centre of the universe.
HENRY DAVID THOREAU (1817–1862), *Journal*

There is no ultimate test of truth besides the testimony borne to truth by the mind itself.
JOHN HENRY NEWMAN, *A Grammar of Assent*, IX, 1870

So long as we are able to distinguish any space whatever between the truth and us we remain outside it.
HENRI AMIEL, *Journal of*, 1882

He who sets out in search of Truth must leave Superstition forever and wander down into the land of Absolute Negation and Denial. He must then go . . . where the mountains of Stern Reality will rise before him. *Beyond* them lies Truth.
OLIVE SCHREINER, *Story of an African Farm*, 1883

It is the customary fate of new truths to begin as heresies and to end as superstitions.
THOMAS HENRY HUXLEY, *The Coming of Age of "The Origin of Species,"* 1893

The key of the world is given into our hands when we throw ourselves unreserv-

edly into the service of the highest truth we know.
G. S. MERRIAM, *The Chief End of Man*, 1897

Truth is given the eternal years of God because she needs them every one.
THOMAS B. REED, *Speech*, July 25, 1902

The truths which are not translated into lives are dead truths, and not living truths.
WOODROW WILSON, *Address*, October, 1904

Be not content to know the Truth; rouse your heart to love it.
B. W. MATURIN, *Self-Knowledge and Self-Discipline*, 1905

Truth is immortal, error is mortal. . . . Truth is intelligent; error is non-intelligent. Moreover Truth is real, and error is unreal.
MARY BAKER EDDY, *Science and Health*, 1908

A thing is not truth until it is so strongly believed in that the believer is convinced that its existence does not depend on him. This cuts off the pragmatist from knowing what truth is.
JOHN JAY CHAPMAN, *Essays*, 1910

The truth may be one, final, determined, but my apprehension of it can never be anything of the kind; it is changing continuously.
BEDE JARRETT, *Meditations for Layfolk*, 1915

Let each of us look for truth where it is most accessible and where it speaks the language he best understands.
L. P. JACKS, *Religious Perplexities*, 1922

We will not believe that the final truth is not *in* us and that it must come *to* us in a singular, external event in history.
EMIL BRUNNER, *The Theology of Crisis*, 1929

I cannot prove scientifically that truth must be conceived as a truth that is valid independent of humanity; but I believe it firmly.

ALBERT EINSTEIN, to Tagore, July, 1930, quoted in Rabindrinath Tagore, *The Religion of Man*, Appendix, II

Eternal truths . . . are . . . tenets which the remotest ancestors of man are reputed to have held, and which his remotest descendants are forbidden to abandon.

GEORGE SANTAYANA, *The Realm of Truth*, 1938

Truth is a kingdom which belongs to those who give themselves to it, lead where it may, cost what it will, use or no use.

RALPH W. SOCKMAN, *The Highway of God*, 1941

It is neither possible for man to know the truth fully nor to avoid the error of pretending that he does.

REINHOLD NIEBUHR, *Human Destiny*, 1943

One of the supreme hours of human experience arrives when a man gets his eye on something concerning which he is persuaded that it is the eternal truth.

HARRY EMERSON FOSDICK, *A Great Time to Be Alive*, 1944

The modern world, because indifferent to dogmatic truth, has logically become indifferent to ethical truth.

BERTRAND L. CONWAY, *The Church and Eugenics*, 1951

Truth is not for or against anything; truth simply is.

AELRED GRAHAM, *Christian Thought and Action*, 1951

Since there is no complete truth, our movement toward it is itself the only form in which truth can achieve completion in existence, here and now.

KARL JASPERS, *Tragedy Is Not Enough*, 1952

Truth is eternal, but there are degrees and varieties in the disclosure of truth, and in the way it is received.

SARVEPALLI RADHAKRISHNAN, *The Philosophy of*, 1952

Ever since the advent of conscienceless perjury under oath, the abuse of the Fifth Amendment, big-time huckstering, the insanity plea and quiz programs—in short, ever since the formal disappearance of truth in our civilization, it has become not only prohibitively difficult to find anyone, even the most impudent and cynical evildoers, guilty of anything.

VINCENT P. McCORRY, *America*, February 20, 1960

Never to have seen the truth is better than to have seen it and not to have acted upon it.

ANONYMOUS

He who dies for the truth finds holy ground everywhere for his grave.

German Proverb

See also Absolutes; Agnosticism; Agnostics; Art and Christianity; Beauty; Belief; Believing; Bible and Doctrine; Christianity; Christians; Conversion; Creeds; Devil; Dhamma; Doctrine; Doubt; Education; Enlightenment; Error; Evolution; Exclusiveness; Faith, False, the; Falsehood; Good; Happiness; Heart; Holy Spirit; Ignorance; Integrity; Justice; Knowledge; Liars and Lies; Man's Quest of God; Mind; Moral Truth; Philosophy; Pragmatism; Reality; Reason; Relativity; Religion; Its Nature and Function; Revelation; Risk; Salvation; Scandal; Scholars; Science; Science and God; Speech; Superstition; Theism; Time; Truth, Definitions of; Truth and Religion; Truths, Conflict of; Understanding; Unity; Veracity; Wisdom.

TRUTH, DEFINITIONS OF

That which is.

PLATO, "Euthydemus," *Dialogues*, 4th century B.C.

Truth is an immortal and eternal thing. It bestows, not a beauty which time will wither, nor a boldness of which the sentence of a judge can deprive us; but [the knowledge of] what is just and lawful, distinguishing from them, and confuting what is unjust.

> Attributed to Epictetus (60–140 A.D.), *Fragments–Morals Discourses*

Truth is indeed one name for Nature, the first cause of all things true.

> MARCUS AURELIUS, *Meditations,* c. 170

Truth is the aristocracy of language.

> SYNESIUS OF CYRENE (died 414), *Essays and Hymns of*

Rightness perceptible to the mind alone. . . . Rightness distinguishes it from every other thing which is called rightness. . . . Truth and rightness and justice define each other.

> ST. ANSELM, *Dialogue on Truth,* c. 1080

Truth is simply one in the divine mind, but many truths flow thence into the human mind, as one face may be mirrored with variety.

> ST. THOMAS AQUINAS, *De Veritate,* 1259

Truth is the daughter of Time.

> ELIZABETH GRYMESTON, *Miscellanea— Meditations,* 1604

I say that as concerns the truth, of which mathematical demonstrations gives us the knowledge, it is the same as that which the Divine Wisdom knows.

> GALILEO, *Dialogue on the Great World Systems,* 1632

Whatever satisfies the soul is truth.

> WALT WHITMAN, *Leaves of Grass* (Preface to edition of 1855)

The deepest truths we can reach, are simply statements of the widest uniformities in our experience of the relations of Matter, Motion, and Force.

> HERBERT SPENCER, *First Principles,* 1862

Where you find the general permanent voice of humanity agreeing with the voice of your conscience, be sure that you hold in your grasp something of absolute truth —gained and forever yours.

> JOSEPH MAZZINI, *Essays,* 1887

Truth is a property of certain of our ideas. It means their "agreement," as falsity means their "disagreement" with "reality." . . . True ideas are those that we can assimilate, validate, corroborate and verify.

> WILLIAM JAMES, *Pragmatism,* 1907

Truth is essentially a relation between two things, an idea, on the one hand, and a reality outside of the idea, on the other.

> WILLIAM JAMES, *The Meaning of Truth,* 1907

Truth is the system of propositions which have an unconditional claim to be recognized as valid.

> A. E. TAYLOR, *Philosophical Review,* XIV, 1908

The conformation of Appearance to Reality. This conformation may be more or less, also direct or indirect. Thus Truth is a generic quality with a variety of degrees and modes.

> ALFRED NORTH WHITEHEAD, *Adventures in Ideas,* 1933

The truth is all things seen under the form of eternity.

> GEORGE SANTAYANA, *The Realm of Truth,* 1938

Truth is a quality belonging primarily to judgments, and whatever our views as to its ultimate nature, I think we might all agree that a judgment is true when and only when it states a fact.

> WILLIAM PEPPERELL MONTAGUE, *Ways of Knowing,* 1940

What we essentially mean by truth is the matching of our human minds with something akin to them.
  D. E. TRUEBLOOD, *The Logic of Belief,* 1942

Truth is God's daughter.
  Proverb

See also Error; Falsehood; Reality; Truth; Wisdom.

TRUTH AND RELIGION

There is no need to seek of others the truth it is so easy to obtain from the Church; since the Apostles, like a rich man depositing his money in a bank, have deposited in her the fullness of all truth, so that who wills may drink of the waters of life.
  ST. IRENAEUS, *Contra Haereses,* lib. III, c. 175

That alone is to be believed as truth which in no way differs from the ecclesiastical and Apostolic tradition.
  ORIGEN, *Liber de Principiis,* c. 254

No one draws closer to a knowledge of the truth than he who has advanced far in the knowledge of divine things, and yet knows that something always remains for him to seek.
  ST. LEO (390?–461), *Sermon in Nativitate Domini,* IX

As what is true cannot contradict what is true, we determine that every proposition which is contrary to the truth of the revealed faith is entirely false.
  Lateran Council, 1512

If we reflect that the Spirit of God is the only fountain of truth, we will be careful, as we would avoid offering insult to Him, not to reject or contemn truth wherever it appears.
  JOHN CALVIN, *Institutes,* II. 536

Truth indeed came once into the world with her Divine Master, and was a perfect shape most glorious to look on.
  JOHN MILTON, *Areopagitica,* 1644

The truth of our religion, like the truth of common matters, is to be judged by all the evidence taken together.
  JOSEPH BUTLER, *The Analogy of Religion,* II, 1736

There is nothing unreasonable in the notion that there may have been heathen poets and sages, or sibyls again, in a certain extent divinely illuminated, and organs through whom religious and moral truth was conveyed to their countrymen.
  JOHN HENRY NEWMAN, *The Arians of the Fourth Century,* 1833

Religious Truth is neither light nor darkness, but both together; it is like the dim view of a country seen in the twilight, with forms half extricated from the darkness with broken lines, and isolated masses.
  JOHN HENRY NEWMAN, *Essays and Sketches,* Vol. I, 1835

Religious truth is not only a presentation, but a condition of general knowledge.
  JOHN HENRY NEWMAN, *The Idea of a University,* 1852

A Revelation is religious doctrine viewed on its illuminated side; a Mystery is the selfsame doctrine viewed on the side unilluminated. Thus Religious Truth is neither light nor darkness, but both together.
  JOHN HENRY NEWMAN, *Essays Critical and Historical,* I, 1871

Man discovers truth by reason only, not by faith.
  LEO TOLSTOY, *On Life,* 1887

If we could grasp the whole truth at a glance, as the Logos does, we should see what now is dark to us.
  JOSIAH ROYCE, *The Spirit of Modern Philosophy,* 1889

The only truth of religion comes from its interpretation of life, from its symbolic rendering of that moral experience which it springs out of and which it seeks to elucidate.

GEORGE SANTAYANA, *Reason in Religion*, 1905

To comprehend the truth rationality itself must conform to all the laws of the spiritual world . . . and be related to all the vital and moral forces of the spirit.

ALEKSEI KHONYSKOV, *Satchineniya*, 1911

Truth is meant to save you first, and the comfort comes afterwards.

GEORGES BERNANOS, *The Diary of a Country Priest*, 1937

Veritas is presupposed in every philosophical argument; and Veritas is God.

PAUL H. TILLICH, *Union Seminary Quarterly Review*, May, 1946

There are men who claim to love the truth. But if a truth comes from God, they reject it and veil their faces like hypocrites and pharisees.

BRUCE MARSHALL, *Father Malachy's Miracle*, 1947

I believe in the message of truth delivered by all the religious teachers of the world.

M. K. (MAHATMA) GANDHI (1869–1948), *The Essential Gandhi*, ed. L. Fischer, 1962

A spiritual truth is valid only when it does not contradict universal reason, one's inner experience, and the experience of other seers of truth.

SWAMI NIKHILANANDA, *Perspectives on a Troubled Decade*, ed. Bryson, Finkelstein and MacIver, 1950

Truth as it exists in God's mind has a royalty of its own; banish it from the earth if you will, by police measures, but it will still reign a monarch in exile.

RONALD A KNOX, *Stimuli*, 1951

Christ likes us to prefer truth to him because, before being Christ, he is truth. If one turns aside from him to go towards the truth, one will not go far before falling into His arms.

SIMONE WEIL, *Waiting for God*, 1951

Man is not free to pick and choose among the truths God has made known either through reason or revelation. His obligation is to accept the whole of God's truth.

Catholic Bishops of U.S., November, 1952

Sunlight shining through a prism is broken into different colors. Likewise the truth radiating from God strikes human minds in varied shades of experience. We cannot therefore expect uniformity of doctrine and worship.

RALPH W. SOCKMAN, *How to Believe*, 1953

Religion lends itself particularly to the pretensions of possessing absolute truth and virtue by finite and sinful men.

REINHOLD NIEBUHR, *The Self and the Drama of History*, 1955

The quiet voice of sober truth wins out in the long run against the strident noise of passion, provided it does not hesitate to appeal to the deepest foundations of our existence, to the work of God Himself.

JOHN LA FARGE, *An American Amen*, 1958

See also Church: Its Nature; Division; Doctrine; Faith; Holy Spirit; Logos; Religion; Tradition; Truth.

TRUTHS, CONFLICT OF

If we want truth, every man ought to be free to say what he thinks without fear. If the advocates of one side are to be rewarded with miters, and the advocates on the other with rope or stake, truth will not be heard.

DESIDERIUS ERASMUS, *Letter to Cardinal Campeggio*, December 6, 1520

And though all the winds of doctrine were let loose to play upon earth, so Truth be in the field, we do injuriously, by licensing and prohibiting, to misdoubt her strength. Let her and falsehood grapple. Whoever knew Truth put to the worse in a free and open encounter?

JOHN MILTON, *Areopagitica,* 1644

Truth often suffers more by the heat of its defenders, than from the arguments of its opposers.

WILLIAM PENN, *Fruits of Solitude,* 1693

The truths of divine revelation and those of nature cannot really be opposed to one another, and . . . whatever is at variance with them must necessarily be false.

POPE LEO XIII, *Libertas Humana,* 1888

The best test of truth is the power of the thought to get itself accepted in the competition of the market.

JUSTICE OLIVER WENDELL HOLMES, Dissenting opinion, *Abrams vs. U.S.,* 1919

There can be no conflict between philosophical and theological truths, although theologians may correct the errors of philosophers who try to answer questions beyond the competence of natural reason, just as philosophers can correct the errors of theologians who violate the autonomy of reason.

MORTIMER ADLER, *Vital Speeches,* December, 1949

There is a tragic clash between Truth and the world. Pure undistorted Truth burns up the world.

NICHOLAS BERDYAEV, *The Divine and the Human,* 1949

See also Bible and History; Conflict; Disputation; Error; Falsehood; Freedom of Thought and Speech; Paths.

TWENTIETH CENTURY

It is the first century since life began when a decisive part of the most articulate section of mankind has not merely ceased to believe in God, but has deliberately rejected God. And it is the century in which this religious rejection has taken a specifically religious form.

WHITTAKER CHAMBERS, *Witness,* 1952

TYRANTS

Nothing is more abhorrent to the tyrant than the service of Christ and a virtuous Christian life. For these are diametrically opposed to his own habits.

GIROLAMO SAVONAROLA, *Sermon Against Tyrants,* 1497

Tyrants of every description have never deceived themselves; since Caiphas and the Caesars, down to the masters of Germany yesterday and those of Russia today, a very sure instinct has taught them to see their deepest and most dangerous enemy in Christianity.

GUSTAVE THIBON, *Christianity and Freedom,* 1952

See also Allegiance; Authoritarianism; Authority; Dictatorship; Kings; Rebellion; Rulers; State, the.

UNBELIEF

To him that believeth not in Christ, not only all his sins are damnable, but even his good works are also sins.

MARTIN LUTHER, *Commentary on Galatians,* 1531

He never truly believed, who was not made first sensible and convinced of unbelief.

SAMUEL TAYLOR COLERIDGE, *Aids to Reflection,* 1825

The history of contemporary unbelief is worthy of note: it is the key to all the remarkable happenings of modern times.
NOVALIS, *Christendom or Europe*, 1826

Alas! the fearful Unbelief is unbelief in yourself.
THOMAS CARLYLE, *Sartor Resartus*, 1836

Jesus is "curtained from the sight of the gross world" by the wilful unbelief of mankind.
CHARLES H. SPURGEON, *The Saint and His Saviour*, 1858

There is no such thing as "unconscious faith," but those who plead it in their own behalf do not possess it. With them it is conscious unbelief.
JOHN KER, *Thoughts for Heart and Life*, 1888

It seems to me there is a great change come over the world since people like us believed in God.
KATHERINE MANSFIELD (1888–1923), *Letters*

In the history of Christianity, just because it is the religion of revelation, the sin is, as it were, committed with a high hand. Yes, sin! For contradiction against grace is unbelief, and unbelief is sin. Indeed it is *the* sin.
KARL BARTH, *Church Dogmatics*, I, 3, 17, 1938

Sin is always unbelief. And unbelief is always man's faith in himself.
KARL BARTH, *Church Dogmatics*, 2nd half-vol., 1938

There is something tragic in the spectacle of a man of intellect who has no fixed religious beliefs and wistfully confesses his longing for them.
GEORGE WHARTON PEPPER, *A Philadelphia Lawyer*, 1944

The waters of the oceans of God's love do come up into the tiny bays of our unbelief.
PETER MARSHALL, quoted by Catherine Marshall in her *A Man Called Peter*, 1951

To the man who is lacking in religious belief, nothing in the end is likely to be sacred, nothing worth preserving. In that direction lies the real danger to our country.
Roman Catholic Bishops of the U.S., 1952

Before seeking union by way of canonical or diplomatic dealings, a psychological and spiritual reconciliation must be sought, and feelings of confidence, and of real sympathy, aroused.
YVES CONGAR, *After Nine Hundred Years*, 1960

The forces of unbelief . . . exist in the free lands and unfortunately are imbued with a cynical and hostile attitude toward all religious beliefs. Even in the free lands their hostility is cloaked in the garment of freedom.
JEROME G. KERWIN, *Catholic Viewpoint on Church and State*, 1960

When we live by and live out the thought that "God is dead," our own self-understanding and our estimate of the being of others suffers radical alteration.
PAUL RAMSEY, *Nine Modern Moralists*, 1962

All religious systems, all faiths which are based upon God's intervention in the natural order are under the same pressure—the vast universal pressure of unbelief.
BARBARA WARD, *Way*, January-February, 1963

See also Agnosticism; Agnostics; Atheism; Atheists; Belief; Despair; Doubt; Existentialism; God, Nonexistence of; Godlessness; Humanism; Man: His Self-Deification; Materialism; Naturalism; Persecution; Religion: Its Decline; Religion, Necessity of; Secularism; Skepticism; Unbelievers.

UNBELIEVERS

We have thrown veils over their [unbelievers'] hearts lest they should understand the Koran, and into their ears a heaviness; and if thou bid them to the guidance, yet even then they will never be guided.
Koran, XVIII, c. 625 A.D.

Nearly all our powerful men in this age of the world are unbelievers; the best of them in doubt and misery; the worst in reckless defiance; the plurality in plodding hesitation.
JOHN RUSKIN, *Modern Painters,* III, 1856

Unbelievers call themselves rational; not because they decide by evidence, but because, after they have made their decision, they merely occupy themselves in sifting it.
JOHN HENRY NEWMAN, *Grammar of Assent,* 1870

It is the high-minded unbeliever, desperately trying in the teeth of repeated disillusions to retain his "faith in human nature" who is really sad.
C. S. LEWIS, *The Problem of Pain,* 1944

We are too ready to assume that we know, better than the unbeliever, what ails him.
THOMAS MERTON, *Way,* May, 1963

See also Unbelief and all the cross-references shown after Unbelief.

UNCERTAINTY

But that dread of something after death,
The undiscover'd country from whose bourn

No traveller returns, puzzles the will
And makes us rather bear those ills we have
Than fly to others that we know not of?
Thus conscience does make cowards of us all;
And thus the native hue of resolution
Is sicklied o'er with the pale cast of thought.
WILLIAM SHAKESPEARE, *Hamlet,* c. 1602

See also Belief; Certainty.

UNCHASTITY

If unchastity in a woman, whom St. Paul calls the glory of man, be such a scandal and dishonor, then certainly in a man, who is both the image and glory of God, it must, though commonly not so thought, be much more deflowering and dishonorable.
JOHN MILTON, *Second Defense of the People of England,* 1654

All forms of unchastity—incontinence and liberties among the married, solitary sin, artificial limitation of offspring, unchastity in thought, imagination and desire—have this in common; they isolate the sex pleasure, the self-centered and selfish elements in the whole love complex from the unselfish and sacred elements.
JOHN M. COOPER, *Religion Outlines for Colleges,* IV, 1930

See also Chastity; Immorality; Sex; Sexual Sin.

UNCONSCIOUS MIND

Immense hidden powers seem to lurk in the unconscious depths of even the most common men—indeed, of all people without exception.
FRITZ KUNKEL, *Creation Continues,* 1924

The modern soul is not going to find peace so long as he is locked up inside himself, mulling around in the scum and sediment of his unconscious mind, a prey of the unconscious forces whose nature and existence he glorifies.

> FULTON J. SHEEN, *Peace of Soul,* 1949

See also Freud; Freudianism; Psychiatrists; Psychiatry; Psychoanalysis.

UNCONVENTIONALITY

The Church cannot do its job without being unconventional from the standpoint of those who are accustomed to the conventions of the world.

> GEDDES MACGREGOR, *The Hemlock and the Cross,* 1963

UNDERSTANDING

If then the understanding is divine in comparison with men, the life of the understanding is divine in comparison with human life.

> ARISTOTLE, *Nicomachean Ethics,* c. 340 B.C.

What is most necessary for understanding divine things is prayer.

> ORIGEN, *Letter to Gregory Thaumaturgus,* c. 235 A.D.

It is the duty of the human understanding to understand that there are things which it cannot understand, and what those things are.

> SÖREN KIERKEGAARD, *Philosophical Fragments,* 1844

I wish to understand in such a way that everything that is inexplicable shall present itself to me as *necessarily* inexplicable.

> LEO TOLSTOY, *My Confession,* 1887

To know a little less and to understand a little more: that, it seems to me, is our greatest need.

> JAMES RAMSEY ULLMAN, *The White Tower,* 1945

Religions are cut off from one another by barriers of mutual incomprehension . . . the sense of the absolute stands on a different plane in each of them.

> FRITHJOF SCHON, *Gnosis,* 1957

See also Belief; Error; Intellect; Knowledge; Light; Mystery; Reality; Reason; Truth; Wisdom.

UNHAPPINESS

Man's Unhappiness, as I construe, comes of his Greatness, it is because there is an Infinite in him, which with all his cunning he cannot quite bury under the Finite.

> THOMAS CARLYLE, *Sartor Resartus,* 1836

See also Adversity; Affliction; Gloom; Happiness; Misery; Pessimism; Sadness.

UNIONS. See LABOR UNIONS

UNITARIANS

The Unitarians, I think, come the nearest to having found a way to adapt the Christian ideas to the world we live in now.

> ALFRED NORTH WHITEHEAD, *Dialogues of,* September, 1945, as recorded by L. Price.

We [Unitarians] neither believe in the unique divinity of Jesus as the supernatural son of God nor in the human depravity which was supposed to make a supernatural savior necessary.

> ROBERT T. WESTON, *Faith Without Fear,* 1949

If to be a Christian is to profess and sincerely seek to practice the religion of Jesus, so simply and beautifully given in the Sermon on the Mount, then Unitarians are Christians.

> KARL M. CHWOROWSKY, "What Is a Unitarian?", *A Guide to the Religions of America,* ed. L. Rosten, 1955

The doctrines of atonement and resurrection, supposedly divinely revealed in the Christian Scriptures, have no meaning for us, since we could not believe that any man could by any act take from us or any others the responsibility for our own sins.
H. B. SCHOLEFIELD, *Guide to Unitarianism,* 1955

UNITED NATIONS. *See* INTERNATIONALISM

UNITED STATES. *See* AMERICA

UNITED STATES CONSTITUTION. *See* CONSTITUTION, U. S.

UNITY

Form all together one choir, so that, with the symphony of your feelings and having taken the tone from God, you may sing with one voice to the Father through Jesus Christ, that He may listen to you.
ST. IGNATIUS OF ANTIOCH, *Letter to the Ephesians,* c. 109

The Church in respect of its unity belongs to the category of things indivisible by nature. . . . The eminence of the Church arises from its unity, as the principle of its constitution—a unity surpassing all else, and having nothing like unto it or equal to it.
ST. CLEMENT OF ALEXANDRIA, *Stromatum,* lib. viii, c. 193

Let us hasten, therefore, to gather ourselves together unto salvation, in the new birth, in the one charity, on the pattern of that perfect unity that is in the one nature of God.
ST. CLEMENT OF ALEXANDRIA (died c. 215), *Protreptic*

In order to manifest unity, He has by His own authority so placed the source of the same unity, as to begin from one. Certainly the other Apostles also were what

Peter was, endued with an equal fellowship both of honor and power; but a commencement is made from unity, that the Church be set before us as one.
ST. CYPRIAN, *On the Unity of the Catholic Church,* to the Council of Carthage, 251

Does anyone believe that this unity [of the Christian association] can be severed in the Church and separated by the divorce of conflicting wills? . . . Who then is so criminal and faithless . . . that he . . . believes that the Church of Christ can be partitioned?
ST. CYPRIAN, *De Unit.,* cap. 6, 251

For when the Lord call his body the bread which is made up of many grains joined together, he means by that the union of all Christian people, which he contained within himself.
ST. CYPRIAN (200–258), *Hom. 46 in Joannem.*

It is impossible to keep men together in one religious denomination, whether true or false, except they be united by means of visible signs or sacraments.
ST. AUGUSTINE, *Contra Faust,* xix, c. 400

All united to the single Christ through his own body, all receiving him, the one and indivisible, into our own bodies, we are the members of this one body and he is thus, for us, the bond of unity.
ST. CYRIL OF ALEXANDRIA, (412–444), *In Joannem. II*

Those whom a holy love unites, even though they do not share the same gifts of grace, enjoy their benefits mutually, however, and that which they love together cannot be foreign to them, for to find joy in the progress of others increases their own riches.
POPE ST. LEO THE GREAT (440–461), quoted by Pope John XXIII, November 11, 1961

Unto the true unity of the Church it is sufficient to agree concerning the doctrine of the Gospel and the administration of the Sacraments: nor is it necessary that human traditions, rites, or ceremonies instituted by men should be alike everywhere.

PHILIP MELANCHTHON, *Augsburg Confession*, 1530

The true unity of the Church is not to be sought in ceremonies and rites, but in the truth and in the catholic faith, as laid down in the Scriptures and summed up in the Apostles' Creed.

HENRY BULLINGER, *The Helvetic Confession*, 1536

The true Church government is to leave the conscience to its full liberty . . . and to seek unity in the Light and in the Spirit, walking sweetly and harmoniously together in the midst of different practices.

ISAAC PENNINGTON (1616–1679), *Works*, Pt. I

The Humble, Meek, Merciful, Just, Pious, and Devout Souls, are everywhere of one religion; and when Death has taken off the Mask, they will know one another, tho' the divers Liveries they wear here make them Strangers.

WILLIAM PENN, *Some Fruits of Solitude*, 1693

I think all Christians, whether papists or Protestants, agree in the essential articles, and that their differences are trivial, and rather political than religious.

SAMUEL JOHNSON, *Boswell's Life of*, June 25, 1763

The totality of the gifts of the Holy Spirit are to be found only in the totality of believers. . . . All believers appear as parts integrating themselves into each other, so that they are perpetually referred to this fundamental law, that it is in unity and charity that the truth is to be found.

J. A. MOEHLER, *Die Einheit*, pt. i, ch. ii, 1825

Christendom must regain its life and vigor, and form itself once again into one visible Church without regard for national frontiers. It must pour out the old cornucopia of blessings on the people once again.

NOVALIS (1772–1801), *Christendom or Europe*, 1826

A clergyman was once asked whether the members of his church were united. He replied that they were perfectly united—frozen together.

Old Farmer's Almanac, 1865

There is one God, and one Christ; and His Church is one and the faith is one; and one the people, joined together in the solid unity of the body in the bond of concord.

POPE LEO XIII, *Satis Cognitum*, 1896

Whereas: in the providence of God the time has come when it seems fitting more fully to manifest the essential oneness of the Christian Churches of America in Jesus Christ as their divine Lord and Savior, and to promote the spirit of fellowship, service and cooperation among them.

Preamble to *Constitution* of Federal Council of Churches of Christ in America, proposed 1905, adopted 1908

One world, waiting surely, for who shall carry to it and place in its empty hands one Faith—the only thing that can ever truly and fundamentally unite it.

W. H. T. GAIRDNER, *Echoes from Edinburgh*, 1910

Any religion that is going to unite men . . . must have room for mystics, prophets, and for priests, and it must be a religion of such a character as will prevent the priests from stoning the prophets.

GEORGE BERNARD SHAW, *The New Commonwealth*, January 2, 1920

We need to find out, not a formula, but a temper—not a Creed, but a Faith—which is common to all, and which underlies all, and supports all, and inspires all.

T. H. BINDLEY, *The Modern Churchman,* September, 1921

The mystic, the authoritarian, the sacramentarian, the radical individualist, these —to mention only a few of the more outstanding types—must be reckoned with in any comprehensive program for Christian unity.

WILLIAM ADAM BROWN, *Christian Unity: Its Principles and Possibilities,* 1921

There is nothing in Christ that any one communion can monopolize. . . . We are coming to a common recognition of the elemental unity of life and experience among the churches.

ROBERT E. SPEER, *Address,* Atlanta, Ga., Federal Council of Churches of Christ in America, in *Report,* 1924

The sins and sorrow, the struggles and losses of the Great War and since have compelled the Christian churches to recognize, humbly and with shame, that the world is too strong for a divided Church.

Message of the Stockholm Conference of Churches, 1925

Nothing save communion with the Roman Pontiff, successor of Peter, provides the true principle of unity, and prevents the Church from splitting up into various national Churches, and, above all, imparts apostolicity of succession to the other Churches.

P. DE LA BRIÈRE, *De Christi Ecclesia,* 1926

At one place only do we stand together— where the religion of Jesus wells up in men of many creeds and churches so that, differing widely in every other respect, they exhibit a like quality and are manifestly baptized by the one Spirit.

HARRY EMERSON FOSDICK, *Adventurous Religion,* 1926

In order to be united we must love one another; in order to love one another we must know one another, in order to know one another we must meet one another.

DESIRÉ JOSEPH MERCIER (1851–1926), quoted in *The Monitor* (of San Francisco Roman Catholic Archdiocese), December, 1960

There is but one way in which the unity of Christians may be fostered and that is by furthering the return to the One True Church of Christ of those who are separated from it.

POPE PIUS XI, *Mortalium Animos,* 1927

In increasingly wide circles men are striving for unity. Lying at the centre of all and providing the only enduring cement is religious unity.

H. N. BATE, *Faith and Order World Conference,* 1928

In such great differences of opinions we do not know how a road may be paved to the unity of the Church save alone through one teaching authority, one sole law of belief and one sole faith among Christians.

POPE PIUS XI, *True Religious Unity,* January, 1928

The road to unity is the road to repentance. It demands resolute turning away from all those loyalties to the lesser values of the self, the denomination, and the nation, which deny the inclusiveness of divine love.

H. RICHARD NIEBUHR, *Social Sources of Denominationalism,* 1929

What is required is that Christians should have one mind as to what has been once for all revealed to the church.

FRANCIS J. HALL, *Christian Reunion in Ecumenical Light,* 1930

While Christians differ deeply about the nature of the Church, they all believe that there is, and can be, only one universal society acknowledging Jesus Christ as Lord.

> W. A. VISSER 'T HOOFT and J. H. OLD-HAM, *The Church and Its Function in Society,* 1937

We believe together that there is a Church in the churches but that we cannot say together how and where it exists, or how and where it functions.

> W. A VISSER 'T HOOFT and J. H. OLD-HAM, *The Church and Its Function in Society,* 1937

We recognize in one another, across the barriers of our separation, a common Christian outlook and a common standard of values.

> Second World Conference on Faith and Order, Edinburgh, 1937

Our unity is of heart and spirit. We are divided in the outward forms of our life in Christ, because we understand differently His will for His Church. . . . We humbly acknowledge that our divisions are contrary to the will of Christ.

> Second World Conference on Faith and Order, Edinburgh, 1937

How the principle of Christian democracy can be reproclaimed for the unity of the distorted and disunited Christendom constitutes one of the gravest problems before us today.

> FRANK GAVIN, *Seven Centuries of the Problem of Church and State,* 1938

To the extent to which the dissident Christianities have preserved the principles of communion with God left by Christ to His Church, there remains in them, with whatever mingling of errors, still something of the Church, some fibre of her being.

> YVES CONGAR, *Divided Christendom,* 1939

Underneath all differences of theological expression, there is a common gospel which makes the Church, in fact, one.

> WILLIAM A. BROWN, *A Teacher and His Times,* 1940

A divided world is seen more and more to call for a united Church if the hurt of that world is to be healed.

> EDWIN LEWIS, *A Philosophy of the Christian Revelation,* 1940

We hold to the unity and catholicity of the Church of Christ, and will unite with all its branches in hearty cooperation, and will earnestly seek, as far as in us lies, that the prayer of Our Lord may be answered that they all may be one.

> G. G. ATKINS and F. L. FAGLEY, *History of American Congregationalism,* 1941

A rapprochement between believers of diverse religious denominations can be accomplished, on the religious and spiritual level itself, only by and in friendship and charity, by and in pure spirituality and freedom of love.

> JACQUES MARITAIN, *Ransoming the Time,* 1941

The cause of Christian unity can best be served neither by religious controversy nor by political action, but by the theological virtues: faith, hope and charity. And these virtues must be applied both in the intellectual and religious spheres.

> CHRISTOPHER DAWSON, *The Judgment of the Nations,* 1942

Unity in worship, unity in doctrine, unity in life and action are necessary if the Christian Church is to be truly Christ's Body in history.

> JOHN A. MACKAY, *Toward World-Wide Christianity,* ed. F. Nolde, 1946

Though Christian faith sanctions no myth about the city of God as realizable on earth, it allies itself strongly with the human hope for unity in the city of man.

JOHN COURTNEY MURRAY, *Address, American Academy of Political and Social Science, Annals of,* March, 1948

We desire unity of religion but not when purchased at the cost of the unity of truth.

FULTON J. SHEEN, *Communism and the Conscience of the West,* 1948

Let them not believe, through false "irenism," that it is possible to bring about the happy return into the bosom of the Church of dissidents and those in error, without teaching to everybody, sincerely, the whole truth in force in the Church, without any corruption or elimination.

POPE PIUS XII, *Humani Generis,* August, 1950

The unity of the Old and the New Testament is not to be found in any naturalistic development, or in any static identity, but in the ongoing redemptive activity of God in the history of one people, reaching its fulfilment in Christ.

ALAN RICHARDSON and W. SCHWEITZER, *Biblical Authority for Today,* 1951

What makes non-Catholic Christians near to us of the Catholic Church is not simply that common brotherhood in a human nature which we share alike, but something much more significant, a "faith in God and in Jesus Christ."

AELRED GRAHAM, *Catholicism and the World Today,* 1952

The penalty when a particular Church loses contact, voluntarily or involuntarily, with that general stream of Christian life is severe. It is fossilizaticn—and ultimately death.

GREGORY DIX, *Jew and Greek,* 1953

Should not our Churches ask themselves . . . whether they should not act together in *all* matters except those in which differ-

ences of conviction compel them to act separately?

Third World Conference on Faith and Order, 1953

The whole notion of Christian solidarity grows out of, and is centered in, the common participation of a common table.

RONALD A. KNOX, *The Window in the Wall,* 1956

In order to have the right to live in separate Churches, we should have to be certain (to put it in broad general terms) that we were unmistakably disunited about the truth.

KARL RAHNER, *Tübinger Theologische Quartalschrift,* 1958

In spite of the existing difficulties, there is still very much common ground. Why then may we not believe that the Holy Spirit will lead to some *unexpected* solution? We all believe in the one Pentecost, why should we not expect a second one to come?

HAMILCAR ALIVISATOS, *Ecumenical Review,* October, 1959

Until the eschatological moment when we can break bread together around the Lord's Table, we must foster a spirit that will at least make it possible for us to break bread together around a dining room table.

ROBERT MCAFEE BROWN, *An American Dialogue,* 1960

The very problem of Christian reconciliation is not that of a *correlation* of parallel traditions, but precisely that of the *reintegration* of a distorted tradition.

GEORGES FLOROVSKY, *Ecumenical Review,* January, 1960

We believe that the unity which is God's will . . . is being made visible as all in each place who are baptized into Jesus Christ and confess him as Lord and Saviour are brought by the Holy Spirit into ONE fully committed fellowship, holding the one apostolic faith, preaching the one Gospel, breaking the one bread, joining in common prayer . . . united with the whole Christian fellowship . . . in such wise that the ministry and members are accepted by all.

> Commission on Faith and Order, World Council of Churches, 1960

If we really believe that our unity in Christ lies at a deeper level than our differences, we will find more and more ways of manifesting it in common action.

> SAMUEL McCREA CAVERT, *On the Road to Christian Unity,* 1961

The great dividing line is not between Christians who interpret Christ in different ways but between men who believe and men who do not believe that in Him God has entered into human history for our redemption.

> SAMUEL McCREA CAVERT, *On the Road to Christian Unity,* 1961

But our appeal for unity is intended to be, above all, an echo of the prayer which Our Savior addressed to His Divine Father at the Last Supper: "That all may be one, even as Thou, Father, in Me and I in Thee; that they may be one in Us."

> POPE JOHN XXIII, *Encyclical,* November 11, 1961

The achievement of unity will involve nothing less than a death and rebirth of many forms of Church life as we have known them. We believe that nothing less can fully suffice.

> *Statement,* Third Assembly of the World Council of Churches, New Delhi, India, 1961

Unity among men in the Church is the result, the reflection, of the event of the Father's Union with Christ by His Spirit realized in the historical Church on the day of Pentecost. . . . Unity is not an *attribute* of the Church, but it is its very *life.*

> N. NISSIOTIS, *Address,* Third Assembly of the World Council of Churches, November 24, 1961

If there cannot be immediate unity of faith, there must be unity of love, expressing itself in common effort in social, economic and political relations.

> JOHN J. WRIGHT, *Address,* Maynooth, Ireland, 1961

The breakdown of Christian unity in the sixteenth century was above all a division of faith; yet the separation was of necessity preceded by a breakdown of charity, and as long as charity founded on truth does not motivate and inspire, no ecumenical movement will succeed.

> JOHN P. DOLAN, *The Unfinished Reformation,* 1962

The Church's solicitude to promote and defend truth derives from the fact that . . . men without the assistance of the whole of revealed doctrine cannot reach a complete and firm unity of minds, with which are associated true peace and eternal salvation.

> POPE JOHN XXIII, October 18, 1962

The world's inability to achieve a unity of thought and to end spiritual divisions is the real reason society is so deeply unhappy, so poor in ideas and enthusiasm, and so lacking in shared spiritual concepts which are its own inner joy, nobility and strength.

> BARRETT McGURN, *A Reporter Looks at the Vatican,* 1962

Christian unity . . . is not an idolatrous competitor to the central affirmations of the faith. It is a precondition for, as well as a result of, the faithful proclamation of the Good News to all men.

> K. R. BRIDSTON and WALTER WAGONER, *Unity in Mid-Career,* 1963

The Ancient Mariner's cry, "Water, water everywhere, Nor any drop to drink," might, without injustice, be paraphrased, "Council, councils, everywhere, But none to make us one."

RALPH HYSLOP, *Unity in Mid-Career,* 1963

Ultimately, the churches themselves must decide what the one great Church is to be, and, in conversation with each other, seek to achieve it. Councils, so long as they last, are always means and never ends.

LEWIS S. MUDGE, JR., *Unity in Mid-Career,* 1963

God is calling all Christian people everywhere, more insistently than ever before, to come together. No portion of the Church in any part of the world can any longer refuse to hear and obey the call.

RAJAIAH D. PAUL, *The Churches and Christian Unity,* ed. by R. J. W. Bevan, 1963

Every quest for unity among men implies first of all that a man who is engaged in it is careful to see that he has this unity in his own person.

ROGER SCHUTZ, *Unity: Man's Tomorrow,* 1963

Christian unity ruthlessly asks all of us to drop our pretensions to squatters' rights on holy land.

WALTER D. WAGONER, *Unity in Mid-Career,* 1963

We look with reverence upon the true religious patrimony we share in common, which has been preserved and in part even well developed among our separated brethren.

POPE PAUL VI, *Homily,* September 29, 1963

Christians must realize that they have one Church, one Cross, one Gospel. Every Church must put its treasures into a safe-deposit box and issue common money, a common money of love, which we need so much.

ATHENAGORAS I, quoted in *Time,* July 5, 1963

It is now clear to everyone that the problem of unity cannot be put on one side. Today the will of Christ is pressing upon us and obliging us to do all that we can, with love and wisdom, to bring all Christians the supreme blessing and honor of a united Church.

POPE PAUL VI, *Address,* Holy Land, January 6, 1964

Nobody can, even for the sake of unity, do violence to his conscience and to truth itself. Whoever in conscience feels obliged to understand the Word of God in a certain way cannot and may not declare he understands it otherwise.

BERNARD ALFRINK, *Address* to Interfederal Assembly of Pax Romana, Washington, D.C., July, 1964

We don't reach Christian unity by riding roughshod over sincere convictions and trying to create, with all possible speed, a superchurch to confront the Goliaths of the modern world.

DAVID H. C. READ, *Sons of Anak,* 1964

An immoderate desire to make peace and sink differences at all costs is, fundamentally, a kind of scepticism about the power and content of the word of God which we desire to preach.

POPE PAUL VI, *Ecclesiam Suam,* August, 1964

The desire to come together as brothers must not lead to a watering-down or subtracting from the truth. Our dialogue must not weaken our attachment to our faith.

POPE PAUL VI, *Ecclesiam Suam,* August, 1964

The Church recognizes that in many ways she is linked with those who, being baptized, are honored with the name of Christian, though they do not profess the faith in its entirety or do not preserve unity of communion with the successor of Peter. . . . In some real way they are joined with us in the Holy Spirit, for to them too He gives His gifts and graces whereby He is operative among them with His sanctifying power.

> SECOND VATICAN COUNCIL, *Constitution on the Church,* November, 1964

Because the human race today is joining more and more into a civic, economic and social unity, it is . . . necessary that priests, . . . under the leadership of the Bishops and the Supreme Pontiff, wipe out every kind of separatedness, so that the whole human race may be brought into the unity of the family of God.

> SECOND VATICAN COUNCIL, *Constitution on the Church,* November, 1964

For a long time we hated one another. Then we ignored one another. Then we began talking about one another. Then we began talking to one another. Then we began praying for one another. And now we are beginning to pray with one another. And when that is a fact, no one can safely erect barriers around where the relationship may go from here.

> ROBERT MCAFEE BROWN, *Address* Pittsburgh, March 4, 1965

Only one thing can give unity in the Church on the human level: the love which allows another to be different even when it does not understand him.

> KARL RAHNER, quoted in *Herder Correspondence Feature Service,* July, 1965

We rejoice to see that our separated brethren look to Christ as the source and center of Church unity.

> SECOND VATICAN COUNCIL, *Decree on Ecumenism,* November, 1965

See also Brotherhood; Catholic and Non-Catholic; Christians; Church, Definitions of; Church: Its Work; Communion of Saints; Community; Democracy, Religion of; Denominationalism; Dialogue; Differences; Discord; Disputation; Division; Ecumenism; Eucharist; Fellowship; Isolation; Luther, Martin; Mystical Body of Christ; Neighbor; Opinions; Paths; Reconciliation; Reunion; Rivalry; Schisms; Sects and Sectarianism; Tolerance; Truth and Religion; Unity of Mankind; Universality.

UNITY OF MANKIND

The human race is most like unto God when it is most one, for the principle of unity dwells in him alone.

> DANTE, *De Monarchia,* Bk. I, ch. 8, c. 1300

All creatures seek after unity; all multiplicity struggles toward it—the universal aim of all life is always this unity. All that flows outward is to flow backward into its source—God.

> JOHANN TAULER (1290–1361), *Life and Sermons*

We are all one, united in our eternal image which is the image of God, and the source in us all of our life and our coming into existence.

> JOHN RUYSBROECK (1293–1381), *The Mirror of Eternal Salvation*

I now understand that my welfare is only possible if I acknowledge my unity with all the people of the world without exception.

> LEO TOLSTOY, *What I Believe,* 1895

The contribution of religion to the unity of all human beings is made, not in the intellectual but in the spiritual realm.

> EDWARD J. JURJI, *The Christian Interpretation of Religion,* 1932

All infidelity to the divine image that man bears in him, every breach with God, is at the same time a disruption of human unity.

> HENRI DE LUBAC, *Catholicism,* 1937

We are bound together by a more primitive and fundamental unity than any unity of thought and doctrine; we all have the same human nature and, considered in their extra-mental reality, the same primordial tendencies.

JACQUES MARITAIN, *Ransoming the Time,* 1944

See also Brotherhood; Eucharist; Humanity; Isolation; Mankind; One World; Rights; Unity.

UNIVERSALITY

The Church is universal because she is born of God, all nations are at home in her, the arms of her crucified Master are stretched above all races, above all civilizations.

JACQUES MARITAIN, *The Things That Are Not Caesar's,* 1930

The universality of the Christian claim implies that there is no religion, not even the most primitive, which has not contributed or will not contribute to the preparation and reception of the new reality in history.

PAUL TILLICH, *Journal of Religion,* January, 1947

Belief in a world religion reduces the sense of cosiness, of neighborliness which makes the atmosphere of a small sect agreeable to our natural prejudices.

RONALD A. KNOX, *Stimuli,* 1951

The Church, surrounded by divine light, spreads her rays over the entire earth. This light, however, is one and unique, and shines everywhere without causing any separation in the unity of the body. She extends her branches over the whole world.

POPE JOHN XXIII, October 18, 1962

See also Catholicism; Christianity; Church, Definitions of; Church: Its Nature; Church: Its Work; Education; Exclusiveness; Mystical Body of Christ; Religion, Definitions of; Unity.

UNIVERSE

Just as light is diffused from a fire which is confined to one spot, so is this whole universe the diffused energy of the supreme Brahman.

Visnu, Puranas, c. 500 B.C.

This vast universe is a wheel. Upon it are all creatures that are subject to birth, death, and rebirth. Round and round it turns, and never stops. It is the wheel of Brahman.

Svetasvatara Upanishad, before 400 B.C.

When we once understand that the universe is a great smelting-pot, and the Creator a great founder, where can we go that will not be right?

CHUANG-TZU (4th century B.C.), *Texts of Taoism,* ed. J. Legge

Cease not to think of the Universe as one living Being, possessed of a single Substance and a single soul.

MARCUS AURELIUS, *Meditations,* c. 170 A.D.

The whole universe together participates in the divine goodness more perfectly, and represents it better than any single creature whatever.

ST. THOMAS AQUINAS, *Summa Theologiae,* I. q. 47, art. 1, 1272

No attack on Christianity is more dangerous than the infinite size and depth of the heavens.

JEROME WOLF, *Letter to Tycho Brahe,* 1575

Every part of the universe, is Body; and that which is not Body, is no part of the Universe: And because the Universe is All, that which is no part of, is Nothing; and consequently *no where.*

THOMAS HOBBES, *Leviathan,* ch. 46, 1651

The universe shows us nothing save an immense and unbroken chain of cause and effect.

P. H. D. D'HOLBACH, *The System of Nature*, 1770

It is not impossible that to some infinitely superior being the whole universe may be as one plain, the distance between planet and planet being only as the pores in a grain of sand, and the spaces between system and system no greater than the intervals between one grain and the grain adjacent.

SAMUEL TAYLOR COLERIDGE, *Omniana*, 1812

Reason is the *substance* of the Universe; viz. that by which and in which all reality has its being and subsistence. On the other hand, it is the *Infinite Energy* of the Universe.

G. W. F. HEGEL, *Philosophy of History*, 1831

The universe is not dead and demoniacal, a charnelhouse with spectres; but godlike, and my Father's!

THOMAS CARLYLE, *Sartor Resartus*, 1836

There is a soul at the center of nature, and over the will of every man, so that none of us can wrong the universe.

RALPH WALDO EMERSON, "Spiritual Laws," *Essays, First Series*, 1841

The plots of God are perfect. The Universe is a plot of God.

EDGAR ALLAN POE, *Democratic Review*, November, 1844

Paley's simile of the watch is no longer applicable to such a world as this. It must be replaced by the simile of the flower. The universe is not a machine, but an organism, with an indwelling principle of life. It was not made, but it has grown.

JOHN FISKE, *Idea of God*, 1887

Our evolutionary conception of the universe allows no place at all for a Creator.

FREDERICK ENGELS, *Introduction to Socialism, Utopian and Scientific*, 1900

Man and Mind are a part and outcome of the universe, and any explanation which left them out would miss one of its greatest wonders.

BORDEN P. BOWNE, *Theism*, 1902

At bottom the whole concern of both morality and religion is with the manner of our acceptance of the universe.

WILLIAM JAMES, *Varieties of Religious Experience*, 1902

He may turn over and explore a million objects, but he must not find that strange object, the universe; for if he does he will have a religion, and be lost.

G. K. CHESTERTON, *Heretics*, 1905

We are impelled by a hidden instinct to reunion with the parts of the larger heart of the universe.

JOHN ELOF BOODIN, *Cosmic Evolution*, 1925

The Universe is all one, but a new aspect will dawn upon our ken, and we shall bound across the gulf, as Emily Bronte says, to reach our home.

OLIVER LODGE, *Science and Human Progress*, 1926

The universe construed solely in terms of efficient causation of purely physical interconnections, presents a sheer, insoluble contradiction.

ALFRED NORTH WHITEHEAD, *The Function of Reason*, 1929

The ultimate realities of the universe are at present quite beyond the reach of science, and may be—and probably are—forever beyond the comprehension of a human mind.

SIR JAMES JEANS, *The Mysterious Universe*, 1930

No theory which represents the universe as merely *pushed up* from below by its own component energy-units without *pull* akin to intelligent purpose to supply pattern or structure can ever permanently hold the philosophic field.

HARRY EMERSON FOSDICK, *As I See Religion*, 1932

A non-purposive universe and the Christian revelation are obviously two utter incompatibilities.

EDWIN LEWIS, *A Philosophy of the Christian Revelation*, 1940

Either we must believe that the universe is ultimately unintelligible because science cannot explain it; or we must accept an explanation which does make the universe intelligible but which is not supplied by science.

GERALD VANN, *The Heart of Man*, 1945

Wonderful and vast as is the universe, man is greater. The universe does not know that it exists; man does. The universe is not free to act; man is.

MARTIN J. SCOTT, *All You Who Are Burdened*, 1946

To believe that the universe and man's mind were caused by anything less than man's mind is simply to abandon science for magic.

EDWARD MCCRADY, *Religious Perspectives in College Teaching*, 1952

In one sense the whole scientific universe is a construction of our own.

C. A. COULSON, *Christianity in an Age of Science*, 1953

The universe is a collector and conservator, not of mechanical energy, as we supposed, but of persons. All round us, one by one, like a continual exhalation, "souls" break away, carrying upwards their incommunicable load of consciousness.

PIERRE TEILHARD DE CHARDIN, *The Phenomenon of Man*, 1955

The universe which science is introducing to modern man . . . leaves no need or place in a rationale of values for the supernatural framework which Jews and Christians projected in the pre-scientific era.

STEWART G. COLE, *This Is My Faith*, 1956

If causality has broken down and events are not rigidly governed by the pushes and pressures of the past, may they not be influenced in some manner by the "pull" of the future—which is a manner of saying that "purpose" may be a concrete physical factor in the evolution of the universe.

ARTHUR KOESTLER, *The Sleepwalkers*, 1959

In all nature, from the vast suns that flame in space to the least infinitesimal of matter, nothing is outlaw. Given such a universe, which interpretation is the more congruous: that it is an idiot's tale in character, or that it is the progressive manifestation of Spirit?

MILTON STEINBERG, *Anatomy of Faith*, 1960

See also Civilization; Creation; Creator; End of the World; Energy; Genesis; Glory of God; God: Considered as Impersonal; God: Finding Him; God: His Existence; God: His Omnipotence; God: His Omnipresence; Nature; Nature and God; Other Worlds; Science; Science and God; Science and Religion; Universe: Its Creation; Universe and God; World, The.

UNIVERSE: ITS CREATION

Did the atoms take counsel together and devise a common plan and work it out? That hypothesis is unspeakably absurd, yet it is rational in comparison with the notion that these atoms combined by mere chance, or by chance produced such a universe as that in which we live.

ROBERT FLINT, *Theism*, 1876

I find no difficulty in imagining that, at some former period, this universe was not in existence, and that it made its appearance in consequence of the volition of some pre-existing Being.

THOMAS HENRY HUXLEY, *Life of Darwin,* 1883

Everything points with overwhelming force to a definite event, or series of events, of creation at some time or times, not infinitely remote. The universe cannot have originated by chance out of its present ingredients, and neither can it have been always the same as now.

JAMES H. JEANS, *Eos, or the Wider Aspects of Cosmogony,* 1928

If the universe is a universe of thought, its creation must have been an act of thought. Time and space must have come into being as a part of this act.

JAMES H. JEANS, *The Mysterious Universe,* 1930

The beginning seems to present insuperable difficulties unless we agree to look on it as frankly supernatural.

A. S. EDDINGTON, *The Expanding Universe,* 1933

If the universe is running down like a clock, the clock must have been wound up at a date which we could name if we knew it. The world, if it is to have an end in time, must have had a beginning in time.

W. R. INGE, *God and the Astronomers,* 1933

See also Creation; Creator; Design; God: His Omnipotence; Mind; Universe; Universe and God.

UNIVERSE AND GOD

Since we preconceive by an indubitable notion that He [God] is a living being and . . . that there is nothing in all nature superior to Him, I do not see that anything can be more consistent . . . than to attribute life and divinity to the universe.

CICERO, *De Natura Deorum,* II, 5, 44 B.C.

The whole universe is but the footprint of the divine goodness.

DANTE, *Of Monarchy,* c. 1300

How could anyone observe the mighty order with which our God governs the universe without feeling himself inclined . . . to the practice of all virtues, and to the beholding of the Creator Himself, the source of all goodness, in all things and before all things?

NICOLAUS COPERNICUS, Preface, *De Revolutionibus Orbium Coelestium,* 1543

This wonderful ordering of the sun, the planets and the comets cannot but be the work of an intelligent, all-powerful Being.

ISAAC NEWTON, *Scholion* of *Principia,* 1687

Then sawest thou that this fair Universe, were it in the meanest province thereof, is in very deed the star-domed City of God: that through every star, through every grass-blade, and most through every Living Soul, the glory of a present God still beams.

THOMAS CARLYLE, *Sartor Resartus,* 1836

The universe, broad and deep and high, is a handful of dust which God enchants. His is the mysterious magic which possesses—not protoplasm, merely, but—the world.

THEODORE PARKER (1810–1860), quoted by Lloyd Morgan, *Interpretation of Nature*

There are, I take it, two master-keys to the secrets of the universe, viewed *sub specie aeternitatis,* the Incarnation of God, and the Personality of Man.

MICHAEL FAIRLESS, *The Roadmender,* 1895

The great central fact of the universe is that Spirit of Infinite Life and Power that is back of all, that animates all, that manifests itself in and through all; that self-existent principle of life from which all has come.

RALPH WALDO TRINE, *In Tune with the Infinite,* 1897

So long as we see the universe in the relation of use to ourselves, it remains cold, indifferent, meaningless to us; but when we see it in relation to God, sharing the life which is God, but sharing it even more imperfectly than ourselves, then the process of nature is no longer a meaningless intimidating mechanism, but pathetic and forgiveable to us even as we are to ourselves.

A. CLUTTON-BROCK, *The Spirit,* ed. B. H. Streeter, 1919

The infinite expanse of the universe, its growth through immeasurable periods of time, the boundless range of its changes, and the rational order that pervades it all, seems to demand an infinite intelligence behind its manifestations.

DAVID STARR JORDAN, *The Relation of Evolution to Religion,* 1926

Faith in God is synonymous with the brave hope that the universe is friendly to the ideals of man.

A. E. HAYDON, *Journal of Religion,* March, 1927

The universe can be best pictured, though still very imperfectly and inadequately, as consisting of pure thought, the thought of what we must describe as a mathematical thinker.

JAMES H. JEANS, *The Mysterious Universe,* 1930

The new physics does not regard the universe as atomic chaos, but, on the contrary, has found strong evidence pointing to the existence of "a directive intelligence."

ARTHUR H. COMPTON, reported in *New York Times,* March 27, 1931

In ultimate analysis, the universe can be nothing less than the progressive manifestation of God.

J. B. S. HALDANE, to interviewer, *The British Weekly,* March 3, 1932

Without God, and the otherworld, and the hope of salvation at the last, without these the universe becomes no sorry jest, as you would courteously deem it, but a purulent cancer on the corpse of nonentity.

PAUL ELMER MORE, *Pages from an Oxford Diary,* 1937

If the universe is so bad, or even half so bad, how on earth did human beings ever come to attribute it to the activity of a wise and good Creator?

C. S. LEWIS, *The Problem of Pain,* 1944

We of the modern West are the only people in the whole history of the world who have refused to find an explanation of the universe in a divine mind and will.

GERALD VANN, *The Heart of Man,* 1945

The universe could not be God because scientists admit that there has been succession in the expansion of the universe. But succession implies a beginning, which would mean that the universe is not eternal and, therefore, could not be God.

J. F. NOLL, *Christian Faith Before the Bar of Reason,* 1948

Order does not emerge out of chaos nor higher forms emerge from lower by pure chance. Except upon the basis of a controlling, creative Mind—God—the ordered law and ascending life of the universe are utterly inexplicable.

> Francis B. Sayre, *Reader's Digest,* July, 1948

The entire universe, as I see it, is the outward manifestation of Mind Energy, of spirit, or to use the older and better word, of God.

> Milton Steinberg, *A Believing Jew,* 1951

The Cosmos (Nature, Universe) is the highest unity that we know. . . . The Cosmos . . . is creative. This does not mean making something from nothing, but rather making the new out of the old. . . . Since the Cosmos is the highest known unity and is creative, we call it God. God and the Cosmos are one.

> John H. Hershey, *Unity,* May–June, 1955

See also Being; Creation; Creator; God: His Omnipotence; Mind; Universe; Universe: Its Creation.

UNIVERSITIES

In a country which has no established church and no dominant sect you cannot build a university on a sect at all—you must build it upon the nation.

> Charles W. Eliot, *Address,* New York, December 22, 1877

To look to theology to unify the modern university is futile and vain.

> Robert M. Hutchins, *The Higher Learning in America,* 1936

The record of religion in the development of great universities in the United States during the past eighty years was not always one to engender confidence in its disinterested concern for the pursuit of truth.

> Nathan M. Pusey, *Religion and Freedom of Thought,* 1954

See also Church, Criticism of; Education.

UNKNOWN

While it is the summit of human wisdom to learn the limit of our faculties, it may be wise to recollect that we have no more right to make denials than to put forth affirmatives about what lies beyond that limit.

> Thomas Henry Huxley, *Hume,* 1878

See also Mystery.

UNPLEASANT

Nothing is more unpleasant than a virtuous person with a mean mind.

> Walter Bagehot, *Literary Studies,* 1879

UNRIGHTEOUSNESS

The difficulty, my friends, is not to avoid death, but to avoid unrighteousness; for that runs faster than any death.

> Plato "Apology," *Dialogues,* 399 b.c.

USELESS

A useless life is only an earlier death.

> J. W. von Goethe, *Iphigenie auf Tauris,* 1787

USURY

If any cleric be found taking usury, he shall be deposed and excommunicated. If, moreover, a layman be proved to have taken usury . . . if he persists in that iniquity, he must be cast out of the Church.

> *Canons of the Council of Elvira,* c. 305

Manifest usurers shall not be admitted to communion, nor, if they die in sin, to Christian burial; and no priest shall accept their alms.

> *Third Council of the Lateran,* 1179

He who takes it goes to hell, and he who does not goes to the poorhouse.

BENNENUTIS DA IMOLA, *Comentum suga Dantis Comoediam*, c. 1331

Usury must be judged not by a particular passage of Scripture, but simply by the rules of equity.

JOHN CALVIN, *Letter on Usury*, 1545

Calvin deals with usurie as the apothecarie doth with poison.

ROGER FENTON, *A Treatise of Usurie*, 1612

The sin of taking interest is so great that whoever commits it is considered as though he denied the God of Israel.

MOSES LUZZATO (1707–1747), *Mesillat Yesharim*

See also Business; Economics and Christianity; Money; Riches; Wealth.

UTILITARIANISM

By the principle of utility is meant that principle which approves or disapproves of every action whatsoever according to the tendency which it appears to have to augment or diminish the happiness of the party whose interest is in question.

JEREMY BENTHAM, *The Principles of Morals and Legislation*, 1789

Nature has placed mankind under the governance of two sovereign masters, "pain" and "pleasure." It is for them alone to point out what we ought to do, as well as to determine what we shall do.

JEREMY BENTHAM, *The Principles of Morals and Legislation*, 1789

See also Philosophy; Pragmatism.

UTOPIAS

Utopias of historical progress cannot seduce those who believe in Christ. Utopias

are straws to which those cling who have no real hope.

EMIL BRUNNER, *The Scandal of Christianity*, 1951

VAINGLORY

Man is often vainglorious about his contempt of glory.

ST. AUGUSTINE, *Confessions*, 397

When all else has been subjugated, only the vice of vainglory lurks in the midst of the virtues.

DESIDERIUS ERASMUS, *Enchiridion*, 1501

See also Conceit; Glory; Man: His Self-Deification; Pride; Righteousness; Self-Contempt; Self-Deception; Self-Knowledge; Self-Love; Self-Praise; Self-Will; Vanity.

VALOR

Perfect valor is to do without witnesses what one would do before all the world.

LA ROCHEFOUCAULD, *Maxims*, 1665

See also Bravery; Courage; Heroism.

VALUES

Values, human values, can survive only if, reaching out toward a metaphysical condition which their dream shapes foreshadow, they *find* it.

WILLIAM E. HOCKING, *Human Nature and Its Remaking*, 1918

Things have in fact just that value which God sees in them, and no other. To Him, the All Holy and All Wise, the pomps and successes of men and what are sometimes called the "substantial rewards of life" are simply of no worth whatever.

EDWARD F. GARESCHE, *The Things Immortal*, 1919

The eternal and absolute values are at least as much parts of reality as atoms and electrons.

W. R. INGE, *Living Philosophies*, 1931

It is precisely because the Church does not desire to intrust the question of values to irreligious hands that Catholic institutions of higher learning exist.

HOWARD MUMFORD JONES, *General Education*, ed. W. S. Gray, 1934

Since no way can be found for deciding a difference in values, the conclusion is forced upon us that the difference is one of tastes, not one as to any objective truth.

BERTRAND RUSSELL, *Religion and Science*, 1935

As long as the Church pretends, or assumes to preach, absolute values, but actually preaches relative and secondary values, it will merely hasten this process of disintegration.

Editorial, *Fortune*, January, 1940

There are no eternal values unless there are eternal valuers.

WILLIAM E. HOCKING, *Living Religions and a World Faith*, 1940

That economic values are the highest, the genuine reality, is not an invention of Karl Marx, but of capitalist society of the 19th century.

EMIL BRUNNER, *Christianity and Civilization*, 1943

The faith we have to build is a faith in the values of this world, not in the values of another.

HAROLD J. LASKI, *Reflections on the Revolution of Our Time*, 1943

Man's chief purpose . . . is the creation and preservation of value; that is what gives meaning to our civilization, and the participation in this is what gives signifi-cance, ultimately to the individual and human life.

LEWIS MUMFORD, *Faith for Living*, 1950

There no longer exists any articulate public consensus in the West on the ultimate values which once formed the living soul of its culture.

NORRIS CLARK, *America*, March 31, 1962

The Christian mind clings to a hierarchy of values. No sane man would ascribe equal value to his brain and his feet, his eye and his fingernail. In the pursuit of knowledge, the Christian intellectual observes a comparable scale of values.

F. X. CANFIELD, *The Catholic Bookman's Guide*, ed. Sr. M. Regis, I.H.M., 1962

See also Absolutes; Civilization; Culture and Religion; Education; Education, Catholic; Education, Parochial; Education, Religious; Good; Goodness; Knowledge; Love; Moral Values; Religion, Definitions of; Rootlessness; Unity; Virtue; Wisdom.

VALUES, SPIRITUAL

The ultimate test of religious values is nothing psychological, nothing definable in terms of *how it happens*, but something ethical, definable only in terms of *what is attained*.

GEORGE A. COE, *The Spiritual Life*, 1900

All Faith consists essentially in the recognition of a world of spiritual values behind, yet not apart from, the world of natural phenomena.

W. R. INGE, *Faith and Its Psychology*, 1910

Man-made values are not only unsatisfying but they are groundless. God alone can give fixity and permanence to values and

hence is to be defined as "The Supreme
Value of the Universe."
　　E. S. BRIGHTMAN, *Religious Values*,
　　1925

Spiritual values have meaning only in human relations and are as much a part of
the evolutionary process as the physical
structure of man.
　　A. EUSTACE HAYDON, *The Quest of the
　　Ages*, 1929

If we accept God's Fatherhood as a true
statement of reality, we cannot think of
human relationships in any other terms.
That, for a Christian, is a real and final
root of world values.
　　BASIL MATTHEWS, *The Clash of World
　　Forces*, 1931

If we are to have values of the intrinsic
and eternal type, we must take by faith as
real the kind of world in which they can
live.
　　RUFUS M. JONES, *Spirit in Man*, 1941

I can see no hope for our unhappy world
save that which lies in the renewal of the
moral and spiritual values which our common ideal of faith has created.
　　SHOLEM ASCH, *One Destiny*, 1945

See also Absolutes; Good; Goodness;
Knowledge; Virtue; Wisdom.

VANDALISM

When a man wantonly destroys one of the
works of man we call him a vandal. When
he wantonly destroys one of the works of
God we call him a sportsman.
　　JOSEPH WOOD KRUTCH, *The Great
　　Chain of Life*, 1956

VANITY

In tricking up themselves men go beyond
women, they wear harlots' colors, and do
not walk, but jet and dance, more like

players, butterflies, baboons, apes, antics,
than men.
　　SENECA (4 B.C.–65 A.D.), *Lib.* 7, cap.
　　31

God hates those who praise themselves.
　　ST. CLEMENT OF ROME, *First Epistle to
　　the Corinthians*, c. 100

No sickness worse than imagining thyself
to be perfect can afflict thy soul.
　　JALLALUDIN RUMI (1207–1273), *Mas-
　　navi*

Account not thyself better than others lest
peradventure thou be held worse in the
sight of God that knoweth what is in
man.
　　THOMAS À KEMPIS, *Imitation of Christ*,
　　1441

What greater vanity can there be, than to
go about by our proportions and conjectures to guess at God? And to govern both
him, and the world according to our capacity and laws?
　　MICHEL DE MONTAIGNE, *Essays*, Bk. 2,
　　ch. 12, 1580

Were it not a sottish arrogance, that we
should think ourselves to be the perfectest
thing of this Universe?
　　MICHEL DE MONTAIGNE, *Essays*, Bk. 2,
　　ch. 12, 1580

What renders the vanity of others insupportable is that it wounds our own.
　　LA ROCHEFOUCAULD, *Maxims*, 1665

If vanity does not entirely overthrow the
virtues, at least it makes them totter.
　　LA ROCHEFOUCAULD, *Maxims*, 1665

Nothing can exceed the vanity of our
existence but the folly of our pursuits.
　　OLIVER GOLDSMITH, *The Good Natr'd
　　Man*, 1768

Vanity is the polite mask of pride.
　　FRIEDRICH NIETZSCHE, *Human, All Too
　　Human*, 1878

Nothing makes one so vain as being told that one is a sinner.

> OSCAR WILDE, *The Picture of Dorian Gray,* 1891

The ugliest vanity is the vanity of one who boasts of his humility.

> JACOB KLATZKIN, *In Praise of Wisdom,* 1943

See also Conceit; Cosmetics; Glory; Intellectuals; Man: His Self-Deification; Pride; Righteousness; Self-Contempt; Self-Deception; Self-Knowledge; Self-Love; Self-Praise; Self-Will; Vainglory.

VENGEANCE

O believers! retaliation for bloodshed is prescribed to you: the free man for the free, and the slave for the slave, and the woman for the woman: but he to whom his brother shall make any remission is to be dealt with equitably. . . . In this law of retaliation is your security for life.

> *Koran,* c 625

How shall one take vengeance on an enemy? By increasing one's own good qualities.

> IBN GABIROL (1021–c. 1058), *Choice of Pearls*

Vengeance is mine, saith the Lord; and that means that it is not the Lord Chief Justice's.

> GEORGE BERNARD SHAW, Preface to S. and B. Webb's *English Prisons,* 1922

See also Anger; Bloodshed; Capital Punishment; Enemy; Hatred; War; War, Condemnation of.

VERACITY

Veracity is a plant of paradise and its seeds have never flourished beyond the walls.

> NICHOLAS MACHIAVELLIA in George Eliot's *Romola,* 1863

See also Error; Falsehood; Honesty; Truth.

VERIFICATION

Faith is verification by the heart; confession by the tongue; action by the limbs.

> A Sufi Saying

VICE

It is not possible to form any other notion of the origin of vice than as the absence of virtue.

> ST. GREGORY OF NYSSA (c. 335–c. 395), *The Great Catechism*

For God who would never have foreknown vice in any work of His, angel or man, but that He knew in like manner, what good use to put it unto, so making the world's course like a fair poem, more gracious by antithetic figures.

> ST. AUGUSTINE, *City of God,* X, 18, 426

There is no vice so completely contrary to our nature that it obliterates all trace of nature.

> ST. AUGUSTINE, *City of God,* XIX, 426

No man is discerned to be vicious as soon as he is so, and vices have their infancy and their childhood, and it cannot be expected that in a child's age should be the vice of a man.

> JEREMY TAYLOR, *Sermons,* 1651

Whatever was passion in the contemplation of man, being brought forth by his will into action, is vice and the bondage of sin.

> JAMES HARRINGTON, *The Commonwealth of Oceana,* 1656

When our vices quit us we flatter ourselves with the belief that it is we who quit them.

> LA ROCHEFOUCAULD, *Maxims,* 1665

The same vices that are gross and insupportable in others we do not notice in ourselves.

JEAN DE LA BRUYÈRE, *Caractères,* 1688

Vice, although triumphant in the world, is still forced to disguise itself under the mask of hypocrisy, that it may secure a regard that it does not hope for when it is known as it is. Thus it renders, in spite of itself, homage to virtue.

FRANÇOIS FÉNELON (1651–1715), *Selections from,* ed. Fellen

Vice makes Virtue shine.

THOMAS FULLER, *Gnomologia,* 1732

Search others for their virtues, thyself for thy vices.

BENJAMIN FRANKLIN, *Poor Richard's Almanac,* 1758

If he does really think there is no distinction between virtue and vice, why, sir, when he leaves our houses let us count our spoons.

SAMUEL JOHNSON, *Boswell's Life of,* 1772

If vices are diseases, they cease to be vices, and theology in sending the drunkard or the gambler to the physician, relinquishes its last connection with reality: the ethical task.

FRITZ KUNKEL, *In Search of Maturity,* 1943

See alos Crime; Immorality; Lust; Malice; Passions; Sensuality; Sex; Virtue.

VICTORY

Victory breeds hatred, for the conquered is unhappy. He who has given up both victory and defeat, he, the contented, is happy.

Dhammapada, c. 5th century B.C.

Not even a God can change into defeat the victory of a man who has vanquished himself.

Dhammapada, c. 5th century B.C.

If victory crowns the arms of the state whose cause was just, it confers no right to exact more than adequate reparations and indemnities, while charity may require those obligations to be postponed or reduced or . . . canceled.

Report, Catholic Association for International Peace, *International Ethics,* 1942

"It is finished." The understanding of these words of Jesus brings final victory of God-self over human-self for others and for us. He held to His faith in God's way as the only way, to the very end.

JAMES W. KENNEDY, *Advance into Light,* 1948

See also Conquest; Failure; Peace; Vengeance; War

VIGILANCE

Eternal vigilance is the price, not only of liberty, but of a great many other things. It is the price of everything that is good. It is the price of one's own soul.

WOODROW WILSON, *Address,* October, 1914

VIOLENCE

Let there be no violence in religion. If they embrace Islam they are surely directed; but if they turn their backs, verily to thee belongs preaching only.

MOHAMMED (570–632), quoted in W. Muir's *Life of Mohammed*

A good portion of the evils that afflict mankind is due to the erroneous belief that life can be made secure by violence.

LEO TOLSTOY, *Confessions,* 1879

One of the great meanings of the Cross was the deliberate repudiation by Christ of violence as a means of overcoming evil.

> Executive Body of London Yearly Meeting [of Quakers], September, 1914

See also Bloodshed; Coercion; Dictatorship; Force; Killing; Murder; Nonresistance; Nonviolence; Nonviolent Resistance; Pacifism; Pacifists; Peace; Punishment; War.

VIRGIN BIRTH

Once the great glove of Nature was taken off His hand. His naked hand touched her. . . . The whole soiled and weary universe quivered at this direct injection of essential life—direct, uncontaminated, not drained through all the crowded history of nature.

> C. S. LEWIS, *Miracles,* 1947

See also Mary, the Mother of Jesus.

VIRGINITY

If anyone shall remain virgin, or observe continence, abstaining from marriage because he abhors it, and not on account of the beauty and holiness of Virginity itself, let him be anathema.

> *Synodical Letter of Council of Gangra,* c. 343 A.D.

If anyone of those who are living a virgin life for the Lord's sake shall treat arrogantly the married, let him be anathema.

> *Synodical Letter of Council of Gangra,* c. 343 A.D.

Virginity stands as far above marriage as the heavens stand above the earth.

> ST. JOHN CHRYSOSTOM, *De Virginitas,* c. 390

Virginity has a special reward hereafter.

> ST. AUGUSTINE, *On Holy Virginity,* c. 402

Virginity is not commanded; it is a free offering to the Lord.

> ST. AUGUSTINE, *On Holy Virginity,* c. 402

Consider the excellency of virgins; marriage replenisheth the earth, but virginity Paradise; Elias, Eliseus, John Baptist were bachelors; virginity is a precious jewel, a fair garland, a never-fading flower.

> ROBERT BURTON, *Anatomy of Melancholy,* III, 1621

Natural virginity, of itself, is not a state more acceptable to God; but that which is chosen and voluntary, in order to the conveniences of religion and separation from worldly encumbrances, is therefore better than the married life.

> JEREMY TAYLOR, *Holy Living,* 1650

The state of virginity consecrated to God is incomparably superior to the married state, not because conjugal love is in any way wrong, but because, instead of being a human love devoted to Jesus Christ, here is a marriage with Jesus Christ Himself.

> A. CARRÉ, *Companions for Eternity,* 1947

Virginity is preferable to marriage . . . above all else because it has a higher aim: that is to say, it is a very efficacious means for devoting oneself to the service of God, while the heart of married persons will remain more or less "divided."

> POPE PIUS XII, *On Holy Virginity,* March, 1954

There is a real threat to marriage, and to the stability of sexual relationships, at work in any society that cannot and does not respect virginity.

> J. V. L. CASSERLEY, *The Bent World,* 1955

Virginity is the virtue which opens up your heart to the truest, greatest, and most encompassing love on earth: the service of Christ and of souls.

Pope John XXIII, *Address,* January 29, 1960

See also Celibacy; Chastity; Continence; Love, Human; Love, Physical; Marriage; Mary, the Mother of Jesus; Modesty; Purity; Self-Conquest; Self-Denial; Self-Sacrifice; Sexual Intercourse; Virtue; Woman.

VIRGINS

There is nothing our Lord delighteth in more than virgins, nor wherein angels more gladly abide, and play with, and talk with.

Lewes Vives, *The Instruction of a Christian Woman,* 1541

The virgin sends prayers to God; but she carries but one soul to him.

Jeremy Taylor, *Twenty-Seven Sermons,* 1651

VIRTUE

Badness . . . you may choose easily. . . . But before Virtue the immortal gods have put the sweat of man's brow; and long and steep is the way of it, and rugged at first.

Hesiod, *Works and Days,* 8th century B.C.

The superior virtue is not conscious of itself as virtue; therefore it has virtue. The inferior virtue never lets off virtue; therefore it has no virtue.

Lao-tzu, *Tao Tê Ching,* c. 500 B.C.

To bring forth and preserve, to produce without possessing, to act without hope of reward, and to expand without waste, this is the supreme virtue.

Lao-tzu, *Tao Tê Ching,* c. 500 B.C.

The virtuous man is happy in this world, and he is happy in the next; he is happy in both. He is happy when he thinks of the good he has done; he is still more happy when going on the good path.

Dhammapada, c. 5th century B.C.

Sweeter than the perfume of sandalwood or of the lotus-flower is the perfume of virtue.

Dhammapada, c. 5th century B.C.

Virtue cannot live in solitude: neighbors are sure to grow up around it.

Confucius, *Analects of,* c. 5th century B.C.

Fine words and an insinuating appearance are seldom associated with true virtue.

Confucius, *Analects of,* c. 5th century B.C.

The determined scholar and the man of virtue will not seek to live at the expense of injuring their virtue. They will even sacrifice their lives to preserve their virtue complete.

Confucius, *Analects of,* 5th century B.C.

Only virtue can compel Heaven, and there is no distance to which it cannot reach.

Shu Ching, c. 490 B.C.

Virtue, like art, constantly deals with what is hard to do, and the harder the task the better success.

Aristotle, *The Nicomachean Ethics,* c. 340 B.C.

The virtue of man will be a state of character which makes a man good and makes him do his work well.

Aristotle, *The Nicomachean Ethics,* c. 340 B.C.

Virtue is a kind of health, beauty and habit of the soul.

Plato, *The Republic,* 270 B.C.

He who dies for virtue's sake does not perish.

Plautus, *Caetivi,* 200 B.C.

If we weigh virtue by the mere utility and profit that attend it, and not by its own merits, the virtue which results will be in fact a species of vice.
> CICERO, *The Laws,* 52 B.C.

In nothing is the uniformity of human nature more conspicuous than in its respect for virtue.
> CICERO, *The Laws,* 52 B.C.

Virtue is the art of the whole life.
> PHILO, *Allegorical Interpretation,* c. 10 A.D.

We do not say as the Stoics do impiously that virtue in man and in God is the same.
> ST. CLEMENT OF ALEXANDRIA, *Miscellanies,* c. 200

Virtue is a will in conformity to God and Christ in life, rightly adjusted to life everlasting.
> ST. CLEMENT OF ALEXANDRIA, *The Instructor,* ch. 13, c. 220

So good a thing is virtue that even its enemies applaud and admire it.
> ST. JOHN CHRYSOSTOM, *Homilies,* c. 388

Where virtue is, there are many snares.
> ST. JOHN CHRYSOSTOM, *Homilies,* c. 388

As to virtue leading us to a happy life, I hold virtue to be nothing else than perfect love of God.
> ST. AUGUSTINE, *The Morals of the Catholic Church,* 388

He who, leaving virtue, ceaseth to be a man, since he cannot be a partaker of the divine condition, is turned into a beast.
> BOETHIUS, *Consolations of Philosophy,* c. 523

A slight failing in one virtue is enough to put all the others to sleep.
> ST. TERESA OF ÁVILA, *Life,* ch. XXXVI, 16, 1565

Now of all the benefits of virtue, the contempt of death is the chiefest.
> MICHEL DE MONTAIGNE, *Essays,* xix, 1580

For growth in virtue the important thing is to be silent and work.
> ST. JOHN OF THE CROSS (1542–1591), *Maxims,* 295

Virtue is like a rich stone,—best plain set.
> FRANCIS BACON, *Essays,* 1597

Virtue ennobles the blood.
> MIGUEL DE CERVANTES, *Don Quixote,* 1605

No beauty leaves such an impression, strikes so deep, or links the souls of men closer than virtue.
> ROBERT BURTON, *Anatomy of Melancholy,* II, 1621

I cannot praise a fugitive and cloistered virtue, unexercised and unbreathed, that never sallies out and sees her adversary.
> JOHN MILTON, *Areopagitica,* 1644

He loves virtue for God's sake and its own that loves and honors it wherever it is to be seen.
> JEREMY TAYLOR, *Holy Living,* 1650

The power of a man's virtue should not be measured by his special efforts, but by his ordinary doing.
> BLAISE PASCAL, *Pensées,* 1670

Those are far astray from a true estimate of virtue who expect for their virtue, as if it were the greatest slavery, that God will adorn them with the greatest rewards.
> BARUCH SPINOZA, *Ethics,* II, 1677

The first step to Virtue, is to love Virtue in another man.
> THOMAS FULLER, *Gnomologia,* 1732

It is nonsense for a woman to consider herself virtuous because she is not a prosti-

tute or a man honest because he does not steal. May the Lord God preserve me from such a poor, starving religion as this.
> JOHN WESLEY, *Character of a Methodist*, 1742

True virtue . . . is that consent, propensity, and union of heart to being in general, which is immediately exercised in a general good-will.
> JONATHAN EDWARDS, *The Nature of True Virtue*, 1758

To be proud of virtue is to poison yourself with the antidote.
> BENJAMIN FRANKLIN, *Poor Richard's Almanac*, 1758

He who will warrant his virtue in every possible situation is either an impostor or a fool.
> C. A. HELVETIUS, *De l'Esprit*, 1758

Can I call virtue anything but that which does good! . . . The prudent man does himself good: the virtuous one does it to other men. . . . If St. Bruno had made peace in families, if he had assisted the indigent, he had been virtuous; having fasted and prayed in solitude, he is only a saint.
> VOLTAIRE, *Philosophical Dictionary*, II, 1764

Virtue is no local thing. It is not honorable because born in this community or that, but for its independent, everlasting beauty. This is the bond of the universal church.
> WILLIAM ELLERY CHANNING, *The Church*, 1841

The less a man thinks or knows about his virtue the better we like him.
> RALPH WALDO EMERSON, "Spiritual Laws," *Essays, First Series*, 1841

The highest proof of virtue is to possess boundless power without using it.
> THOMAS BABINGTON MACAULAY, *Review of Aitkin's Life of Addison*, 1843

There are virtues which become crimes by exaggeration.
> ALEXANDRE DUMAS, *The Count of Monte Cristo*, 1844

Where there is no temptation, there can be little claim to virtue.
> WILLIAM H. PRESCOTT, *The Conquest of Peru*, 1847

As virtue is the business of all men, the first principles of it are written in their hearts in characters so legible that no man can pretend ignorance of them.
> THOMAS REID, *The Works of*, I, 1863

Reverence for superiors, respect for equals, regard for inferiors—these form the supreme trinity of virtues.
> F. ADLER, *Creed and Deed*, 1877

All that unites with the universal is virtue. All that separates is sin.
> VIVEKANANDA (1863–1902), *Works of*

Virtue consists, not in abstaining from vice, but in not desiring it.
> GEORGE BERNARD SHAW, *Man and Superman*, 1903

Each one of the Christian virtues has its own content of joy: each is a little garden harboring flowers of every form and color and fragrance.
> PAUL WILHELM VON KEPPLER, *More Joy*, 1911

A man who is virtuous and a coward has no marketable virtue about him.
> WOODROW WILSON, *Address*, October, 1914

The virtues of man are but the reflections of the goodness of God.
> BEDE JARRETT, *Meditations for Layfolk*, 1915

We need two virtues in our students which are anathema to the high priests of American education. One is discipline, the other is humility.

> ROBERT I. GANNON, *After Black Coffee,* 1946

No justification of virtue will enable a man to be virtuous. Without the aid of trained emotions, the intellect is powerless against the animal organism.

> C. S. LEWIS, *The Abolition of Man,* 1947

A man's virtue is in his behavior in the face of his destiny.

> LYMAN BRYSON, *Perspectives on a Troubled Decade,* ed. Bryson, Finklestein and MacIver, 1950

There are no national virtues. We are alone, each one of us. If we are good, the virtues of others will not make us better. We cannot borrow morals.

> AUBREY MENEN, *Dead Man in the Silver Market,* 1953

We know instinctively what Dorothy Sayers means when she lists the seven virtues as respectability, childishness, mental timidity, dullness, sentimentality, censoriousness, and depression of spirits.

> F. B. SPEAKMAN, *The Salty Tang,* 1954

There is a strange tendency in men and women to lay claim to the more exalted Christian virtues without having acquired the basic ones.

> JOHN MIDDLETON MURRY, *Not as the Scribes,* 1959

See also Beauty; Bureaucracy; Conduct; Courage; Evil; Freedom; Good; Goodness; Happiness; Honesty; Hope; Humilty; Moral Beauty; Morality; Piety; Purity; Religion: Its Nature and Function; Right; Right and Wrong; Selflessness; Sex; Spiritual; Values; Vice; Worship.

VISION

A vision is to be esteemed the more noble the more intellectual it is, the more it is stripped of all image and approaches the state of pure contemplation.

> HENRY SUSO (c. 1295–1365), *Leben,* cap. liv

But it is with man's Soul as it is with Nature; the beginning of Creation is— Light. Till the eye have vision, the whole members are in bonds.

> THOMAS CARLYLE, *Sartor Resartus,* 1836

Methinks we have hugely mistaken this matter of Life and Death. Methinks that what they call my shadow here on earth is my true substance. Methinks that in looking at things spiritual, we are too much like oysters observing the sun through the water, and thinking that thick water the thinnest of air.

> HERMAN MELVILLE, *Moby Dick,* 1851

Progress will be carried forward by a series of dazzling visions.

> VICTOR HUGO, *William Shakespeare,* 1864

The road to Damascus is essential to the march of Progress.

> VICTOR HUGO, *William Shakespeare,* 1864

The high, contemplative, all-commanding vision, the sense of Right and Wrong, is alike in all. Its attributes are self-existence, eternity, intuition and command. It is the mind of the mind.

> RALPH WALDO EMERSON, *North American Review,* April, 1866

The fact of the religious vision, and its history of persistent expansion, is our one ground for optimism. Apart from it, human life is a flash of occasional enjoyments lighting up a mass of pain and misery, a bagatelle of transient experience.

> ALFRED NORTH WHITEHEAD, *Science and the Modern World,* 1925

The vision which converts a saint or illuminates a prophet has a value and quality quite different from a casual dream.

BURNETT H. STREETER, *Reality: a New Correlation of Science and Religions,* 1926

The astonishing thing about the human being is not so much his intellect and bodily structure, profoundly mysterious as they are. The astonishing and least comprehensible thing about him is his range of vision; his gaze into the infinite distance; his lonely passion for ideas and ideals.

W. MACNEILLE DIXON, *The Human Situation,* 1937

Some may be color-blind, but others see the bright hues of sunrise. Some may have no religious sense, but others live and move and have their being in the transcendent glory of God.

WILLIAM CECIL DAMPIER, *A History of Science,* 1942

The great masses without faith are unconscious of the destructive processes going on, because they have lost the vision of the heights from which they have fallen.

FULTON J. SHEEN, *Communism and the Conscience of the West,* 1948

The vision splendid of immortality which uplifted and transfigured the first Christians . . . has grown sadly intermittent in our grey secularized lives.

D. G. M. JACKSON, *Advocate,* Melbourne, Australia, November 3, 1949

Vision looks inward and becomes duty. Vision looks outward and becomes aspiration. Vision looks upward and becomes faith.

STEPHEN S. WISE (1874–1949), *Sermons and Addresses*

Behind every civilization there is a vision.

CHRISTOPHER DAWSON, *Dynamics of World History,* 1957

I am convinced that every human being is capable of catching a vision of the transhuman presence and of entering into communion with It, whether he finds It in Its personal aspect as Brahma or Its impersonal aspect as Brahman or Nirvana.

A. J. TOYNBEE, *A Study of History,* Vol. XII, *Reconsiderations,* 1961

See also Aspiration; Beatific Vision; Brahma; Brahman; Contemplation; Dreams; Experience, Religious; Faith, Definitions of; Inspiration; Intuition; Light; Mind; Mystic; Mystical Experience; Mysticism; Nirvana; Optimism; Progress; Prophets; Reality; Religious; Visionary.

VISIONARY

The visionary is a mystic when his vision mediates to him an actuality beyond the reach of the senses.

EVELYN UNDERHILL, *Practical Mysticism,* 1914

See also Vision.

VOCATION

Each individual has his own kind of living assigned to him by the Lord as a sort of sentry post so that he may not heedlessly wander throughout life.

JOHN CALVIN, *Institutes,* III, 1536

No man can complain that his calling takes him off from religion; his calling itself, and his very worldly employment in honest trades and offices, is a serving of God.

JEREMY TAYLOR, *Holy Living,* 1650

Each man has his own vocation. The talent is the call. . . . This talent and this call depend on his organization, or the mode in which the general soul incarnates itself in him.

RALPH WALDO EMERSON, "Spiritual Laws," *Essays, First Series,* 1841

Each of us has his gift. Let us not imagine that we are disinherited by our heavenly Father, any one of us. Let us be ourselves, as God made us, then we shall be something good and useful.

JAMES FREEMAN CLARKE, *Self-Culture,* 1881

Every vocation is ultimately founded on the salutary selfishness by which an individual, despite the whole world, seeks to save his own immortal soul.

M. RAYMONDS, *The Man Who Got Even With God,* 1941

When you have learned to believe in God's purpose for you as an individual, you are immediately lifted out of the mass and become significant and meaningful in the eyes of God and of man.

JOHN SUTHERLAND BONNELL, *What Are You Living For?,* 1950

There is nothing in the whole world so dangerous as a sense of vocation without a belief in God.

W. R. FORRESTER, *Christian Vocation,* 1951

There is no kind of serviceable labor to increase human happiness and human welfare which may not rightly be called a Christian vocation.

GEORGIA HARKNESS, *The Modern Rival of Christian Faith,* 1953

Without a personal sense of vocation gained in the solitary struggles of the soul with its Maker and Redeemer the minister will always be deficient.

H. RICHARD NIEBUHR, *The Purpose of the Church and Its Ministry,* 1956

The basic sense of vocation which once gave meaning and direction to all walks of life has been the casualty of collectivism, existentialism and sexualism, three of the moods induced by widespread practical atheism.

JOHN J. WRIGHT, *Address,* Rome, Italy, March 11, 1962

A vocation necessarily creates a tension, a crisis, a tug-of-war in the soul. . . . "Fearful lest having Him, one might have naught else besides." He who takes us by the finger may seize the hand.

FULTON J. SHEEN, *Our Sunday Visitor,* March 11, 1962

A vocation is a falling in love with God, a crucifixion which is the prelude to a resurrection.

FULTON J. SHEEN, *Our Sunday Visitor,* March 11, 1962

See also Aspiration; Call; Christian Life; Clergy; Duties; Minister; Ministry; Ordination; Priesthood; Priests; Saints; Service; Work.

VOTING

Reflect that you are accountable not only to society but to God, for the honest and independent and fearless exercise of your own franchise, that it is a trust confided to you not for your private gain but for the public good.

CATHOLIC BISHOPS OF THE U.S., 1840

VOWS

Vows made in storms are forgot in calms.

THOMAS FULLER, *Gnomologia,* 1732

See also Oaths; Promise.

VULGARITY

Vulgarity is, at bottom, the kind of consciousness in which the will completely predominates over the intellect, where the latter does nothing more than perform the service of its master, the will.

ARTHUR SCHOPENHAUER, "The Wisdom of Life," *Essays,* 1851

WAGES

It is said that a dollar a day is not enough for a wife and five or six children. No, not if the man smokes or drinks beer. . . . But is not a dollar a day enough to buy bread with? Water costs nothing; and a man who cannot live on bread is not fit to live. What is the use of a civilization that simply makes men incompetent to live under the conditions which exist?

HENRY WARD BEECHER, 1877 (in midst of railroad worker's strike), quoted in *Protestant Churches and Industrial America,* by H. F. May

Let the workingman and employer make free agreements, and in particular let them agree freely as to wages; nevertheless there underlies a dictate of natural justice more imperious and ancient than any bargain between man and man, namely that wages ought not to be insufficient to support a frugal and well-behaved wage-earner.

POPE LEO XIII, *Rerum Novarum,* 1891

The laborer's right to a decent livelihood is the first moral charge upon industry. The employer has a right to get a reasonable living out of his business, but he has no right to interest on his investment until his employees have obtained at least living wages.

ROMAN CATHOLIC BISHOPS OF THE U.S., January, 1919

A living wage includes not merely a decent maintenance for the present but also a reasonable provision for such future needs as sickness, invalidity, and old age.

Pastoral Letter of Roman Catholic Bishops of U.S., February 22, 1920

It is unjust to demand wages so high that an employer cannot pay them without ruin, and without consequent distress amongst the working people themselves.

POPE PIUS XI, *Quadragesimo Anno,* 1931

The wage-earner is not to receive as alms what is his due in justice. And let no one attempt with trifling charitable donations to exempt himself from the great duties imposed by justice.

POPE PIUS XI, *Atheistic Communism,* 1937

A person may be too puritanical even to mention the seventh commandment and yet pay wages which encourages his sales-girls to break it.

RALPH W. SOCKMAN, *The Highway to God,* 1941

See also Economics and Christianity; Employees; Labor; Labor Unions; Profit; Property; Public Welfare; Rights; Security; Social Conscience; Work.

WAR

Let necessity, and not your will, slay the enemy who fights against you.

ST. AUGUSTINE, *To Publicola,* 398

Peace should be the object of your desire; war should be waged only as a necessity, and waged only that God may by it deliver men from the necessity and preserve them in peace.

ST. AUGUSTINE, *To Publicola,* 398

We shall better overcome the Turks by the piety of our lives than by arms; the empire of Christianity will thus be defended by the same means by which it was originally established.

DESIDERIUS ERASMUS, *Education of a Christian Prince,* 1516

O war! thou son of Hell!

WILLIAM SHAKESPEARE, *Henry VI, Part II,* c. 1591

War is death's feast.

GEORGE HERBERT, *Outlandish Proverbs,* 1640

When war begins, then Hell openeth.

GEORGE HERBERT, *Jacula Prudentum,* 1651

What millions died—that Caesar might be great.

THOMAS CAMPBELL, *The Pleasures of Hope,* 1799

War is a continuation of policy by the use of different means.

KARL VON CLAUSEWITZ, *Vom Kriege,* 1833

The first reason for all wars, and for the necessity of national defenses, is that the majority of persons, high and low, in all European nations, are Thieves, and, in their hearts, greedy of their neighbors's goods, lands, and fame.

JOHN RUSKIN, *Fors Clavigera,* 1871

We must be at war with evil, but at peace with men.

J. E. E. DALBERG-ACTON (Lord Acton), *Address,* 1877

What we need to discover in the social realm is the moral equivalent of war: something heroic that will speak to men as universally as war does, and yet will be compatible with their spiritual selves as war has proved itself to be incompatible.

WILLIAM JAMES, *The Varieties of Religious Experience,* 1902

The powers of this world, founded upon force and forging ever more perfect weapons of death, will always dismiss Him as impossible.

W. G. PECK, *The Divine Revolution,* 1927

It may be that the world must wait for its redemption from warfare until one nation is ready to risk crucifixion at the hands of its possible enemies. It might lose its own national life; but it would set free such a flood of spiritual life as would save the world.

G. H. C. MACGREGOR, *New Testament Basis of Pacifism,* 1936

No sooner has war begun than there automatically follows the prostitution of every conceivable moral value, truth, honesty, decency, upon which all stable personal relationships . . . depend.

G. H. C. MACGREGOR, *New Testament Basis of Pacifism,* 1936

The Christians everywhere have committed themselves to the support of capitalism-industrialism and therefore to wars in its defense, mechanized war to preserve mechanized living.

ERIC GILL, *Autobiography,* 1941

The calm, deliberate judgment of the people rather than the aims of the ambitious few should decide whether war be the only solution.

Report, Catholic Association for International Peace, *International Ethics,* 1942

There is a duty, besides, imposed on all, a duty which brooks no delay, no procrastination, no hesitation, no subterfuge; it is the duty to do everything to ban, once and for all, wars of aggression as a legitimate solution of international disputes.

POPE PIUS XII, *Christmas Address,* 1944

If we do not devise some greater and more equitable system Armageddon will be at our door. The problem basically is theological and involves a spiritual recrudescence and improvement of human character that will synchronize with our almost matchless character in science.

DOUGLAS MACARTHUR, when Japan signed Articles of Surrender, September 2, 1945

The theory of war as an apt and proportionate means of solving international conflicts is now out of date.

POPE PIUS XII, *Christmas Message,* 1948

We often hear it said: "If God existed there would be no wars." But it would be truer to say: If God's laws were observed there would be no wars.

    YVES M. CONGAR, *God, Man and the Universe,* 1950

Every war of the future will be a war of religion, for no country will go to war till it can give its cause the color of a Crusade and so secure for its maintenance absolute loyalty of a heroic quality in the whole population.

    W. R. FORRESTER, *Christian Vocation,* 1951

The world continues to sow wars and reap wretchedness. When wars threaten or come, we complain bitterly. But we live and think things that breed discontent, distrust and fear. . . . We violate, with abandon, many, if not all, of the laws of the Creator, and then call on the atomic bomb to save us from our own folly.

    THOMAS E. MURRAY, *Address,* December 4, 1951

We shall never stop war, whatever machinery we may devise, until we have learned to think always, with a sort of desperate urgency and an utter self-identification, of single human beings.

    VICTOR GOLLANCZ, *From Darkness to Light,* 1956

The verbal Christian belief in the sanctity of life has not been affected by the impersonal barbarism of twentieth century war.

    C. WRIGHT MILLS, *The Causes of World War III,* 1958

Until now it has been a matter of debate whether it is legitimate for a Christian to refuse to fight, but now the question must be whether it is legitimate for him to fight at all.

    BEDE GRIFFITH, *Morals and Missiles: Catholic Essays on the Problem of War Today,* 1959

The axiom "the Church shrinks from bloodshed" was taken so seriously through-out the first thousand years of the Christian era that numerous ecclesiastical synods imposed severe penances for killing in war.

    FRANZISKUS STRATMANN, *Morals and Missiles: Catholic Essays on the Problem of War Today,* 1959

The moral problem of war will never be correctly analyzed unless there is a return to a morality of means as well as ends in warfare that can at all be justified for the Christian.

    PAUL RAMSEY, *War and the Christian Conscience,* 1961

When war begins, the Devil makes Hell bigger.

    Proverb

A great war always creates more scoundrels than it kills.

    ANONYMOUS

He that preaches war is the devil's chaplain.

    Proverb

See also Aggression; Armaments; Atomic Bomb; Bloodshed; Brotherhood; Calamity; Charity; Christianity; Conquest; Conscience; Conscientious Objector; Conscription; Discord; End of the Word; Evil, Problem of; Force; Internationalism; Killing; Love; Loyalty; Machines; Militarism; Military Service; Mobilization; Nonresistance; Nonviolence; Nonviolent Resistance; Nuclear Energy; Nuclear War; Pacifism; Pacifists; Patriotism; Peace; Science; Self-Defense; Soldier; Vengeance; Victory; Violence; War, Condemnation of; War, Defense of; War, Just; War, Unjust.

WAR, CONDEMNATION OF

Where armies have been quartered brambles and thorns grow. . . . He who takes delight in the slaughter of men cannot have his will done in the world.

    LAO-TZU, *Tao Tê Ching,* 5th century B.C.

How could you . . . not grieve at war and delight in peace, being children of one and the same Father?

PHILO, *Confusion of Languages,* c .10 A.D.

In so far as we conquer the demons who stir up war and disturb peace, we perform better service for our ruler than they who bear the sword.

ORIGEN, *Against Celsus,* VIII, 246

The wars of mankind are like children's fights—all meaningless, pitiless and contemptible.

JALLALUDIN RUMI (1207–1273), *Masnavi*

War is so cruel a business that it befits beasts and not men, . . . so pestilential that it brings with it a general blight upon morals, so iniquitous that it is usually conducted by the worst bandits, so impious that it has no accord with Christ.

DESIDERIUS ERASMUS, *The Praise of Folly,* 1511

Bishops, how dare you, who hold the place of the Apostles, teach people things that touch on war at the same time you teach the precepts of the Apostles? . . . There is no peace, even unjust, which is not preferable to the most just of wars.

DESIDERIUS ERASMUS, *The Complaint of Peace,* 1517

War is the greatest plague that can afflict humanity; it destroys religion, it destroys states, it destroys families. Any scourge is preferable to it.

MARTIN LUTHER (1483–1546), *Table Talk*

Can anything be more ridiculous than that a man has a right to kill men because he dwells on the other side of the water, and because his prince has a quarrel with mine, although I have none with him?

BLAISE PASCAL, *Pensées,* 1670

There never was a good war or a bad peace.

BENJAMIN FRANKLIN, *Letter to Josiah Quincy,* September 11, 1773

If we will not be peaceable, let us then at least be honest, and acknowledge that we continue to slaughter one another, not because Christianity permits it, but because we reject her laws.

JONATHAN DYMOND, *Essay on War,* 1823

Under the sky is no uglier spectacle than two men with clenched teeth, and hellfire eyes, hacking one another's flesh; converting precious living bodies, and priceless living souls, into nameless masses of putrescence, useful only for turnip-manure.

THOMAS CARLYLE, *Past and Present,* 1843

What a cruel thing is war: to separate and destroy families and friends; and mar the purest joys and happiness God has granted us in this world: to fill our hearts with hatred instead of love for our neighbors, and to devastate the fair face of this beautiful world.

ROBERT E. LEE, *Letter to his wife,* December 25, 1862

Who can reflect on the sacredness of human life in view of its eternal destinies, without coming to the conclusion that war, with its attendants, hatred, destruction and slaughter, is incompatible with the high dictates of religion?

L. LEVI, *International Law,* 1888

I am tired and sick of war. Its glory is all moonshine. It is only those who have neither fired a shot nor heard the shrieks and groans of the wounded who cry aloud for blood, more vengeance, more desolation. War is hell.

WILLIAM T. SHERMAN, *Address,* June 19, 1879, according to a letter published in *The National Tribune,* Washington, D.C., November 26, 1914

War is the greatest of all the awful and complex moral situations of the world—second only to the final judgment day. . . . It is a moral pestilence. It is wrong on both sides.

> P. T. FORSYTH, *The Christian Ethic of War*, 1916

If war is the collective sin they say it is, let us then collectively quit participating in the sin.

> *Christian Century*, January 31, 1924

The war system is inconsistent with all Christian ideals. . . . Religion should no longer sanction war.

> Federal Council of Churches of Christ in America, *Report*, 1932

To support war is to deny the Gospel which we profess to believe.

> Federal Council of Churches of Christ in America, *Report*, 1932

It is the most colossal and ruinous social sin which afflicts humanity.

> Executive Committee, Federal Council of Churches of Christ in America, *Report*, 1932

Men who in every nation pray to the same God for peace on earth cannot be at the same time bearers of discord among peoples; men who turn in prayer to the Divine Majesty cannot foment that nationalistic imperialism which of each people makes its own god; men who look to the "God of Peace and of Love."

> POPE PIUS XI, *Caritate Christi Compulsi*, 1932

War involves compulsory enmity, diabolical outrage against human personality, and a wanton distortion of truth. War is a particular demonstration of the power of sin in the world, and a defiance of the righteousness of God.

> Oxford Conference on Church, Community and State, in *Reports*, Vol. VIII, *The Churches Survey Their Task*, 1937

War and Christianity are incompatible; you cannot conquer war by war; cast out Satan by Satan; or do the enormous evil of war that good may come of it.

> NORMAN THOMAS, *Letter*, January 31, 1937

An evil so atrocious, and so universal, a course so straight to the abyss of nothingness, cannot be borne with unless it be erected into an absolute in hearts poisoned with hatred.

> GUSTAVE THIBON, *Études; Carmélitaines*, 1939

Our country is at war. Its life is at stake. . . . It is our necessity, an unnecessary necessity, therefore a guilty necessity. . . . Our fighting, though necessary, is not righteous.

> CLAYTON W. MORRISON, *Christian Century*, December, 1941

War is the collapse of the Divine order which God is striving with man's co-operation to establish in the world.

> CHARLES CLAYTON MORRISON, *The Christian and the War*, 1942

There is something appallingly wrong, something tragically wrong with a world in which hundreds of millions of those individuals for whom Christ died to save, are hurled helplessly into bloodshed by half a dozen men whose plans and motives have been completely hidden from all but perhaps another half dozen.

> ALFRED NOYES, *The Edge of Darkness* 1942

There is a duty which is incumbent on all, a duty which tolerates no delay, no postponement, no hesitation, no shuffling; to do everything possible to proscribe and once for all banish a war of aggression as a legitimate solution of international differences and as an instrument of national aspirations.

> POPE PIUS XII, *Broadcast*, December 24, 1943

On the basic principle that the Church cannot acquiesce in the supremacy of military considerations even in war time, nor in the view that modern war may properly, even in the case of extreme peril to the nation, church or culture, become total war, we are agreed.

> Federal Council of Churches (U.S.), *The Relation of the Church to War in the Light of the Christian Faith,* Report of the Committee of Christian Scholars, 1944

Christ bids us love our enemies; governments bid us kill them.

> Statement on Conscription by Friends [Quakers] in Great Britain, 1945

The future of the Church as the Body of Christ cannot be staked in a conflict in which there is no place left for mercy and the individual person counts for nothing at all.

> *The Era of Atomic Power,* British Council of Churches Commission, 1946

War is not "a judgment of God" in the sense that God wills it as a punishment for men. . . . War is in a general sense a crucifixion of both man and God.

> Commission of twenty-six Christian scholars, *The Relation of the Church to War in the Light of the Christian Faith,* Report to Federal Council of Churches of Christ in America, 1946

War as a method of settling disputes is incompatible with the teaching and example of our Lord Jesus Christ.

> *First Assembly of the World Conference of Churches,* 1948

Just as death is preferable to life under some conditions, so, too, victory at any price is not worth having. . . . Military expediency, therefore, cannot be the sole test, but must be subordinated to moral and political considerations.

> Dun Commission Report, *Christianity and Crisis,* December 11, 1950

Any kind of glorification of war must be condemned as an aberration of the intellect and the heart.

> POPE PIUS XII, *Address,* October 19, 1953

If the opposing sides are Christian, they share the sin of caricaturing their Faith; if the one side is Christian, and the other not, Christians sin gravely if they are the aggressors.

> C. C. MARTINDALE, *The Catholic Bedside Book,* 1953

There is no ground for Christians to support a war for the objective of unconditional surrender.

> *Christians and the Prevention of War in an Atomic Age,* World Council of Churches, August, 1958

War and all that goes into the preparation therefor is evil in itself. We cannot adorn it with the title of "good."

> JAMES A. PIKE, *God and the H-Bomb,* ed. D. Keys, 1962

The Church must proclaim categorical condemnation of total, all-out war. Under modern conditions, such war cannot serve any moral or even useful purpose. Every possible moral force must be summoned to prevent its occurrence.

> "The Church's Attitude Toward Questions of War and Peace," Report by Department of Christian Social Relation of Protestant Episcopal Church, October, 1962

The Church declares that the concept of massive retaliation should be rethought and be repudiated.

> "The Church's Attitude Toward Questions of War and Peace," Report by Department of Christian Social Relation of Protestant Episcopal Church, October, 1962

The horror and perversity of war is immensely magnified by the addition of scientific weapons. For acts of war involving these weapons can inflict massive and indiscriminate destruction, thus going far beyond the bounds of legitimate defense.

Second Vatican Council, *The Church in the Modern World,* December, 1965

Any act of war, aimed indiscriminately at the destruction of entire cities or of extensive areas along with their population is a crime against God and the man himself. It merits unequivocal and unhesitating condemnation.

Second Vatican Council, *The Church in the Modern World,* December, 1965

See also Aggression; Armaments; Atomic Bomb; Bloodshed; Conquest; Conscience; Conscientious Objector; Force; Nuclear War; Pacifism; Patriotism; Peace; Vengeance; Violence; War.

WAR, DEFENSE OF

As to killing others in order to defend one's own life, I do not approve of this, unless one happens to be a soldier or public functionary acting, not for himself, but in defense of others or of the city in which he resides, if he act according to the commission lawfully given him, and in the manner becoming his office.

ST. AUGUSTINE, *To Publicola,* 398

Fight for the cause of God against those that fight against you: but commit not the injustice of attacking them first. . . . Kill them whenever ye shall find them and eject them from whatever place they have ejected you.

Koran, c. 625

Lo, Allah loveth those who battle for His cause. . . . swear by Allah . . . that marching about, morning and evening, to fight for religion is better than the world and everything in it; and verily the standing of one of you in the line of battle is better than superrogatory prayers performed in your house for sixty years.

MOHAMMED (570–632), *Speeches and Table Talk of Mohammed,* S. Lane-Poole

War has the deep meaning that by it the ethical health of the nations is preserved and their finite aims uprooted.

G. W. F. HEGEL, *The Philosophy of Law,* 1821

Eternal peace is a dream, and not even a beautiful one. War is a part of God's world order. In it are developed the noblest virtues of man: courage and abnegation, dutifulness and self-sacrifice. Without war the world would sink into materialism.

HELMUTH VON MOLTKE, *Letter to J. K. Bluntschli,* December, 1880

The man who has renounced war has renounced a grand life.

FRIEDRICH NIETZSCHE, *The Twilight of the Idols,* 1889

The grandeur of war lies in the utter annihilation of puny man in the great conception of the State, and it brings out the full magnificence of the sacrifice of fellow-countrymen for one another.

HEINRICH VON TREITSCHKE, *Politics,* 1890

That faith is true and admirable which leads a soldier to throw away his life in obedience to a blindly accepted faith, in a cause which he little understands, in a plan of campaign in which he has little notion, under tactics of which he does not see the use.

OLIVER WENDELL HOLMES, JR., *The Soldier's Faith,* 1895

War is only a sort of dramatic representation, a sort of dramatic symbol of a thousand forms of duty.

WOODROW WILSON, *Speech,* May 11, 1914

Let the Churches of Christ enlist for this great adventure of the soul.

    RAYMOND ROBBINS, *Speech,* Washington, D.C., May, 1917

As citizens of a peace-loving nation, we abhor war. . . . But since, in spite of every effort, war has come, we are grateful that the ends to which we are committed are such as we can approve.

    Federal Council of Churches of Christ in America, May, 1917

The complete representative of the American Church in France is the United States Army overseas. . . . The Army today is the Church in action . . . expressing the moral judgments of the Church in smashing blows. Its worship has its vigil in the trenches. . . . Our Army is preaching the sermon of the American Church to Germany.

    GEORGE PERKINS ATWATER, *Atlantic Monthly,* April, 1918

Although war is a scourge in so far as our life on earth is concerned—a scourge, indeed, of such destructive force that we cannot measure the range of its impact,—it is also an agent of purification for souls, a means of expiation, and a lever enabling many to climb the heights of patriotism and Christian disinterestedness.

    DÉSIRÉ JOSEPH MERCIER, *Voix de la Guerre,* ed. Thone, 1937

We agree that in the outcome of the present conflict moral issues are at stake which as Christians we dare not evade. There are certain political objectives which touch vitally the Christian way of life.

    Federal Council of Churches of Christ in America, *Report,* 1940

The horrors of modern warfare, though ghastly beyond all previous tragedies, are not the worst alternatives now confronting Christendom and Democracy.

    EDMUND A. WALSH, *Address,* July 27, 1952

See also Aggression; Duties; Injustice; Loyalty; Patriotism; Rights; Self-Defense; State, the; War; War, Just.

WAR, JUST

The blood of a nation ought never to be shed except for its own preservation in the utmost extremity.

    FRANÇOIS FÉNELON, *Telemachus,* 1699

We believe that the cause for which our country is standing in this war is directly related to those great truths for which the Church stands.

    ARTHUR JUDSON BROWN, quoted in *President Wilson and the Moral Aims of the War,* ed. F. Lynch, 1917

The war is steadily becoming a conflict between progression and reaction, humanity and savagery, freedom and tyranny, German philosophy and Christianity.

    HENRY CHURCHILL KING, quoted in C. S. Macfarland's *Wartime Activity of the Churches,* 1917

For a war to be just it must, first, be seeking to rectify actual violations of rights or rights that with certainty are in imminent danger of violation. . . . Those rights that a war may protect must be of such primary importance as to balance in the scales the wreck and devastation of war. The war must be necessary; peaceful means must be tried and not abandoned until found utterly hopeless.

    A committee of National Catholic Welfare Council, *The Christian Way to Peace,* 1929

War can be justified only on the ground that it is a necessary means for keeping the peace.

    DÉSIRÉ JOSEPH MERCIER, *Voix de la Guerre,* ed. Thone, 1937

Apart from the question of a defensive war (and that under fixed conditions) through which a state seeks to defend itself against the actual unjustified military aggression of another state, *there is no longer today any possibility of a just war* which permits a state to uphold its rights by proceeding with aggression.

ALFREDO OTTAVIANI, *Public Laws of the Church*, 1947

The real moral line between what may be done and what may not be done by the Christian lies not in the realm of distinction between weapons but in the realm of the motives for using and the consequences of using all kinds of weapons.

DUN COMMISSION, *Christianity and Crisis*, December 11, 1950

The only constraint to wage war is defense against an injustice of the utmost gravity which strikes the entire community and which cannot be coped with by any other means.

POPE PIUS XII, *Address*, October 19, 1953

The occasions to which the concept of the just war can be rightly applied have become highly restricted. A war to "defend the victims of wanton aggression" where the demands of justice join the demands of order, is today the clearer case of a just war. . . . The concept of a just war does not provide moral justification for initiating a war of incalculable consequences to end such oppression.

ANGUS DUN and REINHOLD NIEBUHR, *Christianity and Crisis*, June 13, 1955

The Kingdom of God cannot take the responsibility for defending itself in arms: that is the lesson of the New Testament. But the New Testament nowhere forbids the secular powers to defend the Kingdom of God, when unjustly attacked.

CHARLES JOURNET, *The Church of the Word Incarnate*, Vol. I, 1955

There may come into existence in a nation a situation in which all hope of averting war becomes vain. In this situation a war of efficacious self-defense against unjust attacks, which is undertaken with hope of success, cannot be considered illicit.

POPE PIUS XII, *Christmas Message*, 1956

The morality of the violence will depend on its proportion to the aggression. One will not rout a burglar with an atomic bomb.

JOHN R. CONNEY, *Theology Digest*, Winter, 1957

Always look out, my young friend, when the theologians start talking about a just war. It is such a comprehensive and reasonable phrase that it really ought to be prohibited.

HEINRICH BÖLL, *Letter to a Young Catholic*, 1958

To be finally justified there should be some reasonable expectation that a war can produce more good than evil, or at least achieve a lesser evil than not resorting to arms would lead to.

PAUL RAMSEY, *War and the Christian Conscience*, 1961

See also Aggression; Injustice; Peace; Rights; Self-Defense; War; War, Defense of.

WAR, UNJUST

The one thing a belligerent state can never lawfully do is this: it may not directly intend to kill the innocent.

LAWRENCE L. MCREAVY, *Clergy Review*, February, 1941

A state may make war only to safeguard its rights. Hence a war is not morally justified which aims at extending national territory, enhancing national power and prestige, promoting an international "balance of power" or forestalling some hypothetical or merely probable menace.

Report, Catholic Association for International Peace, *International Ethics*, 1942

Statesmen are not justified in making war if their country is likely to find itself in a worse condition at the end than at the beginning.

> Report, Catholic Association for International Peace, *International Ethics,* 1942

It is true that if we can win the war by use of one means which will incidentally and without intending it mean the death of 100,000 civilians or of another which in the same way will kill one million civilians then we may not use the second and larger since the excess of evil is not required for the defense of our right.

> WILFRED PARSONS, *Ethics of Atomic War,* 1947

To seek the entire subjection of the enemy, or the abolition of his sovereignty, or unrestricted control over his life, labour and property, is not permissible; for such aims transcend the limits set by justifying causes.

> DUN COMMISSION, *Christianity and Crisis,* December 11, 1950

Defending oneself against any kind of injustice is not sufficient reason to resort to war. When the losses it brings are not comparable to those of the "injustice tolerated," one may have the obligation of "submitting to the injustice."

> POPE PIUS XII, *Address,* October 19, 1953

Christians must oppose all policies which give evidence of leading to all-out war. Finally, if all-out war should occur, Christians should urge a cease fire, if necessary, on the enemy's terms, and resort to non-violent resistance.

> *Christians and the Prevention of War in an Atomic Age,* World Council of Churches, 1958

The ancient theory of the just war breaks down when victory is impossible, when the weapons are so undiscriminating as to destroy both sides.

> Editorial, *Christian Century,* August 3, 1960

See also Aggression; Armaments; Conquest; Imperialism; Injustice; Nuclear War; Victory; War; War, Condemnation of.

WAY, THE

The way is like an empty vessel, that yet may be drawn from without even needing to be filled. It is bottomless; the very progenitor of all things in the world. In it all sharpness is blunted, all tangles untied, all glare tempered, all dust smoothed. It is like a deep pool that never dries.

> *Tao Tê Ching,* between 6th and 3rd century B.C.

See also Tao.

WEALTH

No one goes to Hades with all his immense wealth.

> THEOGNIS, *Maxims,* 6th century B.C.

Faith is wealth! Obedience is wealth! Modesty also is wealth! Hearing is wealth, and so is Charity! Wisdom is sevenfold riches.

> *Dhammapada,* c. 5th century B.C.

The hereafter never rises before the eyes of the careless child, deluded by the delusion of wealth. "This is the world," he thinks, "there is no other"—thus he falls again and again under my sway.

> Death speaking in *Katha Upanishad,* before 400 B.C.

The character which results from wealth is that of a prosperous fool.

> ARISTOTLE, *Rhetoric,* c. 322 B.C.

Can you rise superior to your riches? Say so, and Christ does not draw you away from the possession of them.

ST. CLEMENT OF ALEXANDRIA (died c. 215), *The Rich Man's Salvation*

He does not see, poor wretch, that his life is but a gilded torture, that he is bound fast by his wealth, and that his money owns him rather than he owns it.

ST. CYPRIAN OF CARTHAGE, *The World and Its Vanities*, c. 250

But perhaps you are deceived by the fact that many who know not God possess wealth in abundance, are full of honors, and enjoy great authority. These unhappy men are uplifted the higher, that their fall may be greater.

MARCUS MINUCIUS FELIX, *Octavius*, 3rd century

Nothing is more fallacious than wealth. Today it is for thee, tomorrow it is against thee. It arms the eyes of the envious everywhere. It is a hostile comrade, a domestic enemy.

ST. JOHN CHRYSOSTOM, *Homilies*, c. 388

Alas! Before man was, that seductive thing, abundance of wealth, which is the mother of our luxury, began to be. . . . But nature is nowise at fault; she provided our nourishment, she did not prescribe our vices. She gave these things as common possessions, so that you might not claim any of them as your private property.

ST. AMBROSE, *Hexameron*, V, i, 2, c. 389

They lost all they had. Their faith? Their godliness? The possession of the hidden man of the heart, which in the sight of God are of great price? Did they lose these? For these are the wealth of the Christians.

ST. AUGUSTINE, *The City of God*, I, 14, 10, 426

However, if thou shouldst happen to possess such earthly riches, use them not according to thy pleasure, but according to the necessities of the time: in this way thou shalt use them as if using them not.

ST. BERNARD, *De Consideratione*, Lib. ll, cap. vi, c. 1150

Shine in jewels, stink in conditions; have purple robes, and a torn conscience.

ST. BERNARD (1091–1153), *Epistle 113*

When holy men for gold and silver care,
Search somewhere else for holy men than
    there!

SHAIKH SAADI, *Gulistan*, c. 1265

Rich and poor alike
Are bondsmen of the clay;
And they who most possess
Have most from Heaven to pray.

SHAIKH SAADI, *Gulistan*, c. 1265

Man ought to possess external things not as his own but as common, so that he is ready to communicate them to others in their need.

ST. THOMAS AQUINAS, *Summa Theologiae*, 1272

Whatever some people possess in superabundance is due by natural law to the purpose of succoring the poor.

ST. THOMAS AQUINAS, *Summa Theologiae*, 1272

How can true happiness proceed from wealth, which in its acquisition causes pain; in loss, affliction; in abundance, folly.

Hitopadesa, 13th century

He who has enough to satisfy his wants, and nevertheless ceaselessly labors to acquire riches, either in order to obtain a higher social position, or that subsequently he may have enough to live without labor, or that his sons may become men of wealth and importance—all such are incited by a damnable avarice, sensuality and pride.

HENRY OF LANGENSTEIN (1325–1397), *Tractutus Bipartibus de Contractibus*

Where wealth is, there are also all manner of sins; for through wealth comes pride, through pride dissension, through dissension wars, through wars, poverty, through poverty, great distress and misery. Therefore, they that are rich, must yield a strict and great account; for to whom much is given, of him will much be required.

MARTIN LUTHER, *Table Talk*, 1569

All the riches of the world and the glory of creation, compared with the wealth of God, are extreme and abject poverty.

ST. JOHN OF THE CROSS (1542–1591), *The Ascent of Mount Carmel*

Moderate Riches will carry you; if you have more, you must carry them.

THOMAS FULLER, *Gnomologia*, 1732

Many a man would have been worse if his estate had been better.

BENJAMIN FRANKLIN, *Poor Richard's Almanac*, 1751

Wealth tends to corrupt the mind and to nourish its love of power, and to stimulate its oppression.

GOUVERNEUR MORRIS, *Speech*, July, 1788

Wealth desired for its own sake obstructs the increase of virtue, and large possessions in the hands of selfish men have a bad tendency.

JOHN WOOLMAN, *A Word of Remembrance and Caution to the Rich*, 1793

Many men want wealth—not a competence alone, but a five-story competence. Every thing subserves this; and religion they would like as a sort of lightning rod to their houses, to ward off, by and by, the bolts of divine wrath.

HENRY WARD BEECHER, *Life Thoughts*, 1858

It is impossible to conclude, of any given mass of acquired wealth, merely by the fact of its existence, whether it signifies good or evil to the nation in the midst of which it exists.

JOHN RUSKIN, *Unto This Last*, 1860

That which seems to be wealth may in verity be only the gilded index of far-reaching ruin; a wrecker's handful of coin gleaned from the beach to which he has beguiled an argosy.

JOHN RUSKIN, *Unto This Last; The Veins of Wealth*, 1862

Even war and riches, even the Babel life of our great cities, even the high places of ambition and earthly honor, have been touched by His spirit, have found how to be Christian.

R. W. CHURCH, *Sermon* preached at University of Oxford, in *The Gifts of Civilization and Other Sermons and Lectures*, 1867

The heart which haunts the treasure-house where the moth and rust corrupt, will be exposed to the same ravages as the treasure.

GEORGE MACDONALD, *Unspoken Sermons*, 1st Series, 1869

Superior want of conscience . . . is often the determining quality which makes a millionaire out of one who otherwise might have been a poor man.

HENRY GEORGE, *Progress and Poverty*, 1879

If wealth is to be valued because it gives leisure, clearly it would be a mistake to sacrifice leisure in the struggle for wealth.

JOHN LUBBOCK, *The Pleasures of Life*, 1887

Of all the corrupting effects of wealth there is none worse than this, that it makes the wealthy (and their parasites) think in some way divine . . . what is in truth nothing more than their power of luxurious living.

> HILAIRE BELLOC, *The Path to Rome*, 1900

There is to be no leisure class in a Christian society. Interest and profits on investments thus find justification only if a corresponding service is rendered by the recipient of them.

> Federal Council of Churches of Christ in America, quoted in *The Church and Industrial Reconstruction*, 1922

Compromise is as impossible between the Church of Christ and the idolatry of wealth, which is the practical religion of capitalistic societies, as it was between the Church and the State idolatry of the Roman Empire.

> R. H. TAWNEY, *Religion and the Rise of Capitalism*, 1926

Wealth, which is constantly being augmented by social and economic progress, must be so distributed among the various individuals and classes of society that the common good of all . . . be thereby promoted.

> POPE PIUS XI, *Quadragesimo Anno*, 1931

The great fault of modern democracy—a fault that is common to the capitalist and the socialist—is that it accepts economic wealth as the end of society and the standard of personal happiness.

> CHRISTOPHER DAWSON, *The Modern Dilemma*, 1932

The throne and the altar will never be united in the United States; but the pocketbook and the altar can make, if we do not watch out, a quite unholy alliance. A wealthy Catholic with high political influence—be it local or national—can drive some surprisingly hard bargains.

> JOHN LA FARGE, *The Manner Is Ordinary*, 1954

The state of a man's soul has no necessary connection with the state of his bank account. For the prince in the penthouse can become saintly or satanic—and so can the pauper in the pig pen.

> JOHN E. LARGE, *The Small Needle of Doctor Large*, 1962

See also Avarice; Capitalism; Charity; Covetousness; Desires; Ease; Gold; Greed; Happiness; Luxury; Mammon; Money; Ownership; Pleasure; Poor, the; Possessions; Poverty; Profit; Property; Prosperity, Renunciation; Rich, the; Riches; Success; Usury; Work; Worldliness.

WEEKDAYS

Monday is as holy as Sunday, because all our time belongs to God. . . . Doing the duties of life, with hand or with mind is as religious as prayer.

> GEORGE ALBERT COE, *The Religion of a Mature Mind*, 1902

Remember the week-day to keep it holy.

> ELBERT HUBBARD (1859–1915), *Notebook*

See also Day; Days; Sabbath; Sunday.

WEEPING

To weep beyond measure, is to protest against the ways of God and to deny immortality of the soul.

> *Talmud*, c. 4th century A.D.

See also Bereavement; Grief; Laughter; Sorrow; Tears.

WELFARE. See
PUBLIC WELFARE

WELFARE STATE

No doubt the welfare state has come into being largely through Christian inspiration; but the average villager is quite incapable of that kind of historical analysis. For him what has happened is that the State has taken the place of the Church.

> JOHN MIDDLETON MURRY, *Not as the Scribes,* 1959

See also Public Welfare; Social Action; Social Conscience; Social Gospel; Social Order; Socialism.

WICKED, THE

Wicked is he who is good to the wicked.

> YASNA (Zoroastrian), 6th century B.C.

The difficult thing is not to escape death but to escape wickedness.

> SOCRATES, in Plato's *Apology,* 399 B.C.

The success of the wicked is a temptation to many others.

> PHAEDRUS, *Fabulae Aesopiae,* c. 40 A.D.

He who by His providence and omnipotence distributes to every one his own portion, is able to make good use not only of the good, but also of the wicked.

> ST. AUGUSTINE, *City of God,* XIV, 426

While God accomplishes through the wicked what he has decreed by His secret judgment, they are not excusable.

> JOHN CALVIN, *Institutes,* I, 1536

There are wicked people who would be much less dangerous if they were wholly without goodness.

> LA ROCHEFOUCAULD, *Maxims,* 1665

If it be true that men are always miserable because they are wicked, it is likewise true, that many are wicked because they are miserable.

> SAMUEL TAYLOR COLERIDGE, *Aids to Reflection,* 1825

See also Evil; Good; Goodness; Man: His Wickedness; Misery; Predestination.

WIFE

A man who has a bad wife will never see the face of hell.

> *Erubin, Talmud,* between 2nd and 4th century A.D.

If he [a husband] is absent from her she [the wife] wisheth him well in her person by guarding herself from unchastity and taketh care of his property.

> MOHAMMED, *Speeches and Table Talk of,* 7th century A.D.

He who has an old, spiteful, quarrelsome, sickly wife, may fairly reckon himself in Purgatory.

> MARTIN LUTHER (1483–1546), *Table Talk*

There is no joy, no comfort, no sweetness, no pleasure in the world like to that of a good wife.

> ROBERT BURTON, *The Anatomy of Melancholy,* III, 1621

A judicious, diligent, and pious wife is the soul of a great household; she introduces order there for temporal welfare and future salvation.

> FRANÇOIS FÉNELON, *Education of Girls,* 1688

All the blessings of a household come through the wife; therefore should her husband honor her. . . . Let men beware of causing women to weep; God counts their tears.

> Hebrew Proverb, quoted in M. H. HARRIS, *Hebraic Literature*

See also Family; Husband; Husband and Wife; Marriage; Parents; Woman.

WILL

The commander of the forces of a large State may be carried off, but the will of

even a common man cannot be taken from him.
CONFUCIUS, *Analects,* 5th century B.C.

No man is a creature of will. According to what his will is in this world, so will he be when he has departed this life.
Chandogya Upanishad, before 400 B.C.

No inferior thing depraves the will, but the will depraves itself by following inferior things inordinately.
ST. AUGUSTINE, *City of God,* XI.6, 426

I know not in what wicked, yet wonderful way, the will, when turned towards evil by sin, imposes a constraint on itself; so that on the one hand such constraint, since it is voluntary, cannot avail to excuse the will, and, on the other hand, the will, being drawn away and allured, is unable to resist the constraint.
ST. BERNARD (1091–1153), *Serm. in Cant.*

The will can tend to nothing except under the aspect of good. But because the good is of many kinds, for this reason the will is not of necessity determined to one.
ST. THOMAS AQUINAS, *Summa Theologiae,* Pt. I, Q. 82, A. 2, Reply 1, 1272

The human will is like a beast of burden. If God mounts it, it wishes and goes as God wills; if Satan mounts it, it wishes and goes as Satan wills. Nor can it choose its rider. . . . The riders contend for its possession.
MARTIN LUTHER, *De Servo Arbitrio,* 1525

Man's will hath some liberty to work a civil righteousness, and to choose such things as reason can reach into; but it hath no power to work the righteousness of God.
PHILIP MELANCHTHON, *Augsburg Confession,* 1530

The will, being inseparable from the nature of man, is not annihilated; but it is fettered by depraved and inordinate desires, so that it cannot aspire after anything that is good.
JOHN CALVIN, *Institutes,* I, 1536

Will is one of the principal organs of belief, not that it forms belief, but because things are true or false according to the side on which we look at them.
BLAISE PASCAL, *Pensées,* 1670

As we had no part of our will on our entrance into this life, we should not presume to any in our leaving it, but soberly learn to will which He wills.
WILLIAM DRUMMOND, *The Cypress Grove,* 1673

Will signifies nothing but the power, or ability, to prefer or choose.
JOHN LOCKE, *Essay Concerning Human Understanding,* 1690

All things in the world appear plainly to be the most arbitrary that can be imagined. . . . and plainly the product, not of necessity but will.
SAMUEL CLARKE, *Demonstrations,* 1706

The will is that by which the mind chooses anything.
JONATHAN EDWARDS, *The Freedom of the Will,* 1754

In the power of willing . . . nothing is to be found but acts which are purely spiritual and wholly inexplicable by the laws of mechanism.
JEAN JACQUES ROUSSEAU, *Discourse on Inequality,* 1755

As his will cannot be determined but by a motive which is not in his own power, it follows that he is never the master of the determination of his own peculiar will.
P. H. D' HOLBACH, *The System of Nature,* 1770

The determinations of what we call the will are, in fact, nothing more than a particular case of the general doctrine of association of ideas, and therefore a perfectly mechanical thing.

JOSEPH PRIESTLEY, *The Doctrine of Philosophical Necessity*, 1778

The will is a faculty to choose *that only* which reason independent of inclination recognizes as practically necessary, i.e. as good . . . a faculty of determining oneself to action *in accordance with the conception of certain laws.*

IMMANUEL KANT, *Metaphysics of Ethics*, 1785

In this world will alone, as it lies concealed from mortal eyes in the secret obscurities of the soul, is the first link in a chain of consequences that stretches through the whole invisible realm of spirit.

J. G. FICHTE (1762–1814), *The Vocation of Man*

The will is the only permanent and unchangeable element in the mind; . . . it is the will which . . . gives unity to consciousness and holds together all its ideas and thoughts, accompanying them like a continuous harmony.

ARTHUR SCHOPENHAUER, *The World as Will and Idea*, II, 1818

Will . . . is the foundation of all being; it is part and parcel of every creature, and the permanent element in everything.

ARTHUR SCHOPENHAUER, "Further Psychological Observations," *Essays*, 1851

Will is the child of desire, and passes out of the dominion of its parent only to come under that of habit.

JOHN STUART MILL, *Utilitarianism*, 1863

A simple homogeneous mental state, forming the link between feeling and action, and not admitting of subdivisions.

HERBERT SPENCER, *Essays: Political, Scientific, and Speculative*, 1858–1874

Our wills are not ours to be crushed and broken; they are ours to be trained and strengthened.

HAMILTON WRIGHT MABIE, *The Life of the Spirit*, 1898

It is astonishing how the act of placing our own will as far as possible in unison with the Will of God restores our tranquillity.

ARTHUR CHRISTOPHER BENSON, *From a College Window*, 1906

The doctrine that the will alone is the way to power is a most woe-begone theory for the relief of the morally sick.

J. A. HADFIELD, *The Psychology of Power*, 1923

Our wills are the slaves of the accumulated influence of our interior companionships. What we can do is to get new mental images.

HARRY EMERSON FOSDICK, *The Hope of the World*, 1933

Man's sinful will cannot be explained: it must remain as the one completely irrational fact in a world which God created.

J. S. WHALE, *Christian Doctrine*, 1941

Dante said "In God's will lies our peace," but we better first make sure that it is God's will we are obeying, and not that of a frail human being, his whim or prejudice, or our own fear.

GEORGE LAWTON, *Aging Successfully*, 1946

By *will*, or rational appetite in general, we mean the faculty of inclining towards or striving after some object defined simply as the *capacity of self-determination.*

JOHN A. O'BRIEN, *Is the Will Free?*, 1946

See also Action; Acts; Belief; Choice; Commitment; Deeds; Desires; Detachment; Determinism; Election; Fatalism; Fate; Foreknowledge; Free Will; Freedom; God: His Omniscience; Guilt; Judgment,

God's; Mechanism; Necessity; Original Sin; Personality; Positivism; Prayer: Defined and Explained; Predestination; Self-Will; Sin.

WINE

When the wine goes in the murder comes out.
Talmud (*Erubin*), c. 200 A.D.

Toward evening, about supper-time, when the serious studies of the day are over, is the time to take wine.
ST. CLEMENT OF ALEXANDRIA, *Paedagogus*, c. 220

I hear many cry when deplorable excesses happen, "Would there were no wine!" Oh, folly! oh, madness! Is it the wine that causes this abuse? No. It is the intemperance of those who take an evil delight in it.
ST. JOHN CHRYSOSTOM, *Homilies*, c. 388

Wine was given us of God, not that we might be drunken, but that we might be sober; that we might be glad, not that we get ourselves pain.
ST. JOHN CHRYSOSTOM, *Homilies*, c. 388

Wine is the first weapon that devils use in attacking the young.
ST. JEROME, *The Virgin's Profession*, c. 420

O thou invisible spirit of wine, if thou hast no name to be known by, let me call thee Devil!
WILLIAM SHAKESPEARE, *Othello*, 1604

If God forbade drinking would He have made wine so good?
ARMAND RICHELIEU, *Mirame*, c. 1625

Wine . . . is one of the noblest cordials in nature.
JOHN WESLEY, *Journal*, September 9, 1771

Wine gives great pleasure, and every pleasure is of itself a good.
SAMUEL JOHNSON, *Boswell's Life of,* April 28, 1778

See also Abstinence; Alcohol; Drunkenness; Gluttony; Moderation; Pleasure; Sobriety; Temperance.

WISDOM

By thoughtfulness, by restraint and self-control, the wise man may make for himself an island which no flood can overwhelm.
Dhammapada, c. 5th century B.C.

The virtue of wisdom more than anything else contains a divine element which always remains.
PLATO, *The Republic*, c. 370 B.C.

Humbleness, truthfulness and harmlessness
Patience and honor . . .
this is true Wisdom, Prince.
The Song Celestial, Sir Edwin Arnold's translation of the *Bhagavad-Gita*, 5th to 2nd century B.C.

Should it be said that the Greeks discovered philosophy by human wisdom. I reply that I find the Scriptures declare all wisdom to be a divine gift.
ST. CLEMENT OF ROME, *Stromateis*, 200

We maintain that human wisdom is a means of education for the soul, divine wisdom being the ultimate end.
ORIGEN, *Contra Celsus*, c. 230

Watch this only, brethren, that no one of you be found only not speaking or meditating wisdom, but even hating and opposing those who pursue study of wisdom.
ORIGEN (185–254), *Homilies on Psalm XXVI*

The greatest good is wisdom.
> ST. AUGUSTINE, *Soliloquies*, 387

Wisdom without fear of God is despicable.
> *Talmud: Tosefa Derek Eretz*, 1.9., c. 500

Wisdom is the highest virtue, and it has in it four other virtues; of which one is prudence, another temperance, the third fortitude, the fourth justice.
> BOETHIUS, *Consolations of Philosophy*, c. 523

The foundation and pillar of wisdom is to recognize that there is an original Being . . . and that all . . . exist only through the reality of His being.
> MAIMONIDES, *Yad: Yesode HaTorah*, 1180

Of all human pursuits the pursuit of wisdom is the most perfect, the most sublime, the most profitable, the most delightful.
> ST. THOMAS AQUINAS, *Summa contra Gentiles*, c. 1260

A man of truest wisdom will resign his wealth, and e'en his life in a good cause.
> *Hitopadesa*, 13th century

When God lights the soul with wisdom, it floods the faculties, and that man knows more than ever could be taught him.
> MEISTER ECKHART (1260?–1327?), *Meister Eckhart*, R. B. Blakney

All the wisdom of the world is childish foolishness in comparison with the acknowledgement of Jesus Christ.
> MARTIN LUTHER (1483–1546), *Table Talk*

All the wisdom in the world and all human cleverness compared with the infinite wisdom of God is sheer and extreme ignorance.
> ST. JOHN OF THE CROSS (1542–1591), *The Ascent of Mount Carmel*

Wisdom is that olive that springeth from the heart, bloometh on the tongue, and beareth fruit in the actions.
> ELIZABETH GRYMESTON, *Miscellanea— Meditations*, 1604

[Wisdom is] the science of happiness or of the means of attaining the lasting contentment which consists in the continual achievement of a greater perfection or at least in variations of the same degree of perfection.
> G. W. VON LEIBNIZ, *Discourses on Metaphysics and Monadology*, 1714

[Wisdom is] pursuing the best ends by the best means.
> FRANCIS HUTCHESON, *Inquiry Concerning the Origin of Our Ideas of Beauty and Virtue*, 1725

Wisdom rises upon the Ruins of Folly.
> THOMAS FULLER, *Gnomologia*, 1732

All wisdom may be reduced to two words —wait and hope.
> ALEXANDRE DUMAS, *The Count of Monte Cristo*, 1844

Pure wisdom always directs itself towards God; the purest wisdom is knowledge of God.
> LEW WALLACE, *Ben Hur*, 1880

Wisdom consists in the highest use of the intellect for the discernment of the largest moral interest of humanity. It is the most perfect willingness to do the right combined with the utmost attainable knowledge of what is right. . . . Wisdom consists in working for the better from the love of the best.
> FELIX ADLER, *Life and Destiny*, 1913

The fear of God is not the beginning of wisdom. The fear of God is the death of wisdom. Skepticism and doubt lead to study and investigation, and investigation is the beginning of wisdom.

CLARENCE DARROW, *Speech,* Columbus, Ohio, 1929

I heartily scorn that kind of wisdom that is attained only through cooling off or lassitude.

ANDRÉ GIDE, *Journal,* January 25, 1931

When a man is on the point of drowning, all he cares for is his life. But as soon as he gets ashore, he asks "Where is my umbrella?" Wisdom, in life, consists in not asking for the umbrella.

JOHN WU, *Beyond East and West,* 1951

It is not wise to be wiser than it is given man to be wise.

ANONYMOUS

See also Good; Knowledge; Learning; Light; Philosophy; Platitudes; Religion: Its Nature and Function; Thinking; Thought; Truth; Truth, Definitions of; Values; Virtue.

WITCHCRAFT

What then must be His wrath against witchcraft, which we may justly designate high treason against divine majesty,—a revolt against the infinite power of God. . . . Does not witchcraft then, merit death?

MARTIN LUTHER, *Table Talk,* August 25, 1538

I believe in general that there is and has been such a thing as witchcraft, but at the same time can give no credit to any particular instance of it.

JOSEPH ADDISON, *The Spectator,* July 14, 1711

To deny the possibility, nay, actual existence, of witchcraft and sorcery is flatly to contradict the revealed Lord of God.

WILLIAM BLACKSTONE, *Commentaries on the Laws of England,* 1765

See also Superstition.

WITNESS

The soul is its own witness; yea, the soul itself is its own refuge; grieve thou not, O man, thy soul, the great internal Witness.

Code of Manu, between 1200 and 500 B.C.

There is a Witness everywhere.

THOMAS FULLER, *Gnomologia,* 1732

We learn from Holy Scripture that the Church has only one task, which is to bear witness to Him who was and is and is to come. . . . We can do nothing, we have nothing, we are nothing.

LUDWIG IHMELS, *The Stockholm Conference of 1925,* ed. K. A. Bell

The first demand which is made of those who belong to God's Church is . . . that they shall be witnesses of Jesus Christ before the world.

DIETRICH BONHOEFFER, *Ethics,* 1955

See also Church, Definitions of; Conscience, Conversion; Evangelism; Missionaries.

WOMAN

The judgment of God upon your sex endures even today; and with it inevitably endures your position of criminal at the bar of justice. You are the gateway to the Devil.

TERTULLIAN, *Women's Dress,* c. 220 A.D.

Nothing so much casts down the mind of man from its citadel as do the blandishments of women, and that physical contact without which a wife cannot be possessed.

St. Augustine, *Soliloquies,* 387

The beauty of woman is the greatest snare. Or rather, not the beauty of woman, but unchastened gazing.

St. John Chrysostom, *Homilies,* c. 388

Despise not yourselves, ye women; the Son of God was born of a woman.

St. Augustine, *On the Christian Conflict,* c. 397

Women are your fields; therefore go to your fields as you please.

Koran, c. 625

Every woman who dieth, and her husband is pleased with her, shall enter paradise.

Koran, iv, c. 625

The most valuable thing in the world is a virtuous woman.

Mohammed (570–632), *Speeches and Table Talk of Mohammed,* S. Lane-Poole

An evil woman in a good man's home,
It is as if in this life Hell were come.

Shaikh Saadi, *Gulistan,* c. 1265

The woman is subject to the man on account of the weakness of her nature, both of mind and body.

St. Thomas Aquinas, *Summa Theologiae,* suppl. lxxxi, 1272

The evil spirit takes delight (as he did from the beginning with Adam) in using a woman to make a fool of man—if he cannot make him godless, as he much prefers to do.

Martin Luther, *Letter,* November 2, 1525

What defects women have, we must check them for in private, gently by word of mouth, for woman is a frail vessel.

Martin Luther (1483–1546), *Table Talk*

I wish that women would repeat the Lord's Prayer before opening their mouths.

Martin Luther (1483–1546), quoted in R. Bainton's *Here I Stand*

To promote a woman to bear rule, superiority, dominion, or empire above any realm, nation, or city, is repugnant to nature; contumely to God, a thing most contrarious to His revealed will and approved ordinances.

John Knox, *First Blast of the Trumpet Against the Monstrous Regiment of Women,* 1558

Is it not women that ruin or uphold families, that regulate all the details of domestic life, and that decide, consequently, what touches most closely the whole human race?

François Fénelon, *Education of Girls,* 1688

A woman of sense and manners is the finest and most delicate part of God's creation, the glory of her Maker, and the great instances of His singular regard to man.

Daniel Defoe, *An Essay upon Projects,* 1697

The woman was made out of a rib out of the side of Adam; not of his feet to be trampled on by him, but out of his side to be equal with him, under his arms to be protected and, near to his heart to be loved.

Matthew Henry, *Exposition of Genesis,* 1725

Her dignity consists in being unknown to the world; her glory is in the esteem of her husband; her pleasures in the happiness of her family.

Jean Jacques Rousseau, *Emile,* 1762

There is in every true woman's heart a spark of heavenly fire, which lies dormant in the broad daylight of prosperity, but

which kindles up, and beams and blazes in the dark hour of adversity.
WASHINGTON IRVING, *The Sketch Book,* 1819

The new doctrine [of positivism] will institute the Worship of Women, publicly and privately, in a far more perfect way than has ever been possible. It is the first permanent step toward the worship of Humanity.
AUGUSTE COMTE, *Positive Polity,* 1820

Without woman the beginning of our life would be helpless, the middle without pleasure, and the end void of consolation.
VICTOR DE JOUY, *Sylla,* 1823

The happiest women, like the happiest nations, have no history.
GEORGE ELIOT, *The Mill on the Floss,* 1860

Their sensibility is greater, they are more chaste both in thought and act, more tender to the erring, more compassionate to the suffering, more affectionate to all about them.
W. E. H. LECKY, *History of European Morals,* 1869

Morally, the general superiority of women over men is, I think, unquestionable.
W. E. H. LECKY, *History of European Morals,* 1869

Noble-minded women, those in whom the spirit preponderates, succeed somehow in spiritualizing the physical and in developing in themselves an intensity and purity of spiritual love which produces types of mystics, wives, and mothers who are the admiration of mankind.
JACQUES LECLERCQ, *Marriage and the Family,* 1941

The Bible is the only literature in the world up to our century which looks at

women as human beings, no better and no worse than men.
EDITH HAMILTON, *Spokesmen for God: The Great Teachers of the Old Testament,* 1948

I am quite sure that a lot of moral delinquency is caused through the endeavor of women to become something that God never meant them to be.
ANTHONY HOSKYNS-ABRAHALL, quoted in *Look,* June 28, 1955

Since women are becoming ever more conscious of their human dignity, they will not tolerate being treated as mere material instruments, but demand rights befitting a human person both in domestic and in public life.
POPE JOHN XXIII, *Pacem in Terris,* April, 1963

See also Chastity; Daughters; Family; Love, Human, Love, Physical; Marriage; Maternity; Mother; Motherhood; Parents; Sexual Attraction; Sexual Desire; Sexual Intercourse; Virginity.

WOMEN. See WOMAN

WONDER

Men go forth to wonder at the height of mountains, the huge waves of the sea, the broad flow of rivers, the extent of the ọcean, the course of the stars—and forget to wonder at themselves.
ST. AUGUSTINE, *Confessions,* X15, 397

We carry within us the wonders we seek without us.
THOMAS BROWNE, *Religio Medici,* 1635

In wonder all philosophy began; in wonder it ends; and admiration fills up the interspace. But the first wonder is the offspring of ignorance: the last is the parent of adoration.

SAMUEL TAYLOR COLERIDGE, *Aids to Reflection*, 1825

Wonder is the basis of worship.

THOMAS CARLYLE, *Journal*, June 8, 1830

The man who cannot wonder, who does not habitually wonder (and worship), were he President of the innumerable Royal Societies . . . is but a Pair of Spectacles behind which there is no Eye.

THOMAS CARLYLE, *Sartor Resartus*, 1836

The material world, indeed, is infinitely more wonderful than any human contrivance, but wonder is not religion, or we should be worshipping railroads.

JOHN HENRY NEWMAN, *Parochial and Plain Sermons*, 1843

Wonder is the attitude of reverence for the infinite values and meaning of life, and of marveling over God's purpose and patience in it all.

GEORGE WALTER FISKE, *The Recovery of Worship*, 1931

See also Mystery; Reverence; Worship.

WORD, THE

Listening, not to me, but to the Word, it is wise for men to confess that all things are one. Though the Word always speaks, yet men are born without understanding for it, before they hear it, and at first after they have heard it. For though all things are produced according to this Word, men seem to be unaware of it.

HERACLITUS (535–475 B.C.), *Fragments*

The Word, arousing and moving the whole body, the Church, to befitting action, awakens, moreover, each individual member belonging to the Church, so that they do nothing apart from the Word.

ORIGEN, *Against Celsus*, 246 A.D.

Since the Word is in the Father, and the Spirit comes from the Word, we should receive the Spirit, so that possessing the Spirit of the Word who is in the Father, we too may then become one by the Spirit in the Word, and through Him in the Father.

ST. ATHANASIUS, III, *Contra Arianos* XXV, c. 357

The word of God is all those commandments and revelations, those promises and threatenings, the stories and sermons recorded in the Bible; nothing else is the word of God.

JEREMY TAYLOR, *Holy Living*, 1650

Never did there exist a full faith in the Divine Word (by whom light as well as immortality, was brought into the world), which did not expand the intellect, while it purified the heart.

SAMUEL TAYLOR COLERIDGE, *Aids to Reflection*, 1825

That the Word of God is *God's* Word— this is not distinct from *what* it tells us, as form from content; this is itself content, the very plentitude of content.

KARL BARTH, *Dogmatics*, I, 1927

The Church does not say in its preaching: there is a God, this one God: But it says: this one God acts. *He gives His Word.* In his Word he gives his being. In his Word he works. In his Word he exists for the Church.

KARL BARTH, *Christliche Dogmatik*, I, 1927

The Word of God is not based on and contained in Christian faith, but Christian faith is based on and contained in the Word of God.

KARL BARTH, *Christliche Dogmatik*, 1927

Jesus does not merely *have* the Word, He *is* the Word. His teaching reveals God's secret.

 EMIL BRUNNER, *The Word and the World,* 1931

God's Word is not simply a communication or an objective statement, but a positive command which does not permit man to assume the attitude of a spectator or to enjoy mere disinterested research.

 ADOLPH KELLER, *Religion and the European Mind,* 1934

The Word of God is a red-hot iron.

 GEORGES BERNANOS, *The Diary of a Country Priest,* 1937

Herod showed himself much more competent and realistic than Pilate or Caiaphas. He grasped the principle that if you *are* to destroy the Word, you must do so before it has time to communicate itself. Crucifixion gets there too late.

 DOROTHY L. SAYERS, *The Mind of the Maker,* 1941

What is more sublime than to scrutinize, explain, propose to the faithful and defend from unbelievers the very word of God, communicated to men under the inspiration of the Holy Ghost?

 POPE PIUS XII, *Divino Afflante Spiritu,* 1943

No matter what the human intermediaries may be, it is the living and personal Word of God which presents the truths of faith to the soul until the end of time.

 JEAN MOUROUX, *I Believe,* 1960

In the beginning was the Word, it has been piously recorded, and I might venture that the word was hydrogen gas. In the very beginning were hydrogen atoms.

 HARLOW SHAPLEY, *Science Ponders Religion,* 1960

See also Bible; Bible: Its Inspiration; Church, Definitions of; Church: Its Work; Creation; God, Word of; Holy Spirit; Incarnation; Jesus Christ; Literature; Logos; Man Indwelt by God; New Testament; Old Testament; Preachers; Preaching; Preaching and the Bible; Torah.

WORDS

Ill deeds are doubled with an evil word.

 WILLIAM SHAKESPEARE, *The Comedy of Errors,* c. 1591

The Word is well said to be omnipotent in this world; man, thereby divine, can create as by a *Fiat.* Awake, arise! Speak forth what is in thee; what God has given thee, what the Devil shall not take away.

 THOMAS CARLYLE, *Sartor Resartus,* 1836

When man had found names for body and soul, for father and mother, and not till then, did the first act of human history begin. Not till there were names for right and wrong, for God and man, could there be anything worthy of the name of human society.

 F. MAX MÜLLER, *Address,* Congress of Orientalists, 1892

No one means all he says, and yet very few say all they mean, for words are slippery and thought is viscous.

 HENRY ADAMS, *The Education of Henry Adams,* 1906

Why shouldn't we quarrel about a word? What is the good of words if they aren't important enough to quarrel over? Why do we choose one word more than another if there isn't any difference between them?

 G. K. CHESTERTON, *The Ball and the Cross,* 1909

Nowhere more than in ecclesiastical politics and doctrine do words prove themselves the veils of thought.

 VINCENT MCNABB, *From a Friar's Cell,* 1923

Words spoken to God are immeasurably above words spoken about Him. There is a huge difference between saying: "Why hast Thou?" and "Why has He?"

> HENRY SLOANE COFFIN, *Joy in Believing,* 1956

As man who has been given the gift of word, I am deeply conscious of my need for meditation and prayer in my use of word. The Word is of God, and I tremble before it.

> ROBERT RAYNOLDS, *In Praise of Gratitude,* 1961

See also Author; Books; Eloquence; Falsehood; Gossip; Literature; Preachers; Rhetoric; Sermons; Speech.

WORK

Do without attachment the work you have to do; for a man who does his work without attachment attains the Supreme Goal verily. By action alone men like Janaka attained perfection.

> SRI KRISHNA, *in the Bhagavad-Gita,* c. 200 B.C.

Where our work is, there let our joy be.

> TERTULLIAN, *Women's Dress,* c. 220 A.D.

And first of all, whatever good work you begin to do, beg of Him with most earnest prayer to perfect it.

> ST. BENEDICT, *Rule of,* c. 530

Be not proud of good work; for God's judgments are thiswise and man's otherwise; for ofttimes what pleaseth man displeaseth God.

> THOMAS À KEMPIS, *Imitation of Christ,* 1441

One who works conscientiously, not expecting any reward other than virtue, seems to work far more virtuously and more ingenuously than he who expects some reward beyond virtue.

> PIETRO POMPONAZZI, *On the Immortality of the Soul,* 1516

Whatsoever kind the works may be: eating, drinking, working with the hand, teaching, I add that even they are plainly sins.

> PHILIP MELANCHTON, *Common Topics,* 1521

We should accustom ourselves to think of our position and work as sacred and well-pleasing to God, not on account of the position and work, but on account of the word and faith from which the obedience and work flow.

> JOHN CALVIN, *Institutes,* III, 1536

Though the rich have no outward want to urge them, they have as great a necessity to obey God. . . . God has strictly commanded work to all.

> RICHARD BAXTER, *Christian Directory,* I, ch. X, 1673

Next to the saving his soul, his care and business is to serve God in his calling, and to drive it as far it will go.

> RICHARD STEELE, *The Tradesman's Calling,* 1684

The Great Governour of the world hath appointed to every man his proper post and province, and let him be never so active out of his sphere, he will be at a great loss, if he do not keep his own vineyard and mind his own business.

> RICHARD STEELE, *The Tradesman's Calling,* 1684

All speech and rumor is short-lived, foolish, untrue. Genuine WORK alone, what thou workest faithfully, that is eternal.

> THOMAS CARLYLE, *Past and Present,* 1843

All true Work is sacred; in all true Work, were it but true hand-labor, there is something of divineness.

THOMAS CARLYLE, *Past and Present,* 1843

Blessed is he who has found his work; let him ask no other blessedness. He has a work, a life purpose.

THOMAS CARLYLE, *Past and Present,* 1843

The sum of wisdom is, that the time is never lost that is devoted to work.

RALPH WALDO EMERSON, *Success,* 1844

If you would avoid uncleanness, and all the sins, work earnestly, though it be at cleaning a stable.

HENRY DAVID THOREAU, *Walden,* 1854

Thank God every morning when you get up that you have something to do that day which must be done, whether you like it or not.

JAMES RUSSELL LOWELL (1819–1891), *Letters*

If you do your work with complete faithfulness . . . you are making as genuine a contribution to the substance of the universal good as is the most brilliant worker whom the world contains.

PHILLIPS BROOKS, *Perennials,* 1898

The modern world is so out of sympathy with the language and atmosphere of religion that it is hard for most people to recognize religion in work.

RICHARD C. CABOT, *What Men Live By,* 1914

The inner ear of each man's soul hears the voice of Life, "Find your work, and do it!" Only by obedience to this command can he find peace.

FRANK CRANE, *The Looking Glass,* 1917

Any legitimate and beneficial State intervention in the field of work must be such as to preserve and respect its personal character, both in principle and within the limits of possibility, as regards execution.

POPE PIUS XII, *Broadcast,* June 1, 1941

There is dignity in work only when it is work freely accepted.

ALBERT CAMUS, *Notebooks,* 1935–1942

All action must be done in a more and more Godward and finally a God-possessed consciousness; our work must be a sacrifice to the Divine.

AUROBINDO, *Synthesis of Yoga,* 1950

The spiritual driving force transmitted from religion to work has gathered such momentum . . . that work has eventually become an end in itself instead of continuing to be . . . an incidental means of spiritual edification.

A. J. TOYNBEE, *Man at Work in God's World,* ed. G. E. DeMille, 1955

If Christians are also joined in mind and heart with the most Holy Redeemer, when they apply themselves to temporal affairs, their work in a way is a continuation of the labor of Jesus Christ Himself, drawing from it strength and redemptive power.

POPE JOHN XXIII, *Mater et Magistra,* May 15, 1961

The only work of which we are absolute masters and over which we have sovereign power, the only one that we can dominate, encompass in a glance, and organize, concerns our own heart.

FRANÇOIS MAURIAC, *Cain, Where Is Your Brother?,* 1962

See also Business; Call; Commitment; Conscience; Duties; Ease; Idleness; Labor; Prayer: Defined and Explained; Puritan; Religion; Service; Vocation.

WORKS

The way of godliness consists of these two parts, pious dogmas and good works. Neither are the dogmas acceptable to God without good works, nor does God accept works accomplished otherwise than as linked with pious dogmas.
ST. CYRIL OF JERUSALEM, *Catechetical Lectures*, 350

That is the true life on which the rich are exhorted to lay hold by being rich in good works; and in it is the true consolation.
ST. AUGUSTINE, *To Proba*, 412

Our faith in Christ does not free us from works but from false opinions concerning works, that is, from the foolish presumption that justification is acquired by works.
MARTIN LUTHER, *Freedom of a Christian*, 1520

As the soul needs the word alone for life and justification, so it is justified by faith alone, and not by any works.
MARTIN LUTHER, *On Christian Liberty*, 1520

Works, since they are irrational things, cannot glorify God; although they may be done to the glory of God, if faith be present.
MARTIN LUTHER, *On Christian Liberty*, 1520

Men ought to do the good works commanded of God, because it is God's will, and not for any confidence of meriting justification before God by their works.
PHILIP MELANCHTHON, *Augsburg Confession*, 1530

Good works must be done, not to merit thereby eternal life, which is a free gift of God, nor for ostentation or from selfishness, which the Lord rejects, but for the glory of God.
HENRY BULLINGER, *The Helvetic Confession*, 1536

The Gospel preaches nothing of the merit of works; he that says the Gospel requires works for salvation, I say flat and plain he is a liar.
MARTIN LUTHER (1483–1546), *Table Talk*

The Lord does not look so much to the grandeur of our works as to the love with which they are done.
ST. TERESA OF ÁVILA, *The Interior Castle*, 1577

Faith without good works is dead.
MIGUEL DE CERVANTES, *Don Quixote*, 1605

Every man is the son of his own works.
MIGUEL DE CERVANTES, *Don Quixote*, 1605

The works of the just man are not effaced, abolished, or annihilated by supervening sin, but only forgotten. . . . But love, returning to the soul of the penitent, restores life to former good works.
ST. FRANCIS OF SALES (1567–1622), *Consoling Thoughts of*, ed. Huguet

Insolent zeals, that do decry good Works and rely only upon Faith . . . they enforce the condition of GOD, and in a more sophistical way do seem to challenge Heaven.
THOMAS BROWNE, *Religio Medici*, 1635

Works done by unregenerate men—although, for the matter of them, they may be things which God commands . . . are sinful and cannot please God. . . . And yet their neglect of them is more sinful and displeasing unto God.
Westminster Confession of Faith, Formulary of the Presbyterian Church of Scotland, 1643

Religion alone induces men to do good works, and this through the intermediary of the senses, since the virtuous maxims of the philosophers serve only to provide eloquence with the means of persuading the senses.

GIOVANNI VICO, *The New Science,* 1725

One works for social equality, justice, order, brotherhood only because these are expressions of his love for God and his consequent love for men.

W. B. EASTON, JR., *The Faith of a Protestant,* 1946

He who devotes himself to the mere study of religion without engaging in works of love and mercy is like one who has no God.

Proverb

See also Faith; Justification; Predestination; Religion.

WORLD, THE

Come, look at this world, glittering like a royal chariot; the foolish are immersed in it, but the wise do not touch it.

Dhammapada, c. 5th century B.C.

The world is either a welter of alternate combination and dispersion, or a unity of order and providence.

MARCUS AURELIUS, *Meditations,* c. 170 A.D.

Love not the world abidingly, since the world ye love cannot itself abide.

SAINT GREGORY THE GREAT, *Book of Pastoral Rules,* 590 A.D.

The love of the world is the root of all evil.

MOHAMMED (7th century A.D.), *Sayings of, Wisdom of the East Series*

Why blame the world? The world is free Of sin; the blame is yours and mine.

ABU'L-ALA-AL-MA'ARRI (973–1057), in R. A. Nicholson's *Translation of Eastern Poetry and Prose*

It is more philosophical to put our relations with things and men on such a footing as to treat the world as the common country of us all.

DESIDERIUS ERASMUS (1466–1536), *Epistles,* II

Nothing that is without a soul and void of reason, is able to bring forth a living soul capable of reason. The world doth bring us forth, then the world hath both soul and reason.

MICHEL DE MONTAIGNE, *Essays,* Bk. 2, ch. 12, 1580

The world and that infinite variety of pleasing objects in it, do so allure and enamour us, that we cannot so much as look towards God, seek him, or think on him as we should.

ROBERT BURTON, *The Anatomy of Melancholy,* III, 1621

The world is not an inn, but a hospital, and a place, not to live, but to die in.

THOMAS BROWNE, *Religio Medici,* 1635

The world in itself has no value, it is merely zero—but with Heaven before it, it means much.

BALTASAR GRACIÁN, *The Art of Worldly Wisdom,* 1647

All this visible world is but an imperceptible point in the ample bosom of nature.

BLAISE PASCAL, *Pensées,* 1670

The created world is but a small parenthesis in eternity.

THOMAS BROWNE, *Christian Morals,* 1680

The World is a Ladder for some to go up, and some down.

THOMAS FULLER, *Gnomologia,* 1732

The World . . . [is] only the first rude essay of some infant deity, who afterwards abandoned it, ashamed of his lame performance; it is the world only of some dependent inferior deity; and is the object of derision to his superiors; it is the production of old age and dotage in some superannuated deity; and ever since his death, has run on at adventures, from the first impulse and active force which it received from him.

> DAVID HUME, *Dialogues Concerning Natural Religion*, V, 1779

The world is a sum of appearance, and must have some transcendent ground.

> IMMANUEL KANT, *Critique of Pure Reason*, 1781

We see the world piece by piece, as the sun, the moon, the animal, the tree; but the whole, of which these are the shining parts, is the soul.

> RALPH WALDO EMERSON, "The Over-Soul," *Essays, First Series*, 1841

There are two worlds, "the visible and the invisible," as the Creed speaks,—the world we see, and the world we do not see. And the world which we do not see as really exists as the world we do see.

> JOHN HENRY NEWMAN, *Parochial and Plain Sermons*, IV, 1843

I shall walk through this world, with its misery and joy, as a happy pilgrim, and use it only as a bridge to thee, Lord, across the stream of time.

> EICHENDORFF (1788–1857), "The Boatman," *Spiritual Poems*

In the morning, we carry the world, like Atlas; at noon, we stoop and bend beneath it; and at night, it crushes us to the ground.

> HENRY WARD BEECHER, *Life Thoughts*, 1858

The good world is not innocent. It does not ignore evil; it possesses and still conquers evil.

> JOSIAH ROYCE, *Spirit of Modern Philosophy*, 1892

Like many or all of those who have placed their heaven in this earth, I have found in it not merely the beauty of heaven, but the horror of hell also.

> OSCAR WILDE, *De Profundis*, 1896

It is better that the world shall be feared than that it be embraced with a good conscience.

> REINHOLD NIEBUHR, *Christian Century*, April 22, 1926

The world is what I share with others.

> MARTIN HEIDEGGER, *Sein und Zeit*, 1927

The world is just a scaffolding up which souls climb to the kingdom of Heaven.

> FULTON J. SHEEN, *The Life of All Living*, 1929

The partition of the world into a natural order overlaid by a supernatural order which keeps breaking through is to a well-instructed mind impossible.

> HARRY EMERSON FOSDICK, *As I See Religion*, 1932

Perhaps the world *may* suddenly have burst into being one fine day; but if so, it is a world which just as logically might not have been, and it is in that sense a colossal accident, with no necessity of reason behind it.

> A. O. LOVEJOY, *The Great Chain of Being*, 1933

We face the Biblical world made historically vivid over against the modern world presently experienced, and we cannot use the old method of accommodating the one to the other.

> HARRY EMERSON FOSDICK, *The Modern Use of the Bible*, 1934

The Truth about the world and the earthly city is that they are the kingdom at once of man, of God, and of the devil . . . the history of the temporal city . . . leads

. . . at one and the same time to the kingdom of perdition and the Kingdom of God.

JACQUES MARITAIN, *True Humanism,* 1938

The future is hidden from us, but the past warns us that the world in the end belongs to the unworldly.

SARVEPALLI RADHAKRISHNAN, *Eastern Religions and Western Thought,* 1939

The world does not stand or fall with discoveries or inventions, nor with the trample of armed hosts and the thunder of bombing planes. The world stands or falls with the laws of life which Heaven has written in the human conscience.

PIERRE VAN PAASEN, *Days of Our Years,* 1940

The world that is knowable and describable has taken on a greater interest and importance than the realm that is entered by faith and spiritual vision.

RUFUS M. JONES, *A Call to What Is Vital,* 1949

The world is not an illusion; it is not nothingness, for it is willed by God and therefore is real. . . . The reality of the world is not in itself but it is in the thought and being of the Creator. It is what God thought and willed it to be before it was.

SARVEPALLI RADHAKRISHNAN, *Philosophy of,* 1952

The world is the community of those before God who feel rejected by God and reject him; again it is the community of those who do not know God, and seem not to be known by him; or, it is the community of those who knowing God do not worship him.

H. RICHARD NIEBUHR, *The Purpose of the Church and Its Ministry,* 1956

See also Creation; End of the World; Evil; God: Considered as Impersonal; Nature;

Possessions; Providence; Spiritual World; Temporal; Unity; Universe; World, Condemnation of; World, Praise of; World and Christianity; World and the Church; World and God; World and Man; Worldliness.

WORLD, CONDEMNATION OF

Beware of this world with all its wariness; for it is like to a snake, smooth to the touch, but its venom is deadly.

AL-HASAN AL-BASRĪ (died 728 A.D.), quoted in *Sūfism,* translated by A. J. Arberry

If heaven is our country, what is the earth but a place of exile? If the departure out of the world is but an entrance into life, what is the world but a sepulchre? What is a continuance in it but an absorption in death?

JOHN CALVIN, *Institutes,* III, 1536

The world is not only the devil's, but the devil himself.

MARTIN LUTHER, *Letter,* January 10, 1539

You fear to quit the medleys of the world, where vanity reigns, where avarice tarnishes the most beautiful virtues, where infidelity holds dominion with the sway of a despot, where virtue is trampled under foot and vice carries off the prize of honor.

ST. FRANCIS OF SALES (1567–1622), *Consoling Thoughts of,* ed. Huguet

The world?—It is a territory under a curse, where even its pleasures carry with them their thorns and their bitterness. . . . A place where hope, regarded as a passion so sweet, renders everybody unhappy; where those who have nothing to hope for, think themselves still more miserable, where all that pleases, pleases never for long; and where *ennui* is almost the sweetest destiny and the most supportable that one can expect in it.

JEAN BAPTISTE MASSILLON (1663–1742), *Sermons*

The world is a league of rogues against the true people, of the vile against the generous.

GIACOMO LEOPARDI, *Pensieri,* 1838

The world is sweet to the lips, but bitter to the taste. It pleasures us at first, but not at last. It looks gay on the outside, but evil and misery lie within.

JOHN HENRY NEWMAN, *Parochial and Plain Sermons,* 1843

Our natural world is apparently in the victorious grip of the inane for it is dominated by corruptibility and death, animosity and hatred, egoism and discord. Man is overwhelmed by the meaningless evil of the whole of life.

NICHOLAS BERDYAEV, *Freedom and Spirit,* 1944

See also World, the; World, Praise of; World and Christianity; World and the Church; World and God; World and Man; Worldliness.

WORLD, PRAISE OF

The world is the fairest of creations, and the Creator the best of Causes.

PLATO, *The Republic,* c. 370 B.C.

In the world as it is, the richness of the outer stirs us all to the wonder of the inner whose greatness is displayed in acts so splendid.

PLOTINUS, (203–262 A.D.), *The Enneads*

The standing miracle of this visible world is little thought of, because always before us, yet, when we arouse ourselves to contemplate it, it is a greater miracle than the rarest and most unheard-of marvels.

ST. AUGUSTINE, *The City of God,* 426

This world is a most holy Temple, into which man is brought there to behold Statues and Images, not wrought by mortal hands, but such as by the secret thought of God hath made sensible, as intelligible unto us.

MICHEL DE MONTAIGNE, *Essays,* Bk. 2, ch. 12, 1580

A good man finds every place he treads upon holy ground; to him the world is God's temple.

JOHN SMITH (1618–1652), *The Excellence and Nobleness of True Religion*

Your enjoyment of the world is never right, till every morning you awake in Heaven; see yourself in your Father's Palace; and look upon the skies, the earth, and the air as Celestial Joys; having such a reverend esteem of all, as if you were among the Angels.

THOMAS TRAHERNE (1634–1704), *Centuries of Meditation*

The world is certainly a great and stately Volume of natural Things; and may be not improperly styled the Hieroglyphics of a better.

WILLIAM PENN, *Some Fruits of Solitude,* 1718

What a glorious world Almighty God has given us! How thankless and ungrateful we are, and how we labor to mar His gifts.

ROBERT E. LEE, *Letter to his wife,* August 4, 1861

The wonder is not that there should be obstacles and sufferings in this world, but that there should be law and order, beauty and joy, goodness and love.

RABINDRANATH TAGORE, *Sādhanā,* 1913

Just as a hand held before the eyes conceals the greatest mountain, so does petty earthly life conceal from view the vast lights and mysteries of which the world is full.

RABBI NACHMAN OF BRATISLAVA (1772–1811), quoted in Martin Buber, *Die Chassidischen Bücher*

All is not right with the world, but with the grace of God we can in a measure re-create the world into something nobler and more beautiful.

J. E. BOODIN, *God and Creation,* 1934

If in our world there are vales of tears, there are hillsides also of joy and laughter and peaks of splendor shining in the sun.

H. SAMUEL, *Belief and Action,* 1937

There is consolation in the assurance that whatever becomes of this husk of a planet, the inner meaning of it, hope itself, God, man's ideal, continually progresses and develops.

WILLIAM FAULKNER, *Speech,* Accepting Nobel Prize, January, 1951

See also Christianity; Creation; Nature; World, the; World, Condemnation of; World and Christianity; World and the Church; World and God; World and Man; Worldliness.

WORLD AND CHRISTIANITY

The world hateth Christians, though it receiveth no wrong from them, because they set themselves against its pleasures.

Epistle to Diognetus, c. 200

The soul is enclosed in the body, and yet itself holdeth the body together; so Christians are kept in the world as in a prison-house, and yet they themselves hold the world together.

Epistle to Diognetus, c. 200

The excellency of the Christian Religion appears as this, that it puts an end to this state of things, blots out all ideas of worldly wisdom, brings the world itself to ashes and creates all anew.

WILLIAM LAW, *Christian Perfection,* 1726

Death is not more certainly a separation of our souls from our bodies than the Chris-

tian life is a separation of our souls from worldly tempers, vain indulgences, and unnecessary cares.

WILLIAM LAW, *Christian Perfection,* 1726

All Christians are in the world, and of the world, so far as sin has domination over them; and not even the best of us is clean every whit from sin.

JOHN HENRY NEWMAN, *Parochial and Plain Sermons,* VII, 1843

Love of God is hatred of the world. And the day when Christianity and the world become friends Christianity is done away with.

SÖREN KIERKEGAARD (1813–1855), *Living Thoughts of,* ed. W. H. Auden

It is an essential doctrine of Christianity that the world is fundamentally good and practically bad, for it was made by God, but is now controlled by sin.

WALTER RAUSCHENBUSCH, *Christianity and the Social Crisis,* 1907

Christians are living in this sinful world and must bear its burdens, they may not steal away from the battle field.

NICHOLAS BERDYAEV, *Christianity and Class War,* 1933

The world that the Christian detests consists of that mass of disorder, deformity and evil introduced into creation by man's own voluntary defection.

ÉTIENNE GILSON, *The Spirit of Medieval Philosophy,* 1936

The Christian frankly admits that his view of the external world is colored by the mind of Christ, but he maintains that thereby he catches the true colors of creation's handiwork.

RALPH W. SOCKMAN, *The Highway of God,* 1941

The attitude of the Christian in regard to the world is not simple. He cannot follow his tendencies without restraint, but neither can he reject and destroy everything. His attachment should be considered and should be accompanied by constant purifications.

YVES MONTCHEUIL, *For Men of Action*, 1951

The Christian, far from having to flee the world, has as his task to "complete" it and "assume" it.

EMMANUEL SUHARD, *The Church Today*, 1953

If the unity of truth and being in Christ is more than a piece of sentimentalizing, then this identifying of oneself fully with the things and the people of the world is in fact an absolutely necessary step.

RONALD GREGOR SMITH, *The New Man*, 1956

The whole world of nature and human institutions is not only to be healed—it is also to be divinized. It will be divinized only if it is bedewed, not by holy water, but by the sweat of Christians laboring to make the City of Man a fit dwelling place for the sons of God.

PHILIP SCHARPER, *Sheed and Ward Trumpet*, Fall, 1962

If the world thinks itself to be a stranger from Christianity, Christianity does not consider itself a stranger from the world, no matter what attitude the world adopts towards it.

POPE PAUL VI, *Address*, Holy Land, January 6, 1964

See also Christianity; Christians; Civilization and Christianity; Civilization and Religion; Spiritual World; World, the; World, Condemnation of; World, Praise of; World and the Church; World and God; World and Man; Worldliness.

WORLD AND THE CHURCH

The Church so far from being literally, and in fact, separate from the wicked world, is within it. The Church is a body, gathered together in the world, and in a process of separation from it.

JOHN HENRY NEWMAN, *Parochial and Plain Sermons*, VII, 1843

The corrupt world . . . deifies and worships human nature and its impulses, and denies the power and grant of grace. This is the source of the hatred which the world bears to the Church; it finds a whole catalogue of sins brought into light and denounced, which it would fain believe to be no sins at all.

JOHN HENRY NEWMAN, *Discourse to Mixed Congregations*, 1849

It is the peculiarity of the warfare between the Church and the world, that the world seems ever gaining on the Church, yet the Church is really ever gaining on the world. Its enemies are ever triumphing over it as vanquished, and its members ever despairing; yet it abides.

JOHN HENRY NEWMAN, *Sermons on Subjects of the Day*, 1885

To apply the laws of the spirit to the activities of this earth is at once a desecration and denial of religion, and a bewildering and unsettling of the social order.

PAUL ELMER MORE, *Shelburne Essays*, 1904

The Church must either condemn the world and seek to change it, or tolerate it and conform to it. In the latter case it surrenders its holiness and its mission.

WALTER RAUSCHENBUSCH, *Christianity and the Social Crisis*, 1907

It is quite impossible for the Church, for any Church, to mix itself up . . . in the secular controversies of the day without losing more for itself than it can gain for the community.

A. J. BALFOUR, *The Mind of,* ed. W. F. Short, 1918

The church will find itself as it loses itself in the struggle to achieve a warless, just and brotherly world.

Council for Social Action of the Congregational Christian Churches, 1934

Nine-tenths of the work of the Church in the world is done by Christian people fulfilling responsibilities and performing tasks which in themselves are not part of the official system of the Church at all.

WILLIAM TEMPLE, *Christianity and Social Order*, 1942

All the great religions of the world supply, for those who can subscribe to their arguments and affirmations, a world-conception that has logical simplicity and serene majesty.

GORDON W. ALLPORT, *The Individual and His Religion*, 1950

From the list of charges brought by contemporary atheism against the Church let us in honesty accept one fact, the de-Christianization of the world.

EMMANUEL SUHARD, *The Church Today*, 1953

The Church and the Christian are not in the world to hate it but to love it with a redemptive love.

JOHN F. MURPHY, *Sanctity and Success in Marriage*, 1956

Authentic religion has always enabled man to see that the power by which he can endure the world requires him to change the world.

PAUL L. LEHMAN, *Religion and Culture*, ed. W. Leibrecht, 1959

If the church doesn't listen to the world, then the world will never listen to the church.

BERNARD HARING, quoted in *New York Times*, June 14, 1964

See also Christianity; Church: Its Nature; Church: Its Work; Religion; World, the;

World, Condemnation of; World, Praise of; World and Christianity; World and God; World and Man; Worldliness.

WORLD AND GOD

As one body is provided with many members, and is held together by one soul, so I am of opinion, that the whole world also ought to be regarded as some huge and immense animal, which is kept together by the power and reason of God as by one soul.

ORIGEN, *De Principiis*, Bk. IV, ch. 1, par. 3, c. 254 A.D.

The whole world is sustained by God's charity.

Talmud, Berakot, c. 500

In the great body of the world the divine murmur finds as many veins whereby it may come at us as there are creatures over which the very divinity rules.

ST. GREGORY THE GREAT, *Book of Morals*, V, 584

This universe of things is a ladder whereby we may ascend to God, since among these things are God's footprints, some God's image, some corporeal, some spiritual, some temporal, some eternal.

ST. BONAVENTURE, *Journey of the Mind to God*, 1259

He who has gotten the whole world plus God has gotten no more than God by himself.

MEISTER ECKHART (1260?–1327?), *Meister Eckhart*

For this World belongs as well to the Body or Corpus of God the Father, as the Heaven does.

JAKOB BOEHME, *Aurora*, 1612

The World is a kingdom whereof God is the King . . . an absolute monarchy . . . by the title of Creation . . . God is the end as well as the beginning of the divine monarchy of the world.

RICHARD BAXTER, *A Holy Commonwealth,* 1659

A feeble compromise between God and world will satisfy neither. God will reject you, and the world will drag you back into its vortex, and laugh at you for falling into its snares.

FRANÇOIS FÉNELON (1651–1715), *Spiritual Letters*

The notion of the world's being a great machine, going on without the interposition of God . . . is the notion of material and fate, . . . to exclude providence and God's government in reality out of the world.

G. W. VON LEIBNIZ, *A Collection of Papers Which Passed Between the late learned Dr. Leibniz and Dr. Clarke,* 1717

The end of God's creating the world, was to prepare a kingdom for his Son . . . which should remain to all eternity.

JONATHAN EDWARDS, *History of the Work of Redemption, Works,* IV, 1754

The world and all that it contains can exist, but it need not necessarily; only God must exist as He creates all the worlds ex nihilo.

RABBI NAHMAN OF BRATSLAV (1772–1811), quoted in *Judaism,* ed. A. Hertzberg

The light upon all the saints in Heaven is just as much and no more God's work, as the sun which shall shine tomorrow upon this infinitesimal speck of creation.

W. M. THACKERAY, *Letters to Mrs. Brookfield,* November, 1848

We mortals are on board a fast-sailing, never-sinking world-frigate, of which God was the ship-wright; and she is but one craft in a Milky-Way fleet, of which God is the Lord High Admiral. The port we sail from is forever astern.

HERMAN MELVILLE, *White Jacket,* 1850

If I looked into a mirror and did not see my face, I should have the same sort of feeling which actually comes upon me, when I look into this living busy world, and see no reflection of its Creator.

JOHN HENRY NEWMAN, *Apologia pro Vita Sua,* 1864

The world would be consistent without God; it would also be consistent with God; whichever hypothesis a man adopts will fit experience equally well.

W. E. HOCKING, *The Meaning of God in Human Experience,* 1912

In meeting my world divinely it shows itself divine. It supports my postulate. And without such an act of will, no discovery of divinity could take place.

WILLIAM E. HOCKING, *Meaning of God in Human Experience,* 1912

He who thinks to reach God by running away from the world, when and where does he expect to meet him?

RABINDRANATH TAGORE, *Gitanjali,* 1913

If we could look steadily at the world and see it as it is in the eyes of God many of our estimates would be amazingly changed.

EDWARD F. GARESCHE, *The Things Immortal,* 1919

It [the world] is a hymn sung by the creative Logos to the glory of God the Father. Its objects, so far as we can discern, are the manifestation of the nature of God under His three attributes of Wisdom, Beauty and Goodness.

W. R. INGE, *Outspoken Essays,* 1919

God is the binding element in the world. The consciousness which is individual in us is universal in him: the love which is partial in us is all-embracing in him.

ALFRED NORTH WHITEHEAD, *Religion in the Making,* 1927

If we knew all, as God does, the unideal aspects of the world would not seem so entirely out of harmony with an absolute and holy love as they now do.

A. C. KNUDSON, *The Doctrine of God,* 1930

So lies the sick world in the arms of God, who not for an instant leaves it alone, without whom we should not live.

A. MAUDE ROYDEN, *Federal Council Bulletin,* January, 1931

God, it is obvious, if He is to be an object worthy of our adoration must be kept unspotted from the World that adores Him.

C. E. M. JOAD, *Philosophical Aspects of Modern Science,* 1932

Unless the city of God pre-exists in heaven it cannot descend to earth. Therefore those who deny that Divine city cannot build on earth the city of their dreams.

E. I. WATKIN, *Men and Tendencies,* 1937

The great need of the Church today is a flaming conviction of the activity of God in the world.

R. ROBERTS, The Contemporary Christ, 1938

Happy are the Christians who recognize the imprint of God on the outside world!

FRANÇOIS MAURIAC, *The Eucharist,* 1944

To be truly wise is to have learnt to see God, but to see God is also to see and love and labor for the world he has made.

GERALD VANN, *Eve and the Gryphon,* 1946

Underlying everything was Christ's unswerving and rock-foundationed sureness that this world is God's world.

FRANCIS B. SAYRE, *Reader's Digest,* July, 1948

The will of the world is never the will of God.

WILLIAM HAMILTON, *Interpretation,* October, 1957

God the Redeemer does not set out to contradict the work of God the Creator. He uses things of earth to unite and reveal Himself to men of earth. The sacramental man will love earth because it is a sign of heaven.

JAMES H. DEADY, *Address,* Seattle, Wash., August, 1962

The world will not perish just because we cannot do everything. God still has things under control.

HANS URS VON BALTHASAR, *Prayer,* 1962

See also Creation; Creator; End of the World; God: His Intervention in the World; God: His Omnipotence; God: His Omnipresence; God: His Omniscience; Kingdom of God; Logos; Pantheism; Providence; Spiritual World; World, The; World, Condemnation of; World, Praise of; World and Christianity; World and the Church; World and Man; Worldliness.

WORLD AND MAN

All other beings and objects which surround us on the earth were created for the benefit of man, and to be useful to him, as means to his final end; hence his obligation to use, or abstain from the use of, these creatures according as they bring him nearer that end or tend to separate him from it.

ST. IGNATIUS LOYOLA, *Spiritual Exercises,* 1541

God has not made it necessary that the great majority of mankind should be heretics or infidels in order to take care of the earth, and leave us believers free to devote ourselves solely to ascetic exercises and the salvation of our souls.

ORESTES BROWNSON, *Brownson's Quarterly,* July, 1863

God calls on us to become creators, to make the world new and in that sense to bring something into being which was not there before.

J. E. BOODIN, *God and Creation,* 1934

If consciousness means what it claims to mean, not everything of worth in the World is traceable to an origin with Man, reference to Man, or application to Man's use.

M. C. SWABEY, *The Judgment of History,* 1954

See also Man; World, The; World, Condemnation of; World, Praise of; World and Christianity; World and the Church; World and God; Worldliness.

WORLDLINESS

When I am called before the Divine tribunal, what will I wish I had done with my worldly goods? This certainly is what I ought to do at the present moment.

ST. IGNATIUS LOYOLA, *Spiritual Exercises,* 1541

If a man be weighed down with worldliness, he shall sink like an overladen boat in the world's ocean.

AMAR DAS, c. 1565, *The Sikh Religion,* M. A. Macauliffe, I

If a man of this world is attracted by things of this world and is estranged from his Creator, he is corrupted and he can corrupt the entire world along with him.

MOSES LUZZATO (1707–1747), *Mesillat Yesharim*

The world with all its goods cannot content the heart of man; for he was created not for them, but for God alone; hence God alone can make him happy and content.

ST. ALPHONSUS DE LIGUORI, *Preface for Death,* c. 1760

There is no more mistaken path to happiness than worldliness, revelry, high life.

ARTHUR SCHOPENHAUER, *Essays,* 1841

Worldliness is not, in the last analysis, love of possessions, or the habit of courting great personages. It is simply the weakness of fibre which makes us take our standards from the society round us.

RONALD A. KNOX, *Stimuli,* 1951

See also Adversity; Comfort; Desires; Dissipation; Ease; Evil; Gluttony; Greed; Hedonism; Lust; Luxury; Materialism; Money; Pleasure; Poor, the; Possessions; Renunciation; Selfishness; Sensuality; Temporal; Wealth; World, The.

WORRY

The crosses which we make for ourselves by overanxiety as to the future are not Heaven-sent crosses.

FRANÇOIS FÉNELON (1651–1715), *Spiritual Letters of*

See also Anxiety; Fear; Gloom; Pessimism; Sadness.

WORSHIP

Thou [Ahura Mazda] art Divine. I know,
O Lord Supreme,
Since Good found entrance to my heart
through Love.
I asked: "What is Thy Holy Will? To
whom
Daily my utmost homage shall I pay?"
Since then unto Thine Inner Flame I pay
My homage and to Thine Eternal Law.
The Gatha Illumination, Yasna, 7th century B.C.

Among men there is no nation so savage and ferocious as to deny the necessity of worshipping God, however ignorant it may be respecting the nature of his attributes.

CICERO, *The Laws,* 52 B.C.

Follow and worship God in the exercise of virtue, for this way of worshipping God is the most holy.

> FLAVIUS JOSEPHUS, *Against Apion,* c. 93 A.D.

If a Greek is stirred to the remembrance of God by the art of Phidias, an Egyptian by paying worship to animals, and another man by a river, another by fire—I have no anger for their divergences; only let them know, let them love, let them remember.

> MAXIMUS OF TYRE (2nd century), quoted by Gilbert Murray in his *Four Stages of Greek Religion*

Wisdom precedes, religion follows; for the knowledge of God comes first, His worship is the result of knowledge.

> LACTANTIUS, *Divine Institutes,* c. 310

Surely religion is the worship of the true, superstition of the false. And what makes all the difference is what you worship, not how you worship.

> LACTANTIUS, *Divine Institutes,* c. 310

God is to be worshipped by faith, hope, and love.

> ST. AUGUSTINE, *On Faith, Hope and Charity,* c. 421

O my Lord if I worship thee from fear of Hell, burn me in Hell, and if I worship thee from hope of Paradise, exclude me thence; but if I worship thee for Thine own sake, then withhold not from me Thine Eternal Beauty.

> RABIA AL-ADAWIYYA (8th century A.D.), *Readings from the Mystics of Islam,* ed. Margaret Smith, 1950

Who worships God as God, God hears. But he who worships God for worldly goods, worships not God; he worships what he worships God for and employs God as his servant.

> MEISTER ECKHART (1260?–1327?), *Meister Eckhart*

The worship of God is as natural to men, as is neighing to horses or barking to dogs.

> MARSILIO FICINO, *Theologica Platonica,* 1474

Our mind cannot conceive of God without ascribing some worship to Him.

> JOHN CALVIN, *Institutes,* I, 1536

All true and acceptable worship to God is offered in the inward and immediate moving and drawing of His own Spirit, which is neither limited to places, times, or persons.

> ROBERT BARCLAY, *Apology for the Quakers,* 1678

The mind of Man is so made that, at first sight, an attitude of neutrality in the matter of the worship of God is felt to be more violently shocking than the worship of false gods.

> PIERRE BAYLE, *Dictionary,* 1697

Wonder is the basis of Worship.

> THOMAS CARLYLE, *Sartor Resartus,* 1836

The simplest person, who in his integrity worships God, becomes God.

> RALPH WALDO EMERSON, "The Over-Soul," *Essays, First Series,* 1841

Man is made to adore and obey; but . . . if you give him nothing to worship, he will fashion his own divinities and find a chieftain in his own passions.

> BENJAMIN DISRAELI, *Coningsby,* 1844

To know whom you worship, let me see you in your shop, let me hear you in your trade, let me know how you rent your houses, how you get your money, how you kept it and how you spent it.

> THEODORE PARKER, *Sermon, of Conventional and Natural Sacraments,* 1849

Whatever each man worships inwardly is his God, whether he knows it or not. He who has a ruling passion worships one God, good or evil. He who is carried at random by impulses has many gods; perhaps as shiftless, as shapeless, as unworthy, as any heathen divinities.

> F. W. NEWMAN, *Theism,* 1858

Worship is the free offering of ourselves to God; ever renewed, because ever imperfect. It expresses the consciousness that we are His by right, yet have not duly passed into His hand.

> JAMES MARTINEAU, *Hours of Thought,* Vol. II, 1879

True worship is not a petition to God: it is a sermon to ourselves.

> E. G. HIRSCH, *Reform Advocate,* iii, 1892

The language of worship seems far, and yet lies very nigh; for what better note can our frail tongues lisp than the voice of wind and sea, river and stream, those grateful servants giving all and asking nothing, the soft whisper of snow and rain eager to replenish, or the thunder proclaiming a majesty too great for utterance.

> MICHAEL FAIRLESS, *The Roadmender,* 1895

As long as man is man, so long will religion endure, and, with it, the obligation of worship.

> F. HETTINGER, *Natural Religion,* 1898

Bow down and worship where others kneel, for where so many have been paying tribute of adoration the kind Lord must manifest himself, for he is all mercy.

> SRI RAMAKRISHNA, *His Life and Sayings,* ed. F. M. Müller, 1899

The first of all worship is the worship of those all around us. . . . These are all our gods—men and animals; and the first gods we have to worship are our own countrymen.

> VIVEKANANDA (1863–1902), quoted by Romain Rolland in *Prophets of the New India*

Religious worship is only as it were a postern by the side of the great portals of beauty and nobility and truth. One whose heart is filled with a yearning mystery at the sight of the starry heavens, who can adore the splendor of noble actions, courageous deeds, patient affections, who can see and love the beauty so abundantly shed abroad in the world, . . . he can at all these moments draw near to God, and open his soul to the influx of the Divine Spirit.

> ARTHUR CHRISTOPHER BENSON, *From a College Window,* 1906

Worship, or prayer, is the especial sphere of the will in religion.

> WILLIAM E. HOCKING, *The Meaning of God in Human Experience,* 1912

Whenever beauty overwhelms us, whenever wonder silences our chattering hopes and worries, we are close to worship.

> RICHARD C. CABOT, *What Men Live By,* 1915

Worship God as if thou didst see him; for it thou doest not see him, yet he sees thee.

> *Selections from Mohammedan Traditions,* 1923

The act of worship is itself the process by which we first define God.

> WILLARD L. SPERRY, *Reality and Worship,* 1925

The worship of God is not a rule of safety—it is an adventure of the spirit, a flight after the unattainable. The death of religion comes with the repression of the high hope of adventure.

> ALFRED NORTH WHITEHEAD, *Science and the Modern World,* 1925

It is a man listening through a tornado for the Still Small Voice . . . a soul standing in awe before the mystery of the Universe . . . a hungry heart seeking for love . . .

Time flowing into Eternity. . . . It is a man climbing the altar stairs to God.

> DWIGHT BRADLEY, *The Congregationalist,* October, 1928

The first step in the act of worship is to relax and to become aware of that upon which we are dependent, that which sustains us in every breath we breathe.

> HENRY N. WIEMAN, *Methods of Private Religious Living,* 1929

There is something in us which demands, and finds satisfaction in, the act or at least the attitude of worship. But, since there is nothing in the visible creation which has a dignity corresponding to that attitude, we may be very sure that there is more in existence than our visible creation contains.

> RONALD A. KNOX, *Broadcast Minds,* 1932

This solitary response to reality is the deepest religious experience one can have. It is turning from the periphery of life to the core of existence. In this solitary moment it is as if one entered into the scheme of things.

> BERNARD E. MELAND, *Modern Man's Worship,* 1934

Worship arises as spontaneously in the heart of the religious devotee, as love arises in the heart of the youth who has found in the maiden beauty, inspiration, and understanding.

> CHARLES C. JASEY, *Journal of Religion,* XV, October, 1935

Worship is not only the natural expression and language of the Christian soul, but the fountain and source of creative activities.

> W. A. VISSER 'T HOOFT and J. H. OLDHAM, *The Church and Its Function in Society,* 1937

Ecstatic worship which is devoid of charity is for all practical purposes heathen.

> WILLIAM TEMPLE, *Christian Faith and the Common Life,* ed. N. S. Ehrenström, 1938

The world can be saved—by one thing only and that is worship. For to worship is to quicken the conscience by the holiness of God, to feed the mind with the truth of God, to purge the imagination by the beauty of God, to open the heart to the love of God, to devote the will to the purpose of God.

> WILLIAM TEMPLE, *The Hope of a New World,* 1941

In my view it is true to say that we can worship Nature or Humanity or Art, or God. I believe that all of these are the same activity, but that they differ in quality.

> HOWARD E. COLLIER, *The Place of Worship in Modern Medicine,* 1944

The healing effect of worship is greatly assisted by the warm fellowship that invariably springs up between the members of a worshipping group.

> HOWARD E. COLLIER, *The Place of Worship in Modern Medicine,* 1944

Man needs religion because he has an impelling need to worship, and if he does not worship God he will direct his worship to base objects that will pervert his mind and his heart.

> Roman Catholic Bishops of the U.S., 1952

When someone says "Oh, I can worship God anywhere," the answer is, "Do you?"

> JAMES A. PIKE, *Beyond Anxiety,* 1953

Worship is a way of living, a way of seeing the world in the light of God. To worship is to rise to a higher level of existence, to see the world from the point of view of God.

> ABRAHAM J. HESCHEL, *Man's Quest for God,* 1954

Whether the worship of a God is a good thing or not depends on how God is conceived.

RALPH BARTON PERRY, *The Humanity of Man*, 1956

The reality of Christian worship cannot be restored by injection of saccharine. Paul Claudel pillories the procedure: "If the salt hath lost its savour, wherewith shall it be salted? *With sugar!*"

AMOS N. WILDER, *Theology and Modern Literature*, 1958

Worshipers in spirit and truth are to be found in all confessions and all Churches, and they are recognizable by a sign, and they love one another, in a manner of speaking, not in spite of what separates them but in some way or other because of what separates them.

FRANÇOIS MAURIAC, *What I Believe*, 1962

The test of worship is how far it makes us *more sensitive* to "the beyond in our midst," to the Christ in the hungry, the naked, the homeless and the prisoner.

J. A. T. ROBINSON, *Honest to God*, 1963

Yet worship in common is not to be considered as a means to be used indiscriminately for the restoration of Christian unity. . . . Witness to the unity of the Church very generally forbids common worship to Christians, but the grace to be had from it sometimes commends this practice. The course to be adopted, with due regard to all the circumstances of time, place, and persons, is to be decided by local episcopal authority, unless otherwise provided for by the Bishops' Conference according to its statutes, or by the Holy See.

Decree on Ecumenism, Second Vatican Council, November, 1965

See also Abandonment; Adoration; Art and Religion; Brotherhood; Church, Definitions of; Community; Contemplation; Creeds; Demons; Detachment; Devotion; Eucharist; Experience, Religious; Fellowship; Freedom, Religious; Hope; Liturgy; Love of God; Man and God; Mass, the; Meditation; Music; Obedience; Piety; Praise; Prayer; Ritual; Sacrifice; Self-Giving; Selflessness; Self-Sacrifice; Song; Spiritual; Sunday; Superstition; Symbols; Wonder.

WORTH

Worth not by wealth, but merit, guage;
And wits by wise words, not by age.

SHAIKH SAADI, *Gulistan*, c. 1265

YES

But there is in man a reason which demands selection, preference, negation, in conduct and in art. To say "Yes" to everything and everybody is manifestly to have no character at all.

A. O. LOVEJOY, *The Great Chain of Being*, 1933

YOGA

In this [Yoga] there is neither waste of effort nor possibility of evil results. Even a little practice of this [Yoga] delivers one from great fear.

Bhagavad-Gita, c. 2nd century B.C.

Yoga: the control of thought-waves in the mind.

PATANJALI (2nd century B.C.), *Yoga Aphorisms*, I

The Yogi proposes to himself no less a task than to master the whole universe, to control the whole of nature. He wants to arrive at the point where what we call "nature's laws" will have no influence over him, where he will be able to get beyond them all.

SWAMI VIVEKANANDA, *The Yoga Philosophy, Lectures on Raja Yoga*, 1897

YOUTH

There is a feeling of Eternity in Youth, which makes us amends for everything. To be young is to be as one of the Immortal Gods.

WILLIAM HAZLITT, *On the Feeling of Immortality in Youth*, 1807

Like a rustic at a fair, we are full of amazement and rapture, and have no thought of going home, or that it will soon be night.

WILLIAM HAZLITT, *On the Feeling of Immortality in Youth*, 1807

In very early youth the soul can still remember its immortal habitation, and clouds and the edges of hills are of another kind from ours, and every scent and color has a savor of Paradise.

HILAIRE BELLOC, *The Path to Rome*, 1900

Young men have a passion for regarding their elders as senile.

HENRY ADAMS, *The Education of Henry Adams*, 1906

The deepest definition of youth is, life as yet untouched by tragedy.

ALFRED NORTH WHITEHEAD, *Adventures of Ideas*, 1933

The universe is not altogether as God meant it to be. We are here partly to change it. One of his mercies is that as men grow older and used to things, he takes them away and puts the universe in the hands of young, fresh men.

CLELAND B. MCAFEE, *Near to the Heart of God*, 1954

See also Adolescence; Commandments.

ZEAL

Zeal is a great ease to a malicious man, by making him believe he does God service,

whilst he is gratifying the bent of a perverse revengeful temper.

JOSEPH ADDISON, *The Spectator*, 1714

Violent zeal for truth hath an hundred to one odds to be either petulancy, ambition, or pride.

JONATHAN SWIFT, *Thoughts on Religion*, 1728

Zeal is fit only for wise men, but is found mostly in fools.

THOMAS FULLER, *Gnomologia*, 1732

Nothing spoils human Nature more than false Zeal. The *Good-nature* of an Heathen is more God-like than the furious *Zeal* of a Christian.

BENJAMIN WHICHCOTE, *Moral and Religious Aphorisms*, 1753

Zeal, not rightly directed, is pernicious; for as it makes a good cause better, so it makes a bad cause worse.

Old Farmer's Almanac, 1860

If we have learned anything at all in the two thousand years of Christian history, we should have learned that few things are more dangerous than zeal without knowledge.

CHARLES W. KEGLEY, *Religion in Modern Life*, 1957

See also Anger; Fanaticism; Tolerance.

ZEALOTS

The self-righteous zealot relishes playing the role of a merciful, compassionate person. After crushing a sinner under the weight of his indignation, he enjoys condescendingly lifting him up again in a gesture of sham mercy.

DIETRICH VON HILDEBRAND, *True Morality and Its Counterfeits*, 1955

One of the most hideous features of the self-righteous zealot is his abuse of particularly sublime Christian virtues.

DIETRICH VON HILDEBRAND, *True Morality and Its Counterfeits*, 1955

See also Fanaticism; Reformers; Tolerance.

ZIONISM

It belongs completely to the series of messianic movements which have continuously existed within Judaism.

Franz Rosenzweig (1887–1929), *Der Stern der Erlosung*

Zionism is a watered-down, meaningless and ineffectual concept without the influence of traditional and historic Jewish values. . . . Religious Zionism also serves the essential purpose of forging, cementing and unifying the permanent links, bridges and contacts between Israeli and American Jews.

Mordecai Kirshblum, *Interview, New York Times,* August 30, 1964

INDEX OF AUTHORS

INDEX OF AUTHORS